Linux Administration Handbook

Evi Nemeth

Garth Snyder

Trent R. Hein

with Adam Boggs,
Matt Crosby, and Ned McClain

PH
PTR

Prentice Hall PTR
Upper Saddle River, NJ 07458
www.phptr.com

ISBN 0-13-008466-2

Library of Congress Cataloging-in-Publication Data

A CIP catalog record for this book can be obtained from the Library of Congress.

Editorial/production supervisor: *Patti Guerrieri*
Executive editor: *Mary Franz*
Marketing manager: *Dan DePasquale*
Manufacturing manager: *Maura Zaldivar*
Editorial assistant: *Noreen Regina*
Cover design director: *Jerry Votta*
Cover designer: *Anthony Gemmellaro*

© 2002 by Prentice Hall PTR
A division of Pearson Education, Inc.
Upper Saddle River, NJ 07458

Prentice Hall books are widely used by corporations and government agencies for training, marketing, and resale. Volume discounts are available. For more information, contact the corporate sales department:

Prentice Hall PTR   Phone: (800) 382-3419
Corporate sales department Fax: (201) 236-7141
One Lake Street   Email: corpsales@prenhall.com
Upper Saddle River, NJ 07458

The names and logos of all products and services mentioned in this book are the trademarks or service marks of their respective companies or organizations. Red Hat and the Red Hat SHADOW MAN logo are registered trademarks of Red Hat, Inc., and such trademarks are used with permission.

Printed in the United States of America

10 9 8 7 6 5 4 3 2 1

ISBN 0-13-008466-2

Pearson Education LTD.
Pearson Education Australia PTY, Limited
Pearson Education Singapore, Pte. Ltd.
Pearson Education North Asia Ltd.
Pearson Education Canada, Ltd.
Pearson Educación de Mexico, S.A. de C.V.
Pearson Education — Japan
Pearson Education Malaysia, Pte. Ltd.

Table of Contents

Chapter 9   Periodic Processes   152

Chapter 10   Backups   159

NETWORKING

CHAPTER 15   NETWORK HARDWARE   335

BUNCH O' STUFF

CHAPTER 24 PRINTING   **744**

Foreword

I was quite excited to preview this Linux-only edition of the *UNIX System Adminis-tration Handbook*. The third edition of *USAH* included coverage of Red Hat Linux, but it was only one of four very different variants of UNIX. This version of the book covers several major Linux distributions and omits most of the material that's not relevant to Linux. I was curious to see how much of a difference it would make.

A lot, it turns out. Linux distributions draw from a common pool of open-source software, so they're far more similar to one another than are other versions of UNIX. As a result, the text seems to have become considerably more specific. Instead of suggesting various ways your system *might* behave, the authors can now tell you ex-actly how it *does* behave.

At the same time, it's clear that all the richness and variety of UNIX software are still represented here. Just about all of the world's popular software runs on Linux these days, and Linux sites are finding themselves faced with fewer and fewer compro-mises. As big-iron vendors like IBM, Oracle, and Silicon Graphics embrace Linux, it is rapidly becoming the universal standard to which other versions of UNIX are compared (and not always favorably!).

As this book shows, Linux systems are just as functional, secure, and reliable as their proprietary counterparts. Thanks to the ongoing efforts of its thousands of develop-ers, Linux is more ready than ever for deployment at the frontlines of the real world. The authors of this book know that terrain well, and I am happy to leave you in their most capable hands. Enjoy!

Linus Torvalds
April 2002

Preface

Linux is a relatively new operating system in the world of computing. Born in the early 1990s, it has enjoyed tremendous publicity and support from the open source community. In many ways, Linux has come to represent the antimatter of an otherwise Microsoft-centric universe.

Despite Linux's many achievements, it has yet to gain full acceptance in the world of "production computing." Once synonymous with big-iron mainframes, this environment is a world in which a few minutes of downtime can cost millions of dollars, dozens of jobs, or in extreme cases, lives.

We think it's about time that Linux was accepted as a fully ordained member of this community. However, such acceptance can only develop with the help of a cavalry of *professional* Linux system administrators.

We set out to write a book that would be the professional Linux system administrator's best friend. Where appropriate, we've adapted the proven concepts and materials from our popular book, *UNIX System Administration Handbook*. We've added a truckload of Linux-specific material and updated the rest, but much of the coverage remains similar. We hope you agree that the result is a high-quality guide to Linux administration that benefits from its experience in a past life.

There are other books on Linux system administration, but none that provide the breadth and depth of material necessary to effectively use Linux in real-world business environments. Here are the features that distinguish our book:

- We take a practical approach. Our purpose is not to restate the contents of your manuals but rather to summarize our collective experience in system administration. This book contains numerous war stories and a wealth of pragmatic advice.

- This is not a book about how to run Linux at home, in your garage, or on your PDA. We describe the use of Linux in production environments such as businesses, government offices, and universities.

- We cover Linux networking in detail. It is the most difficult aspect of system administration and the area in which we think we can be of most help.

- We do not oversimplify the material. Our examples reflect true-life situations with all their warts and unsightly complications. In most cases, the examples have been taken directly from production systems.

- We cover three major Linux distributions.

OUR EXAMPLE DISTRIBUTIONS

Like so many operating systems, Linux has grown and branched in several different directions. Although development of the kernel has remained surprisingly centralized, packaging and distribution of complete Linux operating systems is overseen by a variety of groups, each with its own agenda.

We cover three Linux distributions in detail:

- Red Hat 7.2
- SuSE 7.3
- Debian 3.0

We chose these distributions because they are among the most popular and because they are representative of the Linux community as a whole. However, much of the material in this book applies to other mainstream distributions as well.

We provide detailed information about each of these example distributions for every topic that we discuss. Comments specific to a particular operating system are marked with the distribution's logo.

THE ORGANIZATION OF THIS BOOK

This book is divided into three large chunks: Basic Administration, Networking, and Bunch o' Stuff.

Basic Administration provides a broad overview of Linux from a system administrator's perspective. The chapters in this section cover most of the facts and techniques needed to run a stand-alone Linux system.

The Networking section describes the protocols used on Linux systems and the techniques used to set up, extend, and maintain networks. High-level network software is also covered here. Among the featured topics are the Domain Name System, the Network File System, routing, **sendmail**, and network management.

Bunch o' Stuff includes a variety of supplemental information. Some chapters discuss optional software packages such as the Linux printing system. Others give advice on topics ranging from hardware maintenance to the politics of running a Linux installation.

Each chapter is followed by set of practice exercises. Items are marked with our estimate of the effort required to complete them, where "effort" is an indicator of both the difficulty of the task and the time required.

There are four levels:

no stars	Easy, should be straightforward
★	Harder or longer, may require lab work
★★	Hardest or longest, requires lab work and digging
★★★★★	Semester-long projects (only in a few chapters)

Some of the exercises require root or **sudo** access to the system; others require the permission of the local sysadmin group. Both requirements are mentioned in the text of the exercise.

OUR CONTRIBUTORS

We're delighted that Adam Boggs, Matt Crosby, and Ned McClain were able to participate as contributing authors. Their deep knowledge of a variety of areas has greatly enriched the content of this book. We owe them special thanks for making this book possible. Adam did a wonderful job delivering more than he promised, Matt was a master of pulling a high-quality rabbit out of a hat, and Ned was our much needed (and always enthusiastic) jack-of-all-trades.

CONTACT INFORMATION

Please send suggestions, comments, typos, and bug reports to sa-book@admin.com. We answer most mail, but please be patient; it is sometimes a few days before one of us is able to respond. To get a copy of our current bug list and other late-breaking information, visit our web site, www.admin.com.

We hope you enjoy this book, and we wish you the best of luck with your adventures in system administration!

Evi Nemeth
Garth Snyder
Trent R. Hein

April 2002

Acknowledgments

Many folks have helped with this book in one way or another, assisting with everything from technical reviews or suggested exercises to overall moral support. These people deserve special thanks for hanging in there with us:

Eric Allman	Robert Gray	Laszlo Nemeth
Piet Barber	Andreas Gustafsson	Gretchen Phillips
Jon Corbet	Cricket Liu	Josh Prismon
Jim Dennis	Paul Lussier	Greg Shapiro
Barbara Dijker	Derek Martin	Paul Vixie
Bill Fenner	Lynda McGinley	

Mary Franz, our editor, is deserving not only of special thanks but also an award for successfully dealing with flaky authors (herding cats comes to mind). Mary was infinitely patient with us, even when we didn't deserve it, and she did everything possible to encourage a continued focus on quality.

Mary Lou Nohr once again did an exceptional job as copy editor. She is a car crushing plant and botanical garden all rolled into one.

We'd like to thank Hank Pantier and Jeff Lindermeier at Hungry Mind Interactive Technologies for helping us update our increasingly eclectic cover cartoon. Robert Gray, David Clements, and Cyrus Hall of Boulder Labs helped with the exercises. Once again, Pat Parseghian came to our rescue with moral support and willingness to be our "special agent." Thanks, Pat!

The computer science department at the University of Colorado deserves many thanks for providing computing resources and numerous "test subjects." The computer science department at Brown University in Providence, RI, provided Evi with a temporary office and Internet access while she was trying to multiplex working on this book with working on her boat.

SECTION ONE
BASIC ADMINISTRATION

1 *Where to Start*

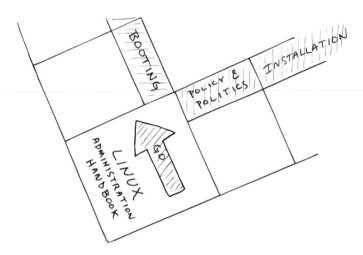

We set out to write a book that could be a system administrator's trusty companion, providing the practical advice, comfort, and basic system administration theory that you can't get from reading manual pages. As a result, this book is designed to complement—not replace—the Linux documentation.

We think this book will help you in five ways:

- It will give you an overview of the major administrative systems, identifying the different pieces of each and explaining how they work together.

- It will introduce general administrative techniques that we have found, through experience, to be worthwhile.

- It will help you choose solutions that continue to work well as your site grows in size and complexity.

- It will help you sort good ideas from bad and educate you about various atrocities of taste committed by distributors.

- It will summarize common procedures so that you don't have to dig through the excessive detail of the manuals to accomplish simple tasks.

It's impossible to perform these functions with perfect objectivity, but we think we've made our biases fairly clear throughout the text. One of the interesting things about system administration is the fact that reasonable people can have dramatically different notions of what constitutes the most appropriate policies and procedures. We offer our subjective opinions to you as raw data. You'll have to decide for yourself how much to accept and to what extent our comments apply to your environment.

1.1 SUGGESTED BACKGROUND

We assume in this book that you have a certain amount of Linux or UNIX experience. In particular, you should have a general concept of how Linux looks and feels from the user's perspective before jumping into administration. Several good books can get you up to speed; see the reading list on page 16.

You perform most administrative tasks by editing configuration files and writing scripts, so you must be familiar with a text editor. To the dismay of many, using Microsoft Word as one's only text editor is a significant impediment to effective system administration.

We strongly recommend that you learn **vi**. It is standard on all Linux systems, and though it may appear a bit pale when compared with glitzier offerings such as **emacs**, it is perfectly usable. We also like **pico**, which is a simple and low-impact "starter editor" that's good for new sysadmins. It's included in many distributions. Be wary of nonstandard editors; if you become addicted to one, you may soon tire of dragging it along with you to install on every new system.

One of the mainstays of system administration (and a theme that runs throughout this book) is the use of scripts to automate administrative tasks. To be an effective administrator, you must be able to read and modify **sh** scripts (which in the Linux world are really **bash** scripts). Scripts that you write from scratch can be written in the shell or scripting language of your choice.

See cpan.org for a complete selection of useful Perl software.

For new scripting projects, we recommend Perl. As a programming language, it is a little strange (OK, more than a little). However, it does include many features that are indispensable for administrators. The O'Reilly book *Programming Perl* by Larry Wall et al. is the standard text; it's also a model of good technical writing. A full citation is given on page 16.

Many administrators prefer Python to Perl, and we know of sites that are making a concerted effort to convert from Perl to Python. Python is a "nicer" language than Perl, and Python scripts are generally more readable and easier to maintain. However, Python doesn't have Perl's massive inertia and broad user base; you'll have to judge what features are most important for your site. A useful set of links that compare Python to other scripting languages (including Perl) can be found at

> http://www.python.org/doc/Comparisons.html

1.2 LINUX'S RELATIONSHIP TO UNIX

Some will call this heresy, but it's a point that really can't be overstressed: Linux is a version of UNIX. It's a bottom-up reimplementation of the POSIX standard, runs on several different hardware platforms, and is compatible with most existing UNIX software. It differs from most other versions of UNIX in that it is free, open source, and cooperatively developed, with contributions having come from hundreds of different individuals and organizations.

The Linux community sometimes downplays Linux's relationship to UNIX to emphasize the independence of the Linux development effort. Linux really *is* different from UNIX in its implementation and in its technical management, and it's understandable that the Linux developers would like to be acknowledged as something more than mere cloners of UNIX. Nevertheless, the differences between UNIX and Linux are largely unimportant from the perspective of users and system administrators. In fact, Linux systems generally behave more like traditional UNIX systems than do oddball UNIX variants such as Sun's Solaris or IBM's AIX.

Linux software *is* UNIX software. Thanks largely to the GNU Project, most of the important software that gives UNIX systems their value has been developed under some form of open source model. The same code runs on Linux and non-Linux systems. The Apache web server, for example, doesn't really care whether it's running on Linux or HP-UX. From the standpoint of proprietary applications, Linux is simply one of the best-supported varieties of UNIX.

It's also worth noting that Linux is not the only free version of UNIX in the world. FreeBSD, NetBSD, and OpenBSD, all offshoots of the Berkeley Software Distribution from UC Berkeley, have ardent followers of their own. These OSes are generally comparable to Linux in their features and reliability, although they enjoy somewhat less support from third-party software vendors.

UNIX systems have been used in production environments for many years. Now, Linux has matured to the point at which it, too, is a production-grade operating system. This book, unlike most others on Linux administration, focuses on the effective use of Linux in a production environment—not just as a single-user desktop.

1.3 LINUX AND UNIX HISTORY

Linux originated in 1991 as a personal project of Linus Torvalds, a Finnish graduate student. He originally conceived the project as a modest offshoot of Minix, a model operating system written by Andrew S. Tanenbaum. However, Linux generated substantial interest in the world at large, and the kernel soon took on a life of its own. By exploiting the power of cooperative development, Linus was able to tackle a much more ambitious agenda. Kernel version 1.0 was released in 1994; as of this writing (early 2002), the most recent stable version of the Linux kernel is 2.4.17.

Because Linux owes much to its UNIX ancestors, it's not quite fair to locate the dawn of the Linux era in 1991. The history of UNIX goes back several decades to 1969, when UNIX originated as a research project at AT&T Bell Labs. In 1976, UNIX was made available at no charge to universities and thus became the basis of many operating systems classes and academic research projects.

Berkeley UNIX began in 1977 when the Computer Systems Research Group (CSRG) at the University of California, Berkeley, licensed code from AT&T. Berkeley's releases (called BSD, for Berkeley Software Distribution) began in 1977 with 1BSD for the PDP-11 and culminated in 1993 with 4.4BSD.

As UNIX gained commercial acceptance, the price of source licenses rose rapidly. Eventually, Berkeley set the long-term goal of removing AT&T's code from BSD, a tedious and time-consuming process. Before the work could be completed, Berkeley lost funding for operating systems research and the CSRG was disbanded.

Before collapsing, the CSRG released its final collection of AT&T-free code, known as 4.4BSD-Lite. Most current versions of BSD UNIX (including BSD/OS, FreeBSD, NetBSD, and OpenBSD) claim the 4.4BSD-Lite package as their grandparent.

Most other major versions of UNIX (including HP-UX, Solaris, and IRIX) are descendants of the original AT&T lineage. Linux systems fall somewhere in the middle.

1.4   LINUX DISTRIBUTIONS

The Linux project differs from other variants of UNIX in that it defines only an OS kernel. The kernel must be packaged together with commands, daemons, and other software to form a usable and complete operating system—in Linux terms, a "distribution." All Linux distributions share the same kernel lineage, but the ancillary materials that go along with that kernel can vary quite a bit among distributions.

Distributions vary in their focus, support, and popularity. Table 1.1 lists the most popular general-purpose distributions.

Table 1.1   Most popular general-purpose Linux distributions[a]

Distribution	Web site	Comments
BestLinux	www.bestlinux.net	Supports several languages, easy installation
Caldera	www.caldera.com	Stability- and business-oriented distribution
Debian	www.debian.org	Most closely associated with the GNU project
Linux Mandrake	www.mandrake.com	Claims to be polished but full-featured
Red Hat Linux	www.redhat.com	Most widely used general-purpose distribution
Slackware Linux	www.slackware.com	Formerly a dominant Linux, less popular now
SuSE Linux	www.suse.com	Particularly strong in Europe, multilingual
TurboLinux	www.turbolinux.com	Strong in Asia, supports Asian languages

a. Distributions are listed in alphabetical order, not in order of preference or popularity.

Many smaller distributions are not listed in Table 1.1, and many unlisted special-purpose distributions are targeted at groups with specialized needs (such as embedded system developers). A more comprehensive guide to distributions, including the many non-English distributions, can be found at www.linux.org/dist.

So what's the best distribution?

A quick search on the net will reveal that this is one of the most frequently asked—and least frequently answered—Linux questions. Unfortunately, we have no ready answer either. The right answer for you depends on how you intend to use the system, the varieties of UNIX that you're familiar with, your political sympathies, and your support needs.

Most Linux distributions can do everything you might ever want to do with a Linux system. Some of them may require the installation of additional software to be fully functional, and some may facilitate certain tasks; however, the differences among them are not cosmically significant. In fact, it is something of a mystery why there are so many different distributions, each claiming "easy installation" and "a massive software library" as its distinguishing feature. It's hard to avoid the conclusion that people just like to make new Linux distributions.

On the other hand, since our focus in this book is the management of large-scale Linux installations, we're partial to distributions such as Red Hat that take into account the management of networks of machines. Some distributions are designed with production environments in mind, and others are not. The extra crumbs of assistance that the production-oriented systems provide can make a significant difference in ease of administration.

When you adopt a distribution, you are making an investment in a particular vendor's way of doing things. Instead of looking only at the features of the installed software, it's wise to consider how your organization and that vendor are going to work with each other in the years to come. Some important questions to ask are:

- Is this distribution going to be around in five years?
- Is this distribution going to stay on top of the latest security patches?
- Is this distribution going to release updated software promptly?
- If I have problems, will the vendor talk to me?

Viewed in this light, some of the more interesting, offbeat little distributions don't sound quite so appealing. On the other hand, the most viable distributions are not necessarily the most corporate. For example, we expect Debian Linux (OK, OK, Debian GNU/Linux!) to remain viable for quite a while despite the fact that Debian is not a company, doesn't sell anything, and offers no support.

LinuxPlanet maintains a list of Linux distributions at www.linuxplanet.com, along with a variety of in-depth reviews. Some of the reviews are a bit out of date, but they still give a good feel for the characteristics of each distribution. There are also some relatively clear and unbiased comments on the major distributions at www.linux.com; see the *Introduction to Linux and Linux.com*.

In this book, we use three popular Linux distributions as our examples: Red Hat Linux 7.2, SuSE Linux 7.3, and Debian GNU/Linux 3.0. These systems represent a cross-section of the enterprise Linux market and account collectively for a majority of the Linux installations in use at large sites today.

Distribution-specific administration tools

Many distributions provide visually oriented tools (such as the Red Hat Network Administration Tool or SuSE's YaST) that help you configure or administer selected aspects of the system. These tools can be very useful, especially for novice administrators, but they do tend to obscure the details of what's actually going on when you make changes. In this book, we cover the underlying mechanisms that the visual tools refer to rather than the tools themselves, for several reasons.

For one, the visual tools tend to be proprietary, or at least distribution-specific—they introduce variation into processes that may actually be quite consistent among distributions at a lower level. Second, we believe that it's important for administrators to have an accurate understanding of how their systems work. When the system breaks, the visual tools are usually not helpful in tracking down and fixing problems. Finally, manual configuration is often just plain better: it's faster, more flexible, more reliable, and easier to script.

1.5 NOTATION AND TYPOGRAPHICAL CONVENTIONS

In this book, filenames, commands, and literal arguments to commands are shown in boldface. Placeholders (e.g., command arguments that should not be taken literally) are in italics. For example, in the command

> **cp** *file directory*

you're supposed to replace *file* and *directory* with the names of an actual file and an actual directory.

Excerpts from configuration files and terminal sessions are shown in a fixed-width font.[1] Sometimes, we annotate interactive sessions with italic text. For example:

```
% grep Bob /pub/phonelist          /* Look up Bob's phone # */
Bob Knowles 555-2834
Bob Smith 555-2311
```

Outside of these specific cases, we have tried to keep special fonts and formatting conventions to a minimum as long as we could do so without compromising intelligibility. For example, we often talk about entities such as the Linux group named daemon and the printer anchor-lw with no special formatting at all.

In general, we use the same conventions as the manual pages for indicating the syntax of commands:

- Anything between square brackets ("[" and "]") is optional.
- Anything followed by an ellipsis ("…") can be repeated.
- Curly braces ("{" and "}") mean that you should select one of the items separated by vertical bars ("|").

---

1. Actually, it's not really a fixed-width font, but it looks like one. We liked it better than the real fixed-width fonts that we tried. That's why the columns in some examples may not all line up perfectly.

For example, the specification

    bork [**-x**] {**on**|**off**} *filename …*

would match any of the following commands:

    bork on /etc/passwd
    bork -x off /etc/passwd /etc/termcap
    bork off /usr/lib/tmac

We use shell-style globbing characters for pattern matching:

- A star (*) matches zero or more characters.
- A question mark (?) matches one character.
- A tilde or "twiddle" (~) means the home directory of the current user.
- *~user* means the home directory of *user*.

For example, we might refer to the Debian startup script directories **/etc/rc0.d**, **/etc/rc1.d**, and so on with the shorthand pattern **/etc/rc*.d**.

Text within quotation marks often has a precise technical meaning. In these cases, we ignore the normal rules of English and put punctuation outside the quotation marks so that there can be no confusion about what's included and what's not.

System-specific information

Information in this book generally applies to all of our example distributions unless a specific attribution is given. Details particular to one distribution are marked with the vendor's logo:

 Red Hat Linux 7.2

 SuSE Linux 7.3

 Debian GNU/Linux 3.0

These logos are used with the kind permission of their respective owners. However, the distributors have neither reviewed nor endorsed the contents of this book.

1.6 WHERE TO GO FOR INFORMATION

Linux documentation is spread over a number of sources, some of which you will find installed on your system and some of which live out on the net. The biggies are:

- Manual pages (man pages), read with the **man** command
- Texinfo documents, read with the **info** command
- HOWTOs, short notes on various subjects (www.linuxdoc.org)
- Guides, longer treatises on various subjects (www.linuxdoc.org)
- Distribution-specific documentation

The man pages and Texinfo documents constitute the traditional "on-line" documentation (though, of course, all of the documentation is on-line in some form or another). These docs are typically installed with the system; program-specific man pages usually come along for the ride whenever you install a new package.

Man pages are concise descriptions of individual commands, drivers, file formats, or library routines. They do not address more general topics such as "How do I install a new device?" or "Why is my system so slow?" For those questions, you must consult the HOWTOs.

Texinfo documents were invented long ago by the GNU folks in reaction to the fact that the **nroff** command used to format man pages was proprietary to AT&T. These days we have GNU's own **groff** to do this job for us and the **nroff** issue is no longer important. Unfortunately, many GNU packages persist in documenting themselves with Texinfo files rather than man pages. In addition to defining an unnecessary second standard for documentation, Texinfo proves to be a rather labyrinthine little hypertext system in its own right. **info info** will initiate you into the dark mysteries of Texinfo.

Fortunately, packages that are documented with Texinfo usually install man page stubs that tell you to go use the **info** command to read about those particular packages. You can safely stick to the **man** command for doing manual searches and delve into **info** land only when instructed to do so.

HOWTOs and guides are maintained by the Linux Documentation Project, reachable on-line at www.linuxdoc.org. The LDP is a central repository for all sorts of useful Linux information. It also centralizes efforts to translate Linux-related documents into additional languages.

Some free, on-line LDP guides of particular relevance to system administrators are *The Linux System Administrators' Guide* by Lars Wirzenius, Joanna Oja, and Stephen Stafford; the *Advanced Bash-Scripting Guide* by Mendel Cooper; *The Linux Network Administrator's Guide, Second Edition,* by Olaf Kirch and Terry Dawson; and *Linux System Administration Made Easy* by Steve Frampton.

Unfortunately, many of the LDP documents are not maintained on an ongoing basis. Since Linux-years are a lot like dog-years in their relation to real time, untended documents are apt to quickly go out of date. Always check the time stamp on a HOWTO or guide and weigh its credibility accordingly.

Many of the most important parts of the Linux software base are maintained by neutral third parties such as the Internet Software Consortium and the Apache Software Foundation. These groups typically provide adequate documentation for the packages they distribute. Distributions sometimes package up the software but skimp on the documentation, so it's often useful to check back with the original source to see if additional materials are available.

Another useful source of information about the design of many Linux software packages is the "Request for Comments" document series, which describes the protocols and procedures used on the Internet. See page 240 for more information.

Organization of the man pages

The Linux man pages are typically divided into nine sections as shown in Table 1.2.

Table 1.2   Sections of the Linux man pages

Section	Contents
1	User-level commands and applications
2	System calls and kernel error codes
3	Library calls
4	Device drivers and network protocols
5	Standard file formats
6	Games and demonstrations
7	Miscellaneous files and documents
8	System administration commands
9	Obscure kernel specs and interfaces

Some sections are further subdivided. For example, section 3M contains man pages for the system's math library. Sections 6 and 9 are typically empty. Many systems have a section of the manuals called "l" for local man pages. Another common convention is section "n" for software-specific subcommands (such as **bash** built-ins).

nroff input for man pages is usually kept in the directories **/usr/share/man/man**X, where X is a digit **1** through **9**, or **l** or **n**. The pages are normally compressed with **gzip** to save space. (The **man** command knows how to uncompress them on the fly.) Formatted versions of the manuals are kept in **/var/cache/man/cat**X. The **man** command will format man pages as they are needed; if the **cat** directories are writable, **man** will also deposit the formatted pages as they are created, generating a cache of commonly read man pages.

The **man** command actually searches a number of different directories to find the manual pages you request. You can determine the search path with the **manpath** command. This path (from Red Hat) is typical:

```
% manpath
/usr/share/man:/usr/man:/usr/X11R6/man:/usr/kerberos/man:/usr/local/man
```

If necessary, you can set your MANPATH environment variable to override the default path. You can also set the system-wide default in **/etc/man.config** (Red Hat) or **/etc/manpath.config** (Debian and SuSE).

man: read manual pages

man *title* formats a specific manual page and sends it to your terminal with **less** (or whatever program is specified in your PAGER environment variable). *title* is usually a command, device, or filename. The sections of the manual are searched in roughly numeric order, although sections that describe commands (sections 1, 8, and 6) are usually searched first.

The form **man** *section title* gets you a man page from a particular section. Thus, **man tty** gets you the man page for the **tty** command and **man 4 tty** gets you the man page for the controlling terminal driver.

man -k *keyword* prints a list of man pages that have *keyword* in their one-line synopses. For example:

```
% man -k translate
mhbuild (1)    - translate MIME composition draft
objcopy (1)    - copy and translate object files
pfbtops (1)    - translate a PostScript font in .pfb format to ASCII
tr (1)         - translate or delete characters
...
```

Other sources of Linux information

There's a great big Linux-lovin' world out there. We couldn't possibly mention every useful collection of Linux information, or even just the major ones, but a few significant sources of information are shown in Table 1.3.

Table 1.3 Linux resources on the web

Web site	Description
www.linux.com	Linux information clearing house (unofficial)
www.linux.org	Another Linux information clearing house (unofficial)
www.linuxdoc.org	The Linux Documentation Project
www.linuxtoday.com	Linux Today on-line magazine
www.linuxplanet.com	Yet another on-line magazine, good sysadmin content
www.freshmeat.com	Large index of Linux and UNIX software
www.linuxhq.com	Compilation of kernel-related info and patches
www.kernel.org	Official Linux kernel site
www.linuxapps.com	Linux software archive
www.tucows.com	Multiplatform software archive with Linux content
www.linuxworld.com	On-line magazine from the Computerworld folks

Don't be shy about accessing general UNIX resources, either—most information is directly applicable to Linux. A wealth of information about system administration is available on the net, in many forms. For example, you can type sysadmin questions into any of the popular search engines, such as www.google.com, www.yahoo.com, www.altavista.com, and www.webopedia.com. A list of other "starter" resources can be found in Chapter 29, *Policy and Politics*.

Many sites cater directly to the needs of system administrators. Here are a few that we especially like:

- www.ugu.com – the UNIX Guru Universe; lots of stuff for sysadmins
- www.stokely.com – a good collection of links to sysadmin resources
- www.tucows.com – Windows and Mac software, filtered for quality
- slashdot.org – "the place" for geek news
- www.cpan.org – a central source for Perl scripts and libraries
- securityfocus.com – security info; huge, searchable vulnerability database

Another fun and useful resource is Bruce Hamilton's "Rosetta Stone" page at

> http://bhami.com/rosetta.html

It provides pointers to the commands and tools used for various system administration tasks on many different operating systems.

1.7 HOW TO FIND AND INSTALL SOFTWARE

Most Linux distributions divide their software into packages that can be installed independently of one another. When you install Linux on a new computer, you typically select a range of "starter" packages to be copied onto the new system.

This architecture simplifies many aspects of system configuration and is one of Linux's key advantages over traditional versions of UNIX. Unfortunately, this design also complicates the task of writing about these distributions because it's never really clear which packages are "part of" a given distribution. Is a package "included" if it's on the installation CDs but isn't part of the default installation? Only if it's on every computer running that distribution? If it's on the "bonus" CDs that come only with the supersize version of the distribution?

In this book, we generally describe the default installation of each of our example distributions. When we say that a particular package isn't included in the default installation, it doesn't necessarily mean that the package won't be on *your* system or that it isn't supported by your distribution. Here's how to find out if you've got it, and if not, how to get it.

First, use the shell's **which** command to find out if a relevant command is already in your search path. For example, the following command reveals that the Apache web server has already been installed on this machine in **/usr/sbin**:

```
% which httpd
/usr/sbin/httpd
```

If **which** can't find the command you're looking for, try **whereis**, which searches a broader range of system directories and is independent of your shell's search path. Be aware also that some systems' **which** will not show you files that you do not have permission to execute. For example:

```
% which ipppd
/usr/bin/which: no ipppd in (/bin:/usr/bin:/sbin:/usr/sbin)
% whereis ipppd
ipppd: /usr/sbin/ipppd
% ls -l /usr/sbin/ipppd
-rwx------   1 root     root      124924 Aug  3  2000 /usr/sbin/ipppd
```

Another alternative is the incredibly useful **locate** command, which consults a pre-compiled index of the filesystem to locate filenames that match a particular pattern. It is not specific to commands or packages, but can find any type of file. For example, if you weren't sure where to find the **signal.h** include file (which is the authoritative source for Linux signal definitions), you could try

```
% locate signal.h
/usr/include/asm/signal.h
/usr/include/linux/signal.h
/usr/include/signal.h
/usr/include/sys/signal.h
```

locate's database is usually regenerated every night by the **updatedb** command, which runs out of **cron**. Therefore, the results of a **locate** don't always reflect recent changes to the filesystem.

If you know the name of a package you're looking for, you can also use your system's packaging utilities to check directly for the package's presence. For example, on a Red Hat or SuSE system, the following command checks for the presence of the Python scripting language:

```
% rpm -q python
python-1.5.2-27
```

See Chapter 23, *Software Installation and Localization*, for more information about our example systems' packaging commands.

If the package you're interested in doesn't seem to be installed, it may be easier to look for it on the Internet than to return to your original installation CDs. You're also more likely to end up with a current version of the package, since many packages are updated frequently.

Most Linux software is developed by independent groups that release the software in the form of source code. Linux distributors then pick up the source code, compile it appropriately for the conventions in use on their particular system, and package the resulting binaries. It's usually easier to install a distribution-specific binary package than to fetch and compile the original source code. However, distributors are often a release or two behind the current version.

The fact that two distributions use the same packaging system doesn't necessarily mean that packages for the two systems are interchangeable. Red Hat and SuSE both use RPM, for example, but their filesystem layouts are somewhat different. It's always best to use packages designed for your particular distribution if they are available.

The first stop on your software search should generally be your distributor's web site. Most distributions provide a web-searchable database of packages, along with a network of FTP mirrors from which the actual packages can be downloaded. If all else fails, try looking for the package at a download site such as freshmeat.com or doing a Google search on the name of the package.

1.8 ESSENTIAL TASKS OF THE SYSTEM ADMINISTRATOR

The sections below give an overview of some tasks that system administrators are typically expected to perform. These duties need not necessarily be performed by one person, and at many sites the work is distributed among several people. However, there does need to be at least one person who understands all of the chores and makes sure that someone is doing them.

Adding and removing users

See Chapter 6 for more information about adding new users.

The system administrator adds accounts for new users and removes the accounts of users that are no longer active. The process of adding and removing users can be automated, but certain administrative decisions (where to put the user's home directory, on which machines to create the account, etc.) must still be made before a new user can be added.

When a user should no longer have access to the system, the user's account must be disabled. All of the files owned by the account must be backed up to tape and disposed of so that the system does not accumulate unwanted baggage over time.

Adding and removing hardware

See Chapters 8, 12, and 24 for more information about these topics.

When new hardware is purchased or when hardware is moved from one machine to another, the system must be configured to recognize and use that hardware. Hardware-support chores can range from the simple task of adding a printer to the more complex job of adding a disk drive.

Performing backups

See Chapter 10 for more information about backups.

Performing backups is perhaps the most important job of the system administrator, and it is also the job that is most often ignored or sloppily done. Backups are time consuming and boring, but they are absolutely necessary. Backups can be automated and delegated to an underling, but it is still the system administrator's job to make sure that backups are executed correctly and on schedule (and that the resulting media can actually be used to restore files).

Installing new software

When new software is acquired, it must be installed and tested, often under several operating systems and on several types of hardware. Once the software is working correctly, users must be informed of its availability and location. Local software should be installed in a place that makes it easy to differentiate from the system software. This organization simplifies the task of upgrading the operating system since the local software won't be overwritten by the upgrade procedure.

Monitoring the system

Large installations require vigilant supervision. Daily activities include making sure that email and web service are working correctly, watching log files for early signs of trouble, ensuring that local networks are all properly connected, and keeping an eye on the availability of system resources such as disk space.

Troubleshooting

Linux systems and the hardware they run on occasionally break down. It is the administrator's job to play mechanic by diagnosing problems and calling in experts if needed.

the problem is often harder than fixing it.

Maintaining local documentation

See page 859 for suggestions regarding documentation.

As the system is changed to suit an organization's needs, it begins to differ from the plain-vanilla system described by the documentation. It is the system administrator's duty to document aspects of the system that are specific to the local environment. This chore includes documenting any software that is installed but did not come with the operating system, documenting where cables are run and how they are constructed, keeping maintenance records for all hardware, recording the status of backups, and documenting local procedures and policies.

Auditing security

See Chapter 21 for more information about security.

The system administrator must implement a security policy and periodically check to be sure that the security of the system has not been violated. On low-security systems, this chore might involve only a few cursory checks for unauthorized access. On a high-security system, it can include an elaborate network of traps and auditing programs.

Helping users

Although helping users with their various problems is rarely included in a system administrator's job description, it claims a significant portion of most administrators' workdays. System administrators are bombarded with problems ranging from "My program worked yesterday and now it doesn't! What did you change?" to "I spilled coffee on my keyboard! Should I pour water on it to wash it out?"

1.9 SYSTEM ADMINISTRATION UNDER DURESS

System administrators wear many hats. In the real world, they are often people with other jobs who have been asked to look after a few computers on the side. If you are in this situation, you may want to think a bit about where it might eventually lead.

The more you learn about your system, the more the user community will come to depend on you. Networks invariably grow, and you may be pressured to spend an increasing portion of your time on administration. You will soon find that you are the only person in your organization who knows how to perform a variety of important tasks.

Once coworkers come to think of you as the local system administrator, it is difficult to extricate yourself from this role. We know several people that have changed jobs to escape it. Since many administrative tasks are intangible, you may also find that you're expected to be both a full-time administrator and a full-time engineer, writer, or secretary.

Some unwilling administrators try to fend off requests by adopting an ornery attitude and providing poor service. We do not recommend this approach; it makes you look bad and creates additional problems.

Instead, we suggest that you document the time you spend on system administration. Your goal should be to keep the work at a manageable level and to assemble evidence that you can use when you ask to be relieved of administrative duties. In most organizations, you will need to lobby the management from six months to a year to get yourself replaced, so plan ahead.

On the other hand, you may find that you enjoy system administration and that you yearn to be a full-time administrator. Your prospects for employment are good. Unfortunately, your political problems will probably intensify. Refer to Chapter 29, *Policy and Politics*, for a preview of the horrors in store.

System Administration Personality Syndrome

One unfortunate but common clinical condition resulting from working as a system administrator is System Administration Personality Syndrome. The onset of this condition usually begins early in the third year of a system administrator's career and the syndrome can last well into retirement. Characteristic symptoms include but are not limited to:

- Acute phantom pagerphobia: the disturbing feeling that your pager has gone off (when it really hasn't) and that your peaceful evening with your significant other is about to abruptly end, resulting in a 72-hour work marathon without food

- User voodoographia: the compulsive creation of voodoo-doll representations of the subset of your user population that doesn't seem to understand that their persistent lack of planning doesn't constitute an emergency in your world

- Idiopathic anal tapereadaplexia: the sudden, late-night urge to mount backup tapes to see if they're actually readable and labeled correctly

- Scientifica inapplicia: the strong desire to violently shake fellow system administrators who seem never to have encountered the scientific method

Many curative therapies can be used to treat this unfortunate condition. The most effective are a well-developed sense of humor and the construction of a small but well-endowed office wine cellar. You might also consider the more meditative approach of silently staring off into space and clicking your heels together whenever the words "Is the server down again?" are spoken in your vicinity. If all else fails, take a vacation.

1.10 RECOMMENDED READING

Although there are lots of introductory Linux books on the market, we find that most of them are pretty … well, bad. In general, you're better off looking for the UNIX "classics." Almost everything you read will apply equally well to Linux.

ANDERSON, GAIL, AND PAUL ANDERSON. *The UNIX C Shell Field Guide*. Englewood Cliffs, NJ: Prentice Hall. 1986.

LAMB, LINDA, AND ARNOLD ROBBINS. *Learning the vi Editor, 6th Edition*. Sebastopol, CA: O'Reilly and Associates. 1998.

ABRAHAMS, PAUL W., AND BRUCE A. LARSON. *UNIX for the Impatient, 2nd Edition*. Reading, MA: Addison-Wesley. 1995.

PEEK, JERRY, TIM O'REILLY, AND MIKE LOUKIDES. *UNIX Power Tools, 2nd Edition*. Sebastopol, CA: O'Reilly & Associates. 1997.

MONTGOMERY, JOHN. *The Underground Guide to Unix: Slightly Askew Advice from a Unix Guru*. Reading, MA: Addison-Wesley. 1995.

REICHARD, KEVIN, AND ERIC FOSTER-JOHNSON. *Unix in Plain English, 3rd Edition*. Foster City, CA: IDG Books Worldwide. 1999.

WALL, LARRY, TOM CHRISTIANSEN, AND JON ORWANT. *Programming Perl, 3rd Edition*. Sebastopol, CA: O'Reilly & Associates. 2000.

CHRISTIANSEN, TOM, NATHAN TORKINGTON, AND LARRY WALL. *Perl Cookbook*. Sebastopol, CA: O'Reilly & Associates. 1998.

WELSH, MATT, MATTHIAS KALLE DALHEIMER, AND LAR KAUFMAN. *Running Linux, 3rd Edition*. Sebastopol, CA: O'Reilly and Associates. 1999.

GANCARZ, MIKE. *The UNIX Philosophy*. Woburn, MA: Digital Press. 1994.

1.11 EXERCISES

E1.1   What command would you use to read about the **sync** system call (*not* the **sync** command)? How would you read a local man page for **sync** that was kept in **/usr/local/share/man**?

E1.2   Is there a system-wide config file that controls the behavior of **man** at your site? What lines would you add to this file if you wanted to store local documentation in **/doc/man**? What directory structure would you have to use in **/doc/man** to make it a full citizen of the man page hierarchy?

E1.3   What are the main differences between **man** and **info**? What are some advantages of each?

★ **E1.4**   What is the current status of Linux development? Who are some of the key players? How is the project managed?

★ **E1.5**   Research several Linux distributions (see page 4 for a starter list) and recommend a distribution for each of the following applications. Explain your choices.

a) A single user working in a home office
b) A university computer science lab
c) A corporate web server

★ **E1.6**   Suppose you discover that a certain feature of Apache **httpd** does not appear to work as documented on Red Hat 7.2.

a) What should you do before reporting the bug?
b) If you decide that the bug is real, who should you notify and how?
c) What information must be included to make the bug report useful?

2 *Booting and Shutting Down*

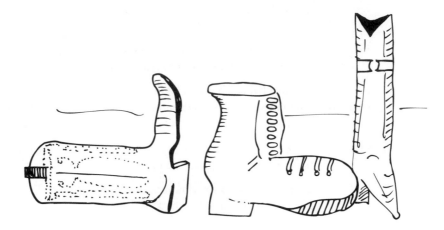

Linux is a complex operating system, and turning Linux systems on and off is more complicated than just flipping the power switch. Both operations must be performed correctly if the system is to stay healthy.

The bootstrapping process is akin to the development of human relationships. It varies widely, as determined by the early development years, and is considered by most to be a "private matter." Watching the process as an observer can occasionally be grotesque and evoke feelings of helplessness or dismay.

Although this chapter appears early in the book, it refers to material that is not discussed in detail until many hundreds of pages later. In particular, familiarity with the material in Chapter 5, *The Filesystem*, Chapter 12, *Drivers and the Kernel*, and Chapter 28, *Daemons*, will prove helpful. If your system already boots without any problem, you may want to skip this chapter and come back to it later.

An additional caveat: the booting process is hardware dependent. The information that follows is generically true but may differ from reality for your system.

2.1 BOOTSTRAPPING

Bootstrapping is the nerd word for "starting up a computer." The normal facilities provided by the operating system are not available during the startup process, so the computer must "pull itself up by its own bootstraps." During bootstrapping, the kernel is loaded into memory and begins to execute. A variety of initialization tasks are performed, and the system is then made available to users.

Boot time is a period of special vulnerability. Errors in configuration files, missing or unreliable equipment, and damaged filesystems can all prevent a computer from coming up. Boot configuration is often one of the first tasks an administrator must perform on a new system. Unfortunately, it is also one of the most difficult, and it requires some familiarity with many other aspects of Linux.

When a computer is turned on, it executes boot code that is stored in ROM. That code in turn attempts to figure out how to load and start your kernel. The kernel probes the system's hardware and then spawns the system's **init** process, which is always PID 1.

Several things must happen before a login prompt can appear. Filesystems must be checked and mounted, and system daemons started. These procedures are managed by a series of shell scripts that are run in sequence by **init**. The startup scripts are often referred to as "rc files" because of the way they are named; the "rc" stands for "runcom" or "run command," a historical remnant of the CTSS operating system circa 1965. The exact layout of the startup scripts and the manner in which they are executed vary among systems. We cover the details later in this chapter.

Automatic and manual booting

Linux systems can boot in either automatic mode or manual mode. In automatic mode, the system performs the complete boot procedure on its own, without any external assistance. In manual mode, the system follows the automatic procedure up to a point but then turns control over to an operator before most initialization scripts have been run. At this point, the computer is in "single-user mode." Most system processes are not running, and other users cannot log in.

In day-to-day operation, automatic booting is used almost exclusively. A typical boot procedure for a modern machine is for a user to turn on the power and wait (and wait ...) for the system to come on-line. Nevertheless, it's important to understand the automatic boot procedure and to know how to perform a manual boot. You'll usually have to boot manually when some problem breaks automatic booting, for example, a corrupted filesystem or an improperly configured network interface.

Steps in the boot process

A typical bootstrapping process consists of six distinct phases:

- Loading and initialization of the kernel
- Device detection and configuration
- Creation of spontaneous system processes
- Operator intervention (manual boot only)
- Execution of system startup scripts
- Multiuser operation

Administrators have little control over most of these steps. We effect most bootstrap configuration by editing the system startup scripts.

Kernel initialization

See Chapter 12 for more information about the kernel.

The Linux kernel is itself a program, and the first bootstrapping task is to get this program into memory so that it can be executed. The pathname of the kernel is usually **/vmlinuz** or **/boot/vmlinuz**.

Linux implements a two-stage loading process. During the first stage, the system ROM loads a small boot program into memory from disk. This program then arranges for the kernel to be loaded. This procedure occurs outside the domain of Linux and so is not standardized among systems.

The kernel performs memory tests to find out how much RAM is available. Some of the kernel's internal data structures are statically sized, so the kernel sets aside a fixed amount of real memory for itself when it starts. This memory is reserved for the kernel and cannot be used by user-level processes. The kernel prints on the console a message that reports the total amount of physical memory and the amount available to user processes.

Hardware configuration

One of the kernel's first chores is to check out the machine's environment to see what hardware is present. When you construct a kernel for your system, you tell it what hardware devices it should expect to find; when the kernel begins to execute, it tries to locate and initialize each device that you have told it about. The kernels prints out a line of cryptic information about each devices it finds.

The device information provided at kernel configuration time is often underspecified. In these cases, the kernel tries to determine the other information it needs by probing the bus for devices and asking the appropriate drivers for information. The drivers for devices that are missing or that do not respond to a probe will be disabled. If a device is later connected to the system, it may also be possible to load or enable a driver for it on the fly. See Chapter 12, *Drivers and the Kernel*, for details.

System processes

Once basic initialization is complete, the kernel creates several "spontaneous" processes in user space. They're called spontaneous processes because they are not created through the normal system **fork** mechanism; see page 50 for more details.

The number and nature of the spontaneous processes vary from system to system. Under Linux, there is no visible PID 0. **init** (always process 1) is accompanied by several memory and kernel handler processes typically including **kflushd**, **kupdate**, **kpiod**, and **kswapd**. Of all of these processes, only **init** is really a full-fledged user process. The others are actually portions of the kernel that have been dressed up to look like processes for scheduling or architectural reasons.

Once the spontaneous processes have been created, the kernel's role in bootstrapping is complete. However, none of the processes that handle basic operations (such as accepting logins) have been created, nor have most of the Linux daemons been started. All of these tasks are taken care of (indirectly, in some cases) by **init**.

Operator intervention (manual boot only)

See Chapter 3 for more information about the root account.

If the system is to be brought up in single-user mode, a command-line flag passed in by the kernel notifies **init** of this fact as it starts up. **init** eventually turns control over to **sulogin**, a special neutered-but-rabid version of **login** that prompts for the root password.[1] If you enter the right password, the system will spawn a root shell. You can type <Control-D>[2] instead of a password to bypass single-user mode and continue to multiuser mode.

See Chapter 5 for more information about file-systems and mounting.

From the single-user shell, you can execute commands in much the same way as when logged in on a fully booted system. However, on SuSE and Debian systems, only the root partition is usually mounted; you must mount other filesystems by hand to use programs that don't live in **/bin**, **/sbin**, or **/etc**. Daemons do not normally run in single-user mode, so commands that depend on server processes (e.g., **mail**) will not work correctly.

The **fsck** command is normally run during an automatic boot to check and repair filesystems. When you bring the system up in single-user mode, you may need to run **fsck** by hand. See page 143 for more information about **fsck**.

When the single-user shell exits, the system will attempt to continue booting into multiuser mode.

Execution of startup scripts

By the time the system is ready to run its startup scripts, it is recognizably Linux. Even though it doesn't quite look like a fully booted system yet, there are no more "magic" steps in the boot process. The startup scripts are just normal shell scripts, and they're selected and run by **init** according to an algorithm that, though sometimes tortuous, is relatively comprehensible.

The care, feeding, and taxonomy of startup scripts merits a major section of its own. It's taken up in more detail starting on page 28.

Multiuser operation

See page 110 for more information about the login process.

After the initialization scripts have run, the system is fully operational, except that no one can log in. For logins to be accepted on a particular terminal (including the console), a **getty** process must be listening on it. **init** spawns these **getty** processes directly, completing the boot process. **init** is also responsible for spawning graphical login systems such as **xdm** or **gdm** if the system is set up to use them.

Keep in mind that **init** continues to perform an important role even after bootstrapping is complete. **init** has one single-user and several multiuser "run levels" that determine which of the system's resources are enabled. Run levels are described later in this chapter, starting on page 29.

1. Actually, this isn't always true on Red Hat systems. Depending on the options you provide to the boot loader, you may or may not be prompted for the root password before entering single-user mode.
2. Linux uses <Control-D> as the default end-of-file (EOF) indicator, so typing it at a single-user shell signifies that you have finished executing user commands.

2.2 BOOTING PCS

At this point we've seen the general outline of the boot process. We now revisit several of the more important (and complicated) steps to fill in some additional details relevant to the PC world.

PC booting is a lengthy ordeal that requires quite a bit of background information to explain. If you don't need to deal with PCs, you might want to jump ahead to page 27.

How a PC is different from proprietary hardware

When a machine boots, it begins by executing code stored in ROMs. The exact location and nature of this code varies, depending on the type of machine you have. On a machine designed explicitly for UNIX or another proprietary operating system, the code is typically firmware that knows how to use the devices connected to the machine, how to talk to the network on a basic level, and how to understand disk-based filesystems. Such omniscient firmware is very convenient for system administrators. For example, you can just type in the filename of a new kernel, and the firmware will know how to locate and read that file.

On PCs, this initial boot code is generally called a BIOS (Basic Input/Output System), and it is extremely simplistic compared to the firmware of a proprietary machine. Actually, a PC has several levels of BIOS: one for the machine itself, one for the video card, and one for the SCSI card if the system has one.

The built-in BIOS knows about some of the devices that live on the motherboard, typically the IDE controller (and disks), keyboard, serial ports, and parallel ports. SCSI cards are usually only aware of the devices that are connected to them. Working out the conflicts and interactions among all these various BIOSes can be a real nightmare. In many cases, mass confusion reigns supreme over which BIOS gets to choose what device to try to boot from.

The PC boot process

Modern BIOSes are a little smarter than they used to be. They usually allow you to enter a configuration mode at boot time by holding down one or two special keys; better BIOSes have even hit upon the innovation of telling you what those special keys are so you don't have to look them up in the manual.

The BIOS will normally let you select which devices you want to try to boot from, which sounds more promising than it actually is. You can usually specify something like "Try to boot off the floppy, then try to boot off the CD-ROM, then try to boot off the hard disk." Unfortunately, the BIOS is generally limited to booting from the first IDE CD-ROM drive or the first IDE hard disk. If you have been very, very good over the previous year, Santa might even provide you with a BIOS that acknowledges the existence of SCSI cards.

We would like to offer you some useful guidance for negotiating this quagmire. Alas, it is impossible; this phase of the boot process is entirely under the control of the hardware manufacturers and their wretched BIOSes. You will have to negotiate with them for assistance.

Once your machine has figured out what device to boot from, it will try to load the first 512 bytes of the disk. This 512-byte segment is known as the Master Boot Record or MBR. The MBR contains a program that tells the computer from which disk partition to load a secondary boot program (the "boot loader"). For more information on PC-style disk partitions and the MBR, refer to Chapter 8, *Adding a Disk*.

The default MBR is a simple program that tells the computer to get its boot loader from the first partition on the disk. Linux provides a more sophisticated MBR that knows how to deal with multiple operating systems and kernels.

Once the MBR has chosen the partition to boot from, it tries to load the boot loader specific to that partition. The boot loader is then responsible for loading the kernel.

2.3   BOOT LOADERS: LILO AND GRUB

What would life be like without choices? These days you can choose between two popular boot loaders: LILO and GRUB. LILO is the traditional Linux boot loader; it is very stable and well documented. GRUB is the upstart newcomer; it is both more flexible and more complex.

LILO: the traditional Linux boot loader

LILO comes with almost all Linux distributions, including Red Hat, SuSE, and Debian. Red Hat systems now give you a choice of boot loaders during the installation process. If you're using LILO, the installation scripts will plonk down a copy of LILO with the generic options; you'll have very little say in the process.

LILO can be installed either into the MBR of the disk or into the boot record of the Linux root partition.

LILO is configured and installed with the **lilo** command. **lilo** bases the installed configuration on the contents of the **/etc/lilo.conf** file. To change your boot configuration, you simply update **/etc/lilo.conf** and rerun **lilo**. LILO must be reconfigured every time the boot process changes—in particular, every time you want to add a new boot partition and every time you have a new kernel to boot.

Here's a basic **lilo.conf** file for a Linux system that has both a production kernel and a backup kernel:

```
boot=/dev/hda           # Put boot loader on MBR
root=/dev/hda1          # Specify root partition
install=/boot/boot.b
map=/boot/map
delay=20                # 2 sec for user interrupt
image=/vmlinuz          # Kernel to boot
    label=linux         # Label to refer to this entry
    read-only
```

```
image=/vmlinuz-backup  # Backup entry
    label=backup
    read-only
```

Each possible boot scenario has a label. At boot time, you can tell LILO which one to use by entering the appropriate label. The first label to appear in **lilo.conf** becomes the default.

The default scenario (named linux) boots the file **/vmlinuz**. The read-only tag specifies that the kernel should mount its root filesystem read-only. This option should always be present; the startup scripts will take care of remounting the partition read-write at the appropriate time. This system is also configured to boot a backup kernel, **/vmlinuz-backup**. It's always a good idea to have such an alternate.

Running **lilo** without any arguments will generate and install the boot loader and tell you which entries are available. It puts a star next to the default image. However, if you have made an error in the **lilo.conf** file, **lilo** usually won't discover the problem until halfway through the installation of the boot loader. When this happens, the boot loader is in a confused state. *Do not reboot* until you've run **lilo** successfully. To avoid getting into this situation, you can run **lilo -t** to test the configuration without really installing it. If everything looks kosher, you can then run **lilo** for real. It is something of a mystery why **lilo** does not run this pretest for you by default.

lilo's output when run with the config file above is:

```
# lilo
Added linux*
Added backup
```

When the system boots, LILO prints the following prompt:

```
LILO:
```

It then waits 2 seconds (20 tenths of a second, set with the delay tag), then boots the **/vmlinuz** kernel and mounts the first partition of the first IDE disk as the root partition. You can see a list of defined boot scenarios by pressing the <Tab> key:

```
LILO: <Tab>
linux   backup
LILO:
```

To boot using an alternate scenario, just enter its label at the prompt.

GRUB: the GRand Unified Boot loader

GRUB is a complete replacement for LILO. It's a common aftermarket option that can be added to any Linux system; it also receives official support from Red Hat. GRUB is particularly popular among users who run a variety of operating systems (such as Windows, OpenBSD, FreeBSD, etc.) on the same machine or who are actively working on kernel development.

GRUB is also useful for folks who change their system configuration frequently. Unlike LILO, which must be reinstalled into the boot record or MBR every time you change the **lilo.conf** file, GRUB reads its configuration file on the fly at boot time, eliminating an extra step.

You install GRUB on your boot drive by running **grub-install**. This command takes the name of the device from which you'll be booting as an argument. Unfortunately, GRUB has its own way of naming physical disk devices which is very different from the standard Linux convention. A GRUB device name looks like this:

```
(hd0,0)
```

The first numeric value indicates the physical drive number (starting from zero), and the second numeric value represents the partition number (again, starting from zero). In this example (hd0,0) is equivalent to the Linux device **/dev/hda1**. Ergo, if you wanted to install GRUB on your primary drive, you would use the command

```
grub-install '(hd0,0)'
```

The quotes are necessary to prevent the shell from trying to interpret the parentheses in its own special way.

By default, GRUB reads its default boot configuration from **/boot/grub/grub.conf**. Here's a sample **grub.conf** file:

```
default=0
timeout=10
splashimage=(hd0,0)/boot/grub/splash.xpm.gz
title Red Hat Linux (2.4.7-10)
        root (hd0,0)
        kernel /boot/vmlinuz-2.4.7-10 ro root=/dev/hda1
```

This example configures only a single operating system, which GRUB will boot automatically (default=0) if it doesn't receive any keyboard input within 10 seconds (timeout=10). The root filesystem for the "Red Hat Linux" configuration is the GRUB device (hd0,0). GRUB will load the kernel from **/boot/vmlinuz-2.4.7-10** and display a splash screen from the file **/boot/grub/splash.xpm.gz** when it is loaded.

Multibooting on PCs

Since many operating systems run on PCs, it is fairly common practice to set up a machine to be able to boot several different systems. To make this work, you need to configure a boot loader to recognize all of the different operating systems on your disks. In the next few sections, we cover some common multiboot stumbling blocks and then review some example configurations.

Every disk partition can have its own second-stage boot loader. However, there is only one MBR. When setting up a multiboot configuration, you must decide which boot loader is going to be the "master." For better or worse, your choice will often be dictated by the vagaries of the operating systems involved. LILO and GRUB are the best options for a system that has a Linux partition. The exceptions to this rule are Windows NT and 2000, which sometimes need to have their own boot loader in the

MBR. We know of systems on which LILO or GRUB can boot Windows from the MBR; we also know of cases in which this just doesn't work.

Note that GRUB really is superior to LILO in this particular situation. It may be worth your time to install GRUB in the hope of minimizing multiboot headaches.

Multibooting gotchas

Installing a multiboot system can make you tear your hair out. This section is meant to prevent you from going bald.

If you're installing a multiboot system that includes a consumer version of Windows (95, 98, or Me), always install Windows before you install anything else. The consumer versions of Windows are very stupid and have no idea that other operating systems may exist on the same machine. They will always want to take partition 1 on your first hard disk and will overwrite other boot loaders during installation.

The same rule applies to Windows NT/2000: always install Windows first. The reasons are slightly different, but the upshot is the same. The NT/2000 boot loader really, really wants to be installed in the MBR and be the One True Boot Loader for the system. Resistance is futile.

To get the NT/2000 boot loader to boot a Linux partition, install Linux and then boot to it using a floppy or CD-ROM. You'll need to peel off the first 512 bytes of the Linux partition (this is the partition boot record), and write them to a file. You can do this with the **dd** command. Here is an example:

```
# dd if=/dev/hda2 of=linux.bin bs=512 count=1
```

*The **mtools** suite of commands is handy for moving files between the Linux and Windows environments.*

You must then copy this file to the NT/2000 partition and add an entry to the NT boot loader configuration that tells it how to boot using this file. We don't describe the NT boot loader in this book, but all you really have to do is add to **C:\boot.ini** a line that contains the file's path along with a label. For Linux, the line would look something like this:

```
C:\linux.bin="Linux"
```

For more information about the format of the **boot.ini** file, see the on-line Microsoft Knowledge Base at support.microsoft.com.

If Linux and Windows NT/2000 are cohabiting and you're using LILO as your boot loader, you will need to install LILO onto Linux's disk partition because the MBR is already spoken for. Point the boot line in the **lilo.conf** file to your Linux partition to make this change. For example, if Linux were on the second partition of the first IDE hard disk, the line would be

```
boot=/dev/hda2
```

You'll need to make this change *before* you copy the second-stage boot loader to a file and transfer it to the NT partition. In fact, you will need to repeat the entire process whenever you rerun **lilo**.

LILO multiboot configuration

To configure a multiboot system that uses LILO in the MBR (e.g., Linux with Windows 98), begin with the standard LILO configuration as outlined on page 23. You can then go back and add entries for the other operating systems to **/etc/lilo.conf**.

Here's the **lilo.conf** entry you need to boot Windows from the first partition of your first IDE disk:

```
other = /dev/hda1
label = windows
table = /dev/hda
```

A complete **lilo.conf** file that boots Windows from partition 1, Linux from partition 2, and FreeBSD from partition 3 would look something like this:

```
boot = /dev/hda          # install on the MBR of 1st IDE drive
delay = 20               # Wait 2 sec. for user's boot choice
default = linux          # If no input, boot linux from 2nd partition
image = /boot/vmlinuz-2.4.17
    root = /dev/hda2
    label = linux
    read-only
other = /dev/hda1        # boot from 1st partition
    label = windows
    table = /dev/hda
other = /dev/hda3        # boot from 3rd partition
    label = freebsd
    table = /dev/hda
```

You'll need to rerun **lilo** after putting these entries into **lilo.conf**. Remember to run **lilo -t** first to test the config file. See page 135 for more partitioning information.

If you find yourself backed into a corner, an alternate multiboot plan is to let the "other" operating system have all the good boot block spaces and boot your Linux partition from a floppy.

2.4 BOOTING SINGLE-USER MODE

You'll usually enter Linux's single-user mode through LILO. How you reach the LILO prompt varies based on the exact hardware of your system. If you're using standard PC hardware, you can reach the LILO prompt by selecting the "command line" option from the fancy full-color boot screen on Red Hat and SuSE systems. On Debian systems, hold down the Shift key immediately after the system has finished its self-test and memory checks.

At the LILO prompt, enter the label of the configuration you want to boot (as specified in **lilo.conf**) followed by **-s** or **single**. For example, the default configuration shipped with Red Hat is called "linux", so to boot that configuration into single-user mode, you'd use

```
LILO: linux single
```

LILO accepts a variety of other command-line options; Table 2.1 shows examples.

Table 2.1 **Examples of LILO's boot time options**

Option	Meaning
root=/dev/foo	Tells the kernel to use **/dev/foo** as the root device
single	Boots to single-user mode
init=/sbin/init	Tells the kernel to use **/sbin/init** as its **init** program
ether=0,0,eth1	Makes the kernel probe for a second Ethernet card
init=/bin/bash	Starts only the **bash** shell; useful for emergency recovery

As a precautionary measure against a possibly unstable system,[3] the filesystem root directory starts off being mounted read-only. This may be counterproductive to your mission if you're trying to fix a problem with a configuration file or command that lives in the root filesystem, or if you need to execute a command that modifies files. To fix this problem, you'll have to begin your single-user session by remounting **/** in read/write mode. The command **mount -o remount -w /** should do the trick.

2.5 STARTUP SCRIPTS

After you exit from single-user mode (or, in the automated boot sequence, at the point at which the single-user shell would have run), **init** executes the system startup scripts. These scripts are really just garden-variety shell scripts that are interpreted by **sh** (well, **bash**, really). The exact location, content, and organization of the scripts vary considerably from system to system.

Some tasks that are often performed in the startup scripts are:

- Setting the name of the computer
- Setting the time zone
- Checking the disks with **fsck** (only in automatic mode)
- Mounting the system's disks
- Removing old files from the **/tmp** directory
- Configuring network interfaces
- Starting up daemons and network services

Most startup scripts are quite verbose and print out a description of everything they are doing. This loquacity can be a tremendous help if the system hangs midway through booting or if you are trying to locate an error in one of the scripts.

On systems of yore, it was common practice to modify startup scripts to make them do the right thing for a particular environment. These days, the scripts supplied with your operating system should be general enough to handle most any configuration. Instead of putting the details of your local configuration in the code of the scripts,

---

3. And against clueless users impersonating a system administrator.

you put them in a separate configuration file (or set of files) that the scripts consult. The config files are normally just mini **sh** scripts that the startup scripts include to define the values of certain shell variables.

init and run levels

Traditionally, **init** defines 7 run levels, each of which represents a particular complement of services that the system should be running:

- Level 0 is the level in which the system is completely shut down.
- Level 1 or S represents single-user mode.
- Levels 2 through 5 are multiuser levels.
- Level 6 is a "reboot" level.

Levels 0 and 6 are special in that the system can't actually remain in them; it shuts down or reboots as a side effect of entering them. On most systems, the normal multiuser run level is 2 or 3. Run level 5 is often used for X Windows login processes such as **xdm**. Run level 4 is rarely used, and run levels 1 and S are defined differently on each system.

Single-user mode was traditionally **init** level 1. It brought down all multiuser and remote login processes and made sure the system was running a minimal complement of software. Since single-user mode provides root access to the system, however, administrators wanted the system to prompt for the root password whenever it was booted into single-user mode. The S run level was created to address this need: it spawns a process that prompts for the root password. On Linux, the S level serves only this purpose and is not a destination in itself.

There seem to be more run levels defined than are strictly necessary or useful. The usual explanation for this is that a phone switch had 7 run levels, so it was thought that a UNIX system should have at least that many. Linux actually supports up to 10 run levels, but levels 7 through 9 are undefined.

The **/etc/inittab** file tells **init** what to do at each of its run levels. Its format varies from system to system, but the basic idea is that **inittab** defines commands that are to be run (or kept running) when the system enters each level.

As the machine boots, **init** ratchets its way up from run level 0 to the default run level set in **/etc/inittab**. To accomplish the transition between each pair of adjacent run levels, **init** runs the actions spelled out for that transition in **/etc/inittab**. The same progression is made in reverse order when the machine is shut down.

Unfortunately, the semantics of the **inittab** file are somewhat rudimentary. To map the facilities of the **inittab** file into something a bit more flexible, Linux systems implement an additional layer of abstraction in the form of a "change run levels" script (usually **/etc/init.d/rc**) that's called from **inittab**. This script in turn executes other scripts from a run-level-dependent directory to bring the system to its new state.

It's usually not necessary for system administrators to deal directly with **/etc/inittab** because the script-based interface is adequate for almost any application. In the remainder of this chapter, we will tacitly ignore the **inittab** file and the other glue that attaches **init** to the execution of startup scripts. Just keep in mind that when we say that **init** runs such-and-such a script, the connection may not be quite so direct.

The master copies of the startup scripts live in the **/etc/init.d** directory. Each script is responsible for one daemon or one particular aspect of the system. The scripts understand the arguments **start** and **stop** to mean that the service they deal with should be initialized or halted. Most also understand **restart**, which is typically the same as a **stop** followed by a **start**. As a system administrator, you can manually start and stop individual services by running their associated **init.d** scripts by hand.

For example, here's a simple startup script that can start, stop, or restart **sshd**:

```
#! /bin/sh
test -f /usr/local/sbin/sshd || exit 0
case "$1" in
    start)
        echo -n "Starting sshd: sshd"
        /usr/local/sbin/sshd
        echo "."
        ;;
    stop)
        echo -n "Stopping sshd: sshd"
        kill `cat /var/run/sshd.pid`
        echo "."
        ;;
    restart)
        echo -n "Stopping sshd: sshd"
        kill `cat /var/run/sshd.pid`
        echo "."
        echo -n "Starting sshd: sshd"
        /usr/local/sbin/sshd
        echo "."
        ;;
    *)
        echo "Usage: /etc/init.d/sshd start|stop|restart"
        exit 1
        ;;
esac
```

Although the scripts in **/etc/init.d** can start and stop individual services, the master control script run by **init** needs additional information about which scripts to run (and with what arguments) to enter any given run level. Instead of looking directly at the **init.d** directory when it takes the system to a new run level, the master script looks at a directory called **rc***level***.d**, where *level* is the run level to be entered (e.g., **rc0.d**, **rc1.d**, and so on).

These **rc***level***.d** directories typically contain symbolic links that point back to the scripts in the **init.d** directory. The names of these symbolic links all start with **S** or **K** followed by a number and the name of the service that the script controls (e.g.,

Booting

S34named). When **init** transitions from a lower run level to a higher one, it runs all the scripts that start with **S** in ascending numerical order with the argument **start**. When **init** transitions from a higher run level to a lower one, it runs all the scripts that start with **K** (for "kill") in descending numerical order with the argument **stop**. Depending on the system, **init** may look only at the **rc***level***.d** directory appropriate for the new run level, or it may also look at the **rc***level***.d** directory for the old run level to see what the differences are.

To tell the system when to start a daemon, you must place symbolic links into the appropriate directory. Most systems seem to start the majority of their networking daemons during run level 2. For example, to tell the system to start **sshd** during run level 2 and to stop the daemon nicely before shutting down, the following pair of links would suffice:

```
# ln -s /etc/init.d/sshd /etc/rc2.d/S99sshd
# ln -s /etc/init.d/sshd /etc/rc0.d/K25sshd
```

The first line tells the system to run the **/etc/init.d/sshd** startup script as one of the last things to do when entering run level 2 and to run the script with the **start** argument. The second line tells the system to run **/etc/init.d/sshd** relatively late when shutting down the system and to run the script with the **stop** argument. Some systems treat shutdown and reboot differently, so we will have to put a symlink in the **/etc/rc6.d/** directory as well to make sure the daemon shuts down properly when the system is rebooted.

Red Hat startup scripts

 Startup scripts are one of the things that distinguish Linux distributions from each other. Red Hat's are a complicated mess; they contain many comments such as

```
# stupid hack, but it should work
```

and

```
# this is broken!
```

At each run level, **init** invokes the script **/etc/rc.d/rc** with the new run level as an argument. **/etc/rc.d/rc** usually runs in "normal" mode, in which it just does its thing, but it can also run in "confirmation" mode, in which it asks you before it runs each individual startup script. Use the **chkconfig** command to manage the links in the run-level directories.

Red Hat also has an **rc.local** script much like that found on BSD systems. **rc.local** is the last script run as part of the startup process. It's best to avoid adding your own customizations to **rc.local** because this file gets overwritten by the install scripts.

Here's an example of a Red Hat startup session:

```
[kernel information]
INIT: version 2.77 booting
           Welcome to Red Hat Linux
         Press 'I' to enter interactive startup.
```

```
Mounting proc filesystem                            [  OK  ]
Setting clock  (utc): Fri Feb 15 07:16:41 MST 2002  [  OK  ]
Loading default keymap                              [  OK  ]
Activating swap partitions                          [  OK  ]
...
```

Once you see the "Welcome to Red Hat Linux" message, you can press the 'i' key to enter confirmation mode. Unfortunately, Red Hat gives you no confirmation that you have pressed the right key. It blithely continues to mount local filesystems, activate swap partitions, load keymaps, and locate its kernel modules. Only after it switches to run level 3 will it actually start to prompt you for confirmation:

```
                   Welcome to Red Hat Linux
               Press 'I' to enter interactive startup.
Mounting proc filesystem                              [  OK  ]
Setting clock  (utc): Fri Feb 15 07:16:41 MST 2002    [  OK  ]
Loading default keymap                                [  OK  ]
Activating swap partitions                            [  OK  ]
Setting hostname redhat.synack.net                    [  OK  ]
Checking root filesystem
/dev/hda1: clean, 73355/191616 files, 214536/383032 blocks [  OK  ]
Remounting root filesystem in read-write mode         [  OK  ]
Finding module dependencies                           [  OK  ]
Checking filesystems                                  [  OK  ]
Mounting local filesystems                            [  OK  ]
Turning on user and group quotas for local filesystems [  OK  ]
Enabling swap space                                   [  OK  ]
INIT: Entering runlevel: 3
Entering interactive startup
Start service kudzu (Y)es/(N)o/(C)ontinue? [Y]
```

Interactive startup and single-user mode both begin at the same spot in the booting process. When the startup process is so broken that you cannot reach this point safely, you can use a rescue floppy to boot.

You can also pass the argument **init=/bin/sh** to LILO to trick it into running a single-user shell before **init** even starts.[4] If you take this tack, you will have to do all the startup housekeeping by hand, including manually **fsck**ing and mounting the local filesystems.

Most configuration of Red Hat's boot process should be achieved through manipulation of the config files in **/etc/sysconfig**. Table 2.2 summarizes the function of the items in the **/etc/sysconfig** directory.

Several of the items in Table 2.2 merit additional comments:

- The **hwconf** file contains all of your hardware information. The obnoxious Kudzu service checks it to see if you have added or removed any hardware

---

4. We once had a corrupted keymap file, and since the keymap file is loaded even in single-user mode, single-user was useless. Setting **init=/bin/sh** was the only way to boot the system to a usable single-user state to fix the problem. This can also be a useful trick in other situations.

Table 2.2   Files and subdirectories of Red Hat's /etc/sysconfig directory

File/Dir	Function or contents
apmd	Lists arguments for the Advanced Power Management Daemon
clock	Specifies the type of clock that the system has (almost always UTC)[a]
console	A mysterious directory that is always empty
hwconf	Contains all of the system's hardware info. Used by Kudzu.
i18n	Contains the system's local settings (date formats, languages, etc.)
init	Configures the way messages from the startup scripts are displayed
keyboard	Sets keyboard type (use "us" for the standard 101-key U.S. keyboard)
mouse	Sets the mouse type. Used by X Windows and **gpm**.
network	Sets global network options (hostname, gateway, forwarding, etc.)
network-scripts	A directory that contains accessory scripts and network config files
pcmcia	Tells whether to start PCMCIA daemons and specifies options
sendmail	Sets options for **sendmail**

a. If you multiboot your PC, all bets are off as to how the clock's time zone should be set.

and asks you what to do about changes. You will probably want to disable this service on a production system because it delays the boot process whenever it detects a change to the hardware configuration, resulting in an extra 30 seconds of downtime for every hardware change made.

- The **network-scripts** directory contains additional material related to network configuration. The only things you should ever need to change are the files named **ifcfg-***interface*. For example, **network-scripts/ifcfg-eth0** contains the configuration parameters for the interface eth0. It sets the interface's IP address and networking options. See page 266 for more information about configuring network interfaces.

- The **sendmail** file contains two variables: DAEMON and QUEUE. If the DAEMON variable is set to yes, the system starts **sendmail** in daemon mode (**-bd**) when the system boots. QUEUE tells **sendmail** how long to wait between queue runs (**-q**); the default is one hour.

SuSE startup scripts

Startup scripts are one area in which SuSE really outshines the other Linux variants. SuSE's startup scripts are well organized, robust, and well documented. The folks that maintain this part of the operating system deserve a gold star.

At each run level, **init** invokes the script **/etc/init.d/rc** with the new run level as an argument. **/etc/rc.config** (which is normally maintained by SuSE's GUI administration tool, YaST) provides the individual startup scripts with configuration data in the form of environment variables. For subsystems that require extraordinary amounts of configuration, individual files in **/etc/rc.config.d** provide the needed parameters.

Booting

The **/etc/rc.config** file is rich with options that you can customize to your particular situation. Basic system parameters such as the hostname and network interfaces (with their associated IP addresses) are defined in this file:

```
FQHOSTNAME="inura.toadranch.com"
IPADDR_0="192.168.1.101"
NETDEV_0="eth0"
IFCONFIG_0="192.168.1.101 broadcast 192.168.1.255 netmask 255.255.255.0
```

There are also options that specify which daemons to start. Helpful tips for most options are provided by the surrounding comments; for example,

```
# start routed (for dynamic routing - see man routed) (yes/no)
# ATTENTION:  starting routed causes net traffic every 30 seconds.
# If your host is connected to internet via dial-up it makes absolutely
# no sense to activate it.
#
START_ROUTED="no"
```

There are also a number of security-related options in the **/etc/rc.config** file that you should examine to determine if they apply to your environment. See Chapter 21, *Security*, for more information about securing your system.

```
# If you want to allow root logins from other machines, set
# ROOT_LOGIN_REMOTE to "yes".
#
ROOT_LOGIN_REMOTE="no"
```

Whether you choose to use YaST or maintain your startup scripts by hand, it's a good idea to look through **/etc/rc.config** and ponder its contents.

Here's what a typical SuSE boot session looks like (this one from an older release):

```
[kernel information]
Inspecting /boot/System.map-2.2.18
Loaded 10080 symbols from /boot/System.map-2.2.18.
Symbols match kernel version 2.2.18.
Loaded 51 symbols from 1 module.
klogd 1.3-3, log source = ksyslog started.
<4>Linux version 2.2.18 (root@Pentium.suse.de) (gcc version 2.95.2 19991024
    (release)) #1 Wed Jan 24 12:28:55 GMT 2001
Checking file systems...
Parallelizing fsck version 1.19a (13-Jul-2000)
/dev/hda3: clean, 105679/2424832 files, 482130/4847613 blocks
/dev/hda1: clean, 31/6024 files, 4052/24066 blocks
Setting up the CMOS clock                              done
Mounting local file systems...
proc on /proc type proc (rw)
devpts on /dev/pts type devpts (rw,mode=0620,gid=5)
/dev/hda1 on /boot type ext2 (rw)                      done
Setting up timezone data                               done
Setting up loopback device                             done
Setting up hostname                                    done
```

```
Configuring serial ports                                        done
Running /etc/init.d/boot.local                                  done
```

As you can see, SuSE runs **/etc/init.d/boot.local** as the last script in the startup process. We don't recommend that you put commands in this file.

Debian startup scripts

If SuSE is the ultimate example of a well-designed, well-executed plan for the management of startup scripts, Debian is the exact opposite. The Debian scripts are fragile, undocumented, and unbelievably inconsistent. Sadly, it appears that the lack of a standard way of setting up scripts has resulted in chaos in this case. Bad Debian!

At each run level, **init** invokes the script **/etc/init.d/rc** with the new run level as an argument. Each script is responsible for finding its own configuration information, which may be in the form of other files in **/etc**, a subdirectory of **/etc**, or somewhere in the script itself.

If you're looking for the hostname of the system, it's stored in **/etc/hostname**, which is read by the **/etc/init.d/hostname.sh** script. Network interface and default gateway parameters are stored in **/etc/network/interfaces**, which is read by the **ifup** command called from **/etc/init.d/networking**. Some network options can also be set in **/etc/network/options**.

Good luck.

2.6 REBOOTING AND SHUTTING DOWN

Linux filesystems buffer changes in memory and write them back to disk only sporadically. This scheme makes disk I/O faster, but it also makes the filesystem more susceptible to data loss when the system is rudely halted.

Traditional UNIX and Linux machines were very touchy about how they were shut down. Modern systems have become less sensitive (especially when you use a robust filesystem such as ext3fs), but it is always a good idea to shut down the machine nicely when possible. Improper shutdown can result in anything from subtle, insidious problems to a major catastrophe.

On consumer-oriented operating systems, rebooting the operating system is an appropriate first course of treatment for almost any problem. On a Linux system, it's better to think first and reboot second. Linux problems tend to be subtler and more complex, so blindly rebooting is effective in a smaller percentage of cases. Linux systems also take a long time to boot, and multiple users may be inconvenienced.

You may need to reboot when you add a new piece of hardware or when an existing piece of hardware becomes so confused that it cannot be reset. If you modify a configuration file that's used only at boot time, you must reboot to make your changes take effect. If the system is so wedged that you cannot log in to make a proper diagnosis of the problem, you obviously have no alternative but to reboot.

Some things can be changed and fixed without rebooting, but whenever you modify a startup script, you should reboot just to make sure that the system will come back up successfully.

Unlike bootstrapping, which can be done in essentially only one way, there are a number of ways to shut down or reboot. They are:

- Turning off the power
- Using the **shutdown** command
- Using the **halt** and **reboot** commands
- Using **telinit** to change **init**'s run level
- Using the **poweroff** command to tell the system to turn off the power

Turning off the power

Even on a small Linux system, turning off the power is not a good way to shut down. You can potentially lose data and leave the system's files in an inconsistent state.

Some machines have a "soft power switch," which means that when you press the power button, the machine actually runs some commands to perform a proper shutdown sequence. If you're not sure whether your machine provides this feature, don't poke the power button to find out! It's better to run the shutdown sequence yourself.

That said, however, powering off is not the end of the world. In the event of a flood or fire, it's OK to turn off the power if you can't afford the time to bring machines down gracefully. Old-style machine rooms often had a panic button that turned everything off at once. Our sysadmins once triggered it with a poorly aimed Nerf football. (Don't ask!)

shutdown: the genteel way to halt the system

shutdown is the safest, most considerate, and most thorough way to initiate a halt or reboot or to return to single-user mode.

You can ask **shutdown** to wait a while before bringing down the system. During the waiting period, **shutdown** sends messages (a la **wall**) to logged-in users at progressively shorter intervals, warning them of the impending downtime. By default, the warnings simply say that the system is being shut down and give the time remaining until the event; you can also supply a short message of your own. Your message should tell why the system is being brought down and should estimate how long it will be before users can log in again (e.g., "back at 11:00 a.m."). Users cannot log in when a **shutdown** is imminent, but they will see your message if you specified one.

shutdown lets you specify whether the machine should halt (**-h**) or reboot (**-r**) after the shutdown is complete. You can also specify whether you want to forcibly **fsck** the disks after a reboot (**-F**) or not (**-f**). By default, Linux automatically skips the **fsck** checks whenever the filesystems were properly unmounted.

For example, a **shutdown** command that reminds users of scheduled maintenance and halts the system at 9:30 a.m. would look something like this:

```
shutdown -h 09:30 "Going down for scheduled maintenance"
```

It's also possible to specify a relative shutdown time. For example, the following command will effect a shutdown 15 minutes from when it is run:

```
shutdown -h +15 "Going down for emergency disk repair."
```

halt: a simpler way to shut down

The **halt** command performs the essential duties required to bring the system down. It is called by **shutdown -h** but can also be used by itself. **halt** logs the shutdown, kills nonessential processes, executes the **sync** system call (called by and equivalent to the **sync** command), waits for filesystem writes to complete, and then halts the kernel.

halt -n prevents the **sync** call. It's used by **fsck** after it repairs the root partition. If **fsck** did not use **-n**, the kernel might overwrite **fsck**'s repairs with old versions of the superblock that were cached in memory.

reboot: quick and dirty restart

reboot is almost identical to **halt**, but it causes the machine to reboot instead of halting. **reboot** is called by **shutdown -r**. Like **halt**, it supports the **-n** flag.

telinit: change init's run level

You can use **telinit** to direct **init** to go to a specific run level. For example,

```
# telinit 1
```

takes the system to single-user mode.

When you use **telinit**, you do not get the nice warning messages or grace period that you get with **shutdown**, so most of the time you'll probably want to avoid it. **telinit** is most useful for testing changes to the **inittab** file.

poweroff: ask Linux to turn off the power

The **poweroff** command is identical to **halt**, except that after Linux has been shut down, **poweroff** sends a request to the power management system (on systems that have one) to turn off the system's main power. This feature makes it easy to turn off machines remotely (for example, during an electrical storm).

Unfortunately, there is no corresponding **poweron** command. The reason for this apparent oversight is left as an exercise for the reader.

2.7 Exercises

E2.1 Why is it important to run **lilo -t** before installing the LILO boot loader? How do you boot a kernel named something other than **vmlinuz**?

E2.2 Why shouldn't a Linux system be turned off with the power button on the computer case? What are some of the alternatives?

E2.3 If you trip over a power cord and crash your Linux system, what steps are necessary to get it up and happy again?

★ **E2.4** Explain the concept of run levels. List the run levels defined in Linux, and provide a short description of each. What is the relationship between run level 1 and run level S?

★ **E2.5** What is bootstrapping? List the steps involved and discuss what happens at each stage.

★ **E2.6** Write a startup script to start the "foo" daemon (**/usr/local/sbin/foo**), a network service. Show how you would glue it into the system to start automatically at boot time.

★ **E2.7** Obtain and install the **mactime** program by Dan Farmer and Wietse Venema (part of the TCT toolkit; see page 670). Run **mactime** to create an initial database of the time stamps associated with your system files. Reboot the machine. Run **mactime** again and determine which files have been modified by booting the machine. Which files were accessed but not modified? (Requires root access.)

★★ **E2.8** If a system is at run level 4 and you run the command **telinit 1**, what steps will be taken by **init**? What will be the final result of the command?

★★ **E2.9** Draw a dependency graph that shows which daemons must be started before other daemons on your Linux system.

★★ **E2.10** List in order the steps used to create a working multi-OS system that includes Linux and Windows XP (or Windows 2000). Use GRUB and the Windows boot loader.

3 *Rootly Powers*

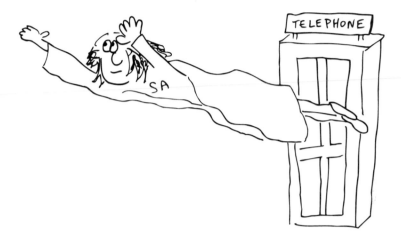

Every file and process on a Linux system is owned by a particular user account. Other users can't access these objects without the owner's permission, so this convention helps protect users against one another's misdeeds, both intentional and accidental.

System files and processes are owned by a fictitious user called "root", also known as the superuser. As with any account, root's property is protected against interference from other users. To make administrative changes, you'll need to use one of the methods of accessing the root account described in this chapter.

The root account has several "magic" properties. Root can act as the owner of any file or process. Root can also perform several special operations that are off-limits to other users. The account is both very powerful and, in untrained or malicious hands, very dangerous.

This chapter introduces the basics of superuser access for administrators. Chapter 21, *Security*, describes how to avoid unwanted and embarrassing superuser access by others. Chapter 29, *Policy and Politics* covers the relevant political and administrative aspects.

3.1 OWNERSHIP OF FILES AND PROCESSES

Every file has both an owner and a "group owner." The owner of the file enjoys one special privilege that is not shared with everyone on the system: the ability to modify the permissions of the file. In particular, the owner can set the permissions on a file so restrictively that no one else can access it.[1] We take up the subject of file permissions in Chapter 5, *The Filesystem*.

*See page 85 for
more information
about groups.*

Although the owner of a file is always a single person, many people can be group owners of the file, as long as they are all part of a single Linux group. Groups are defined in the **/etc/group** file.

The owner of a file gets to specify what the group owners can do with it. This scheme allows files to be shared among members of the same project. For example, we use a group to control access to the source files for the www.admin.com web site.

Both ownerships of a file can be determined with **ls -l** *filename*. For example:

```
% ls -l /staff/scott/todo
-rw-------  1 scott  staff  1258 Jun 4 18:15  /staff/scott/todo
```

This file is owned by the user "scott" and the group "staff."

Linux actually keeps track of owners and groups as numbers rather than as text names. User identification numbers (UIDs for short) are mapped to user names in the **/etc/passwd** file, and group identification numbers (GIDs) are mapped to group names in **/etc/group**.[2] The text names that correspond to UIDs and GIDs are defined only for the convenience of the system's human users. When commands such as **ls** want to display ownership information in a human-readable format, they must look up each name in the appropriate file or database.

Processes have not two but four identities associated with them: a real and effective UID and a real and effective GID. The "real" numbers are used for accounting, and the "effective" numbers are used for the determination of access permissions. Normally, the real and effective numbers are the same. The owner of a process can send the process signals (see page 51) and can also reduce (degrade) the process's scheduling priority.

*See page 73 for more
information about
permission bits.*

While it is not normally possible for a process to alter its four ownership credentials, there is a special situation in which the effective user and group IDs can be changed. When a command is executed that has its "setuid" or "setgid" permissions bit set, the effective UID or GID of the resulting process can be set to the UID or GID of the file containing the program image rather than the UID and GID of the user that ran the command. The user's privileges are thus "promoted" for the execution of that specific command only.

Linux's setuid facility allows programs run by ordinary users to make use of the root account in a limited and tightly controlled way. For example, the **passwd** command that users run to change their login password is a setuid program. It modifies the **/etc/shadow** (or **/etc/passwd**) file in a well-defined way and then terminates. Of

---

1. In fact, the permissions can be set so restrictively that even the owner of a file cannot access it, a feature that is actually more useful than it may seem.
2. Some systems no longer store this information in text files. See Chapter 18, *Sharing System Files*, for more information.

course, even this limited task has potential for abuse, so **passwd** requires users to prove that they know the current account password before it agrees to make the requested change.

3.2 THE SUPERUSER

The defining characteristic of the root account is its UID of 0. Linux does not prevent you from changing the username on this account or from creating additional accounts whose UIDs are 0, but both actions are very bad ideas. Such changes have a tendency to create inadvertent breaches of system security. They also engender confusion and scorn when other people have to deal with the strange way you've configured your system.

Linux permits the superuser (that is, any process whose effective UID is 0) to perform any valid operation on any file or process.[3] In addition, some system calls (requests to the kernel) can be executed only by the superuser. Some examples of such restricted operations are:

- Changing the root directory of a process with **chroot**
- Creating device files
- Setting the system clock
- Raising resource usage limits and process priorities
- Setting the system's hostname
- Configuring network interfaces
- Opening privileged network ports (those numbered below 1,024)
- Shutting down the system

An example of superuser powers is the ability of a process owned by root to change its UID and GID. The **login** program and its window system equivalents are a case in point; the process that prompts you for your password when you log in to the system initially runs as root. If the password and username that you enter are legitimate, the login program changes its UID and GID to your UID and GID and starts up your user environment. Once a root process has changed its ownerships to become a normal user process, it can't recover its former privileged state.

3.3 CHOOSING A ROOT PASSWORD

See page 667 for more information about password cracking.

The root password should be at least eight characters in length; seven-character passwords are substantially easier to crack. On systems that use DES passwords, it doesn't help to use a password longer than eight characters because only the first eight are significant. See the section *Encrypted password* starting on page 83 for information about how to enable MD5 passwords, which can be longer than eight characters.

---

3. "Valid" is an important weasel word here. Certain operations (such as executing a file on which the execute permission bit is not set) are forbidden even to the superuser.

It's important that the root password be selected so as not to be easily guessed or discovered by trial and error. In theory, the most secure type of password consists of a random sequence of letters, punctuation, and digits. But because this type of password is hard to remember and usually difficult to type, it may not be optimally secure if administrators write it down or type it slowly.

Until recently, a password consisting of two randomly selected words separated by a punctuation mark was a pretty good compromise between security and memorability. Unfortunately, such passwords can now be cracked fairly quickly; we now advise against this scheme.

These days, we suggest that you form a root password by boiling down a phrase of "shocking nonsense," defined by Grady Ward in an earlier version of the PGP Passphrase FAQ:

> *"Shocking nonsense" means to make up a short phrase or sentence that is both nonsensical and shocking in the culture of the user. That is, it contains grossly obscene, racist, impossible or otherwise extreme juxtapositions of ideas. This technique is permissible because the passphrase, by its nature, is never revealed to anyone with sensibilities to offend.*
>
> *Shocking nonsense is unlikely to be duplicated anywhere because it does not describe a matter of fact that could be accidentally rediscovered by someone else. The emotional evocation makes it difficult for the creator to forget. A mild example of such shocking nonsense might be, "Mollusks peck my galloping genitals." The reader can undoubtedly make up many far more shocking or entertaining examples for him or herself.*

You can reduce such a phrase to a password by recording only the first letter of each word or by some similar transformation. Password security will be increased enormously if you include numbers, punctuation marks, and capital letters.

You should change the root password

- At least every three months or so
- Every time someone who knows the password leaves your site
- Whenever you think security may have been compromised
- On a day you're not planning to party so hard in the evening that you will have forgotten the password the next morning

3.4 BECOMING ROOT

Since root is just another user, you can log in directly to the root account. However, this turns out to be a bad idea. To begin with, it leaves no record of what operations were performed as root. That's bad enough when you realize that you broke something last night at 3:00 a.m. and can't remember what you changed; it's even worse when an access was unauthorized and you are trying to figure out what an intruder has done to your system. Another disadvantage is that the log-in-as-root scenario leaves no record of who was really doing the work. If several people have access to the root account, you won't be able to tell who used it when.

For these reasons, most systems allow root logins to be disabled on terminals and across the network—everywhere but on the system console. We suggest that you use these features. See *Secure terminals* on page 661 to find out what file you need to edit on your particular system.

su: substitute user identity

A slightly better way to access the root account is to use the **su** command. If invoked without any arguments, **su** will prompt for the root password and then start up a root shell. The privileges of this shell remain in effect until the shell terminates (by <Control-D> or the **exit** command). **su** doesn't record the commands executed as root, but it does create a log entry that states who became root and when.

The **su** command can also substitute identities other than root. Sometimes, the only way to reproduce or debug a user's problem is to **su** to their account so that you re-produce the environment in which the problem occurs.

If you know someone's password, you can access that person's account directly by executing **su** *username*. As with an **su** to root, you will be prompted for the pass-word for *username*. You can also first **su** to root and then **su** to another account; root can **su** to any account without providing a password.

It's a good idea to get in the habit of typing the full pathname to the **su** command (e.g., **/bin/su**) rather than relying on the shell to find the command for you. This will give you some protection against programs called **su** that may have been slipped into your search path with the intention of harvesting passwords.[4]

sudo: a limited su

Since the privileges of the superuser account cannot be subdivided, it is hard to give someone the ability to do one task (backups, for example) without giving that person free run of the system. And if the root account is used by several administrators, you really have only a vague idea of who's using it or what they've done.

Our solution to these problems is a program called **sudo** that is currently maintained by Todd Miller. It's packagized for Linux by Red Hat, SuSE, and Debian but is also available in source code form from www.courtesan.com.

sudo takes as its argument a command line to be executed as root (or as another restricted user). **sudo** consults the file **/etc/sudoers**, which lists the people who are authorized to use **sudo** and the commands they are allowed to run on each host. If the proposed command is permitted, **sudo** prompts for the *user's own* password and executes the command.

---

4. For the same reason, we highly recommend that you *not* include "." (the current directory) in your shell's search path. While convenient, this configuration makes it easy to inadvertently run "special" versions of system commands that a user or intruder has left lying around as a trap. Naturally, this advice goes double for root.

Additional **sudo** commands can be executed without the "sudoer" having to type a password until a five-minute period (configurable) has elapsed with no further **sudo** activity. This timeout serves as a modest protection against users with **sudo** privileges who leave terminals unattended.

sudo keeps a log of the command lines that were executed, the people who requested them, the directory from which they were run, and the times at which they were invoked. This information can be logged by syslog or placed in the file of your choice. We recommend using syslog to forward the log entries to a "secure" central host.

A log entry for randy executing **sudo /bin/cat /etc/sudoers** might look like this:

```
Dec 7 10:57:19 tigger sudo: randy: TTY=ttyp0 ; PWD=/tigger/users/randy;
    USER=root ; COMMAND=/bin/cat /etc/sudoers
```

The **sudoers** file is designed so that a single version can be used on many different hosts at once. Here's a typical example:

```
# Define aliases for machines in CS & Physics departments
Host_Alias    CS = tigger, anchor, piper, moet, sigi
Host_Alias    PHYSICS = eprince, pprince, icarus

# Define collections of commands
Cmnd_Alias  DUMP = /sbin/dump, /sbin/restore
Cmnd_Alias  PRINTING = /usr/sbin/lpc, /usr/bin/lprm
Cmnd_Alias  SHELLS = /bin/sh, /bin/tcsh, /bin/csh, /bin/bash, /bin/ash,
    /bin/bsh

# Permissions
mark, ed    PHYSICS = ALL
herb        CS = /usr/local/bin/tcpdump : PHYSICS = (operator) DUMP
lynda       ALL = (ALL) ALL, !SHELLS
%wheel      ALL, !PHYSICS = NOPASSWD: PRINTING
```

The first five noncomment lines define groups of hosts and commands that are referred to in the permission specifications later in the file. The lists could be included literally in the specs, but the use of aliases makes the **sudoers** file easier to read and understand; it also makes the file easier to update in the future. It's also possible to define aliases for sets of users and for sets of users as whom commands may be run.

Each permission specification line includes information about

- The users to whom the line applies
- The hosts on which the line should be heeded
- The commands that the specified users can run
- The users as whom the commands can be executed

The first permission line applies to the users mark and ed on the machines in the PHYSICS group (eprince, pprince, and icarus). The built-in command alias ALL allows them to run any command. Since no list of users is specified in parentheses, **sudo** will only run commands as root.

The second permission line allows herb to run **tcpdump** on CS machines and dump-related commands on PHYSICS machines. However, the dump commands can only be run as operator, not as root. The actual command line that herb would type would be something like

```
% sudo -u operator /sbin/dump 0u /dev/hda2
```

The user lynda can run commands as any user on any machine, except that she can't run several common shells. Does this mean that lynda really can't get a root shell? Of course not:

```
% cp -p /bin/csh /tmp/csh
% sudo /tmp/csh
```

Generally speaking, any attempt to allow "all commands except…" is doomed to failure, at least in a technical sense. However, it may still be worthwhile to set up the **sudoers** file this way as a reminder that root shells are frowned upon. It may discourage casual use.

The final line allows users in group wheel to run **lpc** and **lprm** as root on all machines except eprince, pprince, and icarus. Furthermore, no password is required to run the commands.

Note that commands in **/etc/sudoers** are specified with full pathnames to prevent people from executing their own programs and scripts as root. Though no examples are shown above, it is possible to specify the arguments that are permissible for each command as well. In fact, this simple configuration only scratches the surface of the beauty and splendor that is the **sudoers** file.

To modify **/etc/sudoers**, you use the **visudo** command, which checks to be sure no one else is editing the file, invokes an editor on it, and then verifies the syntax of the edited file before installing it. This last step is particularly important because an invalid **sudoers** file might prevent you from **sudo**ing again to fix it.

The use of **sudo** has the following advantages:

- Accountability is much improved because of command logging.
- Operators can do chores without unlimited root privileges.
- The real root password can be known to only one or two people.
- It's faster to use **sudo** than to run **su** or to log in as root.
- Privileges can be revoked without the need to change the root password.
- A canonical list of all users with root privileges is maintained.
- There is less chance of a root shell being left unattended.
- A single file can be used to control access for an entire network.

*See page 667 for more information about **crack**.*

There are a couple of disadvantages as well. The worst of these is that any breach in the security of a sudoer's personal account can be equivalent to breaching the root account itself. There is not much you can do to counter this threat other than to caution your sudoers to protect their own accounts as they would the root account. You can also run **crack** regularly on sudoers' passwords to ensure that they are making good password selections.

sudo's command logging can be subverted by tricks such as shell escapes from within an allowed program or by **sudo csh** and **sudo su** if you allow them.

3.5 OTHER PSEUDO-USERS

Root is the only user that has special status in the eyes of the Linux kernel, but several other pseudo-users are defined by the system. It's customary to replace the encrypted password field of these special users in **/etc/shadow** with a star so that their accounts cannot be logged in to.

bin: legacy owner of system commands

On some older UNIX systems, the bin user owned the directories that contained the system's commands and most of the commands themselves as well. This account is often regarded as superfluous these days (or perhaps even slightly insecure), so modern systems (including Linux) generally just use the root account. On the other hand, now that the bin account is "standard," it can't really be done away with either.

daemon: owner of unprivileged system software

Files and processes that are part of the operating system but that need not be owned by root are sometimes given to daemon. The theory was that this convention would help avoid the security hazards associated with ownership by root. A group called "daemon" also exists for similar reasons. Like the bin account, the daemon account is not used much by most Linux distributions.

nobody: the generic NFS user

See page 471 for more information about the nobody account.

The Network File System (NFS) uses the nobody account to represent root users on other systems for purposes of file sharing. For remote roots to be stripped of their rooty powers, the remote UID 0 has to be mapped to something other than the local UID 0. The nobody account acts as the generic alter ego for these remote roots.

Since the nobody account is supposed to represent a generic and relatively powerless user, it shouldn't own any files. If nobody does own files, remote roots will be able to take control of them. Nobody shouldn't own no files!

A UID of -1 or -2 was traditional for nobody, and this convention is still observed in some distributions where nobody has UID 65534 (the 16-bit twos-complement version of -2). Others simply assign a low-numbered UID like any other system login, which makes more sense.

3.6 EXERCISES

★ **E3.1**   Use the **find** command with the **-perm** option to locate five setuid files on your system. For each file, explain why the setuid mechanism is necessary for the command to function properly.

★ **E3.2**   Create three "shocking nonsense" passphrases but keep them to yourself. Run your three passphrases through **md5sum** and report these results. Why is it safe to share the MD5 results?

★ **E3.3**   Enumerate a sequence of commands that modify someone's password entry and show how you could cover your tracks. Assume you had only **sudo** power (all commands allowed, but no shells or **su**).

★ **E3.4**   Create two entries for the **sudoers** configuration file:

a) One entry that allows users matt, adam, and drew to service the printer, unjam it, and restart printer daemons on the machine printserver

b) One entry that allows drew, smithgr, and jimlane to kill jobs and reboot the machines in the student lab

★ **E3.5**   Install **sudo** configured to send its mail tattling about misuse to you. Use it to test the **sudo** entries of the previous question with local usernames and machine names; verify that **sudo** is logging to syslog properly. Look at the syslog entries produced by your testing. (Requires root access; you'll most likely have to tweak **/etc/syslog.conf**, too.)

Rootly Powers

4 *Controlling Processes*

A process is the abstraction used by Linux to represent a running program. It's the object through which a program's use of memory, processor time, and I/O resources can be managed and monitored.

It is part of the Linux and UNIX philosophy that as much work as possible be done within the context of processes, rather than handled specially by the kernel. System and user processes all follow the same rules, so you can use a single set of tools to control them both.

4.1 COMPONENTS OF A PROCESS

A process consists of an address space and a set of data structures within the kernel. The address space is a set of memory pages[1] that the kernel has marked for the process's use. It contains the code and libraries that the process is executing, the process's variables, its stacks, and various extra information needed by the kernel while the process is running. Because Linux supports virtual memory, there is not necessarily a correlation between a page's location within an address space and its location inside the machine's physical memory or swap space.

The kernel's internal data structures record various pieces of information about each process. Some of the more important of these are:

- The process's address space map
- The current status of the process (sleeping, stopped, runnable, etc.)

---

1. Pages are the units in which memory is managed, usually 4K on PCs.

- The execution priority of the process
- Information about the resources the process has used
- The process's signal mask (a record of which signals are blocked)
- The owner of the process

A process also keeps track of which instructions the CPU is currently executing on its behalf. Linux allows more than one process to share an address space, thus achieving the effect of multiple threads of execution. So far, multithreading has not had much impact on system administration.

Many of the parameters associated with a process directly affect its execution: the amount of processor time it gets, the files it can access, and so on. In the following sections, we discuss the meaning and significance of the parameters that are most interesting from a system administrator's point of view. These attributes are common to all versions of UNIX and Linux.

PID: process ID number

The kernel assigns a unique ID number to every process. Most commands and system calls that manipulate processes require you to specify a PID to identify the target of the operation. PIDs are assigned in order as processes are created. When the kernel runs out of PIDs, it starts again at 1, skipping over any PIDs that are still in use.

PPID: parent PID

Linux does not supply a system call that creates a new process running a particular program. Instead, an existing process must clone itself to create a new process. The clone can then exchange the program it is running for a different one.

When a process is cloned, the original process is referred to as the parent, and the copy is called the child. The PPID attribute of a process is the PID of the parent from which it was cloned.[2]

UID and EUID: real and effective user ID

See page 85 for more information about UIDs.

A process's UID is the user identification number of the person who created it, or more accurately, it is a copy of the EUID value of the parent process. Usually, only the creator (aka the "owner") and the superuser are permitted to manipulate a process.

The EUID is the "effective" user ID, an extra UID used to determine what resources and files a process has permission to access at any given moment. For most processes, the UID and EUID are the same, the usual exception being programs that are setuid.

Why have both a UID and an EUID? Simply because it's useful to maintain a distinction between identity and permission, and because a setuid program may not wish to operate with expanded permissions all of the time. The effective UID can be set and reset to enable or restrict the additional permissions it grants.

Linux also keeps track of a "saved UID," which is a copy of the process's EUID at the point at which it first begins to execute. Unless the process takes steps to obliterate

---

2. At least initially. If the original parent dies, **init** (process 1) becomes the new parent. See page 51.

this saved UID, it remains available for use as the real or effective UID. A conservatively written setuid program can therefore renounce its special privileges for the majority of its execution, accessing them only at the specific points when extra privileges are needed.

Linux also defines a nonstandard FSUID process parameter that controls the determination of filesystem permissions. It is infrequently used.

The implications of this multi-UID system can be quite subtle. If you need to delve into the details, two excellent resources are the *Secure UNIX Programming FAQ* maintained by Thamer Al-Herbish at www.whitefang.com/sup and the *Secure Programming for Linux and Unix HOWTO* by David A. Wheeler, which is available from www.linuxdoc.org.

GID and EGID: real and effective group ID

See page 85 for more information about groups.

The GID is the group identification number of a process. The EGID is related to the GID in the same way that the EUID is related to the UID in that it can be "upgraded" by the execution of a setgid program. Linux maintains a saved GID similar in spirit to the saved UID.

On Linux systems, a process can be a member of many groups at once. The complete group list is stored separately from the distinguished GID and EGID. Determinations of access permissions normally take account of the EGID and the supplemental group list, but not the GID.

Niceness

A process's scheduling priority determines how much CPU time it receives. The kernel uses a dynamic algorithm to compute priorities, taking into account the amount of CPU time that a process has recently consumed and the length of time it has been waiting to run. The kernel also pays attention to an administratively set value that's usually called the "nice value" or "niceness," so called because it tells how nice you are planning to be to other users of the system. We take up the subject of niceness in detail on page 55.

Control terminal

Most processes have a control terminal associated with them. The control terminal determines default linkages for the standard input, standard output, and standard error channels. When you start a command from the shell, your terminal normally becomes the process's control terminal. The concept of a control terminal also affects the distribution of signals, which are discussed starting on page 51.

4.2 THE LIFE CYCLE OF A PROCESS

To create a new process, a process copies itself with the **fork** system call. **fork** creates a copy of the original process that is largely identical to the parent. The new process has a distinct PID and has its own accounting information.

fork has the unique property of returning two different values. From the child's point of view, it returns zero. The parent, on the other hand, is returned the PID of the newly created child. Since the two processes are otherwise identical, they must both examine the return value to figure out which role they are supposed to play.

After a **fork**, the child process will often use one of the **exec** family of system calls to begin execution of a new program.[3] These calls change the program text that the process is executing and reset the data and stack segments to a predefined initial state. The various forms of **exec** differ only in the ways in which they specify the command-line arguments and environment to be given to the new program.

*See Chapter 2 for more information about booting and the **init** daemon.*

When the system boots, the kernel autonomously creates and installs several processes. The most notable of these is **init**, which is always process number 1. **init** is responsible for executing the system's startup scripts. All processes other than the ones the kernel creates are descendants of **init**.

init also plays another important role in process management. When a process completes, it calls a routine named **_exit** to notify the kernel that it is ready to die. It supplies an exit code (an integer) that tells why it's exiting. By convention, 0 is used to indicate a normal or "successful" termination.

Before a process can be allowed to disappear completely, Linux requires that its death be acknowledged by the process's parent, which the parent does with a call to **wait**. The parent receives a copy of the child's exit code (or an indication of why the child was killed if the child did not exit voluntarily) and can also obtain a summary of the child's use of resources if it wishes.

This scheme works fine if parents outlive their children and are conscientious about calling **wait** so that dead processes can be disposed of. If the parent dies first, however, the kernel recognizes that no **wait** will be forthcoming and adjusts the process to make the orphan a child of **init**. **init** accepts these orphaned processes and performs the **wait** needed to get rid of them when they die.

4.3 SIGNALS

Signals are process-level interrupt requests. About thirty different kinds are defined, and they're used in a variety of ways:

- They can be sent among processes as a means of communication.
- They can be sent by the terminal driver to kill, interrupt, or suspend processes when special keys such as <Control-C> and <Control-Z> are typed.[4]
- They can be sent by the administrator (with **kill**) to achieve various results.
- They can be sent by the kernel when a process commits an infraction such as division by zero.

---

3. Actually, all but one are library routines, not system calls.
4. The functions of <Control-Z> and <Control-C> can be reassigned to other keys with the **stty** command, but this is rare in practice. In this chapter we refer to them by their conventional bindings.

A core dump is a process's memory image. It can be used for debugging.

When a signal is received, one of two things can happen. If the receiving process has designated a handler routine for that particular signal, the handler is called with information about the context in which the signal was delivered. Otherwise, the kernel takes some default action on behalf of the process. The default action varies from signal to signal. Many signals terminate the process; some also generate a core dump.

Specifying a handler routine for a signal within a program is referred to as "catching" the signal. When the handler completes, execution restarts from the point at which the signal was received.

To prevent signals from arriving, programs can request that they be either ignored or blocked. A signal that is ignored is simply discarded and has no effect on the process. A blocked signal is queued for delivery, but the kernel doesn't require the process to act on it until the signal has been explicitly unblocked. The handler for a newly unblocked signal is called only once, even if the signal was received several times while reception was blocked.

Table 4.1 lists the signals that all administrators should know. The uppercase convention for signal names derives from C language tradition. You might also sometimes see signal names written with a SIG prefix (e.g., SIGHUP) for similar reasons.

Table 4.1   Signals that every administrator should know

#	Name	Description	Default	Can catch?	Can block?	Dump core?
1	HUP	Hangup	Terminate	Yes	Yes	No
2	INT	Interrupt	Terminate	Yes	Yes	No
3	QUIT	Quit	Terminate	Yes	Yes	Yes
9	KILL	Kill	Terminate	No	No	No
a	BUS	Bus error	Terminate	Yes	Yes	Yes
11	SEGV	Segmentation fault	Terminate	Yes	Yes	Yes
15	TERM	Software termination	Terminate	Yes	Yes	No
a	STOP	Stop	Stop	No	No	No
a	TSTP	Keyboard stop	Stop	Yes	Yes	No
a	CONT	Continue after stop	Ignore	Yes	No	No
a	WINCH	Window changed	Ignore	Yes	Yes	No
a	USR1	User-defined	Terminate	Yes	Yes	No
a	USR2	User-defined	Terminate	Yes	Yes	No

a. Varies depending on the hardware architecture; see **man 7 signal**.

There are other signals not shown in Table 4.1, most of which are used to report obscure errors such as "illegal instruction." The default handling for signals like that is to terminate with a core dump. Catching and blocking are generally allowed because some programs may be smart enough to try to clean up whatever problem caused the error before continuing.

The BUS and SEGV signals are also error signals. We've included them in the table because they're so common: 99% of the time that a program crashes, it's ultimately one of these two signals that finally brings it down. By themselves, the signals are of no specific diagnostic value. Both of them indicate an attempt to use or access memory improperly.

Most terminal emulators will send a WINCH signal when their configuration parameters (such as the number of lines in the virtual terminal) change. This convention allows emulator-savvy programs (text editors, mostly) to reconfigure themselves automatically in response to changes. If you can't get windows to resize properly, make sure that WINCH is being generated and propagated correctly.

The signals named KILL and STOP cannot be caught, blocked, or ignored. The KILL signal destroys the receiving process, and STOP suspends its execution until a CONT signal is received. CONT may be caught or ignored, but not blocked.

TSTP is a "soft" version of STOP that might be best described as a request to stop. It's the signal generated by the terminal driver when you type a <Control-Z> on the keyboard. Programs that catch this signal usually clean up their state, then send themselves a STOP signal to complete the stop operation. Alternatively, TSTP may simply be ignored, to prevent the program from being stopped from the keyboard.

The signals KILL, INT, TERM, HUP, and QUIT may all sound as if they mean about the same thing, but their uses are actually quite different. It's unfortunate that such vague terminology was selected for them. Here's a decoding guide:

- KILL is unblockable and terminates a process at the OS level. A process can never actually "receive" this signal.

- INT is the signal sent by the terminal driver when you type <Control-C>. It's a request to terminate the current operation. Simple programs should quit (if they catch the signal) or simply allow themselves to be killed, which is the default if the signal is not caught. Programs that have a command line or input mode should stop what they're doing, clean up, and wait for user input again.

- TERM is a request to terminate execution completely. It's expected that the receiving process will clean up its state and exit.

- HUP has two common interpretations. First, it's understood as a reset request by many daemons. If a daemon is capable of rereading its configuration file and adjusting to changes without restarting, a HUP can generally be used to trigger this behavior. Second, HUP signals are sometimes generated by the terminal driver in an attempt to "clean up" (i.e., kill) the processes attached to a particular terminal. This can happen, for example, when a terminal session is concluded or when a modem connection is inadvertently dropped (hence the name "hangup"). The details vary by system.

Shells in the C shell family (**tcsh** et al.) usually make background processes immune to HUP signals so that they can continue to run after the user logs out. Users of Bourne-ish shells (**ksh**, **bash**, etc.) can emulate this behavior with the **nohup** command.

- QUIT is similar to TERM, except that it defaults to producing a core dump if not caught. A few programs cannibalize this signal and interpret it to mean something else.

The signals USR1 and USR2 have no set meaning. They're available for programs to use in whatever way they'd like. For example, the Apache web server interprets the USR1 signal as a request to gracefully restart.

4.4 KILL AND KILLALL: SEND SIGNALS

As its name implies, the **kill** command is most often used to terminate a process. **kill** can send any signal, but by default it sends a TERM. **kill** can be used by normal users on their own processes or by the superuser on any process. The syntax is

    kill [-signal] pid

where *signal* is the number or symbolic name of the signal to be sent (as shown in Table 4.1 on page 52) and *pid* is the process identification number of the target process. A *pid* of –1 broadcasts the signal to all processes except **init**.

A **kill** without a signal number does not guarantee that the process will die because the TERM signal can be caught, blocked, or ignored. The command

    kill -9 pid

will "guarantee" that the process will die because signal 9, KILL, cannot be caught. We put quotes around "guarantee" because processes can sometimes become so wedged that even KILL does not affect them (usually because of some degenerate I/O vapor lock such as waiting for a disk that has stopped spinning). Rebooting is usually the only way to get rid of these naughty processes.

Most shells have their own built-in implementation of **kill** that obeys the syntax described above. According to the man page for the stand-alone **kill** command, the signal name or number should actually be prefaced with the **-s** flag (e.g., **kill -s HUP** *pid*). But since some shells don't understand this version of the syntax, we suggest sticking with the **-HUP** form, which the stand-alone **kill** also understands. That way, you needn't worry about which version of **kill** you're using.

If you don't know the PID of the process you want to signal, you'd normally look it up with the **ps** command, which is described starting on page 56. Another option is to use the **killall** command, which performs this lookup for you. For example, to make the **xinetd** daemon refresh its configuration, you could run

    % sudo killall -USR1 xinetd

The vanilla **kill** command actually has a similar feature, but it does not seem to be as smart as **killall** at matching command names. Stick with **killall**.

4.5 PROCESS STATES

A process is not automatically eligible to receive CPU time just because it exists. There are essentially four execution states that you need to be aware of; they are listed in Table 4.2.

Table 4.2   Process states

State	Meaning
Runnable	The process can be executed.
Sleeping	The process is waiting for some resource.
Zombie	The process is trying to die.
Stopped	The process is suspended (not allowed to execute).

A runnable process is ready to execute whenever CPU time is available. It has acquired all the resources it needs and is just waiting for CPU time to process its data. As soon as the process makes a system call that cannot be immediately completed (such as a request to read part of a file), Linux will put it to sleep.

Sleeping processes are waiting for a specific event to occur. Interactive shells and system daemons spend most of their time sleeping, waiting for terminal input or network connections. Since a sleeping process is effectively blocked until its request has been satisfied, it will get no CPU time unless it receives a signal. Zombies are processes that have finished execution but not yet had their status collected.

Stopped processes are administratively forbidden to run. Processes are stopped on receipt of a STOP or TSTP signal and are restarted with CONT. Being stopped is similar to sleeping, but there's no way to get out of the stopped state other than having some other process wake you up (or kill you).

4.6 NICE AND RENICE: INFLUENCE SCHEDULING PRIORITY

The "niceness" of a process is a numeric hint to the kernel about how the process should be treated in relationship to other processes contending for the CPU. The strange name is derived from the fact that it determines how nice you are going to be to other users of the system. A high nice value means a low priority for your process: you are going to be nice. A low or negative value means high priority: you are not very nice. The range of allowable niceness values is -20 to +19.

Unless the user takes special action, a newly created process inherits the nice value of its parent process. The owner of the process can increase its nice value but cannot lower it, even to return the process to the default niceness. This restriction prevents processes with low priority from bearing high-priority children. The superuser has complete freedom in setting nice values and may even set a process's niceness so low that no other process can run.

See Chapter 26 for more information about performance.

Manually setting process priorities is quickly becoming a thing of the past. When UNIX ran on the puny systems of the 1970s and 80s, performance was most significantly affected by which process was on the CPU. Today, with more than adequate CPU power on most desktops, the scheduler usually does a good job of servicing all processes. However, I/O performance has not kept up with increasingly fast CPUs, and the major bottleneck on most systems has become the disk drives. Unfortunately, a process's nice value has no effect on the kernel's management of its memory or I/O; high-nice processes can still monopolize a disproportionate share of these resources.

A process's nice value can be set at the time of creation with the **nice** command and can be adjusted during execution with the **renice** command. **nice** takes a command line as an argument, and **renice** takes a PID or a username. Confusingly, **renice** requires an absolute priority, but **nice** wants a priority *increment* that it then adds to or subtracts from the shell's current priority.

Some examples:

```
% nice -n 5 ~/bin/longtask      // Lowers priority (raise nice) by 5
% renice -5 8829                 // Sets nice value to -5
% sudo renice 5 -u boggs         // Sets nice value of boggs's procs to 5
```

To complicate things, a version of **nice** is built into the C shell and some other common shells (but not **bash**). If you don't type the full path to the **nice** command, you'll get the shell's version rather than the operating system's. This can be confusing because shell-**nice** and command-**nice** use different syntax: the shell wants its priority increment expressed as +*incr* or -*incr*, but the stand-alone command wants an **-n** flag followed by the priority increment.[5]

The most commonly **nice**d process in the modern world is **xntpd**, the clock synchronization daemon. Since CPU promptness is critical to its mission, it usually runs at a nice value about 12 below the default (that is, at a higher priority than normal).

If a process goes berserk and drives the system's load average to 65, you may need to use **nice** to start a high-priority shell before you can run commands to investigate the problem. Otherwise, your commands may never get a chance to run.

4.7 PS: MONITOR PROCESSES

ps is the system administrator's main tool for monitoring processes. You can use it to show the PID, UID, priority, and control terminal of processes. It also gives information about how much memory a process is using, how much CPU time it has consumed, and its current status (running, stopped, sleeping, etc.). Zombies show up in a **ps** listing as <defunct>.

---

5. Actually, it's even worse than this: the stand-alone **nice** will interpret **nice -5** to mean a *positive* increment of 5, whereas the shell built-in **nice** will interpret this same form to mean a *negative* increment of 5.

The behavior of **ps** tends to vary widely among UNIX variants, and many implementations have become quite complex over the last few years. In an effort to accommodate people who are used to other systems' **ps** commands, Linux provides a trisexual and hermaphroditic version that understands many other implementations' option sets and uses an environment variable to tell it what personality to assume.

Do not be alarmed by all of this complexity: it's there mainly for kernel developers, not for system administrators. Although you will use **ps** frequently, you only need to know a few specific incantations.

You can obtain a general overview of all the processes running on the system with **ps aux**. Here's an example (we removed the START column to make the example fit the page and selected only a sampling of the output lines):

```
% ps aux
 USER     PID  %CPU %MEM   VSZ   RSS  TTY    STAT  TIME  COMMAND
 root       1   0.0  0.0  1344    76  ?      S     0:05  init [3]
 root       2   0.0  0.0     0     0  ?      SW    0:02  [kflushd]
 root       3   0.0  0.0     0     0  ?      SW    0:01  [kupdate]
 root     477   0.0  0.4  2284   552  ?      S     0:01  xinetd -reuse-pi
 root     567   0.0  0.3  3240   408  ?      S     0:02  sendmail:accepti
 root     770   0.0  0.0  1572   120  ?      S     0:00  crond
 root     966   0.0  0.1  2512   208  ?      S     0:00  /usr/sbin/sshd
 root     307   0.0  1.5  1944  1936  ?      SL    0:00  ntpd
 trent   1330   0.0  1.0  2464  1352  pts/5  S     0:00  -csh
 named   1886   0.0  1.3  3232  1732  ?      S     0:04  named -unamed
 boggs   2148   0.0  0.5  1616   764  pts/3  T     0:00  man iptables
 boggs   2150   0.0  0.7  2060   920  pts/3  T     0:00  sh -c/bin/gunzip
 boggs   2151   0.0  0.3  1680   476  pts/3  T     0:00  /bin/gunzip -c/v
 boggs   2152   0.0  0.6  1868   820  pts/3  T     0:00  /usr/bin/less -is
 garth   5279   0.0  1.1  2616  1472  pts/7  S     0:00  -csh
apache   5392   0.0  4.1  8248  5356  ?      S     0:00  /usr/sbin/httpd -
apache   5400   0.0  4.1  8248  5356  ?      S     0:00  /usr/sbin/httpd -
...
```

The meaning of each field is explained in Table 4.3 on page 58.

As you can see in this example, **ps** carefully trims the commands so that each process takes up only one line. To prevent trimming and see as much information as **ps** can provide, include the **w** (for "wide") option on the command line.

Another useful set of arguments is **lax**, which provides more technical information. It is also faster to run because it doesn't have to translate every UID to a username—efficiency can be important if the system is already bogged down by some other process. **ps** is generally quite expensive to run.

Shown on the next page in an abbreviated example, **ps lax** includes fields such as the parent process ID (PPID), nice value (NI), and resource the process is waiting for (WCHAN).

Table 4.3   **Explanation of ps aux output**

Field	Contents
USER	Username of the process's owner
PID	Process ID
%CPU	Percentage of the CPU this process is using
%MEM	Percentage of real memory this process is using
VSZ	Virtual size of the process
RSS	Resident set size (number of pages in memory)
TTY	Control terminal ID
STAT	Current process status:
	R = Runnable D = In disk (or short-term) wait
	S = Sleeping (< 20 sec) T = Traced or stopped
	Z = Zombie
	Additional Flags:
	W= Process is swapped out
	< = Process has higher than normal priority
	N = Process has lower than normal priority
	L = Some pages are locked in core
START	Time the process was started
TIME	CPU time the process has consumed
COMMAND	Command name and arguments[a]

a. Arguments can be truncated; add the **ww** argument to prevent this. Programs can modify this info, so it's not necessarily an accurate representation of the actual command line.

```
% ps lax
   F   UID    PID   PPID PRI NI   VSZ   RSS  WCHAN  STAT TIME  COMMAND
 100     0      1      0   0  0  1344    76  do_sel  S   0:05  init[3]
 040     0      2      1   0  0     0     0  bdflus  SW  0:02  [kflushd]
 040     0      3      1   0  0     0     0  kupdat  SW  0:01  [kupdate]
 140     0    477      1   0  0  2284   552  do_sel  S   0:01  xinetd-reu
 100  1011   8239   8238   0  0  2608  1496  read_c  S   0:00  -csh
 140    25  11886      1   0  0  3232  1732  do_sel  S   0:04  named-una
 000  1011  12148   8239   0  0  1616   764  do_sig  T   0:00  maniptable
 000  1011  12150  12148   0  0  2060   920  do_sig  T   0:00  sh-c/bin/
 000  1011  12151  12150   0  0  1680   476  do_sig  T   0:00  /bin/gunzip
 000  1011  12152  12150   0  0  1868   820  do_sig  T   0:00  /usr/bin/le
 ...
```

4.8 TOP: MONITOR PROCESSES EVEN BETTER

Since commands like **ps** offer only a one-time snapshot of your system, it is often difficult to grasp the "big picture" of what's really happening. The **top** command provides a regularly updated summary of active processes and their use of resources.

For example:

```
5:45pm  up 30 days, 22:25,  9 users,  load average: 0.00, 0.00, 0.00
74 processes: 69 sleeping, 1 running, 0 zombie, 4 stopped
CPU states:  0.0% user,  0.0% system,  0.0% nice,  0.3% idle
Mem:  127884K av, 122676K used,   5208K free, 73344K shrd, 68260K buff
Swap: 265032K av,   5056K used, 259976K free               21524K cached
```

PID	USER	PRI	NI	SIZE	RSS	SHARE	STAT	%CPU	%MEM	COMMAND
6785	garth	16	4	1056	1056	832	R N	0.9	0.8	top
1	root	0	0	120	76	56	S	0.0	0.0	init
2	root	0	0	0	0	0	SW	0.0	0.0	kflushd
337	root	0	0	496	180	152	S	0.0	0.1	klogd
352	rpc	0	0	508	500	416	S	0.0	0.3	portmap
379	rpcuser	0	0	112	0	0	SW	0.0	0.0	rpc.statd
431	daemon	0	0	116	56	40	S	0.0	0.0	atd
477	root	0	0	636	564	392	S	0.0	0.4	xinetd
507	lp	0	0	128	0	0	SW	0.0	0.0	lpd
567	root	0	0	708	408	304	S	0.0	0.3	sendmail
707	root	0	0	5740	5140	4976	S	0.0	4.0	httpd

...

By default, the display is updated every 10 seconds. The most active processes appear at the top. **top** also accepts input from the keyboard and allows you to send signals and **renice** processes, so you can observe how your actions affect the overall condition of the machine.

top must consume a small portion of the CPU to show an update every 10 seconds. It should generally be used only for diagnostic purposes, not as a "Hey, look what neat tools I run in my spare windows" toy.

Root can run **top** with the **q** option to goose it up to the highest possible priority. This can be very useful when you are trying to track down a process that has already brought the system to its knees.

4.9 RUNAWAY PROCESSES

See page 794 for more information about runaway processes.

Runaway processes come in two flavors: user processes that use excessive amounts of a system resource such as CPU time or disk space, and system processes that suddenly go berserk and exhibit wild behavior. The first type of runaway is not necessarily malfunctioning; it might simply be a resource hog. System processes are always supposed to behave reasonably.

You can identify processes that use excessive CPU time by looking at the output of **top**. If it is obvious that a user process is consuming more CPU than can reasonably be expected, investigate the process. Step one is to contact the process's owner and ask what's going on. If the owner can't be found, you will have to do some poking around of your own. Although you should normally avoid looking into users' home directories, it is acceptable when you are trying to track down the source code of a runaway process to find out what it's doing.

There are two reasons to find out what a process is trying to do before tampering with it. First, the process may be both legitimate and important to the user. It's unreasonable to kill processes at random just because they happen to use a lot of CPU. Second, the process may be malicious or destructive. In this case, you've got to know what the process was doing (e.g., cracking passwords) so you can fix the damage.

If the reason for a runaway process's existence can't be determined, suspend it with a STOP signal and send email to the owner explaining what has happened. The process can be restarted later with a CONT signal. Be aware that some processes can be ruined by a long sleep, so this procedure is not always entirely benign. For example, a process may wake to find that some of its network connections have been broken.

If a process is using an excessive amount of CPU but appears to be doing something reasonable and working correctly, you should **renice** it to a higher nice value (lower priority) and ask the owner to do the nicing in the future.

Runaway processes that produce output can fill up an entire filesystem, causing numerous problems. When a filesystem fills up, lots of messages will be logged to the console and attempts to write to the filesystem will produce error messages.

The first thing to do in this situation is to stop the process that was filling up the disk. If you have been keeping a reasonable amount of breathing room on the disk, you can be fairly sure that something is amiss when it suddenly fills up. There's no command analogous to **ps** that will tell you who's consuming disk space at the fastest rate, but several tools can identify files that are currently open and the processes that are using them. See the info on **fuser** and **lsof** that starts on page 66 for more information.

You may want to suspend all suspicious-looking processes until you find the one that's causing the problem, but remember to restart the innocents when you are done. When you find the offending process, remove the files it was creating.

An old and well-known prank is to start an infinite loop from the shell that does:

```
while 1
    mkdir adir
    cd adir
    touch afile
end
```

This program occasionally shows up running from an unprotected login or from a terminal that was left logged in. It does not consume much actual disk space, but it fills up the filesystem's inode table and prevents other users from creating new files. There is not much you can do except clean up the aftermath and warn users to protect their accounts. Because the directory tree that is left behind by this little jewel is usually too large for **rm -r** to handle, you may have to write a script that descends to the bottom of the tree and then removes directories as it backs out.

If the problem occurs in **/tmp** and you have set up **/tmp** as a separate filesystem, you can reinitialize **/tmp** with **newfs** instead of attempting to delete individual files. See Chapter 8 for more information about the management of filesystems.

4.10 EXERCISES

E4.1   Explain the relationship between a file's UID and a running process's real UID and effective UID. Besides file access control, what is the purpose of a process's effective UID?

E4.2   Suppose that a user at your site has started a long-running process that is consuming a significant fraction of a machine's resources.

a) How would you recognize a process that is hogging resources?

b) Assume that the misbehaving process might be legitimate and doesn't deserve to die. Show the commands you would use to put it "on ice" (stop it temporarily while you investigate).

c) Later, you discover that the process belongs to your boss and must continue running. Show the commands you would use to resume the task.

d) Alternatively, assume that the process needs to be killed. What signal would you send, and why? What if you needed to guarantee that the process died?

E4.3   Use **ps** and **top** with appropriate flags to show all running processes. Compare the results. Which things are easier to determine with **top**, and which with **ps**? How much load does **top** put on the system?

E4.4   Find a process with a memory leak (your own program or **netscape** if you don't have one handy). Use **ps** or **top** to monitor the program's memory use as it runs.

★ **E4.5**   Draw a picture representing the execution of a command from a running shell. With time (t) as the x-axis, start out with a single box representing the running shell at t = 0. Suppose the user types a command to the shell. Show at t = 1 the result of executing the **fork** system call. Next the **exec** system calls occurs; show at t = 2 the effects on the processes involved. The command finally completes when it calls the **exit** routine; show the state of the system at t = 3.

Exercises are continued on the next page.

⭐ **E4.6**   Use the **ps** command and a simple **awk** script (sample given below) to
determine the total VSZ and RSS of your system. How do these numbers
relate to the amount of physical memory and swap space available?
Choose reasonable variable names for your version of the script. (This
example is sneaky, i.e., wrong. Use it as a sample only.)

```
BEGIN {
    sum5=0
    sum6=0
}
{
    sum5 += $5
    sum6 += $6
}
END {
    printf("sum5=%d sum6=%s\n", sum5,sum6);
}
```

5 The Filesystem

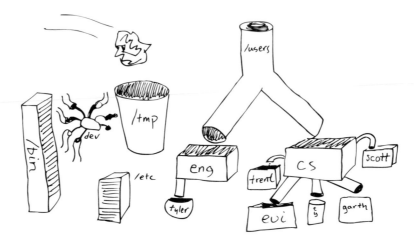

Quick: which of the following would you expect to find in a "filesystem"?

- Processes
- Serial ports
- Interprocess communication channels

If the system is Linux, the answer is "all of the above." And yes, you might find some files in there, too.

While the basic purpose of a filesystem is to represent and organize the system's storage resources, programmers have been eager to avoid reinventing the wheel when it comes to managing other types of objects. Frequently, it has proved to be natural and convenient to map such objects into the filesystem namespace. There are some advantages to this unification (consistent programming interface, easy access from the shell) and some disadvantages (Frankenstein-like filesystem implementations), but like it or not, this is the UNIX (and hence, the Linux) way.

The filesystem can be thought of as comprising four main components:

- A namespace – a way of naming things and organizing them in a hierarchy
- An API[1] – a set of system calls for navigating and manipulating objects
- A security model – a scheme for protecting, hiding, and sharing things
- An implementation – software that ties the logical model to actual hardware

---

1. Application Programming Interface, a generic term for the set of routines that a library, operating system, or software package provides for programmers to call.

Linux defines an abstract kernel-level interface that accommodates many different back-end filesystems. Some portions of the file tree are handled by traditional disk-based implementations; others are fielded by separate drivers within the kernel. For example, NFS filesystems are handled by a driver that forwards the requested operations to a server on another computer.

Unfortunately, the architectural boundaries are not clearly drawn, and there are quite a few special cases. For example, device files provide a way for programs to communicate with drivers inside the kernel. They are not really data files, but they're handled by the basic filesystem driver and their characteristics are stored on disk. Perhaps the details would be somewhat different if the filesystem were reimplemented in light of the last few decades' experience.

See www.namesys.com for more information about ReiserFS.

Another complicating (but ultimately beneficial) factor is that Linux supports more than one type of disk-based filesystem. In addition to the ext2fs filesystem that serves as most systems' default, there are implementations that feature higher performance or easier fault recovery, such as ReiserFS, JFS from IBM, XFS from SGI, and the upcoming ext3fs. There are also many implementations of foreign filesystems such as the FAT filesystem used in Microsoft Windows and the ISO-9660 filesystem used on CD-ROMs. Linux supports more types of filesystem than any other variant of UNIX. Its extensive menu of choices gives you lots of flexibility and makes it easy to share files with other systems.

The filesystem is a rich topic that we approach from several different angles. This chapter tells where to find things on your system and describes the characteristics of files, the meanings of permission bits, and the use of some basic commands that view and set attributes. Chapter 8, *Adding a Disk*, is where you'll find the more technical filesystem topics such as disk partitioning. Chapter 17, *The Network File System*, describes the file sharing systems that are commonly used with Linux.

5.1 PATHNAMES

The filesystem is presented as a single unified hierarchy[2] that starts at the directory **/** and continues downward through an arbitrary number of subdirectories. **/** is also called the root directory.

The list of directories that must be traversed to locate a particular file, together with its filename, form a "pathname." Pathnames can be either absolute (**/tmp/foo**) or relative (**book4/filesystem**). Relative pathnames are interpreted starting at the current directory. You might be accustomed to thinking of the current directory as a feature of the shell, but every process has a current directory.

The terms *file*, *filename*, *pathname*, and *path* are more or less interchangeable (or at least, we use them interchangeably in this book). *Filename* and *path* can be used for both absolute and relative paths; *pathname* generally suggests an absolute path.

2. The single-hierarchy system differs from that used by Windows, which retains the concept of disk-specific namespaces.

The filesystem can be arbitrarily deep. However, each component of a pathname must have a name no more than 255 characters long, and a single path may not contain more than 4,095 characters. To access a file with a pathname longer than this, you must **cd** to an intermediate directory and use a relative pathname.[3]

There are essentially no restrictions on the naming of files and directories, except that names are limited in length and must not contain the "/" character or nulls. In particular, spaces are permitted...kind of. Because of UNIX's long tradition of separating command-line arguments at whitespace, legacy software tends to break when spaces appear within filenames.

Given the amount of file sharing among different types of systems these days, it's no longer safe to assume that filenames will not contain spaces. Even if you don't share files with Macs and PCs, there are plenty of users in the habit of using spaces in filenames.[4] Any software you write that deals with the filesystem must be prepared to deal with spaces.

In the shell and in scripts, spaceful filenames just need to be quoted to keep their pieces together. For example, the command

```
% more "My excellent file.txt"
```

would preserve **My excellent file.txt** as a single argument to **more**.

5.2 MOUNTING AND UNMOUNTING FILESYSTEMS

The filesystem is composed of smaller chunks—also called filesystems—each of which consists of one directory and its subdirectories and files. It's normally apparent from the context which type of "filesystem" is being discussed, but for clarity, we will use the term "file tree" to refer to the overall layout of the filesystem and reserve the word "filesystem" for the chunks attached to the tree.

Most filesystems are disk partitions, but as we mentioned earlier, they can be anything that obeys the proper API: network file servers, kernel components, memory-based disk emulators, etc. Linux even has a nifty "loopback" filesystem that allows you to mount individual files as if they were distinct devices.

Filesystems are attached to the tree with the **mount** command. **mount** maps a directory within the existing file tree, called the mount point, to the root of the newly attached filesystem. The previous contents of the mount point become inaccessible as long as another filesystem is mounted there. Mount points are usually empty directories, however.

---

3. In case this isn't clear: most filesystem disk formats do not themselves impose a limit on the total length of pathnames. However, the system calls that access the filesystem do not allow their string arguments to be longer than 4,095 characters.

4. Annoyingly, even some recent open source projects have begun to use spaces. For example, KDE and GNOME create files and symbolic links with spaces in their names. One of our reviewers wrote, "Most OSes use a space as a delimiter. Using spaces in filenames is *DUMB*—even Windows suffers from this problem at the command line."

For example,

```
# mount /dev/hda4 /users
```

would install the filesystem stored on the disk partition represented by **/dev/hda4** under the path **/users**. You could then use **ls /users** to see that filesystem's contents.

A list of the filesystems that are customarily mounted on a particular system is kept in the **/etc/fstab** file. The information contained in this file allows filesystems to be checked (**fsck -A**) and mounted (**mount -a**) automatically at boot time. It also serves as documentation for the layout of the filesystems on disk and enables short commands such as **mount /usr** (the location of the filesystem to mount is looked up in **fstab**). See page 141 for a complete discussion of the **fstab** file.

Filesystems are detached with the **umount** command. You cannot unmount a filesystem that is "busy"; there must not be any open files or processes whose current directories are located there, and if the filesystem contains executable programs, they cannot be running.

If the kernel complains that a filesystem you are trying to unmount is busy, you can run **fuser** to find out why. When invoked with the **-mv** flags and a mount point, **fuser** displays every process that's using a file or directory on that filesystem:

```
% fuser -mv /usr
          USER   PID    ACCESS   COMMAND
/usr      root   444    ....m    atd
          root   499    ....m    sshd
          root   520    ....m    lpd
          . . .
```

The letter codes in the ACCESS column show what each process is doing to interfere with your unmounting attempt. Table 5.1 describes the meaning of each code.

Table 5.1   Activity codes shown by fuser

Code	Meaning
f	The process has a file open for reading or writing.
c	The process's current directory is on the filesystem.
e	The process is currently executing a file.
r	The process's root directory (set with **chroot**) is on the filesystem.
m	The process has mapped a file or shared library (usually an inactive executable).

To determine exactly what the offending processes are, just run **ps** with the list of PIDs returned by **fuser**. For example,

```
% ps -fp "444 499 520"
       UID   PID  PPID  C  STIME  TTY  TIME       CMD
  daemon   444   1     0  Apr11  ?    00:00:00   /usr/sbin/atd
     root   499   1     0  Apr11  ?    00:00:23   /usr/sbin/sshd
       lp   520   1     0  Apr11  ?    00:00:00   [lpd]
```

The quotation marks force the shell to pass the list of PIDs to **ps** as a single argument.

fuser can also report on the use of specific files (as opposed to entire filesystems); the syntax is **fuser -v** *filename*. **fuser** also accepts the **-k** option to kill (or send a signal to) each of the offending processes. Dangerous—and you must be root (or use **sudo**; see page 43).

An alternative to **fuser** is the free **lsof** utility by Vic Abell of Purdue University. **lsof**'s output is somewhat more verbose than that of **fuser**. **lsof** is available from

ftp://vic.cc.purdue.edu/pub/tools/unix/lsof/

lsof is available for Red Hat and SuSE in RPM format from www.redhat.com. It can be obtained on Debian systems through **apt-get**. Both Linux packagings are somewhat out of date as of this writing, however.

5.3 THE ORGANIZATION OF THE FILE TREE

Filesystems in the UNIX family have never been very well organized. Various incompatible naming conventions are used simultaneously, and different types of files are scattered randomly around the namespace. In many cases, files are divided up by function and not by how likely they are to change, making it difficult to upgrade the operating system. The **/etc** directory, for example, contains some files that are never customized and some that are entirely local. How do you know which files to preserve during the upgrade? Well, you just have to know...

Innovations such as **/var** have helped solve a few problems, but most systems are still a disorganized mess. Nevertheless, there's a culturally correct place for everything. It's particularly important not to mess with the default structure of the file tree under Linux because software packages and their installation tools often make broad assumptions about the locations of files (as do other sysadmins!).

See Chapter 12 for more information about configuring the kernel.

The root filesystem includes the root directory and a minimal set of files and subdirectories. The file containing the kernel lives within the root filesystem in the **/boot** directory; it's normally called (or linked to) **vmlinuz**. Also part of the root filesystem are **/dev** for device files (except **/dev/pts**, which is mounted separately), **/etc** for critical system files, **/sbin** and **/bin** for important utilities, and sometimes **/tmp** for temporary files.

See page 135 for some reasons why partitioning might be desirable and some rules of thumb to guide it.

The directories **/usr** and **/var** are also of great importance. **/usr** is where most standard programs are kept, along with various other booty such as on-line manuals and most libraries. It is not strictly necessary that **/usr** be a separate filesystem, but for convenience in administration it often is. Both **/usr** and **/var** must be available to enable the system to come up all the way to multiuser mode.

/var provides a home for spool directories, log files, accounting information, and various other items that grow or change rapidly and vary on each host. Since **/var** contains log files, which are apt to grow in times of trouble, it's a good idea to put it on its own filesystem if that is practical.

Home directories of users are often kept on a separate filesystem, usually mounted in the root directory. Separate filesystems can also be used to store bulky items such as source code libraries and databases.

Some of the more important standard directories are listed in Table 5.2 (some rows have been shaded to improve readability).

Table 5.2   Standard directories and their contents

Pathname	Contents
/bin	Commands needed for minimal system operability
/boot	Kernel and files needed to load the kernel
/dev	Device entries for terminals, disks, modems, etc.
/etc	Critical startup and configuration files
/lib	Libraries and parts of the C compiler
/opt	Optional, add-on application software packages
/proc	Images of all running processes
/root	Home directory of the superuser (often just /)
/sbin	Commands for booting, repairing, or recovering the system
/tmp	Temporary files that disappear between reboots
/usr	Hierarchy of secondary files and commands
/usr/bin	Most commands and executable files
/usr/include	Header files for C programs
/usr/lib	Libraries; also, support files for standard programs
/usr/local	Local software (stuff you install)
/usr/local/bin	Local executables
/usr/local/etc	Local system configuration files and commands
/usr/local/lib	Local support files
/usr/local/sbin	Statically linked local system maintenance commands
/usr/local/src	Source code for /usr/local/*
/usr/sbin	Less essential commands for system administration and repair
/usr/share	Items that might be common to multiple systems (read-only)
/usr/share/man	On-line manual pages
/usr/src	Source code for (nonlocal) software packages
/usr/src/linux	Kernel-building work area, configuration files
/var	System-specific data and configuration files
/var/adm	Varies: logs, system setup records, strange administrative bits
/var/log	Various system log files
/var/spool	Spooling directories for printers, mail, etc.
/var/tmp	More temporary space (preserved between reboots)

The evolving Filesystem Hierarchy Standard (www.pathname.org/fhs) attempts to codify, rationalize, and explain the standard directories. It's an excellent resource to consult when you're trying to figure out where to put something. We discuss some additional considerations in the design of local hierarchies starting on page 730.

5.4 FILE TYPES

Linux defines seven types of files. Even when developers add something new and wonderful to the file tree (such as the process information listed under **/proc**), it must still be made to look like one of these seven types:

- Regular files
- Directories
- Character device files
- Block device files
- Local domain sockets
- Named pipes (FIFOs)
- Symbolic links

You can determine the type of an existing file with **ls -ld**. The first character of the **ls** output encodes the type. The following example demonstrates that **/usr/include** is a directory:

```
% ls -ld /usr/include
drwxr-xr-x  27 root     root        4096 Jul 15 20:57 /usr/include
```

ls uses the codes shown in Table 5.3 to represent the various types of files.

Table 5.3   FIle-type encoding used by ls

File type	Symbol	Created by	Removed by
Regular file	-	editors, **cp**, etc.	**rm**
Directory	d	**mkdir**	**rmdir, rm -r**
Character device file	c	**mknod**	**rm**
Block device file	b	**mknod**	**rm**
UNIX domain socket	s	**socket**(2)	**rm**
Named pipe	p	**mknod**	**rm**
Symbolic link	l	**ln -s**	**rm**

As you can see from Table 5.3, **rm** is the universal tool for deleting files you don't want anymore. But how would you delete a file named, say, -f? It's a perfectly legitimate filename under most filesystems, but **rm -f** doesn't work because the -f is interpreted as an **rm** flag. The answer is either to refer to the file by a more complete pathname (such as **./-f**) or to use **rm**'s -- argument to tell it that everything that follows is a filename and not an option (i.e., **rm -- -f**).

Filenames that contain control characters present a similar problem, since it can be difficult or impossible to reproduce these names from the keyboard. In this situation, you can use shell globbing (pattern matching) to identify the files to delete. When using pattern matching, it's a good idea to get in the habit of using the **-i** option of **rm** to make **rm** confirm the deletion of each file. This feature will protect you against

The Filesystem

deleting any "good" files that your pattern inadvertently matches. For example, to delete a file named **foo**<Control-D>**bar**, you could use

```
% ls
foo?bar        foose        kde-root

% rm -i foo*
rm: remove `foo\004bar'? y
rm: remove `foose'? n
```

Note that **ls** shows the control character as a question mark, which can be a bit deceptive. If you don't remember that **?** is a shell pattern-matching character and try to **rm foo?bar**, you might potentially remove more than one file (although not in this example). **-i** is your friend!

To delete the most horribly named files, you may need to resort to **rm -i ***.

Regular files

A regular file is just a bag o' bytes; Linux imposes no structure on its contents. Text files, data files, executable programs, and shared libraries are all stored as regular files. Both sequential and random access are allowed.

Directories

A directory contains named references to other files. You can create directories with **mkdir** and delete them with **rmdir** if empty. You can delete nonempty directories with **rm -r**.

The special entries "**.**" and "**..**" refer to the directory itself and to its parent directory; they may not be removed. Since the root directory has no parent directory, the path "**/..**" is equivalent to the path "**/.**" (and both are equivalent to **/**).

A file's name is actually stored within its parent directory, not with the file itself. In fact, more than one directory (or more than one entry in a single directory) can refer to a file at one time, and the references can have different names. Such an arrangement creates the illusion that a file exists in more than one place at the same time.

These additional references ("links") are indistinguishable from the original file; as far as Linux is concerned, they are equivalent. Linux maintains a count of the number of links that point to each file and does not release the file's data blocks until its last link has been deleted. Links cannot cross filesystem boundaries.

References of this sort are usually called "hard links" these days to distinguish them from symbolic links, which are described on page 72. You create hard links with **ln** and remove them with **rm**.

It's easy to remember the syntax of **ln** if you keep in mind that it mirrors that of **cp**. The command **cp oldfile newfile** creates a copy of **oldfile** called **newfile**, and **ln oldfile newfile** makes the name **newfile** an additional reference to **oldfile**.

It is important to understand that hard links are not a distinct type of file. Instead of defining a separate "thing" called a hard link, the filesystem simply allows more than one directory entry to point to a particular file. In addition to the file's contents, the underlying attributes of the file (such as ownerships and permissions) are also shared among links.

Character and block device files

See Chapter 12 for more information about devices and drivers.

Device files allow programs to communicate with the system's hardware and peripherals. When the kernel is configured, modules that know how to communicate with each of the system's devices are linked in.[5] The module for a particular device, called a device driver, takes care of the messy details of managing the device.

Device drivers present a standard communication interface that looks like a regular file. When the kernel is given a request that refers to a character or block device file, it simply passes the request to the appropriate device driver. It's important to distinguish device *files* from device *drivers*, however. The files are just rendezvous points that are used to communicate with the drivers. They are not the drivers themselves.

Character device files allow their associated drivers to do their own input and output buffering. Block device files are used by drivers that handle I/O in large chunks and want the kernel to perform buffering for them. Some types of hardware, such as hard disks, can be represented by both block and character device files. (How do you know which version to use for a given purpose? Unfortunately, there is no rule of thumb—you have to either memorize the common cases or look them up.)

Device files are characterized by two numbers, called the major and minor device numbers. The major device number tells the kernel which driver the file refers to, and the minor device number tells the driver which physical unit to address. For example, major device number 6 on a Linux system indicates the parallel port driver. The first parallel port (**/dev/lp0**) would have major device number 6 and minor device number 0.

Some device drivers use the minor device number in a nonstandard way. For example, tape drivers use the minor device number to determine whether the tape should be rewound when the device file is closed. In some cases, more than one driver can refer to the same physical device. For example, the files **/dev/ttyS0** and **/dev/cua0** have different major device numbers but refer to the same serial port. They implement an interlock scheme for bidirectional modems.

 You can create device files with **mknod** and remove them with **rm**. Most systems provide a script called **/dev/MAKEDEV** that creates the appropriate sets of device files for common devices. Under SuSE, this program is not installed by default. See Chapter 12, *Drivers and the Kernel*, for more information.

---

5. These modules can also be loaded dynamically by the kernel.

The Filesystem

Local domain sockets

Sockets are connections between processes that allow them to communicate in a hygienic manner. Linux provides several different kinds of sockets, most of which involve the use of a network. Local domain sockets are accessible only from the local host and are referred to through a filesystem object rather than a network port. They are sometimes known as "UNIX domain sockets."

See Chapter 11 for more information about syslog.

Although socket files are visible to other processes as directory entries, they cannot be read from or written to by processes not involved in the connection. Some standard facilities that use local domain sockets are the printing system, the X Window System, and syslog.

Local domain sockets are created with the **socket** system call and can be removed with the **rm** command or the **unlink** system call once they have no more users.

Named pipes

Like local domain sockets, named pipes allow communication between two processes running on the same host. They're also known as "FIFO files" (FIFO is short for the phrase "first in, first out"). You can create named pipes with **mknod** and remove them with **rm**.

As with local domain sockets, real-world instances of named pipes are few and far between. They rarely, if ever, require administrative intervention.

Symbolic links

A symbolic or "soft" link points to a file by name. When the kernel comes upon a symbolic link in the course of looking up a pathname, it redirects its attention to the pathname stored as the contents of the link. The difference between hard links and symbolic links is that a hard link is a direct reference, whereas a symbolic link is a reference by name; symbolic links are distinct from the files they point to.

You create symbolic links with **ln -s** and remove them with **rm**. Since they can contain arbitrary paths, they can refer to files on other filesystems or to nonexistent files. Multiple symbolic links can also form a loop.

A symbolic link can contain either an absolute or a relative path. For example,

```
# ln -s ncurses/term.h /usr/include/term.h
```

links **/usr/include/term.h** to **/usr/include/ncurses/term.h** with a relative path; it creates the symbolic link **/usr/include/term.h** with a target of "**ncurses/term.h**". The entire **/usr/include** directory could be moved somewhere else without causing the symbolic link to stop working (not that moving the directory is advisable).

It is a common mistake to think that the first argument to **ln -s** has something to do with your current working directory. It is *not* resolved as a filename by **ln**; it's simply used verbatim as the target of the symbolic link.

5.5 FILE ATTRIBUTES

Every file has a set of nine permission bits that control who can read, write, and execute the contents of the file. Together with three other bits that primarily affect the operation of executable programs, these bits constitute the file's "mode."

The twelve mode bits are stored together with four bits of file-type information. The four file-type bits are set when the file is first created and cannot be changed, but the file's owner and the superuser can modify the twelve mode bits by using the **chmod** (change mode) command. Use **ls -l** (or **ls -ld** for a directory) to inspect the values of these bits. An example is given on page 75.

The setuid and setgid bits

The bits with octal values 4000 and 2000 are the setuid and setgid bits. These bits allow programs to access files and processes that would otherwise be off-limits to the user that runs them. The setuid/setgid mechanism for executables is described on page 40.

When set on a directory, the setgid bit causes newly created files within the directory to take on the group ownership of the directory rather than the default group of the user that created the file. This convention makes it easier to share a directory of files among several users, as long as they all belong to a common group. This interpretation of the setgid bit is unrelated to its meaning when set on an executable file, but there is never any ambiguity as to which meaning is appropriate.

You can also set the setgid bit on nonexecutable plain files to request special locking behavior when the file is opened. However, we've never seen this feature used.

The sticky bit

The bit with octal value 1000 is called the sticky bit. It was of historical importance as a modifier for executable files on early UNIX systems. However, that meaning of the sticky bit is now obsolete and Linux silently ignores it.

If the sticky bit is set on a directory, the filesystem won't allow you to delete or rename a file unless you are the owner of the directory, the owner of the file, or the superuser. Having write permission on the directory is not enough. This convention helps to make directories like **/tmp** a little more private and secure.

The permission bits

The nine permission bits are used to determine what operations may be performed on a file, and by whom. Linux does not allow permissions to be set on a per-user basis. Instead, there are sets of permissions for the owner of the file, the group owners of the file, and everyone else. Each set has three bits: a read bit, a write bit, and an execute bit.

It's convenient to discuss file permissions in terms of octal (base 8) numbers because each digit of an octal number represents 3 bits and there are 3 bits in each group of permission bits. The topmost three bits (with octal values of 400, 200, and 100) control access for the owner. The second three (40, 20, and 10) control access for the group. The last three (4, 2, and 1) control access for everyone else ("the world"). In each triplet, the high bit is the read bit, the middle bit is the write bit, and the low bit is the execute bit.

Each user fits into only one of the three permission sets. The permissions used are those that are most specific. For example, the owner of a file always has access determined by the owner permission bits and never the group permission bits. It is possible for the "other" and "group" categories to have more access than the owner, although this configuration is rarely used.

On a regular file, the read bit allows the file to be opened and read. The write bit allows the contents of the file to be modified or truncated; however, the ability to delete or rename (or delete and then recreate!) the file is controlled by the permissions on its parent directory (because that is where the name-to-dataspace mapping is actually stored).

The execute bit allows the file to be executed. There are two types of executable files: binaries, which the CPU runs directly, and scripts, which must be interpreted by a shell or some other program. By convention, scripts begin with a line of the form

```
#!/bin/csh -f
```

that specifies an appropriate interpreter. Nonbinary executable files that do not specify an interpreter are assumed (by your shell) to be **bash/sh** scripts.[6]

For a directory, the execute bit (often called the "search" or "scan" bit in this context) allows the directory to be entered or passed through while a pathname is evaluated, but not to have its contents listed. The combination of read and execute bits allows the contents of the directory to be listed. The combination of write and execute bits allows files to be created, deleted, and renamed within the directory.

Viewing file attributes

The filesystem maintains about forty separate pieces of information for each file, but most of them are useful only to the filesystem itself. As a system administrator, you will be concerned mostly with the link count, owner, group, mode, size, last access time, last modification time, and type. You can inspect all of these with **ls -l** (or **ls -ld** for a directory).

An attribute change time is also maintained for each file. The conventional name for this time (the "ctime," short for "change time") leads some people to believe that it is the file's creation time. Unfortunately, it is not; it just records the time that the attributes of the file (owner, mode, etc.) were last changed (as opposed to the time at which the file's contents were modified).

---

6. The kernel understands the #! ("shebang") syntax and acts on it directly. However, if the interpreter is not specified completely and correctly, the kernel will refuse to execute the file. The shell then makes a second attempt to execute the script by calling **sh**.

Consider the following example:

```
% ls -l /bin/gzip
-rwxr-xr-x   3 root     root        51388 Jul 13  2000 /bin/gzip
```

The first field specifies the file's type and mode. The first character is a dash, so the file is a regular file. (See Table 5.3 on page 69 for other codes.)

The next nine characters in this field are the three sets of permission bits. The order of groups is owner-group-other, and the order of bits within each group is read-write-execute. Although these bits have only binary values, **ls** shows them symbolically with the letters r, w, and x for read, write, and execute. In this case, the owner has all permissions on the file and everyone else has only read and execute permission.

If the setuid bit had been set, the x representing the owner's execute permission would have been replaced with an s, and if the setgid bit had been set, the x for the group would also have been replaced with an s. The last character of the permissions (execute permission for "other") is shown as t if the sticky bit of the file is turned on. If either the setuid/setgid bit or the sticky bit is set but the corresponding execute bit is not, these bits appear as S or T.

The next field in the listing is the link count for the file. In this case it is 3, indicating that **/bin/gzip** is just one of three names for this file (the others are **/bin/gunzip** and **/bin/zcat**). Every time a hard link is made to a file, the count is incremented by 1.

All directories will have at least two hard links: the link from the parent directory and the link from the special file "." inside the directory itself. Symbolic links do not affect the link count.

The next two fields in the **ls** output are the owner and group owner of the file. In this example, the file's owner is root, and the file also belongs to the group named root. The filesystem actually stores these as the user and group ID numbers rather than as names. If the text versions (names) can't be determined, these fields will contain numbers. This might happen if the user or group that owns the file has been deleted from the **/etc/passwd** or **/etc/group** file. It could also indicate a problem with your NIS database (if you use one); see Chapter 18.

The next field is the size of the file in bytes. This file is 51,388 bytes long, a bit more than 50K.[7] Next comes the date of last modification: July 13, 2000. The last field in the listing is the name of the file, **/bin/gzip**.

ls output is slightly different for a device file. For example:

```
% ls -l /dev/tty0
crw-------   1 root     tty        4,   0 Aug 24  2000 /dev/tty0
```

---

7. K stands for kilo, a metric prefix meaning 1,000; however, computer types have bastardized it into meaning 2^{10} or 1,024. Similarly, a computer megabyte is not really a million bytes but rather 2^{20} or 1,048,576 bytes. The International Electrotechnical Commission is promoting a new set of numeric prefixes (such as kibi- and mebi-) that are based explicitly on powers of 2. At this point, it seems unlikely that common usage will change. To add to the confusion, even the power-of-2 units are not used consistently. RAM is denominated in powers of 2, but network bandwidth is always a power of 10. Storage space is quoted in power-of-10 units by manufacturers and power-of-2 units by everyone else.

Most fields are the same, but instead of a size in bytes, **ls** shows the major and minor device numbers. **/dev/tty0** is the first virtual console, controlled by device driver 4 (the terminal driver).

One **ls** option that's useful for scoping out hard links is **-i**, which makes **ls** show each file's "inode number." Without going into too much detail about the implementation of the filesystem, we'll just say that the inode number is an index into a table that enumerates all the files in the filesystem. Inodes are the "things" that are pointed to by directory entries; entries that are hard links to the same file will have the same inode number. To figure out a complex web of links, you'll need **ls -li** to show link counts and inode numbers along with **find** to search for matches.[8]

The system automatically keeps track of modification time stamps, link counts, and file size information. Conversely, permission bits, ownership, and group ownership change only when they are specifically altered with the **chmod**, **chown**, and **chgrp** commands.

chmod: change permissions

The **chmod** command changes the permissions on a file. Only the owner of the file and the superuser can change its permissions. To use the command on early UNIX systems, you had to learn a bit of octal notation, but current versions accept either octal notation or a mnemonic syntax. The octal syntax is generally more convenient for administrators, but it can only be used to specify an absolute value for the permission bits. The mnemonic syntax can modify some bits while leaving others alone.

The first argument to **chmod** is a specification of the permissions to be assigned, and the second and subsequent arguments are names of files on which permissions should be changed. In the octal case, the first octal digit of the specification is for the owner, the second is for the group, and the third is for everyone else. If you want to turn on the setuid, setgid, or sticky bits, you use four octal digits rather than three, with the three special bits forming the first digit.

Table 5.4 illustrates the eight possible combinations for each set of three bits, where r, w, and x stand for read, write, and execute.

Table 5.4   Permission encoding for chmod

Octal	Binary	Perms	Octal	Binary	Perms
0	000	— — —	4	100	r— —
1	001	— —x	5	101	r—x
2	010	—w—	6	110	rw—
3	011	—wx	7	111	rwx

8. Try **find** *mountpoint* **-xdev -inum** *inode*

For example, **chmod 711 myprog** gives all permissions to the owner and execute-only permission to everyone else.[9]

The full details of **chmod**'s mnemonic syntax can be found in the **chmod** man page. Some examples of mnemonic specifications are shown in Table 5.5.

Table 5.5   Examples of chmod's mnemonic syntax

Spec	Meaning
u+w	Adds write permission for the owner of the file
ug=rw,o=r	Gives r/w permission to owner and group, and read permission to others
a-x	Removes execute permission for all categories (owner/group/other)
ug=srx,o=	Makes the file setuid and setgid and gives r/x permission to the owner and group only
g=u	Makes the group permissions be the same as the owner permissions

The hard part about using the mnemonic syntax is remembering whether **o** stands for "owner" or "other" ("other" is correct). Just remember **u** and **g** by analogy to UID and GID; only one possibility will be left.

You can also specify the modes to be assigned by analogy with an existing file. For example, **chmod --reference=filea fileb** makes **fileb**'s mode the same as **filea**'s.

chmod can update the file permissions within a directory recursively with the **-R** option. However, this is trickier than it looks, since the enclosed files and directories may not all share the same attributes (for example, some might be executable files while others are text files). The mnemonic syntax is particularly useful with **-R** because any bits whose values you don't set explicitly are left alone. For example,

```
% chmod -R g+w mydir
```

adds group write permission to **mydir** and all its contents without messing up the execute bits of directories and programs.

chown: change ownership and group

The **chown** command changes a file's ownership and group ownership. Its syntax mirrors that of **chmod**, except that the first argument specifies the new owner and group in the form *user.group*. Either of *user* or *group* may be left out. If there is no group, you don't need the dot either.

To change a file's group, you must either be the owner of the file and belong to the group you're changing to or be the superuser. You must be the superuser to change a file's owner.

---

9. If **myprog** were a shell script, it would need both read and execute permission turned on. In order for the script to be run by an interpreter, it must be opened and read like a text file. Binary files are executed directly by the kernel and therefore do not need read permission turned on.

Like **chmod**, **chown** offers the recursive **-R** flag to change the settings of a directory and all the files underneath it. For example, the sequence

```
# chmod 755 ~matt
# chown -R matt.staff ~matt
```

might be used to set up the home directory of a new user after you had copied in the default startup files. Make sure that you don't try to **chown** the new user's dot files with a command such as

```
# chown -R matt.staff ~matt/.*
```

The pattern will match **~matt/..** and will therefore end up changing the ownerships of the parent directory and probably the home directories of other users.

Traditional UNIX uses a separate command, **chgrp**, to change the group owner of a file. Linux provides **chgrp** too. It works just like **chown**; feel free to use it if you find it easier to remember.

umask: assign default permissions

You can use the built-in shell command **umask** to influence the default permissions given to the files you create. The **umask** is specified as a three-digit octal value that represents the permissions to take away. When a file is created, its permissions are set to whatever the creating program asks for minus whatever the **umask** forbids. Thus, the digits correspond to the permissions shown in Table 5.6.

Table 5.6   Permission encoding for umask

Octal	Binary	Perms	Octal	Binary	Perms
0	000	rwx	4	100	−wx
1	001	rw−	5	101	−w−
2	010	r−x	6	110	−−x
3	011	r−−	7	111	−−−

For example, **umask 027** allows all permissions for the owner but forbids write permission to the group and allows no permissions for anyone else. The default **umask** value is often 022, which denies write permission to the group and world but allows read permission.

See Chapter 6 for more information about startup files.

There is no way you can force users to have a particular **umask** value, since they can always reset it to whatever they want. However, you can provide a suitable default in the sample **.cshrc** and **.profile** files that you give to new users.

Bonus flags

Linux's ext2fs filesystem defines some supplemental attributes you can turn on to request special filesystem semantics—"request" being the operative word, since many of the flags haven't actually been implemented. For example, one flag makes a file append-only and another makes it immutable and undeletable.

Since these flags don't apply to filesystems other than ext2fs, Linux uses special commands, **lsattr** and **chattr**, to view and change them. Table 5.7 lists the currently defined flags. Information about the implementation status of each flag is sparse, conflicting, and often out of date, so we checked the source code to verify the function of each flag as of kernel version 2.4.5. There is no guarantee that any of the nonworking flags will ever be implemented.

Table 5.7   Ext2fs bonus flags (status as of kernel 2.4.5)

Flag	Meaning	Works?
A	Never update access time (st_atime; for performance)	yes
a	Allow writing only in append mode (only root can set)	yes
c	Keep file contents compressed (transparently)	no
d	No backup—make **dump** ignore this file	yes
i	Make file immutable and undeletable (only root can set)	yes
S	Force changes to be written synchronously (no buffering)	kind of
s	Physically erase (write over) when deleted	no
u	Save contents on deletion to permit recovery	no

With the possible exception of the "no backup" flag, it's not clear that any of these features offer much day-to-day value. The immutable and append-only flags were largely conceived as ways to make the system more resistant to tampering by hackers or hostile code. Unfortunately, they can confuse software and only provide protection against hackers that don't know enough to use **chattr -ia**.[10] Real-world experience has shown that these flags are more often used *by* hackers than *against* them.

The **S** option for synchronous writes also merits a special caution. Since it forces all filesystem pages associated with a file to be written out immediately on changes, it might seem to offer additional protection against data loss in the event of a crash. However, the order of operations for synchronous updates is unusual and has been known to confuse **fsck**; recovery of a damaged filesystem might therefore be made more difficult rather than more reliable.

10. The Linux kernel actually supports a "capability" mechanism that can make it harder to turn off these bits, but the feature is not currently documented or widely used.

5.6 Exercises

E5.1   What is a **umask**? Create a **umask** that would give no permissions to the group or the world.

E5.2   What is the difference between hard links and symbolic (soft) links? When is it appropriate to use one or the other?

★ **E5.3**   Read the man page for the **/etc/fstab** file. Write an entry that automatically mounts a Windows NTFS partition, **/dev/hda1**, at startup. Use the mount point **/mnt/win_c**.

★ **E5.4**   When installing a Linux system, it's important to partition the hard drive so that there is enough space for each filesystem (**/var**, **/usr**, etc.). The "Foobar Linux" distribution uses the following defaults:

/	100MB
/var	50MB
/boot	10MB
<swap>	128MB
/usr	remaining space

What are some potential problems with this arrangement on a busy server box?

★ **E5.5**   Why is it a good idea to put some partitions (such as **/var**, **/home**, and swap) on a separate drive from other data files and programs? What about **/tmp**? Give specific reasons for each of the filesystems listed.

★ **E5.6**   Write a script that finds all the hard links on a filesystem.

★ **E5.7**   Give commands to accomplish the following tasks.

   a) Set the permissions on the file **README** to read/write for the owner and read for everyone else.

   b) Turn on a file's setuid bit without changing (or knowing) the current permissions.

   c) List the contents of the current directory, sorting by modification time and listing the most recently modified file last.

   d) Change the group of a file called **shared** from "user" to "friends".

★ **E5.8**   How would you organize locally installed software on your Linux box if

   a) You were an all-Linux shop?
   b) You supported both Windows and Linux?
   c) You had four other versions of UNIX mixed in with your Linux boxes?

6 *Adding New Users*

The days of centralized servers with logon accounts for hundreds of people are long gone. Nevertheless, adding and removing users is still a bread-and-butter administrative skill. Administrators need a thorough understanding of the Linux account system in order to manage network services and configure accounts appropriately for the local computing environment.

Account hygiene is also a key determinant of system security. Infrequently used accounts are prime targets for hackers, as are accounts with easily guessed passwords. Even if you use your system's automated tools to add and remove users, it's important to understand the underlying changes the tools are making.

In this chapter we'll first examine the underlying model that the automated tools implement, then describe the tools themselves (**useradd**, **userdel**, etc.). The default **useradd** tool is actually quite good and should be sufficient for most sites' needs. Unfortunately, **userdel** is not quite as thorough as we would like.

6.1 THE /ETC/PASSWD FILE

The **/etc/passwd** file is a list of users recognized by the system. The system consults the file at login time to determine a user's UID and to verify the user's password. Each line in the file represents one user and contains seven fields separated by colons:

- Login name
- Encrypted password (unless a shadow password file is used)
- UID number

- Default GID number
- "GECOS" information: full name, office, extension, home phone
- Home directory
- Login shell

For example, the following lines are all valid **/etc/passwd** entries.

```
root:lga5FjuGpZ2so:0:0:The System,,x6096,:/:/bin/csh
jl:x:100:0:Jim Lane,ECT8-3,,:/staff/jl:/bin/sh
dotty:$1$Ce8QpAQI$L.DvJEWiHlWetKTMLXFZO/:101:20::/home/dotty:/bin/csh
```

As computing hardware has become faster, it has become increasingly dangerous to leave encrypted passwords in plain view. Linux allows you to hide the encrypted passwords by placing them in a separate file that is not world-readable. This is known as a shadow password mechanism, and it is the default on most distributions.

The shadow password system makes more sense when explained as an extension of the traditional **/etc/passwd** (as it historically was), so we will defer our discussion of this feature until page 87. A more general discussion of the security implications of shadow passwords can be found on page 657.

The contents of **/etc/passwd** are often shared among systems with a database such as NIS or LDAP. See Chapter 18, *Sharing System Files*, for more information.

The following sections discuss the **/etc/passwd** fields in more detail.

Login name

Login names (also known as usernames) must be unique and no more than 32 characters long. They may contain any characters except colons and newlines.

Some older versions of UNIX limit the permissible characters to alphanumerics and impose an 8-character length limit. If you use NIS, login names are limited to 8 characters regardless of the operating system.

We strongly suggest that you obey the more restrictive limits even under Linux. Such a policy will avert potential conflicts with older software and will guarantee that users can have the same login name on every machine. Remember, the fact that you have a homogeneous environment today doesn't mean that this will be the case tomorrow.

Login names are case sensitive; however, most mail systems (including **sendmail**) pay no attention to case. We are not aware of any problems caused by mixed-case login names, but lowercase names are traditional and also easier to type.

Login names should be easy to remember, so random sequences of letters do not make good login names. We suggest that you avoid "handles" and cutesy nicknames, even if your organization is relatively informal. They're really not that much fun, and they tend to draw scorn; names like DarkLord and QTPie belong in front of @aol.com. Even if your users have no self-respect, at least have some thought for your site's overall credibility.

Since login names are often used as email addresses, it's useful to establish a standard way of forming them. It should be possible for users to make educated guesses about each other's login names. First names, last names, initials, or some combination of these all make reasonable naming schemes.

See page 527 for more information about mail aliases.

Any fixed scheme for choosing login names eventually results in duplicate names or names that are too long, so you will sometimes have to make exceptions. In the case of a long name, you can use the **/etc/mail/aliases** file to equate two versions of the name, at least as far as mail is concerned.

For example, suppose you use an employee's first initial and last name as a paradigm. Brent Browning would therefore be "bbrowning", which is 9 characters and therefore too long. Instead, you could assign the user the login "brentb", leaving "bbrowning" as an **aliases** file entry:

```
bbrowning: brentb
```

If your site has a global mail alias file, each new login name must be distinct from any alias in this file. If it is not, mail will be delivered to the alias rather than the new user.

It's common for large sites to implement a full-name email addressing scheme (e.g., John.Q.Public@mysite.com) that hides login names from the outside world. This is a fine idea, but it really doesn't obviate any of the naming advice given above. If for no other reason than the sanity of administrators, it's best if login names have a clear and predictable correspondence to users' actual names.

If you have more than one machine, login names should be unique in two senses. First, a user should have the same login name on every machine. This rule is mostly for convenience, both yours and the user's.

See page 661 for a discussion of login equivalence issues.

Second, a particular login name should always refer to the same person. Some commands (e.g., **ssh**) can be set up to validate remote users based on their login names. Even if scott@boulder and scott@refuge were two different people, one might be able to log into the other's account without providing a password if the systems were not set up properly.

Experience also shows that duplicate names can lead to email confusion. The mail system might be perfectly clear about which scott is which, but users will often send mail to the wrong address.

Encrypted password

A quick reminder before we jump into the details of passwords: most systems actually keep encrypted passwords in **/etc/shadow** rather than **/etc/passwd**. However, the comments in this section apply regardless of where passwords are actually kept.

/etc/passwd stores passwords in an encrypted form. Unless you can execute encryption algorithms in your head (we want to meet you), you must either set the contents of this field by using the **passwd** command (**yppasswd** if you use NIS) or by copying an encrypted password string from another account.

Adding New Users

If you edit **/etc/passwd** to create a new account, put a star (*) in the encrypted password field. The star prevents unauthorized use of the account until you have set a real password. Never leave this field empty—that introduces a jumbo-sized security hole because no password is required to access the account.[1]

Most Linux distributions (including SuSE and Debian) default to using standard DES encryption for passwords. This standard limits the length of unencrypted passwords to 8 characters. Longer passwords are accepted, but only the first 8 characters are significant. Extra characters are silently ignored.

An alternative password encryption system based on the MD5 secure hashing algorithm is the default in Red Hat and an option on most other versions of Linux. MD5 isn't cryptographically "better" than DES, but the MD5 scheme allows passwords of arbitrary length. Longer passwords are more secure—if you actually use them. Since the use of MD5 won't hurt and might help, we recommend it for all sites.

All major Linux distributions will recognize MD5 passwords in the **passwd** file if they are present. It isn't necessary for all passwords on the system to use the same form of encryption.

 To convince SuSE and Debian to generate MD5 passwords as well as recognize them, you must review *all* of the files in **/etc/pam.d**. Add the keyword md5 to the end of lines that start with password and mention pam_unix.so or pam_pwcheck.so. For example, you would change the Debian line

```
password   required   pam_unix.so nullok obscure min=4 max=8
```

to

```
password   required   pam_unix.so nullok obscure min=4 max=8 md5
```

The max=8 argument sounds like it should limit password length to 8 characters. However, it is not documented and appears to have no effect when MD5 passwords are in effect. Ignore it.

 Under Red Hat, the **authconfig** command accepts the argument **--enablemd5** to turn on the generation of MD5 passwords.[2] Add **--kickstart** to keep the annoying interactive interface from appearing.

Encrypted passwords in the **/etc/passwd** file are normally of constant length (34 characters for MD5, 13 for DES) regardless of the length of the unencrypted password. Passwords are encrypted in combination with a random "salt" so that a given password can correspond to many different encrypted forms (usually 64). If two users happen to select the same password, this fact usually cannot be discovered by inspection of the **passwd** file. MD5 passwords are easy to spot because they always start with 1.

---

1. Even if you are using shadow passwords, it's wise to be a bit anal retentive about password hygiene in the **/etc/passwd** file. You never know when some obsolete program or script is going to peek at it in order to make some kind of security decision.

2. There is also a **--disablemd5** option, although we cannot think of a reason to ever want to use it.

UID number

UIDs are unsigned 32-bit integers that can represent the values 0 to 4,294,967,296. However, because of interoperability issues with older systems, we suggest limiting the largest UID at your site to 32,767 if possible.

By definition, root has UID 0. Most systems also define pseudo-users bin, daemon, and perhaps some others. It is customary to put such fake logins at the beginning of the **/etc/passwd** file and to give them low UIDs. To allow plenty of room for any non-human users you might want to add in the future, we recommend that you assign UIDs to real users starting at 100 (or higher).

*See page 43 for more information about **sudo**.*

It is never a good idea to have multiple accounts with UID 0. While it might seem convenient to have multiple root logins with different shells and/or passwords, this setup just creates more potential security holes and gives you multiple logins to secure. If people need to have alternate ways to log in as root, you are better off if they use a program like **sudo**.

Avoid recycling UIDs for as long as possible, even the UIDs of people that have left your organization and had their accounts permanently removed. This precaution prevents confusion if files are later restored from backups, where users are identified by UID rather than by login name.

See Chapter 17 for more information about NFS.

UIDs should be kept unique across your entire organization. That is, a particular UID should refer to the same login name and the same person on every machine. Failure to maintain distinct UIDs can result in security problems with systems such as NFS and can also result in confusion when a user moves from one workgroup to another.

It can be hard to maintain unique UIDs when groups of machines are administered by different people or organizations. The problems are both technical and political. The best solution is to have a central database that contains a record for each user and enforces uniqueness. (We use a homegrown database for this problem.) A simpler scheme is to assign each group within an organization a range of UIDs and let each group manage its own set. This solution keeps the UID spaces separate (a requirement if you are going to use NFS to share filesystems) but does not address the parallel issue of unique login names.

Default GID number

Like a UID, a group ID number is an unsigned 32-bit integer. GID 0 is reserved for the group called "root". GID 1 is the group "bin" and GID 2 is the group "daemon".

See page 73 for more information about set-gid directories.

Groups are defined in **/etc/group**, with the GID field in **/etc/passwd** providing the default (or "effective") GID at login time. The default GID is not treated specially when access is determined;[3] it is relevant only to the creation of new files and directories. New files are normally owned by the user's effective group. However, in direc-

---

3. Linux allows a user to be in up to 32 groups at once, and all groups are considered when access calculations are performed.

tories on which the setgid bit (02000) has been set and on filesystems mounted with the **grpid** option, new files default to the group of their parent directory.

GECOS field

The GECOS field is commonly used to record personal information about each user. It has no well-defined syntax. The GECOS field originally held the login information needed to transfer batch jobs from UNIX systems at Bell Labs to a mainframe running GECOS (the General Electric Comprehensive Operating System); these days, only the name remains.

Although you can use any formatting conventions you like, **finger** interprets comma-separated GECOS entries in the following order:

- Full name (often the only field used)
- Office number and building
- Office telephone extension
- Home phone number

The **chfn** command lets users change their own GECOS information. **chfn** is useful for keeping things like phone numbers up to date, but it can be misused: a user can change the information to be either obscene or incorrect. Our academic computing center, which caters to hordes of undergraduates, has disabled the **chfn** command.

Home directory

Users' shells are **cd**'d to their home directories when they log in. If a user's home directory is missing at login time, the system prints a message such as "no home directory."[4] Linux systems generally allow the login to proceed and put the user in the root directory. To disallow logins without a valid home directory, set DEFAULT_HOME to no in **/etc/login.defs**.

Be aware that if home directories are mounted over a network filesystem, they may be unavailable in the event of server or network problems.

Login shell

We recommend tcsh as the default shell for new users.

The login shell is normally a command interpreter such as the Bourne shell or the C shell (**/bin/sh** or **/bin/csh**), but it can be any program. **bash** is the default and is used if **/etc/passwd** does not specify a login shell. On Linux systems, **csh** and **sh** are really just links to **tcsh** (a superset of the C shell) and **bash** (the GNU "Bourne again" shell), respectively. Most distributions also provide a public-domain version of the Korn shell, **ksh**.

Users can change their shells with the **chsh** command. The file **/etc/shells** contains a list of "valid" shells that **chsh** will permit users to select; SuSE enforces this list, but

---

4. This message appears when you log in on the console or on a terminal, but not when you log in through a display manager such as **xdm**, **gdm**, or **kdm**. Not only will you not see the message, but you will generally be logged out immediately because of the display manager's inability to write to the proper directory (e.g., ~**/.gnome**).

Red Hat just warns you if the selected shell is not on the list. If you add entries to the **shells** file, be sure to use absolute paths since **chsh** and other programs expect them.

6.2 THE /ETC/SHADOW FILE

The **/etc/shadow** file is readable only by the superuser and serves to keep encrypted passwords safe from prying eyes. It also provides account information that's not available from **/etc/passwd**. The use of shadow passwords is standard on some distributions and configured as an optional package on others. Even when they're optional, it's a good idea to treat them as if they were standard.

When shadow passwords are in use, the old-style password fields in **/etc/passwd** should always contain an x.

The **shadow** file is not a superset of the **passwd** file, and the **passwd** file is not generated from it; you must maintain both files (or use tools such as **useradd** that maintain them both on your behalf). Like **/etc/passwd**, **/etc/shadow** contains one line for each user. Each line contains nine fields, separated by colons:

- Login name
- Encrypted password
- Date of last password change
- Minimum number of days between password changes
- Maximum number of days between password changes
- Number of days in advance to warn users about password expiration
- Number of days after password expiration that account is disabled
- Account expiration date
- A reserved field that is currently always empty

See page 96 for more information about **usermod***.*

The only fields that are required to be nonempty are the username and password. Absolute date fields in **/etc/shadow** are specified in terms of days (*not* seconds) since Jan 1, 1970, which is not a standard way of reckoning time on UNIX systems. Fortunately, you can use the **usermod** program to set the expiration field.

A typical **shadow** entry looks like this:

```
millert:inN0.VRsc1Wn.:11508:0:180:14::12417:
```

Here is a more complete description of each field:

- The login name is the same as in **/etc/passwd**. This field simply connects a user's **passwd** and **shadow** entries.

- The encrypted password is identical in concept and execution to the one previously stored in **/etc/passwd**.

- The last change field indicates the time at which the user's password was last changed. This field is generally filled in by **/usr/bin/passwd**.

- The fourth field sets the number of days that must elapse between password changes. Once users change their password, they cannot change it again until the specified period has elapsed. This feature seems useless, and we think it could be somewhat dangerous when a security intrusion has occurred. We recommend setting this field to 0.

- The fifth field sets the maximum number of days allowed between password changes. This feature allows the administrator to enforce password aging; see page 658 for more information. The actual enforced maximum number of days is the sum of this field and the seventh (grace period) field.

- The sixth field sets the number of days before password expiration that the **login** program should begin to warn the user of the impending expiration.

- The seventh field specifies how many days after the maximum password age has been reached to wait before treating the login as expired. This seems to be a rather pointless feature, and the Linux documentation is extremely vague with respect to its purpose. We had to read the source code to find out what it did.

- The eighth field specifies the day (in days since Jan 1, 1970) on which the user's account will expire. The user may not log in after this date until the field has been reset by an administrator. If the field is left blank, the account will never expire.

- The ninth field is reserved for future use.

Now that we know what each of the fields means, let's look at our example line again:

```
millert:inN0.VRsc1Wn.:11508:0:180:14::12417:
```

In this example, the user millert last changed his password on July 4, 2001. The password must be changed again within 180 days, and millert will receive warnings that the password needs to be changed for the last two weeks of this period. The account expires on December 31, 2003.

You can use the **pwconv** utility to reconcile the contents of the **shadow** file to those of the **passwd** file, picking up any new additions and deleting users that are no longer listed in **passwd**. **pwconv** fills in most of the shadow parameters from defaults specified in **/etc/login.defs**.

6.3 THE /ETC/GROUP FILE

The **/etc/group** file contains the names of UNIX groups and a list of each group's members. For example:

```
wheel:*:10:root,evi,garth,trent
csstaff:*:100:lloyd,evi
student:*:200:dotty
```

Each line represents one group and contains four fields:

- Group name
- Encrypted password (vestigial and rarely used)
- GID number
- List of members, separated by commas (be careful not to add spaces)

As in **/etc/passwd**, fields are separated by colons. Group names should be limited to 8 characters for compatibility reasons, although Linux does not actually require this. While it is possible to enter a group password (to allow users not belonging to a group to change to it by using the **newgrp** command), this is rarely done.[5] Most sites put stars in the password field, but it is safe to leave the password field blank if you wish. The **newgrp** command will not change to a group without a password unless the user is already listed as being a member of that group.

As with usernames and UIDs, group names and GIDs should be kept consistent among machines that share files through a network filesystem. Consistency can be hard to maintain in a heterogeneous environment, since different operating systems use different GIDs for the same group names. We've found that the best way to deal with this issue is to avoid using a system group as the default login group for a user.

If a user defaults to a particular group in **/etc/passwd** but does not appear to be in that group according to **/etc/group**, **/etc/passwd** wins the argument. The group memberships granted at login time are really the union of those found in the **passwd** and **group** files. However, it's a good idea to keep the two files consistent.

To minimize the potential for collisions with vendor-supplied GIDs, we suggest starting local groups at GID 100.

The UNIX tradition has always been to add new users to a group that represents their general category such as "students" or "finance." However, it's worth noting that such a convention increases the likelihood that users will be able to read each others' files because of slipshod permission-setting, even if that is not really the intention of the owner. To avoid this problem, we recommend that you create a unique group for each user. You can use the same name for both the user and the group.

A user's personal group should contain only that user. If you want to let users share files by way of the group mechanism, create separate groups for that purpose. The idea behind personal groups is not to discourage the use of groups per se—it's simply to establish a more restrictive *default* group for each user so that files are not shared inadvertently.

 Red Hat's version of **useradd** defaults to creating personal groups for new users. Although the Linux user maintenance utilities are very similar among distributions, this appears to be a Red Hat-specific feature.

---

5. The only reason we are aware of that someone might want to use the **newgrp** command under Linux is to set the default group of newly created files.

6.4   ADDING USERS

Before you create an account for a new user at a corporate, government, or educational site, it's very important that the user sign and date a copy of your local user agreement and policy statement. (What?! You don't have a user agreement and policy statement? See page 834 for more information about why you need one and what to put in it.)

Users have no particular reason to want to sign a policy agreement, so it's to your advantage to secure their signatures while you still have some leverage. We find that it takes more effort to secure a signed agreement after an account has been released. If your process allows for it, it's best to have the paperwork precede the creation of the account.

Mechanically, the process of adding a new user consists of three steps required by the system, two steps that establish a useful environment for the new user, and several extra steps for your own convenience as an administrator.

Required:

- Edit the **passwd** and **shadow** files to define the user's account.
- Set an initial password.
- Create, **chown**, and **chmod** the user's home directory.

For the user:

- Copy default startup files to the user's home directory.
- Set the user's mail home and establish mail aliases.

For you:

- Add the user to the **/etc/group** file.
- Configure disk quotas.
- Verify that the account is set up correctly.
- Add the user's contact information and account status to your database.

The **useradd** command and its brethren can perform some of these steps for you, but in the next few sections we'll go over the steps as you'd execute them by hand. This is mostly so that you can see what the supplied tools are doing. In real life, it's generally preferable (faster and less error prone) to run **useradd** or a similar home-grown script.

You must perform each step as root or use a program such as **sudo** that allows you to run commands as root.

Editing the passwd and shadow files

To safely edit the **passwd** file, run **vipw** to invoke a text editor on a copy of it. The default editor is **vi**, but you can specify a different editor by setting the value of your EDITOR environment variable. The existence of the temporary edit file serves as a lock; **vipw** allows only one person to edit the **passwd** file at a time, and it prevents users from changing their passwords while the **passwd** file is checked out. When the editor terminates, **vipw** replaces the original **passwd** file with your edited copy.

For example, adding the following line to **/etc/passwd** would define an account called "tyler":

```
tyler:*:103:100:Tyler Stevens, ECEE 3-27, x7919,:/home/staff/tyler:/bin/tcsh
```

We'd also add a matching entry to **/etc/shadow** by running **vipw -s**:

```
tyler:*::::::12417:
```

This **shadow** line for "tyler" has no encrypted password or password aging and sets the account to expire on December 31, 2003.

Setting an initial password

Root can change any user's password with the **passwd** command:

```
# passwd user
```

Rules for selecting good passwords are given on page 655.

passwd prompts you to enter a new password and asks you to repeat it. If you choose a short, all-lowercase, or otherwise obviously unsuitable password, **passwd** will complain and ask you to use something more complex. Red Hat and SuSE check prospective passwords against a dictionary for added security.

The **mkpasswd** utility that comes with Don Libes's **expect** package makes it easy to generate random passwords for new users. For better or worse, the assignment of a random password "forces" new users to change their passwords immediately, as the random ones are difficult to remember. Don't confuse **expect**'s **mkpasswd** with the standard **mkpasswd** command, which simply encodes a given string as a password.

Never leave a new account—or any account that has access to a shell—without a password.

Creating the user's home directory

Any directory you create as root is initially owned by root, so you must change its owner and group with the **chown** command. The following sequence of commands would create a home directory appropriate for our example user:

```
# mkdir /home/staff/tyler
# chown tyler.staff /home/staff/tyler
# chmod 700 /home/staff/tyler
```

Copying in the default startup files

You can customize some commands and utilities by placing configuration files in a user's home directory. Startup files traditionally begin with a dot and end with the letters **rc**, short for "run command," a relic of the CTSS operating system. The initial dot causes **ls** to elide these files from directory listings unless the **-a** option is used; the files are considered "uninteresting." Table 6.1 on the next page lists some common startup files.

Table 6.1   Common startup files and their uses

Command	Filename	Typical uses
csh/tcsh	.login	Sets the terminal type (if needed) Sets up environment variables Sets **biff** and **mesg** switches
	.cshrc	Sets command aliases Sets the search path Sets the **umask** value to control permissions Sets cdpath for filename searches Sets the prompt, history, and savehist variables
	.logout	Prints "to do" reminders Clears the screen
sh	.profile	Similar to **.login** and **.cshrc** for **sh**
bash[a]	.bashrc	Similar to **.cshrc** for **bash**
	.bash_profile	Similar to **.login** for **bash**
vi	.exrc	Sets **vi** editor options
emacs	.emacs	Sets **emacs** editor options Sets **emacs** key bindings
mail/mailx	.mailrc	Defines personal mail aliases Sets mail reader options
xrdb	.Xdefaults	Specifies X11 configuration: fonts, color, etc.
startx	.xinitrc	Specifies the initial X11 environment
	.Xclients	Specifies the initial X11 environment (Red Hat)
xdm	.xsession	Specifies the initial X11 environment

a. **bash** will also read **.profile** or **/etc/profile** in emulation of **sh**.

If you don't already have a set of good default startup files, **/usr/local/lib/skel** is a reasonable place to put them. Copy in some files to use as a starting point and modify them with a text editor. You may wish to start with vendor-supplied files from the **/etc/skel** directory. Be sure to set a reasonable value for the a new user's **umask** (we suggest 077, 027, or 022, depending on the friendliness and size of your site).

Depending on the user's shell, **/etc** may contain system-wide startup files that are processed before the user's own startup files. For example, **sh** (**bash**, really) reads **/etc/profile** before processing ~**/.profile**. For other shells, see the man page for the shell in question for details.

The command sequence for installing startup files for the new user tyler would look something like this:

```
# cp /usr/local/lib/skel/.[a-zA-Z]* ~tyler
# chmod 644 ~tyler/.[a-zA-Z]*
# chown tyler ~tyler/.[a-zA-Z]*
# chgrp staff ~tyler/.[a-zA-Z]*
```

Note that we cannot use

```
# chown tyler ~tyler/.*
```

because tyler would then own not only his own files but also the parent directory ".." (**/home/staff**) as well. This is a very common and dangerous sysadmin mistake.

Setting the user's mail home

It is convenient for each user to receive email on only one machine. This scheme is often implemented with an entry in the global aliases file **/etc/mail/aliases** or the **sendmail** userDB on the central mail server. See Chapter 19 for general information about email; the various ways to implement mail homes are discussed starting on page 525.

Editing the /etc/group file

To continue the processing of the new user tyler, we should add his login name to the list of users in group 100, since that was the default group to which we assigned him in the **/etc/passwd** file. Strictly speaking, tyler will be in group 100 whether he is listed in **/etc/group** or not, because his **passwd** entry has already given him this membership. However, this information should be entered in **/etc/group** so that you always know exactly which users belong to which groups.[6]

Setting disk quotas

If your site uses disk quotas, you should set quota limits for each new account with the **edquota** command. **edquota** can be used interactively, but it is more commonly used in "prototype" mode to model the quotas of the new user after those of someone else. For example, the command

```
# edquota -p proto-user new-user
```

sets *new-user*'s quotas to be the same as *proto-user*'s. This way of using **edquota** is especially useful in scripts.

Since disk space is cheap these days, we're not big proponents of disk quotas. They often seem to cause more problems than they solve, and they impose an additional support burden on administrators. Back when we used quotas (many years ago), we maintained several accounts that existed only to serve as user quota prototypes.

Verifying the new login

To verify that a new account has been properly configured, first log out, then log in as the new user and execute the following commands:

```
% pwd       /* To verify the home directory */
% ls -la    /* Check owner/group of startup files */
```

---

6. The kernel doesn't actually care what's in **/etc/passwd** or **/etc/group**; it only cares about raw UID and GID numbers. **passwd** and **group** store account information for use by high-level software such as **login**. See page 110 for details about the login process.

You will need to notify new users of their login names and initial passwords. Many sites send this information by email, but for security reasons that's usually not a good idea. A new user's account can be compromised and back-doored before they've even logged in. This is also a good time to point users toward additional documentation on local customs if you have any.

See page 834 for more information about written user contracts.

If your site requires users to sign a written contract, be sure this step has been completed before releasing the account. This check will prevent oversights and strengthen the legal basis of any sanctions you might later need to impose.

Be sure to remind new users to change their passwords immediately. (If you wish, you can enforce this by setting the password to expire within a short time. Another option is to check up on new users and be sure their encrypted passwords in the **shadow** file have changed.)

Recording the user's status and contact information

In an environment in which you know all the users personally, it's relatively easy to keep track of who's using a system and why. But if you manage a large and changeable user base, you'll need a more formal way to keep track of accounts. Maintaining a database of contact information and account statuses will help you figure out who someone is and why they have an account once the act of adding them has faded from memory. It's a good idea to keep complete contact information on hand so that you can reach users in the event of problems or misbehavior.

6.5 REMOVING USERS

When a user leaves your organization, that user's login account and files should be removed from the system. This procedure involves removing all references to the login name that were added by you or your **useradd** program. The automated counterpart to **useradd** is **userdel**. If you remove a user by hand, you may want to use the following checklist:

- Set the user's disk quota to zero if quotas are in use.
- Remove the user from any local user databases or phone lists.
- Remove the user from the **aliases** file or add a forwarding address.
- Remove the user's crontab file and any pending **at** jobs.
- Kill any of the user's processes that are still running.
- Remove any temporary files owned by the user in **/var/tmp** or **/tmp** (a bit anal retentive, but helpful in some cases).
- Remove the user from the **passwd**, **shadow**, and **group** files.
- Remove the user's home directory.
- Remove the user's mail spool.

Before you remove a user's home directory, be sure to relocate any files that are needed by other users. Since you often can't be sure which files those might be, it's always a good idea to make an extra tape backup of the user's home directory and mail spool before deleting them.

Once you have removed a user, you may want to verify that the user's old UID owns no more files on the system. To find the paths of orphaned files, you can use the **find** command with the **-nouser** argument. Because **find** has a way of "escaping" onto network servers if you're not careful, it's usually best to check filesystems individually with **-xdev**:

> # **find** *filesystem* -xdev -nouser

If your organization assigns individual workstations to users, it's generally simplest and most efficient to reinstall the entire system from a master template before turning the system over to a new user. Before you do the reinstallation, however, it's a good idea to back up any local files on the system's hard disk in case they are needed in the future.

6.6 DISABLING LOGINS

On occasion, a user's login must be temporarily disabled. Before networking invaded the computing world, we would just put a star in front of the encrypted password, making it impossible for the user to log in. However, users could still log in across the network without entering a password, so this technique no longer works very well.

These days, we replace the user's shell with a program that prints a message explaining why the login has been disabled and providing instructions for rectifying the situation. This pseudo-shell should not be listed in **/etc/shells**; many daemons that provide nonlogin access to the system (e.g., **ftpd**) check to see if a user's login shell is listed in **/etc/shells** and will deny access if it is not (which is the behavior you want). Unfortunately, this message will probably not be seen if logins at your site typically occur through a window system.

There is one problem with this method of disabling logins, however. By default, **sendmail** will not deliver mail to a user whose shell does not appear in **/etc/shells**. It's generally a bad idea to interfere with the flow of mail, even if the recipient is not able to read it immediately. You can defeat **sendmail**'s default behavior by adding a fake shell named **/SENDMAIL/ANY/SHELL/** to the **/etc/shells** file (although there may be unwanted side effects from doing so).

6.7 ACCOUNT MANAGEMENT UTILITIES

The **useradd** command adds users to the **passwd** file (and to the **shadow** file if applicable). It provides a command-line-driven interface that is easy to run by hand or to call from a home-grown **adduser** script. The **usermod** command changes the **passwd** entries of existing users. The **userdel** command removes a user from the system, optionally deleting the user's home directory. The **groupadd**, **groupmod**, and **groupdel** commands also operate on the **/etc/group** file.

For example, to create a new user "hilbert" with **useradd** (using the system defaults), you could simply run:

> # **useradd hilbert**

This command would create the following entry in **/etc/passwd**. Note that **useradd** puts a star in the password field, effectively disabling the account until you assign a real password.

```
hilbert:*:105:20::/home/hilbert:/bin/sh
```

Beware: if you do not specify the groups for the new user explicitly, the user will be assigned to a default group (usually "users") but the **/etc/group** file will not be up-dated to include the new user's name.

useradd is generally more useful when given additional arguments. In the next ex-ample, we specify that hilbert's primary group should be "faculty" and that he should also be added to the "famous" group. We also override the default home directory location and ask **useradd** to create the home directory if it does not already exist:

```
# useradd -c "David Hilbert" -d /home/math/hilbert -g faculty -G famous -m
    -s /bin/tcsh hilbert
```

This command creates the following **passwd** entry:

```
hilbert:x:1005:30:David Hilbert:/home/math/hilbert:bin/tcsh
```

(the assigned UID is one higher than the highest UID on the system) and the corre-sponding **shadow** entry:

```
hilbert:!:11508:0:99999:7:0::
```

It also adds hilbert to the "faculty" and "famous" groups in **/etc/group**, creates the directory **/home/math/hilbert**, and populates it in accordance with the contents of the **/etc/skel** directory.

You can determine the default **useradd** settings with **useradd -D**; you can also use the **-D** flag in combination with other arguments to set those defaults. The defaults are stored in **/etc/default/useradd** and can be edited directly if you prefer.

usermod modifies an account that already exists and takes many of the same flags as **useradd**. For example, we could use the following command to set an expiration date of July 4, 2003 on hilbert's account:

```
# usermod -e "July 4, 2003" hilbert
```

The **userdel** command deletes user accounts, effectively undoing all the changes made by **useradd**. To remove hilbert, we would use the following command:

```
# userdel hilbert
```

This command removes references to hilbert in the **passwd**, **shadow**, and **group** files. By default, it would not remove hilbert's home directory.[7] The **-r** option makes **userdel** remove the user's home directory as well, but even at its most aggressive, **userdel** still performs only the last three tasks from the "user deletion chores" list.

---

7. At our site, we generally preserve deleted users' home directories for a few weeks. This policy mini-mizes the need to restore data from backup tapes if a deleted user should return or if other users need access to the deleted user's work files.

Although the **useradd** and **userdel** commands are convenient, they are usually not sufficient to implement all of a site's local policies. Don't hesitate to write your own **adduser** and **rmuser** scripts; most larger sites do. (Perl is generally the appropriate tool for this task.) Your homebrew scripts can call the standard utilities to accomplish part of their work.

6.8 EXERCISES

E6.1   How is a user's default group determined? How would you change it?

E6.2   Explain the differences among the following umask values: 077, 027, 022, and 755. How you would attempt to implement one of these values as a site-wide default for new users? Can you impose a **umask** standard on your users?

E6.3   What is the purpose of the shadow password file?

★ **E6.4**   List the steps needed to add a user to a system without using the **useradd** program. What extra steps are needed for your local environment?

★ **E6.5**   Determine the naming convention for new users at your site. What are the rules? How is uniqueness preserved? Can you think of any drawbacks? How are users removed?

★★ **E6.6**   Find a list of students' names (from a local on-line telephone directory, perhaps) and use it as the input to a script that forms login names according to the naming convention at your site. How many users can you accommodate before you have a collision? How many collisions are there overall? Use this data to evaluate your site's naming convention and suggest improvements.

★★ **E6.7**   Write a script to help monitor the health of your **/etc/passwd** file. (Parts b and e require root access unless you're clever.)

a) Find any entries that have UID 0.
b) Find any entries that have no password (needs **/etc/shadow**).
c) Find any sets of entries that have duplicate UIDs.
d) Find any entries that have duplicate login names.
e) Find any entries that have no expiration date (needs **/etc/shadow**).

★★★★★ **E6.8**   Design a schema for an LDAP database that stores user information such as login, password, shell, authorized machines, etc. Build a tool that enters new users into the database interactively or obtains from a file a list of users to create. Build a tool that generates from the LDAP database the **passwd**, **group**, and **shadow** files for the machines in your lab. Allow students to have different passwords on each machine if they want. (Not all students are necessarily authorized to use each computer.) Your **adduser** system should be able to print lists of login names for instructors and print login/password pairs for new users.

7 *Serial Devices*

Child left to its own serial devices

Serial ports are one of the handiest I/O facilities available on Linux systems. Although they are not especially fast, they are flexible and cheap.

Serial ports can be used with a variety of devices, including printers, terminals, and other computers. They're also found on a lot of custom-made, hobbyist, and low-volume equipment (media changers, temperature sensors, even sewing machines). A device can be attached to the system either directly (with a cable) or via a telephone line with modems at each end.

This chapter describes how to attach serial devices to your system and explains how to configure your software to take advantage of them. We will often use modems and printers as specific examples, but other devices are essentially similar.

The first few sections address serial hardware and cabling considerations. Then, starting on page 110, we talk about the software infrastructure that has historically been used to support hardware terminals. Terminals are rarely used anymore, but their ghosts live on in Linux's handling of pseudo-terminals and window systems. The rest of the chapter (starting on page 117) provides some general background on modems, serial debugging, parallel ports, and USB (the Universal Serial Bus).

7.1 SERIAL STANDARDS

Most serial ports obey some variant of the standard known as RS-232. This standard specifies the electrical characteristics and meaning of each signal wire, as well as pin assignments on the traditional 25-pin (DB-25) serial connector shown in Exhibit A.

Exhibit A   A male DB-25 connector

Connector	Pin numbers

Full RS-232[1] is overkill for all real-world situations, since it defines numerous signals that are unnecessary for basic communication. DB-25 connectors are also inconveniently large. As a result, a number of alternative connectors have come into widespread use. These are described in the section titled *Alternative connectors* starting on page 102.

Traditional RS-232 uses shielded, twisted-pair cable (STP), usually stranded 22-gauge wire. The original RS-232 signal voltages were ±12 volts DC, but ±5 volts is more common these days. Sometimes, ±3 volts is used. Higher voltages are less susceptible to interference. All of these voltages comply with the RS-232 specification, so it's perfectly OK to connect devices that use different voltage standards.

RS-232 is not an electrically "balanced" system; it uses a single conductor for the data traveling in each direction. Ergo, the special electrical properties of twisted-pair cabling may be less significant for serial communication than they are for, say, Ethernet. In fact, twisted-pair cable can actually reduce the reliability and range of a serial connection if the two data lines (TD and RD) are placed together on a single pair. So don't do that.

There is no commonly agreed-upon standard for which RS-232 signals should be run together on a twisted-pair cable. Some sources recommend pairing signal grounds with both TD and RD, but this pairing costs an extra conductor and provides multiple paths for the signal ground. As far as we know, there is no compelling reason to use this convention.

DB-25 connectors are either male (with pins sticking out, called DB25P) or female (with matching holes, DB25S). There are tiny invisible numbers near the pins or holes which label them from 1 to 25. You can see the numbers best by holding the connector up to the light and viewing it at an angle. Sometimes only pins 1, 13, 14, and 25 are numbered.

---

1. To be technically correct, this standard should now be referred to as EIA-232-E. However, no one will have the slightest idea what you are talking about.

Exhibit A shows a male DB-25. As with all serial connectors, the pin numbers on a female connector are a mirror image of those on a male connector, so that like-numbered pins mate. The diagram is drawn from the orientation shown (as if you were facing the end of the cable, about to plug the connector into your forehead).

Note that in Exhibit A, only seven pins are actually installed. This is typical for the real world. The RS-232 signals and their pin assignments on a DB-25 connector are shown in Table 7.1. Only the shaded signals are ever used in practice (at least on generic computer systems); all others can be ignored.

Table 7.1   RS-232 signals and pin assignments on a DB-25

Pin	Name	Function	Pin	Name	Function
1	FG	Frame ground	14	STD	Secondary TD
2	TD	Transmitted data	15	TC	Transmit clock
3	RD	Received data	16	SRD	Secondary RD
4	RTS	Request to send	17	RC	Receive clock
5	CTS	Clear to send	18	–	Not assigned
6	DSR	Data set ready	19	SRTS	Secondary RTS
7	SG	Signal ground	20	DTR	Data terminal ready
8	DCD	Data carrier detect	21	SQ	Signal quality detector
9	–	Positive voltage	22	RI	Ring indicator
10	–	Negative voltage	23	DRS	Data rate selector
11	–	Not assigned	24	SCTE	Clock transmit external
12	SDCD	Secondary DCD	25	BUSY	Busy
13	SCTS	Secondary CTS			

There are two interface configurations for serial equipment: DTE (Data Terminal Equipment) and DCE (Data Communications Equipment). DTE and DCE share the same pinouts, but they specify different interpretations of the RS-232 signals.

Every device is configured as either DTE or DCE; a few support both, but not simultaneously. Computers, terminals, and printers are generally DTE, and most modems are DCE. DTE and DCE serial ports can communicate with each other in any combination, but different combinations require different cabling.

There is no sensible reason for both DTE and DCE to exist; all equipment could use the same wiring scheme. The existence of two conventions is merely one of the many pointless historical legacies of RS-232.

DTE and DCE can be quite confusing if you let yourself think about the implications too much. When that happens, just take a deep breath and reread these points:

- The RS-232 pinout for a given connector type is always the same, regardless of whether the connector is male or female (matching pin numbers always mate) and regardless of whether the connector is on a cable, a DTE device, or a DCE device.

- All RS-232 terminology is based on the model of a straight-through connection from a DTE device to a DCE device. (By "straight through," we mean that TD on the DTE end is connected to TD on the DCE end, and so on. Each pin connects to the same-numbered pin on the other end.)

- Signals are named relative to the perspective of the DTE device. For example, the name TD (transmitted data) really means "data transmitted from DTE to DCE." Despite the name, the TD pin is an *input* on a DCE device. Similarly, RD is an input for DTE and an output for DCE.

- When you wire DTE equipment to DTE equipment (computer-to-terminal or computer-to-computer), you must trick each device into thinking that the other is DCE. For example, both DTE devices will expect to transmit on TD and receive on RD; you must cross-connect the wires so that one device's transmit pin goes to the other's receive pin, and vice versa.

- Three sets of signals must be crossed in this fashion for DTE-to-DTE communication (if you choose to connect them at all). TD and RD must be crossed. RTS and CTS must be crossed. And each side's DTR pin must be connected to both the DCD and DSR pins of the peer.

- To add to the confusion, a cable crossed for DTE-to-DTE communication is often called a "null modem" cable. You might be tempted to use a null modem cable to hook up a modem, but since modems are DCE, that won't work! A cable for a modem is called a "modem cable" or a "straight cable."

Because the issue of DTE vs. DCE is so confusing, you may occasionally see well-intentioned but ill-advised attempts to bring some sanity to the nomenclature by defining DTE and DCE as if they had separate pinouts (e.g., renaming DCE's TD pin to be RD, and vice versa). In this alternate universe, pinouts vary but cable connections (by signal name) do not. We suggest that you ignore any material that talks about a "DTE pinout" or a "DCE pinout"; it is unlikely to be a reliable source of information.

Originally, DTE devices were supposed to have male connectors and DCE devices were supposed to have female ones. Eventually, hardware designers realized that male connectors are more fragile. Expensive computing hardware now usually has female connectors, and most cables are male on both ends.[2]

Exhibit B on the next page shows pin assignments and connections for both null-modem and straight-through cables. Only signals used in the real world are shown.

2. At Qwest, the terms "male" and "female" are considered inappropriate. Employees are encouraged to use the words "plug" and "receptacle." The standard connector names DB25P and DB25S actually derive from yet a third convention: "pin" and "socket."

Exhibit B   Pin assignments and connections for DB-25 cables

Legend		Straight	Null modem
Frame ground	FG		
Transmitted data	TD		
Received data	RD		
Request to send	RTS		
Clear to send	CTS		
Data set ready	DSR		
Signal ground	SG		
Data carrier detect	DCD		
Data terminal ready	DTR		

Straight: 1–1, 2–2, 3–3, 4–4, 5–5, 6–6, 7–7, 8–8, 20–20

Null modem: 1–1, 2 and 3 crossed, 4 and 5 crossed, 6 and 20 and 7 and 8 crossed

7.2 ALTERNATIVE CONNECTORS

The following sections describe the most common alternative connector systems: mini DIN-8, DB-9, and RJ-45. Despite their physical differences, these connectors all provide access to the same electrical signals as a DB-25. Devices that use different connectors are always compatible if the right kind of converter cable is used.

The mini DIN-8 variant

Mini DIN-8s are found on Macs and on some laptops and workstations. This almost circular and extremely compact connector provides connections for seven signals. It is illustrated in Exhibit C.

Exhibit C   A male mini DIN-8 connector

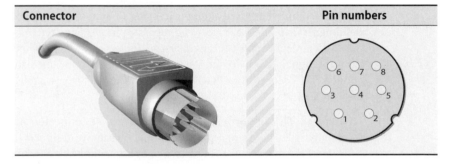

Connector	Pin numbers

Neighborhood computer dealers usually carry injection-molded DB-25 to mini DIN-8 converter cables. Don't try to make them yourself because a mini DIN-8 is so tiny that it defies attempts to secure connections with human fingers. Pin assignments are shown in Table 7.2.

Table 7.2   **Pins for a mini DIN-8 to DB-25 straight cable**

DIN-8	DB-25	Signal	Function
3	2	TD	Transmitted data
5	3	RD	Received data
6	4	RTS	Request to send
2	5	CTS	Clear to send
4,8	7	SG	Signal ground
7	8	DCD	Data carrier detect
1	20	DTR	Data terminal ready

The DB-9 variant

Commonly found on PCs, this nine-pin connector (which looks like a DB-25 "junior") provides the eight most commonly used signals.

Exhibit D   **A male DB-9 connector**

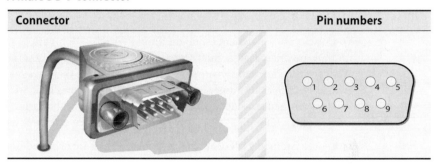

Connector	Pin numbers

PC dealers in your area should carry prefab DB-9 to DB-25 converter cables. Table 7.3 shows the pin assignments.

Table 7.3   **Pins for a DB-9 to DB-25 straight cable**

DB-9	DB-25	Signal	Function
3	2	TD	Transmitted data
2	3	RD	Received data
7	4	RTS	Request to send
8	5	CTS	Clear to send
6	6	DSR	Data set ready
5	7	SG	Signal ground
1	8	DCD	Data carrier detect
4	20	DTR	Data terminal ready

Serial Devices

The RJ-45 variant

An RJ-45 is an eight-wire modular telephone connector. It's similar to the standard RJ-11 connector used for telephone wiring in the United States, but an RJ-45 has eight pins (an RJ-11 has only four[3]). RJ-45 connectors are most commonly used for Ethernet wiring, but they work fine for serial communication, too.

Exhibit E   A male RJ-45 connector

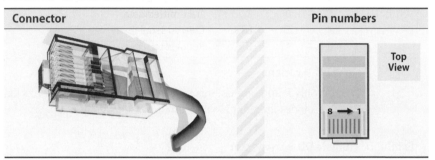

RJ-45 jacks are usually not found on computers or garden-variety serial equipment, but they are often used as intermediate connectors for routing serial lines through patch panels. They can sometimes be found on devices that have many ports in close proximity, such as terminal servers. RJ-45s are sometimes used with flat telephone cable rather than stranded twisted-pair. Either form of cable is acceptable for serial connections, although STP probably gives better signal quality at a distance.

RJ-45s are compact, self-securing, and cheap. They are crimped onto the cable with a special tool. It takes less than a minute to attach one. If you are designing a large cabling system from scratch, RJ-45s are a good choice for intermediate connectors.

There are several systems for mapping the pins on an RJ-45 connector to a DB-25. Table 7.4 shows the official RS-232D standard, which is used only haphazardly.

One alternative way of using RJ-45s is with Dave Yost's system, which adds an RJ-45 socket to every device and uses only a single type of RJ-45 connector cable regardless of whether the devices are DTE or DCE. Dave's system is more than just a pinout; it's a complete cabling system that addresses several different issues. Dave's standard is presented in the next section.

The Yost standard for RJ-45 wiring

This specification was written by Dave Yost (Dave@Yost.com).

Here is a scheme that offers solutions to several RS-232 hassles:

- All cable connectors are of the same sex and type (male RJ-45).
- There is no distinction between DTE and DCE.

---

3. Careful inspection will reveal that an RJ-11 plug actually has six slots where pins might go but that only four conductors are installed. A true 4-conductor telephone connector is an RJ-10. An RJ-11 with all six pins installed is known as an RJ-12.

Table 7.4   Pins for an RJ-45 to DB-25 straight cable

RJ-45	DB-25	Signal	Function
1	6	DSR	Data set ready
2	8	DCD	Data carrier detect
3	20	DTR	Data terminal ready
4	7	SG	Signal ground
5	3	RD	Received data
6	2	TD	Transmitted data
7	5	CTS	Clear to send
8	4	RTS	Request to send

- You need only one kind of connector cable.
- You can mass-produce cables quickly, using only a crimping tool.

Each serial port on every piece of equipment gets its own appropriately wired DB-25 or DB-9 to RJ-45 adaptor. This adaptor is permanently screwed onto the port. The port now presents the same connector interface, female RJ-45, regardless of whether its underlying connector is DB-25 or DB-9, DTE or DCE, male or female. Furthermore, every serial port now transmits and receives data on the same pins.

Once you have put these adaptors on your RS-232 ports, you can connect anything to anything without using null-modems or null-terminals, changing pins on cable connectors, or building special cables. You can connect modem to computer, modem to terminal, terminal to computer, terminal to terminal, computer to computer, etc., all with one kind of cable.

The cables are jacketed, eight-wire ribbon cable. The connectors on each end are squeezed onto the cable with a crimping tool, so there is no soldering or messing with pins.

There are three signal wires (one data and two control) going in each direction, plus a pair of signal grounds. The cables are not wired normally (i.e., with each connector pin connected to the corresponding pin at the other end of the cable). They are wired "with a twist," or "mirror image," or "side-to-side reversed," or whatever you want to call it. That is, pin 1 at one end of the cable goes to pin 8 on the other end, etc. (This meaning of "twist" is distinct from its use in the term "twisted pair.") This scheme works because the layout of the signals on the ribbon cable is symmetrical. That is, each transmit pin has its corresponding receive pin at the mirror-image wire position across the flat cable.[4]

Ready-made RJ-45 cables are usually wired straight through. To use them with this system, you will have to remove the connector from one end and crimp on a new one with the wires reversed. Female-to-female RJ-45 connectors ("butt blocks") are

4. Dave doesn't say this explicitly, but you must in fact wire the cable without a physical twist to achieve the "with a twist" effect. Because the connectors at the ends of a cable point away from each other, their pin numbering is automatically reversed.

available for extending cable lengths, but remember: two twisted cables joined with such a coupler make a straight-through cable.

Many vendors make DB-25 to RJ-45 adaptors. Their internal color coding does not match the cable colors. The adaptors, wire connectors, and wire have become available at electronics stores, sadly without any help on using them for RS-232.

See page 338 for more information about Category 5 cable.

This scheme was intended for use with jacketed ribbon cable, in which all the wires are side by side. Twisted-pair cable, by contrast, has four pairs of wire, each pair twisted against itself along the cable's length. If you use twisted-pair cable (such as Category 5 cable), you should not wire your cables as you normally would for RJ-45 (e.g., for 10BaseT, telephone, etc.). Rather, you should wire them so that wires 3:4 and wires 5:6 make pairs. Other pairings will be susceptible to data signal crosstalk. The pairing of the remaining wires is not important, but 1:2 and 7:8 will be about as good as any.

Inside an adaptor is an RJ-45 socket with eight wires coming out of it. These wires have RS-232 pins (or pin sockets, as appropriate) crimped onto them. You simply push these pins into the proper holes in the RS-232 connector and then snap the adaptor housing on.

Table 7.5   Wiring for a Yost RJ-45 to DB-25 or DB-9 adaptor

RJ-45 Cable			Adaptor	Connect to DCE pins			Connect to DTE pins		
				DB-25	DB-9	Signal	DB-25	DB-9	Signal
1	Brown	(to Gray)	Blue	4	7	RTS	5	8	CTS
2	Blue	(to Orange)	Orange	20	4	DTR	8	1	DCD
3	Yellow	(to Black)	Black	2	3	TD	3	2	RD
4	Green	(to Red)	Red	7	5	GND	7	5	GND
5	Red	(to Green)	Green	7	5	GND	7	5	GND
6	Black	(to Yellow)	Yellow	3	2	RD	2	3	TD
7	Orange	(to Blue)	Brown	8	1	DCD	20	4	DTR
8	Gray	(to Brown)	White	5	8	CTS	4	7	RTS

There is one problem, however: both ground pins have to go into the same DB-25 or DB-9 hole (pin 7 or 5, respectively). You can crimp these wires together so they come out to one pin with a tiny plastic thingy made by AMP called a "Tel-splice connector ½ tap dry," part number 553017-4. So far, this part seems to be available only in quantity 1,000 for $80 or so. Believe me, you want them if you're going to wire more than a few adaptors.

Some DTE devices require the DSR signal to be active before they will send data. This signal is usually provided by the DCE device, but you can fake it by wiring together pins 20 and 6 (4 and 6 on a DB-9 connector). This way, the DTE device will receive the DSR signal from itself whenever it asserts DTR.

On some DCE printers, pin 7 of the RJ-45 adaptor (the brown wire) should be connected to the DSR line (pin 6 on both DB-25 and DB-9). Read your printer documentation to find out if it provides useful handshaking signals on DSR instead of DCD.

Dave Yost
Los Altos, CA
July 1999

Don't use either of these DSR hacks as a matter of course; add them only to specific devices that seem to need them (or that don't seem to work with the standard setup). Some "vanilla" devices tolerate the extra connections, but others become confused.

7.3   HARD AND SOFT CARRIER

Linux expects to see the DCD signal, carrier detect, go high (positive voltage) when a device is attached and turned on. This signal is carried on pin 8 of the standard DB-25 connector. If your serial cable has a DCD line and your computer really pays attention to it, you are using what is known as hard carrier. Most systems also allow soft carrier, where the computer pretends that DCD is always asserted.

For certain devices (particularly terminals), soft carrier is a great blessing. It allows you to get away with using only three lines for each serial connection: transmit, receive, and signal ground. However, modem connections really need the DCD signal. If a terminal is connected through a modem and the carrier signal is lost, the modem should hang up (especially on a long distance call!).

You normally specify soft carrier for a serial port in the configuration file for whatever client software you are using in conjunction with the port (e.g., **/etc/gettydefs** or **/etc/inittab** for a login terminal or **/etc/printcap** for a printer). You can also use **stty -clocal** to enable soft carrier on the fly. For example,

```
# stty -clocal < /dev/ttyS1
```

would enable soft carrier for the port **ttyS1**.

7.4   HARDWARE FLOW CONTROL

The CTS and RTS signals are used to make sure that a device does not send data faster than the receiver can process it. For example, if a modem is in danger of running out of buffer space (perhaps because the connection to the remote site is slower than the serial link between the local machine and the modem), it can tell the computer to shut up until more room becomes available in the buffer.

Flow control is essential for high-speed modems and is also very useful for printers. On systems that do not support hardware flow control (either because the serial ports do not understand it or because the serial cable leaves CTS and RTS disconnected), flow control can sometimes be simulated in software with the ASCII characters XON and XOFF. However, software flow control must be explicitly supported by high-level software, and even then it does not work very well.

XON and XOFF are <Control-Q> and <Control-S>, respectively. This is a problem for **emacs** users because <Control-S> is the default key binding for the **emacs** search

Serial Devices

command. To fix the problem, bind the search command to some other key or use **stty start** and **stty stop** to change the terminal driver's idea of XON and XOFF.

Most terminals ignore the CTS and RTS signals. By jumpering pins 4 and 5 together at the terminal end of the cable, you can fool the few terminals that require a handshake across these pins before they will communicate. When the terminal sends out a signal on pin 4 saying "I'm ready," it gets the same signal back on pin 5 saying "Go ahead." You can also jumper the DTR/DSR/DCD handshake in this way.

As with soft carrier, hardware flow control can be manipulated through configuration files or set with **stty**.

7.5 CABLE LENGTH

The RS-232 standard specifies a maximum cable length of 75 feet at 9,600 bps. Standards are usually conservative, and RS-232 is no exception. We have routinely run RS-232 cables much greater distances, up to about 1,000 feet. We have hit the limit somewhere between 800 and 1,000 feet but have found that the particular brand of devices on each end makes quite a difference.

Line drivers or repeaters are sometimes used with RS-232 to extend the maximum length of a connection. Unfortunately, these devices often boost only the RD and TD pins, so other signals may need to be jumpered.

7.6 SERIAL DEVICE FILES

Serial ports are represented by device files in or under **/dev**. Most computers have two serial ports built in: **/dev/ttyS0** and **/dev/ttyS1**. Linux distributions usually come with a full complement of device files (64 or more) for additional serial ports preinstalled, but until you add more hardware to the system, the extra files are superfluous and should be ignored.

For historical reasons, the system's primary serial ports (**/dev/ttyS0** and **/dev/ttyS1**) are also known as **/dev/cua0** and **/dev/cua1**, respectively. The **cua*** files were formerly used to facilitate the management of modems that handled both incoming and outgoing calls. However, all of the functionality provided by the two-file system is now available through the **ttyS*** files alone, as long as the client software knows how to request it. Use of the **cua*** devices is now strongly discouraged, and Debian does not even create them by default.

If you find yourself stuck with an older software package that does not follow the current conventions, check the file **doc/ttyS-cua.txt** in the **mgetty** package for a description of the relationship between the **ttyS*** and **cua*** files.

As always, the names of the device files do not really matter. Behavior is determined by the major and minor device numbers, and the names of device files are merely a convenience for human users.

7.7 SETSERIAL: TELL THE DRIVER ABOUT SERIAL PORT PARAMETERS

The serial ports on a PC can be set to use several different I/O port addresses and interrupt levels (IRQs). These settings are normally accessed through the system's BIOS at power-on time. The most common reason to change them is to accommodate some cranky piece of hardware that is finicky about its own settings and will only work correctly when it has co-opted the settings normally used by a serial port. Unfortunately, the serial driver may not be able to detect such configuration changes without your help.

The traditional UNIX response to such diversity would be to allow the serial port parameters to be specified when the kernel is compiled. Fortunately, Linux lets you skip this tedious step and change the parameters on the fly with the **setserial** command. **setserial -g** shows the current settings:

```
# setserial -g /dev/ttyS0
/dev/ttyS0, UART: 16550A, Port: 0x03f8, IRQ: 4
```

To set the parameters, you specify the device file and then a series of parameters and values. For example, the command

```
# setserial /dev/ttyS1 port 0x02f8 irq 3
```

sets the I/O port address and IRQ for **ttyS1**. It's important to keep in mind that this command does not change the hardware configuration in any way; it simply informs the Linux serial driver of the configuration. To change the actual settings of the hardware, consult your system's BIOS.

setserial changes only the current configuration, and the settings do not persist across reboots. Unfortunately, there isn't a standard way to make the changes permanent; each of our example distributions does it differently.

 Red Hat's **/etc/rc.d/rc.sysinit** script checks for the existence of **/etc/rc.serial** and executes it at startup time if it exists. No example file is provided, so you must create the file yourself if you want to make use of this feature. Just list the **setserial** commands you want to run, one per line. For completeness, it's probably a good idea to make the file executable and to put **#!/bin/sh** on the first line; however, these *touches d'élégance* aren't strictly required.

 SuSE provides an **/etc/init.d/serial** script that handles serial port initialization. Unfortunately, this script has no configuration file; you must edit it directly to reflect the commands you want to run. Bad SuSE! The script uses its own little metalanguage to construct the **setserial** command lines, but fortunately there are plenty of commented-out example lines to choose from.

 Debian provides a nicely commented configuration file, **/etc/serial.conf**, that is read by **/etc/init.d/setserial**. It provides a variety of advanced features (such as persistent autoconfiguration) that are probably only useful for the designers of the distribution. For simple cases, just uncomment the lines you want or add your own in **setserial** format (omit the command name).

7.8 SOFTWARE CONFIGURATION FOR SERIAL DEVICES

Once a device has been connected with the proper cable, software on the host machine must be configured to take advantage of it. The configuration chores for a new device depend on the type of device and the uses to which it will be put:

- For a hardwired terminal, you must tell the system to listen for logins on the terminal's port. You specify the speed and parameters of the serial connection. Configuration for terminals is described in the next section.

- Dial-in modems are configured similarly to hardwired terminals. However, the exact procedure may be slightly different on some systems.

- To see how to use a modem to connect to a remote network using PPP, refer to page 290.

- See Chapter 24, *Printing*, for information about how to set up a serial printer. Some printers only receive data; others are bidirectional and can return status information to the host computer.

- A custom serial device that you will use only from your own software needs no special configuration. You can simply open the device file to access the device. Refer to the **termios** man page to learn how to set the speed, flag bits, and buffering mode of the serial port.

7.9 CONFIGURATION OF HARDWIRED TERMINALS

Over the last decade, cheap computers have almost entirely replaced ASCII terminals. However, even the "terminal" windows on a graphical display use the same drivers and configuration files as real terminals, so system administrators still need to understand how they work.

Terminal configuration involves two main tasks: making sure that a process is attached to a terminal to accept logins and making sure that information about the terminal is available once a user has logged in. Before we dive into the details of these tasks, however, let's take a look at the entire login process.

The login process

See page 29 for more information about the **init** *daemon.*

The login process involves several different programs, the most important of which is the **init** daemon. One of **init**'s jobs is to spawn a process, known generically as a **getty**, on each terminal port that is turned on in the **/etc/inittab** file. The **getty** sets the port's initial characteristics (such as speed and parity) and prints a login prompt.

The actual name of the **getty** program varies among Linux distributions, and some distributions provide multiple implementations. Red Hat and SuSE use a simplified version called **mingetty** to handle logins on virtual consoles. For the management of terminals and dial-in modems, they provide Gert Doering's **mgetty** implementation. Debian uses a single **getty** written by Wietse Venema et al.; this version is also provided on SuSE systems under the name **agetty**. An older implementation called **uugetty** has largely been superseded by **mgetty**.

To distinguish among this plenitude of **getty**s, think of them in order of complexity. **mingetty** is the simplest and is essentially just a placeholder for a **getty**. It can only handle logins on Linux virtual consoles. **agetty** is a bit more well-rounded and handles both serial ports and modems. **mgetty** is the current king of the hill. It handles incoming faxes as well as logins and does proper locking and coordination so that the same modem can be used as both a dial-in and a dial-out line.

The sequence of events in a complete login is as follows:

- **getty** prints the contents of the **/etc/issue** file, along with a login prompt.
- A user enters a login name at **getty**'s prompt.
- **getty** executes the **login** program with the specified name as an argument.
- **login** requests a password and validates it against **/etc/shadow**.[5]
- **login** prints the message of the day from **/etc/motd** and runs a shell.
- The shell executes the appropriate startup files.[6]
- The shell prints a prompt and waits for input.

When the user logs out, control returns to **init**, which wakes up and spawns a new **getty** on the terminal port.

Most of the configurability in this chain of events is concentrated in **/etc/inittab**, where the system's normal complement of **getty**s is defined, and in **/etc/gettydefs**, where some versions of **getty** look for additional configuration information.

The /etc/inittab file

init supports various "run levels" that determine which system resources are enabled. There are seven run levels numbered 0 to 6, with "s" recognized as a synonym for level 1 (single-user operation). When you leave single-user mode, **init** prompts you to enter a run level unless an initdefault field exists in **/etc/inittab** as described below. **init** then scans the **inittab** file for all lines that match the specified run level.

Run levels are usually set up so that you have one level in which only the console is enabled and another level that enables all **getty**s. You can define the run levels in whatever way is appropriate for your system; however, we recommend that you not stray too far from the defaults.

Entries in **inittab** are of the form

   id:run-levels:action:process

Here are some simple examples of **inittab** entries.

---

5. If shadow passwords are not in use, the password may come directly from **/etc/passwd**. In addition, **/etc/passwd** may be superseded or complemented by an administrative database system such as NIS. See Chapter 18 for more information.

6. **.profile** for **sh** and **ksh**; **.bash_profile** and **.bashrc** for **bash**; **.cshrc** and **.login** for **csh/tcsh**.

```
# Trap CTRL-ALT-DELETE
ca::ctrlaltdel:/sbin/shutdown -t3 -r now

# Run gettys in standard runlevels
1:2345:respawn:/sbin/mingetty tty1
2:2345:respawn:/sbin/mingetty tty2
```

In this format, *id* is a one- or two-character string used to identify the entry; it can be null. For terminal entries, it is customary to use the terminal number as the *id*.

run-levels enumerates the run levels to which the entry pertains. If no levels are specified (as in the first line), then the entry is valid for all run levels. The *action* tells how to handle the *process* field; Table 7.6 lists some of the more commonly used values.

Table 7.6   Common values for the /etc/inittab *action* field

Value	Wait?	Meaning
initdefault	–	Sets the initial run level
boot	No	Runs when **inittab** is read for the first time
bootwait	Yes	Runs when **inittab** is read for the first time
ctrlaltdel	No	Runs in response to a keyboard <Control-Alt-Delete>
once	No	Starts the process once
wait	Yes	Starts the process once
respawn	No	Always keeps the process running
powerfail	No	Runs when **init** receives a power fail signal
powerwait	Yes	Runs when **init** receives a power fail signal
sysinit	Yes	Runs before accessing the console

If one of the *run-levels* matches the current run level and the *action* field indicates that the entry is relevant, **init** uses **sh** to execute (or terminate) the command specified in the *process* field. The Wait? column in Table 7.6 tells whether **init** waits for the command to complete before continuing.

In the example **inittab** lines above, the last two lines spawn **mingetty** processes on the first two virtual consoles (accessed with <Alt-F1> and <Alt-F2>). If you add hardwired terminals or dial-in modems, the appropriate **inittab** lines will look similar to these. However, you must use **mgetty** or **getty** (**agetty** on SuSE) with such devices because **mingetty** is not sophisticated enough to handle them correctly. In general, respawn is the correct action and 2345 is an appropriate set of levels.

The command **telinit -q** makes **init** reread the **inittab** file.

 Different **gettys** require different configuration procedures. The **getty/agetty** version found on both SuSE and Debian is generally a bit cleaner than **mgetty** because it accepts all of its configuration information on the command line (in **/etc/inittab**).

The general model is

　/sbin/getty *port speed termtype*

*See page 113 for more information about the **terminfo** database.*

where *port* is the device file of the serial port relative to **/dev**, *speed* is the baud rate (e.g., 38400), and *termtype* identifies the default terminal type for the port. The *termtype* refers to an entry in the **terminfo** database. Most emulators simulate a DEC VT100, denoted **vt100**. There are many other minor options, most of which relate to the handling of dial-in modems.

  mgetty, provided by Red Hat and SuSE, is a bit more sophisticated than **agetty** in its handling of modems and integrates both incoming and outgoing fax capability. Unfortunately, its configuration is a bit more diffuse. In addition to other command-line flags, **mgetty** can accept an optional reference to an entry in **/etc/gettydefs** that specifies configuration details for the serial driver. Unless you're setting up a sophisticated modem configuration, you can usually get away without a **gettydefs** entry.

On Red Hat systems, use **man mgettydefs** to find the man page for the **gettydefs** file. It's named this way to avoid conflict with an older **gettydefs** man page that no longer exists on any Linux system.

A simple **mgetty** command line for a hardwired terminal looks something like this:

```
/sbin/mgetty -rs speed device
```

The *speed* is the baud rate (e.g., 38400), and the *device* is the device file for the serial port (use the full pathname).

If you want to specify a default terminal type for a port when using **mgetty**, you must do so in a separate file, **/etc/ttytype**, and not on the **mgetty** command line. The format of an entry in **ttytype** is:

```
termtype device
```

device is the short name of the device file representing the port, and *termtype* is the name of the appropriate **terminfo** entry (see the next section). For example:

```
linux      tty1
linux      tty2
vt100      ttyS0
vt100      ttyS1
```

Terminal support: the termcap and terminfo databases

Linux supports many different terminal types through the use of a database of terminal capabilities that specifies the features and programming quirks of each brand of terminal. There have historically been two competing terminal database formats: **termcap** and **terminfo**. For maximum compatibility, Linux distributions generally provide both. The **termcap** database is contained in the file **/etc/termcap**, and the **terminfo** database is stored beneath **/usr/share/terminfo**. The two databases are similar and typically use the same name for each terminal type, so the distinction between them is unimportant.

As shipped, both databases contain entries for hundreds of different terminals. In this terminal-less era, most are completely irrelevant. A good rule of thumb is that

Serial Devices

everything emulates a DEC VT100 until proven otherwise. Many emulators also support "ansi"; "linux" and "xterm" are useful for Linux consoles and **xterm** (X Windows terminal) windows, respectively.

See page 116 for more information about configuring terminals at login time.

Linux programs look at the TERM environment variable to determine what kind of terminal you are using. The terminal can then be looked up in **termcap** or **terminfo**. The system normally sets the TERM variable for you at login time, in accordance with the command-line arguments to **getty/agetty** or the contents of **/etc/ttytype**.

7.10 SPECIAL CHARACTERS AND THE TERMINAL DRIVER

The terminal driver supports several special functions that you access by typing particular keys (usually control keys) on the keyboard. The exact binding of functions to keys can be set with the **tset** and **stty** commands. Table 7.7 lists some of these functions, along with their default key bindings.

Table 7.7 Special characters for the terminal driver

Name	Default	Function
erase	\<Control-?>	Erases one character of input
werase	\<Control-W>	Erases one word of input
kill	\<Control-U>	Erases the entire line of input
eof	\<Control-D>	Sends an "end of file" indication
intr	\<Control-C>	Interrupts the currently running process
quit	\<Control-\>	Kills the current process with a core dump
stop	\<Control-S>	Stops output to the screen
start	\<Control-Q>	Restarts output to the screen
susp	\<Control-Z>	Suspends the current process
lnext	\<Control-V>	Interprets the next character literally

By default, PC versions of the Linux kernel generate a delete character (\<Control-?>) when the backspace key is pressed. (This key may be labeled "backspace" or "delete," or it may show only a backarrow graphic. It depends on the keyboard.) In the past, many UNIX systems used the backspace character (\<Control-H>) for this role. Unfortunately, the existence of two different standards for this function creates a multitude of problems.

You can use **stty erase** (see below) to tell the terminal driver which key code your setup is actually generating. However, some programs (such as text editors and shells with command editing features) have their own idea of what the backspace character should be, and they don't always pay attention to the terminal driver's setting. In a helpful but confusing twist, some programs obey both the backspace and delete characters. You may also find that remote systems that you log in to through the network make very different assumptions from those of your local system.

Solving these annoying little conflicts can be a Sunday project in itself. In general, there is no simple, universal solution. Each piece of software must be individually beaten into submission. Two useful resources to help with this task are the *Linux Backspace/Delete mini-HOWTO* from www.linuxdoc.org and a nifty article by Anne Baretta at www.ibb.net/~anne/keyboard.html.

7.11 STTY: SET TERMINAL OPTIONS

stty lets you directly change and query the various settings of the terminal driver. There are about a zillion options, but most can be safely ignored. **stty** generally uses the same names for driver options as the **termios** man page does, but there are occasional discrepancies.

stty's command-line options can appear in any order and in any combination. A dash before an option negates it. For example, to configure a terminal for 9,600 bps operation with even parity and without hardware tabs, use the command

```
% stty 9600 even -tabs
```

A good combination of options to use for a plain-vanilla terminal is

```
% stty intr ^C kill ^U erase ^? -tabs
```

Here, **-tabs** prevents the terminal driver from taking advantage of the terminal's built-in tabulation mechanism, which is useful because many emulators are not very smart about tabs. The other options set the interrupt, kill, and erase characters to <Control-C>, <Control-U>, and <Control-?> (delete), respectively.

You can use **stty** to examine the current modes of the terminal driver as well as to set them. **stty** with no arguments produces output like this:

```
% stty
speed 38400 baud; line = 0;
-brkint -imaxbel
```

For a more verbose status report, use the **-a** option:

```
% stty -a
speed 38400 baud; rows 50; columns 80; line = 0;
intr = ^C; quit = ^\; erase = ^?; kill = ^U; eof = ^D; eol = <undef>;
eol2 = <undef>; start = ^Q; stop = ^S; susp = ^Z; rprnt = ^R; werase = ^W;
lnext = ^V; flush = ^O; min = 1; time = 0;
-parenb -parodd cs8 -hupcl -cstopb cread -clocal -crtscts
-ignbrk -brkint -ignpar -parmrk -inpck -istrip -inlcr -igncr icrnl ixon -ixoff
-iuclc -ixany -imaxbel
opost -olcuc -ocrnl onlcr -onocr -onlret -ofill -ofdel nl0 cr0 tab0 bs0 vt0 ff0
isig icanon iexten echo echoe echok -echonl -noflsh -xcase -tostop -echoprt
echoctl echoke
```

The format of the output is similar but lists more information. The meaning of the output should be intuitively obvious (if you've written a terminal driver recently).

stty operates on the file descriptor of its standard input, so it is possible to set and query the modes of a terminal other than the current one by using the shell's input redirection character (<). You must be the superuser to change the modes on someone else's terminal.

7.12 TSET: SET OPTIONS AUTOMATICALLY

tset initializes the terminal driver to a mode appropriate for a given terminal type. The type can be specified on the command line; if it is left out, **tset** uses the value of the TERM environment variable.

tset supports a syntax for mapping certain values of the TERM environment variable into other values. This feature is useful if you often log in through a modem or data switch and would like to have the terminal driver configured correctly for the terminal you are really using on the other end of the connection rather than something generic and unhelpful such as "dialup."

For example, suppose that you use **xterm** at home and that the system you are dialing into is configured to think that the terminal type of a modem is "dialup." If you put the command

```
tset -m dialup:xterm
```

in your **.login** or **.profile** file, the terminal driver will be set appropriately for **xterm** whenever you dial in.

Unfortunately, the **tset** command is not really as simple as it pretends to be. To have **tset** adjust your environment variables in addition to setting your terminal modes, you will need lines something like this:

```
set noglob
eval `tset -s -Q -m dialup:xterm`
unset noglob
```

This incantation suppresses the messages that **tset** normally prints (the **-Q** flag), and asks that shell commands to set the environment be output instead (the **-s** flag). The shell commands printed by **tset** are captured by the backquotes and fed to the shell as input with the built-in command **eval**, causing the commands to have the same effect as if they had been typed by the user.

set noglob prevents the shell from expanding any metacharacters such as "*" and "?" that are included in **tset**'s output. This command is not needed by **sh/ksh** users (nor is the **unset noglob** to undo it), since these shells do not normally expand special characters within backquotes. The **tset** command itself is the same no matter what shell you use; **tset** looks at the environment variable SHELL to determine what flavor of commands to print out.

7.13 How to Unwedge a Terminal

Some programs (such as **vi**) make drastic changes to the state of the terminal driver while they are running. This meddling is normally invisible to the user, since the terminal state is carefully restored whenever the program exits or is suspended. However, it is possible for a program to crash or be killed without performing this housekeeping. When this happens, your terminal may behave very strangely: it might fail to handle newlines correctly, to echo characters that you type, or to execute commands properly.

Another common way to confuse a terminal is to accidentally run **cat** or **more** on a binary file. Most binaries contain a delicious mix of special characters that is guaranteed to send some of the less-robust emulators into outer space.

To fix this situation, you can use **reset** or **stty sane**. **reset** is actually just a link to **tset**, and it can accept most of **tset**'s arguments. However, it is usually run without arguments. Both **reset** and **stty sane** restore the correctitude of the terminal driver and send out an appropriate reset code from **termcap/terminfo**, if one is available.

In many cases where a **reset** is appropriate, the terminal has been left in a mode in which no processing is done on the characters you type. Most terminals generate carriage returns rather than newlines when the Return or Enter key is pressed; without input processing, this key generates <Control-M> characters instead of sending the current command off to be executed. To enter newlines directly, use <Control-J> or the line feed key (if there is one) instead of the Return key.

7.14 Modems

A modem converts the digital serial signal produced by a computer into an analog signal suitable for transmission on a standard phone line. Modems are used for a variety of applications. See page 290 for a typical example.

External modems have an RJ-11 jack on the analog side and an RS-232 interface of some type on the digital side—usually a female DB-25. On the front they usually have a series of lights that display the modem's current state and level of activity. These lights are incredibly useful for debugging, so modems should generally be located somewhere in plain sight.

Internal modems are usually seen only on PCs. They plug into an ISA, PCI, or PCM-CIA slot and have an RJ-11 jack that sticks out the back of the computer's case once the modem has been installed. They are cheaper than external modems but more troublesome to configure, and they generally lack indicator lights.

If you are considering an internal modem, you must check to be sure it's supported by Linux. Fast CPUs have made it possible to simplify modem hardware by performing some signal processing tasks on the host processor. Unfortunately, modems that work this way (known generically as Winmodems) require sophisticated drivers and are not universally supported under Linux. See Sean Walbran and Marvin Stodolsky's

Linmodem HOWTO (available from www.linuxdoc.org) for an overview of Winmodem support under Linux. (The *Modem HOWTO* is also very helpful for a broader perspective on the management of modems.)

Internal modems are usually made to appear as though they were connected through a phantom serial port from the perspective of user-level software. This convention helps to insulate the logical function of the modem from its hardware implementation. Standard software packages can drive the modem without having to know anything about its peculiarities.

Modems vary somewhat in general robustness, but this characteristic is hard to judge without direct experience. In the past, we have found some modems to be significantly more tolerant of line noise than others. These days, most designs use a standard chipset from one of several large manufacturers, so it's likely that the variations among modems are not as great as they once were.

High-speed modems require complex firmware, and this firmware is occasionally buggy. Manufacturers share firmware among models when possible, so good or bad firmware tends to run in product lines. For this reason, we still recommend sticking with well-known brands.

Modulation, error correction, and data compression protocols

Long ago, it was important to check the exact protocols supported by a modem because standards were continually changing and modem manufacturers did not always implement a complete suite of protocols. These days, modems all support pretty much the same standards. The only real difference between them is the quality of the firmware, electronics, and support.

A protocol's baud rate is the rate at which the carrier signal is modulated. If there are more than two signal levels, then more than one bit of information can be sent per transition and the speed in bits per second will be higher than the baud rate. Historically, the data speed and signaling speed of modems were the same, leading to a casual confusion of the terms "baud" and "bps" (bits per second).

Today's modems use the "56K" V.90 standard, which doesn't actually provide 56 Kb/s of throughput. At best, it allows 33.6 Kb/s from computer to ISP and 53 Kb/s in the other direction. Nevertheless, V.90 achieves speeds that are very close to the theoretical and legal limits of signaling over ordinary voice telephone lines, and it's not expected to be superseded any time soon.[7]

Line noise can introduce a significant number of errors into a modem connection. Various error correction protocols have been developed to packetize the transmitted data and provide checksum-based correction for errors, insulating the user or application from line faults. You used to have to know something about this to configure your modem correctly, but these days it usually just works.

7. One reviewer wrote, "Isn't that what they said about 110 baud?"

Data compression algorithms can be used to shrink the number of bits that must be transmitted between analog endpoints. The amount of compression varies from worse than none (when transmitting data that has already been compressed) to at most about 4:1. A more typical value is 1.5:1. In general, the average configuration does better with one of these compression algorithms turned on.

minicom: dial out

The traditional UNIX dial-out programs **tip** and **cu** are relatively unpopular on Linux systems, although both have been ported (**cu** is usually packaged with UUCP, an obsolete telephone communication system). More common under Linux are all-in-one packages such as **kermit** and **minicom** that provide terminal emulation and support for data transfer protocols. For debugging and occasional use, we recommend **minicom**, mostly because it's the most likely to be preinstalled. Debian does not install it by default; run **apt-get install minicom** if it seems to be missing.

For better or for worse, **minicom** is a bit more PC-like than most Linux software. If your memories of 1986 include logging in at 1200 baud through an MS-DOS terminal emulator while working your way through a few C-notes' worth of cocaine, **minicom** will make you feel right at home. To configure the software, run **minicom -s** as root and enter the "serial port setup" menu. Set the device file for the modem, turn on hardware flow control, set the coding to 8N1 (8 data bits, odd parity, and 1 stop bit), and make sure the speed looks OK. Return to the main menu and choose "save settings as dfl" to write out your changes.

If you are familiar with the Hayes command language used by most modems, you can simply enter the commands directly (e.g., "ATDT5551212" to dial 555-1212). To have **minicom** do it for you, type <Control-A> and D to enter the dialing menu.

Bidirectional modems

It is often handy to use a single modem for both dial-in and dial-out services, particularly if you want to use fax support. This configuration requires **getty** to handle the serial port in an especially solicitous manner, since it can't just grab hold of the port and lock out all other processes. The exact mechanism by which sharing is achieved is quite subtle and involves both features of the serial driver and files created under **/var/lock** to signal the various participants' intentions. All programs sharing the port must obey the proper protocol.

In the past, configuring a modem for bidirectional use was a big huge deal that required many system-specific tweaks and often did not work very well. Fortunately, the major Linux software packages play pretty well with each other right out of the box as long as you use either **mgetty** or **uugetty**. In general, **mgetty** is preferred; its default behavior is to share, so just plug and go.

Serial Devices

7.15 DEBUGGING A SERIAL LINE

Debugging serial lines is not difficult. Some typical errors are:

- Forgetting to tell **init** to reread its configuration files
- Forgetting to set soft carrier when using three-wire cables
- Using a cable with the wrong nullness
- Soldering or crimping DB-25 connectors upside down
- Connecting a device to the wrong wire because of bad or nonexistent wire maps
- Setting the terminal options incorrectly

A breakout box is an indispensable tool for debugging cabling problems. It is patched into the serial line and shows the signals on each pin as they pass through the cable. The better breakout boxes have both male and female connectors on each side and so are totally flexible and bisexual in their positioning. LEDs associated with each "interesting" pin (pins 2, 3, 4, 5, 6, 8, and 20) show when the pin is active.

Some breakout boxes are read-only and just allow you to monitor the signals; others let you rewire the connection and assert a voltage on a particular pin. For example, if you suspected that a cable needed to be nulled (crossed), you could use the breakout box to override the actual cable wiring and swap pins 2 and 3 and also pins 6 and 20.

See page 355 for more information about Black Box.

A bad breakout box can be worse than no breakout box at all. Our favorite implementation is the BOB-CAT-B made by Black Box. It is an easy-to-use box that costs around $250. You can reach Black Box at (724) 746-5500 or www.blackbox.com.

7.16 OTHER COMMON I/O PORTS

Serial ports used to be the unchallenged standard for attaching low-speed peripherals to UNIX systems, but the PC hardware platform has opened up a variety of new and interesting options.

PC-style parallel ports are similar in concept to serial ports, but they transfer eight bits of data at once rather than just one. They're significantly faster than serial ports but require bulkier cabling and connectors. Parallel interfaces are most commonly found on printers, but in the Windows world they're also used to connect Zip and tape drives, which require more bandwidth than a serial port can deliver. Linux support for parallel devices other than printers is scant, however.

USB, the Universal Serial Bus, is a more recent innovation that puts traditional serial and parallel ports to shame. It's fast (up to 12 Mb/s), architecturally elegant, and uses standardized cables that are both simple and cheap. Unfortunately, it will take years for organizations to get rid of their existing serial and parallel devices. For now, we can only dream of living in the USB promised land (and hope that Microsoft doesn't build on all the good lots first).

Parallel ports

Any Linux system based on PC hardware will have a parallel port, but some manufacturers have also begun to add parallel ports onto dedicated workstations so that Linux wireheads can use printers made for the Windows market.

Parallel ports have adhered to five or six different protocol standards over the years, but contemporary parallel interfaces are compatible with all earlier versions. The best standard now available is IEEE-1284, which incorporates compatibility with most prior standards (both de facto and written).

To achieve the fastest throughput speeds, modern parallel ports can be set to operate in either EPP (Enhanced Parallel Port) mode or ECP (Extended Capability Port) mode, both allowing speeds of 2 MB/s and beyond. The two high-speed modes are more or less equivalent, except that ECP supports DMA. It's unlikely that this feature makes any difference in practice.

Computers usually provide a female DB-25 connector for the parallel port, and peripherals tend to have a female 36-pin Centronics connector. Therefore, most parallel cables are male DB-25 to male Centronics. A third connector type, mini-Centronics, is also permitted by IEEE-1284.

Parallel cables can be up to 10 meters long. Since cable lengths are limited and only two types of connectors are in common use, it's more cost effective to buy prefabricated parallel cables than to make them yourself.

Although many Windows peripherals can connect to a PC's parallel port, only printers are widely and generically supported under Linux. Other peripherals, such as Zip drives and video cameras, need a device-specific driver to be usable. Drivers are available for a number of popular devices, but the drivers must usually be installed by hand. See the Linux parallel port home page at

> www.torque.net/linux-pp.html

for more details. For a useful list of generic parallel port FAQs and related parallel port information, see the entry under "parallel port" at www.webopedia.com.

USB: the Universal Serial Bus

For more information about USB, see the site www.usb.org.

USB is a generic peripheral interconnect system designed by Compaq, DEC, IBM, Intel, Microsoft, NEC, and Northern Telecom. The first USB standard was published in 1996. Acceptance of USB in the Windows world has snowballed rapidly over the last couple of years. All new PCs have USB ports, and most computer peripherals are available in USB versions.

USB is a great system, and we think it's likely to stay in use for many years to come. It has almost all of the properties and features one could wish for in a low-speed bus.

- It's extremely cheap.
- Up to 127 devices can be connected.
- Cables have only four wires: power, ground, and two signal wires.
- Connectors and connector genders are standardized.
- The connectors are small, and the cables are thin and flexible.
- Devices can be connected and disconnected without power-down.
- Signaling speeds up to 12 Mb/s are possible.
- Legacy serial and parallel devices can be connected with adaptors.

USB can even be used as a LAN technology, although it's really not designed for that.

Linux already has fairly broad support for USB devices, although this is still an active area of development. Some configuration is often required to get a particular USB device up and running; the degree of tweaking needed varies by the type of device. The USB standard defines standard interfaces for several classes of common equipment (such as mice, modems, and mass storage devices), so the use of these devices is often relatively straightforward. Devices such as cameras and scanners, on the other hand, can require chipset-specific drivers.

You can verify that your system has USB fully enabled (including support for hot-plugging) by looking for a mounted filesystem of type usbdevfs; the mount point will normally be **/proc/bus/usb**. All of our example systems except Debian are set up by default. If there's no USB filesystem mounted, you may need to either reconfigure your kernel or install the hot-plugging scripts (or both). See the instructions at www.linux-usb.org for explicit details.

The **/proc/bus/usb** filesystem provides a dynamically updated snapshot of the USB bus. Numbered files (such as **001**, which represents the host's own USB controller) correspond to individual USB devices that have been connected to the system. The **/proc/bus/usb/devices** file provides detailed information about the current device census, and the **/proc/bus/usb/drivers** file contains the names of the currently registered USB drivers (whether or not they are being used). Both of these files can be inspected with **more** or your favorite text editor.

Although the **/proc/bus/usb** filesystem is needed to support autoconfiguration and is helpful for debugging, it's generally not used directly by kernel-level drivers. Most USB devices are accessed through traditional UNIX-style device files under **/dev**.

For up-to-date information about supported devices and the drivers needed to make them work, see the device list at www.linux-usb.org.

7.17 EXERCISES

E7.1 What is a null modem cable? How is it used when connecting DCE and DTE serial devices?

E7.2 Can you use a 3-wire serial cable for a serial modem connection? For a serial printer? Why or why not?

E7.3 How does hardware flow control work? What can be done if a system does not understand hardware flow control?

E7.4 What is a pseudo-terminal? What programs use pseudo-terminals?

E7.5 Provide **inittab** entries that

a) Run a program called **server-fallback**, wait for it to finish, and then immediately halt the system if the power fails.

b) Respawn a server called **unstable-srv** if it crashes.

c) Run a script called **clean-temp** that removes all temporary files each time the system is rebooted.

★ **E7.6** Compare the RS-232 and USB serial standards.

★ **E7.7** A friend of yours carelessly left himself logged in overnight in the Linux lab and is now experiencing strange problems when he runs shell applications. Programs quit or suspend, and previous input disappears, when certain commands and input are given; however, some things seem to work normally. What could an unfriendly user have done to cause such behavior? Explain how you could test your answer. How could the problem be fixed? Who would do such a mean thing?

8 *Adding a Disk*

It's hard to believe that with the last few decades' advances in chip, network, and software technology, we're still using essentially the same technology for long-term data storage that was popular 40 years ago. Densities have increased (and prices decreased) by several orders of magnitude, but the basic concepts remain unchanged.

Unfortunately, new uses for disk space have continued to appear, especially as wide area networks have become common. As a result, there is *still* never enough disk space. The minute a new disk is added to the system, it is half full; or so it seems. Getting users to clean up their disk space is as difficult as getting teenagers to clean up their rooms. Therefore, an administrator will occasionally have to install new disk drives.

Most server systems connect their disks through a standard peripheral bus called SCSI (the Small Computer Systems Interface, pronounced "scuzzy"). An alternative interface called Integrated Drive Electronics (IDE) is standard on desktop and laptop PCs. We begin this chapter with a general discussion of the SCSI and IDE standards and the structure of modern hard disks. We then discuss the general mechanisms by which disks are formatted and partitioned and the procedure for initializing filesystems.

8.1 DISK INTERFACES

These days, only a few interface standards are in common use, although several new technologies are on the horizon. It's important to select disk drives that match the interfaces of the system on which they will be installed. If a system supports several different interfaces, you should use the one that best meets your requirements for speed, redundancy, mobility, and price.

- SCSI is one of the most common and widely supported disk interfaces. It comes in several flavors, all of which support multiple disks on a bus and various speeds and communication styles. SCSI is described in more detail in the next section.

- IDE was developed as a simple, low-cost interface for PCs. It was originally called Integrated Drive Electronics because it put the hardware controller in the same box as the disk platters and used a relatively high-level protocol for communication between the computer and the disks. This is now the standard architecture for all modern disks, but the name lives on. IDE disks are medium to fast in speed, high in capacity, and unbelievably cheap. However, the interface design makes IDE a practical option only for workstations with four or fewer devices. See page 130 for more information about IDE.

- Fibre Channel is a serial interface that is gaining popularity in the enterprise environment thanks to its high bandwidth and to the large number of devices that can be attached to it at once. Fibre Channel devices connect together with a fiber optic or twinaxial copper cable. Current speeds are 100 MB/s and up. Common topologies include loops, called Fibre Channel Arbitrated Loop (FC-AL), and fabrics, which are constructed with Fibre Channel switches. Fibre Channel can speak several different protocols, including SCSI and even IP. Fibre Channel devices are identified by a hardwired ID number called a World Wide Name that's similar to an Ethernet MAC address.

- The Universal Serial Bus (USB) has become popular for connecting devices such as keyboards and mice, but it has enough bandwidth to support slower disk devices such as removable hard disks and CD-ROM drives. USB is common on PCs and enables you to easily move a disk among systems.

SCSI and IDE are by far the dominant players in the disk drive arena. They are the only interfaces we discuss in detail.

The SCSI interface

Several chipsets implement the SCSI standard, so vendors sometimes put SCSI support right on the motherboard. SCSI defines a generic data pipe that can be used by all kinds of peripherals. Most commonly, it's used for disks, tape drives, scanners, and printers. The SCSI standard does not specify how a disk is constructed or laid out, only the manner in which it communicates with other devices.

The SCSI standard has been through several revisions, with SCSI-3 being the current version. SCSI-1 was developed in 1986 as an ANSI standard based on the Shugart Associates System Interface (SASI), which was a commercially available system bus. SCSI-2 was developed in 1990. It is backward compatible with SCSI-1 but adds several

Adding a Disk

performance features. These features include command queuing, which allows devices to reorder I/O requests to optimize throughput, and scatter-gather I/O, which permits Direct Memory Access (DMA) from discontiguous memory regions.

You might see the terms "fast" and "wide" applied to SCSI-2 device; these terms mean that the bus speed is doubled or that the number of bits transferred simultaneously is larger, typically 16 or 32 bits instead of the usual 8.[1] Wide SCSI chains can also support up to 16 devices; narrow SCSI allows only 8. Fastness and wideness are separate features that are commonly used together for synergistic increases.

SCSI-3 is actually a family of standards. It includes specifications for various physical media, including the traditional parallel buses and high-speed serial media such as Fibre Channel and IEEE 1394 ("FireWire"). It also defines the SCSI command sets and introduces enhancements to support device autoconfiguration, multimedia applications, and new types of devices.

Although the SCSI-3 specification has not yet been finalized, many of its features have already made their way to the marketplace, often under the name "Ultra SCSI." SCSI-3 encompasses SCSI-2, so a certain degree of backward compatibility is built in. Keep in mind, however, that putting an older device on a newer bus can slow down the entire bus. It will also affect the maximum cable length.

Another feature that is sometimes used in SCSI systems is "differential SCSI." In normal ("single ended") SCSI, every other pin is grounded to help reduce crosstalk among signals.[2] This construction limits the cable length to 6 meters for SCSI-1 and 3 meters for SCSI-2. Ultra SCSI reduces the total bus length even further, to 1.5 meters. Differential signalling puts an inverted signal next to each pin instead of a ground, making the net voltage zero and reducing noise significantly.

Differential signalling increases the cable length limit to 25 meters for SCSI-2 and to 12 meters for Ultra SCSI. The extra length is a big win when all of your disks (or tape libraries) are in a distant external cabinet. However, since differential signalling is completely incompatible with nondifferential devices, you *must* make sure you have a differential controller, disk, cable, and terminator. Label these well to ensure that you do not accidentally mix them up with your single-ended devices, or things will not work at all.

Table 8.1 summarizes the different SCSI versions and their associated bus bandwidths and cable lengths.

The maximum cable length for single-ended Ultra and wide Ultra SCSI depends on the number of devices in use. For 8 devices, 1.5 meters is the maximum; if only 4 devices are used, the bus can be extended to 3 meters. Wide Ultra SCSI supports all 16 devices only in differential mode.

1. 32-bit SCSI buses are not very common. Some may require multiple cables, referred to as the A cable and the B cable.
2. Crosstalk is most significant on a parallel electrical bus. It is not a concern for serial and fiber optic transports such as Fibre Channel, which have a much longer maximum cable length.

Table 8.1   The evolution of SCSI

Version	Freq.	Width	Speed	Length	Diff. length
SCSI-1	5 MHz	8 bits	5 MB/s	6m	25m
SCSI-2	5 MHz	8 bits	5 MB/s	6m	25m
Fast SCSI-2	10 MHz	8 bits	10 MB/s	3m	25m
Fast/wide SCSI-2	10 MHz	16 bits	20 MB/s	3m	25m
Ultra SCSI	20 MHz	8 bits	20 MB/s	1.5m[a]	25m
Wide Ultra SCSI[b]	20 MHz	16 bits	40 MB/s	1.5m[a]	25m
Wide Ultra2 SCSI[b]	40 MHz	16 bits	80 MB/s	–[c]	25m (HVD)[d] 12m (LVD)
Wide Ultra3 SCSI[e]	80 MHz	16 bits	160 MB/s	–[c]	12m (LVD)

a. Varies; see the comments in the text below.

b. Wide Ultra SCSI and wide Ultra2 SCSI are sometimes called Fast-20 wide SCSI and Fast-40 wide SCSI, respectively.

c. These versions of SCSI use only differential signalling.

d. HVD is High Voltage Differential and LVD is Low Voltage Differential. HVD is used for the earlier SCSI versions and is not defined above Ultra2 SCSI.

e. Wide Ultra3 SCSI is sometimes called Ultra-160.

Many types of connectors are used for SCSI devices. They vary, depending on the version of SCSI in use and type of connection: internal or external. Narrow SCSI devices have 50 pins, and wide SCSI devices have 68 pins. Internal devices typically accept a 50-pin header or a 68-pin male mini-micro connector attached to a ribbon cable. External drives usually connect to the computer with a high density 50- or 68-pin mini-micro connector. Apple reduced the 50 pins to 25 by tying all of the ground lines together and shoehorning the bus onto a DB-25 connector.

An interesting variant that's especially useful for hot-swappable drive arrays is the Single Connector Attachment (SCA) plug. It's an 80-pin connector that includes the bus connections, power, and SCSI configuration, allowing a single connector to provide all of the drive's needs.

Exhibit A on the next page shows pictures of the most common connectors. Each connector is shown from the front, as if you were about to plug it into your forehead.

The connectors on SCSI devices are almost always female, and the ends of SCSI cables are male. SCSI buses use a daisy chain configuration, so most external devices have two SCSI ports. The ports are identical and interchangeable, so either one can be the input. For some reason, scanner vendors seem to consider themselves exempt from the normal laws of physics and sometimes provide only one SCSI port. If not internally terminated, these devices require a special type of terminator.

Internal SCSI devices are usually attached to a ribbon cable; only one port is needed on the actual SCSI device because connectors can be clamped onto the middle of the ribbon cable. When using a ribbon cable, make sure pin 1 on the SCSI bus is connected to pin 1 on the hard drive. (Pin 1 is usually marked with a red stripe.)

Exhibit A   Common SCSI connectors (front view, male except where noted)

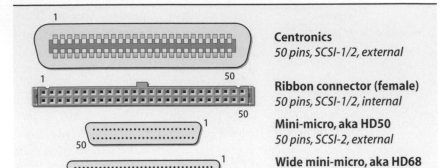

Centronics
50 pins, SCSI-1/2, external

Ribbon connector (female)
50 pins, SCSI-1/2, internal

Mini-micro, aka HD50
50 pins, SCSI-2, external

Wide mini-micro, aka HD68
68 pins, SCSI-2/3, int/ext

SCA-2
80 pins, SCSI-3, internal

Each end of the SCSI bus must have a terminating resistor ("terminator"). These resistors absorb signals as they reach the end of the bus and prevent noise from reflecting back onto the bus. Terminators take several forms, from small external plugs that you snap onto a regular port to sets of tiny resistor packs that install onto a device's circuit boards. Some devices are even autoterminating.

SCSI-1 used a different terminator design from that of later versions of SCSI ("passive" rather than "active"), so very old terminators (and old self-terminating devices) can cause problems on a newer SCSI bus. In practice, we have rarely found such old terminators to be an issue.

One end of the bus normally terminates inside the host computer, either on the SCSI controller or on an internal SCSI drive. The other end usually terminates on an external device, or on the SCSI controller if there are no external devices. If you experience seemingly random hardware problems on your SCSI bus, first check that both ends of the bus are properly terminated. Improper termination is one of the most common SCSI configuration mistakes, and the errors it produces can be obscure and intermittent.

Each device has a SCSI address or "target number" that distinguishes it from the other devices on the bus. Target numbers start at 0 and go up to 7 or 15, depending on whether the bus is narrow or wide. The SCSI controller itself counts as a device and is usually target 7 (even on a wide bus, for backward compatibility). All other devices must have their target numbers set to unique values. It is a common error to forget that the SCSI controller has a target number and to set a device to the same target number as the controller.

A SCSI address is essentially arbitrary. Technically, it determines the device's priority on the bus, but in practice the exact priorities don't make much difference. Some systems pick the disk with the lowest target number to be the default boot disk, and some require the boot disk to be target 0.

If you're lucky, a device will have an external thumbwheel with which the target number can be set. Other common ways of setting the target number are DIP switches and jumpers. If it is not obvious how to set the target number on a device, consult the hardware manual. Most hardware specifications can be found on the manufacturer's web site these days; trying to set up a random disk used to involve quite a lot of trial and error.

The SCSI standard supports a form of subaddressing called a "logical unit number." Each target can have several logical units inside it. A plausible example might be a drive array with several disks but only one SCSI controller. However, logical units are seldom used in real life. When you hear "SCSI unit number," you should assume that it is really a target number that's being discussed until proven otherwise. If a SCSI device contains only one logical unit, the LUN usually defaults to 0.

SCSI buses are generally quite easy to configure, but a variety of things can go wrong:

- Many workstations have internal SCSI devices. Check the listing of current devices before you reboot to add a new device.

- Make sure that a differential SCSI controller has only differential devices and differential terminators connected to it, and make sure that a single-ended SCSI chain does not contain any differential devices. The single-ended and differential signalling techniques are incompatible.

- After you have added a new SCSI device, check the listing of devices discovered by the Linux kernel when it reboots to make sure that everything you expect is there. Most SCSI drivers will not detect multiple devices that have the same SCSI address, which is an illegal configuration. SCSI address conflicts can lead to very strange behavior.

- Some expansion boxes (enclosures with a power supply and one or more SCSI devices) terminate the bus inside the box. If devices are attached after the expansion box, you can have reliability problems with any of the devices on the SCSI chain. Always double-check that you have exactly two terminators and that they are both at the ends of the bus.

- The thumbwheel used to set a device's SCSI address is sometimes connected backwards. When this happens, the thumbwheel will change the SCSI address, but not to the displayed value.

- When figuring the length of your SCSI-2 bus, make sure you count the cables inside devices and expansion boxes. They can be quite long. Also remember that the maximum length can be reduced if older SCSI devices are added to a newer SCSI bus.

- Never forget that your SCSI controller uses one of the SCSI addresses!

Adding a Disk

The IDE interface

IDE, also called ATA (for AT Attachment), was designed to be simple and inexpensive. It is most often found on PCs or low-cost workstations. The controller is built into the disk, which reduces interface costs and simplifies the firmware. IDE became popular in the late 1980s. Shortly thereafter, ATA-2 was developed to satisfy the increasing demands of consumers and hard drive vendors.

ATA-2 adds faster Programmed I/O (PIO) and Direct Memory Access (DMA) modes and extends the bus's Plug and Play features. It also adds a feature called Logical Block Addressing (LBA), which (in combination with an enhanced PC BIOS) overcomes a problem that prevented BIOSes from accessing more than the first 1024 cylinders of a disk. This constraint formerly limited disk sizes to 504MB. Who would have thought a disk could get that big!

Since the BIOS manages part of the bootstrapping process, it was at one time necessary to create a small bootable partition within the first 1024 cylinders to ensure that the kernel could be loaded by an old BIOS. Once the kernel was up and running, the BIOS was not needed and you could access the rest of your disk. This silly maneuver is unnecessary on modern hardware since LBA gets rid of cylinder-head-sector (CHS) addressing in favor of a linear addressing scheme.

ATA-3 adds additional reliability, more sophisticated power management, and self-monitoring capabilities. Ultra-ATA is an attempt to bridge the gap between ATA-3 and ATA-4, adding high-performance modes called Ultra DMA/33 and Ultra DMA/66 that extend the bus bandwidth from 16 MB/s to 33 MB/s and 66 MB/s, respectively. ATA-4 is also a much-needed attempt to merge ATA-3 with the ATA Packet Interface (ATAPI), a protocol that allows CD-ROM and tape drives to work on an IDE bus.The latest additions to the family, ATA-5 and ATA-6, include enhanced performance management and error handling which improve performance, especially in a multiuser environment such as Linux.

IDE disks are almost always used internally (unless you consider a disk hanging out the side of the computer for testing purposes "external"). The maximum cable length for an ATA-2 bus is a mere 18 inches, which can make it difficult even to reach your system's top drive bay. In addition to the short cable length, an IDE bus can accommodate only two devices. To compensate for these shortcomings, most manufacturers provide more than one IDE bus on their motherboards.

IDE devices are accessed in a connected manner, which means that only one device can be active at a time. Therefore, performance is best if you spread the devices over multiple buses. Put fast devices such as hard drives on one bus and tapes or CD-ROMs on another to prevent the slower devices from hindering the faster ones. Historically, SCSI has handled multiple devices on a bus much better than has IDE, but ATA-5 and ATA-6 drives are beginning to compete in the same league.

The IDE connector is a 40-pin header that connects the drive to the interface card with a ribbon cable. Newer IDE standards such as Ultra DMA/66 use a different cable that provides more ground pins and therefore reduces electrical noise. If a cable or drive is not keyed, be sure that pin 1 on the drive goes to pin 1 on the interface card. Pin 1 is usually marked with a small "1" on one side of the connector. If it is not marked, a rule of thumb is that pin 1 is usually the one closest to the power connector. Pin 1 on a ribbon cable is usually marked in red. If there is no red stripe on one edge of your cable, just make sure you have the cable oriented so that pin 1 is connected to pin 1, and mark it clearly for next time.

If you have more than one device on an IDE bus, you must designate one as the master and the other as the slave. Some older IDE drives do not like to be slaves, so if you are having trouble getting one configuration to work, try reversing their roles and make the other device the slave. If things are still not working out, you might be better off making each device a master of its own IDE bus.

When considering IDE hardware, keep in mind the following points:

- New IDE drives work on older cards, and old IDE drives work on newer cards. Naturally, only the features common to both devices are supported.

- The cable length is exceedingly short, which can make adding an extra device to the bus a stretch. If you experience random flakiness, check the cable length. A quality cable can make all the difference.

- Dealing with an old BIOS that does not see past the first 500MB of a disk is a bona fide nightmare. Check to see if the manufacturer has issued a firmware update to fix the problem. If not, you can replace the system's motherboard for $200 or less; it's worth it. Fortunately, BIOSes that old are rarely seen today.

- Well-designed drivers can significantly increase performance and reliability, especially when they support the most recent standards. Find out which features your driver supports (e.g., DMA and PIO modes) and compare those features to the range of options available in the marketplace. This is also good advice when you are shopping for disks.

Which is better, SCSI or IDE?

This is a frequently asked question that's often waved away with talk about how each standard has its own advantages. However, we'll go out on a limb and give you a straight answer: SCSI is better. Usually.

A more accurate answer would be that SCSI beats IDE in every possible technical sense but that SCSI equipment may not be worth the enormous price premium it now commands. For a single-user workstation, a good IDE disk is a simple, high-capacity, dirt-cheap solution that provides 85% of the performance of a SCSI setup. In most cases, upgrading a single-user workstation to SCSI *will not* increase the system's perceived performance.

However, in some situations SCSI is advisable or even mandatory:

- If you absolutely must have the best possible performance, go SCSI. Part of the increased performance will come from SCSI's technical superiority, but an even larger part will come from the fact that disk drive manufacturers use the IDE/SCSI divide to help them stratify the disk drive market. Some IDE drives may outperform SCSI on peak throughput, but SCSI almost always provides better sustained throughput.

- Servers and multiuser systems require SCSI. The SCSI protocol is unparalleled in its ability to manage multiple simultaneous requests in an efficient manner. On a busy system, you'll see a concrete and measurable improvement in performance.

- If you want to connect many devices, SCSI wins again. SCSI devices play well with others; IDE devices hog and fight over the bus.

- You might need some particular feature that only SCSI provides. For example, it's a real challenge (though no longer impossible) to build a hot-pluggable disk array out of IDE drives.

8.2 DISK GEOMETRY

The geometry of a hard disk and the terminology used to refer to its various parts are shown in Exhibit B. This information is provided mainly to improve your general knowledge. Modern disk drives are still based on this same basic design, but the software no longer knows (or needs to know) much about the physical construction of the drive.

A typical hard drive consists of spinning platters coated with a magnetic film. Data is read and written by a small head that changes the orientation of the magnetic particles on the surface of the platters. The data platters are completely sealed so that no dust or dirt can get in. This feature makes fixed hard disks far more reliable than removable media.

In the very early days of computer hardware, disk drives usually had one platter. An increase in storage capacity was provided by an increase in the diameter of the platter. On the wall of one of our user areas is an ancient disk over four feet in diameter that held approximately 280K of data. That's about 25% of the capacity of a modern floppy disk.

Today, hard disks usually have several small platters stacked on top of one another rather than having a single large platter. Both sides of the platters are used to store data, although one side of one platter usually contains positioning information and cannot be used for storage. Single-platter densities are currently up around 30GB, with no end to Moore's Law[3] in sight.

---

3. Moore's Law states that technology (CPU speed, disk sizes, etc.) will double about every 18 months.

Exhibit B   Disk geometry lesson

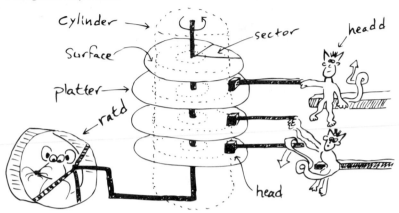

Platters rotate at a constant speed. They are read from and written to by little skating heads that move back and forth like the needle on a record player. The heads float very close to the surface of the platters but do not actually touch them. The distance between the head and the spinning platter can be compared to an F-16 fighter jet flying at full speed 10 feet above the ground. If a head does touch a platter, this event is called a head crash; it can be very destructive.

Rotational speeds have increased dramatically over time. Older disks ran at 3,600 RPM or 5,400 RPM. 7,200 RPM is currently the upper-mass-market standard, and 10,000 RPM and 15,000 RPM drives are becoming popular at the high end. Higher rotational speeds decrease latency and increase the bandwidth of data transfers but may potentially introduce thermal problems stemming from increased heat production. Be sure you have adequate air circulation if you plan to purchase a cutting-edge drive.

At least one head is required for each surface. The heads on early drives had to move huge distances, but the modern geometry of small, stacked platters is more efficient. The diameter of disks continues to decrease, from a standard of 14 inches 20 years ago, to 5-1/4 inches 10 years ago, to 3-1/2 inches and smaller today.

Moving the head to the correct position to read a particular piece of data is called seeking. Each position that a head can occupy as the disk spins under it is called a track. Tracks are further divided into sectors, which are usually 512 bytes long.

A set of tracks on different platters that are the same distance from the spindle is called a cylinder. If all the heads move together, as is typical on most mass-market drives, the data stored in a single cylinder can be read without any additional movement. Although heads move amazingly fast, they still move much slower than the disks spin around. Therefore, any disk access that does not require the heads to seek to a new position will be faster.

The standard Linux filesystems attempt to exploit this fact to improve efficiency. Unfortunately, a now-universal practice known as zone sectoring, in which tracks on the outside of a platter contain more sectors than inner tracks, complicates this matter. To fully optimize the internal workings of the drive, the layout information is not shared with the software. Instead, an artificial cylinder-head-sector (CHS) addressing scheme is made up to fit the size of the disk. Even today, many filesystem optimizations are based on complete fiction.

Although almost any CHS values that multiply out to match the size of the disk can be used, the manufacturer will typically have some suggested values. Some configurations—such as those with more than 1,024 cylinders or more than 255 heads—may cause problems with some operating systems or boot loaders. This is usually only a concern on PCs running old hardware or multiple operating systems.

8.3 AN OVERVIEW OF THE DISK INSTALLATION PROCEDURE

The procedure for adding a new disk involves the following steps:

- Connecting the disk to the computer
- Formatting the disk
- Labeling and partitioning the disk
- Establishing logical volumes
- Creating Linux filesystems within disk partitions
- Setting up automatic mounting
- Setting up swapping on swap partitions

The following sections elaborate on these basic steps. Starting on page 145, we show the complete process from start to finish for an example disk drive.

Connecting the disk

The way a disk is attached to the system depends mostly on the interface that is used. The rest is all mounting brackets and cabling. If the disk is IDE, try to configure the system with only one IDE disk per bus. Double-check your cable orientation and the master/slave settings on each disk. If the disk is SCSI, double-check that you have properly terminated both ends of the SCSI bus, that the cable length is less than the maximum appropriate for the SCSI variant you are using, and that the new SCSI target does not conflict with the controller or another device on the bus. For more details, see the system-specific sections toward the end of this chapter.

Before you can access a new disk, you need device files in **/dev** that point to it. Linux automatically creates files for all possible SCSI devices. See page 226 for general information about device files.

It is possible to destroy a filesystem in seconds by writing randomly on the disk, so you should set the permissions on disk device files quite restrictively. We allow read and write access for the owner (root) and read access for the group owner (operator); this setup allows **dump** to be run by operators without superuser privileges but prevents mere mortals from reading from the raw device.

Formatting the disk

Overeager vendors often quote disk capacities in terms of the number of unformatted bytes. About 10% of that capacity is typically used up to mark the disk surfaces so that the hardware and software can find the data that is written there. When purchasing disks, always think in terms of formatted size and compare prices accordingly.

Another common trick is to quote disk sizes in "megabytes" that are really millions of bytes. In the context of computer systems, a megabyte is actually 2^{20} or 1,048,576 bytes. Using the 1MB = 1,000,000 byte convention overstates the capacity of a disk drive by almost 5%.[4] Be sure to check your units when comparing disk capacities.

The formatting process writes address information and timing marks on the platters to delineate each sector. It also identifies "bad blocks," imperfections in the media that result in areas that cannot be reliably read or written. Modern disks have bad block management built in, so neither you nor the driver need to worry about it.[5]

All hard disks come preformatted, and the factory formatting is often more precise than any formatting you can do in the field. It is best to avoid doing a low-level format if it is not required. If you encounter read or write errors on a disk, first check for cabling, termination, and address problems, which can cause symptoms similar to those of a bad block. If after this procedure you are still convinced that the disk is bad, you might be better off to replace it with a new one rather than waiting long hours for a format to complete.

IDE disks are usually not designed to be formatted outside the factory. However, you may be able to get special formatting software from the manufacturer, usually for Windows. Make sure the software matches the drive you plan to format and follow the manufacturer's directions carefully.

SCSI disks format themselves in response to a command that you send from the host computer. The procedure for sending this command varies from system to system. On PCs, you can often send the command from the SCSI controller's BIOS.

Various utilities let you verify the integrity of a disk by writing random patterns onto it and then reading them back. This process is very time consuming, so unless you suspect that the disk is bad or you bill by the hour, you may want to skip it. Barring that, let the tests run overnight. Don't be concerned about "wearing out" a disk with overuse or aggressive testing. Disks are designed to withstand constant activity.

Labeling and partitioning the disk

After a disk has been formatted and its bad sectors remapped, it must be divided into chunks called *partitions*. Partitioning allows the disk to be treated as a group of independent data areas rather than as one vast expanse of blocks. Partitioning also allows "bonus" items such as the boot blocks and the partition table itself to be hidden from

---

4. Of course, the prefix "mega" really does mean "million," so the practice is not entirely indefensible.
5. However, any bad blocks that appear after a disk has been formatted will not be "handled"; they can manifest themselves in the form of read and write errors and lost data.

high-level software (e.g., the filesystem). Only the device driver knows about the layout of the entire disk; other software works with the cleaned-up abstraction of partitions.

Partitions make backups easier, prevent users from poaching each other's disk space, improve performance, and confine potential damage from runaway programs. The partition table is kept on the disk in a record called the label. The label usually occupies the first few blocks of the disk. Its exact contents vary, but it generally contains enough information to get the system booting.

Partitions are, in concept, distinct and separate from one another. However, Linux also defines one partition (the unnumbered one, e.g., **/dev/sda**) to be an image of the entire disk. This way, user-level commands can access the disk "directly" through a normal device file. For example, a user-level process can write the disk's label or duplicate its contents to a backup disk by using the **dd** command. Of course, this special partition must be used carefully, since it allows every other partition on the disk to be screwed up at once.

Some systems go even farther down this treacherous path and allow you to define multiple overlapping sets of partitions. For example, partitions 1, 2, and 3 might divide up the disk one way, while partitions 4 and 5 do it another way. You're expected to use one set of self-consistent partitions and simply ignore the others. In real life, such overlapping partitions invite operator errors and are a common cause of random data corruption.

Modern systems tend to use fewer partitions than their predecessors, but on most systems you will have at least the following three.

- **The root partition:** Everything needed to bring the system up to single-user mode is kept here. A second copy of this partition is often stored on another disk for emergencies.

- **The swap partition:** A swap area stores pages of virtual memory when not enough physical memory is available to hold them. Every system should have at least one swap partition. See page 788 for more information about virtual memory.

- **The user partition:** Home directories, data files, source code libraries, and other random data files find a home here.

Opinions differ on the best way to split disks into partitions. Here are some hints:

- If you have multiple disks, make a copy of the root filesystem on one of them and verify that you can boot from it.

- As you add memory to your machine, you should also add swap space. For normal use, you should have at least as much swap space as real memory. This amount of swap allows a kernel crash dump to fit in the swap area in the event of a system panic.

- Splitting swap space among several disks increases performance. This technique works for filesystems, too; put the busy ones on different disks. See page 793 for notes on this subject.

- If you intend to back up a partition, don't make it bigger than the capacity of your backup device. See page 161.

- Try to cluster information that changes quickly on a few partitions that are backed up frequently.

- It's a good idea to create a separate filesystem (**/tmp**) for temporary files because it limits the files to a finite size and saves you from having to back them up.

- Since log files are kept in **/var**, it's a good idea for **/var** to be a separate disk partition. Leaving **/var** as part of a small root partition makes it easy to fill the root and bring the machine to a halt.

Establishing logical volumes

The Linux Logical Volume Manager (LVM) is an optional subsystem that provides a sort of supercharged version of disk partitioning. It lets you group individual disks into "volume groups." The aggregate capacity of a volume group can then be allocated to logical volumes, which are accessed as regular block devices. Logical volume management lets you

- Use and allocate disk storage more efficiently
- Move logical volumes among different physical devices
- Grow and shrink logical volume sizes on the fly
- Take "snapshots" of whole filesystems
- Replace on-line drives without interrupting service

The components of a logical volume can be put together in various ways. Concatenation keeps each device's physical blocks together and lines the devices up one after another. Striping interleaves the components so that adjacent virtual blocks are actually spread over multiple physical disks. By reducing single-disk bottlenecks, striping can often provide higher bandwidth and lower latency.

As of this writing (early 2002), LVM is still under active development, having just been incorporated into the 2.4.x kernel line. LVM may not yet provide the "rock solid" volume management features that system administrators may be familiar with on other platforms.[6] If you're interested in learning about the latest LVM developments or you plan to install it, point your browser at www.sistina.com/products_lvm.htm.

Although it is not yet supported by LVM, "mirroring" is another common feature of volume managers. A mirrored volume is associated with another volume of the same size. Whenever data is written to one side of the mirror, it is duplicated on the other.

---

6. Alternate storage systems, such as LVM, must be thoroughly evaluated in a test environment before being used on production servers. Data corruption can often have catastrophic side effects.

Reads are split among the volumes to increase performance. If one volume experiences a hardware failure, the system automatically "fails over" to the other with no interruption in service. Once the original problem has been fixed, the two sides of the mirror must be resynchronized.

Linux filesystems

Linux filesystem support has evolved rapidly over the last few years as Linux has absorbed features from a variety of different operating systems. Linux originally used the filesystem code from Andrew S. Tanenbaum's MINIX operating system. The MINIX filesystem was quite limited, however: it restricted the maximum file size to 64MB and filenames to 14 characters. It soon became clear that Linux would need to support multiple filesystem formats, and a Virtual File System (VFS) layer was introduced into the kernel to support this feature. The VFS layer is particularly handy on PCs because it provides the framework needed to mount "native" filesystems such as the infamous MS-DOS FAT filesystem.

The Second Extended File System, commonly known as ext2fs, is the filesystem that is most commonly used with Linux today. It was designed and implemented primarily by Rémy Card, Theodore Ts'o, and Stephen Tweedie. Although the code for ext2 was written specifically for Linux, it adopts many concepts and file types from the BSD FFS filesystem designed and implemented by Kirk McKusick and team in 1984.

The Third Extended File System, ext3fs, is a remarkable extension to ext2fs originally developed by Stephen Tweedie. It adds journaling capability to the existing ext2fs code, a conceptually simple modification which provides extraordinary functionality. The ext3fs extensions have been seamlessly implemented without changing the fundamental structure of ext2fs. In fact, you can still mount an ext3fs filesystem as an ext2fs filesystem—it just won't have journaling enabled.[7]

The ext3fs filesystem sets aside an area of the disk for the journal file. When a filesystem operation occurs, the required modifications are first written to the journal file. When the journal update is complete, a "commit record" is written to mark the end of the entry. Only then is the normal filesystem modified. If a crash were to occur, the journal log could be used to reconstruct a perfectly consistent filesystem.

Journaling reduces the time needed to perform filesystem consistency checks (see the **fsck** section on page 143) to approximately one second per filesystem. Barring some type of hardware failure, the state of an ext3fs can be almost instantly assessed and restored.

ReiserFS is another up-and-coming filesystem for Linux. Like ext3fs, it is also a journaling filesystem and hence can maintain filesystem consistency despite incidents such as system crashes and unplanned reboots (which may be common in a laptop or desktop workstation environment). The current version of ReiserFS is not opti-

---

7. But don't try this at home.

mized for systems (such as servers) that might experience a large number of simultaneous reads and writes. A new version, Reiser4, is due out in the fall of 2002.

In addition to its journaling capabilities, Reiser4 will provide a modular filesystem interface that allows application developers and system administrators to specify how files should be handled (and secured) at a very granular level. This feature has the potential to increase the security of files in specialized environments.

8.4 THE EXT2 AND EXT3 FILESYSTEMS

Even after a hard disk has been conceptually divided into partitions, it is still not ready to hold files. The filesystem needs to add a little of its own overhead before the disk is ready for use. In this section, we first describe ext2fs and then describe some of the ext3fs extensions.

To install a filesystem within a disk partition, use **mke2fs**. Unless you are doing something strange, you should be able to build the filesystem by specifying nothing but the **mke2fs** command and the partition name.

We cover the exact procedure in more detail later; the rest of this section discusses how files are placed on the disk when you build the filesystem. If you are not interested, just skip ahead to the next section and revel in blissful ignorance.

An ext2fs filesystem consists of five structural components:

- A set of inode storage cells
- A set of scattered "superblocks"
- A map of the disk blocks in the filesystem
- A block usage summary
- A set of data blocks

Each filesystem partition is divided into block groups. Structures such as inode tables are allocated among the block groups so that blocks that are accessed together can be stored close to each other on the disk. This grouping reduces the need to seek all over the disk when accessing blocks in the same file.

Inodes are fixed-length table entries that each hold information about one file. Since space for inodes must be set aside when Linux does its initial structuring of the filesystem, you must decide in advance how many of them to create. It is impossible to predict exactly how many files (inodes) will someday be needed; Linux uses an empirical formula to guesstimate an appropriate number, based on the size of the partition and an average file size.

You can adjust the number of inodes either up or down when you create the filesystem: more inodes for filesystems with lots of small files (such as Usenet news partitions or source code repositories), and fewer inodes for filesystems with a few large files (such as a filesystem containing a database).

A superblock is a record that describes the characteristics of the filesystem. It contains information about the length of a disk block, the size and location of the inode tables, the disk block map and usage information, the size of the block groups, and a few other important parameters of the filesystem. Because damage to the superblock could erase some extremely crucial information, several copies of it are maintained in scattered locations (at the beginning of each block group).

For each mounted filesystem, Linux keeps both an in-memory copy of the superblock and several on-disk copies. The **sync** system call flushes the cached superblocks to their permanent homes on disk, making the filesystem consistent for a split second. This periodic save minimizes the amount of damage that would occur if the machine were to crash when the filesystem had not updated the superblocks. **sync** also flushes modified inodes and cached data blocks. The **update** command is usually run at boot time and starts the **bdflush** daemon, which performs a **sync** every 30 seconds to minimize the amount of data lost in the event of a crash.

A filesystem's disk block map is a table of the free blocks it contains. When new files are written, this map is examined to devise an efficient layout scheme. The block usage summary records basic information about the blocks that are already in use.

Setting up ext3fs extensions

An ext3fs filesystem is simply an ext2fs filesystem with a journal file and its associated options. In fact, on systems where ext3fs is available, it's possible to convert an existing ext2fs filesystem to an ext3fs filesystem with **tune2fs**. For example, if you had an ext2fs filesytem on **/dev/hda4**, you could convert it with

```
# tune2fs -j /dev/hda4
```

You would then need to modify the corresponding entry in **/etc/fstab** to read ext3 rather than ext2 (see page 141 for more information on the **fstab** file).[8]

Note that ext3 filesystems behave slightly differently from ext2 filesystems. One of the most notable changes is that rather than syncing unwritten disk blocks every 30 seconds, ext3 syncs every 5 seconds. You also have a choice of three different trade-offs between performance and functionality in selecting a journaling mode:

- The default mode, "ordered," guarantees that the filesystem is always consistent and that as a result, files will never be corrupted by a crash. This is the best choice for most environments.

- The "writeback" mode can result in corrupted files after a crash but is faster in some cases. This is actually the way most journaling filesystems work, and it isn't substantially riskier than the default ext2 behavior.

- The "journal" mode uses a larger journal file, which may slow down recovery on reboot but can be faster when used with a database application.

---

8. If you are converting your root filesystem, you will also need to tell your boot loader (LILO or GRUB) to load the ext3 modules. See the man page for **mkinitrd** for details.

The ext3 filesystem mode is set with a data=*mode* entry in the **fstab** file, where *mode* is one of ordered, writeback, or journal.

Setting up automatic mounting

A filesystem must be mounted before it becomes available to Linux processes. The mount point for a filesystem can be any directory, but the files and subdirectories beneath it will not be accessible while a filesystem is mounted there. See page 65 for more information about mounting filesystems. Be sure that the partition you are mounting or checking has a valid filesystem on it—if you try to **mount** or **fsck** your swap partition, you can really mess things up.

After installing a new disk, you should mount new filesystems by hand to test that everything is working correctly. For example,

```
# mount /dev/sda1 /mnt
```

would mount the filesystem in the partition represented by the device file **/dev/sda1** on the directory **/mnt**. If the filesystem is brand new, its contents should look something like this:

```
# ls /mnt
lost+found
```

The **lost+found** directory is automatically created when you build a filesystem. It is used by **fsck** in emergencies; do not delete it. The **lost+found** directory has some extra space preallocated so that **fsck** can store "unlinked" files there without having to allocate additional directory entries on an unstable filesystem.

You can verify the size of a filesystem with the **df** command. Here's an example:

```
% df /home
Filesystem      1k-blocks      Used   Available   Use%   Mounted on
/dev/sda5       17212156    1445776    14892044     9%   /home
```

The units reported by **df** are 1K blocks, or you can use the **--block-size** option to specify your units.

An **fstab** file that included the filesystem above might look something like this:

```
/dev/sdb6        /                ext2      defaults          1  1
/dev/sda1        /boot            ext2      defaults          1  1
/dev/sda5        /home            ext2      defaults          1  2
/dev/cdrom       /mnt/cdrom       iso9660   noauto,owner,ro   0  0
/dev/fd0         /mnt/floppy      auto      noauto,owner      0  0
LABEL=/usr       /usr             ext2      defaults          1  2
LABEL=/var       /var             ext2      defaults          1  2
none             /proc            proc      defaults          0  0
/dev/sdb7        swap             swap      defaults          0  0
```

There are six fields per line, separated by whitespace. Each line describes a single filesystem. The fields are traditionally aligned for readability, but alignment is not required.

See Chapter 17 for more information about NFS.

The first field gives the device name or the label that was associated with it by **e2label** (the LABEL= form). The **fstab** file can include mounts from remote systems, in which case the first field contains an NFS path. The notation *server:/export* indicates the */export* directory on the machine named *server.*

The second field specifies the mount point, and the third field indicates the type of filesystem. The exact type name used to identify local filesystems varies, depending on your system configuration. Traditionally, right-out-of-the-box Linux has used ext2, but these days Red Hat and SuSE provide the option of choosing ext3 as the default local filesystem.

In the case of the **/proc** filesystem above, the none in the first column is a place-holder value. The virtual filesystem type is specified by the value proc in the third column; this filesystem exports kernel process information to user utilities.

The fourth field lists the mount options (rw, for read/write, is the default). The fifth field specifies a "dump frequency" value which can theoretically be used by backup products but usually isn't.

fsck is described on page 143.

The sixth field specifies the pass in which **fsck** should check the filesystem. Filesystems with the same value in this field are checked concurrently if possible. Do not set two filesystems on the same disk to the same value or you will cause the disk head to seek back and forth so much that performance will be significantly degraded. Only filesystems on separate disks should be checked in parallel.

mount, **umount**, **swapon**, and **fsck** all read the **fstab** file, so it is important that the data presented there be correct and complete. **mount** and **umount** use the **fstab** file to figure out what you want done if you specify only a partition name or mount point on the command line. For example, using the **fstab** file just shown, the command

```
# mount /mnt/cdrom
```

would be the same as typing

```
# mount -t iso9660 -o ro,noauto,owner /dev/cdrom /mnt/cdrom
```

The command **mount -a** mounts all regular filesystems listed in the **fstab** file; it is usually executed from the startup scripts at boot time. The **-t** flag constrains the operation to filesystems of a certain type. For example,

```
# mount -at ext2
```

would mount all local ext2 disk filesystems on a Linux system. The **mount** command reads **fstab** sequentially; therefore, filesystems that are mounted beneath other filesystems must follow their parent partitions in the **fstab** file. For example, the line for **/var/log** must follow the line for **/var** if **/var** is a separate filesystem.

The **umount** command for unmounting filesystems accepts a similar syntax. On most systems, you cannot unmount a filesystem that a process is using as its current directory or one on which files are open. There are ways of getting around this constraint; see page 66.

Enabling swapping

One of the early advantages of UNIX was its implementation of virtual memory. This feature allows the operating system to pretend that the machine has more memory than it actually does. If processes try to use this "extra" memory, the system's disks are brought into use as a kind of ultra-slow RAM. Juggling the contents of memory to and from disk is known as swapping or paging.[9]

To make swapping efficient, you would normally use raw partitions (partitions without filesystems) as the backing store. Instead of using a filesystem structure to keep track of the swap area's contents, the kernel maintains its own simplified mapping from memory blocks to disk blocks. It's also possible to swap to a file in a filesystem partition, but this configuration is slower than using a dedicated partition.

See page 793 for more information about splitting swap areas.

The more swap space you have, the more virtual memory your processes can allocate. The best swapping performance is achieved when the swap area is split among several drives (or better yet, among several SCSI buses).

You can manually enable swapping to a particular device, but you will generally want to have this function performed automatically at boot time. On most systems, swap areas can be listed in the **fstab** file, the same file that's used to enumerate mountable filesystems. A swap entry looks something like:

```
/dev/sdb7          swap               swap     defaults          0  0
```

During startup, the **swapon** command is run to enable swapping on all swap partitions listed in the **fstab** file.

8.5 FSCK: CHECK AND REPAIR FILESYSTEMS

The traditional Linux filesystem (ext2fs) is surprisingly reliable, and it does a remarkable job of coping with unexpected system crashes and flaky hardware. However, filesystems can become damaged or inconsistent in a number of ways.

Any time the kernel panics or the power fails, small inconsistencies may be introduced into the filesystems that were active immediately preceding the crash. Since the kernel buffers both data blocks and summary information, the most recent image of the filesystem is split between disk and memory. During a crash, the memory portion of the image is lost. The buffered blocks are effectively "overwritten" with the versions that were most recently saved to disk.

There are a couple of approaches to fixing this problem. Minor damage can usually be fixed with the **fsck** command ("filesystem consistency check," spelled aloud or pronounced "fs check" or "fisk"). This isn't a very architecturally elegant way of approaching the issue, but it works pretty well for all the common inconsistencies.

---

9. Swapping and paging are technically distinct. For now, we group them together and call the combination "swapping." For a more detailed description of virtual memory under Linux, see page 788.

Journaling filesystems such as ReiserFS and ext3fs write metadata out to a sequential log file that is flushed to disk before each command returns. The metadata eventually migrates from the log to its permanent home within the filesystem. If the system crashes, the log can be rolled up to the most recent consistency point; a full filesystem cross-check is not required. **fsck** is still run at boot time to ensure that the filesystem is in a consistent state, but it runs much faster than when checking a traditional ext2 filesystem. This feature can save you many hours of boot time on a system with large filesystems.

If some form of journaling is not available, you must wait for **fsck** to work its magic. The five most common types of damage are:

- Unreferenced inodes
- Inexplicably large link counts
- Unused data blocks not recorded in the block maps
- Data blocks listed as free that are also used in a file
- Incorrect summary information in the superblock

fsck can safely and automatically fix these five problems. If **fsck** makes corrections to a filesystem, you should rerun it until the filesystem comes up completely clean.

Disks are normally checked at boot time with **fsck -p**, which examines all local filesystems listed in **/etc/fstab** and corrects the five errors listed above. Linux keeps track of which filesystems were unmounted cleanly and checks only the "dirty" ones. If some form of journaling is enabled, **fsck** simply tells you that the filesystem is journaled and rolls up the log to the last consistent state.

fsck -p can also be run on a particular filesystem. For example:

```
# fsck -p /dev/sda5
```

When **fsck -p** reads the **fstab** file to find out which filesystems to check, it obeys the sequence indicated by the last field of each entry. Filesystems are checked in increasing numeric order. If two filesystems are on different disks, they can be given the same sequence number; this configuration makes **fsck** check them simultaneously, minimizing the time spent waiting for disk I/O. Always check the root partition first.

Errors that do not fall into one of the five categories above are potentially serious. They cause **fsck -p** to ask for help and then quit. In this case, run **fsck** without the **-p** option. When run in manual mode, **fsck** asks you to confirm each of the repairs that it wants to make. The following list shows some of the errors that **fsck** considers dangerous enough to warrant human intervention.

- Blocks claimed by more than one file
- Blocks claimed outside the range of the filesystem
- Link counts that are too small
- Blocks that are not accounted for
- Directories that refer to unallocated inodes
- Various format errors

Unfortunately, it is difficult to patch a disk by hand without extensive knowledge of the implementation of the filesystem. Unless you are attempting to establish yourself as a cult leader in a small town in Texas, you should never attempt to write directly to the filesystem through the device files.

In practice, this state of affairs means that you have little choice but to accept the fixes proposed by **fsck**. You can minimize problems by carefully recording the messages that **fsck** produces, since they will sometimes provide a clue about the file or files that are causing problems. If **fsck** asks for permission to delete a file, you should try to copy it to a different filesystem before allowing **fsck** to proceed. Be aware that any time you attempt to access a damaged filesystem, you risk panicking the system.

See Chapter 10 for information about ***dump*** *and other ways to back up filesystems.*

If a damaged filesystem (one that **fsck** cannot repair automatically) contains valuable data, *do not* experiment with it before making an ironclad backup. You can try to **dump** the disk, but since **dump** expects to be reading an undamaged filesystem, the resulting image may be missing data (or **dump** may crash). The best insurance policy is to **dd** the entire disk to a backup file or backup disk.

If **fsck** finds a file whose parent directory cannot be determined, it will put the file in the **lost+found** directory in the top level of the filesystem. Since the name given to a file is recorded only in the file's parent directory, names for orphan files will not be available and the files placed in **lost+found** will be named with their inode numbers.

8.6 ADDING A DISK TO LINUX: A STEP-BY-STEP GUIDE

After your new disk is installed, it's a good idea to make sure the system can see the new device before you boot up the kernel. If it's an IDE disk, check to be sure the disk is recognized in the BIOS setup display, which you usually access by typing a magic key sequence before the system boots. Consult the manuals that came with your computer or motherboard for specific information on BIOS configuration for IDE devices. In most cases, no special configuration is necessary.

Many SCSI cards also have a BIOS setup screen that you can invoke before the system boots. If this option is available, you scan the SCSI bus to make sure the new device appears. If this procedure hangs or produces a warning message, it's possible that you picked a SCSI ID that was already in use or that you did not install terminators in the right places.

You can also use the SCSI BIOS to low-level format a disk. This operation takes a long time on some disks and cannot be interrupted, so plan ahead.

See page 222 for more information about installing device drivers.

If your SCSI card does not provide its own user interface, you can always just try to boot the system and note the messages displayed by the kernel. If you do not see any messages from a SCSI driver, it is possible that you need to install the driver before the disk can be recognized by the kernel.

In our case, we saw the following messages from our BusLogic SCSI host adaptor.

```
scsi0 : BusLogic BT-948
scsi : 1 host.
  Vendor: SEAGATE    Model: ST446452W        Rev: 0001
  Type:  Direct-Access                ANSI SCSI revision: 02
Detected scsi disk sda at scsi0, channel 0, id 3, lun 0
scsi0: Target 3: Queue Depth 28, Asynchronous
SCSI device sda: hdwr sector=512 bytes. Sectors=91923356 [44884 MB] [44.9 GB]
sda: unknown partition table
```

Ignore warnings about the partition table, since this is the first time the disk has been used. Once the system has finished booting, you can move on to partitioning the disk.

You must first check to see if device files for the disk already exist (they should). In Linux, the names for SCSI disk device files are of the form **/dev/sd**XN, where X is a lowercase letter that identifies the drive (**a** is the lowest numbered SCSI disk, **b** is the second lowest, and so on[10]) and N is the partition number, starting at 1. When referring to the whole disk, simply omit the partition number. There are no character (raw) disk devices in Linux.

In this example, our disk is the first one on the SCSI chain. The first partition is therefore **/dev/sda1**, and the disk as a whole is referred to as **/dev/sda**. If these device files didn't exist, we could create them with the **/dev/MAKEDEV** script:[11]

```
# cd /dev
# ./MAKEDEV sda
```

The disk is now ready to be partitioned. As in most PC operating systems, the tool used for partitioning under Linux is called **fdisk**. Though all versions of **fdisk** do approximately the same thing (they implement Microsoft's standard partitioning system), there are many variations among them. You would be wise to read the man page for your particular system to be sure it matches what we show here.

```
# fdisk /dev/sda
The number of cylinders for this disk is set to 5721.
There is nothing wrong with that, but this is larger than 1024,
and could in certain setups cause problems with:
1) software that runs at boot time (e.g., LILO)
2) booting and partitioning software from other OSs
   (e.g., DOS FDISK, OS/2 FDISK)
```

Since we will be using this disk only on our Linux system, we will ignore the helpful warning. As stated in the geometry discussion on page 130, it is sometimes important to make the first partition small to ensure that it will work with an old BIOS and will work with other operating systems that might be installed on the system.

---

10. Note that this letter refers to the *order* of the target numbers of the SCSI devices, not to the target numbers themselves. If you add or remove a disk, all the drive letters change!

11. **MAKEDEV** is standard on Red Hat and Debian systems, but you'll need to use **mknod** on SuSE systems. See page 226 for more information about creating device files.

The **fdisk** program is interactive; pressing **m** displays a list of all its commands. The ones we use here are:

- **n** or **new** to create a new partition
- **t** or **type** to change the type of a partition
- **p** or **print** to print the partition table
- **w** or **write** to write the partition table to disk

Since our disk does not yet have partitions, we start by creating a new one. If there are old partitions from a disk's former life, you may have to remove them with **fdisk**'s **delete** command before you can create new ones. The **fdisk** program will not change anything on disk until you tell it to write the partition table.

The partition table has room for four "primary" partitions that can be used to hold data. Alternatively, you can create an "extended" partition, which is a primary partition that points to another partition table, giving you another four "logical" partitions. Although the use of extended partitions can overcome the normal four-partition restriction, it is simplest to stick with primary partitions if only a few will be needed, and that's what we'll do in this case:

```
Command (m for help): new
Command action
   e     extended
   p     primary partition (1-4): p
Partition number (1-4): 1
First cylinder (1-5721, default 1): 1
Last cylinder or +size or +sizeM or +sizeK (1-5721, default 5721): +2G

Command (m for help): print
Disk /dev/sda: 255 heads, 63 sectors, 5721 cylinders
Units = cylinders of 16065 * 512 bytes

   Device Boot  Start   End   Blocks   Id  System
/dev/sda1               1    255  2048256   83  Linux
```

We create a swap partition similarly, except that we change the type from Linux to Linux swap. Although the kernel does not care about the partition type, some programs or scripts try to use the type to figure out what each partition is. Linux swap areas cannot currently exceed 2GB, so we specify the maximum size. This is probably overkill for most applications, but since we have disk space to spare, we might as well be generous. **mkswap** will warn us if it cannot use all of the space we have allocated.

```
Command (m for help): new
   e    extended
   p    primary partition (1-4): p
Partition number (1-4): 2
First cylinder (256-5721, default 256): 256
Last cylinder or +size or +sizeM or +sizeK (256-1275, default 1275): 511
```

```
Command (m for help): type
Partition number (1-4): 2
Hex code (type L to list codes): 82
Changed system type of partition 2 to 82 (Linux swap)
```

The third partition, which contains the rest of the disk, is defined in a similar manner. We review the partition table one last time before writing it.

```
Command (m for help): print
Disk /dev/sda: 255 heads, 63 sectors, 5721 cylinders
Units = cylinders of 16065 * 512 bytes
   Device Boot  Start   End    Blocks   Id  System
/dev/sda1            1    255   2048256   83  Linux
/dev/sda2          256    511   2056320   82  Swap
/dev/sda3          512   5721  41849325   83  Linux
```

A star appears next to the number of blocks if the partition does not end on a cylinder boundary. You can either delete the partition and recreate it by entering a number of cylinders (as above), or live with the fact that a small bit of disk space may be unusable. We are happy with the new partition table, so we write the label out to disk:

```
Command (m for help): write
The partition table has been altered!
Calling ioctl() to re-read partition table.
SCSI device sda: hdwr sector=512 bytes. Sectors=91923356 [44884 MB] [44.9 GB]
sda: sda1 sda2 sda3
Syncing disks.
```

Some administrators like to reboot after writing the partition table to make sure everything is stable and consistent before they create the filesystems. It probably isn't really necessary these days, but if you are used to installing Windows, you may feel more comfortable rebooting.

We're now ready to create filesystems. To create a traditional ext2fs filesystem, run **mke2fs** with the device and size of the partition on the command line. (The size can be found in the **fdisk** output above.)

```
# mke2fs /dev/sda1 2048256
Linux ext2 filesystem format
514000 inodes, 2048001 blocks
102412 blocks (5.00%) reserved for the super user
First data block=1
Block size=1024 (log=0)
Fragment size=1024 (log=0)
250 block groups
8192 blocks per group, 8192 fragments per group
2056 inodes per group
Superblock backups stored on blocks:
8193, 16385, 24577, 32769, 40961, 49153, 57345, 65537,
...
Writing inode tables:  250/250 done
Writing superblocks and filesystem accounting information:
done
```

The process for creating the larger filesystem is the same, but it takes significantly longer. If you know that you will not need all of the inodes that **mke2fs** allocates by default, you can reduce the number of inodes per group, speeding up the **mke2fs** and giving you more space for real data. Likewise, you may wish to increase the number of inodes for filesystems that will house a large number of very small files. It's much better to have too many inodes than too few, since running out of inodes will prevent you from creating any more files. You cannot add more inodes after the filesystem has been created. If you run into this situation, you'll need to **dump** the data on the filesystem to tape or to a file on another partition, rerun **mke2fs** with a larger number of inodes (**-i**), and then **restore** the data to the partition. Days of fun!

If you're creating an ext3fs filesystem, you will need to use **mke2fs** with the **-j** flag, which will create a journaled filesystem suitable for most applications. You can also use **-J** to explicitly specify either the size of the journal file that will reside on the new filesystem (**-J size**=x) or the identity of an external device that will contain the journal file (**-J device**=y). Typical installations locate the journal file (which must be between 1,024 and 102,400 filesystem blocks) inside the filesystem itself.

We run **fsck** on our filesystems to make sure they were created properly. The **-f** flag forces **fsck** to check new filesystems rather than assuming that they are clean.

```
# fsck -f /dev/sda1
Pass 1: Checking inodes, blocks, and sizes
Pass 2: Checking directory structure
Pass 3: Checking directory connectivity
Pass 4: Checking reference counts
Pass 5: Checking group summary information
/dev/sda1: 11/514000 files (0.0% non-contiguous), 67014/2048001 blocks
```

New filesystems can be mounted as soon as their mount points are created:

```
# mkdir /bkroot
# mount /dev/sda1 /bkroot
# df /bkroot
Filesystem        1k-blocks      Used    Available   Use%    Mounted on
/dev/sda1          1981000        13     1878575      0%     /bkroot
```

To ensure that the system mounts the new filesystems at boot time, we add a line for each one to the **/etc/fstab** file. Each line should list the name of the device, the mount point, the filesystem type, the mount options, the backup frequency, and the pass number for **fsck**:

```
/dev/sda1        /bkroot        ext2       defaults       0 1
/dev/sda3        /new           ext2       defaults       0 2
```

A boot loader must be written to the disk device to make it bootable. Depending on your installation, either the **lilo** or the **grub** command does the actual installation. See page 23 for more information about configuring and installing a boot loader.

The final step is to create the swap space and add it to the system. Swap partitions must be initialized with **mkswap**, which takes as arguments the device name and the size of the swap partition in sectors. The size can be obtained from **fdisk**, as shown above. You can also pass **mkswap** the **-c** flag, which tells it to clear the sectors before using them. This takes a long time, however, and it isn't really necessary.

With the swap area created, we enable it with the **swapon** command. **swapon** also verifies that the swap area was properly added.

```
# mkswap -c /dev/sda2 2056320
Setting up swapspace version 1, size = 2105667584 bytes
# swapon /dev/sda2
# swapon -s
Filename     Type       Size      Used   Priority
/dev/hda5    partition  133020    688    -1
/dev/sda2    partition  2056316   0      -2
```

As with regular filesystems, you must add the new swap partition to the **/etc/fstab** file if you want the system to remember it the next time you reboot. The following entry would be appropriate for our example disk:

```
/dev/sda2          swap            swap    defaults      0  0
```

Make sure you reboot to test the changes that were made to the **/etc/fstab** file and to make sure that the new filesystems and swap space come on-line correctly.

8.7 EXERCISES

E8.1 List all the variations of SCSI. Which connectors go with which variants? Ignoring the differences in connectors, what are the compatibility issues among the various SCSI versions?

E8.2 What's the difference between formatting a disk and partitioning a disk? What's the difference between partitioning and creating a filesystem?

★ **E8.3** Using print or Internet resources, identify the best-performing SCSI and IDE drives. Do the benchmarks used to evaluate these drives reflect the way that a busy Linux server would use its boot disk? How much of a cost premium would you pay for SCSI, and how much of a performance improvement (if any) would you get for the extra money?

★ **E8.4** Add a disk to your system. Make one partition on the new disk a backup root partition; install a kernel and boot from it. Keep a journal of all the steps required to complete this task. You may find the **script** command helpful. (Requires root access.)

★ **E8.5** What is a superblock and what is it used for? Look up the definition of the ext2fs superblock structure in the kernel header files and discuss what each of the fields in the structure represents.

★   **E8.6**   List the command and arguments you would use to create a filesystem on a disk in each of the following circumstances.

a) The disk will be used as storage for home directories.
b) The disk will be used as swap space.
c) The disk will store the mail queue at a large spam house.
d) The disk will hold an Oracle database.

★★   **E8.7**   What fields are stored in an inode on an ext2fs filesystem? List the contents of the inode that represents the **/etc/motd** file. Where is this file's filename stored? (Tools such as **hexdump** and **ls -i** might help.)

★★   **E8.8**   Examine the contents of a directory file with a program such as **hexdump** or **od**. Each variable-length record represents a file in that directory. Look up the directory entry structure and explain each field using an example from a real directory file. Next, look at the **lost+found** directory on any filesystem. Why are there so many names there when the **lost+found** directory appears to be empty?

★★★★★   **E8.9**   Write a program that traverses the filesystem and prints out the contents of the **/etc/motd** and **/etc/termcap** files. But don't open the files directly; open the raw device file for the root partition and use the **seek** and **read** system calls to decode the filesystem and find the appropriate data blocks. **/etc/motd** is usually short and will probably contain only direct blocks. **/etc/termcap** will probably require you to decode indirect blocks. Hint: when reading the system header files, be sure you have found the filesystem's on-disk inode structure, not the in-core inode structure. (Requires root access.)

Adding a Disk

9 *Periodic Processes*

The key to staying in control of your system is to automate as many tasks as possible. For example, an **adduser** program can add new users faster than you can, with a smaller chance of making mistakes. Almost any task can be encoded in a shell, Perl, or **expect** script.

It's often useful to have a script or command executed without any human intervention. For example, you might want to have a script verify (say, every half-hour) that your network routers and bridges are working correctly and have it send you email when problems are discovered.[1]

9.1 CRON: SCHEDULE COMMANDS

Under Linux, periodic execution is normally handled by the **cron** daemon. **cron** starts when the system boots and remains running as long as the system is up. **cron** reads one or more configuration files containing lists of command lines and times at which they are to be invoked. The command lines are executed by **sh**, so almost anything you can do by hand from the shell can also be done with **cron**.[2]

cron originally appeared in the UNIX family tree in the 1970s, and traditional versions contain lots of cruft and not-so-handy features. Linux is distributed with a

---

1. Many sites go further than this and dial a pager with a modem to summon an administrator as soon as a problem is detected.
2. Actually, **/bin/sh** under Linux is really a link to the **bash** shell, an enhanced (and reimplemented) version of the traditional Bourne shell found on UNIX systems. It's possible to configure **cron** to use other shells as well.

version known as "Vixie-cron," named after its author, Paul Vixie. Vixie-cron is a modern rewrite that provides added functionality without all the mess.

A **cron** configuration file is called a "crontab," short for "cron table." **cron** looks for crontab files in three places: **/var/spool/cron** (or a subdirectory of **/var/spool/cron**, **tabs** on SuSE and **crontabs** on Debian), **/etc/cron.d**, and **/etc/crontab**.

Per-user crontab files are stored in the **/var/spool/cron** directory. Typically, there is (at most) one crontab file per user: one for root, one for jsmith, and so on. Crontab files are named with the login names of the users they belong to, and **cron** uses these filenames to figure out which UID to use when running the commands that each file contains. The **crontab** command transfers crontab files to and from this directory.

Crontab files that schedule system maintenance tasks and other tasks defined by the system administrator are stored in the file **/etc/crontab** and in other files found in the **/etc/cron.d** directory. These files have a slightly different format from the per-user crontab files because they allow commands to be run as an arbitrary user. **cron** treats the **/etc/crontab** and **/etc/cron.d** entries in exactly the same way. In general, **/etc/crontab** is intended as a file for the system administrator to maintain by hand, whereas **/etc/cron.d** is provided as a place where software packages can install any crontab entries they might need.

When **cron** starts, it reads all of its config files, stores them in memory, and then goes to sleep. Once each minute, **cron** wakes up, checks the modification times on the crontab files, reloads any files that have changed, and then executes any tasks scheduled for that minute before returning to sleep.

cron does not compensate for commands that are missed while the system is down or for abrupt changes in the system time (for example, if you notice that the system clock is 20 minutes slow and reset it with the correct time). If you use **cron** for time-sensitive tasks, you might want to investigate **anacron**, a continuous-time version of cron that's supplied on Red Hat and Debian systems. It's conceptually very similar to **cron**, but it makes sure that commands are not skipped because of apparent discontinuities in the flow of time.

 For reasons that are unclear, **cron** has been renamed **crond** on Red Hat systems.

9.2 THE FORMAT OF CRONTAB FILES

All the crontab files on a system share a similar format. Comments are introduced with a pound sign (#) in the first column of a line. Each noncomment line contains six or seven fields and represents one command:

minute hour day month weekday [username] command

The first six fields are separated by whitespace, but within the *command* field, whitespace is taken literally. The *username* is found only in **/etc/crontab** and in files from the **/etc/cron.d** directory; it specifies the user as whom the *command* should be run.

This field is not present or necessary in the user-specific crontab files (those stored in **/var/spool/cron**) because the UID is implied by the filename.

The *minute, hour, day, month,* and *weekday* fields tell when to run the *command*. Their interpretations are shown in Table 9.1.

Table 9.1   Crontab time specifications

Field	Description	Range
minute	Minute of the hour	0 to 59
hour	Hour of the day	0 to 23
day	Day of the month	1 to 31
month	Month of the year	1 to 12
weekday	Day of the week	0 to 6 (0 = Sunday)

Each of the time-related fields may contain

- A star, which matches everything
- A single integer, which matches exactly
- Two integers separated by a dash, matching a range of values
- A comma-separated series of integers or ranges, matching any listed value

For example, the time specification

```
45  10  *  *  1-5
```

means "10:45 a.m., Monday through Friday." A hint: never put a star in the first field unless you want the command to be run every minute.

There is a potential ambiguity to watch out for with the *weekday* and *day* fields. Every day is both a day of the week and a day of the month. If both *weekday* and *day* are specified, a day need satisfy only one of the two conditions in order to be selected. For example,

```
0,30  *  13  *  5
```

means "every half-hour on Friday, and every half-hour on the 13th of the month," not "every half-hour on Friday the 13th."

Vixie-cron also allows step values in crontab time specifications. For example, the series 0,3,6,9,12,15,18,21 can be written more concisely in Vixie-cron as 0-21/3.

See page 42 for more information about su. The *command* is the **sh** command line to be executed. It can be any valid shell command and should not be quoted. *command* is considered to continue to the end of the line and may contain blanks or tabs.

A percent sign (%) is used to indicate newlines within the *command* field. Only the text up to the first percent sign is included in the actual command; the remaining lines are given to the command as standard input.

Here are some examples of legal crontab commands:

```
echo The time is now `date` > /dev/console
write garth % Hi Garth. % Remember to get a job.
cd /etc; /bin/mail -s "Password file" evi < passwd
```

And here are some complete examples of crontab entries:

```
30 2 * * 1     (cd /users/joe/project; make)
```

This entry will be activated at 2:30 each Monday morning. It will run **make** in the directory **/users/joe/project**. An entry like this might be used to start a long compilation at a time when other users would not be using the system. Usually, any output produced by a **cron** command is mailed to the "owner" of the crontab.[3]

```
20 1 * * *       find /tmp -atime +3 -exec rm -f {} ';'
```

This command will run at 1:20 each morning. It removes all files in the **/tmp** directory that have not been accessed in 3 days.

```
55 23 * * 0-3,6 /staff/trent/bin/acct-script
```

This line runs **acct-script** at 11:55 p.m. every day except Thursdays and Fridays.

It is also possible to specify environment variables and their values in a Vixie-cron crontab file. See the **crontab**(5) man page for more details.

9.3 CRONTAB MANAGEMENT

crontab *filename* installs *filename* as your crontab, replacing any previous version. **crontab -e** checks out a copy of your crontab, invokes your editor on it (as specified by the EDITOR environment variable), and then resubmits it to the crontab directory. **crontab -l** lists the contents of your crontab to standard output, and **crontab -r** removes it, leaving you with no crontab file at all.

Most systems allow root to supply a *username* argument so that other users' crontabs can be viewed or edited. For example, **crontab -u jsmith -r** erases the crontab belonging to the user jsmith.

Without command-line arguments, **crontab** will try to read a crontab from its standard input. If you enter this mode by accident, don't try to exit with <Control-D>; doing so will erase your entire crontab. Use <Control-C> instead.

By default, all users can submit crontab files to **cron**. Two config files, **/etc/cron.deny** and **/etc/cron.allow** (on SuSE systems, these files are named **/var/spool/cron/deny** and **/var/spool/cron/allow**), allow you to override this policy. If the allow file exists, then it contains a list of all users that may submit crontabs, one per line. No unlisted person can invoke the **crontab** command. If the allow file doesn't exist, then the deny file is checked. It, too, is just a list of users, but the meaning is reversed: everyone

3. That is, the user after whom the crontab file is named. The actual owner of crontab files is generally root.

except the listed users is allowed access. If neither the allow file nor the deny file exists, only root can submit crontabs.

It's important to note that access control is implemented by **crontab**, not by **cron**. If a user sneaks a crontab file into the appropriate directory by other means, **cron** will blindly execute the commands that it contains.

9.4 SOME COMMON USES FOR CRON

A number of standard tasks are especially suited for invocation by **cron**, and these usually make up the bulk of the material in root's crontab. In this section we look at a variety of such tasks and the crontab lines used to implement them.

Linux systems often come with crontab entries preinstalled, mostly in **/etc/cron.d**. If you want to deactivate the standard entries, comment them out by inserting a pound sign (#) at the beginning of each line. Don't delete them; you might want to refer to them later.

In addition to the **/etc/cron.d** mechanism, Linux distributions also preinstall crontab entries that run the scripts in a set of well-known directories, thereby providing another way for software packages to install periodic jobs without any editing of a crontab file. For example, scripts in **/etc/cron.daily** are run once a day, and scripts in **/etc/cron.weekly** are run once a week.

Cleaning the filesystem

Some of the files on any Linux system are worthless junk (no, not the system files). For example, whenever a program crashes, the kernel writes out a file named **core** that contains an image of the program's address space.[4] Core files are useful for software developers, but for administrators they are usually a waste of space. Users often don't know about core files, so they tend not to delete them on their own.

NFS, the Network File System, is described in Chapter 17.

NFS is another source of extra files. Because NFS servers are stateless, they have to use a special convention to preserve files that have been deleted locally but are still in use by a remote machine. Most implementations rename such files to **.nfs**xxx where xxx is a number. Various situations can result in these files being forgotten and left around after they are supposed to have been deleted.

Many programs create temporary files in **/tmp** or **/var/tmp** that aren't erased for one reason or another. Some programs, especially editors, like to make backup copies of each file they work with.

A partial solution to the junk file problem is to institute some sort of nightly disk space reclamation out of **cron**. Modern systems usually come with something of this sort set up for you, but it's a good idea to review your system's default behavior to

---

4. The word "core" means "memory." This term originated on early computer systems, which used as memory elements little ferrite donuts mounted on a woven mesh.

make sure it's appropriate for your situation. Below are several common idioms implemented with the **find** command.

```
find / -xdev -name core -atime +7 -exec rm -f {} ';'
```

This command removes core images that have not been accessed in a week. The **-xdev** argument makes sure that **find** won't cross over to filesystems other than the root; this restraint is important on networks where many filesystems may be cross-mounted. If you want to clean up more than one filesystem, use a separate command for each (note that **/var** is typically a separate filesystem).

```
find / -xdev -atime +3 '(' -name '#*' -o -name '.#*' -o -name '*.CKP' -o
    -name '*~' -o -name '.nfs*' ')' -exec rm -f {} ';'
```

This command deletes files that begin with **#** or **.#** or **.nfs**, or end with **~** or **.CKP**, and that have not been accessed in three days. These patterns are typical of various sorts of temporary and editor backup files.

```
cd /tmp; find . ! -name . ! -name lost+found -type d -mtime +3
    -exec /bin/rm -rf {} ';'
```

This command recursively removes all subdirectories of **/tmp** not modified in 72 hours. Plain files in **/tmp** are removed at boot time by the system startup scripts, but some systems do not remove directories. If a directory named **lost+found** exists, it is treated specially and is not removed. This is important if **/tmp** is a separate filesystem. See page 145 for more information about **lost+found**.

If you use any of these commands, you should make sure that users are aware of your cleanup policies.

Network distribution of configuration files

See Chapter 18 for more information about sharing configuration files.

If you are running a network of machines, it's often convenient to maintain a single, network-wide version of configuration files such as the mail aliases database (usually **/etc/mail/aliases**). Master versions of these files can be distributed every night with **rsync**, **rdist** or an **expect** script.

Sometimes, postprocessing is required. For example, you might need to run the **newaliases** command to convert a text file of mail aliases to the hashed format used by **sendmail** if the AutoRebuildAliases option isn't set in your **sendmail.cf** file. You might also need to load files into an administrative database such as NIS.

Rotating log files

Linux does a good job of managing most of its log files, but some files grow without bound until they are manually reset. There are various ways to prevent logs from overflowing, the simplest being to simply truncate them at periodic intervals.

A more conservative strategy is to "rotate" log files by keeping several older versions of each one. This scheme prevents log files from getting out of control but never leaves you without any recent log information. Since log rotation is a recurrent and

Periodic Processes

regularly scheduled event, it's an ideal task for **cron**. See *Rotating log files* on page 200 for more details.

9.5 EXERCISES

E9.1   A local user on your system has been abusing his crontab privileges by running expensive tasks at regular intervals. After asking him to stop several times, you are forced to revoke his privileges. List the steps needed to delete his current crontab and make sure he can't add a new one.

★ **E9.2**   Think of three tasks (other than those mentioned in the chapter) that need to be run periodically. Write crontab entries for each task and specify into which crontab files the entries should go.

★ **E9.3**   Write a script that keeps your startup files (~/.[a-z]*) synchronized among all the machines on which you have an account. Schedule this script to run regularly from **cron**.

★ **E9.4**   Locate your Linux system's crontab files and choose three entries. Decode each one and describe when it runs, what it does, and why you think the entry is needed. (Requires root access.)

★ **E9.5**   Using the man pages for the **du**, **sort**, and **head** commands as references, write a script that determines which 10 home directories are the largest on the system. Schedule the script to run every Monday night at 12:00 a.m. and have it mail its output to you. Hint: you'll want to use a reverse numeric sort. (Requires root access.)

10 Backups

At most sites, the information stored on computers is worth more than the computers themselves. It is also much harder to replace. Protecting this information is one of the system administrator's most important (and, unfortunately, most tedious) tasks.

There are hundreds of creative and not-so-creative ways to lose data. Software bugs routinely corrupt data files. Users accidentally delete their life's work. Hackers and disgruntled employees erase disks. Hardware problems and natural disasters take out entire machine rooms.

If executed correctly, backups (aka "dumps") allow an administrator to restore a filesystem (or any portion of a filesystem) to the condition it was in at the time of the last backup. Backups must be done carefully and on a strict schedule. The backup system and backup media must also be tested regularly to verify that they are working correctly.

The integrity of dump tapes directly affects your company's bottom line. Senior management needs to understand what the backups are actually supposed to do, as opposed to what they *want* the backups to do. It may be okay to lose a day's work at a university computer science department, but it probably isn't okay at a commodity trading firm.

We begin this chapter with some general backup philosophy, followed by a discussion of the most commonly used backup devices and media (their strengths, weaknesses, and costs). Next, we discuss Linux backup and archiving commands and give some suggestions as to which commands are best for which situations. We then talk about how to design a backup scheme and review the mechanics of the popular **dump** and

Backups

restore utilities. Finally, we take a look at Amanda, a free network backup package, and then offer some comments on alternatives.

10.1 MOTHERHOOD AND APPLE PIE

Before we get into the meat and potatoes of backups, we want to pass on some general hints that we have learned over time (usually, the hard way). None of these suggestions is an absolute rule, but you will find that the more of them you follow, the smoother your dump process will be.

Perform all dumps from one machine

Many backup utilities allow you to perform dumps over the network. Although there is some performance penalty for doing this, the increase in ease of administration makes it worthwhile. We have found that the best method is to run a script from a central location that executes **rdump** (by way of **rsh** or **ssh**) on each machine that needs to be dumped, or to use a software package (commercial, free, or shareware) that automates this process. All dumps should go to the same backup device (nonrewinding, of course).

If your network is too large to be backed up by a single tape drive, you should still try to keep your backup system as centralized as possible. Centralization makes administration easier and allows you to verify that all machines were dumped correctly. Depending on the backup media you are using, you can often put more than one tape drive on a server without affecting performance. With today's high-performance (12 MB/s and up) tape drives, however, it may be impractical to do this.

Label your tapes

It is essential that you label each dump tape clearly and completely. An unlabeled tape is a blank tape.

The tapes themselves should be labeled to uniquely identify their contents. Detailed information such as lists of filesystems and dump dates can be written on the cases.

You must be able to restore the root and **/usr** filesystems without looking at dump scripts. Label the dump tapes for these filesystems with their format, the exact syntax of the command used to create them, and any other information you would need to restore from them without referring to on-line documentation.

Free and commercial labeling programs abound. Save yourself a major headache and invest in one. If you purchase labels for your laser printer, the label vendor can usually provide (Windows) software that generates labels.

Pick a reasonable backup interval

The more often backups are done, the smaller the amount of data that can be lost in a crash. However, backups use system resources and an operator's time. The sysadmin must provide adequate data integrity at a reasonable cost of time and materials.

On busy systems, it is generally appropriate to back up filesystems with home directories every workday. On systems that are used less heavily or on which the data is less volatile, you might decide that performing backups several times a week is sufficient. On a small system with only one user, performing backups once a week is probably adequate. How much data are your users willing to lose?

Choose filesystems carefully

Filesystems that are rarely modified do not need to be backed up as frequently as users' home directories. If only a few files change on an otherwise static filesystem (such as **/etc/passwd** in the root filesystem), these files can be copied every day to another partition that is backed up regularly.

If **/tmp** is a separate filesystem, it should not be backed up. The **/tmp** directory should not contain anything essential, so there is no reason to preserve it. In case this seems obvious, we know of one large site that does daily backups of **/tmp**.

Make daily dumps fit on one tape

*See Chapter 9 for more information about **cron**.*

In a perfect world, you could do daily dumps of all your user filesystems onto a single tape. High-density media such as DLT and AIT make this goal practical for some sites. You can mount a tape every day before you leave work and run the dumps late at night from **cron**. That way, dumps occur at a time when files are not likely to be changing and the dumps have minimal impact on users.

Unfortunately, this goal is becoming less and less realistic. When users can purchase 40GB disks for $150, there's not much of an economic barrier to the escalation of disk space. Why clean up your disks and enforce quotas when you can just throw a little money at the problem?

If you can't fit your daily backups on one tape, you have several options:

- Buy a higher-capacity tape device.
- Buy a stacker or library and feed multiple pieces of media to one device.
- Change your dump sequence.
- Write a smarter script.
- Use multiple backup devices.

Your automated dump system should always record the name of each filesystem it has dumped. Good record keeping allows you to quickly skip forward to the correct filesystem when you want to restore a file. It is also a good idea to record the order of the filesystems on the outside of the tape. (We've said it before, but it bears repeating: be sure to use the nonrewinding tape device to write tapes with multiple dumps.)

Make filesystems smaller than your dump device

dump and other readily available utilities are perfectly capable of dumping filesystems to multiple tapes. But if a dump spans multiple tapes, an operator must be present to change tapes[1] and the tapes must be carefully labeled to allow restores to

---

1. That is, unless you have a stacker, jukebox, or library, and your backup utility supports it.

be performed easily. Unless you have a good reason to create a really large filesystem, don't do it.

Keep tapes off-site

Most organizations keep backups off-site so that a disaster such as a fire cannot destroy both the original data and the backups. "Off-site" can be anything from a safe deposit box at a bank to the President's or CEO's home. Companies that specialize in the secure storage of backup media guarantee a secure and climate-controlled environment for your archives. Always make sure your off-site storage provider is reputable, bonded, and insured.

The speed with which tapes are moved off-site should depend on how often you need to restore files and on how much latency you can accept. Some sites avoid making this decision by performing two dumps a day (to different tape devices): one that stays on-site and one that is moved immediately.

Protect your backups

Dan Geer, a security consultant, said, "What does a backup do? It reliably violates file permissions at a distance." Hmmm.

Secure your backup tapes. They contain all of your organization's data and can be read by anyone who has physical access to them. Not only should you keep your tapes off-site, but you should also keep them under lock and key. If you use a commercial storage facility for this purpose, the company you deal with should guarantee the confidentiality of the tapes in their care.

Some companies feel so strongly about the importance of backups that they make duplicates, which is really not a bad idea at all.

Limit activity during dumps

Filesystem activity should be limited during dumps because changes can cause your backup utility to make mistakes. You can limit activity either by doing the dumps when few active users are around (at night or on weekends) or by making the filesystem accessible only to the backup utility. (This precaution sounds fine in theory, but it is rarely practiced. Users want 24/7 access to all filesystems. These days it is impossible to do a backup with no disk activity.)

See page 479 for more information about file servers.
Dedicated file servers such as those manufactured by Network Appliance provide on-line backups with snapshots of the filesystem at regular, tunable intervals. This feature enables safe backups to be made of an active filesystem and is one of the important advantages of using a dedicated file server.

Check your tapes

We've heard many horror stories about system administrators who did not discover problems with their dump regime until after a serious system failure. It is essential that you continually monitor your backup procedure and verify that it is functioning correctly. Operator error ruins more dumps than any other problem.

The first check is to have your backup software attempt to reread tapes immediately after it has finished dumping.[2] Scanning a tape to verify that it contains the expected number of files is a good check. It's best if every tape is scanned, but this no longer seems practical for a large organization that uses hundreds of tapes a day. A random sample would be most prudent in this environment.

*See page 174 for more information about **restore**.*

It is often useful to generate a table of contents for each filesystem (**dump** users can use **restore -t**) and to store the results on disk. These catalogs should be named in a way that relates them to the appropriate tape; for example, **okra:usr.Jan.13**. A week's worth of these records makes it easy to discover what tape a lost file is on. You just **grep** for the filename and pick the newest instance.

In addition to providing a catalog of tapes, successfully reading the table of contents from the tape is a reasonable indication that the dump is OK and that you will probably be able to read the tape when you need to. A quick attempt to restore a random file will give you even more confidence in your ability to restore from that tape.[3]

You should periodically attempt to restore from various tapes to make sure that it is still possible to do so. Every so often, try to restore from an old (months or years) dump tape. Drives have been known to wander out of alignment over time and to become unable to read their old tapes. The tapes can be recovered by a company that specializes in this service, but it will be expensive.

A related check is to verify that you can read the tapes on hardware other than your own. If your machine room burns, it does not do much good to know that the dump tapes could have been read on a tape drive that has now been destroyed.

Consider the following story, which circulated through the grapevine a couple of years ago: *A major research firm in California had an operator who was too busy hacking to do dumps. He opened tapes, labeled them, and filed them without ever putting any data on them. This charade went on for two or three months until someone insisted on having a file restored. What happened to him? Fired? No, he was transferred internally, but was eventually arrested and convicted on unrelated electronic fraud charges. Rumor has it he got 40 years.*

Develop a tape life cycle

Tapes have a finite life. It's great to recycle your media, but be sure to abide by the manufacturer's recommendations regarding the life of tapes. Most manufacturers quantify this life in terms of the number of passes that a tape can stand: a backup, a restore, and an **mt fsf** (file skip forward) each represent one pass.

---

2. You can use **restore -C** to verify a dump tape against a directory tree.
3. For example, **restore -t** reads only the table of contents for the dump, which is stored at the beginning of the tape. When you actually restore a file, you are testing a more extensive region of the medium.

Design your data for backups

With disks so cheap and new storage architectures so reliable, it's tempting not to back up all your data. A sensible storage architecture—designed rather than grown willy nilly as disk needs increase—can do a lot to make backups more tractable. Start by taking an inventory of your storage needs:

- The various kinds of data your site will deal with
- The expected volatility of each type of data
- The backup frequency you require to feel comfortable with potential losses
- The political boundaries over which the data will be spread

Use this information to design your site's storage architecture with backups and potential growth in mind. Most sites are not ready to place complete trust in snazzy "black boxes" such as RAID systems or Network Appliance snapshots. Keeping project directories and users' home directories on a dedicated file server can make it easier to manage your data and ensure its safety.

Prepare for the worst

After you have established a backup procedure, explore the worst case scenario: your site is completely destroyed. Determine how much data would be lost and how long it would take to get your system back to life (include the time it would take to acquire new hardware). Then determine whether you can live with your answers.

10.2 BACKUP DEVICES AND MEDIA

Since many types of failure can damage several pieces of hardware at once, backups should be written to some sort of removable media. For example, backing up one hard disk to another (although better than no backup at all) provides little protection against a controller failure. Companies that back up your data over the Internet have entered the scene over the last few years, but most backups are still stored locally.

Many kinds of media store data by using magnetic particles. These media are subject to damage by electrical and magnetic fields. Here are some specific hazards to avoid:

- Audio speakers contain large electromagnets; it's not a good idea to store tapes on or near them. Even small speakers designed for use with computers can be hazardous.

- Transformers and power supplies (including UPS boxes) generate electromagnetic fields. The "wall warts" used to power many peripherals contain transformers.

- Hard disks and tape drives have motors and magnetic heads, and their cases are often unshielded. Drives in metal cases are probably safe.

- Desk fans often contain large, unshielded motors.

- Monitors use transformers and high voltages. Many monitors retain an electrical charge even after being turned off. Color monitors are the worst. Never store tapes on top of a monitor.

- Prolonged exposure to the Earth's background radiation affects the data on magnetic media, limiting its life span. All tapes will become unreadable over a period of years. Most media will keep for three years, but if you plan to store data longer than that, you should either use optical media or re-record the data.

The following sections describe some of the media that can be used for backups. The media are presented roughly in order of increasing capacity.

Many tape drives compress data before writing it to tape, allowing more data to be stored than the tape's nominal capacity would suggest. Manufacturers like to quote tape capacities in terms of compressed data; they often optimistically assume a compression ratio of 2:1 or more. In the sections below, we ignore compression and cite the actual number of bytes that can physically be stored on each piece of media.

The assumed compression ratio of a drive also affects its throughput rating. If a drive can physically write 1 MB/s to tape but the manufacturer assumes 2:1 compression, the throughput magically rises to 2 MB/s. As with capacity figures, we have ignored throughput inflation below.

Although cost and media capacity are both important considerations, it's important to consider throughput as well. Fast media are more pleasant to deal with, and they allow more flexibility in scheduling backups.

Floppy disks

Floppies are the most inconvenient way to store backups. They are slow and do not hold much data. Although the individual disks are cheap, they hold so little data that they are in fact the most expensive backup medium overall. Floppy disks only last for a couple of years; never use them for long-term storage. On the other hand, floppy drives are inexpensive and often come with the system.

Super floppies

Iomega Zip drives are now ubiquitous, and they are often the default external medium on home PCs. The storage capacity of these drives has increased from 100MB to 250MB. The drives are available with parallel, serial, SCSI, and USB connectors.

Imation markets a SuperDisk product that can write both traditional floppy disks and special 120MB media.

Although these products are useful for exchanging data, their high media costs make them a poor choice for backups.

CD-R and CD-RW

The recent decreases in the price of recordable and read/write CDs makes them a far more attractive medium for backups than they were a few years ago. Both forms hold about 650MB. Drives that write these CDs are available in as many varieties as your favorite hard disk: SCSI, IDE, parallel, USB, etc.

CDs are written with a laser through a photochemical process. Although hard data has been elusive, it is widely believed that CDs have a substantially longer shelf life than magnetic media. Write-once CDs, known as CD-Rs, are not quite as durable as normal (stamped) CDs. CD-R is not a particularly good choice for normal backups, but it's good for archiving data you might want to recover a long time in the future.

Recordable DVD technology is just starting to become available. We look forward to its adoption as a medium for data storage. The capacity should be somewhere between 5GB and 10GB.

Removable hard disks

A series of high-capacity removable disks have come onto the market over the last few years. Castlewood Industries has a 2.2GB product called an Orb drive. It comes in internal and external Ultra SCSI, EIDE, and USB varieties. For the gory details, see www.castlewood.com.

Another popular drive is the Iomega Jaz, which holds 2GB and claims an average transfer rate of 8.7 MB/s. The Jaz also claims a data shelf life of 10 years, whereas the Orb sets a more realistic target of 5 years. More information about the Jaz drive can be obtained from www.iomega.com.

The removable disk drive market is becoming very competitive, and prices vary daily. The main advantage of these products is speed: they achieve transfer rates comparable to normal disk drives. They are attractive as backup devices for small systems and home machines, although the disks themselves are somewhat pricey.

8mm cartridge tapes

Several brands of tape drive record to standard 8mm (small-format) videotapes. The drives are often referred to as "Exabytes drives," after the first company that produced them. The original format held 2GB, and the newer formats hold up to 7GB. The hardware compression built into some drives pushes the capacity even higher.

The size of 8mm tapes makes off-site storage very convenient. Originally, the drive mechanisms were somewhat problematic in that they would fall out of alignment every 6-12 months and require a costly repair from the manufacturer. This is no longer the case.

8mm tapes come in both video and data grades. Some manufacturers insist on data grade and void your warranty if you use unapproved media. We have found video grade to be quite acceptable if it does not jeopardize the warranty. Be aware that both grades of tape are susceptible to heat damage.

DAT (4mm) cartridge tapes

DAT (Digital Audio Tape) drives are helical scan devices that use 4mm cartridges. Although these drives are usually referred to as DAT drives, they are really DDS (Digital Data Storage) drives; the exact distinction is unimportant. The original format held about 2GB, but successive generations have improved DDS capacity significantly. The current generation (DDS-4) holds up to 20GB.

DAT drives seek rapidly and transfer data at up to about 2.5 MB/s (for DDS-4), making the systems relatively fast. Their large capacity allows a complete backup to be performed without operator intervention at many sites. The 4mm tapes are compact, reducing the need for storage space and making off-site storage easy. DAT drives do not have a history of alignment problems.

At least one major manufacturer (Sony) has announced end-of-life for DDS, so this technology may not be the best choice for new deployment in an organization.

Travan tapes

Worth a brief mention here is the next generation of QIC tape technology, known as Travan. Travan drives use a linear recording technology and support media from 2.5GB to 10GB. The drives are inexpensive, but the tapes cost slightly more than those of other high-capacity tape systems, about $3/GB. The marketing hype claims a sustained transfer rate of approximately 1 MB/s.

Many manufacturers make Travan drives, but Linux support is patchy. As of this writing, Linux drivers are available for drives from HP, Tandberg, and Tecmar.

DLT

Digital Linear Tapes are a popular backup medium. These drives are reliable, affordable, and capacious. They evolved from DEC's TK-50 and TK-70 cartridge tape drives, which were popular peripherals on the DEC VAXstation. The first generation of DLT drives could read the old TK-70 tapes. DEC sold the technology to Quantum, which popularized the drives by increasing their speed and capacity and by dropping their price. Unfortunately, the mechanical tape transports are essentially the same as those of the original TK-50 design, which was popular in the 1980s. They're due for a redesign.

DLT tapes hold a lot of data, up to 40GB. Transfer rates run about 6 MB/s. Manufacturers boast that the tapes will last 20 to 30 years; that is, if the hardware to read them still exists. How many 9-track tape drives are still functioning and on-line these days?

The downside of DLT is the price of media, which runs about $65 per tape, although the prices are decreasing. For a university, this is a huge expense; for a Wall Street investment firm, it might be OK.

AIT

Advanced Intelligent Tape is Sony's own 8mm product on steroids. In 1996, Sony dissolved its relationship with Exabyte and introduced the AIT-1, an 8mm helical scan device with twice the capacity of 8mm drives from Exabyte. Since the original product release, Sony has introduced a higher-capacity version of AIT-1 and follow-on technologies AIT-2 and (in 2001) AIT-3.

The Advanced Metal Evaporated (AME) tapes used in AIT drives have a long life cycle. They also contain a built-in EEPROM that gives the media itself some smarts. Software support is needed to make any actual use of the EEPROM, however. AIT-2 claims a 6 MB/s native transfer rate with a media capacity of 50GB. AIT-3 claims double those numbers, clocking in at a 12 MB/s native transfer rate and a media capacity of 100GB. Drive and tape prices are both roughly on a par with DLT.

Mammoth

Exabyte's Mammoth is an improved version of the 8mm tape system. Exabyte chose to develop and manufacture its own mechanism after its falling out with Sony. The Mammoth products still rely on Sony for the AME media, but the tapes do not contain a memory chip.

The first generations of the Mammoth line had reliability problems. However, Exabyte listened to their customers and improved the products. They now claim a failure rate of only 1%.

The original tiff between Exabyte and Sony was based on Sony's poor manufacturing quality. Sony ran only one production line for both consumer products and data drives, so your Exabyte was essentially identical to your camcorder in Sony's eyes. However, Sony seems to be ahead of the curve right now.

Jukeboxes, stackers, and tape libraries

With the low cost of disks these days, most sites have so much disk space that a full backup requires multiple tapes, even at 20GB per tape. One solution for these sites is a stacker, jukebox, or tape library.

A stacker is a simple tape changer that is used with a standard tape drive. It has a hopper that you load with tapes; it unloads full tapes as they are ejected from the drive and replaces them with blank tapes from the hopper. Most stackers hold about ten tapes.

A jukebox is a hardware device that can automatically change removable media in a limited number of drives, much like an old-style music jukebox that changed records on a single turntable. Jukeboxes are available for several types of media, including DAT, DLT, AIT, and CD. Jukeboxes are often bundled with special backup software that understands how to manipulate the changer. Storage Technology and Sony are two manufacturers of these products.

Tape libraries are a hardware backup solution for large data sets—terabytes, usually. They are closet-sized mechanisms with multiple tape drives (or CDs) and a robotic arm that retrieves and files media on the library's many shelves. As you can imagine, they are quite expensive to purchase and maintain, and they have special power, space, and air conditioning requirements. Most purchasers of tape libraries also purchase an operations contract from the manufacturer to optimize and run the device. The libraries have a software component, of course, which is what really runs the device. Storage Technology is a leading manufacturer of tape libraries.

Hard disks

We would be remiss if we did not mention the decreasing cost of hard drives as a reason to consider disk-to-disk backups. Although we suggest that you not duplicate one disk to another within the same physical machine, hard disks can be a good, low-cost solution for storage over a network.

One obvious problem is that hard disk storage space is finite and must eventually be reused. However, disk-to-disk backups are an excellent way to protect against the accidental deletion of files. If you maintain a day-old disk image in a well-known place that's shared over NFS or CIFS, users can recover from their own mistakes without involving an administrator.

Summary of media types

Whew! That's a lot of possibilities. Table 10.1 summarizes the characteristics of the media discussed in the previous sections.

Table 10.1   Backup media compared

Medium	Capacity[a]	Speed[a]	Drive	Media	Cost/GB	Reuse?	Random?
Floppy disk	2.8MB	< 100 KB/s	$15	25¢	$91.43	Yes	Yes
SuperDisk	120MB	1.1 MB/s[b]	$200	$8	$68.27	Yes	Yes
Zip 250	250MB	900 KB/s	$200	$15	$61.44	Yes	Yes
CD-R	650MB	2.4 MB/s	$200	75¢	$1.18	No	Yes
CD-RW	650MB	2.4 MB/s	$200	$2	$3.15	Yes	Yes
Jaz	2GB	7.4 MB/s	$350	$100	$50.00	Yes	Yes
Orb	2.2GB	12.2 MB/s[b]	$200	$40	$18.18	Yes	Yes
Exabyte (8mm)	7GB	1 MB/s	$1,200	$8	$1.14	Yes	No
Travan	10GB	1 MB/s	$200	$34	$3.40	Yes	No
DDS-4 (4mm)	20GB	2.5 MB/s	$1,000	$30	$1.50	Yes	No
DLT (1/2 in.)	40GB	6 MB/s	$4,000	$60	$1.50	Yes	No
AIT-2 (8mm)	50GB	6 MB/s	$3,500	$95	$1.90	Yes	No
AIT-3 (8mm)	100GB	12 MB/s	$5,000	$170	$1.70	Yes	No
Mammoth-2	60GB	12 MB/s	$3,500	$80	$1.33	Yes	No

a. Uncompressed capacity and speed
b. Maximum burst transfer rate; the manufacturer does not disclose the true average throughput.

W. Curtis Preston has compiled an excellent reference list of backup devices by manufacturer. It's available from www.backupcentral.com/hardware-drives.html.

Backups

What to buy

When you buy a backup system, you pretty much get exactly what you see in Table 10.1. All of the media work reasonably well, and among the technologies that are close in price, there generally isn't a compelling reason to prefer one over another. Buy a system that meets your specifications and your budget.

DAT and Exabyte drives are excellent solutions for small workgroups and for individual machines with a lot of storage. The startup costs are relatively modest, the media are widely available, and several manufacturers are using each standard. Both systems are fast enough to back up a buttload of data in a finite amount of time.

DLT, AIT, and Mammoth-2 are all roughly comparable. There isn't a clear winner among the three, and even if there were, the situation would no doubt change within a few months as new versions of the formats were deployed. All of these formats work well, and they all address the same market: university and corporate environments that need serious backup hardware (which is to say, pretty much all university and corporate environments).

In the following sections, we use the generic term "tape" to refer to the media chosen for backups. Examples of backup commands are phrased in terms of tape devices.

10.3 Setting up an incremental backup regime with dump

The **dump** and **restore** commands are the most common way to create and restore from backups. These programs have been around for a very long time, and their behavior is well known. At most sites, **dump** and **restore** are the underlying commands used by automated backup software.

You may have to explicitly install **dump** and **restore** on your Linux systems, depending on the options you selected during the original install. An **rpm** (Red Hat Package Manager) file is available for easy installation for both Red Hat and SuSE. Under Linux, nothing is statically linked, so you need the shared libraries in **/lib** to do anything useful (yuck). Static linking makes it easier to recover from a disaster because **restore** is then completely self-contained.

Dumping filesystems

dump builds a list of files that have been modified since a previous dump, then packs those files into a single large file to archive to an external device. **dump** has several advantages over most of the other utilities described in this chapter:

- Backups can span multiple tapes.
- Files of any type (even devices) can be backed up and restored.
- Permissions, ownerships, and modification times are preserved.
- Files with holes are handled correctly.[4]

---

4. Holes are blocks that have never contained data. If you open a file, write one byte, seek 1MB into the file, then write another byte, the resulting "sparse" file will take up only two disk blocks even though its logical size is much bigger. Files created by Berkeley **db** or **ndbm** contain many holes.

- Backups can be performed incrementally (with only recently modified files being written out to tape).

The GNU version of **tar** used in Linux provides all of these features as well. However, **dump**'s handling of incremental backups (discussed later) is a bit more sophisticated than **tar**'s. You may find the extra horsepower useful if your needs are complex.

Actually, the most compelling reason to choose **dump** over **tar** in a Linux environment has nothing to do with Linux at all. Unfortunately, the version of **tar** shipped with most major UNIX distributions can't perform the wondrous feats listed above. If you must support backups for both Linux and UNIX variants, **dump** is your best choice. It is the only command that handles these issues (fairly) consistently across platforms, allowing you to be an expert in one command rather than being familiar with two. If you are lucky enough to be in a completely homogeneous Linux environment, pick your favorite. **dump** is less filling, but **tar** tastes great!

The **dump** command understands the layout of raw filesystems, and it reads a filesystem's inode tables directly to decide which files must be backed up. This knowledge of the filesystem allows **dump** to be very efficient, but it also imposes a few limitations.[5]

See Chapter 17 for more information about NFS.

The first limitation is that every filesystem must be dumped individually. If you have a disk that is partitioned, you must dump each partition separately. The other limitation is that only filesystems on the local machine can be dumped; you cannot dump an NFS filesystem mounted from a remote machine. However, you can dump a local filesystem to a remote tape drive with **dump**'s evil twin, **rdump**.

The most important feature of **dump** is its support for the concept of an "incremental" backup. Although it is possible to back up the entire system each day, it is usually not practical. Incremental dumps make it possible to back up only files that have changed since the last backup.

When you do a dump, you assign it a backup level, which is an integer from 0 to 9. A level N dump backs up all files that have changed since the last dump of level less than N. A level 0 backup places the entire filesystem on the tape. With an incremental backup system, you may have to restore files from several sets of backup tapes to reset a filesystem to the state it was in during the last backup.[6]

Another nice feature of **dump** is that it does not care about the length of filenames. Hierarchies can be arbitrarily deep, and long names are handled correctly.

The first argument to **dump** must be the incremental dump level. **dump** uses the **/etc/dumpdates** file to determine how far back an incremental dump must go. The **-u** flag causes **dump** to automatically update **/etc/dumpdates** when the dump completes. The date, dump level, and filesystem name are recorded. If you never use the

---

5. **dump** requires access to raw disk partitions. Anyone allowed to do dumps can read all the files on the system with a little work.

6. Actually, **dump** does not keep track of files that have been deleted. If you restore from incremental backups, deleted files will be recreated.

Backups

-u flag, all dumps become level 0s because no record of having previously dumped the filesystem will ever be created. If you change a filesystem's name, you can edit the **/etc/dumpdates** file by hand.

See page 223 for information about device numbers.

dump sends its output to some default device, usually the primary tape drive. If you want to use a different device, use the **-f** flag to tell **dump** to send its output elsewhere. If you are placing multiple dumps on a single tape, make sure you specify a nonrewinding tape device (a device file that does not cause the tape to be rewound when it is closed—most tape drives have both a standard and a nonrewinding device entry). Read the man page for the tape device to determine the exact name of the appropriate device file.[7] Linux usually uses **/dev/st0** for the rewinding device and **/dev/nst0** for the nonrewinding device.

If you choose the rewinding device by accident, you will end up saving only the last filesystem dumped. Since **dump** does not have any idea where the tape is positioned, this mistake does not cause errors. The situation only becomes apparent when you try to restore files.

When you use **rdump** to dump to a remote system, you specify the identity of the remote tape drive as *hostname:device*; for example,

```
# rdump -0u -f anchor:/dev/nst0 /spare
```

Permission to access remote tape drives is controlled by the **.rhosts** mechanism. We recommend that you use an SSH tunnel instead. See page 673 for more information.

In the past, you had to tell **dump** exactly how long your tapes were so that it could stop writing before it ran off the end of a tape. Most modern tape drives can tell when they have reached the end of a tape and can report that fact back to **dump**, which then rewinds and ejects the current tape and requests a new one. Since the variability of hardware compression makes the "virtual length" of each tape somewhat indeterminate, it's always best to rely on the end-of-tape indication if your hardware supports it. If not, you can specify the tape length in kilobytes with the **-B** option.

The **-B** flag can also be useful in dire situations when you're forced to use a cartridge that suffers from a media defect late in the tape. For example, suppose you want to do a level 5 dump of **/work** to a DDS-1 (DAT) drive whose native capacity is 1GB. It's Sunday morning at 3:00 a.m. and your supply cabinet contains nothing but a pile of defective DAT tapes and half a baggie of stale Cheetos.[8] The first tape you choose is labeled as having a fault at about the 850MB mark. In this situation, you could use the **-B** option to tell **dump** that the tape length was slightly shorter than it actually is.

---

7. All the entries for a tape unit use the same major device number. The minor device number tells the driver about special behaviors (rewinding, byte swapping, etc.).

8. One symptom of System Administration Personality Syndrome is the habitual stockpiling of partially operational computers and accessories. It's best to label what's wrong with the stuff you throw in the pile so that you can easily ascertain its usefulness in an emergency. Note: if you find yourself unsoldering chips from circuit boards in this "boneyard" pile and transplanting them into machines to keep them running "just another day," it's time to seek psychiatric help. Trust us, we've all been there.

```
# dump -5u -B 800000 -f /dev/st0 /work
DUMP: Date of this level 5 dump: Wed May  8 16:59:45 2002
DUMP: Date of last level 0 dump: the epoch
DUMP: Dumping /dev/hda2 (/work) to /dev/st0
DUMP: mapping (Pass I) [regular files]
DUMP: mapping (Pass II) [directories]
DUMP: estimated 18750003 tape blocks on 1.51 tape(s).
...
```

The flags **-5u** are followed by the flags **-B** (length of the tape in KB: 800MB) and **-f** (tape device: **/dev/st0**). The last argument, which is mandatory, is the name of the filesystem to be dumped (**/work**). The last line of output above verifies that **dump** will switch tapes on its own initiative about two-thirds of the way through the backup process, avoiding the defect in the media.

Dump sequences

Because dump levels are arbitrary (they have meaning only in relation to other levels), dumps can be performed on various schedules. The schedule that is right for you depends on:

- The activity of your filesystems
- The capacity of your dump device
- The amount of redundancy you want
- The number of tapes you want to buy

In the days when it took many tapes to back up a filesystem, complicated dump sequences were useful for minimizing the number of tapes consumed by each day's backups. As tape capacities have grown, it has become less useful to make fine distinctions among dump levels.

Because most files never change, even the simplest incremental schedule eliminates many files from the daily dumps. As you add additional levels to your dump schedule, you divide the relatively few active files into smaller and smaller segments.

A complex dump schedule provides the following three benefits:

- You can back up data more often, limiting your potential losses.
- You can use fewer daily tapes (or fit everything on one tape).
- You can keep multiple copies of each file, to protect against tape errors.

In general, the way to select a sequence is to determine your needs in each of these areas. Given these constraints, you can design a schedule at the appropriate level of sophistication. We describe a couple of possible sequences and the motivation behind them. One of them might be right for your site—or, your needs might dictate a completely different schedule.

A simple schedule

If your total amount of disk space is smaller than the capacity of your tape device, you can use a completely trivial dump schedule. Do level 0 dumps of every filesystem each day. Reuse a group of tapes, but every N days (where N is determined by your site's needs), keep the tape forever. This scheme will cost you

(365/N) * (price of tape)

per year. Don't reuse the exact same tape for every night's dump. It's better to rotate among a set of tapes so that even if one night's dump is blown, you can still fall back to the previous night.

This schedule provides massive redundancy and makes data recovery very easy. It's a good solution for a site with lots of money but limited operator time (or skill). From a safety and convenience perspective, this schedule is the ideal. Don't stray from it without a specific reason (e.g., to conserve tapes or labor).

A moderate schedule

A more reasonable schedule for most sites is to assign a tape to each day of the week, each week of the month (you'll need 5), and each month of the year. Every day, do a level 9 dump to the daily tape. Every week, do a level 5 dump to the weekly tape. And every month, do a level 3 dump to the monthly tape. Do a level 0 dump whenever the incrementals get too big to fit on one tape, which is most likely to happen on a monthly tape. Do a level 0 dump at least once a year.

The choice of levels 3, 5, and 9 is arbitrary. You could use levels 1, 2, and 3 with the same effect. However, the gaps between dump levels give you some breathing room if you later decide you want to add another level of dumps.

This schedule requires 24 tapes plus however many tapes are needed to perform the level 0 dumps. Although it does not require too many tapes, it also does not provide much redundancy.

10.4 RESTORING FROM DUMPS WITH RESTORE

The program that extracts data from tapes written with **dump** is called **restore**. We first discuss restoring individual files (or a small set of files), then explain how to restore entire filesystems.

Restoring individual files

The first step to take when you are notified of a lost file is to determine which tapes contain versions of the file. Users often want the most recent version of a file, but that is not always the case. For example, a user who loses a file by inadvertently copying another file on top of it would want the version that existed before the incident occurred. It's helpful if you can browbeat users into telling you not only what files are missing, but also when they were lost and when they were last modified.

If you do not keep on-line catalogs, you must mount tapes and repeatedly attempt to restore the missing files until you find the correct tape. If the user remembers when the files were last changed, you may be able to make an educated guess about which tapes the files might be on.

After determining which tapes you want to extract from, create and **cd** to a temporary directory such as **/var/restore** where a large directory hierarchy can be created; most versions of **restore** must create all of the directories leading to a particular file before that file can be restored. Do not use **/tmp**—your work could be wiped out if the machine crashes and reboots before the restored data has been moved to its original location.

The **restore** command has many options. Most useful are -**i** for interactive restores of individual files and directories and -**r** for a complete restore of an entire filesystem. You might also need -**x**, which requests a noninteractive restore of specified files— be careful not to overwrite existing files.

restore -**i** reads the table of contents from the tape and then lets you navigate through it as you would a normal directory tree, using commands called **ls**, **cd**, and **pwd**. You mark the files that you want to restore with the **add** command. When you are done selecting, type **extract** to pull the files off the tape.

*See page 180 for a description of **mt**.* If you placed multiple files on a single tape, you must use the **mt** command to position the tape at the correct dump file before running **restore**. Remember to use the nonrewinding device!

For example, to restore the file **/users/janet/iamlost** from a remote tape drive, you might issue the following commands. Let's assume that you have found the right tape, mounted it on **tapehost:/dev/nst0**, and determined that the filesystem containing janet's home directory is the fourth one on the tape.

```
# mkdir /var/restore
# cd /var/restore
# rsh⁹ tapehost mt -f /dev/nst0 fsf 3
# rrestore -i -f tapehost:/dev/nst0
restore> ls
.:
janet/  garth/  lost+found/ lynda/
restore> cd janet
restore> ls
afile bfile cfile iamlost
restore> add iamlost
restore> ls¹⁰
afile bfile cfile iamlost*
restore> extract
You have not read any volumes yet.
Unless you know which volume your files are on you should
start with the last volume and work towards the first.
Specify next volume #: 1
set owner/mode for '.'? [yn] n
```

---

9. You could instead use the **ssh** command here for added security.

10. The star next to **iamlost** indicates that it has been marked for extraction.

Volumes (tapes) are enumerated starting at 1, not 0, so for a dump that fits on a single tape, you specify 1. When **restore** asks if you want to set the owner and mode for ".", it's asking whether it should set the current directory to match the root of the tape. Unless you are restoring an entire filesystem, you probably do not want to do this.

Once the **restore** has completed, you need to give the file to janet:

```
# cd /var/restore
# ls janet
iamlost
# ls ~janet
afile bfile cfile
# cp -p janet/iamlost ~janet/iamlost.restored
# chown janet ~janet/iamlost.restored
# rm -rf /var/restore
# mail janet
Your file iamlost has been restored as requested and has
been placed in /users/janet/iamlost.restored.

Your name, Humble System Administrator
```

Some administrators prefer to restore files into a special directory, allowing users to copy their files out by hand. In that scheme, the administrator must protect the privacy of the restored files by verifying their ownership and permissions. If you choose to use such a system, remember to clean out the directory every so often.

If you created a backup with **rdump** and are unable to restore files from it with **restore**, try running **rrestore** instead. To minimize the chance of problems, use the same host to read the tape as was used to write it.

restore -i is usually the easiest way to restore a few files or directories from a dump. However, it will not work if the tape device cannot be moved backward a record at a time (a problem with some 8mm drives). If **restore -i** fails, try **restore -x** before jumping out the window. **restore -x** requires you to specify the complete path of the file you want to restore (relative to the root of the dump) on the command line. The following sequence of commands repeats the previous example, but with **restore -x**:

```
# mkdir /var/restore
# cd /var/restore
# rsh tapehost mt -f /dev/nst0 fsf 3
# rrestore -x -f tapehost:/dev/nst0 ./janet/iamlost
```

Restoring entire filesystems

With luck, you will never have to restore an entire filesystem after a system failure. However, the situation does occasionally arise. Before attempting to restore the filesystem, you must make sure that whatever problem caused the filesystem to be destroyed in the first place has been taken care of. It's pointless to spend numerous hours spinning tapes only to lose the filesystem once again.

Before you begin a full restore, you must create and mount the target filesystem. See Chapter 8, *Adding a Disk*, for more information about how to prepare the filesystem.

To start the restore, **cd** to the mount point of the new filesystem, put the first tape of the most recent level 0 dump in the tape drive, and type **restore -r**.

restore will prompt for each tape in the dump. After the level 0 dump has been restored, mount and restore the incremental dumps. Restore incremental dumps in the order in which they were created. Because of redundancy among dumps, it may not be necessary to restore every incremental. Here's the algorithm for determining which dumps to restore:

Step 1: Restore the most recent level 0 dump.

Step 2: Restore the lowest-level dump made after the dump you just restored. If multiple dumps were made at that level, restore the most recent one.

Step 3: If that was the last dump that was ever made, you are done.

Step 4: Otherwise, go back to step 2.

Here are some examples of dump sequences. You would need to restore only the levels shown in boldface.

```
0 0 0 0 0 0
0 5 5 5 5
0 3 2 5 4 5
0 9 9 5 9 9 3 9 9 5 9 9
0 3 5 9 3 5 9
```

*See Chapter 8 for more information about **mke2fs** and **mount**.*

Let's take a look at a complete command sequence. If the most recent dump was the first monthly after the annual level 0 in the "moderate" schedule on page 174, the commands to restore **/home**, residing on the physical device **/dev/sda1**, would look like this (the device names are hardware dependent):

```
# /etc/mke2fs /dev/sda1 QUANTUM_PD1050S
# /etc/mount /dev/sda1 /home
# cd /home
/* Mount first tape of level 0 dump of /home. */
# restore -r
/* Mount the tapes requested by restore. */
/* Mount first tape of level 3 monthly dump. */
# restore -r
```

If you had multiple filesystems on one dump tape, you would have to use the **mt** command to skip forward to the correct filesystem before running each **restore**. See page 180 for a description of **mt**.

This sequence would restore the filesystem to the state it was in when the level 5 dump was done, except that all deleted files would be ghoulishly resurrected. This problem can be especially nasty when you are restoring an active filesystem or are restoring to a disk that is nearly full. It is quite possible for a **restore** to fail because the filesystem has been filled up with ghost files.

Backups

10.5   DUMPING AND RESTORING FOR UPGRADES

When you perform an OS upgrade, you must back up all filesystems with a level 0 dump and, possibly, restore them. The restore is needed only if the new OS uses a different filesystem format or if you change the partitioning of your disks. However, you *must* do backups as insurance against any problems that might occur during the upgrade. A complete set of backups also gives you the option of reinstalling the old OS if the new version does not prove satisfactory.

Be sure to back up and restore any system-specific files that are in **/** or **/usr**, such as **/etc/passwd**, **/etc/shadow**, or **/usr/local**. Linux's brain-dead directory organization mixes local files with vendor-distributed files, making it quite difficult to pick out your local customizations.

You should do a complete set of level 0 dumps immediately after an upgrade, too. Most vendors' upgrade procedures set the modification dates of system files to the time when they were mastered rather than to the current time. Ergo, incremental dumps made relative to the pre-upgrade level 0 will not be sufficient to restore your system to its post-upgrade state in the event of a crash.

10.6   USING OTHER ARCHIVING PROGRAMS

dump is not the only program you can use to archive files to tapes; however, it is usually the most efficient way to back up an entire system. **tar**, **cpio**, and **dd** can also move files from one medium to another.

tar: package files

tar reads multiple files or directories and packages them into one file, often a tape file. **tar** is a useful way to back up any files whose near-term recovery you anticipate. For instance, if a user is leaving for six months and the system is short of disk space, you can use **tar** to put the user's files on a tape and then remove them from the disk.

tar is also useful for moving directory trees from place to place, especially if you are copying files as root (**tar** preserves ownership information). For example,

```
tar -cf - fromdir | ( cd todir ; tar -xfp - )
```

creates a copy of the directory tree *fromdir* in *todir*. Avoid using ".." in the *todir* argument, since symbolic links and automounters can make it mean something different from what you expect. We've been bitten several times.

tar does not follow symbolic links by default, but it can be told to do so. **tar** can also be told to include only files that were modified since a given date, which is useful for creating your own incremental backup scheme. Consult the **tar** man page for this and other nifty features.

One problem with some non-Linux versions of **tar** is that pathnames are limited by default to 100 characters. This restriction prevents **tar** from archiving deep hierarchies. If you're creating **tar** archives on your Linux systems and exchanging them with others, remember that people with the standard **tar** may not be able to read the tapes or files you create.

tar's -**b** option lets you specify a "blocking factor" to use when writing a tape. The blocking factor is specified in 512-byte blocks; it determines how much data **tar** buffers internally before performing a write operation. Some DAT devices do not work correctly unless the blocking factor is set to a special value, but other drives do not require this setting.

On some systems, certain blocking factors may yield better performance than others. The optimal blocking factor varies widely, depending on the computer and tape drive hardware. In many cases, you will not notice any difference in speed. When in doubt, try a blocking factor of 20.

Linux **tar** expands holes in files unless you use the -**S** option when creating the original archive. Linux **tar** is relatively intolerant of tape errors.

cpio: archiving utility from ancient times

cpio is similar to **tar** in functionality. It dates from the beginning of time and is rarely used today. Like **tar**, **cpio** can be used to move directory trees. The command

    find *fromdir* -**depth** -**print** | **cpio** -**pdm** *todir*

would make a copy of the directory tree *fromdir* in *todir*. The GNU version of **cpio** used in Linux allows multiple tape volumes, but most versions do not. Only the superuser can copy special files. Even if you are familiar with **cpio** from another system, we recommend that you review the man page carefully, as the options vary greatly among systems.

dd: twiddle bits

dd is a file copying and conversion program. Unless it is told to do some sort of conversion, **dd** just copies from its input file to its output file. If a user brings you a tape that was written on some non-Linux system, **dd** may be the only way to read it.

One historical use for **dd** was to create a copy of an entire filesystem. However, a better option these days is to **mke2fs** the destination filesystem and then run **dump** piped to **restore**. **dd** can sometimes clobber partitioning information if used incorrectly. It can only copy filesystems between partitions of exactly the same size.

dd can also be used to make a copy of a magnetic tape. With two tape drives, say, **/dev/st0** and **/dev/st1**, you'd use the command

    % **dd** if=/dev/st0 of=/dev/st1 cbs=16b

With one drive (**/dev/st0**), you'd use the following sequence:

    % **dd** if=/dev/st0 of=tfile cbs=16b
    /* *Change tapes.* */
    % **dd** if=tfile of=/dev/st0 cbs=16b
    % **rm** tfile

Backups

Of course, if you have only one tape drive, you must have enough disk space to store an image of the entire tape.

volcopy: duplicate filesystems

volcopy is a Linux utility that makes an exact copy of a filesystem on another device, changing the block size as appropriate. You can use **volcopy** to back up a filesystem to a removable disk pack or to make a complete copy of a filesystem on tape. Consult the man page on your system for the appropriate options and syntax.

10.7 USING MULTIPLE FILES ON A SINGLE TAPE

In reality, a magnetic tape contains one long string of data. However, it's often useful to store more than one "thing" on a tape, so tape drives and their Linux drivers conspire to provide you with a bit more structure. When **dump** or some other command writes a stream of bytes out to a tape device and then closes the device file, an end-of-file marker is automatically placed on the tape. This marker separates the stream from other streams that are written subsequently. When the stream is read back in, reading stops automatically at the EOF.

You can use the **mt** command to position a tape at a particular stream or "file set," as **mt** calls them. **mt** is especially useful if you put multiple files (for example, multiple dumps) on a single tape. It also has some of the most interesting error messages of any Linux utility. The basic format of the command is

> **mt** [**-f** *tapename*] *command* [*count*]

There are numerous choices for *command*. They vary from platform to platform, so we discuss only the ones that are essential for doing backups and restores:

rew   rewinds the tape to the beginning.

offl   puts the tape off-line. On most tape drives, this command causes the tape to rewind and pop out of the drive. Most scripts use this command to eject the tape when they are done, giving a clear indication that everything finished correctly.

status   prints information about the current state of the tape drive (whether a tape is loaded, etc.).

fsf [*count*]   fast-forwards the tape. If no *count* is given, **fsf** skips forward one file. With a numeric argument, it skips the specified number of files. Use this command to skip forward to the correct filesystem on a tape with multiple dumps.

bsf [*count*]   should backspace *count* files. The exact behavior of this directive depends on the tape drive hardware and its associated driver. In some situations, the current file is counted. In others, it is not. On some equipment, **bsf** does nothing silently. If you go too far forward on a tape, your best bet is to **rew** it and start again from the beginning.

Consult your manuals for an exact list of commands supported by **mt**.

Robot at your service?

If you're fortunate enough to have a robotic tape library, you may be able to control its tape changer by installing the **mtx** package, an enhanced version of the **mt** command. For example, we use it for unattended tape swapping with our super-groovy HP 6x24 DAT tape cartridge system. Look ma, no hands!

10.8 AMANDA

The Advanced Maryland Automatic Network Disk Archiver, Amanda, is a sophisticated network backup system that can replace the home-grown scripts used by many sites. It can back up all the machines on a LAN to a single server's tape drive. Not only is Amanda free, but it also runs on a variety of UNIX and Linux variants. It is therefore a good choice for backing up sites that use a mix of operating systems.

Amanda was originally written by James da Silva of the University of Maryland in 1991. It's now supported by a team of sysadmins from around the world. The latest information and source code are available from www.amanda.org.

Amanda is not itself a backup program, but rather a wrapper that manages other backup software. Most sites will have Amanda use their systems' native **dump** and **restore** commands as the underlying backup software, but Amanda can also drive **tar** and even Samba's **smbtar** for those pesky Windows machines.

Amanda supports a wide variety of tape drives, and it also takes advantage of jukeboxes and stackers. Amanda can use your tape drives' hardware compression facilities, or it can compress backup images with **compress** or **gzip** on client machines before the data goes over the network.

Another great feature of Amanda is tape management. Amanda writes a header on each tape it uses and so will never overwrite the wrong tape. In addition, Amanda manages dump levels based on configuration parameters and the fullness of tapes. Amanda keeps records of which backups are on which tapes, and it can print out sticky labels showing the contents of each tape. (These labels become very useful when the disk that holds Amanda's database crashes.)

Amanda is one of the most popular free backup solutions in common use. It boasts implementation at about 1,500 sites worldwide. It seems to scale well and is constantly being enhanced to support the latest and greatest backup devices.

The architecture of Amanda

In the Amanda model, tape drives and holding disks are attached to a central server. The server also hosts all the Amanda config files, log files, and databases. Amanda can only write one backup image to each tape at a time, but it can spool multiple dumps to its holding disks simultaneously and then stream them out to tape.

Amanda supports multiple "configurations" on the same server machine. For example, one configuration might perform only level 0s of clients, while another does only incrementals. Each configuration generates its own log files and databases.

The Amanda server looks at its configuration files to determine which filesystems need to be backed up, which tape devices are available, and how much of the system's resources (network bandwidth, tapes, CPU load, etc.) it is allowed to use. It then contacts client machines and asks them to estimate the size of their backup files. Using this information, Amanda schedules the backups.

The Amanda server is actually a collection of programs that implement the various parts of the system. It is best to run the server programs on a fast machine that is not generally busy. If you are backing up large amounts of data, the server should have the best connectivity your network architecture permits. Since the holding disk is used to spool dump images from the network to the tape drive, it should be at least as large as the largest partition you want to back up. Amanda also needs some disk space (< 75MB) for its own logs and databases.

As of this writing, the latest stable release of Amanda is 2.4.2p2; the examples, configuration files, and commands shown in this chapter are taken from that version.

Amanda setup

When you download Amanda, take the latest stable version, not the current development snapshot. We are talking about backups, so you want something stable!

After unpacking the source code, read the **README**, **docs/SYSTEM.NOTES**, and **docs/INSTALL** files. Any architecture-specific gotchas are documented in the file **SYSTEM.NOTES**. The **INSTALL** file gives step-by-step instructions for installation.

Before running **configure**, run **configure --help** to see the complete list of options. In addition to deciding where the software should be installed, you must decide what user and group Amanda should run as. For each partition you intend to back up with **dump**, the corresponding raw device needs to be readable by this user. The device files will already be in the **disk** group, and so adding the Amanda user to that group will provide the necessary access.

After running **configure**, run **make** and **make install** to complete the installation.

Every Amanda client needs to have access to the Amanda binaries. However, it's not a good idea to have every client access the binaries through a network-based filesystem, since there are times when all the clients will need to run simultaneously (in particular, at the beginning of the backup procedure, when Amanda asks the clients to estimate their dump sizes). It's best to install the binaries on each client's local disks, usually somewhere under **/usr/local**.

The following programs should be installed on every client. They should never be run by hand.

amandad   handles all communication between the client and the central server; runs all the other client programs.

selfcheck   checks that the client is set up for Amanda: has correct device permissions, can find **gzip**, can write to **/etc/dumpdates**, etc.

sendbackup   performs the backups.

sendsize   estimates backup sizes at different dump levels.

Client machines need some other configuration as well. Each device that you want to back up must be readable by Amanda's group, and the **/etc/dumpdates** file must be writable by this group as well. Once you think everything has been set up correctly, use **amcheck** to verify the configuration.

A list of the Amanda server commands follows. Most take a command-line argument that tells them which Amanda configuration to use.

amdump   does the nightly dumps; usually run by **cron**.

amflush   flushes the holding disk to tape if there were problems.

amcleanup   cleans up if the master host crashed during dumps.

amrestore   handles restore operations from Amanda dumps.

amlabel   writes Amanda labels on tape; used to avoid mistakes with overwriting wrong tapes, etc.

amadmin   finds the right tape to restore from and performs various other administrative chores.

amcheck   verifies that you are using the correct (expected) tape, that there is enough free space on the holding disk, and that client hosts are set up properly.

amtape   manages stackers and tape changers.

amplot   draws graphs of Amanda activity (e.g., holding disk and network usage) for each dump run.

Each configuration is kept in a separate directory and needs the files **amanda.conf** and **disklist**. The **amanda.conf** file specifies the server's general configuration, and the **disklist** file specifies which clients and filesystems to back up. These files live only on the server.

The amanda.conf file

amanda.conf is quite a large file, so we discuss it in four logical pieces: local information, dump strategy, resource parameters, and dump type definitions. These pieces are purely our invention; neither Amanda nor the Amanda documentation distinguishes the parts of the **amanda.conf** file in this way.

The file format is fairly self-explanatory, so we present it in the form of a long example with commentary on each section. We begin with the local information section, which identifies your organization and dumpmeister, defines log files and other configuration files, and specifies the format of tape labels (the logical labels recorded on the tapes themselves, not sticky labels).

```
##########################################################
# Local parameters
##########################################################

org "Podunk Univ."      # your organization name for reports
mailto "amanda"         # space-separated list of operators at your site
dumpuser "amanda"       # the user to run dumps as
runtapes 1              # number of tapes to use in a single run of amdump
tpchanger "chg-manual"  # tape changer glue script (provided with Amanda)
tapedev "/dev/nst0"     # the no-rewind tape device to be used

labelstr "^Podunk-[0-9][0-9]*$"  # label constraint regex: all tapes must match

infofile "/usr/adm/amanda/podunk/curinfo"   # database directory
logdir "/usr/adm/amanda/podunk"             # log directory
indexdir "/usr/adm/amanda/podunk/index"     # index directory
```

Amanda reads the label from each piece of media and will not use a tape unless its label matches the regular expression specified in labelstr. Therefore, all tapes must be labeled by **amlabel** before they can be used to store backups. Labels cannot contain whitespace characters.

It is up to the system administrator to define a meaningful naming scheme. For example, you might want to have the * in the regex match as a hint to the compression used or the type of machine backed up. In the example above, tapes would have labels Podunk-01, Podunk-02, and so on.

If you try to reuse a tape before the normal rotation cycle has been completed, the server will reject it. This feature prevents you from accidentally overwriting a tape that is still of historical importance in the backup scheme you have defined.

The parameters of that scheme (how often a particular tape can be used, how often each filesystem should get a level 0 dump, when to increase the dump level, etc.) are defined in the second section of **amanda.conf**.

```
##########################################################
# Strategy parameters
##########################################################

dumpcycle 4 weeks # the number of days in the normal dump cycle
bumpdays 2        # minimum days at each level
bumpsize 20 Mb    # minimum savings (threshold) to bump level 1 -> 2
bumpmult 2        # threshold = bumpsize * bumpmult^(level-1)
runspercycle 20   # the number of amdump runs in dumpcycle days
                  # 4 weeks * 5 amdump runs per week (weekdays)
tapecycle 25 tapes # the number of tapes in rotation
                  # 4 weeks (dumpcycle) * 5 tapes per week (weekdays)
                  # plus a few to handle errors that need amflush and
                  # so we do not overwrite the full backups performed
                  # at the beginning of the previous cycle
```

In the Amanda system, dumps are not rigidly scheduled by calendar date. Instead, you give Amanda general information about how much redundancy you want it to maintain. Amanda then tries to spread the work out across the entire dump cycle so that tapes are used efficiently and protection is maximized. Amanda recalculates its daily schedule each night, using real-time information about each client filesystem. It's really not possible to predict the exact dump agenda in advance.

A "dump cycle" is a period in which level 0 dumps will be done at least once on every filesystem. Long cycles increase Amanda's scheduling flexibility, but may also increase the average number of tapes that must be read to complete a restore. Amanda might perform level 0 dumps more often than strictly necessary if tape is available.

The Amanda model assumes that dumps will be done every day. If this isn't true, you should set the runspercycle parameter to the actual number of dump days in a cycle. This example configuration does dumps only on weekdays, which is reasonable if someone must be physically present to change tapes.

Another assumption that's made by default is that one dump tape will be written per day (or per "run," in Amanda terminology). If you're using a stacker or jukebox, you can write multiple tapes per run. Additional configuration is required.

The tapecycle parameter tells how many tapes you plan to use in regular rotation. A minimal value is the number of runs per dump cycle times the number of tapes per run, plus a few extra to handle edge conditions and tape problems. If you allocate at least twice the minimal number of tapes, you are always guaranteed to have on hand at least two level 0 dumps of each filesystem.

The "bump" parameters let you exercise some control over how large an incremental dump must become before Amanda shifts up to the next level of dump. The parameters are specified in a rather mathematical and nonintuitive way. Fortunately, you can use the **bumpsize** option of **amadmin** to make sure that you've really implemented the strategy you intended.

For example, with the parameters shown above and assuming the configuration files are stored in a directory called **podunk**, **amadmin** would report:

```
# amadmin podunk bumpsize
Current bump parameters:
bumpsize 20480 KB    - minimum savings (threshold) to bump level 1 -> 2
bumpdays 2           - minimum days at each level
bumpmult 2           - threshold = bumpsize * (level-1)**bumpmult

Bump ->  To    Threshold
   1  ->  2      20480 KB
   2  ->  3      40960 KB
   3  ->  4      81920 KB
   4  ->  5     163840 KB
   5  ->  6     327680 KB
   6  ->  7     655360 KB
   7  ->  8    1310720 KB
   8  ->  9    2621440 KB
```

Backups

After an initial level 0, Amanda will start by doing level 1 dumps. Once the level 1 dumps become larger than 20MB, Amanda will shift to level 2 dumps. Once the level 2 dumps get larger than 40MB, Amanda will move up to level 3, and so on.

You should carefully tune these parameters to balance your desire for redundancy against the cost of tapes. Too much redundancy will result in high operating costs, and too little redundancy may result in lost data.

The rest of **amanda.conf** is devoted to parameters that specify how much network bandwidth, CPU, and disk space (on the server) to use; the type of tape drive to back up to; and the types of client partitions to be backed up.

```
############################################################
# Resource parameters
############################################################

tapetype EXB-8500      # what kind of tape it is (see tapetypes below)
inparallel 4           # maximum client dumpers that will run in parallel
netusage 600 Kbps      # maximum net bandwidth for Amanda, in KB per sec
etimeout 300           # number of seconds to wait for estimate per filesystem

holdingdisk hd1 {
    comment "main holding disk"
    directory "/dumps/amanda"    # mount point of holding disk
    use 8196 Mb                  # how much space we can use on it
}

define tapetype EXB-8500 {
    comment "Exabyte EXB-8500 drive on decent machine"
    length 4200 mbytes
    filemark 48 kbytes
    speed 474 kbytes
}
```

This example shows the configuration for an Exabyte 8500 tape drive. The tape type parameters are extremely important and should never be guessed. If your tape drive isn't listed in the sample **amanda.conf** file that comes with the distribution, you can probably find it in the **docs/TAPETYPES** file or at

> http://www.cs.columbia.edu/~sdossick/amanda

You might also try asking for an appropriate configuration on one of the Amanda mailing lists. If all else fails, you can use the **tapetype** program that comes with Amanda. It determines the correct parameters for your tape drive by filling a tape with 32KB blocks. However, regard this procedure as a last resort—it can take a very long time (1 or 2 days!) on some tape drives.

The final resource parameters are the dump types, which represent the different types of data (e.g., volatile, important, static, etc.) that filesystems might contain. Each filesystem on a client must be assigned a particular dump type. The dump type also specifies what kind of compression (if any) should be applied when the data is archived. Here are some examples:

```
############################################################
# Dump type definitions
############################################################

define dumptype comp-user {
      comment "partitions on reasonably fast machines"
      compress client fast
      priority medium
}

define dumptype comp-root {
      comment "root partitions on reasonably fast machines"
      compress client fast
      priority low
}

define dumptype nocomp-user {
      comment "partitions on slow machines"
      compress none
      priority medium
}
define dumptype clone-user {
      comment "partitions which should not get incrementals"
      compress client fast
      skip-incr
      priority medium
}

define dumptype comp-high-samba {
      comment "used for Windows filesystems"
      program "GNUTAR"
      compress server fast
}

define dumptype dos-user {
      comment "used for dos partitions that are always mounted"
      program "GNUTAR"
      compress client fast
}
```

These particular dump types are all predefined by Amanda. You can use them directly, customize them for your own purposes, or write your own specifications from scratch. The comment field hints at what each dump type does.

The compress parameter specifies where dump data is to be compressed: on the client, on the server, or nowhere. You specify the compression program (e.g., **compress** or **gzip**) when you initially install Amanda. The possible values for the compress option are none, client best, client fast, server best, and server fast. The default is client fast.

compress none turns compression off. You might want to choose this option if the server's tape drive implements compression in hardware. The client options compress the dumps before they are sent over the network to the server, and the server options compress the dumps once they have reached the server's holding disk. If you want to use software compression, it generally makes more sense to perform the compression on the clients.

The best and fast modifiers tell the compressor how hard to work at squeezing the data; compare with **gzip --best** and **gzip --fast**. We only use fast; best can take much longer, and the compression is not significantly better.

The holdingdisk parameter has two possible values: yes and no. It specifies whether the holding disk should be used to spool this backup. You would want to turn this option off when archiving the holding disk itself. The default value is yes.

The maxdumps parameter specifies the maximum number of concurrent dumps that can be run on a client. The default value is 1, but you could increase it for better performance on beefy file servers that have lots of CPU and network bandwidth.

The priority parameter tells how important the backup is. The possible values are low, medium, and high. The default is medium. If there is not enough tape to store all the dumps that have been scheduled, the lower-priority dumps are skipped. In the event of a tape error, Amanda tries to marshall the higher-priority backups onto the holding disk; if there is room, the lower-priority dumps are put there as well.

We recommend defining a different dump type for each priority. Home directories should be dumped at high priority. Medium priority is good for local software packages (e.g., **/usr/local**), and low priority is appropriate for system files that do not change very often.

The program parameter specifies whether to use **dump** or **tar**. The default is **dump** and is usually a better choice.

The skip-full option instructs Amanda to skip the filesystem when a level 0 dump is due. You would generally select this option when level 0 dumps are performed outside Amanda. For example, you might choose to do level 0s only when the machine is in single-user mode.

The skip-incr option makes Amanda skip all dumps except level 0s. You'd choose this option for archive configurations in which only full dumps are done and the tapes are saved indefinitely.

The disklist file

The **amanda.conf** file tells how to do dumps without actually specifying any clients or filesystems to dump. That information is recorded in the **disklist** file. Each client filesystem is assigned one of the dump types defined in **amanda.conf**.

```
########################################################################
# client    partition      dumptype       # mountpoint
########################################################################

# the dump server
ocean       sd0a           comp-root       # /
ocean       sd0g           comp-user       # /usr
ocean       sd0d           comp-user       # /var
ocean       sd0h           comp-high       # /amanda

# lorien's Windows partition mounted via Samba on ocean
ocean       //lorien/c$    comp-high-samba # c:\

# prototype
squish      yc0t0d0s0      comp-high       # /
squish      yc0t0d0s6      comp-high       # /usr
squish      yc0t0d0s3      comp-high       # /var
squish      yc0t0d0s7      comp-high       # /local

# clone
zamboni     hda1           clone-user      # /
zamboni     hda6           clone-user      # /usr
zamboni     hda5           comp-root       # /var
zamboni     hda3           comp-user       # /local

# slow PC
fuzz        sd1a           nocomp-high     # /
fuzz        sd1f           nocomp-high     # /local
fuzz        sd1e           nocomp-high     # /usr
fuzz        sd1d           nocomp-high     # /var
fuzz        /dos           dos-user        # /dos
```

The first column is the hostname of the client machine to back up. The second column lists the target disk partition. You can use either the device name (as above) or the mount point.

Note that the dump server's (ocean's) holding disk, **/dumps/amanda**, is not mentioned in the **disklist** file. In our case it is not necessary to back up this partition because its contents are limited to dump images stored during Amanda runs. If you keep Amanda logs or other important information on the holding disk, you should back it up by using the holdingdisk dump type parameter.

The skip-incr option (included in the clone-user type defined above) is handy for backing up clones of a prototype machine. At our site, we have one prototype machine for each architecture that's cloned onto other machines of the same architecture. Since the root partitions of the clones are the same as that of their prototype, we don't need to waste tape space backing them up every night.

However, every clone has a few unique files (e.g., config files in **/etc**), so we still do a level 0 once during the dump cycle. If you have a similar setup and choose not to perform nightly backups of certain filesystems, make sure that they are indeed

Backups

identical to something that does get archived every night. In our example, zamboni's **/var** partition holds users' email, so it has to be backed up every night.

See Chapter 27 for more information about Samba.

We've installed the Samba program **smbtar** on our dump server so that we can back up Windows filesystems. In this example configuration, we back up lorien's C: drive. Notice that the client host listed in the **disklist** file is ocean, not lorien. If you're using Samba to access a filesystem, the Amanda client must be the Linux host on which **smbtar** is located rather than the Windows machine. (We don't specify fuzz's **/dos** partition this way because it is always mounted and is not accessed through Samba.) Amanda distinguishes between Samba partitions and regular mount points (e.g., **/usr** or **/dos**) by the number of slashes at the beginning: two for Samba and one for regular mounts.

Amanda log files

Amanda creates two log files on the server for each run. The first is **amdump.***n*, where *n* is the number of additional Amanda runs that have occurred since the log file was created. This file contains a verbose description of the scheduling decisions that Amanda has made. The other log file is **log.***date.n*, where *date* is the date of the run and *n* is the number of runs already made on that day.

Amanda debugging

After every run, Amanda generates a summary report of the run's activities and emails it to the dumpmeister. This report includes information about the amount of tape used, the filesystems that were successfully backed up, and any errors that were encountered. Here is an example from a configuration using a slightly different version of the **disklist** than that shown above:

```
To: amanda@ocean
Subject: Podunk Univ. AMANDA MAIL REPORT FOR September 5, 2001

These dumps were to tape Podunk-481.
Tonight's dumps should go onto 1 tape: Podunk-482.

FAILURE AND STRANGE DUMP SUMMARY:
  fuzz   sd1a   lev 0    FAILED   [no estimate or historical data]
...
  taper: FATAL syncpipe_get: w: unexpected EOF
```

STATISTICS:	Total	Full	Daily	
	--------	--------	--------	
Dump Time (hrs:min)	3:02	0:36	0:04	(0:34 start, 1:49 idle)
Output Size (meg)	2954.6	2666.8	287.8	
Original Size (meg)	7428.1	6292.5	1135.5	
Avg Compressed Size (%)	39.8	42.4	25.3	
Tape Used (%)	70.5	63.5	7.0	(level:#disks ...)
Filesystems Dumped	18	8	10	(1:8 2:2)
Avg Dump Rate (k/s)	105.3	124.5	43.4	
Avg Tp Write Rate (k/s)	1254.2	1251.8	1276.9	

```
NOTES:
   planner: Adding new disk zamboni:hda3.
   driver: WARNING: /dumps/amanda: 8550400 KB requested, but only 1035113
      KB available.
   planner: Forcing full dump of squishy:c0t0d0s0 as directed.
   planner: Request to fuzz timed out.
   planner: Incremental of ocean:sd0h bumped to level 2.
...
   driver: going into degraded mode because of tape error.
...
```

One common problem is that Amanda might be unable to write backups onto a tape. This problem can occur when there isn't a valid tape in the drive or when some kind of tape error occurs during writing (as in the example with host fuzz above). In either case, Amanda still spools the backups to the holding disk. To write these buffered dumps to tape, insert the proper tape in the drive and run **amflush**.

To diagnose other problems, you can investigate either the log files on the server or the debug files on the client. The location of log files on the server is specified in the **amanda.conf** file. The debug files are located in each client's **/tmp/amanda** directory, that is, if you compiled Amanda with **--with-debugging** (the default).

Amanda generates the email report from the log file. For example, here's the log file (**amdump.***n*) from which the email above was derived.

```
SETTING UP FOR ESTIMATES...
dumper: pid 18199 executable dumper version 2.4.1p1, using port 791
...
driver: started dumpersetup_estimates: ocean:sd0d: command 0, options:
   last_level 1 next_level0 6 level_days 16
   getting estimates 0 (20023) 1 (2735) -1 (-1)
...
zamboni:hda1 lev 1 skipped due to skip-incr flag
planner: SKIPPED zamboni hda1 [skip-incr]
...
GETTING ESTIMATES...
got result for host ocean disk sd0a: 0 -> 53797K, 1 -> 1797K, -1 -> -1K
got result for host ocean disk sd0d: 0 -> 19695K, 1 -> 2696K, -1 -> -1K
...
ANALYZING ESTIMATES...
...
pondering ocean:sd0d... next_level0 6 last_level 1 (not due for a full dump,
   picking an incr level)
...
```

Here is the other log file, **log.20010905.0,** that corresponds to the original email:

```
START planner date 20010905
START driver date 20010905
INFO planner Adding new disk depot:dsk/d1.
SUCCESS planner zamboni hda1 1 [skipped: skip-incr]
```

Backups

```
WARNING driver WARNING: /dumps/amanda: 8550400 KB requested, but only
    1035113 KB available.
...
START taper datestamp 20010905 label Podunk-481 tape 0
FAIL planner fuzz sd1a 0 [no estimate or historical data]
...
STATS driver startup time 2019.456
SUCCESS dumper ocean sd0a 0 [sec 418.311 kb 25088 kps 59.97 orig-kb 58087 ]
SUCCESS dumper ocean sd0d 1 [sec 15.867 kb 800 kps 50.42 orig-kb 2719 ]
...
SUCCESS taper ocean sd0a 0 [sec 53.366 kb 25088 kps 474.612 {wr: writes 2
    rdwait 0.000 wrwait 0.032 filemark 38.332 }]
SUCCESS taper ocean sd0d 1 [sec 6.345 kb 800 kps 133.3 {wr: writes 1 rdwait
    1.470 wrwait 0.356 filemark 2.637 }]
...
STRANGE dumper ocean sd0h 1 [sec 82.435 kb 33.4 kps 0.4 orig-kb 155.0 ]
  sendbackup: start [ocean:sd0h level 1 datestamp 20010905]
  | DUMP: Date of this level 1 dump: Wed Sep 05 23:47:54 2001
  | DUMP: Date of last level 0 dump: Mon Aug 27 23:43:23 2001
  | DUMP: Dumping /dev/rsd0h (/amanda) to standard output
  | DUMP: mapping (Pass I) [regular files]
  | DUMP: mapping (Pass II) [directories]
  ? DUMP: (This should not happen) bread from /dev/rsd0h [block 64]:
    count=8192, got=-1
  | DUMP: estimated 38 blocks (19KB) on 0.00 tape(s).
  | DUMP: dumping (Pass III) [directories]
  | DUMP: dumping (Pass IV) [regular files]
  | DUMP: level 1 dump on Wed Sep 05 23:47:54 2001
  | DUMP: 310 blocks (155KB) on 1 volume
  | DUMP: DUMP IS DONE
  sendbackup: size 158720
  sendbackup: end
  ...
```

Each SUCCESS dumper line means that a dump was written to the holding disk, and each SUCCESS taper line means a dump was written to tape. A STRANGE dumper means that Amanda saw error output while running **dump**. When dump errors occur, Amanda saves the output in this log file (it puts a "?" in front of the offending lines) and also includes it in the email summary.

Another common problem occurs when Amanda cannot get an estimate of the dump sizes for a client's filesystems. The first things to check in this situation are that the client is reachable over the network and that its copy of Amanda is set up properly. You can also check the debug files in the client's **/tmp/amanda** directory. Each of Amanda client programs writes debugging output here every time it runs.

When Amanda can't obtain a size estimate, look at **sendsize**'s debug file. **sendsize** parses the output of **dump** and looks for the estimated size line. If it doesn't see it, Amanda reports [no estimate]. Here's an example of a **sendsize.debug** file.

```
sendsize: getting size via dump for sd5c level 1
sendsize: running "/usr/ccs/bin/dump 1sf 100000 - /dev/sd5c"
   DUMP: Date of this level 1 dump: Wed Sep 05 21:59:36 2001
   DUMP: Date of last level 0 dump: Mon Aug 27 05:08:33 2001
   DUMP: Dumping /dev/sd5c (/var) to standard output
   DUMP: mapping (Pass I) [regular files]
   DUMP: mapping (Pass II) [directories]
   DUMP: mapping (Pass II) [directories]
   DUMP: mapping (Pass II) [directories]
   DUMP: estimated 7150 tape blocks on 0.00 tape(s).
   DUMP: dumping (Pass III) [directories]
....
calculating for amname 'sd3d', dirname '/local'
sendsize: getting size via dump for sd3d level 0
sendsize: running "/usr/ccs/bin/dump 0sf 100000 - /dev/sd3d"
   DUMP: Cannot open/stat /dev/sd3d, Permission denied
....
(no size line match in above dump output)
```

In this case, it's obvious that we need to fix the permissions on **/dev/sd3d**.

If you can't solve your problem by looking in the log files or the Amanda documentation, you may want to look over the archives of the Amanda mailing lists. You can search them at

> http://www.egroups.com/list/amanda-users
> http://www.egroups.com/list/amanda-hackers

File restoration from an Amanda backup

To restore from Amanda backups, use the **amadmin** and **amrestore** programs. Let's walk through a complete example. Suppose we have a user who deleted a whole directory and wants it restored. The first step is to find the tapes on which the directory was backed up. To do this, you need the following information:

- The name of the machine and partition on which the directory resided
- The full path to the directory
- The date the directory was lost or corrupted
- The date the directory was last modified

The dates will determine a range of tapes that contain the directory in a state we might want to restore. Let's suppose the directory we want to restore is in zamboni's **/local** partition, and that it was modified on October 5 and deleted on October 12. **amadmin** will determine which tapes we need:

```
% amadmin podunk find zamboni hda3
date          host       disk     lv  tape         file  status
2002-01-26    zamboni    hda3     1   Podunk-795   33   OK
2002-01-25    zamboni    hda3     1   Podunk-794   41   OK
2002-01-23    zamboni    hda3     0   Podunk-792   9    OK
2002-01-22    zamboni    hda3     1   Podunk-791   32   OK
...
```

Backups

```
2001-10-13    zamboni    hda3    1    Podunk-685    38    OK
2001-10-12    zamboni    hda3    1    Podunk-684    37    OK
2001-10-11    zamboni    hda3    1    Podunk-683    39    OK
2001-10-10    zamboni    hda3    1    Podunk-682    72    OK
2001-10-09    zamboni    hda3    1    Podunk-681    44    OK
2001-10-08    zamboni    hda3    1    Podunk-680    88    OK
2001-10-07    zamboni    hda3    1    Podunk-518    35    OK
2001-10-06    zamboni    hda3    1    Podunk-517    33    OK
2001-10-05    zamboni    hda3    1    Podunk-516    33    OK
2001-10-04    zamboni    hda3    1    Podunk-515    51    OK
2001-10-03    zamboni    hda3    1    Podunk-514    16    OK
2001-10-02    zamboni    hda3    1    Podunk-513    19    OK
2001-10-01    zamboni    hda3    1    Podunk-512    36    OK
2001-09-30    zamboni    hda3    1    Podunk-511    15    OK
2001-09-29    zamboni    hda3    1    Podunk-510    78    OK
2001-09-28    zamboni    hda3    0    Podunk-509    99    OK
...
```

The **find** option causes **amadmin** to go through each log file in the **amanda.conf** configuration, searching for the machine and partition we supplied as arguments. To do our restore, we need the level 0 tape Podunk-509 and the level 1 tape Podunk-683 from the day before the deletion. For the level 1, we could theoretically use any tape written after the 5th, since the user claims the directory wasn't modified between the 5th and the 12th. In the absence of a reason to do otherwise, however, it's best to use the latest available tape. Users don't always have perfect memories.

Next, we use **amrestore** to actually restore the data. We'd start with the tape Podunk-509, since it's the level 0. After inserting the tape into the tape drive, we could run

```
% amrestore -p /dev/st0 zamboni hda3 | restore -i -f -
```

to locate the appropriate record and start an interactive restore. **amrestore** looks at each dump image on the tape until it finds the one we're looking for, then splurts that dump image to its standard output to be read by the **restore** command. The actual restore procedure works just as described starting on page 174. After extracting from the level 0 tape, we'd repeat the process with the level 1 tape.

amrestore can recognize the appropriate dump because Amanda put a 32K header in front of each dump that records where it came from and how it was compressed. If compression was used, **amrestore** automatically pipes the tape image through the appropriate decompressor.

Searching all the headers can take quite a long time, since **amrestore** might have to skip over hundreds of filesystems. The output of **amadmin** shows which file set we're looking for, so it is not really necessary to let **amrestore** do all this work. We can simply run **mt fsf** to fast-forward the tape before running **amrestore**.

You must run the **restore** process on the same operating system and architecture that generated the original dump. Amanda doesn't know anything about the actual contents of the dump, and it can't shield you from cross-platform compatibility issues.

If the Amanda logs are deleted, we can always look at the tape labels to find the tapes we need. But what if **amrestore** itself has been deleted? Fear not: **amrestore** doesn't really do anything more than **dd**. If you look at the 32K header of the backup you want to restore, you'll see instructions for restoring it. For example, here's the header from the level 0 tape:

```
# mt -f /dev/nst0 fsf 99
# dd if=/dev/nst0 bs=32k count=1
AMANDA: FILE 20010928 zamboni hda3 lev 0 comp .gz
To restore, position tape at start of file and run:
dd if=<tape> bs=32k skip=1 | gzcat | restore ...f -

1+0 records in
1+0 records out
```

Alternatives to Amanda: other open source backup packages

Several other free or shareware backup tools are available on the Internet for download. A few worth mentioning are:

- Arkeia – a very nice GUI-based tool with excellent support
- BURT – a backup and recovery utility based on Tcl/TK 8.0
- **cddump** – an automated utility designed specifically for CD-Rs
- **star** – a faster implementation of **tar**. Has some additional features such as automatic byte swapping. Won't clobber existing files on restore.

10.9 COMMERCIAL BACKUP PRODUCTS

We would all like to think that Linux is the only OS in the world, but unfortunately, that is not the case. When looking at commercial backup solutions, you should consider their ability to handle any other operating systems that you are responsible for backing up. Most contemporary products take cross-platform issues into consideration and enable you to include UNIX, Windows, and Macintosh workstations in your Linux backup scheme. You must also consider non-Linux storage arrays and file servers.

Users' laptops and other machines that are not consistently connected to your network should also be protected from failure. When looking at commercial products, you may want to ask if each product is smart enough not to back up identical files from every laptop. How many copies of **command.com** do you really need?

There are several common commercial packages that you may want to investigate when choosing a site-wide backup system. Since we find that Amanda works well for us, we don't have much experience with commercial products. We asked some of our big-bucks buddies at commercial sites for quick impressions of the systems they use. Their comments are reproduced here.

Backups

ADSM/TSM

The ADSM product was developed by IBM and later purchased by Tivoli. It is marketed today as the Tivoli Storage Manager (TSM). TSM is a data management tool that also handles backups. More information can be found at www.tivoli.com.

Pros:

- Backed by IBM; it's here to stay
- Attractive pricing and leasing options
- Very low failure rate
- Uses disk cache; useful for backing up slow clients
- Deals with Windows clients
- Excellent documentation (priced separately)

Cons:

- Poorly designed GUI interface
- Every 2 files =1K in the database.
- The design is incremental forever

Veritas

Veritas sells backup solutions for a variety of systems. When you visit their web site (www.veritas.com), make sure you select the product that's appropriate for you.

Pros:

- Decent GUI interface
- Connects directly to Network Appliance filers
- Push install for Linux
- Can write tapes in GNU **tar** format
- Centralized database, but can support a distributed backup system

Cons:

- Some bugs
- Pricing is confusing and annoying
- Windows support is spotty

Legato

Legato backup software is sold directly from Legato, but it's also bundled by some major computer manufacturers, such as Compaq. More information can be found at www.legato.com.

Pros:

- Nice GUI
- Very reasonably priced
- Automatic mail to users informing them of backup status

Cons:

- We've heard of problems with a corrupted index file
- Not recommended for 100+ clients
- May not support heterogeneous clients well (though advertised to do so)
- We've heard of problems with large filesystems
- Poor support

Other alternatives

W. Curtis Preston, author of the O'Reilly backup book, maintains a very useful web page about backup-related topics (disk mirroring products, advanced filesystem products, remote system backup products, off-site data-vaulting products, etc.). Among other resources, it includes an extensive table of just about every piece of commercial backup software known to mankind. We highly recommend both the book and the web site. The address is www.backupcentral.com.

10.10 RECOMMENDED READING

PRESTON, CURTIS W. *Unix Backup and Recovery*. O'Reilly, 1999.

10.11 EXERCISES

E10.1 Investigate the backup procedure used at your site. Which machine(s) perform the backups? What type of storage devices are used? Where are tapes stored? Suggest improvements to the current system.

E10.2 What steps are needed to restore files on a system that uses Amanda? How do you find the right tape?

⭐ **E10.3** Design a backup plan for the following scenarios. Assume that each computer has a 10GB disk and that users' home directories are stored locally. Chose a backup device that balances cost vs. support needs and explain your reasoning. List any assumptions you make.

a) A research facility has 50 machines. Each machine holds a lot of important data that changes often.

b) A small software company has 10 machines. Source code is stored on a central server that has 50GB of disk space. The source code changes continuously throughout the day. Individual users' home directories do not change very often. Cost is of little concern and security is of utmost importance.

c) A home network has two machines. Cost is the most important issue.

⭐ **E10.4** Design a restore strategy for each of the three situations above.

Backups

★ **E10.5** Outline the steps you would use to perform a secure **rdump** through a secure SSH tunnel.

★ **E10.6** Given the following output from **df** and **/etc/dumpdates**, identify the steps needed to perform the three restores requested. Enumerate your assumptions. Assume that the date of the restore request is January 18.

df output from the machine khaya.cs.colorado.edu:

/dev/hda8	256194	81103	161863	33%	/
/dev/hda1	21929	4918	15879	24%	/boot
/dev/hda6	3571696	24336	3365924	1%	/local
/dev/hda10	131734	5797	119135	5%	/tmp
/dev/hda5	1815580	1113348	610004	65%	/usr
/dev/hda7	256194	17013	225953	7%	/var

/etc/dumpdates from khaya.cs.colorado.edu:

/dev/hda8	2	Thu	Jan	17	22:59:23	2002
/dev/hda6	3	Thu	Jan	17	22:51:51	2002
/dev/hda7	3	Thu	Jan	17	22:50:24	2002
/dev/hda5	9	Thu	Jan	17	22:46:25	2002
/dev/hda5	1	Sat	Jan	12	22:45:42	2002
/dev/hda7	0	Sat	Jan	12	23:14:47	2002
/dev/hda6	1	Sat	Jan	12	23:14:32	2002
/dev/hda8	1	Sat	Jan	12	23:14:17	2002
/dev/hda6	0	Thu	Jan	10	22:47:31	2002
/dev/hda1	1	Tue	Jan	8	22:16:05	2002
/dev/hda7	1	Mon	Jan	7	22:08:09	2002
/dev/hda1	4	Thu	Jan	3	22:51:53	2002
/dev/hda7	2	Mon	Dec	24	22:53:52	2001
/dev/hda5	0	Sat	Nov	3	22:46:21	2001
/dev/hda1	0	Fri	Sep	21	22:46:29	2001
/dev/hda8	0	Fri	Aug	24	23:01:24	2001
/dev/hda1	3	Sun	Jul	29	22:52:20	2001
/dev/hda6	2	Sun	Jul	29	23:01:32	2001

a) "Please restore my entire home directory (**/usr/home/clements**) from some time in the last few days. I seem to have lost the entire code base for my senior project."

b) "Umm, I accidentally did a **sudo rm -rf /*** on my machine khaya. Could you please restore all the filesystems from the latest backups?"

c) "All my MP3 files that I have been collecting from Aimster over the last month are gone. They were stored in **/tmp/mp3/**. Could you please restore them for me?"

★★ **E10.7** Write Amanda configuration statements that implement the backup plans you came up with for exercise 10.3. Make sure you specify the backup devices, the partition types, and the **disklist** files.

11 *Syslog and Log Files*

The system daemons, the kernel, and various utilities all emit data that is logged and eventually ends up on your finite-sized disks. Most of that data has a limited useful life and needs to be summarized, compressed, archived, and eventually thrown away.

11.1 LOGGING POLICIES

Logging policies vary from site to site. Common schemes include the following:

- Throw away all data immediately.
- Reset log files at periodic intervals.
- Rotate log files, keeping data for a fixed time.
- Compress and archive logs to tape or other permanent media.

The correct choice for your site depends on how much disk space you have and how security conscious you are. Even sites with an abundance of disk space must deal with the cancerous growth of log files.

Whatever scheme you select, you should automate the maintenance of log files with **cron**. See Chapter 9, *Periodic Processes*, for more information about this daemon.

Throwing away log files

We do not recommend throwing away all logging information. Sites that are subject to security problems routinely find that log files provide important evidence of break-ins. Log files are also helpful for alerting you to hardware and software problems. In general, given a comfortable amount of disk space, you should keep data for at least a month. In the real world, it may take this long for you to realize that your site has been compromised by a hacker and that you need to review the logs. If you need to go back further into the past, you can recover older log files from your backup tapes.

Some administrators allow log files to grow until they become bothersome, then restart them from zero. This plan is better than keeping no data at all, but it does not guarantee that log entries will be retained for any particular length of time. Average disk usage may also be higher than with other management schemes.

Rotating log files

Many sites store each day's log information separately, sometimes in a compressed format. Daily files are kept for a specific period of time and then deleted. It is handy to keep the log files uncompressed so that they can be easily searched with **grep**. At our site we dedicate a disk partition on a central logging host (**/var/log**) to log files. We compress data that's more than a week old with **gzip**.

One common way to keep logging information for a fixed period is known as "rotation." In a rotation system, you keep backup files that are one day old, two days old, and so on. Each day, a script or utility program renames the files to push older data toward the end of the chain.

If a log file is called **logfile**, for example, the backup copies might be called **logfile.1**, **logfile.2**, and so on. If you keep a week's worth of data, there will be a **logfile.7** but no **logfile.8**. Every day, the data in **logfile.7** is lost as **logfile.6** overwrites it.

Suppose a file needs daily attention and you want to archive its contents for three days (to keep the example short). The following script would implement an appropriate rotation policy:

```
#!/bin/sh
cd /var/log
mv logfile.2 logfile.3
mv logfile.1 logfile.2
mv logfile logfile.1
cat /dev/null > logfile
chmod 600 logfile
```

Most Linux distributions (including all of our examples except SuSE) supply a very nice log rotation utility called **logrotate**, which we describe starting on page 205. It's much easier (and more reliable) than writing your own scripts and is worth seeking out and installing if your distribution doesn't include it.

Ownership information is important for some log files. You may need to run your rotation script from **cron** as the log files' owner rather than as root, or you may need to add a **chown** command to the sequence.

Some sites identify log files by date rather than by sequence number; for example, **logfile.tues** or **logfile.aug26**. This system is a little harder to implement, but it can be worth the effort if you frequently refer to old log files. It's much easier to set up in Perl than in **sh**. One useful idiom that doesn't require any programming is

```
mv logfile logfile.`date +%Y.%m.%d`
```

This scheme has the advantage of making **ls** sort the log files chronologically.

Some daemons keep their log files open all the time. Because of the way the filesystem works, our example script cannot be used with such daemons. Instead of flowing to the recreated **logfile**, log data will continue to go to **logfile.1**; the active reference to the original file persists even after the file has been renamed. To install a new log file, you must either signal the daemon or kill and restart it.

Here is an updated example that uses both compression and signals:

```
#!/bin/sh
cd /var/log
mv logfile.2.gz logfile.3.gz
mv logfile.1.gz logfile.2.gz
mv logfile logfile.1
cat /dev/null > logfile
chmod 600 logfile
kill -signal pid
gzip logfile.1
```

signal represents the appropriate signal for the program writing the log file; *pid* is its process ID. The signal can be hardcoded into the script, but you must determine the PID of the daemon dynamically, either by reading a file that the daemon has left around for you (e.g., **/var/run/syslogd.pid**, described below) or by using the **killall** variant of **kill**, which can look up the PID in the process table for you. For example, the command

killall -e -HUP syslogd

is equivalent to

kill -HUP `cat /var/run/syslogd.pid`

Archiving log files

Some sites must archive all accounting data and log files as a matter of policy, perhaps to provide data for a potential audit. In this situation, log files should be first rotated on disk and then written to tape or other permanent media. This scheme reduces the frequency of tape backups and gives you fast access to recent data.

See Chapter 10 for more information about backups.

Log files should always be included as part of your regular backup sequence. Because they contain information that is vital for investigating security incidents, they should be backed up at the highest frequency your dump schedule permits. Log files change frequently, so they can represent a significant portion of the system information that is stored on incremental backups. Keep the interaction between your logging policy and your backup policy in mind when designing both.

Syslog / Log Files

In addition to being stored as part of regular backups, logs can also be archived to a separate tape series. Separate tapes are more cumbersome, but they impose less of a documentation burden and won't interfere with your ability to recycle dump tapes. If you use separate tapes, we suggest that you use **tar** format and write a script to automate your backup scheme.

11.2 LINUX LOG FILES

Traditional UNIX systems are often criticized for their inconsistent and even somewhat bizarre approach to logging. Fortunately, Linux systems are generally a bit more sane, although each distribution has its own way of naming and dividing up the log files. For the most part, Linux packages send their logging information to files in the **/var/log** directory. On some distributions, logs are also stored in **/var/adm**.

The format of the **syslog.conf** *file is described on page 207.*

Most programs these days actually send their log entries to a central clearing system called syslog, which is described later in this chapter. The default syslog configuration typically dumps most of these messages somewhere into **/var/log**. Check syslog's configuration file, **/etc/syslog.conf**, to find out the specifics.

Table 11.1 compiles information about some of the more common log files on our example distributions. Specifically, it lists

- The log files to archive, summarize, or truncate
- The program that creates each
- An indication of how each filename is specified
- The frequency of attention or cleanup that we consider reasonable
- The distributions (among our examples) that use the log file
- A description of the file's contents

Filenames are relative to **/var/log** unless otherwise noted.

The character in the Where column tells how the log file is specified: S for programs that use syslog, F for programs that use a configuration file, and H if the filename is hardwired in code. The Freq column indicates our suggested cleanup frequency.

Log files are generally owned by root, although conventions for the ownership and mode of log files vary among distributions. In our opinion, most logs should be given mode 600 (read and write for the owner only) because their contents are potentially useful to hackers. At the very least, the **secure**, **auth.log**, and **sudo.log** files should be off limits to casual browsing. Never give write permission on any log file to anyone but the owner.

It's worth noting that many of the log files in Table 11.1 are maintained by syslog but that the default syslog configuration varies widely among systems. With a more consistent **/etc/syslog.conf** file, the log files would look relatively similar among Linux distributions.

Table 11.1   **Log files on parade**

File	Program	Where[a]	Freq[a]	Distros[a]	Contents
messages	various	S	W	all	Often the main system log file
syslog	various	S	W	D	Often the main system log file
auth.log	**su**, etc.[b]	S	M	DR	Authorizations
secure	**xinetd**	S	M	R	Private authorization messages
boot.log	**rc** scripts	F[c]	M	R	Output of system startup scripts
dmesg	kernel	H	–	RD	Dump of kernel message buffer
boot.msg	kernel	H	–	S	Dump of kernel message buffer
wtmp	**login**	H	M	all	Login records (binary)
lastlog	**login**	H	–	all	Last login time per user (binary)
setuid.*	**checksecurity**	H	D	D	List of setuid files on the system
debug	various	S	D	D	Debug output (when enabled)
faillog	**login**	H	W	DS	Unsuccessful login attempts
sudo.log	**sudo**	F	W	–	Log of root access through **sudo**

a. Where: S = Syslog, H = Hardwired, F = Configuration file
   Freq: D = Daily, W = Weekly, M = Monthly
   Distros: R = Red Hat, D = Debian, S = SuSE
b. **passwd**, **login**, and **shutdown** also write to the authorization log. It's in **/var/adm** on Red Hat.
c. Actually logs through syslog, but the facility and level are configured in **/etc/initlog.conf**.

Special log files

Most logs are text files to which lines are written as "interesting" events occur. A few of the logs listed in Table 11.1 have a rather different context, however.

/var/log/wtmp contains a record of users' logins and logouts as well as entries that indicate when the system was rebooted or shut down. It's a fairly generic log file in that new entries are simply added to the end of the file. However, the **wtmp** file is maintained in a binary format. Use the **last** command to decode the information. Despite its unusual format, the **wtmp** file should be rotated or truncated like any other log file because its natural tendency is to grow without limit.

See the footnote on page 170 for more info about sparse files.

/var/log/lastlog contains similar information to **/var/log/wtmp**, but it records only the time of last login for each user. It is a sparse, binary file that's indexed by UID. It will stay smaller if your UIDs are assigned in some kind of numeric sequence, although this is certainly nothing to lose sleep over in the real world. **lastlog** doesn't need to be rotated because its size stays constant unless new users log in.

Debian's **checksecurity** utility runs every day (from **/etc/cron.daily/standard**) to enumerate the system's complement of setuid programs. **checksecurity** writes any changes relative to the previous baseline to **/var/log/setuid.changes**; it also maintains the current and previous lists of setuid programs in the files **setuid.today** and

setuid.yesterday. Check the modification time on the **setuid.yesterday** file to see when the most recent change occurred.

Kernel and boot-time logging

The kernel and the system startup scripts present some special challenges in the domain of logging. In the case of the kernel, the problem is to create a permanent record of the boot process and the operation of the kernel without building in dependencies on any particular filesystem or filesystem organization. In the case of the startup scripts, the challenge is to capture a coherent narrative of the startup procedure without permanently tying any of the system daemons to a startup log file, interfering with any program's own logging, or gooping up the startup scripts with double entries or output redirections.

Kernel logging is dealt with by having the kernel store its log entries in an internal buffer of limited size. The buffer is large enough to accommodate messages about all the kernel's activities at boot time. Once the system has come all the way up, a user process can access the kernel's log buffer and make a final disposition of its contents. Distributions typically do this by running the **dmesg** command and redirecting its output to **/var/log/dmesg** (Red Hat and Debian) or **/var/log/boot.msg** (SuSE). This is the best place to look for information about the most recent startup process.

The kernel's ongoing logging is handled by a daemon called **klogd**. The functions of **klogd** are actually a superset of those of **dmesg**; in addition to dumping the kernel log and exiting, it can also read messages out of the kernel buffer as they are generated and pass them along to a file or to syslog. In normal operation, **klogd** runs in this latter mode; syslog processes the messages according to the instructions for the "kern" facility.

Our example distributions' startup scripts do not use **dmesg**'s **-c** flag when they make their initial dump of log messages, so the kernel's message buffer is read but not reset. When **klogd** starts up, it finds the same set of messages seen by **dmesg** in the buffer and submits them to syslog. For this reason, some entries appear in both the **dmesg** or **boot.msg** file and in another, syslog-managed file such as **/var/log/messages**.

Another issue in kernel logging is the appropriate management of the system console. As the system is booting, it's important for all the output to come to the console. However, once the system is up and running, console messages may be more an annoyance than a help, particularly if the console is used for logins.

Both **dmesg** and **klogd** let you set the kernel's console logging level with a command-line flag. For example:

```
% sudo dmesg -n 2
```

Level 7 is the most verbose and includes debugging information. Level 1 includes only panic messages (the lower-numbered levels are the most severe). All kernel messages continue to go to the central buffer (and to syslog) regardless of whether they are forwarded to the console or not.

Logging for the system startup scripts is unfortunately not as well managed as kernel logging. Red Hat uses a command called **initlog** to capture the output of startup commands and submit it to syslog. Unfortunately, **initlog** has to be mentioned explicitly whenever a command is run, so the information capture does come at the cost of some complexity. The entries eventually make their way to **/var/log/boot.log**.

Our other example systems make no coherent effort to capture a history of the startup scripts' output. Some information is logged by individual commands and daemons, but much goes unrecorded.

11.3   LOGROTATE: MANAGE LOG FILES

Erik Troan's excellent **logrotate** utility implements a variety of log management policies and is standard on Red Hat and Debian systems. SuSE users should install the RPM at once.

A **logrotate** configuration file consists of a series of specifications for groups of log files to be managed. Options that appear outside the context of a log file specification (such as errors, rotate, and weekly in the following example) apply to all following specifications; they can be overridden within the specification for a particular log file and can also be respecified later in the file to modify the defaults.

Here's a somewhat contrived example that handles several different log files:

```
# Example log rotation policy
errors sa-book@admin.com
rotate 5
weekly

/var/log/messages {
        postrotate
                /bin/kill -HUP `cat /var/run/syslogd.pid`
        endscript
}

/var/log/samba/*.log {
        notifempty
        copytruncate
        sharedscripts
        postrotate
                /bin/kill -HUP `cat /var/lock/samba/*.pid`
        endscript
}
```

This configuration rotates **/var/log/messages** every week. It keeps five versions of the file and notifies **syslogd** each time the file is reset. The Samba log files (of which there may be several) are also rotated on a weekly schedule, but instead of being moved aside and restarted, they are copied and then truncated. The Samba daemons are sent HUP signals only after all log files have been rotated.

Table 11.2 lists the most useful **logrotate.conf** options.

Table 11.2   logrotate options

Option	Meaning
compress	Compresses all noncurrent versions of the log file
daily, weekly, monthly	Rotates log files on the specified schedule
delaycompress	Compresses all versions but current and next-most-recent
endscript	Marks the end of a prerotate or postrotate script
errors *emailaddr*	Emails error notifications to the specified *emailaddr*
missingok	Doesn't complain if the log file does not exist
notifempty	Doesn't rotate the log file if it is empty
olddir *dir*	Specifies that older versions of the log file be placed in *dir*
postrotate	Introduces a script to be run after the log has been rotated
prerotate	Introduces a script to be run before any changes are made
rotate *n*	Includes *n* versions of the log in the rotation scheme
sharedscripts	Runs scripts only once for the entire log group
size=*logsize*	Rotates if log file size > *logsize* (e.g., 100K, 4M)

logrotate is normally run out of **cron** once a day. Its standard configuration file is **/etc/logrotate.conf**, but multiple configuration files (or directories containing configuration files) can appear on **logrotate**'s command line at once. This feature is used to great effect by Red Hat and Debian, which define the **/etc/logrotate.d** directory as a standard place for **logrotate** config files. **logrotate**-aware software packages (of which there are many) can drop in log management instructions as part of their installation procedure, greatly simplifying administration.

11.4 SYSLOG: THE SYSTEM EVENT LOGGER

Syslog, originally written by Eric Allman, is a comprehensive logging system. It has two important functions: to liberate programmers from the tedious mechanics of writing log files and to put administrators in control of logging. Before syslog, every program was free to make up its own logging policy. System administrators had no control over what information was kept or where it was stored.

Syslog is quite flexible. It allows messages to be sorted by their source and importance ("severity level") and routed to a variety of destinations: log files, users' terminals, or even other machines. Syslog's ability to centralize the logging for a network is one of its most valuable features.

Syslog consists of three parts:

- **syslogd**, the logging daemon (along with its config file, **/etc/syslog.conf**)
- **openlog** et al., library routines that submit messages to **syslogd**
- **logger,** a user-level command that submits log entries from the shell

In the following discussion, we first cover the configuration of **syslogd** and then briefly show how to use syslog from Perl scripts.

syslogd is started at boot time and runs continuously; it cannot be managed with **inetd**. Programs that are syslog-aware write log entries (by using the **syslog** library routine) to the special file **/dev/log**, a UNIX domain socket. **syslogd** reads messages from **/dev/log**, consults its configuration file, and dispatches each message to the appropriate destinations.

The kernel logging daemon, **klogd**, is responsible for retrieving messages from the kernel's internal log buffer and forwarding them to **syslogd**.

A hangup signal (HUP, signal 1) causes **syslogd** to close its log files, reread its configuration file, and start logging again. If you modify **/etc/syslog.conf**, you must send a hangup signal to **syslogd** to make your changes take effect. A TERM signal causes **syslogd** to exit.

syslogd writes its process ID to the file **/var/run/syslogd.pid**. This convention makes it easy to send signals to **syslogd** from a script. For example, the following command sends a hangup signal:

```
# kill -HUP `/bin/cat /var/run/syslogd.pid`
```

Trying to compress or modify a log file that **syslogd** has open for writing is not healthy and has unpredictable results. The proper procedure is to move the old log aside, recreate the log with the same ownerships and permissions, and then send a HUP signal to **syslogd**. This procedure is easily implemented with **logrotate**; see page 205 for an example.

Configuring syslogd

The configuration file **/etc/syslog.conf** controls **syslogd**'s behavior. It is a text file with a relatively simple format. Blank lines and lines with a pound sign (#) in column one are ignored. The basic format is:

```
selector <Tab> action
```

For example, the line

```
mail.info      /var/log/maillog
```

would cause messages from the email system to be saved in the file **/var/log/maillog**.

Selectors identify the program ("facility") that is sending a log message and the message's severity level with the syntax *facility.level*. Both facility names and severity levels must be chosen from a short list of defined values; programs can't make up their own. Facilities are defined for the kernel, for common groups of utilities, and for locally written programs. Everything else is classified under the generic facility "user."

Selectors can contain the special keywords * and none, meaning all or nothing, respectively. A selector can include multiple facilities separated with commas. Multiple selectors can also be combined with semicolons.

In general, selectors are ORed together; a message matching any selector will be subject to the line's *action*. However, a selector with a level of none excludes the listed facilities regardless of what other selectors on the same line may say.

Here are some examples of ways to format and combine selectors:

```
facility.level                      action
facility1,facility2.level           action
facility1.level1;facility2.level2   action
*.level                             action
*.level;badfacility.none            action
```

Table 11.3 lists the valid syslog facility names.

Table 11.3   Syslog facility names

Facility	Programs that use it
*	All facilities except "mark"
auth	Security and authorization-related commands
authpriv	Sensitive/private authorization messages[a]
cron	The **cron** daemon
daemon	System daemons
ftp	The FTP daemon, **ftpd**
kern	The kernel
local0-7	Eight flavors of local message
lpr	The line printer spooling system
mail	**sendmail** and other mail-related software
mark	Time stamps generated at regular intervals
news	The Usenet news system
syslog	**syslogd** internal messages
user	User processes (the default if not specified)
uucp	Reserved for UUCP, which doesn't use it

a. *All* authorization-related messages are sensitive. Neither authpriv messages nor auth messages should be world-readable.

syslogd itself produces time stamp messages, which are logged if the "mark" facility appears in **syslog.conf** to specify a destination for them. Time stamps can help you figure out that your machine crashed between 3:00 and 3:20 a.m., not just "sometime last night." This information can be a big help when you are debugging problems that seem to occur regularly. For example, many sites have experienced mysterious crashes when the housekeeping staff plugged in vacuum cleaners late at night, tripping the circuit breakers.

If your system is quite busy, other log messages often provide adequate time stamp information. But in the wee hours of the morning, that is not always the case.

Table 11.4 lists syslog's severity levels in order of descending importance.

Table 11.4   Syslog severity levels (descending severity)

Level	Approximate meaning
emerg	Panic situations
alert	Urgent situations
crit	Critical conditions
err	Other error conditions
warning	Warning messages
notice	Things that might merit investigation
info	Informational messages
debug	For debugging only

The severity level of a message specifies its importance. In the **syslog.conf** file, levels indicate the *minimum* importance that a message must have in order to be logged. For example, a message from the mail system at level warning would match the selector mail.warning as well as the selectors mail.notice, mail.info, mail.debug, *.warning, *.notice, *.info, and *.debug. If **syslog.conf** specifies that mail.info messages be logged to a file, then mail.warning messages will go there also.

As a refinement of the basic syntax, the Linux version of syslog also allows the characters = and ! to be prefixed to priority levels to indicate "this priority only" and "except this priority and higher." Table 11.5 shows examples.

Table 11.5   Examples of priority level qualifiers in syslog.conf

Selector	Meaning
mail.info	Selects mail-related messages of info prio. and higher
mail.=info	Selects only messages at info priority
mail.info;mail.!err	Selects only priorities info, notice, and warning
mail.debug;mail.!=warning	Selects all priorities except warning

The *action* field tells what to do with a message. Table 11.6 lists the options.

Table 11.6   Syslog actions

Action	Meaning
filename	Writes the message to a file on the local machine
@*hostname*	Forwards the message to the **syslogd** on *hostname*
@*ipaddress*	Forwards the message to the host at IP address *ipaddress*
| *fifoname*	Writes the message to the named pipe *fifoname*[a]
user1,user2,...	Writes the message to users' screens if they are logged in
*	Writes the message to all users who are currently logged in

a. See **info mkfifo** for more information.

See page 498 for more information about how hostnames are translated to IP addresses.

If a *filename* (or *fifoname*) action is used, the name should be an absolute path. If you specify a nonexistent filename, **syslogd** will create the file when a message is first directed to it.[1] You can preface a *filename* action with a dash to indicate that the filesystem should not be **sync**ed after each log entry is written. **sync**ing helps to preserve as much logging information as possible in the event of a crash, but it is expensive in terms of disk throughput.

If a *hostname* is used rather than an IP address, it must be resolvable through a translation mechanism such as DNS or NIS.

Although multiple facilities and levels are allowed in a selector, there is no provision for multiple actions. To send a message to two places (such as to a local file and to a central logging host), you can include in the configuration file two lines with the same selectors.

Because syslog messages can be used to mount a denial of service attack, **syslogd** will not accept log messages from other machines unless it is started with the **-r** flag. By default, **syslogd** also refuses to act as a third-party message forwarder; messages that arrive from one network host cannot be sent on to another. Use the **-h** flag to override this behavior. (If you want these options turned on all the time, add the flags to the **/etc/rc.d/init.d/syslog** script under Red Hat or to **/etc/init.d/sysklogd** under Debian. SuSE Linux provides better syntactic sugar and only requires to you modify the SYSLOGD_PARAMS variable defined in **/etc/rc.config**.)

Config file examples

Syslog configuration is one area in which Linux distributions vary widely. Since it's relatively easy to read a **syslog.conf** file, we will not review our example distributions' config files in detail; they're all pretty straightforward. Instead, we'll look at some common ways that you might want to set up logging if you choose to depart from your system's default.

Below are three sample **syslog.conf** files that correspond to a stand-alone machine on a small network, a client machine on a larger network, and a central logging host on the same large network. The central logging host is called "netloghost."[2]

Stand-alone machine

A basic configuration for a stand-alone machine is shown below:

```
# Small network or stand-alone syslog.conf file

# emergencies: tell everyone who is logged on
*.emerg                                    *
#  important messages
```

---

1. Note that this behavior is opposite to that of the original syslog implementation, which required log files to be created in advance.

2. More accurately, it uses "netloghost" as one of its hostname aliases. This allows the identity of the log host to be modified with little reconfiguration. An alias can be added in **/etc/hosts** or set up with a CNAME record in DNS. See page 417 for more information about DNS CNAME records.

```
*.warning;daemon,auth.info,user.none /var/log/messages
#   printer errors
lpr.debug                                       /var/log/lpd-errs
```

The first noncomment line writes emergency messages to the screens of all current users. An example of emergency-level messages are those generated by **shutdown** when the system is about to be turned off.

The second line writes important messages to **/var/log/messages**. The info level is below warning, so the daemon,auth.info clause includes additional logging from **passwd**, **su**, and daemon programs. The third line writes printer error messages to **/var/log/lpd-errs**.

Network client

A network client typically forwards serious messages to a central logging machine:

```
# CS Department syslog.conf file for nonmaster machines

# Emergencies: tell everyone who is logged on
*.emerg;user.none                        *

# Forward important messages to the central logger
*.warning;lpr,local1.none                @netloghost
daemon,auth.info                         @netloghost

# Send local stuff to the central logger too
local2.info;local0,local7.debug          @netloghost

# cardd logs through facility local1 -- send to boulder
local1.debug                             @boulder.colorado.edu

# Keep printer errors local
lpr.debug                                /var/log/lpd-errs

# sudo logs to local2 - keep a copy here too
local2.info                              /var/log/sudo.log

# Keep kernel messages local
kern.info                                /var/log/kern.log
```

This configuration does not keep much log information locally. It's worth mentioning that if netloghost is down or unreachable, log messages will be irretrievably lost. You may want to keep some additional local duplicates of important messages to guard against this possibility.

At a site with lots of local software installed, lots of messages can be logged inappropriately to facility user, level emerg. In this example, user/emerg has been specifically excluded with the user.none clause in the first line.

*See page 43 for more information about **sudo**.*

The second and third lines forward all important messages to the central logging host; messages from the printing system and the campus-wide card access system are explicitly excluded. The fourth line forwards local logging information to netloghost as well. The fifth line forwards card access logging information to the campus-wide logging host, boulder. The last two entries keep local copies of printer errors and **sudo** log messages.

Central logging host

This example is for netloghost, the central, secure logging host for a moderate-sized network of about 7,000 hosts.

```
# CS Department syslog.conf file, master logging host

# Emergencies to the console and log file, with timing marks
*.emerg                          /dev/console
*.err;kern,mark.debug;auth.notice    /dev/console
*.err;kern,mark.debug;user.none    /var/log/console.log
auth.notice                      /var/log/console.log

# Send non-emergency messages to the usual log files
*.err;user.none;kern.debug       /var/log/messages
daemon,auth.notice;mail.crit     /var/log/messages
lpr.debug                        /var/log/lpd-errs
mail.debug                       /var/log/mail.log

# Local authorization stuff like sudo and npasswd
local2.debug                     /var/log/sudo.log
local2.alert                     /var/log/sudo-errs.log
auth.info                        /var/log/auth.log

# Other local stuff
local4.notice                    /var/log/da.log
local7.debug                     /var/log/tcp.log

# User stuff (the default if no facility is specified)
user.info                        /var/log/user.log
```

Logging data arriving from local programs and from **syslogd**s on the network is written to files. In some cases, the output from each facility is put into its own file.

The central logging host generates the time stamp for each message as it writes the message out. The time stamps do not reflect the time on the originating host. If you have machines in several time zones or your system clocks are not synchronized, the time stamps can be somewhat misleading.

Sample syslog output

Below is a snippet from one of the log files on the master syslog host at the University of Colorado's computer science department. About 200 hosts log to this machine.

```
Dec 18 15:12:42 av18.cs.colorado.edu sbatchd[495]: sbatchd/main: ls_info()
    failed: LIM is down; try later; trying ...
Dec 18 15:14:28 proxy-1.cs.colorado.edu pop-proxy[27283]: Connection from
    128.138.198.84
Dec 18 15:14:30 mroe.cs.colorado.edu pingem[271]: maltese-
    office.cs.colorado.edu has not answered 42 times
```

```
Dec 14 15:14:51 coyote.cs.colorado.edu PAM_unix[17405]: (sshd) session closed
    for user trent
Dec 18 15:15:48 proxy-1.cs.colorado.edu pop-proxy[27285]: Connection from
    12.2.209.183
Dec 18 15:15:50 av18.cs.colorado.edu last message repeated 100 times
```

This example contains entries from several different hosts (av18, proxy-1, coyote, and mroe) and from several programs: **sbatchd**, **pop-proxy**, **pingem**, and the Pluggable Authentication Modules library.

Note the last line of the excerpt, which complains of a message being repeated 100 times. To help keep the logs shorter, syslog generally attempts to coalesce duplicate messages and replace them with this type of summary. However, the machine from which this example was drawn accepts log entries from many other hosts, so this particular message is a bit misleading, It actually refers to the previous log entry from av18, not the entry immediately preceding it in the composite log.

It's a good idea to peruse your log files regularly. Determine what is normal so that when an anomaly occurs, you can recognize it. Better yet, set up a log postprocessor such as **swatch** to trap these cases automatically; see *Condensing log files to useful information* on page 216.

Designing a logging scheme for your site

At a small site it is adequate to configure logging so that important system errors and warnings are kept in a file on each machine, much as was done before we had syslog. The **syslog.conf** file can be customized for each host.

On a large network, central logging is essential. It keeps the flood of information manageable and, with luck, makes auditing data unavailable to a person who violates the security of a machine on the network. Hackers often edit system logs to cover their tracks; if log information is whisked away as soon as it is generated, it is much harder to destroy. But be aware that anyone can call **syslog** and fake log entries from any daemon or utility. Syslog also uses the UDP protocol, which is not guaranteed to be reliable; messages can get lost. Your firewall should not allow external sites to submit messages to your **syslogd**.

See Chapter 18 for more information about distributing files on a network.

Choose a stable machine as your logging server, preferably one that is well secured and does not have many logins. Other machines can use a generic configuration file that is maintained in a central place. Thus, only two versions of the **syslog.conf** file need be maintained. This approach allows logging to be complete but at the same time is not a nightmare to administer.

Some very large sites may want to add more levels to the logging hierarchy. Unfortunately, syslog retains the name of the originating host for only one hop. If host "client" sends some log entries to host "server," which sends them on to host "master," master will see the data as coming from server, not from client.

Syslog / Log Files

Software that uses syslog

Table 11.7 lists some of the programs that use syslog, the facilities and levels they log to, and a brief description of each program. Some rows are shaded to improve readability.

Table 11.7   Software that uses syslog

Program	Facility	Levels	Description
cron	cron	info	System task-scheduling daemon
ftpd	ftp	debug–crit	FTP daemon (**wu-ftpd**)
imapd	mail	info–alert	IMAP mail server
inetd	daemon	err, warning	Internet superdaemon
login	authpriv	info–err	Login programs
lpd	lpr	info–err	Line printer daemon
named	daemon	info–err	Name server (DNS)
passwd	auth	notice, warning	Password-setting program
popper	local0	debug, notice	POP3 mail server
sendmail	mail	debug–alert	Mail transport system
shutdown	auth	notice	Halts the system
su	auth	notice	Switches UIDs
sudo	local2	notice, alert	Limited **su** program
syslogd	syslog, mark	info–err	Internal errors, time stamps
tcpd	local7	debug-err	TCP wrapper for **inetd**
vmlinuz	kern	all	The kernel
xinetd	*configurable*	info (default)	Variant of **inetd** (Red Hat)

With all this information, it should be perfectly clear which messages to keep and which to discard, right? Well, maybe not. In practice, you just have to learn what the useful logging levels are for your system. It's best to start with an excessive amount of logging and gradually winnow out the cases that you don't want. Stop winnowing when you feel comfortable with the average data rate.

Debugging syslog

The **logger** command is useful for submitting log entries from shell scripts. You can also use it to test changes in **syslogd**'s configuration file. For example, if you have just added the line

```
local5.warning          /tmp/evi.log
```

and want to verify that it is working, run

```
% logger -p local5.warning "test message"
```

A line containing "test message" should be written to **/tmp/evi.log**. If this doesn't happen, perhaps you forgot to send **syslogd** a hangup signal.

Be careful about logging to the console device, **/dev/console**, or to any pseudo-terminal or port that supports flow control. If someone has inadvertently typed <Control-S> on the console, output to the console will stop. Each call to **syslog** will block and your system will slow to a crawl. A good way to check for this degenerate condition is to send a syslog message to the console with **logger**. If **logger** hangs, you need to find the offending port, type a <Control-Q>, and rethink your logging strategy.

Another drawback to logging on the console is that the flood of messages sparked by a major problem can make the console unusable at precisely the moment that it is most needed. Depending on how your console is set up and managed (e.g., through a console server), console logging may also have some security implications.

Using syslog from programs

The library routines **openlog**, **syslog**, and **closelog** allow programs to use the syslog system. Versions of these library routines are available for both C and Perl; we describe only the Perl interface here. To import the definitions of the library routines, include the line

```
use Sys::Syslog;
```

at the beginning of your Perl script.

The **openlog** routine initializes logging, using the specified facility name:

```
openlog(ident, logopt, facility);
```

Messages are logged with the options specified by *logopt* and begin with the identification string *ident*. If **openlog** is not used, *ident* defaults to the current username, *logopt* to an empty string, and *facility* to "user." The *logopt* string should contain a comma-separated list of the options shown in Table 11.8.

Table 11.8   Logging options for the openlog routine

Option	Meaning
pid	Include the current process's PID in each log message.
ndelay	Connect to **syslogd** immediately (don't wait until a message is submitted).
cons	Send messages to the system console if **syslogd** is unreachable.
nowait	Do not **wait**(3) for child processes forked to write console messages.

For example, a reasonable invocation of **openlog** might be

```
openlog("adminscript", "pid,cons", "local4");
```

The **syslog** routine sends a *message* to **syslogd**, which logs it at the specified *priority*:

```
syslog(priority, message, ...);
```

The date, time, hostname, and *ident* string from the **openlog** call are prepended to the message in the log file. *message* may be followed by various other parameters to form a **printf**-style output specification that can include text and the contents of other variables; for example,

```
syslog("info", "Delivery to '%s' failed after %d attempts.", $user, $nAttempts);
```

The special symbol %m expands to an error message derived from the current value of **errno** (the most recent error code).

A priority string of the form "*level|facility*" sets both the severity level and the facility name. If you did not call **openlog** and specify an *ident* string, the **syslog** routine also checks to see if your *message* has the form of a standard UNIX error message such as

```
adminscript: User "nobody" not found in /etc/passwd file.
```

If it does, the part before the colon is secretly adopted as your *ident* string. These helpful (but undocumented) features make it unnecessary to call **openlog** at all; however, it is still a good idea. It's better to specify the facility name in one place (the **openlog** call) than to repeat it throughout your code.

The **closelog** routine closes the logging channel:

```
closelog( );
```

You must call this routine if you want to reopen the logging channel with different options. It's good form to call **closelog** when your program exits, but doing so is not strictly necessary.

Here's a complete example:

```
use Sys::Syslog;

openlog("adminscript", "cons,pid", "user");
syslog("warning","Those whom the gods would destroy, they first teach Basic.");
closelog();
```

This scriptlet produces the following log entry (191 is **admincript**'s PID):

```
Dec 28 22:56:24 moet.colorado.edu adminscript[191]: Those whom the gods
    would destroy, they first teach Basic.
```

11.5 CONDENSING LOG FILES TO USEFUL INFORMATION

Syslog is great for sorting and routing log messages, but when all is said and done, its end product is still a bunch of log files. While they may contain all kinds of useful information, those files aren't going to come and find you when something goes wrong. Another layer of software is needed to analyze the logs and make sure that important messages don't get lost amid the chatter.

A variety of free tools are available to fill this niche, and most of them are pretty similar: they scan recent log entries, match them against a database of regular expressions, and process the important messages in some attention-getting way. Some tools mail you a report; others can be configured to make noise, print log entries in different colors, or page you. Tools differ primarily in their degree of flexibility and in the size of their off-the-shelf database of patterns.

Two of the more commonly used log postprocessors are Todd Atkins' **swatch** and Craig Rowland's **logcheck**. **swatch** is available from

> http://www.oit.ucsb.edu/~eta/swatch

and **logcheck** from

> http://www.psionic.com/abacus/logcheck

swatch is a Perl script that gets its marching orders from a configuration file. The configuration syntax is fairly flexible, and it also provides access to the full pattern-matching mojo of Perl. While **swatch** can process an entire file in a single bound, it's primarily intended to be left running so that it can review new messages as they arrive, a la **tail -f**. A disadvantage of **swatch** is that you must build your own configuration pretty much from scratch; it doesn't know about specific systems and the actual log messages they might generate.

logcheck is a more basic script written in **sh**; the distribution also includes a C program that **logcheck** uses to help it record its place within a log file. Since **logcheck** knows how far it has read in a log file, there is perhaps less chance of a message slipping by at startup or shutdown time; in addition, **logcheck** can run at intervals from **cron** rather than running continuously.

logcheck comes with sample databases for several different versions of UNIX (including Linux). Even if you don't want to use the actual script, it's worth looking over the patterns to see if there are any you might want to steal for your own use.

Both of these tools have the disadvantage of working on only a single log file at a time. If your syslog configuration sorts messages into many different files, you might want to duplicate some of the messages into a central file that is frequently truncated, then use that summary file to feed a postprocessing script. That's easier than setting up a complicated network of scripts to handle multiple files.

Another tool worth mentioning is Kirk Bauer's **logwatch**. It's more a log summarizer than an ongoing monitoring and alerting tool, but it has the advantages of being relatively simple and of being available as an RPM package. You can download it from redhat.com or from

> http://www.kaybee.org/~kirk/html/linux.html

No matter what system you use to scan log files, there are a couple of things you should be sure to look for and immediately bring to the attention of an administrator:

- Most security-related messages should receive a prompt review. It's often helpful to monitor failed login, **su**, and **sudo** attempts in order to catch potential break-ins before they happen. If someone has just forgotten his password (as is usually the case), a prompt and proactive offer of help will make a good impression and cement your reputation for clairvoyance.

Syslog / Log Files

- Messages about disks that have filled up should be flagged and acted on immediately. Full disks often bring all useful work to a standstill.

- Messages that are repeated many times deserve attention, if only in the name of hygiene.

11.6 EXERCISES

E11.1 What are the main reasons for keeping old log files?

E11.2 What is the difference between **lastlog** and **wtmp**? What is a reasonable rotation policy for each?

E11.3 Dissect and understand the following **syslog.conf** line:

> *.notice;kern.debug;lpr.info;mail.crit;news.err   /var/log/messages

Does it seem sensible?

E11.4 Run a log file summarizer on your system's largest log file. Did it turn up anything interesting? (May require root access.)

E11.5 Look through your log files for entries from **named**, the DNS name server. Are any machines trying to update your domain files dynamically? Are they succeeding? (May require root access.)

★ **E11.6** Where would you find the boot log for your machine? What are the issues that affect logging at boot time? How does **klogd** solve these issues?

★ **E11.7** Investigate the logging policy in use at your site, including the log file rotation policy. How much disk space is dedicated to logging? How long are log files kept? Can you foresee circumstances in which your site's policy would not be adequate? What solution would you recommend? (Requires root access.)

★ **E11.8** Some log messages are extremely important and should be reviewed by an administrator immediately. What system could you set up to make sure that this happens as quickly as possible?

★ **E11.9** Write a C program or Perl script that submits messages to syslog with facility "user." (May require root access.)

12 *Drivers and the Kernel*

The kernel is the part of the system that's responsible for hiding the system's hardware underneath an abstract, high-level programming interface. It provides many of the facilities that users and user-level programs take for granted. For example, the kernel assembles all of the following concepts from lower-level hardware features:

- Processes (time sharing, protected address spaces)
- Signals and semaphores
- Virtual memory (swapping, paging, mapping)
- The filesystem (files, directories, namespace)
- Interprocess communication (pipes and network connections)

The kernel contains device drivers that manage its interaction with specific pieces of hardware; the rest of the kernel is, to a large degree, device independent. The relationship between the kernel and its device drivers is similar to the relationship between user-level processes and the kernel. When a process asks the kernel to "Read the first 64 bytes of **/etc/passwd**," the kernel might translate this request into a device driver instruction such as "Fetch block 3,348 from device 3." The driver would further break this command down into sequences of bit patterns to be presented to the device's control registers.

The kernel is written mostly in C, with a sprinkling of assembly language to help it interface with hardware- or chip-specific functions that are not accessible through normal compiler directives.

One of the advantages of the Linux environment is that the availability of source code makes it easy, relatively speaking, to roll your own device drivers and kernel modules from scratch. In the early days of Linux, having skills in this area was a necessity because it was difficult to effectively administer Linux systems without being able to "mold" the system to a specific environment.

Today, Linux is so pervasive that sysadmins can be perfectly effective without ever getting their hands soiled with gooey kernel code. In fact, one might argue that such activities are better left to programmers and that administrators should focus more on the overall needs of the user community. System administrators can tune the kernel or add preexisting modules as described in this chapter, but they don't need to take a crash course in C or 80x86 assembly language programming to survive.

The bottom line is that you shouldn't confuse the administration of modern Linux environments with the frontier husbandry of just a few years back.

12.1 KERNEL ADAPTATION

Linux systems live in a world that could potentially include any of tens of thousands of different pieces of computer hardware. The kernel must adapt to whatever hardware is present in the machine on which it's running.

A kernel can learn about the system's hardware in a variety of ways. The most basic is for you to provide the kernel with explicit information about the hardware it should expect to find (or pretend not to find, as the case may be). Some kernels can also prospect for devices on their own, either at boot time or dynamically once the system is running.

On the PC platform, where Linux is popular, the challenge of creating an accurate inventory of the system's hardware is particularly difficult (and sometimes impossible). PC hardware has followed an evolutionary path not unlike our own, in which early protozoa have now given rise to everything from dingos to killer bees. This diversity is compounded by the fact that PC manufacturers usually don't give you much technical information about the systems they sell, so you must often take your system apart and visually inspect the pieces to answer questions such as "What chipset does my Ethernet card use?"

Most modern Linux systems survive on a hybrid diet of static and dynamic kernel components, with the mix between the two being dictated primarily by the limitations of PC hardware. It's likely that at some point during your system administration career you'll need to provide a helping hand in the form of building a new kernel configuration.

12.2 WHY CONFIGURE THE KERNEL?

When the system is installed, it comes with a generic configuration that's designed to run most any application on most any hardware. The generic configuration includes many different device drivers and option packages, and it has tunable parameter values chosen for "general purpose" use. By carefully examining this configuration and adjusting it to your exact needs, you may be able to enhance your system's performance, security, or even reliability.

Modern Linux kernels are better than their ancestors at flushing unwanted drivers from memory, but compiled-in options will always be turned on. Although reconfiguring the kernel for efficiency is less important than it used to be, a good case can still be made for doing so.

Instructions for adding a new driver start on page 222.

Another reason to reconfigure the kernel is to add support for new types of devices (i.e., to add new device drivers). The driver code can't just be mooshed onto the kernel like a gob of Play-Doh; it has to be integrated into the kernel's data structures and tables. On some systems, this procedure may require that you go back to the configuration files for the kernel and add in the new device, rebuilding the kernel from scratch. On other systems, you may only need to run a program designed to make these configuration changes for you.

The kernel is not difficult to configure; it's just difficult to fix once you break it.

12.3 CONFIGURATION METHODS

Four basic methods can be used to configure the Linux kernel. Chances are you'll have the opportunity to try all of them eventually. The methods are:

- Modifying tunable (dynamic) kernel configuration parameters

- Loading new drivers and modules on the fly into an existing kernel

- Building a kernel from scratch (really, this means compiling it from source files, possibly with modifications and additions)

- Providing operational directives at boot time through the kernel loader, LILO, or GRUB. See page 23 for more information about these systems.

These methods are each applicable in slightly different situations. Modifying tunable parameters is the easiest and most common, whereas building a kernel from source files is the hardest and least often required. Fortunately, all of these approaches become second nature with a little practice.

12.4 TUNING A LINUX KERNEL

Many modules and drivers in the kernel were designed with the knowledge that one size doesn't fit all. To increase flexibility, special hooks allow parameters such as an internal table's size or the kernel's behavior in a particular circumstance to be adjusted on the fly by the system administrator. These hooks are accessible through an extensive kernel-to-userland interface represented by files in the **/proc** filesystem. In many cases, a large user-level application (especially an "infrastructure" application such as a database) will require you to adjust parameters to accommodate its needs.

Drivers / Kernel

Special files in **/proc/sys** let you view and set kernel options at run time. These files mimic standard Linux files, but they are really back doors into the kernel. If one of these files has a value you would like to change, you can try writing to it. Unfortunately, not all of the files can be written to (regardless of their apparent permissions), and no documentation tells you which ones can and cannot be written.

For example, to change the maximum number of open files a process can have, try something like

```
# echo 32768 > /proc/sys/fs/file-max
```

Once you get used to this unorthodox interface, you'll find it quite useful, especially for changing configuration options. A word of caution, however: changes are not remembered across reboots. If you want to make permanent changes, you should use the **/etc/sysctl.conf** file documented below. Table 12.1 lists some useful options.

Table 12.1   Files in /proc/sys for some sample tunable kernel parameters

Dir[a]	File	Default	Function
F	**file-max**	4096	Sets max # of open files per process
F	**inode-max**	16384	Sets max # of open inodes per process
N	**ip_forward**	0	Allows IP forwarding when set to 1
N	**icmp_echo_ignore_all**	0	Ignores ICMP pings when set to 1
N	**icmp_echo_ignore_broadcasts**	0	Ignores broadcast pings when set to 1
K	**shmmax**	32M	Sets max shared memory size
K	**ctrl-alt-del**	0	Reboot on Ctrl-Alt-Delete sequence?
C	**autoeject**	0	Auto-eject CD-ROM on dismount?

a. F = **/proc/sys/fs**, N = **/proc/sys/net/ipv4**, K = **/proc/sys/kernel**, C = **/proc/sys/dev/cdrom**

See page 284 in the TCP chapter to learn about additional network parameters that are tunable.

A less kludgy way to modify these same parameters can be found on most systems in the form of the **sysctl** command. **sysctl** can set individual variables either from the command line or by reading a list of *variable=value* pairs from a file. By default, the file **/etc/sysctl.conf** is read at boot time and its contents used to set initial (custom) parameter values.

For example, the command

```
# sysctl net.ipv4.ip_forward=0
```

turns off IP forwarding. Note that you form the variable names used by **sysctl** by replacing the /'s in the **/proc/sys** directory structure with dots.

12.5 Adding device drivers

A device driver is a program that manages the system's interaction with a piece of hardware. The driver translates between the hardware commands understood by the device and the stylized programming interface used by the kernel. The existence of the driver layer helps keep Linux reasonably device independent.

Device drivers are part of the kernel; they are not user processes. However, a driver can be accessed both from within the kernel and from user space. User-level access to devices is usually provided through special device files that live in the **/dev** directory. The kernel transforms operations on these files into calls to the code of the driver.

The PC platform has been a source of chaos in the system administrator's world. A dizzying array of hardware and "standards" with varying levels of operating system support are available. Behold:

- Over 30 different SCSI chipsets are supported by Linux, and each is packaged and sold by at least twice that many vendors.

- Over 200 different network interfaces are out there, each being marketed by several different vendors under different names.

- Newer, better, cheaper types of hardware are being developed all the time. Each will require a device driver in order to work with your Linux of choice.

With the remarkable pace at which new hardware is being developed, it is practically impossible to keep the mainline OS distributions up to date with the latest hardware. It is not at all uncommon to have to add a device driver to your kernel to support a new piece of hardware.

Only device drivers designed for use with Linux (and usually, a specific version of the Linux kernel) can be successfully installed on a Linux system. Drivers for other operating systems (like Windows) will not work, so you will need to purchase new hardware with this in mind. In addition, devices vary in their degree of compatibility and functionality when used with Linux, so it's wise to pay some attention to the results other sites have obtained with any hardware you are considering.

Vendors are becoming more aware of the Linux market, and they even provide Linux drivers on occasion. You may be lucky and find that your vendor will furnish you with both drivers and installation instructions. More likely, you will only find the driver you need on some uncommented web page. In either case, this section shows you what is really going on when you add a device driver.

Device numbers

Many devices have a corresponding file in **/dev**, the notable exceptions on modern operating systems being network devices. By virtue of being device files, the files in **/dev** each have a major and minor device number associated with them. The kernel uses these numbers to map references to a device file to the corresponding driver.

The major device number identifies the driver with which the file is associated (in other words, the type of device). The minor device number usually identifies which particular instance of a given device type is to be addressed. The minor device number is sometimes called the unit number.

You can see the major and minor number of a device file with **ls -l**:

```
% ls -l /dev/sda
brw-rw---- 1 root    disk    8,   0 Mar  3 1999 /dev/sda
```

This example shows the first SCSI disk on a Linux system. It has a major number of 8 and a minor number of 0.

The minor device number is sometimes used by the driver to select the particular characteristic of a device. For example, a single tape drive can have several files in **/dev** representing it in various configurations of recording density and rewind characteristics. In essence, the driver is free to interpret the minor device number in whatever way it wants. Look up the man page for the driver to determine what convention it's using.

There are actually two types of device files: block device files and character device files. A block device is read or written one block (a group of bytes, usually a multiple of 512) at a time; a character device can be read or written one byte at a time. Some devices support access through both block and character device files, although this is extremely rare under Linux.

It is sometimes convenient to implement an abstraction as a device driver even when it controls no actual device. Such phantom devices are known as pseudo-devices. For example, a user who logs in over the network is assigned a PTY (pseudo-TTY) that looks, feels, and smells like a serial port from the perspective of high-level software. This trick allows programs written in the days when everyone used a TTY to continue to function in the world of windows and networks.

When a program performs an operation on a device file, the kernel automatically catches the reference, looks up the appropriate function name in a table, and transfers control to it. To perform an unusual operation that doesn't have a direct analog in the filesystem model (for example, ejecting a floppy disk), a program can use the **ioctl** system call to pass a message directly from user space into the driver.

12.6 ADDING A LINUX DEVICE DRIVER

On Linux systems, device drivers are typically distributed in one of three forms:

- A patch against a specific kernel version
- A loadable module
- An installation script that applies appropriate patches

The most common of all these is the patch against a specific kernel version. These patches can in most cases be applied with the following procedure:[1]

```
# cd /usr/src/linux ; patch -p1 < patch_file
```

Diffs made against a different minor version of the kernel may fail, but the driver should still work. Here, we cover how to manually add a network "snarf" driver to the

---

1. Of course, the kernel source package must be installed before you can modify the kernel tree.

kernel. It's a very complicated and tedious process, especially when compared to other operating systems we've seen.

By convention, Linux kernel source resides in **/usr/src/linux**. Within the **drivers** subdirectory, you'll need to find the subdirectory that corresponds to the type of device you have. A directory listing of **drivers** looks like this:

```
% ls -F /usr/src/linux/drivers
Makefile    cdrom/    i2o/          nubus/      sbus/      telephony/
acorn/      char/     isdn/         parport/    scsi/      usb/
ap1000/     dio/      macintosh/    pci/        sgi/       video/
atm/        fc4/      misc/         pcmcia/     sound/     zorro/
block/      i2c/      net/          pnp/        tc/
```

The most common directories to which drivers are added are **block**, **char**, **net**, **usb**, **sound**, and **scsi**. These directories contain drivers for block devices (such as IDE disk drives), character devices (such as serial ports), network devices, USB devices, sound cards, and SCSI cards, respectively. Some of the other directories contain drivers for the buses themselves (e.g., **pci**, **nubus**, and **zorro**); it's unlikely that you will need to add drivers to these directories. Some directories contain platform-specific drivers, such as **macintosh**, **acorn**, and **ap1000**. Some directories contain specialty devices such as **atm**, **isdn**, and **telephony**.

Since our example device is a network-related device, we will add the driver to the directory **drivers/net**. We'll need to modify the following files:

- **drivers/net/Makefile**, so that our driver will be compiled
- **drivers/net/Config.in**, so that our device will appear in the config options
- **drivers/net/Space.c**, so that the device will be probed on startup

After putting the **.c** and **.h** files for the driver in **drivers/net**, we'll add the driver to **drivers/net/Makefile**. The lines we'd add (near the end of the file) follow.

```
ifeq ($(CONFIG_SNARF),y)
    L_OBJS += snarf.o
else
    ifeq ($(CONFIG_SNARF),m)
    M_OBJS += snarf.o
    endif
endif
```

This configuration adds the snarf driver so that it can be either configured as a module or built into the kernel.

After adding the device to the **Makefile**, we have to make sure we can configure the device when we configure the kernel. All network devices need to be listed in the file **drivers/net/Config.in**. To add the device so that it can be built either as a module or as part of the kernel (consistent with what we claimed in the **Makefile**), we add the following line:

```
tristate 'Snarf device support' CONFIG_SNARF
```

Drivers / Kernel

The tristate keyword means you can build the device as a module. If the device cannot be built as a module, use the keyword bool instead of tristate. The next token is the string to display on the configuration screen. It can be any arbitrary text, but it should identify the device that is being configured. The final token is the configuration macro. This token needs to be the same as that tested for with the ifeq clause in the **Makefile**.

The last file we need to edit to add our device to the system is **drivers/net/Space.c**. **Space.c** contains references to the probe routines for the device driver, and it also controls the device probe order. Here, we'll have to edit the file in two different places. First we'll add a reference to the probe function, then we'll add the device to the list of devices to probe for.

At the top of the **Space.c** file are a bunch of references to other probe functions. We'll add the following line to that list:

```
extern int snarf_probe(struct device *);
```

Next, to add the device to the actual probe list, we need to determine which list to add it to. A separate probe list is kept for each type of bus (PCI, EISA, SBus, MCA, ISA, parallel port, etc.). The snarf device is a PCI device, so we'll add it to the list called pci_probes. The line that says

```
struct devprobe pci_probes[] __initdata = {
```

is followed by an ordered list of devices. The devices higher up in the list are probed first. Probe order does not usually matter for PCI devices, but some devices are sensitive. Just to be sure the snarf device is detected, we'll add it to the top of the list:

```
struct devprobe pci_probes[] __initdata = {
#ifdef CONFIG_SNARF
    snarf_probe, 0},
#endif
```

The device has now been added to the Linux kernel. When we next configure the kernel, the device should appear as a configuration option under "network devices."

12.7 DEVICE FILES

By convention, device files are kept in the **/dev** directory. Large systems, especially those with networking and pseudo-terminals, may support hundreds of devices.

Device files are created with the **mknod** command, which has the syntax

mknod *filename type major minor*

Official Linux device number assignments can be found at www.lanana.org.

where *filename* is the device file to be created, *type* is **c** for a character device or **b** for a block device, and *major* and *minor* are the major and minor device numbers. If you are creating a device file that refers to a driver that's already present in your kernel, check the man page for the driver to find the appropriate major and minor device numbers.

Red Hat and Debian provide a script called **MAKEDEV** (in **/dev**) to automatically supply default values to **mknod**. Study the script to find the arguments needed for your device. For example, to make PTY entries, you'd use the following commands:

```
# cd /dev
# ./MAKEDEV pty
```

Naming conventions for devices

Naming conventions for devices are somewhat random. They are often holdovers from the way things were done under UNIX on a DEC PDP-11, as archaic as that may sound in this day and age.

See Chapter 7 for more information about serial ports. Serial device files are named **ttyS** followed by a number that identifies the specific interface to which the port is attached. TTYs are sometimes represented by more than one device file; the extra files usually provide access to alternative flow control methods or locking protocols.

The names of tape devices often include not only a reference to the drive itself but also an indication of whether the device rewinds after each tape operation and the density at which it reads and writes.

IDE hard disk devices are named **/dev/hd**LP, where L is a letter that identifies the unit (with **a** being the master on the first IDE interface, **b** being the slave on that interface, **c** being the master on the second IDE interface, etc.) and P is the partition number (starting with 1). For example, the first partition on the first IDE disk is typically **/dev/hda1**. SCSI disks are named similarly, but with the prefix **/dev/sd** instead of **/dev/hd**. You can drop the partition number on both types of devices to access the entire disk (e.g., **/dev/hda**).

SCSI CD-ROM drives are referred to by the files **/dev/scd**N, where N is a number that distinguishes multiple CD-ROM drives. Modern IDE (ATAPI) CD-ROM drives are referred to just like IDE hard disks (e.g., **/dev/hdc**).

12.8 LOADABLE KERNEL MODULES

Loadable kernel module (LKM) support allows a device driver—or any other kernel service—to be linked into and removed from the kernel while it is running. This facility makes the installation of drivers much easier, since the kernel binary does not need to be changed. It also allows the kernel to be smaller because drivers are not loaded unless they are needed.

Loadable modules are implemented by one or more documented "hooks" into the kernel that additional device drivers can grab onto. A user-level command communicates with the kernel and tells it to load new modules into memory. There is usually a command that unloads drivers as well.

Although loadable drivers are convenient, they are not entirely safe. Any time you load or unload a module, you risk causing a kernel panic. We don't recommend loading or unloading an untested module when you are not willing to crash the machine.

Drivers / Kernel

Under Linux, almost anything can be built as a loadable kernel module. The exceptions are the root filesystem type, the device on which the root filesystem resides, and the PS/2 mouse driver.

Loadable kernel modules are conventionally stored under **/lib/modules/***version*, where *version* is the version of your Linux kernel as returned by **uname -r**. You can inspect the currently loaded modules with the **lsmod** command:

```
# lsmod
Module          Size    Used by
ppp             21452   0
slhc            4236    0 [ppp]
ds              6344    1
i82365          26648   1
pcmcia_core     37024   0 [ds   i82365]
```

This machine has the PCMCIA controller modules, the PPP driver, and the PPP header compression modules loaded.

Linux LKMs can be manually loaded into the kernel with **insmod**. For example, we could manually insert our example snarf module with the command

```
# insmod /path/to/snarf.o
```

Parameters can also be passed to loadable kernel modules; for example,

```
# insmod /path/to/snarf.o io=0xXXX irq=X
```

Once a loadable kernel module has been manually inserted into the kernel, it will only be removed if you explicitly request its removal or if the system is rebooted. We could use **rmmod snarf** to remove our snarf module.

You can use **rmmod** at any time, but it works only if the number of current references to the module (listed in the Used by column of **lsmod**'s output) is 0.

You can also load Linux LKMs semiautomatically with **modprobe**, a wrapper for **insmod** that understands dependencies, options, and installation and removal procedures. **modprobe** uses the **/etc/modules.conf** file to figure out how to handle each module.

You can dynamically generate an **/etc/modules.conf** file that corresponds to all your currently installed modules by running **modprobe -c**. This command generates a long file that looks like this:

```
#This file was generated by: modprobe -c (2.1.121)
path[pcmcia]=/lib/modules/preferred
path[pcmcia]=/lib/modules/default
path[pcmcia]=/lib/modules/2.3.39
path[misc]=/lib/modules/2.3.39
...
# Aliases
alias block-major-1 rd
alias block-major-2 floppy
```

```
...
alias char-major-4 serial
alias char-major-5 serial
alias char-major-6 lp
...
alias dos msdos
alias plip0 plip
alias ppp0 ppp
options ne io=x0340 irq=9
```

The path statements tell where a particular module can be found. You can modify or add entries of this type if you want to keep your modules in a nonstandard location.

The alias statement provides a mapping between block major device numbers, character major device numbers, filesystems, network devices, and network protocols and their corresponding module names.

The options lines are not dynamically generated. They specify options that should be passed to a module when it is loaded. For example, we could use the following line to tell the snarf module its proper I/O address and interrupt vector:[2]

```
options snarf io=0xXXX irq=X
```

modprobe also understands the statements pre-install, post-install, pre-remove, post-remove, install, and remove. These statements allow commands to be executed when a specific module is inserted into or removed from the running kernel. They take the following form

```
pre-install module command ...
install module command ...
post-install module command ...
pre-remove module command ...
remove module command ...
post-remove module command ...
```

and are run before insertion, simultaneously with insertion (if possible), after insertion, before removal, during removal (if possible), and after removal.

 Debian systems execute **/etc/cron.daily/modutils** once a day to shoo away any modules that have overstayed their welcome in the kernel.

12.9 BUILDING A LINUX KERNEL

Because Linux is evolving so rapidly, it is much more likely that you'll be faced with the need to build a Linux kernel than you would if you were running a big-iron operating system. Kernel patches, device drivers, and new functionality are constantly becoming available. This is really something of a mixed blessing. On one hand, it's convenient to always have support for the "latest and greatest," but on the other hand

---

2. If you're using PC hardware, it can be a challenge to create a configuration in which device interrupt request vectors (IRQs) and I/O ports do not overlap. You can view the current assignments on your system by examining the contents of **/proc/interrupts** and **/proc/ioports**, respectively.

it can become quite time consuming to keep up with the constant flow of new material. But after you successfully build a kernel once, you'll feel empowered and eager to do it again.

It's less likely that you'll need to build a kernel on your own if you're running a "stable" version. Linux has adopted a versioning scheme in which the second part of the version number indicates whether the kernel is stable (even numbers) or in development (odd numbers). For example, kernel version 2.4.3 would be a "stable" kernel, whereas 2.5.3 would be a "development" kernel. Now you know.

Linux kernel configuration has come a long way, but it still feels very primitive compared to the procedures used on some other systems. The process revolves around the **.config** file in the root of the kernel source directory (usually **/usr/src/linux**).[3] All of the kernel configuration information is specified in this file, but its format is somewhat cryptic. Use the decoding guide in **Documentation/Configure.help** to find out what the various options mean.

To save folks from having to edit the **.config** file directly, Linux has several **make** targets that let you configure the kernel with different interfaces. If you are running X Windows, the prettiest configuration interface is provided by **make xconfig**. This command brings up a graphical configuration screen on which you can pick the devices to add to your kernel (or compile as loadable modules).

If you are not running X, you can use a **curses**-based[4] alternative invoked with **make menuconfig**. Finally, there is the older style **make config**, which prompts you to respond to every single configuration option available without letting you later go back and change your mind.

We recommend **make xconfig** if you are running X and **make menuconfig** if you aren't. Avoid **make config**.

These tools are straightforward as far as the options you can turn on, but unfortunately they are painful to use if you want to maintain several versions of the kernel for multiple architectures or hardware configurations.

The various configuration interfaces described above all generate a **.config** file that looks something like this:

```
# Automatically generated make config: don't edit
#
# Code maturity level options

CONFIG_EXPERIMENTAL=y
#
# Processor type and features
#
```

---

3. Again, you will need to install the kernel source package before you can build a kernel on your system; see page 733 for tips on package installation.

4. **curses** is a library from the days of yore used to create text-based GUIs that run in a terminal window.

```
# CONFIG_M386 is not set
# CONFIG_M486 is not set
# CONFIG_M586 is not set
# CONFIG_M586TSC is not set
CONFIG_M686=y
CONFIG_X86_WP_WORKS_OK=y
CONFIG_X86_INVLPG=y
CONFIG_X86_BSWAP=y
CONFIG_X86_POPAD_OK=y
CONFIG_X86_TSC=y
CONFIG_X86_GOOD_APIC=y
...
```

As you can see, the contents are rather cryptic and provide no descriptions of what the CONFIG tags mean. Sometimes you can figure out the meaning. Basically, each CONFIG line refers to a specific kernel configuration option. The value **y** compiles the option into the kernel; **m** enables it, but as a loadable module.

Some things can be configured as modules and some can't. You just have to know which is which; it's not clear from the **.config** file. There is also no easy mapping of the CONFIG tags to meaningful information. However, you can usually extract this information from the **Config.in** file located in each driver directory. The **Config.in** files are difficult and inconvenient to track down, so it's best to just use **make xconfig** or **make menuconfig**.

Once you have a working, running kernel, you may need to pass special configuration options to it at boot time, such as the root device it should use or an instruction to probe for multiple Ethernet cards. The boot loader (typically LILO or GRUB) passes in these options. You add static configuration options to the **/etc/lilo.conf** or **/boot/grub/grub.conf** file, depending on which boot loader you use. See page 23 for more information.

If it's not possible to edit the boot loader configuration file (perhaps you broke something and the machine can't boot), you can pass the options in by hand. For example, at a LILO boot prompt you could type

> LILO: **linux root=/dev/hda1 ether=0,0,eth0 ether=0,0,eth1**

to tell LILO to load the kernel specified by the "linux" tag, to use the root device **/dev/hda1**, and to probe for two Ethernet cards.

A similar example using GRUB would look like this:

> grub> **kernel /vmlinuz root=/dev/hda1 ether=0,0,eth0 ether=0,0,eth1**
> grub> **boot**

Building the Linux kernel binary

Setting up an appropriate **.config** file is the most important part of the Linux kernel configuration process, but you must jump through several more hoops to turn that file into a finished kernel.

Drivers / Kernel

Here's an outline of the entire process:

- **cd** to **/usr/src/linux**.
- Run **make xconfig** or **make menuconfig**.
- Run **make dep**.
- Run **make clean**.
- Run **make bzImage**.
- Run **make modules**.
- Run **make modules_install**.
- Copy **/usr/src/linux/arch/i386/boot/bzImage** to **/boot/vmlinuz**.
- Copy **/usr/src/linux/arch/i386/boot/System.map** to **/boot/System.map**.
- Edit **/etc/lilo.conf** (LILO) or **/boot/grub/grub.conf** (GRUB) to add a configuration line for the new kernel.
- If you're using LILO, run **/sbin/lilo** to install the reconfigured boot loader.

The **make clean** step is not always strictly necessary, but it is generally a good idea to start with a clean build environment. In practice, many problems can be traced back to skipping this step.

12.10 DON'T FIX IT IF IT AIN'T BROKEN

With new Linux kernel versions arriving on the scene every few months and new drivers and patches being released every day, it's easy to become addicted to patching and upgrades. After all, what's more exciting than telling your user community that you just found a new kernel patch and that you'll be taking the mail server down for the afternoon to install it? Some administrators justify their existence this way; everybody likes to be the hero.

A good system administrator carefully weighs needs and risks when planning kernel upgrades and patches. Sure, the new release may be the latest and greatest, but is it as stable as the current version? Could the upgrade or patch be delayed and installed with another group of patches at the end of the month? It's important to resist the temptation to let "keeping up with the joneses" (in this case, the kernel hacking community) dominate the best interests of your user community.

A good rule of thumb is to upgrade or apply patches only when the productivity gains you expect to obtain (usually measured in terms of reliability and performance) will exceed the effort and lost time required to perform the installation. If you're having trouble quantifying the specific gain, that's a good sign that the patch can wait for another day.

12.11 RECOMMENDED READING

BECK, MICHAEL, ET AL. *Linux Kernel Internals, 2nd Edition*. Reading, MA: Addison-Wesley. 1998.

This is an older Linux kernel book, but it's still our favorite. Although it's a bit outdated, it gives a good explanation of the kernel's inner workings.

12.12 Exercises

E12.1 Describe what the kernel does. Explain the difference between a kernel that uses modules and one that doesn't.

E12.2 For each configuration method listed on page 221, give a practical example of a parameter that might need to be changed.

★ **E12.3** Examine the values of several parameters from Table 12.1 on page 222 using both the **/proc** method and the **sysctl** method. Change two of the values with one method and then read them back with the other method. Verify that the system's behavior has actually changed in response to your tuning. Turn in a typescript of your experiment. (Requires root access.)

★ **E12.4** At a local flea market, you get a great deal on a laptop card that gives you Ethernet connectivity through the parallel port. What steps would you need to perform to make Linux recognize this new card? Should you compile support directly into the kernel or add it as a module? Why? (Bonus question: if your hourly consulting fee is $80, estimate the value of the labor needed to get this cheapie Ethernet interface working.)

★ **E12.5** A new release of the Linux kernel just came out, and you want to upgrade all the machines in the student lab (about 50 machines, not all identical). What issues should you consider? What procedure should you follow? What problems might occur, and how would you deal with them?

★★ **E12.6** In the lab, configure a kernel with **xconfig** or **menuconfig** and build a kernel binary. Install and run the new system. Turn in **dmesg** output from the old and new kernels and highlight the differences. (Requires root access.)

SECTION TWO

NETWORKING

13 *TCP/IP Networking*

there is no need
For Microsoft to
Support TCP/IP.

GATES
1994

Microsoft has invented
a new protocol. We're
calling it TCP/IP.

GATES
1995

It would be hard to overstate the importance of networks to modern computing, although that doesn't seem to stop people from trying. At many sites, web and email access are now the main activities for which computers are used. As of mid-2001, the Internet is estimated to have 450 million users, and it still seems to be growing rapidly.[1] Maintenance of local networks, Internet connections, web sites, and network-related software is a bread-and-butter portion of most sysadmins' jobs.

TCP/IP is the networking protocol suite most commonly used with Linux/UNIX, MacOS, Windows, and most other operating systems. It is also the native language of the Internet. TCP stands for Transmission Control Protocol and IP stands for Internet Protocol.

Devices that speak the TCP/IP protocol can exchange data ("interoperate") despite their many differences. IP, the suite's underlying delivery protocol, is the workhorse of the Internet. TCP and UDP (the User Datagram Protocol) are transport protocols built on top of IP to deliver packets to specific applications.

TCP is a connection-oriented protocol that facilitates a conversation between two programs. It works a lot like a phone call: the words you speak are delivered to the person you called, and vice versa. The connection persists even when neither party is speaking. TCP provides reliable delivery, flow control, and congestion control.

UDP is a packet-oriented service. It's analogous to sending a letter through the post office. It does not provide two-way connections, does not have any form of congestion

TCP/IP

---

1. See www.netsizer.com for a current estimate.

control, and does not guarantee that packets will be delivered in the same order they were sent.

TCP is a polite protocol that forces competing users to share bandwidth and generally behave in ways that are good for the productivity of the overall network. UDP, on the other hand, blasts packets out as fast as it can.

As the Internet becomes more popular and more crowded, we need the traffic to be mostly TCP to avoid congestion and effectively share the available bandwidth. Measurements of protocol utilization over the past few years showed UDP traffic increasing from about 5% of the bytes in 1997–1998 to about 7% in 1999–2000. In 2001, TCP was on the upswing again with UDP down to 3%–4% of the bytes and about 12% of the packets. Applications such as games, music, voice, and video are making their presence felt but are overwhelmed by the web and by programs such as Gnutella that are popular bandwidth hogs but use TCP instead of UDP for transport.

This chapter introduces the TCP/IP protocols in the political and technical context of the Internet. Unfortunately, even basic networking is too big a topic to be covered in a single chapter. Other network-related chapters in this book include Chapter 14, *Routing*, Chapter 20, *Network Management and Debugging*, Chapter 16, *The Domain Name System*, and Chapter 21, *Security*.

The next few sections include background material on the protocols and politics of the Internet and are quite opinionated and fluffy. Skip ahead to page 247 to go directly to the gory details of IP, or to page 274 to jump to distribution-specific configuration information.

13.1 TCP/IP AND THE INTERNET

TCP/IP and the Internet share a history that goes back several decades. The technical success of the Internet is due largely to the elegant and flexible design of TCP/IP and to the fact that it is an open and nonproprietary protocol suite. In turn, the leverage provided by the Internet has helped TCP/IP prevail over several competing protocol suites that were favored at one time or another for political or commercial reasons.

A brief history lesson

Contrary to popular belief, the Internet is not a Microsoft product that debuted in 1995, nor is it the creation of a U.S. vice president. The progenitor of the modern Internet was a network called ARPANET that was established in 1969 by DARPA (Defense Advanced Research Project Agency), the R&D arm of the U.S. Department of Defense. The ARPANET eventually became the NSFNET backbone, which connected supercomputer sites and regional networks.

By the end of the 1980s, the network was no longer a research project and it was time for the National Science Foundation to extract itself from the networking business. We transitioned to the commercial Internet over a period of several years; the NSF-

NET was turned off in April of 1994. Today's backbone Internet is a collection of private networks owned by Internet service providers (ISPs) that interconnect at many so-called peering points.

In the mid-1980s, the Internet essentially consisted of the original ARPANET sites and a handful of universities with Digital Equipment Corporation's VAX computers running Berkeley UNIX on 10 Mb/s Ethernets connected by 56 Kb/s leased digital telephone lines. Every September, when students went back to school, the Internet would suffer what became known as congestion collapse. Van Jacobson, then a researcher in the Network Research Group at Lawrence Berkeley Labs, would look at the protocols' behavior under load and fix them. The algorithms we now know as *slow start*, *congestion avoidance*, *fast retransmit*, and *fast recovery* arose from this context.

Moore's law (the rule of thumb that hardware speeds double every 18 months) and market pressure have greatly accelerated the development of the Internet. Since the late 1980s when the current TCP algorithms were stabilized, the speed of network interfaces has increased by a factor of 1,000 (from 6% efficiency on early 10 Mb/s Ethernets to near 90% efficiency on gigabit Ethernets), the speed of leased circuits by a factor of 12,000, and the total number of hosts by a factor of 50,000.

In 1996, Bob Metcalfe, the inventor of Ethernet, predicted that the Internet would collapse because infrastructure would not be installed fast enough to keep up with customer demand, resulting in long outages and a network that was unusable. Fortunately, the Internet gold rush seems to have left us with excess capacity rather than a shortage, at least for the immediate future.

Anyone who has designed a software system and seen it obsoleted by the next generation of hardware or the next release of an operating system knows how amazing it is that our Internet is still alive and kicking, running basically the same TCP/IP protocol suite that was designed 25 years ago for a very different Internet. Our hats are off to Bob Kahn, Vint Cerf, Jon Postel, Van Jacobson, and all the other people who made it happen.

How the Internet is managed today

The development of the Internet has always been a cooperative and open effort. Now that it is a driving commercial force in the world economy, several sectors are worried that the Internet seems to be in the hands of a bunch of computer geeks, with perhaps a little direction from the U.S. government. Like it or not, Internet governance is coming.

Several organizations are involved:

- ICANN, the Internet Corporation for Assigned Names and Numbers: if anyone can be said to be in charge of the Internet, this group is it. (www.icann.org)

- ISOC, the Internet Society: ISOC is a membership organization that represents Internet users. (www.isoc.org)

- IETF, the Internet Engineering Task Force: this group oversees the development and standardization of the technical aspects of the Internet. It is an open forum in which anyone can participate. (www.ietf.org)

Of these groups, ICANN has the toughest job: establishing itself as the authority in charge of the Internet, undoing the mistakes of the past, and foreseeing the future.

Network standards and documentation

The technical activities of the Internet community are summarized in documents known as RFCs; an RFC is a Request for Comments. Protocol standards, proposed changes, and informational bulletins all usually end up as RFCs. RFCs start their lives as Internet Drafts, and after lots of email wrangling and IETF meetings they either die or are promoted to the RFC series. Anyone who has comments on a draft or proposed RFC is encouraged to reply. In addition to standardizing the Internet protocols, the RFC mechanism sometimes just documents or explains aspects of existing practice.

RFCs are numbered sequentially; currently, there are about 3,000. RFCs also have descriptive titles (e.g., *Algorithms for Synchronizing Network Clocks*), but to forestall ambiguity they are usually cited by number. Once distributed, the contents of an RFC are never changed. Updates are distributed as new RFCs with their own reference numbers. By convention, updated RFCs contain all the material that remains relevant, so the new RFCs completely replace the old ones, at least in theory.

The process by which RFCs are published is itself documented in the RFC titled *Internet Official Protocol Standards*. This RFC also includes pointers to the most current RFCs for various protocol standards. Since the information changes frequently, this RFC is reissued every 100 RFCs. The Internet standards process itself is detailed in RFC2026. Another useful meta-RFC is RFC2555, *30 Years of RFCs*, which describes some of the cultural and technical context behind the RFC system.

Don't be scared away by the wealth of technical detail found in RFCs. Most contain introductions, summaries, and rationales that are useful for system administrators. Some are specifically written as overviews or general introductions. RFCs may not be the gentlest way to learn about a topic, but they are authoritative, concise, and free.

Not all RFCs are dry and full of boring technical details. Some of our favorites on the lighter side (often written on April 1st) are RFCs 1118, 1149, 1925, 2324, and 2795:

- RFC1118 – *The Hitchhiker's Guide to the Internet*
- RFC1149 – *A Standard for the Transmission of IP Datagrams on Avian Carriers*[2]
- RFC1925 – *The Twelve Networking Truths*
- RFC2324 – *Hyper Text Coffee Pot Control Protocol (HTCPCP/1.0)*
- RFC2795 – *The Infinite Monkey Protocol Suite (IMPS)*

---

2. A group of Linux enthusiasts from BLUG, the Bergen (Norway) Linux User Group, actually implemented the Carrier Pigeon Internet Protocol (CPIP) as specified in RFC1149. For details, see the web site www.blug.linux.no/rfc1149!

They are a good read and give a bit of insight into the people who are designing and building our Internet.

In addition to being assigned its own serial number, an RFC may also be assigned an FYI (For Your Information) number, a BCP (Best Current Practice) number, or a STD (Standard) number. FYIs, STDs, and BCPs are subseries of the RFCs that include documents of special interest or importance.

FYIs are introductory or informational documents intended for a broad audience. They are usually an excellent place to start research on an unfamiliar topic. STDs document Internet protocols that have completed the IETF's review and testing process and have been formally adopted as standards. BCPs document recommended procedures for Internet sites; they consist of administrative suggestions and for system administrators are often the most valuable of the RFC subseries.

RFCs, FYIs, STDs, and BCPs are numbered sequentially within their own series, so a document can bear several different identifying numbers. For example, RFC1635, *How to Use Anonymous FTP*, is also known as FYI0024.

RFCs are available from numerous sources. There's a list of actively maintained RFC mirrors at www.rfc-editor.org, which is dispatch central for RFC-related matters.

13.2 NETWORKING ROAD MAP

Now that we've provided a bit of context, let's take a look at the TCP/IP protocols themselves. TCP/IP is a "protocol suite," a set of network protocols designed to work smoothly together. It includes several components, each defined by a standards-track RFC or series of RFCs:

- IP, the Internet Protocol, which routes data packets from one machine to another (RFC791)

- ICMP, the Internet Control Message Protocol, which provides several kinds of low-level support for IP, including error messages, routing assistance, and debugging help (RFC792)

- ARP, the Address Resolution Protocol, which translates IP addresses to hardware addresses (RFC823)[3]

- UDP, the User Datagram Protocol, and TCP, the Transmission Control Protocol, which deliver data to specific applications on the destination machine. UDP provides unverified, "best effort" transport for individual messages, whereas TCP guarantees a reliable, full duplex, flow-controlled, error-corrected conversation between processes on two hosts. (RFCs 768 and 793)

TCP/IP is designed around the layering scheme shown in Table 13.1 on the next page.

TCP/IP

---

3. This is actually a little white lie. ARP is not really part of TCP/IP and can be used with other protocol suites. However, it's an integral part of the way TCP/IP works on most LAN media.

Table 13.1   TCP/IP network model

Layer	Function
Application layer	End-user application programs
Transport layer	Delivery of data to applications[a]
Network layer	Basic communication, addressing, and routing
Link layer	Network hardware and device drivers
Physical layer	The cable or physical medium itself

a. Optionally addressing reliability and flow control issues

After TCP/IP had been implemented and deployed, the International Organization for Standardization came up with its own seven-layer protocol suite called OSI. It was a consummate design-by-committee white elephant, and it never really caught on because of its complexity and inefficiency. Some think a financial layer and a political layer should have been added to the original seven OSI layers.[4]

Exhibit A shows how the various components and clients of TCP/IP fit into its general architecture and layering scheme.

Exhibit A   One big happy TCP/IP family

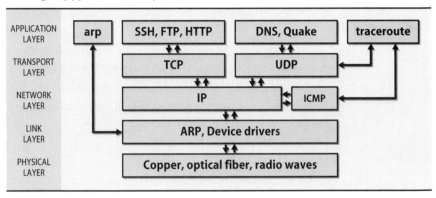

13.3   PACKETS AND ENCAPSULATION

Linux can support a variety of physical networks, including Ethernet, FDDI, token ring, ATM (Asynchronous Transfer Mode), wireless Ethernet, and serial-line-based systems. Hardware is managed within the link layer of the TCP/IP architecture, and higher-level protocols do not know or care about the specific hardware being used.

Data travels on a network in the form of *packets*, bursts of data with a maximum length imposed by the link layer. Each packet consists of a header and a payload. The

4. In fact, a T-shirt showing this extended nine-layer model is available from the computer science department at the University of Colorado. Email tshirt@cs.colorado.edu for details.

header tells where the packet came from and where it's going. It can also include checksums, protocol-specific information, or other handling instructions. The payload is the data to be transferred.

The name of the primitive data unit depends on the layer of the protocol. At the link layer it is called a *frame*, at the IP layer a *packet*, and at the TCP layer a *segment*. Here, we use "packet" as a generic term that encompasses all these cases.

As a packet travels down the protocol stack (from TCP or UDP transport to IP to Ethernet to the physical wire) in preparation for being sent, each protocol adds its own header information. Each protocol's finished packet becomes the payload part of the packet generated by the next protocol. This nesting is known as encapsulation. On the receiving machine, the encapsulation is reversed as the packet travels back up the protocol stack.

For example, a UDP packet being transmitted over Ethernet contains three different wrappers or envelopes. On the Ethernet wire, it is "framed" with a simple header that lists the source and next-hop destination hardware addresses, the length of the frame, and the frame's checksum (CRC). The Ethernet frame's payload is an IP packet, the IP packet's payload is a UDP packet, and the UDP packet's payload is the actual data being transmitted. Exhibit B shows the components of such a frame.

Exhibit B   **A typical network packet**

Ethernet header	IP header	UDP header	Application data	Ethernet CRC
14 bytes	20 bytes	8 bytes	100 bytes	4 bytes

UDP packet (108 bytes)

IP packet (128 bytes)

Ethernet frame (146 bytes)

We use the term "byte" to refer to an 8-bit data unit. In days of yore, "byte" was a more general term, so you will often see the term "octet" used in RFCs instead.

The link layer

In this section, we cover several topics that bridge the gap between the lowest layers of the networking software and the network hardware itself.

Ethernet framing standards

One of the main chores of the link layer is to add headers to packets and to put separators between them. The headers contain the packets' link-layer addressing information and checksums, and the separators ensure that receivers can tell where one packet stops and the next one begins. The process of adding these extra bits is known generically as framing.

TCP/IP

Two different standards for 10 Mb/s Ethernet framing are in common use: DIX Ethernet II and the IEEE 802.2 LLC SNAP.[5] Linux hosts use Ethernet II, as do most UNIX hosts and Cisco routers. Novell or IPX networks and Windows hosts normally use 802.2. Ethernet II and 802.2 differ in some fields of the frame header but do not conflict, so receivers can determine unambiguously which format is being used by each individual packet and decode the header appropriately.

The framing that a machine uses is determined both by its interface card and by the interface card's driver. On PCs running Windows you can choose which style of framing you want, but on Linux you usually cannot. Both types of framing interoperate just fine from Linux's perspective. On the other hand, Windows machines that use different framing on the same network cannot talk to each other. As a sysadmin, you usually don't need to worry about framing mismatches unless you are performing low-level debugging of a mixed network.

Ethernet cabling and signalling standards

The cabling options for the various Ethernet speeds (10 Mb/s, 100 Mb/s, 1 Gb/s, and now 10 Gb/s) are usually specified as part of the IEEE's standardization efforts. Often, a single type of cable with short distance limits will be approved as a new technology emerges. Cheaper media types and more generous limits will be added later.

Refer to Chapter 15, *Network Hardware*, for more information about the various Ethernet standards. Another useful reference to the ins and outs of Ethernet is the web site wwwhost.ots.utexas.edu/ethernet, which is maintained by Charles Spurgeon.

Wireless networking

The IEEE 802.11 standard attempts to define framing and signalling standards for wireless links. Unfortunately, it was originally rather vague and included several parameters and options that were not fully specified. One interoperability issue you may need to pay attention to is that of "translation" vs. "encapsulation."

Translation converts a packet from one format to another; encapsulation wraps the packet with the desired format. Windows systems tend to default to encapsulation and Linux systems to translation; the wireless base stations must be explicitly configured. If you are deploying a wireless network, you must make sure that your base stations and the workstations they talk to are all operating in the same mode.

Maximum transfer unit (MTU)

The size of packets on a network may be limited both by hardware specifications and by protocol conventions. For example, the payload of a standard Ethernet frame can be no longer than 1,500 bytes. The size limit is associated with the link-layer protocol and is called the maximum transfer unit or MTU. Table 13.2 shows typical values for the MTU.

---

5. The link layer is actually divided into two parts: MAC, the Media Access Control sublayer, and LLC, the Link Layer Control sublayer. The MAC layer deals with the media and gets packets onto the wire. The LLC layer handles the framing.

Table 13.2   MTUs for various types of network link layer

Network type	Maximum transfer unit
Ethernet	1,500 bytes (1,492 with 802.2 framing)
FDDI	4,470 bytes (4,352 for IP/FDDI)
Token ring	Configurable[a]
PPP modem link	Configurable, often 512 or 576 bytes
PC stacks	Configurable, usually defaults to 512
Point-to-point WAN links (T1, T3)	Configurable, often 1,500 or 4,500 bytes

a. Common values are 552; 1,064; 2,088; 4,508; and 8,232. Sometimes 1,500 to match Ethernet.

In the TCP/IP suite, the IP layer splits packets to conform to the MTU of a particular network link. If a packet is routed through several networks, one of the intermediate networks may have a smaller MTU than the network of origin. In this case, the router that forwards the packet onto the small-MTU network will further subdivide the packet in a process called fragmentation. Fragmentation is an unwelcome chore for a busy router. The TCP protocol can determine the smallest MTU along the path to the destination and use that size from the outset. UDP is not so nice and is happy to shunt extra work to the IP layer. In IPv6, a new protocol winding its way through the standards process, intermediate routers can no longer perform fragmentation; MTU discovery is required.

Fragmentation problems can be insidious. If you are using a tunneled architecture for a virtual private network, for example, you should look at the size of the packets that are traversing the tunnel. They are often 1,500 bytes to start with, but once the tunneling header is added, they become 1,540 bytes or so and must be fragmented. Setting the MTU of the link to a smaller value will avert fragmentation and increase the overall performance of the tunneled network. Consult the **ifconfig** man page to see how to set an interface's MTU.

Packet addressing

Like letters or email messages, network packets must be properly addressed in order to reach their destinations. Several addressing schemes are used in combination:

- MAC (medium access control) addresses for hardware
- IP addresses for software
- Hostnames for people

A host's network interface usually has a link-layer MAC address that distinguishes it from other machines on the physical network, an IP address that identifies it on the global Internet, and a hostname that's used by humans.

The lowest level of addressing is dictated by network hardware. For example, Ethernet devices are assigned a unique 6-byte hardware address at the time of manufacture.[6] Token ring interfaces have a similar address that is also 6 bytes long. Some

TCP/IP

point-to-point networks (such as PPP, described on page 290) need no hardware addresses at all; the identity of the destination is specified as the link is established.

A 6-byte Ethernet address is divided into two parts: the first three bytes identify the manufacturer of the hardware, and the last three bytes are a unique serial number that the manufacturer assigns. Sysadmins can often identify at least the brand of machine that is trashing the network by looking up the 3-byte identifier in a table of vendor IDs. A current vendor table is available from

http://www.iana.org/assignments/ethernet-numbers

This information used to be published regularly in the RFC series, but it is no longer distributed that way. RFC1700 (1994) was the last *Assigned Numbers* RFC. The official repository of all the Internet's magic numbers is www.iana.org/numbers.htm.

Ethernet hardware addresses should be permanently assigned and immutable; unfortunately, some network interface cards let you specify the hardware address. Wireless cards are especially bad in this respect. Don't assign values in the multicast address range (odd second digit) or use other special values.

Linux lets you change the hardware address of the Ethernet interface, but please don't do that; it can break firewalls and some DHCP implementations. However, this feature can be handy if you have to replace a broken machine or network card and for some reason must use the old MAC address (e.g., all your switches filter it or your DHCP server hands out addresses based on MAC addresses).

At the next level up from the hardware, Internet addressing (more commonly known as IP addressing) is used. Typically, one[7] 4-byte IP address is assigned to each network interface. IP addresses are globally unique[8] and hardware independent. We ramble on for pages about IP addresses in the next section.

See page 262 for more information about ARP.
The mapping between IP addresses and hardware addresses is implemented at the link layer of the TCP/IP model. On networks that support broadcasting (i.e., networks that allow packets to be addressed to "all hosts on this physical network"), the ARP protocol allows mappings to be discovered automatically, without assistance from a system administrator.

Since IP addresses are long, seemingly random numbers, they are hard for people to remember. Linux systems allow one or more hostnames to be associated with an IP address so that users can type yahoo.com instead of 216.115.108.245. This mapping

---

6. Unique at least in theory. At one time, 3Com duplicated Ethernet numbers among cards with different types of network connector; they assumed that customers would order only a single type. This shortcut raised havoc at sites that were transitioning between media and even caused problems on 3Com's own internal network. MAC address conflicts are deadly on the same network but OK on networks that are separated by a router.

7. Network interfaces can actually have more than one IP address associated with them, but this is a specialized configuration that's used in only a few specific circumstances. See *Virtual interfaces* on page 700 for more information.

8. This is a small lie that's true in most situations. See the discussion of NAT starting on page 255 for the skinny on nonunique IP addresses.

can be set up in several ways, ranging from a static file (**/etc/hosts**) to the NIS database system to DNS, the world-wide Domain Name System. Keep in mind that hostnames are really just a convenient shorthand for IP addresses.

Ports

IP addresses identify machines, or more precisely, network interfaces on a machine. They are not specific enough to address particular processes or services. TCP and UDP extend IP addresses with a concept known as a "port." A port is 16-bit number that supplements an IP address to specify a particular communication channel. Standard services such as email, FTP, and the web all associate themselves with "well known" ports defined in **/etc/services**. To help prevent impersonation of these services, Linux systems restrict server programs from binding to port numbers under 1,024 unless they are run as root. (But anyone can communicate with a server running on a low port number; the restriction applies only to taking control of the port.)

Address types

Both the IP layer and the link layer define several different types of addresses:

- Unicast – addresses that refer to a single host (network interface, really)
- Multicast – addresses that identify a group of hosts
- Broadcast – addresses that include all hosts on the local network

Multicast addressing facilitates applications such as video conferencing in which the same set of packets must be sent to all participants. The Internet Group Management Protocol (IGMP) constructs and manages sets of hosts that are treated as one multicast destination. Multicasting is still somewhat experimental. However, the voice-over-IP and video-on-demand markets may speed up its deployment somewhat.

Multicast IP addresses begin with a byte in the range 224 to 239. Broadcast addresses reach all hosts on the local network by using a special wild card form of address in which the binary representation of the host part (defined next) is all 1s.

13.4 IP ADDRESSES: THE GORY DETAILS

An IP or Internet address is four bytes long and is divided into a network part and a host part. The network part identifies a logical network to which the address refers, and the host part identifies a machine on that network.

By convention, IP addresses are written as decimal numbers, one for each byte, separated by periods. For example, the IP address for our machine "boulder" is written as 128.138.240.1. The leftmost byte is the most significant and is always part of the network portion.

When 127 is the first byte of an address, it denotes the "loopback network," a fictitious network that has no real hardware interface and only one host. The loopback address 127.0.0.1 always refers to the current host. Its symbolic name is "localhost".

TCP/IP

An interface's IP address and other parameters are set with the **ifconfig** command. Jump ahead to page 266 for a detailed description of **ifconfig**.

IP address classes

Historically, IP addresses were grouped into "classes," depending on the first bits of the leftmost byte. The class determined which bytes of the address were in the network portion and which were in the host portion. Today, routing systems use an explicit mask to specify the network portion and can draw the line between any two bits, not just on byte boundaries. However, the traditional classes are still used as defaults when no explicit division is provided.

Classes A, B, and C denote regular IP addresses. Classes D and E are used for multicasting and research purposes. Table 13.3 describes the characteristics of each class. The network portion of an address is denoted by N, and the host portion by H.

Table 13.3   Historical Internet address classes

Class	1st byte[a]	Format	Comments
A	1-126	N.H.H.H	Very early networks, or reserved for DOD
B	128-191	N.N.H.H	Large sites, usually subnetted, were hard to get
C	192-223	N.N.N.H	Easy to get, often obtained in sets
D	224-239	–	Multicast addresses, not permanently assigned
E	240-255	–	Experimental addresses

a. The value 0 is special and is not used as the first byte of regular IP addresses. 127 is reserved for the loopback address.

Subnetting and netmasks

It is rare for a single physical network to have more than a hundred computers attached to it. Therefore, class A and class B addresses (which allow for 16,777,214 and 65,534 hosts per network, respectively) are really quite silly and wasteful. For example, the 126 class A networks use up half of the available address space.

Sites that have these addresses use a refinement of the addressing scheme called subnetting, in which part of the host portion of an address is "borrowed" to extend the network portion. For example, the four bytes of a class B address would normally be interpreted as N.N.H.H. If subnetting is used to assign the third byte to the network number rather than the host number, the address would be interpreted as N.N.N.H. This use of subnetting turns a single class B network address into 256 distinct class-C-like networks, each capable of supporting 254 hosts.

See page 266 for more information about **ifconfig**.

This reassignment is effected by use of the **ifconfig** command to associate an explicit "subnet mask" with a network interface. Each bit of the netmask that corresponds to the network portion of an IP address is set to 1, and host bits are set to 0. For example, the netmask for the N.N.N.H configuration would be 255.255.255.0 in decimal or 0xFFFFFF00 in hex. **ifconfig** normally uses the inherent class of an address to figure out which bits are part of the network. When you set an explicit mask, you simply override this behavior.

The division between network part and host part need not fall on a byte boundary. However, the network bits must be contiguous and must appear at the high order end of the address.[9]

Netmasks that do not end at a byte boundary can be annoying to decode and are often written as /XX, where XX is the number of bits in the network portion of the address. This is sometimes called CIDR (Classless Inter-Domain Routing) notation. For example, the network address 128.138.243.0/26 refers to the first of four networks whose first bytes are 128.138.243. The other three networks have 64, 128, and 192 as their fourth bytes. The netmask associated with these networks is 255.255.255.192 or 0xFFFFFFC0; in binary, it's 26 ones followed by 6 zeros. Exhibit C shows the relationships among these numbers in a bit more detail.

Exhibit C   Subnet mask base conversion

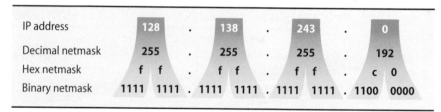

IP address	128 .	138 .	243 .	0
Decimal netmask	255 .	255 .	255 .	192
Hex netmask	f f .	f f .	f f .	c 0
Binary netmask	1111 1111 .	1111 1111 .	1111 1111 .	1100 0000

A /26 network has 6 bits left (32 – 26 = 6) to number hosts. 2^6 is 64, so the network has 64 potential host addresses. However, it can only accommodate 62 actual hosts, because the all-0 and all-1 host addresses are reserved (they are the network and broadcast addresses, respectively).

It's confusing to do all this bit twiddling in your head, but some tricks can make it simpler. The number of hosts per network and the value of the last byte in the netmask always add up to 256:

> last netmask byte = 256 – net size

For example, 256 – 64 = 192, which is the final byte of the netmask in the preceding example. Another arithmetic fact is that the last byte of an actual network address (as opposed to a netmask) must be evenly divisible by the number of hosts per network. We see this fact in action in the current example, where the last bytes are 0, 64, 128, and 192—all evenly divisible by 64.

In our example, the extra two bits of network address obtained by subnetting can take on the values 00, 01, 10, and 11. The 128.138.243.0/24 network has thus been divided into four /26 networks.

---

9. Configurations such as N.N.H.N were once allowed but were uncommon; they are no longer permitted.

- 128.138.243.0/26   (0 in decimal is **00**000000 in binary)
- 128.138.243.64/26   (64 in decimal is **01**000000 in binary)
- 128.138.243.128/26   (128 in decimal is **10**000000 in binary)
- 128.138.243.192/26   (192 in decimal is **11**000000 in binary)

The boldfaced bits of the last byte of each address are the bits that belong to the network portion of that byte.

Given an IP address (say, 128.138.243.100), we cannot tell without the associated netmask what the network address and broadcast address will be. Table 13.4 shows the possibilities for /16 (the default for a class B address), /24 (a sensible value), and /26 (a realistic value if address space is tight).

Table 13.4   Example IP address decodings

IP address	Netmask	Network	Broadcast
128.138.243.100/16	255.255.0.0	128.138.0.0	128.138.255.255
128.138.243.100/24	255.255.255.0	128.138.243.0	128.138.243.255
128.138.243.100/26	255.255.255.192	128.138.243.64	128.138.243.127

Keith Owens has written a wonderful little Perl script called **ipcalc.pl** that helps with binary/hex/mask arithmetic. It's available from ftp.ocs.com.au and requires Perl 5. **ipcalc** displays everything you might need to know about a network address and its netmask, broadcast address, hosts, etc. We've even found a version of **ipcalc** that was ported to the Palm Pilot; see www.ajw.com/ipcalc.htm.

Here's some sample **ipcalc** output, munged a bit to help with formatting:

```
% ipcalc.pl 128.138.243.100/26
IP address    128 . 138 . 243 . 100 / 26     128.138.243.100/26
Mask bits  11111111 11111111 11111111 11000000
Mask bytes    255 . 255 . 255 . 192          255.255.255.192
Address    10000000 10001010 11110011 01100100
Network       128 . 138 . 243 . 64           128.138.243.64
Broadcast     128 . 138 . 243 . 127          128.138.243.127
First Host    128 . 138 . 243 . 65           128.138.243.65
Last Host     128 . 138 . 243 . 126          128.138.243.126
Total Hosts        62
PTR                100.243.138.128.in-addr.arpa
IP Address (hex)   808AF364
```

The output provides both easy-to-understand versions of the addresses and "cut and paste" versions. Cool.

 Red Hat includes a program, also called **ipcalc**, that is pretty lame and for most calculations assumes that IP addresses are in class A, B or C.

The original RFC on IP subnetting (RFC950) did not permit the use of the first or last subnets (all 0s and all 1s). In our example with the /26 networks, this rule would eliminate half of the subnets: the 0 subnet and the 192 subnet. Everyone ignored the

RFC except Novell and Cisco. (In early versions of Cisco's IOS operating system, you had to explicitly enable subnet 0 with the ip subnet zero command. On versions 12.0 and later, subnet 0 is available by default.)

The RFC is wrong, although its intentions were fine. Subnet 0 was disallowed because it was thought that confusion might arise if a subnet address was indistinguishable from an unsubnetted network address. The fear proved groundless, however, and all-0/all-1 subnets are in common use today. It is the host portion that should not be all 0s or all 1s.

The network address and broadcast address steal two hosts from each network, so it would seem that the smallest meaningful network would have four possible hosts: two real hosts—usually at either end of a point-to-point link—and the network and broadcast addresses. To have four values for hosts requires two bits in the host portion, so such a network would be a /30 network with netmask 255.255.255.252 or 0xFFFFFFFC. However, a /31 network is treated as a special case (see RFC3021) and has no network or broadcast address; both of its two addresses are used for hosts, and its netmask is 255.255.255.254.

Although the hosts on a network may agree that they are using subnetted addresses, the rest of the world doesn't know about this and continues to treat addresses according to their implicit class.[10] Rather than advertising every subnet to the outside world, in our 128.138.243.100 example you would need to advertise only a single class B network. Once a packet arrived within the subnetted area, its destination address would be reinterpreted with local netmasks, the real target network "discovered," and the packet routed to its exact destination.

The IP address crisis

The Internet community realized in about 1992 that there were three fundamental problems with the original address allocation scheme:

- First, we were going to run out of class B addresses—the most desirable ones for moderately large organizations—by mid-1995.

- Second, the routing tables of Internet backbone sites were growing so large that they would not fit in the memory of available routers.

- Finally, IP addresses were being allocated on a first-come, first-served basis with no locality of reference; that is, numerically adjacent addresses could be within the same organization or on different continents. Imagine the confusion that would result if phone numbers or zip codes were assigned in this haphazard fashion.

To solve the problem, two solutions were advanced in tandem: one for the immediate future and one for the long term. Classless Inter-Domain Routing (CIDR), the short-term solution, is a different way of managing the existing four-byte address

---

10. Another lie in the name of a simple, as yet incomplete description; see the discussion of Classless Inter-Domain Routing (CIDR) on page 252 for the real scoop.

TCP/IP

space that uses the available addresses more efficiently and allows routing tables to be simplified by accounting for numerical adjacencies. We discuss CIDR in more detail in the next section.

The long-term solution, IPv6, is a revision of the IP protocol that expands the address space to 16 bytes and incorporates several other lessons learned from the use of IP over the last 25 years. It removes several features of IP that experience has shown to be of little value, making the protocol potentially faster and easier to implement. It also integrates security and authentication into the basic protocol and eliminates fragmentation at intermediate routers.

IPv6 is still in the early stages of deployment, but CIDR has been fully operational for years. CIDR is supported and used by the Internet backbone and by the major manufacturers of routing equipment. Network Address Translation (NAT), a scheme for reusing IP addresses that's covered on page 255, also played a large role in reducing the demand for IP addresses.

The complexity of IPv6, the efficiency of CIDR and NAT, and the inertia of an Internet that already works pretty well all combine to suggest that it may be a long time before we move to IPv6, if indeed we ever do. Such a move will likely be driven by countries such as Japan or China that cannot get the IPv4 address space they need or by a new killer application that requires IPv6. A good candidate for such an application might be a new generation of cell phones and other wireless devices that may each have an IPv6 address that would map to a telephone number. Voice-over-IP systems would also benefit from a closer correspondence between phone numbers and IPv6 addresses.

Some additional details on IPv6 addressing are given on page 257.

CIDR: Classless Inter-Domain Routing

CIDR, defined in RFC1519 (September 1993), eliminates the class system that formerly determined the network portion of an IP address. Like subnetting, of which it is a direct extension, it relies on an explicit netmask to define the boundary between the network and host parts of an address. But unlike subnetting, it allows, for purposes of routing, the network portion to be made *smaller* than would be implied by an address's implicit class. Using a shorter netmask has the effect of aggregating several networks. Hence, CIDR is sometimes referred to as supernetting.

With CIDR, several class C networks can be allocated to a site without requiring the Internet to have separate routing table entries for each one. The site could also be allocated a subspace of a class A or B address. For example, suppose a site has been given a block of 8 class C addresses numbered 192.144.0.0 through 192.144.7.0 (in CIDR notation, 192.144.0.0/21). Internally, the site could use them as

- 1 network of length /21, 2,046 hosts,[11] netmask 255.255.248.0
- 8 networks of length /24, 254 hosts each, netmask 255.255.255.0
- 16 networks of length /25, 126 hosts each, netmask 255.255.255.128
- 32 networks of length /26, 62 hosts each, netmask 255.255.255.192

and so on. It's also possible to mix and match regions of different subnet lengths, as long as all the pieces fit together without overlaps. This is called variable length subnetting. For example, an ISP with the 192.144.0.0/21 allocation could define some /30 networks for PPP dial-up customers, some /24s for large customers, and some /27s for smaller folks.

When you mix and match like this, all the hosts on a particular network must be configured with the same netmask. You cannot tell one host on the network that it is a /24 and another host on that same network that it is a /25.

The beauty and value of CIDR is that from the perspective of the Internet, it's not necessary to have 256, 128, or even 32 routing table entries for these addresses. They all refer to the same organization, and the packets all need to go to the same place. A single routing entry for the address 192.144.0.0/21 suffices. In addition, CIDR makes it easy to allocate portions of class A and B addresses and thus increases the number of available addresses manyfold.

With the advent of CIDR, system administrators have gotten good at binary and hex arithmetic, or have discovered that the Linux utility **bc** can do math in any base, using the **ibase** and **obase** directives.[12] You can use Table 13.5 as a cheat sheet.

Table 13.5   Network configurations for various lengths of netmask

Length[a]	Host bits	Hosts/net[b]	Dec netmask	Hex netmask
/20	12	4094	255.255.240.0	0xFFFFF000
/21	11	2046	255.255.248.0	0xFFFFF800
/22	10	1022	255.255.252.0	0xFFFFFC00
/23	9	510	255.255.254.0	0xFFFFFE00
/24	8	254	255.255.255.0	0xFFFFFF00
/25	7	126	255.255.255.128	0xFFFFFF80
/26	6	62	255.255.255.192	0xFFFFFFC0
/27	5	30	255.255.255.224	0xFFFFFFE0
/28	4	14	255.255.255.240	0xFFFFFFF0
/29	3	6	255.255.255.248	0xFFFFFFF8
/30	2	2	255.255.255.252	0xFFFFFFFC

a. The network length + the number of host bits is always 32, since we are dividing up the fixed-size "pie" of a 32-bit IP address.

b. Mathy folks will notice that the number of hosts per net is $2^{\#hostbits} - 2$; the -2 reflects the fact that the all-0 and all-1 host addresses are special.

When CIDR was introduced in 1993, the backbone tables contained approximately 20,000 routes. Despite the exponential growth of the Internet since that time, the

11. The original Ethernet on RG-11 coaxial cable allowed at most 1,024 hosts on a single network; with today's switches, it's possible (but not very sensible) to build really huge networks.

12. But be careful not to back yourself into a corner… This puzzle is left as an exercise for the reader.

TCP/IP

size of the routing tables had grown to only 100,000 routes by the fall of 2001. This modest growth in routing entries is due to extensive aggregation of both old and new address allocations.[13]

An unaggregated region of the address space, called the 192 swamp (and smaller swamps in the 199 and 205 ranges), consists of early class C addresses whose owners cannot aggregate them and do not want to turn them in and then have to renumber. The United States is particularly bad in this regard. Europe and Asia, which started a bit later, learned from our mistakes and did a much better job of allocating addresses. Sites with an unaggregated 192 network should turn it back into the American Registry for Internet Numbers (ARIN) and get a new block from their ISP. Unfortunately, the cost of renumbering (in IPv4 space at least) precludes most sites from doing this.

Although CIDR was only intended as an interim solution, it has proved to be strong enough to handle the Internet's growth problems for the foreseeable future. In fact, CIDR has worked so well that it is unclear if we really need a new IP protocol. An enormous amount of engineering work has gone into the IPv6 specification and production implementations of IPv6. It would be a shame to waste this work, but wholesale deployment of IPv6 will probably require either a new killer application written only for IPv6, a yuppie toy that uses IPv6 addressing, or a decision by Microsoft to obsolete IPv4.

Address allocation

In the early days of the Internet, individual sites applied to the Internet Network Information Center (InterNIC) for address space. ARIN has now replaced the InterNIC in the Americas.[14] Only ISPs who allocate significant amounts of address space per year are eligible to apply to ARIN for IP address space. All other sites must apply to their ISP.

Only network numbers are formally assigned; sites must define their own host numbers to form complete IP addresses. You can subdivide the address space given to you into subnets however you like.

Administratively, ICANN (the Internet Corporation for Assigned Names and Numbers) has delegated blocks of addresses to three regional Internet registries, and these regional authorities are responsible for doling out subblocks to ISPs within their regions (see Table 13.6). These ISPs in turn divide up their blocks and hand out pieces to individual clients. Only large ISPs should ever have to deal directly with one of the ICANN-sponsored address registries.

The delegation from ICANN to ARIN, RIPE, and APNIC and then on to national or regional ISPs has allowed for further aggregation in the backbone routing tables. ISP

---

13. The routing tables were growing hair-raisingly fast throughout 2000, but growth has slowed significantly since then, probably because of the economic climate. Current routing hardware and algorithms can sustain a few percent growth per year, but not the 25% we were seeing in the dotcom heyday. See www.telstra.net/ops/bgptable.html for more information.

14. A new registry is being created for Latin America, but it won't be operational for a while.

Table 13.6   Regional IP address registries

Name	Web address	Region covered
ARIN	www.arin.net	North and South America, sub-Saharan Africa
APNIC	www.apnic.net	Asia/Pacific region
RIPE	www.ripe.net	Europe and surrounding areas

customers who have been allocated address space within the ISP's block do not need individual routing entries on the backbone. A single entry for the aggregated block that points to the ISP suffices.

Originally, address space was not very fairly allocated. The U.S. government reserved about half the address space for itself and gave relatively small blocks to Europe and Asia. But Europe and Asia managed their address space much more wisely than we did in the United States. The address space map at

> http://www.caida.org/outreach/resources/learn/ipv4space

illustrates this fact quite effectively, showing the IP address space as a whole, the portions that have been allocated, the portions that are routed (and therefore reachable), and the addresses for which traffic has been observed at a couple of major exchange points in the United States.

Private addresses and NAT

Another temporary solution to address space depletion is the use of private IP address spaces, described in RFC1918 (February 1996). In the CIDR era, sites normally obtain their IP addresses from their Internet service provider. If a site wants to change ISPs, it may be held for ransom by the cost of renumbering its networks. The ISP gave it the address space as long as it was a customer. If the site now wants to choose a different ISP, it will have to convince the old ISP to let it have the addresses and also convince the new ISP to make the routing work correctly to the new location with the old addresses. Typically, ISPs don't want to bother with these issues and will require customers to renumber.

One alternative to using ISP-assigned addresses is to use private addresses that are never shown to your ISP. RFC1918 sets aside one class A network, 16 class B networks, and 256 class C networks that will never be globally allocated and can be used internally by any site. The catch is that packets bearing those addresses must never be allowed to sneak out onto the Internet. You should filter them at your border router just to make sure. If some packets slip by, you should track down the misconfigurations that allowed them to escape.

Table 13.7 on the next page shows the network numbers reserved for private addressing. (The "CIDR range" column shows the range for each class in the more compact CIDR notation; it does not add any additional information.)

Sites can choose from this set the size of network that best fits their organization.

TCP/IP

Table 13.7   IP addresses reserved for private use

IP class	From	To	CIDR range
Class A	10.0.0.0	10.255.255.255	10.0.0.0/8
Class B	172.16.0.0	172.31.255.255	172.16.0.0/12
Class C	192.168.0.0	192.168.255.255	192.168.0.0/16

To allow hosts that use these private addresses to talk to the Internet, the site's border router runs a system called NAT (Network Address Translation). NAT intercepts packets addressed with these internal-only addresses and rewrites their source addresses, using a real external IP address and perhaps a different source port number. It also maintains a table of the mappings it has made between internal and external address/source-port pairs so that the translation can be performed in reverse when answering packets arrive from the Internet.

NAT's use of port number mapping allows several conversations to be multiplexed onto the same IP address so that a single external address can be shared by many internal hosts. In some cases, a site can get by with only one "real" IP address.

A site that uses NAT must still request address space from its ISP, but most of the addresses thus obtained are used for NAT mappings and are not assigned to individual hosts. If the site later wants to choose another ISP, only the border router and its NAT configuration need to change, not the configurations of the individual hosts.

Several router vendors implement NAT, including Cisco. It is also possible to have a Linux box perform the NAT function, although many sites prefer to delegate that task to their routers or network connection devices. See the vendor-specific sections later in this chapter for details. For some reason, the Linux world used to call NAT "IP masquerading." However, with the introduction of the 2.4 kernel the Linux folks have begun to call it NAT as well.

An incorrect NAT configuration can let private-address-space packets escape onto the Internet. The packets will get to their destinations, but answering packets won't be able to get back. CAIDA,[15] an organization that measures everything in sight about the backbone networks, finds that 0.1% to 0.2% of the packets on the backbone have either private addresses or bad checksums.

This sounds like a tiny percentage, and it is, but it represents about 20,000 packets every 10 minutes on a busy circuit at MAE-West (one of the major public exchanges at which different ISPs meet to exchange traffic). See www.caida.org for other interesting statistics and network measurement tools.

One disadvantage of NAT (or perhaps it's an advantage) is that an arbitrary host on the Internet cannot connect directly to your site's internal machines. Some imple-

---

15. CAIDA, pronounced "kay duh," is the Cooperative Association for Internet Data Analysis at the San Diego Supercomputer Center on the UCSD campus (www.caida.org).

mentations (e.g., Linux and Cisco PIX) let you configure "tunnels" that support direct connections for particular hosts.

Another problem is that some applications embed IP addresses in the data portion of packets; these applications are foiled or confused by NAT. Examples include some routing protocols, streaming programs such as RealVideo and SHOUTcast, some FTP commands such as PORT and PASV, ICQ instant messaging, and many games. NAT sometimes breaks VPNs (virtual private networks), too.

Large corporations that use NAT and RFC1918 addresses must institute some form of central coordination so that all hosts, independently of their department or administrative group, have unique IP addresses. The situation can become complicated when one company that uses RFC1918 address space acquires or merges with another company that's doing the same thing. Parts of the combined organization must often renumber.

NAT hides interior structure. This secrecy feels like a security win, but the security folks say NAT doesn't really help for security and certainly does not replace the need for a firewall. It also foils any attempt to measure the size or topology of the Internet.

IPv6 addressing

An IPv6 address is 128 bits long. These long addresses were originally intended to solve the problem of IP address exhaustion. Now that they're here, however, they are being exploited to help with issues of routing, mobility, and locality of reference. They are also, as of early 2002, in a state of disarray with respect to the DNS records that will be used to map between hostnames and IPv6 addresses.

Two DNS record types for IPv6 addresses are in use: the A6 type, which is described below, and the earlier AAAA type, which was previously considered obsolete but is now making a comeback. Everyone was making do with AAAA until A6 could be deployed, but now folks at the IETF meetings are saying that A6 is too complicated and that we should go back to AAAA. So beware—by the time you read this, these next few sections may just be historical references to a failed standard. See page 422 for more information about the status of IPv6 addresses in DNS.

IP addresses have never been geographically clustered in the way that phone numbers or zip codes are. Now, with the proposed segmentation of the IPv6 address space, they will at least cluster to ISPs. The boundary between the network portion and the host portion of an IPv6 address is fixed at /64; the boundary between public topology and a site's local topology is fixed at /48. Table 13.8 on the next page shows the various parts of an IPv6 address.

Of these pieces, only the SLA ID and the INTERFACE ID belong to the host and its site. The other parts are provided by the upstream ISP. The SLA specifies a local subnet. The 64-bit interface ID identifies the host network interface. It typically contains the 48-bit MAC address with the hex digits 0xFFFE in the middle. A special bit in the MAC address (bit 6 of the first byte, numbering bits from the left, starting at 0) called the universal/local bit must be complemented (see RFC2373). This scheme allows

TCP/IP

Table 13.8   The parts of an IPv6 address

Complete IPv6 address (128 bits)		
ISP prefix	**Subnet**	**Host identifier**
45 bits	16 bits	64 bits

┗ **Address type** 3 bits

Bits	Acronym	Translation
1–3	FP	Format prefix; the type of address, e.g., unicast
4–16	TLA ID	Top-level aggregation ID, like backbone ISP
17–24	RES	Reserved for future use
25–48	NLA ID	Next-level aggregation ID, e.g., regional ISPs and site ID
49–64	SLA ID	Site-level aggregation ID, like local subnet
65–128	INTERFACE ID	Interface identifier (MAC address plus padding)

hosts to be automatically numbered, which is a nice feature for the sysadmin since only the subnet needs to be managed.

In IPv6, the MAC address is seen at the IP layer, which has both good and bad implications. The brand and model of interface card are encoded in the first half of the MAC address, so hackers with code for a particular architecture will be helped along. The visibility of this information has also worried some privacy advocates. The IPv6 folks have responded by pointing out that sites are not actually required to use MAC addresses; they're free to use whatever they want for the host address. A scheme to include a random token in the local part of the address has also been proposed. Too many bits to play with!

On the other hand, assigning IPv6 addresses should be easier than assigning IPv4 addresses since you need only keep track of the subnet address. The hosts can configure themselves—or at least, that's the theory.

The format prefix identifies the type of IPv6 address: unicast, multicast, or anycast. Unicast addresses set FP to 001 (binary). The TLA and NLA IDs identify your top-level IP backbone carrier and the local ISPs up the chain to your backbone provider.

Most vendors have IPv6 stacks either in development or already deployed. Table 13.9 shows the IPv6 readiness of some common OS and router vendors. (Switches don't really care about IPv6 because they don't make routing decisions and don't look inside the IP header.)

To see the full scoop on Linux IPv6 implementations, check the following two sites:

> playground.sun.com/pub/ipng/html/ipng-implementations.html
> www.bieringer.de/linux/IPv6/status/IPv6+Linux-status-distributions.html

The latter site describes five Linux implementations and sports a nifty table that includes not only the basic IPv6 implementations but also various common networking

Table 13.9   IPv6 readiness for some common vendors

System	IPv6?	Comments
Red Hat	yes	IPv6 is in the Linux kernel, versions 2.2 and later
SuSE	yes	Includes an IPv6 version of the OSPF and RIP routing protocols and many utilities
Debian	yes	Fewer utilities in 2.2; better in 3.0, but still missing **inetd**
Windows XP	yes	Research version available (including source code)
Cisco	yes	Implemented in the slow path (CPU)[a]
Juniper	yes	Implemented in the fast path
Nortel/Bay	yes	Shipping since 1997

a. Will probably move to the fast path if customers demand it

utilities. Of our example Linux distributions, SuSE seems to be the most complete in the IPv6 area, followed by Red Hat, with Debian bringing up the rear. According to this site, the most complete Linux IPv6 implementation is the Polish(ed) Linux Distribution from www.ipd.org.pl in Poland.

The address registries have just begun allocating IPv6 address space. At the moment, ARIN will only allocate space to large ISPs who plan to implement an IPv6 network within 12 months. These ISPs can then allocate subspaces to their customers. Even though we have 665,579,793,348,866,943,898,599 IPv6 addresses per square meter of the Earth's surface (really!), allocation seems stingy and is expensive. The minimal charge is $2,500/year, and the maximal charge is $20,000/year; IPv4 subscribers seem to be exempt.

Here are some useful sources of IPv6 information:

- www.6bone.net – the IPv6 testbed; uses tunnels to bypass IPv4 routers
- www.6ren.net – a world-wide IPv6 research and education network
- www.ipv6.org – FAQs and technical information
- www.ipv6forum.com – marketing folks and IPv6 propaganda

One major advantage of IPv6 is that it was designed to solve the renumbering issue.[16] In the IPv4 world, ISPs allocate address space to customers, but the addresses are not portable; when customers leave an ISP, they must return their addresses and renumber with addresses from their new ISP. With IPv6, the new ISP gives you an address prefix that you simply prepend to the local parts of your addresses, probably at your border router. This scheme is similar to that of NAT for IPv4 addressing, but without any of NAT's little problems.

Various schemes have been proposed to ease the transition from IPv4 to IPv6, including the use of NAT to hide IPv6 addresses while packets are tunneled across the existing IPv4 infrastructure.

16. However, as of early 2002, the IETF is waffling between the AAAA and A6 schemes for DNS address records for IPv6 hosts. A6 is more complicated but solves the renumbering problem. AAAA is simpler and could be deployed sooner, but it punts on the renumbering problem.

13.5 ROUTING

Routing is the process of directing a packet through the maze of networks that stand between its source and its destination. In the TCP/IP system, it is similar to asking for directions in an unfamiliar country. The first person you talk to might point you toward the right city. Once you were a bit closer to your destination, the next person might be able to tell you how to get to the right street. Eventually, you get close enough that someone can identify the building you're looking for.

TCP/IP routing information takes the form of rules ("routes") such as, "To reach network A, send packets through machine C." There can also be a default route that tells what to do with packets bound for a network to which there is no explicit route.

Routing information is stored in a table in the kernel. Each table entry has several parameters, including a netmask for each listed network (once optional but now required if the default netmask is not correct). To route a packet to a particular address, the kernel picks the most specific of the matching routes (that is, the one with the longest netmask). If the kernel finds no relevant route and no default route, then it returns a "network unreachable" ICMP error to the sender.

The word "routing" is commonly used to mean two distinct things:

- Looking up a network address in the routing table to forward a packet toward its destination

- Building the routing table in the first place

In this section we examine the forwarding function and look at how routes can be manually added to or deleted from the routing table. We defer the more complicated topic of routing protocols that build and maintain the routing table until Chapter 14.

Routing tables

You can examine a machine's routing table with **netstat -r**. Use **netstat -rn** to avoid DNS lookups and to present all the information numerically. We discuss **netstat** in more detail starting on page 633, but here is a short example to give you a better idea of what routes look like. This host has two network interfaces: 132.236.227.93 (eth0) on the 132.236.227.0/24 net and 132.236.212.1 (eth1) on the 132.236.212.0/26 net.

```
% netstat -rn
Kernel IP routing table
Destination     Genmask          Gateway          Fl   MSS   Iface
132.236.227.0   255.255.255.0    132.236.227.93   U    1500  eth0
default         0.0.0.0          132.236.227.1    UG   1500  eth0
132.236.212.0   255.255.255.192  132.236.212.1    U    1500  eth1
132.236.220.64  255.255.255.192  132.236.212.6    UG   1500  eth1
127.0.0.1       255.255.255.255  127.0.0.1        U    3584  lo
```

The destination field is usually a network address; the gateway must be a host address. For example, the fourth route says that to reach the network 132.236.220.64/26, packets must be sent to the gateway 132.236.212.6 through interface eth1. The second entry is a default route; packets not explicitly addressed to any of the three networks listed (or to the machine itself) will be sent to the default gateway host, 132.236.227.1. Hosts can route packets only to gateway machines that are directly attached to their same network.

See page 270 for more information about the **route** *command.*
Routing tables can be configured statically, dynamically, or with a combination of the two approaches. A static route is one that you enter explicitly with the **route** command. Static routes should stay in the routing table as long as the system is up; they are often set up at boot time from one of the system startup scripts. For example, the Linux commands

```
route add -net 132.236.220.64 netmask 255.255.255.192 gw 132.236.212.6 eth1
route add default gw 132.236.227.1 eth0
```

would add the fourth and second routes displayed by **netstat -rn** above. (The first and third routes in that display were added by **ifconfig** when the eth0 and eth1 interfaces were configured.)

The final route is also added at boot time. It configures a pseudo-device called the loopback interface. The loopback prevents packets sent from the host to itself from going out on the network; instead, they are transferred directly from the network output queue to the network input queue inside the kernel.

In a stable local network, static routing is an efficient solution. It is easy to manage and reliable. However, it requires that the system administrator know the topology of the network accurately at boot time and that the topology not change often.

Most machines on a local area network have only one way to get out to the rest of the network, and so the routing problem is easy. A default route added at boot time suffices to point toward the way out. Hosts that use DHCP (see page 278) to get their IP addresses can also obtain a default route with DHCP.

For more complicated network topologies, dynamic routing is required. Dynamic routing is typically performed by a daemon process that maintains and modifies the routing table. Routing daemons on different hosts communicate to discover the topology of the network and to figure out how to reach distant destinations. Several routing daemons are available. In Chapter 14, we describe the standard Linux daemon, **routed** ("route dee"), and a more full featured daemon called **gated** ("gate dee"), as well as the routing protocols they speak.

ICMP redirects

Although IP generally does not concern itself with the management of routing information, it does define a small damage control feature called an ICMP redirect. When a router forwards a packet to a machine on the same network from which the packet was originally received, something is clearly wrong. Since the sender, the router, and the next-hop router are all on the same network, the packet could have been forwarded in one hop rather than two. The router can conclude that the sender's routing tables are inaccurate or incomplete.

TCP/IP

In this situation, the router can notify the sender of its problem with an ICMP redirect packet. In effect, a redirect says, "You should not be sending packets for host *xxx* to me; you should send them to host *yyy* instead." The ICMP protocol allows redirects to be sent for both individual host addresses and entire networks. However, many implementations generate only host redirects; network redirects are pretty much useless these days because they only apply to class A, B, or C networks.

Upon receiving a redirect, a naive sender updates its routing table so that future packets bound for that destination will take the more direct path. In the early days of multicasting, a few systems generated ICMP routing redirects in response to multicast packets. Modern systems do not have this problem.

The standard ICMP scenario contains no authentication step. Your router receives a redirect that claims to be from another, well-respected router and directs you to send traffic elsewhere. Should you listen? Paying attention to redirects actually creates something of a security problem. Redirects are generally ignored by Linux (for security reasons) and by Cisco routers (because they are routers). It's not a good idea to let untrusted hosts modify your routing tables.

Under Linux, the variable **accept_redirects** in the **/proc** hierarchy controls the acceptance of ICMP redirects. See page 284 for instructions on examining and resetting this variable.

13.6 ARP: THE ADDRESS RESOLUTION PROTOCOL

Even though IP packets are usually thought of in terms of IP addresses, hardware addresses must be used to actually transport data across a network's link layer.[17] ARP, the Address Resolution Protocol, discovers the hardware address associated with a particular IP address. It can be used on any kind of network that supports broadcasting but is most commonly described in terms of Ethernet.

If host A wants to send a packet to host B on the same Ethernet, it uses ARP to discover B's hardware address. If B is not on the same network as A, host A uses the routing system to determine the next-hop router along the route to B and then uses ARP to find that router's hardware address. Since ARP uses broadcast packets, which cannot cross networks,[18] it can only be used to find the hardware addresses of machines connected directly to the sending host's local network.

Every machine maintains a table in memory called the ARP cache, which contains the results of recent ARP queries. Under normal circumstances, many of the addresses a host needs are discovered soon after booting, so ARP does not account for a lot of network traffic.

ARP functions by broadcasting[19] a packet of the form, "Does anyone know the hardware address for 128.138.116.4?" The machine being searched for recognizes its own

---

17. Except on point-to-point links, on which the identity of the destination is sometimes implicit.
18. Routers can often be configured to flood broadcast packets to other networks; don't do this.

IP address and sends back a reply, "Yes, that's the IP address assigned to one of my network interfaces, and the corresponding Ethernet address is 8:0:20:0:fb:6a."

The original query includes the IP and Ethernet addresses of the requestor so that the machine being sought can reply without issuing an ARP query of its own. Thus, the two machines learn each other's ARP mappings with only one exchange of packets. Other machines that overhear the requestor's initial broadcast can record its address mapping, too. This passive inspection of ARP traffic is sometimes called snooping.

The **arp** command examines and manipulates the kernel's ARP cache. **arp** is typically used to add or delete an entry; it can also flush the table or show it. The command **arp -a** displays the contents of the ARP cache. For example:

```
redhat% /sbin/arp -a
sprint-gw (192.168.1.254) at 00:02:4B:5B:26:45 [ether] on eth0
inura-local.toadranch.com (192.168.1.101) at 00:04:76:37:AE:7E [ether] on eth0
```

The **arp** command is generally useful only for debugging and for situations that involve special hardware. Some devices are not smart enough to speak ARP (for example, network-attached printers or special-purpose graphics displays). To support such devices, you might need to configure another machine as a proxy ARP server for your crippled hardware. That's normally done with the **arp** command as well (using the **-s** flag). For example:

```
# /sbin/arp -s printer.toadranch.com  00:50:04:ce:ef:38
```

Linux kernels 2.4 and later do not support proxy ARP service for a whole subnet but will automatically act as a proxy ARP server when a route exists and the interface is configured to forward packets.

If two hosts on a network are using the same IP address, one will have the right ARP table entry and one will be wrong. You can use the **arp** command to track down the offending machine.

Sometimes, hardware addresses need to be translated into IP addresses. A lot of handicapped hardware (e.g., diskless workstations, network computers, printers) needs to perform this translation at boot time. Instead of having an IP address hardwired into a configuration file, a machine can query a central server to discover its own address. The near-obsolete RARP protocol (Reverse ARP) extends ARP to cover reverse translations.

Unlike ARP, RARP requires a central server process to be installed on each network. RARP is not self-configuring; you must supply an explicit mapping between Ethernet addresses and IP addresses. On most systems that support RARP, the server is called **rarpd** and configuration data is drawn from **/etc/ethers** and **/etc/hosts**.

RARP has been largely superseded, first by BOOTP and now by DHCP.

TCP/IP

---

19. ARP uses the underlying link layer's broadcasting conventions, not IP broadcasting.

This ends our coverage of networking background material. In the sections that follow, we address the issues involved in configuring Linux machines for your local network and the Internet.

13.7 ADDING A MACHINE TO A NETWORK

Only a few steps are involved in adding a new machine to an existing local area network, but some vendors hide the files you must modify and generally make the chore difficult. Others provide a setup script that prompts for the networking parameters that are needed, which is fine until you need to undo something or move a machine. Before bringing up a new machine on a network that is connected to the Internet, you should secure it (Chapter 21, *Security*) so that you are not inadvertently inviting hackers onto your local network.

The basic steps to add a new machine to a local network are:

- Assign a unique IP address and hostname.
- Set up the new host to configure its network interfaces at boot time.
- Set up a default route and perhaps fancier routing.
- Point to a DNS name server, to allow access to the rest of the Internet.

Of course, you could add a debugging step to this sequence as well. After any change that might affect booting, you should always reboot to verify that the machine comes up correctly. Six months later when the power has failed and the machine refuses to boot, it's hard to remember what change you made that might have caused the problem. (Refer also to Chapter 20, *Network Management and Debugging*.)

If your network uses DHCP, the Dynamic Host Configuration Protocol, the DHCP server will do these chores for you. Refer to the DHCP section starting on page 278 for general information about DHCP and the specifics of configuring our example distributions to use DHCP at boot time.

We will first cover the general outline of these steps, then return to the details for each distribution in a series of vendor-specific sections. The commands involve the Linux kernel's networking stack and are the same across different distributions. However, each distribution has established its own configuration files for automating network configuration at boot time, as summarized in Table 13.10.

Table 13.10 Network configuration files

System	File	What's set there
Red Hat	**/etc/sysconfig/network** **network-scripts/ifcfg-***ifname*	Hostname, default route IP address, netmask, broadcast address
SuSE	**/etc/rc.config** **/etc/route.conf**	Hostname, IP address, netmask, and more Default route
Debian	**/etc/hostname** **/etc/network/interfaces**	Hostname IP address, netmask, default route

The process of designing and installing a physical network is touched on in Chapter 15, *Network Hardware*. If you are dealing with an existing network and have a general idea of how it is set up, it may not be necessary for you to read too much more about the physical aspects of networking unless you plan to extend the existing network.

We describe the process of network configuration in terms of Ethernet; other technologies are essentially similar.

Assigning hostnames and IP addresses

See Chapter 16 for more information about DNS.

Administrators have various theories about how the mapping from hostnames to IP addresses is best maintained at a local site: through the **hosts** file, NIS, the DNS system, or perhaps some combination of those sources. If multiple systems are used, there must also be a sensible plan for how they are to work together. The conflicting values are scalability and maintainability versus a system that is flexible enough to allow machines to boot when not all services are available (and flexible enough to handle the heterogeneity of your site).

Another longer-term issue that may be relevant is that of renumbering. If your site changes ISPs, you may have to return your old IP addresses and renumber with addresses assigned by the new ISP. That process becomes quite daunting if you must visit each host on the network to reconfigure it. To expedite such renumbering, use hostnames in configuration files and make the hostname-to-IP-address translation only in the DNS database files. On the other hand, using IP addresses in configuration files reduces dependencies during bootup when not all services are available. Damned if you do, damned if you don't.

The **/etc/hosts** file is the oldest and simplest way to map names to IP addresses. Each line starts with an IP address and continues with the various symbolic names by which that address is known. Here is a typical **/etc/hosts** file for the host lollipop:

```
127.0.0.1        localhost
192.108.21.48    lollipop.xor.com lollipop loghost
192.108.21.254   chimchim-gw.xor.com chimchim-gw
192.108.21.1     ns.xor.com ns
192.225.33.5     licenses.xor.com license-server
```

A minimalist version would contain only the first two lines. It is common to have localhost as the first entry in the **/etc/hosts** file.

Because **/etc/hosts** contains only local mappings, most modern systems use it only for mappings that are needed at boot time. DNS is then consulted to find mappings for the rest of the local network and the rest of the world. Sometimes **/etc/hosts** is used to specify mappings that you do not want the rest of the world to know about and therefore do not publish in DNS.

/etc/hosts was once important during the boot process because DNS was not yet available and hostnames were sometimes used in config files instead of IP addresses. Modern Linux distributions don't really need the **/etc/hosts** file, but it should probably contain at least the mappings for the host itself and the loopback address. Map-

TCP/IP

pings for the default gateway machine and a name server might also be helpful. Many sites put all of their really important hosts, servers, and gateways in the **/etc/hosts** file. Others put only the host itself and the loopback interface; still others add in all local hosts and their off-site backup name servers.

Our example Linux systems install only a very basic **/etc/hosts** file. Debian's contains only localhost, Red Hat's contains localhost and the machine itself, and SuSE's contains localhost, the machine itself, and IPv6 addresses for localhost and a few special IPv6 names.

If your **/etc/hosts** file contains all your local data, it must be replicated on every machine that wants to use symbolic names. Various schemes allow a single version of the **hosts** file to be kept in a central location and distributed to or shared by other hosts at your site; see Chapter 18, *Sharing System Files*, for more information. DNS is really the "correct" way to manage the mapping. Chapter 16 describes DNS and BIND, its Linux/UNIX implementation, in detail.

The **hostname** command assigns a hostname to a machine. **hostname** is typically run at boot time from one of the startup scripts, which obtains the name to be assigned from a configuration file. Of course, each vendor names that configuration file differently. See the vendor-specific sections beginning on page 274 for information about your specific distribution. Most systems today assign a fully qualified name (that is, a name that includes both the hostname and the DNS domain name, such as anchor.cs.colorado.edu).

See page 505 for more information about LDAP.

At a small site, you can easily dole out hostnames and IP addresses by hand. But when many networks and many different administrative groups are involved, it helps to have some central coordination to ensure uniqueness. For dynamically assigned networking parameters, DHCP takes care of the uniqueness issues. Some sites are now using LDAP databases to manage their hostnames and IP addresses assignments.

ifconfig: configure network interfaces

ifconfig enables or disables a network interface, sets its IP address and subnet mask, and sets various other options and parameters. It is usually run at boot time (with command-line parameters taken from config files), but it can also make changes on the fly. Be careful if you are making **ifconfig** changes and are logged in remotely; many a sysadmin has been locked out this way and had to drive in to fix things.

An **ifconfig** command most commonly has the form

> **ifconfig** *interface address options ...*

For example:

> **ifconfig** eth0 128.138.240.1 netmask 255.255.255.0 up

interface identifies the hardware interface to which the command applies. On UNIX systems this is usually a two- or three-character device name (derived from the chipset used on the interface card) followed by a number, but for Linux it is almost always something like eth0.[20] The real identity of the hardware and the mapping to an appropriate device driver are stored in the **/etc/modules.conf** file on an alias line. The loopback interface is called lo.

ifconfig *interface* displays the current settings for *interface* without changing them. Many systems understand **-a** to mean "all interfaces," and **ifconfig -a** can therefore be used to find out what interfaces are present on the system. If your system does not understand **ifconfig -a**, try **netstat -i** to find the interface names.

The *address* parameter specifies the interface's IP address. Many versions of **ifconfig** also accept a hostname for the address parameter. We prefer to use the actual IP address; if **ifconfig** is given a hostname (or the output of the **hostname** command), the potential for boot-time problems is increased. If there's a problem resolving the hostname, the machine won't boot or it will boot into a state in which it cannot be accessed from the network, requiring you to physically go to the machine to debug the problem. DNS queries that cannot complete take a long while to time out, making it seem that the machine is hung. On the other hand, if you ever have to renumber your network, finding all those hidden hardwired IP addresses in configuration files can be a nightmare.

The keyword **up** turns the interface on; **down** turns it off. When an **ifconfig** command assigns an IP address to an interface, as in the example above, the **up** parameter is implicit and does not need to be mentioned by name.

ifconfig understands many other options. We cover only the most common ones; as always, consult your man pages for the final word on your particular system. **ifconfig** options all have symbolic names. Some options require an argument, which should be placed immediately after the option name.

The **netmask** option sets the subnet mask for the interface and is required if the network is not subnetted according to its address class (A, B, or C). The mask can be specified in dotted decimal notation or as a 4-byte hexadecimal number beginning with **0x**. In either case, bits set to 1 are part of the network number, and bits set to 0 are part of the host number.

The **broadcast** option specifies the IP broadcast address for the interface, expressed in either hex or dotted quad notation. The correct broadcast address is one in which the host part is set to all 1s, and most systems default to this value; they use the netmask and IP address to calculate the broadcast address.

On Linux, you can set the broadcast address to any IP address that's valid for the network to which the host is attached. Some sites have chosen weird values for the broadcast address in the hope of avoiding certain types of denial of service attacks that are based on broadcast pings. We dislike this approach for several reasons.

---

20. You can assign more than one IP address to an interface by making use of the concept of "virtual network interfaces" or "IP aliases." Administrators often do this to allow one machine to host several web sites. On Linux systems, the virtual interfaces are named eth0:0, eth0:1, and so on. You don't need to declare the interfaces ahead of time, just **ifconfig** them to set them up. See page 700 for more information.

TCP/IP

First, it requires you to reset the broadcast address on every host on the local network, which can be a time-consuming chore on a large net. Second, it requires you to be absolutely sure that you reconfigure every host, or broadcast storms can result in which packets travel from machine to machine until their TTLs expire.

Broadcast storms occur because the same link-layer broadcast address must be used to transport packets no matter what the IP broadcast address has been set to. For example, suppose that machine X thinks the broadcast address is A1 and that machine Y thinks it is A2. If X sends a packet to address A1, Y will receive the packet (because the link-layer destination address is the broadcast address), will see that the packet is not for itself and also not for the broadcast address (because Y thinks the broadcast address is A2), and will then forward[21] the packet back onto the net. If two machines are in Y's state, the packet will circulate until its TTL expires. Broadcast storms can erode your bandwidth, especially on a large switched net.

A better way to avoid problems with broadcast pings is to prevent your border routers from forwarding them and to tell individual hosts not to respond to them. See page 284 for instructions on how to implement these constraints.

In the **ifconfig** example at the beginning of this section, the broadcast address is 128.138.240.255 because the network is a /24, as specified by the netmask value of 255.255.255.0.

Executing **ifconfig** shows the following output:

```
redhat% /sbin/ifconfig eth0
eth0   Link encap:Ethernet  HWaddr 00:02:B3:19:C8:86
       inet addr:192.168.1.13  Bcast:192.168.1.255  Mask:255.255.255.0
       UP BROADCAST RUNNING MULTICAST  MTU:1500  Metric:1
       RX packets:206983 errors:0 dropped:0 overruns:0 frame:0
       TX packets:218292 errors:0 dropped:0 overruns:0 carrier:0
       collisions:0 txqueuelen:100
       Interrupt:7 Base address:0xef00
```

The lack of collisions on the Ethernet interface in this example may indicate a very lightly loaded network or, more likely, a switched network. On a shared network (built with hubs instead of switches), you should check this number to ensure that it is below about 5% of the output packets. Lots of collisions indicate a loaded network that needs to be watched and possibly split into multiple subnets or migrated to a switched infrastructure.

Let's look at some complete examples.

```
# ifconfig lo 127.0.0.1 up
```

This command configures the loopback interface, which doesn't usually require any options to be set. You should never need to change your system's default configuration for this interface. The implied netmask of 255.0.0.0 is correct and does not need to be manually overridden.

---

21. Machine Y must be configured with ip_forwarding turned on for this to happen.

```
# ifconfig eth0 128.138.243.151 netmask 255.255.255.192
    broadcast 128.138.243.191 up
```

This is a typical example for an Ethernet interface. The IP and broadcast addresses are set to 128.138.243.151 and 128.138.243.191, respectively. The network is class B (you can tell from the first byte of the address), but it has been subnetted by an additional 10 bits into a /26 network. The 192 in the netmask is 11000000 in binary and so adds 2 extra bits to the 24 contained in the three 255 octets. The 191 in the broadcast address is 10111111 in binary, which sets all 6 host bits to 1s and indicates that this interface is part of the 3rd network (first two bits 10) in the group of 4 carved out of the 4th octet.

Now that you know how to configure a network interface by hand, you need to figure out how the parameters to **ifconfig** are set when the machine boots, and you need to make sure that the new values are entered correctly. You normally do this by editing one or more configuration files; see the vendor-specific sections starting on page 274 for more information.

mii-tool: configure autonegotiation and other media-specific options

Occasionally, network hardware has configurable options that are specific to its media type. One extremely common example of this is modern-day Ethernet, where an interface card may support 10, 100, or even 1000 Mb/s in both half duplex and full duplex modes. Most equipment defaults to autonegotiation mode, in which both the card and its upstream connection (usually a switch port) try to guess what the other wants to use. Unfortunately, the autonegotiation process usually works about as well as trying to rope a calf while blindfolded. High packet loss rates (especially of large packets) are a common artifact of failed autonegotiation.

The best way to avoid this pitfall is to lock the interface speed and duplex both on servers and on the switch ports they are connected to. Autonegotiation is useful for ports in public areas where roving laptops may stop for a visit, but it serves no useful purpose for statically attached hosts. If you're having problems with mysterious packet loss, turn off autonegotiation everywhere as your first course of action.

Under Linux, the **mii-tool** command queries and sets media-specific parameters such as link speed and duplex. You can query the status of an interface with the **-v** flag. For example, this eth0 interface has autonegotiation enabled:

```
% mii-tool -v eth0
eth0: negotiated 100baseTx-FD flow-control, link ok
  product info: vendor 00:10:5a, model 0 rev 0
  basic mode:   autonegotiation enabled
  basic status: autonegotiation complete, link ok
  capabilities: 100baseTx-FD 100baseTx-HD 10baseT-FD 10baseT-HD
  advertising:  100baseTx-FD 100baseTx-HD 10baseT-FD 10baseT-HD flow-control
  link partner: 100baseTx-FD 100baseTx-HD 10baseT-FD 10baseT-HD flow-control
```

To lock this interface to 100 Mb/s full duplex, use the command

```
# mii-tool -force=100BaseTx-FD eth0
```

TCP/IP

Afterward, the status query returns

```
% mii-tool -v eth0
eth0: 100 Mbit, full duplex, link ok
  product info: vendor 00:10:5a, model 0 rev 0
  basic mode:   100 Mbit, full duplex
  basic status: link ok
  capabilities: 100baseTx-FD 100baseTx-HD 10baseT-FD 10baseT-HD
  advertising:  100baseTx-FD 100baseTx-HD 10baseT-FD 10baseT-HD flow-control
```

route: configure static routes

The **route** command defines static routes, explicit routing table entries that never change (you hope), even if you run a routing daemon.[22] When you add a new machine to a local area network, you usually need to specify only a default route; see the next section for details.

This book's discussion of routing is split between this section and Chapter 14, *Routing*. Although most of the basic information about routing and the **route** command is here, you might find it helpful to read the first few sections of Chapter 14 if you need more information.

Routing is performed at the IP layer. When a packet bound for some other host arrives, the packet's destination IP address is compared with the routes in the kernel's routing table. If it matches or partially matches a route in the table, the packet is forwarded to the "next-hop gateway" IP address associated with that route.

There are two special cases. First, a packet may be destined for some host on a directly connected network. In this case, the "next-hop gateway" address in the routing table will be one of the local host's own interfaces, and the packet is sent directly to its destination. This type of route is added to the routing table for you by the **ifconfig** command when you configure an interface.

Second, it may be that no route matches the destination address. In this case, the default route is invoked if one exists. Otherwise, an ICMP "network unreachable" or "host unreachable" message is returned to the sender. Many local area networks have only one way out, and their default route points to it. On the Internet backbone, the routers do not have default routes—the buck stops there. If they do not have a routing entry for a destination, that destination cannot be reached.

Each **route** command adds or removes one route. The format is

> **route** [*op*] [*type*] *destination* **gw** *gateway* [*metric*] [**dev** *interface*]

The *op* argument should be **add** to add a route, **del** to remove one, and omitted to display the routing tables. *destination* can be a host address (type -**host**), a network address (type -**net**), or the keyword **default**. If *destination* is a network address, you should also specify a netmask.

---

22. However, some versions of the **routed** daemon will overwrite static routes.

The *gateway* is the machine to which packets should be forwarded. It *must* be on a directly connected network; forwarding can only be performed one hop at a time. Linux lets you specify an interface instead of (or along with) the *gateway.* The **dev** keyword in the interface specification is optional and can be omitted.

metric is the number of forwardings (the hop count) required to reach the destination. Linux does not require or use the hop count but keeps the value in the routing tables if you set it, so that routing protocols can use it.

The optional *type* argument supports host routes, which apply to a complete IP address (a specific host) rather than to a network address. The values **-net** and **-host** are accepted for the *type* parameter. If a *type* isn't specified, **route** checks the host part of the destination address to see if it's zero. If the host part is 0 or the address is a network defined in the **/etc/networks** file, then the route is assumed to be a normal network route.[23]

Since **route** cannot magically know which network numbers have been subnetted, you must frequently use the *type* field to install certain routes. For example, the address 128.138.243.0 refers to a subnetted class B network at our site, but to **route** it looks like a class B address of 128.138 with a host part of 243.0; you must specify the **-net** option to deconfuse **route**. In general, it's good hygiene to provide an explicit *type* for all routes that involve subnets.

route del *destination* removes a specific entry from the routing table. Other UNIX systems have an option to **route**, usually **-f** or **-flush**, that completely flushes the routing tables and starts over. Linux does not support this option, so you might be faced with many **route del**s to clean out a large routing table—be sure you are logged in locally or you may end up half done and disconnected!

To inspect existing routes, use the command **netstat -nr** or **netstat -r** if you want to see names instead of numbers. Numbers are often better if you are debugging, since the name lookup may be the thing that is broken.

```
redhat% netstat -nr
Kernel IP routing table
Destination    Gateway        Genmask         Flags  MSS  Window  irtt  Iface
192.168.1.0    0.0.0.0        255.255.255.0   U        0  0          0  eth0
127.0.0.0      0.0.0.0        255.0.0.0       U        0  0          0  lo
0.0.0.0        192.168.1.254  0.0.0.0         UG       0  0          0  eth0

redhat% netstat -r
Kernel IP routing table
Destination    Gateway        Genmask         Flags  MSS  Window  irtt  Iface
192.168.1.0    *              255.255.255.0   U        0  0          0  eth0
127.0.0.0      *              255.0.0.0       U        0  0          0  lo
default        sprint-gw      0.0.0.0         UG       0  0          0  eth0
```

_____

23. **/etc/networks** can be used to map names to network numbers much like the **/etc/hosts** file maps hostnames to complete IP addresses. Many commands that expect a network number can accept a network name if it is listed in the **/etc/networks** file (or in DNS).

TCP/IP

The Genmask is the netmask associated with the destination. The Flags specify the status of the route, how it was learned, and other parameters. Finally, the Iface is the interface through which packets using that route are sent. These examples are from a Red Hat system, but SuSE and Debian are identical except that Debian doesn't show the loopback route by default.

Default routes

A default route causes all packets whose destination network is not found in the kernel's routing table to be sent to the indicated gateway. To set a default route, simply add the following line to your startup files:

route add default gw *gateway-IP-address*

Rather than hardcoding an explicit IP address into the startup files, most vendors have their systems get the gateway IP address from a configuration file. The way that local routing information is integrated into the startup sequence is unfortunately different for each of our Linux systems (hurry LSB,[24] fix this not-invented-here syndrome!). Table 13.11 summarizes the necessary incantations.

Table 13.11   How to set the default route

System	File to change	Variable to change
Red Hat	**/etc/sysconfig/network**	GATEWAY
SuSE	**/etc/route.conf**	add line: default *IP-addr mask interface*
Debian	**/etc/network/interfaces**	gateway

Configuring DNS

To configure a machine as a DNS client, you only need to edit one or two files: all systems require **/etc/resolv.conf** to be modified, and some require you to modify a "service switch" file as well.

The **/etc/resolv.conf** file lists the DNS domains that should be searched to resolve names that are incomplete (that is, not fully qualified, such as anchor instead of anchor.cs.colorado.edu) and the IP addresses of the name servers to contact for name lookups. A sample is shown here; for more details, see page 377.

```
search cs.colorado.edu colorado.edu
nameserver 128.138.242.1
nameserver 128.138.243.151
nameserver 192.108.21.1
```

/etc/resolv.conf should list the "closest" stable name server first because the server in the first position will be contacted first. You can have up to three nameserver entries. If possible, you should always have more than one. The timeout period for a

---

24. LSB is the Linux Standard Base, a standardization effort for Linux; see page 866 for more details.

DNS query to a particular name server seems quite long, so if the first name server does not respond, your users will notice.

You will sometimes see a domain line instead of a search line. Such a line indicates either an ancient **resolv.conf** file that has not been updated to use the search directive or an ancient resolver that doesn't understand search. domain and search are not equivalent; search is preferred. To this day, Red Hat defaults to a **resolv.conf** file that uses domain instead of search.

See Chapter 18 for more information about NIS.

Some systems do not use DNS by default, even if a properly configured **resolv.conf** file exists. These systems have a "service switch" file that determines which mechanisms will be used to resolve hostname-to-IP-address mappings. Prioritization of information sources is covered in more detail starting on page 498, but we mention the topic here as well, since it sometimes foils your attempts to configure a new machine.

The service switch file lets you specify the order in which DNS, NIS, and **/etc/hosts** should be consulted. In most cases, you can also rule out certain sources of data entirely. Your choice of order impacts the machine's ability to boot and the way that booting interacts with the contents of the **/etc/hosts** file.

If DNS is chosen as the first data source to consult, you may need to have a name server on the local network and have its hostname and IP address in the **hosts** file in order for everything to work at boot time.

Table 13.12 lists the location of the relevant config files and the default configuration for host lookups on each of our example systems.

Table 13.12   Service switch files by system

System	Switch file[a]	Default for hostname lookups
Red Hat	**/etc/nsswitch.conf** **/etc/host.conf**	files nisplus nis dns hosts, bind
SuSE and Debian	**/etc/nsswitch.conf** **/etc/host.conf**	files dns hosts, bind

a. Most applications are linked against **libc6**, which uses BIND's resolver and **nsswitch.conf**. A few older applications are linked with **libc4** or **libc5**, which uses **host.conf**.

The Linux networking stack

See page 700 for more information about virtual interfaces.

The networking stack in Linux kernels 2.2 and above includes support for virtual network interfaces, selective acknowledgements (or SACKs, as they are called) as well as a new IP feature, Explicit Congestion Notification (ECN). ECN marks TCP packets to notify the sender of congestion instead of letting the recovery of dropped packets that never made it to the receiver serve as the only indication of problems. ECN was originally specified in RFC2481 (January 1999) and is now a proposed standard documented in RFC3168. RFC2884 (July 2000) includes performance data and

TCP/IP

an evaluation of ECN. In general, it found that ECN is a good thing for both bulk transfers of data and transactional data such as web requests and responses.

Linux is always one of the first networking stacks to include new features. Sometimes, the Linux folks are so quick that the rest of the networking infrastructure cannot interoperate. For example, the Linux ECN feature (which is on by default) collided with incorrect default settings on a Cisco firewall product, causing all packets with the ECN bit set to be dropped. Oops.

The original Linux implementation of selective acknowledgments was wrong, or perhaps more accurately, nonoptimal. When a SACK arrives and specifies, for example, that packets 2, 5, and 6 were lost, the sender's proper behavior is to resend all three packets immediately to facilitate a quick recovery. Linux sends the proper three packets, but does so one at a time, waiting for each packet to be acknowledged before continuing. It's rare for Linux to be accused of being too conservative, but in the case of selective acknowledgements, it's true.

13.8 DISTRIBUTION-SPECIFIC NETWORK CONFIGURATION

Chapter 2 describes the succulent details of our example systems' booting procedures. In the next few sections, we simply summarize the chores that are related to configuring a network. Our example systems configure the loopback interface automatically; you should never need to modify that part of the configuration. Beyond that, each system is a bit different.

One alternative to manual configuration is **linuxconf**, a module-based utility that provides a simple interface for managing a number of system administration tasks, including most network-related configuration. There are three user interfaces: text-based, web, and X Windows. You type in local parameters to various configuration chores and **linuxconf** does the configuration for you.

linuxconf is freely available on the web but is not included in the default installation. www.solucorp.qc.ca/linuxconf has a web-based demo that runs in a **chroot**ed environment so you can try it out without damaging their systems.

Four files are common to each of our example systems: **/etc/hosts**, **/etc/resolv.conf**, **/etc/nsswitch.conf**, and **/etc/host.conf**. These were covered in the generic network configuration sections above and, except for **resolv.conf** and possibly **hosts**, usually do not need to be modified when you add a machine to the network.

After any change to a file that controls network configuration at boot time, you may need to either reboot or bring the network interface down and then up again for your change to take effect. On Red Hat or Debian you can use the **ifup** and **ifdown** commands; on SuSE, just reboot the machine.

Network configuration for Red Hat

Table 13.13 shows the Red Hat configuration files for networking parameters.

Table 13.13   Red Hat network configuration files

File	What's set there
/etc/sysconfig/network	Hostname, default route
/etc/sysconfig/static-routes	Static routes
network-scripts/ifcfg-_ifname_[a]	IP address, netmask, broadcast address per interface

a. Relative to **/etc/sysconfig**

A Red Hat machine's hostname is set in the file **/etc/sysconfig/network**, which also contains lines that specify the machine's DNS domain and default gateway. For example, here is a **network** file for a host that has a single Ethernet interface:

```
NETWORKING=yes
HOSTNAME=redhat.toadranch.com
DOMAINNAME=toadranch.com        ### optional
GATEWAY=192.168.1.254
```

Interface-specific data is stored in **/etc/sysconfig/network-scripts/ifcfg-**_ifname_, where _ifname_ is the name of the network interface. These configuration files let you set the IP address, netmask, network, and broadcast address for each interface. They also include a line that specifies whether the interface should be configured "up" at boot time.

Typically, files for an Ethernet interface (eth0) and for the loopback interface (lo) are present. For example,

```
DEVICE=eth0
IPADDR=192.168.1.13
NETMASK=255.255.255.0
NETWORK=192.168.1.0
BROADCAST=192.168.1.255
ONBOOT=yes
```

and

```
DEVICE=lo
IPADDR=127.0.0.1
NETMASK=255.0.0.0
NETWORK=127.0.0.0
BROADCAST=127.255.255.255
ONBOOT=yes
NAME=loopback
```

are the **ifcfg-eth0** and **ifcfg-lo** files for the machine redhat.toadranch.com described in the **network** file earlier in this section.

Red Hat provides a couple of handy scripts that facilitate interface management. **ifup** and **ifdown** accept the name of a network interface as an argument and bring the specified interface up or down. After changing network information in any of the **/etc/sysconfig** directories, be sure to run **ifdown** _ifname_ followed by **ifup** _ifname_.

TCP/IP

Better yet, reboot the system to be sure your changes don't cause some kind of subtle problem. There are no man pages for **ifup** and **ifdown**, but they are shell scripts (kept in **/sbin**), so you can take a look and see what they do in detail.

If you need to manage all the interfaces at once, the **/etc/rc.d/init.d/network** script accepts the arguments **start**, **stop**, **restart**, and **status**. This script is invoked at boot time with the **start** argument.

The Red Hat startup scripts can also configure static routes. Any routes added to the file **/etc/sysconfig/static-routes** are entered into the routing table at boot time. The entries provide arguments to **route add**, although in mixed-up order (the interface is first instead of last):

```
eth0 net 130.225.204.48 netmask 255.255.255.248 gw 130.225.204.49
eth1 net 192.38.8.0 netmask 255.255.255.224 gw 192.38.8.129
```

The interface is specified first, followed by arguments to **route**: the route type (net or host), the target network, the netmask associated with that network, and finally, the next-hop gateway. The keyword gw is required. Current Linux kernels do not use the metric parameter to **route** but allow it to be entered and maintained in the routing table for routing daemons to use. The **static-routes** example above would produce the following **route** commands:

```
route add -net 130.225.204.48 netmask 255.255.255.248 gw 130.225.204.49 eth0
route add -net 192.38.8.0 netmask 255.255.255.224 gw 192.38.8.129 eth1
```

Network configuration for SuSE

Table 13.14 shows the network configuration files for SuSE Linux.

Table 13.14   SuSE network configuration files

File	What's set there
/etc/rc.config	Hostname, IP address, netmask, and more
/etc/route.conf	Default route, static routes

SuSE Linux sets most configuration options, including those related to networking, in the **/etc/rc.config** file. It also provides a configuration tool, **/sbin/SuSEconfig**, that uses scripts in **/sbin/conf.d** and **/etc/rc.config.d** to do all sorts of careful and sensible configuration stuff behind your back.

/etc/rc.config contains all network-related parameters except routing information and DNS information. In the excerpt below, we have added a comment introduced by ### to explain the less obvious lines. The **rc.config** file itself is mostly comments and does a great job of self-documentation.

```
START_LOOPBACK="yes"    ### start loopback pseudo-device?
NETCONFIG="_0"          ### #of net cards; _0 = 1, _1 = 2, etc.
```

```
IPADDR_0="192.168.1.101"
NETDEV_0="eth0"              ### logical name of first network device
IFCONFIG_0="192.168.1.101 broadcast 192.168.1.255 netmask 255.255.255.0"
FQHOSTNAME="inura.toadranch.com"
DISABLE_ECN="yes"            ### TCP Explicit Congestion Notification
```

Multiple Ethernet interfaces would have their parameters set in variables with the suffixes _1, _2, and _3; for example, IPADDR_1, NETDEV_1, IFCONFIG_1. Up to four interfaces are supported by default.

Static routing information for a SuSE system is stored in the file **/etc/route.conf**. For example, for the host configured above, which has only a default route, it contains

```
default 192.168.1.254 0.0.0.0 eth0
```

where 192.168.1.254 is the IP address of the default gateway host on the local network reached through **/dev/eth0**. The format of **route.conf** is the same as the arguments to the **route** command: destination, gateway, netmask, interface, and optional extra parameters stored in the routing table for the use of routing daemons.

Dynamic routing is configured with the **rc.config** file, using the variables shown below (with their default values). We have added comments to identify them.

```
START_ROUTED="no"  ### RIP (Routing Information Protocol) version 1 daemon
START_ZEBRA="no"   ### zebra routing manager
START_BGPD="no"    ### BGP (Border Gateway Protocol) daemon
START_RIPNG="no"   ### RIP version 2 daemon
START_OSPFD="no"   ### OSPF (Open Shortest Path First) protocol daemon
START_MRTD="no"    ### Multithreaded routing daemon
```

Network configuration for Debian

As shown in Table 13.15, Debian network configuration occurs mostly in the files **/etc/hostname** and **/etc/network/interfaces**, with a bit of help from the **options** file in the **/etc/network** directory.

Table 13.15   Debian network configuration files

File	What's set there
/etc/hostname	Hostname
/etc/network/interfaces	IP address, netmask, default route
/etc/network/options	Low-level network options (IP forwarding, etc.)

The hostname is set in **/etc/hostname**. The name in this file should be fully qualified because its value is used in other contexts where a fully qualified name is expected. However, the standard Debian installation leaves a nonqualified name there. The IP address, netmask, and default gateway are set in the **/etc/network/interfaces** file.

For example:

```
iface lo inet loopback
iface eth0 inet static
        address 192.168.1.102
        netmask 255.255.255.0
        gateway 192.168.1.254
```

The **ifup** and **ifdown** commands read this file and bring the interfaces up or down by calling lower-level commands such as **ifconfig** with the correct parameters. The basic format of the **interfaces** file includes a line beginning with the keyword iface for each interface followed by indented lines that specify more parameters.

The inet keyword in the iface line is the address family; this will always be inet. The keyword static is called a method and specifies that the IP address and netmask for eth0 will be assigned directly. The address and netmask lines are required for static configurations; earlier versions of the Linux kernel also required the network address to be specified, but now the kernel is smarter and can figure out the network address from the IP address and netmask. The gateway line specifies the address of the default gateway and is used to install a default route.

The **options** file allows some networking variables to be set at boot up time. By default, Debian sets IP forwarding off, spoof protection on, and syn cookies off.

Network configuration with a GUI

We have described in gory detail how to configure network interfaces on the command line. If you come from the Windows world and prefer to point and click rather than type, consider the various graphical user interfaces that vendors provide to handle network configuration. Many of them look suspiciously like Windows network configuration, but without the "You must reboot your computer …" step.

 For example, Red Hat includes a tool called **neat** (NEtwork Administration Tool) that can perform Ethernet, modem, ISDN, xDSL, and wireless configuration. To run it, select

```
Main menu --> programs --> system --> network configuration
```

from the GNOME desktop, or just type **neat** in a shell. **neat** replaces Red Hat's earlier attempt at a GUI configuration tool, **netcfg**.

13.9 DHCP: THE DYNAMIC HOST CONFIGURATION PROTOCOL

DHCP is defined in RFCs 2131 and 2132.

Linux hosts have always required manual configuration to be added to a network. When you plug a Mac or PC into a network, it just works. Why can't Linux do that? The Dynamic Host Configuration Protocol (DHCP) brings this reasonable expectation several steps closer to reality.

The protocol enables a DHCP client to "lease" a variety of network and administrative parameters from a central server that is authorized to distribute them. The leasing paradigm is particularly convenient for PCs that are turned off when not in use and for ISPs that have intermittent dial-up customers.

Leasable parameters include

- IP addresses and netmasks
- Gateways (default routes)
- DNS name servers
- Syslog hosts
- WINS servers, X font servers, proxy servers, NTP servers
- TFTP servers (for loading a boot image)

and dozens more (see RFC2132). Real-world use of the more exotic parameters is rare, however. In many cases, a DHCP server supplies only basic networking parameters such as IP addresses, netmasks, default gateways, and name servers.

Clients must report back to the DHCP server periodically to renew their leases. If a lease is not renewed, it eventually expires. The DHCP server is then free to assign the address (or whatever was being leased) to a different client. The lease period is configurable, but it's usually quite long (hours or days).

DHCP can save a formerly hapless sysadmin a lot of time and suffering. Once the server is up and running, clients can use it to obtain their network configuration automatically at boot time. No fuss, no mess.

DHCP software

Table 13.16 shows the DHCP software that is shipped with our example systems.

Table 13.16   DHCP software on our example systems

System	DHCP client	DHCP server
Red Hat	**/usr/sbin/dhcpcd** and **/sbin/pump**	Available as an RPM package
Suse	**/sbin/dhcpcd**	**/usr/sbin/dhcpd** from ISC
Debian	**/sbin/pump** with 2.2	Available with **apt-get**
	/sbin/dhclient with 3.0	

ISC, the Internet Software Consortium, has built a reference implementation of the DHCP protocol. The server, client, and relay agent are available from ftp.isc.org. The ISC server also speaks the BOOTP protocol, which is similar in concept to DHCP but less sophisticated.

We recommend the ISC package over all the vendor-specific implementations. In a typical heterogeneous network environment, administration can be greatly simplified by standardization on a single implementation. The ISC software provides a reliable, open source solution that builds without incident on most systems. Version 3.0 contains many new useful configuration options, including conditional behavior, separate address pools with access control, dynamic DNS updates, and more.

TCP/IP

DHCP clients must initiate a conversation with the DHCP server by using the generic all-1s broadcast address—the clients don't yet know their subnet masks and therefore cannot use the subnet broadcast address.

ISC's DHCP server speaks the DNS dynamic update protocol. Not only does the server give your host its IP address and other networking parameters, but it can also update the DNS database with the correct hostname-to-IP-address mapping. See page 433 for more information about dynamic DNS updates.

In the next few sections, we briefly discuss the DHCP protocol, explain how to set up the ISC server that implements it, and then discuss some client configuration issues.

How DHCP works

DHCP is a backward-compatible extension of BOOTP, a protocol that was originally devised to enable diskless UNIX workstations to boot. BOOTP supplies clients with their IP address, netmask, default gateway, and TFTP booting information. DHCP generalizes the parameters that can be supplied and adds the "lease" concept.

A DHCP client begins its interaction with a DHCP server by broadcasting a "Help! Who am I?" message. If there is a DHCP server on the local network, it negotiates with the client to lease it an IP address and provides other networking parameters (netmask, name server information and default gateway). If there is no DHCP server on the local net, servers on different subnets can also receive the initial broadcast message from a proxy called a "relay agent."

When the client's lease time is half over, it will renew the lease. The server is obliged to keep track of the addresses it has handed out, and this information must persist across reboots. Clients are supposed to keep their lease state across reboots too, although many do not. The goal is to maximize stability in network configuration.

Incidentally, DHCP is normally not used to configure dial-up PPP interfaces. PPP's own PPPCP (PPP Control Protocol) typically fills that role.

ISC's DHCP server

ISC's DHCP server is available from ftp.isc.org or www.isc.org. The details that follow are for version 2 of the package (included in the SuSE distribution). The 3.0 release is imminent, so be sure to check the version you actually download against these instructions.

Unpack the **tar.gz** file and **cd** to the distribution directory. You should see subdirectories for the server, the client, and the relay agent, along with a directory of shared code. Run **./configure** followed by **make** and **make install** to build and install each of the pieces.

 Debian's DHCP is the ISC DHCP, so you can just do **apt-get install dhcp dhcp-relay** to obtain the client, server, and relay agent.

To configure the DHCP server, **dhcpd**, you need to edit the sample **dhcpd.conf** file from the **server** directory and install it in **/etc/dhcpd.conf**.[25] You must also create an empty lease database file called **/var/db/dhcp.leases**; use the **touch** command. Make sure that **dhcpd** can write to this file. To set up the **dhcpd.conf** file, you need the following information:

- The subnets for which **dhcpd** should manage IP addresses, and the ranges of addresses to dole out

- The initial and maximum lease durations, in seconds

- Configurations for BOOTP clients if you have any (they have static IP addresses and must have their MAC-level hardware address listed as well)

- Any other options the server should pass to DHCP clients: netmask, default route, DNS domain, name servers, etc.

The **dhcpd** man page gives an overview of the configuration process. The exact syntax of the config file is covered in the **dhcpd.conf** man page. Both are located in the distribution's **server** subdirectory. SuSE Linux includes a sample **dhcpd.conf** file in the **/etc** directory; change it to match your local site's network configuration.

dhcpd should be started automatically at boot time. You may find it helpful to make the startup of the daemon conditional on the existence of **/etc/dhcpd.conf**.

Here's a sample **dhcpd.conf** file from a Linux box with two interfaces: one internal and one that connects to the Internet. This machine performs NAT translation for the internal network and leases out a range of 10 IP addresses on this network as well. The **dhcpd.conf** file contains a dummy entry for the external interface (required) and a host entry for one particular machine that needs a fixed address.

```
# dhcpd.conf
#
# global options
option domain-name "synack.net";
option domain-name-servers gw.synack.net;
option subnet-mask 255.255.255.0;
default-lease-time 600;
max-lease-time 7200;

subnet 192.168.1.0 netmask 255.255.255.0 {
    range 192.168.1.51 192.168.1.60;
    option broadcast-address 192.168.1.255;
    option routers gw.synack.net;
}

subnet 209.180.251.0 netmask 255.255.255.0 {
}
```

---

25. Be careful: the **dhcpd.conf** file format is a bit fragile. Leave out a semicolon, and you'll receive an obscure, unhelpful error message.

```
host gandalf {
        hardware ethernet 08:00:07:12:34:56;
        fixed-address gandalf.synack.net;
}
```

*See Chapter 16 for
more information
about DNS.*
Addresses assigned by DHCP might potentially be in conflict with the contents of
the DNS database. Sites often assign a generic name to each dynamically leased address (e.g., dhcp1.synack.net) and allow the names of individual machines to "float"
along with their IP addresses. If you are running a recent version of BIND that supports dynamic updates, you can also configure **dhcpd** to update the DNS database
as it hands out addresses. The dynamic update solution is more complicated, but it
has the advantage of preserving each machine's hostname.

dhcpd records each lease transaction in the file **dhcp.leases**. It also periodically
backs up this file by renaming it to **dhcpd.leases~** and recreating the **dhcp.leases**
file from its in-memory database. If **dhcpd** were to crash during this operation, you
might end up with only a **dhcp.leases~** file. In that case, **dhcpd** will refuse to start
and you will have to rename the file before restarting it. *Do not* just create an empty
dhcp.leases file, or chaos will ensue as clients end up with duplicate addresses.

DHCP configuration for Red Hat

Red Hat used to ship the ISC DHCP server, **dhcpd**, but no longer does by default. It is
still available as a package and can be downloaded from one of the Red Hat mirror
sites. Red Hat does ship two different DHCP clients: **pump**[26] and **dhcpcd**. If you're
feeling bored, we suggest that you ignore both of the supplied DHCP clients and install the client from the Internet Software Consortium at www.isc.org. In our experience, it is more reliable, but sometimes a challenge to compile (look at the Linux
hints in the distribution).

pump is Red Hat's default DHCP client. It is started at boot time when requested by
one of the **/etc/sysconfig/network-scripts/ifcfg-***interface* script fragments. For example, to configure interface eth0 automatically with DHCP, you would edit the file
/etc/sysconfig/network-scripts/ifcfg-eth0. Instead of setting the interface's IP address, netmask, and other parameters, you would include the line

```
BOOTPROTO=dhcp
```

If you need to manually start **pump** to manage eth0, run the command

```
# pump -i eth0
```

To stop **pump**'s management of eth0, use

```
# pump -r -i eth0
```

dhcpcd is the supplied alternative to **pump**, but to use it automatically you must
replace calls to **pump** with calls to **dhcpcd** in the **ifup** and **ifdown** startup scripts.
dhcpcd is configured by files in the directory **/etc/dhcpc**, which is empty in the

---

26. A pump, like a boot (as in BOOTP), is a type of footwear.

current Red Hat release. There is also a directory **/etc/dhcpcd** that contains a file that is symbolically linked to itself. We are not sure what was intended here, but it doesn't seem very useful. Performance art, perhaps?

DHCP configuration for SuSE

SuSE ships ISC's DHCP server, **/usr/sbin/dhcpd** and a DHCP client, **/sbin/dhcpcd**, written by Yoichi Hariguchi and Sergei Viznyuk.

Installation and configuration of the ISC server were covered briefly above. Set the following variables from **/etc/rc.config** to automatically start the DHCP server. Use the relay agent if you need to span multiple networks with the same server.

```
START_DHCPD="no"         ### DHCP server, not started, by default
DHCPD_INTERFACE="eth0"   ### server's interface
START_DHCRELAY="no"      ### DHCP relay agent not started, by default
DHCRELAY_SERVERS="127.0.0.1 127.0.0.2"  ### relay agent's IP addresses
```

The DHCP client does not really require configuration. It stores status files for each connection in the directory **/var/state/dhcp**. The files are named after the interfaces they describe. For example, **dhcpcd-eth0.info** would contain all the networking parameters that **dhcpcd** had set for the eth0 interface.

dhcpcd's **-D** option forces it to accept the domain name from the server (the default is not to accept it). Some ISPs require use of the **-h** *hostname* option for authentication. There is also a **-d** debugging option that's useful if you are having trouble getting **dhcpcd** to work correctly. **dhcpcd** logs through syslog to facility LOCAL0 tagged with the program name **dhcpcd**.

To tell an interface to use the DHCP protocol to get its networking parameters, set the corresponding IFCONFIG line in **/etc/rc.config** to the string "dhcpclient". For example,

```
IFCONFIG_0="dhcpclient"
```

would cause interface eth0 to be configured by **dhcpcd**. There are a couple of other DHCP-related variables in **rc.config** as well:

```
DHCLIENT_SLEEP="3"              ### to give tired interfaces time to be init'ed
DHCLIENT_SET_HOSTNAME="no"  ### should hostname be set by DHCP?
```

DHCP configuration for Debian

DHCP is configured on Debian systems as a "method" (akin to static; see page 278) in the **/etc/network/interfaces** file. The method is called dhcp; it supports the options hostname, leasehours/leasetime, vendor, and client. Debian includes both the **pump** DHCP client and the **dhcpcd** client. **pump** uses options hostname and leasehours; **dhcpcd** needs hostname, leasetime, vendor and client. The units of leasetime are seconds, not hours. None of these options are required.

In Debian 3.0, **dhcpcd** is gone, **pump** is available with **apt-get**, and the default DHCP client is the ISC **dhclient**.

TCP/IP

13.10 LINUX DYNAMIC RECONFIGURATION AND TUNING

Linux has its own special way of tuning kernel and networking parameters; we will describe it in detail for Red Hat and then note SuSE and Debian differences. Instead of providing a command that reads and sets the parameters, Linux puts a representation of each variable that can be tuned into the **/proc** filesystem. The networking variables are in **/proc/sys/net/ipv4**:

```
% cd /proc/sys/net/ipv4; ls -F
conf/                              ipfrag_low_thresh      tcp_max_tw_buckets
icmp_destunreach_rate              ipfrag_time            tcp_mem
icmp_echo_ignore_all               ip_local_port_range    tcp_orphan_retries
icmp_echo_ignore_broadcasts        ip_nonlocal_bind       tcp_reordering
icmp_echoreply_rate                ip_no_pmtu_disc        tcp_retrans_collapse
icmp_ignore_bogus_error_responses  neigh/                 tcp_retries1
icmp_paramprob_rate                route/                 tcp_retries2
icmp_timeexceed_rate               tcp_abort_on_overflow  tcp_rfc1337
igmp_max_memberships               tcp_adv_win_scale      tcp_rmem
inet_peer_gc_maxtime               tcp_app_win            tcp_sack
inet_peer_gc_mintime               tcp_dsack              tcp_stdurg
inet_peer_maxttl                   tcp_ecn                tcp_synack_retries
inet_peer_minttl                   tcp_fack               tcp_syncookies
inet_peer_threshold                tcp_fin_timeout        tcp_syn_retries
ip_autoconfig                      tcp_keepalive_intvl    tcp_timestamps
ip_default_ttl                     tcp_keepalive_probes   tcp_tw_recycle
ip_dynaddr                         tcp_keepalive_time     tcp_window_scaling
ip_forward                         tcp_max_orphans        tcp_wmem
ipfrag_high_thresh                 tcp_max_syn_backlog
```

Many of the variables with **rate** and **max** in their names are used to thwart denial of service attacks. The **conf** subdirectory contains variables that are set on a per-interface basis. It contains subdirectories **all** and **default** and a subdirectory for each interface (including the loopback). Each subdirectory contains the same set of files.

```
% cd conf/default; ls -F
accept_redirects      bootp_relay     mc_forwarding   secure_redirects   tag
accept_source_route   forwarding      proxy_arp       send_redirects
arp_filter            log_martians    rp_filter       shared_media
```

If you change something in the **all** subdirectory, your change applies to all interfaces. If you change the same variable in, say, the **eth0** subdirectory, only that interface will be affected. The **defaults** subdirectory contains the default values as shipped.

The **neigh** directory also contains a subdirectory for each interface. The files in each subdirectory control ARP table management and IPv6 neighbor discovery for that particular interface. Here is the list of variables; the ones starting with **gc** (for garbage collection) determine how ARP table entries are timed out and discarded.

```
% cd neigh/default; ls -F
anycast_delay            gc_interval     gc_thresh3     proxy_qlen
app_solicit              gc_stale_time   locktime       retrans_time
base_reachable_time      gc_thresh1      mcast_solicit  ucast_solicit
delay_first_probe_time   gc_thresh2      proxy_delay    unres_qlen
```

To see the value of a variable, use **cat**; to set it, use **echo** redirected to the proper filename. For example, the command

```
% cat icmp_echo_ignore_broadcasts
0
```

shows that this variable's value is 0, meaning that broadcast pings are not ignored. To set it to 1 (and avoid falling prey to smurf-type denial of service attacks), run

```
% sudo sh -c "echo 1 > icmp_echo_ignore_broadcasts"[27]
```

from the **/proc/sys/net** directory. You'll typically be logged in over the same network you are tweaking as you adjust these variables, so be careful! You can mess things up badly enough to require a reboot from the console to recover, which might be inconvenient if the system happens to be in Point Barrow, Alaska, and it's January. Test-tune these variables on your desktop system before you even think of attacking a production machine.

The document **/usr/src/linux/Documentation/proc.txt**, written by the SuSE Linux folks, is a nice primer on kernel tuning with **/proc**.[28] It tells you what the variables really mean and sometimes provides suggested values. The **proc.txt** file is readable only by root so you will have to use **sudo** to see it. It's also a bit out of date, as the Linux coders seem to write faster than the documenters.

 SuSE puts the **proc.txt** documentation file mentioned above in the **filesystems** subdirectory of **/usr/src/linux/Documentation**. A couple of the variables visible in the **/proc** filesystem are configurable in **/etc/rc.config**. For example:

```
IP_TCP_SYNCOOKIES="yes"
IP_FORWARD="no"
```

 Debian also has a few configurable parameters that are listed in the networking configuration files and then set for you in **/proc** during bootup. They are listed in the **/etc/network/options** file. By default, it contains:

```
ip_forward=no
spoofprotect=yes
syncookies=no
```

TCP/IP

27. If you try this command in the form **sudo echo 1 > icmp_echo_ignore_broadcasts**, you'll just generate a "permission denied" message—your shell attempts to open the output file before it runs **sudo**. You want the **sudo** to apply to both the **echo** command and the redirection. Ergo, you must create a root subshell in which to execute the entire command.

28. You must install the kernel source code in order for this file to exist.

13.11 SECURITY ISSUES

We address the topic of security in a chapter of its own (Chapter 21), but several security issues relevant to IP networking merit discussion here. In this section, we briefly look at a few networking features that have acquired a reputation for causing security problems and recommend ways to minimize their impact. The details of our example Linux systems' default behavior on these issues (and appropriate methods for changing them) are covered later in this section.

IP forwarding

If a Linux box has IP forwarding enabled, it can act as a router. Unless your system has multiple network interfaces and is actually supposed to function as a router, it's advisable to turn this feature off. Hosts that forward packets can sometimes be coerced into compromising security by making external packets appear to have come from inside your network. This subterfuge can help naughty packets evade network scanners and packet filters.

ICMP redirects

ICMP redirects can be used maliciously to reroute traffic and mess with your routing tables. Most operating systems listen to them and follow their instructions by default. It would be bad if all your traffic were rerouted to a competitor's network for a few hours, especially while backups were running! We recommend that you configure your routers (and hosts acting as routers) to ignore and perhaps log ICMP redirects.

Source routing

IP's source routing mechanism lets you specify an explicit series of gateways for a packet to transit on the way to its destination. Source routing bypasses the next-hop routing algorithm that's normally run at each gateway to determine how a packet should be forwarded.

Source routing was part of the original IP specification; it was intended primarily to facilitate testing. It can create security problems because packets are often filtered according to their origin. If someone can cleverly route a packet to make it appear to have originated within your network instead of the Internet, it might slip through your firewall. We recommend that you neither accept nor forward source-routed packets.

Broadcast pings and other forms of directed broadcast

Ping packets addressed to a network's broadcast address (instead of to a particular host address) will typically be delivered to every host on the network. Such packets have been used in denial of service attacks; for example, the so-called smurf attacks. Most hosts have a way to disable broadcast pings—that is, they can be configured not to respond to or forward them. Your Internet router can also filter out broadcast pings before they reach your internal network. It's a good idea to use both host and firewall-level security measures if you can.

Broadcast pings are a form of "directed broadcast," in that they are packets sent to the broadcast address of a distant network. The default handling of such packets has been gradually changing. For example, versions of Cisco's IOS up through 11.x forwarded directed broadcast packets by default, but IOS releases since 12.0 do not. It is usually possible to convince your TCP/IP stack to ignore broadcast packets that come from afar, but since this behavior must be set on each interface, this can be a nontrivial task at a large site.

IP spoofing

The source address on an IP packet is normally filled in by the networking libraries and is the IP address of the host from which the packet was sent. However, if the software creating the packet uses a raw socket, it can fill in any source address it likes. This is called IP spoofing and is usually associated with some kind of malicious network behavior. The machine identified by the spoofed source IP address (if it is a real address) is often the victim in the scheme. Error and return packets can disrupt or flood the victim's network connections.

You should deny IP spoofing at your border router by blocking outgoing packets whose source address is not within your address space. This precaution is especially important if your site is a university where students like to experiment and often feel vindictive toward "jerks" on their favorite IRC (Internet Relay Chat) channels.

At the same time, if you are using private address space internally, you can filter to catch any internal addresses escaping to the Internet. Such packets can never be answered (owing to the lack of a backbone route) and usually indicate that your site has an internal configuration error.

Linux-based firewalls, described in the next section, provide a way to implement such filtering on a host-by-host basis. However, most sites prefer to implement this type of filtering at their border routers rather than at each host. This is the approach we recommend as well. We describe host-based firewalls only for completeness and for special situations.

You must also protect against a hacker forging the source address on external packets to fool your firewall into thinking that they originated on your internal network. The kernel parameter **rp_filter** (settable in the **/proc/sys/net/ipv4/conf/***ifname* directory) can help you detect such packets; the **rp** stands for reverse path. If you set this variable to 1, the kernel discards packets that arrive on an interface that is different from the one on which they would leave if the source address were the destination. This behavior is turned on by default.

If your site has multiple connections to the Internet, it may be perfectly reasonable for inbound and outbound routes to be different. In this situation, you will have to set **rp_filter** to 0 to make your routing protocol work properly. If your site has only one way out to the Internet, then setting **rp_filter** to 1 is usually safe and appropriate.

Host-based firewalls

Linux includes packet filtering (aka "firewall") software. Although we describe this software later in this chapter (page 289) and also in the *Security* chapter (page 676), we don't really recommend using a workstation as a firewall. The security of Linux (especially as shipped by our friendly vendors) is weak, and NT's security is even worse. We suggest that you buy a dedicated hardware solution to use as a firewall. Even a sophisticated software solution like Checkpoint's Firewall-1 product (which runs on a Solaris host) is not as good as a piece of dedicated hardware such as Cisco's PIX box—and it's almost the same price!

A more thorough discussion of firewall-related issues begins on page 676.

Virtual private networks

Many organizations that have offices in several parts of the world would like to have all those locations connected to one big private network. Unfortunately, the cost of leasing a transoceanic or even a transcontinental data line can be prohibitive. Such organizations can actually use the Internet as if it were a private data line by establishing a series of secure, encrypted "tunnels" among their various locations. A "private" network that includes such tunnels is known as a virtual private network or VPN.

See page 683 for more information about IPSEC.

Some VPNs use the IPSEC protocol, which was standardized by the IETF in 1998. Others use proprietary solutions that don't usually interoperate with each other. If you need VPN functionality, we suggest that you look at products like Cisco's 3660 router or the Watchguard Firebox, both of which can do tunneling and encryption. The Watchguard device uses PPP to a serial port for management. A sysadmin can dial into the box to configure it or to access the VPN for testing.

For a low-budget VPN solution, see the example on page 299 that uses PPP over an **ssh** connection to implement a virtual private network.

Security-related kernel variables

Table 13.17 shows Linux's default behavior with regard to various touchy network issues. For a brief description of the implications of these behaviors, see page 286. We recommend that you change the values of these variables so that you do not answer broadcast pings, do not listen to routing redirects, and do not accept source-routed packets.

Table 13.17 Security-related network behaviors in Linux

Feature	Host	Gateway	Control file (in /proc/sys/net)
IP forwarding	off	on	**ipv4/ip_forward** for the whole system **ipv4/conf/**_interface_**/forwarding** per interface[a]
ICMP redirects	obeys	ignores	**ipv4/conf/**_interface_**/accept_redirects**
Source routing	ignores	obeys	**ipv4/conf/**_interface_**/accept_source_route**
Broadcast ping	answers	answers	**ipv4/icmp_echo_ignore_broadcasts**

a. The *interface* can be either a specific interface name or **all**.

To change any of these parameters permanently (or more accurately, to reset them every time the system boots), add the appropriate **echo** commands to a script that is run during the boot sequence or use the **sysctl** command.

 On Red Hat you usually do this by adding values to **/etc/sysctl.conf**, which is read by the **sysctl** command at boot time (at the request of the **network** startup script). The format of **sysctl.conf** is *variable=value* rather than **echo value > variable** as you would enter it to change things by hand. Variable names are pathnames relative to **/proc/sys**; you can also use dots instead of slashes if you prefer. For example, either of the lines

```
net.ipv4.ip_forward=0
net/ipv4/ip_forward=0
```

in the **/etc/sysctl.conf** file would cause IP forwarding to be turned off (for this host). You can also control forwarding in **/etc/sysconfig/network**.

 The SuSE distribution includes the **sysctl** command but does not run the command in its boot scripts and does not ship a nicely commented **/etc/sysctl.conf** file like the ones we have become accustomed to. To change the values of kernel variables relevant to networking, you can mimic the handling of the IP_FORWARD variable from **rc.config** (in **/etc/init.d/boot**) or add your own call to the **sysctl** command somewhere in the startup sequence.

 Debian does provide a sample **sysctl.conf** file and also calls **sysctl** with this file during startup. One of the supplied examples sets the kernel to ignore broadcast pings, as we suggested earlier in this section.

13.12 LINUX NAT (IP MASQUERADING)

Linux traditionally implements only a limited form of Network Address Translation (NAT) that is more properly called Port Address Translation, or PAT. Instead of using a range of IP addresses as a true NAT implementation would, PAT multiplexes all connections onto a single address. To add to the confusion, Linux documents often refer to the feature as neither NAT nor PAT but as "IP masquerading." The details and differences aren't of much practical importance, so we will refer to the Linux implementation as NAT for the sake of consistency.[29]

Linux includes some pretty reasonable software for setting up NAT. The predominant software as of this writing is **ipchains**, which all of our example distributions provide. A new and improved user space packet filtering package called **iptables** uses the "netfilter" feature in the Linux 2.4 kernel and is in the current release of Red Hat. We expect that **iptables** will completely replace **ipchains** in relatively short order. On systems that have both, you can use only one of the systems at a time; we suggest **iptables**.

_____

29. The more recent **iptables** software in kernel version 2.4 can in fact provide true NAT, but it remains to be seen whether this feature will become widely used.

Both packages implement not only NAT but also packet filtering. In **ipchains** this was a bit of a mess, but **iptables** makes a much cleaner separation between the NAT and filtering features. Packet filtering features are covered in more detail in the *Security* chapter starting on page 676; here, we restrict our discussion to a few examples of NAT configuration.

For IP masquerading to work, you must enable IP forwarding and build the kernel with CONFIG_IP_MASQUERADE defined. It also helps to set the kernel variable ip_masq_debug to facilitate debugging (see the **sysctl** command or change the contents of **/proc/sys/net/ipv4/ip_masq_debug** to 1).

For example, to set up IP masquerading (aka NAT, aka PAT) to disguise the private address space used on the internal network 192.168.1.0/24, you could use the following command:

```
ipchains -A forward -i ppp0 -s 192.168.1.0/24 -d ! 192.168.1.0/24 -j MASQ
```

Here, we specified in the matching criteria that the source address must be internal and the destination address external (the **!** negates the sense of the test) in order for IP masquerading to occur. Internal traffic that happens to pass through this host is not affected.

Since **ipchains** implements PAT rather than true NAT, there is no need to specify a range of external addresses to be used on the Internet. The Linux gateway uses its own IP address for all external traffic and uses port numbers to multiplex connections from multiple interior hosts.

The **iptables** command to map packets from the 192.168.1.0/24 network to a range of 10 addresses in the routable network 128.138.198.0 would be:

```
iptables -A POSTROUTING SNAT --to-source 128.138.198.1-128.138.198.10
```

You can also specify a range of source ports by appending **:***startport-stopport* to the command. In general, it's best to let **iptables** manage the ports on its own. By default, **iptables** will not modify the source port unless necessary for uniqueness.

13.13   PPP: THE POINT-TO-POINT PROTOCOL

PPP, the Point-to-Point Protocol, has the distinction of being used on both the slowest and fastest Internet links. In its synchronous form, it is the encapsulation protocol used on high-speed circuits that have fat routers at either end. In its asynchronous form, it is a serial line encapsulation protocol that specifies how IP packets must be encoded for transmission on a slow (and often unreliable) serial line. Serial lines simply transmit streams of bits and have no concept of the beginning or end of a packet. The PPP device driver takes care of encoding and decoding packets on the serial line; it adds a link-level header and markers that separate packets.

PPP is sometimes used with the newer home technologies such as DSL and cable modems, but this fact is usually hidden from you as an administrator. Encapsulation is typically performed by the interface device, and the traffic is bridged to Ethernet. You just see an Ethernet connection.

Designed by committee, PPP is the "everything *and* the kitchen sink" encapsulation protocol. It was inspired by the SLIP (Serial Line IP) and CSLIP (Compressed SLIP) protocols designed by Rick Adams and Van Jacobson, respectively. PPP differs from these systems in that it allows the transmission of multiple protocols over a single link. It is specified in RFC1331.

Addressing PPP performance issues

PPP provides all the functionality of Ethernet, but at *much* slower speeds. Normal office LANs operate at 10 Mb/s or 100 Mb/s—that's 10,000–100,000 Kb/s. A dial-up connection operates at about 28–56 Kb/s.[30] To put these numbers in perspective, it takes about 5 minutes to transfer a one-megabyte file across a dial-up PPP line. The speed is OK for email or web browsing with images turned off, but glitzy web sites will drive you crazy. To improve interactive performance, you can set the MTU of the point-to-point quite low. It usually defaults to 512 bytes; try 128 if you are doing a lot of interactive work. If you are using PPP over Ethernet, use **tcpdump** to see the sizes of the packets going over the network and set the MTU accordingly. Ethernet's MTU is 1500, but the PPP encapsulation makes slightly smaller values more efficient. For example, **pppoe** suggests 1412 bytes for hosts behind the PPP connection and 1492 on the PPP link. You certainly don't want each packet to be fragmented because you've set your default MTU too big.

See Chapter 17 for more information about NFS.

Running NFS over a PPP link can be painfully slow. You should consider it only if you can run NFS over TCP instead of UDP.

The X Windows protocol uses TCP, so it's possible to run X applications over a PPP link. Programs like **xterm** work fine, but avoid applications that use fancy fonts or bitmapped graphics.

Connecting to a network with PPP

To connect a host to a network with PPP, you must satisfy three prerequisites:

- Your host's kernel must be able to send IP packets across a serial line as specified by the PPP protocol standard.

- You must have a user-level program that allows you to establish and maintain PPP connections.

- A host on the other end of the serial line must understand the protocol you are using.

---

30. PPP is normally used at speeds over 19,200 bps. Technically, it can be used on slower links, but it becomes insufferably slow.

Making your host speak PPP

*See page 266 for more information about **ifconfig**.*

To establish a PPP connection, your host must be capable of sending and receiving PPP packets. On Linux systems, PPP is a loadable kernel module that places network packets in the serial device output queue, and vice versa. This module usually pretends to be just another network interface, so it can be manipulated with standard configuration tools such as **ifconfig**.

Controlling PPP links

The exact sequence of events involved in establishing a PPP connection depends on your OS and on the type of server you are dialing into. Connections can be initiated either manually or dynamically.

To establish a PPP connection manually, you run a command that dials a modem, logs in to a remote host, and starts the remote PPP protocol engine. If this procedure succeeds, the serial port is then configured as a network interface. This option normally leaves the link up for a long time, which makes it best suited for a phone line dedicated to IP connectivity.

In a dynamic configuration, a daemon watches your serial "network" interfaces to see when traffic has been queued for them. When someone tries to send a packet, the daemon automatically dials a modem to establish the connection, transmits the packet, and if the line goes back to being idle, disconnects the line after a reasonable amount of time. Dynamic dial-up is often used if a phone line carries both voice and data traffic or if the connection involves long distance or connect-time charges.

Software to implement both of these connection schemes is included with most versions of PPP.

Finding a host to talk to

If you're setting up a link between two sites within your own company or, perhaps, between home and work, you can simply install the PPP software on both ends. However, if your intent is to use PPP to obtain an Internet connection, you'll probably need to deal with a commercial ISP. Most ISPs offer dial-up PPP service to the public at a reasonable cost. Many also support either DSL or cable modem connections that use PPP over faster media.

Assigning an address

See page 265 for more information about assigning IP addresses.

Just as you must assign an IP address to a new host on your Ethernet, you need to assign an IP address to each PPP interface. There are a number of ways to assign addresses to these links (including assigning no addresses at all). We discuss only the simplest method here.

Think of a PPP link as a network of its own. That is, a network of exactly two hosts, often called a "point-to-point" network. You need to assign a network number to the link just as you would assign a network number to a new Ethernet segment, using whatever rules are in effect at your site. You can pick any two host addresses on that network and assign one to each end of the link. Follow other local customs, such as subnetting standards, as well. Each host then becomes a "gateway" to the point-to-point network as far as the rest of the world is concerned. (In the real world, you usually do not control both ends of the link; your ISP gives you the IP address you must use at your end.)

DHCP can also be used to assign the IP address at the end of a PPP link. Some ISPs offer home service that uses DHCP and business service that costs more but includes static addresses.

Routing

See Chapter 14 for more information about routing.

Since PPP requires the remote server to act as an IP router, you need to be concerned with IP routing just as you would for a "real" gateway, such as a machine that connects two Ethernets. The purpose of routing is to direct packets through gateways so that they can reach their ultimate destinations. Routing can be configured in several different ways.

A run-of-the-mill PPP client host should have a default route that forwards packets to the PPP server. Likewise, the server needs to be known to the other hosts on its network as the gateway to the leaf machine.

Most PPP packages handle these routing chores automatically.

Ensuring security

See Chapter 21 for more information about security.

Security issues arise whenever you add a host to a network. Since a host connected via PPP is a bona fide member of the network, you need to treat it as such: verify that the system has no accounts without passwords or with insecure passwords, that all appropriate vendor security fixes have been installed, and so on. See the *Security issues* section on page 286 for some specifics on network security. PPP on Linux supports two authentication protocols: PAP, the Password Authentication Protocol, and CHAP, the Challenge Handshake Authentication Protocol.

Using terminal servers

You may find that once you begin offering PPP connections to home users, you have more requests than you have serial ports. A number of terminal servers offer PPP capability, and recent ones also have integrated modems. Our favorite is the Lucent (formerly Livingston) Portmaster 3. The Cisco Access Server AS5x00 series is also popular. These products provide a convenient and easily maintainable source of serial ports complete with PPP software already installed. They allow you to establish a dial-in "pool" of modems that offer PPP service to off-site users.

Using chat scripts

The Linux serial line PPP implementation uses a "chat script" to talk to the modem and also to log in to the remote machine and start up a PPP server. A chat script consists of a sequence of strings to send and strings to expect in return, with a limited

TCP/IP

form of conditional statement that can express concepts such as "expect the string 'Login', but if you don't get it, send a carriage return and wait for it again."

The idea of a chat script originated with the UUCP store-and-forward system of days gone by. In the 1980s, machines would call each other up in the middle of the night, log in through chat scripts, and exchange files. Despite popular demand, UUCP is not quite completely dead yet: the user uucp is the group owner of serial device files on SuSE Linux, and you must be a member of the uucp group to use a dial-out modem for PPP.

Most PPP implementations come with sample chat scripts that you can adapt to your own environment. You'll need to edit the scripts to set parameters such as the telephone number to call and the command to run after a successful login. Most chat scripts contain a cleartext password; set the permissions accordingly.

Linux PPP configuration

Modems (along with printers) have always been a thorn in the side of system administrators. And it's no wonder, when the software to configure a PPP connection over a random modem has over 125 possible options—far too many to weigh and configure carefully.

Red Hat, SuSE, and Debian all ship Paul Mackerras's PPP package, which uses a daemon called **pppd** and keeps most of its configuration files in **/etc/ppp**. Run the command **pppd --version** to see what version of the PPP package has been installed on your particular distribution.

Red Hat and SuSE include a version of PPP from Roaring Penguin Software that's designed for use over Ethernet (for example, on a DSL connection to a local ISP). All three of our reference distributions also include PPP support for ISDN connections. The configuration files for these additional media are co-located with those for PPP over serial links in the directory **/etc/ppp**. Filenames are usually similar but with the addition of **oe** for "over Ethernet" or **i** for ISDN. Table 13.18 shows the locations of the relevant commands and config files.

See page 108 for more information about the names of serial ports.
In our configuration file examples, we call the serial port that has a modem attached to it **/dev/modem**. Some distributions actually have a **/dev/modem** file that is a link to one of the system's serial ports (usually **/dev/ttyS0** or **/dev/ttyS1**), but this practice is now deprecated. You should substitute the device file appropriate for your situation. SuSE helpfully defines a variable called MODEM in **/etc/rc.config** for use in their startup scripts, but doesn't seem to actually use it.

In addition to PPP software, each distribution provides several programs that actually dial the telephone to establish a connection. The examples below use **pppd** with chat scripts and **wvdial**, which is included on all of our example distributions. We do not describe the alternatives to **wvdial**, but Table 13.19 shows where to look and what to look for if you're interested in comparing.

Table 13.18   PPP-related commands and config files by system

System	Commands or config files	Description
Red Hat, SuSE, Debian (serial)	**/usr/sbin/pppd** **/usr/sbin/chat** **/usr/sbin/pppstats** **/usr/sbin/pppdump** **/etc/ppp/options**	PPP daemon program Talks to modem Shows statistics of PPP link Makes PPP packets readable ASCII Config file for **pppd**
Debian (serial extras)	**/usr/bin/pon** **/usr/bin/poff** **/usr/bin/plog** **/usr/sbin/pppconfig** **/etc/ppp/peers/provider** **/etc/chatscripts/provider**	Starts up a PPP connection Shuts down a PPP connection Shows the tail end of **ppp.log** Configures **pppd** Options for **pon** to contact your ISP Chat script for **pon** to talk to the ISP
Red Hat (DSL)	**/usr/sbin/pppoe** **/usr/sbin/pppoe-server** **/usr/sbin/pppoe-sniff** **/usr/sbin/adsl-connect** **/usr/sbin/adsl-setup** **/usr/sbin/adsl-start** **/usr/sbin/adsl-stop** **/usr/sbin/adsl-status** **/etc/ppp/pppoe.conf** **/etc/ppp/pppoe-server-options**	PPP-over-Ethernet client PPP-over-Ethernet server Sniffer that debugs provider's quirks Script that manages link Script that configures **pppoe** Script that brings up **pppoe** link Script that shuts down **pppoe** link Shows the status of **pppoe** link Config file used by **adsl-*** File for extra options to server
SuSE (DSL)	**/usr/sbin/pppoed** **/etc/pppoed.conf**	PPP over Ethernet client Config file for **pppoed**
All (ISDN)	**/usr/sbin/ipppd** **/usr/sbin/ipppstats** **/etc/ppp/ioptions**	PPP over ISDN daemon Shows ISDP PPP statistics Options to **ipppd**

Table 13.19   PPP dialers by system

System	Dialer	Sample configurations
Red Hat	**wvdial** **dip**	– –
SuSE	**wvdial** **diald** **dip**	Well-commented sample **/etc/wvdial.conf** Sample **/etc/diald.conf** and **/usr/lib/diald/*** Sample **/etc/diphosts**
Debian	**wvdial** **diald**	Includes sample configs Sample configs in **/etc/diald**

Now that we've mentioned the modem ports and dialer software, let's talk about how to set up **pppd** to use them. Global options are set in the file **/etc/ppp/options**, and options for particular connections can be stored in the directories **/etc/ppp/peers** and **/etc/chatscripts** (on Debian). Red Hat and SuSE tend to put chat scripts in the

TCP/IP

/etc/ppp directory with names like **chat.***remotehost*. Alternatively, on Red Hat, the file **/etc/sysconfig/network-scripts/ifcfg-***ttyname* can include connection-specific options for a particular PPP interface.

By default, **pppd** consults the **options** file first, then the user's personal **~/.ppprc** startup file, then the connection-specific **options.***ttyname* file (if one exists), and finally, its command-line arguments.

A handy trick suggested by Jonathan Corbet, a Linux old-timer, is to define more than one PPP interface: one for home, one for hotels while traveling, etc. This setup can make it easier to switch contexts.

wvdial is smarter than **chat** and has sensible default behavior if parameters are left unspecified. **wvdial** gets its configuration information from **/etc/wvdial.conf**: modem details, login name, password, telephone number, etc. You can provide information for multiple destinations in the single configuration file. Use the **wvdialconf** program to figure out your modem's characteristics and create an initial **wvdial.conf** file for it.

The configuration files below are drawn from several different PPP setups. The first file, **/etc/ppp/options**, sets global options for **pppd**. The active options for each distribution as shipped are shown below:

Red Hat: **/etc/ppp/options**

```
lock
```

SuSE: **/etc/ppp/options**

```
debug
noauth
crtscts
lock
modem
asyncmap 0
nodetach
lcp-echo-interval 30
lcp-echo-failure 4
idle 600
noipx
```

Debian: **/etc/ppp/options**

```
asyncmap 0
auth
crtscts
lock
hide-password
modem
proxyarp
lcp-echo-interval 30
lcp-echo-failure 4
noipx
```

At the University of Colorado, we like to use the following options file:

```
# Global PPP options
lock                      # Always lock the device you're using
asyncmap 0x00000000  # By default, don't escape anything
crtscts                   # Use hardware flow control
defaultroute              # Add default route thru the ppp interface
mru 552                   # MRU/MTU 512 (data) + 40 (header)
mtu 552
```

 Next is a sample **/etc/sysconfig/network-scripts/ifcgf-ppp0** file from a Red Hat system. This skeletal file was constructed by the **linuxconf** utility.

```
PERSIST=yes
DEFROUTE=yes
ONBOOT=no
INITSTRING=ATZ
MODEMPORT=/dev/modem
LINESPEED=115200
ESCAPECHARS=no
DEFABORT=yes
HARDFLOWCTL=yes
DEVICE=ppp0
PPPOPTIONS=
DEBUG=yes
PAPNAME=remote
REMIP=
IPADDR=
BOOTPROTO=none
MTU=
MRU=
DISCONNECTTIMEOUT=
RETRYTIMEOUT=
USERCTL=no
```

Here is a sample chat script (**chat-ppp0**) that corresponds to the **ifcfg-ppp0** file above (with all of its terse and slightly bizarre syntax):

```
'ABORT' 'BUSY'
'ABORT' 'ERROR'
'ABORT' 'NO CARRIER'
'ABORT' 'NO DIALTONE'
'ABORT' 'Invalid Login'
'ABORT' 'Login incorrect'
'' 'ATZ'
'OK' 'ATDT phone-number'
'CONNECT' ''
'TIMEOUT' '120'
'ogin:' 'account'
'ord:' 'password'
'TIMEOUT' '5'
'~--' ''
```

Several lines in this chat script contain a null parameter indicated by a pair of single quotes, which look similar to double quotes in this font.

You can usually adapt an existing chat script to your environment without worrying too much about exactly how it works. Here, the first few lines set up some general conditions on which the script should abort. The next lines initialize the modem and dial the phone, and the remaining lines wait for a connection and enter the appropriate username and password.

The timeout in the chat script sometimes needs to be adjusted to deal with complicated dialing situations such as those in hotels or businesses with local telephone switches, or to deal with the voice mail signal that some phone companies use before they give you a real dial tone. On most modems, a comma in the phone number indicates a pause in dialing. You may need several commas if you have to dial a particular digit and then wait for a second dial tone before continuing.

PPP logins at our site are just usernames with a P in front of them. This convention makes it easy to remember to whom a particular PPP machine belongs.

The association between **ifcfg-ppp0** and **chat.ppp0** is made by the **ifup** command, which will be run automatically during startup since the **ifcfg** file exists. You can also call **pppd** explicitly with a connection-specific options file as an argument, provided that file contains a connect line that lists the corresponding chat filename.

 Our next dialup example is from a Debian system. It uses the **peers** directory, puts its chat script in the **/etc/chatscripts** directory, and uses the PAP authentication mechanism instead of storing the password in the chat script. First, the options for this connection, **/etc/ppp/peers/my-isp**:

```
/dev/modem              ### fill in the serial port of your modem
debug
crtscts
name username           ### username at my-isp
remotename my-isp
noauth
noipdefault
defaultroute
connect '/usr/sbin/chat -v -f /etc/chatscripts/my-isp'
```

/etc/chatscripts/my-isp contains the following entries:

```
'ABORT' 'BUSY'
'ABORT' 'ERROR'
'ABORT' 'NO CARRIER'
'ABORT' 'NO DIALTONE'
'' 'ATZ'
'OK' 'ATDT phonenumber'
'CONNECT' ''
'TIMEOUT' 15
'~--' ''
```

The authentication file used to connect to the ISP, **/etc/ppp/pap-secrets**, needs to contain the line:

```
login-name my-isp password
```

where *my-isp* is the value of the remotename variable in the options above. To bring up the connection in this scenario, use the command **pppd call my-isp**.

Here is an example that uses PPP over existing generic Internet connectivity, but teams up with **ssh** to create a secure connection through a virtual private network (VPN). We show both the server and client configurations.

Server's **/etc/ppp/options** file:

```
noauth
logfile pppd.log
passive
silent
nodetach
```

Each connection also has an **/etc/ppp/options.***ttyname* file that contains the IP address assignments for the connection:

```
local-IPaddress:remote-IPaddress
```

The PPP user's shell is set to **/usr/sbin/pppd** on the server so that the server daemon is started automatically. All the authentication keys have to be set up in advance with **ssh-agent** so that no password is requested. On the client side, the configuration is done in the **/etc/ppp/peers** directory with a file named for the server—let's call the configuration "my-work". The client's **/etc/ppp/peers/my-work** file would contain:

```
noauth
debug
logfile pppd.log
passive
silent
pty "ssh -t user@remotehost"
```

To log in to work from home on a secure PPP connection, the user would just type **pppd call my-work**.

Finally, we include an example that uses the **wvdial** command and its easy configuration to avoid all the chat script magic that seems to be necessary:

/etc/wvdial.conf:

```
[Dialer Defaults]
Phone = phonenumber
Username = login-name
Password = password
Modem = /dev/ttyS1

[Dialer creditcard]
Phone = long-distance-access-code,,,phone-number,,cc-number
```

TCP/IP

If **wvdial** is invoked with no arguments, it will use the dialer defaults section of the **/etc/wvdial.conf** file or your ~/**.wvdialrc** to make the call and start up PPP. If called with a parameter (for example, **wvdial creditcard**) it will use the appropriate section of the config file to override any parameters specified in the defaults section.

To take a PPP connection down, it's better to use **ifdown** than to just kill the **pppd** daemon. If you kill **pppd** directly, Linux will notice and restart it on you.

```
% sudo ifdown ppp0
```

If your machine is portable and sometimes uses Ethernet instead of PPP, there may be a default route through the Ethernet interface before **pppd** starts up. Unfortunately, **pppd** is too polite to rip out that route and install its own, which is the behavior you'd actually want. To fix the problem, remove the existing default route before you start **pppd**. It's easiest to write yourself a little **ppp.up** script that removes the default route automatically.

Here's what the PPP interface configuration and routing table look like after the PPP connection has been brought up:

```
% ifconfig ppp0
ppp0   Link encap:Point-to-Point Protocol
       inet addr:10.0.0.56  P-t-P:10.0.0.55  Mask:255.255.255.255
       UP POINTOPOINT RUNNING NOARP MULTICAST  MTU:1500  Metric:1
       RX packets:125 errors:0 dropped:0 overruns:0 frame:0
       TX packets:214 errors:0 dropped:0 overruns:0 carrier:0
       collisions:0 txqueuelen:3
       RX bytes:11446 (11.1 Kb)  TX bytes:105586 (103.1 Kb)
```

```
% netstat -nr
Kernel IP routing table
Destination  Gateway     Genmask          Flags  MSS  Window irtt Iface
10.0.0.55    0.0.0.0     255.255.255.255  UH     40   0         0  ppp0
0.0.0.0      10.0.0.55   0.0.0.0          UG     40   0         0  ppp0
```

You can obtain statistics about the PPP connection and the packets it has transferred with the **pppstats** command:

```
% pppstats
    IN  PACK VJCOMP VJUNC VJERR |   OUT  PACK VJCOMP VJUNC NON-VJ
 11862   133      8    96     0 | 110446   226     27    89    110
```

The VJCOMP column counts packets that use Van Jacobson's TCP header compression, and the VJUNC column counts those that don't. See RFC1144 for details.

Debugging a PPP connection can be a real pain because so many players are involved. **pppd** submits log entries to the daemon facility through syslog on Red Hat and Debian systems and to facility local2 on SuSE. You can increase the logging level by using the **debug** flag on **pppd**'s command line or by requesting more logging in the options file. **pppd** also provides detailed exit codes on failure, so if you try to run **pppd** and it balks, run **echo $status** (before you do anything else) to recover the exit code and then look this value up in the **pppd** man page.

SuSE Linux tends to include sample configuration files for each subsystem that are mostly comments but that explain the format and the meaning of available options. The files in SuSE's **/etc/ppp** directory are no exception; they are well documented and contain sensible suggested values for many parameters.

 Debian also has well-documented sample configuration files for PPP. It has a subdirectory devoted to chat scripts, **/etc/chatscripts**. To bring up an interface with PPP, you can include it in the **/etc/network/interfaces** file with the ppp method and the provider option to tie the name of your provider (in our case, my-isp) to a filename in the **/etc/peers** directory (**/etc/peers/my-isp**). For example:

```
iface eth0 inet ppp
    provider my-isp
```

In this case, the Debian-specific commands **pon** and **poff** will be used to manage the connection.

13.14 LINUX NETWORKING QUIRKS

Unlike most kernels, Linux pays attention to the type-of-service (TOS) bits in IP packets and gives faster service to packets that are labeled as being interactive (low latency). Jammin'! Unfortunately, brain damage on the part of Microsoft necessitates that you turn off this perfectly reasonable behavior.

All packets originating on Windows 95, 98, NT, and 2000 are labeled as being interactive, no matter what their purpose. UNIX systems, on the other hand, usually do not mark any packets as being interactive. If your Linux gateway serves a mixed network of UNIX and Windows systems, the Windows packets will consistently get preferential treatment. The performance hit for UNIX can be quite noticeable.

You can turn off TOS-based packet sorting when you compile the Linux kernel. Just say no to the option "IP: use TOS value as routing key."

When IP masquerading (NAT) is enabled, it tells the kernel to reassemble packet fragments into a complete packet before forwarding them, even if the kernel must immediately refragment the packet to send it on its way. This reassembly can cost quite a few CPU cycles, but CPUs are fast enough now that it shouldn't really be an issue on modern machines.

Linux lets you change the MAC-level addresses of certain types of network interfaces:

```
redhat% ifconfig eth1
eth1   Link encap:Ethernet  HWaddr 00:02:B3:19:C8:87
       BROADCAST MULTICAST  MTU:1500  Metric:1
       RX packets:0 errors:0 dropped:0 overruns:0 frame:0
       TX packets:0 errors:0 dropped:0 overruns:0 carrier:0
       collisions:0 txqueuelen:100
       Interrupt:7 Base address:0xee80

redhat% sudo ifconfig eth1 hw ether 00:02:B3:19:C8:21
```

TCP/IP

```
redhat% ifconfig eth1
eth1   Link encap:Ethernet  HWaddr 00:02:B3:19:C8:21
       BROADCAST MULTICAST  MTU:1500  Metric:1
       RX packets:0 errors:0 dropped:0 overruns:0 frame:0
       TX packets:0 errors:0 dropped:0 overruns:0 carrier:0
       collisions:0 txqueuelen:100
       Interrupt:7 Base address:0xee80
```

This is a dangerous feature that tends to break things. It can be handy, but it should be used only as a last resort.

13.15 RECOMMENDED READING

STEVENS, W. RICHARD. *TCP/IP Illustrated, Volume One: The Protocols.* Reading, MA: Addison-Wesley. 1994.

WRIGHT, GARY R., AND W. RICHARD STEVENS. *TCP/IP Illustrated, Volume Two: The Implementation.* Reading, MA: Addison-Wesley. 1995.

These two books are an excellent and thorough guide to the TCP/IP protocol stack. A bit dated, but still solid.

STEVENS, W. RICHARD. *UNIX Network Programming.* Upper Saddle River, NJ: Prentice Hall. 1990.

STEVENS, W. RICHARD. *UNIX Network Programming, Volume 1: Networking APIs—Sockets and XTI.* Upper Saddle River, NJ: Prentice Hall. 1997.

STEVENS, W. RICHARD. *UNIX Network Programming, Volume 2: Interprocess Communications.* Upper Saddle River, NJ: Prentice Hall. 1998.

These books are the student's bibles in networking classes that involve programming. If you need only the Berkeley sockets interface, the original edition is a fine reference. If you need the STREAMS interface too, then the second edition, which became too large to bind in one volume, is a good bet. The second edition also includes IPv6. All three are clearly written in typical Rich Stevens style.

TANENBAUM, ANDREW. *Computer Networks, 3rd Edition.* Upper Saddle River, NJ: Prentice Hall. 1996.

This was the first networking text, and it is still a classic. It contains a very thorough description of all the nitty-gritty details going on at the physical and link layers of the protocol stack. Earlier editions were kind of stuck on the ISO protocols, but the latest edition has been updated to cover the modern Internet.

SALUS, PETER H. *Casting the Net, From ARPANET to INTERNET and Beyond.* Reading, MA: Addison-Wesley. 1995.

This is a lovely history of the ARPANET as it grew into the Internet, written by a historian who has been hanging out with UNIX people long enough to sound like one of them!

COMER, DOUGLAS. *Internetworking with TCP/IP Volume 1: Principles, Protocols, and Architectures, 4th Edition*. Upper Saddle River, NJ: Prentice Hall. 2000.

The Comer books were for a long time the standard reference for the TCP/IP protocols. This new edition has descriptions of modern networking technologies as well as the TCP/IP protocol suite. It is designed as an undergraduate textbook and is a good source of background material.

HEDRICK, CHARLES. "Introduction to the Internet Protocols." Rutgers University.

This document is a gentle introduction to TCP/IP. It does not seem to have a permanent home, but it is widely distributed on the web; search for it.

HUNT, CRAIG. *TCP/IP Network Administration, Second Edition*. Sebastopol, CA: O'Reilly & Associates. 1998.

Like other books in the nutshell series, this book is directed at administrators of UNIX systems. Half the book is about TCP/IP, and the rest deals with higher-level UNIX facilities such as email and remote login.

www.netscan.org maintains a list of "smurf" attack amplifiers (systems that respond to broadcast ICMP). You can type in your network's IP address to verify that it's OK, provided that you subnet on byte boundaries. If your network is on this list, disable directed broadcast as described in this chapter to become a nicer netizen.

An excellent collection of documents about the history of the Internet and its various technologies can be found at www.isoc.org/internet/history.

TCP/IP

13.16 EXERCISES

E13.1 How could listening to (i.e., obeying) ICMP redirects allow an unauthorized user to compromise the network?

E13.2 What is the MTU of a network link? What happens if the MTU for a given link is set too high? Too low?

★ **E13.3** After installing a fresh Linux system, how would you address the security issues mentioned in this chapter? Check to see if any of the security problems have been dealt with on the Linux systems in your lab. (Requires root access.)

★ **E13.4** Explain the concept of subnetting and explain why it is useful. What are netmasks? How do netmasks relate to the split between the network and host sections of an IP address?

★ **E13.5** The network 134.122.0.0/16 has been subdivided into /19 networks.

a) How many /19 networks are there? List them. What is their netmask?
b) How many hosts could there be on each network?
c) Determine which network the IP address 134.122.67.124 belongs to.
d) What is the broadcast address for each network?

★ **E13.6** Host 128.138.2.4 on network 128.138.2.0/24 wants to send a packet to host 128.138.129.12 on network 128.138.129.0/24. Assume that:

- Host 128.138.2.4 has a default route through 128.138.2.1.
- Host 128.138.2.4 has just booted and has not sent or received any packets.
- All other machines on the network have been running for a long time.
- Router 128.138.2.1 has a direct link to 128.138.129.1, the gateway for the 128.138.129.0/24 subnet.

a) List all the steps that are needed to send the packet. Show the source and destination Ethernet and IP addresses of all packets transmitted.

b) If the network were 128.138.0.0/16, would your answer change? How?

c) If the 128.138.2.0 network were a /26 network instead of a /24, would your answer change? How?

★★ **E13.7** What steps are needed to add a new machine to the network in your lab environment? In answering, use parameters appropriate for your network and local situation. Assume that the new machine already runs Linux.

★★ **E13.8** Show the configuration file needed to set up a DHCP server that assigns addresses in the range 128.138.192.[1-55]. Use a lease time of two hours and make sure that the host with Ethernet address 00:10:5A:C7:4B:89 always receives IP address 128.138.192.55.

14 Routing

Keeping track of where network traffic should flow next is no easy task. Chapter 13 provided a short introduction to IP packet forwarding. In this chapter, we examine the forwarding process in more detail and investigate several network protocols that allow routers to discover efficient routes automatically. Routing protocols not only lessen the day-to-day administrative burden of maintaining routing information, but they also allow network traffic to be redirected quickly if a router or network should fail.

It's important to distinguish between the process of actually forwarding IP packets and the management of the routing table that drives this process, both of which are commonly called "routing." Packet forwarding is simple, whereas route computation is tricky; consequently, the second meaning is used more often in practice. This chapter describes only unicast routing; multicast routing involves an array of very different problems and is beyond the scope of this book.

Conventional wisdom says that IP routing is exceptionally difficult, understood only by a few long-haired hippies that live in the steam tunnels under the Lawrence Berkeley Laboratories campus in California. In reality, this is not the case, as long as you understand the basic premise that IP routing is "next hop" routing. At any given point, you only need to determine the *next* host or router in a packet's journey to its final destination. This is a different approach from that of many legacy protocols which determine the exact path a packet will travel before it leaves its originating host, a scheme known as source routing.[1]

14.1 PACKET FORWARDING: A CLOSER LOOK

Before we jump into the management of routing tables, let's take a more detailed look at how the tables are used. Consider the network shown in Exhibit A.

Exhibit A   Example network

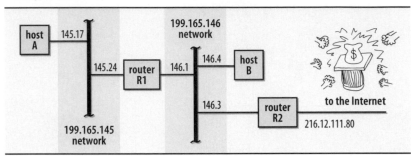

Router R1 connects the two Ethernets, and router R2 connects one of the nets to the outside world. (For now, we'll assume that R1 and R2 are Linux computers rather than dedicated routers.) Let's look at some routing tables and some specific packet forwarding scenarios. First, host A's routing table:

```
A% netstat -rn
Kernel IP routing table
Destination     Gateway          Genmask        Flags MSS Window irtt Iface
199.165.145.0   0.0.0.0          255.255.255.0  U        0   0        0 eth0
127.0.0.0       0.0.0.0          255.0.0.0      U        0   0        0 lo
0.0.0.0         199.165.145.24   0.0.0.0        UG       0   0        0 eth0
```

*See page 266 for more information about **ifconfig**.*

Host A has the simplest routing configuration of the four machines. The first two routes describe the machine's own network interfaces in standard routing terms. These entries exist so that forwarding to directly connected networks need not be handled as a special case. eth0 is host A's Ethernet interface, and lo is the loopback interface, a virtual network interface emulated in software. Entries such as these are normally added automatically by **ifconfig** when a network interface is configured.

The default route on host A forwards all packets not addressed to the loopback address or to the 199.165.145 network to the router R1, whose address on this network is 199.165.145.24. The G flag indicates that this route goes to a gateway, not to one of A's local interfaces. Gateways can be only one hop away.

See page 245 for more information about addressing.

Suppose a process on A sends a packet to B, whose address is 199.165.146.4. The IP implementation looks for a route to the target network, 199.165.146, but none of the routes match. The default route is invoked and the packet is forwarded to R1. Exhibit B shows the packet that actually goes out on the Ethernet (the addresses in the Ethernet header are the MAC addresses of A's and R1's interfaces on the 145 net).

---

1. It is also possible to source-route IP packets, but this is almost never done. The feature is not widely supported because of security considerations.

Exhibit B   Ethernet packet

Ethernet header	IP header	UDP header and data
From: A To: R1 Type: IP	From: 199.165.145.17 To: 199.165.146.4 Type: UDP	1100101011010101110101011011 0101 0111011011011101010001010010 0010 0101111011010101010011101010 000

UDP PACKET

IP PACKET

ETHERNET FRAME

The Ethernet destination hardware address is that of router R1, but the IP packet hidden within the Ethernet frame does not mention R1 at all. When R1 inspects the packet it has received, it will see from the IP destination address that it is not the ultimate destination of the packet. It will then use its own routing table to forward the packet to host B without rewriting the IP header, so that it still shows the packet coming from A.

Here's the routing table for host R1:

```
R1% netstat -rn
Kernel IP routing table
Destination    Gateway        Genmask         Flags MSS  Window  irtt  Iface
127.0.0.0      0.0.0.0        255.0.0.0       U     0    0       0     lo
199.165.145.0  0.0.0.0        255.255.255.0   U     0    0       0     eth0
199.165.146.0  0.0.0.0        255.255.255.0   U     0    0       0     eth1
0.0.0.0        199.165.146.3  0.0.0.0         UG    0    0       0     eth1
```

This table is similar to that of host A, except that there are two physical network interfaces. The default route in this case points to R2, since that's the gateway through which the Internet can be reached. Packets bound for either of the 199.165 networks can be delivered directly.

Like host A, host B has only one real network interface. However, B needs an additional route to function correctly because it has direct connections to two different routers. Traffic for the 199.165.145 net must travel via R1, while other traffic should go out to the Internet via R2.

```
B% netstat -rn
Kernel IP routing table
Destination    Gateway        Genmask         Flags MSS  Window  irtt  Iface
127.0.0.0      0.0.0.0        255.0.0.0       U     0    0       0     lo
199.165.145.0  199.165.146.1  255.255.255.0   U     0    0       0     eth0
199.165.146.0  0.0.0.0        255.255.255.0   U     0    0       0     eth0
0.0.0.0        199.165.146.3  0.0.0.0         UG    0    0       0     eth0
```

Routing

See page 261 for
an explanation of
ICMP redirects.

It is possible to configure host B with initial knowledge of only one gateway, thus relying on the help of ICMP redirects to eliminate extra hops. For example, one possible initial configuration for host B is:

```
B% netstat -rn
Kernel IP routing table
Destination    Gateway        Genmask        Flags MSS Window irtt Iface
127.0.0.0      0.0.0.0        255.0.0.0      U       0  0        0 lo
199.165.146.0  0.0.0.0        255.255.255.0  U       0  0        0 eth0
0.0.0.0        199.165.146.3  0.0.0.0        UG      0  0        0 eth0
```

If B then sends a packet to host A (199.165.145.17), no route will match and the packet will be forwarded to R2 for delivery. R2 (which, being a router, presumably has complete information about the network) will send the packet on to R1. Since R1 and B are on the same network, R2 will also send an ICMP redirect notice to B, and B will enter a host route for A into its routing table:

```
199.165.145.17 199.165.146.1  255.255.255.255 UGHD 0  0        0 eth0
```

This route will send all future traffic for A directly through R1. However, it does not affect routing for other hosts on A's network, all of which will have to be routed by separate redirects from R2.

Some sites have chosen ICMP redirects as their primary routing "protocol," thinking that this approach is very dynamic. Unfortunately, once the kernel learns a route from a redirect, either the route must be manually deleted or the machine must be rebooted if that information changes. Because of this problem and several other disadvantages of redirects (increased network load, increased load on R2, routing table clutter, dependence on extra servers), we don't recommend the use of redirects for configurations such as this. In a properly configured network, redirects should never appear in the routing table.

14.2 ROUTING DAEMONS AND ROUTING PROTOCOLS

In simple networks such as the one shown in Exhibit A, it is perfectly reasonable to configure routing by hand. At some point, however, networks become too complicated to be managed this way (possibly due to their growth rate). Instead of having to explicitly tell every computer on every network how to reach every other computer and network, it would be nice if the computers could just put their heads together and figure it all out. This is the job of routing protocols and the daemons that implement them.

Routing protocols have a major advantage over static routing systems in that they can react and adapt to changing network conditions. If a link goes down, the routing daemons can quickly discover and propagate alternate routes to the networks that link served, if any exist.

Routing daemons collect information from three sources: configuration files, the existing routing tables, and routing daemons on other systems. This information is merged to compute an optimal set of routes, and the new routes are then fed back into the system routing table (and possibly fed to other systems through a routing protocol). Because network conditions change over time, routing daemons must periodically check in with each other to reassure themselves that their routing information is still current.

The exact way that routes are computed depends on the routing protocol. Two types of protocols are in common use: distance-vector protocols and link-state protocols.

Distance-vector protocols

Distance-vector (aka "gossipy") protocols are based on the general idea, "If router X is five hops away from network Y, and I'm adjacent to router X, then I must be six hops away from network Y." You announce how far you think you are from the networks you know about. If your neighbors don't know of a better way to get to each network, they mark you as being the best gateway. If they already know a shorter route, they ignore your advertisement.[2] Over time, everyone's routing tables are supposed to converge to a steady state.

This is really a very elegant idea. If it worked as advertised, routing would be relatively simple. Unfortunately, this type of algorithm does not deal well with changes in topology. In some cases, infinite loops (e.g., router X receives information from router Y and sends it on to router Z, which sends it back to router Y) can prevent routes from converging at all. Real-world distance-vector protocols must avoid such problems by introducing complex heuristics or by enforcing arbitrary restrictions such as the RIP (Routing Information Protocol) notion that any network more than 15 hops away is unreachable.

Even in nonpathological cases, it can take many update cycles for all routers to reach a steady state. Therefore, to guarantee that routing will not jam for an extended period, the cycle time must be made short, and for this reason distance-vector protocols as a class tend to be talkative. For example, RIP requires that routers broadcast all of their routing information every 30 seconds. IGRP and EIGRP send updates every 90 seconds.

On the other hand, BGP, the Border Gateway Protocol, transmits the entire table once and then transmits changes as they occur. This optimization substantially reduces the potential for "chatty" (and mostly unnecessary) traffic.

Table 14.1 on the next page lists the distance-vector protocols that are in common use today.

Link-state protocols

Link-state protocols distribute information in a relatively unprocessed form. The records traded among routers are of the form "Router X is adjacent to router Y, and the

---

2. Actually, it is not quite this simple, since there are provisions for handling changes in topology that may lengthen existing routes. Some DV protocols such as EIGRP maintain information about multiple possible routes so that they always have a fallback plan. The exact details are not important.

Routing

Table 14.1   Common distance-vector routing protocols

Proto	Long name	Application
RIP	Routing Information Protocol	Internal LANs
IGRP	Interior Gateway Routing Protocol	Small WANs
EIGRP	Enhanced Interior Gateway Routing Protocol	WANs, corporate LANs
BGP	Border Gateway Protocol	Internet backbone routing

link is up." A complete set of such records forms a connectivity map of the network from which each router can compute its own routing table. The primary advantage that link-state protocols offer over distance-vector protocols is the ability to quickly converge on an operational routing solution after a catastrophe occurs. The tradeoff is that maintaining a complete "map" of the network at each node requires memory and CPU power that would not be needed by a distance-vector routing system.

Because the communications among routers in a link-state protocol are not part of the actual route-computation algorithm, they can be implemented in such a way that transmission loops do not occur. Updates to the topology database propagate across the network efficiently, at a lower cost in network bandwidth and CPU time.

Link-state protocols tend to be more complicated than distance-vector protocols, but this can be explained in part by the fact that link-state protocols make it easier to implement advanced features such as type-of-service routing and multiple routes to the same destination. Neither of these features is supported on stock Linux systems; you must use dedicated routers to benefit from them.

The common link-state protocols are shown in Table 14.2.

Table 14.2   Common link-state routing protocols

Proto	Long name	Application
OSPF	Open Shortest Path First	Internal LANs, small WANs
IS-IS	Intermediate System to Intermediate System	Insane asylums

Cost metrics

In order for a routing protocol to determine which path to a network is shortest, it has to define what is meant by "shortest".[3] Is it the path involving the fewest number of hops? The path with the lowest latency? The largest minimal intermediate bandwidth? The lowest financial cost?

For routing purposes, the quality of a link is represented by a number called the cost metric. By adding together the costs of each link in a path, a path cost can be computed. In the simplest systems, every link has a cost of 1, leading to hop counts as a

---

3. Fortunately, it does not have to define what the meaning of "is" is.

path metric. But any of the considerations mentioned above can be converted to a numeric cost metric.

Networking mavens have labored long and hard to make the definition of cost metrics flexible, and some modern protocols even allow different metrics to be used for different kinds of network traffic. Nevertheless, in 99% of cases, all this hard work can be safely ignored. The default metrics for most systems work just fine.

You may encounter situations in which the actual shortest path to a destination may not be a good default route for political reasons. To handle these cases, you can artificially boost the cost of the critical links to make them seem less appealing. Leave the rest of the routing configuration alone.

Interior and exterior protocols

An "autonomous system" is a group of networks under the administrative and political control of a single entity. The definition is vague; real-world autonomous systems can be as large as a worldwide corporate network or as small as a building or a single academic department. It all depends on how you want to manage routing. The general tendency is to make autonomous systems as large as possible. This convention simplifies administration and makes routing as efficient as possible.

Routing within an autonomous system is somewhat different from routing between autonomous systems. Protocols for routing among ASs ("exterior" protocols) must often handle routes for many networks, and they must deal gracefully with the fact that neighboring routers are under other people's control. Exterior protocols do not reveal the topology inside an autonomous system, so in a sense they can be thought of as a second level of routing hierarchy that deals with collections of nets rather than individual hosts or cables.

In practice, small to medium sites rarely need to run an exterior protocol unless they are connected to more than one ISP. With multiple ISPs, the easy division of networks into local and Internet domains collapses, and routers must decide which route to the Internet is best for any particular address. (However, that is not to say that *every* router must know this information. Most hosts can stay stupid and route their default packets through an internal gateway that is better informed.)

While exterior protocols are not so different from their interior counterparts, this chapter concentrates on the interior protocols and the daemons that support them. If your site must use an external protocol as well, see the recommended reading list on page 332 for some suggested references.

14.3 PROTOCOLS ON PARADE

Several interior routing protocols are in common use. In this section, we introduce the major players and summarize their main advantages and weaknesses.

RIP: Routing Information Protocol

RIP, defined in RFC1058, is an old Xerox protocol that has been adapted for IP networks. It is the protocol used by **routed**. RIP is a simple distance-vector protocol that uses hop counts as a cost metric. Because RIP was designed in an era when a single computer cost hundreds of thousands of dollars and networks were relatively small, RIP considers any host fifteen or more hops away to be unreachable. Therefore, large local networks that have more than fifteen routers along any single path cannot use the RIP protocol.

Although RIP is a resource hog because of its overuse of broadcasting, it does a good job when a network is changing often or when the topology of remote networks is not known. However, it can be slow to stabilize after a link goes down.

RIP is widely implemented on non-Linux platforms. A variety of common devices from printers to SNMP-manageable network components can listen to RIP advertisements to learn about possible gateways. In addition, **routed** is available for all versions of Linux, so RIP is a de facto lowest common denominator routing protocol. Often, RIP is used for LAN routing and a more featureful protocol is used for wide-area connectivity.

RIP-2: Routing Information Protocol, version 2

See page 252 for information about classless addressing, aka CIDR.

RIP-2 is a mild revision of RIP that adds support for a few features that were missing from the original protocol. The most important change is that RIP-2 distributes netmasks along with next-hop addresses, so it provides better support for subnetted networks and CIDR. A vague gesture towards increasing the security of RIP was also included, but the definition of a specific authentication system has been left for future development.

Many sites use **routed** in its **-q** ("quiet") mode, in which it manages the routing table and listens for routing updates on the network but does not broadcast any information of its own. At these sites, the actual route computations are usually performed with a more efficient protocol such as OSPF (see below). The computed routes are converted to RIP updates for consumption by nonrouter machines. **routed** is lightweight (in **-q** mode) and universally supported, so most machines can enjoy the benefits of dynamic routing without any special configuration.

RIP-2 provides several features that seem targeted for this multiprotocol environment. "Next hop" updates allow broadcasters to advertise routes for which they are not the actual gateway, and "route tags" allow externally discovered routes to be propagated through RIP.

RIP-2 can be run in a compatibility mode that preserves most of the new features of RIP-2 without entirely abandoning vanilla RIP receivers. In most respects, RIP-2 is identical to RIP and should be preferred over RIP if it is supported by the systems you are using. However, Linux distributions generally don't support it out of the box.

OSPF: Open Shortest Path First

OSPF is defined in RFC2328. It's a link-state protocol. "Shortest path first" refers to the mathematical algorithm used to calculate routes; "open" is used in the sense of "nonproprietary."

OSPF was the first link-state routing protocol to be broadly used, and it is still the most popular. Its widespread adoption was spurred in large part by its support in **gated**, a popular multiprotocol routing daemon of which we will have more to say later. Unfortunately, the protocol itself is very complex and hence only worthwhile at sites of significant size (where routing protocol behavior really makes a difference).

The OSPF protocol specification does not mandate any particular cost metric. **gated**'s implementation uses hop counts by default, as does Cisco's. Cisco routers can also be configured to use network bandwidth as a cost metric.

OSPF is an industrial-strength protocol that works well for large, complicated topologies. It offers several advantages over RIP, including the ability to manage several paths to a single destination and the ability to partition the network into sections ("areas") that share only high-level routing information.

IGRP and EIGRP: Interior Gateway Routing Protocol

IGRP and its souped-up successor EIGRP are proprietary routing protocols that run only on Cisco routers. IGRP was created to address some of the shortcomings of RIP before robust standards like OSPF existed. EIGRP is configured similarly to IGRP, though it is actually quite different in its underlying protocol design. IGRP only handles route announcements using traditional IP address class boundaries, whereas EIGRP understands arbitrary CIDR netmasks.

Both IGRP and EIGRP are distance-vector protocols, but they are designed to avoid the looping and convergence problems found in other DV systems. EIGRP in particular is widely regarded as the paragon of distance-vector routing. For most purposes, EIGRP and OSPF are equally functional.

In our opinion, it is best to stick with an established, nonproprietary, and multiply implemented routing protocol such as OSPF. More people are using and working on OSPF than EIGRP, and several implementations are available.

IS-IS: the ISO "standard"

IS-IS, the Intra-domain Intermediate System to Intermediate System Routeing Protocol, is the International Organization for Standardization's answer to OSPF. It was originally designed to manage "routeing" for the OSI network protocols and was later extended to handle IP routing.

Both IS-IS and OSPF were developed in the early 90s at a time when ISO protocols were politically in vogue. Early attention from the IETF helped to lend IS-IS a veneer of legitimacy for IP, but it seems to be falling farther and farther behind OSPF in popularity. Today, IS-IS use is rare. The protocol itself is mired with lots of ISO baggage and generally should be avoided.

MOSPF, DVMRP, and PIM: multicast routing protocols

MOSPF (Multicast OSPF), DVMRP (Distance Vector Multicast Routing Protocol), and PIM (Protocol Independent Multicast) are protocols designed to support IP multicasting, a technology that is not yet widely deployed. You can find pointers to more information about these protocols at www.mbone.com.

Router Discovery Protocol

Router Discovery Protocol uses ICMP messages sent to the IP multicast address 224.0.0.1 to announce and learn about other routers on a network. Unfortunately, not all routers currently make these announcements, and not all hosts listen to them. The hope is that someday this protocol will become more popular.

14.4 ROUTED: RIP YOURSELF A NEW HOLE

You may not be rich. You may not be good looking. But you'll always have **routed**. **routed** was for a long time the standard UNIX routing daemon, and it's still supplied with most versions of UNIX, and Linux.

Linux's **routed** speaks only RIP. If you need RIP-2, you can always use **gated** as a RIP-2 daemon instead. It's just a bit more complicated, especially if you have to install it yourself. (You only really need RIP-2 if you have subnets that have different mask lengths.)

routed can be run in server mode (**-s**) or in quiet mode (**-q**). Both modes listen for broadcasts, but only servers distribute their own information. Generally, only machines with multiple interfaces should be servers. If neither **-s** nor **-q** is specified, **routed** is supposed to run in quiet mode with one interface and in server mode with more. But on many systems, this feature is broken.[4]

See page 270 for more about route.

routed adds its discovered routes to the kernel's routing table. Routes must be reheard at least every four minutes or they will be removed. However, **routed** knows which routes it has added and will not remove static routes that were installed with the **route** command.

routed -t can be used to debug routing. This option makes **routed** run in the foreground and print out all packets it sends or receives.

routed normally discovers routing information dynamically and does not require configuration. However, if your site contains gateways to the Internet or to other autonomous systems, you may have to take some additional steps to make these links work with **routed**.

---

4. **routed** has a reputation for misbehavior on many systems. One of our reviewers went so far as to say, "**routed** is simply not to be trusted."

If you have only a single outbound gateway, you can advertise it as a global default route by running its **routed** with the **-g** flag. This is analogous to setting the default route on a single machine, except that it is propagated throughout your network.

routed also supports a configuration file, **/etc/gateways**, which was designed to provide static information about gateways to "preload" into the **routed** routing table. In modern times, if you find yourself needing this functionality, you should really be running **gated** instead.

14.5 GATED: A BETTER ROUTING DAEMON

gated can be obtained from www.gated.org.

gated is a generic routing framework that allows many different routing protocols to be used simultaneously. **gated** provides pinpoint control over advertised routes, broadcast addresses, trust policies, and metrics. It can share routes among several protocols, allowing routing gateways to be constructed between areas that have standardized on different routing systems. **gated** also has one of the nicest administrative interfaces and configuration file designs of any Linux administrative software.

Many people have contributed to the development of **gated**. Work was originally coordinated by Cornell University. **gated** started out as freely distributable software, but in 1992 it was privatized and turned over to the Merit GateD Consortium. Current versions of **gated** are available only to Consortium members. Membership (ten categories! four product lines! but wait! you also get...) is open to everyone, but it requires the execution of a license agreement, and it's expensive for nonacademic users.

Although the definition of "academic and research use" is quite broad, we recommend steering clear of the bureaucratic quagmire in which **gated** has become mired. Version 3 was the last **gated** to be unencumbered with red tape, and it works just fine. Version 3.6 was the current release (of version 3) as of this writing, and that's the version we describe below.

gated supports RIP (both versions), OSPF, and IS-IS for interior routing and also the exterior protocols EGP and BGP. An older protocol called HELLO is supported for historical reasons.

gated startup and control

gated is normally started at boot time with no arguments. The correct way to do this is system dependent; see Chapter 2, *Booting and Shutting Down*, for information.

gated takes its operating instructions from a single configuration file. The config file is normally **/etc/gated.conf**, but this can be changed with a command-line flag. Once running, **gated** can be manipulated with the **gdc** command, which is installed along with it. Most uses of **gdc** take the form

   gdc *command*

The most common **gdc** commands follow.

interface	signals **gated** to recheck the kernel's list of active network interfaces. **gated** does this periodically on its own, but if you have just changed an interface's configuration, you may want to force an immediate update.
reconfig	makes **gated** reread its configuration file.
checkconf	parses the configuration file and checks it for syntax errors, but does not tell **gated** to load it.
toggletrace	starts or stops logging.
stop	terminates **gated**: gracefully if possible, forcibly if not.
start	spawns a new **gated** if one is not already running.
restart	kills and restarts **gated**. Equivalent to **stop** followed by **start**.

Tracing

gated can be run with debugging (called "tracing") turned on, causing its actions to be archived to a log file. **gated**'s tracing features are very useful when you are first setting up the config file; they also provide a history of routing updates.

Depending on which tracing options have been enabled, the log file may grow quickly and should be restarted or truncated periodically. **gdc toggletrace** will completely close the log file, allowing you to rename or truncate it. A second **gdc toggletrace** turns logging back on.

Trace options can be specified in the configuration file or on the **gated** command line (preceded by **-t** for options, nothing for the log file name). In the config file, different options can be specified for each protocol; on the command line, they are global. The most useful options are listed below.

all	turns on all tracing options.
normal	traces normal events. Abnormal events are always traced.
policy	traces the way that administratively configured policy statements affect the distribution of routes.
route	traces routing table changes.
general	turns on both **normal** and **route**.

An even more detailed level of tracing dumps individual network packets to the log file. However, packet tracing can only be enabled in the config file, not on the command line.

The gated configuration file

Unlike many Linux administrative systems, **gated** has reasonable default behavior. Hundreds of options are supported, but simple networks should need only a few lines of configuration. As you read this rest of this chapter and the **gated** documentation, keep in mind that most features will not apply to you.

The following sections provide a quick look at the most mainstream **gated** configuration options. Because of the way **gated**'s configuration file works, it's necessary to show syntax outlines for many of the options. We've pruned these outlines so that they contain only the parts we want to talk about. If you find yourself thinking that there really ought to be an XYZ option available somewhere, there probably is; we just haven't shown it. Refer to the **gated** documentation for complete coverage.

gated comes with an explanation of the format of its configuration file, but the documentation won't do much to educate you about advanced routing issues. You may need to refer to one of the sources listed on page 332 to really understand the function and purpose of each option.

gated's configuration file consists of a series of statements separated by semicolons. Tokens are separated by whitespace, which may include newlines. Curly braces are sometimes used for grouping, but only in specific contexts.

There are several classes of statement. Statements of each type must appear together in the configuration file, and the sections must appear in the following order:

- Options and definitions (including declarations of network interfaces)
- Configuration of individual protocols
- Static routes
- Import, export, and aggregation controls

It's fine for a section to be empty.

Tracing options can appear anywhere. If they appear within curly braces, they apply only within the context of the option or protocol being configured. The options are specified with a **traceoptions** statement:

traceoptions ["*log*" [**replace**] [**size** *size*[**k**|**m**] **files** *num*]] *trace_options*
    [**except** *trace_options*] ;

The *log* is the filename into which tracing output is stored. If **replace** is specified, the log will be truncated and restarted whenever **gated** restarts; the default is to append. The **size** parameter specifies the maximum size of the log file in kilo or megabytes. When the log gets too big, it will be restarted and the old log renamed *log*.**1**, *log*.**2**, etc., up to the number of files specified by the **files** clause. If you specify **size**, you must also specify **files**.

The possible *trace_options* are those specified above (some additional minor options not listed here are also supported).

Here's an example that creates the file **/var/log/gated.log** and rotates 1MB files up to 3 deep, with all possible tracing options turned on:

    traceoptions "/var/log/gated.log" replace size 1m files 3 all;

Option configuration statements

The most common options are:

    options [**nosend**] [**noresolv**] [**syslog** [**upto**] *log_level*] ;

The arguments have the following meanings:

nosend   prevents **gated** from sending any packets. This argument is useful for debugging, since **gated** can be asked to process information from other routers without interfering with the actual routing of the network.

noresolv   prevents **gated** from attempting to use DNS to translate host-names to IP addresses. DNS queries can fail if not enough routing information is available to process them, leading to a chicken-and-egg deadlock. We recommend against using hostnames in any network configuration context, and this option can be used to help enforce that policy.

See Chapter 11 for more information about syslog.

syslog   controls how much information is logged via syslog. This option is meaningless if your site does not use syslog. The valid *log_levels* are listed in the **syslog.conf** man page. The default is **syslog upto info**.

Example:

```
options noresolv;
```

Network interface definitions

The properties of network interfaces are set with an **interfaces** statement, which has the following format:

```
interfaces {
    options [strictinterfaces] ;
    define address [broadcast addr] | [pointtopoint addr]
    interface iflst [preference prf] [passive] [simplex] ;
    [netmask mask] [multicast] ;
} ;
```

There may be multiple **options**, **interface**, or **define** statements—or none. This is generally true for all clauses throughout the **gated** configuration file.

The **strictinterfaces** option makes it illegal to refer to an interface in the configuration file that cannot be found by the kernel at startup time and that has not been listed in a **define** statement. This is always an error, but without **strictinterfaces** turned on, it is not fatal.

See page 290 for more information about point-to-point links.

The **define** statement describes a network interface that may or may not be present at startup. It's mostly used for dial-up links or for other interfaces that might "appear" at a later time. Another good example is a PCMCIA Ethernet card that might be inserted in a slot sometime down the road.

An **interface** statement (repeated here for clarity)

```
interface iflst [preference prf] [passive] [simplex] ;
```

sets the options for a particular interface or set of interfaces. *iflst* can be an interface name such as **eth0** or **exp1**, a name wild card such as **eth** or **exp** (matching all instances of that type of interface), a hostname or IP address (indicating the interface to which that address is bound), or the literal string **all**.

If an interface is **passive**, routes through it will be maintained even if it does not appear to be properly connected. If it's **simplex**, the interface cannot receive its own broadcast packets. **gated** can normally figure this out for itself, but on some systems you may need to say so explicitly.

The **preference** field requires a more elaborate explanation. Since routing protocols work in different ways and use different cost metrics to determine the "shortest" paths, there's no guarantee that any two protocols will agree about which routes are best. When the results computed by different protocols are incompatible, an administrative policy must be used to decide which routes are propagated to the kernel's routing table and exported to other routers.

To implement this policy, **gated** associates a numeric preference value with each route. When two routes conflict, the one with the lowest preference is the winner of the routing beauty contest.

Preference values can originate from a variety of sources. Every routing protocol has an intrinsic preference value. Preference values can also be assigned to network interfaces and to remote gateways. Since most routes have a protocol of origin *and* a network interface *and* a remote gateway, there may be several candidate preference values. **gated** assigns the most specific of these values. In other words, the path with the lowest numeric preference value (as determined by any of the preference metrics for the path) is the chosen path.

Normally, routes to directly connected networks have a preference value of 0. If it is necessary to prefer one interface over another, you can use **preference** clauses to prioritize them. Some of the other default preference values used by **gated** are shown in Table 14.3.

Table 14.3   Default route preference values

Source of routing information	Preference
Routes to directly connected networks	0
Routes learned via OSPF	10
ICMP redirects	30
Externally defined static routes	40
Static routes defined in **gated.conf**	60
Routes learned from RIP	100
Routes across point-to-point interfaces	110
Routes through interfaces that are down	120

Routing

The following example sets the interface eth0 to be passive, meaning that it will not be used to advertise any routing information:

```
interfaces {
    interface eth0 passive;
};
```

Other miscellaneous definitions

Several other global parameters can be set in the definitions section.

routerid *host* ;

The **routerid** statement sets the router identification number, which is used by the BGP and OSPF protocols. It should be listed in the form of an IP address, and it defaults to the address of the machine's first physical interface. This value is important to the protocols that use it, and other routers may need to refer to it explicitly in their configuration files.

```
martians {
    host host [allow] ;
    network [allow] [exact | refines] ;
    network mask mask [allow] [exact | refines] ;
    network masklen number [allow] [exact | refines] ;
    default [allow] ;
} ;
```

Martian routes are routes to destinations that you would prefer to ignore. There may be misconfigured routers on your network that are broadcasting routes to bogus destinations, or you may simply want to exclude certain destinations from the routing table. Any route to a destination listed in a **martians** statement is simply ignored by **gated**.

Each routing destination has an address and a mask associated with it. The various flavors of specification are all just different ways of providing an address/mask pair against which these can be matched.

A network number with a **mask** or **masklen** specifies the two values explicitly. If no mask is supplied, the mask implied by the address's intrinsic class is used.

exact and **refines** request different flavors of address matching. Actually, there are three. With neither keyword, the mask of the destination is ignored. As long as the portion of the destination address covered by the rule's mask matches the rule's address, the destination is considered a martian.

If **exact** is specified, the destination's address and mask must both match the rule's values exactly in order for the destination to be martian. An exact match selects a network, but not its subnets or supernets.

If **refines** is specified, the destination's mask must be longer than the rule's. If it is longer, then the addresses are compared normally (using the rule's mask only). This has the effect of selecting a network's subnets without selecting the network itself.

The entries

```
host host ;
default ;
```

are equivalent to

```
host mask 255.255.255.255 exact ;
0.0.0.0 mask 0.0.0.0 exact ;
```

The **allow** keyword can be used to reenable certain addresses disabled by a previous, broader specification. For example:

```
martians {
    128.138.0.0 mask 255.255.0.0 ;
    128.138.145.0 mask 255.255.255.0 allow ;
} ;
```

This configuration rejects all information about the class B network 128.138. However, routes to the 128.138.145 subnet are accepted. The most specific rule always has precedence.

Protocol configuration for RIP

Both versions of the RIP protocol are configured with a **rip** statement.

```
rip yes | no | on | off [ {
    broadcast ;
    nobroadcast ;
    preference pref ;
    defaultmetric metric ;
    interface interface_list
       [noripin | ripin] [noripout | ripout]
       [version 1]|[version 2 [multicast|broadcast]] ;
    trustedgateways gateway_list ;
    sourcegateways gateway_list ;
    traceoptions [packets | request | response [detail]] ;
} ] ;
```

yes and **no** are synonymous with **on** and **off**. RIP is enabled by default, so you must include the line

```
rip no ;
```

if you don't want to run RIP at all. The **broadcast** and **nobroadcast** options are similar to the -**s** and -**q** flags of **routed**: **broadcast** forces RIP updates to be sent out even if the host does not appear to be on more than one network. **nobroadcast** prevents RIP from sending out any updates.

The **defaultmetric** clause assigns the cost *metric* to routes learned through other protocols when they are rebroadcast through RIP. This is a very crude form of translation, but there isn't really an elegant solution. By default, this value is set at 16— unreachable—so that other protocol's routes will never go out over RIP. If you want to redistribute these routes, a good value to use is 10.

Per-interface options are set with the same type of interface specification found in the **interfaces** statement earlier in the configuration file. **ripin** accepts RIP updates on an interface, and **noripin** rejects them. **ripout** and **noripout** are essentially interface-specific versions of **broadcast** and **nobroadcast**. **noripout** is the default on point-to-point links such as dial-ups.

The **version** statement tells whether to run RIP-1 or RIP-2 on the specified interfaces. The default when running RIP-2 is to multicast updates rather than broadcast them, which prevents RIP-1 routers from seeing them. You can specify **broadcast** to force broadcasting to occur.

By default, **gated** will listen to RIP updates from anyone who sends them. If a list of **trustedgateways** is present, however, **gated** will only pay attention to the listed hosts. A *gateway_list* is just a series of IP addresses separated by whitespace.

sourcegateways are hosts to which RIP updates should be sent directly, rather than via broadcasting. This feature can be used to reach hosts on different networks or to target routers on a network that does not support broadcasting (or on which broadcasting has been disabled).

traceoptions are specified as described on page 317. Any options included here will apply only to RIP. The RIP-specific packet-tracing options **request**, **response**, and **packets** log requests received, outgoing responses, and all packets, respectively. Packets are normally summarized. If **detail** is specified, a more detailed dump of each packet is included in the log.

An actual RIP configuration clause appears in section 1 of the complete **gated.conf** config file example on page 327.

Some preliminary background on OSPF

Before launching into the gory details of OSPF configuration (which are in truth not really so gory), we need to talk a bit about two more features of OSPF: routing areas and designated routers.

Routing areas

At a large site, it may not be necessary or desirable to distribute a complete set of link states from one corner of the network to another. To cut down on the amount of update traffic, OSPF allows individual networks to be grouped into "areas." Link-state information (i.e., information about the network's physical topology) is propagated only within an area; information about the area is distributed to the outside world in the form of routing summaries.

Every network is a member of exactly one area, and areas can include more than one network. Routers are considered to be members of all the areas on which they have network interfaces. A router that belongs to more than one area is called an area-border router and is responsible for translating link-state records into summary records.

A routing summary is really just a collection of routes: "Router X can send packets to network Y in 3 hops," where X is an area-border router. The routers outside an area combine the declared summary cost with the computed cost to the area-border router to determine a total path cost to the network.

This scheme might sound like a distance-vector routing protocol in disguise, but there are two important differences. First, summaries are propagated exactly as they came from the area-border router that originated them. A router may compute that if it is two hops away from X and X is 3 hops from Y, then it must be 5 hops away from Y. However, it will never reveal the result of this calculation to another router. It will just pass along the original summary route.[5]

The second difference from a distance-vector protocol is that the OSPF scheme does not attempt to deal with arbitrary network topologies. OSPF requires that all routing areas be logically adjacent to a central backbone area known as area 0 (though they may be adjacent to each other as well). Route summaries can travel only from a leaf area to the backbone, and vice versa, not directly between leaf areas.[6] This simple two-level hierarchy forestalls the possibility of loops.

If your real-world network architecture does not match OSPF's two-layer model, all is not lost. You can still represent it as a two-layer hierarchy by using an OSPF concept called "virtual links." Unfortunately, a discussion of virtual links is beyond the scope of this book.

Designated routers

In theory, link-state protocols distribute routing information in the form of records that describe connectivity among routers; for example, "Router A is adjacent to router B, and the cost of the link is 1." If there were 6 routers on a network, 30 different link-state advertisements would potentially need to be propagated, because each router was adjacent to 5 other routers. Even worse, the routers would all have to treat each other as neighbors and make sure that their databases were synchronized.

OSPF reduces the amount of information that is propagated by appointing one of the routers on a network to be the *designated router*.[7] The designated router listens to link-state advertisements from all the other routers and then sends out a digest of what it has learned.

The routers on a network cooperate to elect a designated router based on a per-router priority value that is set administratively. Routers with a priority of 0 are ineligible to be the designated router. Among the remaining routers, the one with the highest priority is declared the winner. If there is a tie, a router is selected pseudo-randomly.

5. This is true only within an area. If the summary record crosses into an adjacent area, the area-border router that forwards it will restate the information relative to itself.

6. OK, this statement isn't entirely true. There are a few special area types, such as the "Not So Stubby Area" (NSSA) that may bridge routing information between leaves, but each route learned in this fashion is specially tagged so that it doesn't accidentally create a loop.

7. Actually, "broadcast domain" would be a better term than "network" here. There is also a mechanism defined to support the concept of a designated router on a nonbroadcast (but multiaccess) network.

A backup designated router is also selected in the same way. Each router on the network maintains an ongoing relationship with both the designated router and the designated router's backup. If the designated router should fail, the backup immediately steps in to assume control and a new backup is elected.

Designated routers handle a bit more protocol traffic than their peers, so they should be selected accordingly.

Protocol configuration for OSPF

In **gated.conf**, you configure OSPF options with the **ospf** statement:

```
ospf yes | no | on | off [ {
    defaults {
        router-prio ;
    } ;
    traceoptions trace_options ;
    backbone | (area area) {
        networks {
            network [exact | refines] [restrict] ;
            network mask mask [exact | refines] [restrict] ;
            network masklen num [exact | refines] [restrict] ;
            host host [exact | refines] [restrict] ;
        } ;
        stubhosts {
            host cost cost ;
        } ;
        interface interface_list [cost cost] {
            enable | disable ;
            priority priority ;
        } ;
    } ;
} ] ;
```

This statement is less complicated than it looks. **on**, **off**, **yes**, and **no** have the obvious meanings; the default is not to run OSPF.

In the **defaults** section, **router-prio** specifies a default router priority (to be used when electing a designated router) of 1 on all interfaces. This value may be overridden on specific interfaces if desired. The default priority is 0, which makes **gated** ineligible to become any network's designated router.

The definition of each area begins with either the **backbone** or the **area** keyword. There must be one area or backbone statement for each area of which the router is a member. The backbone is defined as area 0 in the OSPF protocol specification, but **gated** requires you to use the **backbone** keyword instead of **area 0**.

The *area* may be given as a decimal number or as a four-byte number in IP address format (e.g., 128.138.45.2). The area number is never interpreted as an IP address by **gated**, but the dotted quad format is supported in case you want to label areas with the IP addresses of principal routers or servers.

The list of **networks** defines the networks that compose the area. It is only necessary to enumerate networks in the configuration files of area-border routers. The specification of addresses and masks is done exactly as for **martians**, as described on page 320, except that there is no **allow** keyword. Networks marked with the **restrict** option are not included in route summaries; they are "secret" networks that are reachable only within the area.

stubhosts are directly attached hosts that should be advertised as being reachable via this router with the specified *cost* (1 is usually fine). This feature is used primarily to support links to hosts that are connected via PPP or SLIP.

Finally, the **interface** list specifies the *cost* to the attached networks (usually 1, the default), and the *priority* of this **gated** for becoming the designated router. If an interface is set to **disable**, then no OSPF conversations will take place over this interface.

A real example of an OSPF configuration clause appears in section 2 of the complete **gated.conf** configuration file on page 327.

Protocol configuration for ICMP redirects

gated lets you exert some administrative control over the handling of routes learned through ICMP redirects (see page 261 for an explanation of what these are).

```
redirect yes | no | on | off [ {
    preference preference ;
    interface interface_list [noredirects] | [redirects] ;
    trustedgateways gateway_list ;
    traceoptions trace_options ;
} ] ;
```

These options should all be familiar by now. **preference** sets the route preference for redirect-derived routes in general (the default is 30, which is fairly good). The options **redirects** and **noredirects** enable and disable acceptance of redirects per network interface, and **trustedgateways** enables them only when sent by specific routers. There are no redirect-specific tracing options.

Static routes

Static routes are configured with a **static** statement:

```
static {
    dest gateway gateway_list [interface interface_list] [preference preference]
        [retain] [reject] [blackhole] [noinstall] ;
} ;
```

The *dest* can be specified with any of the usual suspects:

```
host host
default
network
network mask mask
network masklen length
```

The *gateway_list* is the set of routers through which this destination can be reached. If the designated gateway is not on a directly connected network (via one of the interfaces specified in the optional *interface_list*), the route will be ignored.

The route preference defaults to 60, which allows it to be superseded by OSPF-computed routes or by ICMP redirects.

If a route is marked with **retain**, it will be left in the kernel's routing table when **gated** exits. Normally, **gated** cleans up after itself and leaves only interface and preexisting routes. Conversely, the **noinstall** option causes the route not to be installed in the local routing table, but only made available for propagation to other routers. This option is useful on routers that act as "route servers," meaning that they don't actually route traffic but rather coordinate routing information for the network infrastructure (they may have access to an alternate "management traffic only" network that carries their packets).

Routes marked with the **blackhole** and **reject** tags prevent forwarding from occurring on systems that support these features. With **reject**, an ICMP error is returned to the sender; with **blackhole**, the packets just mysteriously disappear without a trace, kind of like Evi's email.

A static route example appears in section 3 of the complete **gated.conf** configuration file example on page 328.

Exported routes

Once **gated** has computed the routes it likes, it defaults to putting them in the kernel's forwarding table. For most applications, this is all that's necessary. Sometimes, however, it's desirable to configure **gated** to act as a kind of translator, accepting information from one protocol and distributing it out another. This is done in the configuration file with an **export** clause:

```
export proto protocol
    [interface interface_list | gateway gateway_list]
    restrict ;
```

or

```
export proto protocol
    [interface interface_list | gateway gateway_list]
    [metric metric] {
        export_list ;
    } ;
```

In this case, *protocol* is the routing protocol that will be advertising the translated information, and *export_list* is what to translate as specified by listing a **proto** clause for each dataset to be translated. Here's a sample *export_list*:

```
proto static {
    ALL metric 1;
} ;
```

This snippet translates all static routes and inserts them into the exported list with a metric of 1.

A complete gated configuration example

The following configuration is for an environment in which both RIP and OSPF are in use. The configuration is for the area-border router shown in Exhibit C.

Exhibit C   Network topology for our sample gated configuration

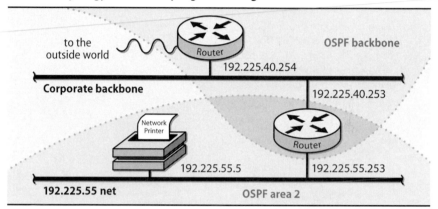

The upstream network (the corporate backbone) has standardized on OSPF, but the downstream LAN has devices (a few network printers) that can only listen to RIP. In this environment, **gated** is used to rebroadcast the OSPF routes via RIP. This is a good configuration for a corporate or campus environment because it lets PCs and network appliances learn information via RIP, yet uses a more sensible protocol to communicate on the backbone among groups, floors, and buildings.

The contents of the configuration file are as follows:

Section 1:
```
rip yes {
     broadcast;
     defaultmetric 10;
     interface 192.225.40.253 noripout;
     interface 192.225.55.253 ripout;
};
```

Section 2:
```
ospf yes {
     area 0.0.0.2 {
          authtype none;
          networks {
               192.225.55.0 mask 255.255.255.0;
          };
          interface 192.225.55.253 cost 1 {
               priority 2;
          };
     };
```

```
            backbone {
                interface 192.225.40.253 {
                    priority 2;
                };
            };
        };
```

Section 3:
```
        static {
            default gateway 192.225.40.254 preference 140 retain;
        };
```

Section 4:
```
        export proto rip {
            proto ospf {
                ALL metric 1;
            };
            proto direct {
                ALL metric 1;
            };
            proto static {
                ALL metric 1;
            } ;
        };
```

Section 5:
```
        export proto ospf {
            proto direct {
                ALL metric 1;
            };
        };
```

In section 1, **gated** is instructed to speak the RIP protocol. It listens for RIP broadcasts from other routers on both interfaces but sends out RIP packets of its own only on the 192.225.55.253 interface. This restriction serves to eliminate undesirable broadcast traffic on the corporate backbone.

Section 2 enables OSPF. The 192.225.40.253 interface is in area 0, the backbone area. It will send out OSPF HELLO messages to other routers on this network to discover who its neighbors are. 192.225.55.253 is in area 2. (There may or may not be other downstream routers that want to share information via OSPF.)

Currently, there is only one way out of this network to the outside world. Hence, for good measure, section 3 includes a static default route to the Internet gateway on the 192.225.40.0 network.

In sections 4 and 5, we tell **gated** what routes to advertise via RIP and OSPF, respectively. We want the RIP advertisements to include any directly connected networks, the static default route, and any routes learned via OSPF. We want the OSPF advertisements to include any directly connected networks (such as the 192.225.55.0 network). Since we are an interior router, we do not want to announce a default route.

14.6 ROUTING STRATEGY SELECTION CRITERIA

There are essentially four levels of complexity at which the routing for a network can be managed:

- No routing
- Static routes only
- Mostly static routes, but clients listen for RIP updates
- Dynamic routing everywhere

The topology of the overall network has a dramatic effect on each individual segment's routing requirements. Different nets may need very different levels of routing support. The following rules of thumb can help you choose a strategy:

- A stand-alone network requires no routing.

- If there is only one way out of a network, clients (nongateway machines) on that network should have a static default route to the lone gateway. No other configuration is necessary, except on the gateway itself.

- A gateway with a small number of networks on one side and a gateway to "the world" on the other side can have explicit static routes pointing to the former and a default route to the latter. However, dynamic routing is advisable if there is more than one routing choice on both sides.

- If you use RIP and are concerned about the network and system load this entails, avoid using **routed** in active mode—it broadcasts everything it knows (correct or not) at short intervals. **gated** allows you to specify what routes may be sent out ("advertised"), thus reducing the flood of routing information. **gated** can also send RIP updates to particular gateways rather than broadcasting them everywhere.

- To have clients listen passively for routing updates without sending out their own information, use **routed -q**. Clients can also listen passively with **gated**, but **gated** has a larger footprint.

- Many people will tell you that RIP is a horrible, terrible protocol and that **routed** is the spawn of Satan. It isn't necessarily so. If it works for you and you are happy with the performance, go ahead and use it. You get no points for spending time on an overengineered routing strategy.

- If RIP is not your primary routing protocol, you can have **gated** broadcast its routing information as RIP purely for the benefit of passive clients.

- **routed** listens to everyone and believes everything it hears. **gated** gives you more control over updates. Even if your site uses RIP, you may want to manage the exchange of routing data with **gated** and run **routed** only on client machines.

- Use dynamic routing at points where networks cross political or administrative boundaries.

Routing

- On dynamically routed networks that contain loops or redundant paths, use OSPF if possible.

- Routers connected to the Internet with multiple upstream providers must use BGP. Most routers connected to the Internet have only one upstream path, and therefore a simple static route is sufficient.

A good routing strategy for a medium-sized site with a relatively stable local structure and a connection to someone else's net is to use a combination of static and dynamic routing. Machines within the local structure that do not have a gateway to external networks can use static routing, forwarding all unknown packets to a default machine that understands the outside world and does dynamic routing.

A network that is too complicated to be managed with this scheme should rely on dynamic routing. Default static routes can still be used on leaf networks, but machines on networks with more than one router should run **routed** in passive mode. All machines with more than one network interface should run **gated** in active mode and broadcast routes with RIP.

14.7 CISCO ROUTERS

Routers made by Cisco Systems, Inc., are the de facto standard for Internet routing today. Having captured over 70% of the router market, Cisco's products are well known, and staff that know how to operate them are relatively easy to find. Before Cisco, UNIX boxes with multiple network interfaces were often used as routers. Today, dedicated routers are the favored gear to put in datacom closets and above ceiling tiles where network cables come together. They're cheaper, faster, and more secure than their UNIX or Linux counterparts.

Most of Cisco's router products run an operating system called Cisco IOS, which is proprietary and unrelated to Linux. Its command set is rather large; the full documentation set fills up about 4.5 feet of shelf space. We could never fully cover Cisco IOS here, but knowing a few basics can get you a long way.

IOS defines two levels of access (user and privileged), both of which are password-protected. By default, you can simply **telnet** to a Cisco router to enter user mode.[8] You'll be prompted for the user-level access password:

```
% telnet acme-gw.acme.com
Connected to acme-gw.acme.com.
Escape character is '^]'.

User Access Verification
Password:
```

Upon entering the correct password, you will receive a prompt from Cisco's EXEC command interpreter.

---

8. A variety of access methods can be configured. If your site already uses Cisco routers, contact your network administrator to find out which methods have been enabled.

acme-gw.acme.com>

At this prompt, you can enter commands such as **show interfaces** to see the router's network interfaces or **show ?** to get help about the other things you can see.

To enter privileged mode, type **enable** and enter the privileged password when it is requested. Once you have reached the privileged level, your prompt will end in a #:

acme-gw.acme.com#

BE CAREFUL—you can do anything from this prompt, including erasing the router's configuration information and its operating system. When in doubt, consult Cisco's manuals or one of the comprehensive books published by Cisco Press.

You can type **show running** to see the current running configuration of the router and **show config** to see the current nonvolatile configuration. Most of the time, these are the same. Here's a typical configuration:

```
acme-gw.acme.com# show running
Current configuration:
version 12.1
hostname acme-gw
enable secret xxxxxxxx
ip subnet-zero

interface Ethernet0
description Acme internal network
ip address 192.108.21.254 255.255.255.0
no ip directed-broadcast
interface Ethernet1
description Acme backbone network
ip address 192.225.33.254 255.255.255.0
no ip directed-broadcast

ip classless
line con 0
transport input none

line aux 0
transport input telnet
line vty 0 4
password xxxxxxxx
login

end
```

The router configuration can be modified in a variety of ways. Cisco offers graphical tools that run under some versions of UNIX/Linux and Windows. Real network administrators never use these; the command prompt is always the "sure bet." It is also possible to **tftp** a config file to or from a router so that you can edit it in your favorite editor.[9]

---

9. Hot tip: Microsoft Word isn't the best choice for this application.

To modify the configuration from the command prompt, type **config term**:

```
acme-gw.acme.com# config term
Enter configuration commands, one per line.  End with CNTL/Z.
acme-gw(config)#
```

You can then type new configuration commands exactly as you want them to appear in the **show running** output. For example, if we wanted to change the IP address of the Ethernet0 interface in the example above, we could enter

```
interface Ethernet0
ip address 192.225.40.253 255.255.255.0
```

When you've finished entering configuration commands, press <Control-Z> to return to the regular command prompt. If you're happy with the new configuration, enter **write mem** to save the configuration to nonvolatile memory.

Here are some tips for a successful Cisco router experience:

- Name the router with the **hostname** command. This precaution helps to prevent accidents caused by changing the configuration on the wrong router. The hostname will always appear in the command prompt.

- Always keep a backup router configuration on hand. You can write a short **expect** script that **tftp**s the running configuration over to a Linux box every night for safekeeping.

- Control access to the router command line by putting access lists on the router's VTYs (VTYs are like PTYs on a Linux box). This precaution prevents unwanted parties from trying to break into your router.[10]

- Control the traffic flowing among your networks (and possibly to the outside world) with access lists on each interface. See *Packet-filtering firewalls* on page 676 for more information about how to set up access lists.

- Keep routers physically secure. It's easy to reset the privileged password if you have physical access to a Cisco box.

14.8 RECOMMENDED READING

HUITEMA, CHRISTIAN. *Routing in the Internet, Second Edition*. Prentice Hall. 2000.

This book is a clear and well-written introduction to routing from the ground up. It covers most of the protocols in common use and also some advanced topics such as multicasting. Amazon.com customers who bought this book also bought the album *The Dirty Boogie* by The Brian Setzer Orchestra.

---

10. The very latest versions of IOS support the SSH protocol. You should use that instead of the standard TELNET interface if it's available in your environment.

Moy, John T. *OSPF: Anatomy of an Internet Routing Protocol*. Addison-Wesley. 1998.

A thorough exposition of OSPF by the author of the OSPF protocol standard and a big chunk of **gated**. Amazon.com customers who bought this book also bought the album *Stunt* by the Barenaked Ladies.

Halabi, Bassam. *Internet Routing Architectures, Second Edition*. Cisco Press. 2000.

This book focuses on BGP, the most widely used exterior gateway protocol. Amazon.com customers who bought this book also bought the soundtrack to the movie *The Matrix*, featuring explicit lyrics.

Stewart, John W. *BGP4 Inter-domain Routing in the Internet*. Addison-Wesley. 1999.

This is a very practical expose of BGP4 and its uses. Amazon.com customers who bought this book only bought other books about routing protocols, and mostly boring ones at that.

There are many routing-related RFCs. The main ones are shown in Table 14.4.

Table 14.4   Routing-related RFCs

RFC	Title	Authors
2328	OSPF Version 2	John T. Moy
1058	Routing Information Protocol	C. Hedrick
2453	RIP Version 2	Gary Scott Malkin
1256	ICMP Router Discovery Messages	Stephen E. Deering
1142	OSI IS-IS Intra-domain Routing Protocol	David R. Oran
1075	Distance Vector Multicast Routing Protocol	D. Waitzman et al.
1519	CIDR: an Address Assignment and Aggregation Strategy	Vince Fuller et al.
1771	A Border Gateway Protocol 4 (BGP-4)	Yakov Rekhter et al.

Routing

14.9 EXERCISES

E14.1 Investigate the Linux **route** command and write a short description of what it does. Using **route**, how would you:

a) Add a default route to 128.138.129.1 using interface eth1?

b) Delete a route to 128.138.129.1?

c) Determine whether a route was added by a program such as **gated** or an ICMP redirect? (Note that this method will work with the output of **netstat -rn** as well.)

E14.2 Compare static and dynamic routing, listing several advantages and disadvantages of each. Describe situations in which each would be appropriate and explain why.

★ **E14.3** Consider the following **netstat -rn** output. Describe the routes and figure out the network setup. Which network, 10.0.0.0 or 10.1.1.0, is closer to the Internet? Which process added each route?

Destination	Gateway	Genmask	Flags	MSS	Window	irtt	Iface
10.0.0.0	0.0.0.0	255.255.255.0	U	40	0	0	eth1
10.1.1.0	0.0.0.0	255.255.255.0	U	40	0	0	eth0
0.0.0.0	10.0.0.1	0.0.0.0	UG	40	0	0	eth1

★ **E14.4** What are martian routes in **gated**, and why is the martian definition useful?

★★ **E14.5** Figure out the routing scheme that is used at your site. What protocols are in use? Which machines connect to the Internet? You can use **tcpdump** to look for routing update packets on the local network and **traceroute** to explore beyond the local net. (Requires root access.)

★★ **E14.6** If you were a medium-sized ISP that provided dial-in accounts and virtual hosting, what sort of routing setup up would you use? Make sure that you consider not only the gateway router(s) between the Internet backbone and the your own network, but also any interior routers that may be in use. Draw a network diagram that outlines your routing architecture.

15 *Network Hardware*

Nothing is influencing our culture today more than the ability to move large amounts of data from one place to another very quickly. We now have world-wide connectivity at a level that only die-hard sci-fi fanatics could have dreamed of just a few years ago. Behind all of this craziness is fancy network hardware and—you guessed it—a whole bunch of stuff that originated in the deep, dark caves of UNIX.

Keeping up with all these fast-moving bits is a challenge. The speed and reliability of your network has a direct effect on your organization's productivity. A poorly designed network is a personal and professional embarrassment. It can also be very expensive to fix.

At least three major factors contribute to a successful installation:

- Development of a reasonable network design
- Selection of high-quality hardware
- Proper installation and documentation

The first sections of this chapter discuss the media that are commonly used for local area and wide area networking, including Ethernet, ATM, frame relay, and DSL. We then cover design issues you are likely to face on any network, be it new or old.

15.1 LAN, WAN, OR MAN?

We're lucky, in a sense, that TCP/IP can be easily transported over a variety of media. In reality, however, the network hardware market is split into a variety of confusing classifications.

Networks that exist within a building or group of buildings are generally referred to as Local Area Networks or LANs. High-speed, low-cost connections prevail. Wide Area Networks—WANs—are networks in which the endpoints are geographically dispersed, perhaps separated by thousands of kilometers. In these networks, high speed usually comes at high cost, but there are virtually no bounds to the sites you can include on the network (Brugge, Belgium to Sitka, Alaska!). MAN is a telecom marketing term for Metropolitan Area Network, meaning a high-speed, moderate-cost access medium used within a city or cluster of cities. In this chapter, we explore some of the technologies used to implement these beasts.

15.2 ETHERNET: THE COMMON LAN

Having captured over 80% of the world-wide LAN market, Ethernet can be found just about everywhere in its many forms. It started as Bob Metcalfe's Ph.D. thesis at MIT. Bob graduated and went to Xerox PARC; together with DEC and Intel, Xerox eventually developed Ethernet into a product. It was one of the first instances in which competing computer companies joined forces on a technical project.[1]

Ethernet was originally specified at 3 Mb/s (mega*bits* per second), but it moved to 10 Mb/s almost immediately. It was developed on the Xerox Alto, which didn't have enough room on the circuit board for an external clock. The Ethernet interface had to use the Alto's clock, which meant that the network speed had to be 2.94 Mb/s. This was rounded up to 3 Mb/s. Metcalfe and other early developers who had worked on the architecture of the ARPANET objected to a roundoff error that exceeded the ARPANET's entire bandwidth, but marketing won out.

Ethernet weathered its early years in the 1980s, a time when a variety of network operating systems, including UNIX, were also gaining basic networking skills and learning to play with each other. When Ethernet hit its mid-teenage years, it was ready to drive. In 1994, Ethernet caught attention as it was standardized at 100 Mb/s. Just after turning 19 years old in 1998, it was ready to fight a new war—at 1 Gb/s. Now an adult in its mid-20s, Ethernet is headed for the new frontier of 10 Gb/s, having eclipsed all of its rivals.[2] Table 15.1 highlights the evolution of the various Ethernet standards.[3]

How Ethernet works

Ethernet can be described as a polite dinner party at which guests (computers) don't interrupt each other but rather wait for a lull in the conversation (no traffic on the network cable) before speaking. If two guests start to talk at once (a collision) they both stop, excuse themselves, wait a bit, and then one of them starts talking again.

---

1. Bob Metcalfe also articulated "Metcalfe's Law," which states that the value of the network expands exponentially as the number of users increases.

2. Current speculation predicts the widespread availability of terabit Ethernet by 2008!

3. We have omitted a few Ethernet standards that have not proved popular, such as 100BaseT4 and 100BaseVG-AnyLAN.

Table 15.1   **The evolution of Ethernet**

Year	Speed	Common name	IEEE#	Dist	Media
1973	3 Mb/s	Xerox Ethernet	–	?	Coax
1980	10 Mb/s	Ethernet 1	–	500m	RG-11 coax
1982	10 Mb/s	DIX Ethernet (Ethernet II)	–	500m	RG-11 coax
1985	10 Mb/s	10Base5 ("Thicknet")	802.3	500m	RG-11 coax
1985	10 Mb/s	10Base2 ("Thinnet")	802.3	180m	RG-58 coax
1989	10 Mb/s	10BaseT	802.3	100m	Category 3 UTP[a] copper
1993	10 Mb/s	10BaseF	802.3	2km	MM[b] Fiber
				25km	SM Fiber
1994	100 Mb/s	100BaseTX ("100 meg")	802.3u	100m	Category 5 UTP copper
1994	100 Mb/s	100BaseFX	802.3u	2km	MM fiber
				20km	SM fiber
1998	1 Gb/s	1000BaseSX	802.3z	260m	62.5-μm MM fiber
				550m	50-μm MM fiber
1998	1 Gb/s	1000BaseLX	802.3z	440m	62.5-μm MM fiber
				550m	50-μm MM fiber
				3km	SM fiber
1998	1 Gb/s	1000BaseCX	802.3z	25m	Twinax
1999	1 Gb/s	1000BaseT ("Gigabit")	802.3ab	100m	Cat 5E and 6 UTP copper
2001	10 Gb/s	10GbE ("10 Gigabit")	802.3ae	65m	MM Fiber
				40km	SM Fiber

a. Unshielded twisted pair
b. Multimode and single-mode fiber

The technical term for this scheme is CSMA/CD:

- Carrier Sense: you can tell whether anyone is talking.
- Multiple Access: everyone can talk.
- Collision Detection: you know when you interrupt someone else.

The actual delay upon collision detection is somewhat random. This convention avoids the scenario in which two hosts simultaneously transmit to the network, detect the collision, wait the same amount of time, and then start transmitting again, thus flooding the network with collisions. This was not always true!

Ethernet topology

The Ethernet topology is a branching bus with no loops; there is only one way for a packet to travel between any two hosts on the same network. Ethernet provides a mechanism to exchange three types of packets on a segment: unicast, multicast, and broadcast. Unicast packets are addressed to only one host. Multicast packets are addressed to a group of hosts. Broadcast packets are delivered to all hosts on a segment.

A "broadcast domain" is the set of hosts that receive packets destined for the hardware broadcast address, and there is exactly one broadcast domain for each logical

Ethernet segment. Under the early Ethernet standards and media (such as 10Base5), physical segments and logical segments were exactly the same since all the packets traveled on one big cable with host interfaces strapped onto the side of it.[4]

Exhibit A   A polite Ethernet dinner party

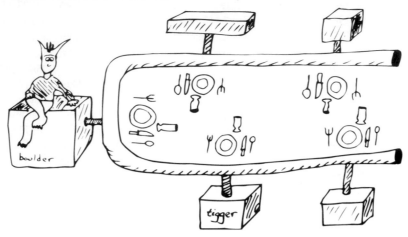

With the advent of modern switches, today's logical segments usually consist of many (possibly dozens or hundreds) physical segments to which only two devices are connected: the switch port and the host. The switches are responsible for escorting multicast and unicast packets to the physical segments on which the intended recipients reside; broadcast traffic is forwarded to all ports in a logical segment.

A single logical segment may consist of physical segments operating at different speeds (10 Mb/s, 100 Mb/s, 1 Gb/s, or 10 Gb/s); hence, switches must have buffering and timing capabilities to eliminate potential conflicts.

Unshielded twisted pair

Unshielded twisted pair (UTP) is the preferred cable medium for Ethernet. It is based on a star topology and has several advantages over other media:

- It uses inexpensive, readily available copper wire. (Sometimes, existing phone wiring can be used.)

- UTP wire is much easier to install and debug than coax or fiber. Custom lengths are easily made.

- UTP uses RJ-45 connectors, which are cheap, reliable, and easy to install.

- The link to each machine is independent (and private!), so a cabling problem on one link is unlikely to affect other hosts on the network.

---

4. No kidding! Attaching a new computer involved boring a hole into the outer sheath of the cable with a special drill to reach the center conductor. A "vampire tap" which bit into the outer conductor was then clamped on with screws.

The general "shape" of a UTP network is illustrated in Exhibit B.

Exhibit B   A UTP installation

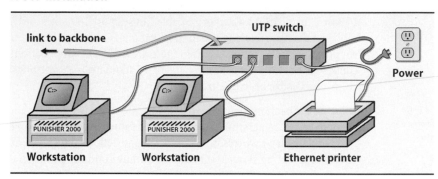

UTP wire suitable for use in modern LANs is commonly broken down into eight classifications. The performance rating system was first introduced by Anixter, a large cable supplier. These standards were formalized by the Telecommunications Industry Association (TIA) and are known today as Category 1 through Category 7, with a special Category 5E in the middle.

The International Organization for Standardization (ISO) has also jumped into the exciting and highly profitable world of cable classification and promotes standards that are exactly equivalent or approximately equivalent to the higher-numbered TIA categories. For example, TIA Category 5 cable is equivalent to ISO Class D cable. For the geeks in the audience, Table 15.2 illustrates the major differences among the various modern-day classifications. This is good information to memorize so you can impress your friends at parties.

Table 15.2   UTP cable characteristics

Parameter	Category 5 Class D[a]	Category 5E	Category 6 Class E	Category 7 Class F
Frequency range	100 MHz	100 MHz	250 MHz	600 MHz
Attenuation	24 dB	24 dB	21.7 dB	20.8 dB
NEXT[b]	27.1 dB	30.1 dB	39.9 dB	62.1 dB
ACR[c]	3.1 dB	6.1 dB	18.2 dB	41.3 dB
ELFEXT[d]	17 dB	17.4 dB	23.2 dB	?[e]
Return loss	8 dB	10 dB	12 dB	14.1 dB
Propagation delay	548 ns	548 ns	548 ns	504 ns

a. Includes additional TIA and ISO requirements TSB95 and FDAM 2, respectively
b. Near-end crosstalk
c. Attenuation-to-crosstalk ratio
d. Equal level far-end crosstalk
e. This parameter is currently unspecified pending further study.

In practice, Category 1 and Category 2 cables are suitable only for voice applications (if that). Category 3 cable is as low as you can go for a LAN; it is the standard for 10 Mb/s 10BaseT. Category 4 cable is something of a orphan, not exactly suited for any particular application. It is occasionally used for 16 Mb/s UTP token ring or for fancy 10BaseT installations. Category 5 cable can support 100 Mb/s and is the most common standard currently in use for data cabling. Category 5E and Category 6 cabling support 1 Gb/s. As of this writing, there are no known applications for Category 7 cable, and not all aspects of the Category 7 standard (e.g., the physical shape of the connectors) have been finalized.

See page 350 for more information about wiring.

10BaseT connections require two pairs of Category 3 wire, and each link is limited to a length of 100 meters; 100BaseTX has the same length limitation but requires two pairs of Category 5 wire. Both PVC-coated and Teflon-coated wire are available. Your choice of jacketing should be based on the environment in which the cable will be installed. Enclosed areas that feed into the building's ventilation system ("return air plenums") typically require Teflon.[5] PVC is less expensive and easier to work with.

RJ-45 connectors wired with pins 1, 2, 3, and 6 are used to make the connections. Although only two pairs of wire are needed for a working 10 Mb/s or 100 Mb/s connection, we recommend that when installing a new network, you use four-pair Category 5E wire and connect all eight pins of the RJ-45 jack.

See page 98 for more information about the RS-232 standard.

For terminating the four-pair UTP cable at patch panels and RJ-45 wall jacks, we suggest that you use the TIA/EIA-568A RJ-45 wiring standard. This standard, which is compatible with other uses of RJ-45 (e.g., RS-232), is a convenient way to keep the wiring at both ends of the connection consistent, regardless of whether you can easily access the cable pairs themselves. The 568A standard is detailed in Table 15.3.

Table 15.3   TIA/EIA-568A standard for wiring four-pair UTP to an RJ-45 jack

Pair	Colors	Wired to	Pair	Colors	Wired to
1	White/Blue	Pins 5/4	3	White/Green	Pins 1/2
2	White/Orange	Pins 3/6	4	White/Brown	Pins 7/8

Existing building wiring may or may not be suitable for network use, depending on how and when it was installed. Many old buildings were retrofitted with new cable in the 1950s and 1960s. Unfortunately, this cable usually won't support even 10 Mb/s.

Connecting and expanding Ethernets

Ethernets can be logically connected at several points in the seven-layer ISO network model. At layer 1, the physical layer, you can use either hardware connectors or repeaters (commonly called hubs in modern times). They transfer the signal directly, much like two tin cans connected by string.

---

5. Check with your fire marshall or local fire department to determine the requirements in your area.

At layer 2, the data link layer, switches are used. Switches transfer frames on the basis of the hardware source and destination addresses, much like delivering a message in a bottle by reading only the label on the outside of the bottle.

At layer 3, the network layer, routers are used. Routers transfer messages to the next hop according to the location of the final recipient, rather like looking at the message in a bottle to see who it's really addressed to.

Hubs and concentrators

Hubs (which are also referred to as concentrators) are active devices that connect physical segments in UTP Ethernet networks. They require external power. Acting as a repeater, a hub retimes and reconstitutes Ethernet frames but does not interpret them; it has no idea where packets are going or what protocol they are using.

The two farthest points on the network must never be more than four hubs apart. Ethernet versions 1 and 2 specified at most two hubs in series per network. The IEEE 802.3 standard extended the limit to four for 10 Mb/s Ethernets. 100 Mb/s Ethernets allow two repeaters, 1000BaseT Ethernets allow only one, and 10GbE networks do not allow them at all. Exhibit C shows both a legal and an illegal configuration for a 10 Mb/s network.

Exhibit C   Count the hubs

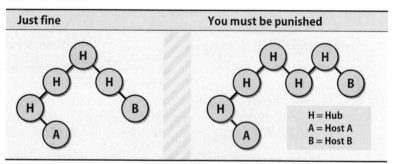

Hubs occasionally require attention from a system administrator, so they should not be kept in obscure or hard-to-reach locations. Power cycling usually allows them to recover from a wedged state.

Switches

Switches connect Ethernets at the data link layer (layer 2) of the ISO model. Their purpose is to join two different physical networks in a way that makes them seem like one big physical network. They do not require software, but rather receive, regenerate, and retransmit packets in hardware.[6] Most switches use a dynamic learning

---

6. Because packets are regenerated and retimed, fully switched networks do not suffer from the "repeater count" limitations shown in Exhibit C.

algorithm. They notice which source addresses come from one port and which come from another. Packets are forwarded between ports only when necessary. At first all packets are forwarded, but in a few seconds the switch has learned the locations of most hosts and can be more selective.

Since not all packets are forwarded between networks, each segment of cable is less saturated with traffic than it would be if all machines were on the same cable. Given that most communication tends to be localized, the increase in apparent bandwidth can be dramatic. And since the logical model of the network is not affected by the presence of a switch, there are few administrative consequences to installing one.

Switches can sometimes become confused if your network contains loops. The confusion arises because packets from a single host appear to be on two (or more) ports of the switch. A single Ethernet cannot have loops, but as you connect several Ethernets together with routers and switches, the topology can include multiple paths to a host. Some switches can handle this situation by holding alternate routes in reserve in case the primary route goes down. They perform a pruning operation on the network they see until the remaining sections present only one path to each node on the network. Some switches can also handle duplicate links between the same two networks and route traffic in a round robin fashion.

Switches keep getting smarter as more functionality is built into their firmware. Some can be used to monitor security on the network. They record any foreign Ethernet addresses they see, thereby detecting and reporting newly connected machines. Since they operate at the Ethernet layer, switches are protocol independent and can handle any mix of high-level packet types (for example, IP, AppleTalk, or NetBEUI).

Switches must scan every packet to determine if it should be forwarded. Their performance is usually measured by both the packet scanning rate and the packet forwarding rate. Many vendors do not mention packet sizes in the performance figures they quote; therefore, actual performance may be less than advertised. Switches are a good but slightly expensive way to connect Ethernets.

Although Ethernet switching hardware is getting faster all the time, it is still not a reasonable technology for connecting more than a hundred hosts in a single logical segment. Problems such as "broadcast storms" often plague large switched networks, since broadcast traffic must be forwarded to all ports in a switched segment. To solve this problem, you should use a router to isolate broadcast traffic between switched segments (thereby creating more than one logical Ethernet).

Large sites can benefit from switches that can partition their ports (through software configuration) into subgroups called Virtual Local Area Networks or VLANs. A VLAN is a group of ports that belong to the same logical segment, as if the ports were connected to their own dedicated switch. Such partitioning increases the ability of the switch to isolate traffic, and that capability has beneficial effects on both security and performance.

Traffic between VLANs is handled by a router, or in some cases, by a routing module or routing software layer within the switch. An extension of this system known as "VLAN trunking" (such as is provided by the IEEE 802.1Q protocol) allows physically separate switches to service ports on the same logical VLAN.

Choosing a switch can be difficult. The switch market is a very competitive segment of the computing industry, and it's plagued with marketing claims that aren't even partially true. When selecting a vendor to buy switches from, you should rely on independent evaluations ("bake offs" such as those that appear in magazine comparisons) rather than any data supplied by vendors themselves. In recent years, it has been common for one vendor to have the "best" product for a few months, but then completely destroy its performance or reliability when trying to make improvements, thus elevating another manufacturer to the top of the heap.

In all cases, make sure that the backplane speed of the switch is adequate—that's the number that really counts at the end of a very long day. A well-designed switch should have a backplane speed that exceeds the sum of the speeds of all its ports.

Routers

Routers are dedicated computers-in-a-box that contain two or more network interfaces; they direct traffic at layer 3 of the ISO protocol stack (the network layer). They shuttle packets to their final destinations in accordance with the information in the TCP/IP protocol headers. In addition to simply moving the packets from one place to another, routers may also perform other functions such as packet filtering (for security reasons), prioritization (for quality of service reasons), and big-picture network topology discovery. See all the gory details of how routing really works in Chapter 14.

Hardware interfaces of many different types (e.g., FDDI, Ethernet, and ATM) can be found on a single router. On the software side, some routers can also handle non-IP traffic such as IPX or AppleTalk. In these configurations, the router and its interfaces must be configured for each protocol you want it to handle.

Routers take one of two forms: fixed configuration and modular. Fixed configuration routers have specific network interfaces permanently installed at the factory. They are usually suitable for small, specialized applications. For example, a router with a T1 interface and an Ethernet interface might be a good choice to connect a small company to the Internet.

Modular routers have a slot or bus architecture to which interfaces can be added by the end user. Although this approach is usually more expensive, it provides for greater flexibility down the road.

Depending on your reliability needs and expected traffic load, a dedicated router may or may not be cheaper than a Linux system configured to act as a router. However, the dedicated router will usually provide superior performance and reliability. This is one area of network design in which it's usually advisable to spend the extra money up front to avoid headaches later.

15.3 WIRELESS: THE NOMAD'S LAN

Wireless networking is a hot growth area, and production-grade products are now becoming available at affordable prices. Given the recent advances in wired network technology, the speeds of wireless networks (usually ranging from 2 Mb/s to 11 Mb/s) may seem a bit inadequate for corporate use. However, these speeds are perfectly adequate for many purposes. An 11 Mb/s wireless network in a home or small business environment can be a system administrator's dream. In addition, wireless access for trade shows, airports, and other public places can really turn an out-of-touch day into a hyper-connected day for many people.

The most promising standards for wireless networking are IEEE's 802.11b wireless LAN standard (which provides LAN-like access at 2 Mb/s to 11 Mb/s at ranges from 100 meters to 40 kilometers, depending on equipment and terrain), and Bluetooth, a standard for short-range (usually less than 10 meter), low-bandwidth (less than 1 Mb/s) communication among PCs, peripherals, mobile phones, and portable devices such as PDAs.

Today, 802.11b networks are becoming commonplace. The cards are inexpensive and available for most laptop and desktop PCs. As with wired Ethernet, the most common architecture for an 802.11b network uses a hub (called an "access point" in wireless parlance) as the connection point for a number of clients. Access points can be connected to traditional wired networks or wirelessly connected to other access points (a configuration known as a "wireless mesh").

You can configure a Linux box to act as an 802.11b access point if you have the right hardware and driver (we know of at least one chipset that supports this, the Intersil Prism II). An excellent standalone 802.11b wireless base station for the home or small office is Apple's AirPort, a spaceship-like product that is inexpensive (around US $300) and highly functional. Buy one today! Various non-MacOS configurators are available for the AirPort, including Freebase (freebase.sourceforge.net) and a Java-based utility by Jonathan Sevy (edge.mcs.drexel.edu/GICL/people/sevy/airport/).

The security of wireless networks is currently very poor. Wired Equivalent Privacy (WEP) is a protocol used in conjunction with 802.11b networks to provide either 40-bit or 128-bit encryption for packets traveling over the airwaves. Unfortunately, the current version of this standard has recently (August 2001) been shown to contain a fatal design flaw (see www.cs.rice.edu/~astubble/wep/wep_attack.html). Until a revised standard has become available, wireless networks—both with and without WEP—should be considered completely insecure. Someone sitting outside your building or house can access your network directly and undetectably.

Debugging a wireless network is also something of a black art, since a wide range of variables come into play when there are problems. In short, wireless is currently a neat and very functional toy for homes, small offices, conferences, or the beach, but it's not going to replace wired corporate backbones anytime soon.

15.4 **FDDI:** THE DISAPPOINTING AND EXPENSIVE **LAN**

At 10 Mb/s, the Ethernet of the 1980s didn't offer enough bandwidth for some networking needs, such as connecting workgroups through a corporate (or campus) backbone. In an effort to provide higher-bandwidth options, the ANSI X3T9.5 committee produced the Fiber Distributed Data Interface (FDDI) standard as an alternative to Ethernet.[7] Designed and marketed as a 100 Mb/s token ring, FDDI once looked like it would be the easy solution to many organizations' bandwidth needs.

Unfortunately, FDDI has been a disappointment in absolutely every way. In the early days of FDDI, the cost of FDDI interfaces often exceeded the cost of the workstations they were installed in (around $10,000 each) and performance was often worse than Ethernet (early DEC boards, for example). Interfaces are still expensive, but the performance is better. Modern interfaces yield around 80 Mb/s of throughput.

See page 244 for more information about maximum transmission units (MTUs).

For good performance, FDDI needs a much higher MTU than the default, which is tuned for Ethernet. An MTU value of 4,352 (set with **ifconfig**) is about right. Until the software used to move files around networks has been tuned for the speed and characteristics of FDDI, mere mortals will probably see performance numbers in the range of one-third to one-half the theoretical maximum.

The FDDI standard specifies a 100 Mb/s token-passing, dual ring, all-singing, all-dancing LAN using a fiber optic transmission medium, as shown in Exhibit D. The dual ring architecture provides for a primary ring that's used for data transmission and a secondary ring that's used as a backup in the event the ring is cut (either physically or electronically).

Exhibit D FDDI dual token ring

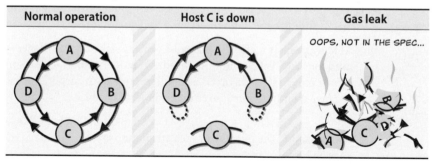

Hosts can either be connected to both rings (they are then referred to as class A or "dual attached" hosts) or just to the primary ring (class B or "single attached" hosts). Most commonly, backbone routers and concentrators are dual attached and workstations are single attached, usually through a "concentrator," a sort of fiber hub.

---

7. FDDI has also been accepted as an ISO standard.

One advantage of token ring systems is that access to the network is controlled by a deterministic protocol. There are no collisions, so the performance of the network does not degrade under high load, as it can with Ethernet. Many token ring systems can operate at 90% to 95% of their rated capacity when serving multiple clients.

For physical media, the FDDI standard suggests two types of fiber: single-mode and multimode. "Modes" are essentially bundles of light rays that enter the fiber at a particular angle. Single-mode fiber allows exactly one frequency of light to travel its path and thus requires a laser as an emitting source.[8] Multimode fiber allows for multiple paths and is usually driven by less expensive and less dangerous LEDs. Single-mode fiber can be used over much longer distances than multimode. In practice, 62.5 µm multimode fiber is most commonly used for FDDI.

Several fiber connector standards are used with FDDI, and they vary from vendor to vendor. Regardless of what connectors you use, keep in mind that a clean fiber connection is essential for reliable operation. Although self-service fiber termination kits are available, we suggest that wherever possible you have a professional wiring firm install the ends on fiber segments.

15.5 ATM: THE PROMISED (BUT SORELY DEFEATED) LAN

ATM stands for Asynchronous Transfer Mode, but some folks insist on Another Technical Mistake. One datacomm industry spokesman describes it as "an attempt by the phone company to turn your networking problem into something they know how to tariff."

ATM is technically "special" because it promotes the philosophy that small, fixed-size packets (called "cells") are the most efficient way to implement gigabit networks. ATM also promises capabilities that haven't traditionally been promised by other media, including bandwidth reservation and quality-of-service guarantees.

ATM was widely marketed as an all-in-one switched network medium that could be used for LAN, WAN, and MAN needs. In modern times, ATM is mostly dead, preserved only in WAN environments where large telco corporations are still trying to leverage their misguided investments in ATM hardware.

On top of ATM's 53-byte cells, five ATM Adaptation Layers (AALs) are described for cell transport. The purpose of each adaptation layer is summarized in Table 15.4 on page 347.

It is unclear how AAL 2 would ever be used in real life. Currently, there is no defined standard for it. AALs 3 and 4 turned out to be very similar and were combined. A group of vendors that had to implement ATM were unhappy with AALs 3 and 4 because of their high overhead. They developed their own solution, the Simple and Efficient Adaptation Layer (SEAL), which soon became AAL 5.

---

8. *Never look directly at the ends of dangling or cut fibers.* If they are laser driven, they can burn your eyes without your immediate knowledge.

Table 15.4   ATM adaptation layers

AAL	Application
1	Constant bit-rate applications, like voice (requires bounded delay)
2	Variable bit-rate applications requiring bounded delay
3	Connection-oriented data applications
4	Connectionless data applications
5	General data transport (especially IP traffic, replaces 3 and 4)

15.6   FRAME RELAY: THE SACRIFICIAL WAN

Frame relay is a WAN technology that offers packet-switched data service, usually for a reasonable cost. Although the claim is not 100% accurate, frame relay is often said to be remarketed X.25, a scary packet-switched technology from the mid-1970s. Fortunately, it's in such widespread use that the equipment, software, and staff that support it have evolved to be robust and to perform well.

Traditionally, users who wished to connect to remote sites would purchase a dedicated circuit from the phone company, such as a 56 Kb/s DDS line or a T1 line. These are point-to-point data circuits that are connected 24 hours a day. Unfortunately, this type of connection is often expensive, as it requires that the phone company dedicate equipment and bandwidth to the link.

In contrast, frame relay is an "economy of scale" approach. The phone company creates a network (often referred to as a "cloud"[9]) that connects its central offices. Users such as yourself provide data for remote sites in small packets. The phone company switches the packets through the appropriate central offices, ultimately delivering them to their destinations. In this model, you and the phone company are gambling that at any given second, the total amount of traffic won't exceed the bandwidth of the network (a condition known euphemistically as "being oversubscribed").

A router encapsulates IP traffic over frame relay connections. Packets are switched over invisible "permanent virtual circuits" (PVCs), which allow your packets to travel only to the sites you've paid for them to reach. These PVCs provide some degree of privacy protection from the other sites connected to the frame relay network.

The biggest advantage of frame relay is that it is usually inexpensive. But in the world of "you get what you pay for," you may find that frame relay's performance is sometimes poor. Frame relay connections have some packet switching overhead, and link speed may degrade during periods of heavy use.

15.7   ISDN: THE INDIGENOUS WAN

Integrated Services Digital Network (ISDN) is a phone company offering that takes many forms. In its most common and usable form, called Basic Rate Interface (BRI)

---

9. Which is an all-too-appropriate name, since it's never quite clear what the weather forecast will be in a frame relay network. Stormy? Rainy? Sleet? Hail?

ISDN, it is essentially an all-digital phone line that provides two dial-up 64 Kb/s "B" channels and a single 16 Kb/s signaling "D" channel. Each B channel can be used for either voice or data (a voice line can be carried on a single 64 Kb/s channel).

ISDN offers a relatively high-speed digital line at a reasonable cost ($30–$150 per month, depending on where you live). Devices called terminal adaptors convert the phone line into a more familiar interface such as RS-232. They are used (and priced) much like modems. Most adaptors can aggregate the two B channels, yielding a 128 Kb/s data channel.

ISDN can be used in place of normal dial-up networking and also as a wide-area technology that uses a router or bridge to connect remote sites across the line.

Although many U.S. phone companies have installed switches that are compatible with ISDN, they still haven't figured out how to market or support them.[10] Only in a few areas can you just call up the phone company and order an ISDN line. Some tips: make sure you deal with the branch of the phone company that handles business services, since that is how ISDN is usually classified. In many regions, you will have to argue your way past several waves of drones before you reach someone who has heard of ISDN before, even if the service really is available.

15.8   DSL AND CABLE MODEMS: THE PEOPLE'S WAN

It's easy to move large amounts of data among businesses and other large data facilities. Carrier-provided technologies such as T1, T3, SONET, ATM, and frame relay provide relatively simple conduits for moving bits from place to place. However, these technologies are not realistic options for connecting individual houses and home offices. They cost too much, and the infrastructure they require is not universally available.

Digital Subscriber Line (DSL) uses ordinary copper telephone wire to transmit data at speeds of up to 7 Mb/s (although typical DSL connections yield between 256 Kb/s and 768 Kb/s). Since most homes already have existing telephone wiring, DSL is a viable way to provide the "last mile" of connectivity from the telephone company to the home. DSL connections are usually terminated in a box that acts as a TCP/IP router and provides an Ethernet connection to other devices within the home. DSL is typically both cheaper and faster than ISDN, so it is now the preferred technology for home users.

Unlike regular POTS (Plain Old Telephone Service) and ISDN connections, which require you to "dial up" an endpoint, DSL is a dedicated network service that is always connected. This feature makes it even more attractive, because there is no setup or connection delay when a user wants to transfer data.

DSL comes in several forms, and as a result it's often referred to as xDSL, with the x representing a specific subtechnology such as A for asymmetric, S for symmetric, H for high speed, or RA for rate adaptive. The exact technology variants and data

---

10. Hence the interpretation: It Still Does Nothing.

transfer speeds available in your area depend on the central office equipment that your telephone company or carrier has chosen to deploy.

The race for "last mile" connectivity to hundreds of millions of homes is a hot one. It's also highly politicized, well capitalized, and overpublicized. The DSL approach leverages the copper infrastructure that is common among the Incumbent Local Exchange Carriers (ILECs), who favored higher profit margins over investments in infrastructure as the networking revolution of the 1980s and 90s passed them by.

Cable television companies, which already have fiber infrastructure in most neighborhoods, are promoting their own "last mile" solutions, which yield similar (though asymmetric) high-bandwidth connections to the home. The cable modem industry has recently become enlightened about data standards and is currently promoting the Data Over Cable Service Interface Specification (DOCSIS) standard. This standard defines the technical specs for both the cable modems and the equipment used at the cable company, and it allows various brands of equipment to interoperate.

All in all, the fight between cable modem and DSL technologies largely boils down to "my marketing budget is bigger than yours." DSL has something of an inherent advantage in that each connection is private to the particular customer; cable modems in a neighborhood share bandwidth and may be able to eavesdrop on each other's traffic.

15.9 WHERE IS THE NETWORK GOING?

When you look closely at the technologies described above, you'll see one thing in common: the simple, inexpensive ones are succeeding, whereas the complex and expensive ones are dying quickly. Where does this put us down the road?

Ethernet has pummeled its rivals because it is incredibly inexpensive. It's so simple to implement that today you can even buy microwave ovens with Ethernet interfaces. Ethernet has scaled well: in many organizations, 10 Mb/s Ethernet infrastructure from the early 1980s is still in production use, connected into 100 Mb/s and 1 Gb/s segments. 10 Gb/s Ethernet has already escaped from the laboratories and should be widely available by 2003. We expect to see this trend continue, with faster and faster switching hardware to connect it all.

On the "connectivity to the home" front, DSL offers new life to the tired old Ma Bell copper plant. The proliferation of cable modems has brought high-speed access (and real security problems) within reach of millions of homes.

What's great about all of these new developments is that regardless of the medium or its speed, TCP/IP is compatible with it.

15.10 NETWORK TESTING AND DEBUGGING

One major advantage of the large-scale migration to Ethernet (and other UTP-based technologies) is the ease of network debugging. Since these networks can be analyzed link by link, hardware problems can often be isolated in seconds rather than days.

The key to debugging a network is to break it down into its component parts and test each piece until you've isolated the offending device or cable. The "idiot lights" on switches and hubs (such as "link status" and "packet traffic") often provide immediate clues to the source of the problem. Top-notch documentation of your wiring scheme is essential for making these indicator lights work in your favor.

As with most tasks, having the right tools for the job is a big part of being able to get the job done right and without delay. The market offers two major types of network debugging tools (although they are quickly growing together).

The first is the hand-held cable analyzer. This device can measure the electrical characteristics of a given cable, including its length (with a groovy technology called "time domain reflectrometry"). Usually, these analyzers can also point out simple faults such as a broken or miswired cable. Our favorite product for LAN cable analysis is the Fluke LanMeter. It's an all-in-one analyzer that can even perform IP pings across the network. High-end versions have their own web server that can show you historical statistics. For WAN (telco) circuits, the T-Berd line analyzer is the cat's meow. The T-Berd and its high-end LAN-testing companion, the FireBERD, are made by TTC (www.ttc.com). Be forewarned: all these products cost as much as a small house in most cities.

The second type of debugging tool is the network sniffer. This device disassembles network packets to look for protocol errors, misconfigurations, and general snafus. It usually requires a substantial amount of training and patience to use such a device effectively, and these days analysis at the network-packet level is rarely necessary. If you must do it, the Cadillac of network sniffers is made by Sniffer Technologies (www.sniffer.com).

15.11 BUILDING WIRING

Whether you're running gigabit Ethernet or just serial cables, we recommend that you use the highest possible quality of wire. It will increase the chances that you can still use the same wire ten years down the road. It's cheapest to wire an entire building at once rather than to wire it one connection at a time.

UTP cabling options

Category 5E wire is relatively new and offers the best price vs. performance tradeoff in today's market. Its normal format is four pairs per sheath, which is just right for a variety of data connections from RS-232 to gigabit Ethernet.

Category 5E specifications require that the twist be maintained to within half an inch of the connection to the punchdown block. This implies that any wire with more than four pairs per sheath will have to be taped or secured to maintain the twist, since it feeds more than one connection.

You must use Category 5E termination parts in addition to Category 5E wire. We've had the best luck using parts manufactured by The Siemon Company of Watertown, Connecticut (www.siemon.com).

Connections to offices

One connection per office is clearly not enough. But should you use two or four? We recommend four, for several reasons:

- They can be used for serial connections (modem, printer, etc.).
- They can be used with voice telephones.
- They can be used to accommodate visitors or demo machines.
- The cost of the materials is typically only 5%–10% of the total cost.
- Your best guess doubled is often a good estimate.
- It's much cheaper to do it once rather than adding wires later.

If you're in the process of wiring your entire building, you might consider installing a few outlets in the hallways, conference rooms, lunch rooms, and bathrooms. Networking is becoming pervasive.

Wiring standards

Modern buildings often require a large and complex wiring infrastructure to support all of the various activities that take place inside. Walking into the average telecommunications closet is usually a shocking experience for the weak of stomach, as identically colored, unlabeled wires often cover the walls.

In an effort to increase traceability and standardize building wiring, the Telecommunications Industry Association released the TIA/EIA-606 Administration Standard for the telecommunication infrastructure of commercial buildings in February 1993. EIA-606 specifies requirements and guidelines for the identification and documentation of telecommunications infrastructure.

Items covered by EIA-606 include:

- Termination hardware
- Cables
- Cable pathways
- Equipment spaces
- Infrastructure color coding
- Symbols for standard components

In particular, it specifies standard colors to be used for wiring. The occult details are revealed in Table 15.5 on page 352.

Pantone now sells software to map between the Pantone systems for ink-on-paper, textile dyes, and colored plastic. Hey, you could color-coordinate the wiring, the uniforms of the installers, and the wiring documentation! On second thought . . .

15.12 NETWORK DESIGN ISSUES

This section addresses the logical and physical design of the network. It's targeted at medium-sized installations. The ideas presented here will scale up to a few hundred hosts but are overkill for three machines and inadequate for thousands. We also

Table 15.5   EIA-606 color chart

Termination type	Color	Code[a]	Comments
Demarcation point	Orange	150C	Central office terminations
Network connections	Green	353C	Also used for aux. circuit terminations
Common equipment[b]	Purple	264C	Major switching/data eqpt. terminations
First-level backbone	White	–	Cable terminations
Second-level backbone	Gray	422C	Cable terminations
Station	Blue	291C	Horizontal cable terminations
Inter-building backbone	Brown	465C	Campus cable terminations
Miscellaneous	Yellow	101C	Maintenance, alarms, etc.
Key telephone systems	Red	184C	–

a. According to the Pantone Matching System®
b. PBXes, hosts, LANs, muxes, etc.

assume that you have an adequate budget and are starting from scratch, which is probably only partially true.

Most of network design consists of the specification of:

- The types of media that will be used
- The topology and routing of cables
- The use of repeaters, bridges, and routers

Another key issue in network design is congestion control. For example, NFS taxes the network quite heavily, and so file serving on a backbone cable is undesirable.

The issues presented in the following sections are typical of those that must be considered in any network design.

Network architecture vs. building architecture

The network architecture is usually more flexible than the building architecture, but the two must coexist. If you are lucky enough to be able to specify the network before the building is constructed, be lavish. For most of us, both the building and a facilities management department already exist and are somewhat rigid.

In existing buildings, the network must use the building architecture, not fight it. Modern buildings often contain utility raceways for data and telephone cables in addition to high-voltage electrical wiring and water or gas pipes. They often use drop ceilings, a boon to network installers. Many campuses and organizations have underground utility tunnels that facilitate network installation.

The integrity of fire walls[11] must be maintained; if you route a cable through a fire wall, the hole must be snug and filled in with a noncombustible substance. Respect

---

11. This type of fire wall is a concrete, brick, or flame-retardant wall that prevents flames from spreading and burning down a building. While much different from a network security firewall, it's probably just as important.

return air plenums in your choice of cable. If you are caught violating fire codes, you may be fined and will be required to fix the problems you have created, even if that means tearing down the entire network and rebuilding it correctly.

Your network's logical design must fit into the physical constraints of the buildings it serves. As you specify the network, keep in mind that it is easy to draw a logically good solution and then find that it is physically difficult or impossible to implement.

Existing networks

Computer networks are the focus of this discussion, but many organizations already have CATV networks and telephone networks capable of transmitting data. Often, these include fiber links. If your organization is ready to install a new telephone system, buy lots of extra fiber and have it installed at the same time.

We had that opportunity several years ago and asked the contractors if they would string some fiber for us. They said, "Sure, no charge" and were a bit miffed when we showed up with a truckload of fiber for them to install.

Expansion

It is very difficult to predict needs ten years into the future, especially in the computer and networking fields. It is important, therefore, to design the network with expansion and increased bandwidth in mind. As cable is being installed, especially in out-of-the-way, hard-to-reach places, pull three to four times the number of pairs you actually need. Remember: the majority of installation cost is labor, not materials.

Even if you have no immediate plans to use fiber, it is wise to install some when wiring your building, especially if it is hard to install cables later. Run both multimode and single-mode fiber; the kind you will need in the future is always the kind you didn't install.

Congestion

A network is like a chain: only as good as its weakest or slowest link. The performance of Ethernet, like that of many other network architectures, degrades as the network gets loaded.

Overtaxed switches, mismatched interfaces, and low-speed links can all lead to congestion. It is helpful to isolate local traffic by creating subnets and by using interconnection devices such as routers. Subnets can also be used to cordon off machines that are used for experimentation; it's difficult to run an experiment that involves several machines if there is no easy way to isolate those machines both physically and logically from the rest of the network.

Maintenance and documentation

We have found that the maintainability of a network correlates highly with the quality of its documentation. Accurate, complete, up-to-date documentation is absolutely indispensable.

Cables should be labeled at all termination points and also every few feet so that they can easily be identified when discovered in a ceiling or wall.[12] It's a good idea to post copies of local cable maps inside communications closets so that the maps can be updated on the spot when changes are made. Once every few weeks, someone should copy down the changes for entry into an electronic database.

Joints between major population centers in the form of switches or routers can facilitate debugging by allowing parts of the network to be isolated and debugged separately. It's also helpful to put joints between political and administrative domains.

15.13 MANAGEMENT ISSUES

If the network is to work correctly, some things need to be centralized, some distributed, and some local. Reasonable ground rules and "good citizen" guidelines need to be formulated and agreed on.

A typical environment includes:

- A backbone network among buildings
- Departmental subnets connected to the backbone
- Group subnets within a department
- Connections to the outside world (e.g., Internet or field offices)

Several facets of network design and implementation must have site-wide control, responsibility, maintenance, and financing. Networks with charge-back algorithms for each connection grow in very bizarre but predictable ways as departments try to minimize their own local costs. Prime targets for central control are:

- The network design, including the use of subnets, routers, switches, etc.
- The backbone cable itself, including the connections to it
- Host IP addresses, hostnames, and subdomain names
- Protocols, mostly to ensure that they interoperate
- Routing policy to the Internet

Domain names, IP addresses, and network names are in some sense already controlled centrally by authorities such as ARIN and ICANN. However, your site's use of these items must be coordinated locally as well.

A central authority has an overall view of the network: its design, capacity, and expected growth. It can afford to own monitoring equipment (and the staff to run it) and to keep the backbone network healthy. It can insist on correct network design, even when that means telling a department to buy a router and build a subnet to connect to the campus backbone network. Such a decision might be necessary so that a new connection does not adversely impact the existing network.

If a network serves many types of machines, operating systems, and protocols, it is almost essential to have a very smart router (e.g., Cisco) as a gateway between nets.

---

12. Some cable manufacturers will prelabel spools of cable every few feet for you.

15.14 RECOMMENDED VENDORS

In the past 15+ years of installing networks around the world, we've gotten burned more than a few times by products that didn't quite meet specs or were misrepresented, overpriced, or otherwise failed to meet expectations. Below is a list of vendors in the United States that we still trust, recommend, and use ourselves today.

Cables and connectors

AMP
P.O. Box 3608
Harrisburg, PA 17105
(800) 522-6752
www.amp.com

Anixter
4711 Golf Rd.
Skokie, IL 60076
(708) 677-2600
www.anixter.com

Belden Cable
P.O. Box 1980
Richmond, IN 47375
(319) 983-5200
www.belden.com

Krone
6950 S. Tucson Way
Englewood, CO 80112
(800) 992-9901
www.krone.com

Black Box Corporation
P.O. Box 12800
Pittsburgh, PA 15241
(412) 746-5500
www.blackbox.com

Newark Electronics
4801 N. Ravenswood Ave.
Chicago, IL 60640
(312) 784-5100
www.newark.com

The Siemon Company
76 Westbury Park Road
Watertown, CT 06795
(203) 274-2523
www.siemon.com

Test equipment

Wavetek
9045 Balboa Ave.
San Diego, CA 92123
(800) 854-2708
www.wavetek.com

Fluke
P.O. Box 9090
Everett, WA 98206
(800) 323-5700
www.fluke.com

The Siemon Company
76 Westbury Park Road
Watertown, CT 06795
(203) 274-2523
www.siemon.com

TTC
20400 Observation Drive
Germantown, Maryland 20876
(800) 638-2049
www.ttc.com

Routers/switches

Cisco Systems
PO Box 3075
1525 O'Brien Drive
Menlo Park, CA 94026-1435
(415) 326-1941
www.cisco.com

15.15 RECOMMENDED READING

GROTH, DAVID, AND JIM MCBEE. *Cabling: The Complete Guide to Network Wiring.* Sybex. 2000.

SEIFERT, RICH. *Gigabit Ethernet.* Reading, MA: Addison-Wesley. 1998.

ANSI/TIA/EIA-568-A, *Commercial Building Telecommunications Cabling Standard,* and ANSI/TIA/EIA-606, *Administration Standard for the Telecommunications Infrastructure of Commercial Buildings,* are the telecommunication industry's standards for building wiring. Unfortunately, they are not free. See www.tiaonline.org.

SPURGEON, CHARLES. "Guide to Ethernet."
http://wwwhost.ots.utexas.edu/ethernet/ethernet-home.html

15.16 EXERCISES

E15.1 Today, most office buildings house computer networks and are wired with UTP Ethernet. Some combination of hubs and switches is needed to support these networks. In many cases, the two types of equipment are interchangeable. List the advantages and disadvantages of each.

★ **E15.2** Draw a simple, imaginary network diagram that connects a machine in your computer lab to Amazon.com. Include LAN, MAN, and WAN components. Show what technology is used for each component. Show some hubs, switches, and routers.

★★ **E15.3** TTCP is a tool that measures TCP and UDP performance (look for it at www.rpmfind.net). Install TTCP on two networked machines and measure the performance of the link between them. What happens to the bandwidth if you adjust buffer sizes up or down? How do your observed numbers compare with the theoretical capacity of the physical medium?

★★ **E15.4** Read the paper mentioned on page 344 that addresses security issues in the Wired Equivalent Privacy protocol. For each type of attack described in the paper, evaluate the potential threat. Which problems are of real-world concern, and in what types of scenarios would you be concerned about them?

16 *The Domain Name System*

Zillions of hosts are connected to the Internet. How do we keep track of them all when they belong to so many different countries, networks, and administrative groups? Two key pieces of infrastructure hold everything together: the Domain Name System (DNS), which keeps track of who the hosts are, and the Internet routing system, which keeps track of how they are connected.

This chapter is about the DNS portion of that system. Although DNS has come to serve several different purposes, its primary job is to map between hostnames and IP addresses. Users and user-level programs like to refer to machines by name, but low-level network software understands only numbers. DNS provides the glue that keeps everyone happy. It has also come to play an important role in the routing of email and web server access.

DNS is a distributed database. "Distributed" means that my site stores the data about its computers, your site stores the data about your computers, and somehow, our sites automatically cooperate and share data when one site needs to look up some of the other's data.

16.1 **DNS** FOR THE IMPATIENT: ADDING A NEW MACHINE

This chapter is almost a mini-book in itself. Before we dive into its mind-numbing depths, let's take a quick breather to answer the most common DNS question: How do you add a new host to a network that's already using DNS? The following recipe shows you how to do it by copying and modifying the existing records for a similar computer—templatehost.my.domain.

Step 1: Choose a hostname and IP address for the new machine in conjunction with local sysadmins or your upstream ISP (Internet service provider).

Step 2: Identify a similar machine on the same subnet. We'll use that machine's records as a model for our new ones.

Step 3: Log in to the master name server machine.

Step 4: Look through **/etc/named.conf** or **/etc/bind/named.conf** (Debian):

- From the options statement, find the directory line that tells where zone data files are kept at your site (see page 384). The zone files contain the actual host and IP address data.

- From the zone statements, find the filenames for the forward zone file and for the reverse zone file of the network your new IP address is on (page 391).

Step 5: Go to the zone file directory and edit the forward zone file (using RCS and **sudo**, of course). Find the records for the template host you identified earlier. They'll look something like this:

```
templatehost       IN    A     128.138.243.100
                   IN    MX    10  mail-hub
                   IN    MX    20  templatehost
```

Step 6: Duplicate those records and change them appropriately for your new host. The zone file might be sorted by hostname; follow the existing convention. Be sure to also change the serial number in the SOA record at the beginning of the file (it's the first of the five numbers in the SOA record). The serial number should only increase; add 1 if your site uses an arbitrary serial number, or set the field to the current date if your site uses that convention.

Step 7: Edit the reverse zone file,[1] duplicate the record for the template host, and update it. It should look something like this:

```
100                IN    PTR   templatehost.my.domain.
```

You must also update the serial number in the SOA record of the reverse zone file.

If your reverse zone file shows more than just the last byte of each host's IP address, you must enter the bytes in reverse order. For example, the record

```
100.243            IN    PTR   templatehost.my.domain.
```

corresponds to the IP address 128.138.243.100 (here, the reverse zone is relative to 138.128.in-addr.arpa rather than 243.138.128.in-addr.arpa).

Step 8: While still logged in to the master name server machine, run **ndc reload** (**rndc reload** for BIND 9).

---

1. The reverse zone might be maintained elsewhere (e.g., at your ISP's site). If so, the reverse entry will have to be entered there.

Step 9: Check the configuration with **dig**; see page 456. You can also try to **ping** or **traceroute** to your new host's name, even if the new host has not been set up yet. A "host unknown" message means you goofed; "host not responding" means that everything is probably OK.

The most common errors are:

- Forgetting to update the serial number and restart the name server; and
- Forgetting to add a dot at the end of the hostname in the PTR reverse entry.

16.2 THE HISTORY OF DNS

In the good old days, the mapping between hostnames and addresses was kept in a single text file that was managed centrally and distributed to all the hosts on the ARPANET. Hostnames were not hierarchical, and the procedure for naming a computer included verifying that no one else in the world had taken the name you wanted. Updates consumed a large portion of the ARPANET's bandwidth, and the file was constantly out of date.

It soon became clear that although a static host table was reasonable for a small network, it was inadequate for the large and growing ARPANET. DNS solves the problems of a static table by using two key concepts: hierarchical hostnames and distributed responsibility. DNS was formally specified by Paul Mockapetris in RFCs 882 and 883 (1983) and updated in RFCs 1034 and 1035 (1987). Paul also wrote an early non-UNIX implementation.

The original UNIX work was done by four graduate students at Berkeley (Douglas Terry, Mark Painter, David Riggle, and Songnian Zhou) in 1984. It was then picked up by Ralph Campbell of Berkeley's Computer Systems Research Group, who started gluing it into BSD. In 1985, Kevin Dunlap, a DEC engineer on loan to Berkeley, took over the project and produced BIND, the Berkeley Internet Name Domain system. Mike Karels, Phil Almquist, and Paul Vixie have maintained BIND over the years. It is shipped with most UNIX or Linux systems and is also available from www.isc.org.

ISC, the Internet Software Consortium, is a nonprofit organization that maintains several crucial pieces of Internet software, including BIND. Paul Vixie and Mark Andrews currently maintain the BIND 8 code tree on ISC's behalf with help from folks on the bind-workers mailing list. ISC developed BIND 9 with funding from several vendors, government agencies, and other organizations.

ISC also provides various types of support for these products, including help with configuration, classes on BIND and DNS, and even custom programming. These services are a boon for sites that must have a support contract before they can use open source software. Several companies use service contracts as a way to contribute to the ISC—they buy expensive contracts but never call for help.

RFCs 1034 and 1035 are still considered the baseline specification for DNS, but more than 30 other RFCs have superseded and elaborated on various aspects of the protocol and data records over the last decade (see the list at the end of this chapter). Currently, no single standard or RFC brings all the pieces together in one place. Historically, DNS has more or less been defined as "what BIND implements," though this is becoming less accurate as other DNS servers emerge.

Although DNS has been implemented on non-UNIX/Linux operating systems, this book discusses only BIND. Nortel ported BIND to Windows and contributed the port back to ISC; since then, BIND version 8.2 has been available for Windows, too. Thanks to the standardization of the DNS protocol, UNIX and non-UNIX DNS implementations can interoperate and share data. Many sites run UNIX servers to provide DNS service to their Windows desktops; the combination works well.

Microsoft provides a DNS server in Windows 2000, but the Microsoft implementation has its own special quirks and differences. It interoperates with BIND but also tends to clutter the net with unnecessary or malformed packets.

16.3 Who needs DNS?

DNS defines:

- A hierarchical namespace for hosts and IP addresses
- A host table implemented as a distributed database
- A "resolver" – library routines that query this database
- Improved routing for email
- A mechanism for finding services on a network
- A protocol for exchanging naming information

To be full citizens of the Internet, sites need DNS. Maintaining a local **/etc/hosts** file with mappings for every host you might ever want to contact is not possible.

Each site maintains one or more pieces of the distributed database that makes up the world-wide DNS system. Your piece of the database consists of two or more text files that contain records for each of your hosts. Each record is a single line consisting of a name (usually a hostname), a record type, and some data values. The name field can be omitted if its value is the same as that of the previous line.

For example, the lines

```
forklift      IN   A     192.108.21.7
              IN   MX    10 chimchim.xor.com.
```

in the "forward" file, and

```
7             IN   PTR   forklift.xor.com.
```

in the "reverse" file associate "forklift.xor.com" with the IP address 192.108.21.7 and reroute email addressed to this machine to the host chimchim.xor.com.

DNS is a client/server system. Servers ("name servers") load the data from your DNS files into memory and use it to answer queries both from internal clients and from clients and other servers out on the Internet. All of your hosts should be DNS clients, but relatively few need to be DNS servers.

If your organization is small (a few hosts on a single network), you can run a server on one host or ask your ISP to supply DNS service on your behalf. Use an authoritative, recursive server if you provide DNS service for yourself, and a caching-only server (or no local server at all) if your ISP supplies service. A medium-sized site with several subnets should run multiple DNS servers to reduce query latency and improve reliability. A very large site can divide its DNS domain into subdomains and run several servers for each subdomain.

16.4   What's new in DNS

Several significant changes have been made to DNS over the last few years. This section gives you the flavor of the major changes and a road map to the places where they are covered in more detail.

Both DNS and BIND are constantly being updated. DNS has new types of resource records, new protocol tweaks, and some new features. BIND has been redesigned and rewritten with support for multithreading and multiprocessor systems. Table 16.1 lists the major changes.

Table 16.1   New features in DNS and BIND

Page	RFCs	Feature
421	2052	SRV records for the location of services
423	–	A6 records for IPv6 addresses
424	2672–3	DNAME records for IPv6 address lookup redirection
418	2317	Classless in-addr delegation (the CNAME hack)
424[a]	–	The ip6.arpa domain for reverse IPv6 mappings
–[a]	–	An IPv6-aware resolver
376	2671	EDNS0, protocol changes and extensions
384	1996	Asynchronous notification of zone changes
433	2136	Dynamic update (for sites that use DHCP)
432	1995	Incremental zone transfers
440	2535–41	DNSSEC, authentication, and security for zone data
438	2845	TSIG/TKEY transaction signatures and key exchange

a. Not covered in this book, or in the case of ip6.arpa, not covered in much detail

Some of these new features are enormous projects that the IETF has not yet finished standardizing. The working groups that are writing the standards have good writers but lack vigilant code warriors; some of the more recent specifications may be difficult or even impossible to implement. The current release of BIND (8.2.5) includes some of the new features; the initial release of BIND 9 (9.2.0) includes almost all of them, but not necessarily in their final form.

IPv6 is described in more detail in Chapter 13.

Two massive new features, IPv6 support and DNSSEC, warrant a bit of commentary. IPv6 increases the length of IP addresses from 32 bits to 128 bits. If ever fully implemented, it will have an enormous impact on the Internet. BIND 9 supports the pieces of IPv6 that have been standardized so far, but it appears unlikely that IPv6 will be widely deployed during the lifetime of this book. Therefore, our coverage of BIND 9's IPv6 support is brief. There's enough in this chapter to give you the general flavor, but not enough to let you migrate your site to IPv6 and configure DNS for it.

The DNSSEC standard attempts to add authentication to the DNS database and its servers. It uses public key cryptography to verify the source and integrity of DNS data and uses DNS to distribute keys as well as host data.

Simpler authentication mechanisms have also been introduced, such as support for authentication through the use of a "shared secret." However, the shared secret must be distributed to each pair of servers that wants to perform mutual authentication. Although that's fine for a local site with a handful of servers, it doesn't scale to the level of the Internet. BIND 9 implements both the DNSSEC public key system and the TSIG (transaction signatures) shared-secret system.

We expect to see some form of authentication used extensively in the next few years, starting with the root zones. Experiments have shown that some top-level zones (e.g., nl and de) can be signed in a few hours. However, the com zone is so large that it would take days to sign with current (circa 2002) technology. Since com is now updated twice a day, a signing process that takes days won't work. Security attacks against the integrity of DNS will no doubt hasten the adoption of authentication measures.

On the horizon for DNS is the introduction of internationalized domain names, which will allow non-English-language countries to define domain names in their native alphabets. Each of these three big issues (IPv6, DNSSEC, and internationalization) significantly increases the size of DNS data records, thereby making it more likely that DNS will bump into limits on UDP packet sizes.

16.5 THE DNS NAMESPACE

In the sections that follow, we first discuss the general anatomy of DNS (the specification) and then describe the configuration files used by BIND (the implementation). If you are familiar with DNS and want to get right to the meat of the chapter, skip ahead to *BIND client issues* on page 376 or *BIND server configuration* on page 380.

In the real world and elsewhere in this book, you will see the terms DNS and BIND used interchangeably. However, in this chapter we attempt (perhaps unsuccessfully) to preserve the distinction between them.

The DNS namespace is a tree of "domains." Each domain represents a distinct chunk of the namespace and is loosely managed by a single administrative entity. The root of the tree is called "." or dot, and beneath it are the top-level (or root-level) domains. The top-level domains have been relatively fixed in the past, but ICANN approved

DNS

seven new ones in 2001: biz, info, name, pro, museum, aero, and coop.[2] As of our publication date (early 2002), museum is operational, pro is available for registration only, and the others are in the DNS system on their way to becoming operational.

One branch of the naming tree maps hostnames to IP addresses, and a second branch maps IP addresses back to hostnames. The former branch is called the "forward mapping," and the BIND data files associated with it are called "forward zone files." The address-to-hostname branch is the "reverse mapping," and its data files are called "reverse zone files."

For historical reasons, two types of top-level domain names are in current use. In the United States, top-level domains originally described organizational and political structure and were given three-letter names such as com and edu. Some of these domains (primarily com, org, and net) are used outside the United States as well; they are called the generic top-level domains or gTLDs for short.

Table 16.2 lists the most important gTLDs along with their original purposes. When good names in the com domain became scarce, the registries began to offer names in org and net without regard to those domains' original restrictions. The domains in the left column of Table 16.2 are the originals, dating from about 1988; the right column includes the new domains added in 2001.

Table 16.2   Generic top-level domains

Domain	What it's for	Domain	What it's for
com	Commercial companies	aero	Air transport industry
edu	Educational institutions	biz	Businesses
gov	Government agencies	coop	Cooperatives
mil	U.S. military agencies	info	Unrestricted use
net	Network providers	museum	Museums
org	Nonprofit organizations	name	Individuals
int	International organizations	pro	Accountants, lawyers, etc.
arpa	Anchor for IP address tree		

For most domains outside the United States, two-letter ISO country codes are used; they are called ccTLDs. Both the geographical and the organizational TLDs coexist within the same global namespace. Table 16.3 on page 364 shows some common country codes.

Some countries outside the United States build an organizational hierarchy with second-level domains. Naming conventions vary. For example, an academic institution might be an edu in the United States and an ac.jp in Japan.

---

2. ICANN is the Internet Corporation for Assigned Names and Numbers, the governing body of the Internet. See page 239 for more information about ICANN.

Table 16.3   Common country codes

Code	Country	Code	Country	Code	Country
au	Australia	fi	Finland	hk	Hong Kong
ca	Canada	fr	France	ch	Switzerland
br	Brazil	jp	Japan	mx	Mexico
de	Germany	se	Sweden	hu	Hungary

The top-level domain "us" is also sometimes used in the United States, primarily with locality domains; for example, bvsd.k12.co.us, the Boulder Valley School District in Colorado. The "us" domain is never combined with an organizational domain—there is no "edu.us" (yet). The advantage of "us" domain names is that they are free or inexpensive to register; see www.nic.us for more details. The restrictions on second-level domains beneath "us" (which was formerly limited to U.S. states) are being relaxed, and domain names like evi-nemeth.us will soon be possible.

Domain mercenaries have in some cases bought an entire country's namespace. For example, the domain for Moldovia, "md", is now being marketed to doctors and residents of the state of Maryland (MD) in the United States. Another example is Tuvalu, for which the country code is "tv". The first such sale was Tonga ("to"), the most active is currently Niue ("nu"), and perhaps the most attractive is "tm" from Turkmenistan. These deals have sometimes been fair to the country with the desirable two-letter code and sometimes not.

Domain squatting is also widely practiced: folks register names they think will be requested in the future and then resell them to the businesses whose names they have snitched. Years ago, all the Colorado ski areas were registered to the same individual, who made quite a bit of money reselling them to individual ski areas as they became web-aware. The going rate for a good name in the com domain is between several thousand and a few million dollars—business.com sold recently for $3.5M. We were offered $50,000 for the name admin.com, which we obtained years ago when sysadmin.com had already been taken by /Sys/Admin magazine.

Domain names are case insensitive. "Colorado" is the same as "colorado", which is the same as "COLORADO" as far as DNS is concerned. Current DNS implementations must ignore case when making comparisons but propagate case when it is supplied.[3] In the past it was common to use capital letters for top-level domains and an initial capital for second-level domains. These days, fingers are weary from typing and all-lowercase is the norm.

Two new features of DNS collide with respect to case sensitivity: internationalization of names and DNSSEC security. Internationalized names require case to be significant and preserved, but DNSSEC maps all names to lower case before computing cryptographic signatures. It's likely that DNS will canonicalize names to lower case

---

3. BIND (the reference implementation used by most sites) preserves case, but some implementations (e.g., Microsoft's and DJB's DNS) change case according their own preference. So much for tight standards.

internally for its cryptographic computations but send the actual data with case preserved. Any international encoding will have to include canonicalization rules. With luck, the IETF standards folks will sort out these issues before either new feature is in widespread use.

An Internet host's fully qualified name is formed by appending its domain name to its hostname. For example, boulder.colorado.edu is the fully qualified name for the host boulder at the University of Colorado. Other sites can use the hostname boulder without colliding because the fully qualified names will be different.

Within the DNS system, fully qualified names are terminated by a dot, for example, "boulder.colorado.edu.". The lack of a final dot indicates a relative address. Depending on the context in which a relative address is used, additional components might be added. The final dot convention is generally hidden from everyday users of DNS. In fact, some systems (such as mail) will break if you supply the dot yourself.

It's common for a host to have more than one name. The host boulder.colorado.edu could also be known as www.colorado.edu or ftp.colorado.edu if we wanted to make its name reflect the services it provides. In fact, it's a good practice to make service hostnames such as www be "mobile," so that you can move servers from one machine to another without changing any machine's primary name. The assignment of extra names is achieved with the CNAME construct; see page 417.

When we were issued the name colorado.edu, we were guaranteed that colorado was unique within the edu domain. We have further divided that domain into subdomains along department lines. For example, the host anchor in the computer science department is called anchor.cs.colorado.edu on the Internet.

The creation of each new subdomain must be coordinated with the administrators of the domain above to guarantee uniqueness. Entries in the configuration files for the parent domain delegate authority for the namespace to the subdomain.

Masters of their domains

Management of the top-level domains com, org, net, and edu was formerly coordinated by Network Solutions, Inc., under contract with the National Science Foundation. This monopoly situation has now changed, and other organizations are allowed to register domain names in those gTLDs. Other top-level domains, such as those for individual countries, are maintained by regional organizations.

There have been various proposals to allow private companies to operate their own top-level domains, and it is likely that additional top-level domains will be available in the near future. Consult www.icann.org for up-to-date information.

Most ISPs offer fee-based domain name registration services. They deal with the top-level domain authority on your behalf and configure their DNS servers to handle name lookups within your domain. Although you can reduce direct expenses by dealing directly with the registrars and running your own DNS servers, you will not necessarily save money. The disadvantage of relying on an ISP's servers is that you lose direct control over the administration of your domain.

See page 252 for more information about CIDR.

Even if you want to manage your own DNS services, you must still coordinate with your ISP. Most ISPs supply reverse DNS mappings for IP addresses within their CIDR blocks. If you take over DNS management of your addresses, make sure that your ISP disables its service for those addresses and delegates that responsibility to you.

A domain's forward and reverse mappings should be managed in the same place whenever possible. Some ISPs are happy to let you manage the forward files but are reluctant to relinquish control of the reverse mappings. Such split management can lead to synchronization problems. See page 418 for an elegant hack that makes delegation work even for tiny pieces of address space.

DNS domains should (must, in fact; see RFC1219) be served by at least two servers. One common arrangement is for a site to operate its own master server and to let the ISP's servers act as a backup. Once the system has been configured, the ISP's servers automatically download their configuration information from your master server. Changes made to the DNS configuration are reflected on the backup servers without any explicit work on the part of either site's administrator.

Don't put all of your DNS servers on the same network. When DNS stops working, the network effectively stops for your users. Spread your DNS servers around so that you don't end up with a fragile system with a single point of failure. DNS is quite robust if configured carefully.

Selecting a domain name

Certain names are taboo; for example, names that are already taken. Others that used to be off-limits have recently been allowed, such as combinations of top-level domains (edu.com) and domains with repeating components (x.x.com[4] or com.com[5]).

Our advice used to be that names should be short and easy to type and that they should identify the organization that used them. These days, the reality is that all the good, short names have been taken, at least in the com domain. It's tempting to blame this state of affairs on squatters, but in fact most of the good names are in actual use.

RFC1032 recommends that the names of second-level domains be no longer than 12 characters, but DNS actually allows up to 63 characters in each component and up to 255 characters in a complete name. The 12-character suggestion is often ignored, and there is no real reason to adhere to it other than to relieve the tedium of typing longer names.

---

4. Not all names with repeated components were illegal. For example, xinet.xinet.com was always a valid name. The domain part is xinet.com and the domain contains a host called xinet.

5. At one point, the servers for com.com were all lame (see page 458). Unfortunately, Windows systems have the habit of adding .com to names they can't find. A common configuration resulted in NT boxes querying the gTLD servers 5,000 times a second for names in the com.com domain. That's a pretty heavy load of bogus queries.

Domain bloat

DNS was designed to map an organization's domain name to a name server for that organization. In that mode it needs to scale to the number of organizations in the world. Now that the Internet has become a conduit of mass culture, however, domain names are being applied to every product, movie, sporting event, English noun, etc. Domain names such as twinkies.com are not (directly) related to the company that makes the product; they're simply being used as advertisements. It's not clear that DNS can continue to scale in this way. The real problem here is that the DNS naming tree is an efficient data structure only when it has some hierarchy and is not totally flat. With each organization naming hundreds or thousands of products at the top level of the tree, hierarchy is doomed.

What we really need is a directory service that maps brand and marketing names to organizations, leaving DNS free to deal with IP addresses. The beginnings of this idea are implemented in most modern web browsers through a service provided by the RealNames Corporation. Unfortunately, RealNames is a proprietary monopoly; only organizations that subscribe and pay a fee can have their keywords listed in the database. Another possible solution is to enforce hierarchy in the system; for example, twinkies.hostess-foods.com. But this will never happen—we've already gone too far down the marketing-domain-name.com path.

Sony does things the right way from DNS's perspective—all of its products are subdomains of sony.com. It might take an extra click or two to find the products you want, but DNS appreciates the hierarchy.

Registering a second-level domain name

To obtain a second-level domain name, you must apply to the authority for the appropriate top-level domain. ICANN is currently accrediting various agencies to be part of its shared registry project for registering names in the gTLDs. As of this writing, you have something like 200 choices of registrar. Check www.icann.org for the definitive list.

In Europe, contact the Council of European National Top-level Domain Registries at www.centr.org to identify your local registry and apply for a domain name. For the Asia-Pacific region, the appropriate body is the Asia-Pacific Network Information Center, www.apnic.net.

To complete the domain registration forms, you must identify a technical contact person, an administrative contact person, and at least two hosts that will be servers for your domain. You'll also have to choose a name that is not already taken.

Creating your own subdomains

The procedure for creating a subdomain is similar to that for creating a second-level domain, except that the central authority is now local (or more accurately, within your own organization). Specifically, the steps are as follows.

- Choose a name that is unique in the local context.
- Identify two or more hosts to be servers for your new domain.
- Coordinate with the administrator of the parent domain.

Parent domains should check to be sure that a child domain's name servers are up and running before performing the delegation. If the servers are not working, a "lame delegation" results, and you might receive nasty email asking you to clean up your DNS act. Page 458 covers lame delegations in more detail.

16.6 THE BIND SOFTWARE

BIND, the Berkeley Internet Name Domain system, is an open source software package from ISC that implements the DNS protocol and provides name service on Linux, UNIX, MacOS, and Windows systems.

Versions of BIND

There have been three main flavors of BIND: BIND 4, BIND 8, and BIND 9. BIND 4 has been around since the late 1980s (roughly corresponding to the release of RFCs 1034 and 1035). BIND 8 was released in 1997, and BIND 9 in mid-2000. There is no BIND 5, 6, or 7; BIND 8 was such a significant update that the authors felt it merited a version number twice as big as the old one.[6] Well, not really... BIND 8 was released with 4.4BSD, for which all version numbers were raised to 8. **sendmail** also skipped a few numbers and went to version 8 at the same time.

BIND 8 incorporated numerous technical advances that improved efficiency, robustness, and security. BIND 9 raises the ante even further with multiprocessor support, thread-safe operation, real security (public key cryptography), IPv6 support, incremental zone transfers, and a host of other features. A new data structure (at least, new to BIND), the red-black tree, stores zone data in memory. BIND 9 is a complete redesign and reimplementation. It isolates the OS-specific parts of the code, making it easier to port BIND to non-UNIX systems. The internals of BIND 9 are significantly different, but its configuration procedure remains the same.

BIND 4 is only maintained with respect to security patches, and it will soon be discontinued. It is expected that a year or two after BIND 9 is stable and in common use, BIND 8 will be discontinued as well. We were tempted to cover only BIND 9 in this book, but since V9's configuration language is a superset of V8's and since we don't yet have much operational experience with V9, we cover both.

Many sites postpone upgrading because they are hesitant to mess with working code. If you are still using BIND 4, the Perl script **named-bootconf.pl** that ships with the V8 and V9 distributions can convert a V4 configuration file to its V8 or V9 equivalent. The actual database of DNS records does not need to change. A configuration file converted from version 4 will not use any of the new BIND 8 and BIND 9 features, but it should provide a good starting point for you to expand upon.

---

6. Who says marketing and engineering can't get along?

Finding out what version you have

It often doesn't seem to occur to vendors to document which version of an external software package they have included with their systems, so you might have to do some sleuthing to find out exactly what software you are dealing with. In the case of BIND, you can sometimes determine the version number with a sneaky query from **dig**, a command that comes with BIND. The command

> **dig @***server* **version.bind txt chaos**

returns the version number unless someone has decided to withhold that information by changing it in the config file. For example, the command works on isc.org:

```
% dig @rc.isc.org version.bind txt chaos
version.bind.          0S CHAOS TXT    "9.2.0rc5"
```

but not on cs.colorado.edu:

```
% dig @mroe.cs.colorado.edu version.bind txt chaos
version.bind.          0S CHAOS TXT "wouldn't you like to know..."
```

Some sites configure BIND to conceal its version number on the theory that this provides some degree of "security through obscurity." We don't really endorse this practice, but it might help fend off some of the script kiddies. See page 384 for a more detailed discussion of this topic.

See Chapter 11 for more information about syslog.

You can also usually tell what BIND version you have by inspecting the log files in **/var/log**. The BIND server daemon, **named**, logs its version number to syslog (facility "daemon") as it starts up. **grep** for lines like this (this one is from Red Hat 7.1):

```
Nov  5 17:17:58 coyote named[8076]: starting (/etc/named.conf).  named 8.2.3-
    REL Sat Jan 27 05:53:47 EST 2001   root@porky.devel.redhat.com:
    /usr/src/bs/BUILD/bind-8.2.3/src/bin/named
```

If **named** is installed but your system does not normally start it at boot time, just run it by hand as root with no arguments. **named** will log its version number, realize that it has no configuration file, and exit.

Table 16.4 shows the versions of BIND that are included with our example distributions. Versions earlier than 8.2.3 have known security problems.

Table 16.4   Versions of BIND on our example systems

System	OS vers	BIND vers
ISC	–	8.2.5/9.2.0
Red Hat	7.2	9.1.0-10
SuSE	7.3	8.2.4-REL
Debian	3.0	8.3.0-REL-NOESW

Red Hat has been known to freeze version numbers and then install patches, thus putting themselves out of sync with the rest of the community. Red Hat's internal version numbers are included in the names of package files and sometimes have an internal bug fix number or patch number appended. For example, the package **bind-9.1.0-10.arch.rpm** is Red Hat's version 10 of isc.org's version 9.1.0. Confusing.

Components of BIND

The BIND system has three components:

- A daemon called **named** that answers queries
- Library routines that resolve host queries by contacting the servers of the DNS distributed database
- Command-line interfaces to DNS: **nslookup**, **dig**, and **host**

In DNS parlance, a daemon like **named** (or the machine on which it runs) is called a "name server," and the client code that contacts it is called a "resolver." We briefly discuss the function of each component below but postpone the actual configuration of BIND until page 376.

named: the BIND name server

named answers queries about hostnames and IP addresses. If **named** doesn't know the answer to a query, it asks other servers and caches their responses. **named** also performs "zone transfers" to copy data among the servers of a domain. (A "zone" is a domain minus its subdomains. Name servers deal with zones, but "domain" is often used where "zone" is really meant.)

Name servers can operate in several different modes. The distinctions among them fall along several axes, so the final categorization is often not very tidy. To make things even more confusing, a single server can play different roles with respect to different zones. Table 16.5 lists some of the adjectives used to describe name servers. Indented entries are loosely classified under their unindented headings.

Table 16.5   A name server taxonomy

Type of server	Description
authoritative	An official representative of a zone
master	The primary server for a zone; gets data from a disk file
slave	Copies its data from the master (also called a secondary server)
stub	Similar to a slave, but copies only name server data (not host data)
distribution	A server that's visible[a] only inside a domain; (aka "stealth server")
nonauthoritative[b]	Answers a query from cache; doesn't know if the data is still valid
caching	Caches data from previous queries; usually has no local zones
forwarder	Performs queries on behalf of many clients; builds a large cache
recursive	Queries on your behalf until it returns either an answer or an error
nonrecursive	Refers you to another server if it can't answer a query

a. A distribution server can be visible to anyone who knows its IP address.
b. Strictly speaking, "nonauthoritative" is an attribute of a DNS query response, not a server.

These categorizations are based on a name server's source of data (authoritative, caching, master, slave), on the type of data saved (stub), on the query path (forwarders), on the type of answers handed out (recursive, nonrecursive), and finally, on the visibility of the server (distribution). The next few sections provide some additional details on the most important of these distinctions; the other distinctions are described elsewhere in this chapter.

Authoritative and caching-only servers

Master, slave, and caching-only servers are distinguished by two characteristics: where the data comes from and whether the server is authoritative for the domain.

Each zone has one master name server. The master server keeps the official copy of the zone's data on disk. The system administrator changes the zone's data by editing the master server's data files.

See page 432 for more information about zone transfers.

A slave server gets its data from the master server through a "zone transfer" operation. A zone can have several slave name servers and *must* have at least one. A stub server is a special kind of slave that loads only the NS (name server) records from the master. See page 430 for an explanation of why you might want this behavior. It's fine for the same machine to be both a master server for your zones and a slave server for other zones. Such cooperation usually makes for good DNS neighbors.

A caching-only name server loads the addresses of the servers for the root domain from a startup file and accumulates the rest of its data by caching answers to the queries it resolves. A caching-only name server has no data of its own and is not authoritative for any zone. See *A university department* on page 403 for an example of a caching-only configuration.

An authoritative answer from a name server is "guaranteed" to be accurate; a nonauthoritative answer might be out of date. However, a very high percentage of nonauthoritative answers are perfectly correct. Master and slave servers are authoritative for their own zones, but not for information they have cached about other domains. Truth be told, even authoritative answers can be inaccurate if a sysadmin changes the master server's data and forgets to update the data's serial number or to run **ndc reload** or **rndc reload** (or if the changes have not yet propagated to slave servers).

The master server should be located on a machine that is stable, does not have many users, is relatively secure, and perhaps is on an uninterruptible power supply. There should be at least two slaves, one of which is off-site. On-site slaves should live on different networks and different power circuits. When name service stops, all normal network access stops, too.

A domain's zone data normally includes the identities of the name servers of all of its subdomains. This name server chaining enables DNS clients to walk down the domain tree to look up any host on the Internet. If a parent domain does not mention certain name servers of a subdomain, those servers become "internal" servers and are not accessible from the outside world.

Although they are not authoritative, caching-only servers can reduce the latency seen by your users and the amount of DNS traffic on your internal networks. Consider putting a caching-only server on each subnet. At most sites, desktop machines typically go through a caching server to resolve queries about hosts on the Internet.

In BIND 4 and BIND 8, it wasn't a good idea to use a single name server as an authoritative server for some zones and as a caching server for others. Each **named** ran with a single in-memory database, and cross-contamination could occur if memory was tight and cached data mixed with authoritative data. BIND 9 has eliminated this problem, so mix away.

Recursive and nonrecursive servers

Name servers are either recursive or nonrecursive. If a nonrecursive server has the answer to a query cached from a previous transaction or is authoritative for the domain to which the query pertains, it provides an appropriate response. Otherwise, instead of returning a real answer, it returns a referral to the authoritative servers of another domain that are more likely to know the answer. A client of a nonrecursive server must be prepared to accept and act on referrals.

Although nonrecursive servers may seem lazy, they usually have good reason not to take on extra work. Root servers and top-level domain servers are all nonrecursive, but at 10,000 queries per second we can excuse them for cutting corners.

A recursive server returns only real answers or error messages. It follows referrals itself, relieving the client of this responsibility. The basic procedure for resolving a query is essentially the same; the only difference is that the name server takes care of handling referrals rather than passing them back to the client.

Resolver libraries do *not* understand referrals; the local name server that clients point to must be recursive.

One side effect of having a name server follow referrals is that its cache acquires information about intermediate domains. On a local network, this caching is often the behavior you want since it allows subsequent lookups from any host on the network to benefit from the name server's previous work. On the other hand, the server for a high-level domain such as com or edu should not save up information requested by a host several domains below it.

Early versions of BIND required source code changes and recompilation to modify a server's recursiveness. This option then moved to a command-line flag (**-r**), and it is now a parameter in the configuration file. A server can even be configured to be recursive for its own clients and nonrecursive for outsiders.

Name servers generate referrals hierarchically. For example, if a server can't supply an address for the host lair.cs.colorado.edu, it refers to the servers for cs.colorado.edu, colorado.edu, edu, or the root domain. A referral must include addresses for the servers of the referred-to domain, so the choice is not arbitrary; the server must refer to a domain for which it already knows the servers.

The longest known domain is generally returned. If the address of lair was not known but the name servers for cs.colorado.edu were known, then those servers' address would be returned. If cs.colorado.edu was unknown but colorado.edu was known, then the addresses of name servers for colorado.edu would be returned, and so on.

Name servers preload their caches from a "hints" file that lists the servers for the root domain. Some referral can always be made, even if it's just "Go ask a root server."

The resolver library

Clients look up hostname mappings by calling the **gethostbyname** family of library routines. The original implementation of **gethostbyname** looked up names in the **/etc/hosts** file. For host mappings to be provided by DNS, these routines must use the resolver library, which knows how to locate and communicate with name servers. Linux has integrated the resolver into the standard libraries.

Linux systems' implementations of **gethostbyname** can draw upon information from several different sources: flat files (such as **/etc/hosts**), DNS, and perhaps a local administrative database system such as NIS. A switch file allows for detailed administrative control over which sources are searched and in what order. See page 498 in Chapter 18, *Sharing System Files*, or page 463 later in this chapter for specifics.

BIND 9 contains the lightweight resolver library that lets sites that do not need to speak IPv6 use a stripped-down resolver library together with a resolver daemon, **lwresd**. If the lwres statement is included in **named**'s configuration file, the name server will also act as a lightweight resolver.

Shell interfaces to DNS

The BIND software distribution includes the **dig**, **host**, and **nslookup** commands, which provide a command-line interface for executing DNS queries. They are useful as debugging aids and as tools for extracting information from DNS. Although the commands are similar in function, they are somewhat different in design. See page 456 for more information.

16.7 How DNS works

Each host that uses DNS is either a client of the system or simultaneously a client and a server. If you do not plan to run any DNS servers, it's not essential that you read the next few sections (skip ahead to *Resolver configuration on page 377*). However, they will help you develop a more solid understanding of the architecture of DNS.

Delegation

All name servers know about the root servers. The root servers in turn know about com, org, edu, fi, de, and other top-level domains. Farther down the chain, edu knows about colorado.edu, com knows about admin.com, and so on. Each zone can delegate authority over its subdomains to other servers.

Let's inspect a real example. Suppose we want to look up the address for the machine vangogh.cs.berkeley.edu from the machine lair.cs.colorado.edu. The host lair asks its local name server, ns.cs.colorado.edu, to figure out the answer. Exhibit A illustrates the subsequent events. We used relative names to reduce clutter and to make the labels more readable. The numbers on the arrows between servers show the order of events, and a letter indicates the type of transaction (query, referral, or answer). We assume that none of the required information was cached before the query, except for the names and IP addresses of the servers of the root domain.

Exhibit A   DNS query process for vangogh.cs.berkeley.edu

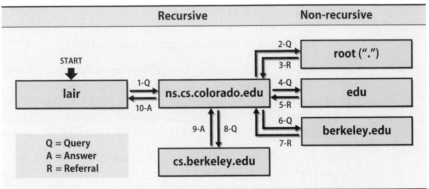

The local name server doesn't know the address; furthermore, it doesn't know anything about cs.berkeley.edu or berkeley.edu or even edu. It does know some servers for the root domain, however, and since it is a recursive server, it queries a root server about vangogh.cs.berkeley.edu.

Root servers used to contain data for both the root zones and for the gTLDs, but these days the gTLDs com, net, and org have their own servers. The edu domain should really have its own servers as well, though in fact, it is currently still served by the root servers. For purposes of this example, we'll assume that we receive a referral to some independent servers of the edu domain in answer to our root-server query about vangogh.cs.berkeley.edu.

The local name server then sends its query to an edu server (asking, as always, about vangogh.cs.berkeley.edu) and gets back a referral to the servers for berkeley.edu. It then repeats the query in the berkeley.edu domain. If the Berkeley server is not recursive and doesn't have the answer cached, it returns a referral to cs.berkeley.edu. The cs.berkeley.edu server is authoritative for the requested information and returns vangogh's address.

When the dust settles, ns.cs.colorado.edu has cached vangogh's address. It has also cached lists of servers for edu, berkeley.edu, and cs.berkeley.edu.

Caching and efficiency

Caching increases the efficiency of lookups: a cached answer is almost free and is usually correct, because mappings change infrequently. Most queries are for local hosts and can be resolved quickly. Users also inadvertently help with efficiency because they repeat many queries; after the first instance of a query, the rest are "free."

For a long time, caching was only applied to positive answers. If a host's name or address could not be found, that fact was not saved. A scheme for negative DNS caching was described in RFC1034, but it was incomplete and was not implemented in most versions of BIND. In 1998, RFC2308 defined an updated scheme for negative caching. This scheme was implemented in BIND 8.2 as an optional feature; it is mandatory in BIND 9.

One measurement at the RIPE root server in Europe showed that 60% of DNS queries were for nonexistent data (many queries were for 127.in-addr.arpa or for Microsoft services as hostnames). Caching this information farther down the DNS tree should dramatically reduce the load on the root servers.

Negative caching saves answers of the following types:

- No host or domain matches the name queried.
- The type of data requested does not exist for this host.
- The server to ask is not responding.
- The server is unreachable because of network problems.

The first two types of negative data are cached for 1–3 hours, and the other types are cached for 5 minutes. Nonauthoritative answers *may* be cached; authoritative negative answers *must* be cached. BIND follows these guidelines from the RFCs, but Windows boxes seem to implement the TTLs selectively, at least for negative caching. They use the minimum from the SOA record the first time a query returns NXDOMAIN (no such domain), then reset the TTL to 15 minutes and let it time out normally from there.

named often receives multiple DNS records in response to a query. For example, a query for the name servers of the root domain would receive a response that listed all 13 root servers. Which one should your server query?

When **named** must choose among several remote servers, all of which are authoritative for a domain, it first determines the network round trip time (RTT) to each server. It then sorts the servers into "buckets" according to their RTTs and selects a server from the fastest bucket. Servers within a bucket are treated as equals and are used in a round robin fashion.

You can achieve a primitive but effective form of load balancing by assigning a single hostname to several IP addresses (which in reality are different machines):

```
www          IN   A     192.168.0.1
             IN   A     192.168.0.2
             IN   A     192.168.0.3
```

Busy web servers such as Yahoo or AltaVista are not really a single machine. They're just a single name in DNS. A name server that has multiple records for the same name and record type returns all of them to the client, but in round robin order. For example, round robin order for the A records above would be 1, 2, 3 for the first query, 2, 3, 1 for the next, 3, 1, 2 for the third, and so on.

The extended DNS protocol

The original DNS protocol definition dates from the late 1980s and uses both UDP and TCP on port 53. UDP is typically used for queries and responses, and TCP for zone transfers between master servers and slave servers. Unfortunately, the maximum packet size that's guaranteed to work in all UDP implementations is 512 bytes, which is much too small for some of the new DNS security features that must include digital signatures in each packet.

The 512-byte constraint also affects the number and names of the root servers. To make all root server data fit in a 512-byte UDP packet, the number of root servers is limited to 13, and each server is named with a single letter of the alphabet.

Many resolvers issue a UDP query first; then, if they receive a truncated response, they reissue the query over TCP. This procedure gets around the 512-byte limit, but it is inefficient. You might think that DNS should just bail on UDP and use TCP all the time, but TCP connections are much more expensive. A UDP name server exchange can be as short as two packets, one query and one response. A TCP exchange involves at least seven packets: a three-way handshake to initiate the conversation, a query, a response, and a final handshake to close the connection.

In the mid-1990s, the DNS protocol was amended to include incremental zone transfers (like a **diff** between old and new zone files, inspired by Larry Wall's **patch** program), asynchronous notifications (to tell slaves when the master's data files have been updated), and dynamic updates (for DHCP hosts). These changes added features but did not really address the fundamental transport problem.

In the late 1990s, EDNS0 (Extended DNS, version 0) addressed some of the shortcomings of the DNS protocol in today's Internet. It lets speakers advertise their reassembly buffer size, supported options, and protocol versions spoken. If the receiving name server responds with an error message, the sender drops back to the original DNS protocol. BIND 9 implements EDNS0 in both the server and the resolver.

16.8 BIND CLIENT ISSUES

See Chapter 18 for more information about distributing files on a network.

Before we dive into the configuration of BIND, let's outline the chores that are associated with using BIND on the Internet. Table 16.6 summarizes what must be done, for whom, and how often. An entry in the "How often" column that includes the word "distribute" means that you do it once per subnet or architecture and then copy the result to the appropriate hosts with a tool like **rdist** or **rsync**. Alternate rows are shaded to improve readability.

Table 16.6   BIND installation and maintenance chores

Chore	For	How often
Obtain domain name	Site	Once
Choose name servers	Site	Once or more
Obtain BIND distribution	Site	Once, but keep current
Configure resolver	Client	Once and distribute
Configure efficient resolver	Client	Each subnet and distribute
Configure services switch	Client	Each architecture and distribute
Start **named** at boot time	Server	Each name server
Set up **named** config file	Server	Each type of server
Configure hints file	Server	Once[a] and distribute to servers
Configure zone files	Master	Once
Update zone files	Master	As needed
Review log files	Log host	At least weekly
Educate users	All hosts	Continuously and repeatedly

a. But must be redone if the root servers change.

Since each host on the network must be a BIND client, we begin our detailed discussion with client-side chores.

Resolver configuration[7]

Each host on the network has a file called **/etc/resolv.conf** that lists the DNS servers the host should query. If your host gets its IP address and network parameters from a DHCP server, the **/etc/resolv.conf** file should be set up for you automatically. Otherwise, you must edit it by hand. The format is:

```
search domainname ...
nameserver ipaddr
```

Up to three name servers can be listed. Here's a complete example:

```
search cs.colorado.edu colorado.edu ee.colorado.edu
nameserver 128.138.243.151    ; ns
nameserver 128.138.204.4      ; piper
nameserver 128.138.240.1      ; anchor
```

Comments were never defined for the **resolv.conf** file. They are somewhat supported in that anything that is not recognized is ignored. It's safe to put comments at the end of nameserver lines because the parser just looks for an IP address and ignores the rest of the line. Because the search line can contain multiple arguments, comments there could cause problems.

---

7. Linux uses a "switch" file (**/etc/nsswitch.conf** or, for much older applications, **/etc/host.conf**) that specifies what sources of data should be used to implement name lookups. Each of our distributions specifies DNS, although not always first.

The search line lists the domains to query if a hostname is not fully qualified. If a user issues the command **ssh foo**, for example, the resolver completes the name with the first domain in the search list (in the **resolv.conf** above, cs.colorado.edu) and looks for foo.cs.colorado.edu. If no such name can be found, the resolver also tries foo.colorado.edu and foo.ee.colorado.edu.

Users in our cs subdomain can use simple hostnames for any local host, but users in the parent domain must use *hostname*.cs to reach a host in the subdomain. If you create new subdomains, you will also have to reconfigure (educate) your users.

A search directive in the **resolv.conf** files of machines in the parent domain could allow simple hostnames to be used in both directions:

```
search colorado.edu. cs.colorado.edu. ee.colorado.edu.
```

Of course, this configuration assumes that hostnames are unique across the three domains. A search directive can specify up to eight domains.

The servers listed in **resolv.conf** must be recursive (since the resolver does not understand referrals), and they should each have a cache. If you are using BIND 4 or BIND 8, the servers should not be authoritative for any zones. Their caches can grow quite large, and since versions 4 and 8 do not manage the cache properly, it can take over the entire memory of the machine. If you must mix cached and authoritative data, see the listen-on configuration option on page 387 for a way to do it safely— by running, on the same machine, two separate servers that listen to different ports.

The servers in nameserver lines are contacted in order; as long as the first one continues to answer queries, the others will be ignored. If a problem occurs, the query times out and the next name server is tried. Each server is tried in turn, up to four times. The timeout interval increases with every failure. When DNS is broken, it feels like the whole network is broken.

Most resolvers allow a maximum of three name servers to be listed. If more are provided, they are silently ignored. If a host is itself a name server, it should be listed first in its own **resolv.conf** file.

Earlier versions of BIND used the domain directive in **resolv.conf** instead of the search directive. It specified a single domain to add to names that were not fully qualified. We recommend replacing domain directives with search directives. The two directives are mutually exclusive, so only one should be present. If you have an older resolver and include both directives in the **resolv.conf** file, the last one listed is used.

From a cross-platform perspective, the default behavior of today's resolvers is a real hodgepodge. Some resolvers are more aggressive with default values than others. Some assume the local machine is a DNS server if no name servers are listed. Some deconstruct a local (fully qualified) hostname to come up with a search list. Some can operate with no **/etc/resolv.conf** file at all. Don't count on any of these misfeatures. Just configure **resolv.conf** normally for each of your hosts, regardless of the version of UNIX or Linux that it's running.

DNS queries arriving from the outside world will come to your authoritative name servers. It's a good idea to provide separate servers for resolving queries from inside your domain. Your internal servers should be caching-only and recursive. A large site should have several name servers running throughout the site and should customize the **resolv.conf** file to spread the load among the servers, minimize network traffic, and reduce the vulnerability of machines to a single point of failure. If name service is broken, your whole site grinds to a halt.

Forwarders are also a good way for a local site to optimize name service. Local name servers point to a forwarder that makes all the external queries for your site and builds a very rich cache. This configuration minimizes the external bandwidth used for name service and allows all local machines to share one large cache. Forwarders are covered in the configuration section starting on page 388.

Exhibit B illustrates the design recommended in the previous paragraphs. It shows a two-level forwarding hierarchy, which is overkill for small sites. Adjust the balance between servers that handle outgoing queries and servers that handle incoming queries so that neither group is too loaded.

Also note the use of the off-site slave server, which is highly recommended. Often, an ISP or local university will be willing run an off-site server for your domain. Companies with multiple offices can designate one location as the master; this location becomes "off site" relative to the rest of the company.

Exhibit B   DNS server architecture

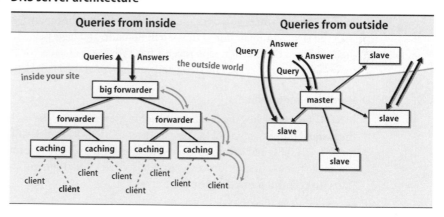

Resolver testing

On Linux systems, all you have to do to start using DNS is add a nameserver line to **/etc/resolv.conf**. The default switch file (**/etc/nsswitch.conf**) does include dns; see page 498 for more information.

After configuring **/etc/resolv.conf** (and assuming that your local network connection is up and running correctly), you should be able to refer to other machines by name rather than by IP address. If you try to reach another local machine and the command just hangs, try referring to the machine by its address. If that works, then your DNS configuration is the problem. Verify that the name server IP addresses in **/etc/resolv.conf** are correct and that the servers you point to allow queries from your network (see page 388).

Impact on the rest of the system

The change from static host tables to DNS creates some potential dependencies in booting and configuration that you need to protect against.

As a host boots, references to hostnames in the startup files might be unresolvable if they are encountered before the network is up. The commands in the startup files will unsuccessfully try to contact DNS. Thanks to the resolver's robustness, they will try multiple times on multiple servers, increasing their timeout period with each attempt. A couple of minutes later, the command needing the hostname will finally fail.

To fix the problem, use only literal IP addresses in the early stages of the boot process. Or, since Linux supports the simultaneous use of both DNS and **/etc/hosts** by way of the switch file, you can install a **hosts** file that contains the server addresses needed at boot time. Be sure the **hosts** file is checked before DNS so you don't have to wait for DNS to time out.

16.9 BIND SERVER CONFIGURATION

In this section, we assume that your political chores have been completed. That is, we assume that you have a domain name (possibly a subdomain), have coordinated with the DNS administrator of the parent domain, and have been delegated your address space in the in-addr.arpa reverse tree. You have chosen your master name server and a couple of secondaries, and you have installed BIND.

Hardware requirements

BIND is a memory hog. Its database is kept in memory, so as the cache grows, so does the **named** process. Some of the new features of BIND 9 are also CPU intensive, most notably DNSSEC and IPv6. To help reduce this burden, BIND 9 is multithreaded and can make full use of multiprocessor systems. BIND 9 also contains configuration options that control **named**'s use of resources.

The best way to determine if a name server machine has enough memory is to run it for a while and watch the size of the **named** process. It takes a week or two to converge on a stable size at which old cache records are expiring at about the same rate that new ones are being inserted. Once stable, the system should not be swapping, and its paging rates should be reasonable.

If your name server runs on a dedicated machine, a good rule of thumb is for the machine to have double the amount of memory consumed by **named** after it has been running for two weeks. The **top** and **vmstat** commands show memory usage; see *Analyzing memory usage* on page 790 for more details.

named startup

named is started at boot time and runs continuously. Each of our Linux distributions has a startup script for **named** that's run through **init**: **/etc/init.d/named** for Red Hat and SuSE and **/etc/init.d/bind** for Debian.

To control a running copy of **named**, you use a command-line interface called **ndc** in BIND 8 and **rndc** in BIND 9. **ndc** and **rndc** are described in more detail in the BIND debugging section that starts on page 453. The usage is just

```
# ndc command
```

Some useful commands are **start**, **stop**, **restart**, and **status**, which have the obvious meanings. We've had bad luck with **ndc start** on Red Hat systems; try the following command instead:

```
# /sbin/service named start
```

The **init** scripts that start **named** on each system provide some extra entry points (such as **reload**) that are intended for use by system administrators. However, the implementation on some distributions is questionable, and it's easier to use **ndc** anyway. We suggest that you leave the startup scripts for **init**—no point in building unnecessary system dependencies into your administrative scripts or your brain.

*See page 812 for more information about **inetd**.*

named uses syslog, and therefore **syslogd** should be started before **named**. Do not use **inetd/xinetd** to manage **named**; it will restart **named** every time it's needed, slowing response times and preventing any useful cache from being developed.

Configuration files

The complete configuration for **named** consists of the config file, the hints file, and, for master servers, the zone data files that contain address mappings for each host. **named**'s config file has its own format; all the other files are collections of individual DNS data records that are formatted according to the DNS specification. We discuss the config file in the next two sections. The format of DNS data records is described beginning on page 408.

named's configuration file specifies the role (master, slave, or stub) of this host relative to each zone and the way in which it should get its copy of the resource records that make up the local part of the database. It's also the place where options are specified—both global options related to the operation of **named** itself and server-specific or zone-specific options that affect particular venues.

The format of **named**'s configuration file changed completely between BIND 4 and BIND 8, with the newer format resembling that of **gated.conf** (see page 316). The name of the config file also changed: in BIND 4, it was **/etc/named.boot**, and in BIND 8 and 9 it is **/etc/named.conf**. Cache files and data files remain the same.

We describe the BIND 8/9 config file and totally ignore BIND 4. As with any software, older versions of BIND may contain security vulnerabilities that have been patched in the current versions.

The file **named.conf** consists of a series of statements, each terminated by a semi-colon. Tokens are separated by whitespace, which can include newlines. Curly braces are sometimes used for grouping, but only in specific contexts. The format is quite fragile—a missing semicolon can wreak havoc.

Fortunately, BIND 9 includes a couple of handy tools to check the syntax of the config file (**named-checkconf**) and the zone data files (**named-checkzone**). They look for both errors and omissions. For example, **named-checkzone** will tell you if you've forgotten to include a $TTL directive. Unfortunately, it doesn't catch everything. For example, missing glue records (see page 429) are not reported and cause heavy loads on the root and gTLD servers.

Comments can appear anywhere that whitespace is appropriate. C, C++, and shell-style comments are all understood:

```
/* This is a comment and can span lines. */
// Everything to the end of the line is a comment.
# Everything to the end of the line is a comment.
```

but you should pick one style and use it consistently.

Each statement begins with a keyword that identifies the type of statement. There can be more than one instance of each type of statement, except for options and logging. Statements and parts of statements can also be left out, invoking default behavior for the missing items. Table 16.7 lists the available statements. Alternate rows have been shaded to improve readability.

Table 16.7   Statement types used in named.conf (BIND 8 and 9)

Statement	Function
include	Interpolates a file (e.g., trusted keys readable only by **named**)
options	Sets global name server configuration options and defaults
server	Specifies per-server options
lwres	Configures the name server as a lightweight resolver too (BIND 9 only)
key	Defines authentication information
acl	Defines access control lists
zone	Defines a zone of resource records
trusted-keys	Uses preconfigured keys
controls	Defines channels used to control the name server with **ndc**
logging	Specifies logging categories and their destinations
view	Defines a view of the namespace (BIND 9 only)

Before describing these statements and the way they are used to configure **named**, we need to describe a data structure that is used in many of the statements: the address match list. An address match list is a generalization of an IP address that can include the following items.

- An IP address (e.g., 199.165.145.4)
- An IP network specified with a CIDR netmask (e.g., 199.165/16)
- The name of a previously defined access control list (see page 389)
- A cryptographic authentication key
- The ! character to negate things

Address match lists are used as parameters to many statements and options. Some examples:

```
{ ! 1.2.3.13; 1.2.3/24; };
{ 128.138/16; 198.11.16/24; 204.228.69/24; 127.0.0.1; };
```

The first of these lists excludes the host 1.2.3.13 but allows the rest of the 1.2.3/24 network; the second defines the networks assigned to the University of Colorado. The braces and final semicolon are not really part of the address match list but are part of the enclosing statement that uses it.

When an IP address or network is compared to a match list, the list is searched in order until a match is found. This "first match" algorithm makes the ordering of entries important. For example, the first address match list above would not have the desired effect if the two entries were reversed, because 1.2.3.13 would succeed in matching 1.2.3/24 and the negated entry would never be encountered.

Now, on to the statements! Some are short and sweet; others almost warrant a chapter unto themselves.

The include statement

To break up or better organize a large configuration, you can put different portions of the configuration in separate files. Subsidiary files are brought into **named.conf** with an include statement:

```
include "path";
```

If the *path* is relative, then it is interpreted relative to the directory specified in the directory option. A common use of the include statement is to bring in cryptographic keys that should not be world-readable. Rather than closing read access to the whole **named.conf** file, some sites keep keys in files with restricted permissions that only **named** can read. Those files are then included into **named.conf**.

The options statement

The options statement specifies global options, some of which may later be overridden for particular zones or servers. The general format is:

```
options {
    option;
    option;
    ...
};
```

If no options statement is present in **named.conf**, then default values are used.

BIND 8 had about 30 options, and BIND 9 has over 50. For a complete list, refer to the BIND documentation or to O'Reilly's *DNS and BIND* by Paul Albitz and Cricket Liu (the third edition covers BIND 8, and the fourth covers both 8 and 9). We have biased our coverage of these options and discuss only the ones whose use we recommend. (We also asked the BIND developers for their suggestions on which options to cover, and took their advice.) The default values are listed in square brackets beside each option.

```
version "string";                       [real version number of the server]
```

There are two schools of thought on the issue of hiding the version number. Some sites believe that their servers will be more vulnerable to attack if hackers can tell what version they are running. Others think that hiding the version information is counterproductive because hackers will try their luck anyway and most newly discovered bugs are present in all versions of the software.

We recommend that you not reset the version string despite the fact that our example site does (we lost the security-through-obscurity argument with the sysadmin group). It is very handy to be able to query your name servers and find out what version they are running (for example, if you want to know if your vendor is shipping a current release or if you need to verify that you have in fact upgraded all your servers to the latest revision).

```
directory "path";                       [directory where the server was started]
```

The directory statement causes **named** to **cd** to the specified directory. Wherever relative pathnames appear in **named**'s configuration files, they are interpreted relative to this directory. The *path* should be an absolute path. Any output files (debugging, statistics, etc.) are also written in this directory.

We recommend putting all BIND-related configuration files (other than **named.conf** and **resolv.conf**) in a subdirectory beneath **/var** (or wherever you keep your configuration files for other programs). We use **/var/named**.

```
notify yes | no;                        [yes]
also-notify servers_ipaddrs;            [empty]
```

If notify is set to yes and this **named** is the master server for one or more zones, **named** automatically notifies those zones' slave servers whenever the corresponding zone database changes. The slave servers can then rendezvous with the master to update their copies of the zone data. The notify option can be used as both a global option and as a zone-specific option. It makes the zone files converge much more quickly after you make changes.

See page 430 for more information about stub zones.

named normally figures out which machines are slave servers of a zone by looking at that zone's NS records. If also-notify is specified, a set of additional servers that are not advertised with NS records can also be notified. This tweak is sometimes necessary when your site has internal servers. Don't also-notify stub servers; they are only interested in the zone's NS records and can wait for the regular update cycle. The target of an also-notify must be a list of IP addresses—an acl won't work.

BIND 4 servers do not understand notification messages. They log an error and wait for the refresh interval prescribed in the zone data (page 411) to expire before updating themselves. The localhost reverse zone is a good place to turn notification off.

```
recursion yes | no;                        [yes]
allow-recursion { address_match_list };   [all hosts]
```

The recursion option specifies whether **named** queries other name servers on behalf of clients, as described on page 372. It's fairly unusual to configure a name server with recursion off. However, you might want to allow recursion for your own clients but not for outside queries.

Recursion can be controlled at a finer granularity with the allow-recursion option and an address list that includes the hosts and networks on whose behalf you are willing to perform recursive queries.

```
use-id-pool yes | no;                      [no (V8 only)]
```

In BIND V8, this option causes **named** to keep track of outstanding query IDs so that it doesn't issue duplicates and so that the sequence of IDs it issues can be more random. It helps prevent DNS spoofing. If you turn it on, expect **named** to use a bit more memory. The feature is worth the extra memory cost, however; we recommend that you use this option. In BIND 9, the use-id-pool option is gone and **named** always manages its query IDs this way.

```
maintain-ixfr-base yes | no;        [no (V8 only)]
ixfr-base "filename"                 [(V8 only)]
ixfr-tmp-file "filename"             [(V8 only)]
```

Incremental zone transfers (see RFC1995) allow servers to send out "patches" to a zone when it changes instead of resending the entire zone. For a zone like com, this incrementality is very important. The current release of BIND 8 allows incremental zone transfers for any zone that does dynamic updates; it keeps a transaction log file if maintain-ixfr-base is set to yes. BIND 9 always maintains a log.

In BIND 8, you can meddle with the default names for the IXFR transaction log and temporary file with the ixfr-base and ixfr-tmp-file options. *Zone transfers* on page 432 covers incremental zone transfers in more detail.

```
check-names { master|slave|response action }     [see text (V8 only)]
```

BIND 8 includes code to check the validity of hostnames—not in the sense of "Does this host exist?" but in the sense of "Does this hostname actually follow the rules specified in the RFCs for hostnames?" A surprising number of them don't.

A name is valid if it contains only letters, numbers, and dashes and is no longer than 64 characters per component (including the dot) and 256 characters overall. The rules for names and the distinction between the host portion and the domain portion are subjects of current debate. Internationalization of the DNS system and support for non-ASCII character sets might change all the naming rules.

You can specify the check-names behavior globally and also individually for each zone; a zone specification overrides the global values. You can apply the option to master servers, to slave servers, or to the answers returned in response to queries.[8] Each type has three possible action values:

- ignore – do no checking
- warn   – log bad names but continue processing
- fail   – log and reject bad names

The default for the master is to fail, since errors on the master are likely to be typos or noncompliant names that the sysadmin should fix. A site should not knowingly propagate noncompliant names. The default for slave servers is to warn, and the default for responses is to ignore. The default values are just right; you should not need to change them.

check-names logging data is a prime candidate for tuning with the infinitely flexible logging system that is covered beginning on page 448.

BIND 9, in anticipation of internationalized domain names, does not implement the check-names option.

```
transfer-format one-answer | many-answers;      [see text]
```

This option affects the way in which DNS data records (described starting on page 408) are replicated from master servers to their slaves. The actual transmission of data records used to take place one record at a time, which is a recipe for sloth and inefficiency. An option to combine many records into one packet (many-answers) was added in BIND 8.1; it is the default in BIND 9. Use this option only if all the servers with which you share zone data are running at least 8.1, since BIND 4 servers do not understand it. If you have a mixed environment, you can specify a transfer format in individual server statements to override the global option. Your mix of servers will dictate whether you choose many-answers globally and override it for specific servers, or vice versa.

```
transfers-in number;            [10]
transfers-out number;           [10 (V9 only)]
transfers-per-ns number;        [2]
transfer-source IP-address;     [system dependent]
serial-queries number;          [4 (V8 only)]
```

A large site—one that serves a very large zone (such as com, which currently is over two gigabytes), or one that serves thousands of zones—may need to tune some of these zone transfer options.

The transfers-in and transfers-out options limit the number of inbound or outbound zone transfers that can happen concurrently.[9] The transfers-per-ns option sets the maximum number of inbound zone transfers that can be running concur-

---

8. BIND 8 slave servers that are using check-names do not seem to recognize bad names in zone transfers, and they allow the bad data to propagate. However, the feature works fine for master servers.
9. The BIND code enforces a hard-wired limit of 20 for the transfers-in parameter.

rently from the same remote server. Large sites may need to increase transfers-in or transfers-out; be careful that you don't run out of file descriptors for the **named** process. transfers-per-ns should probably not be changed; it controls how many resources the master server is willing to devote to us. It should only be increased if all remote master servers are willing to handle more than two simultaneous zone transfers. Changing it on a per-server basis with the transfers clause of the server statement is a better way to fine-tune the convergence of slave zones.

The transfer-source option lets you specify the IP address of the interface you want to use for incoming transfers. It must match the address specified in the master's allow-transfer statement.

In BIND 8 you can limit the number of simultaneous inquiries for the serial number of a zone with the serial-queries option. Each such inquiry keeps state on the local server; if thousands of queries are being received, this limit can help the server maintain its sanity. The default value is four, which is way too low for a big site; raise it to several hundred or even a thousand. In BIND 9 this parameter is currently ignored; it will be replaced by a query rate in the future.

As with any parameter that you change drastically, you should watch things carefully after changing one of these throttle values to be sure the machine is not thrashing. The log files are your friends.

```
files number;                        [unlimited]
```

The files option sets the maximum number of files the server is allowed to have open concurrently. The default value, unlimited, means as close as possible to the number of open files the kernel can support. (To change the number of open files that the kernel can support, set the value of **/proc/sys/fs/file-max**. See page 221.)

```
listen-on port ip_port address_match_list;    [53 all]
query-source address ip_addr port ip_port;    [random]
```

The listen-on option specifies the network interfaces and ports on which **named** listens for queries. The query-source option specifies the interface and port that **named** uses to query other name servers. The values of these options default to the standard **named** behavior: listening on port 53 on all interfaces and using a random, high-numbered UDP port and any interface for queries.

See page 700 for more information about virtual interfaces.

The listen-on option lets you run multiple name servers on one host. For example, you might want to do this because it's best not to configure a BIND 4 or BIND 8 server to be both authoritative and caching—those versions of **named** keep all their data in one giant database. **named** can run out of memory, and the data can become corrupted. To avoid this risk, you can run two separate **named** processes: one as an authoritative server and the other as a caching server that uses the listen-on statement and a different virtual IP address. The authoritative and caching servers can interact just as if they ran on separate machines. Put only the caching server's IP address in the **resolv.conf** file. (Using **ndc** to control multiple instances of **named** running on the same machine can be challenging and nearly impossible.)

If your site has a firewall, you can use the query-source option to give external DNS queries a specific, recognizable profile. You typically set **named** to use port 53 as the source port so that the firewall can recognize outbound DNS traffic as trustworthy packets from one of your name servers. Don't set the source port to zero—that's an illegal port and **named** will log the query as an error and not answer it. One large ISP has a sysadmin who likes port 0 and has rendered many of their name servers ineffective through his use of the query-source clause. It's curious that their customers don't notice and complain.

```
forwarders { in_addr; in_addr; ... };            [empty list]
forward only | first;                            [first]
```

Instead of having every name server perform its own external queries, you can designate one or more servers as *forwarders*. A run-of-the-mill server can look in its cache and the records for which it is authoritative; if it doesn't find the answer it's looking for, it can then send the query on to a forwarder host. That way, the forwarders build up caches that benefit the entire site. Forwarders reduce the load on your network, limit CPU and memory use on weaker servers, increase performance for users, and reduce your reliance on external Internet connectivity. Many sites designate their more powerful and memory-rich servers as forwarders.

A medium-sized site can construct a very efficient DNS system with a series of caching servers that point to just one or two forwarders. Large sites may need a hierarchy of forwarders. The example on page 403 uses a two-level forwarding scheme.

The forwarders option lists the IP addresses of the servers you want to use as forwarders. They are queried in turn. The use of a forwarder circumvents the normal DNS procedure of starting at a root server and following the chain of referrals. Be careful not to create forwarding loops.

A forward only server caches values and queries forwarders, but it never queries anyone else. If the forwarders do not respond, queries will fail. A forward first server prefers to deal with forwarders but will process queries directly if need be.

Since the forwarders option has no default value, forwarding does not occur unless it has been specifically configured. You can turn on forwarding either globally or within individual zone statements.

```
allow-query { address_match_list };       [all hosts]
allow-transfer { address_match_list };    [all hosts]
blackhole { address_match_list };         [empty]
```

These options let you specify which hosts (or networks) can query your name server and request block transfers of your zone data. The blackhole address list identifies servers that you never want to talk to; **named** will not accept queries from these servers and will not ask them for answers.

```
sortlist { address_match_list };          [should die, don't use]
```

We mention the sortlist option only to warn you away from it. sortlist should really go away and die. Its purpose was to help primitive resolvers that don't sort record sets properly. It lets you specify the order in which multiple answers are returned and works against current BINDs' internal smarts.

Other BIND options that meddle with the order of things are the rrset-order statement, which specifies whether to return multiple answers in cyclic (round robin), fixed, or random order, and the topology statement, which tries to second-guess BIND's system for selecting remote servers to query. In most cases there is no need to use these statements, either.

The acl statement

An access control list is just an address match list with a name:

```
acl acl_name {
    address_match_list
};
```

You can use an access control list anywhere that an address match list is called for, with the exception of the also-notify statement.

An acl must be a top-level statement in **named.conf**, so don't try sneaking it in amid your other option declarations. **named.conf** is read in a single pass, so access control lists must be defined before they are used. Four lists are predefined:

- any – all hosts
- localnets – all hosts on the local network
- localhost – the machine itself
- none – nothing

The localnets list includes all of the networks to which the host is directly attached. In other words, it's a list of the machine's network addresses modulo their netmasks.

The server statement

named can potentially talk to many servers, not all of which are running the latest version of BIND, and not all of which are even nominally sane. The server statement tells **named** about the characteristics of its remote peers.

```
server ip_addr {
    bogus yes | no;                                      [no]
    provide-ixfr yes | no;                               [yes (V9 only)]
    request-ixfr yes | no;                               [yes (V9 only)]
    support-ixfr yes | no;                               [no (V8 only)]
    edns yes | no;                                       [yes]
    transfers number;                                    [2 (V9 only)]
    transfer-format one-answer | many-answers;   [V8: one, V9: many]
    keys { key-id; key-id; ... };
};
```

You can use a server statement to override the values of server-related configuration options. Just list the ones for which you want nondefault behavior.

If you mark a server as being bogus, **named** won't send any queries its way. This directive should generally be reserved for servers that really are bogus.

The ixfr clauses changed between V8 and V9, though both sets are similar. V8 has support-ixfr, and V9 has provide-ixfr and request-ixfr. The server statements in the config file of a server running V8 can set support-ixfr to yes if the remote server understands incremental zone transfers. A V9 server acting as master for a zone will do incremental zone transfers if provide-ixfr is set to yes. Likewise, a V9 server acting as a slave will request incremental zone transfers from the master if request-ixfr is set to yes.

The edns clause determines whether the local server will try to use the extended DNS protocol when contacting the remote server. Many of the newer features in BIND (IPv6 and DNSSEC, for example) generate packets bigger than 512 bytes and therefore require the use of the EDNS protocol to negotiate a larger UDP packet size.

The transfers clause limits the number of concurrent inbound zone transfers from the remote server. It is a server-specific version of transfers-in, but because it applies to only one server, it acts like a per-server override of the transfers-per-ns option. The name is different to preserve compatibility with BIND 8.

The transfer-format clauses are the server-specific forms of the options discussed on page 386. Use transfer-format if you talk to both BIND 8/9 and BIND 4 servers or if you have Microsoft name servers on your network. NT cannot handle anything but the original one-answer format; Windows 2000 is OK with either format.

The keys clause identifies a key ID that has been previously defined in a key statement for use with TSIG transaction signatures (see page 438). Any requests sent to the remote server are signed with this key. Requests originating at the remote server are not required to be signed, but if they are, the signature will be verified.

The logging statement

named is the current holder of the "most configurable logging system on Earth" award. Syslog put the prioritization of log messages into the programmer's hands and the disposition of those messages into the sysadmin's hands. But for a given priority, the sysadmin had no way to say, "I care about this message but not about that message." BIND 8 added categories that classify log messages by type, and channels that broaden the choices for the disposition of messages. Categories are determined by the programmer, and channels by the sysadmin.

Since the issue of logging is somewhat tangential (especially given the amount of explanation required), we discuss it in the debugging section later in this chapter. It starts on page 448.

The zone statement

zone statements are the heart of the **named.conf** file. They tell **named** about the zones for which it is authoritative and set the options that are appropriate for managing each zone. A zone statement is also used to preload the root server hints (the names and addresses of the root servers, which bootstrap the DNS lookup process).

The exact format of a zone statement varies, depending on the role that **named** is to play with respect to that zone (for example, master server or slave server). We examine each possibility in turn. Many of the global options covered earlier can become part of a zone statement and override the previously defined values. We have not repeated those options here except to mention certain ones that are frequently used.

Configuring the master server for a zone

Here is the format you need for a zone of which this **named** is the master server:

```
zone "domain_name" {
    type master;
    file "path";
};
```

Other server-specific attributes are also frequently specified. For example:

```
allow-query { address_match_list };      [all]
allow-transfer { address_match_list };   [all]
allow-update { address_match_list };     [none]
ixfr-base "path";                        [domain_name.ixfr (V8 only)]
zone-statistics yes | no                 [no]
```

The *domain_name* in a zone specification must always be in double quotes.

The zone's data is kept on disk in a human-readable (and human-editable) file. Since there is no default for the filename, you must provide a file statement when declaring a master zone. A zone file is just a collection of DNS resource records; the format description begins on page 408.

The access control options are not required, but it's a good idea to use them. If dynamic updates are used for this zone, the allow-update clause must be present with an address match list that limits the hosts from which updates can occur. Dynamic updates apply only to master zones; the allow-update clause cannot be used for a slave zone (in BIND 9). Be sure that this clause includes just your local DHCP servers and not the whole Internet.[10]

If incremental zone transfers are to be used with this zone, BIND 8 keeps a transaction log in a file called *domain_name*.**ixfr** in **named**'s home directory. If you want to change the name, use the ixfr-base clause to specify a new filename. This file is maintained by **named** and needs no attention from you.

---

10. You also need ingress filtering at your firewall; see page 676. Better yet, use TSIG for authentication.

In BIND 9, the transaction log is used for both dynamic updates and IXFR. Its name ends with **.jnl** and is not configurable. Both dynamic updates and incremental zone transfers are relatively new features of BIND. They are discussed in more detail starting on page 432.

The zone-statistics option makes **named** keep track of query/response statistics such as the number and percentage of responses that were referrals, demanded recursion, or resulted in errors. See the examples for BIND 8 and BIND 9 on page 453.

With all these zone-specific options (and about 30 more we have not covered), the configuration is starting to sound complicated. However, a master zone declaration consisting of nothing but a pathname to the zone file is perfectly reasonable. In BIND 4, that's all you could specify. Here is an example from the BIND documentation that we have modified slightly:

```
zone "example.com" {
    type master;
    file "forward/example.com";
    allow-query { any; };
    allow-transfer { my-slaves; };
}
```

my-slaves is an access control list that was previously defined.

Configuring a slave server for a zone

The zone statement for a slave is very similar to that of a master:

```
zone "domain_name" {
    type slave | stub;
    file "path";
    ixfr-base "path";                       [V8 only]
    masters { ip_addr; ip_addr; ... };      [no default]
    allow-query { address_match_list };     [all]
    allow-transfer { address_match_list };  [all]
};
```

Slave servers normally maintain a complete copy of their zone's database. However, if the type is set to stub instead of slave, only NS (name server) records are transferred. Stub zones allow the **named**s for the parent zone to automatically discover which machines provide DNS service for their delegated child zones, just in case the administrator of the child zone is not conscientious about informing the parent of changes. The parent needs this information to make appropriate referrals or recursive queries. We revisit this topic in greater detail on page 429.

The file statement specifies a local file in which the replicated database can be stored. Each time the server fetches a new copy of the zone, it saves the data in this file. If the server crashes and reboots, the file can then be reloaded from the local disk without being transferred across the network.

You shouldn't edit this cache file, since it's maintained by **named**. However, it can be interesting to look at if you suspect you have made an error in the master server's data file. The slave's disk file shows you how **named** has interpreted the original zone data; relative names and origin directives have all been expanded. If you see a name in the data file that looks like one of these

> 128.138.243.151.cs.colorado.edu.
> anchor.cs.colorado.edu.cs.colorado.edu.

you can be pretty sure that you forgot a trailing dot somewhere.

The masters statement lists the IP addresses of one or more machines from which the zone database can be obtained. We have said that only one machine can be the master for a zone, so why is it possible to list more than one address? Two reasons.

First, the master machine might have more than one network interface and therefore more than one IP address. It's possible for one interface to become unreachable (because of network or routing problems) while others are still accessible. Therefore, it's a good practice to list all of the master server's topologically distinct addresses.

Second, **named** really doesn't care where the zone data comes from. It can pull the database just as easily from a slave server as from the master. You could use this feature to allow a well-connected slave server to serve as a sort of backup master, since the IP addresses will be tried in order until a working server is found. In theory, you can also set up a hierarchy of servers, with one master serving several second-level servers, which in turn serve many third-level servers.

We suggest that you list only bona fide master server addresses on the masters line.

Setting up the root hints

Another form of zone statement points **named** toward a file from which it can prime (preload) its cache with the names and addresses of the root name servers:

```
zone "." {
    type hint;
    file "path";
};
```

The "hints" are a set of DNS records that list servers for the root domain ("."). They're needed to give **named** a place to start searching for information about other sites' domains. Without them, **named** would only know about the domains it actually serves and their subdomains.

The hints file is often called **root.cache**; it contains the response you would get if you queried a root server for the name server records in the domain ".". We discuss how to set up a proper hints file, starting on page 460.

BIND 9 has root server hints compiled into its code, so no configuration of the root zone is really needed. If you provide a hints file, however, BIND 9 will use it. We recommend that you do supply explicit hints; politics have entered the DNS arena, making root name servers and their IP addresses more volatile.

Setting up a forwarding zone

A zone of type forward overrides **named**'s global forwarding settings (described on page 388) for a particular domain:

```
zone "domain_name" {
    type forward;
    forward only | first;
    forwarders { ip_addr; ip_addr; ... };
};
```

You might use a forward zone if your organization had a strategic working relationship with some other group or company and you wanted to funnel traffic directly to that company's name servers, bypassing the standard query path. You could use such an arrangement to access name servers that were invisible to the outside world, as is done in the example on page 400.

The key statement

The key statement defines a named encryption key to be used for authentication with a particular server. Background information about BIND's support for cryptographic authentication is given in the *Security issues* section starting on page 435. Here, we just touch briefly on the mechanics of the process.

To build a key record, you specify both the cryptographic algorithm that you want to use and a "shared secret," represented as a base-64-encoded string:

```
key key-id {
    algorithm string;
    secret string;
};
```

As with access control lists, the *key-id* must be defined before it is used. To associate the key with a particular server, just include *key-id* in the keys clause of that server's server statement. The key is used both to verify requests from that server and to sign the responses to those requests.

The trusted-keys statement

The trusted-keys statement is for DNSSEC security, specified in RFC2065. Each entry is a 5-tuple that identifies the domain name, flags, protocol, algorithm, and key that are needed to talk securely to a name server for that domain. The format is:

```
trusted-keys {
    domain flags protocol algorithm key;
    domain flags protocol algorithm key;
    ...
}
```

Each line represents the trusted key for a particular domain. The *flags*, *protocol*, and *algorithm* are nonnegative integers. The *key* is a base-64 encoded string.

The trusted-keys construct is intended to be used when a zone is signed but its parent zone is not, so you cannot be sure that the public key for the zone that you get from DNS is really kosher. Entering a trusted key with a trusted-keys statement (using out-of-band methods) ensures that you really have the appropriate key for the domain in question.

DNSSEC is covered in more detail starting on page 440.

The controls statement

The controls statement specifies how **ndc** (**rndc** on BIND 9) controls a running **named** process. **ndc** can start and stop **named**, dump its state, put it in debug mode, etc. **ndc** is a network program, and without proper configuration it might let anyone on the Internet mess around with your name server. The syntax is:

```
BIND 8: controls {
     inet ip_addr port port# allow { address_match_list | key ... };
     unix permission owner group;                              [0600 0 0]
}

BIND 9: controls {
     inet ip_addr allow { address_match_list } keys { key_list };   [see text]
}
```

BIND 9 also allows the port to be specified but defaults to port 953 if the port clause is not present. If the unix line is present, BIND 9 ignores it.

Allowing your name server to be controlled remotely sounds both handy and dangerous. Strong authentication via a key entry in the allow clause was optional in BIND 8. BIND 9 requires strong authentication, ignores keys in the address match list, and uses the keys explicitly stated in the keys clause of the controls statement.

In BIND 9, you can use the **rndc-confgen** command to generate an authentication key for use between **rndc** and **named**. There are essentially two ways to set this up: you can have both **named** and **rndc** consult the same configuration file to learn the key (**/etc/rndc.key**), or you can inform each program of the key in its own configuration file (**/etc/rndc.conf** for **rndc** and **/etc/named.conf** for **named**). The latter option is more complicated, but it's necessary when **named** and **rndc** will be running on different computers.

When no controls statement is present, BIND 9 defaults to the loopback address for the address match list and looks for the key in **/etc/rndc.key**. Because strong authentication is mandatory in BIND 9, you cannot use the **rndc** command to control **named** if there is no key. This may seem a bit draconian, but consider: even if **rndc** worked only from localhost (127.0.0.1) and this address was blocked from the outside world at your firewall, you would still be trusting all local users to not mess with your name server. Any user could **telnet** to the control port and type "stop"—quite an effective denial of service attack.

Here is an example of the output (to standard out) from **rndc-confgen** when a 256-bit key is requested (we chose 256 because it fits on the page!). You would normally redirect the output to **/etc/rndc.conf**. The comments at the bottom of the output show the lines that need to be added to **named.conf** to make **named** and **rndc** play together.

```
% ./rndc-confgen -b 256
# Start of rndc.conf
key "rndc-key" {
    algorithm hmac-md5;
    secret "orZuz5amkUnEp52zlHxD6cd5hACldOGsG/elP/dv2IY=";
};

options {
    default-key "rndc-key";
    default-server 127.0.0.1;
    default-port 953;
};
# End of rndc.conf

# Use with the following in named.conf, adjusting the allow list as needed:
# key "rndc-key" {
#       algorithm hmac-md5;
#       secret "orZuz5amkUnEp52zlHxD6cd5hACldOGsG/elP/dv2IY=";
# };
#
# controls {
#       inet 127.0.0.1 port 953
#               allow { 127.0.0.1; } keys { "rndc-key"; };
# };
# End of named.conf
```

"Automatic" mode, used to generate a shared configuration file, is simpler. Run as root, **rndc-confgen -a -b 256** produces the file **/etc/rndc.key**, which contains

```
key "rndc-key" {
    algorithm hmac-md5;
    secret "laGbZj2Cobyc0m/jFVNCu8OJzsLKNH+CCb2JCWY6yJw=";
};
```

The file has mode 600 and should be owned by the **named** user or root.

In BIND 8, **ndc** can also contact **named** through a UNIX domain socket called **/var/run/ndc**. The unix configuration line sets the permissions and ownerships on that socket and hence restricts access to it. The *permission* parameter should be an octal number that represents the desired mode of the socket; the *owner* and *group* parameters are the UID and GID of the owner of the socket. The defaults are read and write permission only for root.

Split DNS and the BIND 9 view statement

See page 255 for more information about private address spaces.

Many sites want the internal view of their network to be different from the view seen from out on the Internet. This type of configuration (sometimes called "split DNS") seems to be increasingly popular.

For example, you might reveal all of a zone's hosts to internal users but restrict the external view to a few well-known servers. Or, you might expose the same set of hosts in both views but supply additional (or different) records to internal users. For example, the MX records for mail routing might point to a single mail hub machine from outside the domain but point to individual workstations from the perspective of internal users.

A split DNS configuration is especially useful for sites that use RFC1918 private IP address spaces on their internal networks. For example, a query for the hostname associated with IP address 10.0.0.1 can never be answered by the global DNS system, but it is meaningful within the context of the local network. Of the queries arriving at the root name servers, 4-5% are either *from* an IP address in one of the private address ranges or *about* one of these addresses. Neither can be answered; both are the result of misconfiguration, either of BIND's split DNS or Microsoft's "domains."

To create a split DNS configuration with BIND 8, you set up separate servers for the internal and external versions of reality. Names are divided into internal and external zones. Local clients point at servers that dish out the internal version of the zone; the parent zone's NS records point at servers that hold the external version. Transfers and recursive queries are limited. Table 16.8 illustrates the differences in configuration between the internal and external name servers.

Table 16.8   Internal and external server configurations for BIND 8 split DNS

Parameter	External	Internal
directory	/var/named/external	/var/named/internal
listen-on	*external interface*	*internal interface*
recursion	no	yes
allow-query	any	*internal nets only*
forward	*not used*	forward only ; forwarders *external_ns*;

BIND 9's view statement simplifies the setup of split DNS configurations by putting both sets of data inside the same copy of **named**. The view statement packages up an access list that controls which clients see which view, some options that apply to all the zones in the view, and finally, the zones themselves. The syntax is:

```
view view-name {
    match-clients { address_match_list } ;
    view_option; ...
    zone_statement; ...
} ;
```

The `match-clients` clause controls who can see the view. Views are processed in order, so put the most restrictive views first. Zones in different views can have the same names. Views are an all-or-nothing proposition; if you use them, all zone statements in your **named.conf** file must appear in the context of a view.

Here is an example from the BIND 9 documentation that mimics the split DNS scheme described above. The two views define the same zone, but with different data.

```
view "internal" {
    match-clients { our_nets; };     // only internal networks
    recursion yes;                   // internal clients only
    zone "example.com" {             // complete view of zone
        type master;
        file "example-internal.db";
    };
};
view "external" {
    match-clients { any; };          // allow all queries
    recursion no;                    // but no recursion
    zone "example.com" {             // only "public" hosts
        type master;
        file "example-external.db";
    }
};
```

If the order of the views were reversed, no one would ever see the internal view. Internal hosts would match the any value in the `match-clients` clause of the external view before they reached the internal view.

Our second DNS configuration example (starting on page 400) uses split DNS to enforce a single incoming mail gateway via MX records, to hide several subnets of private addresses, and to make HINFO and TXT records that contain sensitive information inaccessible from the outside world.

16.10 BIND CONFIGURATION EXAMPLES

Now that we have explored the wonders of **named.conf**, let's look at some complete examples. In the following sections, we show three sample configurations:

- A student's home Linux box
- A small security company that uses split DNS
- A university department that uses a three-level forwarding hierarchy

A home Linux box

Rob Braun, a student, has a Linux box at home that provides DNS name service for his domain, synack.net, and for the domains of a couple of friends. He is running BIND 8.2.3. His **named.conf** file is below. We have added a few comments to the ends of lines.

Rob's configuration is pretty straightforward. The options are mostly the defaults: a recursive server, files in the usual places, queries and transfers OK, a one-answer transfer format, speaking on port 53, etc. Some control is exercised over the configuration of individual zones. For example, the synack.net and xinetd.org zones allow transfers to only one host, and they do not allow dynamic updates.

This name server is the master server for two domains: synack.net and xinetd.org. It's also a slave server for two friends' domains: teich.net and rmtai.com. As might be expected in a computer science student's configuration, the logging section is not the default. It includes mild debugging and curiosity channels modeled after the sample config file shipped with BIND.

```
/* named.conf file, gw.synack.net */

options {
    directory "/var/named";
    pid-file "/var/named/named.pid";
};

zone "synack.net" {
    type master;
    file "synack.forw";
    allow-transfer { 198.11.19.15; };
};

zone "xinetd.org" {
    type master;
    file "xinetd.forw";
    allow-transfer { 198.11.19.15; };
};

zone "1.168.192.in-addr.arpa" {
    type master;                        // reverse, for private addresses
    file "named.rev";
};

zone "." {
    type hint;
    file "cache.db";
};

zone "teich.net" {
    type slave;
    file "teich.net.sec";
    masters { 216.103.220.218; };
};

zone "rmtai.com" {
    type slave;
    file "rmtai.com.sec";
    masters { 216.103.220.218; };
};
```

```
// Define three logging channels (important syslog messages,
// moderate debugging, and loading zone messages) and
// then map categories to them.

logging {
    channel syslog_errors {
        syslog local1;
        severity error;
    };
    channel moderate_debug {
        severity debug 3;        // level 3 debugging
        file "foo";              // to file foo
        print-time yes;          // time stamp log entries
        print-category yes;      // print category name
        print-severity yes;      // print severity level
    };
    channel no_info_messages {
        syslog local2;
        severity notice;
    };

    category parser {
        syslog_errors;
        default_syslog;
    };
    category lame-servers { null; };        // don't log these
    category load { no_info_messages; };
    category default {
        default_syslog;
        moderate_debug;
    };
};    // end of logging clause
```

This configuration has no reverse localhost zone; localhost must be mapped in the **/etc/hosts** file.

A small security company

Our next example is for a small company that specializes in security consulting. They run BIND 9 on Red Hat 7.2 and use views to implement a split DNS system in which internal and external users see different host data. They also use private address space internally; queries about those addresses should never escape to the Internet to clutter up the global DNS system. Here is their **named.conf** file, reformatted and commented a bit:

```
options {
    directory "/var/domain";
};

controls {
    inet 127.0.0.1 allow { 127.0.0.1; } keys { atkey; };
};
```

```
include "atrust.key";                          // def of atkey in mode 600 file

view "atrust" {                                // internal view

    match-clients { 192.168.1.0/24; 192.168.2.0/24; };
    recursion yes;

    zone "." {                                 // root hints zone
        type hint;
        file "named.ca";
    };
    zone "localhost" {                         // localhost forward zone
        type master;
        file "localhost.zone";
        allow-update { none; };
    };
    zone "0.0.127.in-addr.arpa" {              // localhost reverse zone
        type master;
        file "named.local";
        allow-update { none; };
    };
    zone "atrust.com" {                        // internal forward zone
        type master;
        file "atrust.com-internal";
    };
    zone "2.168.192.in-addr.arpa" {            // internal reverse zone
        type master;
        file "192.168.2.rev";
        allow-update { none; };
    };
    zone "1.168.192.in-addr.arpa" {            // internal reverse zone
        type master;
        file "192.168.1.rev";
        allow-update { none; };
    };
    zone "kalos-strategy.com" IN {             // zone we are secondary for
        type forward;
        forwarders { 127.0.0.1; };
    };
};                                             // end of internal view

view "world" {                                 // external view

    match-clients { any; };
    recursion no;

    // zone statements for dot and localhost as above, omitted for brevity

    zone "atrust.com" {                        // external forward zone
        type master;
        file "atrust.com-external";
    };
```

DNS

```
zone "kalos-strategy.com" IN {          // zone we are secondary for
    type slave;
    file "kalos-strategy.com";
    masters { 66.1.239.14; };
};
zone "198.168.206.in-addr.arpa" {       // external reverse zone
    type master;
    file "206.168.198.rev";
    allow-update { none; };
};
};                                       // end of external view
```

The file **atrust.key** contains the definition of the key named "atkey":

```
key "atkey" {
    algorithm hmac-md5;
    secret "shared secret key goes here";
};
```

Two entries for kalos-strategy.com, a company for which atrust.com runs a slave server, are necessary. If the zone were mentioned only in the external view, queries from outside the atrust.com domain would be fine, but queries from inside would go out on the network to ask a question for which atrust.com's own name server is authoritative. A solution to this inefficiency is to mention kalos-strategy.com in the internal view, but to list it as a forward zone so that the name server sees the query with its external hat on as well.

The zone files **atrust.com-internal** and **atrust.com-external** define the separate views. Snippets of them are shown below. First, the internal file:

```
; atrust.com-internal file
$TTL 86400
$ORIGIN com.
atrust                  3600    SOA  ns1.atrust.com. trent.atrust.com. (
                                        2001110500 10800 1200 3600000 3600 )
                        3600    NS   NS1.toadranch.com.
                        3600    NS   NS2.toadranch.com.
                        3600    MX   10 mailserver.atrust.com.
                        3600    A    206.168.198.209

$ORIGIN atrust.com.
www                             A    192.168.2.1
mailserver                      A    192.168.2.1
bull                            A    192.168.1.1
superg                          A    192.168.1.249
airport                         A    192.168.1.250
superg                          A    192.168.1.252
at-dmz-gw                       A    192.168.1.254
bark                            A    192.168.2.1
at-dmz-outside-gw               A    192.168.2.253
at-external-gw                  A    192.168.2.254
at-external-outside-gw          A    206.168.198.220
indras-gw                       A    206.168.198.222
```

And here is the external view of that same domain, atrust.com:

```
; atrust.com-external file
$TTL 86400
$ORIGIN com.
atrust                      3600  SOA  ns1.atrust.com. trent.atrust.com. (
                                       2001110601 10800 1200 3600000 3600 )
                            3600  NS   NS1.toadranch.com.
                            3600  NS   NS2.toadranch.com.
                            3600  MX   10 mailserver.atrust.com.
                            3600  A    206.168.198.209

$ORIGIN atrust.com.
www                         A    206.168.198.209
mailserver                  A    206.168.198.209
ns1                         A    206.168.198.209
bark                        CNAME www

; reverse maps              ### delegated with CNAME from
;                           ### 168.198.209.in-addr.arpa servers

exterior1           IN  A    206.168.198.209
209.198.168.206     IN  PTR  exterior1.atrust.com.
exterior2           IN  A    206.168.198.213
213.198.168.206     IN  PTR  exterior2.atrust.com.
exterior3           IN  A    206.168.198.220
220.198.168.206     IN  PTR  exterior3.atrust.com.
```

Notice that when multiple names for the same machine are needed, they are presented as additional A records rather than CNAME records. A client searching for the name www.atrust.com would incur an extra lookup if www were mapped to the actual server via a CNAME, thus potentially doubling the time it took to look up the IP address.

The TTL in these zone files is set to default to a day (86,400 seconds) but is reset to an hour (3,600 seconds) for the SOA and NS records. Most individual records in zone files are not assigned an explicit TTL value. The TTL is optional; it can be added to any individual line in the zone file just before the record type.

The bizarre PTR records at the end of the external file allow atrust.com's ISP to delegate the reverse mapping of a very small piece of address space. CNAME records at the ISP's site make this variation of the CNAME hack work; see page 418 for more information.

A university department

The computer science department at the University of Colorado runs BIND 8 in a **chroot**ed jail and implements split DNS by running two instances of **named** on the same machine. The internal zone contains all the local hosts, including some located in private address space. The external zone also includes most hosts but has MX records pointing to the externally visible mail hub rather than to each individual machine. Of course, the external view does not list any machines that live in the private address space. Here are the commands used to start the two instances:

/usr/local/sbin/named -t /var/named -u named -c /etc/named-internal.conf
/usr/local/sbin/named -t /var/named -u named -c /etc/named-external.conf

The configuration files are not really called **/etc/named-*.conf** as shown, but rather **/var/named/etc/named-*.conf** since the process is **chroot**ed to the **/var/named** directory. Internally, Colorado uses caching servers on each subnet; the caching servers forward to a list of slave servers. The slaves themselves forward to a master server that contacts the Internet on their behalf. Each forwarding server is configured to forward first. Below, we show all three configurations: the caching-only servers, the slave servers, and the master. All servers are running a current version of BIND 8.

The caching-only configuration is appropriate for a subnet that wants a local server but doesn't want to soil its hands with data files. We need only set up the **named.conf** file and the hints file and start **named** at boot time. No real local zones are in the config file, only the root server hints and the reverse localhost zone. The caching-only servers are part of the internal view and do not run in a **chroot**ed environment.

```
// bind 8.2 conf file - caching server

// Global options
options {
    directory "/var/named";
    named-xfer "/usr/local/sbin/named-xfer";   // bind 8 only
    // build a rich cache on our master and official slaves
    forwarders {
        128.138.243.151;   // mroe
        128.138.243.140;   // anchor
        128.138.243.137;   // moet
        128.138.243.138;   // vulture
        128.138.236.20;    // piper
    };
    forward first;
    query-source address * port 53;
};

// Logging, syslog to local3, no lame servers
logging {
    channel syslog_info {
        syslog local3;
        severity info;
    };
    category lame-servers { null; };
    category default { syslog_info; };
};

zone "." {   // Root servers cache
    type hint;
    file "named.cache";
};
```

```
// Master server for localhost reverse zone
zone "0.0.127.in-addr.arpa" {
    type master;
    file "localhost";
    notify no;
};
```

The config file for slave servers includes the cs.colorado.edu forward zone and several reverse zones that we have cut down to one or two for illustration. In this example, the reverse zones are not subdivided on a byte boundary (they are mostly /26s), but because all four subnets are controlled by the same administrative authority, they are kept in the same file and the CNAME hack described on page 418 is not necessary. Slave servers are also in the internal view and are not **chroot**ed.

```
// bind 8.2 conf file - slave server

acl CUnets { 128.138/16; 198.11.16/24; 204.228.69/24; 127.0.0.1; };
acl rfc1918 { 10/8; 172.16/12; 192.168/16; };

options {
    directory "/var/named";
    named-xfer "/usr/local/sbin/named-xfer";   // bind 8 only
    forwarders { 128.138.242.197; };           // master's internal IP address
    forward first;
    query-source address * port 53;
    allow-transfer { none; };
};

// Logging, root server hints, and localhost reverse zone are the
// same as for a caching server, so they're not shown here.

// Slave zones
zone "cs.colorado.edu" {
    type slave;
    file "forward/cs.colorado.edu";
    masters { 128.138.242.197; };
};

zone "250.138.128.in-addr.arpa" {
    type slave;
    file "reverse/250.138.128";
    masters { 128.138.242.197; };
};

zone "1.168.192.in-addr.arpa" in {              // private address zones
    type slave;
    file "reverse/1.168.192";
    allow-query { CUnets; rfc1918; };
    masters { 128.138.242.197; };
};

// ... many, many reverse slave zones omitted
```

The next configurations are for the server that is the master for both the internal and external halves of cs.colorado.edu as well as being the forwarder through which all local queries flow. This setup builds a nice cache but breaks the don't-mix-authoritative-and-caching-servers rule.

This configuration sets a preference for local servers with a topology statement. Several servers are not listed in the parent domain's delegations; these are notified of changes with an also-notify clause.

The master server keeps its DNS database in several files. Reverse-mapping zones are organized by subnet number. Each subnet (in our case, the third octet of a class B address) has its own file. This organization is not strictly necessary, but it keeps the files to a manageable size and makes updating them easy. However, it does presuppose either that subnets are divided on a byte boundary or that if subnets are further subdivided, each piece remains under our administrative control.

If a single file were used for all reverse mappings, the records could be organized by network and the $ORIGIN directive could be used at the beginning of each section to reset the identity of the default domain. See page 427.

```
# bind 8.x conf file - internal view, master server for cs.colorado.edu
# $Id: named.conf,v 1.28 2000/01/12 00:20:34 root Exp $

acl CUnets { 128.138/16; 198.11.16/24; 204.228.69/24; 127.0.0.1; };
acl rfc1918 { 10/8; 172.16/12; 192.168/16; };

# Global options
options {
        directory "/";                          # inherits the chroot prefix, /var/named
        pid-file "/named-internal.pid";
        named-xfer "/named-xfer";               # V8 only, program copied to /var/named
        notify yes;
        also-notify {
            128.138.192.205;   # suod
            128.138.244.9;     # riker
            128.138.243.70;    # squid
            128.138.241.12;    # goober
            128.138.244.100;   # av-server
            128.138.202.19;    # nago
        };

        # Since this daemon serves internal hosts, we bind to the
        # internal address, 128.138.242.197 (and localhost).

        listen-on { 127.0.0.1; 128.138.242.197; };   # use internal addresses
        transfer-source 128.138.242.197;
        query-source address 128.138.242.197 port 53;
        forward first;                          # to access external zones that
        forwarders { 128.138.243.151; };        # are secondary for our external IP
        topology { localhost; localnets; CUnets; };
};
```

```
# Logging, root hints, and localhost zone are the same and are not shown

# CS
zone "cs.colorado.edu" {
    type master;
    file "forward/cs.colorado.edu";
};

# CS reverse records (128.138.X.X)
zone "250.138.128.in-addr.arpa" {
    type master;
    file "reverse/250.138.128";
};
zone "1.168.192.in-addr.arpa" in {          # private address space nets
    type master;
    file "reverse/1.168.192";
    allow-query { CUnets; rfc1918; };
};

# ... many, many reverse zones omitted

# Slaves
zone "colorado.edu" {  # colorado.edu top level
    type slave;
    file "secondary/colorado.edu";
    allow-transfer { none; };
    masters { 128.138.240.1; };
};
zone "openbsd.org" {   # openbsd project
    type slave;
    file "secondary/openbsd.org";
    masters { 199.45.131.58; };
};
zone "233.in-addr.arpa" {# experimental multicast addresses
    type slave;
    file "secondary/233.in-addr.arpa";
    masters { 128.223.32.35; };
};

# lots more zones omitted
```

And finally, we have the configuration file for the external view of the master name server for the cs.colorado.edu domain. The internal data files contain private address space records and also MX records that point to each host first and to the central mail hub machine as a backup. Internal mail normally flows directly and does not involve the mail hub. The external view data files include a single MX record for all hosts that points to the mail hub machine.

Instead of repeating many of the same configuration statements below, we list only those that are different.

```
# Snippets from the external version of config, master server, cs.colorado.edu

directory "/";                        # external server also chrooted to /var/named
pid-file "/named-external.pid";
named-xfer "/named-xfer";
listen-on { 128.138.243.151; };  # external IP address
transfer-source 128.138.243.151;
query-source address 128.138.243.151 port 53;

zone "cs.colorado.edu" in {
    type master;
    file "forward-external/cs.colorado.edu";   # external version of zone
};

zone "245.138.128.in-addr.arpa" in {
    type master;
    file "reverse/245.138.128";                # same as internal version
};
```

So much for configuration! Now let's look at the actual zone data files.

16.11 THE DNS DATABASE

A domain's DNS database is a set of text files maintained by the system administrator on the domain's master name server. These text files are often called zone files. They contain two types of entries: parser commands (things like $ORIGIN and $TTL) and "resource records," or RRs as they are sometimes called. Only the resource records are really part of the database; the parser commands just provide some shorthand ways to enter records.

We start this section by describing the DNS resource records, which are defined in RFCs 882, 1035, 1183, 2065, 2181, 2308, and 2535. We defer discussion of the parser commands until page 427.

Resource records

Each zone of the DNS hierarchy has a set of resource records associated with it (the set might be empty). The basic format of a resource record is

[name] [ttl] [class] type data

Fields are separated by whitespace (tabs or spaces) and can contain the special characters shown in Table 16.9.

The *name* field identifies the entity (usually a host or domain) that the record describes. If several consecutive records refer to the same entity, the name can be left out after the first record. The name field if present must begin in column one.

A name can be either relative or absolute. Absolute names end with a dot and are complete. Internally, the software deals only with absolute names; it appends the current domain and a dot to any name that does not already end in a dot. This feature allows names to be shorter, but it also invites mistakes.

Table 16.9   Special characters used in RRs

Character	Meaning
;	Introduces a comment
@	The current domain name
( )	Allows data to span lines
*	Wild card[a] (*name* field only)

a. See page 417 for some cautionary statements.

For example, in the cs.colorado.edu domain, the name "anchor" would be interpreted as "anchor.cs.colorado.edu.". If the name were entered as "anchor.cs.colorado.edu", the lack of a final dot would still imply a relative name, and the default domain would be appended, resulting in the name "anchor.cs.colorado.edu.cs.colorado.edu.". This is a very common mistake.

The *ttl* (time to live) field specifies the length of time, in seconds, that the data item can be cached and still be considered valid. It is often omitted, except in the root server hints file. It defaults to the value set by the $TTL directive at the top of the data file for the zone. In BIND 9, the $TTL directive is required. If there is no $TTL directive in BIND 8, the *ttl* defaults to a per-zone value set in the zone's SOA record.

See Chapter 18 for more information about NIS.

Increasing the value of the *ttl* parameter to about a week reduces network traffic and DNS load substantially. However, once records have been cached outside your local network, you cannot force them to be discarded. If you plan a massive renumbering, set the $TTL value low (e.g., an hour) so that stale records that have been cached elsewhere on the Internet expire quickly.

DNS scales because it uses local caching to distribute the load and the data along the naming tree. Don't set your TTL value to a ridiculously low value just to keep your data fresh. How often do you rename hosts or renumber them? Probably not every second, minute, or even hour. Yet some sites—yp.qwestdex.com, for example—set their TTL to 5 minutes so that almost every query for a phone number involves a full DNS lookup, thus killing the performance of their web site. The politically correct units for TTLs are days or weeks, not 300 seconds. Geez.

The *class* specifies the network type. Three values are recognized:

- IN for the Internet
- CH for ChaosNet
- HS for Hesiod

ChaosNet is an obsolete network protocol formerly used by Symbolics Lisp machines. Hesiod is a database service built on top of BIND. The default value for the class is IN. It is often specified explicitly in zone data files even though it is the default. Today, only one piece of data is normally tucked away in the Chaos class: the version number of the running **named**, which can be extracted with **dig**, as shown on page 369.

Many different types of DNS records are defined, but fewer than 10 are in common use; IPv6 adds a few more. We divide the resource records into four groups:

- Zone records – identify domains and their name servers
- Basic records – map names to addresses and route mail
- Security records – add authentication and signatures to zone files
- Optional records – provide extra information about hosts or domains

The contents of the *data* field depend on the record type. Table 16.10 lists the various record types.

Table 16.10   DNS record types

	Type	Name	Function
Zone	SOA	Start Of Authority	Defines a DNS zone
	NS	Name Server	Identifies zone servers, delegates subdomains
Basic	A	IPv4 Address	Name-to-address translation
	AAAA	Original IPv6 Address	Was obsolete, but being resurrected
	A6	IPv6 Address	Name-to-IPv6-address translation (V9 only)[a]
	PTR	Pointer	Address-to-name translation
	DNAME	Redirection	Redirection for reverse IPv6 lookups (V9 only)
	MX	Mail Exchanger	Controls email routing
Security	KEY	Public Key	Public key for a DNS name
	NXT	Next	Used with DNSSEC for negative answers
	SIG	Signature	Signed, authenticated zone
Optional	CNAME	Canonical Name	Nicknames or aliases for a host
	LOC	Location	Geographic location and extent[b]
	SRV	Services	Gives locations of well-known services
	TXT	Text	Comments or untyped information

a. Now considered "experimental"
b. The LOC record is not well supported in NT (querying for LOC records crashes NT servers).

Some record types are obsolete, experimental, or not widely used. See the BIND documentation for a complete list.

The order of resource records is almost arbitrary. The SOA record for a zone should be first. The subsequent records can be in any order, but NS records usually come right after the SOA. The records for each host are usually kept together. It's a common practice to sort by the *name* field.

As we describe each type of resource record in detail, we inspect some sample records from cs.colorado.edu's data files. The default domain is "cs.colorado.edu." throughout, so a host specified as "anchor" really means "anchor.cs.colorado.edu.".

The SOA record

An SOA record marks the beginning of a zone, a group of resource records located at the same place within the DNS namespace. This node of the DNS tree is also called a delegation point or zone cut. As we discuss in greater detail on page 414, the data for a DNS domain usually includes at least two zones: one for translating hostnames to IP addresses and others that map in the reverse direction. The DNS tree has a forward branch organized by name and a reverse branch organized by IP address.

Each zone has exactly one SOA record. The zone continues until another SOA is encountered. The SOA record includes the name of the zone, a technical contact, and various timeout values. An example:

```
; Start of authority record for cs.colorado.edu
@               IN   SOA  ns.cs.colorado.edu. hostmaster.cs.colorado.edu. (
                         2001111300     ; Serial number
                         7200           ; Refresh    (2 hours)
                         1800           ; Retry      (30 minutes)
                         604800         ; Expire     (1 week)
                         7200 )         ; Minimum    (2 hours)
```

Here, the *name* field contains the symbol @, which is shorthand for the name of the current zone. In this example, "cs.colorado.edu." could have been used instead. The value of @ is the domain name specified in the zone statement in the **named.conf** file; it can be changed from within the zone file with the $ORIGIN parser directive (see page 427).

This example has no *ttl* field. The class is IN for Internet, the type is SOA, and the remaining items form the *data* field.

"ns.cs.colorado.edu." is the zone's master name server.

"hostmaster.cs.colorado.edu." is the email address of the technical contact in the format *"user.host."* rather than the standard *user@host.* Just replace that first dot with an @ and remove the final dot if you need to send mail to a domain's administrator. Sites often use an alias such as admin or hostmaster in place of an actual login name. The sysadmin responsible for hostmaster duties may change, and it's easier to change one entry in the **aliases** file (see page 527) than to change all your zone files when you need to update the contact person.

The parentheses continue the SOA record over several lines. Their placement is not arbitrary in BIND 4 or 8—we tried to shorten the first line by splitting it before the contact address, but then **named** failed to recognize the SOA record. In some implementations, parentheses are only recognized in SOA and TXT records. BIND 9 has a better parser and parentheses can be used anywhere.

The first numeric parameter is the serial number of the zone's configuration data. The serial number is used by slave servers to determine when to get fresh data. It can be any 32-bit integer and should be incremented every time the data file for the zone is changed. Many sites encode the file's modification date in the serial number. For example, 2001111300 is the first change to the zone on November 13, 2001.

Serial numbers need not be continuous, but they must increase monotonically. If by accident you set a really large value on the master server and that value is transferred to the slaves, then correcting the serial number on the master will not work. The slaves request new data only if the master's serial number is larger than theirs.

There are three ways to fix this problem.

- BIND 4.9 and BIND 8 include a hack that lets you set the serial number to zero for one refresh interval and then restart the numbering. The zero always causes a reload, so don't forget to set it to a real value after each of the slaves has reloaded the zone with serial number 0.

- A sneaky but more tedious way to fix the problem is to change the serial number on the master, kill the slave servers, remove the slaves' backup data files so they are forced to reload from the master, and restart the slaves.

- A third way to fix the problem is to exploit properties of the sequence space in which the serial numbers live. This procedure involves adding a large value (2^{31}) to the bloated serial number, letting all the slave servers transfer the data, and then setting the serial number to just what you want. This weird arithmetic, with explicit examples, is covered in detail in the O'Reilly DNS book; RFC1982 describes the sequence space.

It is a common mistake to change the data files but forget to update the serial number. **named** will punish you by failing to propagate your changes to slave servers.

The next four entries in the SOA record are timeout values, in seconds, that control how long data can be cached at various points throughout the world-wide DNS database. Times can also be expressed in units of minutes, hours, days, or weeks by addition of a suffix of m, h, d, or w, respectively. For example, 1h30m means 1 hour and 30 minutes. Timeout values represent a tradeoff between efficiency (it's cheaper to use an old value than to fetch a new one) and accuracy (new values should be more accurate).

The first is the *refresh* timeout, which specifies how often slave servers should check with the master to see if the serial number of the zone's configuration has changed. Whenever the zone changes, slaves must update their copy of the zone's data. The slave compares the serial numbers, and if the master's serial number is larger, requests a zone transfer to update the data. Common values for the *refresh* timeout range from one to six hours (3,600 to 21,600 seconds).

Instead of just waiting passively for slave servers to time out, BIND servers now notify their slaves every time a zone changes, unless the notify parameter is specifically turned off in the configuration file. Slaves that understand the notification immediately refresh themselves.

If a slave server tries to check the master's serial number but the master does not respond, the slave tries again after the *retry* timeout period has elapsed. Our experience suggests that 20–60 minutes (1,200–3,600 seconds) is a good value.

If a master server is down for a long time, slaves will try to refresh their data many times but always fail. Each slave should eventually decide that the master is never coming back and that its data is surely out of date. The *expire* parameter determines how long the slaves will continue to serve the domain's data authoritatively in the absence of a master. The system should be able to survive if the master server is down for a week, so this parameter should have a longish value. We recommend a week to a month.

The *minimum* parameter in the SOA record sets the time to live for negative answers that are cached.[11] The default for positive answers (i.e., actual records) is specified at the top of the zone file with the $TTL directive. Experience suggests values between a few hours and several days for $TTL and an hour or two for the *minimum*. The *minimum* cannot be more than three hours.

The $TTL, *expire*, and *minimum* parameters eventually force everyone that uses DNS to discard old data values. The design of DNS relied on the fact that host data was relatively stable and did not change often. However, DHCP and mobile hosts have changed the rules. BIND is desperately trying to cope by providing the dynamic update and incremental zone transfer mechanisms described starting on page 432. For more information about TTLs and a concept called TTL harmonization, see page 428.

NS records

NS (name server) records identify the servers that are authoritative for a zone (that is, all the master and slave servers) and delegate subdomains to other organizations. NS records usually follow the SOA record.

The format is

zone [*ttl*] IN NS *hostname*

For example:

```
cs.colorado.edu.   IN   NS   ns.cs.colorado.edu.
cs.colorado.edu.   IN   NS   anchor.cs.colorado.edu.
cs.colorado.edu.   IN   NS   ns.cs.utah.edu.
```

Since the zone name is the same as the *name* field of the SOA record that precedes these NS records, it can be left blank. Thus, the lines

```
                   IN   NS   ns.cs.colorado.edu.
                   IN   NS   anchor.cs.colorado.edu.
                   IN   NS   ns.cs.utah.edu.
```

immediately following the SOA record for cs.colorado.edu would be equivalent.

---

11. Prior to BIND 8.2, the *minimum* parameter set the default time to live for resource records. It was included with each record and used to expire the cached records on nonauthoritative servers.

Every authoritative name server for cs.colorado.edu that you want visible to the outside world should be listed both in the zone file for cs.colorado.edu and also in the file for the parent zone, colorado.edu. Caching-only servers cannot be authoritative; do not list them. No parameter in the NS records specifies whether a server is a master or a slave. That information is specified in the **named.conf** file.

named uses a zone's NS records to identify slave servers when it wants to send out notifications of changes to the zone. Those same NS records inside the parent zone (colorado.edu) define the cs subdomain and delegate authority for it to the computer science department's name servers. If the list of name servers in the parent zone is not kept up to date with those in the zone itself, any new servers that are added become stealth servers and are not used to answer queries from the outside world. This situation happens sometimes through design and sometimes through forgetfulness.

See page 429 for more information about delegation.
A quick look at our own delegations revealed a major server for colorado.edu that the edu domain knew nothing about. Do as we say and not as we do: check your delegations with **dig** to be sure they specify an appropriate set of servers.

A records

A (address) records are the heart of the DNS database. They provide the mapping from hostnames to IP addresses that was formerly specified in the **/etc/hosts** file. A host must have one A record for each of its network interfaces. The format is

    hostname [*ttl*] IN A *ipaddr*

For example:

    anchor   IN   A   128.138.243.100

A machine with multiple network interfaces can use a single hostname associated with all interfaces or have separate hostnames for each interface.

PTR records

PTR (pointer) records perform the reverse mapping from IP addresses to hostnames. As with A records, a host must have one PTR record for each network interface. Before we describe PTR records, however, we need to digress and talk about a special top-level domain called in-addr.arpa.

Fully qualified hostnames can be viewed as a notation in which the "most significant part" is on the right. For example, in the name anchor.cs.colorado.edu, anchor is in cs, cs is in colorado, and colorado is in edu. IP addresses, on the other hand, have the "most significant part" on the left. In the address 128.138.243.100, host 100 is on subnet 243, which is part of network 128.138.

The in-addr.arpa domain was created to allow one set of software modules and one naming tree to map from IP addresses to hostnames as well as from hostnames to IP addresses. Domains under in-addr.arpa are named like IP addresses with their bytes reversed. For example, the zone for our 243 subnet is 243.138.128.in-addr.arpa.

The general format of a PTR record is

addr [*ttl*] IN PTR *hostname*

For example, the PTR record in the 243.138.128.in-addr.arpa zone that corresponds to anchor's A record above is

    100   IN   PTR   anchor.cs.colorado.edu.

The name 100 does not end in a dot and therefore is relative. But relative to what? Not "cs.colorado.edu.". For this sample record to be accurate, the default domain has to be "243.138.128.in-addr.arpa.".

You can set the domain by putting the PTR records for each subnet in their own file, as in this example. The default domain associated with the file is set in **named**'s configuration file. Another way to do reverse mappings is to include records such as

    100.243   IN   PTR   anchor.cs.colorado.edu.

with a default domain of 138.128.in-addr.arpa. Some sites put all reverse records in the same file and use $ORIGIN directives to specify the subnet. Note that the hostname anchor.cs.colorado.edu must end with a dot to prevent 138.128.in-addr.arpa from being appended to its name.

Since cs.colorado.edu and 243.138.128.in-addr.arpa are different regions of the DNS namespace, they constitute two separate zones. Each zone must have its own SOA record and resource records. In addition to defining an in-addr.arpa zone for each real network, you also need a zone that takes care of the loopback network, 127.0.0.0.

This all works fine if the subnets are on byte boundaries. But how do you handle the reverse mappings for a subnet such as 128.138.243.0/26? An elegant hack defined in RFC2317 exploits CNAME resource records to accomplish this feat; see page 418.

The reverse mappings provided by PTR records are used by any program that authenticates inbound network traffic. For example, **sshd** may allow remote logins without a password if the machine of origin is listed, by name, in a user's ~/**.shosts** file. When the destination host receives a connection request, it knows the source machine only by IP address. It uses DNS to convert the IP address to a hostname, which is then compared to the appropriate file. **netstat**, **tcpd**, **sendmail**, **sshd**, X Windows, **syslogd**, **fingerd**, **ftpd**, and **rlogind** all do reverse mappings to get hostnames from IP addresses.

It is important that A records match their corresponding PTR records. Mismatched and missing PTR records cause authentication failures that can slow your system to a crawl. This problem is annoying in itself; it can also facilitate denial of service attacks against any application that requires the reverse mapping to match the A record.

MX records

See Chapter 19 for more information about email.

The mail system uses mail exchanger records to route mail more efficiently. An MX record preempts the destination of a message, in most cases directing it to a mail hub at the recipient's site rather than to the recipient's own workstation.

The format of an MX record is

name [*ttl*] IN MX *preference host ...*

Two examples are shown below, one for a host that, unless it is down, receives its own mail, and one for a host that can't receive mail at all:

```
piper       IN   MX   10 piper
            IN   MX   20 mailhub
            IN   MX   50 boulder.colorado.edu.
xterm1      IN   MX   10 mailhub
            IN   MX   20 anchor
            IN   MX   50 boulder.colorado.edu.
```

Hosts with low preference values are tried first: 0 is the most desirable, and 65,535 is as bad as it gets. In this example, mail addressed to bob@xterm1 would be sent to mailhub if it were accessible, to anchor as a second choice, and if both mailhub and anchor were down, to boulder. Note that boulder's name must be fully qualified since it is not a member of the default domain (here, "cs.colorado.edu.").

The list of preferences and hosts can all be on the same line, but separate lines are easier to read. Leave numeric "space" between preference values so you don't have to renumber if you need to squeeze in a new destination.

MX records are useful in many situations:

- When you have a central mail hub
- When the destination host is down
- When the destination isn't reachable from the Internet
- When the destination host doesn't speak SMTP
- When the local sysadmin knows where mail should be sent better than your correspondents do

In the first of these situations, mail is routed to the mail hub, the machine where most users read mail. In the second case, mail is routed to a nearby host and forwarded when the destination comes back up.

Hosts that are not directly on the Internet can't have A records, but they can have MX records. **sendmail** can't connect directly to the destination, but it can get the mail closer by connecting to one of the destination's MX hosts. Such MX-only hosts might be machines behind a firewall, domain names hosted by an ISP or hosting service, or machines that are not turned on all the time.

The final reason to use MX records is that the local sysadmins probably know the mail architecture much better than your correspondents. They need to have the final say on how your site channels its mail stream.

Every host should have MX records. For minor hosts, one or two alternates is enough. A major host should have several records. For example, the following set of records might be appropriate for a site at which each host sends and receives its own mail.

- One for the host itself, as first choice
- A departmental mail hub as second choice
- A central mail hub for the domain or parent domain as a backup

The domain itself should have an MX record to a mail hub machine so that mail to *user@domain* will work. Of course, this configuration does require that user names be unique across all machines in the domain. For example, to be able to send mail to evi@cs.colorado.edu, we need a machine called cs, MX records in cs.colorado.edu, or perhaps both.

```
cs           IN   MX   10 mailhub.cs.colorado.edu.
             IN   MX   20 anchor.cs.colorado.edu.
             IN   MX   50 boulder.colorado.edu.
```

A machine that accepts mail for another host must list that other host in its **sendmail** configuration files; see page 559 for a discussion of **sendmail**'s use_cw_file feature and the file **local-host-names**.

Wild card MX records are also sometimes seen in the DNS database:

```
*            IN   MX   10 mailhub.cs.colorado.edu.
```

At first glance, this record seems like it would save lots of typing and add a default MX record for all hosts. But wild card records don't quite work as you might expect. They match anything in the *name* field of a resource record that is *not* already listed as an explicit name in another resource record.

Thus, you *cannot* use a star to set a default value for all your hosts. But perversely, you can use it to set a default value for names that are not your hosts. This setup causes lots of mail to be sent to your hub only to be rejected because the hostname matching the star really does not belong to your domain. Ergo, avoid wild card MX records. Wild cards are not yet implemented in BIND 9 and may never be.

CNAME records

CNAME records assign additional names to a host. These nicknames are commonly used either to associate a function with a host or to shorten a long hostname. The real name is sometimes called the canonical name (hence, "CNAME").

Some examples:

```
ftp          IN   CNAME   anchor
kb           IN   CNAME   kibblesnbits
```

The format of a CNAME record is

```
nickname [ttl] IN CNAME hostname
```

When the DNS software encounters a CNAME record, it stops its query for the nickname and switches to the real name. If a host has a CNAME record, other records (A, MX, NS, etc.) for that host must refer to its real name, not its nickname. For example, the following lines are OK.

```
colo-gw      IN   A       128.138.243.25
moogie       IN   CNAME   colo-gw
www          IN   CNAME   moogie
```

However, assigning an address or mail priority (with an A or MX record) to either www or moogie in this example would be wrong.

CNAME records can nest eight deep in BIND. That is, a CNAME record can point to another CNAME, and that CNAME can point to a third CNAME, and so on, up to seven times; the eighth target must be the real hostname and A record.

Some sites use CNAME records in a weak attempt at load balancing. They map the public name of their web server to several different machines:

```
www          IN   CNAME   web1
www          IN   CNAME   web2
www          IN   CNAME   web3
```

This use of CNAME records is nonstandard. In fact, it is illegal. An option in BIND 8 allowed you to use this against-the-spec mechanism. BIND 9 is pickier, so it's really not a good idea to use multiple CNAMEs. A better way to achieve the same result is to provide the web server with multiple A records that point to different machines.

The CNAME hack

See page 252 for more information about CIDR.

CNAMEs are also used to torture the existing semantics of DNS into supporting reverse zones for networks that are not subnetted on a byte boundary. Before CIDR addressing was commonplace, most subnet assignments were on byte boundaries or within the same organization, and the reverse delegations were easy to manage. For example, if the class B network 128.138 was subnetted into a set of class C-like networks, each subnet would make a tidy package for the in-addr.arpa domain. The reverse zone for the 243 subnet would be 243.138.128.in-addr.arpa.

But what happens if the 243 subnet is further divided into, say, four pieces as a /26 network? If all four pieces are assigned to the same organization, there is actually no problem. The four subnets can still share a single file that contains all their PTR records. However, if the 243 subnet is assigned to an ISP that wants to delegate each /26 network to a different customer, a more complicated solution is necessary. The ISP must either maintain the reverse records on behalf of each client, or it must find a way to take the third octet of the IP address (243 in this case) and divide it into four different pieces that can be delegated independently.

When an administrative boundary falls in the middle of a byte, you have to be sneaky. You must also work closely with the domain above or below you. The trick is this: for each possible host address in the natural in-addr.arpa zone, add a CNAME that deflects the lookup to a zone controlled by the owner of the appropriate subnet. This scheme makes for messy zone files on the parent, but it does let you delegate authority to the actual users of each subnet.

Here is the scheme in gory detail. The parent organization (in our case, the ISP) creates CNAME records for each possible IP address with an extra fake component (dot-separated chunk) that represents the subnet. For example, in the /26 scenario just described, the first quarter of the addresses would have a "0-63" component, the second quarter would have a "64-127" component, and so on. Here's what it looks like:

```
$ORIGIN 243.138.128.in-addr.arpa.
1            IN   CNAME   1.0-63
2            IN   CNAME   2.0-63
...
63           IN   CNAME   63.0-63
64           IN   CNAME   64.64-127
65           IN   CNAME   65.64-127
...
```

To delegate the 0-63 piece of the reverse zone to the customer that has been assigned that subnet, we'd add the following NS records:

```
0-63         IN   NS      ns1.customer1.com.
0-63         IN   NS      ns2.customer1.com.
...
```

customer1.com's site would have a zone file that contained the reverse mappings for the 0-63.243.138.128.in-addr.arpa zone. For example:

```
1            IN   PTR     host1.customer1.com.
2            IN   PTR     host2.customer1.com.
...
```

By adding this extra component, we create a new "cut" at which to perform delegation. When someone looks up the reverse mapping for 128.138.243.1, for example, the CNAME record at 1.243.138.128.in-addr.arpa refocuses the search to the name 1.0-63.243.138.128.in-addr.arpa, and that name is controlled by the customer.

The customer's files are clean; it's only the ISP that must deal with an inelegant configuration mess. But things can get even more complicated. Customer1 could itself be an ISP that wants to further subdivide its addresses. But that's OK: BIND supports CNAME chains up to 8 links long, and since a byte has only eight bits, we can never run out. CNAME chains are discouraged but not forbidden in the RFCs; they do slow down name resolution since each link in a CNAME chain causes the link to be followed and a new query for the target to be initiated.

This whole scheme is a blatant misuse of the CNAME record, but it's so powerful and useful that a variant of it has become the official standard for the handling of IPv6 reverse zones. See the information about DNAME records on page 424 for more information.

Very early in the life of the CNAME hack, the $GENERATE command (see page 427) was added to **named**'s repertoire to facilitate the creation of resource records in the parent zone.

For example, to produce the records for the first subnet, the following lines suffice:

```
$ORIGIN 243.138.128.in-addr.arpa.
$GENERATE 0-63 $ CNAME $.0-63
0-63           NS  ns1.customer1.com.
0-63           NS  ns2.customer1.com.
```

The $ in the $GENERATE command iterates from 0 to 63 and creates 64 different CNAME records. The other three /26 networks would be handled similarly.

The CNAME hack works fine for BIND 8 and 9. Some older BIND 4 resolvers don't expect to get a CNAME when they query for a PTR record, so they fail. Yet another good reason to upgrade.

LOC records

LOC records are defined in RFC1819.

An LOC record describes the geographic location and, optionally, the physical size (diameter) of a DNS object. LOC records currently have no effect on the technical operation of the Internet, and no standard software looks for them. However, a number of interesting potential uses for the information have been suggested, including route tracing and optimization, automated mapping, and network research.

The format is:

name [ttl] IN LOC *lat lon [alt [size [hp [vp]]]]*

The latitude and longitude are given as space-separated degrees, minutes, and seconds followed by N, S, E, or W. Seconds can be omitted; if they are, minutes can also be omitted.

The other fields are all specified in centimeters (no suffix) or meters (m). *alt* is the object's altitude, *size* is the diameter of the object's bounding sphere, *hp* is the horizontal precision of the measurement, and *vp* is the vertical precision. The default size is one meter, and the default horizontal and vertical precisions are 10 meters and 10 kilometers, respectively.

Here is an example for caida.org in San Diego, California:

caida.org.   IN   LOC   32 53 01 N 117 14 25 W 107m 30m 18m 15m

Many of the graphical visualization tools written by CAIDA (the Cooperative Association for Internet Data Analysis) require latitude and longitude data, and sites are encouraged to include it in their DNS. However, if you are paranoid and run a high-visibility server or ISP, you may not want the general public to know the exact location of your machines. In such situations, we recommend that you use inexact values with a large horizontal precision parameter. Imprecise LOC records are still of value to the network research folks but offer some anonymity.

Another noteworthy feature of LOC records is that they appear to crash NT 4.0's name server; take precautions.

SRV records

An SRV record specifies the location of services within a domain. For example, the SRV record allows you to query a remote domain directly and ask for the name of its FTP server. Until now, you mostly had to guess. To contact the FTP server for a remote domain, you had to hope that the remote sysadmins had followed the current custom and added a CNAME for "ftp" to their server's DNS records.

SRV records make more sense than CNAMEs for this application and are certainly a better way for sysadmins to move services around and control their use. However, SRV records must be explicitly sought and parsed by clients, so it will be a while before their effects are really felt.

SRV records resemble generalized MX records with fields that let the local DNS administrator steer and load-balance connections from the outside world. The format is

```
service.proto.name [ttl] IN SRV pri wt port target
```

where *service* is a service defined in the IANA assigned numbers database (see page 246 or www.iana.org/numbers.htm), *proto* is either tcp or udp, *name* is the domain to which the SRV record refers, *pri* is an MX-style priority, *wt* is a weight used for load balancing among several servers, *port* is the port on which the service runs, and *target* is the hostname of the server that provides this service. The A record of the target is usually returned automatically with the answer to a SRV query. A value of 0 for the *wt* parameter means that no special load balancing should be done. A value of "." for the target means that the service is not run at this site.

Here is an example, snitched from RFC2052 (where SRV is defined) and adapted for the cs.colorado.edu domain:

```
ftp.tcp             SRV  0  0  21  ftp-server.cs.colorado.edu.

; don't allow finger anymore (target = .)
finger.tcp          SRV  0  0  79  .

; 1/4 of the connections to old box, 3/4 to the new one
ssh.tcp             SRV  0  1  22  old-slow-box.cs.colorado.edu.
                    SRV  0  3  22  new-fast-box.cs.colorado.edu.
; main server on port 80, backup on new box, port 8000
http.tcp            SRV  0  0  80  www-server.cs.colorado.edu.
                    SRV  10  0 8000 new-fast-box.cs.colorado.edu.

; so both http://www.cs.colo... and http://cs.colo... work
http.tcp.www        SRV  0  0  80  www-server.cs.colorado.edu.
                    SRV  10  0 8000 new-fast-box.cs.colorado.edu.

; block all other services (target = .)
*.tcp               SRV  0  0   0  .
*.udp               SRV  0  0   0  .
```

This example illustrates the use of both the weight parameter (for SSH) and the priority parameter (HTTP). Both SSH servers will be used, with the work being split between them. The backup HTTP server will only be used when the principal server

DNS

is unavailable. The **finger** service is not included, nor are other services that are not explicitly mentioned. The fact that the **finger** daemon does not appear in DNS does not mean that it is not running, just that you can't locate the server through DNS.

WKS (well-known services) was an earlier service-related DNS record that did not catch on. Instead of pointing you to the host that provided a particular service for a domain, it listed the services provided by a particular host. WKS seems sort of useless and was also deemed a security risk. It was not widely adopted.

TXT records

A TXT record adds arbitrary text to a host's DNS records. For example, we have a TXT record that identifies our site:

```
IN                TXT  "University of CO, Boulder Campus, CS Dept"
```

This record directly follows the SOA and NS records for the "cs.colorado.edu." zone and so inherits the *name* field from them.

The format of a TXT record is

```
name [ttl] IN TXT info ...
```

All *info* items must be quoted. You can use a single quoted string or multiple strings that are individually quoted. Be sure the quotes are balanced—a missing quote will wreak havoc with your DNS data because all the records between the missing quote and the next occurrence of a quote will mysteriously disappear.

TXT records have no intrinsic order. If you use several of them to add a paragraph of information to your DNS, they may all be scrambled by the time **named** and UDP are done with them.

IPv6 resource records

See Chapter 13 for a more detailed discussion of IPv6.

IPv6 is a new version of the IP protocol. It has spent nearly 10 years in the specification process and still isn't done. IPv6 was originally motivated by a perceived need for more IP network addresses. However, the stopgap solutions to this problem—CIDR, NAT, and stricter control of addresses—have been so successful that a mass migration to IPv6 is unlikely to happen any time soon. Unless someone comes up with a new killer app that runs only on IPv6 (or some future version of Microsoft Windows defaults to it), sysadmins are unlikely to have to deal with IPv6 for a few more years. Some folks think that the next generation of cell phones, which may have IP addresses, might just tip the scales in favor of IPv6.

Even though we don't expect to see IPv6 deployed anytime soon, we think it's worthwhile to describe the impact of 128-bit IP addresses on the DNS system. Both the address records and the pointer records have to change, but those changes are relatively simple compared to the task of supporting one of IPv6's totally new concepts: shared ownership of addresses.

The host interface to which an IPv6 address corresponds owns some of the address bits but not all of them. Other bits are delegated to the site's upstream ISPs in an attempt to make renumbering and changing ISPs an easy task. This design adds a lot of complexity. After looking at all the hoops that DNS has had to jump through to support the standards, we wonder if the standards' authors have written any code lately. Probably not.

The IPv6 equivalents of DNS A records were originally called AAAA records, because IPv6 addresses were four times longer than IPv4 addresses. As the split-control scheme for IPv6 addresses evolved, the IETF obsoleted AAAA records and standardized on two new record types: A6 records for name-to-address mappings and DNAME records for delegation of address portions to different organizations. The DNAME records were inspired by the CNAME hack (see page 418), which allows delegation on bit boundaries. A6 records specify an address, but with the possibility that some of the high-order prefix bits must be obtained from another source.

In the summer of 2001, the IETF, frustrated with the slow deployment of IPv6, realized that the complexity of shared addresses with A6 and DNAME records was the stumbling block. They moved A6 and DNAME from the standards track to experimental status and reinstated the AAAA address records and the nibble form of PTR record. There is still controversy regarding the best address format. AAAA is (much) simpler but destroys easy renumbering, which was formerly a key IPv6 goal.

Since we don't expect IPv6 to be widely deployed soon, in either the AAAA or A6 form, we defer detailed descriptions of the IPv6 lookup mechanisms until they have been better defined by the IETF and we have some operational experience with them. In the meantime, the following sections outline the gist of the two plans. You can skip ahead to *Commands in zone files* on page 427 if you'd rather not read about IPv6.

IPv6 address records

The format of an AAAA record is

hostname [*ttl*] IN AAAA *ipaddr*

For example:

anchor   IN   AAAA   3ffe:8050:201:9:a00:20ff:fe81:2b32

Each colon-separated chunk is 4 hex digits, with leading zeros usually omitted. Two adjacent colons stand for "enough zeros to fill out the 128 bits for a complete IPv6 address." An address can contain at most one such double colon.

The format of an A6 record is similar, but with a little twist:

hostname [*ttl*] IN A6 *#-bits-deferred ipaddr referral*

For example:

```
anchor        IN    A6     0  3ffe:8050:201:9:a00:20ff:fe81:2b32 .
anchor        IN    A6     48 ::9:a00:20ff:fe81:2b32 prefix.myisp.net.
```

These two A6 records specify the same IPv6 address for the host anchor; one is fully specified with no prefix bits deferred, and the other has 48 prefix bits deferred to the host prefix.myisp.net. Note the dot as the referral parameter in the first form of the A6 record; it signifies that no further referral is needed.

Forward A6 name lookups might have to talk to many name servers up the A6 chain to assemble a complete 128-bit address. For example, with the second line above, the next level up could defer 47 bits, the next level could defer 46 bits, and so on. 48 queries might be needed to get the full answer. Add to that number the DNSSEC queries needed to verify each piece of the address and you have a 100-fold increase in DNS traffic to resolve one name. Design by committee is not always simple and efficient.

Those 48 potential levels will in practice be more like 2 or 3, but the concept may present interesting avenues for denial of service attacks. For more complete (and less prejudiced) documentation, see the BIND 9 **doc** directory.

IPv6 reverse records

In IPv4, reverse mappings live in the in-addr.arpa domain and forward mappings live in the other branches of the domain tree (under com or edu, for example). In IPv6, the reverse mapping information corresponding to an AAAA address record is a PTR record in the ip6.int top-level domain. The reverse record for an A6 address record is a bit more scattered. Some of it lives under the ip6.arpa domain and the rest is stored among the forward domains.

The "nibble" format reverses an AAAA address record by expanding each colon-separated address chunk to the full 4 hex digits and then reversing the order of those digits and tacking on ip6.int at the end. For example, the PTR record that corresponds to our sample AAAA record for anchor would be

```
2.3.b.2.1.8.e.f.f.f.0.2.0.0.a.0.9.0.0.0.1.0.2.0.0.5.0.8.e.f.f.3.ip6.int PTR anchor.cs.colorado.edu.
```

It certainly doesn't look friendly for a sysadmin to have to type or debug or even read. Of course, in your actual DNS zone files, the $ORIGIN statement would hide some of the complexity.

However, the competing format for reverse lookups makes this nibble format look like a first grader's arithmetic homework by comparison. The alternate format lives in a new top-level branch of the DNS naming tree, ip6.arpa, and uses both traditional PTR records and records of a new, IPv6-specific type, DNAME. PTR records resolve the local bits of an IPv6 address to a particular hostname, and DNAME records determine which parts of the rest of the address are delegated to which organizations.

The components of names in the in-addr.arpa hierarchy represent the bytes of an IP address. For IPv6, we generalize this scheme and allow name components to represent arbitrary sections of an address. Address sections can be any number of bits wide (for values of "any number" between 1 and 128) and are known as bitstrings.

Bitstrings are represented with a peculiar syntax known as a bitstring label. Let's look at an example. All IPv6 unicast A6 addresses begin with the three bits 001. To express this prefix in the language of bitstrings, we start with the binary number 001 and pad it out to a multiple of four bits: 0010. This computation give us the hex digit 2; the digit has three valid bits and one discard bit. The final bitstring is:

    \[x2/3]

The backslash, square brackets, and x delimit every bitstring. The important parts are a series of hex digits (just one in this case, 2) and the length qualifier, /3. The length qualifier, which tells how many of the bits represented by the hex digits are really valid, is optional. If omitted, the bitstring defaults to its natural length as determined by the number of hex digits (here, 4 bits).

Even if your bitstrings end at a hex-digit boundary, it's a good idea to include the length qualifier. Otherwise, the readers of your DNS files will go blind from counting long strings of tiny little hex digits.

The leftmost bits of a hex string are the significant ones. Extra bits used to pad out the rightmost hex digit are simply discarded. Pad bits must be 0s.

Because all unicast IPv6 addresses share the same 001 prefix, the effective top-level domain for A6 reverse mappings is \[x2/3].ip6.arpa.

Here is a more complete example. The lines below show three different representations of the same address: the first undivided, the second divided into three pieces (3/45/80 bits), and the third divided into four pieces (3/13/32/80).[12] As address chunks get shifted around, their hex representations change completely—it's still the same bits underneath, however. **bc** is your friend for bit twiddling.[13]

    \[x3ffe8050020100090a0020fffe812b32/128].ip6.arpa.
    \[x00090a0020fffe812b32/80].\[xfff402801008/45].\[x2/3].ip6.arpa.
    \[x00090a0020fffe812b32/80].\[x80500201/32].\[xfff0/13].\[x2/3].ip6.arpa

As with IPv4 in-addr.arpa zones, individual numbers read from left to right and components (dot-separated chunks) read from right to left. The first component on the second and third lines above is the local part of the address. It represents the low-order 80 bits of the address and consists of the hex digits 00090a0020fffe812b32. Here are the same three lines again with the local part of the address boldfaced:

    \[x3ffe80500201**00090a0020fffe812b32**/128].ip6.arpa.
    \[x**00090a0020fffe812b32**/80].\[xfff402801008/45].\[x2/3].ip6.arpa.
    \[x**00090a0020fffe812b32**/80].\[x80500201/32].\[xfff0/13].\[x2/3].ip6.arpa

---

12. While poking around at the level of bits, it's easy to lose sight of the fact that IPv6 addresses have some internal structure of their own. See page 257 for a discussion of the boundaries and meanings of the regions into which an IPv6 address is conventionally divided.

13. **bc**, the Linux calculator utility, includes the concept of number bases; you can specify the input number base with ibase and the output number base with obase. For example ibase=16 and obase=2 would translate any number typed into **bc** from hexadecimal to binary. Once you have changed the input base, it's easiest to restart **bc** to get back to normal because **bc** interprets all input according to the current base, even new ibase commands.

The /3 in the second line says that the first three of the four bits in the hex digit 2 are valid parts of the address. The /45 in the second line means that the first 45 of the 48 bits present in the hex string fff402801008 are valid in the middle piece of the address. Aren't all these fragments going to be easy to type into your DNS files without making mistakes? Geez.

DNAME records delegate address chunks to other name servers. Their format is:

> bitstring-label [ttl] IN DNAME domain-delegated-to

The idea is that different organizations can control the different pieces of an address or address prefix. You control the local 80 bits, your ISP controls a chunk, your ISP's ISP controls a chunk, and so on. The excerpts below demonstrate the delegation that DNAME records can do. We use the address above in its four-pieces incarnation, in which the delegation path is from the root to my-isp to my-domain.

In this example, the $ORIGIN statements identify the context of each record. These excerpts are from the zone files at three different sites: the root of the ip6.arpa tree, my-isp.net, and my-domain.com—they do not represent a consistent configuration for a single site.

The root of the ip6.arpa tree, \[x2/3].ip6.arpa, delegates a particular 13-bit address to my-isp.net by entering the following lines into its zone file:

```
; delegate prefix to my-isp.net
$ORIGIN \[x2/3].ip6.arpa.
\[xfff0/13]        IN  DNAME  ip6.my-isp.net.
```

These records create a sort of nickname for \[xfff0/13].\[x2/3].ip6.arpa that points to the string "ip6.my-isp.net.". The ISP in turn delegates a 32-bit segment of address space to my-domain.com by including these lines in its ip6.my-isp.net zone file:

```
; delegate prefix to my-domain.com
$ORIGIN ip6.my-isp.net.
\[x80500201/32] IN  DNAME  ip6.my-domain.com.
```

This line forms a name, "\[x80500201/32].ip6.my-isp.net.", which when expanded from the previous DNAME record becomes the 48-bit prefix of the IPv6 address. Those 48 bits are nicknamed ip6.my-domain.com.

In the zone files for ip6.my-domain.com, the rest of the address is mapped with a PTR record:

```
$ORIGIN ip6.my-domain.com.
\[x00090a0020fffe812b32/80]   IN  PTR   host.my-domain.com.
```

We suggest that you not bother with the DNAME delegations if you have only one ISP and are not multihomed. Just list the whole 128-bit address in both forward and reverse zones. You still get some bits from your upstream ISP, but you can put them in your own zone files as long as your ISP tells you when it changes the prefix.

IPv6 is still young, at least from the deployment point of view. The registries are just starting to assign addresses, and the process will become smoother with experience. The local part of the IPv6 address never needs to change, and that's great—no renumbering. But at many organizations, upstream ISPs don't change frequently either, and so putting the ISP's bits into your own data files seems like a good thing. A quick Perl script could change the prefix of all your addresses if you ever switched ISPs.

Once the IETF makes up its mind about which scheme it will actually use, we can consider deployment. However, there will certainly be more changes, so it is really still too early to start dealing with IPv6 in DNS. The root servers do not yet (at the start of 2002) speak IPv6 or handle delegations in the ip6.int or ip6.arpa domains. The gTLD servers are thinking about AAAA IPv6 records for later this year.

Commands in zone files

Now that we have looked at all the basic resource records, let's look at the commands that can be embedded in a zone file to modify the records that follow them. There are four:

```
$ORIGIN domain-name
$INCLUDE filename
$TTL default-ttl
$GENERATE lots-of-args
```

Commands *must* start in the first column and be on a line by themselves.

As **named** reads a zone file, it adds the default domain (or "origin") to any names that are not already fully qualified. The origin is initially set to the domain name specified in the corresponding zone statement in **named.conf**. However, you can set the origin by hand within a zone file by using the $ORIGIN directive.

The use of relative names where fully qualified names are expected saves lots of typing and makes zone files much easier to read. For example, the reverse records for a subnetted class B site might all be in one zone file, with $ORIGIN statements setting the context for each subnet. A statement such as

```
$ORIGIN 243.138.128.in-addr.arpa
```

could precede the records for the 243 subnet.

Many sites use the $INCLUDE directive in their zone database files to separate overhead records from data records, to separate logical pieces of a zone file, or to keep cryptographic keys in a file with restricted permissions. The syntax of the $INCLUDE directive is

```
$INCLUDE filename
```

The specified file is read into the database at the point of the $INCLUDE directive. If *filename* is not an absolute path, it is interpreted relative to the directory specified in the **named.conf** file as **named**'s home.

The $TTL directive sets a default value for the time to live field of the records that follow it. Previously, the only way to set the default was in the SOA record (described on page 411). BIND 8 likes to have a $TTL at the beginning of zone files; BIND 9 requires it and refuses to load zone files that do not set a default $TTL.

The $TTL statement should precede the SOA record for the zone. The default units for the $TTL value are seconds, but you can also qualify numbers with h for hours, m for minutes, d for days, or w for weeks. For example, the lines

```
$TTL 86400
$TTL 24h
$TTL 1d
```

all set the $TTL to one day.

The value of $TTL should be on the order of days or weeks to let caching help DNS scale to an ever-expanding Internet. Legal values range from 0 to 2,147,483,647 seconds (about 65 years). That's too long! If you are planning to move machines around and know that you will be changing the hostnames or IP addresses of your existing fleet, set the TTL to a smaller value (say, an hour) a week before you schedule the renumbering party. That way, stale data will not be cached for long and your new DNS data will propagate more rapidly. (Don't forget to change the TTL back when you are done!)

BIND 9 enforces a concept known as TTL harmonization; it forces all records in an RRset (that is, all records of the same type that pertain to a single node) to have the same TTL. The value that's actually used is that of the first resource record for the node/type pair.

$GENERATE, a relatively new BIND 8 construct, provides a simple way to generate a series of similar records. It serves mostly to help with generating RFC2317-style classless in-addr.arpa mappings (the CNAME hack for reverse zone files), for cases in which the boundaries of administrative authority do not match the boundaries of bytes in an IP address.

The format of the $GENERATE directive is

```
$GENERATE start-stop/[step] lhs type rhs [comment]
```

and the generated lines are of the form

```
lhs type rhs
```

The *start* and *stop* fields specify the range of values for a single numeric iterator. One line is generated for each value in the interval. The iterator value is incorporated into *lhs* and *rhs* with the $ character. If you also specify a *step*, the iteration is by *step*-size increments. *type* is the record type. Currently, only CNAME, PTR, and NS are supported in BIND 8, and those types plus DNAME, A, and AAAA are supported in BIND 9. See page 420 for an example.

DNS

The localhost zone

The address 127.0.0.1 refers to a host itself and should always be mapped to the name "localhost.*localdomain*.", for example, localhost.cs.colorado.edu. Some sites map the address to just plain "localhost." as though it were part of the root domain; this configuration is incorrect.

If you forget to configure the localhost zone, your site may end up querying the root servers for localhost information. The root servers are currently receiving so many of these queries that the operators are considering adding a generic mapping between localhost and 127.0.0.1 at the root level.

See page 461 for an example of a complete and correct localhost configuration.

Glue records: links between zones

Each zone stands alone with its own set of data files, name servers, and clients. But zones need to be connected together to form a coherent hierarchy: cs.colorado.edu is a part of colorado.edu, and we need some DNS linkage between them.

Since DNS referrals occur only from parent domains to child domains, it is not necessary for a name server to know anything about the domains (or more accurately, zones) above it in the DNS hierarchy. However, the servers of a parent domain must know the IP addresses of the name servers for all of its subdomains. In fact, *only* the name servers known to the parent zone can be returned as referrals in response to external queries.

In DNS terms, the parent zone needs to contain the NS records for each delegated zone. Since NS records are written in terms of hostnames rather than IP addresses, the parent server must also have a way to resolve the hostnames, either by making a normal DNS query (if this does not create a dependency loop) or by having copies of the appropriate A records.

There are two ways in which you can meet this requirement: by including the necessary records or by using stub zones.

With the first method, you can simply include the necessary NS and A records in the parent zone. For example, the colorado.edu zone file could contain these records:

```
; subdomain information

cs          IN  NS  ns.cs.colorado.edu.
            IN  NS  piper.cs.colorado.edu.
            IN  NS  ns.xor.com.
ee          IN  NS  ns.ee.colorado.edu.
            IN  NS  ns.cs.colorado.edu.

; glue records

ns.cs       IN  A   128.138.243.151
piper.cs    IN  A   128.138.204.4
ns.ee       IN  A   128.138.200.1
```

The "foreign" A records are called glue records because they don't really belong in this zone. They're only reproduced here to connect the new domain to the Internet naming tree. Missing or incorrect glue records will leave part of your namespace inaccessible, and users trying to reach it will get "host unknown" errors.

It is a common error to include glue records for hostnames that don't need them. For example, ns.xor.com in the example above can be resolved with a normal DNS query. An A record would initially just be unnecessary, but it could later become downright misleading if ns.xor.com's address were to change. The rule of thumb is to include A records only for hosts that are within the current domain or any of its subdomains. Current versions of BIND 8 and 9 ignore unnecessary glue records and log their presence as an error.

The scheme just described is the standard way of connecting zones, but it requires the child to keep in touch with the parent and tell the parent about any changes or additions to its name server fleet. Since parent and child zones are often run by different sites, updates are often a tedious manual task that requires coordination across administrative boundaries. A corollary is that in the real world, this type of configuration is often out of date.

The second way to maintain links is to use stub zones. Stub zones are fully supported in BIND 8, but were also available in BIND 4 (though documented as being experimental). A stub zone is essentially the same thing as a slave zone, but it includes only the zone's NS records.

Stub zones work fine in BIND 8, which mixes different zones' data in memory, but they don't work as well with BIND 9. In BIND 9, the stub zones must be configured identically on both the master and slave servers of the parent, something that is in itself hard to keep consistent. Your best bet is to just keep in touch with your parent domain and to verify its configuration at least a couple of times a year.

You can use the **dig** command to see which of your servers your parent domain is currently advertising. First run

> **dig** *parent-domain* **ns**

to determine the name servers for your parent domain. Pick one and run

> **dig** @*name-server.parent-domain* *child-domain* **ns**

to see your list of public name servers. Here is an actual example with some of **dig**'s wordiness deleted:

```
% dig colorado.edu ns
;;      ...
;; ANSWER SECTION:
colorado.edu.        5h9m22s IN NS   ns1.westnet.net.
colorado.edu.        5h9m22s IN NS   rs0.netsol.com.
colorado.edu.        5h9m22s IN NS   boulder.colorado.edu.
colorado.edu.        5h9m22s IN NS   cujo.colorado.edu.
```

```
% dig @boulder.colorado.edu cs.colorado.edu ns
;;; ANSWER SECTION:
cs.colorado.edu.       6H IN NS      cs.colorado.edu.
cs.colorado.edu.       6H IN NS      huizil.cs.colorado.edu.
cs.colorado.edu.       6H IN NS      xor.com.
cs.colorado.edu.       6H IN NS      pacifier.com.
```

Only four servers for the cs.colorado.edu domain are visible from the outside world. A **dig** from within the department yields a different list:

```
;; ANSWER SECTION:
cs.colorado.edu.       2H IN NS      cs.colorado.edu.
cs.colorado.edu.       2H IN NS      moet.cs.colorado.edu.
cs.colorado.edu.       2H IN NS      piper.cs.colorado.edu.
cs.colorado.edu.       2H IN NS      anchor.cs.colorado.edu.
cs.colorado.edu.       2H IN NS      vulture.cs.colorado.edu.
```

Only the main cs.colorado.edu server is used both inside and outside the department.

One situation in which stub zones are very useful is when your internal addressing uses the RFC1918 private address space and you need to keep the RFC1918 delegations in sync. The BIND 8 distribution contains an example in **src/conf/recursive**.

A couple of stub zone subtleties are worth mentioning:

- Stub zones are not authoritative copies of the zone's data, and stub servers should not be listed among the zone's NS records.

- Since stub servers are not listed in NS records, they are not notified automatically when the zone's data changes. To update stub servers, you can either add an also-notify clause to the configuration of the master servers or you can simply wait for the zone to be updated at the end of the refresh interval specified in the zone's SOA record. The timeout option should work just fine in most cases, though it can potentially result in transitory lame delegations (see page 458).

- Theoretically, it's of no use for **named** to have copies of a zone's NS records if it cannot also obtain the matching A records. However, **named** can bootstrap itself by using the master's IP address, which is given in **named.conf**.

- Why limit yourself to NS records? Why not just be a secondary server for the subdomains? This works, too. However, if every server of the parent domain is also a server of a child domain, then no referrals will ever be made to downstream servers. The parent domain's servers will be providing all the DNS service for the subdomain. Perhaps this is what you want, and perhaps not.

16.12 UPDATING ZONE FILES

When you make a change to a domain (such as adding or deleting a host), the data files on the master server must be updated. You must also increment the serial number in the SOA record for the zone and then run **ndc reload** (**rndc reload** in BIND 9) to signal **named** to pick up the changes. You can also kill and restart **named** (**ndc restart**), but this operation causes cached data from other domains to be discarded.

Earlier versions of BIND used signals and the Linux **kill** command to control **named**, but just as the developers started running out of signal numbers, **ndc** came along and fixed it all. Most of the historical signal stuff in BIND (except for the HUP signal to reread the configuration file and the TERM signal to die) is likely to go away in future releases, so we recommend sticking with **ndc**.

The updated zone data is propagated to slave servers right away because the notify option is on by default. If you have inadvertently turned this option off, your slave servers do not pick up the changes until after *refresh* seconds, as set in the zone's SOA record (typically one to six hours later). If you want a more timely update when the notify option is turned off, **ndc reload** on a slave causes it to check with the master, see that the data has changed, and request a zone transfer.

Don't forget to modify both the forward and reverse zones when you change a hostname or IP address. Forgetting the reverse files leaves sneaky errors: some commands work and some won't.

Changing the data files but forgetting to change the serial number makes the changes take effect on the master server (after a reload) but not on the slaves.

It is improper to edit data files belonging to slave servers. These files are maintained by **named**; sysadmins should not meddle with them. It's fine to look at the data files as long as you don't make changes.

BIND allows zone changes to be made through a programmatic API, as specified in RFC2136. This feature, called dynamic update, is necessary for autoconfiguration protocols like DHCP. The dynamic update mechanism is described on page 433.

Zone transfers

DNS servers are synchronized through a mechanism called a zone transfer. The original DNS specification (and BIND 4) required all zone data to be transferred at once. Incremental updates were eventually defined in RFC1995 and implemented in BIND 8.2. Original and incremental-style zone transfers are sometimes referred to as AXFR and IXFR, respectively. Once configured, they're supposed to be equivalent.

A slave that wants to refresh its data requests a zone transfer from the master server and makes a backup copy of the zone data on disk. If the data on the master has not changed, as determined by a comparison of the serial numbers (not the actual data), no update occurs and the backup files are just touched (that is, their modification time is set to the current time).

Zone transfers use the TCP protocol on port 53 and log information through syslog with the tag "named-xfer." IXFR as specified by the IETF can use either TCP or UDP, but BIND has only implemented it over TCP.

Both the sending and receiving server remain available to answer queries during a zone transfer. Only after the transfer is complete does the slave begin to use the new data. BIND 8 actually calls a separate **named-xfer** program to perform the transfer, but BIND 9's **named** handles the transfers directly. Therefore, the named-xfer option that specified the path to the **named-xfer** program is no longer part of the configuration language for BIND 9.

When zones are huge (like com) or dynamically updated (see the next section), changes are typically small relative to the size of the entire zone. With IXFR, only the changes are sent (unless they are larger than the complete zone, in which case a regular AXFR transfer is done). The IXFR mechanism is like the **patch** program in that it applies differences to an old database to bring it into sync with a new database.

In BIND 8, you enable IXFR by telling **named** to keep a transaction log in the global options section and then turning it on in the server statements for any servers that use it. The relevant configuration lines are:

```
maintain-ixfr-base true ;       # in BIND 8 options section
use-ixfr true ;                 # in BIND 8 server statement
```

If you want to change the default names for the transaction log and temporary file used by IXFR, do it in the zone statements with:

```
ixfr-base "filename" ;          # in BIND 8 zone statements
ixfr-tmp-file "filename" ;      # in BIND 8 zone statements
```

In BIND 9, IXFR is the default for any zones configured for dynamic update, and **named** always maintains a transaction log called *zonename*.**jnl**. You can set the options provide-ixfr and request-ixfr in the server statements for individual peers. provide-ixfr enables or disables IXFR service for zones for which this server is the master. request-ixfr requests IXFRs for zones for which this server is a slave.

```
provide-ixfr yes ;              # in BIND 9 server statement
request-ixfr yes ;              # in BIND 9 server statement
```

BIND cannot cope with a zone being both dynamically updated and edited by hand. BIND 9 provides outgoing IXFR for changes that resulted from dynamic updates or from incoming IXFRs, but not for changes that resulted from edits to the master zone files. This feature will likely be added in a later release.

A lot of work has gone into the IXFR mechanism to ensure that a server crash during an update does not leave the zones with trashed data. An IXFR request to a server that does not support it automatically falls back to the standard AXFR zone transfer.

Dynamic updates

The DNS system is built on the premise that name-to-address mappings are relatively stable and do not change frequently. However, a site that uses DHCP to dynamically assign IP addresses as machines boot and join the network breaks this rule constantly. There are two classical solutions: add generic entries to the DNS database or continually edit the DNS files. For many sites, neither solution is satisfactory.

The first solution should be familiar to anyone who has used a dial-up ISP. The DNS configuration looks something like this:

```
dhcp-host1.domain.    IN   A    192.168.0.1
dhcp-host2.domain.    IN   A    192.168.0.2
...
```

Although this is a simple solution, it means that hostnames are permanently associated with particular IP addresses and that computers therefore change hostnames whenever they receive a new IP address. Hostname-based logging or security measures become very difficult in this environment.

The dynamic update feature in recent versions of BIND provides an alternative solution. It allows the DHCP daemon to notify BIND of the address assignments it makes, thus updating the contents of the DNS database on the fly. A shell interface is also provided for making dynamic updates by hand.

Dynamic updates can add, delete, or modify resource records. The granularity at which dynamic updates are regulated is the zone. It's a bit scary to allow dynamic updates to your site's entire DNS database, so many sites create a subdomain (perhaps dhcp.*site*) and allow dynamic updates only within that subdomain.

Once a zone has been dynamically updated, you cannot edit it by hand without first stopping BIND with **ndc stop** (**rndc stop** in BIND 9) so that the current copy of the database can be written out to disk. You can then edit the zone file by hand. Of course, the original formatting of the zone file will be destroyed (the file will look like those maintained by **named** for slave servers).

While dynamic updates are occurring, a journal file (*zonename*.**jnl**) is kept in case of a server crash. This file must be removed after you stop **named** and before you start editing the zone file by hand. It's really best not to meddle with dynamic DNS zones, though, because inconsistent data can result.

Incremental zone transfers are the default for zones that use dynamic updates. They use the same journaling mechanism as the dynamic updates.

The **nsupdate** program supplied with BIND 9 provides a command-line interface to dynamic updates. It runs in batch mode, taking commands from the keyboard or a file. Two blank lines signal the end of the input. The command language includes a primitive "if" statement to express constructs such as "if this hostname does not exist in the DNS, add it." As predicates for an **nsupdate** action, you can require a name to exist or not exist, or require a resource record set to exist or not exist.

For example, here is a simple **nsupdate** script that adds a new host and also adds a nickname for an existing host if the nickname is not already in use:

```
% nsupdate
> update add newhost.cs.colorado.edu 86400 A 128.138.243.16
>
> prereq nxdomain gypsy.cs.colorado.edu
> update add gypsy.cs.colorado.edu CNAME evi-laptop.cs.colorado.edu
```

Dynamic updates to DNS are scary. They can potentially provide uncontrolled write access to your important system data. Don't try to use IP addresses for access control—they are too easily forged. TSIG authentication with a shared-secret key is better; it's available and is easy to configure. Both BIND 8 and 9 support

> % **nsupdate -k keydir:keyfile**

and BIND 9 also understands

> % **nsupdate -y keyname:secretkey**

For more details on TSIG, see the section starting on page 438.

Dynamic updates to a zone are enabled in **named.conf** with an allow-update or update-policy clause. allow-update grants permission to update any records in accordance with source IP address or key-based authentication. update-policy is a BIND 9 extension that allows fine-grained control for updates according to the hostname or record type. It requires key-based authentication.

Use update-policy to allow clients to update their A records or PTR records but not to change the SOA record, NS records, or KEY records. You can even use it to allow a host to update only its own records. The parameters let you express names explicitly, as a subdomain, as a wild card, or as the keyword self, which sets a general policy for machines' access to their own records. Resource records are identified by class and type. Here's an example:

```
update-policy { grant dhcp-key subdomain dhcp.cs.colorado.edu A } ;
```

This configuration allows anyone who knows the key dhcp-key to update address records in the dhcp.cs.colorado.edu subdomain. This statement would appear in the **named.conf** file under the zone statement for dhcp.cs.colorado.edu. There would have to be a key statement to define dhcp-key as well. See the BIND documentation for all the bells and whistles associated with the update-policy statement.

16.13 SECURITY ISSUES

Two things hold the Internet together: the DNS system and the routing system. In the good old days, the Internet was small, friendly, and used mostly by geeks. Now it is a hostile environment as well as a crucial piece of infrastructure. This section covers several security-related topics in a manner that may appear to be draconian and paranoid. Unfortunately, these topics and precautions are important and sadly necessary in today's Internet.

DNS started out as an inherently open system, but it has steadily grown more and more secure—or at least, securable. By default, anyone on the Internet can investigate your domain with individual queries from tools like **dig**, **host**, or **nslookup**. In some cases, they can dump your entire DNS database.

To address such vulnerabilities, BIND now supports various types of access control based on host and network addresses or on cryptographic authentication. Table 16.11

summarizes the security features that are configured in **named.conf**. The Page column shows where in this chapter to look for more information.

Table 16.11 Security features in named.conf

Feature	Statements	Page	What it specifies
allow-query	options, zone	388	Who can query a zone or server
allow-transfer	options, zone	388	Who can request zone transfers
allow-update	zone	391	Who can make dynamic updates
update-policy	zone	435	What updates are allowed
blackhole	options	388	Which servers to completely ignore
bogus	server	390	Which servers should never be queried
acl	various	389	Access control lists

named can run in a **chroot**ed environment under an unprivileged UID to minimize security risks. It can use transaction signatures to control dynamic updates, and of course, it also supports the whole DNSSEC hairball. These topics are taken up in the next few sections.

Access control lists revisited

ACLs are named address match lists that can appear as arguments to statements such as allow-query, allow-transfer, and blackhole. ACLs can help with two major DNS security issues: spoofing and denial of service attacks. Their basic syntax was described on page 389.

Every site should at least have one ACL for bogus addresses and one ACL for local addresses. For example:

```
acl bogusnets {          // ACL for bogus networks
      0.0.0.0/8 ;        // default, wild card addresses
      1.0.0.0/8 ;        // reserved addresses
      2.0.0.0/8 ;        // reserved addresses
      169.254.0.0/16 ;   // link-local delegated addresses[14]
      192.0.2.0/24 ;     // sample addresses, like example.com
      224.0.0.0/3 ;      // multicast address space
      10.0.0.0/8 ;       // private address space (RFC1918)[15]
      172.16.0.0/12 ;    // private address space (RFC1918)
      192.168.0.0/16 ;   // private address space (RFC1918)
} ;
```

14. The link-local address is used by Macs and PCs that have been told to use IP but cannot find a DHCP server. These machines just assign themselves an address on the 169.254.0.0/16 network. Addresses in this range should be aggressively filtered so that they never escape from the local wire. Cable and DSL modems are starting to use this address range as well.

15. Don't make private addresses bogus if you use them and are configuring your internal DNS servers!

```
acl cunets {                    // ACL for University of Colorado networks
    128.138.0.0/16 ;            // main campus network
    198.11.16/24 ;
    204.228.69/24 ;
};
```

In the global options section of your config file, you could then include

```
allow-recursion { cunets; } ;
blackhole { bogusnets; } ;
```

It's also a good idea to restrict zone transfers to legitimate slave servers. An ACL makes things nice and tidy.

```
acl ourslaves {
    128.138.242.1 ;            // anchor
    ...
} ;

acl measurements {
    128.9.160.157 ;            // bill manning's measurements
    198.32.4.0/24 ;           // bill manning's measurements
    192.5.5.0/24 ;            // mark lottors's measurements
} ;
```

The actual restriction is implemented with a line such as:

```
allow-transfer { ourslaves; measurements; } ;
```

Transfers are limited to our own slave servers and to the machines of two Internet measurement projects that walk the reverse DNS tree to determine the size of the Internet and the percentage of misconfigured servers. Limiting transfers in this way makes it impossible for other sites to dump your entire database with **nslookup**, **dig**, or **host**.

For example, using **dig @**_server domain-to-dump_ **axfr**:

```
% dig @128.138.143.151 cs.colorado.edu axfr
;; connect: Operation timed out

; <<>> DiG 8.3 <<>> @128.138.143.151 cs.colorado.edu axfr
; (1 server found)
;; FROM: chateau.caida.org to SERVER: 128.138.143.151
;; WHEN: Tue Feb 19 17:16:53 2002
```

You should still protect your network at a lower level through router access control lists and normal security hygiene on each host. If those measures are not possible, you can refuse DNS packets except to a gateway machine that you monitor closely.

Confining named

To confine the damage that someone could do if they compromised your server, you can run **named** in a **chroot**ed environment and/or run it as an unprivileged user. The **-t** flag specifies the directory to **chroot** to, and the **-u** and **-g** flags specify the

UID and GID under which to run. BIND 9 supports the **-u** flag, but not the **-g** flag. For example, the commands

```
# named -u 53 -g 53 -t /var/named     /* BIND 8 */
# named -u 53 -t /var/named           /* BIND 9 */
```

starts **named** with UID 53, GID 53 (BIND 8), and a root directory of **/var/named**.

The **chroot** directory cannot be an empty directory since it must contain all the files that **named** normally requires in order to run: **/dev/null**, shared libraries, the zone files, **named.conf**, **named-xfer**, syslog target files and UNIX domain socket, **/var**, etc. If you can compile **named** to statically link its libraries, you don't have to figure out which library files to copy to **/var/named**. See

> http://www.psionic.com/papers/dns/dns-linux

for step-by-step instructions for confining BIND 8's **named** in a **chroot**ed jail under Linux. The O'Reilly DNS book also provides similar instructions. SuSE has its own how-to page on **chroot**ed environments

/usr/share/doc/howto/en/html/Chroot-BIND-HOWTO.html

BIND 9 is easier to configure to run **chroot**ed because **named-xfer** is built in and the **chroot** system call is done after all libraries have been loaded.

If hackers compromise your **named**, they can potentially gain access to the system as whatever user **named** runs as. If this user is root and you do not use a **chroot**ed environment, such a breach can be quite destructive. Many sites don't bother to use the **-u**, **-g**, and **-t** flags, but they must then be faster to upgrade than the hackers are to attack when a new vulnerability is announced.

Secure server-to-server communication with TSIG and TKEY

While DNSSEC (covered in the next section) was being specified, the IETF developed a simpler mechanism called TSIG (RFC2845) to allow secure communication among servers through the use of transaction signatures. Access control based on transaction signatures is more secure than access control based on IP source addresses. The transaction signature authenticates the sender/receiver and verifies that the data has not been tampered with. It is typically used for secure zone transfers between a master server and its slaves and for secure dynamic updates.

Transaction signatures use a symmetric encryption scheme. That is, the encryption key is the same as the decryption key. This single key is called a shared-secret key. You should use a different key for each pair of servers that wants to communicate securely. TSIG is much less expensive computationally than public key cryptography, but it is only appropriate for a local network on which the number of pairs of communicating servers is small. It does not scale to the global Internet.

TSIG signatures sign DNS queries and responses to queries. They are used only between servers, not between servers and resolvers. TSIG signatures are checked at the time a packet is received and are then discarded; they are not cached and do not become part of the DNS data. Although the TSIG specification allows multiple encryption methods, BIND implements only one, the HMAC-MD5 algorithm.

BIND's **dnssec-keygen**[16] utility generates a key for a pair of servers. For example, to generate a shared-secret host key for two servers, *serv1* and *serv2*, use

```
# dnssec-keygen -a HMAC-MD5 -b 128 -n HOST serv1-serv2
```

to create a 128-bit key. Two files are produced: **K***serv1-serv2***.+157+09068.private** and **K***serv1-serv2***.+157+09068.key**. The **157** stands for the HMAC-MD5 algorithm; the **09068** is a random number used as a key identifier in case you have multiple keys for the same pair of servers. The **.private** file looks like this:

```
Private-key-format: v1.2
Algorithm: 157 (HMAC_MD5)
Key: jxopbeb+aPc71Mm2vc9R9g==
```

and the **.key** file like this:

```
serv1-serv2. IN KEY 512 3 157 jxopbeb+aPc71Mm2vc9R9g==
```

Both of these files should have mode 600 and should be owned by the **named** user.[17] You don't actually need the **.key** file at all—it's produced because the **dnssec-keygen** program is also used to generate public key pairs in which the public key (**.key** file) is inserted into the DNS zone file as a KEY resource record.

The generated key is really just a long random number. You could generate the key manually by writing down an ASCII string of the right length and pretending that it's a base-64 encoding of something or by using **mmencode** to encode a random string. (**mmencode** is in the default installation for the Red Hat and SuSE distributions, but you must **apt-get** it for Debian.) The way you create the key is not important; it just has to exist on both machines.

scp is part of the SSH suite. See page 673 for details.

Copy the key to both *serv1* and *serv2* with **scp**, or cut and paste it. *Do not* use **telnet** or **ftp** to copy the key; even internal networks may not be secure. The key must be included in both machines' **named.conf** files. Since **named.conf** is usually world-readable and keys should not be, put the key in a separate file that is included into **named.conf**. For example, you could put the snippet

```
key serv1-serv2 {
    algorithm hmac-md5 ;
    secret "shared-key-you-generated" ;
} ;
```

in the file **serv1-serv2.key**. The file should have mode 600 and its owner should be **named**'s UID. In the **named.conf** file, add the line

```
include "serv1-serv2.key"
```

near the top.

---

16. This command is called **dnskeygen** in BIND 8.

17. BIND 8's **nsupdate** fails silently (no indication, no error message) if the **.key** file is not readable.

This part of the configuration simply defines the keys. To make them actually be used to sign and verify updates, each server needs to identify the other with a keys clause. For example, you might add the lines

```
server serv2's-IP-address {
    keys { serv1-serv2 ; } ;
} ;
```

to serv1's **named.conf** file and

```
server serv1's-IP-address {
    keys { serv1-serv2 ; } ;
} ;
```

to serv2's **named.conf** file. Any allow-query, allow-transfer, and allow-update clauses in the zone statement for the zone should also refer to the key. For example:

```
allow-transfer { key serv1-serv2 ;} ;
```

When you first start using transaction signatures, run **named** at debug level 1 (see page 447 for information about running **named** in debug mode) for a while to see any error messages that are generated. Older versions of BIND do not understand signed messages and complain about them, sometimes to the point of refusing to load the zone.

TKEY is a BIND 9 mechanism that allows two hosts to generate a shared-secret key automatically without phone calls or secure copies to distribute the key. It uses an algorithm called the Diffie-Hellman key exchange in which each side makes up a random number, does some math on it, and sends the result to the other side. Each side then mathematically combines its own number with the transmission it received to arrive at the same key. An eavesdropper might overhear the transmission but will be unable to reverse the math.[18]

DNSSEC

DNSSEC is a set of DNS extensions that authenticate the origin of zone data and verify its integrity by using public key cryptography. That is, the extensions permit DNS clients to ask the questions "Did this DNS data really come from the zone's owner?" and "Is this really the data sent by that owner?"

DNSSEC provides three distinct services: key distribution by means of KEY resource records stored in the zone files, origin verification for servers and data, and verification of the integrity of zone data. DNSSEC relies on a cascading chain of trust: the root servers provide validation information for the top-level domains, the top-level domains provide validation information for the second-level domains, and so on.

Public key cryptosystems use two keys: one to encrypt (sign) and a different one to decrypt (verify). Publishers sign their data with a secret "private" key. Anyone can

---

18. The math involved is called the discrete log problem and relies on the fact that for modular arithmetic, taking powers is easy but taking logs to undo the powers is close to impossible.

verify the validity of a signature with a matching "public" key that is widely distributed. If a public key correctly decrypts a zone file, then the zone must have been encrypted with the corresponding private key. The trick is to make sure that the public keys you use for verification are authentic. Public key systems allow one entity to sign the public key of another, thus vouching for the legitimacy of the key; hence the term "chain of trust."

The data in a DNS zone is too voluminous to be encrypted with public key cryptography—the encryption would be too slow. Instead, since the data is not secret, a secure hash (e.g., an MD5 checksum) is run on the data and the results of the hash are signed (encrypted) by the zone's private key. The results of the hash are like a fingerprint of the data. The signed fingerprint is called a digital signature.

Digital signatures are usually appended to the data they authenticate. To verify the signature, you decrypt it with the public key of the signer, run the data through the same secure hash algorithm, and compare the computed hash value with the decrypted hash value. If they match, you have authenticated the signer and verified the integrity of the data.

In the DNSSEC system, each zone has its own public and private keys. The private key signs each RRset (that is, each set of records of the same type for the same host). The public key verifies the signatures and is included in the zone's data in the form of a KEY resource record.

Parent zones sign their child zones' public keys. **named** verifies the authenticity of a child zone's KEY record by checking it against the parent zone's signature. To verify the authenticity of the parent zone's key, **named** can check the parent's parent, and so on back to the root. The public key for the root zone would be included in the root hints file.

Before we jump into the mechanics of generating keys and signing zones, we need to be honest about the current status of DNSSEC and its impact on sysadmins. Many applications are crying for a public key infrastructure ("PKI"), and DNS is a prime candidate for supplying it. However, we have a bit of a chicken and egg problem. We need to be sure that DNS is secure before we can trust it with our keys for other Internet transactions. But, we need a public key infrastructure in order to secure DNS.

Systems such as PGP (Pretty Good Privacy by Phil Zimmermann) rely on a "web of trust" concept. You will believe that something is my key if someone you trust says it is. The thought with DNSSEC is to build the web of trust from parent zone to child zone by signing keys and putting the signatures into the DNS data. We just need to bootstrap the process and allow for partial deployment.

Sysadmins may need to deal with DNSSEC in a year or two, but it is certainly not on the must-do-this-week list. Enough politics, now back to the mechanics of generating keys and signing your zones ...

Several steps are required to create and use signed zones. First, you generate a key pair for the zone. For example, in BIND 9,

```
# dnssec-keygen -a DSA -b 768 -n ZONE mydomain.com.
```

or in BIND 8,

```
# dnskeygen -D768 -z -n mydomain.com.
```

Table 16.12 shows the meanings of the arguments to these commands.

Table 16.12   Decoding guide for dnssec-keygen and dnskeygen arguments

Argument	Meaning
For **dnssec-keygen**	
-a DSA	Uses the DSA algorithm
-b 768	Creates a 768-bit key pair
-n ZONE mydomain.com.	Creates keys for a zone named mydomain.com
For **dnskeygen**	
-D768	Uses the DSA algorithm, with a 768-bit key
-z	Creates a zone key
-n mydomain.com.	Creates keys for a zone named mydomain.com

dnssec-keygen and **dnskeygen** return the following output:

```
alg = 003
key identifier = 12345         # a random key id string
flags = 16641
```

They also create files containing the public and private keys:

```
Kmydomain.com.+003+12345.key         # public key
Kmydomain.com.+003+12345.private     # private key
```

The private key is used for signing a zone's data records, and the public key is used for verifying signatures. The public key is typically put in the zone file right after the SOA record.

DNSSEC requires a chain of trust, so a zone's public key must be signed by its parent to be verifiably valid. BIND 8 had no mechanism to get a parent zone to sign a child zone's key other than out-of-band cooperation among administrators. BIND 9 provides a program called **dnssec-makekeyset** to help with this process.

dnssec-makekeyset bundles the keys you want signed (there may be more than just the zone key), a TTL for the resulting key set, and a signature validity period, then sends the bundle to the parent for signing. For example, the command

```
# dnssec-makekeyset -t 3600 -s +0 -e +864000 Kmydomain.com.+003+12345
```

bundles the public zone key that you just generated with a TTL of 3,600 seconds (one hour) and requests that the parent's signature be valid for 10 days starting from now.

dnssec-makekeyset creates a single output file, **keyset.mydomain.com**. You must then send the file to the parent zone for signing. It contains the public key and signatures generated by the zone keys themselves so that the parent can verify the child's public key.

In BIND 9, the parent zone uses the **dnssec-signkey** program to sign the bundled set of keys:

```
# dnssec-signkey keyset.mydomain.com Kcom.+003+56789
```

This command produces a file called **signedkey.mydomain.com**, which the parent (com) sends back to the child (mydomain.com) to be included in the zone files for mydomain.com. In BIND 8, the parent uses the **dnssigner** command.

Once you have obtained the parent's signature, you are ready to sign the zone's actual data. The signing operation takes a normal zone data file as input and adds SIG and NXT records immediately after every set of resource records. The SIG records are the actual signatures, and the NXT records support signing of negative answers.

In BIND 8, you use the **dnssigner** program in the **contrib** directory of the distribution to sign a zone; in BIND 9, you use the **dnssec-signzone** command. For example, the commands

```
# dnssigner -or mydomain.com -zi db.mydomain -zo
      db.mydomain.signed -k1 mydomain.com dsa 12345 -st   # BIND 8
# dnssec-signzone -o mydomain.com db.mydomain            # BIND 9
```

read the zone file **db.mydomain** and produce a signed version of the zone file called **db.mydomain.signed**. The BIND 8 command shows several statistics about the signing operation (requested by the **-st** parameter). In particular, it shows how long it took to sign the zone and shows what records were added or deleted. It can take a long time to sign a zone.

The zone signing process adds SIG and NXT records to each resource record set. The next example shows before and after views. Here's the before:

```
anchor       IN   A     128.138.242.1
             IN   A     128.138.243.140
             IN   MX    10 anchor
             IN   MX    99 @
awesome      IN   A     128.138.236.20
...
```

And the after:

```
$ORIGIN mydomain.com.
anchor              SIG    MX 3 3 3600 20001008023531 (20000908023531 12345
                           mydomain.com. BFEtOCT+y0dQPx7Am7gpxD9SjEl+
                           USuaE7qExUOrX22X7wjqJFJbqdo= )
                    SIG    A 3 3 3600 20001008023531 (20000908023531 12345
                           mydomain.com.BDwfBm2j6xFLoXttzvtuln9ZD+9q
                           UWBAwSBJVB06WJ/Rc6+F1ubj/fs= )
```

```
$TTL 7200 ; 2 hours
            SIG    NXT 3 3 7200 20001008023531 (20000908023531 12345
                   mydomain.com.BIMwxryI8NyfWupBe4JJmeRCCj1/
                   FnyPjxAuBOQKTRXX4FsaDrma1X4= )
            NXT    awesome ( A MX SIG NXT )
$TTL 3600 ; 1 hour
            A      128.138.242.1
            A      128.138.243.140
            MX     10 anchor
            MX     99 mydomain.com.
     ...
```

Signed zones are ugly. They are typically four times larger than the original zone, and your nice logical ordering is lost. Basically, a signed zone file is no longer human-readable and cannot be edited by hand because of the SIG and NXT records. No user-serviceable parts inside!

A SIG record contains a wealth of information:

- The type of record set being signed
- The signature algorithm used (in our case, it's 3, the DSA algorithm)
- The TTL of the record set that was signed
- The time the signature expires (as *yyyymmddhhssss*)
- The time the record set was signed (also *yyyymmddhhssss*)
- The key identifier (in our case, 12345)
- The signer's name (mydomain.com.)
- And finally, the digital signature itself

To use the signed zone, change the file parameter in the **named.conf** zone statement for mydomain.com to point at **db.mydomain.signed** instead of **db.mydomain**. In BIND 8, you must also include a pubkey statement in the zone statement; BIND 8 verifies the zone data as it loads and so must know the key beforehand. BIND 9 does not perform this verification. It gets the public key from the KEY record in the zone data and does not need any other configuration. Whew! That's it.

Digital signatures are fine for positive answers like "Here is the IP address for the host anchor.cs.colorado.edu, along with a signature to prove that it really came from cs.colorado.edu and that the data is valid." But what about negative answers like "No such host?" Such negative responses typically do not return any signable records.

In DNSSEC, this problem is handled by NXT records that list the next record in the zone in a canonical sorted order.[19] If the next record after anchor in cs.colorado.edu was awesome.cs.colorado.edu and a query for anthill.cs.colorado.edu arrived, the response would be a signed NXT record such as

```
anchor.cs.colorado.edu.    IN   NXT   awesome.cs.colorado.edu A MX NXT
```

---

19. The ordering is sort of alphabetical, but with names higher up the DNS tree coming first. For example, in the cs.colorado.edu zone, cs.colorado.edu comes before any host.cs.colorado.edu. Within a level of the hierarchy, the ordering is alphabetical.

This record says that the name immediately after anchor in the cs.colorado.edu zone is awesome and that anchor has at least one A record, MX record, and NXT record. The last NXT record in a zone wraps around to the first name in the zone. For example, the NXT record for zamboni.cs.colorado.edu would point back to the first record, that of cs.colorado.edu itself:

```
zamboni.cs.colorado.edu.  IN  NXT  cs.colorado.edu A MX NXT
```

NXT records are also returned if the host exists but the record type queried for does not exist. For example, if the query was for an LOC record for anchor, anchor's same NXT record would be returned and would show only A, MX, and NXT records.

NXT records supply an easy way to walk the zone, giving a persistent querier a complete zone transfer, one record at a time. Not good for security/privacy.

The material in this section describes DNSSEC as of BIND v9.2 (November, 2001). Judging from the significant changes that occurred since the first release of BIND 9, this information may not be correct for long. As always, consult your manuals and the documentation that comes with BIND for the exact details. That said, let's look at some potential problems with the current DNSSEC design.

DNSSEC is at odds with the notions of caching and forwarders. DNSSEC assumes that queries contact the root zone first and then follow referrals down the domain chain to get an answer. Each signed zone signs its children's keys, and the chain of trust is unbroken and verifiable. When you use a forwarder, however, the initial query is diverted from the root zone and sent to your forwarding server for processing. A caching server that is querying through a forwarder will recheck signatures, so responses are guaranteed to be secure. But, for the query to succeed, the forwarder must be capable of returning all the SIGs and KEYs needed for the signature checking. Non-DNSSEC servers don't know to do this, and the RFCs ignore the whole issue of forwarding.

BIND 9 implements some extra features beyond those required by RFC2535 so that a BIND 9 caching server can use DNSSEC through a BIND 9 forwarder. If you are using forwarders and want to use DNSSEC, you might have to run BIND 9 throughout your site.

Unfortunately, those busy sites that use forwarders and caching are probably the sites most interested in DNSSEC. Alas, the standards writers didn't quite think through all of the implications for the other parts of the DNS system.

DNSSEC also relies on the existence of a public key infrastructure that isn't quite a reality yet. There is no smooth way to get the parent to sign a child's keys; we cannot send mail to the hostmaster@com and get signed keys back. In the next few years we should start to see DNSSEC deployed, probably beginning with signed versions of the root zone and top-level country code zones in Europe. Sysadmins need to keep an eye on DNSSEC developments, but it's still too early (early 2002) to really worry about DNSSEC for now.

Another troubling issue with DNSSEC is that it increases the size of response packets because for each data response, we need to include SIG and NXT records too. That 512-byte UDP limit will start to come much earlier. As EDNS0 is deployed and more name servers can negotiate larger packet sizes, this issue should become progressively less menacing.

Transaction signatures (TSIG/TKEY) use less CPU time and network bandwidth than does public key authentication, but they guarantee only that you know where your responses came from, not that the responses are correct. A combination of a TSIG relationship with a server known to do full DNSSEC might provide a reasonable degree of security. It is not possible to have a TSIG relationship with every server you might ever want to talk to, since TSIG relationships must be manually configured.

Microsoft bad, Linux good

Windows 2000 uses SRV resource records to discover everything: name servers, printers, filesystems, and so forth. They have followed the IETF specs in their implementation of SRV records, but the way that they insert the records into DNS by using a secure dynamic update is nonstandard. Microsoft uses a variation of transaction signatures called GSS-TSIG that is also based on a shared secret. The shared secret is obtained through Kerberos from the Kerberos KDC (Key Distribution Center). At the moment, Microsoft's implementation uses the vendor extensions field and therefore is not compatible with the open source version of Kerberos 5. (Hmm... Embrace, extend, exterminate.)

If you want to run Win2K and use SRV records, you'll have to nuke your existing Kerberos realm and run a Win2K Kerberos server on your networks. For some sites with a rich Kerberos infrastructure, this problem is a showstopper. Microsoft seems to be using open protocols just enough to sneak past companies' purchasing checklists, but not enough to allow anyone else to interoperate and sell into their market. Hopefully, Microsoft will document their extensions without the currently required nondisclosure agreement so that ISC can make its TSIG and Microsoft's GSS-TSIG interoperate.

About a week after Win2K was released, the query load on the DNS root servers increased significantly. A bit of digging revealed that misconfigured Win2K boxes were trying to dynamically update the root or top-level zones. The number of UDP queries to the A root server more than doubled as a result. To make matters worse, when their update requests were refused, the Win2K boxes asked for a KEY record to try an authenticated update. This also failed, so they tried one final time by opening a TCP connection to attempt an authenticated dynamic update. A root server does not have time for the zillions of TCP connection requests that resulted. As we go to press, the situation is somewhat better now but still not completely resolved, with root server operators pointing fingers at Microsoft and Microsoft saying "No, no, not us!"

To stop Win2K boxes from attempting to update the root zones and make them play more nicely with your Linux name servers, try the following procedure.

- Right-click on My Network Places and select Properties, which displays a window labeled Network and Dial-up Connections.

- Right-click on each connection in turn and select Properties.

- Click on Internet Protocol (TCP/IP), then click the Properties button.

- Click the Advanced... button at the bottom of the properties page.

- Click the DNS tab at the top.

- Toward the bottom of the page remove the check from the "Register this connection's address in DNS" line.

- Click OK all the way out.

You may also find your Win2K systems flooding your network with DNS queries. Win2K doesn't follow the specification and query one source at a time but rather sends parallel queries asking the same question, with very low timeouts. By default, every Win2K box is configured to be a caching name server with nasty habits. You can turn off this behavior with the following sequence of steps:

- Select Settings->Control Panel from the Start menu.

- In the control panel, double-click Administrative Tools.

- On the Administrative Tools page, double-click Computer Management.

- On the left side, click the "+" next to Services and Applications to expand it.

- Select Services on the left side and double-click DNS Client on the right side.

- Click the pull-down menu beside "Startup type" and select Manual.

- Click the Stop button to halt the already running DNS client.

- Click OK all the way out.

At this point, it's best to avoid Microsoft's DNS implementation as much as possible. You will probably want to point your Win2K boxes at a Linux name server to gain full DNS functionality without the shotgun blasts of unnecessary traffic generated by Microsoft's "creativity."

Microsoft servers raise a ruckus when they query a zone whose servers are all lame. If your site delegates to servers that appear to be lame, it's good practice to at least install an empty zone file that substitutes for the missing servers. This measure will prevent Microsoft servers that query for the lame name from becoming confused and pummeling the root and gTLD servers.

16.14 TESTING AND DEBUGGING

named provides several built-in debugging aids, foremost among which is its voluptuously configurable logging. You can specify debug levels on the command line or set them with **ndc/rndc**. You can also instruct **named** to dump its operating statistics to a file and verify name lookups with external tools such as **dig**.

Logging

*See Chapter 11 for
more information
about syslog.*

named's logging facilities are flexible enough to make your hair stand on end. BIND 4 used syslog to report error messages and anomalies. BIND 8 generalizes the concepts of syslog by adding another layer of indirection and support for logging directly to files. Before we dive in, let's take a look at the mini-glossary of BIND logging terms shown in Table 16.13.

Table 16.13   A BIND logging lexicon

Term	What it means
channel	A place where messages can go: syslog, a file, or **/dev/null**
category	A class of messages that **named** can generate; for example, messages about dynamic updates or messages about answering queries
module	The name of the source module that generates a message (BIND 9 only)
facility	A syslog facility name. DNS does not have its own specific facility, but you have your pick of all the standard ones.
severity	The "badness" of an error message; what syslog refers to as a priority

You configure BIND logging with a logging statement in **named.conf**. You first define channels, the possible destinations for messages. You then tell various categories of message to go to particular channels.

When a message is generated, it is assigned a category, a module (in BIND 9), and a severity at its point of origin. It is then distributed to all the channels associated with its category and module. Each channel has a severity filter that tells what severity level a message must have in order to get through. Channels that lead to syslog are also filtered according to the rules in **/etc/syslog.conf**.

Here's the outline of a logging statement:

```
logging {
    channel_def;
    channel_def;
    …
    category category_name {
        channel_name;
        channel_name;
        …
    };
};
```

A *channel_def* looks slightly different depending on whether the channel is a file channel or a syslog channel. You must choose file or syslog for each channel; a channel can't be both at the same time.

```
channel channel_name {

    file path [versions numvers | unlimited] [size sizespec];
    syslog facility;

    severity severity;
    print-category yes | no;
    print-severity yes | no;
    print-time yes | no;
};
```

For a file channel, *numvers* tells how many backup versions of a file to keep, and *sizespec* specifies how large the file should be allowed to grow (examples: 2048, 100k, 20m, 15g, unlimited, default) before it is automatically rotated. If you name a file channel **mylog**, then the rotated versions will be **mylog.0**, **mylog.1**, and so on.

See page 208 for a list of syslog facility names. In the syslog case, *facility* specifies what facility name is used to log the message. It can be any standard facility. In practice, only daemon and local0 through local7 are reasonable choices.

The rest of the statements in a *channel_def* are optional. *severity* can have the values (in descending order) critical, error, warning, notice, info, or debug (with an optional numeric level, e.g., severity debug 3). The value dynamic is also recognized and matches the server's current debug level.

The various print options add or suppress message prefixes. Syslog prepends the time and reporting host to each message logged, but not the severity or the category. In BIND 9, the source filename (module) that generated the message is also available as a print option. It makes sense to enable print-time only for file channels; no need to duplicate syslog's time.

The four channels listed in Table 16.14 are predefined by default. The default channels should be fine for most installations.

Table 16.14   Predefined logging channels in BIND

Channel name	What it does
default_syslog	Sends to syslog, facility daemon, severity info
default_debug	Logs to file **named.run**, severity set to dynamic
default_stderr	Sends to standard error of the **named** process, severity info
null	Discards all messages

Table 16.15 on page 450 shows the current list of message categories for BIND 8 and 9. BIND 9 categories are in a bit of flux; see the source code files

lib/dns/include/dns/log.h
bin/named/include/named/log.h

for a list of current categories.

Table 16.15   BIND logging categories

Category	Vers	What it includes
cname	8	Messages of the form "… points to a CNAME"
eventlib	8	Debugging info from the event system [a]
insist	8	Internal consistency check failures
load	8	Zone loading messages
maintenance	8	Periodic maintenance events
ncache	8	Messages about negative caching
os	8	Operating system problems
packet	8	Dumps of packets received and sent [a]
panic	8	Fatal errors (duplicated onto this category)
parser	8	Low-level configuration file processing
response-checks	8	Commentary on malformed or invalid response packets
config	8/9	Configuration file parsing and processing
db/database	8/9	Messages about database operations
default	8/9	Categories with no explicit channel assignments [b]
lame-servers	8/9	Servers that are supposed to be serving a zone, but aren't [c]
notify	8/9	Messages about the "zone changed" notification protocol
queries	8/9	A short log message for every query the server receives (!)
security	8/9	Approved/unapproved requests
statistics	8/9	Name server aggregate statistics
update	8/9	Messages about dynamic updates
xfer-in	8/9	Zone transfers that the server is receiving
xfer-out	8/9	Zone transfers that the server is sending
client	9	Client requests
dnssec	9	DNSSEC messages
general	9	Unclassified messages
network	9	Network operations
resolver	9	DNS resolution, e.g., recursive lookups for clients

a. Must be a single file channel.
b. The default category is also the catchall category for unclassified messages in BIND 8.
c. Either the parent zone or the child zone could be at fault; it's impossible to tell without investigating.

The default logging configuration for BIND 8 is

```
logging {
     category default { default_syslog; default_debug; };
     category panic { default_syslog; default_stderr; };
     category eventlib { default_debug; };
     category packet { default_debug; };
};
```

and for BIND 9 it is

```
logging {
    category default { default_syslog; default_debug; };
};
```

You should watch the log files when you make major changes to BIND and perhaps increase the logging level. Then, reconfigure to preserve only serious messages once **named** is stable.

Query logging can be quite educational. You can verify that your allow clauses are working, see who is querying you, identify broken clients, etc. Writing to syslog is less efficient than writing to a file directly, so use a file channel on a local disk when you are logging every query. Have lots of disk space and be ready to turn query logging off once you get enough data. Query logging is a good check to perform after major reconfigurations, especially if you have archived what your query load used to look like before the changes. To start query logging, just direct the queries category to a channel. **rndc querylog** toggles query logging on and off in BIND 9.

Some common log messages are listed below:

- *Lame server.* If you get this message about one of your own zones, you have configured something incorrectly. The message is relatively harmless if it's about some zone out on the Internet; it's someone else's problem. A good one to throw away by directing it to the null channel.

- *Bad referral.* This message indicates a miscommunication among a zone's name servers.

- *Not authoritative for.* A slave server is unable to get authoritative data for a zone. Perhaps it's pointing to the wrong master, or perhaps the master had trouble loading the zone in question.

- *Rejected zone.* **named** rejected a zone file because it contained errors.

- *No NS RRs found.* A zone file did not have NS records after the SOA record. It could be that the records are missing, or it could be they don't start with a tab or other whitespace. In the latter case, the records are not attached to the zone of the SOA record and are therefore misinterpreted.

- *No default TTL set.* The preferred way to set the default TTL is with a $TTL clause at the top of the zone file. This error message indicates that the $TTL is missing. In BIND 8 it defaults to the value of the *minimum* parameter from the SOA record.[20] In BIND 9, the $TTL is required; **named** refuses to load zone files that do not specify a $TTL.

- *No root nameserver for class.* Your server is having trouble finding the root name servers. Check your hints file and the server's Internet connectivity.

---

20. The meaning of *minimum* changed in BIND 8.2 from the default TTL for all records to the default TTL for negative caching.

- *Address already in use.* The port on which **named** wants to run is already being used by another process, probably another copy of **named**. If you don't see another **named** around, it might have crashed and left an **ndc** control socket open that you'll have to track down and remove.[21] A good way to fix it is to stop and restart the **named** process:

  ```
  % sudo /etc/init.d/named stop (or /sbin/service named stop)
  % sudo /etc/init.d/named start (or /sbin/service named start)
  ```

- *Dropping source port zero packet from …* Recent versions of BIND let you set the query source port number, and sysadmins use this feature to add rules to their firewalls that can recognize their DNS packets by source port. However, 0 is an illegal value for a TCP/UDP port number. If the error message relates to one of your hosts, you should change the query-source directive in that host's **named.conf** file to fix this error.

- *Denied update from […] for …* A dynamic update for a zone was attempted and denied because of the allow-update or update-policy clause in **named.conf** for this zone.

You can find a nice table of BIND error messages at

> http://www.acmebw.com/askmrdns/bind-messages.html

Debug levels

named debug levels are indicated by integers from 0 to 11. The higher the number, the more verbose the output. Level 0 turns debugging off. Levels 1 and 2 are fine for debugging your configuration and database. Levels beyond about 4 are appropriate for the maintainers of the code.

You invoke debugging on the **named** command line with the **-d** flag. For example,

```
# named -d2
```

would start **named** at debug level 2. By default, debugging information is written to the file **named.run** in the current working directory from which **named** is started. The **named.run** file grows very fast, so don't go out for a beer while debugging or you will have bigger problems when you return.

You can also turn on debugging while **named** is running with **ndc trace**, which increments the debug level by 1. **ndc notrace** turns debugging off completely. (Unfortunately, **rndc** does not support these commands.) You can also enable debugging by defining a logging channel that includes a severity specification such as

```
severity debug 3
```

which sends all debugging messages up to level 3 to that particular channel. Other lines in the channel definition specify the destination of those debugging messages. The higher the severity level, the more information is logged.

---

21. On a gTLD server, this message probably means that com is still loading. :-)

Watching the logs or the debugging output illustrates how often DNS data is miscon-figured. That pesky little dot at the end of names (or rather, the lack thereof) accounts for an alarming amount of DNS traffic. Theoretically, the dot is required at the end of each fully qualified domain name.

Debugging with ndc

The **ndc** command (called **rndc** in BIND 9) is a useful tool for manipulating **named**. Table 16.16 shows some of the options it accepts. Commands that produce files put them in the directory specified as **named**'s home in **named.conf**.

Table 16.16   Useful ndc and rndc commands

Command	Function
help	Lists the available **ndc** commands
status	Displays current status of the running **named**
start (V8)	Starts **named**
stop	Halts **named** and in V9, saves pending updates
halt (V9)	Halts **named** without doing pending updates
trace	Increments the debug level by 1[a]
notrace	Turns off debugging[a]
dumpdb	Dumps DNS database to **named_dump.db**
stats	Dumps statistics to **named.stats**
flush (V9)	Flushes server's cache
reload	Reloads **named.conf** and zone files
reload *zone*	Reloads only the specified *zone*
reconfig	Reloads config file and any new zones
querylog	Toggles tracing of incoming queries

a. Not in **rndc**

ndc reload makes **named** reread its configuration file and reload zone files. The **ndc reload** *zone* command is handy, especially on a busy server, when only one zone has changed and you don't want to reload all zones.

ndc dumpdb makes **named** dump its database to **named_dump.db**. The dump file is big and includes not only local data but also any cached data that the name server has accumulated. A recent dump of the database cache on our primary colorado.edu name server was over 16MB, but the zone data loaded was less than 200K. Lots of caching there.

In split DNS situations where you have one **named** process handling the internal zone and another handling the external zone, **ndc** does not give you enough control. You cannot specify the PID of the **named** you want to control. Also, if you are running **named** in a **chroot**ed environment, you will have to give **ndc** the path to the **ndc** socket because it will not be in **/var/run** where **ndc** expects it. Use something like:

```
# sudo ndc -l /var/named/var/run/ndc
```

In BIND 9, it's important to make sure that the version of **named** and the version of **rndc** match, lest you get an error message about a protocol version mismatch. Just install both when you upgrade. Each new release moves **rndc** closer to the functionality of **ndc** in BIND 8. Signals in BIND 9 no longer work for controlling **named**. SIGHUP will reload the configuration file and zone files; any other signal will kill the running **named**.

Statistics for BIND 8

The BIND 8 version of **named** keeps a record of query statistics that you can access with **ndc stats.** Running this command makes **named** write the statistics to the file **named.stats**. A sample stats file from a cs.colorado.edu server that has been up for 83 days is shown below. This information is normally printed in one long column, but we compressed it a bit by deleting entries for obsolete or unused resource record types. We also reformatted the lower section; it's normally one long line of values.

```
+++ Statistics Dump +++ (1008202999) Wed Dec 12 17:23:19 2001

2612979    time since boot (secs)
2612979    time since reset (secs)
9          Unknown query types
1230669    A queries
7          NS queries
0          CNAME queries
8075       SOA queries
705639     PTR queries
41366      MX queries
384370     TXT queries
7198       AAAA queries
6          SRV queries
353057     ANY queries

++ Name Server Statistics ++
```

RR	RNXD	RFwdR	RDupR	RFail	RFErr	RErr	RAXFR	RLame
428444	33365	163125	21179	112775	0	450	0	27388

ROpts	SSysQ	SAns	SFwdQ	SDupQ	SErr	RQ	RIQ	RFwdQ
0	84483	2587274	273517	520533	0	2730553	0	273517

RDupQ	RTCP	SFwdR	SFail	SFErr	SNaAns	SNXD
3272	26671	163125	0	0	753041	166469

The number of TXT queries seems abnormally high. At first we thought someone was trolling for addresses to spam or machines to hack into. But then we remembered that the campus uses the Hesiod class to store mail home and mail name (*first.last*) information for each user in TXT records.

The cryptic data at the end counts things like the number of duplicate queries, duplicate responses, and lame delegations seen by this server. The initial letter in the abbreviations stands for received (R) or sent (S); the final letter indicates query (Q) or response (R). The real meaning of these headings is documented in the code, where a brief comment identifies each abbreviation—see the file **ns_stats.c** beneath the **bin/named** directory in the BIND 8 distribution. A less painful way to decode these abbreviations is to read the statistics section in the O'Reilly DNS book.

Any query that results in an error is logged, counted in one or more statistics buckets, and dropped. The category Unknown query types includes any query for a resource record type that the server does not recognize. As new record types are standardized, they show up in this column until the name servers have been upgraded to include the new record types. The ANY bucket is not a real resource record type; it counts queries that ask for any and all information a server might have about a particular name. The Dup entries in the bottom half of the output represent duplicate queries or responses. Duplicates normally occur when a query times out before its answer has been received; the querier then resubmits the query.

In BIND 8, **ndc stats** also produces memory statistics in the file **named.memstats** if deallocate-on-exit is set. BIND 9 memory statistics can be accessed only through **named**'s debug mode.

Statistics for BIND 9

BIND 9 does not gather query statistics to the same extent that BIND 8 does, but it does maintain some summary information. **named** dumps the information to the file **named.stats** in its working directory on receipt of a nudge from **rndc**:

```
% sudo rndc stats
```

Here's an example of the output:

```
+++ Statistics Dump +++ (1008196810)
success 30647
referral 18
nxrrset 1405
nxdomain 6833
recursion 13630
failure 1699
--- Statistics Dump --- (1008196810)
```

The statistics show the success vs. failure of lookups and categorize the various kinds of errors. This server answered 30,647 queries successfully and failed to answer 9,937 times. The biggest contributor to the failures was the nxdomain error, which occurs when the requested hostname is unknown.

The 6,833 nxdomain errors would be way too many if their primary source were user typos and spelling errors. In this case, the errors actually derive from a bug in Microsoft's resolver[22] that sends out many queries for A (address) records with the data field set to an IP address rather than a hostname as required by the DNS specification. These bizarre queries have an apparent top-level domain of something like 56 (or whatever the last byte of the IP address string was), so they send the local DNS

---

22. Microsoft has fixed this for Win2K in Service Pack 2.

server scurrying off to nag the root servers about this nonexistent domain, ultimately yielding an nxdomain error.[23]

The failure entry counts the failures that are neither nxdomain (no such domain) nor nxrrset (no such resource record set).

Debugging with nslookup, dig, and host

Three tools can be used from the shell to query the DNS database: **nslookup**, **dig**, and **host**. Each is distributed with BIND 8. **nslookup** is the oldest of these tools and has always been part of the BIND distribution. **dig**, the domain information groper, was originally written by Steve Hotz; it has been rewritten for BIND 9 by Michael Sawyer and is shipped with BIND 9 as well. **host**, by Eric Wassenaar, is another open source tool; it features user-friendly output and functions to check the syntax of your zone files.

We discuss each of these tools below but recommend **dig** over **nslookup**; we like **host**, too. You might sometimes get different results from these tools because of the different resolver libraries that they use. **dig** and **host** use BIND's resolver, and **nslookup** has its own.

nslookup is a user-level command that queries the DNS database. It expects fully qualified names ending in a dot and appends the default domain if you forget the dot. For local names, this behavior is often what you want. Table 16.17 gives a short list of **nslookup** commands.

Table 16.17   Commands understood by nslookup

Command	Function
name	Prints info about the host or domain *name*
help or **?**	Shows a complete list of commands
exit	Quits
server *host*	Sets the default server, using the current server
lserver *host*	Sets the default server, using the initial server
set type=*xxx*	Sets the record types to query for[a]
set debug	Turns on debugging
set d2	Turns on lots of debugging
ls *domain*	Lists all host/address mappings

a. **any** is a good value that means "all record types."

dig provides the same rough functionality as **nslookup**, but it has more sensible defaults, provides more information, and has a nicer user interface (especially when compared to older versions of **nslookup**).

---

23. The severity of the problem is even more apparent when you consider that in this instance, all of the bogus queries were generated by a *single* machine running Windows 2000.

For example, to ask for anchor's MX records, use

> % **dig anchor.cs.colorado.edu. mx**

The command

> % **dig @ns1.berkeley.edu vangogh.berkeley.edu. any**

obtains vangogh's complete records from a berkeley.edu server, and

> % **dig -x 128.32.33.5**

performs a reverse query for vangogh. Be careful with the *@nameserver.somewhere* syntax; if the server does not exist, **dig** uses its local server and returns the answer to you. This is good backup behavior, but not always what you want.

Here is an example that uses **host**, **dig**, and **nslookup** to obtain the same data:

```
% nslookup
Default Server:  bb.rc.vix.com
Address:  204.152.187.11
> set type=any
> amazon.com.
Server:  bb.rc.vix.com
Address:  204.152.187.11
Non-authoritative answer:
amazon.com          nameserver = AUTH00.NS.UU.NET
amazon.com          nameserver = NS2.PNAP.NET
amazon.com          nameserver = NS1.PNAP.NET
amazon.com          nameserver = NS-1.amazon.com
amazon.com          preference = 10, mail exchanger = service-4.amazon.com
amazon.com          preference = 10, mail exchanger = service-5.amazon.com
amazon.com          internet address = 208.216.182.15
Authoritative answers can be found from:
amazon.com          nameserver = AUTH00.NS.UU.NET
amazon.com          nameserver = NS2.PNAP.NET
amazon.com          nameserver = NS1.PNAP.NET
amazon.com          nameserver = NS-1.amazon.com
AUTH00.NS.UU.NET    internet address = 198.6.1.65
NS2.PNAP.NET        internet address = 206.253.194.97
NS1.PNAP.NET        internet address = 206.253.194.65
NS-1.amazon.com     internet address = 209.191.164.20
service-4.amazon.com internet address = 209.191.164.50
service-5.amazon.com internet address = 209.191.164.51
```

nslookup returns four NS records, two MX records, and an A record. It also provides the IP addresses of the name servers and MX hosts.

```
% dig amazon.com. any
; <<>> DiG 8.3 <<>> amazon.com any
;; res options: init recurs defnam dnsrch
;; got answer:
;; ->>HEADER<<- opcode: QUERY, status: NOERROR, id: 4
;; flags: qr rd ra; QUERY: 1, ANSWER: 7, AUTHORITY: 4, ADDITIONAL: 6
```

```
;; QUERY SECTION:
;;      amazon.com, type = ANY, class = IN
;; ANSWER SECTION:
amazon.com.              1h27m11s  IN  NS  AUTH00.NS.UU.NET.
amazon.com.              1h27m11s  IN  NS  NS2.PNAP.NET.
amazon.com.              1h27m11s  IN  NS  NS1.PNAP.NET.
amazon.com.              1h27m11s  IN  NS  NS-1.amazon.com.
amazon.com.              59m22s    IN  MX  10 service-4.amazon.com.
amazon.com.              59m22s    IN  MX  10 service-5.amazon.com.
amazon.com.              1h59m29s  IN  A   208.216.182.15
;; AUTHORITY SECTION:
amazon.com.              1h27m11s  IN  NS  AUTH00.NS.UU.NET.
amazon.com.              1h27m11s  IN  NS  NS2.PNAP.NET.
amazon.com.              1h27m11s  IN  NS  NS1.PNAP.NET.
amazon.com.              1h27m11s  IN  NS  NS-1.amazon.com.
;; ADDITIONAL SECTION:
AUTH00.NS.UU.NET.        13h11m20s IN  A   198.6.1.65
NS2.PNAP.NET.            20h51m44s IN  A   206.253.194.97
NS1.PNAP.NET.            20h51m44s IN  A   206.253.194.65
NS-1.amazon.com.         59m22s    IN  A   209.191.164.20
service-4.amazon.com.    59m22s    IN  A   209.191.164.50
service-5.amazon.com.    59m22s    IN  A   209.191.164.51
;; Total query time: 7 msec
;; FROM: bb.rc.vix.com to SERVER: default -- 204.152.187.11
;; WHEN: Sun Jul  2 12:45:59 2000
;; MSG SIZE  sent: 28  rcvd: 338
```

dig is verbose. Its output includes not only the same domain information but also the number of queries sent and the answers' round trip time. The output is formatted correctly to be used in a zone file, which is particularly handy when you are querying for the root servers for your hints file.

host provides terse-but-friendly output by default, but it can be made more verbose with the **-v** option (although not as verbose as **dig**). It expects the domain you are querying to end in a dot. If you look up a relative name, **host** first tries appending the domains in your **resolv.conf** file; if none of them work, **host** simply appends the dot.

```
% host amazon.com.
amazon.com has address 208.216.182.15
amazon.com mail is handled (pri=10) by service-4.amazon.com
amazon.com mail is handled (pri=10) by service-5.amazon.com
```

When testing a new configuration, be sure that you look up data for both local and remote hosts. If you can access a host by IP address but not by name, DNS is probably the culprit.

Lame delegations

When you apply for a domain name, you are asking for a part of the DNS naming tree to be delegated to your primary name server and your DNS administrator. If you never use the domain or you change the name servers without updating the parent domain's glue records, a "lame delegation" results.

The effects of a lame delegation can be very bad. If a user tries to contact a host in your lame domain, your name server will refuse the query. DNS will retry the query several hundred times, pummeling both your master server and the root servers. BIND uses a lame server "penalty box" to help with the load created by lameness, but Microsoft servers do not implement it.

In one log file that was 3.5MB (at level info) after almost a week, over one-third of the entries were lame delegations. Of those, 16% involved queries to the root servers, presumably for nonexistent domains. One persistent user queried the root servers for tokyotopless.net hundreds of times. Sigh. Here is an example:

```
Jan 29 05:34:52 ipn.caida.org named[223]: Lame server on 'www.games.net' (in
     'GAMES.net'?): [207.82.198.150].53 'NS2.EXODUS.net'
```

Here's how we'd track down the problem with **dig**; we truncated some of **dig**'s verbose output:

```
% dig www.games.net.
;; ...
;; QUESTIONS:
;;      www.games.net, type = A, class = IN
;; ANSWERS:
www.games.net.        3600    A    209.1.23.92
;; AUTHORITY RECORDS:
games.net.            3600    NS   ns.exodus.net.
games.net.            3600    NS   ns2.exodus.net.
games.net.            3600    NS   ns.pcworld.com.
;; ADDITIONAL RECORDS: ...
```

The first query at the local server returns the address record for www.games.net and a list of authoritative servers.

The server at ns.exodus.net worked fine when we queried it (not shown), but ns2.exodus.net is another story:

```
% dig @ns2.exodus.net www.games.net.
;; QUESTIONS:
;;      www.games.net, type = A, class = IN
;; AUTHORITY RECORDS:
net.              244362 NS   F.GTLD-SERVERS.net.
net.              244362 NS   J.GTLD-SERVERS.net.
net.              244362 NS   K.GTLD-SERVERS.net.
net.              244362 NS   A.GTLD-SERVERS.net.
;; ...
```

ns2 is listed as an authoritative server for the domain, but it returns no records and refers us to the servers for the net top-level domain. Therefore, we can conclude that ns2.exodus.net is configured incorrectly. Sometimes when you **dig** at an authoritative server in an attempt to find lameness, **dig** returns no information; try it again with the **+norecurse** flag so you can see exactly what the server in question knows.

16.15 LOOSE ENDS

This section includes a few loose ends and examples that should have come earlier in the chapter, but for which we just couldn't find the right place. We collect them here, in no particular order.

The hints file

The hints file primes **named**'s cache with information about the servers of the root domain. Putting the root servers in the cache bootstraps the lookup process for all other names. If you don't provide a hints file, BIND 9 uses a list of root servers hardwired into its code and will be able to load the root zone anyway as long as the addresses of the root servers don't all change between when you installed BIND 9 and when you need the root zone's name servers. All earlier versions of BIND require a hints file. (If you supply a hints file for BIND 9, it overrides the hardwired hints.)

The root name servers change from time to time, but it's easier to track them down than it used to be because they are all assigned hostnames in the root-servers.net domain. Use the sample file below for reference only.

If you already have access to a system with a running name server, you can have **dig** contact a root name server and generate the hints file for you. The master server is currently a.root-servers.net, but any of the root servers will do:

```
% dig @f.root-servers.net . ns > root.cache
```

Mind the dot. If f.root-servers.net is not responding, you can run the query without specifying a particular server:

```
% dig . ns > root.cache
```

The output will be similar; however, you will be obtaining the list of root servers from the cache of a local name server, not from an authoritative source. That should be just fine. Even if you have not rebooted or restarted your name server for a year or two, it has been refreshing its root server records periodically as their TTLs expire. When **named** starts, it reloads the hints from one of the root servers. Ergo, you'll be fine as long as your hints file contains at least one valid reachable root server.

Here's what the cache file looks like:

```
; <<>> DiG 8.2 <<>> @f.root-servers.net . ns
; Lots of detailed dig info formatted as comments here...

.                        1d1h42m  IN  NS  E.ROOT-SERVERS.NET.
.                        1d1h42m  IN  NS  D.ROOT-SERVERS.NET.
.                        1d1h42m  IN  NS  A.ROOT-SERVERS.NET.
.                        1d1h42m  IN  NS  H.ROOT-SERVERS.NET.
...
```

```
E.ROOT-SERVERS.NET.   2d1h42m  IN   A    192.203.230.10
D.ROOT-SERVERS.NET.   2d1h42m  IN   A    128.8.10.90
A.ROOT-SERVERS.NET.   2d1h42m  IN   A    198.41.0.4
H.ROOT-SERVERS.NET.   2d1h42m  IN   A    128.63.2.53
...
```

Note the dots that begin the first set of records; they are not fly specks but rather they define the domain (the root) to which the NS records apply. Some versions of **dig** show the TTL in seconds instead of days, minutes, and seconds.

A current hints file can also be obtained by anonymous FTP from rs.internic.net in the file domain/named.root. Comments in this version of the root hints file show the old names of the root servers, which hint at their historic locations. This file is also mirrored at ftp://ftp.nic.mil/domain/named.root.

Localhost configuration

The forward mapping for the name localhost or localhost.*domain* is done in the forward zone file for the domain. Each server is usually the master for its own reverse localhost domain, however. Here is a sample zone file:

```
@           IN   SOA  cs.colorado.edu. hostmaster.cs.colorado.edu. (
                      1996110801  ; Serial number
                      3600        ; Refresh
                      900         ; Retry
                      3600000     ; Expire
                      14400 )     ; Minimum
            IN   NS   cs.colorado.edu.
1           IN   PTR  localhost.cs.colorado.edu.
```

The reverse mapping for the localhost address (127.0.0.1) never changes, so the timeouts can be large. Note the serial number, which encodes the date; the file was last changed in 1996. Also note that only the master name server is listed for the localhost domain. The meaning of @ here is "0.0.127.in-addr.arpa.".

Host management tools

DNS database files often span local administrative and political domains. In many cases, tight central control is unfeasible. This situation presents a common administration problem: How do you manage critical (but fragile) data files that many untrained people may need to edit at random times? It would also be nice if the physics department could not change the engineering department's records, and vice versa.

If a political domain contains several hosts and has an administrative staff, then a subdomain is a good way to distribute control. But for a small department with only a few hosts, a subdomain is not necessary.

addhost is available from ftp.xor.com.

This data is a good candidate for an LDAP database that holds organization-wide host data and for tools that build individual departments' zone files. We use an ancient, crufty, home-grown tool called **addhost**, but we intend to change to LDAP as soon as we can assign it as a student project.

DNS for systems not on the Internet

See page 676 for more information about firewalls.

If you are not part of the Internet but want to use DNS, you can declare your primary name server to be authoritative for the root domain. This configuration might be appropriate for either a small company that is not yet on the Internet or for an organization that hides its local structure behind a firewall.

In this setup, your hints file should point to local name servers, not to the root servers of the Internet. You should still get a registered domain name and legitimate IP addresses or perhaps use the RFC1918 private addresses described on page 255.

16.16 DISTRIBUTION SPECIFICS

Each of our reference Linux distributions ships BIND as its default name server software. This section describes the details of each distribution's software and its default configuration.

Versions

Table 16.4 on page 369 summarizes the versions of BIND that each distribution includes. The current ISC distributions (8.2.5 and 9.2.0) both build on Linux just fine if you are inclined to upgrade. If you are using BIND 9, upgrading to the latest stable release is a good idea; new features are being added regularly, bugs are being fixed, and performance is being enhanced. BIND 9 is still slower than BIND 8 or 4, however.

BIND files

A Linux box that is a BIND client specifies its default domain, the other domains to search when names are not fully qualified, and the IP addresses of its local name servers in the file **/etc/resolv.conf**. A Linux host that acts as a BIND server also uses the **named** files listed in Table 16.18.

Table 16.18   BIND files in Linux

File	Directory	Description
resolv.conf	**/etc**	Resolver library configuration file
named	**/usr/sbin**	Name server daemon
named-xfer	**/usr/sbin**	Zone transfer code
named.conf	**/etc**	Config file for name server in Red Hat and SuSE
named.conf	**/etc/bind**	Config file for name server in Debian Linux
named.pid	**/var/run**	Process ID of the running **named**
named.run	*directory*[a]	Output from debug mode
named.stats	*directory*[a]	Statistics output
named.memstats	*directory*[a]	Memory usage statistics (BIND 8 only)
named_dump.db	*directory*[a]	Dump of the entire database

a. The directory specified in **/etc/named.conf** as the home for BIND files

The man page for **named** says that the debugging and statistics files are located in **/var/tmp**. This is a lie, probably a remnant of the man page distributed with the BIND package from ISC.

The name server switch file

Linux includes a switch file, **/etc/nsswitch.conf,** that specifies how hostname-to-IP-address mappings should be done and whether DNS should be tried first, last, or not at all. If there is no switch file present, the default behavior is

```
hosts:  dns [!UNAVAIL=return] files
```

The !UNAVAIL clause means that if DNS is available but a name is not found there, the lookup attempt should fail rather than continuing to the next entry (in this case, the **/etc/hosts** file). If no name server were running (as might be the case during the boot process), the lookup process *would* consult the **hosts** file.

Our example distributions use various defaults for host lookups:

```
hosts:  db files nisplus nis dns    # Red Hat
hosts:  files dns                   # SuSE
hosts:  files dns                   # Debian
```

There is really no "best" way to configure the lookups. It depends on how your site is managed. In general, we prefer to keep as much host information as possible in DNS rather than NIS or flat files. Therefore, we like the default when there is no switch file (dns if **named** is running; otherwise, files). The SuSE and Debian defaults are also OK, provided that the **hosts** file is not too large.

Configuration files

Red Hat and SuSE provide sample **/etc/named.conf** files with good comments. They seem to restate the BIND defaults in many cases, but they also comment on what the various options mean and where their settings vary from the defaults. Both Red Hat and SuSE use the default home directory, **/var/named**, for **named**. Red Hat includes the ISC distribution's documentation and sample zone files in **/usr/doc/bind-9.1.0**. SuSE has them in **/usr/share/doc/packages/bind8**. SuSE includes DNS documentation from the Linux documentation project in

/usr/share/doc/howtoen/html/DNS-HOWTO.html.

Debian provides a sample **named.conf** file and zone files for localhost in the directory **/etc/bind**. Debian sets BIND's default directory to **/var/cache/bind**; as shipped, the directory exists but is empty. Debian's sample **named.conf** file does not need to be modified if you want to run a caching-only server. If you are authoritative for some zones, you must add them to the supplied **named.conf** file.

The directory **/usr/share/doc/bind** contains several useful references. Check out the **README.Debian** file there to understand Debian's strategy for configuring BIND.

16.17 RECOMMENDED READING

DNS and BIND are described by a variety of sources, including the documentation that comes with the distribution, chapters in several books on Internet topics, an entire book in the O'Reilly Nutshell series, and various on-line resources.

Mailing lists and newsgroups

The following mailing lists are associated with BIND:

- bind-announce – mail bind-announce-request@isc.org
- namedroppers – mail namedroppers-request@internic.net

and specifically for BIND 8:

- bind-users – mail bind-users-request@isc.org to join
- bind-workers – mail bind-workers-request@isc.org (for code warriors)

and BIND 9:

- bind9-users – mail bind-users-request@isc.org to join
- bind9-workers – mail bind-workers-request@isc.org (for code warriors)

Send bug reports to bind-bugs@isc.org or bind9-bugs@isc.org.

Books and other documentation

THE NOMINUM BIND DEVELOPMENT TEAM. *BINDv9 Administrator Reference Manual.* Available in the BIND distribution (**doc/arm**) from www.isc.org.

This document outlines the administration and management of BIND 9. An earlier document, the *Bind Operations Guide*, or BOG as it is called, describes in detail the operation and configuration of BIND 4. The BOG is included in BIND distributions up through version 8.

ALBITZ, PAUL, AND CRICKET LIU. *DNS and BIND, 4th Edition.* Sebastopol, CA: O'Reilly, 2001.

This popular and well-respected book about BIND includes coverage of both BIND 8 and BIND 9, with a bit of BIND 4 thrown in for good measure. It is very complete.

On-line resources

The DNS Resources Directory, www.dns.net/dnsrd, is a useful collection of resources and pointers to resources maintained by András Salamon.

Cricket Liu's "Ask Mr. DNS" archive is searchable and includes about a zillion questions and their answers; see

http://www.acmebw.com/askmrdns/archive.php

Google has indexed DNS resources at

http://directory.google.com/Top/Computers/Internet/Protocols/DNS

The FAQ for comp.sys.tcp-ip.domains includes a lot of BIND information, mostly about BIND 4. It's maintained by Chris Peckham and is available from

> http://www.intac.com/~cdp/cptd-faq

The comp.protocols.dns.bind newsgroup also contains good information.

The RFCs

The RFCs that define the DNS system are available from www.rfc-editor.org. Early and evolving ideas appear first in the Internet-Drafts series and later move into the RFC series. A selected subset of the RFCs, including those that have caused BIND 9 to be such a major undertaking, are listed below.

The original, definitive standards

- 1034 – Domain Names: Concepts and Facilities
- 1035 – Domain Names: Implementation and Specification.

Proposed standards

- 1995 – Incremental Zone Transfer in DNS
- 1996 – A Mechanism for Prompt Notification of Zone Changes
- 2136 – Dynamic Updates in the Domain Name System
- 2181 – Clarifications to the DNS Specification
- 2308 – Negative Caching of DNS Queries

Newer standards-track RFCs

- 2535 – Domain Name System Security Extensions
- 2671 – Extension Mechanisms for DNS (EDNS0)
- 2672 – Non-Terminal DNS Name Redirection (DNAME)
- 2673 – Binary Labels in the Domain Name System

Miscellaneous RFCs

- 1535 – A Security Problem … with Widely Deployed DNS Software
- 1536 – Common DNS Implementation Errors and Suggested Fixes
- 1982 – Serial Number Arithmetic
- 2536–2541, 3007 – Various DNSSEC RFCs

Resource record types

- 1183 – New DNS RR Definitions: AFSDB, RP, X25, ISDN, RT
- 1706 – DNS NSAP Resource Records
- 1876 – A Means for Expressing Location Information in DNS
- 2052 – A DNS RR for Specifying the Location of Services (SRV)
- 2168 – Resolution of Uniform Resource Identifiers using DNS
- 2230 – Key Exchange Delegation Record for the DNS

DNS and the Internet

- 1101 – DNS Encoding of Network Names and Other Types
- 1123 – Requirements for Internet Hosts: Application and Support
- 1591 – Domain Name System Structure and Delegation
- 2317 – Classless in-addr.arpa Delegation

DNS operations

- 1537 – Common DNS Data File Configuration Errors
- 1912 – Common DNS Operational and Configuration Errors
- 2182 – Selection and Operation of Secondary DNS Servers
- 2219 – Use of DNS Aliases for Network Services

Other DNS-related RFCs

- 1464 – Using DNS to Store Arbitrary String Attributes
- 1713 – Tools for DNS Debugging
- 1794 – DNS Support for Load Balancing
- 2240 – A Legal Basis for Domain Name Allocation
- 2345 – Domain Names and Company Name Retrieval
- 2352 – A Convention for Using Legal Names as Domain Names

16.18 EXERCISES

E16.1 What is Split DNS? Why is it useful? Is your site using it?

E16.2 Explain the function of each of the following DNS records: SOA, PTR, A, MX, and CNAME.

E16.3 What are glue records and why are they needed? Use **dig** to find the glue records that connect your local zone to its parent.

E16.4 Why are the name servers in **/etc/resolv.conf** specified with IP addresses instead of names?

E16.5 What are the implications of negative caching? Why is it important?

★ **E16.6** What steps are needed to set up a new second-level domain? Include both technical and procedural factors.

★ **E16.7** What is the difference between an authoritative and a nonauthoritative answer to a DNS query? How could you ensure that an answer was authoritative?

★ **E16.8** What machine is your local name server? What steps must it take to resolve the name www.admin.com, assuming that no information about this domain is cached anywhere in DNS?

★ **E16.9** What is a lame delegation? Use **dig** to determine if there are any lame delegations at your site. Be sure to query from outside the site, starting at the root servers, so that you see what the rest of the world sees.

★ **E16.10** Explain the significance for DNS of the 512-byte limit on UDP packets. What work-arounds are used to address potential problems?

★★ **E16.11** Explore your site's DNS implementation.

a) What version of BIND is running?
b) Are any forwarders set up?
c) Which machines are the master and slave servers?
d) Are they on different networks?
e) Where are caches maintained?
f) Draw a network map of the system.

★★ **E16.12** Copy the zone file for your local site and sign it using the DNSSEC tools distributed with BIND 8 or 9. How long did the signing process take? Change one record and resign the zone—how long did that take? Compare the "before" and "after" size of the signed and unsigned zones. Using **dig** to see what is actually returned in a DNS answer packet, determine the size of a corresponding return packet from a signed and unsigned zone. Is the 512-byte UDP limit a showstopper for the deployment of DNSSEC?

★★★★★ **E16.13** Running repeated **dig** queries on a name server will show you how that implementation handles issues such as caching and expiration of records. Build a tool that determines what version of name server software is running on a server. Where possible, use **tcpdump** to see the queries that actually go out and review all the traffic, not just what **dig** reports. **dig** options such as **+norecurse** may be helpful.

Try to obtain profiles for the various versions of the Microsoft name server (NT, 2000, XP). Use **nmap** to confirm your suspicions if you cannot ask a local sysadmin about the architecture and software running on a particular machine. **nmap** is considered unfriendly by many sites; you might name your machine dns-measurements.*your.domain* while you are working on this project.

17 *The Network File System*

The Network File System, commonly known as NFS, allows you to share filesystems among computers. NFS is almost transparent to users and is "stateless," meaning that no information is lost when an NFS server crashes. Clients can simply wait until the server returns and then continue as if nothing had happened.

NFS was introduced by Sun Microsystems in 1985. It was originally implemented as a surrogate filesystem for diskless clients, but the protocol proved to be well designed and very useful as a general file-sharing solution. In fact, it's difficult to remember what life was like before NFS. Nearly all modern Linux distributions have at least minimal support for NFS.

17.1 GENERAL INFORMATION ABOUT NFS

NFS consists of a number of components, including a mounting protocol and mount server, daemons that coordinate basic file service, and several diagnostic utilities. A portion of both the server-side and client-side software resides in the kernel. However, these parts of NFS need no configuration and are largely transparent from an administrator's point of view.

NFS protocol versions

The NFS protocol has been remarkably stable over time. The original public release of NFS was version 2. In the early 1990s, a collection of changes was integrated into the protocol to produce version 3, which increases performance and provides better support for large files.

Since NFS version 2 clients cannot assume that a write operation is complete until they receive an acknowledgment from the server, version 2 servers must commit each modified block to disk before replying to avoid discrepancies in the event of a crash. This constraint introduces a significant delay in NFS writes, since modified blocks would normally be written only to the in-memory buffer cache.

NFS version 3 eliminates this bottleneck with a coherency scheme that makes writes safely asynchronous. It also updates several other aspects of the protocol that were found to have caused performance problems. The net result is that NFS version 3 is quite a bit faster than version 2.

Version 3 software is always capable of interoperating with version 2, although it simply falls back to using the earlier protocol. Linux has supported NFS version 2 since the 1.2 kernel series. NFS version 3 was not introduced until kernel 2.2.18. Other interoperability enhancements and file locking support were also added at that point, so a kernel version of 2.2.18 or above is highly recommended if you use NFS.

NFS version 4 is still under development and is not yet supported by Linux.

Choice of transport

NFS runs on top of Sun's RPC (Remote Procedure Call) protocol, which defines a system-independent way for processes to communicate over a network. One advantageous side effect of this architecture is that it's possible to use either UDP or TCP as the underlying transport protocol.

NFS originally used UDP because that was what performed best on the LANs and computers of the 1980s. Although NFS does its own packet sequence reassembly and error checking, UDP and NFS both lack the congestion control algorithms that are essential for good performance on a large IP network.

To remedy these potential problems, most UNIX systems now allow you to use TCP instead of UDP as the transport for NFS. This option was first explored as a way to help NFS work through routers and over the Internet. However, the current consensus seems to be that TCP is usually the best option for local NFS traffic as well. Over time, most of the original reasons for preferring UDP over TCP have evaporated in the warm light of fast CPUs, cheap memory, and smarter network controllers.

Most servers that support TCP will generally accept connections on either transport, so the choice between TCP and UDP is made by the client. Linux supports NFS over TCP on the client side, but at this point, server-side TCP support is considered experimental or is altogether nonexistent. You should consider trying out TCPNFS in a lab and keeping an eye on others' experiences before putting it into production.

File locking

File locking (as provided by the **flock** and/or **lockf** systems calls) has been a sore point on UNIX systems for a long time. On local filesystems, it has been known to work less than perfectly. In the context of NFS, the ground is shakier still. By design,

NFS servers are stateless: they have no idea which machines are using any given file. However, this information is needed to implement locking. What to do?

The traditional answer has been to implement file locking separately from NFS. Most systems provide two daemons, **lockd** and **statd**, that try to make a go of it. Unfortunately, the task is difficult for a variety of subtle reasons, and NFS file locking has generally tended to be flaky.

Disk quotas

Access to remote disk quota information can be provided by a similar out-of-band server, **rquotad**. An NFS server will enforce disk quotas, but users cannot view their quota information unless **rquotad** is running on the remote server. We consider disk quotas to be largely obsolete, so we won't discuss **rquotad** any further.

Cookies and stateless mounting

A client must explicitly mount an NFS filesystem before using it, just as a client must mount a filesystem stored on a local disk. However, because NFS is stateless, the server does not keep track of which clients have mounted each filesystem. Instead, the server simply discloses a secret "cookie" at the conclusion of a successful mount negotiation. The cookie identifies the mounted directory to the NFS server and so provides a way for the client to access its contents.

Unmounting and remounting a filesystem on the server normally changes its cookie. As a special case, cookies persist across a reboot so a server that crashes can return to its previous state. But don't try to boot single-user, play with filesystems, then boot again; this procedure will revoke cookies and make clients unable to access the filesystems they have mounted until they either reboot or remount.

Once a client has a magic cookie, it uses the RPC protocol to make requests for filesystem operations such as creating a file or reading a data block. Because NFS is stateless, the server doesn't care what requests the client has or hasn't made before. In particular, the client is responsible for making sure that the server acknowledges write requests before it deletes its own copy of the data to be written.

Naming conventions for shared filesystems

It is easier to manage NFS if you have a standard naming scheme. Names that include the server (such as **/anchor/tools** for a filesystem that lives on anchor) are useful, since they allow users to translate announcements such as "anchor will be down all day Saturday for an upgrade" into "I won't be able to use **/anchor/tools/TeX** on Saturday to finish my thesis, so I should go skiing instead."

Unfortunately, this scheme requires the directory **/anchor** to exist in the root directory of all client machines. If a client gets filesystems from several other hosts, the root can get cluttered. Consider providing a deeper hierarchy (e.g., **/home/anchor**, **/home/rastadon**, etc.). We recommend implementing such a scheme with one of the automounter daemons described starting on page 479.

Security and NFS

NFS provides a convenient way to access files on a network, and thus it has great potential to cause security problems. In many ways, NFS is a poster child for everything that is or ever has been wrong with UNIX security. The protocol was originally designed with essentially no concern for security—convenience has its price. Fortunately, Linux supports a number of features designed to reduce and isolate the security problems from which NFS has traditionally suffered.

See page 473 for more information about the **exports** *file.*

Access to NFS volumes is granted by a file called **/etc/exports** which enumerates the hostnames (or IP addresses) of systems that should have access to a server's filesystems. Unfortunately, this is a weak form of security because the server trusts the clients to tell it who they are. It's easy to make clients lie about their identities, so this mechanism cannot be fully trusted. Nevertheless, you should only export filesystems to clients that you trust, and you should always check that you have not accidentally exported filesystems to the whole world.

The TCP wrappers package can help limit the hosts that can access NFS filesystems. We recommend that you deny access to the **portmap** service to everyone by editing **/etc/hosts.deny**; enable access for trusted hosts and subnets in the **/etc/hosts.allow** file. You should never put anything but IP addresses on the portmap lines in these files because the hostname lookups themselves may require access to the **portmap** daemon, resulting in a loop.

As on local filesystems, file-level access control on NFS filesystems is managed according to UID, GID, and file permissions. But once again, the NFS server trusts the client to tell it who is accessing files. If mary and bob share the same UID on two separate clients, they will have access to each other's NFS files. In addition, users that have root access on a system can change to whatever UID they want; the server will happily give them access to the corresponding files. For these reasons, we strongly recommend the use of globally unique UIDs and the root_squash option described in the next section.

If your site has installed a network firewall, it's a good idea to block access to TCP and UDP ports 2049, which are used by NFS. You should also block access to the **portmap** daemon, which normally listens on TCP and UDP ports 111. It's implicit in these precautions but perhaps worth saying explicitly that NFS filesystems should not be exported to nonlocal machines.

Root access and the nobody account

Although users should generally be given identical privileges wherever they go, it's traditional to prevent root from running rampant on NFS-mounted filesystems. By default, the Linux NFS server intercepts incoming requests made on behalf of UID 0 and changes them to look as if they came from some other user. This modification is called "squashing root." The root account is not entirely shut out, but it is limited to the abilities of a normal user.

A placeholder account named "nobody" is defined specifically to be the pseudo-user as whom a remote root masquerades on an NFS server. The traditional UID for nobody is 65534 (the twos-complement equivalent of UID -2).[1] You can change the default UID and GID mappings for root with the anonuid and anongid export options. You can use the all_squash option to map all client UIDs to the same UID on the server. This configuration eliminates all distinctions among users and creates a sort of public-access filesystem. At the other end of the spectrum, the no_root_squash option turns off UID mapping for root. This option is sometimes needed to support diskless clients or software that requires root access to the filesystem. It's generally a bad idea to turn this feature off, but the option is there nonetheless.

The intent behind these precautions is good, but their ultimate value is not as great as it might seem. Remember that root on an NFS client can **su** to whatever UID it wants, so user files are never really protected. System logins such as "bin" and "sys" aren't UID-mapped, so any files they own, such as the occasional system binary or third-party application, may be vulnerable to attack. The only real effect of UID mapping is to prevent access to files that are owned by root and not readable or writable by the world.

17.2 SERVER-SIDE NFS

A server is usually said to "export" a directory when it makes the directory available for use by other machines.

The process used by clients to mount a filesystem (that is, to learn its secret cookie) is completely separate from the process used to access files. The operations use separate protocols, and the requests are served by different daemons: **mountd** for mount requests and **nfsd** for actual file service. These daemons are actually called **rpc.nfsd** and **rpc.mountd** as a reminder that they rely on RPC as an underlying protocol (and hence require **portmap** to be running; see page 818). We will omit the **rpc** prefix for readability.

On an NFS server, both **mountd** and **nfsd** should start when the system boots, and both should remain running as long as the system is up. The system startup scripts will typically run the daemons for you automatically if you have any exports configured. The names of the NFS server startup scripts for each platform are shown in Table 17.1.

mountd and **nfsd** share a single access control database that tells which filesystems should be exported and which clients may mount them. The operative copy of this database is usually kept in a file called **/usr/lib/nfs/xtab** in addition to tables internal to the kernel. Since **xtab** isn't meant to be human-readable, you use a helper command to add and modify entries: **exportfs**. To remove entries from the exports table, use **exportfs -u**.

---

1. While the Red Hat NFS server defaults to UID -2, the nobody account in the **passwd** file uses UID 99. You can leave it alone, add a **passwd** entry for UID -2, or change anonuid and anongid to 99 if you wish. The other distributions use UID -2 for the nobody and nogroup accounts in the **passwd** file, as expected.

Table 17.1   NFS server startup scripts

Distribution	Paths to startup scripts
Red Hat	**/etc/init.d/nfs**
SuSE	**/etc/init.d/nfsserver**[a]
Debian	**/etc/init.d/nfs-kernel-server**
	/etc/init.d/nfs-common

a. **/etc/init.d/nfs** mounts the NFS client filesystems on SuSE.

On most systems, **/etc/exports** is the canonical, human-readable list of exported directories. By default, all filesystems in **/etc/exports** are exported at boot time. You can manually export all of the filesystems listed in **/etc/exports** by using **exportfs -a**, which should be run after you make changes to the **exportfs** file. You can also export filesystems on a one-time basis by specifying the client, path, and options directly on the **exportfs** command line.

NFS deals with the logical layer of the filesystem. Any directory can be exported; it doesn't have to be a mount point or the root of a physical filesystem. However, for security reasons, NFS does pay attention to the boundaries between filesystems and does require each device to be exported separately. For example, on a machine that has a **/users** partition, you could export the root directory without exporting **/users**.

Clients are usually allowed to mount subdirectories of an exported directory if they wish, although the protocol does not require this feature. For example, if a server exports **/chimchim/users**, a client could mount only **/chimchim/users/joe** and ignore the rest of the **users** directory. Most versions of UNIX don't let you export subdirectories of an exported directory with different options, but Linux is an exception.

The exports file

In the Linux **exports** file, the clients that may access a given filesystem are presented in a whitespace-separated list. Each client is followed immediately by a parenthesized list of comma-separated options. Lines can be continued with a backslash.

Here's what the format looks like:

```
/home/boggs        inura(rw,no_root_squash) lappie(rw)
/usr/share/man     *.toadranch.com(ro)
```

There is no way to list multiple clients for a single set of options, although some client specifications actually refer to multiple hosts. Table 17.2 on page 474 lists the four types of client specifications that can appear in the **exports** file.

Table 17.3 on page 474 shows the most common export options.

Linux's NFS server has the unusual feature of allowing subdirectories of exported directories to be exported with different options. The noaccess option is provided to "unexport" subdirectories that you would rather not share.

Table 17.2   Client specifications in the /etc/exports file

Type	Syntax	Meaning
Hostname	*hostname*	Individual hosts
Netgroup	*@groupname*	NIS netgroups; see page 497 for details
Wild cards	* and ?	FQDNs[a] with wild cards. "*" will not match a dot.
IP networks	*ipaddr/mask*	CIDR-style specifications (e.g., 128.138.92.128/25)

a. Fully qualified domain names

Table 17.3   Common export options

Option	Description
ro	Exports read-only
rw	Exports for reading and writing (the default)
rw=*list*	Exports read-mostly. *list* enumerates the hosts allowed to mount for writing; all others must mount read-only.
root_squash	Maps ("squashes") UID 0 and GID 0 to the values specified by anonuid and anongid. This is the default.
no_root_squash	Allows normal access by root. Dangerous.
all_squash	Maps all UIDs and GIDs to their anonymous versions. Useful for supporting PCs and untrusted single-user hosts.
anonuid=*xxx*	Specifies the UID to which remote roots should be squashed
anongid=*xxx*	Specifies the GID to which remote roots should be squashed
secure	Requires remote access to originate at a privileged port
insecure	Allows remote access from any port
noaccess	Prevents access to this dir and its subdirs (used with nested exports)

For example, the configuration

```
/home            *.toadranch.com(rw)
/home/boggs      (noaccess)
```

allows hosts in the toadranch.com domain to access all of the contents of **/home** except for **/home/boggs**. The absence of a client name on the second line means that the option applies to all hosts; it's perhaps somewhat more secure this way.

Don't forget to run **exportfs -a** after updating the **exports** file to make your changes take effect.

nfsd: serve files

Once a client's mount request has been validated by **mountd**, the client can request various filesystem operations. These requests are handled on the server side by **nfsd**, the NFS operations daemon.[2] **nfsd** need not be run on an NFS client machine unless the client exports filesystems of its own.

---

2. In reality, **nfsd** simply makes a nonreturning system call to NFS server code embedded in the kernel.

nfsd takes a numeric argument that specifies how many server threads to fork. Selecting the appropriate number of **nfsd**s is important and is unfortunately something of a black art. If the number is too low or too high, NFS performance can suffer.

The performance of older systems could degrade quite a bit as a result of having too many **nfsd**s because the kernel would wake up all the idle **nfsd**s in response to each incoming request. Linux systems are better about this because they use threads instead of separate processes, so it's OK to err a bit on the side of generosity.

Generally speaking, 8 **nfsd** threads is adequate for a server that is used infrequently and is few enough that performance problems won't really arise. On a production server, somewhere between 12 and 20 is a good number. If you notice the load average (as reported by **uptime**) rising as you add **nfsd**s, you've gone too far; back off a bit from that threshold. You should also run **nfsstat** regularly to check for performance problems that might be associated with the number of **nfsd** threads. See page 478 for more information about **nfsstat**.

On a loaded NFS server with a lot of UDP clients, UDP sockets can overflow if requests arrive while all **nfsd** threads are already in use. You can monitor the number of overflows with **netstat -s**. Add more **nfsd**s until UDP socket overflows drop to zero. Overflows indicate a severe undersupply of server daemons, so you should probably add a few more than this metric would indicate.

You can change the number of **nfsd** processes by editing the appropriate startup script in **/etc/init.d**. See Table 17.1 on page 473 for the name of the script to edit.

17.3 CLIENT-SIDE NFS

NFS filesystems are mounted in much the same way as local disk filesystems. The **mount** command understands the notation *hostname:directory* to mean the path *directory* on the host *hostname*. As with local filesystems, **mount** will map the remote *directory* on the remote *host* into a directory within the local file tree. After mounting, an NFS-mounted filesystem is accessed in the same way as a local file system. The **mount** command and its associated NFS extensions represent the most significant concerns to a system administrator of an NFS client.

Before an NFS file system can be mounted, it must be properly exported (see *Server-side NFS* on page 472). To verify that a server has properly exported its filesystems from the client's perspective, you can use the client's **showmount** command:

```
% showmount -e coyote
Export list for coyote:
/home/boggs inura.toadranch.com
```

This example indicates that the directory **/home/boggs** on the server coyote has been exported to the client system inura.toadranch.com. **showmount** output should be the first thing you check if an NFS mount is not working and you have already verified that the filesystems have been properly exported on the server with **exportfs**. (You might have just forgotten to run **exportfs -a** after updating the **exports** file.)

If the directory is properly exported on the server but **showmount** returns an error or an empty list, you might double-check that all the necessary processes are running on the server (**portmap**, **mountd**, **nfsd**, **statd**, and **lockd**), that the **hosts.allow** and **hosts.deny** files allow access to those daemons, and that you are on the right client system.

To actually mount the filesystem, you would use a command such as this:

```
# mount -o rw,hard,intr,bg coyote:/home/boggs /coyote/home/boggs
```

The options after **-o** indicate that the filesystem should be mounted read-write, that operations should be interruptible, and that retries should be done in the background. These flags are pretty standard; other common flags are listed in Table 17.4.

Table 17.4   NFS mount flags

Flag	Description
rw	Mounts the filesystem read-write (must be exported that way)
ro	Mounts the filesystem read-only
bg	If the mount fails (server doesn't respond), keeps trying it in the background and continues with other mount requests
hard	If a server goes down, causes operations that try to access it to block until the server comes back up
soft	If a server goes down, causes operations that try to access it to fail and return an error. This feature is useful to avoid processes "hanging" on inessential mounts.
intr	Allows users to interrupt blocked operations (and make them return an error)
nointr	Does not allow user interrupts
retrans=n	Specifies the number of times to repeat a request before returning an error on a soft-mounted filesystem
timeo=n	Sets the timeout period (in tenths of a second) for requests
rsize=n	Sets the read buffer size to n bytes
wsize=n	Sets the write buffer size to n bytes
nfsvers=n	Selects NFS protocol version 2 or 3 (normally automatic)
tcp	Selects transport via TCP. UDP is the default.[a]

a. Note that most NFS servers for Linux do not support TCP as the transport.

Filesystems mounted hard (the default) can cause processes to hang when their servers go down. This behavior is particularly bothersome when the processes in question are standard daemons, so we do not recommend serving critical system binaries over NFS. In general, the use of the soft and intr options will reduce the number of NFS-related headaches. However, these options can have their own undesirable side effects, such as aborting a 20-hour simulation after it has run for 18 hours just because of a transient network glitch.[3] Automount solutions such as autofs and **amd**, discussed later in this chapter, also provide some remedies for mounting ailments.

The read and write buffer sizes apply to both UDP and TCP mounts, but the optimal values differ. Because you can trust TCP to transfer data efficiently, the values should be higher; 32K is a good value. For UDP, good values when server and client are on the same network is 8K.[4] The default is 1K, though even the man page recommends increasing it to 8K for better performance.

However, on Linux 2.2 and 2.4 kernels, the default input queue size is 64K. With eight **nfsd** threads running on the NFS server, only one request can be outstanding on each instance of **nfsd** before requests start getting dropped. Therefore, you might consider increasing the receive queue size for **nfsd** only, returning it to the default value after running **nfsd** so that other processes are not negatively affected by the change. You can change the input queue size in your system startup scripts by using procfs. This example sets the queue size to 256K, which is a reasonable default:

```
rmem_default=`cat /proc/sys/net/core/rmem_default`
rmem_max=`cat /proc/sys/net/core/rmem_max`
echo 262144 > /proc/sys/net/core/rmem_default
echo 262144 > /proc/sys/net/core/rmem_max
```

Run or restart **rpc.nfsd**, then return the settings to their original values:

```
echo $rmem_default > /proc/sys/net/core/rmem_default
echo $rmem_max > /proc/sys/net/core/rmem_max
```

The mount can be tested with **df** just as you would test a local filesystem:

```
% df /coyote/home/boggs
Filesystem          1k-blocks    Used  Available  Use%  Mounted on
coyote:/home/boggs 17212156  1694128   14643692   11%  /coyote/home/boggs
```

NFS partitions can be unmounted with the **umount** command. If the NFS filesystem is in use when you try to unmount it, you will get an error such as

```
umount: /coyote/home/boggs: device is busy
```

Like any other filesystem, an NFS filesystem cannot be unmounted while it is in use. Use **lsof** to find processes with open files on the filesystem; kill them or change directories in the case of shells. If all else fails or your server is down, try **umount -f** to force the filesystem to be unmounted.

Mounting remote filesystems at boot time

See page 479 for more information about autofs and **amd**.

You can use the **mount** command to establish temporary network mounts, but you should list mounts that are part of a system's permanent configuration in **/etc/fstab** so that they are mounted automatically at boot time. Alternatively, mounts can be

---

3. Jeff Forys, one of our technical reviewers, remarked, "Most mounts should use hard, intr, and bg, because these options best preserve NFS's original design goals (reliability and statelessness). soft is an abomination, an ugly Satanic hack! If the user wants to interrupt, cool. Otherwise, wait for the server and all will eventually be well again with no data lost."

4. If you use **ipchains** or **iptables**, you might have to add a rule to accept fragments because 8K is above the MTU for Ethernet. Accepting fragments may make you more vulnerable to a denial of service attack.

handled by an automatic mounting service such as **automount** or **amd**; see *Automatic mounting* on page 479.

The following **fstab** entries mount the filesystems **/home** and **/usr/local** from the hosts coyote and inura:

```
# filesystem       mountpoint      fstype   flags             dump fsck
coyote:/home       /coyote/home    nfs      rw,bg,intr,hard    0    0
inura:/usr/local   /usr/local      nfs      ro,bg,intr,soft    0    0
```

See page 141 for more information about the fstab file.

When you add entries to **fstab**, be sure to create the appropriate mount point directories with **mkdir**. You can make your changes take effect immediately (without rebooting) by running **mount -a -t nfs** to mount all file systems of type nfs in **fstab**.

The flags field of **/etc/fstab** specifies options for NFS mounts; these options are the same ones you would specify on the **mount** command line.

Secure port restrictions

NFS clients are free to use any TCP or UDP source port they like when connecting to an NFS server. However, Linux servers may insist that requests come from a privileged port (a port numbered lower than 1024) if the filesystem is exported with the secure export option, which is on by default. In the world of PCs and desktop Linux boxes, the use of privileged ports provides little actual security.

Linux NFS clients adopt the traditional (and still recommended) approach of defaulting to a privileged port, to avert the potential for conflict. To accept mounts from unprivileged source ports, export the filesystem with the insecure export option.

17.4 NFSSTAT: DUMP NFS STATISTICS

Linux provides a command called **nfsstat** that can display various statistics kept by the NFS system. **nfsstat -s** displays statistics for NFS server processes, and **nfsstat -c** shows information related to client-side operations.[5] For example:

```
% nfsstat -s
Server rpc stats:
calls          badcalls      badauth      badclnt      xdrcall
24314112       311           9            302          0
Server nfs v2:
getattr        null          setattr      root         lookup        readlink
8470054 34%    58      0%    55199 0%     0       0%   1182897 4%    917      0%
read           wrcache       link         create       remove        rename
6602409 27%    0       0%    7452  0%     61544   0%   46712   0%    11537    0%
write          symlink       mkdir        rmdir        readdir       fsstat
7785789 32%    744     0%    3446  0%     2539    0%   13614   0%    69201    0%
```

This example is from a relatively healthy NFS server. If more than 3% of calls are bad, it's likely that there is a problem with your NFS server or network. Check the output

---

5. At the time of this writing, the man page for **nfsstat**(8) states that the NFS client does not yet log statistics. However, actually running **nfsstat** reports nonzero client statistics. Your mileage may vary.

of **netstat -s** for general network statistics. It may reveal problems with dropped packets, fragment reassembly, or network queue overruns that will affect your NFS performance. See page 633 for more on debugging your network with **netstat**.

Running **nfsstat** and **netstat** occasionally and becoming familiar with their output will help you discover NFS problems before your users do.

17.5 DEDICATED **NFS** FILE SERVERS

Fast, reliable file service is one of the most important elements of any production computing environment. Although you can certainly roll your own file server from a Linux workstation and a handful of off-the-shelf hard disks, doing so is often not the best-performing or easiest-to-administer solution (though it is often the cheapest).

Dedicated NFS file servers have been around for more than a decade. They offer a host of potential advantages over the homebrew approach:

- They are optimized for file service and typically provide the best possible NFS performance.

- As storage requirements grow, they can scale smoothly to support terabytes of storage and hundreds of users.

- They are more reliable than Linux boxes thanks to their simplified software, redundant hardware, and use of disk mirroring.

- They usually provide file service for both Linux and Windows clients. Some even contain integral web and FTP servers.

- They are often easier to administer than Linux file servers.

- They often provide backup and checkpoint facilities that are superior to those found on vanilla Linux systems.

Of the current offerings, our favorites are those made by Network Appliance, Inc. (www.netapp.com). Their servers run the gamut from very small to very large, and their pricing is OK. Auspex and EMC are players in the high-end server market. They make good products, but be prepared for sticker shock and build up your tolerance for marketing buzzwords.[6]

17.6 AUTOMATIC MOUNTING

Mounting filesystems one at a time by listing them in **/etc/fstab** introduces a number of problems in large networks.

First, maintaining **/etc/fstab** on a few hundred machines can be tedious. Each one may be slightly different and thus require individual attention.

---

6. Speaking of buzzwords, one of the main ones you'll hear in this context is "network attached storage," also known as NAS. It's just a fancy way of saying "file service."

Second, if filesystems are mounted from many different hosts, chaos ensues when one of those servers crashes. Every command that accesses the mount points will hang.

Third, when an important server crashes, it may cripple users by making important partitions like **/usr/share/man** unavailable. In this situation, it's best if a copy of the partition can be mounted temporarily from a backup server.

An automount daemon mounts filesystems when they are referenced and unmounts them when they are no longer needed. This procedure minimizes the number of active mount points and is mostly transparent to users. With most automounters, it is also possible to supply a list of "replicated" (identical) filesystems so that the network can continue to function when a primary server becomes unavailable.

To implement this behind-the-scenes mounting and unmounting, the automounter mounts a virtual filesystem driver on the directories you've designated as locations for automatic mounting to occur. In the past, the automounter did this by posing as an NFS server, but this scheme suffers from several significant limitations and is rarely found on contemporary systems. These days, a kernel-resident filesystem driver called autofs is used.

Instead of mirroring an actual filesystem, an automounter "makes up" a filesystem hierarchy according to the specifications you list in its configuration file. When a user references a directory within the automounter's virtual filesystem, the automounter intercepts the reference and mounts the actual filesystem the user is trying to reach.

The idea of an automounter originally comes from Sun. The Linux automounter, called **automount**, is designed to mimic Sun's automounter, although it is an independent implementation of the concept and is different in a number of ways.

amd, originally written by Jan-Simon Pendry of Imperial College in London, is the product of a doctoral thesis that expanded upon Sun's original idea. **amd** corrected many of the problems in Sun's original automounter. It also had the advantage of being free and installable on a wide variety of UNIX systems, and it can be compiled or installed from a package to run on Linux.

automount configuration is relatively simple and concise. **amd** is more complicated, more powerful, and more portable. It also includes some features that are largely experimental. You might want to check out **amd**'s feature list and see if there's anything that you can't live without.

17.7 AUTOMOUNT

automount is a background process that configures a single mount point for autofs, the kernel portion of the Linux automounter. The startup script **/etc/init.d/autofs** parses a master file (usually **/etc/auto.master**) and runs **automount** for each of the listed mount points. It's typical to see a running instance of **automount** for each automatic mount point that has been configured.

You will rarely need to run the **automount** command directly, as almost all administration of the automounter is performed through the **/etc/init.d/autofs** script.[7] As with most startup scripts, the **autofs** script accepts a single parameter on the command line that can be **start**, **stop**, **reload**, **restart**, or **status**. Whenever changes are made to the automounter configuration, you must run **autofs reload** in order for the changes to take effect. **autofs status** gives you the status of existing automounts.

The **auto.master** file associates a mount point with a "map." A map translates the directory name accessed—known as the "key"—into a command line that **mount** can use to perform the real mount. A map can be a text file, an executable program, or an NIS or LDAP database.

When a user references a directory that has been mounted with the autofs kernel filesystem module, it notifies the user-land **automount** process of the access. The **automount** process figures out which filesystem to mount by consulting a map file or program, then performs the mount before returning control to the user who triggered the lookup.

You can see the autofs filesystems and the **automount** processes they are attached to by running **mount** and **ps**:

```
% mount
/dev/hda3 on / type ext2 (rw)
proc on /proc type proc (rw)
/dev/hda1 on /boot type ext2 (rw)
automount(pid8359) on /misc type autofs          // automounter filesystem
     (rw,fd=5,pgrp=8359,minproto=2,maxproto=4)
automount(pid8372) on /net type autofs           // automounter filesystem
     (rw,fd=5,pgrp=8372,minproto=2,maxproto=4)

% ps auxw | grep automount
root     8359 0.0  1.0  1360  652 ?     S   Dec27  0:00
     /usr/sbin/automount /misc file /etc/auto.misc
root     8372 0.0  1.0  1360  652 ?     S   Dec27  0:00
     /usr/sbin/automount /net program /etc/auto.net
```

Here we can see two autofs filesystems mounted on **/misc** and **/net**. These virtual filesystems are attached to the **automount** processes with PIDs 8359 and 8372, respectively. The **automount** commands run by the **/etc/init.d/autofs** script can be seen in the **ps** output. **auto.misc** is a regular map file, and **auto.net** is an executable program. These maps are described in more detail below.

The master file

The master file lists the directories that should have autofs filesystems mounted on them and associates a map with each directory. In addition to providing the root directory for the map and the map name, you can also specify additional options in the "**-o**" format used by the **mount** command. These options will apply to each entry in

---

7. Don't confuse the **autofs** script with the autofs filesystem. The relationship between them is that the script tells the kernel how to configure the filesystem.

the map. The Linux conventions vary from Sun's in that the master file's options are cumulative with those of the map; both sets of options are handed to mount.

A simple master file that makes use of the map file shown in the next section would look something like this:

```
# Directory      Map              Options
/chimchim        /etc/auto.chim   -secure,hard,bg,intr
```

The master file can be replaced or augmented by a version shared through NIS. The source of the system's automount information is specified by the automount field in **/etc/nsswitch.conf**. See *Prioritizing sources of administrative information* on page 498 for more information about the **nsswitch.conf** file.

Map files

Map files (known as "indirect maps" on other systems) automount several filesystems underneath a common directory. The path of the directory is specified in the master file, not in the map itself. For example, a map for filesystems that get mounted under **/chimchim** (corresponding to the example above) might look like this:

```
users    chimchim:/chimchim/users
devel    -soft,nfsproto=3 chimchim:/chimchim/devel
info     -ro chimchim:/chimchim/info
```

The first column names the subdirectory where each automount should be installed, and subsequent items list the mount options and source path of the filesystem. This example (stored in **/etc/auto.chim**) tells **automount** that it can mount the directories **/chimchim/users**, **/chimchim/devel**, and **/chimchim/info** from the host chimchim, with **info** being mounted read-only and **devel** being mounted soft with NFS protocol version 3.

In this configuration the paths on chimchim and the local host will be identical, but this correspondence is not required.

Executable maps

If an indirect map file is executable, it's assumed to be a script or program that dynamically generates automounting information. Instead of reading the map as a text file, the automounter will execute it with an argument (the key) that indicates which subdirectory a user has attempted to access. The script is responsible for printing out an appropriate map entry; if the specified key is not valid, the script can simply exit without printing anything.

This feature is very powerful and makes up for many of the potential deficiencies in **automounter**'s rather strange configuration system. In effect, it allows you to easily define a site-wide automount configuration file in a format of your own choice. You can write a simple Perl script to decode the global configuration on each machine. Some systems are shipped with a handy **/etc/auto.net** executable map that takes a hostname as a key and mounts all exported file systems on that host.

17.8 AMD: A MORE SOPHISTICATED AUTOMOUNTER

amd is an elaborate riff on the automounter concept. It became something of an orphan when its original author stopped maintaining it. It's now kept up by Erez Zadok at Columbia University as a component of the **am-utils** package. The current URL is

> http://www.cs.columbia.edu/~ezk/am-utils

amd offers the following advantages over **automount**:

- **amd** sends "keep alive" queries to remote servers at regular intervals and maintains a list of servers that are accessible. **amd** will mount, unmount, and replace filesystems based on this information. If a server crashes, future filesystem accesses return an "operation would block" error rather than hanging.

- **amd** contains no proprietary source code and has been ported to over 20 versions of UNIX, including Linux.

- **amd** offers support for a number of mount types, such as the "union" mount, that are not supported by **automount**.

- The **amd** distribution includes a query-and-manipulation tool, **amq**, that lets you monitor **amd**'s status and send it hints and commands (such as forced unmount requests).

- **amd**'s map syntax is more generic than that of **automount**. You can create a single file for all hosts at your site and distribute it with **rdist** or **rsync**.

- **amd** is based on the concept that each server has one or more filesystems, with each filesystem containing one or more volumes (a coherent set of files). This makes the handling of subdirectories more straightforward than with **automount**.

- **amd** won't eat all the popcorn or send you out to get Milk Duds.

amd maps

The **amd** map format is extremely flexible and allows the same configuration file to be used on many machines. Map entries can contain conditionals that activate them only in specific contexts (e.g., on a specific host or type of machine). Conditionals use built-in "selector variables" that are filled in with various pieces of information about the environment in which **amd** is running. The most commonly used selector variables are listed in Table 17.5 on page 484.

The entry for a mount point can describe several different things that might be mounted there. For example, the following map file tells **amd** about two filesystems: **/usr/man** and **/cs/tools**. Each filesystem has one set of options that controls mounting on the machine where the filesystem actually lives and another that mounts the filesystem over the network.

Table 17.5 amd selector variables

Variable	Description
arch	Architecture of the current machine
autodir	Default directory under which to mount filesystems
byte	CPU byte sex (big-endian or little-endian)
cluster	Name of local cluster of machines, defaults to domain
domain	Local NIS domain name
host	Local hostname
hostd	Hostname concatenated with local DNS domain name
karch	Kernel architecture (defaults to value of arch selector)
key	Volume name being resolved
map	Name of mount map being used
network	Matches network name or number of any net interface
os	Operating system
osver	Operating system version

/default	opts:=rw,soft,timeo=10,retrans=5
usr/man	host==chimchim;type:=ufs;dev:=/dev/sd1f \
	host!=chimchim;rhost=chimchim;rfs:=/${key};\
	type=nfs;fs:=${autodir}/${key}
cs/tools	host==anchor;type:=ufs;dev:=/dev/sd3c \
	host!=anchor;rhost=anchor;rfs:=/${key};\
	type=nfs;fs:=${autodir}/${key}

Elements of the form name:=value define various attributes of the mount. For example, the first line sets the default mount options to "rw,soft,timeo=10,retrans=5". Elements of the form name==value or name!=value are conditionals; subsequent elements are only used if the conditional evaluates to true. Notations like ${autodir} and ${key} insert the value of the appropriate variable.

The /default clause specifies defaults that apply to all map entries unless they are explicitly overridden. Table 17.6 describes the various options.

Table 17.6 amd map options

Option	Description
rhost	Remote host on which the volume lives
rfs	Remote filesystem name
type	Type of mount, usually nfs or ufs (local disk)
fs	Local mount point
opts	Mount options
addopts	Options to be added to the default options
remopts	Options to use if server is nonlocal (e.g., smaller read/write sizes)

Starting amd

A running copy of **amd** manages one virtual filesystem directory beneath which all of its automounting action occurs. The name of the virtual directory and the map file that tells what to mount within it are specified on the command line.

amd can be started with a script such as this:

```
#!/bin/csh -f
cd /usr/local/etc/amd
exec /usr/local/bin/amd -x fatal,error,user -r -l syslog -a /tmp_mnt
    /amd amd.master.map >& /dev/console
```

The options used in this script are described in Table 17.7.

Table 17.7   amd command-line options

Option	Description
-x	Sets run-time logging options
-r	"Adopts" existing mounts
-l	Specifies log file or **syslog** for error messages
-a	Specifies alternate location for mount points[a]
/amd	Sets the virtual (automount) directory
amd.master.map	Specifies the map file containing the mount options

a. The default is **/a**.

When a user references one of the filesystems defined in **amd**'s map file, **amd** mounts the filesystem and monitors subsequent use of the mount. After it has been inactive for a period of time (usually 5–15 minutes), **amd** unmounts the filesystem until it is referenced again.

Use the **amq** command to see the status of mounts.

Stopping amd

amd needs to be stopped gracefully so that it has a chance to untangle itself from the filesystem structure. Sending **amd** a SIGTERM is the polite way to ask it to leave.

17.9 RECOMMENDED READING

ZADOK, EREZ. *Linux NFS and Automounter Administration.* Sybex. 2001.

Erez Zadok is the maintainer of **amd**, and his book covers **amd** as well as the Linux NFS environment.

CALLAGHAN, BRENT. *NFS Illustrated.* Addison-Wesley. 1999.

PENDRY, JAN-SIMON, AND NICK WILLIAMS. "AMD: The 4.4BSD Automounter Reference Manual." 4.4BSD System Manager's Manual, Usenix and O'Reilly. 1994.

S<small>TERN</small>, H<small>AL</small>, M<small>IKE</small> E<small>ISLER</small>, <small>AND</small> R<small>ICARDO</small> L<small>ABIAGA</small>. *Managing NFS and NIS, Second Edition*. Sebastopol: O'Reilly & Associates, 2001.

Table 17.8 lists the various RFCs for the NFS protocol.

Table 17.8   NFS-related RFCs

RFC	Title	Author	Date
1094	Network File System Protocol Specification	Sun Microsystems	Mar 1989
1813	NFS Version 3 Protocol Specification	B. Callaghan et al.	Jun 1995
2623	NFS Version 2 and Version 3 Security Issues	M. Eisler	Jun 1999
2624	NFS Version 4 Design Considerations	S. Shepler	Jun 1999

17.10 E<small>XERCISES</small>

★ **E17.1** What are the benefits of automounting? Provide configuration files for **automount** and **amd** for the situation presented in E17.4.

★ **E17.2** Explore your local NFS setup. Is NFS used, or is a different solution in place? Is automounting used? What tradeoffs have been made?

★ **E17.3** What is the relationship between **mountd**, **nfsd**, and **portmap**? What does NFS's dependency upon **portmap** mean in terms of security?

★★ **E17.4** What are some of the design ramifications of NFS being a stateless protocol? In particular, discuss any effects statelessness has on file locking, access permissions, and security. How would a stateful network filesystem differ from NFS?

★★ **E17.5** Your employer needs you to export **/usr** and **/usr/local** through NFS. Give the following information.

a) Because of office politics, you want only your department (local subnet 192.168.123.0/24) to be able to use these exported filesystems. What lines must be added to what files to implement this configuration? Pay attention to the proper export options.

b) List the steps needed to make **mountd** and **nfsd** recognize these new shared filesystems. How could you verify that the directories were being shared without mounting them?

c) Outline a strategy that would make all machines on your local subnet mount the exported directories automatically using the mount points **/mnt/usr** and **/mnt/usr/local**.

18 *Sharing System Files*

A properly functioning system depends on tens, perhaps hundreds, of configuration files all containing the right pieces of information. When you multiply the number of configuration files on a host by the number of hosts on a network, the result can be thousands of files—too many to manage by hand.

In the real world, machines are often similar from an administrative point of view. Instead of editing text files on each machine, you will find it more efficient to combine machines into groups that share configuration information. You can combine machines in several different ways.

The simplest way is to keep a master copy of each configuration file in one place and distribute it to members of the group whenever it changes. This solution has the advantages of being simple and working on every Linux (and UNIX) system.

Another approach is to eliminate text files altogether and have each machine obtain its configuration information from a central server. This is more complicated than copying files, but it solves some other problems as well. For example, clients can't miss updates, even if the clients are down when a change is made. It may also be faster to obtain information from a server than from a file, depending on the speed of the local disk and the amount of caching performed by the server. On the other hand, the entire network can hang when the central server goes down.

Several attempts have been made to develop administrative databases for large networks, and they are all interesting systems. However, none of the current products seems exactly right in its approach. Some are simple but not secure and not scalable. Others are functional but unwieldy. Some look promising but are not yet fully baked.

All the systems seem to have limitations that can prevent you from setting up the network the way you want to, and none of them will manage all the information you may want to share across your machines.

In this chapter we first discuss some basic techniques for keeping files synchronized on a network. We then talk about the most widely used database system, NIS, and briefly mention its big brother NIS+ (which is not used much under Linux and is slated to be discontinued). Finally, we address LDAP, a relatively new system that may become widely deployed over the next few years. Large sites often end up using several of these methods and systems in combination.

18.1 WHAT TO SHARE

Of the many configuration files on a Linux system, only a subset can be usefully shared among machines. The most commonly shared files are listed in Table 18.1.

Table 18.1   System files that are commonly shared

Filename	Function
/etc/passwd	User account information database
/etc/shadow[a]	Shadow password file
/etc/group	UNIX group definitions
/etc/hosts	Maps between hostnames and IP addresses
/etc/networks	Associates text names with IP network numbers
/etc/services	Lists port numbers for well-known network services
/etc/protocols	Maps text names to protocol numbers
/etc/ethers	Maps between hostnames and Ethernet addresses
/etc/mail/aliases	Contains electronic mail aliases
/etc/rpc	Lists ID numbers for RPC services
/etc/netgroup	Defines collections of hosts, users, and networks
/etc/printcap	Printer information database

a. Not necessarily sharable with other flavors of UNIX, since the type of encryption can vary; see page 87.

Many other configuration files can potentially be shared among systems, depending on how similar you want machines at your site to be. For the most part, these other configuration files are associated with specific applications (e.g., **/etc/sendmail.cf** for **sendmail**) and are not supported by administrative database systems such as NIS and LDAP; you must share the files by copying them.

See page 656 for more information about PAM.

Historically, many of the files in Table 18.1 have been accessed through routines in the standard C library. For example, the **/etc/passwd** file can be searched with the **getpwuid**, **getpwnam**, and **getpwent** routines. These routines take care of opening, reading, and parsing the **passwd** file so that user-level programs don't have to do it themselves. Modern Linux distributions also use Pluggable Authentication Modules (PAM), which provide a standard programming interface for performing security-related lookups. The PAM modules allow authentication systems such as Kerberos to be easily integrated into Linux.

Administrative database systems complicate matters by providing alternative sources for much of this information. The traditional C library routines (**getpwent**, etc.) are aware of the common database systems and can access them in addition to (or instead of) the standard flat files. The exact complement of data sources that are consulted is set by the system administrator; see *Prioritizing sources of administrative information* on page 498 for details.

nscd: cache the results of lookups

On some distributions (among our examples, only SuSE), another finger in the system file pie belongs to **nscd**, the somewhat misleadingly titled name service cache daemon. **nscd** works in conjunction with the C library to cache the results of library calls such as **getpwent**. **nscd** is simply a wrapper for these library routines; it knows nothing about the actual data sources being consulted. **nscd** should in theory improve the performance of lookups, but it usually doesn't yield much of a subjective improvement from the user's perspective.

See Chapter 16 for more information about DNS.

'Name service cache daemon" is potentially misleading because the term "name service" typically refers to DNS, the distributed database system that maps between hostnames and Internet addresses. **nscd** does in fact cache the results of DNS lookups (because it wraps **gethostbyname**, etc.), but it also wraps the library routines that access information from the **passwd** and **group** files and their network database equivalents. (For security reasons, lookups to **/etc/shadow** are not cached.)

In concept, **nscd** should have no effect on the operation of the system other than to speed up repeated lookups. In practice, it can cause unexpected behavior because it maintains its own copy of the lookup results. Lookups are stored in the cache for a fixed amount of time (set in **nscd**'s configuration file, **/etc/nscd.conf**), and there is always the possibility that recent changes will not be reflected in **nscd**'s cache until the previous data has timed out. **nscd** is smart enough to monitor local data sources (such as **/etc/passwd**) for changes, so local updates should propagate within 15 seconds. For remote entries, such as those retrieved through NIS, you may have to wait for the full timeout period before changes take effect.

On systems that use it, **nscd** starts at boot time and runs continuously. The default **/etc/nscd.conf** specifies a timeout of 10 minutes for **passwd** data and an hour for **hosts** and **group**, with a 20-second negative timeout (the amount of time before an unsuccessful lookup will be retried). In practice, these values rarely need changing. If you find yourself wondering why a change you recently made doesn't seem to show up, **nscd** is probably the reason.

18.2 COPYING FILES AROUND

We use brute-force file copying to maintain the University of Colorado's Engineering network. It is not an elegant solution, but it works on every kind of machine and is easy to set up and maintain. It's also a reliable system because it minimizes the interdependencies among machines (although it may also make it easier for machines to fall out of sync). File copying also offers the most flexibility in terms of what can be distributed and how. Indeed, it is also often used to keep applications and data files up to date as well as system files.

Quite a few configuration files are not supported by any of the common database services. (Some examples are **/etc/sendmail.cf**, which determines how **sendmail** delivers mail, and **/etc/ntp.conf**, which determines how hosts keep their clocks synchronized.) If you wish to keep such files in sync (which is usually wise), you really have no choice but to use some sort of brute-force copying system even if you distribute other information with NIS or LDAP.

It's often assumed in manuals and in Linux culture that you will use a system such as NIS if one is available. But if your needs aren't complex, you don't need a complex solution. Sometimes the dumbest, most straightforward solution is the best one.

Our site consists of several connected but independent fiefdoms. Only a little bit of administrative data is shared everywhere. In our distribution scheme, each fiefdom has one or two servers that store master copies of its system files. This is the sort of environment in which file copying works well, since the task is simply to pump the data around, not to tailor it for particular machines or networks.

File copying systems can use either a "push" model or a "pull" model. With push, the master server periodically distributes the freshest files to each client, whether the client wants them or not. Files may be pushed explicitly whenever a change is made or may simply be distributed on a regular schedule (perhaps with some files being transferred more often than others).

The push model has the advantage of keeping the distribution system centralized on one machine. Files, lists of clients, update scripts, and timetables are all stored in one place, making the scheme easy to control. One disadvantage is that each client must allow the master to modify its system files, creating a security hazard.

In a pull system, each client is responsible for updating itself from the server. This is a less centralized way of distributing files, but it is also more adaptable and more secure. A pull system is especially attractive when data is shared across administrative boundaries because the master and client machines need not be run by the same political faction.

rdist: push files

The **rdist** command is the easiest way to distribute files from a central server. It has something of the flavor of **make**: you use a text editor to create a specification of the files to be distributed, and then you use **rdist** to bring reality into line with your specification. **rdist** copies files only when they are out of date, so you can write your specification as if all files were to be copied and let **rdist** optimize out unnecessary work.

rdist preserves the owner, group, mode, and modification time of files. When **rdist** updates an existing file, it first deletes the old version before installing the new. This feature makes **rdist** suitable for transferring executables that might be in use during the update.[1]

Unfortunately, **rdist** has historically had some security issues. It traditionally ran on top of **rsh** and used **rsh**-style authentication to gain access to remote systems. Under this scheme, root access is permitted from any host listed in a target system's **/.rhosts** file. This scheme was acceptable on the relatively open and isolated networks of the past, but it's too dangerous to use in the context of the modern Internet. If one host is broken into, the security of all hosts that trust it is automatically compromised.

Since you are distributing administrative files such as **/etc/passwd**, it's pretty much a given that root access on the master server can be parlayed into root access on clients. That's not the problem. The problem is that by running **rlogind** (the server for **rsh** and also **rlogin** and **rcp**), client machines leave themselves open to other types of attack.

Current versions of **rdist** are better in that they allow any other command that understands the same syntax to be substituted for **rsh**. In practice, the substitute is **ssh**, which uses cryptography to verify the identity of hosts and to prevent network eavesdroppers from obtaining copies of your data. The downside is that you must run remote **ssh** servers in a mode that does not require a password. This is a less secure configuration than we would normally recommend, but it is still a huge improvement over **rsh**. See page 673 for more information about **sshd** and its authentication modes.

Now that we've belabored the perils of **rdist**, let's look at how it actually works. Like **make**, **rdist** looks for a control file (**Distfile** or **distfile**) in the current directory. **rdist -f** *distfile* explicitly specifies the control file's pathname. Within the **Distfile**, tabs, spaces, and newlines are used interchangeably as separators. Comments are introduced with a pound sign (#).

The meat of a **Distfile** consists of statements of the form

```
label: pathnames -> destinations commands
```

The *label* field associates a name with the statement. From the shell, you can run **rdist** *label* to distribute only the files described in a particular statement.

The *pathnames* and *destinations* are lists of files to be copied and hosts to copy them to, respectively. If there is more than one entry in a list, it must be surrounded with parentheses and the elements must be separated with whitespace. The *pathnames* can include shell-style globbing characters (e.g., **/usr/man/man[123]** or **/usr/lib/***). The notation *~user* is also acceptable, but it is evaluated separately on the source and destination machines.

---

1. Though the old version disappears from the filesystem namespace, it continues to exist until all references have been released. You must also be aware of this effect when managing log files. See page 201 for more information.

By default, **rdist** copies the files and directories listed in *pathnames* to the equivalent paths on each destination machine. You can modify this behavior by supplying a sequence of commands and terminating each with a semicolon.

The following commands are understood:

```
install options [destdir];
notify namelist;
except pathlist;
except_pat patternlist;
special [pathlist] string;
```

The install command sets options that affect the way **rdist** copies files. Options typically control the treatment of symbolic links, the correctness of **rdist**'s difference-checking algorithm, and the way that deletions are handled. The options should be preceded by -o and consist of a comma-separated list of option names. For example, the line

```
install -oremove,follow ;
```

makes **rdist** follow symbolic links (instead of just copying them as links) and removes existing files on the destination machine that have no counterpart on the source machine. See the man page for **rdist** for a complete list of options. The defaults are almost always what you want.

The name "install" is somewhat misleading, since files are copied whether or not an install command is present. Options are specified as they would be on the **rdist** command line, but when included in the **Distfile**, they apply only to the set of files handled by that install command.

The optional *destdir* specifies an installation directory on the destination hosts. By default, **rdist** uses the original pathnames.

The notify command takes a list of email addresses as its argument. **rdist** sends mail to these addresses whenever a file is updated. Any addresses that do not contain an at sign (@) are suffixed with the name of the destination host. For example, **rdist** would expand "pete" to "pete@anchor" when reporting a list of files updated on host anchor.

The except and except_pat commands remove pathnames from the list of files to be copied. Arguments to except are matched literally, and those of except_pat are interpreted as regular expressions. These exception commands are useful because **rdist**, like **make**, allows macros to be defined at the beginning of its control file. You might want to use a similar list of files for several statements, specifying only the additions and deletions for each host.

The special command executes an **sh** command (the *string* argument, which should be quoted) on each remote host. The command is executed after each file is copied. There is unfortunately no way to execute a command only after all files have been copied.

Here's a simple example of a **Distfile**:

```
SYS_FILES = (/etc/passwd /etc/group /etc/mail/aliases)
GET_ALL   = (chimchim lollipop barkadon)
GET_SOME  = (whammo spiff)

all: ${SYS_FILES} -> ${GET_ALL}
    notify barb;
    special /etc/mail/aliases "/usr/bin/newaliases";

some: ${SYS_FILES} -> ${GET_SOME}
    except /etc/mail/aliases;
    notify eddie@spiff;
```

*See page 534 for more information about **newaliases**.*
This configuration replicates the three listed system files on chimchim, lollipop, and barkadon and sends mail to barb@*destination* describing any updates or errors that occur. After **/etc/mail/aliases** is copied, **rdist** runs **newaliases** on each destination. Only two files are copied to whammo and spiff. **newaliases** is not run, and a report is mailed to eddie@spiff.

To get **rdist** working among machines, you must also make **sshd** on the recipient hosts trust the host from which you are distributing files. To do this, you generate a plaintext key for the master host and store a copy of the public portion in the file **~root/.ssh/authorized_keys** on each recipient. It's probably also wise to restrict what this key can do and where it can log in from. See the description of "method B" on page 674 for more information.

rsync: transfer files more securely

***rsync** is available from rsync.samba.org.*
rsync, written by Andrew Tridgell and Paul Mackerras, is similar in spirit to **rdist** but with a somewhat different focus. It does not use a file-copying control file in the manner of **rdist** (although the server side does have a configuration file). **rsync** is a bit like a souped-up version of **rcp** that is scrupulous about preserving links, modification times, and permissions. It is more network efficient than **rdist** because it looks inside individual files and attempts to transmit only the differences between versions. Most Linux distributions provide **rsync**, including Red Hat, SuSE, and Debian.

From our perspective, the main advantage of **rsync** is the fact that receiving machines can run the remote side as a server process out of **inetd**. The server (actually just a different mode of **rsync**, which must be installed on both the master and the clients) is quite configurable: it can restrict remote access to a set of given directories and can require the master to prove its identity with a password. Since no **rsh** access is necessary, you can set up **rsync** to distribute system files without making too many security compromises. (However, if you prefer to use **rsh** or **ssh** instead of an **inetd**-based server process, **rsync** lets you do that too.) What's more, **rsync** can also run in pull mode (pulling files down from the **rsync** server rather than pushing them to it), which is even more secure (see the section on pulling files, page 495).

Unfortunately, **rsync** isn't nearly as flexible as **rdist**, and its configuration is less sophisticated than **rdist**'s **distfile**. You can't execute arbitrary commands on the clients, and you can't **rsync** to multiple hosts at once.

As an example, the command

```
# rsync -gopt --password-file=/etc/rsync.pwd /etc/passwd lollipop::sysfiles
```

transfers the **/etc/passwd** file to the machine lollipop. The **-gopt** options preserve the permissions, ownerships, and modification times of the file. The double colon in **lollipop::sysfiles** makes **rsync** contact the remote **rsync** directly on port 873 instead of using **rsh**. The password stored in **/etc/rsync.pwd** authenticates the connection.[2]

This example transfers only one file, but **rsync** is capable of handling multiple files at once. In addition, the --**include** and --**exclude** flags let you specify a list of regular expressions to match against filenames, so you can set up a fairly sophisticated set of transfer criteria. If the command line gets too unwieldy, you can also read the patterns from separate files with the --**include-file** and --**exclude-file** options.

 Red Hat ships with **rsync** ready to go, but turned off. To turn it on, edit the file **/etc/xinetd.d/rsync** and change the line that says disable=yes to disable=no.

 SuSE includes a line for **rsyncd** in **/etc/inetd.conf**, but it is commented out by default. Uncomment the line (remove the leading #) to enable **rsyncd**.

 The Debian **rsync** package does not set up the **rsync** server by default; you have to create an appropriate **rsyncd.conf** file and add an entry to **/etc/inetd.conf**. For example, the following line in **inetd.conf** will run the server (with TCP wrappers):

```
rsync stream tcp nowait root /usr/sbin/tcpd /usr/bin/rsyncd --daemon
```

See page 668 for more information about TCP wrappers.

If you use TCP wrappers, you may want to configure **tcpd** to block access from all hosts except the one that will be distributing your system files. Host rejection can also be specified in **rsyncd.conf**, but it never hurts to erect multiple barriers.

Once you have enabled **rsync**, you need to set up a couple of config files to tell the **rsync** server how to behave. The main file is **/etc/rsyncd.conf**, which contains both global configurations parameters and a set of "modules," each of which is a directory tree to export or import. A reasonable configuration for a module that you can push to (i.e., that will accept incoming file transfers initiated by the connecting client) looks something like this:

```
# sysfiles is just an arbitrary title for the particular module.
[sysfiles]
# This is the path you allow files to be pushed to. It could be just /.
path = /etc
```

---

2. Although the password is not sent in plaintext across the network, the transferred files are not encrypted. If you use **ssh** as the transport (**rsync -gopt -e ssh /etc/passwd /etc/shadow lollipop:/etc** – note the single colon), the connection will be encrypted, but **sshd** will have to be configured not to require a password. Name your poison!

```
# This is the secrets file containing the username/password pair for
    authenticating the module
secrets file = /etc/rsyncd.secrets
# Can be read only if you are pulling files
read only = false
# UID and GID under which the transfer will be done
uid = root
gid = root
# List of hosts that are allowed to connect
hosts allow = distribution_master_hostname
```

Many other options can be set, but the defaults are reasonable. This configuration limits operations to the **/etc** directory and allows access only by the listed host. From the user's or client's point of view, you can **rsync** files to the server with the destination *hostname*::**sysfiles**, which maps to the module above. If you want to set up **rsync** in pull mode (pulling files from a central **rsync** server), the configuration above will still work, although you may want to tighten things up a bit (e.g., by setting the transfer mode to read-only).

The last thing you need to do is set up an **rsyncd.secrets** file. It's generally kept in **/etc** (although you can put it elsewhere) and contains the passwords that clients can use to authenticate themselves. For example:

root:*password*

rsync passwords should as a general rule be different from actual passwords. Because the passwords are shown in plaintext, **rsyncd.secrets** must be readable only by root.

Pulling files

There are several ways to implement a pulling system. The most straightforward and simplest is to make the files available on a central FTP or web server and to have the clients automatically download files as needed. In historical times, administrators would roll their own utilities to do this (often scripting **ftp** with a system such as **expect**), but there are now standard utilities that do this for you.

A popular one that ships with most Linux distributions is **wget**. It's a straightforward little program that fetches the contents of a URL (either FTP or HTTP). For example, to FTP a file with **wget**, just run

wget **ftp**://*user*:*password*@*hostname*/*path*/*to*/*file*

The specified *file* will be deposited in the current directory.

An alternative option for FTP only is **ncftp**, which also ships with most distributions. It's really just an enhanced FTP client that allows for easy scripting.

Some sites distribute files by publishing them on a networked filesystem such as NFS. This is perhaps the simplest technique from an automation point of view—all you need is **cp**, at least in theory. In practice, you would probably want to be a little more sophisticated and check for signs of security problems and corrupted content before blindly copying system files. Publishing sensitive system files over NFS has some disadvantages from a security point of view, but it's a simple and effective way of moving the bits.

A final option is to use **rsync**. If you run an **rsync** server on your central distribution host, clients can simply **rsync** the files down. This method is perhaps slightly more complex than using FTP, but it gives you access to all of **rsync**'s features.

Whatever system you use, be careful not to overload your data server. If a lot of machines on the network try to access your server simultaneously (e.g., if everyone runs an update out of **cron** at the same time), you can cause an inadvertent denial of service attack. Large sites should keep this problem in mind and provide for time staggering or randomization. A simple way to do this is to wrap **cron** jobs in a Perl script such as this:

```
#!/usr/bin/perl
sleep rand() * 600; # sleep between 0 and 600 seconds (ie, 10 minutes)
system(copy_files_down);
```

18.3   NIS: THE NETWORK INFORMATION SERVICE

NIS, released by Sun in the 1980s, was the first "prime time" administrative database. It was originally called the Sun Yellow Pages, but eventually had to be renamed for legal reasons. NIS commands still begin with the letters **yp**, so it's hard to forget the original name. NIS was widely adopted among UNIX vendors and is supported by virtually every Linux distribution.

The unit of sharing in NIS is the record, not the file. A record usually corresponds to one line in a config file. A master server maintains the authoritative copies of system files, which are kept in their original locations and formats and are edited with a text editor just as before. A server process makes the contents of the files available over the network. A server and its clients constitute an NIS "domain".[3]

Data files are preprocessed into database files by the **gdbm** hashing library to improve the efficiency of lookups. After editing files on the master server, you tell NIS to convert them to their hashed format with **make**.

Only one key can be associated with each entry, so a system file may have to be translated into several NIS "maps." For example, the **/etc/passwd** file is translated into two different maps called **passwd.byname** and **passwd.byuid**. One map is used to look up entries by username and the other to look up entries by UID. Either map can be used to enumerate the entries in the **passwd** file. However, because hashing libraries do not preserve the order of records, there is no way to reconstruct an exact duplicate of the original file (unless it was sorted).

NIS allows you to replicate the network maps on a set of slave servers. Providing more than one server helps to relieve the load on the master and to keep clients working

---

3. Do not confuse NIS domains with DNS domains. They are completely separate and have nothing to do with each other.

even when some servers become unavailable. Whenever a file is changed on the master server, the corresponding NIS map must be pushed out to the slaves so that all servers provide the same data. Clients do not distinguish between the master server and the slaves.

In the traditional NIS implementation, you must place at least one NIS server on every physical network. Clients use IP broadcasting to locate servers, and broadcast packets are not forwarded by routers and gateways. The **ypset** command can be used to point a client at a particular server; however, at the first hint of trouble, the client will attempt to locate a new server by using broadcasting. Unless there is a server on the client's network, this sequence of events may cause the client to hang.

This system causes a lot of problems, not least of which is that it is extremely insecure. An intruder can set up a rogue NIS server that responds to broadcasts and either provides bogus data or delivers a denial of service attack by allowing binding and then blocking on actual requests. These days, the preferred management technique is to give each client an explicit list of its legitimate NIS servers. This system also has the advantage that the servers need not be on the local subnet.

Under Linux, servers are listed in **/etc/yp.conf**. Here's an example:

```
domain  we.luv.nis  server  10.2.2.3
domain  we.luv.nis  server  10.2.2.4
```

There is one line for each server; if one server goes down, NIS will fail over to another. Note that the servers are given in the form of IP addresses. **yp.conf** accepts hostnames, but these hostnames must then be resolvable at boot time (e.g., enumerated in the **/etc/hosts** file).

If you *must* use broadcast mode, the syntax is

```
domain  we.luv.nis  broadcast
```

Netgroups

NIS introduced a popular abstraction known as netgroups. Netgroups name sets of users, machines, and nets for easy reference in other system files. They are defined in **/etc/netgroup** and are also shared as an NIS map.

The format of a **netgroup** entry is

groupname list-of-members

Members are separated by whitespace. A member is either a netgroup name or a triplet of the form

(hostname, username, nisdomainname)

Any empty field in a triplet is a wild card; thus the entry (boulder,,) refers to all users in all domains on the host boulder (or to the host boulder itself, depending on the context in which the netgroup is used). A dash in a field indicates negation, so the entry (boulder,-,) refers to the machine boulder and no users. Netgroup definitions can nest.

Here's a simple example of an **/etc/netgroup** file:

```
bobcats        (snake,,) (headrest,,)
servers        (anchor,,) (moet,,) (piper,,) (kirk,,)
anchorclients  (xx,,) (watneys,,) (molson,,)
beers          (anchor,,) (anchor-gateway,,) anchorclients
allhosts       beers bobcats servers
```

These netgroups are all defined in terms of hosts; that's typical for real-world use.

See Chapter 17 for more information about NFS.

Netgroups can be used in several system files that define permissions. The most common application these days is for configuring NFS exports. Netgroups can be mentioned in the **/etc/exports** file to specify groups of hosts that are allowed to mount each filesystem. This feature is very handy when you are exporting to a lot of hosts, particularly on systems that require fully qualified domain names and that limit lines in the **exports** file to 1,024 characters.

Netgroups are a nice idea. They simplify system files, making them more understandable. They also add a layer of indirection that permits the status of a user or machine to be changed in one file rather than fifteen.

Prioritizing sources of administrative information

Configuration information can be distributed in several ways. Every system understands flat files and knows how to use DNS to look up hostnames and Internet addresses. Most also understand NIS. Since there may be several potential sources for a given piece of information, Linux provides a way for you to specify the sources that are to be checked and the order in which the checks are made.

In the original (pre-Linux) implementation of NIS, some configuration files (the **/etc/passwd** and **/etc/group** files in particular) had to be configured to "invite in" the contents of the corresponding NIS maps. The invitation was extended by inclusion of special incantations in the files themselves. A lone "+" at the beginning of a line would include the entire NIS map, "+@*netgroup*" would include only entries relevant to a given netgroup, and "+*name*" would include a single entry.

This approach was never very well liked, and it has been superseded by a central config file, **/etc/nsswitch.conf**, that allows an explicit search path to be specified for each type of administrative information. The original behavior can be emulated by use of a compatibility mode, but it's unlikely you would ever want to actually perform this emulation. (Unfortunately, emulation is most distributions' default.)

A typical **nsswitch.conf** file looks something like this:

```
passwd:  files nis
hosts:   files dns
group:   files
...
```

Each line configures one type of information (usually, one flat-file equivalent). The potential sources are nis, nisplus, ldap, hesiod, files, dns, and compat; they refer to NIS, NIS+, LDAP, MIT's Hesiod directory service, vanilla flat files (ignoring to-kens such as "+"), DNS, and NISified flat files (honoring "+"), respectively. DNS is only a valid data source for host and network information. Another source (unfor-tunately not very well documented) is db, which reads a hashed (**gdbm**) version of the map from **/var/db** (for example, **/var/db/passwd.db**). If your flat files are large, the use of hashed versions could increase lookup speed substantially.

Sources are tried from left to right until one of them produces an answer for the query. In the example above, the **gethostbyname** routine would first check the **/etc/hosts** file, and if the host was not listed there, would then check DNS. Queries about UNIX groups, on the other hand, would check only the **/etc/group** file.

If necessary, you can define the "failure" of a source more specifically by putting bracketed expressions after it. For example, the line

```
hosts:   dns [NOTFOUND=return] nis
```

causes DNS to be used exclusively if it is available; a negative response from the name server makes queries return immediately (with a failure code) without checking NIS. However, NIS will be used if no name server is available. The various types of failures are shown in Table 18.2; each may be set to return or continue, indicating whether the query should be aborted or forwarded to the next source.

Table 18.2   Failure modes recognized in /etc/nsswitch.conf

Condition	Meaning
UNAVAIL	The source doesn't exist or is down.
NOTFOUND	The source exists, but couldn't answer the query.
TRYAGAIN	The source exists but is busy.
SUCCESS	The source was able to answer the query.

By default, Linux distributions all ship with **nsswitch.conf** files that are reasonable for a stand-alone machine without NIS. All entries go to the flat files, with the excep-tion of host lookups, which first consult flat files and then DNS. Our example distri-butions all default to compat mode for **passwd** and **group**, which is probably worth changing. If you really use NIS, just put it in the **nsswitch.conf** file.

 Debian ships with protocols, services, ethers, and rpc going to db and then files. This is slightly odd, since Debian doesn't, in fact, include **/var/db** or any mechanism to maintain it. Presumably it would be slightly more efficient to go directly to files; you can modify the settings to do that if you want.

Advantages and disadvantages of NIS

One nice feature of NIS is that it can be understood by mere mortals. NIS is analo-gous to copying files around; in most cases, it's unnecessary for administrators to be aware of NIS's internal data formats. Administration is performed with the same old flat files, and only one or two new procedures need to be learned.

Since there is no way to link NIS domains, NIS is not suitable for managing a large network of machines unless a single configuration is to be applied to every machine. You can divide a large network into several NIS domains, but each domain must be administered separately. Even if a large network does use a single configuration, limitations on the scaling of slave servers mean that in practice these sites usually come up with some other mechanism to keep their NIS servers in sync. They often end up rolling their own back-end databases and making their NIS servers fetch their data from this central source.

*See Chapter 9 for more information about **cron**.*

If a slave server is down or inaccessible when a map is changed, the slave's copy will not be updated. Slaves must periodically poll the master to be sure that they have the most recent version of every map. Although basic tools for polling are provided with NIS, you must implement the polling scheme you want by using **cron**. Even so, there is the possibility that two different versions of a map will be served simultaneously for a while, with clients randomly seeing one or the other.

NIS is not secure. Broadcast mode is particularly bad; any host on a network can claim to serve a particular domain and feed bogus administrative data to NIS clients. You can avoid this problem by explicitly enumerating the permissible NIS servers for each client.

You can restrict the hosts that are able to read a server's maps by explicitly listing them in the file **/var/yp/securenets**; however, this is not 100% secure. You can also improve the security of your system by distributing your shadow password file with some other technique (such as **rdist** or **rsync**); we don't recommend using NIS to serve shadow passwords.

Older versions of Linux NIS (including those in pre-7.* SuSE and Red Hat) contain known security holes. If you are running an older system, make sure you get the latest upgrades before starting NIS.

How NIS works

NIS's data files are stored in the directory **/var/yp**. Each NIS map is stored in a hashed format in a subdirectory of the NIS directory named for the NIS domain. There is one file for each key by which a file can be searched. For example, in the domain cssuns, the **gdbm** files for the **/etc/passwd** maps might be

```
/var/yp/cssuns/passwd.byname
/var/yp/cssuns/passwd.byuid
```

The **passwd** file is searchable by both name and UID, so two maps are derived from it.

The **makedbm** command generates NIS maps from flat files. However, you need not invoke this command directly. There is a **Makefile** in **/var/yp** that generates all the common NIS maps. After you modify a system file, **cd** to **/var/yp** and run **make**. The **make** command checks the modification time of each file against the modification times of the maps derived from it and runs **makedbm** for each map that needs to be rebuilt.

Maps are copied from the master server to the slave servers by the **ypxfr** command. **ypxfr** is a pull command; it must be run on each slave server to make that server import the map. Slaves usually execute **ypxfr** every so often just to verify that they have the most recent maps; you can use **cron** to control how often this is done.

The default implementation of map copying is somewhat inefficient. Linux provides a daemon called **ypxfrd** that can be run on the master server to respond in a speedier fashion to **ypxfr** requests. **ypxfrd** sidesteps the normal NIS protocol and simply hands out copies of the map files.

yppush is a "push" command that's used on the master server. It actually does not transfer any data but rather instructs each slave to execute a **ypxfr**. The **yppush** command is used by the **Makefile** in the NIS directory to ensure that newly updated maps are propagated to slaves.

The special map called **ypservers** does not correspond to any flat file. This map contains a list of all the servers of the domain. It's constructed automatically when the domain is set up with **ypinit** (see *Configuring NIS servers* on page 502). Its contents are examined whenever the master server needs to distribute maps to slaves.

After initial configuration, the only active components of the NIS system are the **ypserv** and **ypbind** daemons. **ypserv** runs only on servers (both master and slave); it accepts queries from clients and answers them by looking up information in the hashed map files.

ypbind runs on every machine in the NIS domain, including servers. The C library contacts the local **ypbind** daemon whenever it needs to answer an administrative query (provided that **/etc/nsswitch.conf** says to do so). **ypbind** locates a **ypserv** in the appropriate domain and returns its identity to the C library, which then contacts the server directly. The query mechanism is illustrated in Exhibit A.

Exhibit A   NIS query procedure

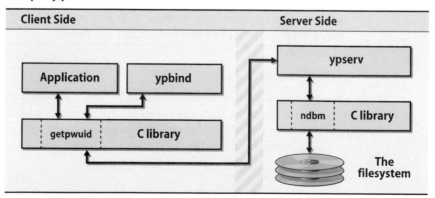

Once **ypbind** locates a server, it continues to rely on that server for all queries until the server goes down or some other communication problem occurs. A **ypbind** on a server machine does not give itself preferential treatment, so servers don't necessarily bind to themselves.

In some circumstances (for example, when all servers but one are simultaneously rebooted), clients can fixate on one server and refuse to let go even after other servers become available. This situation can slow response time considerably.

NIS includes a number of minor commands that examine maps, find out which version of a map each server is using, and control the binding between clients and servers. A complete list of NIS commands and daemons is given in Table 18.3. (Rows have been shaded to improve readability.)

Table 18.3   NIS commands and daemons

Program	Description
ypserv	NIS server daemon, started at boot time
ypbind	NIS client daemon, started at boot time
domainname	Sets the NIS domain a machine is in (run at boot time)
ypxfr	Downloads current version of a map from master server
ypxfrd	Serves requests from **ypxfr** (runs on master server)
yppush	Makes slave servers update their versions of a map
makedbm	Builds a hashed map from a flat file
ypmake	Rebuilds hashed maps from flat files that have changed
ypinit	Configures a host as a master or slave server
ypset	Makes **ypbind** connect to a particular server
ypwhich	Finds out which server the current host is using
yppoll	Finds out what version of a map a server is using
ypcat	Prints the values contained in an NIS map
ypmatch	Prints map entries for a specified key
yppasswd	Changes a password on the NIS master server
ypchfn	Changes GECOS information on the NIS master server
ypchsh	Changes a login shell on NIS master server
yppasswdd	Server for **yppasswd**, **ypchsh**, and **ypchfn**

Setting up an NIS domain

NIS must be initialized on the master server, on the slave servers, and on each client. You do this in two steps. First, run **ypinit** on each server. Second, on every machine in the domain, set the domain name from one of the system startup files and configure **/etc/nsswitch.conf** to import NIS data.

Configuring NIS servers

ypinit initializes both the master and slave servers for a domain. On the master, you use the following commands.

```
# cd /var/yp          /* The NIS directory, wherever it is */
# domainname foo      /* Name the new domain. */
# ypinit -m           /* Initialize as master server. */
# ypserv              /* Start the NIS server. */
```

The **-m** flag tells **ypinit** that it's configuring a master server; it will prompt you to enter a list of slave servers. Once the master is up and running, you should prime each slave server by running **ypinit** with the **-s** (slave) flag:

```
# cd /var/yp
# ypinit -s master    /* Argument is  master's hostname. */
# ypserv
```

ypinit -s makes a local copy of the master's current data; the presence of the domain's data files is enough to let **ypserv** know that it should serve the domain.

*See Chapter 9 for more information about **cron**.*

On each slave, you should set up crontab entries to pull fresh copies of all maps from the master. The command **ypxfr** *map*, where *map* is a name such as **passwd.byuid**, will transfer the specified map from the master server. You must run the command once for each map. Maps tend to change at different rates, and if network bandwidth is precious, you may want to transfer some maps more often than others. In most circumstances, transferring all the maps once or twice a day (perhaps late at night) is good enough. The following script transfers every map:

```
#!/bin/sh
mydomain = `/bin/domainname`
cd /var/yp/$mydomain    # the NIS directory
for map in `/bin/ls`; do
    /usr/lib/yp/ypxfr $map
done
```

There are also prefabricated scripts in **/usr/lib/yp** that transfer NIS maps at various frequencies (**ypxfr_1perday**, **ypxfr_2perday**, and **ypxfr_1perhour**).

If you want users to be able to change their passwords with **yppasswd**, you must run the **yppasswdd** daemon on the master NIS server. The Linux version of this server has been known to crash frequently, so be sure to verify that it is still running if the **yppasswd** command doesn't seem to be working.

Configuring NIS clients

After setting up servers, you must inform each client machine that it is a member of the new domain. The servers of a domain are generally clients as well.

See Chapter 2 for more information about the system startup scripts.

The **domainname** command sets a machine's NIS domain. It's usually run at boot time from one of the startup scripts. The exact contortions necessary to configure this vary by distribution; distribution-specific details are given below.

Each client must have at least a minimal private version of the **passwd**, **group**, and **hosts** files. **passwd** and **group** are needed to allow root to log in when no NIS server is available. They should contain the standard system accounts and groups: root, bin, daemon, etc. The **hosts** file (or DNS) must be present to answer boot-time queries that occur before NIS is up and running.

 Under Red Hat, you set the NIS domain name in **/etc/sysconfig/network** by setting the variable NISDOMAIN. **ypbind**, **ypserv**, and **yppasswdd** are enabled and disabled with **chkconfig**; for example,

> # chkconfig ypbind on

 Under SuSE, turn on **ypbind** by editing **rc.config**. Set YP_DOMAINNAME to your domain name and change START_YPBIND to "yes". You can also (optionally) enumerate a list of servers in the YP_SERVER variable. To run an NIS server (**ypserv**), set START_YPSERV to "yes"; other server parameters are set in the file

> **/etc/rc.config.d/ypserv.rc.config**.

 Debian stores the name of the NIS domain in **/etc/defaultdomain**. The rest of the configuration information comes from **/etc/ypbind.config**. Debian starts **ypbind** automatically if **/etc/defaultdomain** exists. You can make the box a server by changing the line NISSERVER=false in the **/etc/init.d/nis** file to true.

18.4 NIS+: SON OF NIS

NIS+, aka "NIS on steroids whose face nobody is Ever Going to Kick Sand in Again," was designed to correct the deficiencies of NIS and introduce deficiencies of its own. It handles large networks of machines. It has security features built in. It permits multiple domains to be administered from anywhere on a network. It transfers updates efficiently. It's a distributed database *and* a dessert topping; it sings, it dances, it leaps capital T in a single bound.

Sun released NIS+ in the early 90s. Despite their similar names, NIS and NIS+ do not really have much to do with each other. NIS+ is considerably more complex than NIS, and it has not enjoyed the same degree of popular support. Sun has announced plans to discontinue support for NIS+, and we expect that it will gradually disappear over time.[4]

Although Linux can act as an NIS+ client, there is no NIS+ server for Linux and no one is working to implement one. As a Linux administrator, you almost certainly won't have to deal with NIS+ unless you are integrating your systems into an established UNIX environment that has already standardized on it. If you're in that camp, you are probably already familiar with NIS+.

NIS+ is a good example of what Frederick P. Brooks, Jr. calls "the second system effect" in his classic book on software engineering, *The Mythical Man-Month*. It attempts to build on the success of its progenitor while avoiding all of the mistakes and pitfalls of the previous design. It devotes substantial effort to the system's formal architecture. In theory it should be perfect. In practice it's somewhat clunky, over-

---

4. But who knows—there were still several active Multics sites in 1996.

engineered, and adrift from everyday reality. We've been told that even Sun does not use NIS+ internally.

From a client's perspective, NIS+ looks mostly the same as NIS. Most data is accessed through the same library routines as always, and NIS+'s complex world of domains, tables, permissions, and search paths is in the end rendered down to an analog of the original UNIX flat files.

There is a NIS+ client for Linux, but it is not very well integrated into the distributions. There are some instructions in the *NIS HOWTO* (see www.linuxdoc.org); they are a bit too involved to be reproduced in this book, but they work moderately well.

 Red Hat includes the basic software necessary for NIS+, but no documentation. You will have to roll your own **rc** script to start the necessary daemons. Follow the directions in the *NIS HOWTO*.

 A guide to setting up NIS+ under SuSE can be found at

> http://www.suse.de/~kukuk/nisplus/SuSE-Linux.html

 A set of NIS+ packages for Debian is available from

> http://www.realbodo.de/debian

(Then follow the instructions in the *NIS HOWTO*.)

18.5 LDAP: THE LIGHTWEIGHT DIRECTORY ACCESS PROTOCOL

UNIX sites need a good way to distribute their administrative configuration data; however, the problem is really more general than that. What about nonadministrative data such as telephone and email directories? What about information that you want to share with the outside world? What everyone really needs is a generalized directory service.

A directory service is just a database, but one that makes a few assumptions. Any data set that has characteristics matching the assumptions is a candidate for inclusion. The basic assumptions are as follows:

- Data objects are relatively small.
- The database will be widely replicated and cached.
- The information is attribute based.
- Data are read often but written infrequently.
- Searching is a common operation.

The current IETF standards-track system designed to fill this role is the Lightweight Directory Access Protocol (LDAP). The LDAP specifications don't really speak to the database itself, just the way that it's accessed through a network. But because they specify how the data is schematized and how searches are performed, they imply a fairly specific data model as well.

LDAP's history is quite sordid. The story begins with the OSI networking system, a cradle-to-grave network protocol suite that was misguidedly adopted as an international standard in the mid-1980s. The OSI system as a whole proved to be a big flop, but several of its component protocols (LDAP among them) have enjoyed a macabre afterlife in mutant forms adapted to life in the TCP/IP world.

LDAP was originally designed as a simple gateway protocol that would allow TCP/IP clients to talk to the X.500 directory servers that ran on OSI systems. Over time, it became apparent both that X.500 was going to die out and that UNIX really needed a standard directory of some sort. These factors have led to LDAP being developed as a full-fledged directory system in its own right (and perhaps to its no longer being quite so deserving of the L).

At this point (in the year 2001), we are still somewhere in the middle of the development process. The most widely implemented version of LDAP, version 2, lacks many features that will be needed to get LDAP to the same level of functionality and reliability as, say, DNS. Even version 3 of the protocol, which is not yet standardized, appears to have some substantial gaps. Outside of a few specific domains (Internet phone books, **sendmail** alias configuration, some calendaring applications), real-world experience with LDAP has been limited. People are slowly beginning to push LDAP into other domains, so with luck this situation will improve.

Unfortunately, LDAP has become chum for an industry-wide feeding frenzy of sorts, with everybody and their dog pledging undying support for the protocol. Like Java technology in the mid-1990s, the swirling waters have thrown off a lot of press releases but relatively little actual software. We will just have to wait and see if a beautiful Venus eventually rises from the waves.

Our sense of LDAP is that it may or may not develop further in the direction of helping sysadmins. LDAP hasn't really found its niche yet. We advise a policy of "watchful waiting" for now. That said, most Linux distributions do ship with support for LDAP as a directory service (just specify it in **nsswitch.conf**) and sites *are* running it in the real world.

LDAP documentation and specifications

Currently, the best introduction to LDAP is a booklet called *Understanding LDAP* written by Heinz Johner et al. for IBM's International Technical Support Organization. It's available for download as an Acrobat file from www.redbooks.ibm.com. The parts about the C language programming API can be ignored; all the rest is useful information for system administrators. And don't say IBM never did anything for you.

The LDAP-related RFCs are many and varied. Some of the high points are listed in Table 18.4. Most of the listed RFCs have version 2 equivalents that are not shown. As this table suggests, most LDAP objects and transactions can be represented in plaintext, which is one of the protocol's nicer features. It's easy to generate queries from a script or to set up gateways to other protocols, such as HTTP.

Table 18.4   LDAP-related RFCs

RFC	Title
1777	Lightweight Directory Access Protocol (v2)
2251	Lightweight Directory Access Protocol (v3)
2252	LDAPv3: Attribute Syntax Definitions
2253	LDAPv3: UTF-8 String Representation of Distinguished Names
2254	The String Representation of LDAP Search Filters
2255	The LDAP URL Format
2256	A Summary of the X.500 User Schema for Use with LDAPv3
2307	An Approach for Using LDAP as a Network Information Service

RFC2307 suggests ways of mapping traditional UNIX data sets such as the **passwd** and **group** files into the LDAP namespace. This RFC is still classified as "experimental" but is widely followed.

Hands-on LDAP

See page 538 for more information about using LDAP with **sendmail**.

LDAP has been implemented by the University of Michigan, by Netscape, and by others. The best source today is the OpenLDAP group at www.openldap.org, which took over and enhanced the University of Michigan code base. OpenLDAP is shipped with Red Hat, SuSE, Debian, and many other Linux distributions. Some docs are provided, including an administrator's guide (at openldap.org) and an *LDAP HOWTO* (www.linuxdoc.org).

In the OpenLDAP distribution, **slapd** is the standard server daemon and **slurpd** handles replication, sort of like an NIS slave server. This scheme adds hierarchy to the server network independently of whether the data is truly hierarchical. When version 3 of the LDAP protocol is fully deployed, we will have true hierarchy in both the data and the infrastructure.

Configuring an OpenLDAP server

Assuming that you installed the OpenLDAP server as part of your general Linux installation, setting it up is a matter of tweaking some config files.

First, create an **/etc/openldap/slapd.conf** file. A sample is installed with the OpenLDAP server. You need to change the following lines:

```
suffix "dc=mydomain, dc=com"
rootdn "cn=admin, dc=mydomain, dc=com"
rootpw {crypt}abJnggxhB/yWI
```

The suffix is your "LDAP basename." It's the root of your portion of the LDAP namespace, similar in concept to your DNS domain name. In fact, the common practice is to use your DNS domain name as your LDAP basename (as indicated above). Unlike DNS, LDAP requires that complex names such as mydomain.com be broken out into domain components (the dc= entries of the example).

The rootdn is your administrator's name, and the rootpw is the administrator's UNIX-format (DES) password. Note that the domain components leading up to the administrator's name must be specified as well. You can either copy and paste the password from **/etc/shadow** (if you don't use MD5 passwords) or generate it with a simple Perl one-liner

```
perl -e "print crypt('password','salt');"
```

where *password* is the desired password and *salt* is an arbitrary two-character string. Because of the presence of this password, make sure that the permissions on your **slapd.conf** file are 600 and that it's owned by root.

You also need to edit both **/etc/ldap.conf** and **/etc/openldap/ldap.conf** to change the name of your LDAP server and your basename. It's pretty straightforward—just set the argument of the HOST entry to your server and set the BASE to the same value as the suffix in **slapd.conf**. (Make sure both lines are uncommented.) At this point, you should be able to start up **slapd** by simply running it with no arguments.

 Under Red Hat, make LDAP run at startup by enabling it with **chkconfig**:

```
# chkconfig ldap on
```

 Under SuSE, you set LDAP to run at boot time by finding the START_LDAP entry in **/etc/rc.config** and setting it to "yes".

 Under Debian, installing the OpenLDAP package should automatically arrange for the server to start up at boot time.

Populating your server

You can populate your LDAP database the hard way or the easy way. The hard way is to do it by hand. However, once you've seen an LDAP schema you'll never want to do this—LDAP brings verbosity to a new level. For example, a single group entry looks like this:

```
dn: cn=staff,ou=groups,dc=domainname,dc=com
cn: staff
objectclass: posixGroup
userPassword: {crypt}*
gidNumber: 10
memberuid: root
memberuid: matthew
memberuid: evi
```

This is the LDAP equivalent of the following **/etc/group** line:

```
staff:*:10:root,matthew,evi
```

Type in a few of those and you'll soon be begging for NIS+. Fortunately, there are a number of tools out there for managing LDAP data. In particular, Padl Software provides a free set of Perl scripts that migrate existing flat files or NIS maps over to LDAP. They're available from www.padl.com/tools.html and are straightforward to run.

You may encounter some issues; for example, the default **services** file cannot be migrated because there are + symbols in some services' names. This is fixable with a little bit of editing but shows yet again just how bleeding edge this LDAP stuff is. Once a database has been imported, you can verify that the transfer worked correctly by running the **slapcat** utility, which displays the entire database.

LDAP can be an extraordinarily complicated system, and there is much more you can do to embellish the system in terms of security, replication, and general bells and whistles. If you desire job security, you can implement an LDAP setup with a complexity that defies belief. Because of both the obvious maintainability reasons and the immature nature of LDAP as a directory service, we recommend that you keep things fairly simple.

Setting up an LDAP client

Once you have a running server, it's easy to set up the clients. Edit the LDAP config files (**/etc/ldap.conf** and **/etc/openldap/ldap.conf**) to specify the identity of the server and your site's basename.

You can verify that you are connecting to the LDAP server correctly by running **ldapsearch -x**, which dumps the entire database. The **-x** is important because it turns off authentication.

Finally, change the appropriate lines in **/etc/nsswitch.conf** to use the LDAP server as a data source.

LDAP and security

At its worst, LDAP contains enough security issues to make any vaguely conscientious security administrator wince. In particular (ignoring the client-to-server authentication issues), data is sent across the network as plaintext, so shadow passwords and such are not protected. We strongly recommend that you *not* use LDAP to distribute shadow passwords, for much the same reasons that we don't recommend distributing them with NIS. Use **rsync** or some other method.

On the other hand, there is a lot more hope with LDAP than there is with NIS. For example, since LDAP runs on a known port, you could run it over SSL or even SSH to provide protection against sniffing. (SSL support for LDAP is being developed.) In addition, LDAP servers (including OpenLDAP) contain fairly fine-grained support for access control lists (ACLs).

A system as complex and with as many moving parts as LDAP will inevitably contain a lot of potential for accidental misconfiguration that weakens security, not to mention good old security holes. Caveat administrator.

18.6 EXERCISES

E18.1 Why is **rsync** considered more secure than **rdist**?

★ **E18.2** Why is a pull method of updating a local machine's files more secure than a push method?

★ **E18.3** Explain the following excerpt from an **rdist** distfile:

```
LINUX_PASSWD = ( redhatbox debianbox susebox )

passwd:
    ( /etc/passwd ) -> ( ${LINUX_PASSWD} )
    install /etc/passwd.rdist;
    cmdspecial /etc/passwd.rdist "/usr/local/sbin/mkpasswd";
```

★ **E18.4** Explain the differences between **rdist** and **rsync**. In what situations would it be better to use one than the other?

★ **E18.5** Compare and contrast NIS and LDAP. When would you use one and not the other? Would you ever use both?

★ **E18.6** What method does your site use to share system files? What are the security issues related to that method? Suggest an alternative way to share system files at your site and detail the concerns that it addresses. Are there any drawbacks?

★★ **E18.7** Outline the steps needed to secure LDAP by using SSL, the Secure Socket Layer (or TLS, as it is now called; Transport Layer Security).

19 Electronic Mail

Each time we tackle the job of updating this chapter, we underestimate both the complexity of a full-service mail system and the speed at which software is evolving. The major changes since our last rewrite include serious performance enhancements for very busy mail hubs, new security features, and spam fighting tools.

Today, electronic mail is absolutely essential to business and personal communication. Many of the recent changes in **sendmail** respond to the scaling and flexibility issues faced by ISPs with millions of email-hungry customers. Spam has inspired additional changes and increasingly stringent enforcement of the existing rules. The IETF has been busy issuing new email-related RFCs. And hackers have been busy beating on any system that trusts user-supplied content to be reasonable and follow the rules.

A social aspect of email that has become prevalent in the United States over the last few years is unsolicited commercial email, colloquially called spam, the junk mail of the Internet. Sending email on the Internet is cheap—much cheaper than sending stamped snail mail. The sender is typically billed a flat rate, so it costs the same to send one message as to send 25 million. But to the ISP who must provide enough bandwidth to handle the influx of spam—estimated to be as much as 30% of the incoming mail at America Online—spam is certainly not free. Attempts to control spam through laws and the courts have so far had minimal success. Technical solutions in the form of mail filters and black hole lists have been more effective. We cover the current state of the art in spam fighting starting on page 588.

The sheer bulk of this chapter—more than 100 pages—attests to the complexity of email systems. The chapter contains both background information and details of software configuration, in roughly that order.

We tried to divide this chapter into four smaller ones (on mail systems, **sendmail** configuration, spam, and Exim), but that left it confusing, full of chicken-and-egg problems, and, we think, less useful. Instead, we offer the annotated table of contents shown in Table 19.1.

Table 19.1   A road map for this chapter

	Section	Page	Contents
Background	1	513	Mail systems and their various pieces
	2	517	Addressing, address syntax, mail headers
	3	523	Philosophy, client/server design, mail homes
	4	527	Aliases, mail routing, mailing list software, LDAP
sendmail configuration	5	541	**sendmail**: installation, startup, the mail queue
	6	550	Introduction to configuring **sendmail**, **m4** macros
	7	554	Basic **sendmail** configuration primitives
	8	558	Fancier **sendmail** configuration primitives
	9	573	Examples: home machine, company, Linux defaults, etc.
	10	588	Spam, **sendmail** access database
	11	603	Security
	12	611	Performance
	13	615	Collecting statistics, testing, and debugging
Other	14	620	Exim, an alternative to **sendmail** (simpler, not as flexible)
	15	623	Additional sources of information

This organization makes the flow a bit smoother when the chapter is read straight through, but it sometimes separates the items relevant to a particular email-related task. The postmaster for a medium-sized organization might need to read the entire chapter, but a sysadmin setting up PC email support for a typical business client surely does not.

Table 19.2 provides a navigation guide for several common sysadmin chores.

Most of this chapter deals with the configuration of **sendmail**, the standard program that parses and routes electronic mail. **sendmail** was originally written by Eric Allman at the University of California, Berkeley. There have been three major versions: version 5, IDA, and version 8. Version 9 is looming on the horizon. Version 5 and IDA are no longer in common use; version 8 has replaced them. In this chapter we cover version 8 (8.12, to be precise) and look ahead to the features expected in version 9.

sendmail is being developed commercially by Sendmail, Inc., which also maintains a free, open source version. The commercial versions feature a graphical configuration

Table 19.2   Sections of this chapter relevant to various chores

Chore	Sections
Upgrading **sendmail**	5, 6
Configuring **sendmail** for the first time	3, 6, 7, 8, 9, 11, 13
Changing the config file	6
Designing a mail system for a site	3, 4, 6, 7, 8, 9, 11
Fighting spam	10
Auditing security	11
Setting up a PC to get mail	1, 3
Setting up a mailing list	4
Performance tuning	3, 8, 12
Virtual hosting	8, 9
Using Exim instead of **sendmail**	14

tool and centralized monitoring and reporting (features that are especially useful at high-volume mail sites).

19.1 MAIL SYSTEMS

In theory, a mail system consists of four distinct components:

- A "mail user agent" (MUA) that lets users read and compose mail
- A "mail transport agent" (MTA) that routes messages among machines
- A "delivery agent" that places messages in a local message store;[1] it is sometimes called a Local Delivery Agent (LDA)
- An optional "access agent" that connects the user agent to the message store (e.g., through IMAP or POP)

Some sites also use a mail submission agent that speaks SMTP (the mail transport protocol) and does some of the work of the transport agent. Exhibit A on page 514 shows the relationship of these components.

User agents

Email users employ a user agent to read and compose messages. Email messages originally consisted only of text, but a standard known as Multipurpose Internet Mail Extensions (MIME) is now used to encode text formats and attachments (including many viruses) into email. It is supported by most user agents. Since it does not affect the addressing or transport of mail, we do not discuss it further in this chapter.[2]

One chore of user agents is to make sure that any text embedded in the contents of a mail message that might be misunderstood by the mail system gets protected. An example is the string "From " that serves as a record separator between messages.

---

1. The receiving users' mailboxes or, sometimes, a database.
2. Some feel that the primary effect of the MIME standard has been to convert the Internet's open email format into a morass of proprietary subformats. The dust is still settling.

Exhibit A   Mail system components

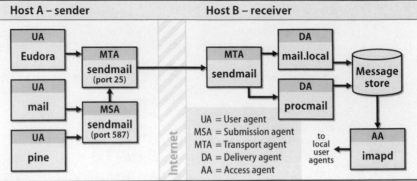

/**bin/mail** was the original user agent. Several alternatives now exist. The popular user agents are listed below, along with their original sources. Individual Linux distributions may include several of these programs (among the default installations of our example systems, SuSE is the richest in user agents and Debian the leanest). Don't fret if an agent you need isn't preinstalled—versions of all of these packages are readily available for Linux, so you can easily install any user agent your users request.

- /**bin/mail** on Red Hat is the BSD version of the original UNIX **mail** command; on SuSE and Debian, it's in /**usr/bin/mail**[3]
- **mh** and **nmh** ("new **mh**") based on software from the Rand Corporation, plus the **exmh** front end by Brent Welch of Scriptics
- **pine** from the University of Washington, www.washington.edu/pine
- **elm** by David Taylor, now maintained by the Elm Development Group and Kari Hurrta, available from ftp.virginia.edu
- **mutt** by Michael Elkins, available from ftp.mutt.org
- **rmail** and **VM**, mail user agents that are part of **emacs** and **XEmacs**; see www.wonderworks.com/vm and www.xemacs.org
- Mulberry from Cyrusoft International, Inc., (www.cyrusoft.com/mulberry) for a variety of platforms
- Messenger from Netscape Communications, for a variety of platforms
- Eudora from Qualcomm for Macs or PCs running Windows
- Outlook from Microsoft for Windows

Some user agents support a system-wide configuration file that sets defaults for all users. Individual users can override these defaults by setting up a personal configuration file in their home directories. User agents from the Windows and Mac worlds are configured from the application's UI, although most also support some form of global or automatic configuration for use at large sites.

---

3. This user agent is sometimes called **Mail** or **mailx** on other systems. Accordingly, Red Hat provides a link called **Mail**, and SuSE and Debian provide links called **Mail** and **mailx**.

Table 19.3 shows the features of the various user agents and the locations of their startup files. The locations and even the names of the global configuration files are sometimes vendor-specific; many are in **/etc**.

Table 19.3   User agent features and configuration files

User agent	Sys. prefs	User prefs	MIME	POP	IMAP	SMTP
[usr]/bin/mail	**mail.rc**	**.mailrc**				
***mh**	–	**.mh_profile** **.maildelivery**	✔	✔		✔
pine	**pine.conf**	**.pinerc**	✔	✔	✔	✔ [a]
elm	**lib/elm.rc**	**.elm/elmrc**	✔	✔ [b]	✔ [b]	
mutt	**Muttrc**	**.muttrc**	✔	✔	✔	
Mulberry	–	–	✔	✔	✔	✔
Netscape	–	–	✔	✔	✔	✔
Eudora	–	–	✔	✔	✔ [c]	✔
Outlook	–	–	✔	✔	✔	✔

a. **pine** calls **sendmail** by default, but it can also speak SMTP.
b. Not supported in the standard release, but a patch is available.
c. Included in the commercial version but not in the free version.

The SMTP column refers to the way the user agent conveys mail to the transport agent or mail submission agent. A check means that the user agent opens a network connection directly to the transport or submission agent. No check means that the user agent executes the transport or submission agent as a subcommand.

Transport agents

A transport agent must accept mail from a user agent, understand the recipients' addresses, and somehow get the mail to the correct hosts for delivery. Most transport agents also act as message submission agents for the initial injection of new messages into the mail system. Transport agents speak the Simple Mail Transport Protocol (SMTP) defined in RFC2821 (originally defined in RFC821) or the Extended SMTP protocol (ESMTP) defined in RFCs 1869, 1870, 1891, and 1985.

Several transport agents are available for UNIX and Linux systems (PMDF, Postfix, **smail**, **qmail**, Exim, and **zmailer**, among others), but **sendmail** is the most comprehensive, most flexible, and most widely used. A recent survey[4] of mail systems reported that **sendmail** was used by 60% of the domains, Exim by 8%, Microsoft Exchange Server by 4%, and Postfix by 2%. Others (about 50 of them) were in the noise.

Red Hat and SuSE Linux ship with **sendmail** installed. Debian pretends to include **sendmail**, but if you look closely you'll find that **sendmail** is really a link to the Exim mail transport agent. Exim has been carefully crafted to understand **sendmail's**

---

4. Private study by Matrix.net for Sendmail, Inc.

command-line flags. User agents that call "**sendmail**" explicitly to submit email should be none the wiser.

Delivery agents

A delivery agent accepts mail from a transport agent and actually delivers it to the appropriate local recipients. Mail can be delivered to a person, to a mailing list, to a file, or even to a program.

Each type of recipient may require a different agent. **/bin/mail** is the delivery agent for local users. **/bin/sh** is the original delivery agent for mail going to a program; delivery to a file is handled internally. Recent versions of **sendmail** ship with safer local delivery agents called **mail.local** and **smrsh** (pronounced "smursh"). **procmail** from www.procmail.org can also be used as a local delivery agent; see page 570.

Message stores

As email grew from servicing the computer science department at a university to servicing sites such as America Online with millions of subscribers, the filesystem became inadequate as a message store. Searching a directory that contains a million mailboxes is prohibitively expensive.

The message store is the spot on the local machine where email is stored. It used to be the directory **/var/spool/mail** or **/var/mail**, with mail being stored in files named after users' login names. That's still the most common message store, but ISPs with thousands or millions of email clients are looking to other technologies for the message store (databases, usually).

On systems that use the **/var/spool/mail** or **/var/mail** store, the mail directory is created during the installation of the operating system. It should have permissions set to mode 775, with group owner mail,[5] unless you use **mail.local** as your local mailer, in which case the mode can be 755. Our Linux platforms vary a bit:

```
Red Hat: drwxrwxr-x  2  root  mail  1024 Dec  5 2000   /var/spool/mail
SuSE:    drwxrwxrwt  2  root  root  4096 Aug  2 23:25  /var/spool/mail
Debian:  drwxrwsr-x  2  root  mail  4096 Aug  3 16:17  /var/mail
```

See page 73 for more information about the sticky bit.

SuSE's permissions are a bit generous, but files inside the mail spool directory are mode 660 with group root. Directories with the sticky bit set (the t in the permissions) do not allow users to delete each other's files even though they have write permission on the directory. However, a malicious user could fill the mail spool, use it as a scratch partition, or create another user's mailbox.

Access agents

Programs such as **imapd** and **spop** are access agents for PC, Mac, or Linux users whose mail is delivered to a Linux server and then downloaded with the Internet

---

5. Systems that deliver mail by giving away files with a nonroot **chown** need to have group write permission to the directory as well. In general, nonroot **chown** is a bad idea.

Message Access Protocol (IMAP) or the Post Office Protocol (POP), respectively. IMAP and POP are covered starting on page 526.

Mail submission agents

Another newcomer to the mail arena that was necessitated by high-volume sites is the mail submission agent. The transport agent at a busy mail hub spends lots of time preprocessing mail messages: ensuring that all hostnames are fully qualified, modifying headers inherited from lame mail user agents, logging errors, rewriting headers, and so forth. RFC2476 introduced the idea of splitting the mail submission agent (MSA) from the mail transport agent (MTA) to spread out the workload and maximize performance.

The idea is to use the MSA, which runs on a different port, as a sort of "receptionist" for new messages injected into the mail system by local user agents. The MSA does all the prep work and error checking that must be done before a message can be sent out by the transport agent. It's a bit like inserting a sanity checker between the MUA and the MTA.

In particular, the MSA ensures that all hostnames are fully qualified; it verifies that local hostnames are legitimate before adding the local domain portion. The MSA also fixes message headers if they are missing or nonconformant. Often, the MSA adds a From or Date header or adjusts the Message-Id header. One final chore that an MSA can do is to rewrite the sender's address from a login name to a preferred external form such as *First_Last*.

To make this scheme work, user agents must be configured to connect to the MSA on port 587 instead of to port 25, which is the traditional port for mail. If your user agents cannot be taught to use port 587, you can still run an MSA on port 25, but on a system other than the one that runs your MTA. You must also configure your transport agent so that it doesn't duplicate the work done by the MSA. Duplicate processing won't affect the correctness of mail handling, but it does represent useless extra work.

sendmail can act as an MSA as well as an MTA. Starting with **sendmail** 8.10, a single instance of the program listens on both port 25 and port 587. User agents often call **sendmail** directly with flags that ask it to accept a mail message (**-bs** or **-bm**) or with no flags at all, in which case **sendmail**'s behavior defaults to **-bm**. The **sendmail** process keeps track of how it was called and becomes an MSA if called with flags **-bs** or **-bm** or an MTA if called with **-bd**.

User agents that open an SMTP connection directly must be modified to use port 587 to take advantage of an MSA.

19.2 THE ANATOMY OF A MAIL MESSAGE

A mail message has three distinct parts that we must understand before we become embroiled in **sendmail** configuration.

- The envelope
- The headers
- The body of the message

The envelope determines where the message will be delivered or, if the message can't be delivered, to whom it should be returned. The envelope addresses generally agree with the From and To lines of the header for an individual recipient but do not agree if the message is sent to a mailing list. The addresses are supplied separately to the MSA. The envelope is invisible to users; it's used internally by **sendmail** to figure out where to send the message.

The headers are a collection of property/value pairs formatted according to RFC2822. They record a variety of information about the message, such as the date and time it was sent and the transport agents through which it passed on its journey. The headers are a bona fide part of the mail message, although user agents often hide some of the less interesting ones when displaying messages for the user.

The body of the message is the actual content to be sent. It must consist of plain text, although that text often represents a mail-safe encoding of various binary content.

As we get into the configuration section, we sometimes speak of the envelope sender and recipients and sometimes speak of the header sender and recipients. We try to specify which addresses we are referring to if it's not clear from the context.

Mail addressing

Local addressing is simple because a user's login name is a unique identifier. An Internet address is also simple: *user@host.domain* or *user@domain*. In the deep dark past of email and the Internet, addresses such as those shown in Table 19.4 were common.

Table 19.4   Examples of obsolete address types

Address type	Example address	Modern form
UUCP	mcvax!uunet!ucbvax!hao!boulder!lair!evi	evi@lair
Route-based	<@site1,@site2,…,@siteN:user@final-site>	user@final.site
"Percent hack"	user%host1%host2@host3	user@host1

Much of the complexity of **sendmail** configuration stems from the early requirement to handle such addresses. Each of these forms of addressing relies on relaying, and thanks to spammers, sites are slowly turning relaying off. The percent hack (last line in Table 19.4) is a favorite tool of spammers who are trying to hide their identity or to relay mail through your machines. If you need to deal with any of these address forms, see the **sendmail** documentation or the O'Reilly **sendmail** book for help.

Reading mail headers

Every mail message starts with several lines called headers that contain information about the message. Each header begins with a keyword such as To, From, or Subject, followed by a colon and the contents of the header. The format of the standard headers is defined in RFC2822; however, custom headers are allowed, too. Any header beginning with "X-" is ignored by the mail system but propagated along with the message. Ergo, you can add a header such as X-Joke-of-the-Day to your email messages without interfering with the mail system's ability to route them.[6]

Some headers are added by the user agent and some by the transport agent. Several headers trace the path of a message through the mail system. Many user agents hide these "uninteresting" headers from you, but there is usually an option to make the agent reveal them all. Reading headers is becoming an important skill as we are bombarded with spam and must sometimes try to trace a message back to its source. Here is the header block from a simple message:

```
From evi Wed Jan 19 19:01:11 2000
Received: (from evi@localhost) by xor.com (8.9.3/8.9.3) id TAA17820; Wed, 19
    Jan 2000 19:01:11 -0700 (MST)
Date: Wed, 19 Jan 2000 19:01:11 -0700 (MST)
From: Evi Nemeth <Evi.Nemeth@xor.com>
Message-Id: <200001200201.TAA17820@xor.com>
To: trent@xor.com
Subject: xor.mc
Cc: evi@xor.com
Status: R

------ body of the message was here ---
```

This message stayed completely on the local machine; the sender was evi and the recipient was trent. The first From line was added by **mail.local**, which was the local delivery agent in this case. The Subject and Cc header lines were added by evi's mail user agent, which probably added the To, From, and Date headers as well. The Status header was added by trent's mail reader. **sendmail**, the mail transport agent, will add To, From, and Date headers if they are not supplied by the MUA. Each machine (or more precisely, each MTA) that touches a message adds a Received header.

The headers on a mail message tell a lot about where the message has been, how long it stayed there, and when it was finally delivered to its destination. Below is a more complete dissection of a mail message sent across the Internet. It is interspersed with comments that describe the purpose of the various headers and identify the programs that added them. The line numbers at the left are for reference in the following discussion and are not part of the message. Some lines have been folded to allow the example to fit the page.

---

6. Technically speaking, you can add any header you like because mail routing uses only the envelope and ignores the headers.

```
1: From eric@knecht.sendmail.org
```

Line 1 was added by **/bin/mail** or **mail.local** during final delivery to separate this message from others in the recipient user's mailbox. Some mail readers recognize message boundaries by looking for a blank line followed by the characters "From "; note the trailing space. This line does not exist until the message is delivered, and it is distinct from the "From:" header line. Many mail readers don't display this line, so you may not see it at all.

```
2: Return-Path: eric@knecht.Neophilic.COM
```

Line 2 specifies a return path, which may be a different address from that shown on the From: line later in the mail header. Error messages should be sent to the address in the Return-Path header line; it contains the envelope sender address.

```
3: Delivery-Date: Mon, 06 Aug 2001 14:31:07 -0600
```

Line 3 shows the date that the mail was delivered to evi's local mailbox. It includes the offset from UTC for the local time zone (MDT, mountain daylight time).

```
4: Received: from anchor.cs.colorado.edu (root@anchor.cs.colorado.edu
   [128.138.242.1]) by rupertsberg.cs.colorado.edu (8.10.1/8.10.1) with ESMTP
   id f76KV7J25997 for <evi@rupertsberg.cs.colorado.edu>; Mon, 6 Aug 2001
   14:31:07 -0600 (MDT)
5: Received: from mroe.cs.colorado.edu (IDENT:root@mroe.cs.colorado.edu
   [128.138.243.151]) by anchor.cs.colorado.edu (8.10.1/8.10.1) with ESMTP id
   f76KV6418006 for <evi@anchor.cs.colorado.edu>; Mon, 6 Aug 2001 14:31:06
   -0600 (MDT)
6: Received: from knecht.Neophilic.COM (knecht.sendmail.org [209.31.233.176])
   by mroe.cs.colorado.edu (8.10.1/8.10.1) with ESMTP id f76KV5Q17625 for
   <evi@anchor.cs.colorado.edu>; Mon, 6 Aug 2001 14:31:05 -0600 (MDT)
7: Received: from knecht.Neophilic.COM (localhost.Neophilic.COM [127.0.0.1])
   by knecht.Neophilic.COM (8.12.0.Beta16/8.12.0.Beta17) with ESMTP id
   f76KUufp084340 for <evi@anchor.cs.colorado.edu>; Mon, 6 Aug 2001 13:30:
   56 -0700 (PDT)
```

Lines 4–7 document the passage of the message through various systems en route to the user's mailbox. Each machine that handles a mail message adds a Received line to the message's header. New lines are added at the top, so in reading them you are tracing the message from the recipient back to the sender. If the message you are looking at is a piece of spam, the only Received line you can really believe is the one generated by your local machine.

Each Received line includes the name of the sending machine, the name of the receiving machine, the version of **sendmail** (or whatever transport agent was used) on the receiving machine, the message's unique identifier while on the receiving machine, the recipient (if there is only one), the date and time, and finally, the offset from Universal Coordinated Time (UTC, previously called GMT for Greenwich Mean Time) for the local time zone. This data is collected from **sendmail**'s internal macro variables. In the next few paragraphs, we trace the message from the sender to the recipient (backwards, from the point of view of header lines).

See page 415 for more information about MX records.

Line 7 shows that the message went from knecht's localhost interface (which Eric's particular mail user agent chose for its initial connection) to knecht's external interface via the kernel loopback pseudo-device. Line 6 documents the fact that knecht then sent the message to mroe.cs.colorado.edu, even though the message was addressed to evi@anchor.cs.colorado.edu (see header line 9). A quick check with **dig** or **nslookup** shows that the host anchor has an MX record that points to mroe, causing the delivery to be diverted. The machine knecht was running **sendmail** version 8.12.0Beta16.

The machine mroe was running **sendmail** version 8.10.1, and it identified the message with queue ID f76KV5Q17625 while it was there. mroe then forwarded the message to anchor.cs.colorado.edu as addressed (line 5), which may seem strange given that the original transmission from knecht was diverted from anchor to mroe because of MX records. The reason for this apparent inconsistency is that the cs.colorado.edu domain uses a "split DNS" configuration. The MX record for anchor that is visible to the outside world points to the incoming master mail machine (mroe). However, a different record is seen within the cs.colorado.edu domain itself. The internal version of the record points first to anchor itself and then to mroe as a backup.

As soon as the mail arrived on anchor, it was immediately forwarded again, this time to rupertsberg. The cause of this hop was aliasing, a mail handling feature that is described in detail starting on page 527.

Aliases play an important role in the flow of mail. An alias maps a username to something else; for example, to the same user at a different machine, to a group of users, or even to an alternative spelling of the user's name. You cannot determine why the message was diverted by examining only the example headers. As with MX records, you must seek external sources of information.

Received lines 5 and 6 include the "for <evi@anchor.cs.colorado.edu>" phrase, which identifies how the mail was addressed when it arrived at the local site. This information is very helpful when you are trying to unsubscribe from a mailing list that requires you to either send the unsubscribe message from the same host that you subscribed from (sometimes years earlier) or to know that address and use it as a parameter in your unsubscribe message.

The final Received line (line 4) shows "for <evi@rupertsberg.cs.colorado.edu>"; the value of **sendmail**'s destination address macro has been changed by the alias lookup on the machine anchor. The local mail delivery agent on rupertsberg put the mail in evi's mailbox.

```
8: Message-Id: <200108062030.f76KUufp084340@knecht.Neophilic.COM>
```

Line 8 contains the message ID, which is different from a queue ID and is unique within the world-wide mail system. It is added to the message when the message is initially submitted to the mail system.

```
9: To: evi@anchor.cs.colorado.edu
10: From: Eric Allman <eric@Sendmail.ORG>
11: X-URL: http://WWW.Sendmail.ORG/~eric
12: Subject: example message for Evi
13: Date: Mon, 06 Aug 2001 13:30:56 -0700
14: Sender: eric@knecht.Neophilic.COM
```

Lines 9, 10, 12, 13, and 14 are standard. Although a Subject header is not required, most user agents include it. The To line contains the address of the primary recipient or recipients. The From line lists the sender as eric@sendmail.org; however, the Received lines list the sending machine as being in the neophilic.com domain—Eric's machine knecht has several virtual domains tied to it in addition to sendmail.org.

The Date line shows the date and time the message was sent. In this case the send time matches the dates in the Received lines pretty closely, even though each was measured with a different clock.

Line 11 identifies the URL of Eric's home page. Notice that it begins with an X, making it an unofficial header. When mail was first specified, there was no such thing as the web or URLs.

The Received lines are usually added by the transport agent (unless they are forged), and the other headers are added by the user agent. Some user agents are lame and do not add proper headers; in this case, **sendmail** steps in to add the missing headers.

The first Received line that is added (usually on the sending machine, when the mail is transferred to the outgoing interface) sometimes includes an "ident" clause that gives the sender's login name. It should be the same as the name on the From line, but it won't be if the From line is forged. In our example, Eric's machine knecht was not running the daemon that implements this feature (**identd**), so there is no clause that lists the sender's login name.

Exhibit B illustrates this message's journey through the mail system. It shows what actions were taken, where they happened, and what programs performed them.

Exhibit B **A message from Eric**

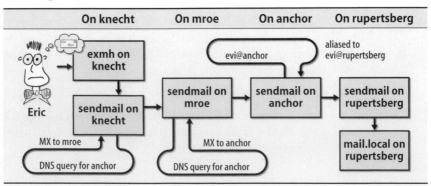

As you can see, **sendmail** is the workhorse in this process. It handles the message from the time it leaves **exmh** in Berkeley until it arrives on rupertsberg for delivery.

See *Spam examples* on page 599 for more practice reading headers.

19.3 MAIL PHILOSOPHY

The mail philosophy we outline in this chapter is almost mandatory for keeping the administration of medium and large sites manageable. However, it is also appropriate for small sites. The main concepts that lead to easy administration are:

- Servers for incoming and outgoing mail; or for really large sites, a hierarchy
- A mail home for each user at a physical site
- IMAP or POP[7] to integrate PCs, Macs, and remote clients

See page 415 for more information about MX records.

We discuss each of these key issues below and then give a few examples. Other subsystems must cooperate with the design of your mail system as well: DNS MX records must be set correctly, Internet firewalls must let mail in and out, the message store machine(s) must be identified, and so on.

Mail servers have four functions:

- To accept outgoing mail from user agents and inject it into the mail system
- To receive incoming mail from the outside world
- To deliver mail to end-users' mailboxes
- To allow users to access their mailboxes with IMAP or POP

At a small site, the servers that implement these functions might all be the same machine wearing different hats. At larger sites, they should be separate machines. It is much easier to configure your network firewall rules if incoming mail arrives at only one machine and outgoing mail appears to originate at only one machine.

Some sites use a proxy to receive mail from the outside world. The proxy doesn't really process mail; it just accepts and spools it. A separate process then forwards the spooled mail to **sendmail** for transport and processing. **smtpd** and **smtpfwdd** from www.obtuse.com are examples of such proxies for **sendmail**; **smtpd** can also filter incoming mail with access lists. Both are open source products. None of our Linux distributions include them in the standard installation package.

Using mail servers

Pick stable, reliable machines to use as your mail servers. Here, we outline a mail system design that seems to scale well and is relatively easy to manage and secure. It centralizes the handling of both incoming and outgoing mail on servers dedicated to those purposes. Exhibit C on page 524 illustrates one form of this system.

The mail system depicted in Exhibit C has a single point of exposure to the outside world: the mail server that receives messages from the Internet. The outgoing mail

----

7. IMAP is preferred over POP these days.

Electronic Mail

server is also directly connected to the Internet, but it is less exposed because it initiates connections rather than accepting connections from external sites. The incoming mail server should be carefully monitored, should be upgraded with security patches, and should run the latest version of **sendmail** with spam filters for incoming mail.

Exhibit C   Mail system architecture

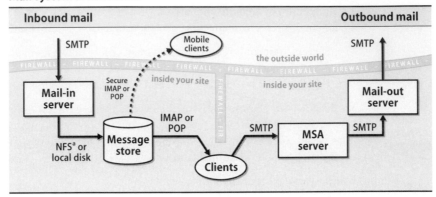

a. We don't recommend using NFS for the message store because of the potential for locking problems.

The server that handles outgoing mail must also be well maintained. It can include spam filters of its own to verify that no local user is contributing to the spam problem. If your site has concerns about the leakage of proprietary information, establishing a single server through which all outgoing mail must pass makes it easier to implement or enforce content policies. If your site manages large mailing lists, the outgoing mail server can be configured to take advantage of some of **sendmail**'s performance-oriented features; see page 611 for details.

Both the incoming and outgoing mail servers can be replicated if your mail load requires it. For example, multiple inbound mail servers can hide behind a load balancing box or use DNS MX records to crudely balance the load. Different client machines can route mail through different outbound servers. Don't pass any mail directly between the incoming servers and the outgoing servers, however; they should be separated from each other by an internal firewall.

At really large sites, incoming and outgoing mail servers would be replicated. An additional routing layer could be added to look up users' mailboxes (perhaps through LDAP) and route the mail to the appropriate message store. The routing layer could also do spam and virus filtering before delivering messages to users' mailboxes.

ISPs who are designing a mail system for customers should add another server that acts as the target of customers' backup MX records and handles mailing lists. This machine has to accept mail and relay it back out, but it must be heavily filtered to make sure that it only relays the mail of actual customers. It, too, should be separated from the incoming and outgoing mail servers by a firewall.

See page 489 for a discussion of file distribution issues.

Garden-variety Linux hosts can be given a minimal **sendmail** configuration that forwards outgoing mail to the server for processing. They do not need to accept mail from the Internet. Some sites may want to relax this funneling model a bit and allow arbitrary hosts to send mail directly to the Internet. In either case, nonserver machines can all share the same **sendmail** configuration. You might want to distribute the configuration with a tool such as **rdist** or **rsync**.[8]

Sites that use software such as Microsoft Exchange and Lotus Notes but are not comfortable directly exposing these applications to the Internet can use a design modeled on that shown in Exhibit D.

Exhibit D   Mail system architecture diagram #2

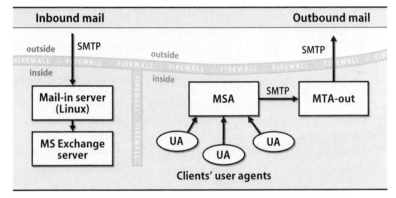

Whatever design you choose, make sure that your **sendmail** configuration, your DNS MX records, and your firewall rules are all implementing the same policy with respect to mail.

Using mail homes

It is convenient for users to receive and keep their mail on a single machine, even if they want to access that mail from several different systems. You can implement mail homes by using the **aliases** file or an LDAP database (see page 538). You can provide remote access to each user's mailbox with IMAP or POP.

The aliasing scheme we use lets the alias files be the same on all machines within an administrative domain. This uniformity is a big win from the administrator's point of view. (We assume that login names and UIDs are unique across all machines, a policy we recommend highly.)

Some sites centralize mail by exporting **/var/spool/mail** over NFS. Locking problems with NFS files can cause users to lose mail or to have their spool files garbled. Finger-pointing among NFS, **sendmail**, and the delivery agents with regard to proper

---

8.   **rsync** is included with Red Hat and SuSE and is only an **apt-get** away for Debian.

locking does not help the poor user whose mailbox has been corrupted (however, **sendmail** is always innocent, since it never actually delivers mail).

Some NFS implementations (such as those on dedicated NFS file servers) include a lock manager that works correctly. Most implementations either do not support locking or support it improperly. Some sites just ignore the locking problem and hope for the best, and others require users to read mail on the file server.

Our advice is not to use an NFS-shared **/var/spool/mail**. LMTP, the Local Mail Transport Protocol, is a good alternative to NFS for communicating with a file server that stores mail.

Using IMAP or POP

IMAP and POP are protocols that download email to a user's desktop machine when it joins the network. It is the ideal way to manage mail, especially for hosts that are not always connected, either because they are turned off when not in use or because they are at home and share the phone line with teenagers. A password is required; be sure to use a version that does not transmit this password in cleartext over the Internet.

We like IMAP, the Internet Message Access Protocol, better than POP. It delivers your mail one message at a time rather than all at once, which is much kinder to the network (especially on a slow link) and better for someone traveling from location to location. It is especially nice for dealing with the giant attachments that some folks like to send: you can browse the headers of your mail messages and not download the attachments until you are ready to deal with them. IMAP manages mail folders among multiple sites, for example, between your mail server and your PC. Mail that stays on the Linux server can be part of the normal backup schedule. www.imap.org contains lots of information about IMAP and a list of available implementations.

POP, the Post Office Protocol, is similar but assumes a model in which all the mail is downloaded from the server to the PC. It can be either deleted from the server (in which case it might not be backed up) or saved on the server (in which case your mail spool file grows larger and larger). The "whole mailbox at a time" paradigm is hard on the network and less flexible for the user. It can be really slow on dial-up lines if you are a pack rat and have a large mail spool file. Mail ends up getting scattered around with POP.

Both of these protocols can become resource hogs if users never delete any messages. In the case of IMAP, it takes forever to load the headers of all the mail messages; POP transmits the whole mailbox. Make sure your users understand the value of deleting messages or filing them in local folders.

A reasonable implementation of POP3, the current version of the protocol, is available from Qualcomm at www.eudora.com/qpopper. **qpopper** is a POP server that includes TLS/SSL authentication between server and client and encrypted messages. Several other Linux POP servers and clients are listed at

www.ibiblio.org/pub/Linux/system/mail/pop

Make sure you choose one that is being actively maintained.

IMAP server software is available from www.washington.edu/imap. No configuration is needed except to put the proper IMAP entries in the files **/etc/services** and **/etc/inetd.conf** and to make sure that your firewall (if any) doesn't prevent IMAP from working. IMAP has been guilty of security problems in the past; see the CERT advisories and be sure to obtain the latest version of IMAP, especially if there are security bulletins that postdate your Linux distribution. Carnegie Mellon University has developed an IMAP server called Cyrus IMAP that supports the POP protocol as well. We like it better than the UW IMAP implementation.

All three of our example Linux distributions include an IMAP server called **imapd** and a client, **fetchmail**, that speaks both IMAP and POP. Red Hat's **imapd** is the Cyrus IMAP server from CMU; SuSE and Debian use the University of Washington version. Red Hat also includes **pop3d**, a POP server. Not to be outdone, SuSE includes three: **qpopper** (which SuSE renames **popper**), **pop2d**, and **pop3d**. Debian has several tools for managing mailboxes with IMAP; **man -k imap** will tell you their names.

19.4 MAIL ALIASES

Aliases allow mail to be rerouted either by the system administrator or by individual users.[9] They can define mailing lists, forward mail among machines, or allow users to be referred to by more than one name. Alias processing is recursive, so it's legal for an alias to point to other destinations that are themselves aliases.

sendmail supports several aliasing mechanisms: LDAP (the Lightweight Directory Access Protocol), NIS and NIS+ from Sun, NetInfo from NeXT/Apple, mail routing databases, and various alias files that users and system administrators can set up.

See page 538 for more information about LDAP.

If you want to use the mail homes concept and you have a large, complex site, we recommend that you implement mail homes by storing your aliases in an LDAP server. The alternatives have several disadvantages. Flat alias files usually must be maintained by root. Their database representation must be rebuilt with every change, and they must be replicated on every mail-delivering machine. A small or simple site is better off just using the **/etc/mail/aliases** flat file and the **newaliases** command. Some sites that have lots of virtual domains maintain separate alias file fragments for each domain and merge them with a script to form the actual alias file.

LDAP does not work for mailing list aliases directly. However, it can be used to return aliases that point to programs such as **majordomo** or to :include: files. These features let LDAP work fine in environments that must support mailing lists.

sendmail uses an LDAP server much like it uses the DNS name server. It calls on the DNS server to resolve names into IP addresses so that messages can be sent. It calls on the LDAP server to look up aliases to reroute messages to the right place. In both

---

9. Technically, aliases are configured only by sysadmins. The user's control of mail routing by use of a **.forward** file is not really aliasing, but we have lumped them together here.

cases, the lookups have moved from flat files (**/etc/hosts** and **/etc/aliases**) to databases, with servers managing the queries.

We cover LDAP in more detail in three places in this chapter, and we also mention it in Chapter 18, *Sharing System Files*. We introduce and explain LDAP on page 538. We then describe LDAP's interaction with **sendmail** and with **sendmail**'s configuration file (page 565). Our first example (page 573) uses LDAP to implement aliasing and virtual hosting.

Before diving into LDAP, however, we first describe the traditional aliasing mechanisms. Aliases can be defined in the following three places (unfortunately, with three different syntaxes):

- In a user agent's configuration file (by the sending user)
- In the system-wide **/etc/mail/aliases** file (by the sysadmin)
- In a user's forwarding file, ~**/.forward** (by the receiving user)[10]

The user agent looks for aliases in the user's config files and expands them before injecting the message into the mail system. The transport agent, **sendmail**, looks for aliases in the global **aliases** file and then in the recipients' forwarding files. Aliasing is applied only to messages that **sendmail** considers to be local.[11]

Here are some examples of aliases in the **aliases** file format:

```
nemeth: evi
evi: evi@mailhub
authors: evi,garth,trent
```

The first line says that mail sent to "nemeth" should be delivered to the user evi on the local machine. The second line says that all mail to evi should be delivered on the machine mailhub, and the third line says that mail addressed to "authors" should be delivered to the users evi, garth, and trent. Recursion is supported, so mail sent to nemeth actually ends up going to evi@mailhub.

See Chapter 18 for more information about NIS.

The path to the global **aliases** file is specified in **sendmail**'s configuration file—it's **/etc/aliases** on both Red Hat and SuSE. **/etc/mail/aliases** is actually the "standard" location. Sites can have multiple **aliases** files, and they can also use alternate ways of storing alias mappings such as NIS or database files.

The format of an entry in the **aliases** file is

```
local-name: recipient1,recipient2,...
```

where *local-name* is the original address to be matched against incoming messages and the recipient list contains either recipient addresses or the names of other aliases. Indented lines are considered continuations of the preceding lines.

---

10. ~**/.forward** is the default place that **sendmail** looks. However, you can override this path by setting **sendmail**'s ForwardPath option.

11. Actually, this is not completely true. If you add the F=A flag to the SMTP mailer, you can implement aliasing for remote addresses as well.

From mail's point of view, the **aliases** file supersedes **/etc/passwd**, so the entry

```
david: david@somewhere-else.edu
```

would prevent the local user david from ever getting any mail. Therefore, administrators and **adduser** tools should check both the **passwd** file and the **aliases** file when selecting new user names.

The **/etc/mail/aliases** file should always contain an alias named "postmaster" that forwards mail to whoever maintains the mail system. An alias for automatic messages from **sendmail** must also be present; it's usually called Mailer-Daemon and is often aliased to postmaster.

You should redirect root's mail to your site administrators or to someone who logs in every day. The bin, sys, daemon, nobody, and hostmaster accounts (and any other pseudo-user accounts you set up) should also have aliases that forward mail to a human. The file **sendmail/aliases** in the distribution is a good template for the system-wide aliases that should be included. It also includes security suggestions and an example of how some common user requests are routed at Berkeley.

sendmail detects loops that would cause mail to be forwarded back and forth forever by counting the number of Received lines in a message's header and returning it to the sender when the count reaches a preset limit (usually 25).[12] Each visit to a new machine is called a "hop" in **sendmail** jargon; returning a message to the sender is known as "bouncing" it. The previous sentence, properly jargonized, would be, "Mail bounces after 25 hops."[13]

In addition to a list of users, aliases can refer to:

- A file containing a list of addresses
- A file to which messages should be appended
- A command to which messages should be given as input

Since the sender of a message totally determines its content, these delivery targets were often abused by hackers. **sendmail** has gotten very fussy about the ownership and permissions on such files and commands. To override **sendmail**'s paranoia, you must set one of the DontBlameSendmail options, so named to discourage you from doing it. Unfortunately, the error messages that **sendmail** produces when it encounters unsafe permissions or ownerships are not always clear.

Getting mailing lists from files

The :include: directive is a great way to let users manage their own mailing lists. It allows the members of an alias to be taken from an external file rather than listed

---

12. The default hop limit is 25, but you can change it in the config file.

13. We have been inconsistent with terminology in this chapter, sometimes calling a returned message a "bounce" and sometimes calling it an "error." What we really mean is that a Delivery Status Notification (DSN) has been generated. Such a notification usually means that a message was undeliverable and is therefore being returned to the sender.

directly in the **aliases** file. The file can also be changed locally without intervention by the system administrator who is responsible for the global **aliases** file.

When setting up the list, the sysadmin must enter the alias into the global **aliases** file, create the included file, and **chown** the included file to the user maintaining the mailing list. For example, the **aliases** file might contain

```
sabook: :include:/usr/local/mail/usah.readers
```

The file **usah.readers** should be on a local filesystem, not an NFS-mounted filesystem,[14] and should be writable only by its owner. To be really complete, we should also include aliases for the mailing list's owner so that errors (bounces) are sent to the owner of the list and not to the sender of a message addressed to the list:

```
owner-sabook: evi
```

See page 535 for more about mailing lists and their interaction with the **aliases** file.

Mailing to files

If the target of an alias is an absolute pathname (double-quoted if it includes special characters), messages are appended to the specified file. The file must already exist. For example:

```
complaints: /dev/null
```

It's useful to be able to send mail to files and programs, but this feature introduces security concerns and is therefore restricted. This syntax is only valid in the **aliases** file and in a user's **.forward** file (or in a file that's interpolated into one of these files with :include:). A filename is not understood as a normal address, so mail addressed to /etc/passwd@host.domain will bounce.

Some user agents let you save mail to a local file (such as an outbox folder). However, that copy of the message is saved by the user agent and is never really processed by the mail system.

If the destination file is referenced from the **aliases** file, it must be world-writable (not advisable), setuid but not executable, or owned by **sendmail**'s default user. The identity of the default user is set with the DefaultUser option. It is normally mailnull, sendmail, daemon, or UID 1, GID 1.

If the file is referenced in a **.forward** file, it must be owned and writable by the original message recipient, who must be a valid user with an entry in the **/etc/passwd** file and a valid shell that's listed in **/etc/shells**. For files owned by root, use mode 4644 or 4600, setuid but not executable.

---

14. If the NFS filesystem is mounted "hard" and NFS fails, **sendmail** will block with several file handles open and several waiting processes. You may eventually run out of process IDs or file handles and have to reboot the machine to clear things.

Mailing to programs

An alias can also route mail to the standard input of a program. This behavior is specified with a line such as

```
autoftp: "|/usr/local/bin/ftpserver"
```

It's even easier to create security holes with this feature than with mailing to a file, so once again it is only permitted in **aliases**, **.forward**, or :include: files. In the **aliases** file, the program runs as **sendmail**'s default user; otherwise, the program runs as the owner of the **.forward** or :include: file. That user must be listed in the **/etc/passwd** file with a valid shell (in **/etc/shells**).

The program mailer changes its working directory to the user's home directory (or, if that directory is inaccessible, to the root directory) before running the command that is to receive the mail. The default used to be **sendmail**'s queue directory, but some **csh**-based shells objected.

Mailing to programs is a major potential security hole. To be safe, don't use **/bin/sh** as your program mailer; use **sendmail**'s restricted shell, **smrsh**, instead. See *Security and sendmail* on page 603 for more information about **smrsh**.

Examples of aliases

Here are some typical aliases that a system administrator might use.

```
# Required aliases[15]

postmaster: trouble, evi
postmistress: postmaster
MAILER-DAEMON: postmaster
hostmaster: trent
abuse: postmaster
webmaster: trouble, trent
root: trouble, trent

# include for local trouble alias
trouble: :include:/usr/local/mail/trouble.alias
troubletrap: "/usr/local/mail/logs/troublemail"
tmr: troubletrap,:include:/usr/local/mail/tmr.alias

# sysadmin conveniences
diary: "/usr/local/admin/diary"
info: "|/usr/local/bin/sendinfo"

# class aliases that change every semester
sa-class: real-sa-class@nag
real-sa-class: :include:/usr/local/adm/sa-class.list
```

In this example, we would like users from all over campus to be able to send mail to a single alias "trouble" whenever problems occur. Problem reports should always be

---

15. A white lie. Only postmaster and MAILER-DAEMON are really required (by the RFCs), but it is conventional to include hostmaster, abuse, and webmaster as well.

routed to an appropriate group of local system administrators. In particular, we'd like to set up the mail aliases so that

- Trouble mail always goes to an appropriate group.
- A single version of the aliases file is used on all hosts.
- Individual admin groups control their own distribution lists.
- A copy of all trouble mail goes to a local log file for each group.

The configuration above satisfies these goals by taking the definition of the trouble alias from a file on each machine. Mail sent to the addresses trouble@anchor and trouble@boulder would end up in different places even though anchor and boulder use the same **/etc/mail/aliases** file.

Trouble mail is usually handled on one particular machine in each locale. For example, the **trouble.alias** file on a slave machine could contain the address

    trouble@*master*

to make trouble mail go to the appropriate master machine.

When a trouble message is resolved, it is sent to the alias tmr, which stands for "trouble mail readers." The tmr alias archives the message to the troubletrap alias and also sends it to a list of users taken from a file on the master machine. Adding novice administrators to the tmr list is a great way to let them see the support questions that arise, the administrators' replies, and the proper sycophantic tone that should be used with users (i.e., customers).

This mechanism is just the tip of the iceberg of a complete trouble ticket tracking system called **queuemh**, which is based on the **mh** user agent.

The sa-class alias has two levels so that the data file containing the list of students only needs to be maintained on a single machine, nag. The sabook alias example on page 530 should really have this same type of indirection so that the include file does not need to be replicated.

The diary alias is a nice convenience and works well as a documentation extraction technique for squirrelly student sysadmins who bristle at documenting what they do. Sysadmins can easily memorialize important events in the life of the machine (OS upgrades, hardware changes, crashes, etc.) by sending mail to the diary file. Don't put the file on a filesystem that contains your log files; that would allow hackers to fill up the filesystem and prevent syslog from writing log entries (thus covering their tracks).

Mail forwarding

The **aliases** file is a system-wide config file that should be maintained by an administrator. If users want to reroute their own mail (and your site doesn't use POP or IMAP to access mail), they can do so by creating **.forward** files in their home directories. **sendmail** always looks in a user's home directory for a **.forward** file unless the ForwardPath variable is set and overrides the default location. It's convenient to use a **.forward** file when a user wants to receive mail on a particular host or when someone leaves your site and wants to have mail forwarded to a new location.

A **.forward** file consists of a list of comma-separated addresses on a single line or several entries on separate lines. For example,

```
evi@ipn.caida.org
evi@xor.com
```

or

```
\mcbryan, "/home/mcbryan/archive", mcbryan@f1supi1.gmd.de
```

In the first example, mail for evi is not delivered on the local machine, but is instead forwarded to the machine ipn at CAIDA in San Diego and to xor.com. The second entry is from a user who does not trust mail systems and wants his mail replicated in three places: the regular mail spool on the local machine, a permanent archive of all incoming mail, and a temporary address in Germany where he is traveling at the moment. The backslash before his username says to deliver mail locally no matter what the aliases or forward files might say.

For temporary changes in mail routing, use of a **.forward** file is preferable to use of the global **aliases** file. The overhead (computer time and people time) required to change the system-wide aliases is quite high.

A user's **.forward** file must be owned by the user and must not be group- or world-writable. If **sendmail** thinks the directory path to the **.forward** file is safe (i.e., the permissions from the root all the way down are OK), it can be a link; otherwise, it cannot be a link. **sendmail** ignores forwarding files on which the permissions look suspicious; the permissions on the parent directory must also be safe (writable only by the user who owns the files).

Naturally, **sendmail** must be able to access a user's home directory on the machine where mail is delivered to determine whether it contains a **.forward** file. Permanent changes of address should be put in the **/etc/mail/aliases** file because a user's home directory and files will eventually be removed.

sendmail has a nifty feature, FEATURE('redirect'), that helps with the management of permanent email changes. If an alias points to user@newsite.REDIRECT, mail will be returned to the sender with a notification of the new address. The message is not forwarded to the new address, so the sender must update his address book and re-send the message.

You can configure **sendmail** to support a central directory for **.forward** files, but users do not expect this configuration. The location of **.forward** files is controlled by the ForwardPath option, which usually points to that central directory and then to the user's home directory. The **generic.m4** domain file illustrated on page 557 contains an example of a central location for **.forward** files.

An entry in the global **aliases** file takes precedence over an entry in a **.forward** file. Since these files are maintained by different people, users must be careful not to inadvertently create mail loops. If a user on a network has a mail home (and therefore an entry in the global **aliases** file), that user cannot use a **.forward** file to reroute mail to another machine that shares the same aliases. For example, at the University of Colorado, where we use a site-wide **aliases** file, an entry such as

```
evi:  evi@boulder
```

and a **.forward** file on the machine boulder containing

```
evi@anchor.cs
```

would create a loop. Mail addressed to evi would be forwarded to boulder, where the **.forward** file would cause it to be sent to anchor in the cs subdomain. The **aliases** file on anchor would cause it to be forwarded back to boulder, and so on. After 25 hops, the mail would be returned to the sender.

Notifying a user of a mail loop is challenging if your primary mode of communication is email. Mail to \user[16] delivers the message on the local machine, regardless of what the system-wide **aliases** file or the user's **.forward** file might say. If the local machine is where the user expects to read mail, fine; otherwise, send mail to the postmaster to report the loop or pick up the phone!

The hashed alias database

Since entries in the **aliases** file are in no particular order, it would be inefficient for **sendmail** to search this file directly. Instead, a hashed version is constructed with either the Berkeley DB database system or the **ndbm** database system that is standard on most versions of UNIX. This hashing significantly speeds alias lookups, especially when the file gets big.

The files derived from **/etc/mail/aliases** are called **aliases.db** for DB and **aliases.dir** and **aliases.pag**, for **ndbm**. The **dir** file is an index for the **pag** file, in which the data actually resides. Every time you change the **aliases** file, you must rebuild the hashed database with the **newaliases** command. **newaliases** is really just **sendmail** in disguise with command-line flags (**-bi**) that tell it to rebuild the database. Save the error output if you run **newaliases** automatically—you might have introduced formatting errors.

See Chapter 18 for more information about NIS.

When you compile **sendmail**, you should include database library support for the **dbm/ndbm** routines, the new Berkeley DB routines, or both. If both are included and **sendmail** needs to create a database file but the type is not specified, **sendmail** uses DB. If you are using NIS, **sendmail** *creates* both but *uses* the DB version if the path to the **aliases** file includes **/yp/**.

The DB library, written and maintained by Keith Bostic and Margo Seltzer, is available at www.sleepycat.com. It is much better (faster access, smaller database files) than the **ndbm** system. DB is open source and free unless you ship it in a proprietary product; then, you need a license.

---

16. You may have to use two or more backslashes to get one of them past the shell and into **sendmail**.

Mailing lists and list wrangling software

A mailing list is a giant alias that sends a copy of each message posted to it to each person who has joined the list. It's like a Usenet newsgroup that is delivered by email. Some mailing lists have thousands of recipients.

Mailing lists are usually specified in the **aliases** file but maintained in an external file. Some standard naming conventions are understood by **sendmail** and most mailing list software. Experienced users have come to rely on them as well. Most common are the "-request" suffix and the "owner-" prefix, which are used to reach the maintainers of the list. The conventions are illustrated by the following aliases:

```
mylist: :include:/etc/mail/include/mylist
owner-mylist: mylist-request
mylist-request: evi
owner-owner: postmaster
```

In this example, mylist is the name of the mailing list. The members are read from the file **/etc/mail/include/mylist**. Bounces from mailing to the list are sent to its owner, evi, as are requests to join the list. The indirection from "owner" to "request" to evi is useful because the owner's address (in this case, mylist-request) becomes the Return-Path address on each message sent to the list. mylist-request is a bit better than the actual maintainer for this field. Errors in messages to the owner-mylist alias (evi, really) would be sent to owner-owner.

Other conventions exist; for example, sendmail.com would use:

```
mylist: :include:/etc/mail/include/mylist
owner-mylist: mylist-owner
mylist-owner: evi
mylist-request: evi
```

The case in which a message is undeliverable is called a bounce. The case in which the error message sent about the bounce cannot be delivered is a double bounce. So in our example, double bounces are sent to owner-owner or postmaster.

If you use a site-wide aliases file, you need to add an extra level of indirection pointing mylist to myreallist@master so that the data file containing the list of members only needs to exist in one place.

Several software packages automate the maintenance of mailing lists. They typically allow users to add and remove themselves from the list, obtain information about the list, and obtain files through email. A few of the popular mailing list managers (and their download sources) are

- Majordomo, from www.greatcircle.com (included with SuSE)
- Mailman, the GNU mailing list processor, from www.list.org
- ListProc, from www.cren.net
- SmartList, from ftp.informatik.rwth.aachen.de
- **listmanager** from www.listmanager.org
- LISTSERV Lite, from www.lsoft.com (free version of the commercial LISTSERV)

A good FAQ by Norm Aleks on mailing list software is available from rtfm.mit.edu through FTP (look under comp.answers/mail/list-admin). Unfortunately, the FAQ is no longer maintained and so might be a bit out of date. However, it still includes useful information to help you choose the best mailing list software for your needs.

In general, SmartList is small and simple, ListProc is large and complex, and the others are in between. They differ in their philosophies of list maintenance, with some leaning toward sysadmins as administrators (ListProc) and others leaning toward users as maintainers (Majordomo, Mailman, SmartList, LISTSERV Lite). Majordomo, Mailman, **listmanager**, and LISTSERV Lite support remote administration; the list maintainer does not even need to have a login on the machine where the list is located because all transactions take place through email. Most of the list packages allow information posted to the list to be assembled into digests, some automatically (ListProc, Mailman, **listmanager**, and LISTSERV Lite) and some through manual configuration (SmartList and Majordomo).

Mailman is our favorite list manager. It's a joy to administer and lets list maintainers tweak all the features of their own lists. ListProc and LISTSERV Lite are proprietary: the first expensive, the other binary-only and crippled. We have not tried SmartList, but we like **procmail**, on which it depends.

We describe each of these packages briefly below. For more detail, see the documentation with each package or the O'Reilly book *Managing Mailing Lists* by Alan Schwartz and Paula Ferguson.

Majordomo

Majordomo is a Perl/C package available from www.greatcircle.com. It was originally written by Brent Chapman. Development of Majordomo has ceased; Majordomo 2 is a total rewrite but is still in beta test, so we describe only the original. Among our example distributions, only SuSE ships Majordomo. Despite what the man page says (**/usr/lib/mail/majordomo**), it's hidden in the directory **/usr/lib/majordomo**.

See page 603 for more information about trusted users.

Majordomo runs as an unprivileged user, typically with username majordom or mdom and default group daemon. Since Linux supports long user names (more than 8 characters), you can also use majordomo as the login name. The user must be one that **sendmail** recognizes as "trusted" and so must be mentioned in your **sendmail** configuration, usually in a confTRUSTED_USERS declaration.[17]

Majordomo is configured through the **majordomo.cf** file, which consists of valid Perl commands that initialize variables, define the directories where things are (or where they should be put), specify the lists to be supported, and configure the handling of bounced mail. A helper program, **config-test**, will test your configuration file for missing variables or bad syntax. SuSE puts the config file in **/etc** and leaves **config-test** with the Majordomo distribution in **/usr/lib/majordomo**.

---

17. A "trusted" user is allowed to change the From header line of a message and rebuild the **aliases** file.

Majordomo requires special aliases to be installed in **sendmail**'s **aliases** file. The cleanest way to integrate these aliases is to create a separate alias file used just for Majordomo (recent versions of **sendmail** support multiple alias files). The file contains a set of aliases for Majordomo itself and a set for each mailing list that it manages. The distribution contains a sample aliases file, **majordomo.aliases**.

The most common user question about mailing lists is "How do I unsubscribe?" For lists managed by Majordomo, the answer for listname@host is to send mail to the address majordomo@host with the words "unsubscribe listname" or "unsubscribe listname email-address" in the body of the message (not on the subject line).

With the first form, you need to send the unsubscribe message from the same host that you used when you subscribed to the list; in the second form, that host is part of the email address. See page 519 for hints on how to glean this information from the mail headers so that you can unsubscribe properly, even if you have forgotten which machine you used when you joined the list. Some mailing lists also accept mail to listname-request@host with just the word "unsubscribe" in the body.

Never, ever, send an unsubscribe message to the list itself. If you do, your message announces to all the recipients of the list that you don't know what you're doing.

Mailman

Mailman, a fairly recent addition to the mailing list software fleet (version 1.0 released in July 1999), is available from www.list.org or the GNU archives. It was originally written by John Viega and is currently being developed in collaboration with Ken Manheimer, and Barry Warsaw. Like Majordomo, Mailman is primarily written in a scripting language with C wrappers, but in this case the language is Python (available from www.python.org).

Mailman was inspired by its authors' use of Majordomo and their frustration with bounce errors, tricky configuration of advanced features such as digests and moderated lists, and performance difficulties with bulk mailings. Mailman provides a script that imports Majordomo lists. It also has some ability to detect and control spam.

Mailman's big claim to fame is its web interface, which makes it easy for the moderator or postmaster to manage a list and also easy for users to subscribe, unsubscribe, and configure their options.

ListProc

ListProc is an old-timer in mailing list management software. It was written in 1991 by Anastasios Kotsikonas and maintained until about 1994. It then lay idle for a few years but was resurrected with a new beta release in 1998. It used to be available from the computer science department at Boston University for free, but with somewhat strange licensing rules. Now it is available from www.cren.net for a hefty licensing fee ($2,000 per copy, even for universities). Forget ListProc and go with one of the free, open source packages.

SmartList

SmartList was originally written by Stephen R. van den Berg, who is also the original author of the **procmail** package. It's available from ftp.informatik.rwth-aachen.de or www.mindwell.com/smartlist. It uses **procmail**, so you will need to download both **procmail.tar.gz** and **SmartList.tar.gz**. It's probably easiest to just grab the Linux package appropriate to your system.

SmartList is small and simple. It's a combination of C code, **procmail** rules, and shell scripts. Bounces, the maintenance headache of mailing lists, are automatically dealt with by the software. Users are automatically removed from a list after a certain number of bounces to their address. SmartList requires a login entry in the **passwd** file ("smart" or perhaps "list") that is a trusted user in **sendmail**'s configuration file.

The installation includes **led**, a lock wrapper for editing that tries to protect SmartList against being left with an incoherent, partially edited configuration file.

listmanager

listmanager by Murray Kucherawy is written in C and so is faster than the packages built on top of a scripting language such as Perl or Python. **listmanager** also improves speed by using the DB database package from sleepycat.com rather than flat files and the filesystem. Its feature list is about a page long and includes a web interface, digests, and several security enhancements.

listmanager really seems like a killer list manager—the only downside is that source code is not yet being distributed. According to the www.listmanager.org web page, the code is being withheld until the author finishes a cleanup pass to avoid possible embarrassment. A Linux binary is available.

LISTSERV Lite

LISTSERV Lite by Eric Thomas is a crippled version of LISTSERV, the commercial product from L-Soft International, Inc. Some of the features of the real version are missing, and the software is limited to managing 10 mailing lists of up to 500 people. LISTSERV Lite needs to run as the pseudo-user listserv, which must own its files. It also likes to have a listserv group. LISTSERV Lite provides a web interface both for subscribing to a list and for maintaining it.

The distribution is available from www.lsoft.com. Source code is not distributed, but precompiled binaries and stubs for many versions of UNIX and Linux are provided. If you already are familiar with LISTSERV and have lists that use it, you might be able to justify running a binary-only, crippled list manager. If you're starting from scratch, choose one of the open source, unrestricted alternatives mentioned above.

LDAP: the Lightweight Directory Access Protocol

LDAP is a protocol that provides access to a generic administrative directory service. It has been around for a few years, but it has just recently started to become popular.

Administrators are discovering that LDAP is good for lots of things:

- **sendmail** configuration: aliases, virtual domains, mail homes, the access database, and tables
- User management: login names, passwords, hosts (e.g., Stanford University)
- Administrative config files (e.g., SuSE Linux)
- As a replacement for NIS
- As a calendar server
- For use with Pluggable Authentication Modules (PAM)

It's envisioned that LDAP will eventually become a global directory system used for many different purposes. Unfortunately, tools for automating typical sysadmin tasks with LDAP are still missing.

LDAP grew out of the ISO protocols and the X.500 directory service. That heritage immediately suggests complex, bloated, verbose, bad, etc., but the L in LDAP is supposed to take care of all that. Protocol versions 1 and 2 have been standardized. Version 3 is close. Fortunately, all versions are backward compatible. Version 3 of the LDAP protocol supports hierarchical servers; querying one server for a piece of data can result in a referral to another server. Version 2 supported hierarchical data, but hierarchical servers are only in version 3.

Mail aliases are a particularly good match for LDAP, especially now that **sendmail** supports LDAP internally. **sendmail** can query the LDAP server for alias lookups instead of doing them directly. LDAP can also manage mail routing and virtual domains. LDAP support must be compiled into the **sendmail** binary.

If you are looking for an LDAP implementation, we recommend the server produced by the OpenLDAP group at www.openldap.org. This group took over and enhanced the code of an earlier server that was developed at the University of Michigan. For a bit more information about LDAP-related software, see page 507.

LDAP database entries resemble a termcap entry with longer variable names. The attributes (variable names) in the LDAP database are not yet fully standardized, and this fact can result in incompatibilities among different implementations.

The attributes on the first line of a database entry are defined by the LDAP configuration file. The examples in this section assume that the LDAP server daemon (**slapd**, in the OpenLDAP case) was configured with a root distinguished name (rootdn) of:

```
"cn=root, dc=synack, dc=net"
```

The dc attribute appears twice because the domain component values cannot contain a dot; to express the domain synack.net, two entries are necessary. Further attributes, or variable names, can be whatever you want. They are case insensitive. **sendmail** (whose code looks for specific attribute names and assigns them predetermined interpretations), the LDAP server, and the builder of the LDAP database must all cooperate and use the same naming conventions.

Some possible attributes that can appear on the first line of a database entry (the database keys) are dn for a domain name, dc for a domain component, o for an organization name, c for a country name, and uid for a unique ID (e.g., a login name).

By default, **sendmail** recognizes the following LDAP data tags:

```
mailLocalAddress
mailRoutingAddress
mailHost
```

Version 8.12 expands this default set extensively (see **cf/sendmail.schema**) and also lets you define your own schema to use any LDAP tags you like.

Here is an example of the OpenLDAP implementation's **slapd ldap.conf** file

```
# LDAP Defaults, ldap.conf file, should be world-readable.
#
BASE     dc=synack, dc=net
HOST     gw.synack.net
PORT     389
```

that supports database entries of the form

```
dn: uid=jon, dc=synack, dc=net
objectClass: inetLocalMailRecipient
mailLocalAddress: jon@synack.net
mailRoutingAddress: stabilej@cs.colorado.edu
uid:jon
```

When FEATURE(ldap_routing) has been specified in the **sendmail** configuration file, the incoming recipient is matched against the mailLocalAddress field. If it matches, the mail is redirected to the mailRoutingAddress. The objectClass line has to be there—it comes from the draft RFC that defines the interaction of LDAP and mail systems.

On the host gw.synack.net, this database entry corresponds to the alias:

```
jon: stabilej@cs.colorado.edu
```

A bit long-winded, isn't it? These database entries could replace the typical entries in the **aliases** file for defining a mail home for each user. But until tools are widely available for adding, changing, and deleting LDAP entries—that is, tools that do not require you to type ten times as many characters as an alias line—the performance benefits do not come close to justifying the extra time spent by sysadmins to keep the LDAP database up to date.

The **aliases** file is also still the best way to define mailing lists (with the :include: directive). Mailing list software typically pipes the message to a wrapper script and resends it. An LDAP query can return a local address that handles the mailing list (by way of the **aliases** file), but it cannot directly call a program.

As of version 8.12, LDAP can also be used to store the contents of some of **sendmail**'s other data (for example, tables and classes). See page 565 for more information about configuring **sendmail** to use LDAP and page 573 for a slightly contrived example that uses LDAP to implement aliases and virtual hosting.

19.5 SENDMAIL: RINGMASTER OF THE ELECTRONIC MAIL CIRCUS

All three of our Linux reference platforms ship a mail transport agent. Red Hat and SuSE provide **sendmail**, and Debian uses Exim. We describe Exim briefly starting on page 620. Many of the Exim constructs and configuration knobs have analogs within the **sendmail** world. Since this chapter is already far too long, we cover only **sendmail** in detail. We describe Exim in terms of the equivalent **sendmail** facilities.

sendmail can adapt to the whims of standards-makers thanks in part to the flexibility of its configuration file, which allows **sendmail** to meet the needs of a diverse community of users. The rest of this chapter is primarily devoted to the understanding and construction of this configuration file, the infamous **sendmail.cf**.

sendmail is a transport agent, a program that interfaces between user agents and delivery agents. It speaks the SMTP protocol and delivers messages to peers on remote machines through the Internet. **sendmail**'s list of chores includes:

- Controlling messages as they leave the user's keyboard
- Understanding the recipients' addresses
- Choosing an appropriate delivery or transport agent
- Rewriting addresses to a form understood by the delivery agent
- Reformatting headers as required
- Passing the transformed message to the delivery agent

sendmail also generates error messages and returns messages to the sender if they are undeliverable.

The history of sendmail

sendmail V5 was written by Eric Allman in 1983. One branch was enhanced by Lennart Lövstrand at the University of Linköping in Sweden in 1987 and called IDA **sendmail**.[18] It was maintained by Neil Rickert and Paul Pomes. Another branch, King James Sendmail, was developed by Paul Vixie at DECWRL during 1989–1993. It was based on IDA **sendmail** but had a far greater emphasis on throughput and performance for commercial sites. IDA and KJS pioneered several of the features that are now included in **sendmail** V8, Eric's major rewrite of 1993.

As of this writing, most Linux vendors ship versions of **sendmail** derived from V8. They are typically a release or two behind the master version from Sendmail, Inc., however. Vendors often customize a particular version of **sendmail** and are then reluctant to upgrade their base system to include current revisions. See Table 19.5 for information about the versions of **sendmail** that are shipped with various systems.

---

18. Lennart was a student in the computer science department, which in Swedish is the Institutionen för Datavetenskap; hence the name IDA.

We base our discussion of **sendmail** on V8.12 and totally ignore both V5 and IDA, which are obsolete. V8 uses the **m4** macro processor to allow easy configuration of the standard cases. This "config lite" is all that most sites need.

Unfortunately, if your configuration has a problem, you may have to base your debugging on an understanding of the raw config file, which we've heard described as unapproachable, daunting, picky, cryptic, onerous, infamous, boring, sadistic, confusing, tedious, ridiculous, obfuscated, and twisted. We talked quite a bit about the raw config file in older versions of this book, but since its relevance to modern administrators has waned, we now refer you to the O'Reilly **sendmail** book by Bryan Costales and Eric Allman (titled *sendmail*) or the *Sendmail Installation and Operations Guide* that is included in the **sendmail** distribution.

Vendor-supplied versions of sendmail

Table 19.5 lists the version of **sendmail** shipped with Red Hat and SuSE systems or available with **apt-get** for Debian systems. It also shows where our friendly vendors have stashed the **sendmail** binary and its config files, **sendmail.cf** and **submit.cf**. We list sendmail.org as a vendor so that you can match their defaults if you replace your vendor's version. Rather than ignore **sendmail** on Debian, which ships with Exim as its mail transport agent, we installed **sendmail** by using **apt-get** and include those details.

Table 19.5   Vendors' versions of sendmail (circa 2001)

System	Code	Config	Binary dir	Config dir
sendmail.org	8.12.2	Level 10	–	**/etc/mail**
Red Hat 7.2	8.11.6	Level 9	**/usr/sbin**	**/etc**
SuSE 7.3	8.11.2	Level 9	**/usr/sbin**	**/etc**
Debian 3.0	8.9.3	Level 8	**/usr/sbin**	/etc/mail

New releases of **sendmail** are sometimes issued to address security problems; we suggest that you check the release notes from www.sendmail.org and upgrade if you have missed any security-related patches. You'll need a C compiler and the **m4** macro preprocessor (both of which are usually included in Linux distributions).

Sometimes it's difficult to determine the actual **sendmail** base release, but if the vendor hasn't meddled too much, you can run

```
% /usr/sbin/sendmail -d0.1 -bt < /dev/null
```

to make **sendmail** disclose its version, the options that were compiled into it, and who it thinks it is after reading the config file. The **-d** flag sets a debug level (see page 616 for more info on debugging levels in **sendmail**), the **-bt** flag puts **sendmail** into address test mode, and the redirect from **/dev/null** gives it no addresses to test. Here is some sample output (slightly truncated) from a Red Hat system.

```
Version 8.11.6
 Compiled with: LDAPMAP MAP_REGEX LOG MATCHGECOS MIME7TO8
     MIME8TO7 NAMED_BIND NETINET NETINET6 NETUNIX NEWDB NIS
     QUEUE SASL SCANF SMTP TCPWRAPPERS USERDB
=========== SYSTEM IDENTITY (after readcf) ============
         (short domain name) $w = coyote
 (canonical domain name) $j = coyote.toadranch.com
          (subdomain name) $m = toadranch.com
               (node name) $k = coyote.toadranch.com
=======================================================
```

sendmail should always use DNS MX (mail exchanger) records and will do so if compiled with the NAMED_BIND option (as in the preceding example). The one-letter variables such as $w are from the raw config file or determined at run time.

sendmail installation from sendmail.org

The installation environment of **sendmail** version 8.12 has changed a bit. **sendmail** no longer runs setuid to root but instead is setgid to the sendmail group, smmsp. Before installing **sendmail**, you must create both the user smmsp and the group smmsp (the mysterious name stands for **s**end**m**ail **m**ail **s**ubmission **p**rogram). We use UID and GID 25 to match the SMTP mail protocol's well-known port number. The smmsp user should have smmsp as its default login group, which is typically set in the **/etc/passwd** file. The addition of a dedicated sendmail user and group lets **sendmail** run with reduced privileges and enhances security.

The second major change from a sysadmin's point of view is that **sendmail** now uses two configuration files: **submit.cf** and **sendmail.cf**. The file **submit.cf** controls the handling of mail that originates on the local machine (and is being initially submitted to the mail system), and **sendmail.cf** controls incoming mail and mail queued during the submission process. **submit.cf** is supplied with the distribution and is the same for all sites; there's usually no need to customize it.

This section briefly describes the installation process; refer to the installation notes in the **sendmail** distribution for the gory details and for issues related to particular architectures or operating systems. The next section describes **sendmail** installation on a Debian system with **apt-get**. If you are replacing your vendor's original version of **sendmail**, some of the configuration chores (such as installing help files) may already have been done for you.

The players:

- The **sendmail** binary, usually installed in **/usr/sbin**.

  ```
  -r-xr-sr-x    root    smmsp    /usr/sbin/sendmail
  ```

- The configuration files **/etc/mail/sendmail.cf** and (in versions 8.12 and later) **/etc/mail/submit.cf**, installed by the sysadmin:

  ```
  -rw-r--r--    root    bin      /etc/mail/sendmail.cf
  -rw-r--r--    root    bin      /etc/mail/submit.cf
  ```

- The mail queue directories, **/var/spool/mqueue** and (in versions 8.12 and later) **/var/spool/clientmqueue**, created by the sysadmin or the installation process:

```
drwxrwx--- smmsp smmsp    /var/spool/clientmqueue
drwx------ root  wheel    /var/spool/mqueue
```

- Various links to the **sendmail** binary (**newaliases**, **mailq**, **hoststat**, etc.)[19]

- **sendmail**'s safer local delivery agents, **smrsh** and **mail.local** (usually installed in **/usr/libexec**)

You can download the latest version of **sendmail** from www.sendmail.org. To compile and install the package, follow the directions in the top level **INSTALL** file. Start by adding the smmsp user and group; do not give this user a real shell. Here is a typical **/etc/passwd** entry:

```
smmsp:x:25:25:Sendmail Mail Submission Prog:/nonexistent:/bin/false
```

And here is a typical **/etc/group** entry:

```
smmsp:*:25:smmsp
```

To compile the software, change to the distribution's **sendmail** directory, run the **Build** script and then run **Build install**. The file **devtools/OS/Linux** contains the assumptions used to build **sendmail** on Linux systems. Linux distributions have not standardized where things are, so **devtools/OS/Linux** contains best guesses and may not be exactly right for your distribution.

Before you start compiling, however, you must decide on a database format and a strategy for interfacing **sendmail** with administrative databases such as NIS. For on-disk databases, we recommend the Berkeley DB package specified in the **Makefile** as NEWDB (the default). Linux ships with an ancient version of Berkeley DB (vintage 1994). Although **sendmail** works with this old version, we recommend that you get a current version from sleepycat.com. The licensing terms are quite generous: as long as you do not distribute the DB software, no license is necessary and there is no fee.

To customize the Makefile, don't edit it; create your own **site.config.m4** file and put it in the directory **devtools/Site** to tweak it for your operating system and local environment. For example, if you intend to use LDAP and the new mail filtering library for spam, create in that directory a **site.config.m4** file containing the lines

```
APPENDDEF(`confMAPDEF', `-DLDAPMAP')
APPENDDEF(`confLIBS', `-lldap -llber')
APPENDDEF(`conf_sendmail_ENVDEF', `-DMILTER')
```

A define replaces the current definition of an attribute; the APPENDDEF macro appends to the current definition.

---

19. Be careful here. Some vendors use hard links, with the result that when you upgrade, you might end up with the version of **sendmail** not matching the version of **newaliases**, creating subtle and hard-to-find support headaches.

Compiling **sendmail** with

  % **sh ./Build**

will automatically include the site-specific entries. To install **sendmail** in the proper place, run

  % **sudo sh ./Build install**

sendmail should *not* normally be set up to be controlled by **inetd/xinetd**, so it must be explicitly started in the **rc** files at boot time. A typical sequence is something like:

```
if [-f /usr/sbin/sendmail -a -f /etc/mail/sendmail.cf];
then
    (cd /var/spool/clientmqueue; rm -f [tTx]f*)
    (cd /var/spool/mqueue; rm -f [tTx]f*)
    /usr/sbin/sendmail -bd -q30m     ### queue runner for regular queue
    /usr/sbin/sendmail -Ac -q30m &  ### queue runner for client queue (8.12)
    echo -n ' sendmail' > /dev/console
fi
```

These lines check for the **sendmail** binary and its configuration file and then start the program in daemon mode.

Several user agents explicitly run **sendmail** (sometimes with the **-bm** or **-bs** flags) when they submit a user's message to the mail system rather than speaking the SMTP protocol directly. In this situation, **sendmail** uses the config file **submit.cf** and puts messages in the **/var/spool/clientqueue** queue directory. Calling **sendmail** with the **-Am** or **-Ac** flags forces messages to the **mqueue** or **clientqueue**, respectively.

 Red Hat has a **sendmail** startup script (**/etc/init.d/sendmail**) that does not clean cruft out of the **mqueue** directories (as shown in the example above). However, it does rebuild the database maps. With **sendmail** 8.12 and later, LDAP can be used for the database maps, and rebuilding the maps after changes is not necessary. Parameters defined in **/etc/sysconfig/sendmail** determine whether **sendmail** should start in daemon mode and how often it should run the queue, so that is where you should set the **sendmail** startup behavior for your site. Red Hat, as shipped, starts **sendmail** in daemon mode and runs the queue every 30 minutes.

 SuSE's startup script (**/etc/init.d/sendmail**) just checks for the binary and config file and then starts **sendmail** with the arguments defined in the SENDMAIL_ARGS environment variable; these are set in the file **/etc/rc.config.d/sendmail.rc.config**. SuSE also defaults to daemon mode and runs the queue every 30 minutes.

The **sh** fragment above (or one like it) should be added to **/etc/init.d/sendmail** if your Linux distribution does not include a **sendmail** startup script. A fancier script in the installation guide tries to clean up previously interrupted queue runs. Mix and match as you like.

Historically, **sendmail**'s supporting files have wandered around the filesystem to glamorous destinations such as **/usr/lib**, **/etc**, **/usr/ucblib**, and **/usr/share**. With the

8.10 release of **sendmail**, all files (except the queue directories) are expected to be kept beneath the **/etc/mail** directory.[20] Let's hope that vendors take the hint and leave them together in one consistent place.

Installing sendmail on Debian systems

You can use Debian's **apt-get** program to install **sendmail**. It installs **sendmail** (version 8.9.3) and **m4** and also uninstalls Exim. After **apt-get** has downloaded and installed the Debian **sendmail** package, it will offer to configure the package. Saying yes invokes a script that asks you questions (20 or so) about the **sendmail** configuration you want. Each question shows the default answer in square brackets and with a few exceptions provides a reasonable configuration file. The only question that you really have to answer differently from the default value is "mail name"; the default answer is the unqualified hostname (e.g., lappie), but it needs to be the fully qualified name (e.g., lappie.toadranch.com).

Answering the questions posed by the script will make more sense if you are familiar with **sendmail**'s various options and features, which are discussed in more detail later in this chapter. The configuration script does not take into account the contents of the generic domain file that it includes by default. As a result, you can decline a feature but ending up with it turned on anyway (for example, the redirect feature).

The switch file

The service switch is covered in more detail in Chapter 18.

Linux systems have a "service switch" configuration file, **/etc/nsswitch.conf**, that enumerates the methods that can be used to satisfy various standard queries such as user and host lookups. If more than one resolution method is listed for a given type of query, the service switch also determines the order in which methods are consulted.

The use of the service switch is normally transparent to software. However, **sendmail** likes to exert fine-grained control over its lookups, so it currently ignores the system switch file and uses its own internal one (**/etc/mail/service.switch**) instead.

Two fields in the switch file impact the mail system: aliases and hosts. The possible values for the hosts service are dns, nis, nisplus, and files. For aliases, the possible values are files, nis, nisplus, and ldap. Support for all the mechanisms you use (except files) must be compiled into **sendmail** before the service can be used.

sendmail's internal service switch contains:

```
aliases   files nisplus nis    # if compiled with nis/nis+
hosts     dns nisplus nis files
```

Modes of operation

You can run **sendmail** in several modes, selected with the **-b** flag. **-b** stands for "be" or "become" and is always used with another flag that determines the role **sendmail** will play. Table 19.6 lists the legal values.

---

20. Well, it's not quite totally true yet that all files are kept under **/etc/mail**. The **sendmail.pid** file and sometimes the statistics file are still kept elsewhere.

Table 19.6   Command-line flags for sendmail's major modes

Flag	Meaning
-bd	Run in daemon mode, listening for connections on port 25
-bD	Run in daemon mode, but in the foreground rather than the background[a]
-bh	View recent connection info (same as **hoststat**)
-bH	Purge disk copy of outdated connection info (same as **purgestat**)
-bi	Initialize hashed aliases (same as **newaliases**)
-bm	Run as a mailer, deliver mail in the usual way (default)
-bp	Print mail queue (same as **mailq**)
-bP	Print the number of entries in queues via shared memory (8.12 and later)
-bs	Enter SMTP server mode (on standard input, not port 25)
-bt	Enter address test mode
-bv	Verify mail addresses only; don't send mail

a. This mode is used for debugging, so that you can see error and debugging messages.

If you expect incoming mail to arrive from the Internet, run **sendmail** in daemon mode (**-bd**). In this mode, **sendmail** listens on network port 25 and waits for work.[21] You will usually specify the **-q** flag, too—it sets the interval at which **sendmail** processes the mail queue. For example, -q30m runs the queue every thirty minutes, and -q1h runs it every hour.

sendmail normally tries to deliver messages immediately, saving them in the queue only momentarily to guarantee reliability. But if your host is too busy or the destination machine is unreachable, **sendmail** queues the message and tries to send it again later. **sendmail** used to fork a child process every time it processed the queue, but it now supports persistent queue runners that are usually started at boot time. RFC1123 recommends at least 30 minutes between runs. **sendmail** does locking, so multiple, simultaneous queue runs are safe.

sendmail 8.12 has added a new feature to help with large mailing lists and large queues: queue groups with envelope splitting. It is covered in more detail starting on page 611.

sendmail reads its configuration file, **sendmail.cf**, only when it starts up. Therefore, you must either kill and restart **sendmail** or send it a HUP signal when you change the config file. **sendmail** creates a **sendmail.pid** file that contains its process ID and the command that started it. You should start **sendmail** with an absolute path because it re**exec**s itself on receipt of the HUP signal. The **sendmail.pid** file allows the process to be HUPed with:

```
# kill -HUP `head -1 sendmail.pid`
```

The location of the PID file used to be a compile-time parameter, but it can now be set in the **.mc** config file with the confPID_FILE option.

21. The ports that **sendmail** listens on are determined by DAEMON_OPTIONS; port 25 is the default.

```
define(confPID_FILE, `/var/run/sendmail.pid')
```

The default value is OS dependent but is usually either **/var/run/sendmail.pid** or **/etc/mail/sendmail.pid**. Red Hat and Debian use **/var/run/sendmail.pid** and SuSE keeps it in the directory **/var/run/sendmail**.

The mail queue

Mail messages are stored in the queue directory when the machine is too busy to deliver them immediately or when a destination machine is unavailable. **sendmail** serves as a mail submission agent listening on port 587 as well as fulfilling its usual role as a daemon listening on port 25 and using the queue **/var/spool/mqueue**. Some user agents (**mh** and **/bin/mail**, for example) use port 587, the mail submission port, but others (Eudora, Outlook, etc.) speak SMTP directly to the **sendmail** running on port 25. Beginning with version 8.12, mail submission programs inject new messages into the mail system by using the queue directory **/var/spool/clientmqueue** and the configuration file **submit.cf**. All messages go into the queue briefly as they arrive.

sendmail allows you to have more than one mail queue and to identify subsets of the queues as belonging to a queue group. For example, if the **mqueue** directory contained the subdirectories **q1**, **q2**, and **q3** and you specified the queue directory as **/var/spool/mqueue/q***, then all three queues would be used. **sendmail**'s ability to handle multiple queues increases performance under high load.[22] If a site is running a large mailing list, **sendmail** will split the envelope recipient list into several smaller lists and assign them to different queue groups. This trick can greatly enhance performance because the smaller recipient lists can be processed in parallel.

Queue groups are new in version 8.12 and give fine-grained control over individual types of messages. Any of the parameters associated with queues can also be set on a particular queue group, including execution priority (with the **nice** system call). Mail is submitted to a queue group according to the address of the first recipient of the message. The default queue group is called mqueue and is automatically defined and available for use without further configuration. Queue groups are covered in detail starting on page 611.

When a message is queued, it is saved in pieces in several different files. Each filename has a two-letter prefix that identifies the piece, followed by a random ID built from **sendmail**'s process ID. This ID is not fixed because **sendmail** is constantly forking and each copy gets a new process ID. Table 19.7 shows the six possible pieces.

If subdirectories **qf**, **df**, or **xf** exist in a queue directory, then those pieces of the message are put in the proper subdirectory. The **qf** file contains not only the message header but also the envelope addresses, the date at which the message should be returned as undeliverable, the message's priority in the queue, and the reason the

---

22. Directories are an efficient storage mechanism if they do not contain too many files. If you have a busy mail server with lots of mailing lists that get out of date, the queue directory can easily get so large that it cannot be dealt with efficiently.

Table 19.7   Prefixes for files in the mail queue

Prefix	File contents
qf	The header of the message and control file
df	The body of the message
tf	A temporary version of the **qf** file while the **qf** file is being updated
Tf	Signifies that 32 or more failed locking attempts have occurred
Qf	Signifies that the message bounced and could not be returned
xf	Temporary transcript file of error messages from mailers

message is in the queue. Each line begins with a single-letter code that identifies the rest of the line.

Each message that is queued must have a **qf** and **df** file. All the other prefixes are used by **sendmail** during attempted delivery. When a machine crashes and reboots, the startup sequence for **sendmail** should delete the **tf**, **xf**, and **Tf** files from each queue directory. The sysadmin responsible for mail should check occasionally for **Qf** files in case local configuration is causing the bounces.

The mail queue provides several opportunities for things to go wrong. For example, the filesystem can fill up (avoid putting **/var/spool/mqueue** and **/var/spool/news** on the same partition), the queue can become clogged, and orphaned mail messages can get stuck in the queue.

sendmail has a configuration option (confMIN_FREE_BLOCKS) to help manage disk space. When the filesystem that contains the mail queue gets too full, mail is rejected with a "try again later" error until more space has been made available. This option leaves a bit of slop space so mail starts being rejected before the filesystem is totally full and everything wedges.

See page 415 for more information about DNS MX records.
If a major mail hub goes down, its MX backup sites can become overloaded with thousands of messages. **sendmail** can fork too many copies of itself and thrash a machine to death. Several options help with performance on very busy machines; we have collected these in the performance section starting on page 611. To handle a temporarily clogged queue before version 8.12, you would move the clog aside, continue processing new mail as usual, and run a separate copy of **sendmail** on the clogged queue after things quieted down. For example, the procedure for handling a single queue directory would look like this:

```
# kill `head -1 sendmail.pid`
# mv mqueue cloggedqueue          /* To another FS if necessary */
# mkdir mqueue                    /* Set owner/perms, too */
# chown root mqueue
# chmod 700 mqueue
# /usr/sbin/sendmail -bd -q1h &
```

When things settle down, run **sendmail** with the following flags:

```
# /usr/sbin/sendmail -oQ/var/spool/cloggedqueue -q
```

Electronic Mail

These flags point **sendmail** at the clogged queue directory and specify that **sendmail** should process it immediately. Repeat this command until the queue empties. Starting with version 8.12, **sendmail** uses hard links in ways that will break if you move a queue. A better way to deal with clogged queues is to use a fallback machine and MX records; see the performance section for details.

The point at which the queue becomes clogged depends on the site and the hardware on which **sendmail** is running. Your system and the mail hub for aol.com, which processes millions of messages a day, will have different definitions of a clogged queue. See page 615 for information about measuring your traffic levels.

19.6 SENDMAIL CONFIGURATION

Before version 8.12, **sendmail**'s actions were controlled by a single configuration file, **/etc/mail/sendmail.cf** (it was formerly found in **/etc** or **/usr/lib**). We call it the config file for short. Version 8.12 introduced a second instance of the configuration file called **submit.cf** (also in the **/etc/mail** directory). The flags that **sendmail** is started with determine which config file it will use: **-bm**, **-bs**, and **-bt** use **submit.cf** if it exists, and all other modes use **sendmail.cf**. Of course, there are command-line flags and config file options that change the names of the configuration files, but it is best to leave the names alone. The config file determines the following for **sendmail**:

- Choice of delivery agents
- Address rewriting rules
- Mail header formats
- Options
- Security precautions
- Spam resistance

The raw config file format was designed to be easy to parse. This focus has made it a bit lacking in warm, user-friendly features. Maintenance of the config file is the most significant administrative chore related to electronic mail and scares the pejeebers out of even seasoned sysadmins.

Every version of **sendmail** uses a config file, but modern versions make the configuration process easier through the use of **m4** macros, which disguise much of the underlying complexity. It might be said that the raw config file is at the level of assembly language, whereas **m4** configuration is more at the level of Perl.[23]

When the **m4** macros were first introduced, it was hoped that they would handle 80%–90% of cases. In fact, the coverage rate turned out to be much higher, probably closer to 98%. In this book, we cover only the **m4**-based "config lite." You need delve into the low-level config file only if you are debugging a thorny problem, growing your mail site in bizarre ways, or running a very high volume mail hub.

---

23. The **sendmail** config language is "Turing complete," which means that it can be used to write any possible computer program. Readers who have experienced the raw config file will realize what a frightening concept this is …

Three key pieces of documentation are the O'Reilly book *sendmail* by Bryan Costales and Eric Allman, the paper *Sendmail Installation and Operations Guide* by Eric Allman (included in the **doc/op** directory of the distribution), and the **README** file (in the **cf** directory). We often refer to *sendmail* as a source for more information and refer to it as "the **sendmail** book." Likewise, we refer to the installation paper as "the installation guide" and the README file as **cf/README**.

Using the m4 preprocessor

We first describe a few **m4** features, show how to build a configuration file from an **m4** master file, and finally describe some of the important prepackaged **m4** macros that come with the **sendmail** distribution. Neither Red Hat nor SuSE includes the man page for **m4** in their distributions, although the command is there. Debian installs both **m4** and its man page when you install **sendmail** with **apt-get**.

We conclude this section with example configurations for three distinct sites:

- A computer science student's home Linux box
- A medium-sized company that knows how to configure **sendmail** properly
- A site that does lots of web hosting

We also show the default configurations provided with the Red Hat, SuSE, and Debian Linux distributions.

m4 was originally intended as a front end for programming languages that would let the user write more readable (or perhaps more cryptic) programs. **m4** is powerful enough to be useful in many input transformation situations, and it works nicely for **sendmail** configuration files.

m4 macros have the form

```
name(arg1, arg2, ..., argn)
```

There should be no space between the name and the opening parenthesis. Left and right single quotes are used to quote strings as arguments. **m4**'s quoting conventions are different from those of other languages you may have used, since the left and right quotes are different characters.[24] Quotes nest, too. With today's compiler building tools, one wonders how **m4** survived with such a rigid and exotic syntax.

m4 has some built-in macros, and users can also define their own. Table 19.8 on page 552 lists the most common built-in macros used in **sendmail** configuration.

Some sites add a dnl macro to the end of every line to keep the translated **.cf** file tidy; without dnl, **m4** adds extra blank lines to the configuration file. These blank lines don't affect **sendmail**'s behavior, but they make the config file hard to read. We have omitted the dnls from our examples. Other sites use dnl at the beginnings of lines that are intended as comments.

---

24. You could change the quote characters with the changequote macro, but doing so would totally break the use of **m4** in **sendmail** because various macros make assumptions about the quote characters.

Table 19.8   m4 macros commonly used with sendmail

Macro	Function
define	Defines a macro named *arg1* with value *arg2*
undefine	Discards a previous definition of macro named *arg1*
include	Includes (interpolates) the file named *arg1*
dnl	Discards characters up to and including the next newline
divert	Manages output streams

m4 does not really honor comments in files. A comment such as:

```
# And then define the ...
```

would not do what you expect because define is an **m4** keyword and would be expanded. Instead, use the m4 dnl keyword (for "delete to newline"). For example,

```
dnl # And then define the ...
```

would work. You must follow dnl with a space or punctuation mark for it to be recognized as an **m4** command.

The sendmail configuration pieces

The **sendmail** distribution includes a **cf** subdirectory that contains all the pieces necessary for **m4** configuration: a **README** file and several subdirectories, listed in Table 19.9.

Table 19.9   Configuration subdirectories

Directory	Contents
cf	Sample **.mc** (master configuration) files
domain	Sample **m4** files for various domains at Berkeley
feature	Fragments that implement various features
hack	Special features of dubious value or implementation
m4	The basic config file and other core files
ostype	OS-dependent file locations and quirks
mailer	**m4** files that describe common mailers (delivery agents)
sh	Shell scripts used by **m4**

The **cf/cf** directory contains examples of **.mc** files. In fact, it contains so many examples that yours will get lost in the clutter. We recommend that you keep your own **.mc** files separate from the distributed **cf** directory. Either create a new directory named for your site (**cf/***sitename*) or move the **cf** directory aside to **cf.examples** and create a new **cf** directory. If you do this, copy the **Makefile** and **Build** script over to your new directory so the instructions in the **README** file still work. It's best to also copy all the configuration **.mc** files to a central location rather than leaving them inside the **sendmail** distribution. The **Build** script uses relative pathnames that will have to be changed if you try to build a **.cf** file from a **.mc** file and are not in the distribution hierarchy.

Building a configuration file from a sample .mc file

Before we dive into pages and pages of details about the various configuration macros, features, and options, we put the cart before the horse and create a "no frills" configuration to illustrate the process. Our example is for a leaf node, foo.com; the master configuration file is called **foo.mc**.

We'll put **foo.mc** in our shiny new **cf** directory. The translated (by **m4**) configuration file will be **foo.cf** in the same directory, and we'll ultimately install it as **sendmail.cf** in **/etc** or **/etc/mail**. **/etc/mail** is the **sendmail** standard for the location of the config file, but many distributions use **/etc**.

Some boilerplate should go in each new **.mc** file:

```
divert(-1)
#### basic .mc file for foo.com
divert(0)
VERSIONID(`$Id$')
```

If you want to put comments at the start of your file, the first line is usually a divert statement, which throws away any spurious garbage on the **m4** output streams and alleviates the need for dnl in #-style comments. The comments come next, followed by another divert. A VERSIONID line (here, in RCS format) completes the boilerplate. It is described in detail in the next section.

In many cases, specifying an OSTYPE (see page 555) to bring in operating-system-dependent paths or parameters and also a set of MAILERs (see page 557) will complete the configuration:

```
OSTYPE(`linux')
define(`confCOPY_ERRORS_TO', `postmaster')
MAILER(`local')
MAILER(`smtp')
```

Here, we also set an option (confCOPY_ERRORS_TO) that sends a copy of the headers of any bounced mail to the local postmaster. This notification allows the postmaster to intervene when the problem is at the local site.

To build the real configuration file, just run the **Build** command you copied over to the new **cf** directory:

```
# ./Build foo.cf
```

or

```
# make foo.cf
```

Finally, install **foo.cf** in the right spot—normally **/etc/mail/sendmail.cf**, but both Red Hat and SuSE stash it in **/etc/sendmail.cf**.

A larger site can create a separate **m4** file to hold site-wide defaults in the **cf/domain** directory; individual hosts can then include the contents of this file. Not every host needs a separate config file, but each group of similar hosts (same architecture and same role: server, client, etc.) will probably need its own configuration.

Changing the sendmail configuration

You will often find that your existing **sendmail** configuration is almost right, but that you just want to try out a new feature, add a new spam rule, or make a simple change. To do that:

- Edit the **.mc** file and enter your changes.
- Rebuild the config file with the **Build** script in the configuration directory.
- Install the resulting **cf** file as **sendmail.cf** in the right directory.
- Send **sendmail** a HUP signal to make it reread its config file.[25]

Even with **sendmail**'s easy new configuration system, you still have to make several configuration decisions for your site. As you read about the features described below, think about how they might fit into your site's organization. A small site will probably have only a hub node and leaf nodes and thus will need only two versions of the config file. A larger site may need separate hubs for incoming and outgoing mail and, perhaps, a separate POP/IMAP server.

Whatever the complexity of your site and whatever face it shows to the outside world (exposed, behind a firewall, or on a virtual private network, for example), it's likely that the **cf** directory contains some appropriate ready-made configuration snippets just waiting to be customized and put to work.

19.7 BASIC SENDMAIL CONFIGURATION PRIMITIVES

sendmail configuration commands are case sensitive. By convention, the names of predefined macros are all caps (e.g., OSTYPE), **m4** commands are all lower case (e.g., define), and configurable variable names start with a lowercase conf and end with an all-caps variable name (e.g., confCOPY_ERRORS_TO). Macros usually refer to an **m4** file called **../*macroname*/*arg1*.m4**. For example, the macro OSTYPE('linux') causes **../ostype/linux.m4** to be included.

In this section we cover the basic configuration commands and leave the fancier features for later.

The VERSIONID macro

You should maintain your config files with CVS or RCS, not only so that you can back out to an earlier config version if necessary but also so that you can identify the

---

25. Use the **kill** command to do this. The **sendmail.pid** file makes it easy to find **sendmail**'s process ID; unfortunately, its location is not consistent among distributions (try **/var/run/sendmail.pid**). See page 547 for an example of how to use it.

versions of the **m4** files that go into making up the config file. Use the VERSIONID macro to automatically embed version information. The syntax is

VERSIONID(`Id')

The actual version information will be filled in by RCS as you check in the file. It will appear in the final **sendmail.cf** file as a comment. This information can also be useful if you forget where you put the **sendmail** distribution; often, the location of files is dictated by available disk space and not by filesystem design logic.

The OSTYPE macro

Files in the **ostype** directory are named for the operating system whose default values they contain. An OSTYPE file packages up a variety of vendor-specific information, such as the expected locations of mail-related files, paths to commands that **sendmail** needs, flags to mailer programs, etc.

By convention, OS-specific information is interpolated into the config file with the OSTYPE macro.[26] Every config file must include an OSTYPE macro near the top, typically just after VERSIONID.

OSTYPE files do their work primarily by defining other **m4** variables. For example,

define(`ALIAS_FILE', `/etc/aliases')

specifies the location of the system-wide aliases file. You can override the default values for your OS later in the **.mc** file if you wish, but don't change the distributed OSTYPE file unless it's actually wrong, in which case you should also submit a bug report to sendmail-bugs@sendmail.org. Some sites want a consistent location for the **aliases** file across platforms and so redefine its location in their DOMAIN file.

The **README** file in the **cf** directory lists all the variables that can be defined in an OSTYPE file. Some of the important ones are shown in Table 19.10 on page 556, along with several that you may want to configure for spam abatement (but which are undefined by default). The default values are what you get if your OSTYPE file doesn't specify something else.

See Chapter 18 for more information about NIS.
sendmail supports the use of multiple alias files and NIS maps, both to allow the simultaneous use of files and NIS and to facilitate the division of aliases between global and local files. For example,

define(`ALIAS_FILE', `/etc/aliases,nis:mail.aliases")

would search the file **/etc/aliases** first and, if that failed, would then try the NIS map called mail.aliases.

If you install **sendmail** on a new OS release or architecture, be sure to create a corresponding OSTYPE file and give it to sendmail.org so that it can be included in the next release. Just model your new file after those already there and check it against

---

26. So where is the OSTYPE macro itself defined? In a file in the **cf/m4** directory, which is magically prepended to your config file when you run the **Build** script.

Table 19.10   Default values of some variables set in OSTYPE files

Variable	Default value
ALIAS_FILE	**/etc/mail/aliases**
HELP_FILE	**/etc/mail/helpfile**
STATUS_FILE	**/etc/mail/statistics**
QUEUE_DIR	**/var/spool/mqueue**
MSP_QUEUE_DIR	/var/spool/clientmqueue
LOCAL_MAILER_PATH	**/bin/mail**
LOCAL_SHELL_PATH	**/bin/sh**
LOCAL_MAILER_MAX	*undefined*
LOCAL_MAILER_MAXMSGS	*undefined*
SMTP_MAILER_MAX	*undefined*
SMTP_MAILER_MAXMSGS	*undefined*

the table of defaults in the **cf/README** file. If the value of a variable on your new system is the same as the default value, you don't need to include an entry for it (but it doesn't hurt to protect yourself in case the default changes).

Table 19.11 shows the OSTYPE files for our reference platforms. Only Red Hat uses the **linux.m4** file from the standard **sendmail** distribution.

Table 19.11   OSTYPE files for Linux systems

System	File	Directory	Usage
Red Hat	**linux.m4**	**/usr/share/sendmail-cf**	OSTYPE(`linux')
SuSE	**suse-linux.m4**	**/usr/share/sendmail**	OSTYPE(`suse-linux')
Debian	debian.m4	**/usr/share/sendmail/sendmail.cf**	OSTYPE(`debian')

SuSE puts the **sendmail** distribution in **/usr/share/sendmail**. The **suse-linux.m4** OSTYPE file is in the **ostype** directory there and not part of the **sendmail** distribution from sendmail.org. That file is very long (over 80 lines) and contains numerous FEATUREs and other macros that are usually found in a site's master configuration file (the **.mc** file) and not in the OSTYPE file. This hides the real configuration from the sysadmin—a mixed blessing, perhaps, but *not* a practice we recommend.

Debian hides the config files beneath **/usr/share/sendmail/sendmail.cf/**. The directory **sendmail.cf** (confusing choice of names from the Debian folks) corresponds to the **cf** directory in the **sendmail** distribution and contains all the config pieces you need, including a Debian-specific OSTYPE file, **ostype/debian.m4**. The OSTYPE file is 50 lines long and consists mostly of pathnames and comments, as it should. Many are identical to the current defaults from sendmail.org and so don't really need to be explicitly restated. However, restating them protects Debian against changes in defaults that might otherwise introduce inconsistencies or errors. The only Debian sin in the **sendmail** OSTYPE style department is the inclusion of the generic DOMAIN file shipped with the **sendmail** distribution. A DOMAIN statement should appear early in the actual **.mc** file rather than being hidden in the OSTYPE file.

The DOMAIN macro

The DOMAIN directive allows site-wide generic information to be specified in one place (**cf/domain/***filename***.m4**) and then referred to in each host's individual config file with

DOMAIN(`filename')

The filename is usually chosen to describe your site. For example, our file for the computer science department is called **cs.m4** and appears in our **.mc** files as:

DOMAIN(`cs')

Like OSTYPE, DOMAIN is really just a nice way of doing an include. But it makes the structure of the config file clearer and provides a hook for future tweaks. It is most useful when you centralize and build all your site's **.cf** files from **.mc** files kept in a single location.

Small sites do not usually need a domain file, but larger sites often use them for references to relay machines, site-wide masquerading or privacy options, and references to tables for mailers, virtual domains, and spam databases.

The generic DOMAIN file included with the distribution shows the types of entries that are usually put in site-wide domain files. Its contents (with comments and dnls removed) are shown below.

```
VERSIONID(`$Id: generic.m4,v 8.15 1999/04/04 00:51:09 ca Exp $')
define(`confFORWARD_PATH', `$z/.forward.$w+$h:$z/.forward+$h:
    $z/.forward.$w:$z/.forward')
define(`confMAX_HEADERS_LENGTH', `32768')
FEATURE(`redirect')
FEATURE(`use_cw_file')
EXPOSED_USER(`root')
```

The files sets the path for the locations of users' forward files, limits header lengths,[27] includes the redirect feature for users who have left your organization, and turns on the use_cw_file feature for the handling of equivalent machine names. If your **.mc** file includes masquerading, the root user will not be masqueraded. Each of these constructs is described in more detail later in the chapter.

The MAILER macro

You must include a MAILER macro for every delivery agent you want to enable. You'll find a complete list of supported mailers in the directory **cf/mailers** in the **sendmail**

---

27. Hackers have used very, very long headers as a way of causing a denial of service in older versions of **sendmail**. This line is there in case you are still running any of these vulnerable versions (pre-8.9.3).

distribution. Currently, the options are local, smtp, fax, usenet, procmail, qpage, cyrus, pop, phquery, and uucp. Typically, you need at least:

```
MAILER(`local')
MAILER(`smtp')
```

The first line includes the local and prog mailers. The second line includes smtp, esmtp, dsmtp, smtp8, and relay. Support for *user+details@site.domain* email addresses was added to the local mailer starting with version 8.7.[28] The *user* defines the mailbox to which message should be delivered and the *details* provide an extra parameter that a local mail program such as **procmail** can use to sort incoming mail.

If you plan to tune any mailer-related macros (such as USENET_MAILER_ARGS or FAX_MAILER_PATH), be sure that the lines that set these parameters *precede* the line that invokes the mailer itself; otherwise, the old values will be used. For this reason, MAILER declarations usually come toward the bottom of the config file.

The pop mailer interfaces to the **spop** program that is part of the **mh** mail handler package and implements the Post Office Protocol defined in RFC1460. It's used by PCs and Macs that need to access mail on a UNIX host. The cyrus mailer is for use with CMU's IMAP server and comes in two flavors: cyrus to deliver mail to users' mailboxes and cyrusbb to deliver mail to a central bulletin board. The cyrus mailer also understands the user+details syntax; its MAILER specification must come after that of the local mailer.

HylaFAX is available from www.hylafax.org.

The fax mailer integrates Sam Leffler's HylaFAX package into the mail system. SuSE includes it as **/usr/bin/faxmail**; Red Hat and Debian do not include HylaFAX by default. Mailing to *user@destination*.fax sends the body of the message as a fax document. The *destination* is typically a phone number. To allow symbolic names (rather than just phone numbers) as destinations, use a keyed database file.

ghostscript is available from www.gnu.org.

You must glue HylaFAX and **sendmail** together by installing a script from the Hyla-FAX distribution in **/usr/local/bin**. You also might need to change the value of the macro FAX_MAILER_PATH. Human intervention is still needed to deliver incoming faxes from the spool area to a user's mailbox. You can convert fax documents to Post-Script (with HylaFAX) and view them with the GNU package **ghostscript**.

The qpage mailer interfaces to QuickPage software to deliver email to your pager. See www.qpage.org for more information about QuickPage.

The macros VERSIONID, OSTYPE, and MAILER are all you need to build a basic *hostname***.mc** file.

19.8 FANCIER SENDMAIL CONFIGURATION PRIMITIVES

In the next sections, we describe a few more macros and some of the most common FEATUREs used to modify **sendmail**'s default behavior. We also discuss some policy

---

28. The user+details syntax originated at Carnegie Mellon University, where it is used with local tools for routing and sorting mail.

issues in the context of **sendmail** configuration: security, privacy, spam, and the technique of hiding information by the use of masquerading and virtual domains.

The FEATURE macro

With the FEATURE macro you can enable several common options by including **m4** files from the **feature** directory. In the discussion below, we intermix our presentation of FEATUREs and some of **sendmail**'s other macros, as they are occasionally intertwined. When **m4** configuration was first added to **sendmail**, describing the FEATURE macro became a big section of our mail chapter. Now, so many features have been added that FEATURE almost needs its own chapter. The syntax is:

```
FEATURE(keyword, arg, arg, ...)
```

where *keyword* corresponds to a file *keyword*.**m4** in the **cf/feature** directory and the *args* are passed to it. See the directory itself or the **cf/README** file for a definitive list of features. A few commonly used ones are described below.

The use_cw_file feature

The **sendmail** internal class w (hence the name **cw**) contains the names of all local hosts for which this host accepts and delivers mail. A client machine might include its hostname, its nicknames, and localhost in this class. If the host being configured is your mail hub, then the w class should also include any local hosts and virtual domains for which you accept email.

The use_cw_file feature defines class w from the file **/etc/mail/local-host-names** (which used to be called **sendmail.cw**). The exact filename is configurable with the confCW_FILE option, discussed later. Without this feature, **sendmail** delivers mail locally only if it is addressed to the machine on which **sendmail** is running. An incoming mail server must list in the **local-host-names** file all the machines and domain names for which it will handle mail. If you change the file, you must send **sendmail** a HUP signal to make your changes take effect because **sendmail** reads this file only when it starts.

```
FEATURE(`use_cw_file')
```

invokes the feature and uses the **local-host-names** file as the data source; here is an example **local-host-names** file:

```
# local-host-names - include all aliases for your machine here.
toadranch.com
coyote.toadranch.com
hein.tv
coyote.hein.tv
big-tr.com
yoherb.com
herbmorreale.com
appliedtrust.com
applied-trust.com
atrust.com
```

In this example, the entries are all virtual domains that are hosted locally.

The redirect feature

When people leave your organization, you usually either forward their mail or let mail to them bounce back to the sender with an error. The redirect feature provides support for a more elegant way of bouncing mail. If Joe Smith has graduated from oldsite.edu to newsite.com, then enabling redirect with

```
FEATURE(`redirect')
```

and adding the line

```
smithj:  joe@newsite.com.REDIRECT
```

to the **aliases** file causes mail to smithj to be returned to the sender with an error message which suggests that the sender try the address joe@newsite.com instead. The message itself is not automatically forwarded.

The always_add_domain feature

This feature makes **sendmail** add the local hostname to local destination addresses that are not fully qualified. For example, suppose lynda@cs.colorado.edu sends a message to the local users barb and evi. Without always_add_domain, the mail headers would show sender and recipient addresses as simple login names. With always_add_domain turned on, all addresses would become fully qualified before the message left lynda's machine.

Use always_add_domain when you share spool directories among machines that do not share an alias file or that do not have the same **passwd** file (incidentally, you probably shouldn't do such sharing). Mail to an alias or user that is not known everywhere would be fully qualified on the originating machine and therefore could be replied to.

Another selling point for this feature is that unqualified names are often rejected as spam. We recommend that you always use it (unless you are sending spam!).

If you are using MASQUERADE_AS (see page 566), always_add_domain adds the name of the host you are masquerading as, not the local hostname. This convention can cause problems if the **aliases** file or **passwd** file on the local host is not a subset of the equivalent file on the MASQUERADE_AS host.

The nocanonify feature

sendmail typically verifies that the domain name portion of an address is fully qualified and not a DNS CNAME. If this is not so, **sendmail** rewrites the address. This process is called canonification and is usually done by running a DNS lookup on the hostname. The nocanonify feature says not to do this rewriting, and the DNS lookup that is necessary to deliver a message is postponed. For example, at a site with a master mail hub and client machines that forward all their mail through the master, the clients might use

```
FEATURE(`nocanonify')
```

to avoid doing the DNS lookups locally. **sendmail** does not keep track of whether DNS lookups have been done as a message moves from machine to machine within a local site—it can't. The nocanonify feature lets you control the timing of these lookups. See our second sample configuration (page 575) for an example.

nocanonify can also be used in an MSA/MTA scheme such as might be used at a very large mail site. In this scenario, the MSA does all the DNS lookups and the master machine running the MTA specifies nocanonify.

You sometimes want to avoid DNS lookups that are potentially expensive but you are willing to do the lookups for the local domain. You can exempt specific domains from the nocanonify specification by including either the CANONIFY_DOMAIN or CANONIFY_DOMAIN_FILE macros, which take a list of domains or a filename as an argument, respectively. For example, the lines

```
FEATURE('nocanonify')
CANONIFY_DOMAIN('cs.colorado.edu cs')
```

would defer DNS lookups except for addresses of the form *user*@cs.colorado.edu or *user*@cs. These exception macros were first introduced in version 8.12.

Tables and databases

sendmail has several FEATUREs that use a construct called a "table" to figure out where mail should be routed. A table is usually a text file of routing, aliasing, policy, or other information that is converted to a database format externally with the **makemap** command and then used as an internal database for **sendmail**'s various lookups. Although the data usually starts as a text file, that is not required; data for **sendmail** tables can come from DNS, NIS, LDAP, or other sources. The use of a centralized IMAP or POP server relieves **sendmail** of the chore of chasing down users and obsoletes some of the tables discussed below. Table 19.12 on page 569 summarizes the available tables.

Two database libraries are supported: the **dbm/ndbm** library that is standard with most versions of Linux; and Berkeley DB, a more extensible library that supports multiple storage schemes. Your choice of database libraries must be specified at compile time. We recommend DB if you can install it; it's faster than **dbm** and creates smaller files. DB is available from sleepycat.com.

Three database map types are available:

- dbm – uses an extensible hashing algorithm (**dbm/ndbm**)
- hash – uses a standard hashing scheme (DB)
- btree – uses a B-tree data structure (DB)

For most table applications in **sendmail**, the hash database type—the default—is the best. Use the **makemap** command to build the database file from a text file; you specify the database type and the output file base name. The text version of the database should appear on **makemap**'s standard input, for example:

```
# makemap hash /etc/mail/access < /etc/mail/access
```

At first glance this command looks like a mistake that would cause the input file to be overwritten by an empty output file. However, **makemap** tacks on an appropriate suffix, so the actual output file is **/etc/mail/access.db** and in fact there is no conflict. Each time the text file is changed, the database file must be rebuilt with **makemap** (but **sendmail** need not be HUPed).

In most circumstances, the longest possible match is used for database keys. As with any hashed data structure, the order of entries in the input text file is not significant. FEATUREs that expect a database file as a parameter default to hash as the database type and **/etc/mail/**tablename**.db** as the filename for the database. To override this behavior, either specify the desired database type to both the **makemap** command and the FEATURE or reset the default by defining a different value for the variable DATABASE_MAP_TYPE. For example:

```
define(`DATABASE_MAP_TYPE', `dbm')
```

To use your new **access.db** database, you'd add the following line to your **.mc** file:

```
FEATURE(`access_db', `hash /etc/mail/access')
```

Since this line uses the default type and naming scheme, you could just write

```
FEATURE(`access_db')
```

You can specify the database filename either with or without the suffix (**.db**); without is preferred.

Don't forget to rebuild the database file with **makemap** every time you change the text file, or your changes will not take effect.

We cover the mailertable, genericstable, and virtusertable FEATUREs in the next few sections. The access_db is covered later in the spam section. The user_db is not covered at all because it has been deprecated and will eventually be removed.

Starting with version 8.12, all maps and classes can specify LDAP as the source of their data, so you can have **sendmail** contact the LDAP server to determine mail routing and header rewriting. Just specify LDAP as the second parameter:

```
FEATURE(`access_db', `LDAP')
```

This line will cause the access_db to use the default LDAP schema that is defined in the file **cf/sendmail.schema** in the **sendmail** distribution. You can also define your own database schema with additional arguments to the FEATURE directive; see the **cf/README** file for details.

The mailertable feature

The mailertable feature redirects mail addressed to a particular host or domain to an alternate destination through a particular mailer. It is applied as the mail goes out from a site. The mailertable feature looks only at the host portion of the address, not the user portion. The header address is not rewritten, so the mail continues to be addressed to the same user but is sent to a different host through a different mailer. mailertable was originally designed to deal with other mail systems such as UUCP, DECnet, and BITNET, but today is often used to redirect mail from a gateway machine to an internal server.

To use a mailertable, include the following line in your **.mc** file.

```
FEATURE(`mailertable')
```

An entry in the mailertable has the form:

```
old_domain          mailer:destination
```

A leading dot in front of the key on the left side is a wild card that means any host in that domain. Only host and domain names are allowed as mailertable keys; usernames are not allowed. The *destination* value on the right side can be a domain, a user@domain clause, or even null, in which case the envelope is not changed. The *mailer* value must be the name of a mailer defined in a MAILER clause; see page 557.

As an example, suppose you used MS Exchange as your main internal mail server but were reluctant to have it facing the Internet. You could put a Linux box on the Internet as your mail gateway and then forward all mail to the Exchange server after virus scanning or whatever preprocessing you liked. Here is the mailertable entry that would do it, assuming that the Exchange server had the internal IP address shown:

```
my-domain       esmtp:[192.168.1.245]
```

However, this is a form of relaying, which, as we will see on page 590, needs to be controlled. To complete this example, you would need to put the line

```
To: my-domain  RELAY
```

in your access database to allow relaying for all mail to any user at my-domain.

The genericstable feature

The genericstable feature ("generics table," not "generic stable") is like aliasing for outgoing mail. For example, it can map trent@xor.com to trent.hein@xor.com on outbound mail. It is the headers that are rewritten, not the envelope. Mail delivery is not affected, only replies.

Several mechanisms can be used to map hostnames, but the genericstable is the only one that includes both the username and the hostname in the mapping key. The masquerade_envelope and allmasquerade features discussed later in this section can also apply to addresses in the genericstable.

To use the genericstable, make sure that your domain is in the generics class. To put a domain in the generics class, you can either list it in the GENERICS_DOMAIN macro or put it in the file specified by the GENERICS_DOMAIN_FILE macro.

For example, to use the genericstable with the defaults for the database, add

```
GENERICS_DOMAIN_FILE('/etc/mail/local-host-names')
FEATURE(`genericstable')
```

to your **.mc** configuration file. In this example, any host you accept mail for is included. Enabling the genericstable feature slows down **sendmail** slightly because every sender address must be looked up.

The virtusertable feature

The virtual user table supports domain aliasing for incoming mail. This feature allows multiple virtual domains to be hosted on one machine and is common at web hosting sites.

The key field of the table contains either an email address (*user@host.domain*) or a domain specification (*@domain*). The value field is a local email address or an external email address. If the key is a domain, the value can either pass the *user* field along as the variable %1 or route the mail to a different user. If the user specification has the form *user+details*, then the variable %2 will contain the *details* and variable %3 will contain *+details*; use whichever form you want.

Let's look at some examples (we have added the comments):

```
info@foo.com    foo-info                # route to a local user
info@bar.com    bar-info                # another local user
joe@bar.com     error:No such user      # to return an error
@baz.org        jane@elsewhere.com      # all mail to jane
@zokni.org      %1@elsewhere.com        # to the same user, different domain
```

All the host keys on the left side of the data mappings must be listed in the **cw** file, **/etc/mail/local-host-names**, (or the VirtHost class); otherwise, **sendmail** tries to find the host on the Internet and to deliver the mail there. If DNS points **sendmail** back to this server, you get a "local configuration error" message in bounces. Unfortunately, **sendmail** cannot tell that the error message for this instance should really be "virtusertable key not in cw file."

Several pieces are actually involved here:

- DNS MX records must exist so that mail is routed to the right host in the first place, then

- **cw** entries must be present or VIRTUSER_DOMAIN specified (or equivalently, VIRTUSER_DOMAIN_FILE) to allow the local machine to accept the mail, and finally

- the virtual user table must tell **sendmail** what to do with the mail.

The feature is invoked with:

```
FEATURE(`virtusertable')
```

The examples starting on page 573 use virtusertable to implement virtual hosting.

The ldap_routing feature

As a final chunk floating in this cesspool of aliasing, rewriting, and falsification, we have LDAP, the Lightweight Directory Access Protocol. LDAP (see page 538 for general information) can be used as a substitute for the virtusertable with respect to routing email and accepting mail for virtual domains. It can also manage aliases, maps, and classes. And as of version 8.12, it can do a decent job with mailing lists.

To use LDAP in this way, you must include several statements in your config file, and you must have built **sendmail** to include LDAP support. In your **.mc** file you need the lines

```
define(`confLDAP_DEFAULT_SPEC', `-h server -b searchbase')
FEATURE(`ldap_routing')
LDAPROUTE_DOMAIN(`my_domain')
```

to tell **sendmail** that you want to use an LDAP database for routing incoming mail addressed to the specified domain. The LDAP_DEFAULT_SPEC option identifies the LDAP server and database search base name.

In the following example, the search base is o=sendmail.com, c=US. If you run LDAP on a custom port (not 389), add -p ldap_port# to the LDAP_DEFAULT_SPEC.

sendmail uses the values of two tags in the LDAP database:

- mailLocalAddress for the addressee on incoming mail
- mailRoutingAddress for the alias to send it to

sendmail also supports the tag mailHost, which if present routes mail to the MX records for the specified host, with the mailRoutingAddress as recipient.

For example, the LDAP entry (for a server configured with a root distinguished name of cn=root, o=sendmail.com, c=US)

```
dn: uid=eric, o=sendmail.com, c=US
objectClass: inetLocalMailRecipient
mailLocalAddress: eric@sendmail.org
mailRoutingAddress: eric@eng.sendmail.com
```

would cause mail addressed to eric@sendmail.org (which DNS MX records caused to be delivered to sendmail.com) to be sent to eric@eng.sendmail.com. If the entry also contained the line

```
mailHost: mailserver.sendmail.com
```

then mail to eric@sendmail.org would be addressed to eric@eng.sendmail.com and sent to the host mailserver.sendmail.com after MX lookups.

LDAP database entries support a wild card entry, *@domain*, that reroutes mail addressed to anyone at the specified domain (as was done in the virtusertable).

In versions 8.12 and later, a bit more flexibility was added in the form of a configuration primitive, LDAPROUTE_EQUIVALENT (or LDAPROUTE_EQUIVALENT_FILE), that allows you to define equivalent versions of the domain name you are rerouting with LDAP. For example, mail coming to user@host1.mydomain would normally be queried literally in the LDAP database and then queried as @host1.mydomain. Including the line

```
LDAPROUTE_EQUIVALENT(`host1.mydomain')
```

would also try the keys user@mydomain and @mydomain. This feature allows a single database to be used to route mail at a complex site.

Additional arguments to the ldap_routing feature now enable you to specify more details about the LDAP schema to use and to specify the handling of user names that have a +detail part. As always, see the **cf/README** file for exact details.

Masquerading and the MASQUERADE_AS macro

With the MASQUERADE_AS macro, you can specify a single identity that other machines hide behind. All mail appears to emanate from the designated machine or domain. The sender's address is rewritten to be *user@masquerading-name* instead of *user@original-host.domain*. Of course, those masqueraded addresses must be valid so that people can reply to the mail.

This configuration permits all users at a site to use a generic email address. For example, if all hosts at xor.com masquerade behind the domain xor.com, then mail from *user@host*.xor.com will be stamped as being from *user@xor.com*, with no mention of the actual hostname from which the user sent the mail. The machine that represents xor.com must know how to deliver all users' mail, even mail for users that do not have a login on the incoming mail server. Naturally, login names must be unique across the whole domain.

Some users and addresses (such as root, postmaster, hostmaster, trouble, operations, Mailer-Daemon, etc.) should be exempted from this behavior. They can be explicitly excluded with the EXPOSED_USER macro. For example, the sequence

```
MASQUERADE_AS(`xor.com')
EXPOSED_USER(`root')
EXPOSED_USER(`Mailer-Daemon')
```

would stamp mail as coming from user@xor.com unless it was sent by root or the mail system; in these cases, the mail would carry the name of the originating host.

A feature introduced in 8.12 enables you to exempt mail for the local domain (or mail to specific hosts listed as exceptions) from the masquerading. For example, this feature might be handy for a site that uses an unregistered private domain name locally and wants masquerading only on messages bound for the Internet.

The syntax is:

```
FEATURE('local_no_masquerade')
MASQUERADE_EXCEPTION('host.domain')
MASQUERADE_EXCEPTION_FILE(`filename')
```

There are several extensions to the basic MASQUERADE_AS macro, both through other macros and through FEATUREs:

- The MASQUERADE_DOMAIN macro
- The MASQUERADE_DOMAIN_FILE macro
- The MASQUERADE_EXCEPTION macro
- The MASQUERADE_EXCEPTION_FILE macro
- The limited_masquerade FEATURE
- The allmasquerade FEATURE
- The masquerade_envelope FEATURE
- The masquerade_entire_domain FEATURE

We recommend using the MASQUERADE_AS macro described above along with the allmasquerade and masquerade_envelope features. The limited_masquerade feature modifies the behavior of MASQUERADE_DOMAIN and is useful for virtual hosting environments. MASQUERADE_DOMAIN lets you list domains that you want to masquerade; the list is preloaded from the w class that is typically defined with the use_cw_file feature and lists the hosts in your domain. limited_masquerade does not preinitialize the list with class w. All those domains will be hidden by the domain you are masquerading as.

The allmasquerade feature extends masquerading to the recipients of the message (as opposed to just the sender), and the masquerade_envelope feature extends it to the envelope as well as to the header addresses.[29] With these two extensions, all addresses are hidden in a consistent fashion. The masquerade_entire_domain feature extends masquerading to all hosts in a specified list of other domains.

If you want to use other masquerading techniques, you can read about their behavior in the **cf/README** file or in the **sendmail** book. Read carefully; some of the masquerading primitives can hide too much.

The MAIL_HUB and SMART_HOST macros

Masquerading makes all mail appear to come from a single host or domain by rewriting the headers and, optionally, the envelope. Some sites may want all mail to really come from (or go to) a single machine. You can achieve this configuration with the macros MAIL_HUB for incoming mail and SMART_HOST for outgoing mail.

---

29. The header addresses are the To, From, Cc, and Bcc addresses that appear in the header of a message. The envelope addresses are the addresses to which the mail is actually delivered. The envelope addresses are originally built from the header addresses by the user agent, but they are processed separately by **sendmail**. Many of **sendmail**'s masquerading and redirection features would be impossible to implement if the distinction between header and envelope addresses was not maintained.

If you want to route all incoming mail to a central server for delivery, set MAIL_HUB to the value *mailer:host*, where *mailer* is the agent to use to reach the designated *host*. If no delivery agent is specified, relay is used. For example:

```
define(`MAIL_HUB', `smtp:mailhub.cs.colorado.edu')
```

The SMART_HOST designation causes a host to deliver local mail but to punt external mail to SMART_HOST. This feature is useful for machines behind a firewall that cannot use DNS directly. Its syntax parallels that of MAIL_HUB; the default delivery agent is again relay. For example:

```
define(`SMART_HOST', `smtp:mailhub.cs.colorado.edu')
```

In these examples, the same machine acts as the server for both incoming and outgoing mail. A larger site might split these into separate machines. The SMART_HOST must allow relaying so that client machines can send mail through it. mailertable entries override the SMART_HOST designation.

Masquerading and routing

With all these features and macros ready and waiting to massage your email addresses, we thought it might be nice to try to compare the various mechanisms in terms of whether they change the headers, the envelope, or the delivery of a message, whether they apply to incoming or outgoing messages, sender or recipient addresses, etc. If the page were double or triple width, we might have succeeded in really illustrating the differences among the various constructs.

Instead, we give you just a hint; you will have to look up the details in the **sendmail** documentation to get all the nuances of the different variations.

Entries in Table 19.12 that are all capital letters are **m4** macros. Lowercase entries are the names of features that are invoked with the FEATURE macro. Indented items depend on the items above; for example, a feature that modifies the MASQUERADE_AS behavior does nothing unless MASQUERADE_AS has been turned on. In the table, the feature would be indented to indicate this dependency. Masquerading affects the header addresses on outgoing mail and whether a message can be replied to; routing affects the actual delivery of the mail.

The nullclient feature

nullclient is used for a host that should never receive mail directly and that sends all its mail to a central server. The **.mc** file for such a host has only two lines.

```
OSTYPE(`ostype')
FEATURE(`nullclient', `mail_server')
```

The nullclient feature overrides many other features. All mail, without exception, is delivered to *mail_server* for processing.[30] Note that the server must allow the client

---

30. If you configure a client this way and then test the configuration with **sendmail -bt**, the client will appear to locally deliver local mail. The reason is that the nullclient directive is processed later, in ruleset 5 of the raw config file.

Table 19.12   Comparison of masquerading and routing features

	Construct	Dir	Affects[a]	Which piece
Masquerading	MASQUERADE_AS	out	SH	host.domain
	allmasquerade	out	RH[b]	host.domain
	MASQUERADE_DOMAIN[_FILE]	out	SH	host.domain
	masquerade_entire_domain	out	SH	host.sub.domain
	limited_masquerade	out	SH	host.domain
	masquerade_envelope	out	SE[c]	host.domain
	genericstable	out	SH	user@host.domain
Routing	mailertable	out	MAD	host.domain
	virtusertable	in	RD	user@host.domain
	ldap	in	RD	user@host.domain
	mailhub	in	RD	local mail
	smarthost	out	RD	remote mail

a. S = sender, R = recipient, D = delivery, H = header, E = envelope, M = mailer, A = address

b. Once recipient rewriting has been enabled with the allmasquerade feature, all other masquerading constructs rewrite not only the sender but also the recipient.

c. Once envelope rewriting has been enabled with the masquerade_envelope feature, all other masquerading constructs rewrite not only the header but the envelope as well.

to relay through it if users regularly originate mail on the client and don't use a separate server for outgoing mail. Recent versions of **sendmail** have relaying turned off by default. See the spam section (page 588) for details on how to control relaying. A nullclient configuration masquerades as *mail_server*, so you might want to include an EXPOSED_USER clause for root.

The client that uses the nullclient feature must have an associated MX record that points to the server. It must also be included in the server's **cw** file, which is usually **/etc/mail/local-host-names**. These settings let the server accept mail for the client.

A host with a nullclient configuration should not accept incoming mail. If it did, it would just forward the mail to the server anyway. Starting **sendmail** without the **-bd** flag so that it doesn't listen for SMTP connections on port 25 is one way to avoid receiving mail. However, some user agents (MUAs) attempt the initial submission of a mail message through port 25 and so will be foiled if your **sendmail** is not listening. A better way to disallow incoming mail is to run **sendmail** with the **-bd** flag, but to use DAEMON_OPTIONS to listen only on the loopback interface. Either way, leave the **-q30m** flag on the command line so that if *mail_server* goes down, the client can queue outgoing mail and try to send it to *mail_server* later.

nullclient is appropriate for leaf nodes at sites that have a central mail machine. At larger sites, consider the mail load on the hub machine. You may want to separate the incoming and outgoing servers or adopt a hierarchical approach.

Electronic Mail

SuSE Linux ships with a sample nullclient **mc** file in **/etc/mail/linux.nullclient.mc**. Just fill in the name of your *mail_server*, run **m4** on it to build the **sendmail.cf** file, and you are done.

The local_lmtp and smrsh features

By default, the local mailer uses **/bin/mail** as the local delivery agent for users and files and **/bin/sh** as the delivery agent for programs. **sendmail** now provides better alternatives, especially for delivery to programs. Both are available with the feature macro.

If the local_lmtp feature is specified, then its argument is a local mailer capable of speaking LMTP, the Local Mail Transport Protocol (see RFC2033). The default is the **mail.local** program from the **sendmail** distribution. It's usually installed in the directory **/usr/libexec**, but you can specify the install directory with the confEBINDIR option. Red Hat's default installation does not include **mail.local** at all. SuSE puts it in **/usr/lib/sendmail.d/bin** and Debian puts it in **/usr/lib/sm.bin**.

The smrsh feature specifies the path to the program to use for mail delivery to programs; it defaults to **/usr/libexec/smrsh**, the **sendmail** restricted shell. Red Hat installs the **smrsh** binary in **/usr/sbin**, SuSE puts it in **/usr/lib/sendmail.d/bin**, and Debian puts it in **/usr/lib/sm.bin**. **smrsh** enables the local system administrator to control which commands can be run by email.

See page 605 for a more detailed discussion of both **mail.local** and **smrsh**.

The local_procmail feature

You can use Stephen van den Berg's **procmail** as your local mailer by enabling the local_procmail feature. It takes up to three arguments: the path to the **procmail** binary, the argument vector to call it with, and flags for the mailer. The default values are OK, but the default path (**/usr/local/bin/procmail**) conflicts with most distributions' usual **procmail** location (**/usr/bin**).

procmail can do fancier things for the user than plain **/bin/mail** or **mail.local**. In addition to delivering mail to users' mailboxes, it can sort messages into folders, save them in files, run programs, and filter spam. Use of the local_procmail feature largely nullifies the security enhancements provided by **smrsh** (described on page 605). However, if you don't need to restrict the programs your users run (that is, you trust *all* your users), then **procmail** can be very handy. **procmail** is not distributed with **sendmail**; get it from www.procmail.org if it is not installed by your vendor. Red Hat, SuSE, and Debian all include **procmail** and put it in **/usr/bin**.

You can use other mail processing programs in conjunction with this feature just by lying to **sendmail** and saying that you are just showing it the local copy of **procmail**:

```
FEATURE(`local_procmail', `/usr/local/bin/mymailer')
```

If you use **procmail**, check out **/usr/bin/mailstat** for some handy **procmail** statistics (not to be confused with **/usr/sbin/mailstats**, which shows **sendmail** statistics). It is installed on all of our example distributions and can be used to summarize

procmail log files. There is no man page on Red Hat and a very marginal one on SuSE; your best bet on these platforms is to read the source code (it's a Bourne shell script). Or try **mailstat -h** and experiment from there. Debian includes a proper man page for **mailstat**.

The LOCAL_* macros

If you really need to get your hands dirty and write some exotic new rules to deal with special local situations, you use a set of macros prefaced by LOCAL_. The section on spam, later in this chapter, has some examples of this low-level construct.

Configuration options

Config file options and macros (the O and D commands in the raw config language) can be set with the define **m4** command. A complete list of options accessible as **m4** variables and their default values is given in the **cf/README** file. The default values are OK for most sites.

Some examples:

```
define(`confTO_QUEUERETURN', `7d')
define(`confTO_QUEUEWARN', `4h')
define(`confPRIVACY_FLAGS', `noexpn')
```

The queue return option determines how long a message will remain in the mail queue if it cannot be delivered. The queue warn option determines how long a message will sit before the sender is notified that there might problems with delivery. The first two lines set these to 7 days and 4 hours, respectively.

See page 606 for more information about privacy options.

The next line sets the privacy flags to disallow the SMTP EXPN (expand address) command. The confPRIVACY_FLAGS option takes a comma-separated list of values. Some versions of **m4** require two sets of quotes to protect the commas in a field with multiple entries, but the GNU **m4** shipped with Linux is smarter and doesn't require the extra quotes:

```
define(`confPRIVACY_FLAGS', ``noexpn, novrfy'')
```

The default values for most options are about right for a typical site that is not too paranoid about security or too concerned with performance. In particular, the defaults try to protect you from spam by turning off relaying, requiring addresses to be fully qualified, and requiring that addresses resolve to an IP address. If your mail hub machine is very busy and services lots of mailing lists, you may need to tweak some of the performance values.

Table 19.13 on page 572 lists some options that you might need to adjust (about 15% of the almost 175 configuration options), along with their default values. To save space, the option names are shown without their conf prefix; for example, the FALLBACK_MX option is really named confFALLBACK_MX. We divided the table into subsections that identify the kind of issue the variable addresses: generic, resources, performance, security and spam abatement, and miscellaneous. Some options clearly fit in more than one category, but we listed them only once.

Table 19.13   Basic configuration options

	Option name	Description and (default value)
Generic	COPY_ERRORS_TO	Addresses to Cc on error messages (none)
	DOUBLE_BOUNCE_ADDRESS	Catches a lot of spam; some sites use **/dev/null**, but that can hide serious problems (postmaster)
Resources	MIN_FREE_BLOCKS	Minimum filesystem space to accept mail (100)
	MAX_MESSAGE_SIZE	Max size in bytes of a single message (infinite)
	TO_*lots_of_stuff*	Timeouts for all kinds of things (various)
	TO_IDENT	Timeout for ident queries to check sender's identity; if 0, ident checks are not done (5s)
	MAX_DAEMON_CHILDREN	Max number of child processes[a] (no limit)
Performance	MCI_CACHE_SIZE	# of open outgoing TCP connections cached (2)
	MCI_CACHE_TIMEOUT	Time to keep cached connections open (5m)
	HOST_STATUS_DIRECTORY	See page 614 for description (no default)
	FALLBACK_MX	See page 613 for description (no default)
	FAST_SPLIT	Suppresses MX lookups as recipients are sorted and split across queues; see page 613 (1 = true)
	QUEUE_LA	Load average at which mail should be queued instead of delivered immediately (8 * #CPUs)
	REFUSE_LA	Load avg. at which to refuse mail (12 * #CPUs)
	DELAY_LA	Load avg. to slow down deliveries (0 = no limit)
	MIN_QUEUE_AGE	Minimum time jobs must stay in queue; makes a busy machine handle the queue better (0)
Security/spam	TRUSTED_USERS	For mailing list software owners; allows forging of the From line and rebuilding of the aliases database (root, daemon, uucp)
	PRIVACY_FLAGS	Limits info given out by SMTP (authwarnings)
	INPUT_MAIL_FILTERS	List of filters for incoming mail (empty)
	MAX_MIME_HEADER_LENGTH	Max size of MIME headers (no limit)[b]
	CONNECTION_RATE_THROTTLE	Slows DOS attacks by limiting the rate at which mail connections are accepted (no limit)
	MAX_RCPTS_PER_MESSAGE	Slows spam delivery; defers extra recipients and sends a temporary error msg (infinite)
	DONT_BLAME_SENDMAIL	Overrides **sendmail**'s security and file checking; don't change casually! (safe)
	AUTH_MECHANISMS	SMTP auth mechanisms for Cyrus SASL ([c])
Misc	LDAP_DEFAULT_SPEC	Map spec for LDAP database, including the host and port the server is running on (undefined)

a. More specifically, the maximum number of child processes that can run at once. When the limit is reached, **sendmail** refuses connections. This option can prevent (or create) denial of service (DOS) attacks.

b. This option can prevent user agent buffer overflows. "256/128" is a good value to use—it means 256 bytes per header and 128 bytes per parameter to that header.

c. The default value is "EXTERNAL GSSAPI KERBEROS_V4 DIGEST-MD5 CRAM-MD5"; don't add PLAIN LOGIN unless you want to reduce security.

19.9 CONFIGURATION FILE EXAMPLES

We haven't really finished with all the configuration options (a spam section, a security section, and a performance section are coming up), but it's time to look at some example configuration files. This order may be a bit like putting the cart before the horse, but of the arrangements that we've tried, it seems to work the best. The essential configuration feature that we have not yet covered is the access database, which is used primarily to filter and control spam. It's covered starting on page 592.

In documenting the config files in use at various sites, we invariably run into some cruft left over from bygone days that is either wrong or not needed. We have cleaned up these inconsistencies, spelling errors, etc., before using the config files as examples, so they are not shown here exactly as they appeared on the original servers. Nevertheless, they reflect real-world configurations.

A computer science student's home machine

Our first example is a student, Rob Braun, who has a Linux box (gw.synack.net) at home and does virtual hosting for a few friends' domains: xinetd.org, teich.net, and cubecast.com.

He also hosts his own domain, synack.net. Rob maps all incoming mail to the correct person with LDAP. He uses the virtusertable to handle the virtual hosting mappings, and the genericstable to handle outgoing mail. Of the many table types that affect outgoing mail, genericstable is the only one that can rewrite the username as well as the destination host.

Rob's genericstable file (which he actually calls **outmap**) contains:

```
bbraun      rob@synack.net
stabilej    jon@synack.net
teich       oren@teich.net
```

Rob uses the Mail Abuse Prevention Service (dnsbl) for spam control. He also uses masquerading features to stamp any outgoing mail that is not already rewritten by the genericstable as coming from user@synack.net instead of user@gw.synack.net. Here is the complete **gw.mc** file:

```
divert(0)
VERSIONID(`@(#)synack.net.mc 8.7 (Berkeley)5/19/1998')
OSTYPE(linux)
DOMAIN(generic)
FEATURE(dnsbl)
FEATURE(virtusertable, `hash /etc/mail/inmap')
FEATURE(genericstable, `hash /etc/mail/outmap')
GENERICS_DOMAIN_FILE(`/etc/mail/local-host-names')
MASQUERADE_AS(synack.net)
FEATURE(`masquerade_envelope')
FEATURE(`ldap_routing')
LDAPROUTE_DOMAIN(`synack.net')
define(`confLDAP_DEFAULT_SPEC', `-h gw.synack.net -b dc=synack,dc=net')
```

```
MAILER(local)
MAILER(smtp)
```

The **/etc/mail/local-host-names** file contains the hosts and domains for which this host accepts mail. The use_cw_file feature that would invoke the file is hidden in the generic domain file; see page 578 for a listing of its contents. Relaying is turned off by default because the file **/etc/mail/relay-domains** is normally empty. Here, that file contains the domains that are virtually hosted by gw.synack.net. The LDAP database is configured with an **ldap.conf** file that sets the LDAP root distinguished name, server host, and port:

```
BASE dc=synack, dc=net
HOST gw.synack.net
PORT 389
```

The LDAP database is then built from a text file with entries such as:

```
dn: uid=rob, dc=synack, dc=net
objectClass: inetLocalMailRecipient
mailLocalAddress: rob@synack.net
mailRoutingAddress: bbraun@synack.net
uid:rob

dn: uid=webmaster, dc=synack, dc=net
objectClass: inetLocalMailRecipient
mailLocalAddress: webmaster@synack.net
mailRoutingAddress: bbraun@synack.net
uid:webmaster

dn: uid=teich, dc=synack, dc=net
objectClass: inetLocalMailRecipient
mailLocalAddress: teich@synack.net
mailRoutingAddress: oren@teich.net
uid:teich

dn: uid=xinetd, dc=synack, dc=net
objectClass: inetLocalMailRecipient
mailLocalAddress: xinetd@synack.net
mailRoutingAddress: xinetd
uid:xinetd
```

The first three entries map the login names rob, webmaster, and oren to their aliases. The fourth is a mailing list that maps to a local alias and is handled from there by Majordomo by means of these entries in the **/etc/mail/aliases** file:

```
xinetd: "|/usr/local/majordomo/wrapper resend -l test xinetd-list"
xinetd-list: :include:/usr/local/majordomo/lists/xinetd
xinetd-owner: bbraun
owner-xinetd: bbraun
xinetd-request: bbraun
xinetd-approval: bbraun
```

We have shown several supporting files and sample contents for this example. Our next examples keep closer to the point of illustrating how **sendmail** configuration works and do not show peripheral files.

Keep in mind that in any **sendmail** example, DNS MX records play a crucial role and need to agree with the assumptions made by your configuration.

A small but sendmail-clueful company

As our next example, we look at the config files for a small but very **sendmail**-savvy company, Sendmail, Inc. Their mail design includes a master mail hub machine for both incoming mail and outgoing mail. All incoming mail is accepted and immediately routed to a set of internal IMAP servers that check each message for viruses before delivering it to a user's mailbox. The mail hub machine also checks each outgoing message for viruses so that Sendmail, Inc. is never responsible for spreading viruses by email. We look at the clients' configuration first, then inspect the more complicated master machines.

In all of the examples, we have modified the originals slightly, leaving out the copyright notices, adding occasional comments, and removing the **m4** dnl directive at the ends of lines. If you use any of our examples as a model for your **.mc** file, be sure to remove the comments from the ends of lines.

Client machines at sendmail.com

The **smi-client.mc** file for client machines is quite simple. It uses the master machine smtp.sendmail.com, which is really just another name for foon.sendmail.com. Using an MX record (or a CNAME[31]) to point to the mail server is a good idea; it's easy to change when you want to move your master mail machine.

Note that the date on this file is October 1998. **sendmail** has been upgraded many times since then, but the configuration file did not need to change.

```
divert(-1)
#####  This file contains definitions for a Sendmail,
#####  Inc. client machine's .mc file.
divert(0)
VERSIONID(`@(#)smi-client.mc 1.0 (Sendmail) 10/14/98')
OSTYPE(`bsd4.4')
FEATURE(`nocanonify')
undefine(`ALIAS_FILE')
define(`MAIL_HUB', `smtp.sendmail.com')
define(`SMART_HOST', `smtp.sendmail.com')
define(`confFORWARD_PATH', `')
MAILER(`local')
MAILER(`smtp')
```

---

31. An MX record is actually more efficient than a CNAME; CNAMEs require a second lookup on the real name to get the IP address.

The MAIL_HUB and SMART_HOST lines direct incoming and outgoing mail to the host smtp.sendmail.com. MX records in DNS should cooperate and list that host with higher priority (lower number in MX record) than the individual client machines. The path for **.forward** files is set to null, and the alias file is also set to null; all alias expansion occurs on the master machine. The nocanonify feature is specified here to save time, since DNS lookups are done on the master anyway.

Master machine at sendmail.com

The master machine at sendmail.com may be one of the most attacked **sendmail** installations around. It must be secure from all the twisty mailer attacks that people come up with and must protect the machines behind it. Here is its configuration file:

```
divert(-1)
# Created with Sendmail Switch, sendmail.com's commercial product.
divert(0)
ifdef(`COMMERCIAL_CONFIG', `INPUT_MAIL_FILTER(`mime-filter', `S=local:
    /var/run/mime-filter/mime-filter.sock')')
LDAPROUTE_DOMAIN(`sendmail.com sendmail.net sendmail.org')
MASQUERADE_AS(`sendmail.com')
MASQUERADE_DOMAIN(`sendmail.com')
RELAY_DOMAIN(`sendmail.com sendmail.net sendmail.org')
define(`MAIL_HUB', `internal-hub.sendmail.com')
define(`QUEUE_DIR', `/var/spool/mqueue/q*')
define(`SMART_HOST', `virus-scan.sendmail.com')
ifdef(`COMMERCIAL_CONFIG', `define(`confCACERT', `/local/certs/cacert.pem')')
ifdef(`COMMERCIAL_CONFIG', `define(`confCACERT_PATH', `/local/certs/trustedcerts')')
define(`confCHECK_ALIASES', `True')
ifdef(`COMMERCIAL_CONFIG', `define(`confCLIENT_CERT', `/local/certs/cert.pem')')
ifdef(`COMMERCIAL_CONFIG', `define(`confCLIENT_KEY', `/local/certs/key.pem')')
define(`confEIGHT_BIT_HANDLING', `mimify')
define(`confLDAP_DEFAULT_SPEC', `- h "ldap.sendmail.com ldap2.sendmail.com"
    -b "dc=sendmail,dc=com" -p 1389')
define(`confREFUSE_LA', `99')
define(`confRUN_AS_USER', `mailnull')
ifdef(`COMMERCIAL_CONFIG', `define(`confSERVER_CERT', `/local/certs/cert.pem')')
ifdef(`COMMERCIAL_CONFIG', `define(`confSERVER_KEY', `/local/certs/key.pem')')
define(`confTO_IDENT', `0s')
define(`confTO_QUEUEWARN', `2d')
ifdef(`confPOP_TO', `', `define(`confPOP_TO', `900')')
FEATURE(`accept_unqualified_senders')
FEATURE(`accept_unresolvable_domains')
FEATURE(`allmasquerade')
FEATURE(`always_add_domain')
FEATURE(`domaintable')
FEATURE(`ldap_routing', `ldap -1 -v mailHost -k ldap -1 -v mailhost -k
    (&(objectclass=mailRecipient)(|(mail=%0)(|(mailAlternateAddress=%0))))',
    `ldap -1 -v mail -k
    (&(objectclass=mailRecipient)(|(mailalternateaddress=%0)))', `passthru')
FEATURE(`mailertable')
FEATURE(`masquerade_entire_domain')
```

```
FEATURE(`masquerade_envelope')
FEATURE(`relay_entire_domain')
FEATURE(`use_cw_file')
MAILER(`local')
MAILER(`smtp')

LOCAL_RULESETS
SLocal_check_rcpt
R$*     $: $&{verify}
ROK    $# OK
```

The master machine's job is to route incoming mail to the correct internal server and to serve as the smart relay host for outgoing mail.

Because of the following two lines,

```
FEATURE(`accept_unqualified_senders')
FEATURE(`accept_unresolvable_domains')
```

all incoming mail is accepted, even mail from unqualified senders and unresolvable domains. This way, potential customers who have **sendmail** or DNS misconfigured can still get through. These rules undo the defaults that catch lots of spam with forged headers. Ident is turned off (timeout set to 0) to speed up delivery of incoming mail.

This master mail machine first checks incoming messages for certain types of MIME attachments that are frequently used by viruses (INPUT_MAIL_FILTER statement). The **mime-filter** called there contains lines such as:

```
*:anniv.doc:*  error:Your email was not accepted by Sendmail, it appears to be
         infected with the Melissa-X virus.
*:.vbs:*        error:For security and virus protection reasons, Sendmail does
         not accept messages with VBS files attached.  Please retransmit your
         message without the VBS file.
```

MIME attachments of type **.vba**, **.dot**, **.exe**, **.com**, **.reg**, and so on are rejected, but a full virus scan is not done here because it would slow down the processing of incoming mail. The master uses LDAP (with a site-specific schema) to look up the recipient of each message and route it to the correct internal IMAP/POP server. If the recipient is not found in the LDAP database, the mail is sent to an internal master machine (the MAIL_HUB statement) for further processing. Both the IMAP/POP servers and the internal master machine do full virus scanning before delivering a message to a user's mailbox.

Outgoing mail is also routed through this master machine by SMART_HOST statements on the client machines. To send a message through the sendmail.com mail servers, hosts outside the sendmail.com domain must present a certificate signed by the sendmail.com certificate authority. Employees visiting a customer site can relay email to a third party through sendmail.com with this mechanism, but others cannot. This convention authenticates each user and prevents forged email from transiting sendmail.com.

After accepting email destined for the Internet, the master machine passes it to the SMART_HOST for virus scanning. The master mail machine is not too busy to do this virus scanning itself, but if the scanning were done there, users sending mail would have to wait for the scanning to complete before their message was really sent. Queueing it for the virus scanning machine keeps the users happy—their messages seem to zip off instantaneously.

The LOCAL_CONFIG rules at the end of the config file are where header checking for various viruses and known spammers is usually put. Good examples can be found in the **knecht.mc** example file in the **sendmail** distribution. We have included a sample below.

*See page 597 for more details about **libmilter**.* During the summer of 2001, the destructive SirCam worm was circulating wildly. The following fragment from the **knecht.mc** file in the **sendmail** distribution catches it. SirCam is one of the first nastygrams to have random headers. The usual tools to catch it would have failed, except that its authors made an error that differentiates a SirCam message from a real Outlook Express message. The message's content is quite regular (it asks for your advice on the enclosed attachment) and would therefore be a candidate for the new **libmilter** filtering abilities in version 8.12. Without product liability guarantees in the software world, it seems the only solution to all these Microsoft viruses and worms is to dump Windows and install Linux everywhere!

```
LOCAL_RULESETS

KSirCamWormMarker regex -f -aSUSPECT multipart/mixed;boundary=----
        .+_Outlook_Express_message_boundary
HContent-Type: $>CheckContentType

SCheckContentType
R$+            $: $(SirCamWormMarker $1 $)
RSUSPECT       $#error $: "553 Possible virus, see http:
        //www.symantec.com/avcenter/venc/data/w32.sircam.worm@mm.html"

HContent-Disposition:$>CheckContentDisposition

SCheckContentDisposition
R$-            $@ OK
R$- ; $+       $@ OK
R$*            $#error $: "553 Illegal Content-Disposition"
```

Clients at sendmail.com have no spam control in their config files because all mail coming into the site comes through the external mail hub and an internal hub and the spam is winnowed there. Some of the features and other constructs in this example are not covered in our configuration section, but you can find documentation on them in the **cf/README** file.

Another master/client example

XOR Inc. is a medium-sized company with a single master mail machine. Although XOR's overall mail design is similar to that of sendmail.com, it's implemented with slightly different configuration primitives.

Here is the client configuration:

```
divert(-1)
##### xor-client.mc, all clients to relay to xor.com
divert(0)
VERSIONID(`@(#)tcpproto.mc8.5 (Berkeley) 3/23/96')
OSTYPE(`bsdi')
define(`confPRIVACY_FLAGS', `noexpn')
FEATURE(`nullclient', `xor.com')
```

It's really minimal, but fine for a mail design in which the server does all the fancy stuff and the clients are just able to send mail. Even mail to local users is forwarded to xor.com, the machine specified in the nullclient feature. No mailers are specified; **sendmail** is not run in daemon mode.

Below is the master configuration that goes with this client setup. XOR does a lot of web hosting and accepts and manages mail for many virtual domains. Our first example, the student machine, managed three virtual domains with LDAP and the genericstable. XOR manages about 1,000 virtual domains with the virtusertable. It uses the genericstable for mapping login names to *first.last* for outgoing mail. It implements aliases with the standard **aliases** file, which is 3,000 lines long and contains many mailing lists, some with several thousand recipients (and one with over 100,000). All this on a slightly tired, old SunOS sun4m box that doesn't get replaced by a spiffy new Linux box because of inertia and a bit of "it works, don't touch it."

Note that the divert statements and comments that are usually present at the beginning of a **.mc** file are missing. They are only necessary if you use shell-style (#) comments at the beginning of your config file.

This site is running **sendmail** 8.9.3 and uses some of the old (pre-8.10) constructs for configuration lines. Its mail load has caused many of the performance parameters to be set quite a bit higher than their default values.

```
VERSIONID(`@(#)xor.mc3.0 (trent) 10/7/01')
OSTYPE(`sunos4.1')

define(`confPRIVACY_FLAGS', `noexpn,novrfy')
define(`confMESSAGE_TIMEOUT',`5d/72h')
define(`LOCAL_MAILER_PATH', `/usr/bin/mail.local')

dnl ##### increase values for performance and heavy load
define(`confMCI_CACHE_SIZE', `16')
define(`confMCI_CACHE_TIMEOUT', `10m')
define(`confCHECK_ALIASES', `False') ### default value, not needed
define(`confDOMAIN_NAME', `xor.com')
define(`confMAX_MESSAGE_SIZE', `5000000')
define(`confDAEMON_OPTIONS',`Port=NNN') ### NNN must be in /etc/services
define(`confQUEUE_LA', 25)
define(`confREFUSE_LA', 30)

FEATURE(always_add_domain)
FEATURE(use_cw_file)
```

```
FEATURE(virtusertable)
GENERICS_DOMAIN(`xor.com')
FEATURE(genericstable)
FEATURE(`masquerade_envelope')
FEATURE(`redirect')
FEATURE(`access_db', `hash -o /etc/mail/access')

MAILER(local)
MAILER(smtp)

LOCAL_RULESETS
# Kludgey Melissa virus checking routine that checks headers for pattern.
# Instructional note: the format for the rule is
#                RExactly the thing you want to quote
# No quote marks, no tabs, absolutely nothing in paretheses, then after the
# exact thing, then a tab, and the $#error that chooses the mailer to use.
# Note, the $* matches anything, so it's useful for wildcarding; sendmail must
# scan all messages so there is a small performance hit.

HSubject:          $>local_check_header
D{MelissaMessage}"553 Your message may contain the Melissa virus.  Please
     email postmaster@$j if you have questions."
D{LoveVirus}"553 Your message probably contains the LOVELETTER virus -
     Please email postmaster@$j if you have questions"
D{virus}"553 We think your message contains a VIRUS so we will reject it"

Slocal_check_header
RPeace between America and Islam!$*          $#error $: ${virus}
RPEACE BETWEEN AMERICA AND ISLAM!$*          $#error $: ${virus}
RPeace Between America and Islam!$*          $#error $: ${virus}
RPeace Between America And Islam!$*          $#error $: ${virus}
Rpeace between america and islam!$*          $#error $: ${virus}
RWar Vote$*                                  $#error $: ${virus}
Rwar vote$*                                  $#error $: ${virus}
RImportant Message From $*                   $#error $: ${MelissaMessage}
RRe: Important Message From $*               $#error $: ${MelissaMessage}
RILOVEYOU                                    $#error $: ${LoveVirus}
RI LOVE YOU                                  $#error $: ${LoveVirus}
Rfwd: Joke                                   $#error $: ${virus}
RSusitikim$*                                 $#error $: ${virus}
R$*Jokes text                                $#error $: ${virus}
R$*Jokes                                     $#error $: ${virus}
R$*Funny text                                $#error $: ${virus}

dnl ##### deleted a few hundred lines matching viruses and spam

R$*The declaration of independence$*          $#error $: ${spam}
R$*Affordable Benefits$*                      $#error $: ${spam}
R$*Do your own Criminal Background Checks$*   $#error $: ${spam}
R$*Are YOU Ready For Wealth & Freedom ????$*  $#error $: ${spam}
```

The virus and spam rules at the end of the **.mc** file reject specific messages on the basis of their subject lines. While these work fine, the variations of upper and lower case are not necessary; rulesets are case insensitive. Some of the targeted subject lines (for example, $\$^*$Jokes) could possibly match legitimate email.

These rules impact **sendmail**'s performance a bit and, at the rate that spam comes in, might end up making the config file huge. If you have a very busy site, it is probably best to do the spam filtering on a machine other than your main mail gateway.

To drop all mail from specific sites, use the access database and the keyword REJECT. The access file at xor.com contains more than 800 domains from which to reject mail, mostly pornography or spam sites judging from the domain names. Here is a snippet:

```
adult-megasite.com       REJECT
adult-zone.com           REJECT
adult10000.com           REJECT
adultage.com             REJECT
. . .
vivarebates.com          REJECT
vividnet.com             REJECT
vjs.org                  REJECT
vmadmin.com              REJECT
vnuemedia.com            REJECT
. . .
```

As you can see from the diversity of these examples, there is no single right way to set up your configuration file. **sendmail** contains many constructs for routing mail and munging headers. To some degree, the ones you choose depend on personal preference or on whatever the person from whom you copied the file did.

Now that we've seen some examples of real-world configurations, let's take a look at the default configurations shipped with each of our reference Linux distributions.

Red Hat sendmail configuration

Red Hat ships with **sendmail** installed. By default, it uses a configuration built from **/etc/mail/sendmail.mc** and snags the other parts of the config tree from the directory **/usr/lib/sendmail-cf**, which seems to be the **cf** directory from the **sendmail** distribution.

The Red Hat **.mc** file uses the old names and locations for **sendmail** files rather than the current defaults in **/etc/mail**. The configuration includes several of the databases that control the routing of email. However, these files need to be populated with local data; **mailertable**, **virtusertable**, and **access** exist but are empty. One file, **userdb**, is configured but missing.

We have removed some of the comments (lines beginning with dnl) to save space and have also added comments (beginning with ###) on unusual lines. You would have to remove our comments before using the example as a real **.mc** file. Here is the Red Hat **.mc** file as shipped in early 2002:

```
divert(-1)
include(`/usr/lib/sendmail-cf/m4/cf.m4')            ### old way to build cf file
```

```
VERSIONID(`linux setup for Red Hat Linux')
OSTYPE(`linux')
define(`confDEF_USER_ID',``8:12")                         ### uid/gid for user 'mail'
undefine(`UUCP_RELAY')                                    ### not needed,default
undefine(`BITNET_RELAY')                                  ### not needed,default
define(`confAUTO_REBUILD')                                ### deprecated, see below
define(`confTO_CONNECT', `1m')
define(`confTRY_NULL_MX_LIST',true)                       ### bad and dangerous
define(`confDONT_PROBE_INTERFACES',true)                  ### weird, see below
define(`PROCMAIL_MAILER_PATH',`/usr/bin/procmail') ### duplicate, in ostype
define('ALIAS_FILE','/etc/aliases')
dnl define(`STATUS_FILE', `/var/log/statistics')          ### commented out, RH
     7.1 had filename error here
define(`UUCP_MAILER_MAX', `2000000')                      ### uucp mailer not used
define(`confUSERDB_SPEC', `/etc/mail/userdb.db')          ### deprecated, see below
define(`confPRIVACY_FLAGS', `authwarnings,novrfy,noexpn,restrictqrun')
define(`confAUTH_OPTIONS', `A')
FEATURE(`no_default_msa',`dnl')                           ### kills default MSA but
     no replacement specified with DAEMON_OPTIONS
FEATURE(`smrsh',`/usr/sbin/smrsh')
FEATURE(`mailertable',`hash -o /etc/mail/mailertable.db')
FEATURE(`virtusertable',`hash -o /etc/mail/virtusertable.db')
FEATURE(redirect)
FEATURE(always_add_domain)
FEATURE(use_cw_file)
FEATURE(use_ct_file)
FEATURE(local_procmail,`',`procmail -t -Y -a $h -d $u')
FEATURE(`access_db',`hash -o /etc/mail/access.db')
FEATURE(`blacklist_recipients')
EXPOSED_USER(`root')
dnl This changes sendmail to only listen on the loopback device 127.0.0.1
dnl and not on any other network devices. Comment this out if you want
dnl to accept email over the network.
DAEMON_OPTIONS(`Port=smtp,Addr=127.0.0.1, Name=MTA')
dnl NOTE: binding both IPv4 and IPv6 daemon to the same port requires
dnl      a kernel patch
dnl DAEMON_OPTIONS(`port=smtp,Addr=::1, Name=MTA-v6, Family=inet6')
dnl We strongly recommend to comment this one out if you want to protect
dnl yourself from spam. However, the laptop and users on computers that do
dnl not have 24x7 DNS do need this.
FEATURE(`accept_unresolvable_domains')     ### should be deleted, see below
dnl FEATURE(`relay_based_on_MX')           ### too trusting, see spam section
MAILER(smtp)
MAILER(procmail)
Cwlocalhost.localdomain                    ### should use local-host-names
```

The confAUTO_REBUILD option is deprecated and will go away in future releases. It causes **sendmail** to rebuild its aliases database if it has changed before handling any email.

The confDONT_PROBE_INTERFACES define is strange; it causes **sendmail** not to list the interfaces of the local machine in its w class (**/etc/mail/local-host-names**). Mail must then be handled specifically by a mailertable entry or it will bounce with a configuration error. Even if confDONT_PROBE_INTERFACES is set, the loopback interface is always included, so local mail should work. (However, no local mailer is defined, so maybe not.)

Red Hat 7.1 specified **sendmail.st** as the STATUS_FILE but created the file **statistics**, so no statistics were ever gathered. Red Hat 7.2 corrects the filename but comments the line out.

The userdb feature is deprecated and also is not used in this configuration, so the confUSERDB_SPEC line is strange, perhaps a leftover from earlier times. Both the accept_unresolvable_domains and the relay_based_on_MX features should be removed if possible; the first creates spam havens, and the second lets the spammer steal service.

SuSE sendmail configuration

SuSE ships with two configs, both in **/etc/mail**: **linux.mc** and **linux.nullclient.mc**. One is for use on a master mail machine and the other is for client machines. The big difference in the SuSE versions as shipped is the OSTYPE file, **suse-linux.m4**, which contains way too much stuff.

The **.mc** files and the database sample files contain lots of comments to help you understand what features are included and the format for local information. The **linux.mc** file shown below shrank from 220 lines to 22 lines after we removed the comments.

The list of mailers includes some that are not part of the regular **sendmail** distribution. They can be found in the shipped version in **/usr/share/sendmail/mailers**.

SuSE's **.mc** file violates **sendmail**'s expected order of configuration statements by putting the DOMAIN statement (which is usually near the beginning) after the mailers (which are usually last). If a statement in the DOMAIN file modifies a mailer parameter, that modification won't take effect because of the ordering of the statements. It's best to follow the suggested ordering in the **cf/README** file. Although the SuSE files look nice and clean and simple, most of the configuration is hidden in the **suse-linux** OSTYPE file. Here is **linux.mc**:

```
divert(-1)
# Copyright (c) 1997-1999,2000 SuSE GmbH Nuernberg, Germany.
# Author: Florian La Roche
#         Werner Fink <werner@suse.de>

# After the `divert(0)' all lines starting with `dnl' are
# comments until the next newline character.
# Putting words into `'-pairs disables macro expansion
```

```
### should be done in ./Build, must be after divert(0)
include(`/usr/share/sendmail/m4/cf.m4')
divert(0)
VERSIONID(`@(#)Setup for SuSE Linux     8.11.0-0.4 (SuSE Linux) 04/09/2000')
OSTYPE(`suse-linux')
FEATURE(`always_add_domain')
MAILER(`local')
MAILER(`smtp')
MAILER(`procmail')
MAILER(`uucp')
MAILER(`bsmtp')
MAILER(`fido')
DOMAIN(`generic')
LOCAL_CONFIG        ### useless, does nothing
```

And here is **linux.nullclient.mc**; you must replace mailhub.domain.notused with the name of your actual mail hub machine. We have removed dnl from the ends of lines to make the example easier to read.

```
divert(-1)
# Copyright (c) 1999 SuSE GmbH Nuernberg, Germany.
# Author: Werner Fink <werner@suse.de>

# This is a special case -- it creates a stripped down configuration
# file containing nothing but support for forwarding all mail to a
# central hub via a local SMTP-based network.  The argument is the
# name of that hub.

### should be done in ./Build, must be after divert(0)
include(`/usr/share/sendmail/m4/cf.m4')
divert(0)
VERSIONID(`@(#)Setup for SuSE Linux     8.11.0-0.2 (SuSE Linux) 28/03/2000')
OSTYPE(`suse-linux')
FEATURE(`nullclient', `mailhub.domain.notused')
FEATURE(`nocanonify')
LOCAL_CONFIG        ### useless
```

OSTYPE files are typically about 10 lines and contain the path to various programs whose location is operating system dependent. SuSE Linux has gone way overboard; we have again added comments beginning with ### to lines that are unusual. The single line OSTYPE(`suse-linux') causes the following file to be included in these simple configurations:

```
divert(-1)
#  Copyright (c) 1999,2000 SuSE GmbH Nuernberg, Germany.
#  Author: Werner Fink <werner@suse.de>

divert(0)
VERSIONID(`@(#) suse-linux.m4   8.11.1-0.5 (SuSE Linux) 22/11/2000')
define(`confCF_VERSION', `SuSE Linux 8.11.1-0.5')

define(`confDEF_USER_ID', `daemon:daemon')        ### insecure if anything
    else uses daemon uid/gid
```

```
define(`confCOPY_ERRORS_TO', `Postmaster')
define(`UUCP_MAILER_MAX', `2000000')
define(`confMAX_MIME_HEADER_LENGTH', `256/128')
define(`confMAX_HEADERS_LENGTH', `32768')        ### default
define(`confQUEUE_LA', `12')
define(`confREFUSE_LA', `18')
define(`MAX_DAEMON_CHILDREN', `30')
define(`confTO_ICONNECT', `30s')
dnl Many sysadmins have disabled IDENT
define(`confTO_IDENT', `0s')
dnl Should we set noreceipts aka disable DSN?
define(`confPRIVACY_FLAGS',`authwarnings,needmailhelo,novrfy,noexpn,noverb')
define(`confTRUSTED_USERS', `mdom wwwrun root uucp daemon')
define(`confNO_RCPT_ACTION', `add-to-undisclosed')
dnl Note: RFC1891 says that, but often misused
dnl define(`confRRT_IMPLIES_DSN', `True')
FEATURE(`always_add_domain')

define(`PROCMAIL_MAILER_PATH', `/usr/bin/procmail')
define(`PROCMAIL_MAILER_ARGS', `procmail -m $h $f $u')
FEATURE(`local_procmail')
define(`LOCAL_SHELL_FLAGS', `u09')
define(`LOCAL_MAILER_ARGS', `procmail -a $h -d $u')
define(`LOCAL_MAILER_FLAGS', `SPfhn09')
define(`USENET_MAILER_PATH', `/usr/bin/inews')

define(`DATABASE_MAP_TYPE', `hash')              ### default

define(`SMLIBDIR', `/usr/lib/sendmail.d')
define(`MAIL_SETTINGS_DIR', `/etc/mail/')        ### default
define(`confDEAD_LETTER_DROP', `/var/log/dead.letter')

syscmd(`test -f /etc/SuSE-release')
ifelse(sysval, 0,
`define(`STATUS_FILE', `/var/log/sendmail.st')'
`define(`QUEUE_DIR', `/var/spool/mqueue')'       ### default
`define(`STATUS_FILE', `/etc/mail/sendmail.st')' ### old name for stats file
`define(`QUEUE_DIR', `/var/mqueue')'
)
define(`confHOST_STATUS_DIRECTORY', `.hoststat')
define(`HELP_FILE', SMLIBDIR`/helpfile')
define(`ALIAS_FILE', `/etc/aliases')
define(`confHOSTS_FILE', `/etc/hosts')                   ### default
define(`confCT_FILE', `-o /etc/mail/sendmail.ct %[^\#]')   ### %[^\#] not needed
define(`confCW_FILE', `-o /etc/mail/sendmail.cw %[^\#]') ### %[^\#] not needed
define(`confCR_FILE', `-o /etc/mail/relay-domains %[^\#]')### %[^\#] not needed
define(`confUSERDB_SPEC', `/etc/mail/userdb.db')        ### userdb is deprecated
define(`confSERVICE_SWITCH_FILE', `/etc/mail/service.switch')### default
define(`confEBINDIR', SMLIBDIR`/bin')
define(`confDONT_BLAME_SENDMAIL', `AssumeSafeChown,TrustStickyBit') ###
    dangerous
define(`confCONTROL_SOCKET_NAME', `/var/run/sendmail/control')
```

```
FEATURE(`no_default_msa')    ### weird, see below

FEATURE(`mailertable', `hash -o /etc/mail/mailertable.db')
FEATURE(`genericstable', `hash -o /etc/mail/genericstable.db')
FEATURE(`virtusertable', `hash -o /etc/mail/virtusertable.db')
FEATURE(`access_db', `hash -o /etc/mail/access.db')
dnl
LOCAL_CONFIG                  ### useless
```

This is a total mess. Most of it belongs in the **.mc** file (or in a domain file of configuration primitives for your site) where you can see it easily, not hidden behind a layer of OSTYPE indirection. OSTYPE files should be reserved for operating-system-dependent parameters such as the path to a particular program. The **cf/README** file in the **sendmail** distribution includes a list of the definitions that should go in the OSTYPE file—perhaps someone should send SuSE a highlighted copy.

In spite of this ridiculous OSTYPE file, SuSE has provided a pretty sensible initial configuration file to build on. All the tables referred to have corresponding files in **/etc/mail** with comments to indicate the format and typical entries. This configuration just needs a little reorganization into a proper OSTYPE file and perhaps a SuSE DOMAIN file, with the real meat—the features used—staying in the **.mc** file where they belong. The no_default_msa feature is a bit strange; it disables port 587, which all the newer user agents use to submit messages to the mail system. It's unclear why SuSE does this.

Notice the conditional definitions (introduced by the **m4** keyword ifelse) for the location of the statistics file and the queue directory. The file **/etc/SuSE-release** does exist, so the syscmd **m4** directive succeeds and returns 0 in sysval, resulting in the ifelse **m4** construct choosing the first alternative rather than the second. SuSE does not include a man page for **m4** in their distribution, so you may have to go to another machine to really figure out the details of these conditionals.

Debian sendmail configuration

Debian's **sendmail.mc** file is generated by the installation script and by default includes masquerading and not much else. It uses OSTYPE(debian), which pulls in the file **/usr/share/sendmail/sendmail.cf/ostype/debian.m4** shown here:

```
divert(0)
VERSIONID(`@(#)debian.m4      8.9.3-21 (Debian) 20000309')
define(`confCF_VERSION', `Debian 8.9.3-21')

# changes made herein *must* be reflected in parsemc,updatedb,debian.m4

# paths
define(`_USE_ETC_MAIL_',              `True')   # a bit late for some items ;-{
define(`DATABASE_MAP_TYPE',           `hash')   ### default
define(`STATUS_FILE',                 `/var/lib/sendmail/sendmail.st')
define(`confHOST_STATUS_DIRECTORY',`/var/lib/sendmail/host_status')
define(`HELP_FILE',                   `/usr/share/sendmail/sendmail.hf')
```

```
define(`confCR_FILE',                    `-o /etc/mail/relay-domains %[^\#]')
    ### %[^\#] not needed
define(`confCT_FILE',                    `-o /etc/mail/trusted-users %[^\#]')
define(`confCW_FILE',                    `-o /etc/mail/local-host-names %[^\#]')
    ### %[^\#] not needed
define(`confUSERDB_SPEC',                `/etc/mail/users')        ### deprecated
define(`ALIAS_FILE',                     `/etc/mail/aliases')      ### default
define(`confSERVICE_SWITCH_FILE',        `/etc/mail/service.switch')### default
define(`confEBINDIR',                    `/usr/lib/sm.bin')

# flags
define(`confCON_EXPENSIVE', `True')
define(`confDIAL_DELAY', `45')
define(`confMAX_DAEMON_CHILDREN', `30')
define(`confNO_RCPT_ACTION', `add-to-undisclosed')
define(`confQUEUE_SORT_ORDER', `Host')
define(`confSAFE_FILE_ENV')
define(`confSAFE_QUEUE', `True')
define(`confTEMP_FILE_MODE', `600')
define(`confTO_ICONNECT', `30s')

define(`LOCAL_MAILER_PATH', `/usr/lib/sm.bin/sensible-mda')
define(`LOCAL_MAILER_FLAGS', `hnPu90')
define(`LOCAL_MAILER_ARGS', `sensible-mda $g $u $h ${client_addr}')
define(`LOCAL_SHELL_FLAGS', `u90')
define(`PROCMAIL_MAILER_PATH', `/usr/bin/procmail')
define(`USENET_MAILER_PATH', `/usr/bin/inews')
define(`confMAX_MIME_HEADER_LENGTH', `256/128')
define(`confMAX_HEADERS_LENGTH', `32768')

# Debian users have group writable directories/files by default...
define(`confDONT_BLAME_SENDMAIL',
    `ClassFileInUnsafeDirPath,ForwardFileInGroupWritableDirPath,GroupWritab
    leAliasFile,GroupWritableForwardFileSafe,GroupWritableIncludeFileSafe,Incl
    udeFileInGroupWritableDirPath,MapInUnsafeDirPath') ### trashes security
#
DOMAIN(generic)
LOCAL_CONFIG      ### useless, not needed
```

This is way too much stuff to hide away in the OSTYPE file—it's almost as egregious as the 90-odd line SuSE file. In particular, the DOMAIN line should go in the **.mc** file, as should many of the defines that influence **sendmail**'s behavior. Many of the lines in the OSTYPE file would not be necessary if Debian shipped a more current version of **sendmail** and took advantage of **sendmail**'s defaults.

The DONT_BLAME_SENDMAIL line is curious. It totally trashes security and is overkill; most of the entries have nothing to do with home directories. This file also uses # for a comment character, which won't work.

The **.mc** file generated by the installation script follows. Each line is the script's default except that we requested smrsh and always_add_domain.

```
divert(0)
VERSIONID(`@(#)sendmail.mc        8.9.3-21 (Debian) 20000309')
OSTYPE(debian)
LOCAL_CONFIG                      ### doesn't belong in the middle of an mc file
FEATURE(masquerade_envelope)
FEATURE(always_add_domain)
Cwlappie.toadranch.com           ### should be at the end under LOCAL_CONFIG
FEATURE(use_cw_file)
FEATURE(use_ct_file)
FEATURE(nouucp)
FEATURE(smrsh, `/usr/lib/sm.bin/smrsh')
MAILER_DEFINITIONS               ### doesn't belong
MAILER(local)
MAILER(smtp)

LOCAL_CONFIG
MASQUERADE_AS(lappie.toadranch.com)  ### should be above MAILERs
## Custom configurations below (will be preserved)
```

This **.mc** file has a variety of problems, including weird statements that don't seem to belong and statements listed in the wrong order. It's amazing that **m4** is still able to cope and figure it all out.

In general, hiding most of the configuration in the OSTYPE file adds complexity and makes debugging harder as you try to figure out how all the features that you haven't turned on are magically part of your eventual config file. For example, the installation script chose not to include the REDIRECT feature, but it is still listed in the DOMAIN file. Even if you say no to the script during configuration, you will get that feature anyway.

19.10 SPAM-RELATED FEATURES IN SENDMAIL

Spam is the jargon word for junk mail, also known as unsolicited commercial email. It has become a serious problem, primarily because the senders (at least in the United States) do not pay by the byte, but rather pay a flat rate for connectivity. Or if they do pay per byte, they send a single message with many thousands of recipients and relay it through another machine. The other machine pays the big per-byte cost and the spammer pays for only one copy. In many countries, end users pay for bytes received and get pretty angry at having to pay to receive spam.

Spam seems to be primarily a U.S. problem. The U.S. marketing culture has found a gold mine and continues to exploit it.

ISPs in the United States are starting to feel the effects of spam as their support lines have to deal with more and more instances of spam abuse originating from their customers. One ISP in Colorado with about 150 downstream T1 customers (many of them ISPs) needs a half-time person just to deal with spam complaints.

From the marketing folks' point of view, spam works well. Response rates are high, costs are low, and delivery is instantaneous. A list of 30 million email addresses costs about $40.

Many spammers try to appear innocent by suggesting that you answer their email with a message that says "remove" if you want to be removed from their mailing list. Although they may remove you, you have just verified for them that they have a valid, current email address; this fact can land you on other lists. Spammers also like to mess with their mail headers in an attempt to disguise who the mail is from and on which machine it originated.

Folks that sell email addresses to spammers have recently started to use a form of dictionary attack to ferret out unknown addresses. Starting with a list of common last names, the scanning software adds different first initials in hopes of hitting on a valid email address. To check the addresses, the software connects to the mail servers at, say, 50 large ISPs and does a VRFY or RCPT on each of zillions of addresses.

This probing has a huge impact on your mail server and its ability to deliver your customers' legitimate mail. **sendmail** can deal with this situation through the use of the PrivacyOption goaway which is covered starting on page 606. But the smarter spam programs are very robust; if VRFY is blocked, they try EXPN, and if both are blocked they try RCPT. They can try millions of addresses that way and never send a single message—they sure keep your mail server busy, though.

sendmail has an option to foil such behavior, the BAD_RCPT_THROTTLE. If the number of rejected addresses in a message's envelope exceeds the value of this option, **sendmail** starts to sleep for one second after each rejected RCPT command.

sendmail has added some very nice features to help with spam control and also to help with the occasional mail-borne computer virus. Unfortunately, most ISPs must pass along all mail, so these features may be too draconian for customer policy (or then again, maybe they aren't). However, the features can be used to great effect at the end user's site.

There are four types of spam control features:

- Rules that control third-party or promiscuous relaying, which is the use of your mail server by one off-site user to send mail to another off-site user. Spammers often use relaying in an attempt to mask the true source of their mail and therefore avoid detection by their ISPs. It also lets them use *your* cycles and save their own. That's the killer.

- The access database, which allows mail to be filtered by address, rather like a firewall for email.

- Blacklists containing open relays and known spam-friendly sites that **sendmail** can check against.

- Header checking and input mail filtering by means of a generic mail filtering interface called **libmilter**. It allows arbitrary scanning of message headers *and content* and lets you reject messages that match a particular profile.

We describe these new features here and then look at a couple of pieces of spam we received recently to see how we might have tuned our mail system to recognize and reject them automatically.

Relaying

sendmail and other mail transport agents accept incoming mail, look at the envelope addresses, decide where the mail should go, and then pass it along to an appropriate destination. That destination can be local or it can be another transport agent farther along in the delivery chain. When an incoming message has no local recipients, the transport agent that handles it is said to be acting as a relay.

Before **sendmail** version 8.9, promiscuous relaying (also called open relaying) was on by default. **sendmail** would accept any message presented to it on port 25 and try its best to make the delivery. It was the neighborly Internet thing to do.

Unfortunately, spammers started to abuse relaying; they exploited it to disguise their identities and, more importantly, to use your bandwidth and cycles instead of their own. It is now considered very bad to configure your mail server as an open relay. Nevertheless, many, many servers are still configured as open relays (15%–50% in some estimates).

Only hosts that are tagged with RELAY in the access database (see page 592) or that are listed in **/etc/mail/relay-domains** are allowed to submit mail for relaying. The proportion of open relays should fall over the next few years as a result of this change in default behavior, along with increasing public awareness and the help of proactive screening that uses the various black hole lists.

So, promiscuous relaying is bad. At the same time, some types of relaying are useful and legitimate. How can you tell which messages to relay and which to reject? Relaying is actually necessary in only two situations:

- *When the transport agent acts as a gateway for hosts that are not reachable any other way*; for example, hosts that are not always turned on (PPP hosts, Windows PCs) and virtual hosts. In this situation, all the recipients for which you want to relay lie within the same domain.

- *When the transport agent is the outgoing mail server for other, not-so-smart hosts.* In this case, all the senders' hostnames or IP address will be local (or at least enumerable).

Any other situation that appears to require relaying is probably just an indication of bad design (with the possible exception of support for mobile users). You can obviate the first use of relaying (above) by designating a centralized server to receive mail (with POP or IMAP used for client access). The second case should always be allowed, but only for your own hosts. You can check IP addresses or hostnames; hostnames are easier to fake, but **sendmail** verifies that they are not forgeries.

Although **sendmail** comes with relaying turned off by default, several features have been added to turn it back on, either fully or in a limited and controlled way. These features are listed below for completeness, but our recommendation is that you be careful about opening things up too much. Most sites do not need any of the really dangerous features in the second bulleted list below. The access_db feature, covered in the next section, is the safest way to allow limited relaying.

- FEATURE(`relay_entire_domain')   – allows relaying for just your domain
- RELAY_DOMAIN(`*domain*, …')   – adds more domains to be relayed
- RELAY_DOMAIN_FILE(`*filename*')   – same, but takes domain list from a file
- FEATURE(`relay_hosts_only')   – affects RELAY_DOMAIN, accessdb

You will need to make an exception if you use the SMART_HOST or MAIL_HUB designations to route mail through a particular mail server machine. That server will have to be set up to relay mail from local hosts. It should be configured with:

FEATURE(`relay_entire_domain')

Sites that do virtual hosting may also need RELAY_DOMAIN to allow relaying for their virtual names, although

FEATURE(`use_cw_file')

effectively opens relays for those domains or hosts.

There are a few other possibilities, but they are fraught with problems:

- FEATURE('promiscuous_relay')   – allows all relaying; don't use
- FEATURE('relay_based_on_MX')   – relays for anyone that MXes to you
- FEATURE('loose_relay_check')   – allows "percent hack" addressing
- FEATURE('relay_local_from')   – relays based on the From address

The promiscuous_relay feature allows relaying from any site to any other site. Using it is a one-way ticket to the black hole lists. *Do not* use this feature on a machine reachable through the public Internet.

The relay_based_on_MX feature is bad because you do not control what sites are allowed to point their MX records at you. Typically, the only hosts that have an MX record pointing to your mail server are your own, but nothing prevents other sites from changing their MX records to point to you. Spammers do not usually have the ability to change MX records, but shady sites certainly could.

The loose_relay_check feature allows the "% hack" form of addressing (see page 518) that spammers love to use.

The relay_local_from feature trusts the sender address on the envelope of the message and relays messages that appear to be from a local address. Of course, both the envelope and the headers of mail messages are trivial to forge, and spammers are forgery experts.

If you consider turning on relaying in some form, consult the **sendmail** documentation in **cf/README** to be sure you don't inadvertently become a friend of spammers. When you are done, have one of the relay checking sites verify that you did not inadvertently create an open relay—try spam.abuse.net.

There are mismatched configurations in which your host might be convinced to relay weird addresses that misuse the UUCP addressing syntax. Just to be sure, if you have no UUCP connectivity, you can use

```
FEATURE(`nouucp', `reject')
```

to forestall this possibility. Current **sendmail** does not default to supporting any of the ancient networking technologies such as UUCP, BITNET, or DECnet.

Another common relay is the LUSER_RELAY for local users who do not exist. It is defined by default as

```
define(`LUSER_RELAY', `error:No such user')
```

A site with **sendmail** misconfigured sometimes leaks unqualified local user names to the Internet (usually on the Cc line). Someone who replies to the mail will be addressing the response to an apparently local user who does not exist. This relay is often called the "loser relay" and is directed to the error mailer. There is no need to change this configuration unless you want to return a different message or implement some kind of special treatment. Some sites redirect "loser" mail to a person or program that does fuzzy matching in case the sender made a typo or just has the login name slightly wrong.

The access database

sendmail includes support for an access database that you can use to build a mailspecific firewall for your site. It checks mail coming in from the outside world and rejects it if it comes from specific users or domains. You can also use the access database to specify which domains a machine is willing to relay for.

The access database is enabled with the line

```
FEATURE(`access_db', `type filename')
```

If *type* and *filename* are not specified, the database defaults to type hash (if DB databases are used—depends on the DATABASE_MAP_TYPE setting) built from the file **/etc/mail/access**. DBM databases don't use the *type* field. As always, create the database with **makemap**:

```
# makemap hash /etc/mail/access < /etc/mail/access
```

The key field of the access file can contain email addresses, user names, domain names, or network numbers.

For example:

```
cyberspammer.com            550 Spam not accepted
okguy@cyberspammer.com      OK
badguy@aol.com              REJECT
sendmail.org                RELAY
128.32                      RELAY
170.201.180.16              REJECT
hotlivesex@                 550 Spam not accepted
friend@                     550 You are not my friend!
```

The value part must contain one of the items shown in Table 19.14. The value RELAY is the most permissive; it simply accepts the message and forwards it to its final destination. OK accepts the message but will not allow relaying. REJECT will not accept the message at all. SKIP allows you to make exceptions. For example, if you want to relay mail for all hosts except two in a certain domain, you could list the two hosts with the SKIP action and then list the domain with the RELAY action. The order does not matter.

Table 19.14   Things that can appear in the value field of the access database

Value	What it does
OK	Accepts mail and delivers it normally
RELAY	Accepts the mail as addressed and relays it to its destination; enables per-host relaying
SKIP	Allows for exceptions to more general rules
REJECT	Rejects the mail with a generic error message
DISCARD	Silently discards the message
FRIEND	For spam, used by delay-checks feature; if matched, skips other header checks
HATER	For spam, used by delay-checks feature; if matched, applies other header checks
xxx message	Returns an error; *xxx* must be an RFC821 numeric code[a]
ERROR:*xxx message*	Same as above, but clearly marked as an error message
ERROR:*x.x.x message*	*x.x.x* must be an RFC1893-compliant delivery status notification (a generalization of the 550 error code)

a. For example, 550 is the single-error code.

The preceding database file would allow messages from okguy at cyberspammer.com but would reject all other mail from cyberspammer.com with the indicated error message. Mail from either sendmail.org or 128.32.0.0/16 (UC Berkeley's network) would be relayed. Mail from badguy at AOL and from hotlivesex or friend at any domain would also be rejected.

IPv6 addresses in their colon-separated form can be used on the left hand side as well, but they must be prefaced with "IPv6:". The @ after the usernames hotlivesex and friend is required to differentiate them from domain names.

550 is an RFC821 error code. The RFC1893 error codes (or "delivery status notification messages," as they are called) are more extensive. First digit 4 indicates a temporary error; 5 means a permanent error. We've listed a few in Table 19.15.

Table 19.15   RFC1893 delivery status codes

Temporary	Permanent	Meaning
4.2.1	5.2.1	Mailbox is disabled
4.2.2	5.2.2	Mailbox is full
4.2.3	5.2.3	Message is too long
4.2.4	5.2.4	List expansion problem
4.3.1	5.3.1	Mail system is full
4.4.4	5.4.4	Unable to route
4.4.5	5.4.5	Mail congestion
4.7.*	5.7.*	Site policy violation

For even finer control, the key field (left side) can contain the tags Connect, To, From, and in 8.12 and later, Spam to control the way in which the filter is applied. Connect refers to connection information such as client IP address or client hostname. To and From refer to the envelope addresses, not the headers. The Spam tag allows exceptions to global rules through the "spam friend" and "spam hater" tests. It is enabled with the delay_checks feature:

```
FEATURE('delay_checks', 'friend')
FEATURE('delay_checks', 'hater')
```

The first feature skips other rulesets that might reject the message if there is a matching entry in the access_db with FRIEND as the right hand side of the mapping. The second applies the other rulesets if the access_db value is HATER. These four tags provide finer control over relaying and rejection of mail; they can be used to override other restrictions as well. Individual users who complain about your site-wide spam policy can be accommodated with the spam FRIEND or HATER tags.

If one of these tags is used, the lookup is tried first with the tag info and then without, to maintain backward compatibility with older access databases.

Here are some examples:

```
From:spammer@some.domain        REJECT
To:good.domain                  RELAY
Connect:good.domain             OK
Spam:abuse@                     FRIEND
```

Mail from spammer@some.domain would be blocked, but you could still send mail to that address, even if it was blacklisted. Mail will be relayed to good.domain, but not from it (assuming that relaying has been disabled elsewhere). Connections from good.domain would be allowed even if it was in one of the DNS-based rejection lists.

Mail to abuse@localdomain would get through, even from spammer@some.domain whose email would have been rejected by the first access database line.

Many sites use an access database to control spam or policy. Our incoming master mail machine in the computer science department at the University of Colorado rejects mail from over 500 known spammers identified by addresses, domains, or IP networks by using the `access_db` feature.

Blacklisting users or sites

If you have local users or hosts to which you want to block mail, use

```
FEATURE(`blacklist_recipients')
```

which supports the following types of entries in your access file:

```
To:nobody@                    550 Mailbox disabled for this user
To:printer.mydomain.edu       550 This host does not accept mail
To:user@host.mydomain.edu     550 Mailbox disabled for this user
```

These lines block incoming mail to user nobody on any host, to host printer, and to a particular user's address on one machine. The use of the To: tag lets these users send messages, just not receive them; some printers have that capability.

To include the black hole lists from MAPS (the Mail Abuse Prevention System; see mail-abuse.org)—or any other DNS-style blocking list—use the dnsbl feature:

```
FEATURE(`dnsbl')
FEATURE(`enhdnsbl')
```

See Chapter 16 for more information about DNS.

This feature causes **sendmail** to reject mail from any site whose IP address is in the Realtime Blackhole List of known spammers maintained by MAPS. Other lists catalog known dial-up spammers and sites that run open relays. The enhanced version of the dnsbl feature takes up to five parameters and allows different behaviors depending on the return value from the lookup.

These blacklists are distributed through a clever tweak of the DNS system; hence the name dnsbl. For example, a special DNS resource record of the form

```
IP-address.blackholes.mail-abuse.org  IN  A  127.0.0.2
```

put into the DNS database of the blackholes.mail-abuse.org domain would block mail from that host if the dnsbl feature was enabled (because **sendmail** would check explicitly to see if such a record existed). The *IP-address* in this example is a host address in its dotted quad form with the order of the octets reversed.

You can include the dnsbl feature several times to check different lists of abusers: just add a second argument to specify the blacklist name server and a third argument with the error message that you would like returned. If the third argument is omitted, a fixed error message from the DNS database containing the records is returned. Here are examples of three lists: blackholes (the default), the dialups list of dial-up users, and the relays list of open relays.

```
FEATURE(`dnsbl', `blackholes.mail-abuse.org', `Rejected - see www.mail-abuse.org')
FEATURE(`dnsbl', `dialups.mail-abuse.org', `Dialup - see www.mail-abuse.org')
FEATURE(`dnsbl', `relays.mail-abuse.org', `Relay - see www.mail-abuse.org')
```

Access to the MAPS lists used to be free, but the service has become so popular (with large email providers requesting millions of records per day) that it is no longer possible for the MAPS folks to supply the needs of the entire Internet without any financial support. As of August 2001, the service is no longer free. The rates are scaled to the size and nature of an organization. Big commercial users must pay a subscription fee. Universities, little guys, and nonprofit organizations pay less, and individuals can still use the service without charge. See www.maps.org for details.

The intent is not to deny the service to anyone, but just to have the big users help pay for it. The costs are real: bigger servers, more bandwidth, lawyers' bills as spammers sue (and always lose), staff to keep the lists up to date, etc. Now all users must register and officially opt in.

The cost of the extra DNS lookup at the MAPS servers can be expensive if your site handles large amounts of mail. Most large sites run a secondary DNS server for the MAPS zones so that the queries can be resolved by a local server.

Header checking

Spammers often try to hide their identities. Since **sendmail** 8.9, if the envelope From address is not of the form *user@valid.domain*, mail is rejected. This behavior can be waived by the following features:

```
FEATURE(`accept_unresolvable_domains')
FEATURE(`accept_unqualified_senders')
```

The first of these features allows mail from domains that do not exist or do not resolve in the DNS naming tree. The second allows From addresses that contain only a user name with no host or domain portion. Don't use either of these features unless you are behind a firewall and have only local DNS data available there. If you find yourself wanting to turn these features on, you should probably think about redesigning your **sendmail** and DNS environments instead. Requiring a valid envelope sender address reduces spam significantly.

Detailed header checking is a powerful spam-fighting mechanism that makes use of the low-level **sendmail** configuration file syntax, which we do not cover here. By using header checking, **sendmail** can look for specified patterns in headers (e.g., "To: friend@public.com") and reject messages before they are delivered to your users' mailboxes.

Header checking can also be used to recognize viruses carried by email provided that they have a distinctive header line. For example, the Melissa virus of 1999 contained the subject line "Important Message From ...". Within hours of the Melissa virus being released and recognized, sendmail.com posted a local ruleset to identify it and discard it. When the fingerprint of a virus is distinctive and easy to express in

sendmail rules, sendmail.com typically posts a fix for it (at both the sendmail.com and sendmail.org web sites) very quickly.

For a representative sample of filtering rules for spam and viruses, see the **sendmail** configuration for Eric Allman's home machine, knecht. This configuration is included in the **sendmail** distribution as **cf/cf/knecht.mc**. Steal the spam-filtering rules and add them to the end of your **.mc** file.

In looking at various examples, we have seen header checking rules for

- Mail addressed to any user in the domain public.com
- Mail addressed to "friend" or "you"
- Mail with the X-Spanska header, which indicates the Happy99 worm
- Mail with subject "Important Message From …" (the Melissa virus)
- Mail with subject "all.net and Fred Cohen …" (the Papa virus)
- Mail with subject "ILOVEYOU" (the iloveyou virus and variants)
- Zillions of marketing hype spam messages
- Mail with a broken Outlook Express header (the SirCam worm)

All of the header checking rules go under LOCAL_CONFIG and LOCAL_RULESETS statements at the end of the **.mc** configuration file. With the help of **m4**'s divert command, **sendmail** just knows where to put them in the raw config file.

To some degree, any spam abatement that you implement blocks some spammers but raises the bar for the remaining ones. Use the error mailer with a "user unknown" error message instead of the discard mailer, because many spammers clean up their lists. Clean lists are more valuable, so you might get removed from some if you can intercept the spam, filter it, and respond with an error message.

Miltering: mail filtering

sendmail version 8.12 introduced a generalization of header filtering that could develop into a very effective spam-fighting tool. It is a mail filtering API (application programming interface) that folks can use to develop their own mail filtering programs. These filtering programs sit between **sendmail** and incoming messages and can be used to recognize the profile of a virus or spam message and discard or log it (or take whatever other action you feel is appropriate). Both metadata and message content can be targeted.

Miltering is potentially a powerful tool both for fighting spam and for violating users' privacy. Managers who want to know exactly what information is leaving the company by email may be early adopters. Miltering for outgoing mail is not available in 8.12, but it is on the to do list.

The miltering library is called **libmilter**. **sendmail** invokes input filtering with the INPUT_MAIL_FILTER or MAIL_FILTER configuration directives and controls the miltering action with options named MILTER_MACROS_* that allow fine-grained control over the filters applied at each stage of the SMTP conversation.

For example, the line:

```
INPUT_MAIL_FILTER('filtername', 'S=mailer:/var/run/filtername.socket')
```

passes each incoming message to the **/etc/mail/filtername** program through the socket specified in the second argument.

For more information, see **libmilter/README** or the HTML documentation in the **libmilter/docs** directory of the **sendmail** distribution. The **README** file gives an overview and simple example of a filter that logs messages to a file. The files in the **docs** describe the library interface and tell how to use the various calls to build your own mail filtering programs. The attachment filtering done in the sample configuration from sendmail.com's master mail machine (page 576) is also an example of miltering.

Handling spam

Fighting spam can be a difficult and frustrating job. Past a certain point, it's also quite futile. Don't be seduced into chasing down individual spammers, even though lots will get through your anti-spam shields. Time spent analyzing spam headers and fretting about spammers is wasted time. Yes, it's fighting the good fight, but time spent on these issues will probably not reduce the amount of spam coming into your site.

You can nail stationary spammers pretty quickly by ratting them out to their ISP, but hit-and-run spammers that use an ISP account once and then abandon it are hard to hold accountable. If they advertise a web site, then the web site is responsible; if it's a telephone number or postal address, it's harder to identify the perpetrator, but not impossible. Mobile spammers seem to be essentially immune from punishment.

The various black hole lists have been somewhat effective at blocking spam and have reduced the number of open relays dramatically. Being blacklisted can seriously impact business, so some ISPs and companies are careful to police their users. Our main recommendation regarding spam is that you use the preventive measures and publicly maintained blacklists that are available.

Advise your users to simply delete the spam they receive. Many spam messages contain instructions on how recipients can be removed from the mailing list. If you follow those instructions, the spammers may remove you from the current list, but they immediately add you to several other lists with the annotation "reaches a real human who reads the message." Your email address is then worth even more.

If you'd like to take a seat on the spam-fighting bandwagon, some web sites can help. Two awesome sites are mail-abuse.org and www.abuse.net. The spamrecycle.com site asks that you email them your spam; they forward it to your state representative, who might choose to do something politically at the state level. This site also has a nice set of guidelines for protecting yourself against spam. The site analyzes the spam and uses it to help improve anti-spam filters.

Two other web sites of note are spamcop.net, and cauce.org. SpamCop has tools that help parse mail headers and determine the real sender. The cauce.org site has good information on spam laws. The web site www.orbs.org, which formerly maintained open relay databases, went off the net in June 2001 and should no longer be used.

Spam examples

Though we don't recommend analyzing spam as a matter of course, it is sometimes useful to know how to do it. For example, you may be called upon to explain why the CEO of your company received a solicitation for pornography (and to verify that it did not come from a company employee!).

In the next few pages we analyze the headers from some recent spam. These examples illustrate how hard it is to determine the actual sender and how easy it is to fake mail headers. First, some key points:

- Received headers should chain together from the top of a message to the bottom of the message.

- Any Received headers below the Date header are probably fake.

- Take note of any Received headers in which the two hostnames don't match. The mail is probably being relayed through the first host (the parenthesized host is the real origin).

- A Received header with an old date or a future date is probably forged.

- The host part of the From header should agree with the last Received header unless the message was sent to a mailing list.

- The Message-Id header's domain should match the From header's domain unless masquerading at the sender's site changes things.

- Check to see whether the Received headers show that the message was relayed through an unrelated host. Sometimes this is OK; for example, a company relaying for an employee's home machine, or vice versa.

- Check all listed hosts to be sure they exist in DNS. Use an MX lookup, not an A record lookup, because local firewalls or split DNS may make the A lookup fail.

Our first example is a message selling a CD of 10,000,000 email addresses for future spammers. The spam CD was interesting—it guaranteed no duplicate addresses and no "poison" addresses (presumably, addresses that automatically submit the sender to one of the black hole lists).

We numbered the lines of the header to facilitate the commentary; the numbers are not really there.

```
1: From mrktnet77@kayak.msk.ru Thu Nov  4 22:10:48 1999
2: Received: from gaia.es ([195.55.166.66]) by xor.com (8.9.3/8.9.3) with ESMTP
      id WAA26343 for <evi@xor.com>; Thu, 4 Nov 1999 22:10:42 -0700 (MST)
3: From: mrktnet77@kayak.msk.ru
4: Received: from default by gaia.es (8.8.8+Sun/SMI-SVR4) id GAA03907; Fri, 5
      Nov 1999 06:31:10 -0100 (Etc/GMT)
```

```
5: Date: Fri, 5 Nov 1999 06:31:10 -0100 (Etc/GMT)
6: Received: from login_011556.wgukas.com (mail.wgukas.com  [233.214.241.87])
      by  (8.8.5/8.7.3) with SMTP id XAA01510 for fraklin321@thaxghklo.um.de;
      Thu, 4 November 1999 00:21:59 -0700 (EDT)
7: To: mrktnet77@kayak.msk.ru
8: Subject: Just Released!  Millions CD Vol. 6A
9: Comments: Authenticated Sender is <user11556@wgukas.com>
10:Message-Id: 02202108722648597456@sa_ghklo.um.de

/* Several pages of marketeering removed here */
************************************************************
Do not reply to this message -
To be removed from future mailings:
mailto:greg1148@usa.net?Subject=Remove
************************************************************
```

Line 1 was added by **/bin/mail** during local delivery. The domain msk.ru exists, but host kayak.msk.ru does not; this could be legitimate if split DNS was in use at that site. Line 2 is a valid Received line—it's the only Received line whose accuracy is guaranteed, because it was added by our own host (in this case, xor.com). Line 3 is a From header added by **sendmail** along the way because the message did not originally have one.

Line 4 is a valid Received line from an unsuspecting scapegoat host (gaia.es) running sendmail 8.8, under which relaying is allowed by default (and which Sun shipped that way). The "from default" in Line 4 is a clue that the next Received line is a forgery.

Line 6 is a fake Received line. It's below the Date line and was either missing or already in place when **sendmail** received the message. In addition, the format is wrong, which is often a very good indication of tampering. The IP address 233.214.241.87 has no reverse DNS entry. In bygone days of the research and academic Internet, this too would have been a clue that something was wrong. Today, many hosts do not have reverse DNS entries.

Line 7, the To line, is bogus. The recipients' addresses were on the envelope only.

Line 9 purports to identify the authenticated sender, which is sometimes a clue to a message's provenance. This one implies that the sender is from wgukas.com, but that domain does not exist. This line was actually added by a PC mail user agent and so it could well be forged.

Line 10 implies that the sending machine was actually sa_ghklo.um.de, but it has the wrong format (missing angle brackets, < >) and so is probably forged.

It's impossible to tell where this message came from. It was relayed through gaia.es, probably without permission. gaia.es is not yet in the MAPS black hole list but may end up there soon. greg1148 could be the spammer himself, or he could be a user who complained about previous spam. In the latter case, greg1148 assumes the victim role in this message and may receive hundreds or thousands of angry messages from folks asking to be removed from the list.

The body of the message required you to call or fax your order to an 800 number. It is typical to have all the information needed to respond to the spammer and buy his product in the actual body of the message. Note that the address on the From line is the same as the address on the To line; both are probably forged.

Another piece of spam from this same day offered to make us rich if we faxed them a check for $40 by November 15, after which the price went up to $195. Are faxed copies of a check legal tender? Or are the senders just interested in obtaining a bank account routing number and a signature so they can print their own checks? Protect your identity.

```
1: From jimdelno@apexmail.com Thu Nov 11 10:31:41 1999
2: Received: from saturn.globalcon.com (saturn.globalcon.com [209.5.99.8]) by
      xor.com (8.9.3/8.9.3) with ESMTP id KAA15479; Thu, 11 Nov 1999
      10:31:30 -0700 (MST)
3: Received: from hamilton ([168.191.61.20]) by saturn.globalcon.com
      (Post.Office MTA v3.1.2 release (PO205-101c) ID# 0-35881U1500L100S0)
      with SMTP id AAA148; Thu, 11 Nov 1999 12:33:24 -0500
4: Date: Thu, 11 Nov 1999 02:39:57 +0000
5: Subject: Free Information On "Debt Reduction!"
6: Message-Id: <yjsul.lnmqgaasnjymgqaac@hamilton>
7: From: F.Pepper@pmail.net
8: To: benfranklin@onehundred.net
```

Line 2 is a valid Received header. Line 3 is also valid, but **traceroute**s from xor.com, the destination, to hamilton (168.191.61.20) and saturn.globalcon.com (209.5.99.8) show that those two sites have nothing to do with each other. 168.191.61.20 is on Sprint's dial-up network, and judging from the time zone indication (which unfortunately is trivially forgeable), it might be in Europe. 209.5.99.8 is a company in Ontario, Canada. saturn.globalcon.com is probably an open relay. They are not running **sendmail**, but rather version 3.1.2 of the Post.Office mail transport agent from Openwave.com (formerly software.com).

On line 4, the date added by the sender's user agent is about 2:00 a.m. in Europe, 2 hours before it was received on the machine saturn.globalcon.com. Perhaps the recipient list was very long and took 2 hours to process. Or perhaps the message was composed off-line on the spammer's PC and then submitted to the Internet at a later time. The time zone indication (if it isn't forged) is 5 hours different—the same as the difference between Europe and the East Coast of the United States.

On line 6, the host portion of the Message-Id should be a fully qualified domain name, not just the local part "hamilton". This is probably the spammer's machine and it is probably not named hamilton. The portion of the Message-Id to the left of the @ sign typically consists of numbers, but letters are also allowed, so it may be OK.

Line 8 is clearly forged. The actual recipients' addresses were only on the envelope of the message and do not appear anywhere in the headers.

This message might actually be from F.Pepper@pmail.net. The hostname pmail.net resolves to a valid IP address, and **whois** says pmail.net is a British telecom company.

Among the 20 or so spam messages we examined for this section, this one alone might have contained enough information to make up a reasonable complaint (to the hostmaster indicated in DNS for the IP address in line 3 of the header). Never complain directly to the spammer or the spammer's domain.

SpamCop is a software package that parses mail headers and identifies which lines are real, which are probably forged, and which are totally bogus. It provides users who submit spam messages through email or the web (spamcop.net) with a blow-by-blow description of the headers and tells which pieces check out and which don't. This site also makes it easy to submit a spam complaint. The complaint includes all the relevant information that you gleaned from parsing your headers. SpamCop was written by Julian Haight.

We ran SpamCop on our first spam example above, which tried to sell us a CD full of address lists. It determined that the gaia.es Received line was OK, but that the domain wgukas.com was fake. It then determined that gaia.es did not have the IP address the mail said it did and that the real culprit was probably at a site called ttd.net. Clearly, SpamCop's analysis was much better than ours, and it took only a few seconds.

Here's a small snippet of a SpamCop analysis for some fresher spam:

```
Received: from sun1.cskwam.mil.pl (cskwam.mil.pl) [148.81.119.2] by
    mail1.es.net with smtp (Exim 1.81 #2) id 12oBHL-000494-00; Sat, 6 May
    2000 13:34:23 -0700
Possible spammer: 148.81.119.2
"nslookup cskwam.mil.pl" (checking ip) [show] ip not found; cskwam.mil.pl
    discarded as fake.
"dig cskwam.mil.pl mx" (digging for Mail eXchanger) [show] "nslookup
    cskwam.mil.pl" (checking ip) [show] cskwam.mil.pl not 148.81.119.2,
    discarded as fake.
"nslookup sun1.cskwam.mil.pl" (checking ip) [show] ip = 148.81.119.2
Taking name from IP...
"nslookup 148.81.119.2" (getting name) [show] 148.81.119.2 =
    sun1.cskwam.mil.pl
"nslookup sun1.cskwam.mil.pl" (checking ip) [show] ip = 148.81.119.2
"nslookup 2.119.81.148.rbl.maps.vix.com." (checking ip) [show] not found
"nslookup 2.119.81.148.relays.orbs.org." (checking ip) [show] ip = 127.0.0.2
blocked by ORBS
Chain test:mail1.es.net =? mail1.es.net
Chain verified mail1.es.net = mail1.es.net
148.81.119.2 has already been sent to ORBS
Received line accepted
```

Each of the [show] words are links on SpamCop's web page. They show you the actual command that was executed and its output.

SpamAssassin

SpamAssassin is a **procmail** filter that is very effective at identifying spam. It uses a point system for evaluating a message's sins, rarely has false positives, and catches all the real spam. If a message gets too many points (configurable), SpamAssassin refiles it in a spam folder that you can check as you are setting it up and tuning the parameters. Check it out at spamassassin.taint.org.

19.11 SECURITY AND SENDMAIL

With the explosive growth of the Internet, programs such as **sendmail** that accept arbitrary user-supplied input and deliver it to local users, files, or shells have frequently provided an avenue of attack for hackers. **sendmail**, along with DNS and even IP, is flirting with authentication and encryption as a built-in solution to some of these fundamental security issues.

Recent softening of the export laws of the United States regarding encryption has allowed **sendmail** to be shipped with built-in hooks for encryption. Versions 8.11 and later support both SMTP authentication and encryption with TLS, Transport Layer Security (previously known as SSL, the Secure Socket Layer). **sendmail** uses the term TLS in this context and has implemented it as an extension, STARTTLS, to the SMTP protocol. TLS brought with it six new configuration options for certificate files and key files. New actions for access database matches can require that authentication must have succeeded.

In this section, we describe the evolution of **sendmail**'s permissions model, ownerships, and privacy protection. We then briefly discuss TLS and SASL (the Simple Authentication and Security Layer) and their use with **sendmail**.

sendmail has gradually tightened up its security over time, and it is now very picky about file permissions before it believes the contents of, say, a **.forward** or **aliases** file. Although this tightening of security has generally been welcome, it's sometimes necessary to relax the tough new policies. To this end, **sendmail** has introduced the DontBlameSendmail option, so named in hopes that the name will suggest to sysadmins that what they are doing is considered unsafe.

This option has many possible values—55 at last count. The default is safe. For a complete list of values, see **doc/op/op.ps** in the **sendmail** distribution. The values are not listed in the second edition of the O'Reilly **sendmail** book, but will surely be in the third. Or just leave the option set to safe.

Ownerships

Three user accounts are important in the **sendmail** universe: the DefaultUser, the TrustedUser, and the RunAsUser.

By default, all of **sendmail**'s mailers run as the DefaultUser unless the mailer's flags specify otherwise. If a user mailnull, sendmail, or daemon exists in the **/etc/passwd** file, DefaultUser will be that. Otherwise, it defaults to UID 1 and GID 1. We recommend the use of the mailnull account and a mailnull group. Add it to **/etc/passwd** with a star as the password, no valid shell, no home directory, and a default group of mailnull. You'll have to add the mailnull entry to the **/etc/group** file too. The mailnull account should not own any files. If **sendmail** is not running as root, the mailers will have to be setuid.

If RunAsUser is set, **sendmail** ignores the value of DefaultUser and does everything as RunAsUser. If you are running **sendmail** setgid (to smmsp), then the submission **sendmail** just passes messages to the real **sendmail** through SMTP. The real **sendmail** does not have its setuid bit set, but it runs as root from the startup files.

sendmail's TrustedUser can own maps and alias files. The TrustedUser is allowed to start the daemon or rebuild the **aliases** file. This facility exists mostly to support GUI interfaces to **sendmail** that need to provide limited administrative control to certain users. If you set TrustedUser, be sure to guard the account that it points to because this account can easily be exploited to gain root access. The TrustedUser is different from the TRUSTED_USERS class, which determines who can rewrite the From line of messages.[32]

The RunAsUser is the UID that **sendmail** runs under after opening its socket connection to port 25. Ports numbered less than 1,024 can only be opened by the superuser; therefore, **sendmail** must initially run as root. However, after performing this operation, **sendmail** can switch to a different UID. Such a switch reduces the risk of damage or access if **sendmail** is tricked into doing something bad. Don't use the RunAsUser feature on machines that support user accounts or other services; it is meant for use on firewalls or bastion hosts only.

By default, **sendmail** does not switch identities and continues to run as root. If you change the RunAsUser to something other than root, you must change several other things as well. The RunAsUser must own the mail queue, be able to read all maps and include files, be able to run programs, etc. Expect to spend a few hours finding all the file and directory ownerships that must be changed.

Permissions

File and directory permissions are important to **sendmail** security. Use the settings listed in Table 19.16 to be safe.

Table 19.16   Owner and permissions for sendmail-related directories

Path	Owner	Mode	What it contains
/var/spool/clientmqueue	smmsp	770	Mail queue for initial submissions[a]
/var/spool/mqueue	RunAsUser	700	Mail queue directory
/, /var, /var/spool	root	755	Path to **mqueue**
/etc/mail/*	TrustedUser	644	Maps, the config file, aliases
/etc/mail	TrustedUser	755	Parent directory for maps
/etc	root	755	Path to **mail** directory

a. Version 8.12 and later

---

32. The TRUSTED_USERS feature is typically used to support mailing list software. For example, if you use Majordomo, you must add the "majordom" user to the TRUSTED_USERS class. The users root and daemon are the default members of the class.

sendmail will not read files that have lax permissions (for example, files that are group- or world-writable or that live in group- or world-writable directories). Some of **sendmail**'s rigor with regard to ownerships and permissions was motivated by operating systems that allow users to give their files away with **chown** (those derived from System V, mostly).

Linux systems by default have a sane version of **chown** and do not allow file give-aways. However, an #ifdef in the code (CAP_CHOWN) can be set to give System V semantics to **chown**. You would then have to rebuild the kernel. But this behavior is evil; don't coerce your sensible Linux **chown** to behave in the broken System V way.

In particular, **sendmail** is *very* picky about the complete path to any alias file or forward file. This pickiness sometimes clashes with the way sites like to manage Majordomo mailing list aliases. If the Majordomo list is in **/usr/local**, for example, the entire path must be trusted; no component can have group write permission. This constraint makes it more difficult for the list owner to manage the alias file. To see where you stand with respect to **sendmail**'s ideas about permissions, run

```
# sendmail -v -bi
```

The **-bi** flag initializes the alias database and warns you of inappropriate permissions.

sendmail will no longer read a **.forward** file that has a link count greater than 1 if the directory path to it is unsafe (has lax permissions). This rule bit Evi recently when her **.forward** file, which was typically a hard link to either **.forward.to.boulder** or **.forward.to.sandiego**, silently failed to forward her mail from a small site at which she did not receive much mail. It was months before she realized and understood that "I never got your mail" was her fault and not a valid excuse anymore.

You can turn off many of the restrictive file access policies mentioned above with the DontBlameSendmail option. But don't do that.

Safer mail to files and programs

We recommend that you use **smrsh** instead of **/bin/sh** as your program mailer and that you use **mail.local** instead of **/bin/mail** as your local mailer. Both programs are included in the **sendmail** distribution. To incorporate them into your configuration, add the lines

```
FEATURE(`smrsh', `path-to-smrsh')
FEATURE(`local_lmtp', `path-to-mail.local')
```

to your **.mc** file. If you omit the explicit paths, the commands are assumed to live in **/usr/libexec**. You can use **sendmail**'s confEBINDIR option to change the default location of the binaries to whatever you want. Red Hat provides **/usr/sbin/smrsh** but no **mail.local**. SuSE provides both in **/usr/lib/sendmail.d/bin**, and Debian stashes them in **/usr/lib/sm.bin**.

smrsh is a restricted shell that will only execute the programs contained in one directory (**/usr/adm/sm.bin** by default). **smrsh** ignores user-specified paths and tries to find any requested commands in its own known-safe directory. **smrsh** also blocks the use of certain shell metacharacters such as "<", the input redirection symbol. Symbolic links are allowed in **sm.bin**, so you don't need to make duplicate copies of the programs you allow.[33]

 SuSE builds **smrsh** to use the directory **/usr/lib/sendmail.d/bin**.

 Debian's **smrsh** is compiled to use **/usr/lib/sm.bin** directory, which contains the programs **deliver**, **procmail**, and **vacation** (all symbolic links). The **deliver** link is broken and **procmail** should not be there. Sigh.

Here are some example shell commands and their possible **smrsh** interpretations:

```
vacation eric                 # executes /usr/adm/sm.bin/vacation eric
cat /etc/passwd               # rejected, cat not in sm.bin
vacation eric < /etc/passwd   # rejected, no < allowed
```

sendmail's SafeFileEnvironment option controls where files can be written when email is redirected to a file by an **aliases** or **.forward** file. It causes **sendmail** to execute a **chroot** system call, making the root of the filesystem no longer **/** but rather **/safe**, or whatever path you specified in the SafeFileEnvironment option. An alias that directed mail into the **/etc/passwd** file, for example, would really be written to **/safe/etc/passwd**.

The SafeFileEnvironment option also protects device files, directories, and other special files by allowing writes only to regular files. Besides increasing security, this option helps to ameliorate the effects of user mistakes. Some sites set the option to **/home** to allow access to home directories while keeping system files off-limits.

Mailers can also be run in a **chroot**ed directory. This option must be specified in the mailer definition at the moment, but it should soon be configurable with **m4**.

Privacy options

sendmail also has privacy options that control

- What external folks can determine about your site from SMTP
- What you require of the host on the other end of an SMTP connection
- Whether your users can see or run the mail queue

Table 19.17 lists the possible values for the privacy options as of this writing; see the file **doc/op/op.ps** in the distribution for current information.

We recommend conservatism; use

```
define(`confPRIVACY_OPTIONS', ``goaway, authwarnings, restrictmailq,
    restrictqrun'')
```

in your **.mc** file. **sendmail**'s default value for the privacy options is authwarnings; the line above would reset that value. Notice the double sets of quotes; some versions of **m4** require them to protect the commas in the list of privacy option values. Red

---

33. Don't put programs such as **procmail** that can spawn a shell in **sm.bin**. And don't use **procmail** as the local mailer because users can run any program they want from their ~/**.procmailrc** file. It's not secure.

Table 19.17   Values of the PrivacyOption variable

Value	Meaning
public	Does no privacy/security checking
needmailhelo	Requires SMTP HELO (identifies remote host)
noexpn	Does not allow the SMTP EXPN command
novrfy	Does not allow the SMTP VRFY command
needexpnhelo	Does not expand addresses (EXPN) without a HELO
needvrfyhelo	Does not verify addresses (VRFY) without a HELO
noverb[a]	Does not allow verbose mode for EXPN
restrictmailq	Allows only **mqueue** directory's group to see the queue
restrictqrun	Allows only **mqueue** directory's owner to run the queue
restrictexpand	Restricts info displayed by the **-bv** and **-v** flags[b]
noetrn[c]	Does not allow asynchronous queue runs
authwarnings	Adds Authentication-Warning header (this is the default)
noreceipts	Turns off delivery status notification for success return receipts
nobodyreturn	Does not return message body in a DSN
goaway	Disables all SMTP status queries (EXPN, VRFY, etc.)

a. Verbose mode follows **.forward** files when an EXPN command is given and provides more information on the whereabouts of a user's mail. Use noverb or, better yet, noexpn on any machine exposed to the outside world.

b. Unless executed by root or the TrustedUser.

c. ETRN is an ESMTP command designed for use by dial-up hosts. It requests that the queue be run just for messages to that host.

Hat defaults to authwarnings and SuSE to authwarnings, needmailhelo, novrfy, noexpn, and noverb.

Running a chrooted sendmail (for the truly paranoid)

If you are worried about the access that **sendmail** has to your filesystem, you can start it in a **chroot**ed jail. Make a minimal filesystem in your jail, including things like **/dev/null**, **/etc** essentials (**passwd**, **group**, **resolv.conf**, **sendmail.cf**, any map files, **mail/***), the shared libraries that **sendmail** needs, the **sendmail** binary, the mail queue directory, and any log files. You will probably have to fiddle with the list to get it just right. Use the **chroot** command to start a jailed **sendmail**. For example:

```
# chroot /jail /usr/sbin/sendmail -bd -q30m
```

Denial of service attacks

Denial of service attacks are difficult to prevent because there is no a priori way to determine that a message is an attack rather than a valid piece of email. Attackers can try various nasty things, including flooding the SMTP port with bogus connections, filling disk partitions with giant messages, clogging outgoing connections, and mail bombing. **sendmail** has some configuration parameters that can help slow down or limit the impact of a denial of service attack, but these parameters can also interfere with legitimate mail. The new (with version 8.12) mail filtering library may help sys-admins thwart a prolonged denial of service attack.

The `MaxDaemonChildren` option limits the number of **sendmail** processes. It prevents the system from being overwhelmed with **sendmail** work, but it also allows an attacker to easily shut down SMTP service. The `MaxMessageSize` option can help prevent the mail queue directory from filling, but if you set it too low, legitimate mail will bounce. (You might mention your limit to users so that they aren't surprised when their mail bounces. We recommend a fairly high limit anyway, since some legitimate mail is huge.) The `ConnectionRateThrottle` option, which limits the number of permitted connections per second, can slow things down a bit. And finally, setting `MaxRcptsPerMessage`, which controls the maximum number of recipients allowed on a single message, might help.

sendmail has always been able to refuse connections (option `REFUSE_LA`) or queue email (`QUEUE_LA`) according to the system load average. A variation that was introduced in 8.12, `DELAY_LA`, allows the mail to continue flowing, but at a reduced rate. See page 613 in the performance section for details.

In spite of all these knobs to turn to protect your mail system, someone mail bombing you will still interfere with legitimate mail. Mail bombing can be quite nasty.

The University of Colorado provides an email account for each student (25,000), with **pine** as the default mail reader. A few years ago, a student with a new job at a local computer store was convinced to give a copy of the password file to his employer. The company then sent an advertisement to everyone in the password file, in batches of about 1,000 recipients at a time (which made for a very long To line).

pine had been compiled with the default reply mode set to reply to all recipients as well as the sender. Many students replied with questions such as, "Why did you send me this junk?", and of course it went to everyone else on the To line. The result was total denial of service on the server—for email or any other use. **sendmail** took over all the CPU cycles, the mail queue was enormous, and all useful work ground to a halt. The only solution seemed to be to take the machine off-line, go into the mail queues and every user's mailbox, and remove the offending messages. (A header check on the Subject line could have been used as well.)

Forgeries

Forging email has in the past been trivial. **sendmail** 8.10 and later includes SMTP authentication that verifies the identity of the sending machine. Before 8.10, any user could forge mail to appear as though it came from your domain. Authentication checking must be turned on with the `AuthMechanisms` option. Unfortunately, **sendmail** authentication is not end-to-end but just between adjacent servers. If a message is handled by several servers, the authentication helps but cannot guarantee that the message was not forged.

Likewise, it is possible to impersonate any user in mail messages. Be careful if mail messages are your organization's authorization vehicle for things like keys, access cards, and money. You should warn administrative users of this fact and suggest that if they see suspicious mail that appears to come from a person in authority, they should verify the validity of the message. This is doubly true if the message asks that unreasonable privileges be given to an unusual person. Mail authorizing a grand master key for an undergraduate student might be suspect!

The authwarnings privacy option flags local attempts at forgery by adding an Authentication-Warning header to outgoing mail that appears to be forged. However, many user agents hide this header by default.

If forged mail is coming from a machine that you control, you can actually do quite a bit to thwart it. You can use the **identd** daemon to verify a sender's real login name. **sendmail** does a callback to the sending host to ask the **identd** running there for the login name of the user sending the mail. If **identd** is not running on the remote host, **sendmail** learns nothing. If the remote machine is a single-user workstation, its owner could configure **identd** to return a bogus answer. But if the remote host is a multiuser machine such as that found at many university computing centers, **identd** returns the user's real login name for **sendmail** to put in the message's header.

Many sites do not run **identd**; it's often blocked by firewalls. **identd** is only really useful within a site, since machines you don't control can lie. At a large site with somewhat irresponsible users (e.g., a university), it's great—but also a performance hit for **sendmail**.

Several years ago, when we were first experimenting with **identd**, a student at our site became frustrated with the members of his senior project team. He tried to send mail to his teammates as his instructor, telling them he knew that they were not pulling their weight and that they should work harder. Unfortunately, he made a syntax error and the message bounced to the instructor. **sendmail**'s use of the IDENT protocol told us who he was. **sendmail** included the following lines in the bounced message:

The original message was received at Wed, 9 Mar 1994 14:51 -0700 from
    student@benji.Colorado.EDU [128.138.126.10]

But the headers of the message itself told a different story:

From: *instructor*@cs.Colorado.EDU

Moral: avoid syntax errors when sneaking around. Our policy on forging mail caused the student's login to be disabled for the rest of the semester, which actually accomplished exactly what the student wanted. He was unable to work on the project and his partners had to pick up the slack.

Message privacy

See page 672 for more information about PGP.

Message privacy basically does not exist unless you use an external encryption package such as Pretty Good Privacy (PGP) or S/MIME. By default, all mail is sent unencrypted. End-to-end encryption requires support from mail user agents.

Both S/MIME and PGP are documented in the RFC series, with S/MIME being on the standards track. However, we prefer PGP; it's more widely available and was designed by an excellent cryptographer, Phil Zimmermann, whom we trust. These emerging standards offer a basis for email confidentiality, authentication, message integrity assurance, and nonrepudiation of origin. Traffic analysis is still possible since the headers and envelope are sent as plaintext.

Tell your users that they must do their own encryption if they want their mail to be private.

SASL: the Simple Authentication and Security Layer

sendmail 8.10 and later support the SMTP authentication defined in RFC2554. It's based on SASL, the Simple Authentication and Security Layer (RFC2222). SASL is a shared secret system that is typically host-to-host; you must make explicit arrangements for each pair of servers that are to mutually authenticate.

SASL is a generic authentication mechanism that can be integrated into a variety of protocols. So far, **sendmail**, Cyrus's **imapd**, Netscape, Outlook, Mulberry, and some versions of Eudora use it. The SASL framework (it's a library) has two fundamental concepts: an authorization identifier and an authentication identifier. It can map these to permissions on files, account passwords, Kerberos tickets, etc. SASL contains both an authentication part and an encryption part, but because of U.S. export laws, **sendmail** used only the authentication part in version 8.10. Because U.S. export regulations were relaxed in early 2000, the encryption portion that was originally slated to be in the commercial **sendmail** product has become available to everyone in versions 8.11 and later.

To use SASL with **sendmail**, get Cyrus SASL from

> ftp://ftp.andrew.cmu.edu/pub/cyrus-mail

TLS, another encryption/authentication system is specified in RFC2487. It is implemented in **sendmail** as an extension to SMTP called STARTTLS. You can even use both SASL and TLS.

TLS is a bit harder to set up and requires a certificate authority. You can pay VeriSign big bucks to issue you certificates (signed public keys identifying an entity) or set up your own certificate authority. Strong authentication is used in place of a hostname or IP address as the authorization token for relaying mail or for accepting a connection from a host in the first place. An entry such as

```
TLS_Srv:secure.example.com      ENCR:112
TLS_Clt:laptop.example.com      PERM+VERIFY:112
```

in the access_db indicates that STARTTLS is in use and that email to the domain secure.example.com must be encrypted with at least 112-bit encryption keys. Email from a host in the laptop.example.com domain should be accepted only if the client has authenticated itself.

Claus Assmann of Sendmail, Inc., has produced some great web pages describing how to set up SASL and TLS for use with **sendmail**:

www.sendmail.org/~ca/email/auth.html   (SASL)
www.sendmail.org/~ca/email/starttls.html   (TLS)

These instructions are particularly useful for SASL, since the package's own instructions are rather cryptic.

Gregory Shapiro, also of Sendmail, Inc., has created some nifty tutorials about security and **sendmail**, available from www.sendmail.org/~gshapiro.

19.12 SENDMAIL PERFORMANCE

sendmail has several configuration options that are designed to improve performance. Although we have scattered them throughout the chapter, we try to expand on the most important ones in this section. These are options and features you should consider if you run a high-volume mail system (in either direction). Actually, if you really need to send 1,000,000 mail messages an hour and you aren't a spammer, your best bet might be to use the commercial side of **sendmail**, Sendmail, Inc.

Delivery modes

sendmail has four basic delivery modes: background, interactive, queue, and defer. Each represents a tradeoff between latency and throughput. Background mode delivers the mail immediately but requires **sendmail** to fork a new process to do it. Interactive mode also delivers immediately, but delivery is done by the same process and makes the remote side wait for the results. Queue mode queues incoming mail for delivery by a queue runner at some later time. Defer mode is similar to queue mode, but it also defers all map, DNS, alias, and forwarding lookups. Interactive mode is rarely used. Background mode favors lower latency, and defer or queueing mode favors higher throughput. The delivery mode is set with the option confDELIVERY_MODE and defaults to background.

Queue groups and envelope splitting

Queue groups are a new feature of **sendmail** 8.12 that enable you to create multiple queues for outgoing mail and to control the attributes of each queue group individually. Queue groups can contain a single queue directory or several directories. For example, if your Linux box is the mail hub for an ISP, you might define a queue group for your dial-up users and then give dial-up users permission to initiate a queue run (using the SMTP command ETRN) when they connect to download their email. Queue groups are used with an envelope-splitting feature that allows an envelope with many recipients to be split across queue groups. This feature and the use of multiple queue directories per queue group help to ameliorate performance problems caused by having too many files in a single filesystem directory.

When a message enters the mail system, it is assigned to one or more queue groups. The queue group for each recipient is determined independently. Envelopes are rewritten to correspond to queue group assignments. If multiple queue directories are used, messages are assigned randomly to the queues in the correct queue group.

If a queue group has a limit on the maximum number of recipients per envelope, **sendmail** splits the envelope of the message into several smaller envelopes that fit within the queue group's parameters.

Queue groups are declared with directives in the **.mc** file but are really configured in the raw config file language by LOCAL_RULESETS, which we don't describe at all in this book. The example below will get you started if you want to use queue groups to improve performance or to give different quality of service to different destinations.

Table 19.18 lists the attributes that can be specified for a queue group. Only the first letter of the attribute name need be specified when the queue group is defined.

Table 19.18   Queue group attributes

Attribute	Meaning
Flags	Mostly for future knobs; must set **f** flag to have multiple queue runners
Nice	Priority for this queue group; lowers priority a la the **nice** system call
Interval	Time to wait between queue runs
Path	Path to the queue directory associated with the queue group (required)
Runners	Number of **sendmail** processes to run concurrently on the queue group
recipients	Maximum number of recipients per envelope

Here is an example that has queue groups for local mail, for mail to aol.com, for mail to other remote sites, and a default queue for all the rest of the mail. The following lines go in the regular part of the **.mc** file:

```
dnl ##### -- queues
QUEUE_GROUP(`local', `P=/var/spool/mqueue/local')
QUEUE_GROUP(`aol', `P=/var/spool/mqueue/aol, F=f, r=100')
QUEUE_GROUP(`remote', `P=/var/spool/mqueue/remote, F=f')
```

And then at the end of the **.mc** file:

```
LOCAL_RULESETS
Squeuegroup
R<$+>                     $1
R$*@aol.com               $# aol
R$*@mydomain.com          $# local
R$*@$*                    $# remote
R$*                       $# mqueue
```

In this example, we specified a limit of 100 recipients per message when we defined the AOL queue group. If an outgoing message had 10,000 recipients, of whom 1,234 were at AOL, envelope splitting would put 13 messages in the aol queue group, 12 of 100 recipients each and 1 with the remaining 34 recipients.

To speed things up even more, try fast splitting, which defers MX lookups during the sorting process:

```
define('confFAST_SPLIT', '1')
```

Queue runners

sendmail forks copies of itself to perform the actual transport of mail. You can control how many copies of **sendmail** are running at any given time and even how many are attached to each queue group. This feature allows sysadmins to strike a balance between **sendmail** and the operating system on their busy mail hub machines.

Three **sendmail** options control the number of queue runner daemons processing each queue:

- The MAX_DAEMON_CHILDREN option specifies the total number of copies of the **sendmail** daemon that are allowed to run at any one time, including those running queues and those accepting incoming mail.

- The MAX_QUEUE_CHILDREN option sets the maximum number of queue runners allowed at one time.

- The MAX_RUNNERS_PER_QUEUE option sets the default runner limit per queue if no explicit value is set with the Runners= (or R=) parameter in the queue group definition.

If you set values that can conflict (for example, a maximum of 50 queue runners total, but 10 for the local queue, 30 for the mydomain queue, and 50 for the AOL queue), **sendmail** will batch the queues into workgroups and round robin between workgroups. In this example, the local and mydomain queues would be one workgroup and the AOL queues would be a second workgroup. If you choose limits that must conflict (e.g., max=50 but AOL=100), **sendmail** will use MAX_QUEUE_CHILDREN as its absolute limit on the number of queue runners.

Load average controls

sendmail has always been able to refuse connections or queue messages instead of delivering them when the system load average goes too high. Unfortunately, the load average has only a one-minute granularity, so it's not a very finely honed tool for smoothing out the resources consumed by **sendmail**. The new DELAY_LA primitive lets you set a value of the load average at which **sendmail** should slow down; it will sleep for one second between SMTP commands for current connections and before accepting new connections. The default value is 0, which turns the mechanism off.

Undeliverable messages in the queue

Undeliverable messages in the mail queue can really kill performance on a busy mail server. **sendmail** has several features that help with the issue of undeliverable messages. The most effective is the FALLBACK_MX option, which hands a message off to another machine if it cannot be delivered on the first attempt. This feature lets your primary machine crank out the messages to good addresses and shunts the problem children to a secondary fallback machine. Another feature that helps is the host status directory, which stores the status of remote hosts across queue runs.

The FALLBACK_MX option is a big performance win for a site with large mailing lists that invariably contain addresses that are temporarily or permanently undeliverable. To use it you must specify the host that will handle the deferred mail. For example,

```
define(`confFALLBACK_MX', `mailbackup.xor.com')
```

would forward all messages that fail on their first delivery attempt to the central server mailbackup.xor.com for further processing. As of 8.12, there can be multiple fallback machines if multiple MX records are used in DNS for the designated hosts.

On the fallback machines you can use the HOST_STATUS_DIRECTORY option to help with multiple failures. This option directs **sendmail** to maintain a status file for each host to which mail is sent and to use that status information to prioritize the hosts each time the queue is run. This status information effectively implements negative caching and allows information to be shared across queue runs. It's a performance win on servers that handle mailing lists with a lot of bad addresses, but it can be expensive in terms of file I/O.

Here is an example that uses the directory **/var/spool/mqueue/.hoststat** (create the directory first):

```
define(`confHOST_STATUS_DIRECTORY', `/var/spool/mqueue/.hoststat')
```

If the **.hoststat** directory is specified with a relative path, it will be stored beneath the queue directory. **sendmail** creates its own internal hierarchy of subdirectories based on the destination hostname.

For example, if mail to evi@anchor.cs.colorado.edu were to fail, status information would go into the **/var/spool/mqueue/.hoststat/edu./colorado./cs./** directory in a file called **anchor** because the host anchor has an MX record with itself as highest priority. If the DNS MX records had directed anchor's email to host foo, then the filename would have been **foo**, not anchor.

A third performance enhancement for busy machines involves setting a minimum queue age so that any message that cannot be delivered on the initial try is queued and stays in the queue for a minimum time between tries. This technique is usually coupled with command-line flags that run the queue more often (e.g., **-q5m**). If a queue runner hangs on a bad message, another one will start in 5 minutes, improving performance for the messages that can be delivered. The entire queue is run in batches determined by which messages have been there for the required minimum time. Running **sendmail** with the flags **-bd -q5m** and including the option

```
define('confMIN-QUEUE_AGE', '27m')
```

in the config file could result in a more responsive system.

Kernel tuning

If you plan to use a Linux box as a high-volume mail server, you should modify several of the kernel's networking configuration parameters and perhaps even build a custom kernel (depending on your hardware configuration and expected load). Remove any unnecessary drivers so you start with a streamlined kernel that is just right for your hardware configuration.

The custom kernel should include support for multiple processors if the host machine has more than one processor (SMP). (We realize that for true Linux geeks, this comment is analogous to a reminder not to forget to breathe. But since Linux users' kernel-building skills vary, we have ignored reviewers' comments and left this reminder in.)

To reset the parameters of the networking stack, use the shell's **echo** command redirected to the proper variable in the **/proc** filesystem. Chapter 13, *TCP/IP Networking*, contains a general description of this procedure starting on page 284. Table 19.19 shows the parameters to change on a high-volume mail server along with their suggested and default values. These changes should probably be put in a shell script that runs at boot time and performs the corresponding **echo**s.

Table 19.19   Kernel parameters to change on high-volume mail servers

Variable (relative to /proc/sys)	Default	Suggested
net/ipv4/tcp_fin_timeout	180	30
net/ipv4/tcp_keepalive_time	7200	1800
net/core/netdev_max_backlog	300	1024
fs/file_max	4096	16384
fs/inode_max	16384	65536

For example, you could use the command

```
echo 30 > /proc/sys/net/ipv4/tcp_fin_timeout
```

to change TCP's FIN timeout value.

19.13 SENDMAIL STATISTICS, TESTING, AND DEBUGGING

sendmail can collect statistics on the number and size of messages it has handled. You can display this data with the **mailstats** command, which organizes the data by mailer. **sendmail**'s STATUS_FILE option (in the OSTYPE file) specifies the name of the file in which statistics should be kept. The existence of the specified file turns on the accounting function.

The default location for **sendmail**'s statistics file is **/etc/mail/statistics**, but some vendors call the file **sendmail.st** and put it in **/var/log**.

The totals shown by **mailstats** are cumulative since the creation of the statistics file. If you want periodic statistics, you can rotate and reinitialize the file from **cron**.

Here is an example:

```
% mailstats
Statistics from Wed Aug  1 02:13:30 2001
 M   msgsfr  bytes_from   msgsto   bytes_to   msgsrej   msgsdis   Mailer
 4       12         25K       63       455K         0         0   esmtp
 7        0          0K       18        25K         0         0   relay
 8       54        472K        0         0K         0         0   local
=============================================================
 T       66        497K       81       480K         0         0
 C       66                   81                    0
```

If the mail statistics file is world-readable, you don't need to be root to run **mailstats**.

Six values are shown: messages and kilobytes received (msgsfr, bytes_from), messages and kilobytes sent (msgsto, bytes_to), messages rejected (msgsrej), and messages discarded (msgsdis). The first column is a number identifying the mailer, and the last column lists the name of the mailer. The T row is total messages and bytes, and the C row is connections. These values include both local and relayed mail.

Testing and debugging

m4-based configurations are to some extent pretested. You probably won't need to do low-level debugging if you use them. One thing the debugging flags cannot test is your design. While researching this chapter, we found errors in several of the configuration files and designs that we examined. The errors ranged from invoking a feature without the prerequisite macro (e.g., using masquerade_envelope without having turned on masquerading with MASQUERADE_AS) to total conflict between the design of the **sendmail** configuration and the firewall that controlled whether and under what conditions mail was allowed in.

You cannot design a mail system in a vacuum. You must be synchronized with (or at least not be in conflict with) your DNS MX records and your firewall policy.

sendmail provides one of the world's richest sets of debugging aids, with debug flags that are not simple Booleans or even integers but are two-dimensional quantities $x.y$, where x chooses the topic and y chooses the amount of information to display. A value of 0 gives no debugging and 127 wastes many trees if you print the output. Topics range from 0 to 99; currently, about 80 are defined.

The file **sendmail/TRACEFLAGS** in the distribution lists the values in use and the files and functions in which they are used. All debugging support is at the level of the raw config file. In many cases, it's helpful to look at the **sendmail** source along with the debug output.

If **sendmail** is invoked with a **-d**$x.y$ flag, debugging output comes to the screen (standard error). Table 19.20 shows several important values of x and some suggested values for y. Be careful if you turn on debugging for a **sendmail** running as a daemon

(**-bd**) because the debug output may end up interjected into the SMTP dialogue and cause odd failures when **sendmail** talks to remote hosts.

Table 19.20   Debugging topics

Topic	Meaning and suggestions
0	Shows compile flags and system identity (try y = 1 or 10)
8	Shows DNS name resolution (try y = 8)
11	Traces delivery (shows mailer invocations)
12	Shows local-to-remote name translation
17	Lists MX hosts
21	Traces rewriting rules (use y = 2 or y = 12 for more detail)
27	Shows aliasing and forwarding (try y = 4)
44	Shows file open attempts in case things are failing (y = 4)
60	Shows database map lookups

checksendmail is
available from
www.harker.com.

Gene Kim and Rob Kolstad have written a Perl script called **checksendmail** that invokes **sendmail** in address test mode on a file of test addresses that you supply. It compares the results to those expected. This script lets you test new versions of the configuration file against a test suite of your site's typical addresses to be sure you haven't inadvertently broken anything that used to work.

Verbose delivery

Many user agents that invoke **sendmail** on the command line accept a **-v** flag, which is passed to **sendmail** and makes it display the steps taken to deliver the message. The example below uses the **mail** command. The words in bold were typed as input to the user agent, and the rest is **sendmail**'s verbose output.

```
% mail -v trent@toadranch.com
Subject: just testing, please ignore
hi
.
Cc:
trent@toadranch.com... Connecting to coyote.toadranch.com. via esmtp...
220 coyote.toadranch.com ESMTP Sendmail 8.11.0/8.11.0; Tue, 7 Aug 2001 20:
    08:51 -0600
>>> EHLO anchor.cs.colorado.edu
250-coyote.toadranch.com Hello anchor.cs.colorado.edu [128.138.242.1], pleased
    to meet you
250-ENHANCEDSTATUSCODES
250-EXPN
250-VERB
250-8BITMIME
250-SIZE
250-DSN
250-ONEX
250-ETRN
```

```
250-XUSR
250-AUTH DIGEST-MD5 CRAM-MD5
250 HELP
>>> MAIL From:<evi@anchor.cs.colorado.edu> SIZE=65
250 2.1.0 <evi@anchor.cs.colorado.edu>... Sender ok
>>> RCPT To:<trent@toadranch.com>
250 2.1.5 <trent@toadranch.com>... Recipient ok
>>> DATA
354 Enter mail, end with "." on a line by itself
>>> .
250 2.0.0 f7828pi03229 Message accepted for delivery
trent@toadranch.com... Sent (f7828pi03229 Message accepted for delivery)
Closing connection to coyote.toadranch.com.
>>> QUIT
221 2.0.0 coyote.toadranch.com closing connection
```

The **sendmail** on anchor connected to the **sendmail** on toadranch.com. Each machine used the ESMTP protocol to negotiate the exchange of the message.

Talking in SMTP

You can make direct use of SMTP when debugging the mail system. To initiate an SMTP session, **telnet** to TCP port 25 or use **sendmail -bs**. By default, this is the port on which **sendmail** listens when run in daemon (**-bd**) mode; it uses port 587 when running as the mail submission agent. Table 19.21 shows the most important SMTP commands.

Table 19.21   SMTP commands

Command	Function
HELO *hostname*	Identifies the connecting host if speaking SMTP
EHLO *hostname*	Identifies the connecting host if speaking ESMTP
MAIL From: *revpath*	Initiates a mail transaction (envelope sender)
RCPT To: *fwdpath*[a]	Identifies envelope recipient(s)
VRFY *address*	Verifies that *address* is valid (deliverable)
EXPN *address*	Shows expansion of aliases and **.forward** mappings
DATA	Begins the message body[b]
QUIT	Ends the exchange and closes the connection
RSET	Resets the state of the connection
HELP	Prints a summary of SMTP commands

a. There can be multiple RCPT commands for a message.
b. You terminate the body by entering a dot on its own line.

The whole language has only 14 commands, so it is quite easy to learn and use. It is not case sensitive. The specification for SMTP can be found in RFC821 (also, see RFC1123). RFCs 1869, 1870, 1891, and 1985 extend SMTP to ESMTP. Next-generation versions of these references exist in the form of RFCs 2821 and 2822; the earlier ones will become obsolete when the new ones are formally adopted as standards.

Most transport agents, including **sendmail**, speak both SMTP and ESMTP; **smap** is the lone exception these days. Unfortunately, many firewalls boxes that provide active filtering do not speak ESMTP.

ESMTP speakers start the conversation with the EHLO command instead of HELO. If the process at the other end understands and responds with an OK, then the participants negotiate supported extensions and arrive at a lowest common denominator for the exchange. If an error is returned, then the ESMTP speaker falls back to SMTP.

Logging

See Chapter 11 for more information about syslog.

sendmail uses syslog to log error and status messages with syslog facility "mail" and levels "debug" through "crit"; messages are tagged with the string "sendmail." You can override the logging string "sendmail" with the **-L** command-line option, which is handy if you are debugging one copy of **sendmail** while other copies are doing regular email chores.

The confLOG_LEVEL option, specified on the command line or in the config file, determines the severity level that **sendmail** uses as a threshold for logging. High values of the log level imply low severity levels and cause more info to be logged.

Recall that a message logged to syslog at a particular level is reported to that level and all those above it. The **/etc/syslog.conf** file determines the eventual destination of each message. On Red Hat systems the **sendmail** logs go to **/var/log/maillog** by default. For SuSE it's **/var/log/mail**, and for Debian it's **/var/log/mail.log**. Wouldn't it be nice if the Linux standardization efforts could sort out some of these random and apparently meaningless differences so our scripts could be more portable?

Table 19.22 gives an approximate mapping between **sendmail** log levels and syslog severity levels.

Table 19.22   sendmail log levels vs. syslog levels

L	Levels	L	Levels
0	No logging	4	notice
1	alert or crit	5–11	info
2	crit	>=12	debug
3	err or warning		

A nice program called **mreport** by Jason Armstrong is available from

> ftp://ftp.datrix.co.za/pub/mreport

It can be used to summarize log files written by **sendmail**. It builds out of the box with just **make** and then **make install**. Here is a sample of **mreport**'s output from a Red Hat system:

```
# mreport -f -i /var/log/maillog -o mreport.out
[redhat.toadranch.com] [/var/log/maillog]

* [   7]  592601  herb@yoherb.com                    trent@toadranch.com
* [   8]  505797  SNYDERGA@simon.rochester.edu        trent@toadranch.com
  [   1]  179386  steph@toadranch.com                bennettr@ci.boulder.co.us
  [   1]   65086  herb@yoherb.com                    ned@xor.co
  [   7]   19029  evi@anchor.cs.colorado.edu         trent@toadranch.com
  [  11]   17677  lunch-request@moose.org            trent@toadranch.com
  [   2]   16178  trent@toadranch.com                ned@camelspit.org
  [   3]   15229  reminders@yahoo-inc.com            herb@toadranch.com
  [   2]    4653  trent@toadranch.com                garth@cs.colorado.edu
  [   2]    1816  UNKNOWN                            trent@toadranch.com

. . . many lines deleted . . .

======================
Total Bytes           : 7876372
Number of Records     : 192
----------------------
User Unknown          : 125
----------------------
Host Name             : redhat.toadranch.com
Input File            : maillog
Output File           : mreport.out
First Record          : Aug  5 04:47:31
Last Record           : Aug  7 18:16:25
----------------------
Time Taken            : 24317 µs
======================
```

You must use **sudo** or be root to run **mreport** if your mail log files are only readable by root (as they should be). Flags and options are documented in the **mreport** man page. The **-f** flag in this instance says to aggregate and sort by sender; an analogous **-t** flag lets you sort by recipient. The **-i** argument is the input file and **-o** the output file.

If you intend to run **mreport** regularly, you should inform your users. They might feel it was an invasion of their privacy for sysadmins to be browsing the mail logs with such a nice tool.

19.14 THE EXIM MAIL SYSTEM

Debian Linux ships with the Exim mail transport agent instead of **sendmail**. It's a simpler system with fewer bells and whistles, but it also features easier configuration for sites that don't bear a heavy mail load and don't have a bizarre mail system design. Exim's functionality maps to the most commonly used features of **sendmail**.

History

Exim was written in 1995 by Philip Hazel of the University of Cambridge and is distributed under the GNU Public License. Philip Hazel has also written a book called *Exim: The Mail Transfer Agent* which was published by O'Reilly in July 2001. We defer to that book and to the Exim documentation at www.exim.org for the details of Exim configuration and give only a brief description of Debian's release here.

Exim on Debian

Debian 3.0 includes Exim as its mail transport program.

As shipped, Debian sort of pretends to use **sendmail**; however, **/usr/sbin/sendmail** and **/usr/lib/sendmail** are links to the **exim** binary, and **man sendmail** brings up the **exim** man page. The command-line flags understood by **exim** match those of **sendmail**, so user agents that call **sendmail** explicitly with the **-bm** or **-bs** flags still work properly with **exim** as the underlying mail transport agent.

As in the **sendmail** suite, Debian provides some separate commands that perform specific mail functions. These are actually implemented by a call to **exim** with certain command-line flags. Table 19.23 shows the behaviors and their equivalent flags.

Table 19.23   Debian mail utilities (with equivalent exim flags)

Command	Flag	Function
mailq	**-bp**	Shows the mail queue
rsmtp	**-bS**	Batched SMTP connection
rmail	**-i**	For compatibility with **smail**[a]
runq	**-q**	Runs the mail queue

a. Accepts a message terminated by a dot on a line by itself

Exim configuration

Exim contains three logical pieces: directors, routers, and transports. Directors handle local addresses—that is, addresses inside the home domain. Routers handle remote addresses, and transports do the actual delivery.

Exim is configured much like **smail3** or Postfix with the configuration language taking the form *keyword = value*. Debian ships with a Perl script that helps you configure Exim by asking you questions and building Exim's config file, **/etc/exim.conf**, in accordance with your answers.

Unfortunately, a few of the default values leave you with a mail system configured to think that your hostname is a top-level domain. Needless to say, this doesn't work. Even outgoing mail is affected because sender addresses then look like *user@host;* because of spam concerns, most installations reject mail from senders whose email addresses are not fully qualified (that is, they reject addresses that do not contain at least one dot). To get mail working correctly, you must edit **exim.conf** by hand or run **eximconfig** to do the real initial configuration for you.

The **exim.conf** file is very well documented, with comments preceding each variable that describe what the variable does, what the usual value is, and what (bad) things might happen if you fail to define it. The default **exim.conf** file has about 100 variables defined, but this is largely boilerplate that invokes much of the **sendmail** behavior documented in previous sections.

On our testbed system we had to set just four variables to get basic email working. Actually, two of those variables related to privacy concerns and were not absolutely required. Here are the four variables, with our comments on the side:

```
qualify_domain = domain-name       ### by default set to unqualified hostname
local_domains = localhost:domain-name
smtp_verify = false                ### default is on, off disables SMTP VRFY
modemask = 002                     ### default 022 assumes a group for each user
```

We do not cover the details of Exim configuration further but will instead refer you to a nice article by Exim's author at sysadmin.oreilly.com/news.exim_0701.html, as well as to **/usr/doc/exim** (be sure to include the **exim-doc** package when you install the operating system) and to the other sources mentioned above.

Below, we describe a few of Exim's features in **sendmail** terms so you can compare the two system's functionality and decide if you want to install the real **sendmail** instead of Exim.

Exim/sendmail similarities

exim runs setuid to root much like **sendmail** used to (before 8.12), so you need to be careful to stay up to date on security patches. The Exim concept of trusted users matches that of **sendmail** and is used primarily to help facilitate the management of mailing lists, for which From lines are routinely rewritten. Exim also lets you define administrative users who are allowed to initiate queue runs. The SMTP verify command (VRFY) is allowed by default.

exim must be sent the SIGHUP signal with the **kill** command when its config file changes. It stores its process ID in **/var/spool/exim/exim-daemon.pid**. It typically logs to files in the **/var/log/exim** directory but can also use syslog. By default, Debian ships with **exim** logging to its own files and ignoring syslog, yet **syslog.conf** is configured with several mail log files that are empty and are rotated and compressed every day. (Empty files are larger after compression than before!)

Exim does not understand UUCP addresses. It can be configured to accept percent-hack addressing but does not do so by default.

Exim allows you to forward outgoing mail to a smart host and to filter inbound mail at both the host and user levels. It supports virtual domains and has a retry database similar in functionality to **sendmail**'s host status directory for keeping track of difficult deliveries. A system-wide (not per-user) filtering mechanism can screen for Microsoft attachments, worms, viruses, etc.

Exim can use the real-time black hole lists but has the old URL for them; you will need to change the path from vix.com to mail-abuse.org.

Exim includes a nice feature that is not available in **sendmail**, namely, recognition of alias and forwarding loops and sensible handling of them.

Finally, **man -k exim** yields several useful tools to help keep the mail system tidy.

19.15 RECOMMENDED READING

COSTALES, BRYAN, and ERIC ALLMAN. *sendmail, 2nd Edition*. Sebastopol, CA: O'Reilly, 1997.

This book is the definitive tome—1,000 pages' worth. It includes a tutorial as well as a very complete reference section. The book reads well in the open-to-a-random-page mode, which we consider an important feature for a reference book. It has a good index too. The third edition is in progress and should be out around the middle of 2002. The tutorial will be dropped, but the book will still be about 1000 pages long!

CLAYTON, RICHARD. "Good Practice for Combating Unsolicited Bulk Email." RIPE/Demon Internet. 2000. http://www.ripe.net/ripe/docs/ripe-206.html

This document is aimed at ISPs. It has lots of policy information and some good links to technical subjects.

SCHWARTZ, ALAN, AND PAULA FERGUSON. *Managing Mailing Lists*. O'Reilly, 1998.

This book is a good reference on mailing lists.

The man page for **sendmail** describes its command-line arguments. See *Sendmail: An Internetwork Mail Router*, by Eric Allman, for an overview.

Installation instructions and a good description of the configuration file are covered in *Sendmail Installation and Operation Guide*, which can be found in the **doc/op** subdirectory of the **sendmail** distribution. This document is quite complete, and in conjunction with the **README** file in the **cf** directory, it gives a good nuts-and-bolts view of the **sendmail** system.

www.sendmail.org, www.sendmail.org/~ca, and www.sendmail.org/~gshapiro all contain **sendmail**-related documents, HOWTOs, and tutorials.

RFC2822, which obsoletes RFC822, describes the syntax of messages and addresses in a networked mail system, and RFC1123 describes host requirements. These are, in a sense, the functional specifications to which **sendmail** was built.

RFC2821, which obsoletes RFC821, defines the Simple Mail Transport Protocol (SMTP), and RFCs 1869, 1870, 1891, and 1985 extend it to ESMTP.

RFC974 describes MX records in the Domain Name System and their relationship to mail routing.

Other mail-related RFCs include:

- RFC1869 – SMTP service extensions
- RFCs 1891-1894 – Delivery status notifications (bounce messages)
- RFC1985 – Remote queueing
- RFC2033 – LMTP, the Local Mail Transport Protocol
- RFC2034 – SMTP error codes
- RFC2045 – MIME extensions
- RFC2476 – MSA, Mail Submission Agent specifications
- RFC2487 – Secure SMTP over TLS
- RFCs 2554 and 2222 – SMTP authentication and SASL

RFCs 2821 (SMTP) and 2822 (Internet Message Format) tidy up some of the most commonly referred-to Internet email RFCs; they obsolete RFCs 821, 822, 974, and 1869. RFCs 2821 and 2822 were first published in April 2001, and are proposed standards.

HAZEL, PHILIP. *Exim: The Mail Transfer Agent.* Sebastopol, CA: O'Reilly, 2001.

Exim documentation and information can be found at www.exim.org.

19.16 EXERCISES

E19.1 Briefly list the differences and similarities between the genericstable and the virtusertable. In what situations would you use each?

E19.2 Compare the use of **/etc/mail/aliases** with the use of an LDAP server to store mail aliases. What are the advantages and disadvantages of each?

E19.3 Briefly explain the difference between a mail user agent (MUA), a delivery agent (DA), and an access agent (AA). Then explain the difference between a mail transport agent (MTA) and a mail submission agent (MSA).

E19.4 What is **smrsh**, and why should you use it instead of **/bin/sh**? If **smrsh** is in use at your site, what programs are allowed to run as the program mailer? Are any of them dangerously insecure?

☆ **E19.5** Write a brief description of the following email header. What path did the email take? Who was it addressed to, and who was it delivered to? How long did it take the email to go from the sender to the destination?:

```
From clements@boulderlabs.com Fri Dec 28 17:06:57 2001
Return-Path: <clements@mail.boulderlabs.com>
Received: from boulder.Colorado.EDU (boulder.Colorado.EDU
    [128.138.240.1]) by ucsub.colorado.edu (8.11.6/8.11.2/ITS-5.0/student)
    with ESMTP idfBT06vF10618 for <hallcp@ucsub.Colorado.EDU>; Fri,
    28 Dec 2001 17:06:57-0700 (MST)
Received: from mail.boulderlabs.com (mail.boulderlabs.com
    [206.168.112.48]) by boulder.Colorado.EDU
    (8.10.1/8.10.1/UnixOps+Hesiod (Boulder)) with ESMTP id
    fBT06uL13184; Fri, 28 Dec 2001 17:06:56 -0700 (MST)
Received: from ath.boulderlabs.com (cpe-24-221-212-162.co.sprintbbd.net
    [24.221.212.162]) by mail.boulderlabs.com (8.11.6/8.11.6) with ESMTP
    id fBT06oQ29214 for <booklist@boulderlabs.com>; Fri, 28 Dec 2001
    17:06:50 -0700 (MST) (envelope-from
    clements@mail.boulderlabs.com)
From: David Clements <clements@boulderlabs.com>
Received: (from clements@localhost) by ath.boulderlabs.com
    (8.11.6/8.11.4) id fBT06ma01470 for booklist@boulderlabs.com; Fri,
    28 Dec 2001 17:06:48 -0700 (MST) (envelope-from clements)
Date: Fri, 28 Dec 2001 17:06:48 -0700 (MST)
Message-Id: <200112290006.fBT06ma01470@ath.boulderlabs.com>
To: boolist@boulderlabs.com
Subject: Book Questions
```

☆ **E19.6** Write a small **/etc/mail/aliases** file that demonstrates three different types of aliases. Talk briefly about what each line does and why it could be useful.

⭐ **E19.7** List and explain what the prefixes for files in the mail queue directory mean. Why is it important to delete some of them but very wrong to delete others? How can some of the prefixes be used to debug **sendmail** configuration mistakes? Look at the **mailq** on your campus mail server. Is there any cruft in the directory? Are there any messages with no control files or control files with no messages? What is the oldest message in the queue? (Requires root access.)

⭐ **E19.8** Explain the purpose of each of the following **m4** macros. If the macro includes a file, provide a short description of what the contents of the file should be.

a) VERSIONID
b) OSTYPE
c) DOMAIN
d) MAILER
e) FEATURE

⭐ **E19.9** Explain what an MX record is. Why are MX records important for mail delivery? Give an example in which a misconfigured MX record might make mail undeliverable.

⭐ **E19.10** What are some of the implications of being blacklisted on MAPS or a similar spam black hole list? Outline some techniques used to stay off such lists.

⭐ **E19.11** If your site allows **procmail** (even though we say it shouldn't), and if you have permission from your local sysadmin group, set up your personal **procmail** configuration file to illustrate how **procmail** can compromise security.

⭐⭐ **E19.12** Explore the current **sendmail** configuration at your site. What are some of the special features of **sendmail** that are in use? Can you find any problems with the configuration? In what ways could the configuration be made better?

⭐⭐ **E19.13** Find a piece of spam in your mailbox and inspect the headers. Report any signs that the mail has been forged. Then run some of the tools mentioned in this chapter, such as SpamCop or SpamAssassin, and report their findings. How did you do at recognizing faked headers? Submit the spam and your conclusions about the sender, the validity of the listed hosts, and anything else that looks out of place.

20 Network Management and Debugging

Because networks increase the number of interdependencies among machines, they tend to magnify problems. As the saying goes, "Networking is when you can't get any work done because of the failure of a machine you have never even heard of."

Network management is the art and science of keeping a network healthy. It generally includes the following tasks:

- Fault detection for networks, gateways, and critical servers
- Schemes for notifying an administrator of problems
- General monitoring, to balance load and plan expansion
- Documentation and visualization of the network
- Administration of network devices from a central site

On a single network segment, it is generally not worthwhile to establish formal procedures for network management. Just test the network thoroughly after installation, and check it occasionally to be sure that its load is not excessive. When it breaks, fix it.

As your network grows, management procedures should become more automated. On a network consisting of several different subnets joined with switches or routers, you may want to start automating management tasks with shell scripts and simple programs. If you have a WAN or a complex local network, you should consider installing a dedicated network management station.

In some cases, your organization's reliability needs will dictate the sophistication of your network management system. A problem with the network can bring all work to a standstill. If your site cannot tolerate downtime, it may well be worthwhile to obtain and install a high-end enterprise network management system.

Unfortunately, even the best network management system cannot prevent all failures. It is critical to have a well-documented network and a high-quality staff available to handle the inevitable collapses.

20.1 TROUBLESHOOTING A NETWORK

Several good tools are available for debugging a network at the TCP/IP layer. Most give low-level information, so you must understand the main ideas of TCP/IP and routing in order to use the debugging tools.

On the other hand, network issues can also stem from problems with higher-level protocols such as DNS, NFS, and HTTP. You might want to read through Chapter 13, *TCP/IP Networking*, and Chapter 14, *Routing*, before tackling this chapter.

In this section, we start with some general troubleshooting strategy. We then cover several essential tools, including **ping**, **traceroute**, **netstat**, **tcpdump**, and Ethereal. We don't discuss the **arp** command in this chapter, though it, too, is a useful debugging tool—see page 262 for more information.

When your network is broken, chances are that you'll be in quite a rush to repair it. Stop right there! It's important to take a moment and consider how to approach the problem before jumping into action. The biggest mistake you can make is to introduce poorly planned changes into an already failing network.

Before you attack your network, consider these principles:

- Make one change at a time, and test each change to make sure that it had the effect you intended. Back out any changes that have an undesired effect.

- Document the situation as it was before you got involved, and document every change you make along the way.

- Start at one "end" of a system or network and work through the system's critical components until you reach the problem. For example, you might start by looking at the network configuration on a client, work your way up to the physical connections, investigate the network hardware, and finally, check the server's physical connections and software configuration.

- Communicate regularly. Most network problems involve or affect lots of different people: users, ISPs, system administrators, telco engineers, network administrators, etc. Clear, consistent communication will prevent you from hindering one another's efforts to solve the problem.

- Work as a team. Years of experience show that people make fewer stupid mistakes if they have a peer helping out.

- Use the layers of the network to negotiate the problem. Start at the "top" or "bottom" and work your way through the protocol stack.

This last point deserves a bit more discussion. As described on page 241, the architecture of TCP/IP defines several layers of abstraction at which components of the network can function. For example, HTTP depends on TCP, TCP depends on IP, IP depends on the Ethernet protocol, and the Ethernet protocol depends on the integrity of the network cable. You can dramatically reduce the amount of time spent debugging a problem if you first figure out which layer is misbehaving.

Ask yourself questions like these as you work up (or down) the stack:

- Do you have physical connectivity and a link light?
- Is your interface configured properly?
- Is DNS configured properly?[1]
- Do your ARP tables show other hosts?
- Can you ping the localhost address (127.0.0.1)?
- Can you ping other local hosts by IP address?
- Can you ping other local hosts by hostname?
- Can you ping hosts on another network?
- Do high-level commands like **telnet** and **ssh** work?

Once you've identified where the problem lies, take a step back and consider the effect your subsequent tests and prospective fixes will have on other services and hosts.

20.2 PING: CHECK TO SEE IF A HOST IS ALIVE

The **ping** command is embarrassingly simple, but in many situations it is all you need. It sends an ICMP ECHO_REQUEST packet to a target host and waits to see if the host answers back. Despite its simplicity, **ping** is one of the workhorses of network debugging.

You can use **ping** to check the status of individual hosts and to test segments of the network. Routing tables, physical networks, and gateways are all involved in processing a ping, so the network must be more or less working for **ping** to succeed. If **ping** doesn't work, you can be pretty sure that nothing more sophisticated will work either. However, this rule does not apply to networks that block ICMP echo requests with a firewall. Make sure that a firewall isn't interfering with your debugging before you conclude that the target host is ignoring a **ping**. You might consider disabling a meddlesome firewall for a short period of time to facilitate debugging.

Every vendor provides a **ping**. Most versions of **ping** run in an infinite loop unless a packet count argument is given. Once you've had your fill of pinging, type the interrupt character (usually <Control-C>) to get out.

Here's an example:

```
% ping beast
PING beast (10.1.1.46): 56 data bytes
```

---

1. If your machine hangs at boot time, boots very slowly, or hangs on inbound **telnet** connections, DNS should be your prime suspect.

```
64 bytes from 10.1.1.46: icmp_seq=0 ttl=255 time=0.808 ms
64 bytes from 10.1.1.46: icmp_seq=1 ttl=255 time=0.400 ms
64 bytes from 10.1.1.46: icmp_seq=2 ttl=255 time=0.390 ms
^C
--- beast ping statistics ---
3 packets transmitted, 3 packets received, 0% packet loss
round-trip min/avg/max/stddev = 0.390/0.533/0.808/0.195 ms
```

The output for beast shows the host's IP address, the ICMP sequence number of each response packet, and the round trip travel time. The most obvious thing that the output above tells you is that the server beast is alive and connected to the network.

On a healthy network, **ping** can allow you to determine if a host is down. Conversely, when a remote host is known to be up and in good working order, **ping** can give you useful information about the health of the network. Ping packets are routed by the usual IP mechanisms, and a successful round trip means that all networks and gateways lying between the source and destination are working correctly, at least to a first approximation.

The ICMP sequence number is a particularly valuable piece of information. Discontinuities in the sequence indicate dropped packets. Despite the fact that IP does not guarantee the delivery of packets, a healthy network should drop very few of them. Lost-packet problems are important to track down because they tend to be masked by higher-level protocols. The network may appear to function correctly, but it will be much slower than it ought to be, not only because of the retransmitted packets but also because of the protocol overhead needed to detect and manage them.

To track down the cause of disappearing packets, first run **traceroute** (see the next section) to discover the route that packets are taking to the target host. Then ping the intermediate gateways in sequence to discover which link is dropping packets. To pin down the problem, you need to send a statistically significant number of packets. The network fault will generally lie on the link between the last gateway that you can ping without significant loss of packets and the gateway beyond it.

The round trip time reported by **ping** gives you insight into the overall performance of a path through a network. Moderate variations in round trip time do not usually indicate problems. Packets may occasionally be delayed by tens or hundreds of milliseconds for no apparent reason; that's just the way IP and Linux work. You should expect to see a fairly consistent round trip time for the majority of packets, with occasional lapses. Many of today's routers implement rate-limited responses to ICMP packets, which means that a router may delay responding to your ping if it is already dealing with a lot of ICMP traffic.

The **ping** program allows you to send echo request packets of any size. By using a packet larger than the MTU of the network (1,500 bytes for Ethernet), you can force fragmentation to take place. This practice will help you identify media errors or other low-level issues such as problems with a congested ATM network. It's surprising how many problems you can expose this way.

You can specify the desired packet size in bytes with the **-s** flag:

```
# ping -s 1500 cuinfo.cornell.edu
```

Use the **ping** command with the following caveats in mind. First, it is hard to distinguish the failure of a network from the failure of a server with only the **ping** command. A failed ping just tells you that *something* is wrong.

Second, a ping does not guarantee much about the target machine's state. Echo request packets are handled within the IP protocol stack and do not require a server process to be running on the probed host. A response guarantees only that a machine is powered on and has not experienced a kernel panic. You'll need higher-level methods to verify the availability of individual services such as HTTP and DNS.

20.3 TRACEROUTE: TRACE IP PACKETS

traceroute, written by Van Jacobson, lets you discover the sequence of gateways through which an IP packet travels to reach its destination.

The syntax is simply

traceroute *hostname*

There are a variety of options, most of which are not important in daily use. As usual, the *hostname* can be specified either symbolically or numerically. The output is simply a list of hosts, starting with the first gateway and ending at the destination.

For example, a **traceroute** from the host jaguar to the host drevil produces the following output:

```
% traceroute drevil
traceroute to drevil (192.225.55.137), 30 hops max, 38 byte packets
 1  xor-gw2 (192.108.21.254)  0.840 ms  0.693 ms  0.671 ms
 2  xor-gw4 (192.225.56.10)  4.642 ms  4.582 ms  4.674 ms
 3  drevil (192.225.55.137)  7.959 ms  5.949 ms  5.908 ms
```

From this output we can tell that jaguar is exactly three hops away from drevil, and we can see which gateways are involved in the connection. The round trip time for each gateway is also shown—three samples for each hop are measured and displayed. A typical **traceroute** between Internet hosts can include ten or twenty hops.

traceroute works by setting the time to live field (TTL, actually "hop count to live") of an outbound packet to an artificially low number. As packets arrive at a gateway, their TTL is decreased. When a gateway decreases the TTL to 0, it discards the packet and sends an ICMP "time exceeded" message back to the originating host.

See page 414 for more information about reverse DNS lookups.

The first few **traceroute** packets have their TTL set to 1. The first gateway to see such a packet (xor-gw2 in this case) determines that the TTL has been exceeded and notifies jaguar of the dropped packet by sending back an ICMP message. The sender's IP address in the header of the error packet identifies the gateway; **traceroute** looks up this address in DNS to find the gateway's hostname.

To identify the second-hop gateway, **traceroute** sends out a second round of packets with TTL fields set to 2. The first gateway routes the packets and decreases their TTL by 1. At the second gateway, the packets are then dropped and ICMP error messages generated as before. This process continues until the TTL is equal to the number of hops to the destination host and the packets reach their destination successfully.

Most routers send their ICMP messages from the interface "closest" to your host. If you run **traceroute** backwards from the destination host, you will probably see different IP addresses being used to identify the same set of routers. You might also see completely different paths; this configuration is known as "asymmetric routing."

Since **traceroute** sends three packets for each value of the TTL field, you may sometimes observe an interesting artifact. If an intervening gateway multiplexes traffic across several routes, the packets might be returned by different hosts; in this case, **traceroute** simply prints them all.

Let's look at a more interesting example from a host at colorado.edu to xor.com:

```
rupertsberg% traceroute xor.com
traceroute: Warning: xor.com has multiple addresses; using 192.225.33.1
traceroute to xor.com (192.225.33.1), 30 hops max, 40 byte packets
 1  cs-gw3-faculty.cs.colorado.edu (128.138.236.3)  1.362 ms  2.144 ms  2.76 ms
 2  cs-gw-dmz.cs.colorado.edu (128.138.243.193)  2.720 ms  4.378 ms  5.052 ms
 3  engr-cs.Colorado.EDU (128.138.80.141)  5.587 ms  2.454 ms  2.773 ms
 4  hut-engr.Colorado.EDU (128.138.80.201)  2.743 ms  5.643 ms  2.772 ms
 5  cuatm-gw.Colorado.EDU (128.138.80.2)  5.587 ms  2.784 ms  2.777 ms
 6  204.131.62.6 (204.131.62.6)  5.585 ms  3.464 ms  2.761 ms
 7  border-from-BRAN.coop.net (199.45.134.81)  5.593 ms  6.433 ms  5.521 ms
 8  core-gw-eth-2-5.coop.net (199.45.137.14)  53.806 ms  *  19.202 ms
 9  xor.com (192.225.33.1)  16.838 ms  15.972 ms  11.204 ms
```

This output shows that packets must traverse five of our internal gateways before leaving the colorado.edu network (cs-gw3-faculty to cuatm-gw). The next-hop gateway on the BRAN network (204.131.62.6) doesn't have a name in DNS. After two hops in coop.net, we arrive at xor.com.

At hop 8, we see a star in place of one of the round trip times. This notation indicates that no response (error packet) was received in response to the probe. In this case, the cause is probably congestion, but that is not the only possibility. **traceroute** relies on low-priority ICMP packets, which many routers are smart enough to drop in preference to "real" traffic. A few stars shouldn't send you into a panic.

If you see stars in all of the round trip time fields for a given gateway, no "time exceeded" messages are arriving from that machine. Perhaps the gateway is simply down. Sometimes, a gateway will be configured to silently discard packets with expired TTLs. In this case, you will still be able to see through the silent host to the gateways beyond. Another possibility is that the gateway's error packets are slow to return and that **traceroute** has stopped waiting for them by the time they arrive.

Some firewalls block ICMP "time exceeded" messages entirely. If there's one of these firewalls along the path, you won't get information about any of the gateways beyond it. However, you can still determine the total number of hops to the destination because the probe packets will eventually get all the way there. Also, some firewalls may block the outbound UDP datagrams that **traceroute** sends to trigger the ICMP responses. This problem causes **traceroute** to report no useful information at all.

A slow link does not necessarily indicate a malfunction. Some physical networks have a naturally high latency. Sluggishness can also be a sign of congestion on the receiving network, especially if the network uses a CSMA/CD technology that makes repeated attempts to transmit a packet (Ethernet is one example). Inconsistent round trip times would support such a hypothesis, since collisions increase the randomness of the network's behavior.

Sometimes, you may see the notation !N instead of a star or round trip time. It indicates that the current gateway sent back a "network unreachable" error, meaning that it doesn't know how to route your packet. Other possibilities include !H for "host unreachable" and !P for "protocol unreachable." A gateway that gives you any of these error messages will usually be the last hop you can get to. That host usually has a routing problem (possibly caused by a broken link): either its static routes are wrong or dynamic protocols have failed to propagate a usable route to the destination.

If **traceroute** doesn't seem to be working for you (or is working incredibly slowly), it may be timing out while trying to resolve the hostnames of gateways by using DNS. If DNS is broken on the host you are tracing from, use **traceroute -n** to request numeric output. This option prevents the use of DNS; it may be the only way to get **traceroute** to function on a crippled network.

20.4 NETSTAT: GET TONS O' NETWORK STATISTICS

netstat provides a wealth of information about the state of your computer's networking software, including interface statistics, routing information, and connection tables. There isn't really a unifying theme to the different sets of output, except for the fact that they all relate to the network.

Here, we discuss the four most common uses of **netstat**:

- Monitoring the status of network connections
- Inspecting interface configuration information
- Examining the routing table
- Getting operational statistics for various network protocols

Monitoring the status of network connections

With no arguments, **netstat** displays the status of active TCP and UDP ports. Inactive ("listening") servers waiting for connections aren't normally shown; they can be seen with **netstat -a**. (Connections for "UNIX domain sockets" are also shown, but since they aren't related to networking, we do not discuss them here.)

The output looks like this:

```
% netstat -a
Active Internet connections (including servers)
Proto   Recv-Q  Send-Q  Local Address  Foreign Address   (state)
tcp       0       0     *.6013         *.*              LISTEN
tcp       0       0     *.6013         *.*              LISTEN
tcp       0       0     nimi.ssh       xor.com.4105     ESTABLISHED
tcp       0      20     nimi.ssh       xor.com.1612     ESTABLISHED
tcp       0       0     *.13500        *.*              LISTEN
tcp       0       0     nimi.ssh       135.197.2.114.883  ESTABLISHED
tcp       0       0     nimi.1599      xor.com.telnet   ESTABLISHED
tcp       0       0     *.ssh          *.*              LISTEN
tcp       0       0     *.ssh          *.*              LISTEN
tcp       0       0     nimi.ssh       135.197.2.114.776  ESTABLISHED
tcp       0       0     *.cvsup        *.*              LISTEN
udp       0       0     *.syslog       *.*
udp       0       0     *.ntalk        *.*
...
```

The preceding example was run on the host nimi. It shows several inbound SSH connections, an outbound **telnet** connection, and a bunch of ports listening for other connections.

Addresses are shown as *hostname.service*, where the *service* is a port number. For well-known services, **netstat** shows the port symbolically, using the mapping defined in **/etc/services**. You can obtain numeric addresses with the **-n** option. Remember, if your DNS is broken, **netstat** will be painful to use without the **-n** flag.

Send-Q and Recv-Q show the sizes of the send and receive queues for the connection on the local host; the queue sizes on the other end of a TCP connection might be different. They should tend toward 0 and at least not be consistently nonzero. Of course, if you are running **netstat** over a network terminal, the send queue for your connection will probably never be 0.

The connection state has meaning only for TCP; UDP is a connectionless protocol. The most common states you'll see are ESTABLISHED for currently active connections, LISTEN for servers waiting for connections (not normally shown without **-a**), and TIME_WAIT for connections in the process of closing.

This display is primarily useful for debugging higher-level problems once you have determined that basic networking facilities are working correctly. It lets you verify that servers are set up correctly and facilitates the diagnosis of certain types of miscommunication, particularly with TCP. For example, a connection that stays in state SYN_SENT identifies a process that is trying to contact a nonexistent or inaccessible network server.

See Chapter 12 for more information about kernel tuning.

If **netstat** shows a lot of connections in the SYN_WAIT condition, your host is probably unable to handle the number of connections being requested. This inadequacy may be due to kernel tuning limitations or even to malicious flooding.

Inspecting interface configuration information

netstat -i shows the status of network interfaces. For example, here is output from **netstat -i** on the machine evolve:

```
% netstat -i
Kernel Interface table
eth0      Link encap:Ethernet  HWaddr 00:02:B3:19:C8:82
          inet addr:192.168.2.1 Bcast:192.168.2.255  Mask:255.255.255.0
          UP BROADCAST RUNNING MULTICAST  MTU:1500  Metric:1
          RX packets:1121527 errors:0 dropped:0 overruns:0 frame:0
          TX packets:1138477 errors:0 dropped:0 overruns:0 carrier:0
          collisions:0 txqueuelen:100
          Interrupt:7 Base address:0xef00

eth1      Link encap:Ethernet  HWaddr 00:02:B3:19:C6:86
          inet addr:192.168.1.13  Bcast:192.168.1.255  Mask:255.255.255.0
          UP BROADCAST RUNNING MULTICAST  MTU:1500  Metric:1
          RX packets:67543 errors:0 dropped:0 overruns:0 frame:0
          TX packets:69652 errors:0 dropped:0 overruns:0 carrier:0
          collisions:0 txqueuelen:100
          Interrupt:5 Base address:0xed00

lo        Link encap:Local Loopback
          inet addr:127.0.0.1  Mask:255.0.0.0
          UP LOOPBACK RUNNING  MTU:3924  Metric:1
          RX packets:310572 errors:0 dropped:0 overruns:0 frame:0
          TX packets:310572 errors:0 dropped:0 overruns:0 carrier:0
          collisions:0 txqueuelen:0
```

This host has two network interfaces: one for regular traffic plus a "backlan" connection. RX packets and TX packets report the number of packets that have been received and transmitted on each interface since the machine was booted. Many different types of errors are counted in the error buckets, and it is normal for a few to show up.

Errors should be less than 1% of the associated packets. If your error rate is high, compare the rates of several neighboring machines. A large number of errors on a single machine suggests a problem with that machine's interface or connection. An error rate that is high everywhere most likely indicates a media or network problem.

Collisions indicate a loaded network; errors often indicate cabling problems. Although a collision is a type of error, it is counted separately by **netstat**. The field labeled Collisions gives the number of collisions that were experienced while packets were being sent.[2] Use this number to calculate the percentage of output packets (TX packets) that result in collisions. On a properly functioning network, collisions should be less than 3% of output packets, and anything over 10% indicates serious congestion problems.

---

2. This field has meaning only on CSMA/CD-based networks such as Ethernet.

You can also run **netstat** with the **-c** flag to continuously report statistics about network interfaces. This mode is especially useful for tracking down the source of errors. **netstat -i** can alert you to the existence of problems, but it can't tell you whether the errors came from a continuous, low-level problem or from a brief but catastrophic event. Observing the network over time under a variety of load conditions will give you a much better impression of what's going on. Try running **ping** with a large ping packet size while you watch the output of **netstat**.

Examining the routing table

netstat -r displays the kernel's routing table. Here is a sample from a machine with two network interfaces:

```
% netstat -r -n
Kernel IP routing table
Destination     Gateway         Genmask       Flags MSS Window irtt Iface
192.168.1.0     0.0.0.0         255.255.255.0 U       0 0         0 eth1
192.168.2.0     0.0.0.0         255.255.255.0 U       0 0         0 eth0
127.0.0.0       0.0.0.0         255.0.0.0     U       0 0         0 lo
0.0.0.0         192.168.1.254   0.0.0.0       UG      0 0         0 eth1
```

Destinations and gateways can be displayed either as hostnames or as IP addresses; the **-n** flag requests numeric output.

See page 260 for more information about the routing table.

The Flags characterize the route: U means up (active), G is a gateway, and H is a host route. The D flag (not shown) indicates a route resulting from an ICMP redirect. G and H together indicate a host route that passes through an intermediate gateway. The remaining fields give statistics on the route: the current number of TCP connections using the route, the number of packets sent, and the interface used. Remember that this output varies slightly among operating systems.

Use this form of **netstat** to check on the health of your machine's routing table. It's particularly important to verify that the system has a default route and that this route is correct. The default route is represented by an all-0 destination address (0.0.0.0).

Viewing operational statistics for various network protocols

netstat -s dumps the contents of counters that are scattered throughout the network code. The output has separate sections for IP, ICMP, TCP, and UDP. Below are pieces of **netstat -s** output from a gateway machine; they have been edited to show only the tastiest pieces of information.

```
ip:
    1396128 total packets received
    0 forwarded
    0 incoming packets discarded
    139221 incoming packets delivered
    1422181 requests sent out

icmp:
    7917 ICMP messages received
    30 input ICMP message failed.
```

```
ICMP input histogram:
    destination unreachable: 3093
    timeout in transit: 64
    source quenchs: 2
    echo requests: 4704
4848 ICMP messages sent
0 ICMP messages failed
ICMP output histogram:
    destination unreachable: 144
    echo replies: 4704
```

The number of echo requests, responses generated, and echo replies all match. Note that "destination unreachable" messages can still be generated even when all packets are apparently forwardable. Bad packets can eventually reach a gateway that rejects them, and error messages are then sent back along the gateway chain.

```
tcp:
    10753 active connections openings
    0 passive connection openings
    106 failed connection attempts
    0 connection resets received
    4 connections established
    1248990 segments received
    1276311 segments send out
    35946 segments retransmited
    13 bad segments received.
    3080 resets sent
```

It's a good idea to develop a feel for the normal ranges of these statistics so that you can recognize pathological states.

20.5 Packet sniffers

tcpdump and Ethereal belong to a class of tools known as packet sniffers. They listen to the traffic on a network and record or print packets that meet certain criteria specified by the user. For example, all packets sent to or from a particular host or TCP packets related to one particular network connection could be inspected.

Packet sniffers are useful both for solving problems you know about and for discovering entirely new problems. It's a good idea to take an occasional sniff of your network to make sure the traffic is in order.

Since packet sniffers need to be able to intercept traffic that the local machine would not normally receive (or at least, pay attention to), the underlying network hardware must allow access to every packet. Broadcast technologies such as Ethernet work fine, as do some types of token ring network on which the sender of a packet removes it from the ring after it has made a complete circuit.

See page 340 for more information about network switches.

Since packet sniffers need to see as much of the raw network traffic as possible, they can be thwarted by network switches, which by design try to limit the propagation of "unnecessary" packets. However, it can still be informative to try out a sniffer on

Network Management

a switched network. You may discover problems related to broadcast or multicast packets. Depending on your switch vendor, you may be surprised at how much traffic you can see.

In addition to having potential access to all network packets, the interface hardware must provide a way to actually transport those packets up to the software layer. Packet addresses are normally checked in hardware, and only broadcast/multicast packets and those addressed to the local host are relayed to the kernel. In "promiscuous mode," an interface lets the kernel read all packets on the network, even the ones intended for other hosts.

Packet sniffers understand many of the packet formats used by standard daemons, and they can often print out these packets in a human-readable form. This capability makes it easier to track the flow of a conversation between two programs. Some sniffers print the ASCII contents of a packet in addition to the packet header, which can be useful for investigating high-layer protocols. Since some of these protocols send information (and even passwords) across the network as cleartext, you must exercise caution to avoid invading the privacy of your users.

Sniffers must read data from a raw network device, so they must run as root. Although the root limitation serves to decrease the chance that normal users will listen in on your network traffic, it is really not much of a barrier. Some sites choose to remove sniffer programs from most hosts to reduce the chance of abuse. If nothing else, you should check your systems' interfaces to be sure they are not running in promiscuous mode without your knowledge or consent. On Linux systems, an interface in promiscuous mode will show the flag PROMISC in its **ifconfig** status output. You can also check your network for interfaces running in promiscuous with tools such as PromiScan (available from www.securityfriday.com).

tcpdump: king of sniffers

tcpdump, yet another amazing network tool by Van Jacobson, is distributed with most Linux distributions. It has long been the industry-standard sniffer; most other network analysis tools read and/or write trace files in "tcpdump format."

By default, **tcpdump** tunes in on the first network interface that it comes across. If it chooses the wrong interface, you can force an interface with the **-i** flag. If DNS is broken or you just don't want **tcpdump** doing name lookups, use the **-n** option. This option is important because slow DNS service can cause the filter to start dropping packets before they can be dealt with by **tcpdump**. The **-v** flag increases the information you see about packets, and **-vv** gives you even more data. Finally, **tcpdump** can store packets to a file with the **-w** flag and can read them back in with the **-r** flag.

For example, the following output comes from the machine jaguar.xor.com. The filter specification **host jaguar** limits the display of packets to those that directly involve the machine jaguar, either as source or as destination.

```
# tcpdump host jaguar
13:40:23 jaguar.xor.com.1697 > xor.com.domain: A? cs.colorado.edu.
13:40:23 xor.com.domain > jaguar.xor.com.1697: A mroe.cs.colorado.edu
13:40:23 jaguar.xor.com.1698 > xor.com.domain: PTR? 5.96.138.128.in-addr.arpa.
13:40:23 xor.com.domain > jaguar.xor.com.1698: PTR mroe.cs.colorado.edu.
```

The first packet shows jaguar sending a DNS lookup request about cs.colorado.edu to xor.com. The response is the actual name of the machine for which that name is an alias, which is mroe.cs.colorado.edu. The third packet is a reverse lookup of mroe's IP address, and the fourth packet contains the expected response.

The **tcpdump** man page contains several good examples of advanced filtering along with a complete listing of primitives.

Ethereal: visual sniffer

If you're more inclined to use a point-and-click program for packet sniffing, then Ethereal may be for you. Available under the GNU General Public License from www.ethereal.com, Ethereal is a GTK+ (GIMP tool kit)-based GUI packet sniffer that has more functionality than most commercial sniffing products. You can run Ethereal on your Linux desktop, or if your laptop is still painfully suffering in the dark ages of Windows, you can download binaries for that too.

In addition to sniffing packets, Ethereal has a couple of features that make it extra handy. One nice feature is that Ethereal can read and write a large number of other packet trace file formats, including (but not limited to):

- **tcpdump**
- NAI's Sniffer™
- Sniffer™ Pro
- NetXray™
- **snoop**
- Shomiti Surveyor
- Microsoft's Network Monitor
- Novell's LANalyzer
- Cisco Secure IDS iplog

The second extra-handy feature is that you can click on one packet in a TCP stream and ask Ethereal to "reassemble" (splice together) the payload data of all the packets in the stream. This feature is useful if you want to quickly examine the data transferred during a complete TCP conversation, such as a connection carrying an email message across the network.[3]

20.6 NETWORK MANAGEMENT PROTOCOLS

Networks have grown rapidly in size and value over the last decade, and along with that growth has come the need for an efficient way to manage them. Commercial

---

3. You can use the **tcpflow** utility to perform a similar feat on the command line from a **tcpdump** trace.

vendors and standards organizations have approached this challenge in many different ways. The most significant developments have been the introduction of several standard device management protocols and a glut of high-level products that exploit those protocols.

Network management protocols provide a standard way of probing a device to discover its configuration, health, and network connections. In addition, they allow some of this information to be modified so that network management can be standardized across different kinds of machinery and performed from a central location.

The most common management protocol used with TCP/IP is the Simple Network Management Protocol, SNMP. Despite its name, SNMP is actually quite complex. It defines a hierarchical namespace of management data and a way to read and write the data at each node. It also defines a way for managed entities ("agents") to send event notification messages ("traps") to management stations. The protocol itself is simple; most of SNMP's complexity lies above the protocol layer in the conventions for constructing the namespace and the conventions for formatting data items within a node. SNMP is widely supported.

Several other standards are floating around out there. Many of them originate from the Distributed Management Task Force (DMTF), which is responsible for concepts such as WBEM (Web-Based Enterprise Management), DMI (Desktop Management Interface), and the CIM (Conceptual Interface Model). Some of these concepts, particularly DMI, have been embraced by several major vendors and may become a useful complement to (or even a replacement for) SNMP. For now, however, the vast majority of network management takes place over SNMP.

Since SNMP is only an abstract protocol, you need both a server program ("agent") and a client ("manager") to make use of it. (Perhaps counterintuitively, the server side of SNMP represents the thing being managed, and the client side is the manager.) Clients range from simple command-line utilities to dedicated management stations that graphically display networks and faults in eye-popping color.

Dedicated network management stations are the primary reason for the existence of management protocols. Most products let you build a topographic model of the network as well as a logical model; the two are presented together on-screen, along with a continuous indication of the status of each component.

Just as a chart can reveal the hidden meaning in a page of numbers, a network management station can summarize the state of a large network in a way that's easily accepted by a human brain. This kind of executive summary is almost impossible to get any other way.

A major advantage of management-by-protocol is that it promotes all kinds of network hardware onto a level playing field. Linux systems are all basically similar, but routers, switches, and other low-level components are not. With SNMP, they all speak a common language and can be probed, reset, and configured from a central location. It's nice to have one consistent interface to all the network's hardware.

20.7 SNMP: THE SIMPLE NETWORK MANAGEMENT PROTOCOL

When SNMP first became widely used in the early 1990s, it started a mini gold rush. Hundreds of companies have come out with SNMP management packages. Also, many hardware and software vendors ship an SNMP agent as part of their product.

Before we dive into the gritty details of SNMP, we should note that the terminology associated with it is some of the most wretched technobabble to be found in the networking arena. The standard names for SNMP concepts and objects will actively lead you away from an understanding of what's going on. The people responsible for this state of affairs should have their keyboards smashed.

SNMP organization

SNMP data is arranged in a standardized hierarchy. This enforced organization allows the data space to remain both universal and extensible, at least in theory. Large portions are set aside for future expansion, and vendor-specific additions are localized to prevent conflicts. The naming hierarchy is made up of "Management Information Bases" (MIBs), structured text files that describe the data accessible through SNMP. MIBs contain descriptions of specific data variables, which are referred to with names known as object identifiers, or OIDs.

Translated into English, this means that SNMP defines a hierarchical namespace of variables whose values are tied to "interesting" parameters of the system.

The basic data types that an SNMP variable can contain are integer, string, and null. These can be combined into sequences of the basic types, and a sequence can be instantiated repeatedly to form a table. Most implementations support a variety of other data types as well.

The SNMP hierarchy is very much like a filesystem. However, a dot is used as the separator character, and each node is given a number rather than a name. By convention, nodes are also given text names for ease of reference, but this naming is really just a high-level convenience and not a feature of the hierarchy (it is similar in principle to the mapping of hostnames to IP addresses).

For example, the OID that refers to the uptime of the system is 1.3.6.1.2.1.1.3. This OID is also known by the human readable name

> iso.org.dod.internet.mgmt.mib-2.system.sysUpTime

The top levels of the SNMP hierarchy are political artifacts and generally do not contain useful data. In fact, useful data can currently be found only beneath the OID iso.org.dod.internet.mgmt (numerically, 1.3.6.1.2).

The basic SNMP MIB for TCP/IP (MIB-I) defines access to common management data: information about the system, its interfaces, address translation, and protocol operations (IP, ICMP, TCP, UDP, and others). A later and more complete reworking of this MIB (called MIB-II) is defined in RFC1213. Most vendors that provide an

SNMP server support MIB-II. Table 20.1 presents a sampling of nodes from the MIB-II namespace.

Table 20.1   Selected OIDs from MIB-II

OID[a]	Type	Contents
system.sysDescr	string	System info: vendor, model, OS type, etc.
system.sysLocation	string	Physical location of the machine
system.sysContact	string	Contact info for the machine's owner
system.sysName	string	System name, usually the full DNS name
interfaces.ifNumber	int	Number of network interfaces present
interfaces.ifTable	table	Table of infobits about each interface
ip.ipForwarding	int	1 if system is a gateway; otherwise, 2
ip.ipAddrTable	table	Table of IP addressing data (masks, etc.)
ip.ipRouteTable	table	The system's routing table
icmp.icmpInRedirects	int	Number of ICMP redirects received
icmp.icmpInEchos	int	Number of pings received
tcp.tcpConnTable	table	Table of current TCP connections
udp.udpTable	table	Table of UDP sockets with servers listening

a. Relative to iso.org.dod.internet.mgmt.mib-2.

In addition to the basic MIB, there are MIBs for various kinds of hardware interfaces and protocols. There are MIBs for individual vendors and MIBs for particular hardware products. A MIB for you, a MIB for me, catch that MIB behind the tree.

A MIB is only a convention about the naming of management data. To be useful, a MIB must be backed up with agent-side code that maps between the SNMP namespace and the device's actual state. Code for the basic MIB (now MIB-II) comes with the standard Linux agent. Some agents are extensible to include supplemental MIBs, and some are not.

SNMP protocol operations

There are only four basic SNMP operations: get, get-next, set, and trap.

Get and set are the basic operations for reading and writing data to a node identified by a specific OID. Get-next is used to step through a MIB hierarchy, as well as to read the contents of tables.

A trap is an unsolicited, asynchronous notification from server (agent) to client (manager) that reports the occurrence of an interesting event or condition. Several standard traps are defined, including "I've just come up" notifications, traps that report the failure or recovery of a network link, and traps for various routing and authentication problems. Many other not-so-standard traps are in common use, including some that simply watch the values of other SNMP variables and fire off a message when a specified range is exceeded. The mechanism by which the destinations of trap messages are specified depends on the implementation of the agent.

Since SNMP messages can potentially modify configuration information, some security mechanism is needed. The simplest version of SNMP security is based on the concept of an SNMP "community name," which is really just a horribly obfuscated way of saying "password." There's usually one community name for read-only access and another that allows writing.

Version 3 of the SNMP standard introduced access control methods with higher security. Although support for these schemes is still somewhat limited in production network hardware, it is reasonable to expect this situation to change soon.

RMON: remote monitoring MIB

The RMON MIB permits the collection of generic network performance data (that is, data not tied to any one particular device). Network sniffers or "probes" can be deployed around the network to gather information about utilization and performance. Once a useful amount of data has been collected, statistics and interesting information about the data can be shipped back to a central management station for analysis and presentation. Many probes have a packet capture buffer and can provide a sort of remote **tcpdump** facility.

RMON is defined in RFC1757, which became a draft standard in 1995. The MIB is broken up into nine "RMON groups." Each group contains a different set of network statistics. If you have a large network with many WAN connections, you should consider buying probes to reduce the SNMP traffic across your WAN links. Once you have access to statistical summaries from the RMON probes, there's usually no need to gather raw data remotely. Many switches and routers support RMON and will store at least some network statistics.

20.8 THE NET-SMNP AGENT

When SNMP was first standardized, Carnegie Mellon University and MIT both produced implementations. CMU's implementation was more complete and quickly became the de facto standard. When active development at CMU died down, researchers at UC Davis took over the software. After stabilizing the code, they transferred the ongoing maintenance to the SourceForge repository. The package is now known as NET-SNMP.

The NET-SNMP distribution is now the authoritative free SNMP implementation for Linux. It includes an SNMP agent, some command-line tools, and even a library for developing SNMP-aware applications. We discuss the agent in some detail here, and on page 645 we take a look at the command-line tools. The latest version is available from the web at net-snmp.sourceforge.net.

As in other implementations, the agent collects information about the local host and serves it to SNMP managers across the network. The default installation includes

MIBs for network interface, memory, disk, process, and CPU statistics. The agent is easily extensible since it can execute an arbitrary Linux command and return the command's output as an SNMP response. You can use this feature to monitor almost anything on your system with SNMP.

By default, the agent is installed as **/usr/sbin/snmpd**. It is usually started at boot time and reads its configuration information from files in the **/etc/snmp** directory. The most important of these files is **snmpd.conf**, which contains most of the configuration information and comes with a bunch of sample data collection methods enabled. Although the intention of the NET-SNMP authors seems to have been for users to edit only the **snmpd.local.conf** file, you must edit the **snmpd.conf** file at least once to disable any default data collection methods that you don't plan to use.

The NET-SNMP **configure** script lets you specify a default log file and a couple of other local settings. You can use **snmpd -l** to specify an alternate log file or **-s** to direct log messages to syslog. Table 20.2 shows a list of **snmpd**'s most important flags. We recommend that you always use the **-a** flag. For debugging, you should use the **-V**, **-d**, or **-D** flags, each of which gives progressively more information.

Table 20.2   Useful flags for NET-SNMP snmpd

Flag	Function
-l *logfile*	Logs information to *logfile*
-a	Logs the addresses of all SNMP connections
-d	Logs the contents of every SNMP packet
-V	Enables verbose logging
-D	Logs debugging information (lots of it)
-h	Displays all arguments to **snmpd**
-H	Displays all configuration file directives
-A	Appends to the log file instead of overwriting it
-s	Logs to syslog (uses the daemon facility)

It's worth mentioning that many useful SNMP-related Perl modules are available. Look on CPAN[4] for the latest information if you are interested in writing your own network management scripts.

20.9 NETWORK MANAGEMENT APPLICATIONS

We begin this section by exploring the simplest SNMP management tools: the commands provided with the NET-SNMP package. These commands are useful for familiarization with SNMP, and they're also great for one-off checks of specific OIDs. Next, we look at MRTG, a program that generates historical graphs of SNMP values,

---

4. CPAN, the Comprehensive Perl Archive Network, is an amazing collection of useful Perl modules. Check it out at www.cpan.org.

and NOCOL, an event-based monitoring system. We conclude with some recommendations of what to look for when purchasing a commercial system.

The NET-SNMP tools

Even if your system comes with its own SNMP server, you may still want to compile and install the client-side tools, listed in Table 20.3, from the NET-SNMP package.

Table 20.3   Command-line tools in the NET-SNMP package

Command	Function
snmpdelta	Monitors changes in SNMP variables over time
snmpdf	Monitors disk space on a remote host via SNMP
snmpget	Gets the value of an SNMP variable from an agent
snmpgetnext	Gets the next variable in sequence
snmpset	Sets an SNMP variable on an agent
snmptable	Gets a table of SNMP variables
snmptranslate	Searches for and describes OIDs in the MIB hierarchy
snmptrap	Generates a trap alert
snmpwalk	Traverses a MIB starting at a particular OID

In addition to their value on the command line, these programs are tremendously handy in simple scripts. It is often helpful to have **snmpget** save interesting data values to a text file every few minutes. (Use **cron** to implement the scheduling; see Chapter 9, *Periodic Processes*.)

snmpwalk is another useful tool. Starting at a specified OID (or at the beginning of the MIB, by default), this command repeatedly makes "get next" calls to an agent. This behavior results in a complete list of available OIDs and their associated values. Here's a sample **snmpwalk** of the host jaguar ("public" is the community string):

```
% snmpwalk jaguar public
system.sysDescr.0 = Linux jaguar 2.2.12-20 #1 Mon Sep 27 10:40:35 EDT 1999
system.sysUpTime.0 = Timeticks: (88516617) 10 days, 5:52:46.17
system.sysName.0 = jaguar
system.sysLocation.0 = Second Floor Machine Room
interfaces.ifNumber.0 = 2
interfaces.ifTable.ifEntry.ifIndex.1 = 1
interfaces.ifTable.ifEntry.ifIndex.2 = 2
interfaces.ifTable.ifEntry.ifDescr.1 = "lo0" Hex: 6C 6F 30
interfaces.ifTable.ifEntry.ifDescr.2 = "eth0" Hex: 65 74 68 30
interfaces.ifTable.ifEntry.ifType.1 = softwareLoopback(24)
interfaces.ifTable.ifEntry.ifType.2 = ethernet-csmacd(6)
interfaces.ifTable.ifEntry.ifMtu.1 = 3924
interfaces.ifTable.ifEntry.ifMtu.2 = 1500
interfaces.ifTable.ifEntry.ifInOctets.1 = 12590602
interfaces.ifTable.ifEntry.ifInOctets.2 = 2287718531
interfaces.ifTable.ifEntry.ifInErrors.1 = 0
```

```
interfaces.ifTable.ifEntry.ifInErrors.2 = 218
interfaces.ifTable.ifEntry.ifOutOctets.1 = 12591593
interfaces.ifTable.ifEntry.ifOutOctets.2 = 3374588125
...
```

In this example, we see some general information about the system, followed by statistics about the host's network interfaces, lo0 and eth0. Depending on the MIBs supported by the agent you are managing, a complete dump can run to hundreds of lines.

MRTG: the Multi-Router Traffic Grapher

MRTG, written by Tobi Oetiker at ETH in Zurich, collects SNMP data over time and then graphs it. It's written mostly in Perl. MRTG is invaluable for analyzing the historical use of system and network resources.

MRTG runs regularly from **cron** and can collect data from any SNMP source. Each time the program runs, new data is stored and new graph images are created.

MRTG is free and offers several attractive features. First, it maintains a zero-maintenance, statically sized database; the software stores only enough data to create the necessary graphs. For example, MRTG could store one sample every minute for a day, one sample every hour for a week, and one sample every week for a year. This consolidation scheme lets you maintain important historical information without having to store unimportant details or to consume your time with database administration.

Second, MRTG can record and graph any SNMP variable. You're free to collect whatever data you want. When combined with the NET-SNMP agent, MRTG can provide a historical perspective on almost any system or network resource.

Exhibit A shows some examples of the graphs created by MRTG. These graphs show the traffic on a network interface over periods of a day and a week.

The future of MRTG lies in a new package, RRDtool, by the same author. RRDtool is similar in concept to MRTG, but with improved data consolidation and graphing features. Unlike MRTG, RRDtool does not offer any data collection methods of its own. Instead, a separate piece of software must collect the data.

Currently, Jeff Allen's Cricket tool is the best choice for this role. Cricket is not limited to collecting SNMP data; it can pull in data from almost any network source. Since it is written in Perl, you can easily add new data sources.

Tobi Oetiker's home page at ee-staff.ethz.ch/~oetiker provides links to the current versions of MRTG, RRDtool, and Cricket.

NOCOL: Network Operation Center On-Line

NOCOL is an event-driven management tool that's currently maintained by Vikas Aggarwal. Although it will not help you determine how much your bandwidth utilization has increased over the last month, it will page you when your web server goes down. Actually, NOCOL can be configured to page (or email) your operations staff after many kinds of events.

Exhibit A   Examples of MRTG graphs

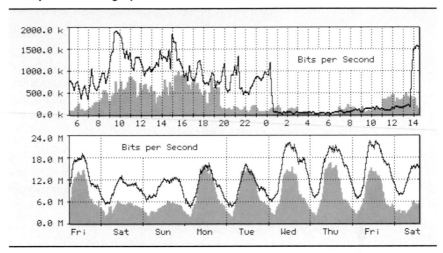

The distribution includes monitor programs that supervise a variety of common points of failure. You can whip up new monitors in Perl, or even in C if you are feeling ambitious. For notification methods, the distribution can send email, generate web reports, view status with a **curses** interface, and use a dial-up modem to page you. As with monitor programs, it's easy to roll your own.

If you cannot afford a commercial network management tool, we suggest giving strong consideration to NOCOL. The software works very well for networks of fewer than 100 hosts and devices. You can read more at www.netplex-tech.com.

Commercial management platforms

Hundreds of companies sell network management software, and new competitors enter the market every week. Instead of recommending the hottest products of the moment (which may no longer exist by the time this book is printed), we'll try to identify the features you should look for in a network management system.

Data gathering flexibility: It's important for management tools to be able to collect data from sources other than SNMP. Many packages include the ability to gather data from almost any network service. For example, some packages can make SQL database queries, check DNS records, and connect to web servers.

User interface quality: Expensive systems often offer a custom GUI or a web interface. Most well-marketed packages today tout the ability to understand XML templates for data presentation. Although the UI often seems like just more marketing hype, it is important to have an interface that relays information clearly, simply, and comprehensibly.

Value: Some management packages come at a stiff price. HP's OpenView is both one of the most expensive and one of the most widely adopted network management systems. For many corporations, there is a definite value in being able to say that their site is managed by a high-end commercial system. If that isn't so important to your organization, you should look at the other end of the spectrum for free tools like MRTG and NOCOL.

Automated discovery: Many systems offer the ability to "discover" your network. Through a combination of broadcast pings, SNMP requests, ARP table lookups, and DNS queries, they are able to identify all your local hosts and devices. All the discovery implementations we have seen work pretty well, but none are very accurate on a complex (or heavily firewalled) network.

Reporting features: Many products can send alert email, activate pagers, and automatically generate tickets for popular trouble-tracking systems. Make sure that the platform you choose allows for flexible reporting; who knows what electronic devices you will be dealing with in a few years?

Configuration management: Some vendors step far beyond monitoring and alerting. They offer the ability to manage actual host and device configurations. For example, CiscoWorks provides an interface that lets you change a router's configuration in addition to monitoring its state with SNMP. Because device configuration information allows for a deeper analysis of network problems, we predict that many packages will develop along these lines in the future.

20.10 RECOMMENDED READING

CISCO ONLINE. *Internetworking Technology Overview: SNMP.* http://www.cisco.com/univercd/cc/td/doc/cisintwk/ito_doc/snmp.htm.

HUNT, CRAIG, AND GIGI ESTABROOK. *TCP/IP Network Administration, Second Edition.* Sebastopol: O'Reilly & Associates. 1998.

STALLINGS, WILLIAM. *Snmp, Snmpv2, Snmpv3, and Rmon 1 and 2, Third Edition.* Reading, MA: Addison-Wesley. 1999.

You may find the following RFCs to be useful as well. Instead of citing the actual titles of the RFCs, we have described their contents. The actual titles are an unhelpful jumble of buzzwords and SNMP jargon.

- RFC1155 – Characteristics of the SNMP data space (data types, etc.)
- RFC1156 – MIB-I definitions (description of the actual OIDs)
- RFC1157 – Simple Network Management Protocol
- RFC1213 – MIB-II definitions (OIDs)
- RFCs 1901-1910 – SNMPv2
- RFC2011 – SNMPv2 MIB for IP
- RFC2012 – SNMPv2 MIB for TCP
- RFC2013 – SNMPv2 MIB for UDP
- RFC2021 – RMON Version 2 using SMIv2
- RFC2570 – Introduction to SNMPv3

20.11 EXERCISES

E20.1 You are troubleshooting a network problem and **netstat -rn** gives you the following output. What is the problem and what command would you use to fix it?

Destination	Gateway	Genmask	Flags	MSS	Window	irtt	Iface
128.138.202.0	0.0.0.0	255.255.255.0	U	40	0	0	eth0
127.0.0.0	0.0.0.0	255.0.0.0	U	40	0	0	lo

⋆ **E20.2** Write a script that monitors a given set of machines and notifies an administrator by email if a machine becomes unresponsive to pings for some set amount of time. Don't hardcode the list of machines, the notification email address, or the amount of time used to determine unresponsive behavior.

⋆ **E20.3** Experiment with changing the netmask on a machine on your local network. Does it still work? Can you reach everything at your site? Can other machines reach you? Do broadcasts work (e.g., ARP requests or DHCP discover packets)? Explain your findings. (Requires root access.)

⋆ **E20.4** Use the **traceroute** command to discover routing paths on your network.

a) How many hops does it take to leave your facility?
b) Are there any routers between machines that you have accounts on?
c) Can you find any bottlenecks?
d) Is your site multihomed?

⋆⋆ **E20.5** Design a MIB that includes all the variables you might want to query or set as a Linux sysadmin. Leave ways for the MIB to be extended to include that important new sysadmin variable you forgot.

⋆⋆ **E20.6** Use the **tcpdump** command to capture traffic that illustrates the following protocols. For TCP sessions, include and indicate the initial and final packets. Submit clean, well formatted **tcpdump** output. (Requires root access.)

a) ARP
b) ICMP echo request and reply
c) SMTP
d) FTP and FTP-DATA
e) DNS (called domain)
f) NFS

⋆⋆ **E20.7** Set up MRTG graphs that show the packets transmitted to and from a local router. This project requires an SNMP package to query the router; you must know the read-only community string for the router.

21 *Security*

In 1988, the world of computer and network technology entered a new era when the Robert Morris, Jr., "Internet Worm" was unleashed on mankind. Before that event, the Internet (and computing in general) lived in an "age of innocence." Security was a topic that administrators thought about mostly in the "what if" sense. A big security incident usually consisted of something like a user gaining administrative access to read another user's mail, often just to prove that he could.

In reality, the Morris worm caused little actual damage and greatly increased security awareness on the Internet. Once again, we were painfully reminded that good fences make good neighbors. A number of excellent tools for use by system administrators (as well as a formal organization for handling incidents of this nature) came into being as a result.

Unfortunately, as evidenced by the recent CSI/FBI Computer Crime Survey (April 2001), 91% of organizations have reported security breaches in the past 12 months. It's interesting to note that this alarming statistic isn't due to a complete lack of installed security technology, since at least 95% of the survey respondents reported using tools such as commercially available firewalls. This data at least teaches us that firewalls are not by themselves an adequate protection against intruders.

In general, security is not something that you can buy in a box or as a service from some third party. Commercial products and services can be part of a solution for your site, but they are not a panacea. Achieving an acceptable level of security at your site requires an enormous amount of patience, vigilance, knowledge, and persistence—not only from you and other administrators, but from your entire user and management communities as well. As the system administrator, you must personally take responsibility for ensuring that your systems are secure and that you and your users are properly educated. You should ensure that you are familiar with current security technology, actively monitor security mailing lists, and hire professional security experts to help when the problems exceed your knowledge.

21.1 IS LINUX SECURE?

Nope. Linux is not secure. Nor is any other operating system that communicates on a network. If you really must have absolute, total, unbreachable security, then you need a measurable air gap[1] between your computer and any other device (and arguably, you probably also need to enclose your computer in a special room that blocks electromagnetic radiation as designed by retired Soviet intelligence operatives). How fun is that?

There are some steps you can take to make your system somewhat more resistant to attack. Even so, several fundamental flaws in the Linux model ensure that you will never reach security nirvana:

- Like UNIX, Linux is optimized for convenience and doesn't make security easy or natural. The Linux philosophy stresses easy manipulation of data in a networked, multiuser environment.

- Linux security is effectively binary: you are either a powerless user, or you're root. Linux facilities such as setuid execution tend to confer total power all at once. Slight lapses in security can compromise entire systems.

- Linux is developed by a large community of programmers. They range in experience level, attention to detail, and knowledge about the Linux system and its interdependencies. As a result, even the most well-intended or cool new features may introduce gaping security holes. On the other hand, since Linux source code is available to everyone, thousands of people can scrutinize each line of code for a possible security threat. This arrangement is widely believed to result in significantly better security than that of closed operating systems, where a limited number of people have the opportunity to carefully examine the code for holes.

Many known security holes in Linux will never be fixed, and others have been fixed in some versions but not in all. In addition, many sites are a release or two behind, either because localization is too troublesome or because they do not subscribe to a vendor's software maintenance plan. When a fix for a security hole is made available, the window of opportunity for hackers does not disappear overnight.

It might seem that Linux security should gradually improve over time as security problems are discovered and corrected, but unfortunately this does not seem to be

Security

---

1. Of course, the advent of wireless networking technology introduces a whole new set of problems. Air gap in this context means "no networking whatsoever."

the case. System software is growing ever more complicated, hackers are becoming better and better organized, and computers are connecting more and more intimately on the Internet. Security is an ongoing battle that can never really be won.

Remember, too, that

$$\text{Security} \;=\; \frac{1}{(1.072)(\text{Convenience})}$$

The more secure your system, the more miserable you and your users will tend to be.

21.2 LINUX SECURITY, THE CLIFFSNOTES VERSION

This chapter discusses a wide variety of security concerns. Ideally, you should address all of them within your environment. If you're short on time or patience, however, here are the six all-around most important security issues to consider, plus some bonus rules to live by. (Most administrators should really digest the contents of this entire chapter, probably more than once.)

Packet filtering

If you're connecting a Linux system to a network with Internet access, you *must* have a packet filtering router or firewall between the Linux system and the outside world. As an alternative, you can configure packet filtering by using **iptables** on the Linux system itself (discussed starting on page 679). Whatever the implementation, the packet filter should only pass traffic destined for essential services that you specifically want to provide from the Linux system.

Unnecessary services

Various versions of Linux differ widely on what network services are turned on as part of the default installation. It's up to you to examine the services that are enabled on your system and turn off any that aren't absolutely necessary. Examining the contents of **/etc/inetd.conf** (or, on Red Hat, the files in **/etc/xinetd.d**) should be your first step.

Software patches

All of the major Linux distributors regularly release security-related software packages, usually a couple of times every month. You *must* vigilantly watch for patches relevant to your version of Linux (and any software packages you're running) and install them immediately. Keep in mind that once a patch is available, the "bad guys" have known about the hole for weeks, and it may already be too late.

Backups

Put down that RAID array and back away from the data center, cowboy. You *must* perform regular backups of all your systems so that you can recover effectively from a security incident, if one should occur. No amount of mirroring, RAID, or "hot standby" technology eliminates the need for backups. Information on performing backups is provided in Chapter 10.

Passwords

We're simple people with simple rules. Here's one: every account *must* have a password, and it needs to be something that can't easily be guessed. Sadly, it's no longer secure to send plaintext reusable passwords across the Internet, so if you allow remote logins to your system, you must use SSH or some other fancy authentication system (discussed starting on page 673).

Vigilance

To ensure the security of your system, you must monitor its health, network connections, process table, and overall status regularly (usually, daily). Security problems tend to start small and grow quickly, so the earlier you identify an anomaly the better off you'll be.

General philosophy

Effective system security has its roots in common sense and is a lot like dealing with an infestation of mice in your house. Here are some rules you might use:

- Don't leave things that are likely to be interesting to mice lying on the kitchen table overnight. Cheese and peanut butter are excellent mouse getters.

- Don't provide places within the house for mice to build nests. Piles of dirty clothes on the floor make good nests.

- Set traps along walls where you often see mice out of the corner of your eye.

- Check the traps daily to rebait them and to dispose of squashed mice. Full traps don't catch mice, and they smell.

- Avoid using commercial bait-and-kill poisons to deal with the situation. These can leave you with dead mice in your walls or kill your dog. Traditional snap traps are best.

- Get a cat!

You can use these same rules (well, slightly modified) to secure your Linux systems. Here's how you might rewrite them:

- Don't put files on your system that are likely to be interesting to hackers or to nosy employees. Trade secrets, personnel files, payroll data, election results, etc., must be handled carefully if they're on-line. Securing such information cryptographically will provide a far higher degree of security than simply trying to prevent unauthorized users from accessing the files that contain the juicy tidbits.

  Your site's security policy should specify how sensitive information is handled. See Chapter 29, *Policy and Politics*, and RFC2196 (the *Site Security Handbook*) for some suggestions.

Security

- Don't provide places for hackers to build nests on your system. Hackers often break into one system and then use it as a base of operations to get into others. World-writable anonymous FTP directories, group accounts, and accounts with poorly chosen passwords all encourage nesting activity.

- Set traps to detect intrusions and attempted intrusions. Tools such as **trip-wire**, **tcpd**, and **crack** (described starting on page 664) will help keep you abreast of potential problems.

- Monitor the reports generated by these security tools. A minor problem that is ignored in one report may grow into a catastrophe by the time the next report is sent.

- Teach yourself about Linux system security. Traditional know-how, user education and common sense are the most important parts of a site security plan. Bring in outside experts to help fill in gaps, but only under your close supervision and approval.

- Prowl around looking for unusual activity. Investigate anything that seems unusual, such as odd log messages or changes in the activity of an account (more activity, activity at strange hours, or perhaps activity while the owner is on vacation).

21.3 How security is compromised

The sections below discuss some common Linux security problems and their standard countermeasures. But before we leap into the details, we should take a more general look at how real-world security problems tend to occur. Most security lapses stem from one of the following types of problems:

- **Unreliable wetware:** The human users (and administrators) of a computer system are often the weakest links in the chain of security. For example, America Online used to be notorious for being infested by hackers who posed as AOL employees. The hackers sent email to potential victims asking them to send back their passwords as part of a "system test" or "to verify your account." Unsophisticated users often didn't (and still don't) know any better than to comply.

  There are countless variations on this ploy. As an administrator, part of your job includes teaching users about proper security hygiene. Many users are still new to the Internet, and they often have no idea how many scams and freaks are afoot. Tell them how to select and defend good passwords, how to protect their work, and how not to talk to strangers. Make sure your instructions cover non-email communication, too; a telephone can be a hacker's best friend.

- **Software bugs:** Over the years, countless security-sapping bugs have been discovered in Linux software (including software from third parties, both commercial and free). By exploiting subtle programming errors or context dependencies, hackers have been able to manipulate Linux into doing whatever they want. What can you as an administrator do to prevent this? Very little, at least until a bug has been identified and addressed in a patch. Keeping up with patches and security bulletins is an important part of most administrators' jobs.

- **Open doors:** Many pieces of software can be configured securely or not-so-securely. Unfortunately, not-so-securely is often the default. Hackers frequently gain access by exploiting software features that would be considered helpful and convenient in less treacherous circumstances: accounts without passwords, disks shared with the world, and remote logins equivalenced among machines, to name a few. One of the most important parts of securing a system is just making sure that you haven't inadvertently put out a welcome mat for hackers.

Problems in the last of these categories are the easiest to find and fix, although there are potentially a lot of them and it's not always obvious what to check for.

21.4   SECURITY PROBLEMS IN THE /ETC/PASSWD AND /ETC/SHADOW FILES

See page 81 for more information about the ***passwd****file.*

Poor password management is a common security weakness. The contents of the **/etc/passwd** and **/etc/shadow** files determine who can log in and what they can do once they get inside. These files are the system's first line of defense against intruders. They must be scrupulously maintained and free of errors, security hazards, and historical baggage.

Password checking and selection

It is important to continually verify (preferably daily) that every login has a password. Entries in the **/etc/shadow** file (or **/etc/passwd** file if your site does not use shadow passwords) that describe pseudo-users such as "daemon" who own files but never log in should have a star (*) in their encrypted password field. The star will not match any password and will thus prevent use of the account.

Several specialized software packages exist to check **/etc/shadow** for security problems, but the command[2]

```
perl -F: -ane 'print if not $F[1];' /etc/shadow
```

suffices just as well for finding null passwords. A script that performs this check and mails you the results can be run out of **cron**. You can add extra security by writing a script that **diff**s the **passwd** file against a version from the previous day and emails any differences to you. You can then verify that any modifications are legitimate.

/etc/passwd and **/etc/group** must be readable by the world but writable only by root. If your system has an **/etc/shadow** file, the world should have no access to it.

---

2. This command requires Perl 5 or higher.

Security

Linux allows users to choose their own passwords, and although this is a great convenience, it leads to many security problems. When you give users their logins, you should also provide them with instructions for choosing a good password. Tell them not to use their name or initials, the name of a child or spouse, or any word that can be found in a dictionary. Passwords derived from personal data such as telephone numbers or addresses are also easily broken.

Passwords should be at least eight characters long and should include numbers, punctuation, or changes in case. Nonsense words, combinations of simple words, or the first letters of words in a memorable phrase make the best passwords. Of course, "memorable" is good but "traditional" is risky. Make up your own phrase. The comments in the section *Choosing a root password* on page 41 are equally applicable to user passwords.

On a few systems (depending on the authentication libraries you're using), only the first eight characters of a password are significant. More can be entered, but characters beyond the first eight will be silently ignored. See page 83 for details.

PAM: cooking spray or authentication wonder?

Pluggable Authentication Modules, aka PAM, was originally invented by Sun as a flexible way to authenticate users. For many years, authentication in the UNIX environment was as simple as associating users with their entry in the **/etc/passwd** file. Lately, the need for stronger security and support for a wider variety of authentication mechanisms (like smart cards) has created a need for a more flexible approach.

Linux-PAM is shipped with Red Hat, SuSE, and Debian and is unrelated to Sun's current implementation of the PAM standard. The concept is simple: programs that require authentication only need to know that there is a module available that will perform the authentication for them. PAM is set up so that modules can be added, deleted, and reconfigured at any time—it is not necessary for modules to be linked in (or even exist) at the time a utility is compiled. As a result of this architecture, PAM has become an incredibly powerful tool for system administrators.

PAM modules are configured through files in the **/etc/pam.d** directory. Per-service files in this directory contain entries of the form

> *module-type control-flag module-path arguments*

The *module-type* field can have the values auth, account, session, or password. An auth entry establishes who the user is and possibly grants group membership. The account tag performs non-authentication-based decisions, such as access based on time of day. Tasks that need to be performed before or after a user is given service are implemented with the session tag. Finally, the password tag is used when authentication information (such as a password) is requested from the user.

The *control-flag* field has four possible values: required, requisite, sufficient, and optional. required and optional are most commonly used, indicating that a module must succeed in order for execution to continue, or that it doesn't matter if the module succeeds or not, respectively.

The third and fourth fields are the pathname and the arguments for the dynamically loadable module object. If the first character of the path is **/**, it is assumed to be an absolute path. Otherwise, the contents of the field are appended to the default path, **/lib/security**.

*See page 667 for more information about **crack**.*

For example, additions to **/etc/pam.d/passwd** to enable the **passwd** program to perform strong password checking by using a PAM module derived from the **crack** library might look like this:

```
password required pam_cracklib.so retry=3
password required pam_pwdb.so use_authtok
```

With these lines in place, PAM will check users' proposed new passwords against a **crack** dictionary and ruleset. (This setup requires the presence of the system library **libcrack** and also a system dictionary, **/usr/lib/cracklib_dict**.) The retry=3 argument specifies that the user will be given three tries at entering a strong password. The line with use_authtok connects the layers of the password module together.

Dozens of PAM modules are available. You can download specialized modules and their documentation from www.kernel.org/pub/linux/libs/pam.

Shadow passwords

See page 667 for more information about password guessing.

Traditionally, each line in **/etc/passwd** consists of seven fields. The second field contains a string that represents the user's encrypted password. Since **/etc/passwd** must be world-readable for commands like **ls** to work, the encrypted password string is available to all users on the system. Evildoers can encrypt selected dictionaries or words and compare the results with the strings in **/etc/passwd**. If the encrypted strings match, a password has been found.

How much of a threat is this? In the 80s, there was at least one way to decrypt passwords posthaste,[3] but run-of-the-mill hackers had to be content with using the **crypt** library routine[4] to encrypt dictionary words for comparison. A "fast" machine in the 80s could do a few hundred encryptions a second. In 1998, John Gilmore of the Electronic Frontier Foundation and cryptographer Paul Kocher cracked a 56-bit DES key in 56 hours, using a brute force search. Recent proposals suggest that a $1 million special-purpose computer could crack any 56-bit DES key in just a few hours.

These results are frightening, and they suggest that user access to encrypted password strings really ought to be restricted. The standard way to impose restrictions is to put passwords in a separate file that is readable only by root, leaving the rest of

---

3. Evi Nemeth broke the Diffie-Hellman key exchange often used with DES in 1984, using a HEP supercomputer. Although DES is thought to be mathematically secure, the short key lengths in common use offer relatively little security.

4. Don't confuse the **crypt** library routine with the **crypt** command, which uses a different and less secure encryption scheme.

Security

/etc/passwd intact. The file that contains the actual password information is then called the shadow password file, **/etc/shadow**. Most Linux distributions use shadow passwords in their default configuration, and those that don't, should.

Group logins and shared logins

Any login that is used by more than one person is bad news. Group logins (such as "guest" or "demo") are sure terrain for hackers to homestead. Don't allow them at your site.

See page 832 for some additional comments on shared logins.

Likewise, don't allow users to share logins with family or friends. If little Johnny needs a login to work on his science project, give him one with that stated purpose. It's much easier to take away Johnny's login when he abuses it than to get rid of Dad and his account, especially at government sites.

At most sites, "root" is a group login. Dangerous! We recommend using the **sudo** program to control access to rootly powers. See page 43.

Password aging

The Linux shadow password system also allows you to compel users to change their passwords periodically, through a facility known as password aging. This may seem like a good idea at first glance, but it has several problems. Users often become resentful at having to change their passwords, and since they don't want to forget the new password, they choose something simple that is easy to type and remember. Many users switch between two passwords each time they are forced to change, defeating the purpose of password aging.

*See page 43 for more information about **sudo**.*

Nevertheless, passwords should be changed regularly, especially the root password. A root password should roll easily off the fingers so that it can be typed quickly and cannot be guessed by someone watching the movement of fingers on the keyboard. At our site most people use **sudo** rather than the real root password, but we select the root password carefully all the same.

User shells

Do not use a script as the shell for an unrestricted (passwordless) login. Password-less logins should be used only as a facility for running small, noninteractive utilities such as **date**, **sync**, or **lpq**.

Rootly entries

The only distinguishing feature of the root login is its UID of zero. Since there can be more than one entry in the **/etc/passwd** file that uses this UID, there can be more than one way to log in as root.

A common way for hackers to install a back door once they have obtained a root shell is to edit new root logins into **/etc/passwd**. Programs like **who** and **w** refer to the name stored in **/var/run/utmp** rather than the UID that owns the login shell, so they cannot expose hackers that appear to be innocent users but are really logged in as UID 0.

The defense against this subterfuge is a mini-script similar to the one used for finding logins without passwords:[5]

```
perl -F: -ane 'print if not $F[2];' /etc/passwd
```

This script prints out any lines in the **passwd** file that have null or 0 UIDs. You could easily adapt it to find entries with suspicious groups or UIDs that are the same as those of key people within your organization.

You should also check for **passwd** entries that have no username or that have punctuation as a username. These entries may seem nonsensical, but they will often allow a hacker to log in.

21.5 SETUID PROGRAMS

Programs that run setuid, especially ones that run setuid to root, are prone to security problems. The setuid commands distributed with Linux are theoretically secure; however, security holes have been discovered in the past and will undoubtedly be discovered in the future.

The surest way to minimize the number of setuid *problems* is to minimize the number of setuid *programs*. Think twice before installing a software package that needs to run setuid, and avoid using the setuid facility in your own home-grown software.

Setuid shell scripts are especially apt to cause security problems. Under at least one common shell, they are automatically and entirely insecure. Shells tend to be highly customizable, which makes them relatively easy to trick. Although a shell spawned to execute a script doesn't necessarily read the user's shell configuration files, it can be influenced by the user's environment, by the contents of the current directory, or by the manner in which the script is invoked.

There's no rule that says setuid programs must run as root. If all you need to do is restrict access to a particular file or database, you can add a pseudo-user to the **passwd** file whose only reason for existence is to own the restricted resources. Follow the normal pseudo-user conventions: use a low UID, put a star in the password field, and make the pseudo-user's home directory be **/dev/null**.

You can disable setuid and setgid execution on individual filesystems through use of the **-o nosuid** option to **mount**. It's a good idea to use this option on filesystems that contain users' home directories or that are mounted from less trustworthy administrative domains.

It's useful to scan your disks periodically to look for new setuid programs. A hacker who has breached the security of your system will sometimes create a private setuid

---

5. This command requires Perl 5 or higher.

shell or utility to facilitate repeat visits. Some of the tools discussed starting on page 664 will locate such files, but you can do just as well with **find**. For example,

```
/usr/bin/find / -user root -perm -4000 -print |
    /bin/mail -s "Setuid root files" netadmin
```

will mail a list of all setuid root files to the "netadmin" user.

21.6 IMPORTANT FILE PERMISSIONS

Many files on a Linux system must have particular permissions if security problems are to be avoided. Some distributors ship software with permissions set for their own "friendly" development environment. These permissions may not be appropriate for you.

The device file **/dev/kmem** allows access to the kernel's own virtual address space. It is used by programs such as **ps** that need to look at kernel data structures. This file should only be readable by the owner and group, never by the world. Programs that need to access this file should be setgid to the group that owns the file, usually kmem.

In the past, some systems have been carelessly distributed with **/dev/kmem** publicly readable. This is a major security problem because a competent programmer can then look for things like unencrypted passwords in the kernel data structures and buffers. If your system has **/dev/kmem** publicly readable, change that immediately. If the change causes any programs to stop working, make those programs setgid to the group that owns **/dev/kmem**.

/etc/passwd and **/etc/group** should not be world-writable. They should have owner root and mode 644. **/etc/shadow** should have mode 640—no permissions for the world. The group of all these files should be set to some system group, usually root. The **passwd** command runs setuid to root so that users can change their passwords without having write permission on **/etc/passwd** or **/etc/shadow**.

See page 704 for information about setting up a secure FTP server.

Directories that are accessible through anonymous FTP should not be publicly writable. Such directories create a nest for hackers to distribute illegally copied software and other sensitive files. If you manage an FTP archive that allows submissions, be sure to screen the submissions directory regularly.

Setting up anonymous FTP usually involves copying a skeleton password file into **~ftp/etc/passwd** so that **ls** will work correctly. Make sure to remove the encrypted password strings.

Device files for hard disk partitions are another potential source of problems. Having read or write permission on a disk device file is essentially the same as having read or write permission on every file in the filesystem it represents. Only root should have both read and write permission. The group owner is sometimes given read permission to facilitate backups, but there should be no permissions for the world.

21.7 Miscellaneous security issues

The sections below present some miscellaneous security-related topics. Most are either features that are useful to you as an administrator or misfeatures that can provide nesting material for hackers if not kept in check.

Remote event logging

See Chapter 11 for more information about syslog.

The syslog facility allows log information for both the kernel and user processes to be forwarded to a file, a list of users, or another host on your network. Consider setting up a secure host that acts as a central logging machine and prints out security violations (the auth facility) on an old line printer. This precaution prevents hackers from covering their tracks by rewriting or erasing log files.

Secure terminals

Linux can be configured to restrict root logins to specific "secure" terminals. It's a good idea to disable root logins on channels such as dial-up modems. Often, network pseudo-terminals are also set to disallow root logins.

The secure channels are specified as a list of TTY devices in the configuration file **/etc/securetty**. It's also possible to restrict nonroot logins to particular locations with entries in the file **/etc/security/access.conf** or to particular times with entries in the file **/etc/security/time.conf**.

/etc/hosts.equiv and ~/.rhosts

The **hosts.equiv** and **~/.rhosts** files define hosts as being administratively "equivalent" to one another, allowing users to log in (with **rlogin**) and copy files (with **rcp**) between machines without typing their passwords.[6] Use of this facility was once common during the party days of UNIX, but everyone eventually woke up with a nasty headache and realized that it wasn't such a good idea.

We recommend that **rshd** and **rlogind**, the server processes that read **.rhosts** and **hosts.equiv**, be disabled. These days, **telnetd** should be disabled as well. On most systems, you disable these servers by commenting them out of **/etc/inetd.conf** (or, on Red Hat, disabling them in the **/etc/xinetd.d** files). Once the server daemons have been disabled, the host will no longer be reachable by **telnet**, **rlogin**, **rsh**, or **rcp**. However, the functionality of these commands can be replaced with higher-security equivalents such as SSH; see page 673.

Some of the replacements for **rlogin** (including SSH!) pay attention to **.rhosts** and **/etc/hosts.equiv** if they are not configured properly. For added safety, you can create the **/etc/hosts.equiv** file and a **~/.rhosts** file for each user (including root) as an unwritable, zero-length file. It's easier to assess what the state of a file was at 3:00 a.m. if it exists and is untouched than to assess the state of a nonexistent file. This distinc-

---

6. These files are also used by the printing software to authorize remote printer access. See Chapter 24, *Printing*, for details.

tion can be crucial when you are tracking intruders and their attempts to compromise your system.

rexecd and tftpd

rexecd is yet another remote command execution daemon. It is the server for the **rexec** library routine. Requests sent to **rexecd** include a plaintext password, so anyone listening on the network can learn passwords and gain access to the target system. Disable this daemon.

tftpd is a server for the Trivial File Transfer Protocol, an easy-to-implement protocol that's sometimes used to download firmware or boot code into network devices. Because it allows machines on the network to request files from your hard disk, it's a potential security hole. It's best left disabled if you are not using it.

fingerd

finger is a Linux command that prints a short report about a particular user:

```
% finger evi
Login: evi                      Name: Evi Nemeth
Directory: /home/evi            Shell: /usr/bin/tcsh
Last login Thu Nov 29 12:32 (MST) on pts/0 from natted.sendmail.com
No Mail.
No Plan.
```

Without an argument, **finger** prints a summary of all logged-in users.

When supported by the **fingerd** daemon on a remote host, **finger** can also be run in the form **finger** *user@host* or just **finger** *@host*. Unfortunately, the information returned is potentially useful to hackers, so we recommend that you disable **fingerd** in **/etc/inetd.conf** (or in the **fingerd** file in **/etc/xinetd.d** on Red Hat).[7]

Security and NIS

See Chapter 18 for more information about NIS.

Other than the title of this section, these words should never be used together. The Network Information Service (NIS, formerly the Yellow Pages) is a Sun database distribution tool that many sites use to maintain and distribute files such as **/etc/group**, **/etc/passwd**, and **/etc/hosts**. Unfortunately, its very nature of "easy information access" makes it tasty hacker bait. A later replacement for NIS called NIS+ makes a feeble attempt to address the security problems of NIS. You'd be safer not to run either form of NIS at your site.

A more secure and reliable way to distribute these files is to create a login such as "netadmin" and to place the most recent copies of these files in ~**netadmin**. You can then run a script out of **cron** on each client machine to **scp**, sanity check, and install the files. See page 673 for more information about SSH, of which **scp** is a part.

---

7. It's also worth noting that a number of security-related bugs have been discovered in **fingerd** over the years, which is unusual for such a simple program.

Security and NFS

See page 471 for more information about NFS security. You can use **showmount -e** to see which filesystems are being exported and to whom. Every exported filesystem should have an access list, and all hostnames should be fully qualified.

Security and sendmail

*See Chapter 19 for more information about **sendmail**.*

sendmail is a massive network system, a large part of which runs as root. As a result, it has often been subject to the attacks of hackers, and numerous vulnerabilities have been exposed over time. Make sure that you're running the most up-to-date version of **sendmail** on all your systems. Since security problems are one of the most likely issues to spark new software releases, it's probable that all versions of **sendmail** but the most current have them. Specific details about **sendmail** security are covered in the sendmail chapter starting on page 603, and information about the security of your current release is available from www.sendmail.org.

Security and backups

See Chapter 10 for more information about backups.

Regular system backups are an essential part of any site security plan. Make sure that all partitions are regularly dumped to tape and that you store some backups off-site. If a significant security incident occurs, you'll have an uncontaminated checkpoint to restore.

Backups can also be a security hazard. Since anyone can read the contents of a tape once it's mounted on a drive, you must keep all backup tapes under lock and key.

Trojan horses

Trojan horses are programs that aren't what they seem to be. An example of a Trojan horse was a program called **turkey** that was distributed on Usenet a long time ago. The program said it would draw a picture of a turkey on your terminal screen, but it actually deleted files from your home directory.

Given the number of security-related escapades the Linux community has seen over the last few years, it is remarkable how few Trojan horse incidents there have been. In fact, we are not aware of a single documented instance of a program that

- Purported to have some useful purpose,
- Was not distributed as part of an operating system,
- Was supplied in source code form, and
- Was widely available

that contained intentionally malicious code or that intentionally circumvented system security. Don't misunderstand us: we're sure it must have happened. But the risk to the average administrator is very low.

Credit for this state of affairs is due largely to the comity of the Internet. Obvious security problems tend to be discovered quickly and widely discussed. Malicious packages don't stay available for very long on well-known Internet servers.

Security

You can be certain that any software that has been discovered to be malicious will be widely discussed on the Internet. If you want to do a quick check before installing something, type the name of the software package at your favorite search engine.

21.8 SECURITY POWER TOOLS

Some of the nest-avoidance chores mentioned in the previous sections can be automated with freely available tools. Here are a few of the tools you'll want to look at.

nmap: scan network ports

nmap is a network port scanner. Its main function is to check a set of target hosts to see which TCP and UDP ports have servers listening on them.[8] Since most network services are associated with "well known" port numbers, this information tells you quite a lot about the software a machine is running.

Running **nmap** is a great way to find out what a system looks like to someone who is trying to break in. For example, here's a report from a run-of-the-mill, relatively unsecured machine:

```
% nmap -sT host1.uexample.com
Starting nmap V. 2.12 by Fyodor (fyodor@dhp.com, www.insecure.org/nmap/)
Interesting ports on host1.uexample.com (10.10.2.1):

Port    State    Protocol    Service
7       open     tcp         echo
9       open     tcp         discard
13      open     tcp         daytime
19      open     tcp         chargen
21      open     tcp         ftp
23      open     tcp         telnet
25      open     tcp         smtp
...
513     open     tcp         login

Nmap run completed -- 1 IP address (1 host up) scanned in 1 second
```

The **-sT** argument asks **nmap** to try and connect to each TCP port on the target host in the normal way.[9] Once a connection has been established, **nmap** immediately disconnects, which is impolite but not harmful to a properly written network server.

From the example above, we can see that host1.uexample.com is running several servers that have historically been associated with security problems: **ftpd** (ftp), **rlogind** (login), and probably **sendmail** (smtp). Several potential lines of attack have been made clear.

---

8. As described in Chapter 13, a port is a numbered communication channel. An IP address identifies an entire machine, and an IP address + port number identifies a specific server or network conversation on that machine.

9. Actually, only the privileged ports (those with port numbers under 1,024) and the well-known ports are checked by default. Use the **-p** option to explicitly specify the range of ports to scan.

The state column in **nmap**'s output shows "open" for ports with servers, "unfiltered" for ports without servers, and "filtered" for ports that cannot be probed because of an intervening firewall. Unfiltered ports are the typical case and are normally not shown unless there are relatively few of them. For example, here's a dump from a more secure commercial web server, www.aexample.com:

```
% nmap -sT www.aexample.com
Starting nmap V. 2.12 by Fyodor (fyodor@dhp.com, www.insecure.org/nmap/)
(Not showing ports in state: filtered)

Port    State        Protocol    Service
53      unfiltered   tcp         domain
80      open         tcp         http
179     unfiltered   tcp         bgp
443     open         tcp         https

Nmap run completed -- 1 IP address (1 host up) scanned in 122 seconds
```

In this case, it's clear that the host is set up to handle web traffic only. A firewall blocks access to other ports. DNS and BGP traffic is allowed through, but no servers are running to receive it. Ideally, the firewall at this site should block traffic to all unused services (such as BGP and DNS in this case) so that these ports cannot be hijacked for other purposes.

In addition to straightforward TCP and UDP probes, **nmap** also has a repertoire of sneaky ways to probe ports without initiating an actual connection. In most cases, these probes send packets that look like they come from the middle of a TCP conversation (rather than the beginning) and wait for diagnostic packets to be sent back. The stealth probes may be effective at getting past a firewall or at avoiding detection by a network security monitor on the lookout for port scanners. If your site uses a firewall (see *Firewalls* on page 676), it's a good idea to probe it with these alternate scanning modes to see what they turn up.

nmap has the magical and useful ability to guess what OS a remote system is running by looking at the particulars of its implementation of TCP/IP. The **-O** option turns on this behavior. For example:

```
% nmap -O disaster mrhat lollipop
Starting nmap V. 2.12 by Fyodor (fyodor@dhp.com, www.insecure.org/nmap/)

Interesting ports on disaster.xor.com (192.108.21.99):
...
Remote operating system guess: HP-UX 11.00

Interesting ports on mrhat.xor.com (192.108.21.2):
...
Remote operating system guess: BSDI 4.0

Interesting ports on lollipop.xor.com (192.108.21.48):
...
Remote operating system guess: Solaris 2.6 - 2.7

Nmap run completed -- 3 IP addresses (3 hosts up) scanned in 5 seconds
```

This feature can be very useful for taking an inventory of a local network. Unfortunately, it is also very useful to hackers, who can base their attacks on known weaknesses of the target OS. Keep in mind, too, that most administrators usually don't appreciate your efforts to scan their network and point out its vulnerabilities, however well intended your motive. *Never* run **nmap** on someone else's network without permission from one of that network's administrators.

ndiff: create nmap baselines and look for suspicious changes

A window into the past can be a system administrator's best friend when it comes to identifying security breaches. Building on **nmap**'s functionality, **ndiff** provides a way to watch for interesting changes in port states and visible hosts. The **ndiff** command itself is very simple: it compares two **nmap** scans and displays the differences. In much the same way that the **tripwire** system discussed later in this chapter records a baseline image of your filesystem and then warns you when file permissions or checksums change, the **ndiff** system records a baseline of the responsive ports and hosts within your network.

Two commands distributed with **ndiff** help make all this very easy: **ngen** and **nrun**. **ngen** allows you to create a baseline based on wishful thinking (what you'd like your network to look like). **nrun** executes **nmap**, stores the results in machine-readable form, and then **ndiff**s them against a real or imagined baseline. **nrun** can be easily run from **cron** on a regular basis.

The **ndiff** distribution includes an HTML translator for the results, so you can easily put them up on a web page (not one accessible to the outside world, we hope, unless your intent is to publish a hacker's guide to your site). You can learn more about or obtain **ndiff** from www.vinecorp.com/ndiff.

SAINT: check networked systems for vulnerabilities

SAINT is an updated version of SATAN, a network security checker released in 1995 amid much hand-wringing about how it would bring about the end of the world. The original SATAN was written by Dan Farmer and Wietse Venema; SAINT is now maintained by World Wide Digital Security, Inc., from whose web site it can be downloaded (www.wwdsi.com). It's free.

Like **nmap**, SAINT probes computers on a network to find out what servers they are running. But unlike **nmap**, SAINT knows quite a lot about the actual server programs and their historical vulnerabilities. It looks for common misconfigurations that degrade security, and it also checks for the presence of known bugs.

Because a SAINT report essentially provides instructions for breaking into a system, a small but vocal minority of system administrators feel that you would be wise to run SAINT—or a similar program such as Nessus, below—on your systems before the hackers do.

SAINT's user interface is entirely web based, and it requires that a web browser be installed on the same machine as SAINT. Fortunately, SAINT makes good use of HTML and can present its results in a variety of well-designed formats. SAINT does not require that **nmap** be installed but will use **nmap** if it is available. SAINT also claims to make use of the utilities supplied with Samba for checking Windows hosts if they have been installed. See www.samba.org or Chapter 27, *Cooperating with Windows*, for more information about Samba.

Nessus: next generation network scanner

Renaud Deraison has recently released an impressive and powerful package called Nessus that provides many of the same features as SAINT, but in a more architecturally clean and more easily extensible way. It's available from www.nessus.org.

Nessus prides itself on being the security scanner that does not take anything for granted. Instead of assuming that all web servers run on port 80, for instance, it will scan for web servers running on any port and then check them for vulnerabilities. Instead of using the version number reported by the service it has connected to, it attempts to exploit known vulnerabilities to see if the service is susceptible.

Although a substantial amount of setup time is required to get Nessus running on your machine the first time (it requires a number of packages that aren't installed with the typical default distribution), it's well worth the effort. At the time of this writing, Nessus could scan for over 800 common vulnerabilities across the network.

The Nessus system includes a client and a server. The server acts as a database, and the client handles the GUI presentation. You must run the server on a UNIX or Linux system, but a variety of clients are available to control and display Nessus on other platforms.

One of the great advantages of Nessus is its modular design, which makes it easy for third parties to add new security checks. If the user community begins to write and collect script databases for Nessus, it could stay current for a long time without constant updates from the original developers.

crack: find insecure passwords

One way to thwart poor password choices is to try to break the passwords yourself and to force users to change passwords that you have broken. **crack** is a sophisticated tool by Alec D. E. Muffett that implements several common password-guessing techniques.

Even though the vast majority of Linux systems use a shadow password file to hide encrypted passwords from public view, it's still wise to verify that your users' passwords are **crack**-resistant. Knowledge of a user's password can be useful because people tend to use the same password over and over again. A single password might provide access to another system, decrypt files stored in a user's home directory, and allow access to financial accounts on the web. (Needless to say, it's not very security-smart to reuse a password this way. But nobody wants to remember ten passwords.)

As of this writing, the current version of **crack** is 5.0a. It's available from ftp.cert.org. Since **crack**'s output contains the passwords it has broken, you should carefully protect it and delete it as soon as you are done.

tcpd: protect Internet services

tcpd, often referred to as the "TCP wrappers" package, allows you to log connections to TCP services such as **telnetd**, **ftpd**, and **fingerd**. In addition, it allows you to restrict which systems can connect to these services. Both of these features can be very handy when you are tracking or controlling unwanted guests. **tcpd** was written by Wietse Venema; updates are available from ftp.porcupine.org. It comes standard with all Linux distributions.

*See page 812 for more information about **inetd**.*

tcpd does not require modifications to existing network programs. It piggybacks on top of **inetd**; you simply modify your **/etc/inetd.conf** file to execute **tcpd** instead of the actual network server program. In addition, many programs that don't run out of **inetd** (such as SSH or **sendmail**) can be compiled to check connections with **tcpd** in addition to their own access control files. **tcpd** then performs any necessary logging and security checks before executing the server.

For example, if your **/etc/inetd.conf** originally contained the line

```
telnet stream tcp      nowait root    /usr/sbin/in.telnetd   in.telnetd
```

you could change this to

```
telnet stream tcp      nowait root    /usr/sbin/tcpd         in.telnetd
```

For Red Hat users, the functionality of **tcpd** is already compiled into **xinetd** and **ssh**.

The resulting log file (configured in **/etc/syslog.conf**) would look something like:

```
Nov 12 08:52:43 chimchim in.telnetd[25880]: connect from tintin.Colorado.EDU
Nov 12 19:19:44 chimchim in.telnetd[15520]: connect from catbelly.com
Nov 12 23:48:45 chimchim in.telnetd[19332]: connect from atdt.xor.com
Nov 13 20:14:57 chimchim in.telnetd[2362]: connect from 130.13.13.11
```

COPS: audit system security

The Computer Oracle and Password System, COPS, is a set of programs, originally written by Dan Farmer, that monitor several aspects of Linux security. It's a pretty crufty package, originally written in the days before Linux, but it still serves a very useful purpose. Sometimes old habits die hard. You can run COPS every night out of **cron** to search through the filesystem for security problems.

By standardizing and streamlining a variety of simple checks, COPS can save you many hours of manual labor. Although it is no longer under active development, COPS is a classic tool that identifies many classic security problems. Run it before one of your users does.

COPS warns you of potential problems by sending email; it makes no attempt to fix the problems it has discovered. A list of the items monitored includes

- File, directory, and device permissions and modes
- The contents of **/etc/passwd** and **/etc/group**
- The contents of system startup and crontab files
- The writability of users' home directories

Once you install COPS, you will receive a nightly security report similar to this one:

```
ATTENTION:
Security Report from host raja.xor.com

Warning!  Root does not own the following file(s): /etc
Warning!  "." (or current directory) is in root's path!
Warning!  /var/spool/mail is _World_ writable!
Warning!  /var/run/utmp is _World_ writable!
Warning!  User randy's home directory /home/staff/randy is mode 0777!
Warning!  Password file, line 8, no password:
runmailq::33:10:,,,:/home/staff/runmailq:/bin/csh
Warning!  Password Problem: Guessed: beth shell: /bin/csh
```

COPS includes the Kuang expert system, which attempts to intuit devious ways that regular users could attempt to become root. More information about COPS is available from www.cerias.purdue.edu.

tripwire: monitor changes to system files

tripwire, written by Gene Kim and Gene Spafford of Purdue, monitors the permissions and checksums of important system files so that you can easily detect files that have been replaced, corrupted, or tampered with. For example, **tripwire** makes it easy to determine that an intruder has replaced your copy of **/bin/login** with one that records passwords in a clandestine file.

tripwire checks files against a database that records their characteristics and checksums at the time the database was built. The general idea is to make a baseline database from a trusted state of the system and then regularly **diff** the filesystem against that historical database. Files that are expected to change (such as **/var/run/utmp**) can be marked in **tripwire**'s configuration file so that they do not generate warnings. When the configuration of the system is changed or new software is installed, the database should be rebuilt so that real problems do not disappear among a flood of spurious **tripwire** warnings.

If possible, **tripwire's** database and config file should be mounted from a secure server that exports it read-only.[10] This configuration makes it harder for hackers to cover their tracks and remain undetected.

tripwire should be set up to mail you a nightly report. A typical **tripwire** report looks like this:

```
# tripwire
Tripwire(tm) ASR (Academic Source Release) 1.3.1
File Integrity Assessment Software
(c) 1992, Purdue Research Foundation, (c) 1997, 1999 Tripwire
Security Systems, Inc. All Rights Reserved. Use Restricted to
Authorized Licensees.
### Phase 1:   Reading configuration file
```

---

10. Keeping the database on a write-protected floppy or Zip disk is a popular approach that provides a moderate level of protection.

```
### Phase 2:    Generating file list
### Phase 3:    Creating file information database
### Phase 4:    Searching for inconsistencies
###
###                Total files scanned:   20344
###                        Files added:       0
###                      Files deleted:       0
###                      Files changed:       1
###
###                Total file violations:     1
###
changed: -rwxr-xr-x root      262184 Jan 22 12:04:42 2000 /bin/tcsh
### Phase 5:    Generating observed/expected pairs for changed files
###
### Attr          Observed (what it is)        Expected (what it should be)
### ===           =================            ========================
/bin/tcsh
      st_ctime:   Sat Jan 22 12:04:42 2000     Fri May 14 05:11:41 1999
```

In this example, **tripwire** reports that the inode change time of **/bin/tcsh** is different from what it was when the database was generated. This may be an indication that a wily hacker has replaced the vendor's version of **/bin/tcsh** with one that contains a surprise waiting to be found the next time the shell is executed by root. Comparing the checksum of the executable with the version on the distribution tape (use the **siggen** utility that comes with **tripwire** to do this) can confirm or deny this as potential hacker droppings. Since some hackers are wily enough to rig the checksums on modified files, **tripwire** uses two different checksum methods.

tripwire is a bit unusual in that it started out as free software but was later privatized and turned into a commercial product. However, it's not really possible to unrelease something that was formerly free. Tripwire, Inc., has graciously continued to make the free version available and has even released commercial-quality documentation and updates for it. It's available from their web site, www.tripwiresecurity.com.

Forensic tools

One up-and-coming security power tool (tool *kit*, actually) is The Coroner's Toolkit (TCT) from Dan Farmer and Wietse Venema. TCT is a collection of utilities that help to analyze the system after a security breach has occurred.

TCT helps you to identify both *what* happened and *how* it happened. In some cases, it will even recover data that was destroyed during the break-in. One particularly interesting utility is **mactime**, a program that tracks the modification, access, and change times for all files on the system. **mactime** and many other utilities from the TCT tool kit are available from www.fish.com/security.

21.9 CRYPTOGRAPHIC SECURITY TOOLS

Most of the network protocols in common use on Linux systems date from a time before the deployment of the Internet and before the invention of modern cryptography. Security was simply not a factor in the design of many protocols; in others, security concerns were waved away with the transmission of a plaintext password or with a vague check to see if packets originated from a trusted host or port.

These protocols now find themselves operating in the shark-infested waters of large corporate LANs and the Internet, where, it must be assumed, all traffic is open to inspection. Not only that, but there is little to prevent anyone from actively interfering in network conversations. How can you be sure who you're really talking to?

Cryptography provides a solution to many of these problems. It has been possible for a long time to scramble messages so that an eavesdropper cannot decipher them, but this is just the beginning of the wonders of cryptography. Developments such as public key cryptography and secure hashing have allowed the design of cryptosystems that meet almost any conceivable need.[11]

Unfortunately, these mathematical developments have largely failed to translate into secure, usable software that is widely embraced and understood. The developers of cryptographic software systems tend to be very interested in provable correctness and absolute security and not so interested in whether a system makes practical sense for the real world. Most current software tends to be rather overengineered, and it's perhaps not surprising that users run away screaming when given half a chance. Today, the cryptography-using population consists largely of hobbyists interested in cryptography, black-helicopter conspiracy theorists, and those who have no choice because of administrative policy.

We may or may not see a saner approach to cryptography developing over the next few years. In the meantime, some current offerings discussed in the following sections may help out.

Kerberos: a unified approach to network security

The Kerberos system, designed at MIT, attempts to address some of the issues of network security in a consistent and extensible way. Kerberos is an authentication system, a facility that "guarantees" that users and services are in fact who they claim to be. It does not provide any additional security or encryption beyond that.

Kerberos uses DES to construct nested sets of credentials called "tickets." Tickets are passed around the network to certify your identity and to provide you with access to network services. Each Kerberos site must maintain at least one physically secure machine (called the authentication server) to run the Kerberos daemon. This daemon issues tickets to users or services that request authentication based on credentials they provide, such as passwords.

In essence, Kerberos improves upon traditional Linux password security in only two ways: it never transmits unencrypted passwords on the network, and it relieves users

---

11. Two excellent resources for those interested in cryptography are "RSA Labs' Frequently Asked Questions about Today's Cryptography" at www.rsasecurity.com/rsalabs/faq and the sci.crypt FAQ available by FTP from rtfm.mit.edu.

from having to type passwords repeatedly, making password protection of network services somewhat more palatable.

The Kerberos community boasts one of the most lucid and enjoyable documents ever written about a cryptosystem, Bill Bryant's "Designing an Authentication System: a Dialogue in Four Scenes." It's required reading for anyone interested in cryptography and is available at

> http://web.mit.edu/kerberos/www/dialogue.html

There's also a good FAQ:

> http://www.nrl.navy.mil/CCS/people/kenh/kerberos-faq.html

Kerberos offers a better network security model than the "ignoring network security entirely" model. However, it is neither perfectly secure nor painless to install and run. It does not supersede any of the other security measures described in this chapter. In our opinion, most sites are better off without it. Good system hygiene and a focused cryptographic solution for remote logins such as SSH (see page 673) should provide a more-than-adequate level of security for your users.

Unfortunately, the Kerberos system distributed as part of Windows 2000 uses proprietary, undocumented extensions. As a result, it does not interoperate well with a distribution based on the MIT code.

PGP: Pretty Good Privacy

Philip Zimmermann's PGP package provides a tool chest of bread-and-butter cryptographic utilities focused primarily on email security. It can be used to encrypt data, to generate signatures, and to verify the origin of files and messages.

Attempts to regulate or stop the distribution of PGP have given it a rather checkered history. It now exists in several versions, including a set of commercial products from Network Associates (www.nai.com). A governmentally vetted version of PGP is a available for use in the United States, and an international version with somewhat stronger and more varied encryption is available from www.pgpi.org. The international archive sites do not seem to screen out U.S. addresses, so American users must be very careful not to accidentally go to www.pgpi.org and download the full-featured version of PGP.

PGP is the most popular cryptographic software in common use. Unfortunately, the UNIX/Linux version is nuts-and-bolts enough that you have to understand a fair amount of cryptographic background in order to use it. Fortunately (?), PGP comes with an 88-page treatise on cryptography that can help to set the stage. While you may find PGP useful in your own work, we don't recommend that you support it for users, as it has been known to spark many puzzled questions. We have found the Windows version of PGP to be considerably easier to use than the Linux **pgp** command with its 38 different operating modes.

Software packages on the Internet are often distributed with a PGP signature file that purports to guarantee the origin and purity of the software. Unfortunately, it is difficult for people who are not die-hard PGP users to validate these signatures—not because the validation process is complicated, but because true PGP security can only come from having collected a personal library of public keys from people whose identities you have directly verified. Downloading a single public key along with a signature file and software distribution is approximately as secure as downloading the distribution alone.

Unfortunately, there are some patent issues associated with the technology that PGP is based upon. GnuPG (aka GPG) is an alternative to PGP that provides the same basic functionality without using the patented IDEA algorithm. It maintains a reasonable level of compatibility with modern PGP implementations and is readily available for Linux.

SSH: the secure shell

The SSH system, written by Tatu Ylönen, is a secure replacement for **rlogin**, **rcp**, and **telnet**. It uses cryptographic authentication to confirm a user's identity and encrypts all communications between the two hosts. The protocol used by SSH is designed to withstand a wide variety of potential attacks. It has been well studied and is being standardized by the IETF.

Like **tripwire**, SSH morphed from being a freely distributed open source project (SSH1) to being a commercial product using a slightly different (and more secure) protocol (SSH2). Fortunately, the open source community has responded by releasing OpenSSH, which now implements both protocols.

It's important to note that a number of vulnerabilities have been discovered in the original SSH, the once-free-then-commercial SSH, and also OpenSSH. As a result, it's very important to verify that you're running the latest and "most secure" version. A paper published at USENIX in December 2001 included statistics demonstrating that over 30% of sites currently running SSH are running a vulnerable version. In general, we recommend the OpenSSH release, available from www.openssh.com.

The main components of SSH are a server daemon, **sshd**, and two user-level commands: **ssh** for remote logins and **scp** for copying files. Other components are an **ssh-keygen** command that generates public key pairs and a couple of utilities that help support secure X Windows.

sshd can authenticate user logins in several different ways. It's up to you as the administrator to decide which of these methods are acceptable:

- **Method A:** If the name of the remote host from which the user is logging in is listed in **~/.rhosts**, **~/.shosts**, **/etc/hosts.equiv**, or **/etc/shosts.equiv**, then the user is logged in automatically without a password check. This scheme mirrors that of the old **rlogin** daemon and in our opinion is *not* acceptable for normal use.

- **Method B:** As a refinement of method A, **sshd** can also use public key cryptography to verify the identity of the remote host. For that to happen, the remote host's public key (generated at install time) must be listed in the local host's **/etc/ssh_known_hosts** file or the user's **~/.ssh/known_hosts** file. If the remote host can prove that it knows the corresponding private key (normally stored in **/etc/ssh_host_key**, a world-unreadable file), then the user is logged in without being asked for a password. Method B is more restrictive than method A, but we think it's still not quite secure enough. If the security of the originating host is compromised, the local site will be compromised as well.

- **Method C: sshd** can use public key cryptography to establish the user's identity. At login time, the user must have access to a copy of his or her private key file and must supply a password to decrypt it. This method is the most secure, but it's somewhat annoying to set up. It also means that you cannot log in when traveling unless you bring a copy of your private key file with you (perhaps on your laptop).

- **Method D:** Finally, **sshd** can simply allow the user to enter his or her normal login password. This makes **ssh** behave very much like **telnet**, except that the password and session are both encrypted. The main drawbacks of this method are that system login passwords are relatively weak (often limited to 8 significant characters) and that there are ready-made tools (like **crack**) designed to break them. However, this method is probably the best choice for normal use.

Authentication policy is set in the **/etc/sshd_config** file. You will see at once that this file has been filled up with configuration garbage for you, but most of it can be safely ignored. The options relevant to authentication are shown in Table 21.1.

Table 21.1   Authentication-related options in /etc/sshd_config

Option	Meth[a]	Dflt	Meaning when turned on
RhostsAuthentication	A	no	Allows login via **~/.shosts**, **/etc/shosts.equiv**, etc.
RhostsRSAAuthentication	B	yes	Allows **~/.shosts** et al., but also requires host key
IgnoreRhosts	A,B	no	Ignores the **~/.rhosts** and **hosts.equiv** files[b]
IgnoreRootRhosts	A,B	no[c]	Prevents **rhosts**/**shosts** authentication for root
RSAAuthentication	C	yes	Allows per-user public key crypto authentication
PasswordAuthentication	D	yes	Allows use of normal login password

a. The authentication methods to which this variable is relevant
b. But continues to honor **~/.shosts** and **shosts.equiv**
c. Defaults to the value of IgnoreRhosts

Our suggested configuration, which allows methods C and D but not methods A or B, is as follows.

```
RhostsAuthentication no
RhostsRSAAuthentication no
RSAAuthentication yes
PasswordAuthentication yes
```

OPIE: One-time Passwords in Everything

One of the problems with systems such as SSH is that both ends of a connection must support a special protocol to secure the connection. This is normally not a problem, but users can sometimes find themselves stranded. SSH clients are not available for all operating systems (at least, not for free), and users may occasionally want to log in through other people's computers when on the road.

The one-time password (OTP) standard defined in RFC1938 takes a somewhat different approach to password security: instead of encrypting passwords, you just make sure that they only work once. Plaintext passwords can then be entered over the net with impunity, since it does not matter if anyone overhears them. Users typically print out a series of one-time passwords to carry around with them. Unlike regular passwords, one-time passwords are generated on your behalf; you don't get to select them.

OPIE is the most commonly used OTP system today. It's an offshoot of an earlier system called S/Key from Bellcore (now Telcordia Technologies) that was further developed at the U.S. Naval Research Laboratories. OPIE's main features are OTP-compatible versions of **telnetd** and **ftpd** and utilities for generating and administering password lists. It's available from www.inner.net/pub/opie.

It's important to note that OTP systems address only the issue of password snooping. They cannot and do not encrypt the actual content of a conversation. Someone listening in on your **telnet** session might not be able to obtain a usable password, but they could certainly find out a lot about your account. Any passwords you typed after logging in (to **sudo**, for example) would be completely exposed.[12]

Given the growing availability of systems such as SSH, there is less and less need for OPIE. If you don't really need it, don't use it—it's troublesome to install and maintain, and the procedures that users must follow are somewhat confusing.

Hardware tokens

These days, the most common sightings of one-time passwords are in commercial security products. A number of vendors offer one-time password systems based on small "key chain"-sized (or credit card-sized) devices with LCD displays that generate passwords on the fly for user logins. At the very least, distributing and replacing the little hardware devices will keep your administrative assistant busy for a few hours a week.

---

12. In particular, users should not try to obtain a list of more OTP passwords after having logged in with OTP; the passwords will all be transmitted without protection.

21.10 FIREWALLS

In addition to protecting individual machines, you can also implement security precautions at the network level. The basic tool of network security is the "firewall." There are three main categories of firewalls: packet-filtering, service proxy, and stateful inspection.

Packet-filtering firewalls

A packet-filtering firewall limits the types of traffic that can pass through your Internet gateway (or through an internal gateway that separates domains within your organization) based on information in the packet header. It's much like driving your car through a customs checkpoint at an international border crossing. You specify which destination addresses, port numbers, and protocol types are acceptable, and the gateway simply discards (and in some cases, logs) packets that don't meet the profile.

Packet filtering is supported by dedicated routers such as those made by Cisco. It may also be available in software, depending on the machine you're using as a gateway and its configuration. In general, packet-filtering firewalls offer a significant increase in security with little cost in performance or complexity.

Linux includes packet filtering software (see the details beginning on 679 for more information). It's also possible to buy commercial software to perform this function. These packages all have entertainment value, and they can provide a reasonably secure firewall for a home or small office. However, you should refer to the comments at the beginning of this chapter before you consider a Linux system as a production-grade corporate firewall.[13] This is one case in which you should really spend the money for a dedicated network appliance, such as Cisco's PIX firewall.

How services are filtered

Most well-known services are associated with a network port in the **/etc/services** file or its vendor-specific equivalent. The daemons that provide these services bind to the appropriate ports and wait for connections from remote sites.[14] Most of the well-known service ports are "privileged," meaning that their port numbers are in the range 1 to 1,023. These ports can only be used by a process running as root. Port numbers 1,024 and higher are referred to as nonprivileged ports.

Service-specific filtering is based on the assumption that the client (the machine that initiates a TCP or UDP conversation) will use a nonprivileged port to contact a privileged port on the server. For example, if you wanted to allow only inbound SMTP connections to a machine with the address 192.108.21.200, you would install a filter that allowed TCP packets destined for that address at port 25 and that permitted outbound TCP packets from that address to anywhere.[15] The exact way that such a filter would be installed depends on the kind of router you are using.

---

13. We assume you already know not to consider something like Windows as a firewall platform. Does the name "Windows" evoke images of security? Silly rabbit, Windows is for desktops.

14. In many cases, **inetd** does the actual waiting on their behalf. See page 812 for more information.

15. Port 25 is the SMTP port as defined in **/etc/services**.

*See page 704 for more information about setting up an **ftp** server.*

Some services, such as FTP, add a twist to the puzzle. The FTP protocol actually uses two TCP connections when transferring a file: one for commands and the other for data. The client initiates the command connection, and the server initiates the data connection. Ergo, if you want to use FTP to retrieve files from the Internet, you must permit inbound access to all nonprivileged TCP ports, since you have no idea what port might be used to form an incoming data connection.

This tweak largely defeats the purpose of packet filtering, since some notoriously insecure services (for example, X11 at port 6000) naturally bind to nonprivileged ports. This configuration also creates an opportunity for curious users within your organization to start their own services (such as a **telnet** server at a nonstandard and nonprivileged port) that they or their friends can access from the Internet.

The most secure way to use a packet filter is to start with a configuration that allows nothing but inbound SMTP. You can then liberalize the filter bit by bit as you discover useful things that don't work.

Some extremely security-conscious sites use two-stage filtering. In this scheme, one filter is a gateway to the Internet, and a second filter lies between the outer gateway and the rest of the local network. The idea is to leave the outer gateway relatively open and to make the inner gateway very conservative. If the machine in the middle is administratively separate from the rest of the network, it can provide a variety of services on the Internet with reduced risk.

A reasonable approach to the FTP dilemma is to allow FTP to the outside world only from this single, isolated host. Users can also log in to the FTP machine when they need to perform other network operations that are forbidden from the inner net. Since replicating all user accounts on the FTP "server" would defeat the goal of administrative separation, you may want to create FTP accounts by request only. Naturally, the FTP host should run a full complement of security-checking tools.

Service proxy firewalls

Service proxies intercept connections to and from the outside world and establish new connections to services inside your network, acting as a sort of shuttle or chaperone between the two worlds. It's much like driving to the border of your country, walking across the border, and renting a sanitized, freshly washed car on the other side of the border to continue your journey.

Because of their design, service proxy firewalls are much less flexible (and much slower) than pure packet filters. Your proxy must have a module that decodes and conveys each protocol you want to let through the firewall. In the early 1990s this was relatively easy because there were only a few protocols in common use. Today, Internauts might use several dozen protocols in an hour of web surfing. As a result, service proxies are relatively unpopular in organizations that use the Internet as a primary medium of communication.

Stateful inspection firewalls

The theory behind stateful inspection firewalls is that if you could carefully listen to and understand all the conversations (in all the languages) that were taking place in a crowded airport, you could make sure that someone wasn't planning to bomb a plane later that day. Stateful inspection firewalls are designed to inspect the traffic that flows through them and compare the actual network activity to what "should" be happening. For example, if the packets exchanged in an FTP command sequence name a port to be used later for a data connection, the firewall should expect a data connection to occur only on that port. Attempts by the remote site to connect to other ports are presumably bogus and should be dropped.

Unfortunately, reality usually kills the cat here. It's no more realistic to keep track of the "state" of the network connections of thousands of hosts using hundreds of protocols than it is to listen to every conversation in every language in a crowded airport. Someday, as processor and memory capacity increase, it may eventually be feasible.

So what are vendors really selling when they claim to provide stateful inspection? Their products either monitor a very limited number of connections or protocols or they search for a particular set of "bad" situations. Not that there's anything wrong with that; there is clearly some benefit to be obtained from any technology that can detect traffic anomalies. In this particular case, however, it's important to remember that the claims are *mostly* marketing hype.

Firewalls: how safe are they?

A firewall should not be your primary means of defense against intruders. It's only appropriate as a supplemental security measure. The use of firewalls often provides a false sense of security. If it lulls you into relaxing other safeguards, it will have had a *negative* effect on the security of your site.

Every host within your organization should be individually secured and regularly monitored with tools such as **crack**, **tcpd**, **nmap**, COPS, and **tripwire**. Likewise, your entire user community needs to be educated about basic security hygiene. Otherwise, you are simply building a structure that has a hard crunchy outside and a soft chewy center. On the Internet, it doesn't take many licks to get to the center of that bonbon.

Ideally, local users should be able to connect to any Internet service they want, but machines on the Internet should only be able to connect to a limited set of local services. For example, you may want to allow FTP access to a local archive server and allow SMTP (email) connections to your mail server.

If you want to maximize the value of your Internet connection, we recommend that you emphasize convenience and accessibility when deciding how to set up your network. At the end of the day, it's the system administrator's vigilance that makes a network secure, not a fancy piece of firewall hardware.

21.11 LINUX FIREWALL FEATURES: IP TABLES

We normally don't recommend the use of Linux (or UNIX, or NT) systems as firewalls because of the general insecurity of running a full-fledged operating system. Embedded devices designed specifically for routing and packet filtering (such as a Cisco PIX box) make the best firewalls. However, a Linux firewall is better than no firewall at all for a home site or a site with no budget for appropriate hardware, so we will describe Linux's packet filtering software in this section.

If you are set on using a Linux machine as a firewall, please at least make sure that it's up to date with respect to security configuration and patches. A firewall machine is an excellent place to put into practice all of this chapter's recommendations. (The section that starts on page 676 discusses packet-filtering firewalls in general. If you are not familiar with the basic concept of a firewall, it would probably be wise to read that section before continuing.)

Version 2.4 of the Linux kernel introduced an all-new packet handling engine called Netfilter. The tool used to control Netfilter, **iptables**, is the big brother of the older **ipchains** command used with Linux 2.2 kernels. **iptables** applies ordered "chains" of rules to network packets. Sets of chains make up "tables" and are used for handling specific kinds of traffic.

For example, the default **iptables** table is named "filter". Chains of rules in this table are used for packet-filtering network traffic. The filter table contains three default chains. Each packet that is handled by the kernel is passed through exactly one of these chains. Rules in the FORWARD chain are applied to all packets that arrive on one network interface and need to be forwarded to another. Rules in the INPUT and OUTPUT chains are applied to traffic addressed to or originating from the local host, respectively. These three standard chains are usually all you need for firewalling between two network interfaces. If necessary, you can define a custom configuration to support more complex accounting or routing scenarios.

In addition to the filter table, **iptables** includes the "nat" and "mangle" tables. The nat table contains chains of rules that control Network Address Translation (here, "nat" is the name of the **iptables** table and "NAT" is the name of the generic address translation scheme). The section *Private addresses and NAT* on page 255 discusses NAT, and an example of the nat table in action is shown on page 290. Later in this section, we use the nat table's PREROUTING chain for anti-spoofing packet filtering.

The mangle table contains chains that modify or alter the contents of network packets outside the context of NAT and packet filtering. Although the mangle table is handy for special packet handling, such as resetting IP time to live values, it is not typically used in most production environments. We discuss only the filter and nat tables in this section, leaving the mangle table to the adventurous.

Each rule that makes up a chain has a "target" clause that determines what to do with matching packets. As soon as a packet matches a rule, its fate is sealed and no more rules will be checked. Although many targets are defined internally to **iptables**, it is possible to specify another chain as a rule's target.

The targets available to rules in the filter table are ACCEPT, DROP, REJECT, LOG, MIRROR, QUEUE, REDIRECT, RETURN, and ULOG. When a rule results in an ACCEPT, matching packets are allowed to proceed on their way. DROP and REJECT both drop their packets. DROP is silent, and REJECT returns an ICMP error message. LOG provides a simple way to track packets as they match rules, and ULOG provides extended logging.

REDIRECT shunts packets to a proxy instead of letting them go on their merry way. You might use this feature to force all your site's web traffic to go through a web cache such as Squid. RETURN terminates user-defined chains and is analogous to the return statement in a subroutine call. The MIRROR target swaps the IP source and destination address before sending the packet. Finally, QUEUE hands packets to local user programs through a kernel module.

A Linux firewall is usually implemented as a series of **iptables** commands contained in an **rc** startup script. Individual **iptables** commands usually take one of the following forms:

```
iptables -F chain-name
iptables -P chain-name target
iptables -A chain-name -i interface -j target
```

The first form (**-F**) flushes all prior rules from the chain. The second form (**-P**) sets a default policy (aka target) for the chain. We recommend that you use DROP for the default chain target. The third instance (**-A**) appends the current specification to the chain. Unless you specify a table with the **-t** argument, your commands will apply to chains in the filter table. The **-i** parameter applies the rule to the named interface, and **-j** identifies the target. **iptables** accepts many other clauses, some of which are shown in Table 21.2.

Table 21.2   Command-line flags for iptables filters

Clause	Meaning or possible values
-p *proto*	Matches by protocol: **tcp**, **udp**, or **icmp**
-s *source-ip*	Matches host or network source IP address (CIDR notation is OK)
-d *dest-ip*	Matches host or network destination address
--sport *port#*	Matches by source port (note the double dashes)
--dport *port#*	Matches by destination port (note the double dashes)
--icmp-type *type*	Matches by ICMP type code (note the double dashes)
!	Negates a clause
-t *table*	Specifies the table to which a command applies (default is **filter**)

Below we break apart a complete example. We assume that the ppp0 interface goes to the Internet and that the eth0 interface goes to an internal network. The ppp0 IP address is 128.138.101.4, the eth0 IP address is 10.1.1.254, and both interfaces have a netmask of 255.255.255.0. This example uses stateless packet filtering to protect the web server with IP address 10.1.1.2, which is the standard method of protecting Internet servers. Later in the example, we'll show how to use stateful filtering to protect desktop users.

Before you can use **iptables**, you must enable IP forwarding and make sure that various **iptables** modules have been loaded into the kernel. For more information on enabling IP forwarding, see *Tuning a Linux kernel* on page 221 or *Security-related kernel variables* on page 288. All distributions that ship with **iptables** also come with startup scripts to achieve this enabling and loading.

Our first set of rules initializes the filter table. First, all chains in the table are flushed, then the INPUT and FORWARD chains' default target is set to DROP. As with any other network firewall, the most secure strategy is to drop any packets that you have not explicitly allowed.

```
iptables -F
iptables -P INPUT DROP
iptables -P FORWARD DROP
```

Since rules are evaluated in the order in which they sit in a chain, we'll put our busiest rules at the front.[16] The first three rules in the FORWARD chain allow connections through the firewall to network services on 10.1.1.2. Specifically, we allow SSH (port 22), HTTP (port 80), and HTTPS (port 443) through to our web server. The first rule allows all connections through the firewall that originate from within the trusted net.

```
iptables -A FORWARD -i eth0 -p ANY -j ACCEPT
iptables -A FORWARD -d 10.1.1.2 -p tcp --dport 22 -j ACCEPT
iptables -A FORWARD -d 10.1.1.2 -p tcp --dport 80 -j ACCEPT
iptables -A FORWARD -d 10.1.1.2 -p tcp --dport 443 -j ACCEPT
```

The only TCP traffic we will allow to our firewall host is SSH, which will be useful for managing the firewall. The second rule listed below allows loopback traffic, which stays local to our firewall host. Our administrators get nervous when they can't **ping** their default route, so the third rule here allows ICMP ECHO_REQUEST packets from internal IP addresses.

```
iptables -A INPUT -i eth0 -d 10.1.1.1 -p tcp --dport 22 -j ACCEPT
iptables -A INPUT -i lo -d 127.0.0.1 -p ANY -j ACCEPT
iptables -A INPUT -i eth0 -d 10.1.1.1 -p icmp --icmp-type 8 -j ACCEPT
```

For any TCP/IP host to work properly on the Internet, certain types of ICMP packets must be allowed through the firewall. The following eight rules allow a minimal set of ICMP packets to the firewall host, as well as to the network behind it.

```
iptables -A INPUT -p icmp --icmp-type 0 -j ACCEPT
iptables -A INPUT -p icmp --icmp-type 3 -j ACCEPT
iptables -A INPUT -p icmp --icmp-type 5 -j ACCEPT
```

---

16. However, you must be careful that reordering rules for performance doesn't modify functionality.

```
iptables -A INPUT -p icmp --icmp-type 11 -j ACCEPT
iptables -A FORWARD -d 10.1.1.2 -p icmp --icmp-type 0 -j ACCEPT
iptables -A FORWARD -d 10.1.1.2 -p icmp --icmp-type 3 -j ACCEPT
iptables -A FORWARD -d 10.1.1.2 -p icmp --icmp-type 5 -j ACCEPT
iptables -A FORWARD -d 10.1.1.2 -p icmp --icmp-type 11 -j ACCEPT
```

We next add rules to the PREROUTING chain in the nat table. Although the nat table is not intended for packet filtering, its PREROUTING chain is particularly useful for anti-spoofing filtering. If we put DROP entries in the PREROUTING chain, they do not need to be present in the INPUT and FORWARD chains, since the PREROUTING chain is applied to all packets that enter the firewall host. It's cleaner to put the entries in a single place rather than duplicating them.

```
iptables -t nat -A PREROUTING -i ppp0 -s 10.0.0.0/8 -j DROP
iptables -t nat -A PREROUTING -i ppp0 -s 172.16.0.0/12 -j DROP
iptables -t nat -A PREROUTING -i ppp0 -s 192.168.0.0/16 -j DROP
iptables -t nat -A PREROUTING -i ppp0 -s 127.0.0.0/8 -j DROP
iptables -t nat -A PREROUTING -i ppp0 -s 224.0.0.0/4 -j DROP
```

Finally, we end both the INPUT and FORWARD chains with a rule that forbids all packets not explicitly permitted. Although we already enforced this behavior with the **iptables -P** commands above, the LOG target lets us see who is knocking on our door from the Internet.

```
iptables -A INPUT -i ppp0 -j LOG
iptables -A FORWARD -i ppp0 -j LOG
```

Optionally, we could set up IP NAT to disguise the private address space used on the internal network. See *Linux NAT (IP masquerading)* on page 289 for more information about NAT.

One of the most powerful features that Netfilter brings to Linux firewalling is stateful packet filtering. Instead of allowing specific incoming services, a firewall for clients connecting to the Internet needs to allow incoming responses to the client's requests. The simple stateful FORWARD chain below allows all traffic to leave our network but only allows incoming traffic that's related to connections initiated by our hosts.

```
iptables -A FORWARD -i eth0 -p ANY -j ACCEPT
iptables -A FORWARD -m state --state ESTABLISHED,RELATED -j ACCEPT
```

Certain kernel modules must be loaded to enable **iptables** to track complex network sessions such as those of FTP and IRC. If these modules are not loaded, **iptables** simply disallows those connections. Although stateful packet filters can increase the security of your site, they also add to the complexity of the network. Be sure you need stateful functionality before implementing it in your firewall.

Perhaps the best way to debug your **iptables** rulesets is to use **iptables -L -v**. These options will tell you how many times each rule in your chains has matched a packet. We often add temporary **iptables** rules with the LOG target when we want more information about the packets that get matched. You can often solve trickier problems by using a packet sniffer such as **tcpdump**.

21.12 VIRTUAL PRIVATE NETWORKS (VPNs)

One of the most interesting developments of the last few years has been the advent of the virtual private network or VPN. This technology has been made possible mostly by the increased processing power that is now available on a single chip (and on users' workstations). In its simplest form, a VPN is a connection that makes a remote network appear as if it is directly connected, even if it is physically thousands of miles and many router hops away. For increased security, the connection is not only authenticated in some way (usually with a "shared secret" such as a password), but the end-to-end traffic is also encrypted. Such an arrangement is usually referred to as a "secure tunnel."

Here's a good example of the kind of situation in which a VPN is handy: Suppose that a company has offices in Chicago, Boulder, and Miami. If each office has a connection to a local Internet service provider, the company can use VPNs to transparently (and, for the most part, securely) connect the offices across the untrusted Internet. The company could achieve a similar result by leasing dedicated lines to connect the three offices, but that option would be considerably more expensive.

Another good example would be a company whose employees telecommute from their homes. VPNs would allow those users to reap the benefits of their high-speed and inexpensive cable modem service while still making it appear that they are directly connected to the corporate network.

Because of the convenience and popularity of this functionality, everyone and his brother is offering some type of VPN solution. You can buy it from your router vendor, as a plug-in for your operating system, or even as a dedicated VPN device for your network. Depending on your budget and scalability needs, you may want to consider one of the many commercial VPN solutions in the marketplace.

If you're without a budget and looking for a quick fix, SSH will do secure tunneling for you. SSH is normally used to provide one-port-at-a-time connectivity, but it can also supply pseudo-VPN functionality as shown in the example on page 299, which runs PPP through an SSH tunnel.

IPSEC tunnels

If you're a fan of IETF standards (or of saving money) and need a real VPN solution, you should take a look at IPSEC (Internet Protocol SECurity). IPSEC was originally developed for IPv6, but it has also been widely implemented for IPv4. IPSEC is an IETF-approved, end-to-end authentication and encryption system. Almost all serious VPN vendors ship a product that has at least an IPSEC compatibility mode.

IPSEC uses strong cryptography to provide both authentication and encryption services. Authentication ensures that packets are from the right sender and have not been altered in transit, and encryption prevents the unauthorized examination of packet contents. Unfortunately, IPSEC's deployment has been somewhat hampered by the U.S. encryption laws, which prohibit the export of strong encryption software.

Security

In its current form, IPSEC encrypts the transport layer header, which includes the source and destination port numbers. Unfortunately, this scheme conflicts directly with the way that most firewalls work. A proposal to undo this feature is making its way through the IETF.

Table 21.3 shows the status of IPSEC implementations for our example distributions. Note that although IPSEC runs on each system, no U.S. version includes it in the basic installation. For availability and configuration information, visit www.freeswan.org.

Table 21.3   IPSEC implementation status for various Linux distributions

System	Got it?	Comments
Red Hat	not quite	FreeS/WAN IPSEC was developed on Red Hat but is not shipped by default because of U.S. export laws
SuSE	yes	FreeS/WAN IPSEC, since 1999
Debian	sort of	FreeS/WAN IPSEC is part of Gibralta, a Linux firewall product based on Debian

Note that there's a gotcha around IPSEC tunnels and MTU size. It's important to ensure that once a packet has been encrypted by IPSEC, nothing fragments it along the path the tunnel traverses. To achieve this feat, it may be necessary to lower the MTU on the devices in front of the tunnel (in the real world, 1,400 bytes usually works). See page 244 in the TCP chapter for more information about MTU size.

All I need is a VPN, right?

Sadly, there's a downside to VPNs. Although they do provide a (mostly) secure tunnel across the untrusted network between the two endpoints, they don't usually address the security of the endpoints themselves. For example, if you set up a VPN between your corporate backbone and your CEO's home, you may be inadvertently creating a path for your CEO's 15-year-old daughter to have direct access to everything on your network. Hopefully, she only uses her newly acquired access to get a date with the shipping clerk.

Bottom line: you need to treat connections from VPN tunnels as external connections and grant them additional privileges only as absolutely necessary and after careful consideration. You may want to consider adding a special section to your site security policy that covers what rules apply to VPN connections.

21.13 SOURCES OF SECURITY INFORMATION

Half the battle of keeping your system secure consists of staying abreast of security-related developments in the world at large. If your site is broken into, it probably won't be through the use of a novel technique. More likely, the chink in your armor will have been widely discussed on security-related newsgroups and mailing lists.

CERT: a registered service mark of Carnegie Mellon University

In response to the uproar over the 1988 Internet worm, the Defense Advanced Research Projects Agency (DARPA) formed an organization called CERT, the Computer Emergency Response Team, to act as a clearing house for computer security information. CERT is still the best-known point of contact for security information, though it seems to have grown rather sluggish and bureaucratic of late. CERT also now insists that the name CERT does not stand for anything and is merely "a registered service mark of Carnegie Mellon University."

Although CERT's charter includes some degree of problem solving, in reality CERT lacks the ability to investigate problems or to discipline offenders, and so it is really little more than a repository for vendor security patches and security tool announcements. These patches and announcements are called "CERT advisories." New advisories are posted to www.cert.org, emailed to the cert-advisory mailing list, and submitted to the newsgroup comp.security.announce. To subscribe, see

> http://www.cert.org/contact_cert/certmaillist.html.

SecurityFocus.com and the BugTraq mailing list

SecurityFocus.com is a site that specializes in security-related news and information. The news includes current articles on general issues and on specific problems; there's also an extensive technical library of useful papers, nicely sorted by topic.

SecurityFocus's archive of security tools includes software for a variety of operating systems, along with blurbs and user ratings. It is the most comprehensive and detailed source of tools that we are aware of.

The BugTraq list is a moderated forum for the discussion of security vulnerabilities and their fixes. To subscribe, send email to listserv@securityfocus.com with the following message body:

> SUBSCRIBE BUGTRAQ *lastname, firstname*

Traffic on this list can be fairly heavy, however. A database of BugTraq vulnerability reports is also available from the web site.

Crypto-Gram newsletter

The monthly Crypto-Gram newsletter is a valuable and sometimes entertaining source of information regarding computer security and cryptography. It's produced by Bruce Schneier, author of the well-respected books *Secrets and Lies* and *Applied Cryptography*. You can subscribe to Crypto-Gram at

> http://www.counterpane.com/crypto-gram.html

SANS: the System Administration, Networking, and Security Institute

SANS is a professional organization that sponsors security-related conferences and training programs, as well as publishing a variety of security information. Their web site, www.sans.org, is a useful resource that occupies something of a middle ground between SecurityFocus and CERT: neither as frenetic as the former nor as stodgy as the latter.

SANS offers several weekly and monthly email bulletins that you can sign up for on their web site. The weekly NewsBites are nourishing, but the monthly summaries contain a lot of boilerplate. Neither is a great source of late-breaking security news.

Distribution-specific security resources

Because security problems have the potential to generate a lot of bad publicity, vendors are often eager to help customers keep their systems secure. Most large vendors have an official mailing list to which security-related bulletins are posted, and many maintain a web site about security issues as well. It's common for security-related software patches to be distributed for free, even by vendors that normally charge for software support.

There are also security portals on the web, such as www.securityfocus.com, that contain vendor-specific information and links to the latest official vendor dogma.

 A list of Red Hat security advisories can be found at www.redhat.com/support/errata. As of this writing, no official security mailing list is sponsored by Red Hat. However, there are a variety of Linux security resources on the net; most of the information applies directly to Red Hat.

 You can find SuSE security advisories at

  http://www.suse.com/us/support/security/index.html

You can join the official SuSE security announcement mailing list by visiting

  http://www.suse.de/en/support/mailinglists/index.html

 Check out www.debian.org to view the latest in Debian security news, or join the mailing list at

  http://www.debian.org/MailingLists/subscribe#debian-security-announce

Security information about Cisco products is distributed in the form of field notices, a list of which can be found at www.cisco.com/warp/public/770. To subscribe to Cisco's security mailing list, send mail to majordomo@cisco.com with the line "subscribe cust-security-announce" in the message body.

Other mailing lists and web sites

The contacts listed above are just a few of the many security resources available on the net. Given the volume of info that's now available and the rapidity with which resources come and go, we thought it would be most helpful to point you toward some meta-resources.

One good starting point is the X-Force web site (xforce.iss.net) at Internet Security Systems, which maintains a variety of useful FAQs. One of these is a current list of security-related mailing lists. The vendor and security patch FAQs provide useful contact information for a variety of vendors.

www.yahoo.com has an extensive list of security links; be sure to look under the general "computers and Internet" security section since the Linux-specific section is somewhat anemic. Another good source of links on the subject of network security can be found at www.about.com.

21.14 HARDENED LINUX DISTRIBUTIONS

Fortunately (?), we've been blessed with a variety of initiatives to produce "hardened" versions of Linux that provide a broader range of security features than are found in the mainstream releases. The hardening usually takes the form of special access controls and auditing capabilities. These features are probably particularly useful if you're planning to use Linux in some type of custom network appliance product. However, it's not clear that they provide substantial advantages to mainstream users. They still require good hygiene, a good packet filter, and all the other things discussed in this chapter. Perhaps they're good for added peace of mind.

Table 21.4 lists some of the better known hardening projects so you can check out what they have to offer.

Table 21.4   Hardened Linux distributions

Project name	Web site
Bastille Linux	www.bastille-linux.org
Engarde Linux	www.engardelinux.com
Linux Intrusion Detection System	www.lids.org
NSA's Security Enhanced Linux	www.nsa.gov/selinux

21.15 WHAT TO DO WHEN YOUR SITE HAS BEEN ATTACKED

The key to handling an attack is simple: Don't panic. It's very likely that by the time you discover the intrusion, most of the damage has already been done. In fact, it has probably been going on for weeks or months. The chance that you've discovered a break-in that just happened an hour ago is slim to none.

In that light, the wise owl says to take a deep breath and begin developing a carefully thought out strategy for dealing with the break-in. You need to avoid tipping off the intruder by announcing the break-in or performing any other activity that would seem abnormal to someone who may have been watching your site's operations for many weeks. Hint: performing a system backup is usually a good idea at this point and (hopefully!) will appear to be a normal activity to the intruder.[17]

---

17. If system backups are not a "normal" activity at your site, you have much bigger problems than the security intrusion.

This is also a good time to remind yourself that some studies have shown that 60% of security incidents involve an insider. Be very careful who you discuss the incident with until you're sure you have all the facts.

Here's a quick 9-step plan that may assist you in your time of crisis:

Step 1: Don't panic. In many cases, a problem isn't noticed until hours or days after it took place. Another few hours or days won't affect the outcome. The difference between a panicky response and a rational response will. Many recovery situations are exacerbated by the destruction of important log, state, and tracking information during an initial panic.

Step 2: Decide on an appropriate level of response. No one benefits from an over-hyped security incident. Proceed calmly. Identify the staff and resources that must participate and leave others to assist with the post-mortem after it's all over.

Step 3: Hoard all available tracking information. Check accounting files and logs. Try to determine where the original breach occurred. Perform a backup of all your systems. Make sure that you physically write-protect backup tapes if you put them in a drive to read them.

Step 4: Assess your degree of exposure. Determine what crucial information (if any) has "left" the company, and devise an appropriate mitigation strategy. Determine the level of future risk.

Step 5: Pull the plug. If necessary and appropriate, disconnect compromised machines from the network. Close known holes and stop the bleeding. The Compromise FAQ from ISS provides some good technical suggestions on what to actually do with the systems that were broken into. It can be found at

> http://xforce.iss.net/library/faqs/compromise.php3

Step 6: Devise a recovery plan. With a creative colleague, draw up a recovery plan on nearby whiteboard. This procedure is most effective when performed away from a keyboard. Focus on putting out the fire and minimizing the damage. Avoid assessing blame or creating excitement. In your plan, don't forget to address the psychological fallout your user community may experience.

Step 7: Communicate the recovery plan. Educate users and management about the effects of the break-in, the potential for future problems, and your preliminary recovery strategy. Be open and honest. Security incidents are part of life in a modern networked environment. They are not a reflection on your ability as a system administrator or on anything else worth being embarrassed about. Openly admitting that you have a problem is 90% of the battle, as long as you can demonstrate that you have a plan to remedy the situation.

Step 8: Implement the recovery plan. You know your systems and networks better than anyone. Follow your plan and your instincts. Speak with a colleague at a similar institution (preferably one who knows you well) to keep yourself on the right track.

Step 9: Report the incident to authorities. If the incident involved outside parties, you should report the matter to CERT. They can be reached by fax at (412) 268-6989 or by email at cert@cert.org. Provide as much information as you can.

A standard form is available from www.cert.org to help jog your memory. Here are some of the more useful pieces of information you might provide.

- The names, hardware types, and OS versions of the compromised machines
- The list of patches that had been applied at the time of the incident
- A list of accounts that are known to have been compromised
- The names and IP addresses of any remote hosts that were involved
- Contact information if you know it for the administrators of remote sites
- Relevant log entries or audit information

If you believe that a previously undocumented software problem may have been involved, you should report the incident to your vendor as well.

21.16 RECOMMENDED READING

BRYANT, WILLIAM. "Designing an Authentication System: a Dialogue in Four Scenes." web.mit.edu/kerberos/www/dialogue.html

CERT COORDINATION CENTER. "Intruder Detection Checklist." www.cert.org/tech_tips/intruder_detection_checklist.html

CERT COORDINATION CENTER. "UNIX Configuration Guidelines." www.cert.org/tech_tips/unix_configuration_guidelines.html

CHESWICK, WILLIAM R., AND STEVEN M. BELLOVIN. *Firewalls and Internet Security, 2nd Edition.* Reading, MA; Addison-Wesley. 2000.

CURTIN, MATT, AND MARCUS RANUM. "Internet Firewalls: Frequently Asked Questions." www.interhack.net/pubs/fwfaq

FARMER, DAN, AND WIETSE VENEMA. "Improving the Security of Your Site by Breaking Into it." 1993. www.fish.com/security

FARROW, RIK, AND RICHARD POWER. *Network Defense article series.* 1998-2001. www.spirit.com/Network

FRASER, B., EDITOR. *RFC2196: Site Security Handbook.* www.rfc-editor.org.

GARFINKEL, SIMSON, and GENE SPAFFORD. *Practical UNIX and Internet Security.* Sebastopol: O'Reilly & Associates. 1996.

KERBY, FRED, ET AL. "SANS Intrusion Detection and Response FAQ." SANS. www.sans.org/newlook/resources/IDFAQ/ID_FAQ.htm

MANN, SCOTT, AND ELLEN L. MITCHELL. *Linux System Security: The Administrator's Guide to Open Source Security Tools.* Upper Saddle River, NJ: Prentice Hall PTR. 2000.

Security

MORRIS, ROBERT, AND KEN THOMPSON. "Password Security: A Case History." Communications of the ACM, 22 (11): 594-597, November 1979. Reprinted in *UNIX System Manager's Manual*, 4.3 Berkeley Software Distribution. University of California, Berkeley. April 1986.

PICHNARCZYK, KARYN, STEVE WEEBER, AND RICHARD FEINGOLD. "UNIX Incident Guide: How to Detect an Intrusion." Computer Incident Advisory Capability, U.S. Department of Energy. 1994. http://ciac.llnl.gov/ciac/documents

RITCHIE, DENNIS M. "On the Security of UNIX." May 1975. Reprinted in *UNIX System Manager's Manual*, 4.3 Berkeley Software Distribution. University of California, Berkeley. April 1986.

SCHNEIER, BRUCE. *Applied Cryptography: Protocols, Algorithms, and Source Code in C.* New York, NY: Wiley, 1995.

THOMPSON, KEN. "Reflections on Trusting Trust." in *ACM Turing Award Lectures: The First Twenty Years 1966-1985.* Reading, MA: ACM Press (Addison-Wesley). 1987.

ZIMMERMANN, PHILIP R. *The Official PGP User's Guide.* Cambridge: MIT Press, 1995.

SONNENREICH, WES, AND TOM YATES. *Building Linux and OpenBSD Firewalls.* New York, NY: J.W. Wiley. 2000.

This is an awesome little book: it's easy to read, has good examples, shows a good sense of humor, and is just generally excellent. Our only gripe with this book is that it argues against the use of **sudo** for root access, claiming that it's too hard to use and not worth the trouble. We strongly disagree.

21.17 EXERCISES

E21.1 Discuss the strength of SSH authentication with Linux passwords vs. SSH authentication with a passphrase and key pair. If one is clearly more secure than the other, should you automatically require the more secure authentication method?

★ **E21.2** **tripwire** identifies files that have changed.

a) What is required to set up and use **tripwire** on your machine?

b) What recent Internet diseases would **tripwire** be effective against?

c) What recent Internet diseases would **tripwire** be helpless against?

d) Given physical access to a system, how could **tripwire** be circumvented?

e) What can you conclude if **tripwire** says that **/bin/login** has changed, but it seems to have the same size and modification date as before? What if the **sum** program gives the same values for old and new versions?

★ **E21.3** SSH tunneling is often the only way to tunnel traffic to a remote machine on which you don't have administrator access. Read the **ssh** man page and provide a command line that tunnels traffic from localhost port 113 to mail.remotenetwork.org port 113. The forwarding point of your tunnel should also be the host mail.remotenetwork.org.

★ **E21.4** Pick a recent security incident and research it. Find the best sources of information about the incident and find patches or workarounds that are appropriate for the systems in your lab. List your sources and the actions you propose for protecting your lab.

★★ **E21.5** With permission from your local sysadmin group, install **crack**, the program that searches for logins with weak passwords. Modify the **crack** source code so that it outputs only the login names with which weak passwords are associated, not the passwords themselves. Run **crack** on your local lab's password file (you will need access to **/etc/shadow**) and see how many breakable passwords you find. Set your own password to a dictionary word and give **crack** just your own entry in **/etc/shadow**. How long does **crack** take to find it? Try other patterns (capital letter, number after dictionary word, single-letter password, etc.) to see exactly how smart **crack** is.

★★ **E21.6** In the computer lab, set up two machines: a target and a prober. Install **nmap** and Nessus on the prober. Attack the target with these tools. How could you detect the attack on the target? Set up a firewall on the target using **iptables** to defend against the probes. Can you detect the attack now? How? What other defenses can be set up against the attacks? (Requires root access.)

⋆⋆ **E21.7** A security team recently found a large hole in many current and older **sshd** servers. Find a good source of information on the hole and discuss the issues and the best way to address them.

⋆⋆ **E21.8** Setuid programs are sometimes a necessary evil. However, setuid shell scripts should be avoided. Why?

⋆⋆ **E21.9** What do the rules in the following **iptables** output allow and disallow? What would be some very easy additions that would enhance security and privacy? (Hint: the OUTPUT and FORWARD chains could use some more rules.)

```
Chain INPUT (policy ACCEPT)
target     prot opt source      destination
block      all  --   anywhere   anywhere

Chain FORWARD (policy ACCEPT)
target     prot opt source      destination
           all  --   anywhere   anywhere

Chain OUTPUT (policy ACCEPT)
target     prot opt source      destination

Chain block (1 references)
target     prot opt source          destination
ACCEPT     all  --   anywhere        anywhere     state RELATED,ESTABLISHED
ACCEPT     tcp  --   anywhere        anywhere     state NEW tcp dpt:www
ACCEPT     tcp  --   anywhere        anywhere     state NEW tcp dpt:ssh
ACCEPT     tcp  --   128.138.0.0/16  anywhere     state NEW tcp dpt:kerberos
ACCEPT     icmp --   anywhere        anywhere
DROP       all  --   anywhere        anywhere
```

⋆⋆ **E21.10** Inspect a local firewall's rulesets. Discuss what you find in terms of policies. Are there any glaring security holes? (This exercise may require the cooperation of the administrators responsible for your local site's security.)

⋆⋆⋆⋆⋆ **E21.11** Write a tool that determines whether any network interfaces at your site are in promiscuous mode. Run it regularly on your networks to try to spot such an intrusion quickly. How much load does the tool generate? Do you have to run it on each machine, or can you run it from afar? Can you design a sneaky packet that would tell you if an interface was in promiscuous mode? (Requires root access.)

22 Web Hosting and Internet Servers

The last few years have been a wild ride in computing. UNIX was the amino acid-laden tidal pool that gave rise to modern client/server computing and the Internet itself. When the World Wide Web appeared on the scene as the ultimate distributed client/server application in the early 1990s, UNIX was there as its ready-made platform, and a new era was born. In the late 1990s, Linux became a popular hosting platform because of its cost (or lack thereof), speed, variety of supported hardware platforms, and flexibility.

Today, there are a variety of Internet-centric services that you might want to "host," either at your site or at one of the many co-location outsourcing providers. In this chapter, we address the two most common services: the web and FTP.

22.1 WEB HOSTING

In the early 1990s, UNIX was (literally) the only choice for serving content to the web. As the web's popularity grew, an increasing number of parties—ranging from advertising agencies to zoos—developed an interest in having their own presence on the net. However, UNIX and Linux represented a foreign culture to many of these folks.

Seizing the opportunity, companies large and small jumped into the ring with their own server solutions. In many cases, these solutions involved substantial reengineering of operating systems that, unlike Linux, were not built from the ground up with true preemptive multitasking in mind. Nevertheless, a new industry segment known as "web hosting" or "Internet hosting" was born around the task of serving content to the web. Web hosting servers not only deliver raw web (HTML) pages but also provide supporting services such as FTP, SSL, and streaming audio or video.

These days we have a variety of web hosting platforms to choose from, and a number of specialized web servers have been developed to meet the needs of specific market channels. Microsoft's once and future flagship product, Windows, has been widely marketed as a web hosting platform. But for folks looking for extreme reliability, maintainability, security, and performance, Linux is still way ahead of the pack in the web hosting game.

The industry press has published countless articles that ask the question "Which web hosting platform is best?", usually positioning Windows and Linux at opposite corners of the ring. Although some of this brouhaha is akin to the "Less filling!" "Tastes great!" battle, there are concrete reasons why Linux is usually a better choice for production sites.

The foremost advantages of Linux are its maintainability and performance. Linux was designed from the start as a multiuser, interactive operating system. On a Linux box, one administrator can maintain a database while another looks at I/O performance and a third maintains the web server. Under Windows, the person in control of the console (either physically or remotely, using a tool such as PC-Anywhere or the software included with Windows XP) is the only one who can perform critical administration tasks. As for performance, a good administrator can tune Linux to perform at least two to three times faster than Windows on identical hardware.

22.2 WEB HOSTING BASICS

Hosting a web site isn't substantially different from providing any other network service. The foundation of the World Wide Web is the Hyper-Text Transfer Protocol (HTTP), a simple TCP-based protocol that's used to format, transmit, and link documents containing a variety of media types, including text, pictures, sound, animation, and video. HTTP behaves much like the other client/server protocols used on the Internet, for example, SMTP (for email) and FTP (for file transfer).

A web server is simply a system that's configured to answer HTTP requests. To convert your generic Linux system into a web hosting platform, you need to install a daemon that listens for connections on TCP port 80 (the HTTP standard), accepts requests for documents and transmits them to the requesting user.

Web browsers such as Netscape, Opera, and Internet Explorer contact remote web servers and make requests on behalf of users. The documents thus obtained can contain hypertext pointers (links) to other documents, which may or may not live on the server that the user originally contacted. Since the HTTP protocol standard is well defined, clients running on any operating system or architecture can connect to any HTTP server. This platform independence, along with HTTP's ability to transparently pass a user from one server to another, has helped spark its amazing success.

There is life beyond straight HTTP, however. Many enhanced protocols have now been defined for providing everything from encryption to streaming video. These additional services are often managed by separate daemons, even if they are provided by the same physical server. For example, one of the most popular enhanced services is Secure HTTP, aka HTTPS. It's handled by a daemon that understands the Secure Socket Layer (SSL) protocol and listens for requests on TCP port 443.

Uniform resource locators

A uniform resource locator (URL) is a pointer to an object or service on the Internet. It describes how to access an object by means of five basic components:

- Protocol or application
- Hostname
- TCP/IP port (optional)
- Directory (optional)
- Filename (case sensitive; often ends in ".htm" or ".html")

Exhibit A illustrates a typical URL and its components.

Exhibit A   Parts of a URL

Table 22.1 shows the protocols that are commonly used in URLs.

Table 22.1   URL protocols

Proto	What it does	Example
http	Accesses a remote file via HTTP	http://admin.com/index.html
https	Accesses a remote file via HTTP/SSL	https://admin.com/order.shtml
ftp	Accesses a remote file via FTP	ftp://ftp.xor.com/adduser.tar.gz
mailto	Sends email to a designated address	mailto:sa-book@admin.com
news	Accesses Usenet newsgroups	news:alt.cooking
telnet	Logs in to a remote computer	telnet://spot.acme.com
ldap	Accesses LDAP directory services	ldap://ldap.bigfoot.com:389/cn=Herb
file	Accesses a local file (no Internet)	file://etc/syslog.conf

How HTTP works

HTTP is the protocol that makes the World Wide Web really work, and to the amazement of many, it is an extremely basic, stateless, client/server protocol. In the HTTP paradigm, the initiator of a connection is always the client (usually a browser). The client asks the server for the "contents" of a specific URL. The server responds with either a spurt of data or with some type of error message. In HTTP versions 0.9 and 1.0, the connection is then closed; in HTTP 1.1, the client can go on to request another object.

Because HTTP is so simple, you can easily make yourself into a crude web browser by using **telnet**. Since the standard port for HTTP service is port 80, just **telnet** directly to that port on your web server of choice. Once you're connected, you can issue HTTP commands. The most common command is GET, which requests the contents of a document. Usually, GET / is what you want, since it requests the root document (usually, the home page) of whatever server you've connected to. HTTP is case sensitive, so make sure you type commands in capital letters.

```
% telnet localhost 80
Trying 127.0.0.1...
Connected to localhost.atrust.com.
Escape character is '^]'.
GET /
<contents of your index.html file appear here>
Connection closed by foreign host.
```

CGI scripting: generating content on the fly

In addition to serving up static documents, an HTTP server can provide the user with content that has been created on the fly. For example, if you wanted to provide the current time and temperature to users visiting your web site, you might have the HTTP server execute a script to obtain this information. This amaze-the-natives trick is normally accomplished with the Common Gateway Interface, or CGI.

CGI is not a programming language, but rather a specification that allows an HTTP server to exchange information with other programs. Most often, CGI scripts are Perl, Python, or C programs that have been written specifically to interface with an HTTP server. But really, almost any programming language that can perform real-time I/O is acceptable. Just think of all those lonely FORTRAN programmers that can now reapply their skills to the Internet!

For the most part, CGI scripts are the concern of web developers and programmers. Unfortunately, CGI scripting collides with the job of the system administrator in one important area: security. Because CGI scripts have access to files, network connections, and other methods of moving data from one place to another, their execution can potentially affect the security of the machine on which the HTTP server is running. Ultimately, a CGI script gives anyone in the world the ability to run a program (the CGI script) on your server. Therefore, CGI scripts need to be just as secure as any other network-accessible program.

For a good source of information on the secure handling of CGI scripts, see the file www.w3.org/Security/Faq/www-security-faq.html.

Load balancing

It's difficult to predict how many hits (requests for a single object, such as a text file or image) or page views (requests for all the objects on a single viewable page) a single server will be able to handle. The exact capacity of a server depends on the operating system it is running, the extent of system tuning, the system's hardware architecture (including subsystems), and the construction of the site (for instance, is it purely static HTML pages, or are there database calls and numeric calculations to be made?). Only direct benchmarking and measurement of your actual site running on your actual hardware can answer the "how many hits?" question. Sometimes, people who have built similar sites on similar hardware may be able to give you a wild-ass guess that will be useful for planning purposes. In no case should you believe the numbers quoted by commercial system suppliers.

That said, instead of single-server hit counts, a better parameter to focus on is scalability. Make sure that you and your web design team have a plan that allows you to spread the load of a heavily trafficked site across multiple servers. The easiest way to spread the traffic is to use commercial third-party load balancing hardware, such as the Big-IP Controller from F5 Networks, or the Alteon ACEswitch (now sold and marketed by Nortel). These products distribute the work as specified by a variety of administrator-configurable parameters such as individual server response time and availability. Load balancing adds both performance and redundancy to your network—don't leave home without it.

22.3 HTTP SERVER INSTALLATION

Installing and maintaining a web server is easy! Web services rank far below email and DNS in complexity and difficulty of administration.

Choosing a server

Several excellent HTTP servers are available for Linux, but you'll most likely want to start with the Apache server.[1] This is the default web server on Red Hat, SuSE, and Debian systems and is well known in the industry for its flexibility and performance. As of December 2001, 56.5% of web servers on the Internet were running Apache. Exhibit B on page 698 shows the market share trends over time.

The Apache HTTP server is "free to a good home" and full source code is available from the Apache Group site at www.apache.org. The less adventurous may want to install the binary-only Apache package that comes as part of your Linux distribution. (But chances are that it's already installed on your system.)

---

1. The Apache group was formed by several people who provided patch files for NCSA **httpd**, a popular web server in the "early days," circa 1993. The end result was "a patchy" server. Giddit?

Exhibit B **Web server market share through December 2001 (all domains)**[a]

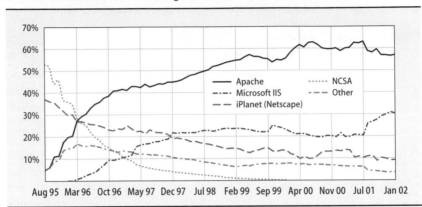

a. Courtesy of Netcraft. See www.netcraft.com/survey for the latest version.

You can find a useful comparison of all the currently available HTTP servers at the site webcompare.internet.com. Here are some of the factors you may want to consider in making your selection:

- Robustness
- Performance
- Timeliness of updates and bug fixes
- Availability of source code
- Cost
- Access control and security
- Ability to act as a proxy
- Ability to handle encryption

Installing Apache

If you do decide to download the source code and compile it yourself, you'll need to execute the **configure** script included with the distribution. This script automatically detects the type of system that you use and sets up the appropriate makefiles. You need to use the **--prefix** option to specify where in your directory tree the Apache server should live. For example:

```
% ./configure --prefix=/etc/httpd/
```

You can include in or remove from your server some of Apache's features by invoking the **-enable-module=** and **-disable-module=** options to **configure**. Although the default set of modules is reasonable, you may also want to enable the modules shown in Table 22.2.

Likewise, you may want to disable the modules listed in Table 22.3. For security and performance, it's a good idea to disable modules that you know you will not be using.

Table 22.2   Useful Apache modules that are not enabled by default

Module	Function
auth_dbm	Uses a DBM database to manage user/group access (recommended)[a]
auth_db	Uses a DB database to manage user/group access (recommended)[a]
usertrack	Enables click-trail tracking of browsers that support "cookie" technology
rewrite	Rewrites URLs using regular expressions
expires	Lets you attach expiration dates to documents
proxy	Uses Apache as a proxy server (more on this later)

a. We recommend that you use one of these modules, but there's no need to enable both.

Table 22.3   Apache modules we suggest removing

Module	Function
asis	Allows designated file types to be sent without HTTP headers
autoindex	Indexes directories that don't have a default HTML file (e.g., **index.html**)
env	Lets you set special environment variables for CGI scripts
include	Allows server-side includes, an obsolete on-the-fly content creation scheme
userdir	Allows users to have their own HTML directories

For a complete list of standard modules, see the **src/Configuration** file in your Apache distribution or http://www.apache.org/docs/mod/index.html.

When **configure** has finished executing, run **make** and then run **make install** to actually compile and install the appropriate files.

Configuring Apache

Once the server has been installed, you'll need to configure it for your application. All configuration files are kept in the **conf** directory (e.g., **/etc/httpd/conf**). You will need to examine and customize three different configuration files to meet your site's needs: **httpd.conf**, **srm.conf**, and **access.conf**.

httpd.conf specifies how the Apache daemon (**httpd**) interacts with your system. In this file, you can set the TCP port on which the HTTP server listens for queries (usually port 80, though you can choose another—and yes, you can run multiple HTTP servers on different ports on a single machine), the location of log files, and various network and performance parameters. **httpd.conf** is also the file in which you can configure **httpd** to respond to virtual interface connections; see page 702 for details.

Resources that the server needs to access are controlled in the **srm.conf** file. This file includes the all-important DocumentRoot definition, which defines the root of the directory tree in which servable documents are located. The file also addresses issues such as the handling of "special" URLs like http://www.atrust.com/~steve.

You manage security concerns through the **access.conf** file. This file contains directives that control access on a per-file or per-directory basis. These permissions prevent access to sensitive files via **httpd**, whether from the outside world or from inside your site.

You should specify at least two access controls: one that covers the entire document directory and one that applies only to the **cgi-bin** directory. Only the designated **cgi-bin** directory should allow script execution. That way, individual users cannot create security holes—accidentally or otherwise—with their own scripts. Use the option ExecCGI in **srm.conf** to enable this restriction.

Running Apache

You can start **httpd** by hand or from your machine's **rc** scripts. The latter is preferable, since this configuration will ensure that the web server restarts whenever the machine reboots. To start the server by hand, you would type something like

```
% /usr/sbin/httpd -f /etc/httpd/conf/httpd.conf
```

*See Chapter 2 for more information about **rc** scripts.*

If you want to start **httpd** automatically at boot time, you'll need to make a link in your **rc** directory that points to the **/etc/init.d/httpd** file (which is installed as part of the **httpd** package). It's best if you start **httpd** late in the booting sequence, after daemons that manage functions such as routing and time synchronization have started.

High-performance hosting

One of the many things the hosting community has learned over the last few years is that the key to high-performance hosting is to optimize servers for static content. Linux now offers unique functionality in this space through the TUX web server.

TUX is a kernel-based web server that runs in conjunction with a traditional web server such as Apache. Whenever possible, TUX serves up static pages without ever leaving kernel space, in much the same way that **rpc.nfsd** serves files. This architecture eliminates the need to copy data between kernel and user space and minimizes the number of context switches. Although TUX is not recommended for beginners, it's an excellent choice for sites that need to serve up content with lightning speed.

Although TUX was developed by Red Hat (and is available from www.redhat.com), it's been released under the GPL and can be used with other Linux distributions. However, configuring TUX can be somewhat of a challenge. For details, see

> http://www.redhat.com/docs/manuals/tux

22.4 VIRTUAL INTERFACES

In the early days, a machine typically acted as the server for a single web site (e.g., www.acme.com). As the web's popularity grew, everybody wanted to have a web site, and overnight, thousands of companies became web hosting providers.

Providers quickly realized that they could achieve significant economies of scale if they were able to host more than one site on a single server. This trick would allow www.acme.com, www.ajax,com, www.toadranch.com, and many other sites to be transparently served by the same hardware. In response to this business need, virtual interfaces were born.

Virtual interfaces allow a daemon to identify connections based not only on the destination port number (e.g., port 80 for HTTP) but also on the connection's destination IP address. Today, virtual interfaces are in widespread use and have proved to be useful for other applications besides web hosting.

The idea is simple: a single Linux machine responds on the network to more IP addresses than it has physical network interfaces. Each of the resulting "virtual" network interfaces can be associated with a corresponding domain name that users on the Internet might want to connect to. This feature allows a single Linux machine to serve literally hundreds of web sites. (By comparison, a competing Intel-centric operating system supports virtual interfaces but can only be practically used to host about a dozen sites. Of course, we could never name names.)

The HTTP 1.1 protocol defines a form of virtual-interface-like functionality (officially called "non-IP virtual interfaces") that eliminates the need to assign unique IP addresses to web servers or to configure a special interface at the OS level. This approach conserves IP addresses and is useful for some sites, especially sites at which a single server is home to hundreds or thousands of home pages (such as universities). However, the scheme isn't very practical for commercial sites; it reduces scalability (you must change the IP address of the site to move it to a different server) and may also have a negative impact on security (if you filter access to a site at your firewall according to IP addresses). It appears that true virtual interfaces will be around for a while.

Configuring virtual interfaces

Setting up a virtual interface involves two steps. First, you must create the virtual interface at the TCP/IP level. Second, you must tell the Apache server about the virtual interfaces you have installed. We cover this second step starting on page 702.

Linux virtual interfaces are named with *interface:instance* notation. For example, if your Ethernet interface is eth0, then the virtual interfaces associated with it would be eth0:0, eth0:1, and so on. All interfaces are configured with the **ifconfig** command. For example, the command

```
# ifconfig eth0:0 128.138.243.150 netmask 255.255.255.192 up
```

configures the interface eth0:0 and assigns it an address on the 128.138.243.128/26 network. To make virtual address assignments permanent, you modify the system startup files.

Web Hosting

For Red Hat, you'll need to create a separate file for each virtual interface in the directory **/etc/sysconfig/network-scripts**. For example, the file **ifcfg-eth0:0** corresponding to the **ifconfig** command shown above would contain

```
DEVICE=eth0:0
IPADDR=128.138.243.150
NETMASK=255.255.255.192
NETWORK=128.138.243.128
BROADCAST=128.138.243.191
ONBOOT=yes
```

On SuSE systems you can either create virtual interfaces with YaST or you can hand-edit the **/etc/rc.config** script to create them. For example, your **rc.config** file might contain the following entries to define both eth0 and eth0:0

```
# IP Adresses

IPADDR_0="128.138.243.149"
IPADDR_1="128.138.243.150"

# network device names (e.g. "eth0")

NETDEV_0="eth0"
NETDEV_1="eth0:0"

# ifconfig parameters

IFCONFIG_0="128.138.243.149 broadcast 128.138.243.191 netmask
    255.255.255.192"
IFCONFIG_1="128.138.243.150 broadcast 128.138.243.191 netmask
    255.255.255.192"
```

Debian's approach is similar to Red Hat's, but the interface definitions must appear in the file **/etc/network/interfaces**. The entries corresponding to the eth0:0 interface in our example above would be

```
iface eth0:0 inet static
    address 128.138.243.150
    netmask 255.255.255.192
    broadcast 128.138.243.191
```

Telling Apache about a virtual interface

In addition to creating the virtual interfaces with **ifconfig**, you need to tell Apache what documents to serve when a client tries to connect to each interface. You do this with a VirtualHost clause in the **httpd.conf** file, one VirtualHost clause for each virtual interface that you've configured. Here's an example:

```
<VirtualHost 128.138.243.150>
ServerAdmin webmaster@www.company.com
DocumentRoot /var/www/htdocs/company
ServerName www.company.com
ErrorLog logs/www.company.com-error_log
TransferLog logs/www.company.com-access_log
</VirtualHost>
```

A client that connects to the virtual host 128.138.243.150 will be served documents from the directory **/var/www/htdocs/company**, which should be unique to this site.

22.5 CACHING AND PROXY SERVERS

The Internet and the information on it are growing rapidly. Ergo, the bandwidth and computing resources required to support it are growing rapidly as well. How can this state of affairs continue?

The only way to deal with this growth is to use replication. Whether it's on a national, regional, or site level, Internet content needs to be more readily available from a closer source as the Internet grows. It just doesn't make sense to transmit the same popular web page from Australia across a very expensive link to North America millions of times each day. There should be a way to store this information once it's been sent across the link once. Fortunately, there is.

One answer is the freely available Squid Internet Object Cache.[2] This package is both a caching and a proxy server that runs under Linux and supports several protocols, including HTTP, FTP, and SSL.

Here's how it works. Client web browsers (such as Netscape and Internet Explorer) contact the Squid server to request an object from the Internet. The Squid server then makes a request on the client's behalf (or provides the object from its cache, as discussed in the following paragraph) and returns the result to the client. Proxy servers of this type are often used to enhance security or to filter content.

In a proxy-based system, only one machine needs to have direct access to the Internet through the organization's firewall. At organizations such as K-12 schools, a proxy server can also filter content so that inappropriate material doesn't fall into the wrong hands. Many commercial and freely available proxy servers (some based on Squid, some not) are available today.

Proxy service is nice, but it's the caching features of Squid that are really worth getting excited about. Squid not only caches information from local user requests, but it also allows a hierarchy of Squid servers to be constructed.[3] Groups of Squid servers use the Internet Cache Protocol (ICP) to communicate information about what's in their caches.

This feature allows administrators to build a system in which local users contact an on-site caching server to obtain content from the Internet. If another user at that site has already requested the same content, a copy can be returned at LAN speed (usually, 10 or 100 Mb/s). If the local Squid server doesn't have it, perhaps it contacts the regional caching server. As in the local case, if anyone in the region has requested the object, it is served immediately. If not, perhaps the caching server for the country or

Web Hosting

---

2. Why "Squid"? According to the FAQ, "all the good names were taken."

3. Unfortunately, some sites mark all their pages as being uncacheable, which prevents Squid from working its magic. In a similar vein, Squid isn't able to cache dynamically generated pages.

continent can be contacted, and so on. Users perceive a performance improvement, so they are happy.

For many, Squid offers economic benefits. Because users tend to share web discoveries, significant duplication of external web requests can occur at a reasonably sized site. One study has shown that running a caching server can reduce external bandwidth requirements by up to 40%. This extra efficiency can be a big win at sites that pay for usage by the minute or the megabyte. Unfortunately, effective use of Squid may require that you mandate all your users to configure their desktops to use your Squid server as their proxy—not always an easy task.

Setting up Squid

Squid is easy to install and configure. Since Squid needs space to store its cache, you should run it on a dedicated machine that has a lot of free memory and disk space. A reasonable configuration would be a machine with 256MB of RAM and 20GB of disk.

You can grab the Squid package in RPM or **apt-get** format from your distribution vendor, or you can download a fresh copy of Squid from www.squid-cache.org. If you choose the roll-your-own path, you will need to run the **configure** script at the top of the source tree after you unpack the distribution. This script assumes that you want to install the package in **/usr/local/squid**. If you prefer some other location, use the --**prefix=***dir* option to **configure**. After **configure** has completed, run **make all** and then **make install**.

Once you've installed Squid, you must localize the **squid.conf** configuration file. See the **QUICKSTART** file in the distribution directory for a list of the changes you need to make to the sample **squid.conf** file.

You must also run **squid -z** by hand to build and zero out the directory structure in which cached web pages will be stored. Finally, you can start the server by hand with the **RunCache** script; you will eventually want to call this script from your system's **rc** files so that they start the Squid server when the machine boots.

To test Squid, configure your desktop web browser to use the Squid server as a proxy. This option is usually found in browser's preferences panel.

22.6 Anonymous FTP server setup

FTP is one of the oldest and most basic services on the Internet, yet it continues to be widely used today. Although FTP has a variety of internal uses at a site, the most common use on the Internet is "anonymous FTP," which lets users that do not have accounts at your site download files you have made available.

FTP is useful for distributing bug fixes, software, document drafts, and the like. Its main advantage over HTTP (for this purpose) is that it allows users to inspect the tree of available materials for themselves and to see the sizes and modification dates of files. You don't need to write any HTML to point to new files—just drop them into the target zone and you're done.

To enable anonymous FTP, you create an account for the fake user "ftp", configure its home directory, and set up the FTP server daemon, **ftpd**. Because of the public nature of anonymous FTP, it is important to configure it correctly so that sensitive files are not accidentally made available to the whole world.

*See page 812 for more information about **inetd**.*

ftpd is managed by **inetd** and therefore must have an entry in the **/etc/inetd.conf** and **/etc/services** files. (If your system uses **xinetd** instead of **inetd**, you'll need to create a file in **/etc/xinetd.d** for **ftpd** instead of creating an **/etc/inetd.conf** entry.) When an FTP users logs in anonymously, **ftpd** executes a **chroot** system call to make files outside of the ~**ftp** directory invisible and inaccessible. The enhanced security provided by this precaution is important because **ftpd** must run setuid to root to manipulate privileged socket ports.

To allow anonymous **ftp** from your site, take the following steps:

- Add the user "ftp" to your regular password file.
- Create subdirectories **bin**, **etc**, **lib**, and **pub** beneath ~**ftp**.
- Copy the **ls** program to the ~**ftp/bin** directory.
- Copy or hard-link the shared libraries needed by **ls** to ~**ftp/lib**.[4]
- Copy **/etc/passwd** and **/etc/group** to ~**ftp/etc**.
- Edit the **passwd** and **group** files as described below.
- Replace all passwords in ~**ftp/etc/passwd** with stars.
- Set the proper permissions on files and directories under ~**ftp**.

No one needs to log in to the ftp account, so use a star as ftp's password. It's also a good idea to specify **/bin/false** as ftp's login shell.

Since an anonymous **ftp** session runs **chroot**ed to ~**ftp**, the subdirectories **bin** and **etc** must provide a copy of all the commands and configuration information needed by **ftpd**. After the **chroot**, ~**ftp/bin** and ~**ftp/etc** will masquerade as **/bin** and **/etc**.

In most cases, **ftpd** uses only the **ls** command and skeletal copies of **/etc/passwd** and **/etc/group** from ~**ftp/etc**.

See page 655 for more information about password security.

The **passwd** file under ~**ftp** should only contain the users root, daemon, and ftp. You must replace the passwords with stars, since this copy of the **passwd** file will be available to people who use your **ftp** server. Even if the passwords are encrypted, there is still a risk that other people could decode them.

For added security, make ~**ftp/bin/ls** execute-only by setting its mode to 111. This tweak prevents clients from copying away the binary and studying it for weaknesses.

Put the files you want to make available in ~**ftp/pub**.

Permissions on the various files and directories are quite important. We recommend that permissions be set as shown in Table 22.4 on page 706.

Web Hosting

---

4. Check the documentation for your distribution to find out which files are required; the default installations of Red Hat, SuSE, and Debian have already done this step for you. Note that hard linking only works if the files live within the same disk partition.

Table 22.4   Recommended permissions under ~ftp

File/Dir	Owner	Mode	File/Dir	Owner	Mode
~ftp	root	555	**~ftp/etc/passwd**	root	444
~ftp/bin	root	555	**~ftp/etc/group**	root	444
~ftp/bin/ls	root	111	**~ftp/pub**	root	755
~ftp/etc	root	555	**~ftp/lib**	root	755

Note that in the Red Hat and SuSE distributions, anonymous FTP is turned on by default. Although the default configuration makes anonymous FTP setup easy, it does pose a risk to the unsuspecting system administrator who is unaware of its presence. Remove the ftp user from the **passwd** file if you do not wish to provide anonymous FTP service.

One of the biggest security risks of anonymous FTP results from allowing users to deposit files in FTP directories. World-writable directories, no matter how obscure, will quickly become "nests" where hackers and kids looking to trade warez will store files, sucking up all your bandwidth and putting you right in the middle of a chain of activities that's probably undesirable, if not downright illegal. Don't be part of the problem; never allow writable anonymous FTP directories on your system.

22.7 EXERCISES

⭐ **E22.1** Configure a virtual interface on your workstation. Run **ifconfig** before and after to see what changed. Can you ping the virtual interface from another machine on the same subnet? From a different network? Why or why not? (Requires root access.)

⭐ **E22.2** With a packet sniffer (**tcpdump**) capture a two-way HTTP conversation that uploads information (e.g., filling out a form or a search field). Annotate the session to show how your browser conveyed information to the Web server. (Requires root access.)

⭐ **E22.3** Use a packet sniffer to capture the traffic when you open a busy web page such as the home page for amazon.com or cnn.com. How many separate TCP connections are opened? Who initiates them? Is this the most efficient way to use the TCP protocol? (Requires root access.)

⭐ **E22.4** Locate log files from an Internet-accessible web server, perhaps the main server for your site. Examine the log files. What can you say about the access patterns over a period of a few hours? What errors showed up during that period? What privacy concerns are illustrated by the contents of the log files? (May require root access.)

⭐⭐ **E22.5** Install Apache on your system and create a couple of content pages. From other machines, verify that your web server is operating. Find the Apache log files that let you see what browsers are hitting your server. Configure Apache to serve some of its content pages to the virtual interface created in E22.1. (Requires root access.)

⭐⭐ **E22.6** Use **tcpdump** to capture FTP traffic for both active and passive FTP sessions. How does the need to support an anonymous FTP server affect the a site's firewall policy? What would the firewall rules need to allow? (Requires root access.)

Web Hosting

SECTION THREE

BUNCH O' STUFF

23 Software Installation and Localization

Linux doesn't just appear on a computer by magic; someone needs to put it there. Although more and more vendors these days are offering to ship preconfigured Linux systems, it's inevitable that at some point you will need to install Linux yourself. Likewise, you will almost always need to make some changes to handle the particular needs of your local environment. Administrators must typically perform all of the following tasks:

- Installing Linux
- Automating mass installations
- Localizing systems
- Keeping systems updated
- Managing software packages

This chapter explores some techniques and applications that help reduce the pain of software installation and make these tasks scale effectively.

23.1 BASIC LINUX INSTALLATION

For the most part, basic installation of a Linux box is straightforward. You boot a CD-ROM or floppy disk, answer a few questions, and your distribution's installer copies the packages you select onto your hard drive. Almost all distributions have very good installation guides. A useful collection of vendor-independent installation guides is at

http://linux.com/learn/installguide

The boxed version of Red Hat includes the installation manual. It can also be found on-line at:

> http://www.redhat.com/docs/manuals/linux

The boxed SuSE set also includes installation manuals. SuSE doesn't appear to be very good about putting their docs online, perhaps in an effort to motivate sales of the retail release. A pity.

The Debian installation manual is at

> http://www.debian.org/releases/stable/installmanual

23.2 AUTOMATING INSTALLATION

If you ever install more than one computer at a time, you will find that you quickly reach the limits of interactive installation. To begin with, it is not very reproducible. Do you remember exactly which packages to install, for example? This sort of problem can be skirted with a localization checklist (see page 729), but even a checklist won't solve all problems.

Interactive installation takes a lot of time and effort. Even if you can afford to hire enough people to install 1,000 machines by hand, there are better uses for that money.

The installers for our example distributions are all scriptable, so another option is to create a floppy that contains the configuration you want. This solution solves the reproducibility problem, but it still doesn't scale very well. If you are installing hundreds of machines, building and using hundreds of configuration floppies is the height of tedium.

Red Hat's Kickstart and SuSE's YaST (both of which are advanced methods of scripting the distributions' standard installers) can both be made to support automatic network installation. There are also several open source development projects striving to produce third-party network installers; for example, SystemImager.

Debian users may feel a little hurt that we don't cover the Debian installer. Although it nominally supports NFS as a source of packages, the Debian installer unfortunately lacks many features that are needed to support proper network installs. A major redesign of the installer is in progress. A project called FAI (Fully Automatic Installation) aims to provide automation for Debian installations. See

> http://www.informatik.uni-koeln.de/fai

for more information. Alternatively, consider using a third-party installer such as SystemImager (see page 719).

Netbooting PCs

Netbooting allows you to boot a computer completely over the net, instead of from a hard disk, floppy, or CD-ROM. It's very convenient for installation because it means that you can sit at your desk and netboot a machine somewhere else without having to walk to the machine and insert a CD-ROM or floppy disk. Unfortunately, the network technique supported by most distributions is to boot from a floppy or CD-ROM and then get everything else from the network.

The Etherboot project (etherboot.sourceforge.net) creates open source boot PROMs for commonly used NICs that support network-only booting. However, since most people don't have EEPROM burners in their office, the actual utility of this solution is not clear. Support is gathering behind a new, open standard for netbooting Intel-based systems: PXE.

PXE: the PC netbooting standard

PXE (Preboot Execution Environment) is a somewhat crufty standard that embraces and extends DHCP to offer a netboot facility for the PC. PXE is being actively promoted by Intel and seems to be gradually taking over the market. Most new PCs support it. Although PXE isn't perfect, an ugly standard is better than none.

The PXE protocol is straightforward (and similar to the netboot procedures used on other architectures). A host broadcasts a DHCP "discover" request with the PXE option set, and a DHCP server or proxy responds with a DHCP packet that includes PXE options (the name of a boot server and a boot file). The client downloads its boot file through TFTP (or, optionally, multicast TFTP) and then executes it.

Although the PXE spec is not totally backward compatible with generic DHCP, in practice many modern DHCP servers can provide PXE booting service. Even servers that don't support the PXE protocol directly can interact with it by means of a proxy mechanism.

Several PXE-based netboot systems are in development, including PXELinux (an extension of Syslinux, see syslinux.hackerdojo.com/pxe.php) and PXEGRUB (an extension to the GRUB boot loader, see www.gnu.org). Intel also provides a PXE package for Linux:

> http://www.intel.com/ial/wfm/index.htm

Setting up PXE for Linux

The ISC (Internet Software Consortium) DHCP server, which ships with our example distributions, supports PXE. If you're using a different DHCP server, install the proxy from Intel's PXE package.

Unfortunately, current Linux distributions don't integrate PXE beyond the point of providing server-side DHCP support. They offer even less support for using PXE as a client; the installers typically don't support it out of the box. Of the installers that we describe in this chapter, only SystemImager is PXE-aware.

Nevertheless, netbooting is the right way to go for large installations, and you don't have to sit around waiting for distributors to get their act together. Documents that describe PXE are available from a variety of sources. A good place to start is the *Remote Boot HOWTO* available from www.linuxdoc.org.

Installation

Although the Red Hat folks don't yet officially support PXE, they do make some PXE stuff available and ship the Intel PXE software as part of their distribution. Kickstart can be made to work over PXE; see

> http://www.stanford.edu/~alfw/PXE-Kickstart

 SuSE doesn't ship with any PXE packages, but you can borrow the ones from Red Hat. YaST can easily be made to work with PXE, although this configuration isn't officially supported.

 Unfortunately, Debian doesn't yet have much in the way of PXE packages or documentation. You are on your own.

Netbooting non-PCs

PXE is an Intel product and is limited to IA-32 and IA-64 hardware. Other architectures have their own methods of booting over the net (almost always more elegant than PXE). Discussion of the many differences among architectures is really beyond the scope of this book, but a variety of resources on the web can help.

Alpha boxes generally use SRM to boot Linux, and the *SRM HOWTO* describes how to use this feature. SPARC machines and most PowerPC boxes use Open Firmware, which is easy to netboot (type **boot net**). The UltraLinux FAQ (www.ultralinux.org) has a useful guide to netbooting Linux on SPARC processors. For Macs, RS/6000s, and other PowerPC-based machines, the netboot procedure is specific to both your hardware and the boot loader you are using, so check your boot loader's docs.

Kickstart: Red Hat's automated installer

Kickstart is Red Hat's tool for performing automated installations. Kickstart is really a scripting interface to the standard Red Hat installer, Anaconda, and is dependent on both the Red Hat distribution and RPM packages. Unlike SystemImager and other raw image copiers, Kickstart is flexible and quite smart about autodetecting a system's hardware.

See page 733 for more information about packages. If you need lots of localization, you can make whatever changes are needed as part of a postinstall script. This works, but the postinstall scripts tend to become large and unmaintainable. Another option is to create an RPM package that contains your local customizations. We recommend the RPM route; it makes versioning easy, facilitates later upgrades, and provides you with dependency support and all the other goodies that come with a packaging system.

If you want to make major changes to the way that Red Hat looks out of the box, you'll probably find Kickstart suboptimal for your needs. In this situation, you're probably better off using an installation tool such as SystemImager.

Setting up a Kickstart configuration file

Kickstart's behavior is controlled by a single configuration file, generally called **ks.cfg**. The format of this file is straightforward. If you're visually inclined, Red Hat includes a handy GUI tool called **ksconfig** that lets you point and click your way to **ks.cfg** heaven.

The **ks.cfg** file is also quite easy to generate programmatically. For example, suppose that you wanted to install a different set of packages on servers and clients and that you also needed to handle slightly different installs customized for multiple offices. You could write a small Perl script that used a master set of parameters to generate a config file for the servers and clients in each office. Changing the complement of packages would become just a matter of changing this one Perl script rather than changing every config file. There may even be some cases in which you need to generate an individualized config file for each host. In this situation, you would certainly want the files to be automatically generated.

A nice manual for Kickstart (including a list of all the available options) is in *The Official Red Hat Linux Customization Guide* for Red Hat 7.2:

> http://www.redhat.com/docs/manuals/linux/RHL-7.2-Manual/custom-guide

One word of warning regarding the config file: if you make an error, the diagnostics consist of an unintelligible Python traceback that may or may not contain a hidden message that points you toward the mistake. It's easier to use **ksconfig**, which should generate a config file that is at least syntactically valid (although when we tried it, the partition commands it gave us didn't work...).

A Kickstart config file consists of three ordered parts. The first part is the command section, which specifies options such as the language, keyboard, and time zone. This section also specifies the source of the distribution with the url option (in the example below, it's a host called installserver).

Here's an example of a complete command section:

```
text
lang en_US                    # lang is used during the installation...
langsupport en_US             # ...and langsupport at run time.
keyboard us                   # Use an American keyboard .
timezone --utc America/EST    # --utc means hardware clock is on UTC (GMT)
mouse
rootpw whatever
reboot                        # Reboot after installation. You pretty much
                              #    always want to do this.
bootloader --location=mbr     # Install default boot loader in the MBR.
install                       # Install a new system instead of upgrading.
url --url http://installserver/redhat
clearpart --all --initlabel
part / --fstype ext3 --size 4096
part swap --size 1024
part /var --fstype ext3 -size 1 --grow
network --bootproto dhcp
auth --useshadow --enablemd5
firewall --disabled
xconfig --defaultdesktop=GNOME --startxonboot --resolution 1280x1024 --depth 24
```

The directives in the command section specify a list of partitions with sizes. You can also designate one of the partitions to grow to fill any remaining space on the disk.

The rootpw option sets the new machine's root password. The default is to specify the password in cleartext, which presents something of a security problem. You can use the --iscrypted flag to specify an already-encrypted password; however, MD5 passwords are not supported.

Kickstart uses graphical mode by default, which defeats the goal of unattended installation. The text keyword at the top of the example fixes this.

The second section is a list of packages to install, beginning with a %packages directive. The list can contain individual packages, collections such as @ GNOME, or the notation @ Everything to include the whole shebang. When selecting individual packages, specify only the package name, not the version or the **.rpm** extension. Here's an example:

```
%packages
@ Networked Workstation
@ X Window System
@ GNOME
mylocalpackage
```

In the third section of the Kickstart configuration file, you can specify arbitrary shell commands for Kickstart to execute. There are two possible sets of commands: one introduced with %pre that runs before installation and one introduced with %post that runs afterward. Both sections have some restrictions on the ability of the system to resolve hostnames, so it's safest to use IP addresses if you want to access the network. In addition, the postinstall commands are run in a **chroot**ed environment, so they cannot access the installation media.

Building a Kickstart server

Kickstart expects its files to be laid out as they are on the CD. It wants to have its packages stored in a directory called **RedHat/RPMS** on the server. You can easily add your own packages to this directory. There are, however, a couple of issues.

First, if you tell Kickstart to install all packages (with an @ Everything in the packages section of your **ks.cfg**), it will install the add-on packages in alphabetical order after the base packages have been laid down. If your package depends on other packages that are not in the base set, you may want to call your package something like **zzmypackage.rpm** to make sure that it gets installed last.

If you don't want to install all packages, either list your supplemental packages individually in the %packages section of the **ks.cfg** file or add your packages to one or more of the collection lists. Collection lists are specified by entries such as @ GNOME and stand for a predefined set of packages whose members are enumerated in the file **RedHat/base/comps** on the server. Unfortunately, the **comps** file format is not well documented. The collections are the lines that begin with 0 or 1 (the number specifies whether the collection is selected by default). In general, it's not a good idea to tamper with the standard collections. We suggest that you leave them as Red Hat defined them and explicitly name all your supplemental packages in the **ks.cfg** file.

Pointing Kickstart at your config file

Once you've created a config file, you have a couple of ways to get Kickstart to use it. The Red Hat-sanctioned method is to boot with a Red Hat boot floppy or CD-ROM and ask for a Kickstart installation by specifying **linux ks** at the initial boot: prompt. If you don't provide any additional arguments, the system will determine its network address by using DHCP. It will then obtain the DHCP boot server and boot file options, attempt to mount the boot server with NFS, and use the value of the boot file option as its **ks.cfg**. If no boot file has been specified, the system will look for a file called **/kickstart/***hostipaddress***-kickstart**.

Alternatively, Kickstart can be told to get its configuration file in some other way by providing a path as an argument to the **ks** option. There are several possibilities. The instruction

> boot: **linux ks=http:***server***:/path**

tells Kickstart to use HTTP to download the file instead of NFS. Using **ks=floppy** tells Kickstart to look for **ks.cfg** on the local floppy drive.

To eliminate the use of boot media entirely, you'll need to graduate to PXE. See page 713 for more information about that.

YaST: SuSE's installation tool

YaST is SuSE's all-in-one installation and configuration tool. The installation portion is more or less equivalent to Red Hat's Anaconda/Kickstart combination. Like Kickstart, YaST operates by installing RPM packages; it can also be automated with a configuration file.

YaST is smarter than Kickstart about hardware detection, and it makes customization easier as well. It's less flexible from a booting point of view and supports only NFS. A YaST white paper at

> http://www.suse.de/en/support/whitepapers/yast/index.html

provides most of the information that you'll need to use YaST. You might also want to read the paper "Automated Installation of Linux Systems Using YaST" that Dirk Hohndel and Fabian Herschel presented at USENIX's LISA conference:

> http://www.usenix.org/events/lisa99/full_papers/hohndel/hohndel_html

YaST doesn't support PXE out of the box, but getting it to work with PXE is quite a bit easier than the equivalent procedure with Kickstart. For details, see Anas Nashif's instructions for automating YaST installs at

> http://www.suse.de/~nashif/autoyast1/html/index.html

Installation

Creating a YaST server

The SuSE documentation describes how to set up an NFS-based YaST server by copying the SuSE CDs onto a hard disk and setting up a tree of symlinks. What they really mean is that YaST looks for a tree of packages and a config file in a directory called **suse**. If you copy these, you'll be fine. You can also insert your own packages into this directory.

Creating a YaST install

YaST is scripted by means of hierarchical **info** files. The base **info** file on your YaST server or CD-ROM can be overridden by one designed for a particular class of machines. Classes are specified by means of IP address ranges or hostname patterns; for example, *.cs.colorado.edu. In turn, class files can be overridden by host-specific files. Even better, YaST can use DHCP to determine parameters such as the host's IP addresses. If you use DHCP, you don't even need a host-specific **info** file to set network parameters.

Officially, YaST supports only booting from a floppy disk or CD-ROM. However, you can use PXE with YaST by installing PXELinux and using the SuSE-supplied **initrd** on the boot floppy as the PXELinux **initrd**.

One issue with using a boot floppy is that the standard SuSE boot disks are not very intelligent about configuring network interfaces. In theory, adding an appropriate **insmod** command to your **info** file (such as **insmod 3c59x**) to identify the model number of your network card helps solve this problem. Alternatively, you can build your own kernel for the boot floppy that includes the necessary network (and disk) devices. See Chapter 12, *Drivers and the Kernel*, for more information on building kernels (it's easy!).

info files live in **suse/setup/descr/info**, both on the install server and on the boot floppy. Configure the defaults in the **info** file on your NFS server and leave host-specific modifications to the host-specific **info** file.

Here's an example of a host **info** file:

```
Language: English
Bootmode: Net                    # Needed for network installation
Keytable: us
IP: 172.16.10.27
Netmask: 255.255.255.0
Gateway: 172.16.10.1
Server: 172.18.5.9               # NFS server from which to get packages
Serverdir: /susedir
Nameserver: 172.18.5.2
Netdevice: eth0
```

Each of these parameters can be configured with DHCP. Server and Serverdir are specified by the DHCP bootserver and bootpath options.

There are also installation parameters that specify the level of interactivity you want, but they are not consistent. Some use 2 to mean noninteractive, some use 1, and some use 0. The following configuration snippet shows how to turn off all the interactivity:

```
FAST_INSTALL 2    # Assume user wants an automatic install.
AUTO_FDISK 2      # 2 means to automatically partition the disk.
AUTO_LILO 2       # 2 means to automate LILO.
INSTALL_WAIT 0    # Don't wait for user input after package installation.
NO_ASK_SWAP 1     # Don't ask about swap.
NEVER_STOP 1      # Don't stop if there's a problem.
```

To tell YaST to use DHCP set:

```
AUTO_NAMESERVER 1
AUTO_NAME 1
AUTO_NET 1        # automatically install network stuff based on install
```

YaST learns which packages to install by means of an AUTO_INSTALL option. The argument to this option is the path to a "selection file," which is a list of packages to be installed. The format of a selection file is essentially a list; add your packages after the Toinstall line. If you start the path with $I:, YaST uses the install path. For example, to install the list of packages specified in the (SuSE-supplied) file **Minimal.sel**:

```
AUTO_INSTALL $I:suse/setup/descr/Minimal.sel
```

The PRE_INSTALL and POST_INSTALL options specify selection files for packages to be installed before or after AUTO_INSTALL. The PRE_SCRIPT and POST_SCRIPT options tell YaST about scripts that are to be run before or after the installation.

The last segment of the **info** file lets you turn services on or off in the **rc.config** file of the newly constructed system; this is one area in which YaST is significantly superior to Kickstart. Each RC_CONFIG_0 line specifies a variable name and its value. All RC_CONFIG_0 lines will be used to construct the **rc.config** file. See *SuSE startup scripts* on page 33 for more information about **rc.config**.

For example, to have **named** started at boot time on the newly installed system, add:

```
RC_CONFIG_0 START_NAMED yes
```

to the end of the **info** file.

SystemImager

SystemImager (www.systemimager.org) is an open source tool that uses a different approach from that of Kickstart or YaST. It installs complete OS images rather than individual packages and is faster than the package-based installers. In addition, you can easily make radical changes to the way you want your systems to look. SystemImager can operate over SSH, which is useful if you are installing Linux in a hostile environment. Its support for PXE is by far the best among the common installers.

SystemImager is simple and easy to customize, but brittle. It doesn't support much automatic configuration of the system image during installation; you need relatively homogenous machines for each system image.

SystemImager lacks the hardware configuration logic of Kickstart and YaST. Getting an image to install on multiple types of hardware can sometimes take a fair amount of tweaking. For example, with the current version you must provide separate images for systems with SCSI disks vs. IDE disks. SystemImager does not understand the concept of networks that are not associated with interface eth0. It also doesn't handle X Windows configuration; however, XFree86 version 4's support for mostly automatic configuration makes this less important. See www.xfree86.org for more information about XFree86.

Since it's possible to have as many images as you want, one option is to build a different image for each type of hardware you support. Too many images will create a maintenance nightmare, but for a cluster of identical machines, SystemImager is the easiest way to exactly duplicate an installation.

SystemImager has an active support group and will soon merge with LUI, an installer that originated at IBM, to produce "a complete suite of applications to manage all your system building needs." VA Software, the company that originally produced SystemImager, is no longer supporting it commercially, but a large open source community still uses it.

How SystemImager works

SystemImager provides a simple SYSLINUX boot image that you can boot from a floppy or CD-ROM or download through PXE. This install image contains a single **rc** script that obtains and executes an installation script from the image server. The installation script partitions the primary disk and then runs a second **rsync** to copy the system image from the server to the client.

SystemImager performs a minimal amount of localization: it sets the hostname and IP address (if you are not using DHCP), runs **lilo**, reboots the box, and leaves you with a freshly installed and (hopefully) operational computer.

A system image is a directory hierarchy on the installation server which is modifiable with standard file manipulation commands. Changes are more convenient than with the package-based systems, which may require you to add packages or insert postinstall scripts. Unfortunately, this feature also makes it tempting to sneak in quickie localizations without documenting them. If you don't painstakingly record the process of building the images, you have little hope of reproducing them when the time comes to upgrade.

If you need to make customizations for individual machines, add code to the install script to implement your changes. Another option is to create your own **rc** scripts that run the first time a new system is booted. For example, one of the authors of SystemImager has written code to supports both SCSI and IDE installation from a single script.

Setting up SystemImager

The SystemImager boot environment is documented at the following site:

http://systemimager.org/manual/html/theactualstep-by-stephowto.html

SystemImager scripts are short Perl or shell scripts. They are well documented.

SystemImager expects you to provide a reference system to use as a template—its "golden client." You must install the SystemImager client package on the golden client and install the server package on your installation server. Both of these packages are available from the SystemImager home base at www.systemimager.org.

The fact that the golden client's configuration is copied verbatim to new machines is actually not as problematic as it might first seem to be. As long as the golden client's kernel contains drivers for all the hardware used at your site, new machines do not have to be identical. In practice, the largest issues concern disk (SCSI/IDE) and network devices. SystemImager expects the network interface to be eth0; to change it, you need to modify the SystemImager installation scripts.

*See page 493 for more information about **rsync**.*

Once you have the golden client configured, run the **prepareclient** command. Then set up the image server by installing the **systemimager-server** package. SystemImager prefers your DHCP server and image server to be the same machine. Use the **makedhcpserver** script to create a DHCP server control file that corresponds to your SystemImager installation.

Create the installation image by running **getimage** on the image server. This script uses **rsync** to install the golden client image on the server and builds a corresponding installation script. Four methods of IP address assignment are supported: static DHCP, dynamic DHCP, static IP addresses or "replicant" (always give the same IP address).

getimage stores the installation script in **/tftpboot/systemimager**. This is an interesting choice, since the script is fetched with **rsync** rather than TFTP. Perhaps SystemImager's authors decided that because the PXE bootstrap materials (which *are* fetched with TFTP) also go in **/tftpboot**, it was best to keep everything together.

SystemImager clients need to be added to the DHCP configuration (or given a boot disk) and have appropriate links set up in the **tftpboot** directory so that they can obtain their basic network information. The SystemImager **addclients** command will automatically perform these steps for you.

To actually install clients, all you need to do is pop in some boot media (see the **mkautoinstallcd** and **mkautoinstalldiskette** commands) or start a PXE boot.

See page 731 for more discussion of the issues relating to ongoing updates.

SystemImager comes with a tool, **updateclient**, that updates a client to match the current version of the golden client. Another tool, **pushupdate**, can be run on the server to make all the SystemImager clients run **updateclient**. The default **rsync** exception list is quite aggressive, and you will probably have to expand it to achieve the desired behavior.

Installation

Customizing SystemImager installation

If your image server and DHCP server are separate machines, you will need to customize the installation process to inform SystemImager of this fact. Create a file called **local.cfg** on the boot floppy to set the parameters you need to change. The floppy is a standard FAT floppy, so you can read it or write to it by mounting it as a FAT volume or by using **mtools**. The **local.cfg** file is really just a shell script that gets run by the **rcS** script in the SystemImager hierarchy. Environment variables are used to specify options. For example, to specify your image server, put the line

```
export IMAGESERVER=imageserver.toadranch.com
```

in the **local.cfg** file.

Obtaining a config file with PXE is currently unsupported. It would be nice if you could specify the identity of the image server as a DHCP option. Instead, you must hack the **rcS** script in the boot image (in **/tftpboot/initrd.gz** on the image server) to fix these issues.

The server side may also need some customization, for example, if you want to change the way that SystemImager lays out disks.

23.3 LOCALIZATION

Installing a new computer is only half the battle. It's almost inevitable that changes will need to be made to the generic configuration for each machine. Following a specific set of guidelines in your localizations can make things easier for you and your users and allow for the safe construction of environments that support thousands of computers.

Many localization issues are really procedural rather than technical, and you should probably consider them even before you start installing computers. An entire forest of issues must be faced, and the correct solutions will depend on the nature of your site. Is your organization very centralized, or do different groups need to have some degree of control over their computers? Are your users technically savvy or are they neophytes? What degree of security and privacy does your site require? Many of these macro-scale issues are taken up in Chapter 29, *Policy and Politics*.

You should consider in particular how you will prevent every box at your site from looking different from every other. You must also be able to guarantee that your plan facilitates easy recovery from sysadmin screwups and system failures.

It's helpful to think of your Linux environment as a software product, one that consists of your chosen distribution, your local applications, your administrative customizations, and whatever software you use for administration. The key to avoiding many problems is adherence to sound software engineering practices: use version control, define a quality assurance procedure, and document your procedures and releases.

If you have only a few systems, some of the stickier issues can be ignored. However, it's never too early to consider how you might manage growth. Your organization can grow much more smoothly if your procedures scale to handle the additional load.

Automation

A localization scheme that requires manual intervention on every new host will not scale. Despite their best intentions, administrators make mistakes and skip steps. In accordance with Murphy's Law, these omissions have a way of coming back to haunt you just at the point when you can least afford it.

Localization procedures are an excellent candidate for automation. No matter how rusty your coding skills are, a Perl script will usually prove to be less error prone than an 8-page checklist. Automation is the "magic" that lets site plans scale to hundreds or thousands of hosts—make changes once rather than repeating them thousands of times.

Versioning your build

If your site has a thousand computers and each computer has its own configuration, you will spend a major portion of your working time figuring out why one box has a particular problem and another doesn't. Clearly, the solution is to make every computer the same, right? Not so fast, Chester!

Individual hosts have individual needs for currency, stability, and uptime. A prudent system administrator should never roll out new software releases en masse. Instead, rollouts should be staged according to a gradual plan that accommodates other groups' needs and allows time for the discovery of problems while their potential to cause damage is still limited. Never update critical servers until you have some confidence in the changes you are contemplating.[1]

Unfortunately, most administrators find themselves supporting multiple software configurations. However, there's a big difference in administrability between *multiple* configurations and *countless* configurations. The trick is to keep tight control over the former so that they don't surreptitiously morph into the latter.

Your primary weapon in this battle is a versioning system. Treat your local OS installation as an independent software release with its own release numbering system and testing procedures. This approach affords many advantages: you can test a new release before deploying it on your production boxes; you can easily roll back systems to a "safe" release in case of problems; and most importantly, you can limit the number of configurations in your environment to a small, manageable number.

An internal release should consist of an OS platform, applications, customizations for the local operating environment, and any necessary patches for these components. Every release should be accompanied by release notes (see *Documentation* on page 729) and by a proper validation procedure.

---

1. Security patches are a possible exception to this rule. It's important to plug security holes as soon as they are found. On the other hand, security patches *do* sometimes introduce bugs.

There are several ways to implement versionized releases. New installations can use a system such as SystemImager that defines a separate image for each release. If you use a package-based installer such as Kickstart or YaST, you can simply enumerate the specific packages (and package versions) that compose each release. Package-based systems work particularly well when local customizations are themselves packaged.

Think carefully about the number of releases you want to keep around. The more releases in existence, the more balls you'll have to keep in the air. On the other hand, don't fix what isn't broken. Upgrading systems for gratuitous reasons costs time and money, and "cutting edge" often means "bleeding edge."

Consider also the costs and drawbacks of a highly formalized release control system. Be prepared to make the cost/benefit tradeoff that's appropriate for your site, and to justify the decisions you make. Release control procedures can make your administrative team less agile and hinder your ability to respond quickly to emergencies. (If you have a security patch that has to go out *right now*, for example, you may not have time to follow proper release management procedures.) However, these costs can usually be minimized and are typically small in comparison with the long-term benefits.

Rogue users and departments

The process of standardizing software configurations often causes conflict. Technically inclined users (and sometimes entire departments) may feel that a centralized release control system cannot adequately accommodate their configuration needs or their need for autonomous control over the computers they use.

Your first impulse may be to try and strong-arm such "rogue" users into accepting standard configurations in order to minimize the cost and time required to support them. However, such an iron-fist approach usually ends up creating both unhappy users and unhappy sysadmins. Keep in mind that rogue users' desires are often perfectly legitimate and that it is the sysadmins' job to support *them*—or at least, to refrain from making their lives more difficult.

The most desirable (but often infeasible) solution is to integrate the rogue users into the process of defining the content of releases. If they have a formal, institutionalized, well-known channel through which they can affect the content of the standard releases (or a sysadmin-supervised release of their own), they may not need as much local control. This communication channel must be easy to use and above all responsive; if suggestions are accumulated for six months before being integrated, no one will have confidence in the system's ability to address individual needs.

The alternative to the integration strategy is to trade support for autonomy. Allow rogue users or groups to do whatever they want, with the explicit understanding that they must also take on responsibility for keeping the customized systems running. Make it clear that you will not be available to clean up messes, but be careful how you propose such an arrangement. It should be presented as an inevitable and regrettable consequence of limited sysadmin resources, never as a peevish "do it my way or I'm taking my ball and going home" power play.

You may need to take steps to protect the systems you control from the wild and lawless autonomous regions of your organization. For example, some sites locate the autonomous regions behind an internal firewall so that the "self motivated" can accidently crash each other while the rest of the network cheerfully ignores them.

Whatever you do, don't let yourself go down the road of picking up the pieces of someone else's creativity. It's not a good use of your time, and it sets a dangerous precedent. In a pinch, you might offer to reinstall the machine with one of the supported configurations; let the user weigh the costs and benefits of receiving help versus preserving a custom environment.

Testing

It's important to test changes before unleashing them on the world. At a minimum, this means that you need to test your own changes (such as new versions of config files like **sendmail.cf**); however, you should really test the software that your vendor ships to you as well. A famous UNIX (not Linux...yet) vendor once released a patch which, when applied a certain way, would perform an **rm -rf /**. Imagine installing this patch throughout your organization without testing it first—we suspect that you would be looking for a new job.

Testing is an especially pertinent issue if you use a service such as **apt-get** or the Red Hat Network that offers an automatic patching capability. You wouldn't want your mission-critical boxes downloading a broken patch, so these systems should never be directly connected to an update service. A reasonable mechanism is to keep an auto-updated machine around for use as a gold master. Periodically build new releases based on snapshots from the gold master, test them, and then roll them out slowly to the rest of the organization.

Be sure to arm-twist your users into cooperating with your testing regime. They will usually not be particularly eager to do so, but their participation is vital—it's the only way that all the components they actually use can be covered. You should of course have your own checklist of testing procedures, but there will inevitably be omissions and lapses in coverage. If that small but critical app that you forgot about doesn't work with the new **glibc** you just rolled out, you will be faced with a painful recovery procedure.

Make sure that users have an easy way to report bugs. If filing bug reports is a pain in the neck, users will typically ignore problems and assume that "someone else will get to that." See page 849 for more information about bug tracking ("trouble ticket") systems.

If your organization is global, make sure that other offices help with testing. International participation is particularly valuable in multilingual environments. If no one in the U.S. office speaks Japanese, for example, you had better get the Tokyo office to test anything that might affect kanji support. A surprising number of system parameters vary with location. Does the U.S. office test changes to the printing infrastructure with A4 paper, or will the non-U.S. offices be in for a surprise?

Making changes undoable

Mistakes are a fact of life. Therefore, it's important to keep track of the changes you make, so that if—horror of horrors—you do make an error, you can easily revert to a known-good configuration. If your site uses a formal versionized release system, rollbacks can be as easy as reinstalling the previous release. But even if you lack this kind of infrastructure, there are ways to make rollbacks easier.

The simplest way to support rollbacks is to keep around a backup copy of any files that you change. For example, you might copy **syslog.conf** to **syslog.conf.old** before making changes. Keeping a backup copy also allows you to **diff** the current and previous versions of a config file if you begin to lose track of the changes you have made.

If you use this manual backup system, pick a naming convention for backup files and try to get all the admins at your site to use it consistently. Some sites use minus signs (e.g., **syslog.conf-**), some use a **.old** or **.bak** suffix, and others use multiversion numbering schemes.

Systems that are regularly backed up to tape can still benefit from the use of manually created backup files. Recovery from a backup file is faster and easier than recovery from a tape, and manual backups preserve an additional layer of history.

Manual backups work up to a point, but they can rapidly become a hassle if you are making a number of changes (do you keep multiple copies with different names? or just keep just the most recent one?). Fortunately, the programming community long ago developed a solution to this problem: revision control.

Revision control

If several different people might edit a file, two potential problems must be overcome. First, there must be some way to make sure that no more than one person edits the file at once; simultaneous edits can result in a race condition that causes some editors' changes to be permanently lost.[2] Second, there must be some organized way to trace the history of modifications so that changes can be understood in context and so that earlier versions of the file are not lost forever. To solve these problems, programmers developed revision control systems.

In the old days of UNIX, the original revision control system was called SCCS. It worked well enough but cost money; RCS (Revision Control System) was developed by Walter Tichy as an open source alternative. Today, RCS has become the de facto standard for UNIX and Linux, and SCCS is pretty much a historical footnote. Every Linux distribution ships with RCS, and it's simple and easy to use.

Several commercial revision control systems are also available. If you work in a development shop, you may already have one of these available. However, in our experience, the commercial systems are generally overkill for sysadmin use.

---

2. For example, suppose that sysadmins Alice and Bob both edit the same file and that each makes some changes. Alice saves first. When Bob saves his copy of the file, it overwrites Alice's version. If Alice has quit from the editor, her changes are completely gone and unrecoverable.

Another option is an open source system called CVS (Concurrent Versions System) that adds some functionality on top of RCS. It supports a distributed model (for use with a remote server) and better multideveloper support. A number of sites have been using CVS for sysadmin tasks; the client/server capability in particular can be quite useful. But if you are starting from scratch, we'd recommend beginning with RCS.

RCS: the Revision Control System

RCS is one of the oldest UNIX applications around. It's actually a fairly simple system. It operates on the level of individual files (as opposed to CVS, which can operate on trees) and stores each file's revision history in a separate shadow file. The shadow file's name is the same as the original, but with the characters **,v** appended to it. For example, if you placed **/etc/syslog.conf** under RCS control, RCS would keep its revisions in **/etc/syslog.conf,v**.

To reduce clutter, RCS looks for a directory called **RCS** in the same directory as the original file. If it exists, RCS will sequester the **,v** file there instead of leaving it in plain view. Directory listings become much cleaner this way because many files can share an **RCS** directory. This is a terrific feature and one that we recommend highly.

The basic concept of RCS is that you "check out" files that you intend to modify and "check in" your changes to store them. The only RCS commands you really need to know are **ci** to check in, **co** to check out, and **rcs**, which performs various housekeeping chores.

To start keeping a file under RCS, run **ci** on it like this:

```
% ci -u syslog.conf
RCS/syslog.conf,v <-- syslog.conf
enter description, terminated with single '.' or end of file:
NOTE: This is NOT the log message!
>> This is the syslog configuration file.
```

The **-u** flag makes **ci** immediately check out the **syslog.conf** file in an unlocked (uneditable) state. If you were to omit this flag, **ci** would check in the file and delete the original copy, which is probably not what you want.

You could **chmod** the **syslog.conf** file to be writable and modify it that way, but this procedure would subvert and confuse RCS. Every time you want to change an RCS-controlled file, you must check it out and lock it with **co -l**:

```
% co -l syslog.conf
RCS/syslog.conf,v --> syslog.conf revision 1.2 (locked)
done
```

This operation tells RCS that you are about to modify the file; RCS will not let anyone else check out the file until you have checked it back in.

In theory, the lock prevents two different people from modifying the file at the same time. In practice, you have to be root to modify system files, so anyone with **sudo** privileges can modify a file once it has been checked out as root. However, if a second administrator attempts another **co -l**, RCS will notice that a writable version already exists. Sysadmins should get in the habit of always trying to check out the RCS-controlled files that they want to modify. The fact that a file is writable means "Stop! Someone else already has this file checked out."

Once you are happy with your changes to a checked-out file, check it back in with **ci -u**. You will be asked to provide a comment describing what you just did. Although it's tempting to skip this step or to write something useless such as "made a change," resist the urge. In a couple of years' time when you are trying to work out why you did something, useful comments can save your life.

```
% ci -u syslog.conf
RCS/syslog.conf,v <-- syslog.conf
new revision: 1.3; previous revision: 1.2
enter log message, terminated with single '.' or end of file:
>> Started logging debug messages to track down problem
>> ^D
done
```

You can look at a file's revision history with the **rlog** command:

```
$ rlog syslog.conf
RCS file: RCS/syslog.conf,v
Working file: syslog.conf
head: 1.3
branch:
locks: strict
access list:
symbolic names:
keyword substitution: kv
total revisions: 3; selected revisions: 3
description:
----------------------------
revision 1.3
date: 2002/01/10 00:44:58; author: adam; state: Exp; lines: +1 -0
Started logging debug messages to track down problem
----------------------------
revision 1.2
date: 2000/07/19 08:23:10; author: evi; state: Exp; lines: +2 -0
Changed log destination to new logmaster
----------------------------
revision 1.1
date: 1998/03/14 11:13:00; author: matthew; state: Exp;
Initial revision
============================================
```

If you want to see what the file looked like before you changed to the new log master, you could check out revision 1.2 of the file with **co**'s **-r** option:

```
% co -r1.2 syslog.conf
RCS/syslog.conf,v --> syslog.conf
revision 1.2
done
```

This command replaces the current **syslog.conf** file with the older version, so make sure you do a regular **co** when you are finished or you (and **syslogd**) may become very confused! Never check out locked copies of older revisions (with **co -l**), since this operation creates branches in the version tree. Version branches are occasionally useful for source code but are almost never used for sysadmin work; just ignore all of the RCS documentation that deals with them to make your life simpler.

You may occasionally find that someone else has changed a file and left it locked— or even worse, overridden RCS and changed the file without locking it. You can review the changes made by the perpetrator with **rcsdiff**, which is an RCS-aware version of **diff**:

```
% rcsdiff syslog.conf
============================================================
RCS file: RCS/syslog.conf,v
retrieving revision 1.3
diff -r1.3 syslog.conf 4c4
< define(LOGHOST,moonbase)
---
> define(LOGHOST,spacelounge)
%
```

As a last resort, you can break the lock with the command **rcs -u** *filename.* This command prompts you to enter an explanation of your actions and sends mail to the user who had previously locked the file.

More information about RCS can be found at

> http://www.cs.purdue.edu/homes/trinkle/RCS/

For CVS information, see www.cvshome.org.

Documentation

Proper documentation of software configurations is absolutely crucial to the smooth functioning of your site. If you make formal releases of your local configuration, it is vital to provide usable release notes with each new release. Even if your site is too small to merit formal releases, it's important to let other sysadmins and your user community know what you change. You don't want someone from another office calling at 4:00 a.m. because they can't figure out why their software breaks on the current release.

In addition, it's useful to maintain a summary document that describes the ways in which your site differs from the standard distribution. This document can be most usefully maintained in the form of a localization checklist that describes both how to set up your local environment (i.e., what changes to make to the base install) and how to install a new box (if the two procedures differ, which they often do).

Documentation issues are covered in more detail in Chapter 29, *Policy and Politics.*

Installation

Where to put local software

In the old days of UNIX, when there were many different architectures, programs were generally distributed in the form of source archives, usually **.tar.Z** files that you would **uncompress** and then compile. Once the program was built, you would then install the software in a location such as **/usr/local**. Today, the use of package management systems means that fewer programs need to be installed this way. It also means that administrators make fewer decisions, since packages specify where their contents are installed.

Even with easy package management, many people still prefer to compile their own software. Running your own build gives you more control over the software's compiled-in options. It also lets you be more paranoid because you can inspect the source code you are compiling. Some people think that this is important, but unless you've got the time and skill to inspect every line of a 20,000-line software package, we suspect that the added security value is probably minimal.

Since not every piece of software in the world has been packaged for every Linux distribution, it's pretty likely that you will run across at least a few programs that you need to install yourself, especially if your Linux boxes are not IA-32 based. What's more, if yours is a development site, you will have to consider where to put your site's own locally developed software.

Historically, the most common location for local software has been **/usr/local**, and this convention is still widely followed today. The UNIX/Linux Filesystem Hierarchy Standard (FHS) specifies that **/usr/local** be present and empty after the initial OS installation, and many packages expect to install themselves there. A depressingly large number of other packages (particularly commercial applications) expect to be installed in **/usr**, which is a bad idea and should be avoided; to the extent that you can, keep **/usr** more or less as your distribution installed it. If you do have an application that insists on putting files in **/usr**, we suggest that you actually put the files somewhere else and just put symlinks to them in **/usr**.

Although **/usr/local** is traditional, many sites find it to be an unmanageable dumping ground. The traditional way that it's laid out (basically the same as **/usr**, with binaries in **/usr/local/bin**, man pages in **/usr/local/man**, and so on) creates a whole raft of problems: it's hard to have multiple versions of the same software installed, the directories can be large, it's a pain to manage multiple architectures, etc.

A useful tool for maintaining hierarchies is Stow; look for it at www.gnu.org.

Larger sites often resort to creating their own namespace conventions for software. This namespace is often mounted through a network file system such as NFS or Coda (the capabilities of both are often used to support multiple architectures). A common technique is to use a three-level hierarchy with a vendor or collection at the top level, an application level beneath that, and a version level beneath that. The top-level grouping can be based on vendor, on function, or, for internal apps, on the group that developed the product. For example, if you group by function, there might be a **graphics** directory that contains **gimp**, **xv**, and other graphics tools.

```
/tools/graphics/bin/gimp (symlink to ../gimp/1.2.3/bin/gimp)
/tools/graphics/gimp/1.04
/tools/graphics/gimp/1.2.3
/tools/graphics/xv/3.1.0/
/tools/editors/xemacs/21.4
```

You could then create a directory **/tools/graphics/bin** that contained symlinks to the most current binaries for each package. If someone needed to use **gimp** 1.0.4, for example, they could run it directly. One of the disadvantages of this approach is that "old tools never die." Consider announcing "end of life" timelines for old versions of packages once you've made a newer version available.

How much to install on client machines

Where should local software actually be installed: on individual clients or on a central file server from which it can be shared over NFS? The NFS solution makes updates much quicker (it's faster to update 10 NFS servers than 1,000 clients), saves disk space on clients (although in the world of 50GB disks, this hardly seems to matter anymore), and allows easier backup (if there is any local state, it's easier to back up 10 servers than 1,000 clients).

The question really boils down to manageability versus speed and reliability. Remote access is centralized and easier to manage, but accessing the network will always be slower than accessing a local disk. In addition, the remote server model adds dependencies on the network and the remote file server.

Diskless workstations were common in the old days of UNIX when hard disks were very expensive. These machines had no disk whatsoever and obtained all their files (including their root partitions and swap space) over the network. We don't recommend this configuration (diskless workstations died for a reason), but the FHS does allow all of **/usr** to be shared remotely, and many sites take advantage of this feature.

23.4 KEEPING YOUR SYSTEMS UP TO DATE WITH RSYNC OR RDIST

OK, you've got the "centralized release" religion and you've defined some specific configurations that you're willing to support. How do you now make all your individual boxes look like the masters, and how will you update them in the future?

See Chapter 18, for a review of some of the ways to keep system files synchronized.

There are two common ways: copy files directly from a master host to your individual boxes by using a tool such as **rsync**, or use the package management system built into your distribution to install new or upgraded packages. The latter option can be automated with a system such as **apt-get**.

Some sites update on a regular schedule; this plan defines an upper bound on the out-of-dateness of client systems. Other sites update their boxes at boot time; this plan is safe but can mean that a long time passes between updates. Some sites with technically savvy users let the users themselves choose when to update their machines. This is a cooperative and unintrusive plan, but you may find that some users never update without being goaded.

Installation

The use of **rsync** or **rdist** is by far the oldest and most traditional technique for keeping systems synchronized. On the server, you simply define a nightly (or hourly, or weekly...) **cron** job that **rsync**s or **rdist**s files to the client machines. With such a system, you guarantee that machines are kept up to date as long as they are up.

As an alternative, you may want to consider using a "pull" mechanism in which the clients are responsible for asking for the update. A pull system affords clients better control over their own update schedules. For example, at a site that updates "every night," the proper update time will vary depending on time zone; a nightly upgrade in the United States would be a middle-of-the-workday upgrade in Asia. You can easily implement pull updates by running **rsync** in daemon mode on the server and making each of the clients kick off its own **rsync** job. SystemImager also facilitates pull updates by providing the **updateclient** tool.

rsync is generally a better protocol than **rdist**, but both are easy to set up; see page 490 for details. Depending on how many machines you have and how large a geographical area they cover, you might want to set up only a single distribution server or a hierarchy of distribution servers. For example, you could have one central master server that distributes to a slave in each building in which you have machines, and that slave in turn could distribute to clients. This type of hierarchical arrangement can really reduce your consumption of WAN bandwidth.

Using **rsync**/**rdist** to keep a filesystem like **/tools** up to date is straightforward; there are few hidden gotchas. However, it's harder to use these tools to update your core OS installations. First, you will need to maintain a list of files that are to be left alone during the update. This list should include files that define a host's personal information (such as **/etc/sysconfig/network** on Red Hat), files created by daemons (such as most anything ending in **.pid**), temporary files (**/tmp** and **/var/tmp**), and files that relate to running processes (such as **/proc**). Most of **/var** should be left alone. Depending on how much consistency you want to enforce, you may or may not want some parts of **/etc** to be copied.

Special procedures must be used to accommodate updates of certain files. For example, you must rerun **lilo** when you install a new kernel. This is actually the one respect in which **rdist** is better than **rsync**: it has a special action that accommodates these considerations. However, the same effect can be achieved with **rsync** with a little extra hacking. You might need to run a shell script after the **rsync** that does cleanup or add a **cron** job that runs **lilo** every night.

The following is an example list of exclusions that will keep a Red Hat machine from being hosed by an **rsync**. You will almost certainly have to add other files that you don't want copied (for example, **/etc/resolv.conf** if you don't want to share it everywhere), but this is a good list to start with.

```
/proc/*
/var/lock/*
/var/log/*
/var/run/*
```

```
/var/spool/*
/dev/*
/var/adm/*
/var/tmp/*
/tmp/*
/etc/sysconfig/*
/etc/modules.conf/*
/etc/HOSTNAME
/etc/X11/XF86Config
```

Let's say that you store this list in **/etc/rsync.excludes**. To copy the files on your machine to the host desthost, you could run the following command:

rsync --exclude-from=/etc/rsync.excludes / desthost:/

Another big issue with keeping the core OS up to date is how you manage packages. One way (shown in the exclusions file above) is to simply copy the package data (**/var/lib/rpm** on RPM-based systems, **/var/lib/dpkg** on Debian) along with the rest of the OS. This means that in practice your clients *will not* be able to add packages of their own; if they do, the package data will be overwritten. Viewed in a certain light, this could actually be a feature—if clients have packages added to them, they are nonstandard, which increases the burden of administration and causes problems with reproducibility. If you feel that it's useful to let clients have different sets of packages installed, you will probably want to manage updates by means of packages.

23.5 PACKAGE MANAGEMENT

These days, most Linux distributions (including all of our example distributions) use some sort of packaging system. Packages are used to distribute applications and sometimes configuration files. They have several advantages over the traditional unstructured **.tar.gz** archives. Perhaps most importantly, they try to make the installation process as atomic as possible. If an error occurs, the package can be backed out or reapplied.

Package installers also back up files that they change. If you find that a newly installed package breaks something on your system, you can in theory back it out to restore your system to its original state.

Packaging systems define a dependency model that allows package maintainers to ensure that all the libraries and support infrastructure on which their applications depend are properly installed. Packages can also run scripts at various times during the installation, so they can do much more than just install new files. (This feature probably accounts for much of the observed failure of packages to restore the system to its original state after uninstallation.)

Two package formats are in common use. SuSE, Red Hat, and most other distributions use RPM, the Red Hat Package Manager. Debian uses **.deb**-format packages. The two package formats are functionally identical, and therefore enormous flame wars are waged over which is better. In practice, RPM has won the war; however, you are best off sticking to the native package mechanism used by your distribution. It's easy to convert between the two package formats with a tool such as Alien from

> http://kitenet.net/programs/alien

Packages can be a nice way to distribute your own localizations because of all the advantages they offer over **.tar.gz** files. You can easily create a package that, when installed, reads localization information about a machine (or gets it from central database) and uses that information to set up configuration files. You can also bundle up your local apps as packages, complete with dependencies, and make packages from third-party apps that aren't normally distributed as packages. You can versionize your packages and use the dependency mechanism to upgrade the machine when the new version of your localization package is installed. For example, it's possible to create a package that installs nothing of its own but depends on many other patches. Installing the package with dependencies turned on will result in all the patches being installed.

Creating new packages is fairly easy, and some excellent documents describe the process. For information about RPM packages, see www.rpm.org or Ed Bailey's book *Maximum RPM*.

 For information about creating Debian-style **.deb** packages, see the *Debian New Maintainers' Guide* at

> http://www.debian.org/doc/maint-guide

It contains instructions for building packages together with useful guidelines for making them manageable. General information about the format of **.deb** packages can be found in Chapter 6 of the Debian FAQ at

> http://www.debian.org/doc/FAQ/ch-pkg_basics.html

RPM packages

You manage RPM packages with the **rpm** command. This one command does pretty much everything that relates to RPMs, including building them. **rpm --help** gives you a list of all the options.

If you are not building packages, the only options you really need to pay attention to are **--install**, **--upgrade**, and **--erase**; the **--query** flag determines the status and content of packages and it, too, is indispensable. The **--query** option actually just puts **rpm** into query mode. You must supply an additional option that poses your specific question. The command **rpm --query --all** shows a complete list of the packages installed on the system.

Suppose you need to install a new version of OpenSSH because a security fix was recently published. First, you need to find the updated package. If the package is part of the core OS, there will most likely be a copy on your distribution's FTP site; the security advisory will tell you where to get it. If the package is more obscure, your first method of searching should be to check rpmfind.net. This web site provides a nifty RPM search engine that tells you exactly where various versions of an RPM for various distributions can be found.

Once you've downloaded the package to your local computer, installing it takes only a simple **rpm --upgrade**:

```
# rpm --upgrade openssh-2.9p2-12.i386.rpm
error: failed dependencies:
openssh = 2.9p2-7 is needed by openssh-askpass-2.9p2-7
openssh = 2.9p2-7 is needed by openssh-askpass-gnome-2.9p2-7
openssh = 2.9p2-7 is needed by openssh-clients-2.9p2-7
openssh = 2.9p2-7 is needed by openssh-server-2.9p2-7
```

Oops! Well, perhaps it's not so simple after all. Here we see that the currently installed version of OpenSSH, 2.9p2-7, is required by a number of other packages. The **rpm** command won't let us upgrade OpenSSH because the change might affect other packages. We could force the upgrade with the --**force** option, but that's usually a bad idea. Instead, we'll grab the rest of the packages. (The original security advisory that we used for this example did in fact list the other packages—behold the power of documentation!)

We could also have determined that other packages depended on OpenSSH this way:

```
# rpm --query --whatrequires openssh
openssh-askpass-2.9p2-7
openssh-askpass-gnome-2.9p2-7
openssh-clients-2.9p2-7
openssh-server-2.9p2-7
```

Now suppose that we've obtained updated copies of all the packages. We could install them one at a time, but **rpm** is smart enough that we can install them all at one time.[3] If you list multiple RPMs on the command line, **rpm** will sort them by dependency before installing them.

```
# rpm --upgrade openssh-*
```

Cool! Looks like it succeeded, and sure enough:

```
# rpm --query openssh
openssh-2.9p2-12
```

Debian packages

Just as RPM packages have the **rpm** command, Debian packages have the **dpkg** command. **dpkg** does pretty much everything you as an end user need to do with Debian packages, including installing them (the --**install** option) and removing them (the --**remove** option). You can list the packages on your system with **dpkg -l**.

Suppose that the Debian security team recently released a fix to **nvi** to patch a potential security problem. After grabbing the patch, we run **dpkg** to install it. As you can see, it's much chattier then **rpm** and tells us exactly what it's doing.

---

3. Actually, earlier versions of **rpm** required that you specify them in the correct order.

```
# dpkg --install ./nvi_1.79-16a.1_i386.deb
(Reading database ... 24368 files and directories currently installed.)
Preparing to replace nvi 1.79-14 (using ./nvi_1.79-16a.1_i386.deb) ...
Unpacking replacement nvi ...
Setting up nvi (1.79-16a.1) ...
Checking available versions of ex, updating links in /etc/alternatives ...
(You may modify the symlinks there yourself if desired - see 'man ln'.)
Leaving ex (/usr/bin/ex) pointing to /usr/bin/nex.
Leaving ex.1.gz (/usr/share/man/man1/ex.1.gz) pointing to
     /usr/share/man/man1/nex.1.gz.
...
```

We can now use **dpkg -l** to see if the installation worked. The **-l** flag accepts an op-tional search pattern, so we can search just for **nvi**:

```
% dpkg -l nvi
Desired=Unknown/Install/Remove/Purge
| Status=Not/Installed/Config-files/Unpacked/Failed-config/Half-installed
|/ Err?=(none)/Hold/Reinst-required/X=both-problems (Status,Err: uppercase=bad)
||/ Name          Version           Description
+++-===========-===============-=================================
ii  nvi           1.79-16a.1        4.4BSD re-implementation of vi.
```

Our installation seems to have gone smoothly.

Automating package installation

Several programs let you upgrade packages automatically. The two most polished and most popular of these are the Red Hat Network and Debian's **apt-get**.

The Red Hat Network is intimately tied to the Red Hat distribution. It's a commer-cial service that costs money and offers a lot more in terms of attractive GUIs and automation ability than does **apt-get**. Unfortunately, it's pretty much a mysterious black box underneath the covers.

apt-get is better documented than the Red Hat Network, is significantly more porta-ble, and is free. It's also more flexible in terms of what you can do with it. **apt-get** is most tightly integrated with Debian and **dpkg**, but there is a version that uses RPMs and works with Red Hat and SuSE. We suggest that you use this version of **apt-get** if you want to set up your own automated package distribution network. See the sec-tion *Setting up an internal APT server* on page 740 for more information.

In addition to the automated package-pullers, there are some tools that are not spe-cifically package oriented but that allow you to easily perform package-related tasks on client machines. One of the best known is **cfengine**, which is a tool that lets you run tasks on many hosts. It's useful for quite a few sysadmin tasks, not just package installation. See

     http://www.iu.hio.no/cfengine

for more information.

The Red Hat Network

One could describe the Red Hat Network as an attempt to provide a reason for you to actually buy the official boxed version of Red Hat Linux rather than download it from the net. You pay a monthly or annual subscription fee, and in return you stay up to date with the Red Hat master tree. Since "rental software" seems to be all the rage these days, it's nice to see Red Hat bringing Linux onto the cutting edge of software charging models.

At it's simplest, you can just use the Red Hat Network as a glorified web portal and mailing list. Used in this way, it's not very different from the patch notification mailing lists that have been run by various UNIX vendors for years. But more features are available if you're willing to pay for them.

The Red Hat Network provides a pretty GUI interface for downloading new packages (there is also a command-line alternative). It even lets you download and install new packages without any human intervention. Once you register, your machines get all the patches and bug fixes that they need without you ever having to leave your Quake session. The downside of automatic registration is that Red Hat decides what updates you need. You might consider how much you really trust Red Hat (and the software maintainers whose products they package) not to screw things up. Given some of the interesting choices Red Hat has made in the past when it comes to little things like which compiler to ship, some folks might remain skeptical. A reasonable compromise might be to sign up one machine in your organization for automatic updates. You can take snapshots from that machine at periodic intervals to test as possible candidates for internal releases.

To register for the Red Hat network, either run the **rhn_register** program that comes with Red Hat or use the web interface at rhn.redhat.com. If you are behind a firewall, run **rhn_register --configure** to set up a proxy; otherwise, use Red Hat's GUI to get up and running.

Once you have registered your system, run **up2date**, the Red Hat update agent, to manage your subscriptions, download packages, and change your configuration. You might also notice a new daemon, **rhnsd**, running on your machine. This is the daemon that polls the Red Hat site for new updates.

Unfortunately, the Red Hat Network doesn't yet offer every feature that you might want from an update service. Most obviously, you cannot use it to upgrade to new releases of Red Hat (for example, to upgrade from 7.1 to 7.2). RHN's Debian counterpart **apt-get** has provided this feature for a while, and it seems to work quite well. **apt-get** is in general a more mature product than RHN, but RHN is evolving rapidly.

23.6   APT-GET: AUTOMATE DOWNLOADING AND INSTALLATION

apt-get is one of the nicest features of Debian. It automates the downloading and installation of updates and new packages. If a new packages depends on other packages, **apt-get** will obtain and install them for you. In fact, with **apt-get** it's possible to upgrade your box to the latest version of Debian with a single command or even have your boxes keep themselves up to date without human intervention. The system as a whole is known as APT, the Advanced Packaging Tool.

Since it originated in the Debian universe, the original **apt-get** supported only **.deb** format packages. However, it has now been ported to the RPM package mechanism. This version, known as **apt-rpm**, is available from

> http://distro.conectiva.com/projetos/42

Unfortunately, **apt-rpm** is less useful than the original **apt-get** because its server-side infrastructure is less well developed. To get **apt-get** up and running under Debian, just point your **/etc/apt/sources.list** file at the closest Debian mirror (by default, it points at the master distribution). This level of integration is not necessarily present on other distributions; you will probably have to set up your own repository and do some tweaking to get **apt-get** to work properly for your organization. However, if you just want to implement your own local package distribution mechanism, **apt-get** and **apt-rpm** have much to offer.

The first rule of using **apt-get** on Debian systems (and indeed all management of Debian packages) is to ignore the existence of **dselect**, which acts as a front end for the system. It's not a bad idea, but the user interface is poor.

If you are using **apt-get** to manage a stock Debian installation from a standard Debian mirror, the easiest way to see what packages are available is to visit the web site packages.debian.org. This site also provides a useful search interface. If you set up your own **apt-get** server (see page 740), then of course you will know what packages are available and can provide a list in whatever way you want.

Debian provides several empty packages (most with names that begin with **task-**) that exist only to list other packages as prerequisites. Since **apt-get** automatically downloads and upgrades prerequisite packages as needed, the **task-*** packages make it easy to install or upgrade several packages as a block. For example, installing the **task-gnome-desktop** package will ensure that you have all the packages necessary to run GNOME.

Once you have set up your **sources.list** file and know the name of a package that you want, the only remaining task is to run **apt-get update** to refresh **apt-get**'s cache of package information. After that, just run **apt-get install** *package-name* to install the package. The same command will update a package that has already been installed.

Suppose we want to install a new version of the **sudo** package that fixes a security bug. First, it's always wise to do an **apt-get update**:

```
% sudo apt-get update
Get:1 http://http.us.debian.org potato/main Packages [824kB]
Get:2 http://non-us.debian.org potato/non-US/main Release [102B]
...
```

Now we can actually fetch the package. Note that we are using **sudo** as we fetch the new **sudo** package—**apt-get** can even upgrade packages that are in use!

```
% sudo apt-get install sudo
Reading Package Lists... Done
Building Dependency Tree... Done
1 packages upgraded, 0 newly installed, 0 to remove and 191 not upgraded.
Need to get 0B/122kB of archives. After unpacking 131kB will be used.
(Reading database ... 24359 files and directories currently installed.)
Preparing to replace sudo 1.6.1-1 (using .../sudo_1.6.2p2-2_i386.deb) ...
Unpacking replacement sudo ...
Setting up sudo (1.6.2p2-2) ...
Installing new version of config file /etc/pam.d/sudo ...
```

We're done! What could be easier?

Configuring apt-get

Configuring **apt-get** is straightforward, and it is one area in which the sometimes spotty Debian documentation is OK; pretty much everything you need to know can be found in the *APT HOWTO:*

> http://www.debian.org/doc/manuals/apt-howto

The most important **apt-get** configuration file is **/etc/apt/sources.list**, which tells **apt-get** where to get its packages. Each line specifies the following: a type of package, currently deb or deb-src; a URL that points to a file, CD-ROM, HTTP server, or FTP server from which to fetch packages; a "distribution" that lets you deliver multiple versions of packages (Debian uses this field to versionize its distributions, but you can also use it for your internal versions); and a potential list of components—in essence, categories of packages within a distribution.

Unless you want to set up your own APT repository or cache, the default configuration generally works fine. If you have a reasonable network connection, you will probably want to comment out the lines for your Debian CD-ROMs. If you want to download source code, uncomment the lines that specify deb-src. As long as you're editing the file, you should change the identity of the Debian mirror to one that is close to you; a full list of mirrors can be found at

> http://www.debian.org/misc/README.mirrors

To make things incredibly easy, Debian proves a tool called **netselect-apt** that will automatically generate a **sources.list** file for you; it selects the closest mirror it can find, based on ping time. **netselect-apt** is part of the **netselect** package, which is available from your nearest Debian mirror.

You should also make sure that security.debian.org is listed as a source so that you will have access to the latest security patches.

Installation

An example /etc/apt/sources.list file

The following example uses http.us.debian.org for the stable archive but also adds non-us.debian.org as a source for non-U.S. packages (cryptographic materials that can't be exported from the United States). We've added security.debian.org, the source of all security patches, and our local APT server, debserver. Finally, we've turned on downloading of source code.

```
deb http://http.us.debian.org/debian stable main contrib non-free
deb http://non-us.debian.org/debian-non-US stable/non-US main contrib non-free
deb http://security.debian.org stable/updates main contrib non-free
deb http://debserver/mypackages/ ./
deb-src http://http.us.debian.org/debian stable main contrib non-free
deb-src http://non-us.debian.org/debian-non-US stable/non-US main contrib non-free
deb-src http://security.debian.org stable/updates main contrib non-free
```

This example uses the stable repository. In practice, the stable Debian distributions are not released as often as the other distributions. If you need packages from the testing or unstable distributions, just copy the stable lines and replace stable with unstable (or testing). Lines are consulted in order, so put the unstable and testing lines at the end of the file to give stable versions precedence.

Using proxies to make apt-get scale

If you plan to use **apt-get** on a large number of boxes, you will probably want to cache packages locally—downloading a copy of each package for every machine is not a sensible use of bandwidth. You may also need to direct your **apt-get** through a proxy if your firewall requires this additional protection. Since **apt-get** uses vanilla HTTP and FTP, you can use any existing web proxy that you might happen to have installed. **apt-get** honors the http_proxy environment variable; likewise, it's possible to set an explicit proxy with a line in the **/etc/apt/apt.conf** file:

```
Acquire::http::Proxy "http://proxy.server.here:8080/
```

An alternative to a generic web proxy is a small application called **apt-proxy**. Despite the name, it is not a true proxy but rather an app that builds a cache of packages by **rsync**ing them from the real APT server. **apt-proxy** is available from

http://sourceforge.net/projects/apt-proxy

Setting up an internal APT server

Instead of using a proxy, you can also set up your own autonomous APT server and point your internal clients at it. This model lets you tweak the packages you offer to your clients, push out upgrades easily (just install new versions on the server), distribute your own applications as packages, and most importantly, provide your own versions of distributions.

Since **apt-get** uses standard protocols (HTTP and FTP) to download its packages, all you need to do to set up an APT server is establish a web or FTP server. Setting up an NFS server or a walking a CD-ROM around to individual machines is also viable;

apt-get is very flexible. Given the widespread support for HTTP proxying and firewalling, HTTP is probably the easiest protocol to use with APT. Instructions for setting up the Apache web server are given on page 697.

To turn a generic HTTP server into an APT server, all you need is a directory that contains packages. The packages can all be in one directory, or they can be arranged in a hierarchy as on the Debian mirrors.

You must also generate two package summary files: **Packages.gz** and **Contents.gz**. **Packages.gz** is a **gzip**ped list of the packages on the server and their dependencies. **apt-get update** uses the list to determine the available complement of packages. The **Contents.gz** file maps raw files to the packages that contain them; it is not actually used by **apt-get** itself.

The **apt-ftparchive** command, which is included in the **apt-utils** package, generates both of the summary files automatically. Once you have created the summary files, the rest is easy. A line such as

```
deb http://debserver/mypackages/ ./
```

in the **/etc/apt/sources.list** files of the clients will connect **apt-get** to your local server. Run **apt-get update** on each client, then use **apt-get** normally.

To distribute source code as well as binary packages, just put the source packages on the server. Unlike RPM, which has an SRPM equivalent for source packages, Debian distributes the source packages in three parts: the vanilla **.tar.gz** file, an optional **.diff.gz** file (which is used by package maintainers to show the changes they have made relative to the original distribution of the code), and a **.dsc** file that contains a package description. The source code equivalent of **Packages.gz** is **Sources.gz**; it is also generated by **apt-ftparchive**.

The preceding example does not specify a "distribution" parameter. If you want to use your own distribution names to allow internal versioning, place each version in a subdirectory and change the ./ to the version name or number. The versioning capability is very useful; it's possible to have different "test" and "production" releases that are just symlinks to the actual versions. You may want to maintain some test boxes that point to your test distribution. When you are happy with the release, upgrade your production machines by pointing the production symlink to the new release.

Automating apt-get

You can run **apt-get** on a regular schedule from **cron**. Even if you don't install packages automatically, you may want to run **apt-get update** regularly to keep your package summaries up to date.

apt-get dist-upgrade will download and install new versions of any packages that are installed on the local machine. **dist-upgrade** is similar to **upgrade** but has slightly more intelligent dependency handling. If you want to play with fire, have machines perform this upgrade automatically—use the **-yes** option for unattended operation; it answers any confirmation questions that **apt-get** might ask with an enthusiastic "Yes!".

It is probably not a good idea to perform automated upgrades directly from the Debian mirrors. However, if you have your own APT servers, packages, and release control system, this is a perfect way to keep clients in sync. A quickie shell script like the following will keep a box up to date with its APT server:

```
#!/bin/sh
apt-get update
apt-get -yes dist-upgrade
```

Call this script from a **cron** job if you want to run it nightly. You can also refer to it from a system startup script to make the machine update at boot time. See Chapter 9, *Periodic Processes*, for more information about **cron**; see Chapter 2, *Booting and Shutting Down*, for more information about startup scripts.

If you run updates out of **cron** on many machines, you should use time randomization to make sure that everyone doesn't try to update at once. The short Perl script on page 496 can help with this task.

If you don't quite trust your source of packages, consider automatically downloading all changed packages without installing them. Use **apt-get**'s **--download-only** option to request this behavior, then review the packages by hand and install the ones you want to update. Downloaded packages are put in **/var/cache/apt**, and over time this directory can grow to be quite large. Clean out the unused files from this directory with **apt-get autoclean**.

23.7 RECOMMENDED READING

BAILEY, ED. *Maximum RPM*. Indianapolis: SAMS. 1997.

BURGESS, MARK. "Cfengine: A Site Configuration Engine." USENIX Computing Systems, Vol 8, No 3. 1995.

INTEL CORPORATION AND SYSTEMSOFT. *Preboot Execution Environment (PXE) Specification*. ftp://download.intel.com/ial/wfm/pxespec.pdf

MINTHA, JIM AND PIETER KRUL. "UltraLinux FAQ." www.ultralinux.org/faq.html

OETIKER, TOBIAS. "SEPP: Software Installation and Sharing System." LISA 1998 proceedings.

"PXELinux Questions." syslinux.hackerdojo.com/pxe.php

RODIN, JOSIP. *Debian New Maintainers' Guide*. www.debian.org/doc/maint-guide
This document contains good information about **.deb** packages.

SILVA, GUSTAVO NORONHA. "APT HOWTO."
www.debian.org/doc/manuals/apt-howto

STÜCKELBERG, MARC VUILLEUMIER, AND DAVID CLERC. "Linux Remote-Boot mini-HOWTO: Configuring Remote-Boot Workstations with Linux, DOS, Windows 95/98 and Windows NT." www.linuxdoc.org/HOWTO/mini/Remote-Boot.html

WACHSMANN, ALF. "How to Install Red Hat Linux via PXE and Kickstart." www.stanford.edu/~alfw/PXE-Kickstart/PXE-Kickstart.html

23.8 EXERCISES

E23.1 Outline the differences between Kickstart, YaST, and SystemImager. When would you chose SystemImager over one of the distribution-specific installers?

E23.2 Suppose that you and another member of your elite homework squad were using RCS to manage a software project. Your partner has forgotten to check in a critical file that you now need to modify. How could you break the lock and not lose any of your partner's changes?

★ **E23.3** Outline the steps needed to create an RPM package. Use this procedure to package a software product from one of your other computer science classes.

★ **E23.4** Repeat exercise E23.3, but create a Debian-format **.deb** package.

E23.5 Review the way that local software is organized at your site. Will the system scale? Is it easy to use? Discuss.

★★ **E23.6** Set up the network installer of your choice and install a new machine by using your server. Outline all the steps needed to perform this task. What were some of the stumbling blocks? What are some of the scalability issues you discovered with the installer that you chose?

Installation

24 *Printing*

Printing is often one of the most annoying and difficult Linux functions to support as a system administrator. Users often take printing for granted, but delivering perfectly rendered pages to a printer six feet from the user can require a string of challenging administrative contortions.

Years ago, the most common printers were ASCII line printers. Laser printers were new, expensive, and rare. High-resolution output devices required custom driver software and formatting programs.

By the close of the millennium, line printers had practically become antiques. Numerous standards had been established for page description and printing languages. Laser printers had permeated the market and were widely used.

Today, laser printers often connect to an Ethernet network instead of a serial or parallel port. They have largely lost the low-end market to inkjet printers.

With all of these changes in technology, you might expect the Linux printing systems to be extremely flexible, and indeed they are. Unfortunately, the most popular systems are still based on the older software used for line printers of yore. They have been hacked and overloaded in an attempt to support the new technologies, and the result is often somewhat unsightly.

In this chapter, we start with general discussions of printing terminology and the Linux printing systems, then provide instructions for configuring printers on each of our reference systems. Finally, we conclude with a brief guide to printer debugging, a discussion of common printing software, and some general printing hints.

24.1 MINI-GLOSSARY OF PRINTING TERMS

Although an overview of current printing technology is beyond the scope of this book, we will try to give you enough information to respond when someone begins haranguing you in printer jargon.

spooler A spooler is a piece of software that receives print jobs, stores them, prioritizes them, and sends them out sequentially to a printer. A user-level command submits jobs to the spooler for printing. A spooler is often called a print server. Some printers have their own internal spoolers.

PDL Most printers accept input in one or more "page description languages" that specify the images to be placed on the page in an abstract way. PDL descriptions are more efficient to transmit than raw images, and they are easier for applications to generate. They also have the benefit of being device and resolution-independent. The best-known PDLs are PostScript, PCL, and PDF.

bitmap Sometimes you need to print images that are not easily described in a PDL. In these cases, you use a bitmap, which is a set of data that specifies which dots are filled in and which are not (or what color each dot is, in the case of a color or grayscale image).

As with PDLs, there are several competing formats for storing bitmaps. Every PDL supports at least one format. Since bitmaps are usually very large, they are often compressed. Common bitmap formats include JPEG, PNG, TIFF, and GIF.

RIP A Raster Image Processor (RIP) is a software system that accepts documents in one or more PDLs and converts them to a bitmap format appropriate for a particular output device. PDL-to-bitmap conversion is often performed by a RIP within the printer.

filters Filters are programs that modify print jobs en route from the spooler to the printer. Filters translate file formats, maintain accounting records, and often handle communications with the printer. Filters are usually not necessary with simple text printers, but they are essential for sending jobs to printers that require nonstandard PDLs. Some PostScript printers can deal with unfiltered input, but the majority prefer specially filtered print jobs. See page 757 for more information about filters.

PostScript PostScript is by far the most common PDL found on Linux systems. It was originally developed by Adobe Systems, and most PostScript printers use an interpreter licensed from Adobe. Almost all page layout programs can generate PostScript.

PostScript is actually a full-fledged programming language. You can read PostScript programs with a text editor or **more**. The programs contain a multitude of parentheses, curly braces, and slashes and often start with the characters %!PS. Although these starting characters are not required by the language itself, Linux printing software usually looks for them when attempting to classify print jobs.

PCL   Printer Command Language is HP's alternative to PostScript. It's found almost exclusively on HP printers and is quite common in the PC world. Linux applications usually cannot generate PCL directly, so they require a filter for conversion.

PDF   Adobe's Portable Document Format is commonly produced by and used with Adobe Acrobat. It's a platform-independent format that is often used to exchange documents electronically for both on-line and off-line (printed) use. A free reader application (for Linux and many other operating systems) is available from www.adobe.com.

24.2 LINUX PRINTING SYSTEMS

Several different printing systems are available for use under Linux. We review the most common options in this chapter. For additional information, check the web site www.linuxprinting.org, which maintains a vast collection of Linux printing resources.

The LPD (Line Printer Daemon) printing system is based on the Berkeley (BSD) printing system, which has been a mainstay of the UNIX environment for many years. Most other versions of UNIX still use some form of the LPD system today. LPD is the standard printing system under SuSE Linux.

LPRng is a next-generation version of LPD with added flexibility and functionality designed for the modern printing world. This system is the default for Red Hat and Debian systems.

LPD and LPRng are extremely similar in approach and configuration, and they are certainly the most commonly used printing systems in professional environments. We cover these systems in gory detail later in this chapter.

Two other printing systems available for Linux are worth mentioning. PDQ, available from pdq.sourceforge.net, takes the unique and innovative approach of decentralizing control over printers (the LPD/LPRng approach is more akin to a government bureaucracy). PDQ can provide much-needed flexibility in dynamic environments and is said to be simpler and more reliable than the traditional systems.

Another up-and-coming system, CUPS (the Common UNIX Printing System), has been ported to Linux and may be suitable for environments that support cross-platform printing among a wide range of UNIX variants. Information about CUPS is available from www.cups.org.

24.3 TYPES OF PRINTERS

Linux lets you spool jobs to almost any type of printer. At the most basic level, printers are classified by their connection interface (network, serial, parallel) and by the type of data they understand (text, PostScript, PCL, or something else entirely).

Many of the "el cheapo" printers used on Windows systems (known collectively as WinPrinters) cannot be used with Linux. These printers have very little built-in intelligence and cannot understand any PDL. Some of the information necessary to communicate with these printers has been hidden in proprietary driver code. Such secrecy hinders efforts to develop Linux support for these devices, although the Linux community has demonstrated a remarkable aptitude for reverse engineering. Many WinPrinters *are* well supported in Linux, but check first, purchase second.

Serial and parallel printers

Serial printers require some extra configuration. The spooler software needs to know the appropriate values for the baud rate and other serial options so that it can communicate properly with the printer. See page 759 for information on how to specify these details, and see Chapter 7, *Serial Devices*, for a broader overview.

Parallel ports are faster than standard serial ports, and fortunately for sysadmins, they require fewer options to be configured. Although the standard has not aged gracefully, it does provide us with ports that require relatively little tinkering. Under Linux, the first (and usually only) parallel port is **/dev/lp0**.

A faster and better serial technology called the Universal Serial Bus (USB) has also made its way into the Linux world. USB has become wildly popular under Windows, but Linux support is still a bit spotty. Check the database of supported USB devices at www.qbik.ch/usb/devices or www.linux-usb.org to see the status of your hardware.

Network printers

Some printers contain full-fledged network interfaces, which allow them to sit directly on a network and accept jobs through one or more network or printing protocols. Data can be sent to network-attached printers much more quickly than it can be sent to printers on serial or parallel ports.

Because any computer on the network can potentially spool directly to the network printer, contention issues arise. Administrative control is often lacking.

To simplify administration, you should try to set up your network so that a few hosts control all of your printers. Other machines should simply transmit jobs to these print server machines. This setup can save you work because you will not have to keep a close eye on the printing system on every machine. In addition, you will have relatively few configurations to investigate when a printing problem occurs.

Many network laser printers include an LPD server that runs inside the printer. This feature allows Linux clients to spool files to the printer in exactly the same manner they would spool files to another Linux server. Since most any variant of UNIX and Linux can spool to an LPD server, we like these printers a lot.

Older network printers required that print jobs be sent to TCP port 9100. This configuration is difficult to support with the LPD printing system (shipped with SuSE), but it's easy with LPRng (shipped with Red Hat and Debian).

Another network printing option is to use CIFS, the Common Internet File System, which is often known as Samba in honor of its most popular UNIX and Linux implementation. CIFS allows printers to be shared from UNIX, Linux, and Windows servers, so any of these boxes can act as a network print server.[1] CIFS is especially useful when you need to share UNIX printers with Windows desktops. See Chapter 27, *Cooperating with Windows*, for more information about CIFS.

Life without PostScript

PostScript printers are well supported by the Linux printing systems, and configuration of these printers is relatively easy. Unfortunately, non-PostScript printers such as inkjets and some cheap laser printers are slightly more difficult to deal with.

*See page 767 for more information about **ghostscript**.*

To print to a non-PostScript printer, you often need special software to convert the print job into the printer's preferred PDL. Some vendors can provide the appropriate Linux software; this is generally your best option if it is available. A popular alternative is the **ghostscript** package, which can convert PostScript to the proprietary PDLs of hundreds of printers. You will need to specify a printing filter to properly invoke **ghostscript** on the fly.

24.4 LPD: THE GOOD OL' PRINTING SYSTEM

The LPD printing system was designed specifically for use with line printers. Fortunately, its design has allowed the system to scale to support most of today's printers and PDLs. The network portion of the LPD printing system also extends well to large, heterogeneous networks and permits many computers to share printers. The LPD print spooler has become such a de facto standard that it has found its way inside many network printers.[2]

An overview of the printing process

Access to printers is controlled by the **lpd** daemon, which lives in **/usr/sbin** and is normally started at boot time. **lpd** is responsible for accepting print jobs from users and other (remote) **lpd**s, processing these jobs, and forwarding them to an actual printer. To accomplish these tasks, **lpd** reads printer configuration information from **/etc/printcap**, the system's printer information database.

---

1. However, we don't recommend this configuration for extremely high-volume printers because of the potential for file locking challenges.
2. The LPD standard has been documented (after the fact) in RFC1179. A newer standard, the Internet Printing Protocol (IPP), is detailed in RFC2568 and friends. It is similar but has not yet been widely adopted. The CUPS printing system uses IPP.

Users invoke the **lpr** program to submit their print jobs to **lpd**. These two processes communicate through the named pipe **/dev/printer**.

When determining what printer to send the job to, **lpr** first looks at the command line. If a **-P***printer* argument is passed to **lpr**, *printer* becomes the destination. Otherwise, **lpr** checks the environment to see if the PRINTER variable is defined, and if so, **lpr** uses the variable's value. If all else fails, the job is submitted to the system-wide default printer, which is the printer named lp, or if there is no lp, to the first entry in the **/etc/printcap** file. Almost all printing-related commands, including **lpq** and **lprm**, understand the PRINTER environment variable and the -**P** argument.

As soon as **lpr** knows where the current job is headed, it looks up the printer in the **/etc/printcap** file. This file designates the directory where **lpr** should place print jobs for that printer. This "spool directory" is often **/var/spool/lpd/***printername*.

lpr creates two files in the spool directory for each job. The first file's name consists of the letters **cf** (control file) followed by a number that identifies the job.[3] This file contains reference and handling information for the job, such as the identity of the user who submitted it. The numeric portion of the filename allows space for only three digits, so the printing system becomes confused if more than 999 jobs are queued. The second file's name begins with **df** (data file) followed by the same number. This file contains the actual data to be printed. After the file has been spooled, **lpr** notifies the **lpd** daemon of the job's existence.

When **lpd** receives this notification, it consults the **printcap** file to determine if the destination is local or remote. If the printer is connected locally, **lpd** checks to be sure a printing daemon is running on the appropriate printer's queue and creates one (by forking a copy of itself) if necessary.

If the requested printer is connected to a different machine, **lpd** opens a connection to the remote machine's **lpd** and transfers both the data and the control file. **lpd** then deletes the local copies of these files.

Scheduling for print jobs is done on a first-in, first-out basis, but the system administrator can modify the printing agenda by using **lpc** on individual jobs. Unfortunately, there is no way to permanently instruct the printing system to give preferential treatment to jobs spooled by a particular user or machine.

When the job is ready to print, **lpd** creates a series of Linux pipes between the spool file and the printing hardware that transports the data to be printed. In the middle of this channel **lpd** installs a filter process that can review and edit the contents of the data stream before it reaches the printer.

Filter processes can perform various transformations on the data or do nothing at all. Their chief purposes are to provide formatting and to support any device-specific protocols that may be required for dealing with a particular printer. A printer's

Printing

---

3. The **cf** file is actually called **tf** ("temporary file") while **lpr** is in the process of accepting a job. After the file has been written, **lpr** changes the file's name from **tf***xxx* to **cf***xxx*.

default filter is specified in **/etc/printcap**, but the default filter can be overridden on the **lpr** command line.

Controlling the printing environment

For day-to-day maintenance of the printing system, you need only three commands: **lpq**, **lprm**, and **lpc**. **lpq** examines the queue of jobs waiting to be printed on a particular printer. **lprm** deletes one or more of these jobs, erasing their stored data files and removing any references to them from within the printing system. Both of these commands are available to users, and both work across a network (if you're lucky).

lpc lets you make a number of changes to the printing environment, such as disabling printers and reordering print queues. Although some of its functions are available to users, **lpc** is primarily an administrative tool. Table 24.1 shows some other commands and daemons associated with the LPD print system.

Table 24.1   LPD printing commands

Command	Location	Function
lpq	**/usr/bin**	Shows print queue contents and status
lpr	**/usr/bin**	Queues jobs for printing
lprm	**/usr/bin**	Cancels a queued or printing job
lpc	**/usr/sbin**	Controls a printer or queue
lpd	**/usr/sbin**	Schedules and prints jobs
lptest	**/usr/bin**	Generates an ASCII test pattern
lpunlock	**/usr/bin**	Unlocks stuck printers

lpd: the print spooler

When **lpd** first starts, it reads the **/etc/printcap** file, in which the system's printers are defined. It then starts printing any jobs that are waiting in the spool directory and starts listening for new print requests.

If you start **lpd** with the **-l** flag, it logs print requests through syslog under the "lpr" facility. Without the **-l** flag, **lpd** logs only printing system errors.

See page 661 for more information about the ***hosts.equiv*** *file.*

Access control is defined for each host; the LPD printing system cannot support access control for specific remote users.[4] Only hosts whose names appear in the files **/etc/hosts.equiv** or **/etc/hosts.lpd** are allowed to spool print jobs.

Remember that adding a hostname to **/etc/hosts.equiv** indicates complete trust in that host. We recommend that you stick to the **/etc/hosts.lpd** file for printer access control. LPRng provides a finer-grained security model.

---

4. Actually, it is possible for printing filters to do this kind of authentication. But because most systems use a variety of filters, maintaining uniform access control among them is impractical.

lpr: submit print jobs

lpr is the only program on an LPD system that can queue files for printing. Other programs that cause files to be printed (for example, **enscript** and Acrobat) must do so by calling **lpr**.

Several useful options can be specified as arguments to **lpr**. The -#*num* flag produces *num* copies, and the **-h** flag suppresses the header page. Reminiscent of the days of slow printers, the **-m** flag requests that email be sent to the owner when the print job is complete.

For example, to print two copies of a file named **thesis** to a printer called **howler-lw**, you could type

```
% lpr -Phowler-lw -#2 thesis
```

lpq: view the printing queue

lpq is normally used with just a -**P** option to select a printer, although the -**l** flag is available to produce more detailed output. Output from **lpq** looks like this:

```
% lpq
anchor-lj is ready and printing
Rank    Owner    Job  Files                Total Size
active  garth    314  domain.2x1.ps        298778 bytes
1st     kingery  286  standard input       17691 bytes
2nd     evi      12   appendices           828 bytes
3rd     garth    13   proc                 43229 bytes
4th     scott    14   periodic             16676 bytes
5th     garth    16   standard input       489 bytes
```

The first column tells you the order in which the jobs will be printed. This information is rather superfluous because the output lines are always in order, with the active job on top and the last job to be printed on the bottom. If the first job is listed as 1st rather than active, no printing daemon is running on the queue.

The second column tells you which user spooled each job. The third column gives the job identification number for each job; this number is important to know if you intend to manipulate the job later with **lprm** or **lpc**. The fourth column shows the filenames that were listed on the **lpr** command line used to spool the job. If the data came in through a pipe (as the first and fifth jobs did above), the entry in this column will be standard input. The fifth and final column tells you the size of the job. This number is the size of the job before it is sent to the filter program and gives no information about how many pages a job will be or how long it will take to print.

lprm: remove print jobs

The most common form of **lprm** is **lprm** *jobid*, where *jobid* is the job identification number reported by **lpq**. **lprm** *user* removes all jobs belonging to *user*. **lprm** without arguments removes the active job. **lprm** - removes all the jobs you submitted; if you are root, it removes every job in the queue. No ordinary user can remove another user's jobs, but the superuser can remove any job.

Printing

The printing system maintains a notion of the origin of a job as well as the user who spooled it, and **lprm**'s matching process takes both into account. Thus, garth@sigi is not equivalent to garth@boulder, and neither can remove the other's jobs.

Trying to **lprm** the active job can cause problems on some printers. The filter process for the job is not properly notified of the termination, causing the whole system to come to a grinding halt, with the filter process holding an exclusive lock on the printer's port and preventing other processes from using the printer.

The only way to fix this situation is to use **ps** to identify the filter processes and kill them off by hand. **lpc** is not of use in this situation. Rebooting the system will always cure a hung printer, but this is a drastic measure. Before you resort to a reboot, kill and restart the master copy of **lpd** and manually remove jobs from the spool directory with the **rm** command.

lpc: make administrative changes

The **lpc** command can perform the following functions:

- Enable or disable queuing for a particular printer
- Enable or disable printing on a particular printer
- Remove all jobs from a printer's queue
- Move a job to the top of a printer's queue
- Start, stop, or restart the **lpd** daemon
- Get printer status information

When the printing system is running smoothly, **lpc** works just fine. But as soon as a filter gets stuck or some other minor problem appears, **lpc** wigs out completely. And it lies: it sometimes claims to have fixed everything when in reality, it has done nothing at all. You may have to fix things up by hand or even power-cycle your equipment when printing gets badly snarled.

lpc cannot be used across a network; you must log in to the machine that owns the printer you want to manipulate. **lpc** is normally used interactively, although you can also invoke it in a one-shot mode by putting one of the interactive commands on **lpc**'s command line. Once you have activated **lpc**, the various commands described below are available:

> **help** [*command*]

help without arguments shows you a short list of all available **lpc** commands. With an argument, it shows a one-line description of a particular command.

> **enable** *printer*
> **disable** *printer*

These commands enable or disable spooling of jobs to the named printer. Users who attempt to queue files are politely informed that spooling has been disabled. Jobs that are already in the queue are not affected. You perform this operation by simply setting or clearing group execute permission on **/var/spool/lpd/***printer***/lock**.

> **start** *printer*
> **stop** *printer*

start enables and **stop** disables printing on the named printer. Print jobs can still be spooled when a printer has been stopped, but they will not be printed until printing is restarted. **start** and **stop** operate by setting or clearing owner execute permission on **/var/spool/lpd/***printer***/lock**. They also start and kill the appropriate daemons for the printer. **stop** allows the active job to complete before disabling printing.

> **abort** *printer*

abort is just like **stop**, but it doesn't allow the active job to complete. When printing is reenabled, this job will be printed again.

> **down** *printer message*
> **up** *printer*

These commands affect both spooling and printing. Use them when a printer is really broken or has to be taken off-line for an extended period. The *message* parameter supplied to **down** can be as long as you like (on one line) and need not be quoted; it will be put in the printer's **/var/spool/lpd/***printer***/status** file and shown to users who run **lpq**. You'll normally want to use this feature to register a short explanation of why the printer is unavailable and when it will be back in service. The **up** command reverses the effect of a **down**.

> **clean** *printer*

This command removes all jobs from the printer's queue, including the active job. Because the printing daemon for the queue will still hold references to the files of the current job, Linux will not really delete them and the current job will complete.

> **topq** *printer jobid*
> **topq** *printer username*

The first form moves the specified job to the top of the printer's queue. The second form promotes all jobs belonging to *username*.

> **restart** *printer*

The **restart** command restarts a printing daemon that has mysteriously died. You'll know that the daemon is dead when **lpq** tells you "no daemon present." Although you might think **restart** would have the same effect as a **stop** followed by a **start**, it does not; **restart** will fail to restart a printer that still has a filter running.

> **status** *printer*

The **status** command shows you four things about a printer: whether spooling is enabled, whether printing is enabled, the number of entries in the queue, and the status of the daemon for that printer. If no entries are in the queue, you'll see something like the following.

Printing

```
lpc> status cer
cer:
queuing is enabled
printing is enabled
no entries
no daemon present
```

The fact that no daemon is present is not a cause for concern; printer-specific daemons go away after the queue is empty and aren't restarted by the master copy of **lpd**
until another job is spooled.

The /etc/printcap file

/etc/printcap is the LPD printing system's master database. It contains information
necessary for printing to local and remote printers. A printer must be described in
the **printcap** file before jobs can be submitted to it.

The first item in each **printcap** entry is a list of names for the printer, separated by
vertical bars. The names are followed by a number of configuration settings separated by colons. Configuration options are of the form xx, xx=*string*, or xx#*number*,
where xx is the two-character name of a parameter and *string* and *number* are values
to be assigned to it. When no value is assigned, the variable is Boolean and its presence indicates "true."

The null statement is acceptable, so you can place two colons side by side. It is helpful to begin and end each line with a colon, to make subsequent modifications easier.
Comments in **/etc/printcap** start with a pound sign (#). Entries can span several
lines if intermediate lines are terminated with a backslash. Continuation lines are,
by convention, indented.

The syntax of the **printcap** file is illustrated in the following example, which defines
a remote printer attached to the machine anchor:

```
# HP LaserJet 5M remote printcap. CS Department.

anchor-lj|cer|1-56|LaserJet 5M in cer lab:\
    :lp=/var/spool/lpd/anchor-lj/.null:\
    :sd=/var/spool/lpd/anchor-lj:\
    :lf=/var/adm/lpd-errs:\
    :rw:mx#0:rm=anchor:rp=anchor-lj:
```

From the first line, we can see that "cer", "anchor-lj", "1-56", and "LaserJet 5M in cer
lab" are all equivalent names for the same printer. These names are the printer's given
name, a well-known abbreviation, the room number of the printer's location, and a
full description. Although you can give your printers as many names as you like, you
should include at least three forms of the primary name:

- Short name – three or four characters, easy to type (e.g., "cer")
- Full name – hostname and type of printer (e.g., "anchor-lj")
- Descriptive name – other information (e.g., "LaserJet 5M in cer lab")

The next three lines in our example contain configuration settings for device name (lp), spool directory (sd), and error log file (lf). The last line specifies a read-write connection with the printer (rw), the maximum file size (mx, unlimited in this case), the remote machine name (rm), and the remote printer name (rp).

Jobs submitted to the printing system without a specific destination are routed to the first printer that has "lp" as one of its aliases. You should not use lp as a printer's primary name; that makes it difficult to change the default printer. If no printer has the name lp, the first printer in the **printcap** file is the system-wide default printer.

printcap variables

The flexibility of the **printcap** file is largely responsible for the LPD printing system's adaptability. The details are documented in the **printcap** man page, so we discuss only the most common variables here. They're shown in Table 24.2.

Table 24.2   Commonly used printcap variables

Name	Type	Meaning	Example
sd	string	Spool directory	sd=/var/spool/lpd/howler-lw
lf	string	Error log file	lf=/var/log/lpd-errors
lp	string	Device name	lp=/dev/lp0
af	string	Accounting file	af=/var/adm/lpr.acct
rm	string	Remote machine name	rm=beast.xor.com
rp	string	Remote printer name	rp=howler-lw
of	string	Output filter	of=/usr/libexec/lpr/lpf
if	string	Input filter	if=/usr/sbin/stylascii
mx	number	Maximum file size	mx#0
sh	bool	Suppress headers	sh

All **printcap** entries should include at least a specification of the spool directory (sd), the error log file (lf), and the printing device (lp). If you have a modern printer, you should specify that the printer be opened for reading and writing (rw) so that the printer can send error and status messages back to the host.

sd: spool directory

Each printer should have its own spool directory. All spool directories should be in the same parent directory (usually **/var/spool/lpd**) and should have the same name as the full name of the printer they serve (anchor-lj in the preceding example). A spool directory is needed even if the printer being described lives on a different machine; spooled files are stored locally until they can be transmitted to the remote system for printing.

When you install a new printer, you must create its spool directory by hand. Permissions should be 775, with both owner and group daemon.

The spool directory for a printer also contains two status files: **status** and **lock**. The **status** file contains a one-line description of the printer's state. This information is maintained by **lpd** and viewed with the **lpq** command. The **lock** file prevents multiple invocations of **lpd** from becoming active on a single queue and holds information about the active job. The permissions on the **lock** file are manipulated by **lpc** to control spooling and printing on the printer.

lf: error log file

See Chapter 11 for more information about log files.

Errors generated by print filters are logged to the file named in this variable. One error log can be shared by all printers, and it can be placed anywhere you like. When a log entry is made, the name of the offending printer will be included. Even remote printers should have log files, just in case of a communication problem with the remote machine.

Keep in mind that **lpd** sends error messages to syslog. Some filters send their error messages to syslog as well, leaving nothing in their **printcap**-specified log file. Check both of these locations when problems arise.

lp: device name

The device name for a printer must be specified if the printer is local. This name is usually the file in the **/dev** directory that represents the port to which the printer is attached. If the **printcap** entry addresses a network printer (that is, a printer on your LAN, not just a "remote" Linux printer; see page 747), the lp variable should be a pointer to a dummy file. (We like to use **/var/spool/lpd/***printer***/.null** for our dummy files.) This variable does not have to be defined for remote printers, but if it is defined, the file must exist.

lpd uses an advisory lock on the lp file to determine if the printer is in use. Even if the printer is really accessed through a network connection, you should provide a value for the lp variable. Specify a unique file that already exists on a local disk.

rw: device open mode

If a printer can send status information back to the host through its device file, the Boolean variable (rw) should be specified to request that the device be opened for both reading and writing. Read-write mode is useful for accounting and status reporting, and some filters require it.

af: accounting file

Even if you don't intend to charge for printer use, printer accounting can give you a good feel for how your printing resources are being consumed. We recommend that you enable accounting for all shared printers. You do that simply by specifying an accounting file. The file need only be specified and present on the machine to which the printer is physically connected, since accounting records are not written until a job is actually printed.

By convention, printer accounting data files are usually called **/var/adm/***printer*-**acct**. They list the number of pages printed for each job (usually a lie), the hostnames where the jobs originated, and the usernames of the jobs' owners.

It is the responsibility of the printer's input filter to generate accounting records. On PostScript printers, unless the filter actually queries the printer for its page count before and after the job, the page counts are extremely suspect.

mx: file size limits

The mx variable sets a limit on the amount of data that can be spooled at one time. File sizes are meaningless for printers other than line printers, however. Small Post-Script or PCL files could print hundreds of pages of garbage. This disconnect between file size and page length is particularly evident when students try to print the compiled binary versions of their programming assignments.

On some systems, mx defaults to some value other than 0 (no limit), and an explicit mx#0 entry is necessary to allow large jobs. Note that mx is a numeric field, so the entry mx=0 is incorrect.

If you really need to control how many pages people can print, you will need to use custom filters or switch to LPRng.

rm and rp: remote access information

In most situations, you will want to access a printer from more than one machine on the network. Even if the printer is a network device, you should pick a single machine to be responsible for communicating with it. All other machines should forward jobs to the designated handler. This setup allows **lpd** to take care of queuing the jobs in order rather than having several machines constantly squabbling over control of the printer. It also gives you a single place to look when printing is not working.

Remote machines (machines that are not directly connected to the printer) have a simple **printcap** entry that tells where to send the job, as in the example on page 765. The rm variable specifies the machine to which jobs should be sent, and the rp variable gives the name of the printer on that machine. The details of remote printing are described on page 765.

The fact that **printcap** entries are different for local and remote printers necessitates a bit of subterfuge on the part of the system administrator if one **printcap** file is to be shared among several machines. The fix is to make the local and remote names for a printer distinct; for example, howler-lw-local and howler-lw. This configuration makes howler-lw a "remote" printer even on the machine where it actually lives, but that's perfectly OK. You will have to refer to howler-lw-local if you want to use the **lpc** command, however.

of, if, nf: printing filters

Filters serve a number of purposes. The default printing filter (usually **/usr/lib/lpf**) fixes up various nonprinting sequences and writes out an accounting record, if ap-

Printing

propriate. Unfortunately, filters are not standardized. Any of several filter packages could do the same job, but each vendor tends to have unique filters.

If you have a character-only printer, you don't really need to be concerned with filters. But if you have an inkjet, laser, or PCL printer, you may need to use a filter to perform the appropriate format conversion.

Filters are usually just shell scripts that call a series of translation programs. The filter program must accept the print job on standard input, translate the job to a format appropriate for the device, and send the result to standard output.

If the user does not specify a filter when executing **lpr**, either the if (input filter) or the of (output filter) will be used. The names are deceptive—both actually send data to a printer.

If the **printcap** entry lists an input filter but does not specify an output filter, the device will be opened once for each job. The filter will be expected to send one job to the printer and then exit.

Conversely, if an output filter is specified without an input filter, **lpd** will open the device once and call the filter program once, sending all the jobs in the queue in a big clump. This convention is OK for devices that take a long time to connect to; however, such devices are rare.

If both an input filter and an output filter are specified, the banner page will be sent to the output filter (and the output filter will be called even if banners are turned off). The input filter will be called to process the rest of the job. This combination of options is really too confusing for mere mortals. Avoid it. Use LPRng if you have complex filtering requirements.

If you have to write new filters, stick to using input filters—they are easier to debug.

Input filters are called with numerous arguments. The most interesting are the username, host of origin, and accounting file name. If you want to do accounting for the printer, the input filter must generate the accounting records and append them to the accounting file. If you want to restrict access to a printer (for example, to deny printing to the user "guest"), the input filter must also take care of that since **lpd** has no built-in way to prevent individual users from printing.

To clarify the uses of filters, let's look at a simple example of an input (if) filter. The example is for a PostScript printer connected to a serial line on the local machine:

```
#!/bin/csh -f
/usr/local/bin/textps $* | /usr/local/bin/psreverse
```

Because the printer is serially connected, **lpd** takes care of opening the device with the correct modes, as specified in **/etc/printcap**. The first program called is **textps**, which looks at the input and decides if it is PostScript (which our printer expects), and if not, converts it to PostScript. **textps** gets all the filter arguments that were passed (the $*) and is expected to generate accounting records from that information.

The second program, **psreverse**, reverses the order of the pages so that they come out in a proper stack.

printcap variables for serial devices

The next few **printcap** variables are useful only for local serial printers. If you are setting up a network printer, skip the rest of this section. Otherwise, open your manual, look up your printer's communication specifications, and read on.

You control three types of communication settings through **printcap**: the baud rate, the "flag" bits, and the "local mode" bits.

br: baud rate

If your printer is connected to a serial port, you will need a br entry. A serial printer is like any other piece of hardware: for correct operation, it and its host computer must agree on a common set of communication parameters such as speed, parity, and flow control. Configuration of a printer is much like the configuration of a terminal. See Chapter 7 for general information about serial devices and cabling.

The baud rate is the speed at which communication occurs (in bits per second) and is a simple integer. Since it is a numeric value, you use the pound sign (#) to set it. For example, br#38400 sets the baud rate to 38,400 bps.

fc and fs: flag bits

Mucking with the flag bits is usually only necessary if you are trying to set up an old impact printer such as a Teletype. Like local mode bits (below), flag bits are integers, but each bit within the number modifies the behavior of the port in its own special way. Correctly setting up these parameters requires that you look up the meaning of each bit in the **termios** man page (look at the section for c_cflag constants) and add up the values for the bits you want to set or clear from **/usr/include/bits/termios.h**. Settings need only be specified on the machine to which the printer is connected.

You can assign two variables when adjusting the flag bits: fc and fs. fc (flag clear) specifies the bits that should be turned off, and fs (flag set) specifies the ones that should be turned on. Bits assigned to neither variable assume default values. It is meaningless to both set a bit and clear it.

The **termios** man page explains the meaning of each flag bit in detail. The flag bits may seem scary, but as long as you know what the communication settings of your printer should be, it's actually quite easy to set the bits.

xc and xs: local mode bits

The local mode bits are useful only for serial line printers. The xc and xs variables clear and set individual mode bits in much the same way that fc and fs clear and set flags bits. The difference between the two sets of bits is that local mode bits configure the serial driver, whereas the flag bits configure the actual communication link. Most of the mode bits are intended for use on interactive video terminals and so are not relevant to printer configuration.

printcap extensions

A nice feature of the **lpr/lpd** system is that it does not mind if you supply values for nonstandard **printcap** variables. Often, when a particular printer needs more configuration information than the base system defines, you can put extra variables in **printcap** for the printer's filters to use.

For example, the output filter for a network printer might need to know the network name of the device. The **printcap** entry for the printer might contain an entry such as

```
:nn=laser.colorado.edu:\
```

The use of **printcap** extensions allows all of the configuration information for a printer to be stored in one convenient place. If you see variables in the **printcap** file that are not discussed in the **printcap** manual page, check the documentation for the printer filters for the meanings of the variables.

Our site has taken advantage of this feature to document the physical location of each printer. Our printers have entries such as

```
:lo=Room 423, Engineering building:\
```

We have scripts that monitor paper and toner levels in the printers and send mail to support staff with instructions such as "take more paper to room 423 in the Engineering building" when necessary. For more information about monitoring network devices, see Chapter 20, *Network Management and Debugging*.

Printing to something besides a printer

We recently saw an instance of "creative misuse" by Sean McCreary in which the LPD printing system was used to spool MP3 music to a software jukebox. If nothing else, this is a great testimonial to the flexibility of the printing system.

The printcap entry looked something like this:

```
mp3-local:\
      :sd=/var/spool/lpd/mp3-local:\
      :lf=/var/log/lpd-errs:\
      :if=/usr/local/lib/mp3-play:\
      :lp=/dev/null:\
      :mx#0:
```

The actual MP3 player, **amp**, does not read from stdin by default, so a one-line script called **mp3-play** interfaced it to the printing system:

```
#!/bin/sh
exec /usr/local/bin/amp -
```

24.5 LPRng

LPRng is a relatively new print spooler that is based on the LPD system, and it's the default printing system shipped with the Red Hat and Debian distributions. Currently maintained by Patrick Powell at AStArt Technologies, LPRng successfully merges the best features of the traditional Berkeley and UNIX System V printing schemes.

One of the most significant problems with the LPD printing system is the need for most of the printing software to run as root. In addition to having **lpr** clients run setuid to root, LPD filters also run as root. Because filters are often shell scripts, this is a frightening prospect.

LPRng solves the problem by allowing clients to run as normal users. In cases in which LPRng doesn't have to interact with non-LPRng clients, even the printing daemon can run as a nonroot user. The package also adds lots of new security checking that is lacking in most LPD systems.

One of the more useful features of LPRng is its ability to produce verbose diagnostics and error messages. Instead of silently failing or returning a cryptic message, programs in this package give descriptive and helpful explanations of what went wrong.[5]

Although LPD supports access control through the **/etc/hosts.lpd** file, no authentication is available. LPRng supports Kerberos 5, SSL, and PGP authentication methods.

Finally, LPRng offers some great queue management features, most of which come from UNIX System V. LPRng includes dynamic redirection of print queues, support for multiple printers on one queue, and even load balancing across several printers.

It's easy to install LPRng on Linux distributions that don't include it by default. Even if you don't want to install LPRng everywhere on your network, consider using LPRng on your print server. This simple step will buy you much of the security and functionality of a network-wide deployment with very little hassle.

The LPRng commands

LPRng's version of **lpr** maintains backward compatibility with most other **lpr** implementations. The only exception is the **-s** flag, which is silently ignored by LPRng's **lpr**. This flag was originally used to create a symbolic link to the file to be printed instead of making a new copy, which was useful for printing large files.

The LPRng version of **lpr** provides a wealth of new functionality. Particularly useful are the verbose flag (**-V**) and the debugging flag (**-D5** for the most detail).

LPRng commands let you specify a printer's host and port in addition to its name. This feature allows users to print to remote printers that are not defined in the local **printcap** file.

To specify the host to which a printer is attached, append @*hostname* to the printer's name. A port is specified by further appending %*port*. For example:

```
% lpr -Phowler-lw@beast%8552 filename
```

This method of specifying a printer works for the LPRng versions of **lpr**, **lpq**, **lprm**, and **lpc**, which means that print clients often don't need a **printcap** file at all.

---

5. Perhaps the Linux standards committee was on vacation the day that LPRng came up for review…

If a printer isn't specified on the command line, the value of the PRINTER environment variable is used. If the PRINTER environment variable is not set, the first entry of the **/etc/printcap** file is used. If no **printcap** file exists, the default printer specified in the **lpd.conf** file is used.

LPRng builds several new features into **lpq**. Several alternative output formats are available with the short (**-s**), long (**-l**), and verbose long (**-L**) flags. These options can be useful with scripts that depend on the output of **lpq**. The command now accepts a flag to make periodic repeated queries (**-t** *seconds*). Finally, the debugging flag described above is supported. With the flag **-D5**, the command output will include detailed status messages from local and remote printers and print spoolers.

Perhaps the greatest addition to LPRng's **lpc** is its ability to prioritize queue entries based on something more useful than the order in which they were submitted. The rules for queuing priority can be made complex enough to accommodate almost any desired policy. Unlike the traditional **lpc**, LPRng's **lpc** can be run across a network.

LPRng's **lprm** allows job removal according to any of several criteria. In the traditional system, the job ID or username was required. With LPRng, jobs can also be removed from a spool by a regular expression that is matched against the job ID.

/etc/lpd.conf: configure lpd

The LPRng **lpd** server is highly configurable through the **/etc/lpd.conf** file. In fact, as of this writing, 185 different parameters can be set in this file. Most of the parameters set directory and operating system defaults. Also provided is a mechanism by which you provide default values for unspecified **/etc/printcap** variables.

The best way to create an **lpd.conf** file for your site is to copy the **lpd.conf** file in the root of the LPRng distribution. This file contains an option-by-option description with examples. If you do not have time to wade through this long list of options, refer to the on-line man page for **lpd.conf**, which contains explanations of all the settings and even an example.

/etc/lpd.perms: configure access control

With **/etc/lpd.perms**, you can establish very complex printing policies. Rules for controlling print access are applied to print jobs in the order in which they appear in the **lpd.perms** file.

Rules are made up of two parts. The first part is simply an ACCEPT or REJECT token that determines whether the specified operation will be allowed. It's followed by a series of clauses that specify which people, hosts, printers, or operations the rule should apply to.

For example, the following line tells the printing system that the user evi on the remote host beast can print jobs, spool jobs, remove jobs, and check the status of jobs on the printer howler-lw.

```
ACCEPT SERVICE=P,R,M,Q REMOTEHOST=beast REMOTEUSER=evi
    PRINTER=howler-lw
```

The one-letter codes in the SERVICE clause determine which operations the rule is referring to. Table 24.3 shows the values the SERVICE clause can contain.

Table 24.3   SERVICE codes in /etc/lpd.perms

Code	Action	What it refers to
P	Print	Printing a job from a queue
C	Control	Using **lpc** (lets secretaries unjam the printer)
R	Spool	Submitting jobs to the spool queue with **lpr**
M	Remove	Removing jobs from the queue with **lprm**
Q	Status	Obtaining status information with **lpq**
X	Connect	Connecting to **lpd**

The best way to set up your site's **lpd.perms** file is to modify the example version included with the package (installed in **/etc**). This file describes the ACCEPT and REJECT lines in detail and includes several enlightening examples. All possible configuration flags are described in this file.

Setting up the printcap file

The most important thing to remember about the LPRng **printcap** file is that it is completely backward compatible with the traditional LPD **printcap** file. That is, all traditional **printcap** files are also valid LPRng **printcap** files.

However, LPRng provides many new **printcap** features as well. Lines can be continued simply by indentation instead of an appended backslash. Variable names are no longer limited to two characters. Several macros are available to help simplify configuration. Entries can be targeted at particular hosts.

Probably the coolest configuration tool LPRng brings us is the **checkpc** program. **checkpc** checks the validity and consistency of the **printcap** file. It warns of missing spool directories, missing files, and incorrect permissions. If you run **checkpc** with the **-f** flag, it attempts to fix simple problems (such as making a directory or changing the permissions of a file). Running **checkpc** with the **-D5** flag produces verbose diagnostics.

Filters

In addition to providing LPD filter functionality, LPRng allows filters to be applied to jobs that are sent to remote printers. This feature allows customized data formatting for a host instead of for a printer.

The output filter (of) and input filter (if) printcap variables act a little differently in LPRng. The output filter under traditional LPD **lpr** is applied to both the document and the banner. Under LPRng, the output filter is used only for the banner. The

LPRng input filter is used only for printing text. Filters for other file types are specified with tags named *x*f, where *x* is a one-letter type abbreviation. You can completely disable filters for a job by adding **-Y** to the **lpr** command line.

Included in LPRng are the **lpbanner**, **pclbanner**, and **psbanner** commands. These commands create text, PCL, and PostScript banners, respectively. Each accepts command-line arguments that specify the banner name, login name, and job title.

LPRng comes with one particularly useful filter, **ifhp**, which prints to a tremendous variety of printers. Although it was designed primarily to support HP printers, it can handle most printers out of the box. Printers that are not supported internally can usually be made to work without too much hassle.

Accounting

In the days of line printers, accounting was a simple task. You could get an accurate page count for any job simply by counting lines. However, this method fails completely on PostScript and other types of files.

The only accurate way to account for the number of pages used for a job is to actually count those pages as they leave the printer. Fortunately, many modern printers keep a counter of the number of pages they have printed over their lifetime. By checking this counter before and after a print job, the printer driver can determine the true page count.

24.6 ADDING A PRINTER

In this section we discuss the overall process of printer configuration. We examine several scenarios:

- Setting up a local serial or parallel printer
- Accepting **lpd** print jobs from the network
- Printing to a network **lpd** print server

In the discussions that follow, we assume that the printer hardware has already been physically connected to a host or the network. See Chapter 7, *Serial Devices*, for information about connecting serial printers, and Chapter 15, *Network Hardware*, for general information about connecting devices to a network.

Network printers require a bit of extra configuration. In particular, they have to be assigned an IP address. That's usually accomplished by one of two methods.

See page 278 for more information about DHCP. First, most modern printers support the ability to boot across the network from a BOOTP or DHCP server. This method works well in environments with many homogeneous printers.

Alternatively, all network printers allow you to set their IP address from the console. Sometimes the "console" is a serial port, but often it's just a scheme for using buttons on the front of the printer. After your printer is on the network and you can ping it, make sure to secure it as discussed on page 769.

Tools available for Linux can help you configure other printer features, such as paper trays. One such tool is XPP, available at cups.sourceforge.net/xpp.

To make the following sections more fluid, we talk about a consistent set of hardware. The server machine runs a generic **lpd** spooler attached to a PostScript laser printer named howler-lw.

Setting up a local printer

For every local printer, you'll need to create an entry in **/etc/printcap**. A **printcap** entry typically looks like this:

```
howler-lw|howl|laserjet:\
    :sd=/var/spool/lpd/howler-lw:\
    :mx#0:\
    :lp=/dev/lp0:\
    :sh:
```

This entry defines three names for the printer, specifies a spool directory and port device, eliminates maximum job sizes, and suppresses print headers.

We can tell from the device file that this is a parallel printer. Serial printers are configured similarly. The device would probably be **/dev/ttyS0** (or **S1** for your second serial port) instead of **/dev/lp0**, and parameters such as baud rate would probably need to be specified. Look up relevant settings in the **printcap** man page.

Accepting network print jobs

Once you have successfully attached a printer locally, you can print to it from other machines on the network. First, make sure you can print locally without any difficulty. Then, to your **/etc/hosts.lpd** file, add the names of the client machines from which you want to accept print jobs. See the next section for client-side configuration.

Printing to a network print server

As with all LPD printing systems, new network printers need an **/etc/printcap** entry on the client machine. For our LaserJet, we'd add something like this:

```
howler-lw|lp|8-6|"LaserJet 5M, called howler-lw on beast":
    :lp=/var/spool/lpd/howler-lw/.null:\
    :rm=beast:rp=howler-lw:\
    :sd=/var/spool/lpd/howler-lw:mx#0:
```

We would then create the spool directory and the **.null** file on the client:

```
# mkdir /var/spool/lpd/howler-lw
# touch /var/spool/lpd/howler-lw/.null
# chown -R daemon /var/spool/lpd/howler-lw
# chgrp -R daemon /var/spool/lpd/howler-lw
# chmod 775 /var/spool/lpd/howler-lw
```

If the **lpd** server is a real machine (and not just a smart printer), make sure you can print jobs from that machine before configuring network clients.

Printing

To test printing from the client, use a sequence of commands similar to the following:

```
# lpc start howler-lw
# lpr -Phowler-lw /etc/motd
# lpq -Phowler-lw
```

Distribution-specific details

Printer setup is one area in which the various flavors of Linux differ substantially. Wherever possible, you are probably best off using the GUI configuration tools supplied by the vendor to set up printers.

 Red Hat's default printing system is a fairly vanilla implementation of LPRng. Some of Red Hat's tools are very useful, especially the graphical **printtool**, which automates editing of the **/etc/printcap** file, and the **lpunlock** script, which rescues locked print servers. The beloved **printtool** holds your hand during the configuration of a variety of types of printers, including local, remote LPD, CIFS (Windows), and NetWare (NCP) printers. Be forewarned that **printtool** requires the format of the **printcap** file to be very precise; if you edit the file by hand, you may not be able to open it in **printtool** anymore. Local printer definitions must be placed in **/etc/printcap.local**; they are moved to **/etc/printcap** automatically when **lpd** starts. **checkpc -f** creates printer spool directories for you.

 The default printing system shipped with SuSE is the stock BSD version of LPD. The **lpd** daemon must be enabled by inclusion of the line START_LPD=yes in the **/etc/rc.config** file before printing will work. YaST, SuSE's GUI system administration tool, includes functions that will generate extremely basic **/etc/printcap** entries for you. However, chances are that you'll need to further refine these entries by editing the **printcap** file by hand.

 Debian defaults to the LPRng package with no extra bells or whistles. You'll have to edit the configuration files (such as **/etc/printcap**) directly to add or change printer configurations (or download the **printtool** GUI configurator by using **apt-get**).

24.7 DEBUGGING PRINTING PROBLEMS

Network **lpd** print jobs are delivered on TCP port 515. Unless you want to be printing jobs for strangers, your firewall should block all traffic to this port from the Internet. To test your connectivity to a remote **lpd** server, **telnet** from the client to port 515 of the server. If you can establish a connection, you can at least verify that the network is working and that **lpd** is running on the server.

If you have problems debugging a remote printer connection, you need to look in six (yes, six) places to track down the problem:

- The system log file (as specified in **/etc/syslog.conf**) on the machine hosting the printer, for messages about permission problems

- The system log files on the sending machine, for name resolution and permission problems

- The print daemon log file on the server machine, for messages about bad device names, incorrect formats, etc. (as specified in **/etc/syslog.conf** for the "lpr" syslog facility)

- The print daemon log file on the sending machine, for missing filters, unknown printers, missing directories, etc.

- The printer log file on the printing machine, for errors in transmitting the job (as specified by the lf variable in the **/etc/printcap** file)

- The printer log file on the sending machine, for errors about preprocessing or queuing the job

When debugging remote printers, always keep in mind that there must be a queue for the job on the requesting machine, a way to decide where to send the job, and a method of sending the job to the remote machine. On the printing machine, there must be a place to queue the job, sufficient permissions to allow the job to be printed, and a way to output to the device.

Before you start tracking down a network printing problem, make sure you can print from the machine that actually hosts the printer. You may not have a network problem at all.

24.8 COMMON PRINTING SOFTWARE

Although LPD and LPRng both provide adequate systems for queuing, monitoring, and outputting print jobs, neither of them provides much of the format translation necessary to drive modern printers. Additional tools that sit on top of the printing system can provide these features.

Our purpose in this section is not to tell you everything you need to know about these packages but just to let you know about the functionality they advertise.

ghostscript

ghostscript is a freely distributed PostScript interpreter that enables you to view PostScript files on your screen. It's also good for driving raster output devices (such as inexpensive WinPrinters). Even if your particular printer is not supported out of the box, you can use **ghostscript** as a starting point for building your own driver. Be forewarned that building a driver can be a very complicated process.

Several different versions of **ghostscript** are available; see www.ghostscript.com for information about the differences among them. Red Hat and SuSE ship the slightly commercial Aladdin (www.aladdin.com) version of **ghostscript**, which contains a wealth of support for WinPrinters.

mpage

mpage is a text-to-PostScript converter that places multiple logical pages on a single physical page. This trick is a great tree saver when you are printing things like source code for which you don't need big type and large margins.

Printing

enscript

Adobe originally developed a product called **enscript** to convert text files to Post-Script for printing. This software, or something like it, makes text output look nice on PostScript printers. **enscript** provides page formatting features such as fancy page headers and "two up" printing (two pages printed at half-size on one sheet).

Although the Adobe version of this program is no longer maintained, a good alternative exists. GNU **enscript** is a free, open source version of **enscript** that is completely backward compatible with Adobe's version. GNU **enscript** offers a wealth of new features, including language-sensitive highlighting, support for various paper sizes, PostScript font downloading, and user-defined headers.

You can download the GNU **enscript** from the web at people.ssh.fi/mtr/genscript. Since most of the work on this project is done in Finland by Markku Rossi, the default paper type is A4. A4 paper is slightly longer than letter, just enough to cut off vital slivers of your documents such as headers, footers, or page numbers. To Americanize GNU **enscript**, run the **configure** command with the following argument when you are first installing it:

```
# ./configure --with-media=Letter
```

The paper type can also be set on the **enscript** command line. If you forget to change the media type and use **enscript** to print to a high-end printer that knows what kinds of paper it has loaded, the printer may refuse to print at all.

24.9 PRINTER PHILOSOPHY

The main things to expect when dealing with printers are troubles and frustrations. If all else fails, just be glad it's not MS-DOS.

Use printer accounting

You should enable printer accounting even if you don't plan to charge for printer use. The overhead is very slight and you get to see exactly who is using the printer. Printer accounting also gives good information about the various sources of print jobs, which is good information to know when you are situating new printers.

Use banner pages only when necessary

The printing system can preface each job with a page showing the title of the job and the user who submitted it. This banner page can be helpful on printers used by many different people, but it's a waste of time and paper in most office situations. If you don't need banner pages, suppress them by setting the Boolean **printcap** variable sh.

Provide recycling bins

All kinds of computer paper are recyclable. You can use the boxes that paper comes in as recycling bins. Post a sign asking that no foreign material (such as staples, paper clips, and newspaper) be discarded there.

Provide previewers

Users will often print a document, find a small error in the formatting, and end up reprinting the whole job. This waste of paper can easily be avoided with software that allows users to see how the printed output will look on their screens.

Previewing is built into many modern WYSIWYG editors, but if your users are addicted to an older typesetting system, you will need to provide some other way to preview documents.

For random PostScript documents, you can use **ghostscript**; for **roff**, pipe the output of **groff** into **ghostview**. After you have provided the necessary previewers, train your users to use them. A good use of accounting records is to check for cases in which the same document has been printed repeatedly.

Buy cheap printers

Printer technology is mature. You don't need to spend a lot of money for great output and reliable mechanics.

Don't splurge on an expensive "workgroup" printer unless you really need it. There's no difference in the output, and a medium-grade "personal" printer can often be just as fast and just as reliable, not to mention tens of pounds lighter. A 10-page-a-minute printer can serve about five full-time writers. In most cases, you'd be better off buying five $500 printers for a group of 25 writers than one $2,500 printer.

In general, never buy a printer (or a hard disk, or memory) from a computer manufacturer. Their printers are usually just rebranded commodity printers at twice the price. The best bet is to invest in PostScript printers manufactured for the PC and Macintosh markets. We have had particularly good luck with HP and Lexmark laser printers. They are superior products that can spool network **lpd** print jobs, and they work pretty well with the generic Linux PostScript drivers.

Secure your printer

Most newer network printers support some form of remote management. Remote management is nice for sysadmins because it allows for convenient configuration without a lot of walking. Some common ways to remotely access a printer include **telnet**, HTTP, and SNMP. Through the remote interface, you can set the printer's IP address, default gateway, syslog server, SNMP community name, protocol options, and most importantly, password.

By default, most remotely administrable printers are unprotected and must have a password (or perhaps a "set" SNMP community name) assigned as part of the installation process. Refer to the installation manuals from your printer manufacturer to learn how to do this on your particular printer. Some vendors only distribute Windows-based configurators, but you can configure most modern HP network printers by using a web browser.

Printing

24.10 EXERCISES

E24.1 How would you turn on printer accounting for LPD? Why is printer accounting important?

E24.2 What steps are needed before you take a printer down for maintenance? Using your procedure, what happens to queued print jobs after the printer is brought back up?

E24.3 Read the **hosts.equiv** man page. Note that the **hosts.lpd** has the same format, except that it does not support the *username* parameter. Write your own **hosts.lpd** that explicitly rejects all print jobs from the machine "rouge" and accepts them from the machine "doc-print".

E24.4 When using a network-connected printer that can spool its own files, why is it still a good idea to use a print server to manage all print jobs?

★ **E24.5** List the steps needed to add a new serial printer named "slow-bro" to your Linux system. The printer's baud rate is 9600, and it is connected to the second serial port of a PC.

★★ **E24.6** Pick a current printer model (e.g., an HP LaserJet 6MP) and investigate how to support it under Linux. Do you need to set up filters? Do you need **ghostscript**? Or is the printer completely unsupported? If the printer is supported, give a brief overview of the steps that would be needed to install it. You get style points if the retail price of your chosen printer is under $200.

25 *Maintenance and Environment*

Once upon a time, dozens of programmers shared a single system, such as the now-famous VAX. In that era, a tremendous amount of effort went into maintaining equipment and providing a nurturing environment for it. Seasoned system administrators often knew as much about ethylene glycol cooling systems as they did about account management.

The 90s brought an influx of desktop workstations and a move away from "big iron" computing platforms. For a while, it appeared that the days of the central machine room might be numbered. Recently, the client/server computing paradigm has resulted in an increased dependence on server platforms running an operating system that provides flexibility, reliability, security, and performance. Linux and UNIX have moved in to fill that marketplace, and as a result, herds of servers have moved into those once-abandoned machine rooms (though in many cases, the machine rooms themselves have been downsized). Providing a healthy, well-maintained environment for these servers is as important as ever.

This chapter offers some hints on handling and maintaining hardware, as well as on giving it a good home.

25.1 MAINTENANCE BASICS

Hardware maintenance was traditionally something that was covered by an expensive annual maintenance contract. Although such contracts are still readily available, today it is more common to use the "fly by the seat of your pants" approach to hardware maintenance.

See page 861 for more information about retiring hardware.

If you keep a log book, a quick glance at the records for the last six to twelve months will give you an idea of your failure rates. It's a good idea to keep a careful record of failures and replacements so that you can accurately evaluate the different maintenance options available to you. Some parts fail more often than anticipated by the manufacturer, so contracts are sometimes not only convenient but also financially advantageous. But remember, there comes a time when all hardware should be replaced, not maintained. Know your hardware and let it go gracefully when its time has finally come. You might even consider donating outdated equipment to your local university or school. For them, equipment is rarely too old to be useful.

The best maintenance scheme is probably the "selective warranty" strategy. Disk drive manufacturers offer warranties up to five years long, and some memory modules even come with a lifetime guarantee. Many workstations have at least a year of warranty. When purchasing new equipment, shop around for the best warranty—it will save you money in the long run.

25.2 MAINTENANCE CONTRACTS

Several major companies offer hardware maintenance on computer equipment that they do not sell. These vendors are often anxious to displace the original manufacturer and get their foot in the door, so to speak. You can sometimes negotiate very attractive maintenance contracts by playing a manufacturer against a third-party provider. If possible, get references on all potential maintenance vendors, preferably from people you know and trust.

On-site maintenance

If you have an on-site maintenance contract, a service technician will bring spare parts directly to your machine. Guaranteed response time varies between 4 and 24 hours; it's usually spelled out in the contract. Response times during business hours may be shorter than at other times of the week.

If you are considering a quick-response maintenance contract, it's usually worth calculating the cost of keeping a couple of complete backup systems around that you can swap in to replace malfunctioning computers. A whole-system swap usually provides faster repair than even the most deluxe maintenance contract, and with today's low hardware prices, the investment is often minimal.

Board swap maintenance

A board swap program requires you and your staff to diagnose problems, perhaps with the help of hotline personnel at the manufacturer's site. After diagnosis, you call a maintenance number, describe the problem, and order the necessary replacement board. It is usually shipped immediately and arrives the next day. You then install the board, get the hardware back up and happy, and return the old board in the same box in which the new board arrived.

The manufacturer will usually want to assign a "return merchandise authorization" (RMA) number to the transaction. Be sure to write that number on the shipping documents when you return the bad board.

Warranties

The length of the manufacturer's warranty should play a significant role in your computation of a machine's lifetime cost of ownership. A year's warranty is standard for computers, but warranties of several years or more are not uncommon.

In a university environment, it seems to be easier to get federal funding for capital equipment than for support personnel or maintenance. We have occasionally paid for an "extended warranty" option on new hardware (which could also be described as prepaid maintenance) to convert equipment dollars to maintenance dollars.

If you order the pieces of a major computer system from several vendors, the parts will not necessarily arrive at the same time. With many pieces of hardware, the biggest maintenance and reliability problems occur quite soon after installation. Hardware failures that occur within a day or two of installation are referred to as "infant mortality."

25.3 BOARD-HANDLING LORE

PC-based systems seem to require at least four or five add-on boards to reach workstation standards (SCSI, sound, video, network, memory… Hmm, what's on that motherboard anyway?). Circuit boards should be handled gently, not dropped, not have coffee spilled on them, not have books piled on them, etc. Most customer engineers (those friendly repair people that come with your maintenance contract) are ten times rougher on boards than seems reasonable.

Static electricity

Electronic parts are sensitive to static electricity. To handle boards safely, you must ground yourself before and during installation. A ground strap worn on the wrist and attached to a special mat that you kneel on (most computers require you to show proper respect!) will ground you properly.

Remember that you need to worry about static when you first open the package containing a printed circuit board and anytime the electronic component is handled—not just when you perform an installation. Be especially careful if the office where you receive your mail (and where you might be tempted to open your packages) is carpeted; carpet generates more static electricity than does a hard floor.

One way to reduce static on carpeted floors is to purchase a spray bottle at your local Wal-Mart and fill it with one part Downy fabric softener to 10 parts water. Spray this on the carpet (but not on computing equipment) once every month to keep static levels low. This procedure also leaves your office area with that all-important April-fresh scent.

Reseating boards

You can occasionally fix a hardware problem by simply powering down the equipment, cleaning the contacts on the edge connectors of the interface cards (SCSI, Ethernet, etc.), reseating the cards, and powering the system back up. If this works temporarily but the same problem comes back a week or a month later, the electrical contact between the card and the motherboard is probably poor.

Contacts can be cleaned with a special cleaning solution and cleaning kit or with an ordinary pencil eraser. Don't use an eraser that is old and hard. If your eraser doesn't work well erasing pencil marks from paper, it won't work well on electrical contacts either. Try to keep your fingers off the contacts. Just "erase" them with the pencil eraser (a mild abrasive), brush off the eraser droppings, and reinstall the card.

Some motherboards still have socketed ICs, although this is increasingly rare. Over time, the connections in the sockets can deteriorate, mostly because of vibrations from fans. You can press firmly on the top of the chips with your thumb (after you've donned a grounding strap, of course) to tuck them in.

25.4 MONITORS

The monitor is often the least reliable component of modern computer systems. Many monitors have brightness and convergence adjustments that are accessible only from the circuit board. Unfortunately, monitors often use internal charges of tens of thousands of volts that can persist long after the power has been disconnected. Because of the risk of electric shock, we recommend that you always have your monitors adjusted by a qualified technician. *Do not attempt the job yourself.*

25.5 MEMORY MODULES

Today's hardware accepts memory in the form of SIMMs (Single Inline Memory Modules), DIMMs (Dual Inline Memory Modules), or RIMMs (Rambus Inline Memory Modules) rather than individual chips. These modules range in size from 32MB to 512MB, all on one little card.

If you need to add memory to a workstation or server, you can usually order it from a third-party vendor and install it yourself. Be cautious of buying memory from workstation vendors; their prices are often quite imaginative. When adding memory, think big. The price of memory is continually decreasing, but so is the standard allotment of expansion slots on a typical motherboard.

It's worth double-checking your system documentation before ordering memory to make sure you have a clear idea of the types of memory modules that your systems will accept. You can often increase performance by installing memory that supports a higher bus rate or special features such as DDR (Double Data Rate). Make sure that you know how many memory slots each system has available and whether there are any restrictions on the addition of new modules. Some systems require modules to be added in pairs; others do not strictly require this but can yield higher performance when modules are paired.

Make sure that you understand how old and new memory modules will interact with each other. In most cases, only the features or speeds common to all modules can actually be used. It may sometimes be worthwhile to remove a system's original memory when upgrading.

If you install your own memory, keep these two rules in mind:

- Memory is more sensitive than anything else to static electricity. Make sure you're well grounded before opening a baggie full of memory.

- The connector that's used to attach the module to the motherboard varies from machine to machine. Most usually snap in easily enough, but you need a special tool to remove them once they've been installed. It's always tempting to use a ballpoint pen or a paper clip to release the fasteners, but this approach often ends up damaging the connector.

Memory modules are frequently a candidate for the pencil eraser cleaning technology described earlier in this chapter.

25.6 PREVENTIVE MAINTENANCE

Some pieces of hardware have filters that must be regularly cleaned or changed. Clogged filters impede the flow of air and may result in overheating, a major cause of equipment failure. It's important to keep the air vents on all equipment open and unobstructed. It is not uncommon to find books or newspapers lying on top of a computer's vents; in these cases, we recommend repeatedly punching the perpetrator on the shoulder until it really starts to hurt.

Anything with moving parts may need regular lubrication, cleaning, and belt maintenance. Listen for squeaks from your older equipment and pamper it accordingly.

On server systems, the part that most frequently fails is the fan and power supply module—especially on PCs, where it is often a single field-replaceable unit (FRU). Periodically check your servers to make sure their main fans are spinning fast and strong. If not, you must usually replace the entire power supply assembly—otherwise, you run the risk of overheating your equipment. *Do not* try to lubricate the fan itself; this procedure might postpone the inevitable breakdown, but it could also accelerate the problem or cause damage to other components.

Many PC cases provide a convenient mounting location for a second fan (and electrical connections to power it). If noise is not a consideration, it's always advisable to install the second fan. In addition to lowering the operating temperature of the components, the extra fan acts as a backup if the primary fan fails. Extra fans are cheap; keep a couple around as spares.

A computer in a dusty environment will burn out components much more frequently than one whose environment is relatively clean. Dust clogs filters, dries out lubrication, jams moving parts (fans), and coats components with a layer of dusty "insulation" that reduces their ability to dissipate heat. All of these effects tend to increase operating temperatures. Check and clean dust filters regularly. You may also need to give your systems' innards an occasional housecleaning in bad environments. (Any environment that features carpeting is likely to be bad.)

Vacuuming is the best way to remove dust, but be sure to keep the motor at least five feet from system components and disks to minimize magnetic field interference. Your machine room should be vacuumed regularly, but make sure this task is performed by people who have been trained to respect proper distances and not harm equipment (office janitorial staff are usually not acceptable candidates for this task).

Tape drives usually require regular cleaning as well. You clean most cassette-type drives by inserting a special cleaning cassette.

25.7 ENVIRONMENT

Just like humans, computers work better and longer if they're happy in their environment. Although they don't care much about having a window with a view, they do want you to pay attention to other aspects of their home.

Temperature

The ideal operating temperature for computer equipment is 64° to 68°F (17° to 20°C), with about 45% humidity. Unfortunately, this temperature does not coincide with the ideal operating temperature of a computer user. Ambient temperatures above 80°F (27°C) in the computer room imply about 120°F (49°C) inside machines. Commercial-grade chips have an operational range up to about 120°F, at which point they stop working; beyond about 160°F (71°C), they break.

Humidity

The ideal humidity for most computer hardware is in the range of 40% to 60%. If the humidity is too low, static electricity becomes a problem. If it is too high, condensation can form on the boards, causing shorting and oxidation.

Office cooling

These days, many computers live in people's offices and must survive on building air conditioning (often turned off at night and on weekends) and must overcome a healthy dose of papers and books on cooling vents. When you put a computer in an office, keep in mind that it will steal air conditioning that is intended for humans. If you are in a role in which you can influence cooling capacity, a good rule of thumb is that each human in the room produces 300 BTUH worth of heat, whereas your average office PC produces about 1,100 BTUH. Don't let the engineers forget to add in solar load for any windows that receive direct sunlight.

Machine room cooling

If you are "lucky" enough to be moving your herd of servers into one of those fancy raised-floor machine rooms built in the 1980s that has enough capacity to cool all of your equipment *and* the state of Oklahoma, then your biggest concern will likely be to find some remedial education in primitive cooling system maintenance. For the rest of us, correctly sizing a cooling system is what makes the difference in the long term. A well-cooled machine room is a happy machine room.

We have found that it's a good idea to double-check the cooling load estimates provided by the HVAC folks, especially when installing a system for a machine room. You'll definitely need an HVAC engineer to help you with calculations for the cooling load that your roof, walls, and windows (don't forget solar load) contribute to your environment. HVAC engineers usually have a lot of experience with those components and should be able to give you an accurate estimate. The part you need to check up on is the internal heat load for your machine room.

You will need to determine the heat load contributed by the following components:

- Roof, walls, and windows (see your HVAC engineer for this estimate)
- Electronic gear
- Light fixtures
- Operators (people)

Electronic gear

You can estimate the heat load produced by your servers (and other electronic gear) by determining their power consumption. Direct measurement power consumption is by far the best method to obtain this information. Your friendly neighborhood electrician can often help you with this. Alternatively, most equipment is labeled with its maximum power consumption in watts, though typical consumption tends to be less than the maximum. You can convert this figure to the standard heat unit, BTUH, by multiplying by 3.412 BTUH/watt. For example, if we wanted to build a machine room that would house 25 servers rated at 450 watts each, the calculation would be:

$$\left(25 \text{ servers}\right) \left(\frac{450 \text{ watts}}{\text{server}}\right) \left(\frac{3.412 \text{ BTUH}}{\text{watt}}\right) = 38{,}385 \text{ BTUH}$$

Light fixtures

As with electronic gear, you can estimate light fixture heat load based on power consumption. Typical office light fixtures contain four 40-watt fluorescent tubes. If your new machine room had six of these fixtures, the calculation would be:

$$\left(6 \text{ fixtures}\right) \left(\frac{160 \text{ watts}}{\text{fixture}}\right) \left(\frac{3.412 \text{ BTUH}}{\text{watt}}\right) = 3{,}276 \text{ BTUH}$$

Operators

At one time or another, humans will need to enter the machine room to service something. Allow 300 BTUH for each occupant. If you want to allow for four humans in the machine room at the same time:

$$\left(4 \text{ humans}\right) \left(\frac{300 \text{ BTUH}}{\text{human}}\right) = 1{,}200 \text{ BTUH}$$

Total heat load

Once you have calculated the heat load for each component, add them up to determine your total heat load. For our example, we assume that our HVAC engineer estimated the load from the roof, walls, and windows to be 20,000 BTUH.

20,000	BTUH for roof, walls, and windows
38,385	BTUH for servers and other electronic gear
3,276	BTUH for light fixtures
1,200	BTUH for operators
62,861	BTUH total

Cooling system capacity is typically expressed in tons. You can convert BTUH to tons by dividing by 12,000 BTUH/ton. You should also allow at least a 50% slop factor to account for errors and future growth:

$$\left(62{,}681 \text{ BTUH}\right)\left(\frac{1 \text{ ton}}{12{,}000 \text{ BTUH}}\right)\left(1.5\right) = 7.86 \text{ tons of cooling required}$$

See how your estimate matches up with the one provided by your HVAC folks.

Temperature monitoring

If you are supporting a mission-critical computing environment, it's a good idea to monitor the temperature (and other environmental factors, such as noise and power) in the machine room even when you are not there. It can be very disappointing to arrive on Monday morning and find a pool of melted plastic on your machine room floor. Fortunately, automated machine room monitors can watch the goods while you are away. We use and recommend the Phonetics Sensaphone product family. These inexpensive boxes monitor environmental variables such as temperature, noise, and power, and they telephone you (or your pager) when a problem is detected. You can reach Phonetics in Aston, PA at (610) 558-2700 or visit them on the web at www.sensaphone.com.

25.8 POWER

Computer hardware would like to see nice, stable, clean power. In a machine room, this means a power conditioner, an expensive box that filters out spikes and can be adjusted to provide the correct voltage levels and phases. In offices, surge protectors placed between machines and the wall help insulate hardware from power spikes.

Servers and network infrastructure equipment should be placed on an Uninterruptible Power Supply (UPS). Good UPSs have an RS-232, Ethernet, or USB interface that can be attached to the machine to which they supply power. This connection enables the UPS to warn the computer that the power has failed and that it should shut itself down cleanly before the batteries run out.

See page 33 for more information about shutdown procedures.

One study has estimated that 13% of the electrical power consumed in the United States is used to run computers. Traditionally, UNIX boxes were based on hardware and software that expected the power to be on 24 hours a day. These days, only servers and network devices really need to be up all the time. Desktop machines can be powered down at night if there is an easy way for users to turn them off (and if you trust your users to do it correctly).

At the very least, ask users to turn off monitors and laser printers when they go home; these are the biggest power hogs. When buying new equipment, look for an Energy Star certification. It signifies that an item complies with EPA guidelines for energy-efficient operation. For example, Energy Star monitors must be able to automatically shut off their displays after a certain period of inactivity.

Remote power control

You may occasionally find yourself in a situation in which you have to regularly power-cycle[1] a server because of a kernel or hardware glitch. Or perhaps you have non-Linux servers in your machine room that are more prone to this type of problem. In either case, you may want to consider installing a system that will allow you to power-cycle problem servers by remote control.

One inexpensive and popular solution is the X-10 power control system, which includes a box that will answer a phone line and will power-cycle machines based on touch-tone codes. The basic X-10 product line is described and sold on-line at the site www.x10.com. If you're really serious about this approach, be sure to check out what's available at www.smarthome.com, which primarily focuses on home automation but includes higher-quality X10-compatible gear.

A more deluxe (and expensive) solution is manufactured by American Power Conversion (APC). Their MasterSwitch product is similar to a power strip, except that it can be controlled by a web browser through its built-in Ethernet port. You can reach APC at (401) 789-0204 or on the web at www.apcc.com.

25.9 RACKS

Much to the dismay of the folks on Wall Street who once viewed raised floors as a corporate status symbol akin to owning a Lamborghini, the days of the true raised-floor machine room are over. Have you ever tried to trace a cable that runs under the floor of one of these behemoths? Our experience is that while it looks nice through glass, "raised floor" is a synonym for "rat's nest." If you *must* put in a raised floor, use it to hide electrical power feeds and *nothing else*.

If your goal is to operate your computing equipment in a professional manner, a dedicated machine room for server-class machines is essential. A server room not only provides a cozy, temperature-controlled environment for your machines but also addresses their physical security needs.

---

1. Power-cycling is the process of turning a machine off, waiting 30 to 60 seconds for the capacitors to drain, and then turning the machine back on again.

Maintenance

In a dedicated machine room, storing equipment in racks (as opposed to, say, setting it on tables or on the floor) is the only maintainable, professional choice. Today, the best storage schemes use racks that are interconnected with an overhead track system for routing cables. This approach provides that irresistible high-tech feel without sacrificing organization or maintainability.

The best overhead track system is manufactured by Chatsworth Products (Chatsworth, CA, (818) 882-8595). Using standard 19" single-rail telco racks, you can construct homes for both shelf-mounted and rack-mounted servers. Two back-to-back 19" telco racks make a high-tech-looking "traditional" rack (for cases in which you need to attach rack hardware both in front of and in back of equipment). Chatsworth provides the racks, cable races, and cable management doodads, as well as all the hardware necessary to mount them in your building. Since the cables lie in visible tracks, they are easy to trace, and you will naturally be motivated to keep them tidy.

25.10 TOOLS

A well-outfitted system administrator is an effective system administrator. Having a dedicated tool box is an important key to minimizing downtime in the event of an emergency. Table 25.1 lists some items you should probably keep in your tool box, or at least within easy reach.

Table 25.1   A system administrator's tool box

General tools	
Phillips-head screwdrivers: #0, #1, and #2	Tweezers
Slot-head screwdrivers: 1/8", 3/16", and 5/16"	Scissors
Electrician's knife or Swiss army knife	Socket wrench kit
Pliers, both flat-needlenose and regular	Small flashlight or penlight
Teensy tiny jeweler's screwdrivers	Hex wrench kit
Ball-peen hammer, 4oz.	Torx wrench kit
Computer-related specialty items	
Wire stripper (with an integrated wire cutter)	Fluke network analyzer
Cable ties (and their Velcro cousins)	IC chip extractor
Spare Category 5 RJ-45 crossover cables	RJ-45 end crimper
Spare RJ-45 connectors (solid core and stranded)	SCSI terminators
Digital multimeter (DMM)	Breakout box
Static grounding strap	
Miscellaneous	
List of emergency maintenance contacts[a]	Q-Tips
Home phone and pager #s of on-call support staff	Electrical tape
First-aid kit	Dentist's mirror
Six-pack of good beer	Cellular telephone

a. And maintenance contract numbers if applicable.

25.11 EXERCISES

E25.1 Why would you want to mount your computers in a rack?

★ **E25.2** Environmental factors affect both people and machines. Augment the factors listed in this book with some of your own (e.g., dust, noise, light, clutter, etc). Pick four factors and evaluate the suitability of your lab for man and machine.

★ **E25.3** A workstation draws 0.8 A, and its monitor draws 0.7 A @ 120V.

   a) How much power does this system consume in watts? (Hint: $P = EI$)

   b) With electricity going for about \$0.10/kWh, what does it cost to leave this system on year-round?

   c) How much money can be saved annually by turning off the monitor for an average of 16 hours a day (either manually, or by using Energy Star features such as Display Power Management Signaling)?

   d) What is the annual cost of cooling this system? (State your assumptions regarding cooling costs and show your calculations.)

★★ **E25.4** Design a new computing lab for your site. State your assumptions regarding space, numbers of machines, and type and power load of each machine. Then compute the power and cooling requirements for the lab. Include both servers and client workstations. Include the layout of the room, the lighting, and the expected human load as well.

Maintenance

26 *Performance Analysis*

Performance is one of the most visible characteristics of any system, and it's often high on the list of complaints from users. Many users are convinced that their computers could run twice as fast if only the administrator knew how to properly tune the system to release its vast, untapped potential. In reality, this is almost never true.

One common fantasy involves tweaking the kernel variables that control the paging system and the buffer pools. Once upon a time, there were situations in which this tweaking was necessary and prudent. These days, it is usually a bad idea. The most likely result is that you will *reduce* your system's overall performance and not even be aware of what you've done, all the while congratulating yourself on being such a wily administrator.

Major distributions' kernels are pretuned to achieve reasonable (though admittedly, not optimal) performance under a variety of load conditions. If you try to optimize the system on the basis of one particular measure of performance, the chances are high that you will distort the system's behavior relative to other performance metrics and load conditions. It seems easy to get results, but the gains are often illusory.

In particular, take everything you read on the web with a tablespoon of salt. In the area of system performance, you will see superficially convincing arguments on all sorts of topics. However, most of the proponents of these theories do not have the knowledge, discipline, and time required to design valid experiments. Popular support means very little; for every hare-brained proposal, you can expect to see a Greek chorus of, "I increased the size of my buffer cache by a factor of ten just like Joe said, and my system feels MUCH, MUCH faster!!!" Right.

System performance is not entirely out of your control. It's just that the road to good performance is not paved with magic fixes and romantic kernel patches. The basic rules are these:

- Collect and review *historical* information about your system. If it was performing fine a week ago, an examination of the aspects of the system that have recently changed is likely to lead you to a smoking gun. Keep regular baselines and trends in your hip pocket to pull out in an emergency.

- Don't overload your systems or your network. Linux gives each process an illusion of infinite resources. But once 100% of the system's resources are in use, Linux has to work very hard to maintain that illusion, delaying processes and often consuming a sizable fraction of the resources itself.

This chapter focuses on the performance of systems that are used as servers. Desktop systems typically do not experience the same types of performance issues that servers do, and the answer to the question of how to improve performance on a desktop machine is almost always "Upgrade the hardware." Users like this answer, because it means they get fancy new systems on their desk more often.

26.1 WHAT YOU CAN DO TO IMPROVE PERFORMANCE

Here are some specific things can you do to improve performance:

- You can make sure that the system has enough memory. As we will see below, memory size has a major influence on performance. Memory is so inexpensive these days that you can usually afford to load every performance-sensitive machine to the gills.

- You can double-check the configuration of the system and of individual applications. Many applications can be tuned in ways that yield tremendous performance improvements (e.g., by spreading data across disks, by not performing DNS lookups on the fly, or by running more instances of a popular server).

- You can correct problems of usage, both those caused by users (too many jobs run at once, inefficient programming practices, jobs run at excessive priority, and large jobs run at inappropriate times of day) and those caused by the system (quotas, CPU accounting, unwanted daemons).

- For cases in which you are using Linux as a web server or as some other type of network application server, you may want to spread traffic among a number of systems with a commercial load balancing appliance such as Cisco's Content Services Switch (www.cisco.com) or Nortel's Alteon Web Switch (www.nortelnetworks.com).[1] These boxes make several physical servers appear to be one logical server to the outside world. They balance

---

1. A free, though somewhat less stable, alternative is the Linux Virtual Server software available from linuxvirtualserver.org.

the load according to one of several user-selectable algorithms such as "most responsive server" or "round robin."

These load balancers also provide useful redundancy should a server go down. They're really quite necessary if your site must handle unexpected traffic spikes.

- You can organize the system's hard disks and filesystems so that load is evenly balanced, maximizing I/O throughput. For specific applications such as databases, you can use a fancy multidisk technology such as RAID to optimize data transfers. Consult with your database vendor for recommendations.

  It's important to note that different types of applications and databases respond differently to being spread across multiple disks. RAID comes in many forms, and you will need to put effort into determining which form (if any) is appropriate for your particular application.

- You can monitor your network to be sure that it is not saturated with traffic and that the error rate is low. A wealth of network information is available from the **netstat** command, described on page 633. See also Chapter 20, *Network Management and Debugging*.

- You can configure the kernel to eliminate unwanted drivers and options and to use tables of an appropriate size. These topics are covered in Chapter 12, *Drivers and the Kernel*.

- You can identify situations in which the system is fundamentally inadequate to satisfy the demands being made of it.

These steps are listed in rough order of effectiveness. Adding memory and balancing traffic across multiple servers can make a huge difference in performance. You might see some improvement from organizing the system's disks correctly and from correcting network problems. The other factors may not make any difference at all.

The optimization of software data structures and algorithms almost always leads to significant performance gains. But unless you have a substantial base of local software, this level of design is usually out of your control.

26.2 FACTORS THAT AFFECT PERFORMANCE

Perceived performance is determined by the efficiency with which the system's resources are allocated and shared. The exact definition of a "resource" is rather vague. It can include such items as cached contexts on the CPU chip and entries in the address table of the memory controller. However, to a first approximation, only the following four resources have much effect on performance:

- CPU time
- Memory
- Hard disk I/O
- Network I/O

All processes consume a portion of the system's resources. If resources are still left after active processes have taken what they want, the system's performance is about as good as it can be.

If there are not enough resources to go around, processes must take turns. A process that does not have immediate access to the resources it needs must wait around doing nothing. The amount of time spent waiting is one of the basic measures of performance degradation.

CPU time is one of the easiest resources to measure. A constant amount of processing power is always available. In theory, that amount is 100% of the CPU cycles, but overhead and various inefficiencies make the real-life number more like 95%. A process that's using more than 90% of the CPU is entirely CPU-bound and is consuming most of the system's available computing power.

Many people assume that the speed of the CPU is the most important factor affecting a system's overall performance. Given infinite amounts of all other resources or certain types of applications (e.g., numerical simulations), a faster CPU *will* make a dramatic difference. But in the everyday world, CPU speed is relatively unimportant.

The most common performance bottleneck on Linux systems is actually disk bandwidth. Because hard disks are mechanical systems, it takes many milliseconds to locate a disk block, fetch its contents, and wake up the process that's waiting for it. Delays of this magnitude overshadow every other source of performance degradation. Each disk access causes a stall worth millions of CPU instructions.

Because Linux provides virtual memory, disk bandwidth and memory are directly related. On a loaded system with a limited amount of RAM, you often have to write a page to disk to obtain a fresh page of virtual memory. Unfortunately, this means that using memory is often just as expensive as using the disk. Paging caused by bloated software is performance enemy #1 on most workstations.

Network bandwidth resembles disk bandwidth in many ways, due to the latencies involved. However, networks are atypical in that they involve entire communities rather than individual computers. They are also susceptible to hardware problems and overloaded servers.

26.3 SYSTEM PERFORMANCE CHECKUP

Most performance analysis tools tell you what's going on at a particular point in time. However, the number and character of loads will probably change throughout the day. Be sure to gather a cross-section of data before taking action. The best information on system performance often becomes clear only after a long period (a month or more) of data collection. It is particularly important to collect data during periods of peak use. Resource limitations and system misconfigurations are often only visible when the machine is under heavy load.

Analyzing CPU usage

You will probably want to gather three kinds of CPU data: overall utilization, load averages, and per-process CPU consumption. Overall utilization can help identify systems on which the CPU's speed itself is the bottleneck. Load averages give you an impression of overall system performance. Per-process CPU consumption data can identify specific processes that are hogging resources.

You can obtain summary information with the **vmstat** command. **vmstat** takes two arguments: the number of seconds to monitor the system for each line of output and the number of reports to provide. If you don't specify the number of reports, **vmstat** runs until you press <Control-C>. The first line of data returned by **vmstat** provides averages since the system was booted. The following lines are averages within the previous sample period, which defaults to five seconds. For example,

```
% vmstat 5 5
procs           memory            swap    io      system      cpu
 r  b  w  swpd  free  buff  cache   si  so   bi  bo   in   cs   us  sy  id
 2  0  0  5288  1896  9352  17868    0   0    0   1   27   12    2   0  98
 0  0  0  5392  1360  8300  18804    0   0    0   0   21   80    1   1  98
 0  0  1  5812  1032  9172  18668    0  18    9  31  219   31   79  20   1
 1  0  0  5304   900  3604  17660    0   0    0  18   96   16   35  59   7
 2  0  0  5268  1440  4148  20056    0   0    3  11  314   48   52  48   0
```

User, system, and idle time are shown in the us, sy, and id columns on the far right. CPU numbers that are heavy on user time generally indicate computation, and high system numbers indicate that processes are making a lot of system calls or performing I/O. A rule of thumb that has served us well over the years is that the system should spend approximately 50% of its nonidle time in user space and 50% in system space; the overall idle percentage should be nonzero.

The cs column shows context switches per interval, the number of times that the kernel changed which process was running. The number of interrupts per interval (usually generated by hardware devices or components of the kernel) is shown in the in column. Extremely high cs or in values typically indicate a misbehaving or misconfigured hardware device. The other columns are useful for memory and disk analysis, which we discuss later.

Long-term averages of the CPU statistics allow you to determine whether there is fundamentally enough CPU power to go around. If the CPU usually spends part of its time in the idle state, there are cycles to spare. Upgrading to a faster CPU won't do much to improve the overall throughput of the system, though it may speed up individual operations.

As you can see from this example, the CPU generally flip-flops back and forth between full-on use and complete idleness. Therefore, it's important to observe these numbers as an average over time. The smaller the monitoring interval, the less consistent the results.

On multiprocessor machines, most Linux tools present an average of processor statistics across all processors. The **mpstat** command gives **vmstat**-like output for each individual processor. The -**P** flag lets you specify a specific processor to report on. **mpstat** is useful for debugging software that supports symmetric multiprocessing (SMP)—it's also enlightening to see how (in)efficiently your system uses multiple processors.

On a workstation with only one user, the CPU generally spends 99% of its time idle. Then, when you go to scroll one of the windows on your bitmap display, the CPU is floored for a short period. In this situation, information about long-term average CPU usage is not meaningful.

The second CPU statistic that's useful for characterizing the burden on your system is the "load average," the average number of runnable processes. In general, the load average includes processes waiting for disk and network I/O, so it is not a pure measure of CPU use. However, it does give you a good idea of how many pieces the CPU pie is being divided into. The load average is obtained with the **uptime** command:

```
% uptime
11:10am  up 34 days, 18:42, 5 users, load average: 0.95, 0.38, 0.31
```

Three values are given, corresponding to the 5, 10, and 15-minute averages. In general, the higher the load average, the more important the system's aggregate performance becomes. If there is only one runnable process, that process will usually be bound by a single resource (commonly disk bandwidth or CPU). The peak demand for that one resource becomes the determining factor in performance.

When more processes share the system, loads may or may not be more evenly distributed. If the processes on the system all consume a mixture of CPU, disk, and memory, the performance of the system is less likely to be dominated by constraints on a single resource. In this situation, it becomes most important to look at average measures of consumption such as total CPU utilization.

See page 50 for more information about priorities.

Linux systems are busy with a load average of 3 and do not deal well with load averages over about 6. A load average of this magnitude is a hint that you should start to look for ways to artificially spread the load, such as asking users to run long processes at night or using **nice** to set process priorities.

The system load average is an excellent metric to track as part of a system baseline. If you know your system's load average on a normal day and it is in that same range on a bad day, this is a hint that you should look elsewhere for performance problems (such as the network). A load average above the expected norm suggests that you should look at the processes running on the Linux system itself.

Another way to view CPU usage is to run the **ps** command with the **aux** arguments, which show you how much of the CPU each process is using. On a busy system, at least 70% of the CPU will often be consumed by just one or two processes. (Remember that **ps** consumes some CPU itself.) Deferring the execution of the CPU hogs or reducing their priority will make the CPU more available to other processes.

Performance Analysis

*See page 58 for more information about **top**.*

An excellent alternative to **ps** is a program called **top**. **top** presents about the same information as **ps**, but in a "live" format that lets you watch the status of the system change over time.[2]

How Linux manages memory

Before jumping into the specifics of Linux's memory management, it's worth mentioning once again that the Linux kernel evolves rapidly, faster than most any other operating system. At the time of this writing, the Linux memory management system is in a period of especially rapid flux, even by Linux standards. The entire memory management system was replaced between kernel versions 2.2.x and 2.4.0, and it was again scrapped for new code in kernel version 2.4.10. We've seen further changes in the latest 2.4.x kernels, and kernel version 2.5 is supposed to use a whole new memory management system. This section provides a description of current Linux memory management concepts that should be useful in understanding your Linux kernel regardless of version-specific details.

Like other UNIX systems, Linux manages memory in units called pages. The size of a memory page is currently 4K on PC hardware. The Linux kernel allocates virtual pages to processes as they request memory. Each virtual page is mapped to real storage, either RAM or swap space on disk. Linux uses a "page table" to keep track of the mapping between these made-up virtual pages and real pages of memory. Linux can effectively allocate as much memory as processes ask for by augmenting real RAM with swap space. Since processes expect their virtual pages to map to real memory, Linux is constantly busy shuffling pages between RAM and swap. This activity is known as paging.

Linux tries to manage the system's memory so that pages that have been recently accessed are kept in memory and less active pages are paged out to disk. This scheme is known as an LRU system since the least recently used pages are the ones that get bumped. It would be very inefficient for the kernel to actually keep track of all memory references, so Linux uses a page cache to decide which pages to move out. This system is much cheaper than a true LRU system but produces similar results.

Linux keeps track of an "age" for each page of virtual memory. Every time Linux examines a page and finds it to have been recently referenced, it increments the page's age. (The term "age" is somewhat misleading because the value really indicates frequency and recency of access. The higher the age, the fresher the page.) Meanwhile, Linux runs the **kswapd** process, which regularly decreases the ages of unreferenced pages by chopping them in half.

The kernel maintains several lists of memory pages. Pages with an age greater than zero are marked as "active" and are contained in the page cache "active list." If a page's age reaches zero, **kswapd** swaps the page to the "inactive list." **kswapd** removes inactive pages from the page table and considers them eligible to be paged to disk. Although inactive pages are no longer immediately accessible through the page

---

2. Refreshing **top**'s output too rapidly can itself be quite a CPU hog, so be judicious in your use of **top**.

table, the kernel will recover them from memory or disk and stick them back into the page table on demand.

When memory is low, the kernel tries to guess which pages on the inactive list were least recently used. If those pages have been modified by a process, Linux considers them "dirty" and must page them out to disk before the memory can be reused. Pages that have been laundered in this fashion or that were never dirty to begin with are "clean" and can be recycled by Linux for use elsewhere.

When a page on the inactive list is referenced by a process, the kernel returns its memory mapping to the page table, resets the page's age, and transfers it from the inactive list to the active list. Pages that have been written to disk must be paged in before they can be reactivated. A "soft fault" occurs when a process references an in-memory inactive page, and a "hard fault" results from a reference to a nonresident (paged-out) page. In other words, a hard fault requires a page to be read from disk and a soft fault does not.

Demand for memory varies, so the kernel can run **kswapd** at different speeds. When the demand for memory is extreme, **kswapd** is run very often and pages must be referenced more often to avoid being paged out because their age decreases to zero.

The virtual memory (VM) system depends on the lag between the time a page is placed on the inactive list and the time it's actually paged out to sort active pages from inactive pages. Therefore, the VM system has to predict future paging activity to decide how often to run **kswapd**. If **kswapd** doesn't run often enough, there might not be enough clean inactive pages to satisfy demand. If **kswapd** runs too often, the kernel spends excessive time processing soft page faults.

Since the paging algorithm is predictive, there is not necessarily a one-to-one correspondence between page-out events and page allocations by running processes. The goal of the system is to keep enough free memory handy that processes don't have to actually wait for a page-out each time they make a new allocation. If paging increases dramatically when your system is busy, you will probably benefit from more RAM.

If the kernel fills up both RAM and swap, all VM has been exhausted. Linux uses an "out of memory killer" to handle this condition. This function selects and kills a process in order to free up memory. Although the kernel attempts to kill off the least important process on your system, running out of memory is always something to avoid. In this situation, it's likely that a substantial portion of the system's resources are being devoted to memory housekeeping rather than to useful work.

Even processes running at a low CPU priority can be sneaky page thieves. For example, suppose you're running a SETI[3] client at very low priority (high nice value) on your workstation while at the same time reading mail in a terminal window. As you pause to read a message, your CPU use falls to zero and the simulation is allowed to run. It brings in all of its pages, forcing out your shell, your window server, your mail reader, and your terminal emulator. When you go on to the next message, there is a

3. The Search for Extraterrestrial Intelligence; see www.seti.org/science/setiathome.html.

delay as a large chunk of the system's memory is turned over. In real life, a high nice value is no guarantee that a process won't cause performance problems.

Analyzing memory usage

Basically, three numbers quantify memory activity: the total amount of active virtual memory and the swapping and paging rates. The first number tells you the total demand for memory, and the next two suggest the proportion of that memory that is actively used. The goal is to reduce activity or increase memory until paging remains at an acceptable level. Occasional paging is inevitable, so don't worry about trying to eliminate it completely.

You can use the **free** command to determine the amount of memory and swap space that are currently in use. Use it with the **-t** flag to automatically calculate the total amount of virtual memory:

```
% free -t
              total      used      free    shared   buffers    cached
Mem:         127884     96888     30996     46840     57860     10352
-/+ buffers/cache:       28676     99208
Swap:        265032      3576    261456
Total:       392916    100464    292452
```

The free column indicates the number of kilobytes on the system's free list; values lower than 3% of the system's total memory generally indicate problems. You can use the **swapon** command to determine exactly what files and partitions are being used for swap space:

```
% swapon -s
Filename              Type        Size     Used    Priority
/dev/sdb7            partition    265032   3576    -1
```

This system uses one disk partition, sdb7, for swap. Since paging activity can be a significant drain on disk bandwidth, it is almost always better to spread your swap space across multiple physical disks if possible. The use of multiple swap disks lowers the amount of time that any one disk has to spend dealing with swapped data and increases swap storage bandwidth.

On traditional UNIX systems, the **vmstat** command provides information about paging and swapping. However, the **procinfo** command shipped with most Linux distributions is a better source of information. Although **procinfo** comes with all of our example systems, it isn't necessarily included in the default installation, so you may need to add the **procinfo** package by hand.

See page 221 for more information about the /proc filesystem.

procinfo doesn't have a special way of getting information about your system; it simply formats the data from the files in your **/proc** filesystem. Without it, interpreting the **/proc** files can present a considerable challenge. For continuous updates every five seconds, you can run **procinfo -n5**.

```
% procinfo
Linux 2.2.16-22 (root@porky) (gcc egcs-2.91.66) #1 Tue Aug 22 16:49:06 EDT
    2000 1CPU [redhat]

Memory:    Total    Used     Free   Shared  Buffers  Cached
Mem:       37960    30320    7640    12136    5312    14536
Swap:      81964     5236   76728

Bootup: Sat Jul 28 16:28:13 2001    Load average: 0.10 0.14 0.09 1/50 15406

user   : 3d   6:56:45.34    0.0%   page in  : 1408236  disk 1: 255812r 2126666w
nice   :      0:00:00.00    0.0%   page out : 5880596  disk 2: 345755r 1276809w
system: 1d   11:55:07.27    4.0%   swap in  :   34087
idle   : 32d  4:58:45.62   87.1%   swap out :   17825
uptime: 36d  23:50:38.22          context  :54303486

irq  0:   241327308  timer          irq 10:   3032801  eth0
irq  1:         538  keyboard       irq 12:      2100  PS/2 Mouse
irq  2:           0  cascade [4]     irq 13:         1  fpu
irq  6:           3                 irq 14:   1905415  ide0
irq  8:           2                 irq 15:         5  ide1
```

Some of the information in **procinfo**'s output overlaps that of **free**, **uptime**, and **vmstat**. In addition, **procinfo** provides information about your kernel distribution, memory paging, disk access, and IRQ assignments. You can use **procinfo -a** to see even more information from your **/proc** filesystem, including kernel boot options, kernel loadable modules, character devices, and filesystems.

Any apparent inconsistencies among the memory-related columns are for the most part illusory. Some columns count pages and others count kilobytes. All values are rounded averages. Furthermore, some are averages of scalar quantities and others are average deltas. For example, you can't compute the next value of Free from the current Free and paging information because the paging events that determine the next average value of Free have not yet occurred.

Use the page in/out and the swap in/out fields to evaluate the system's paging and swapping behavior. A page-in does not necessarily represent a page being recovered from the swap area. It could be executable code being paged in from a filesystem or a copy-on-write page being duplicated, both of which are normal occurrences that do not necessarily indicate a shortage of memory. On the other hand, page-outs always represent data being forcibly ejected by the kernel.

If your system has a constant stream of page-outs, you need more memory. But if paging happens only occasionally and does not produce annoying hiccups or user complaints, you can ignore it. If your system falls somewhere in the middle, further analysis should depend on whether you are trying to optimize for interactive performance (e.g., a workstation) or to configure a machine with many simultaneous users (e.g., a compute server).

If half the operations are page-outs, you can figure that every 50 page-outs cause about one second of latency. If 75 page-outs must occur to let you scroll a window,

Performance Analysis

you will wait for about 1.5 seconds. A rule of thumb used by interface researchers is that an average user perceives the system to be "slow" when response times are longer than seven-tenths of a second.

It's also worth pointing out that **procinfo** provides some CPU information that is not visible with **vmstat** or **uptime**. In addition to reporting the load average over 5, 10 and 15 minute periods, **procinfo** lists the instantaneous number of running processes, the total number of processes, and the process ID of the last process that ran. For example, here's an excerpt of **procinfo**'s output on a busy server:

```
Load average:  2.37  0.71  0.29  3/67  26941
```

This server has 67 total processes, of which one was runnable. The last process to run had PID 26941 (in this case, it was the shell process from which **procinfo** was run).

Analyzing disk I/O

You can monitor disk performance with the **iostat** command. Like **vmstat**, it accepts optional arguments to specify an interval in seconds and a repetition count, and its first line of output is a summary since boot. Like **vmstat**, it also tells you how the CPU's time is being spent. Here is a quick example that omits some output not specific to disks:

```
% iostat
...
Disks:       tps   Blk_read/s   Blk_wrtn/s   Blk_read   Blk_wrtn
hdisk0      0.54         0.59         2.39     304483    1228123
hdisk1      0.34         0.27         0.42     140912     216218
hdisk2      0.01         0.02         0.05       5794      15320
hdisk3      0.00         0.00         0.00          0          0
```

iostat gathers information from the **/proc** filesystem to produce a row of output for each physical disk in your system. Unfortunately, Linux keeps only minimal disk statistics, and even the information that is kept is of limited use. Each hard disk has the columns tps, Blk_read/s, Blk_wrtn/s, Blk_read, and Blk_wrtn, indicating I/O transfers per second, blocks read per second, blocks written per second, total blocks read, and total blocks written. Rows of zeros will be reported if you have fewer than four disks.

Disk blocks are typically 1K is size, so you can readily determine the actual disk throughput in kilobytes. Transfers, on the other hand, are fairly nebulously defined. One transfer request can include several logical I/O requests over several sectors, so this data is also mostly useful for identifying trends or irregular behavior.

The cost of seeking is the most important factor affecting disk drive performance. To a first approximation, the rotational speed of the disk and the speed of the bus it's connected to have relatively little impact. Modern disks can transfer dozens of megabytes of data per second if they are read from contiguous sectors, but they can only perform about 100 to 300 seeks per second. If you transfer one sector per seek, you can easily realize less than 5% of the drive's peak throughput.

Seeks are more expensive when they make the heads travel a long distance. If you have a disk with several filesystem partitions and files are read from each partition in a random order, the heads will have to travel back and forth a long way to switch between partitions. On the other hand, files within a partition will be relatively local to one another. When partitioning a new disk, you may want to consider the performance implications and put files that are accessed together in the same filesystem.

To really achieve maximum disk performance, you should put filesystems that are used together on different disks. Although it depends on the bus architecture and device drivers, most computers can manage multiple disks independently, dramatically increasing throughput. For example, it is often worthwhile to split frequently accessed web server data and logs among multiple disks.

On systems that have more than a couple of disks, consider using SCSI disks with a specialized controller. This technique will only scale to a limited capacity and depends primarily on your hardware architecture. Check your hardware documentation or consult your vendor.

It's especially important to split the swap area among several disks if possible, since paging tends to slow down the entire system. This configuration is supported through the use of the **swapon** command. The Linux kernel can use both dedicated swap partitions and swap files on a formatted filesystem. Dedicated partitions are more efficient; do not use swap files if you have a choice.

Modern Linux systems allow you to set up multiple "memory based filesystems," which are essentially the same thing as PC RAM disks. A special driver poses as a disk but actually stores data in high-speed memory. Many sites use a RAM disk for their **/tmp** filesystem or for other busy files such as web server logs or email spools. Using a RAM disk may reduce the memory available for general use, but it makes the reading and writing of temporary files blindingly fast. It's generally a good deal.

Most Linux kernels have been compiled with RAM disk support. On systems that support RAM disks, the **/dev** directory contains multiple RAM disk device files such as **/dev/ram0** and **/dev/ram1**. The number of devices may vary, but there are usually at least five.

To use a RAM disk, first format the filesystem on an unused RAM disk device, then mount it on an existing directory:

```
# mke2fs /dev/ram12
# mount /dev/ram12 /tmp/fastdisk
```

The default RAM disk size is only 4MB, which really isn't large enough for **/tmp**. Unfortunately, the procedure for changing the size is a bit painful because it is set as a kernel variable. You can either add a line such as ramdisk_size=100000 to your boot loader configuration to pass in the new value at boot time (the size is given in 1K blocks) or set up the RAM disk driver as a dynamically loadable module. In the latter case, you would add the necessary argument to the **/etc/modules.conf** file or pass it in as an argument to **insmod**.

Performance Analysis

Some packages degrade the system's performance by delaying basic operations. Two examples are disk quotas and CPU accounting. Quotas require a disk usage summary to be updated as files are written and deleted. CPU accounting writes a data record to an accounting file whenever a process completes. Disk caching helps to soften the impact of these features, but they may still have a slight effect on performance and should not be enabled unless you really use them.

26.4 HELP! MY SYSTEM JUST GOT REALLY SLOW!

In previous sections, we've talked mostly about issues that relate to the average performance of a system. Solutions to these long-term concerns generally take the form of configuration adjustments or upgrades.

However, you will find that even properly configured systems are sometimes more sluggish than usual. Luckily, transient problems are often easy to diagnose. Ninety percent of the time, they are caused by a greedy process that is simply consuming so much CPU power, disk, or network bandwidth that other processes have been stalled. On occasion, malicious processes hog available resources to intentionally slow a system or network, a scheme known as a "denial of service" or DOS attack.

You can often tell which resource is being hogged without even running a diagnostic command. If the system feels "sticky" or you hear the disk going crazy, the problem is most likely a disk bandwidth or memory shortfall.[4] If the system feels "sluggish" (everything takes a long time, and applications can't be "warmed up"), the problem may be CPU.

The first step in diagnosis is to run **ps auxww** or **top** to look for obvious runaway processes. Any process that's using more than 50% of the CPU is likely to be at fault. If no single process is getting an inordinate share of the CPU, check to see how many processes are getting at least 10%. If there are more than two or three (don't count **ps** itself), the load average is likely to be quite high. This is, in itself, a cause of poor performance. Check the load average with **uptime**, and use **vmstat** or **top** to check whether the CPU is ever idle.

If no CPU contention is evident, check to see how much paging is going on with **vmstat** or **procinfo**. All disk activity is interesting: a lot of page-outs may indicate contention for memory, and disk traffic in the absence of paging may mean that a process is monopolizing the disk by constantly reading or writing files.

There's no direct way to tie disk operations to processes, but **ps** can narrow down the possible suspects for you. Any process that is generating disk traffic must be using some amount of CPU time. You can usually make an educated guess about which of the active processes is the true culprit.[5] Use **kill -STOP** to suspend the process and test your theory.

---

4. That is, it takes a long time to switch between applications, but performance is acceptable when an application is repeating a simple task.

Suppose you do find that a particular process is at fault—what should you do? Usually, nothing. Some operations just require a lot of resources and are bound to slow down the system. It doesn't necessarily mean that they're illegitimate. It is usually acceptable to **renice** an obtrusive process that is CPU-bound. But be sure to ask the owner to use the **nice** command in the future. Sometimes, application tuning can dramatically reduce a program's demand for CPU resources; this effect is especially visible with custom network server software such as web applications.

Processes that are disk or memory hogs can't be dealt with so easily. **renice** generally will not help. You do have the option of killing or stopping a process, but we recommend against this if the situation does not constitute an emergency. As with CPU pigs, you can use the low-tech solution of asking the owner to run the process later.

The Linux kernel allows a process to restrict its own use of physical memory with the **setrlimit** system call. This facility is also available in the C shell through the built-in **limit** command. For example, the command

```
% limit memoryuse 32m
```

causes all subsequent commands that the user runs to have their use of physical memory limited to 32 megabytes. This feature is roughly equivalent to **renice** for memory-bound processes. You might tactfully suggest that repeat offenders put such a line in their **.cshrc** files.

If a runaway process doesn't seem to be the source of poor performance, there are two other possible causes to investigate. The first is an overloaded network. Many programs are so intimately bound up with the network that it's hard to tell where system performance ends and network performance begins. See Chapter 20 for more information about the tools used to monitor networks.

Some network overloading problems are hard to diagnose because they come and go very quickly. For example, if every machine on the network runs a network-related program out of **cron** at a particular time each day, there will often be a brief but dramatic glitch. Every machine on the net will hang for five seconds, and then the problem will disappear as quickly as it came.

Server-related delays are another possible cause of performance crises. UNIX systems are constantly consulting remote servers for NFS, NIS, DNS, and any of a dozen other facilities. If a server is dead or some other problem makes it expensive to communicate with, the effects can ripple back through client systems.

For example, on a busy system, some process may use the **gethostent** library routine every few seconds or so. If a DNS glitch makes this routine take two seconds to complete, you will likely perceive a difference in overall performance. DNS forward and

5. A large virtual address space or resident set used to be a suspicious sign, but shared libraries have made these numbers less useful. **ps** is not very smart about separating system-wide shared library overhead from the address spaces of individual processes. Many processes wrongly appear to have megabytes of active memory.

Performance Analysis

reverse lookup configuration problems are responsible for a surprising number of server performance issues.

26.5 RECOMMENDED READING

LOUKIDES, MIKE, AND GIAN-PAOLO D. MUSUMECI. *System Performance Tuning, 2nd Edition.* Sebastopol: O'Reilly & Associates. 2002.

FINK, JASON R., AND MATTHEW D. SHERER. *Linux Performance Tuning and Capacity Planning.* Indianapolis, IN: SAMS. 2001.

KILLELEA, PATRICK, AND LINDA MUI. *Web Performance Tuning: Speeding Up the Web.* Sebastopol: O'Reilly & Associates. 1998.

26.6 EXERCISES

E26.1 Make an educated guess as to the problem in each of the following cases:

a) When switching between applications, the disk thrashes and there is a noticeable lag.

b) A numerical simulation program takes more time than normal, but system memory is mostly free.

c) Users on a very busy LAN complain of slow NFS access, but the load average on the server is very low.

d) Running a command (any command) often says "out of memory".

E26.2 Run **procinfo** on an available Linux machine and discuss the results. What, if any, resources appear to be in heavy use? What resources appear to be unused? Include the IRQ listing in your analysis.

★ **E26.3** Load balancing can have dramatic impact on server performance as seen from the outside world. Without mentioning specifics, discuss several mechanisms that could be used to perform load balancing.

★ **E26.4** List the four main resources that can affect performance. For each resource, give an example of an application that could easily lead to the exhaustion of that resource. Discuss ways to alleviate some of the stress associated with each scenario.

★ **E26.5** Using the web and/or man pages, look into the command **hdparm**. What options does it provide to test disk access speeds? How can **hdparm** improve disk access speeds in some cases?

★★ **E26.6** Choose two programs that use a noticeable amount of system resources. Use **vmstat** and the other tools mentioned in the chapter to profile both applications. Make a claim as to what each program does that makes it a resource hog. Back up your claims with data.

27 *Cooperating with Windows*

windows   System administrator   Microsoft

It's a fact of life that Windows is not going away. We can't ignore it. We must peacefully coexist with it. One way to look at the situation is that UNIX and Linux have brought TCP/IP and the Internet to the table, while Windows has brought millions of users. The challenge for system administrators is to host the resulting Satanic banquet.[1]

Fortunately, modern medicine (administrative tools) can significantly reduce the chance of Windows-inspired indigestion. It really is the case that both platforms have their strengths and that they can be made to work together. Windows is a popular and featureful desktop platform, capable of bridging the gap between the user and the network cable coming out of the wall. Linux, on the other hand, is a reliable and scalable infrastructure platform.

This chapter addresses a variety of topics faced by administrators in this postmodern, PCs-and-UNIX-living-together world.

27.1 FILE AND PRINT SHARING

Perhaps the most powerful level of Windows/Linux integration is achieved by the sharing of directories that live on a Linux host (or a dedicated Linux-like file server) with desktop PCs that run Windows. The shared directories can be made to appear transparently under Windows, either as drives or as extensions of the regular Windows network file tree. You can mount Windows-resident filesystems under Linux as well, but this arrangement is less common. NFS or CIFS can be used to implement either of these file sharing systems.

1. As the saying goes, "Who sups with the devil must use a long spoon."

See Chapter 17 for more information about NFS.

NFS: the Network File System

NFS was designed to share files among UNIX hosts, where file locking and security paradigms are significantly different from those of Windows. Although a variety of products that mount NFS-shared directories on Windows clients are available, their use should be aggressively avoided, both because of the paradigm mismatch and because CIFS just works better. If you are stuck with Windows file servers, it's reasonable to use Windows NFS server software to share Windows filesystems with Linux clients. However, the Linux SMBFS filesystem described below is usually an easier way to achieve the same effect.

CIFS: the Common Internet File System

CIFS is based on protocols that were formerly referred to as Server Message Block or SMB. SMB was an extension that Microsoft added to DOS in its early days to allow disk I/O to be redirected to a system known as NetBIOS (Network Basic Input/Output System). Designed by IBM and Sytec, NetBIOS was a crude interface between the network and an application.

In the modern world, SMB packets are carried in an extension of NetBIOS known as NBT, NetBIOS over TCP. While this all sounds very convoluted, the result is that these protocols have become widespread and are available on platforms ranging from MVS and VMS to our friends Linux and Windows. Everybody dance now.

SMBFS: mount remote CIFS shares

The SMBFS filesystem allows Linux to treat network CIFS file servers as just another foreign filesystem type, much like it treats NFS servers. SMBFS has been built into the Linux kernel for several years. Originally written by Pal-Kristian Engstad, the code is now maintained by Samba author Andrew Tridgell. Because the filesystem support is built into the kernel, you can use the plain old **mount** command to attach a remote CIFS share to a local mount point. Here is a simple example:

```
# mount -t smbfs -o username=ned //engserver/admin /home/ned/engadmin
```

The **-t smbfs** parameter tells **mount** that it should use the SMBFS filesystem code to mount the CIFS share. We specifiy a username after the **-o** option flag. Finally, we tell **mount** to look for the "admin" service on the server "engserver" and attach it to the existing local directory ~**ned/engadmin**.

You can specify many other CIFS-specific mount options after the **-o** flag for SMBFS mounts, including login password, workgroup, and debugging flags. The man page for **smbmount** lists all the options. However, we recommend that you don't use the **smbmount** command directly, since **mount** provides a more consistent and easier-to-remember interface (**mount** calls **smbmount** for you).

Samba: CIFS server for Linux

Samba is an enormously popular software package, available under the GNU public license, that implements the server side of CIFS on Linux hosts. It was originally created by Andrew Tridgell, an Australian, who reverse-engineered the SMB protocol and published the resulting code in 1992.

Today, Samba is well supported and actively under development to expand its functionality. It provides a stable, industrial-strength mechanism for integrating Windows machines into a Linux network. The real beauty of Samba is that you only need to install one package on the Linux machine; no special software is needed on the Windows side.[2]

CIFS provides five basic services:

- File sharing
- Network printing
- Authentication and authorization
- Name resolution
- Service announcement (file server and printer "browsing")

Samba not only serves Linux files through CIFS, but it can also perform all the basic functions of a Windows NT 4.0 primary domain controller. Samba supports some advanced features, including Windows NT domain logins, roaming Windows user profiles, and CIFS print spooling. Samba makes file sharing easy between Linux and every version of Windows from Windows 95 onward.

Microsoft doesn't share information about how it implements technologies such as CIFS, NT domains, and Active Directory, so the ingenious folks on the Samba project must actually reverse-engineer running Microsoft servers to figure out how to make Samba work. Unfortunately, this constraint introduces a time lag before new Microsoft features can be implemented in Samba. As of this writing, Samba lacks most Windows 2000 domain controller features, such as Kerberos, Active Directory, domain trusts, and replication with NT domain controllers. Samba is a first-rate solution for a large number of organizations; however, the advanced features might not work as well in complex Windows 2000 or Active Directory networks.

Most of Samba's functionality is implemented by two daemons: **smbd** and **nmbd**. **smbd** implements file and print services, as well as authentication and authorization. **nmbd** provides the other major CIFS components, name resolution, and service announcement.

Unlike NFS, which is deeply intertwined with the kernel, Samba requires no kernel modifications and runs entirely as a user process. It binds to the sockets used for NBT requests and waits for a client to request access to a resource. Once the request has been made and authenticated, **smbd** forks an instance of itself that runs as the user who is making the requests. As a result, all normal Linux file access permissions (including group permissions) are obeyed. The only special functionality that **smbd** adds on top of this is a file locking service that provides client PCs with the locking semantics they are accustomed to.

---

2. Provided that the Windows machine has already been configured for "Microsoft networking."

Installing and configuring Samba

Samba is shipped with all Linux distributions covered in this book. Patches, documentation, and other goodies are available from www.samba.org. Versions older than 2.2.0a have known security holes and should be upgraded immediately.

On all systems, you'll need to edit the **smb.conf** file (**/etc/samba/smb.conf** on Red Hat and Debian, **/etc/smb.conf** on SuSE) to tell Samba how it should behave. In this file, you specify the directories and printers that should be shared, their access rights, and Samba's general operational parameters. All of the options are documented in the **smb.conf** man page, which you'll definitely need to consult when integrating Samba into a network on which Microsoft file sharing is already in use. The Samba package comes with a well-commented sample **smb.conf** file that is generally a good starting place for new configurations.

It's important to be aware of the security implications of sharing files or resources across a network. Samba allows fine-grained control over security, but it only works if you actually use it. For a typical site, you need to do two things to ensure a basic level of security:

- In the **smb.conf** file, the hosts allow clause controls which clients can access the resources shared by Samba. Make sure that it contains only the IP addresses (or address ranges) that it should.

- You *must* block access from the Internet to the CIFS TCP ports with a packet-filtering firewall. These are TCP ports 137 through 139. More information on how to do this is given on page 676.

Here's a complete **smb.conf** example for a simple network:

```
[global]

# workgroup = NT-Domain-Name or Workgroup-Name

  workgroup = MYGROUP

# List the hosts that may access Samba-shared objects.
# Here, only hosts on two class C nets are allowed.

  hosts allow = 192.168.1. 192.168.2.

# Automatically load your printer list from a file.³

  printcap name = /etc/printcap
  load printers = yes

# Use a separate log file for each machine, and limit size to 500K each.

  log file = /var/log/samba/log.%m
  max log size = 500
```

---

3. Printers must already be set up on the Linux host. See Chapter 24 for more details.

```
# Set the security mode. Most people will want user-level security. See
# security_level.txt in the Samba doc for details.

  security = user

# We recommend that you use password encryption. Please read
# ENCRYPTION.txt, Win95.txt and WinNT.txt in the Samba documentation.
# Do not enable this option unless you have read those documents.

;  encrypt passwords = yes
;  smb passwd file = /etc/smbpasswd

# Most people will find that this option gives better performance. See
# speed.txt and the manual pages for details.

  socket options = TCP_NODELAY

# Share home directories. For instance, ~trent under Linux will appear
# as the share "trent" in the PC browser.

[homes]
  comment = Home Directories
  browseable = no
  writable = yes

# Share all printers.

[printers]
  comment = All Printers
  path = /var/spool/samba
  browseable = no
  guest ok = no
  writable = no
  printable = yes

# Share a specific directory.

[devel]
  comment = Staff Development Shared Directory
  path = /devel/shared
  public = no
  writable = yes
  printable = no
  create mask = 0775
```

As you can see from the comments, this **smb.conf** file is set up so that when users
log in to their PCs, their home directories and the **/devel/shared** directory are both
available. They can also print to all the printers that the server knows about.

Debugging Samba

Samba usually runs without requiring much attention. However, if you do have a
problem, you can consult two primary sources of debugging information: the per-
client log files and the **smbstatus** command.

The location of log files is specified in the **smb.conf** file, and in that directory you will find a file for each client that has attempted a connection. **smbd** grooms these files so that they do not exceed their specified maximum sizes.

These following abbreviated log entries show a couple of successful connections after one mistyped password:

```
[2002/01/13 11:48:24] smbd/reply.c Rejecting user 'ned': authentication failed
[2002/01/13 11:48:26] smbd/service.c klum (192.168.1.51) connect to service ned
    as user ned (uid=500, gid=500) (pid 1275)
[2002/01/13 13:04:19] smbd/service.c klum (192.168.1.51) closed connection to
    service ned
[2002/01/13 13:04:20] smbd/service.c klum (192.168.1.51) connect to service
    admin as user ned (uid=500, gid=500) (pid 1275)
```

smbstatus enables you to examine currently active connections and open files. This information can be especially useful when you are tracking down locking problems ("Which user has file **xyz** open read-write exclusive?"). The first section of output lists the resources that a user has connected to. The second part lists any active file locks, and the third part displays **smbd**'s resource usage.[4]

```
Samba version 2.0.7
Service   uid    gid    pid    machine
-------------------------------------------------
ned       ned    ned    1275   klum       (192.168.1.51)
goldmine  trent  trent  1279   adminpc    (192.168.1.50)
admin     ned    ned    1275   klum       (192.168.1.51)

Locked files:
Pid    DenyMode      R/W      Oplock           Name
----------------------------------------------------------------------------
1275   DENY_WRITE    RDONLY   EXCLUSIVE+BATCH  /home/admin/doc/ips.txt
1275   DENY_NONE     RDWR     NONE             /home/ned/install_notes.txt

Share mode memory usage (bytes):
   1048336(99%) free + 168(0%) used + 72(0%) overhead = 1048576(100%) total
```

When Windows applications crash, they often leave files locked, thereby causing trouble when the application is restarted. You can force a lock to be released by killing the **smbd** that "owns" the lock; the PID for each lock is shown in the output of **smbstatus**. Don't tell your users you know how to do this, and be aware that breaking locks can lead to corrupted files. Sometimes you gotta do what you gotta do.

Unified Windows and Linux login authentication

See page 498 for more information about the name service switch.

The latest versions of Samba ship with an optional tool called Winbind. By plugging into the low-level name service switch library modules, Winbind lets a Linux server obtain its user and group information from a Windows Domain Controller. Winbind also lets users change their Windows Domain passwords from Linux. Additionally, Winbind includes a PAM module (see page 656 for more information about PAM)

---

4. **smbstatus** output contains some very long lines; we have condensed it here for clarity.

that uses the Windows Domain to authenticate local Linux logins. Although Winbind is a relatively new part of the Samba tool set, it could be the ideal solution for wedging a few Linux boxes into a predominantly Windows network.

27.2 SECURE TERMINAL EMULATION WITH SSH

Some users may find themselves wanting to leave Windows behind and head for the snow-covered slopes of a good C shell or **bash** session. Of course, the easiest way to accomplish this is to use the **telnet** program that Microsoft ships with Windows. Unfortunately, it lacks a few creature comforts such as direct cut and paste. Also, like any implementation of the TELNET protocol, it has no concept of security. (But hey, who needs a command line, anyway?) Fortunately, a variety of terminal emulators are available for Windows that are significantly more comfortable than Microsoft's **telnet**.

See page 673 for more information about SSH.

Our favorite terminal emulator is SecureCRT from VanDyke Technologies, Inc. This inexpensive commercial product supports SSH 1 and 2, TELNET, **rlogin**, and serial consoles. It provides four different ciphers for data encryption and can also provide port forwarding for X11 and other applications, such as mail. Learn more about SecureCRT at www.vandyke.com.

Another commercial emulator is the Windows SSH client produced by F-Secure Corporation. Information about their products is available at www.fsecure.com.

If you're looking for a free emulator, we suggest using PuTTY. PuTTY is simple and effective and also comes with Windows **scp** and **sftp** clients. You can find PuTTY at

> http://www.chiark.greenend.org.uk/~sgtatham/putty/

Another alternative is TeraTerm, a close competitor of PuTTY. Although the Tera-Term emulator doesn't come with SSH support by default, it's easy to add this functionality with the TTSSH plug-in. You can find TeraTerm at

> http://hp.vector.co.jp/authors/VA002416/teraterm.html

The plug-in lives at

> http://www.zip.com.au/~roca/ttssh.html

Together, these tools provide a very reasonable and secure environment.

27.3 X WINDOWS EMULATORS

X Windows is a windowing system that is in no way related to the Windows operating systems from Microsoft. The X Window System was developed at MIT in the 1980s and has been adopted by UNIX workstation manufacturers as their standard windowing environment (sometimes, with substantial modifications). Never fear, X emulators are here.

Cooperating with Windows

X Windows emulators work by implementing the X11 protocol on a Windows PC. The server provides a conduit between client applications (such as the **xterm** terminal emulator) and the Windows desktop. Once the X11 server has been started on the PC, clients can be run from the UNIX or Linux environment and displayed on the Windows desktop. For those of you who lived through the early 1990s, this basically turns your Windows machine into an X terminal on steroids. X applications displayed in this fashion can coexist with other Windows applications on the desktop. With some emulators, it is also possible to use a window manager from the Linux environment.

There are dozens of X emulators out there. The two that we have been impressed by are Labtam's X-ThinPro (www.labtam-inc.com) and Frontier Technologies' SuperX (www.frontiertech.com). We've used both extensively without trouble. Labtam offers an improved version called X-SecurePro that bundles secure SSH tunneling software. SuperX does a good job of ensuring that cutting and pasting between X applications and Windows applications works correctly, and its font mapping is particularly easy.

27.4 PC MAIL CLIENTS

The first thing users want to do at their PCs is check email. Providing a stable email environment is essential to most organizations; fortunately, this is one area in which Windows PCs on desktops and central Linux servers really shine together.

Windows mail clients such as Microsoft Outlook, Netscape Messenger, and Qualcomm's Eudora are packed with groovy features and far outshine the UNIX mail readers of yore. They let users exchange regular email, encrypted email, email with attachments, and email with specially formatted or even colored text. These are essential tools of the Internet world—long gone are the days of **/usr/ucb/mail** and other text-only mail tools.

See page 526 for more information about IMAP and POP.

Organizations need to be able to provide reliable mail service to hundreds or sometimes thousands of users. That's where Linux comes in. Linux provides a scalable, secure, and configurable environment for the receipt and transmission of email on the Internet. Messages can be stored on a Linux server and accessed by Windows mail clients via SSL-encrypted protocols such as IMAPS and POPS. This is the best of all worlds.

Another advantage of this approach, especially when you are using IMAP, is that mail is stored on the server. If the Windows machine crashes and burns, the user's mail folders are not lost. IMAP also allows users to access their mail from a variety of locations, such as from home or from a kiosk when on the road. There are tons of different IMAP clients on the market, including web-based HTTP-to-IMAP gateways.

If email security is at all important to your organization, it is critical to use SSL-encrypted services such as IMAPS, POPS, and HTTPS to protect user passwords. In addition, it's a good idea to enable the filtering add-ons that are available for every popular Linux SMTP server; they do a good job of catching Windows email viruses.

27.5 PC BACKUPS

See Chapter 10 for general information about backups.

Backing up the data on desktop PCs can be a formidable problem, especially now that typical desktop storage capacity exceeds 20GB. There are a number of approaches to this problem, including industrial-strength network backup tools from vendors such as Veritas and IBM. Of course, there's always the handy local tape drive approach. If you have the money and the patience, this is an area where commercial products really are head and shoulders above the rest.

But what about the rest of us? It is possible to back up a Windows machine's drive (all or part) to a Linux server with the **smbtar** utility included in the Samba package. **smbtar** uses Samba's **smbclient** to connect to a remote CIFS share and dump it to a local **tar** file. Unfortunately, this approach is very high maintenance and typically requires custom scripting. Hence, we don't recommend it.

The best solution here seems to be *not* to back up Windows PCs. Sites that get away without PC backups have carefully educated their users and configured PC software such that all important files are stored on a shared network drive. In addition to having users save their files on a network drive, it's important to make sure that each application is configured to store its irreplaceable data (such as email client files, encryption keys, window profiles, address books, and application preferences) on a network drive. The individual PCs can then be configured identically (in terms of installed applications, desktop configuration, etc.) throughout the organization.[5] If one PC fails, another can be swapped in with just a few minutes of work. Crazy? Maybe. Resource smart? Yes!

27.6 DUAL BOOTING

Thank goodness for geeks. It may have occurred to you to "make the most of your life" by harnessing the power of more than one operating system on your PC. Fortunately, it is possible to "dual boot," meaning that you can choose one of several operating systems at boot time. Linux and Windows are a popular combo, especially among desktop users who must switch between environments. Read all about setting up a dual boot configuration on page 25.

Mounting foreign filesystems with Linux

Linux comes with support for a wealth of filesystems, so you can mount and use local disk partitions that were formatted by other operating systems. The Linux **mount** command knows how to mount Windows filesystems such as FAT, FAT32, and NTFS; all you need to know is what device is associated with the Windows partition you want to mount. FAT and FAT32 partitions are specified with the **-t vfat** argument, and NTFS partitions use the **-t ntfs** argument instead. As of this writing, Linux NTFS support is safe only in read-only mode. The software that lets Linux write to NTFS filesystems is still in beta release.

---

5. Two products that can help with this process are Symantec's Norton Ghost and PowerQuest's Drive Image Pro. A standard disk image file can be kept on the network or written to a rescue CD-R.

The following example mounts the Windows FAT32 "C" drive found on **/dev/hda3** on the Linux directory **/mnt/windows**:

```
# mount -t vfat /dev/hda3 /mnt/windows
```

27.7 RUNNING WINDOWS APPLICATIONS UNDER LINUX

Many versions of Linux can run Windows applications…kind of. It's done in a variety of ways, but they all generally boil down to creating some kind of "virtual machine environment" that, to the application, looks like good ol' Windows. These virtual environments are typically a bit fragile, but they tend to work reasonably well for most mainstream applications.

The commercial product VMware (www.vmware.com) turns your entire PC into a virtual machine with the ability to run multiple operating systems at once. VMware runs guest virtual machines on top of a host operating system, which can be either Linux or Windows NT/2000/XP. Regardless of the host operating system, you can install as guests as many Intel-compatible operating systems as you want. Since you can run several virtual machines (and thus several operating systems) at once, VMware is an ideal tool for development or testing environments. It even comes with a feature that networks your virtual operating systems so that they can communicate with each other and share your real Ethernet connection.

Wine (www.winehq.com) provides a Windows API in the Linux environment, allowing you to run Windows applications on top of Linux and X. This free software translates native Windows API calls to their Linux counterparts and can do so without using any Microsoft code. Wine provides support for TCP/IP networking, serial devices, and sound output. Unfortunately, it supports very few hardware drivers. The Wine project was started in 1993 by Bob Amstadt. At the time of this writing, however, Wine's current maintainer, Alexandre Julliard, claims that "Wine is still under development and is not suitable for general use."

Win4Lin is a commercial alternative to Wine from NeTraverse. Win4Lin claims to be more stable than Wine and to support a few more Microsoft applications. However, it requires kernel modifications. which Wine does not. Win4Lin is available from www.netraverse.com.

Finally, Sun has graciously released StarOffice, a Microsoft Office-like package for Linux and Solaris, free of charge. It includes basic business tools such as a spreadsheet, a word processor, and a simple database application. These tools can read and write files generated by Microsoft Word, Excel, and PowerPoint. See

http://www.sun.com/products/staroffice

for more information.

Linux (and UNIX) on Windows

It's possible to make a Windows desktop fairly Linux-friendly. As we mentioned above, VMware is a great way to run Linux on top of your existing Windows installation. In many cases, it's also fairly easy to port simple Linux applications or services to the Windows platform. An extensive list of Linux and UNIX software now runs natively on Windows, including Apache, Perl, BIND, PHP, VIM, MySQL, Ethereal, and Python.

Windows users who are homesick for a UNIX command line should download the Cygwin environment from www.cygwin.com. This package, distributed under the GNU Public License, contains an extensive complement of common UNIX commands as well as a porting library that implements the POSIX APIs under Windows. Cygwin's way of reconciling the UNIX and Windows command-line and filesystem conventions is well thought out and manages to bring many of the creature comforts of a UNIX shell to native Windows commands. In addition to making Linux users feel at home, Cygwin makes it easy to get Linux and UNIX software running under Windows. See the web site for details.

The MKS Toolkit is a commercial alternative to Cygwin. It includes literally hundreds of UNIX shells, scripting languages, network servers, and utilities. See MKS's web site at www.mkssoftware.com for more information.

27.8 PC HARDWARE TIPS

One of the really great things about PC hardware is that it's usually inexpensive. Unfortunately, PC hardware doesn't come to us from an alien planet where the motto is "You pay less, you get more!" Instead, as with most things here on Earth, you get what you pay for. But there are some gotchas to watch out for, even when you're paying for the extra-nice gear.

First of all, if you're planning to run an operating system other than Windows on a PC, make sure you check to see what hardware devices are supported. Device manufacturers typically provide Windows drivers for all their fancy new widgets, but those won't do you much good under Linux. Some vendors are starting to get a clue and are starting to distribute Linux drivers. In particular, fully Linux-compatible laptops have finally become available over the last couple of years.

Second, keep in mind that performance is based on a variety of factors. These days, processor clock rate is not the limiting factor. It's usually I/O performance that will bring your system to a crawl first. Choose PC hardware that supports the latest and greatest high-performance bus and transfer rates. Pay special attention when buying devices such as disk controllers; make sure that they're designed for true multiuser operating systems and can process more than one "command" simultaneously. Instead of shopping for maximum GB per dollar, look for disks that have good warranties, high transfer rates, and high rotation speeds.

Another gotcha is inexpensive modems that require software on the host computer to do some signal processing. A few of these WinModems are supported by Linux, but many are not. Since it's unlikely that the WinModem vendors will release enough technical information about their products for the software to be ported to Linux, it's best to choose modems that do all their own thinking. Some network, video, and sound cards also fit into this category. Your best bet is to check your distribution's hardware compatibility list before picking up any new hardware.

Finally, be aware that prepackaged systems from places like CompUSA are usually designed and optimized to run the operating system that is installed at the factory, right down to special chips on the motherboard. These machines are usually not the best candidates to reinstall with some Linux distribution and to use for hosting your startup dotcom web site. Consider purchasing production-quality PC hardware from high-end vendors who sell hardware certified for Linux, such as IBM and Dell. Additionally, many boutique vendors produce very nice Linux boxes. The following site has a useful list of such vendors:

> http://www.linuxhardware.net/cgi-bin/viewvendor.cgi

All of these vendors offer industrial-strength hardware with redundant power supplies, extra fans, hot-swappable drives, etc., and will guarantee their systems to work with various Linux distributions. In addition, they typically provide generous maintenance agreements.

27.9 RECOMMENDED READING

ECKSTEIN, ROBERT, DAVID COLLIER-BROWN, AND PETER KELLY. *Using Samba*. Sebastopol: O'Reilly & Associates. 1999.

27.10 EXERCISES

E27.1 How does Linux gain access to CIFS shares as a client? How does Linux act as a CIFS share server?

E27.2 Why would you want to block Internet access to ports 137–139 on a Samba server?

★ **E27.3** Install one of the emulator programs that lets you run Windows applications on your Linux box. Try a windows application. Is the functionality OK? The performance? Can you find an application that refuses to run? Why won't it run?

★★ **E27.4** In the lab, compare the performance of a client that accesses files through Samba with one that accesses files from a native CIFS server (i.e., a Windows machine). If your two test servers have different hardware, devise a way to adjust for the hardware variation so that the comparison is more indicative of the performance of the server software. (May require root access.)

★★ **E27.5** In the lab, using a packet sniffer (**tcpdump**), monitor a telnet session between Windows and Linux. Obtain and install the PuTTY software and repeat the monitoring. In each case, what can you see with the packet sniffer? (Requires root access.)

★★ **E27.6** Configure Samba to share files with a Windows PC on your local network. Explore the idea of exporting your home directory to a PC and storing your data files from the PC on the Linux box. Is a Linux box running Samba a good alternative to keeping files locally on a Windows PC? Are there Windows applications that require data to be on the Microsoft side?

28 *Daemons*

A daemon is a background process that performs a specific function or system-related task. In keeping with the UNIX and Linux philosophy of modularity, daemons are programs rather than parts of the kernel. Many daemons start at boot time and continue to run as long as the system is up. Other daemons are started when needed and run only as long as they are useful.

"Daemon" was first used as a computer term by Mick Bailey, a British gentleman who was working on the CTSS programming staff at MIT during the early 1960s.[1] Mick quoted the Oxford English Dictionary in support of both the meaning and the spelling of the word. The words "daemon" and "demon" both come from the same root, but "daemon" is an older form and its meaning is somewhat different. A daemon is an attendant spirit that influences one's character or personality. Daemons are not minions of evil *or* good; they're creatures of independent thought and will. Daemons made their way from CTSS to Multics to UNIX to Linux, where they are so popular that they need a superdaemon (**inetd** or **xinetd**) to manage them.

This chapter presents a brief overview of the most common Linux daemons. Not all of the daemons listed here are supplied with all Linux distributions, and not every daemon supplied with some Linux distribution is listed here. Besides making you more aware of how Linux works, a knowledge of what all the various daemons do will make you look really smart when one of your users asks, "What does **klogd** do?"

---

1. This bit of history comes from Jerry Saltzer at MIT, via Dennis Ritchie.

Before **inetd** was written, all daemons started at boot time and ran continuously (or more accurately, they blocked waiting for work to do). Over time, more and more daemons were added to the system. The daemon population became so large that it began to cause performance problems. In response, the Berkeley gurus developed **inetd**, a daemon that is responsible for starting other daemons as they are needed. **inetd** was so successful that all versions of UNIX and Linux now include it and most new daemons run under its control.

There are many daemons that system administrators should be intimately familiar with, either because they require a lot of administration or because they play a large role in the day-to-day operation of the system. Some daemons that are described here in one or two lines have an entire chapter devoted to them elsewhere in this book. We provide cross-references where appropriate.

We start this chapter by introducing a couple of very important system daemons (**init** and **cron**) and then move on to a discussion of **inetd** and **xinetd**. Finally, we briefly describe most of the daemons a system administrator is likely to wrestle with on our three example systems.

28.1   INIT: THE PRIMORDIAL PROCESS

init is the first process to run after the system boots, and in many ways it is the most important daemon. It always has a PID of 1 and is an ancestor of all user processes and all but a few system processes.

At startup, **init** either places the system in single-user mode or begins to execute the scripts needed to bring the system to multiuser mode. When you boot the system into single-user mode, **init** runs the startup scripts after you terminate the single-user shell by typing **exit** or <Control-D>.

See Chapter 7 for more information about TTYs.

In multiuser mode, **init** is responsible for making sure that processes are available to handle logins on every login-enabled device. Logins on serial ports are generally handled by some variant of **getty** (e.g., **agetty**, **mgetty**, or **mingetty**; see page 112 for details). On many systems, **init** also supervises a graphical login procedure that allows users to log directly in to X Windows.

In addition to its login management duties, **init** also has the ghoulish task of exorcising undead zombie processes that would otherwise accumulate on the system. **init**'s role in this process is described on page 51.

*See page 111 for more information about the **inittab** file.*

init defines several "run levels" that determine what set of system resources should be enabled. There are seven levels numbered 0 to 6. The name "s" is recognized as a synonym for level 1 (single-user mode). The characteristics of each run level are defined in the **/etc/inittab** file.

init is usually passed its initial run level as an argument from the boot loader. If "s" is specified, **init** enters single-user mode. Otherwise, it scans **/etc/inittab** for entries that apply to the requested run level and executes their corresponding commands.

Daemons

The **telinit** command changes **init**'s run level once the system is up. For example, **telinit 4** forces **init** to go to run level 4. **telinit**'s most useful argument is **-q**, which causes **init** to reread the **/etc/inittab** file.

Linux distributions generally implement an additional layer of abstraction on top of the basic run level mechanism provided by **init**. The extra layer allows individual software packages to install their own startup scripts without modifying the system's generic **inittab** file. Bringing **init** to a new run level causes the appropriate scripts to be executed with the arguments **start** or **stop**.

A more complete discussion of **init** and startup scripts begins on page 29.

28.2 CRON AND ATD: SCHEDULE COMMANDS

The **cron** daemon (known as **crond** on Red Hat) is responsible for running commands at preset times. It accepts schedule files ("crontabs") from both users and administrators.

cron is frequently employed for administrative purposes, including management of log files and daily cleanup of the filesystem. In fact, **cron** is so important to system administrators that we have devoted an entire chapter to it. That chapter, *Periodic Processes*, begins on page 152.

The **atd** daemon runs commands scheduled with the **at** command.

28.3 INETD AND XINETD: MANAGE DAEMONS

inetd is a daemon that manages other daemons. It starts up its client daemons when there is work for them to do and allows them to die gracefully once their tasks have been completed.

inetd only works with daemons that provide services over the network. To find out when someone is trying to access one of its clients, **inetd** attaches itself to the network ports that would normally be managed by the quiescent daemons. When a connection occurs, **inetd** starts up the appropriate daemon and connects its standard I/O channels to the network port. Daemons must be written with this convention in mind to be compatible with **inetd**.

*See page 668 for more information about **tcpd**.*

Some Linux distributions have replaced the traditional **inetd** with Panos Tsirigotis's **xinetd**, a souped-up alternative that incorporates security features similar to those formerly achieved through the use of **tcpd**, the "TCP wrappers" package. **xinetd** also provides better protection against denial of service attacks, better log management features, and a more flexible configuration language. Unfortunately, **inetd**'s configuration file is not forward-compatible to **xinetd**. We first discuss the traditional **inetd** and then take a look at **xinetd** in a separate section.

Among our example Linux systems, SuSE and Debian use the standard **inetd** and Red Hat defaults to **xinetd**. You can convert any system to use the nondefault daemon manager, but there's really no compelling reason to do so.

Some daemons (such as those associated with NIS and NFS) rely on a further layer of indirection known as the Remote Procedure Call (RPC) system. RPC was originally designed and implemented by Sun as a way of promoting the sharing of information in a heterogeneous networked environment. Port assignments for daemons that use RPC are managed by the **portmap** daemon, discussed later in this chapter.

Some daemons can be used in either the traditional way (in which they are started once and continue to run until the system shuts down) or with **inetd**. Daemons discussed in this chapter are marked with an ⓣ if they are **inetd**-compatible.

Configuring inetd

inetd consults **/etc/inetd.conf** to determine which network ports it should listen to. Here's a (pared-down) example from a SuSE system:

```
# Example /etc/inetd.conf file - from a SuSE system
#
time      stream  tcp  nowait      root  internal
time      dgram   udp  wait        root  internal
ftp       stream  tcp  nowait      root  /usr/sbin/tcpd in.ftpd
# telnet  stream  tcp  nowait      root  /usr/sbin/tcpd in.telnetd
# login   stream  tcp  nowait      root  /usr/sbin/tcpd in.rlogind
# exec    stream  tcp  nowait      root  /usr/sbin/tcpd in.rexecd
pop3      stream  tcp  nowait      root  /usr/sbin/tcpd /usr/sbin/popper -s
# imap    stream  tcp  nowait      root  /usr/sbin/tcpd imapd
# finger  stream  tcp  nowait      nobody/usr/sbin/tcpd in.fingerd -w
# swat is the Samba Web Administration Tool
swat      stream  tcp  nowait.400 root  /usr/sbin/swat swat
rsync     stream  tcp  nowait      root  /usr/sbin/tcpd /sbin/rsyncd --daemon
...
```

The first column contains the service name. **inetd** maps service names to port numbers by consulting either the **/etc/services** file (for TCP and UDP services) or the **/etc/rpc** file and **portmap** daemon (for RPC services). RPC services are identified by names of the form *name/num* (where *num* is the protocol version number) and the designation rpc in column three. The only RPC service that is commonly managed by **inetd** is **mountd**, the NFS mount daemon. Linux distributions seem to run this daemon the old-fashioned way (by starting it at boot time), so you may have no RPC services at all in your **inetd.conf** file.

On a host with more than one network interface, you can preface the service name with a list of comma-separated IP addresses or symbolic hostnames to indicate the interfaces on which **inetd** should listen for service requests. For example, the line

```
inura:time   stream   tcp   nowait  root    internal
```

provides the time service only on the interface associated with the name inura in DNS, NIS, or the **/etc/hosts** file.

The second column determines the type of socket that the service will use and is invariably stream or dgram. stream is used with TCP (connection-oriented) services, and dgram is used with UDP.

The third column identifies the communication protocol used by the service. The allowable types are listed in the **protocols** file (usually in **/etc**). The protocol is almost always tcp or udp. RPC services prepend rpc/ to the protocol type.

If the service being described can process multiple requests at one time (rather than processing one request and exiting), column four should be set to wait. This option allows the spawned daemon to take over management of the port as long as it is running; **inetd** waits for the daemon to exit before resuming its monitoring of the port. The opposite of wait is nowait; it makes **inetd** monitor continuously and fork a new copy of the daemon each time it receives a request. The selection of wait or nowait must correspond to the daemon's actual behavior and should not be set arbitrarily. When configuring a new daemon, check the **inetd.conf** file for an example configuration line or consult the man page for the daemon in question.

The form nowait.400, used in the configuration line for **swat**, means that **inetd** should spawn at most 400 instances of the server daemon per minute. The default is more conservative, 40 instances per minute. Given the nature of this service (a web administration tool for Samba), it's not clear why the throttle threshold was raised.

The fifth column gives the username under which the daemon should run. If you do not trust a particular program or you know that it has security problems, you can run it as someone other than root to reduce your exposure. Of course, this technique works only for daemons that do not require rootly powers. In the example above, **in.fingerd** runs as the user "nobody."

The remaining fields give the fully qualified pathname of the daemon and its command-line arguments. The keyword internal indicates services whose implementations are provided by **inetd** itself.

*See page 668 for more information about **tcpd**.*

Most of the service entries in this example run their daemons by way of **tcpd** rather than executing them directly. **tcpd** logs connection attempts and implements access control based on the source of the connection attempt. In general, all services should be protected with **tcpd**. This example configuration presents a potential security problem in that **swat**, a file sharing configuration utility, is not protected.[2]

Because **inetd** is responsible for managing many common network-based services, it plays an important role in securing your system. It's important to verify that only services you need and trust have been enabled in **inetd.conf**. On a new system, you will almost certainly need to modify **inetd.conf** to disable services that are unnecessary or undesirable in your environment. A good rule of thumb is to enable only the services that you absolutely need and turn everything else off.

Note that in this example, the servers for **rlogin**, **telnet**, **finger**, and **rexec** have all been disabled. We recommend that these services be disabled on all production

---

2. If you are not using **tcpd** to protect a service, the daemon's first command-line argument should always be the short name of the daemon itself. This requirement is not a peculiarity of **inetd** but a traditional UNIX convention that is normally hidden by the shell.

systems. See the section *Miscellaneous security issues* on page 661 for a more detailed explanation.

See Chapter 11 for more information about syslog.

Changes to **/etc/inetd.conf** do not take effect until you tell **inetd** to reread it, which you do by sending **inetd** a hangup signal. After signalling, wait a minute and then check the log files for error messages related to your changes (**inetd** logs errors to syslog under the "daemon" facility). Test out any new services you have added to be sure they work correctly.

Configuring xinetd

Some distributions provide both **inetd** and **xinetd**, although only one is enabled by default. Use whichever you feel more comfortable with. **xinetd** is standard on Red Hat systems.

xinetd's main configuration file is **/etc/xinetd.conf**. It includes much the same information as the **inetd.conf** file, but it uses an attribute/value list (rather than tabular) format. Below is an example that defines some system defaults and an FTP service, then includes the files in the **/etc/xinetd.d** directory (as on Red Hat). Individual packages can drop **xinetd.conf**-format config files in the **xinetd.d** directory and have them picked up automatically by the system—an elegant feature.

```
defaults
{
    log_type        = SYSLOG local4 info
    log_on_success  = HOST EXIT
    log_on_failure  = HOST ATTEMPT RECORD
    instances       = 2
}

service ftp
{
    # Unlimited instances because wu.ftpd does its own load management
    socket_type     = stream
    protocol        = tcp
    wait            = no
    user            = root
    server          = /usr/sbin/wu.ftpd
    server_args     = -a
    instances       = UNLIMITED
    only_from       = 128.138.0.0/16
    log_on_success  += DURATION
}

includedir /etc/xinetd.d
...
```

Table 28.1 on page 816 provides a mini-glossary of parameters.

Some **xinetd** parameters can accept assignments of the form += or -= (as seen in the log_on_success value for the FTP server) to modify the default values rather than replacing them outright. Broadly speaking, this syntax is allowed wherever it makes

Table 28.1   xinetd configuration parameters (not an exhaustive list)

Parameter	Value	Meaning
bind	*ipaddr/host*	Interface on which to make this service available
cps	*num*	Limits overall connections per second
disable	yes/no	Disables service; easier than commenting it out
include	*path*	Reads listed path as a supplemental config file
includedir	*path*	Reads all files in the specified directory
instances	*num*/UNLIMITED	Maximum number of simultaneous instances
log_on_failure	*special*	Information to log for failures or access denials[a]
log_on_success	*special*	Information to log for successful connections[a]
log_type	*special*	Configures log file or syslog parameters
max_load	*num*	Disables service if load average > threshold
nice	*num*	Nice value of spawned server processes
no_access	*matchlist*	Denies service to specified IP addresses
only_from	*matchlist*	Accepts requests only from specified addresses
per_source	*num*	Limits number of instances per remote peer
protocol	tcp/udp	Service protocol
server	*path*	Path to server binary
server_args	*string*	Command-line arguments for server[b]
socket_type	stream/dgram	Uses stream for TCP services, dgram for UDP
user	*username*	User (UID) as whom the service should run
wait	yes/no	Should **xinetd** butt out until the daemon quits?

a. Note that the USERID directive used with these parameters will cause xinetd to perform IDENT queries on connections, often resulting in significant delays.

b. Unlike **inetd**, **xinetd** does not require the server command to be the first argument.

sense. Only a few parameters are really required for each service; they correspond to the same pieces of information found in the **inetd.conf** file.

Address match lists for the only_from and no_access parameters can be specified in several formats. Most useful are CIDR-format IP addresses with an explicit mask (as shown in the example) and host or domain names such as boulder.colorado.edu and .colorado.edu—note the preceding dot. Multiple specifications can be separated with a space (as in all **xinetd** lists).

xinetd can either log directly to a file or submit log entries to syslog. Since the volume of log information can potentially be quite high on a busy server, it may make sense to use direct-to-file logging for performance reasons. Keep in mind that logging to a file is less secure than logging to a remote server through syslog because a hacker that gains access to the local system can doctor the log files.

xinetd can provide some interesting services such as forwarding of requests to an internal host that is not visible to the outside world. It's worth reviewing **xinetd**'s man page to get an idea of its capabilities.

The services file

After adding a new service to **inetd.conf** or **xinetd.conf**, you may also need to make an entry for it in the **/etc/services** file. This file is used by several standard library routines that map between service names and port numbers. **xinetd** actually allows you to specify the port number directly, but it's always a good idea to maintain a master list of ports in the **services** file.

For example, when you type the command

% `telnet anchor smtp`

telnet looks up the port number for the "smtp" service in the **services** file. Most systems ship with all the common services already configured; you need only edit the **services** file if you add something new.

The **services** file is used only for bona fide TCP/IP services; similar information for RPC services is stored in **/etc/rpc**.

Here are some selected lines from a **services** file (the original is about 70 lines long):

```
tcpmux      1/tcp                         # TCP port multiplexer
echo        7/tcp
echo        7/udp
...
smtp        25/tcp      mail
time        37/tcp      timserver
time        37/udp      timserver
rlp         39/udp      resource          # resource location
name        42/tcp                        # IEN 116
whois       43/tcp      nicname
...
```

The format of a line is

```
name        port/proto aliases           # comment
```

Services are generally listed in numerical order, although this order is not required. *name* is the symbolic name of the service (the name you use in the **inetd.conf** file). The *port* is the port number at which the service normally listens; if the service is managed by **inetd**, it is the port that **inetd** will listen on.[3]

The *proto* indicates the protocol used by the service; in practice, it is always tcp or udp. If a service can use either UDP or TCP, a line for each must be included (as with the time service above). The *alias* field contains additional names for the service (for example, whois can also be looked up as nicname).

---

3. Port numbers are not arbitrary. All machines must agree about which services go with which ports; otherwise, requests will constantly be directed to the wrong port. If you are creating a site-specific service, pick a high port number (greater than 1023) that is not already listed in the **services** file.

Daemons

portmap/rpcbind: map RPC services to TCP and UDP ports

portmap maps RPC service numbers to the TCP/IP ports on which their servers are listening. When an RPC server starts up, it registers itself with **portmap**, listing the services it supports and the port at which it can be contacted. Clients query **portmap** to find out how to get in touch with an appropriate server.

This system allows a port to be mapped to a symbolic service name. It's basically another level of abstraction above the **services** file, albeit one that introduces additional complexity (and security issues) without solving any real-world problems.

If the **portmap** daemon dies, all the services that rely on it (including **inetd** and NFS) must be restarted. In practical terms, this means that it's time to reboot the system. **portmap** must be started before **inetd** for **inetd** to handle RPC services correctly.

28.4 KERNEL DAEMONS

For architectural reasons, a few parts of the Linux kernel are managed as if they were user processes. These processes can usually be identified by their low PIDs and names that start with **k**, such as **kflushd**, **kupdate**, **kpiod**, and **kswapd** in 2.2 kernels and **keventd**, **kapm-idled**, **kreclaimd**, **kupdated** in kernel 2.4. For the most part, these processes deal with various aspects of memory management and synchronization of the disk cache. They cannot be manipulated by the system administrator and should generally be left alone.

Another system daemon in this category, albeit one with a nonstandard name, is **mdrecoveryd**. It's part of the "multiple devices," implementation, more commonly known as RAID.

klogd: read kernel messages

klogd is responsible for reading log entries from the kernel's message buffer and forwarding them to syslog so they can be routed to their final destination. See *Kernel and boot-time logging* on page 204 for more information.

28.5 FILE SERVICE DAEMONS

The following daemons are part of the NFS file sharing system. We give only a brief description of their functions here; Chapter 17 describes them in detail.

rpc.nfsd: serve files

rpc.nfsd runs on file servers and handles requests from NFS clients. In most NFS implementations, **nfsd** is really just a part of the kernel that has been dressed up as a process for scheduling reasons. Linux actually sports two different implementations, one of which follows this convention and one of which runs in user space. The kernel implementation is more popular and is most distributions' default.

rpc.nfsd accepts a single argument that specifies how many copies of itself to fork. Some voodoo is involved in picking the correct number of copies; see page 474.

rpc.mountd: respond to mount requests

rpc.mountd accepts filesystem mount requests from potential NFS clients. It verifies that each client has permission to mount the requested directories. **rpc.mountd** consults the **/var/state/nfs/xtab** file to determine which applicants are legitimate.

amd and automount: mount filesystems on demand

amd and **automount** are NFS automounters, daemons that wait until a process attempts to use a filesystem before they actually mount it. The automounters later unmount the filesystems if they have not been accessed in a specified period of time.

The use of automounters is very helpful in large environments where dozens or hundreds of filesystems are shared on the network. Automounters increase the stability of the network and reduce configuration complexity, since all systems on the network can share the same **amd** or **automountd** configuration. We cover the use of these daemons in detail, starting on page 479.

rpc.lockd and rpc.statd: manage NFS locks

Although these two are distinct daemons, they always run as a team. **rpc.lockd** maintains advisory locks (a la **flock** and **lockf**) on NFS files. **rpc.statd** allows processes to monitor the status of other machines that are running NFS. **rpc.lockd** uses **rpc.statd** to decide when to attempt to communicate with a remote machine.

rpciod: cache NFS blocks

rpciod caches read and write requests on NFS clients. It performs both read-ahead and write-behind buffering and greatly improves the performance of NFS. This daemon is analogous to the **biod** and **nfsiod** daemons found on other systems, although it is structurally somewhat different.

rpc.rquotad: serve remote quotas

rpc.rquotad lets remote users check their quotas on filesystems they have mounted with NFS. The actual implementation of quota restrictions is still performed on the server; **rpc.rquotad** just makes the **quota** command work correctly.

smbd: provide file and printing service to Windows clients

smbd is the file and printer server in the Samba suite. It provides file and printer sharing service through the Windows protocol known variously as SMB or CIFS. See page 798 for more details.

nmbd: NetBIOS name server

nmbd is another component of Samba. It replies to NetBIOS name service requests generated by Windows machines. It also implements the browsing protocol that Windows machines use to populate the Network Neighborhood folder and makes disks shared from the local host visible there. **nmbd** can also be used as a WINS server.

28.6 ADMINISTRATIVE DATABASE DAEMONS

Several daemons are associated with Sun's NIS administrative database system, which is described in Chapter 18, *Sharing System Files*. Although NIS originated at Sun, it is now used on many other vendors' systems as well, including Linux.

ypbind: locate NIS servers

The **ypbind** daemon runs on all NIS clients and servers. It finds an NIS server to which queries can be directed. **ypbind** does not actually process requests itself; it just tells client programs which server to use.

ypserv: NIS server

ypserv runs on all NIS servers. **ypserv** accepts queries from clients and responds with the requested information. See page 502 for information on how to configure the machines that run **ypserv**.

rpc.ypxfrd: transfer NIS databases

rpc.ypxfrd transfers NIS databases to slave servers in an efficient manner. A slave initiates a transfer with the **ypxfr** command. Whenever a database is changed on the master, it should immediately be pushed out to all the slaves so that the NIS servers remain consistent with one another.

nscd: name service cache daemon

nscd caches the results of calls to the standard C library routines in the **getpw***, **getgr***, and **gethost*** families, which look up data that was traditionally stored in the **passwd**, **group**, and **hosts** files. These days, the range of potential sources is larger and includes options such as NIS and DNS. **nscd** does not actually know where the data comes from; it simply caches results and uses them to short-circuit subsequent library calls. Caching policy is set in the **/etc/nscd.conf** file.

28.7 INTERNET DAEMONS

We define "Internet daemons" very loosely to mean daemons that use Internet protocols to handle requests. Many Internet daemons actually spend the majority of their time servicing local requests.

talkd: connect to network chat service

Connection requests from the **talk** program are handled by **talkd**. When it receives a request, **talkd** negotiates with the other machine to set up a network connection between the two users who have executed **talk**.

ⓘ sendmail: transport electronic mail

sendmail's tasks include accepting messages from users and remote sites, rewriting addresses, expanding aliases, and transferring mail across the Internet. **sendmail** is an important and very complex daemon. Refer to Chapter 19, *Electronic Mail*, for the complete scoop.

snmpd: provide remote network management service

snmpd responds to requests that use the Simple Network Management Protocol (SNMP) protocol. SNMP standardizes some common network management operations. See page 641 for more information about SNMP.

rwhod: maintain remote user list

rwhod is a leftover from "the early days" (the 1980s) and maintains information about the users that are logged in to machines on the network. **rwhod** collects this information for the local machine and broadcasts it; when it receives information from other hosts, it verifies that the information is reasonable and then puts it in the file **/var/spool/rwho/whod.**hostname, where *hostname* is the name of the host that sent the information. The programs **rwho** and **ruptime** refer to these files.

By default, **rwhod** broadcasts every three minutes, so the information reported by **rwho** and **ruptime** is only approximately correct. **rwhod** is very inefficient, so unless you have network bandwidth to burn or you actually use the information, you should turn it off.

ⓘ ftpd: file transfer server

*See page 704 for more information about **ftpd**.*

ftpd is the daemon that handles requests from **ftp**, the Internet file transfer program. Many sites disable it, either because it is a resource hog or because they are worried about security. **ftpd** can be set up to allow anyone to transfer files to and from your machine.

A variety of **ftpd** implementations are available for Linux systems. If you plan to run a high-traffic server or need advanced features such as load management, it might be wise to investigate the alternatives to your distribution's default **ftpd**.

WU-FTPD, developed at Washington University, is one of the most popular alternatives to the standard **ftpd**. See www.wu-ftpd.org for more information.

ⓘ popper: basic mailbox server

The **popper** daemon implements the Post Office Protocol (POP). This protocol is commonly used by non-Linux systems to receive electronic mail.

ⓘ imapd: deluxe mailbox server

The **imapd** daemon implements the Internet Mail Access Protocol, IMAP, which is a more festive and featureful alternative to POP. It allows PC-based users (or Linux users with IMAP-enabled mail readers) to access their email from a variety of loca-

Daemons

tions, with mail folders being stored on the Linux server. Check out www.imap.org for more information about IMAP.

ⓘ in.rlogind: remote login server

in.rlogind handles remote logins. When invoked by **inetd**, it tries to automatically authenticate the remote user by examining **/etc/hosts.equiv** and the user's **~/.rhosts** file. If automatic authentication is successful, the user is logged in directly. Otherwise, **in.rlogind** executes the **login** program to prompt the user for a password. Because of its cheap 'n' easy authentication, **in.rlogind** is something of a security hazard. See page 661 for more comments on this subject.

ⓘ in.telnetd: yet another remote login server

in.telnetd is similar to **in.rlogind**, except that it uses the TELNET protocol. This protocol allows the two sides (client and server) to negotiate flow control and duplex settings, making it a better choice than **in.rlogind** for links that are slow or unreliable. Like **rlogin**, **telnet** transmits plaintext passwords across the network. Its use is therefore discouraged in modern networks. However, many non-Linux systems support **telnet**.

ⓘ sshd: secure remote login server

sshd provides services that are similar to **in.rlogind**, but its sessions are transported (and authenticated) across an encrypted pipeline. A variety of encryption algorithms are available. Because of the harsh environment of the Internet today, you must allow shell access from the Internet *only* through a daemon such as this—*not* **in.rlogind** or **in.telnetd**. You can find more information about **sshd** starting on page 673.

ⓘ in.rshd: remote command execution server

in.rshd handles remote command execution requests from **rsh** and **rcmd**. The authentication process enforced by **in.rshd** is similar to that of **in.rlogind**, except that if automatic authentication does not work, **in.rshd** denies the request without allowing the user to supply a password. **in.rshd** is also the server for **rcp** (remote **cp**). Like **in.rlogind**, **in.rshd** has become something of a pariah in recent years for security reasons. See page 661 for more information.

ⓘ in.rexecd: yet another command execution server

in.rexecd is similar to **in.rshd**, except that it does not perform automatic authentication; all requests must be accompanied by a username and a password. This server was used by some early networking programs, but it is no longer in widespread use. Because the username and password are transmitted in plaintext across the network, **in.rexecd** is an extremely poor method of managing remote execution.

ⓘ rsyncd: synchronize files among multiple hosts

rsyncd is really just a link to the **rsync** command; the **--daemon** option turns it into a server process. **rsyncd** facilitates the synchronization of files among hosts. It's essentially an efficient and security-aware version of **rcp**. **rsync** is a real treasure trove for system administrators, and in this book we've described its use in a couple of different contexts. See page 493 for general information and some tips on using **rsync** to share system files. **rsync** is also a large part of many sites' internal installation processes. See page 731 for more details about this application.

routed: maintain routing tables

routed maintains the routing information used by TCP/IP to send and forward packets on a network. **routed** deals only with dynamic routing; routes that are statically defined (that is, wired into the system's routing table with the **route** command) are never modified by **routed**. **routed** is relatively stupid and inefficient, and we recommend its use in only a few specific situations. See page 314 for a more detailed discussion of **routed**.

gated: maintain complicated routing tables

gated understands several routing protocols, including RIP, the protocol used by **routed**. **gated** translates routing information among various protocols and is very configurable. It can also be much kinder to your network than **routed**. See page 315 for more information about **gated**.

named: DNS server

named is the most popular server for the Domain Name System. It maps hostnames into network addresses and performs many other feats and tricks, all using a distributed database maintained by **named**s everywhere. Chapter 16, *The Domain Name System*, describes the care and feeding of **named**.

syslogd: process log messages

See page 206 for more information about syslog.

syslogd acts as a clearing house for status information and error messages produced by system software and daemons. Before **syslogd** was written, daemons either wrote their error messages directly to the system console or maintained their own private log files. Now they use the **syslog** library routine to transfer the messages to **syslogd**, which sorts them according to rules established by the system administrator.

ⓘ in.fingerd: look up users

in.fingerd provides information about the users that are logged in to the system. If asked, it can also provide a bit more detail about individual users. **in.fingerd** does not really do much work itself: it simply accepts lines of input and passes them on to the local **finger** program.

finger can return quite a bit of information about a user, including the user's login status, the contents of the user's GECOS field in **/etc/passwd**, and the contents of the user's ~/**.plan** and ~/**.project** files.

If you are connected to the Internet and are running **in.fingerd**, anyone in the world can obtain this information. **in.fingerd** has enabled some really neat services (such as the Internet white pages), but it has also enabled people to run a variety of scams, such as finding people to cold-call and prospecting for spammable addresses. Some sites have responded to this invasion by turning off **in.fingerd**, while others just restrict the amount of information it returns. If you choose to run **in.fingerd**, you should install a current version; a security hole in older **fingerd**s was exploited by the original Internet worm in 1988.

httpd: World Wide Web server

httpd lets your site become a web server. **httpd** can send text, pictures, and sound to its clients. See Chapter 22, *Web Hosting and Internet Servers*, for more information about serving up web pages.

lpd: manage printing

See page 750 for more information about lpd.

lpd is responsible for the print spooling system. It accepts jobs from users and forks processes that perform the actual printing. **lpd** is also responsible for transferring print jobs to and from remote systems. **lpd** can sometimes hang and need to be manually restarted.

Your system might have either the original flavor of **lpd** or the extra-crispy version that's part of the LPRng package. See Chapter 24, *Printing*, for more information about these alternatives.

28.8 TIME SYNCHRONIZATION DAEMONS

As computers have grown increasingly interdependent, it has become more and more important for them to share a consistent idea of time. Synchronized clocks are essential for correlating log file entries in the event of a security breach, and they're also important for a variety of end-user applications, from joint development of software projects to the processing of financial transactions.

timed: synchronize clocks

There are several different time synchronization systems, and more than one time daemon is named **timed**. Most systems use essentially the same scheme. One or more machines are designated as time masters. Their clocks are considered authoritative, and they negotiate with each other to agree on the "correct" time. Other machines are slaves; they periodically converse with a master to learn the time and then adjust their internal clocks.

The time between settings of a slave's clock is short enough that only slight adjustments are usually needed. Slaves use the **adjtimex** system call to smooth the adjustment of the system's clock and prevent large time leaps backward or forward.[4] It is especially harmful to set the clock back suddenly; time should be a monotonically increasing function.

---

4. **adjtimex** biases the speed of the system's clock so that it gradually falls into correct alignment. When the system time matches the current objective time, the bias is cancelled and the clock runs normally.

The notion of "correct" time is rather nebulously defined. Some systems poll the network to compute an average time, whereas others declare one master correct by fiat.

ntpd and xntpd: synchronize clocks even better

ntpd and **xntpd** are daemons that use the Network Time Protocol defined in RFC-1119 to synchronize a number of "peer" clocks to within milliseconds of each other. Servers are arranged in a hierarchal tree, each level of which is called a "stratum." Clients can access a number of reference time standards, such as those provided by WWV and GPS. As a result, NTP provides a much more accurate way to set the clock on your machine than does **timed**; clocks are not only synchronized but are also accurate within a few milliseconds.

28.9 BOOTING AND CONFIGURATION DAEMONS

In the 1980s, the UNIX world was swept by a wave of diskless workstation mania. These machines booted entirely over the network and performed all their disk operations through a remote filesystem technology such as NFS. As disk prices dropped and speeds increased, interest in diskless workstations quickly faded. They could come back into fashion at any moment, however, like the platform shoes of the 1970s. The two main remnants of the diskless era are a plethora of daemons designed to support diskless systems and the bizarre organization of most vendors' filesystems.

Although diskless workstations are not common anymore, their booting protocols have been usurped by other devices. Most manageable network hubs and network printers boot by using some combination of the services listed in this section.

dhcpd: dynamic address assignment

The Dynamic Host Configuration Protocol (DHCP) provides PCs, laptops, and other "mobile" platforms with information about their IP address, default gateway, and name server at boot time. **dhcpd** is the daemon that implements this service under Linux. You can find more information about DCHP on page 278. A fancier elaboration of DHCP called PXE helps compatible machines boot from the network without the need for a local boot device; see page 713 for more details.

in.tftpd: trivial file transfer server

in.tftpd implements a file transfer protocol similar to that of **ftpd**, but much, much simpler. Many diskless systems use TFTP to download their kernels from a server. **in.tftpd** does not perform authentication, but it is normally restricted to serving the files in a single directory (usually **/tftpboot**). Since anything placed in the TFTP directory is accessible to the entire network, the directory should contain only boot files and should not be publicly writable.

rpc.bootparamd: advanced diskless life support

rpc.bootparamd uses the **/etc/bootparams** file to tell diskless clients where to find their filesystems. **rpc.bootparamd** service is often used by machines that get their IP addresses by using RARP and that use NFS to mount their filesystems.

28.10 EXERCISES

★ **E28.1** Determine which daemons are running on your Linux system using **ps**. Also determine which daemons are available to run through **inetd.conf** or **xinetd.conf**. Combine the lists and describe what each daemon does, where it is started, whether multiple copies can (or do) run at the same time, and any other attributes you can glean from **inetd.conf** and the output of **ps**.

★ **E28.2** In the lab, enable the network time daemon, **ntpd**.

   a) How do you tell if your system has the correct time?

   b) Manually set your system time to be 15 seconds slow with the **date** command. How long does it (or will it) take for the time become correct?

   c) Manually set your system time a month ahead. How does **ntpd** respond to this situation?

   (Requires root access.)

★★ **E28.3** In the lab, use a tool such as **netstat** to determine what ports are in a "listening" state on your machine.

   a) How can you reconcile the **netstat** information with what is found in **inetd.conf**? If there is a discrepancy, what else is going on?

   b) Install the **nmap** tool on a different machine. Run a port scan targeting your system to verify what you learned in part a. What (if any) additional information did you learn from **nmap** that wasn't obvious from **netstat**? (See page 664 for more information about **nmap**.)

29 *Policy and Politics*

This chapter covers some nontechnical topics that are often included in a system administrator's repertoire. In addition to discussing various issues of law and policy, we talk about some of the interpersonal aspects of system administration and the political intrigues that occur at Linux sites.

Linux and computer networks are both quite young—Linux a mere 11 years old, and networks maybe 25—yet they are a microcosm of social issues that have existed for thousands of years. In many cases, the legal and social institutions of the real world have been slow to adapt to the implications of new technology.

The Internet is well on its way to replacing or at least greatly altering several large pieces of economic infrastructure: the publishing industry, the telecommunications industry, the entertainment industry, the postal service, and middlemen of every stripe and color—travel agents, book sellers, music retailers, stockbrokers, and on and on. In many of these contexts, our technological and financial capabilities seem to have leaped far ahead of the policy infrastructure that's needed to support them.

For example, well-defined laws and conventions exist regarding the privacy, use, and misuse of paper mail. But what about email? Is it private, or does the owner of the disk on which it is stored have a right to read it? If a computer forwards a message, is the computer's owner liable when the message turns out to be libelous or obscene?

The lines regarding intellectual property seem to be getting fuzzier and fuzzier. It's well established that you can let someone listen to your new CD or even loan that CD to a friend. And it's fine to transfer the music to your computer and listen to it that way. But what if you want to play the CD over the Internet from work? What if you let your friend listen that way, too? What if only one of you listens at a time?

Applications such as Napster (napster.com) and all of the new peer-to-peer networking applications that it spawned have pushed this concept of sharing via the Internet to extremes. Napster hit college campuses in the fall of 1999 and instantly doubled many sites' Internet service bills. The music industry sued Napster for violation of copyright laws and won. Their case was based on the Digital Millennium Copyright Act of 1998, a new law that many feel treads heavily on the rights of free of speech and expression which are fundamental in the United States.

As might be expected given the uncertainty surrounding these issues, many sites (not to mention governments) lack a well-defined policy for dealing with them.

29.1 LINUX CULTURE

In the 1980s and 90s you could differentiate PC users from Mac users by their level of intensity. PC users found their computers a useful tool, but Mac users loved theirs. A Mac user's computer was a member of the family, like a favorite pet.

The same intensity that pervaded the Mac world is now very strong in the Linux community. Linux users don't just like their systems—they are ready to do battle to defend them, fix them, and make them better and faster and more secure than a Windows box ever dreamed of being. Energy is pouring into Linux at an amazing rate, and Linux culture has its own ethics, myths, gods, and heroes.

A group of Linux enthusiasts from the Bergen Linux User Group in Bergen, Norway, were intrigued by one of the April Fools Day RFCs from the IETF: RFC1149, *A Standard for the Transmission of IP Datagrams on Avian Carriers.* This RFC defines the Carrier Pigeon Internet Protocol (CPIP), which the team implemented with a neighbor's flock of pigeons. Here is a test of their implementation (taken from the project site at blug.linux.no/rfc1149):

```
Script started on Sat Apr 28 11:24:09 2001
vegard@gyversalen:~$ /sbin/ifconfig tun0
tun0     Link encap:Point-to-Point Protocol
         inet addr:10.0.3.2  P-t-P:10.0.3.1  Mask:255.255.255.255
         UP POINTOPOINT RUNNING NOARP MULTICAST  MTU:150  Metric:1
         RX packets:1 errors:0 dropped:0 overruns:0 frame:0
         TX packets:2 errors:0 dropped:0 overruns:0 carrier:0
         collisions:0
         RX bytes:88 (88.0 b)  TX bytes:168 (168.0 b)

vegard@gyversalen:~$ ping -i 900 10.0.3.1[1]
PING 10.0.3.1 (10.0.3.1): 56 data bytes
64 bytes from 10.0.3.1: icmp_seq=0 ttl=255 time=6165731.1 ms
64 bytes from 10.0.3.1: icmp_seq=4 ttl=255 time=3211900.8 ms
```

1. Note the appropriate use of RFC1918 private address space. Clearly, a pigeon-based NAT implementation would be needed to connect the test network to the outside world.

```
64 bytes from 10.0.3.1: icmp_seq=2 ttl=255 time=5124922.8 ms
64 bytes from 10.0.3.1: icmp_seq=1 ttl=255 time=6388671.9 ms

--- 10.0.3.1 ping statistics ---
9 packets transmitted, 4 packets received, 55% packet loss
round-trip min/avg/max = 3211900.8/5222806.6/6388671.9 ms
vegard@gyversalen:~$ exit

Script done on Sat Apr 28 14:14:28 2001
```

Linux rocks. One might say that these folks had too much time on their hands, but it's exactly this kind of creativity and enthusiasm that make the open source movement (and Linux's part in it) so powerful and so much fun.

Mainstream Linux

It used to be common to hear statements such as "Oh, we can't use Linux—it's not supported!" in corporate circles. But the world has been changing fast enough to worry Microsoft. Linux is sneaking its way into the business world. It often arrives first with newly hired students who have used Linux in college and who run it either openly or surreptitiously on their desktop machines. After establishing a beachhead, Linux often becomes the preferred platform for mail or web servers, where its security, performance, and scalability make it preferable to proprietary solutions from Microsoft.

Linux is currently the fastest growing operating system. It runs on everything from mainframes to wristwatches. In 2001, there were 2,300 business applications available for Linux, up 30% from the year before.

Some major corporate players are now shipping and supporting the development of Linux: IBM, Hewlett-Packard, Compaq, Silicon Graphics, and Sun, to name a few. It has been interesting to observe the marriage between these huge, sluggish software shops and a Linux culture driven by young, inexperienced software engineers whose energy often more than makes up for their rough edges. IBM has had to undergo a major paradigm shift to acclimate to life in the anarchistic open source world of Linux. It has been able to contribute by porting its extensive libraries of well-tested code. See the following sites for more information:

> http://ibm.com/linux
> http://oss.software.ibm.com/developerworks/opensource/linux

SGI and other vendors have contributed to Linux by creating the Linux Test Project, a series of test suites and stress testing methods that validate the reliability, robustness, and stability of Linux. At least one provider of computer intrusion insurance recognizes this quality in its pricing and charges 5% to 15% less to insure Linux web servers than to insure equivalent Microsoft systems. An August, 2001, ZDNet article made the following comments.[2]

---

2. http://www.zdnet.com/zdnn/stories/news/0,4586,2805929,00.html

"Insurance broker J.S. Wurzler Underwriting Managers has started charging up to 15 percent more in premiums to clients that use Microsoft's Internet Information Server software, which the Code Red worm feasted on...Wurzler, who has been selling hacker insurance since 1998, based his decision on more than 400 security analyses done by his firm over the past three years. Wurzler found that system administrators working on open source systems tend to be better trained and stay with their employers longer than those at firms using Windows software."

For some companies, cost of ownership is important too. Linux is essentially free to start with, and it's also easier to maintain thanks to its inherent manageability over the network. Microsoft XP Professional currently costs about $275/seat just for the OS. Once the relevant applications are added, the price tag for a large company can be daunting. For example, google.com (the web's best search engine, in our opinion) currently runs on 12,000 Linux boxes and will upgrade to 27,000 (give or take a few) over the next year. That's just under $7.5 million in basic OS software alone. Yikes.

Linux is used by many branches of the U.S. government within organizations such as NASA, NERSC, NIH, NOAA, and USGS. It's also used at the Fermilab, Los Alamos, Oak Ridge, and Sandia National Laboratories. The most powerful computers today are still big-iron systems—but Beowulf clusters (see www.beowulf.org) of Linux machines are catching up.

Linux has come of age.

Linux projects

In addition to the Linux Test Project mentioned above, two other important efforts in the Linux community merit reference here: the Linux Standard Base (LSB) and the Linux Documentation Project (LDP). The LSB (www.linuxbase.org) attempts to iron out the differences between different distributions of Linux from the application programmer's point of view. We talk a bit more about the LSB on page 866.

The LDP (www.linuxdoc.org) provides documentation at many levels of technical expertise, including longish introductory booklets called guides, specific HOWTOs for various common chores, FAQs on many topics, and man pages for all the Linux core commands and packages. The LDP also supports two online magazines, Linux Gazette and Linux Focus. All the documentation is available without charge over the Internet. We discuss the LDP resources in a bit more detail on page 8.

29.2 POLICY AND PROCEDURE

While researching this chapter, we talked to bigshots in the system administration world, in computer security, in the standards community, and in computer law. We were surprised that they all mentioned "signed, written policy" as being essential to a healthy organization.

Policies and procedures should be written down, approved by management, and checked by lawyers. It's preferable that this preparation be completed *before* the documents need to be used to deal with a thorny problem. Several different policy documents should exist:

- Administrative service policies
- Rights and responsibilities of users
- Policies regarding sysadmins (users with special privileges)
- Guest account policy

Procedures in the form of checklists or recipes can be used to codify existing practice. They are useful both for new sysadmins and for old hands. Better yet are procedures in the form of executable scripts. Several benefits of standard procedures are:

- The chores are always done in the same way.
- Checklists reduce the likelihood of errors or forgotten steps.
- It's faster for the sysadmin to work from a recipe.
- The changes are self-documenting.
- Written procedures provide a measurable standard of correctness.

Today, Linux is replacing the big mainframes of the past and performing mission-critical functions in the corporate world. In big shops, checklists, often called "run books," serve as the documentation for common tasks. They're usually kept on-line and also in the form of printed manuals. The sysadmins that write and maintain the run books are often a layer away from the support crew that uses them, but such organization and standardization pays off in the long run.

Here are some common tasks for which you might want to set up procedures:

- Adding a host
- Adding a user
- Localizing a machine
- Setting up TCP wrappers on a machine
- Setting up backups for a new machine
- Securing a new machine
- Restarting a complicated piece of software
- Reviving a web site that is not responding or not serving any data
- Unjamming and restarting a printer
- Upgrading the operating system
- Installing a software package
- Installing software from the net
- Upgrading critical software (**sendmail**, **gcc**, **named**, etc.)
- Backing up and restoring files
- Expiring backup tapes
- Performing emergency shutdowns (all hosts, all but important hosts, etc.)

Many issues sit squarely between policy and procedure. For example:

- Who can have an account?
- What happens when they leave?

The resolutions of such issues need to be written down so that you can stay consistent and avoid falling prey to the well-known, four-year-old's ploy of "Mommy said no, let's go ask Daddy!" Often, the "if" portion is the policy and the "how" portion is the procedure.

Some policy decisions will be dictated by the software you are running or by the policies of external groups, such as ISPs. Some policies are mandatory if the privacy of your users' data is to be protected. We call these topics "nonnegotiable policy."

In particular, we believe that Internet addresses, hostnames, UIDs, GIDs, and user-names should all be managed on a site-wide basis. Some sites (multinational corporations, for example) are clearly too large to implement this policy, but if you can swing it, site-wide management makes things a lot simpler. Tools that facilitate the management of hosts and user accounts across administrative domains are available from the net. Our crufty old versions, **addhost** and **adduser**, are not sterling examples of the genre, but they're still in use and are available from

> ftp://ftp.cs.colorado.edu/sysadmin/utilities

if you can't find anything better.

We strongly believe that logins should *never* be shared. It is a lot easier to enforce this policy if the temptation to share is removed. We used to maintain a guest machine with a liberal account creation policy as an easy alternative to clandestine sharing, but now with free email accounts available from several sources (AOL, Hotmail, Yahoo, et al.) and public terminals everywhere (libraries, Internet cafes, etc.), we no longer find this service to be necessary.

Other important policy issues that may have a larger scope than just your local sysadmin group are:

- Handling of security break-ins
- Filesystem export controls
- Password selection criteria
- Removal of logins for cause
- Copyrighted material (MP3s and DVDs, for example)
- Software piracy

Maintaining good channels of communication among administrative groups at a large site can prevent problems and help to develop trust and cooperation. Consider throwing a party as a communication vehicle. Some sysadmin groups use an IRC-like MUD or MOO as a communication vehicle. It can get very chatty, but if used properly can make your organization run more smoothly, especially if some staff work off-site or from home.

Security policies

What do you want to protect? Your data? Your hardware? Your ability to recover quickly after a disaster? You must consider several tradeoffs when designing a security policy for your site:

- Services offered vs. security provided (more services = less secure)
- Ease of use and convenience vs. security (security = 1/convenience)
- Cost of security vs. risk (cost) of loss

RFC2196, the *Site Security Handbook*, is a 75-page document written in 1997 by a subgroup of the Internet Engineering Task Force (IETF). It advises sysadmins on various security issues, user policies, and procedures. It does not include a recipe for securing an Internet site, but it does contain some valuable information. The last 15 pages are a wonderful collection of both on-line and published references.

RFC2196 suggests that your policy documents include the following points:

- *Purchasing guidelines* for hardware and software. It can be a big win to involve sysadmins in the procurement process because they often know about hardware quirks, software limitations, and support issues that are not advertised by the vendors' marketing teams.

- A *privacy policy* that sets expectations regarding the monitoring of users' email and keystrokes and sets policies for dealing with user files.

- An *access policy*: who can have access, what they can do with their access, what hardware and software they can install, etc. This document should include the same warnings about authorized use and line monitoring that are included in the privacy policy.

- An *accountability policy* that spells out the responsibilities of both users and sysadmins.

- An *authentication policy* that sets guidelines for passwords and remote access.

- An *availability policy* that describes when the system is supposed to be up, lists scheduled maintenance times, gives instructions for reporting problems, and sets expectations regarding response times.

- A *maintenance policy* that includes rules about outsourcing and specifies procedures for giving access to third-party maintenance personnel.

Noticeably missing from the RFC2196 list is an authorization policy that specifies who can authorize new accounts and extended privileges. The original *Site Security Handbook*, RFC1244, contained lists of concrete issues rather than types of policies, which might be a bit more useful from the sysadmin's point of view. The newer RFC includes recommendations for each type of service a machine might run and describes the problems of the services and potential solutions.

Whatever policies you adopt, they must be explicit, written down, understood, and signed by all users and sysadmins. Enforcement must be consistent, even when users are customers who are paying for computing services. Failure to apply policies uniformly weakens their legal and perceived validity.

User policy agreements

At the University of Colorado's computer science department, user policy is delivered in the form of an initial shell that prints the policy and requires users to agree to and "sign" it before they can get a real shell and use their accounts. This scheme saves time and hassle, but check with *your own* lawyers before implementing it at your site.

Here are some explicit issues that should be addressed in a user policy agreement:

- Sharing accounts with friends and relatives
- Running password crackers[3] on the local system's passwords
- Running password crackers on other sites' passwords
- Disrupting service
- Breaking into other accounts
- Misusing or forging electronic mail
- Looking at other users' files (if readable? writable? invited?)
- Importing software from the net (never? always? if the user checks?)
- Using system resources (printers, disk space, modems, CPU)
- Copying licensed software
- Allowing others to copy licensed software
- Copying copyrighted material (music, movies, etc.)
- Conducting illegal activities (fraud, libel, etc.)
- Engaging in activities illegal in some states but not in others (e.g., porn)

Two sample policy agreements are included on our web site, www.admin.com. One is aimed at undergraduate students in a laboratory where a login is a privilege and not a right. It is the more militant of the two. The other document is for faculty, staff, and graduate students.

As an example of a short and simple policy agreement, we here include the agreement that the computer science department at the University of Melbourne requires students to sign in order to use the university's computers:

I, the undersigned, HEREBY DECLARE that I will abide by the rules set out below:

- *I will use the Department's computing and network facilities solely for academic purposes directly related to my study of Computer Science subjects.*

- *I understand that the Department grants computer accounts for the exclusive use of the recipient. Therefore, I will not authorise or facilitate the use of my account or files by any other person, nor will I divulge my password to any other person.*

---

3. For example, **crack**, which is a program for guessing passwords. See page 667 for more information.

- *I will not access, or attempt to gain access to any computer, computer account, network or files without proper and explicit authorisation. Such access is illegal under State and Federal laws, and is contrary to University regulations. I will inform the Computer Science Office immediately should I become aware that such access has taken place.*

- *I understand that some software and data that reside on file systems that I may access are protected by copyright and other laws, and also by licenses and other contractual agreements; therefore, I will not breach these restrictions.*

- *I will not use University facilities for obtaining, making, running or distributing unauthorised copies of software.*

- *I will undertake to keep confidential any disclosure to me by the University of software (including methods or concepts used therein) licensed to the University for use on its computers and I hereby indemnify and hold harmless the University against claims of any nature arising from any disclosure on my part to another of the said software in breach of this undertaking.*

- *I undertake to maintain the highest standard of honesty and personal integrity in relation to my usage of the Department's computing and network facilities. I further warrant that I will avoid any actions in relation to my usage of the Department's computing or network facilities that may bring any disrepute upon the Department or the University.*

I understand that I am bound by Regulation 8.1.R7 of the University of Melbourne (set out in the Student Diary), which also governs and regulates my use of University computing and network facilities.

I understand that acting in breach of any of the principles set out above will incur severe penalties including failure in an assignment or a subject, the suspension or withdrawal of access to University computing facilities, suspension or expulsion from the University, imposition of fines, and/or legal action taken under the Crimes (Computer) Act 1988.[4]

Take special note of the weasel words about honesty, personal integrity, and not bringing the University into disrepute. Vague requirements such as these give you some room for later maneuvering and help to cover any specifics that may have been inadvertently left out of the policy. Although their true legal weight is probably negligible, it's a good idea to include such requirements in your policy agreements.

Sysadmin policy agreements

A policy document for sysadmins (and others with special status) must set guidelines for using root privileges and for honoring users' privacy. It is hard to respond to a user's complaint that mail is broken without looking at messages that have bounced. But a copy of the headers is often sufficient to characterize and fix the problem.

---

4. Keep in mind that this is an Australian law, although similar computer and software-related legislation has been passed in the United States. See page 839.

*See page 43 for more information about **sudo**.*

If your site uses a tool such as **sudo** for root access, it is essential that your sysadmins use good passwords and not share their logins with *anyone*. Consider running **crack** on sysadmins' passwords regularly. It's also essential that they not execute **sudo tcsh** (token use of **sudo**) because that defeats **sudo**'s logging feature.

For some sysadmins, the urge to show off rootly powers overcomes common sense. Gently suggest other career alternatives.

At some sites, having the root password is a status symbol, perhaps more valuable than a key to the executive washroom. Often, the people that have the password are engineers that don't need it or should not have it. One site we know offered all engineers the root password, but stipulated that any takers would have to wear a beeper and help others when necessary. Requests plummeted.

Another technique that we have used with good success is to seal the root password in an envelope and hide it in a spot known to the sysadmin staff. Sysadmins generally use **sudo** to do their work; if they actually need the root password for some reason, they open the envelope. The root password is then changed and a new envelope is stashed. It's not difficult to steam open an envelope, but only sysadmins have physical access to the hiding place, and we trust our staff to respect the system.

Policy and procedures for emergency situations

Decide ahead of time who will be in charge in the event of a security incident. Set up a chain of command and keep the names and phone numbers of the principals off-line. It may be that the best person to put in charge is a sysadmin from the trenches, not the IT director (who is usually a poor choice for this role). We keep a little laminated card with important names and phone numbers printed in microscopic type. Very handy—and it fits in your wallet.

We are accustomed to using the network to communicate and to access documents. However, these facilities may be unavailable or compromised after an incident. Store all the relevant contacts and procedures off-line. Know where to get recent dump tapes and what **restore** command to use without looking at **/etc/dumpdates**. Avoid talking to the media, especially if the incident is unfolding in real time.

Web site hijacking is the latest craze in security break-ins. For the sysadmin at a web hosting company, a hijacking can be a serious event. Phone calls stream in from customers, from the media, from the company VIPs who just saw the news of the hijacking on CNN. Who will take the calls? What should that person say? Who is in charge? What role does each person play? If you are in a high-visibility business, it's definitely worth thinking through this type of scenario, coming up with some preplanned answers, and perhaps even having a practice session to work out the details.

Procedures for dealing with a security break-in are outlined in Chapter 21, *Security*, starting on page 687.

Disaster planning

Planning for a disaster is best accomplished before the disaster hits. An unfortunate disaster fact is that most disasters occur on managers' laptops, and from the sysadmin's point of view, they can yell the loudest. In this section we look at various kinds of disasters, the data you need to gracefully recover, and the important elements of a disaster plan.

There are several kinds of disasters:

- Security breaches: before the year 2000, about 60% originated from within the organization. By 2001, the sheer number of external attacks had driven the percentage down to more like 30%.

- Environmental problems: power spikes and outages, cooling failures, floods, hurricanes, earthquakes, meteors, terrorist or alien invasions

- Human error: deleted or damaged files and databases, lost configuration information (Does your mirroring system respond so quickly that an error propagates everywhere before you realize what's happened?)

- Spontaneous hardware meltdowns: dead servers, fried hard disks, malfunctioning networks

In all of these situations, you will need access to both on-line and off-line copies of essential information. The on-line copies should be kept on an independent machine if possible, one that has a fairly rich complement of tools, has key sysadmins' environments, runs its own name server, has a complete local **/etc/hosts** file, has no file sharing dependencies, has a printer attached, etc. Here's a list of handy data to keep on the backup machine and in printed form;

- An outline of the disaster procedure: people to call, when to call, what to say
- Service contract phone numbers and customer numbers
- Key local phone numbers: staff, police, fire, boss, employment agency
- Data on hardware and software configurations: OS version, patch levels, partition tables, PC hardware settings, IRQs, DMAs, and the like
- Backup tapes[5] and the backup schedule that produced them
- Network maps
- Software serial numbers, licensing data, and passwords
- Vendor contact info for that emergency disk you need immediately

An important but sometimes unspoken assumption made in most disaster plans is that sysadmin staff will be available to deal with the situation. Unfortunately, people get sick, graduate, go on vacation, leave for other jobs, and in stressful times may even turn hostile. It's worth considering what you'd do if you needed extra emergency help. (Not having enough sysadmins around can sometimes constitute an emergency in its own right if your systems are fragile or your users unsophisticated.)

---

5. Backups can be subpoenaed; you might want to expire some backup images.

You might try forming a sort of NATO pact with a local consulting company or university that has shareable system administration talent. Of course, you must be willing to share back when your buddies have a problem. Most importantly, don't operate close to the wire in your daily routine. Hire enough system administrators and don't expect them to work 12-hour days.

Test your disaster recovery plan before you need to use it. If you amassed a lot of Y2K supplies, some items (such as flashlights) may still be useful for more generic disasters. We found a really neat kind of flashlight that plugs into a wall socket. While the power is on, it stays at full charge. When the power goes out, it lights up so you can find it in the dark.

Test your generators and UPSs. Verify that everything you care about is plugged into a UPS, that the UPS batteries are healthy, and that the failover mechanism works. To test an individual UPS, just unplug it from the wall. To make sure that your critical equipment is properly UPSified, you may have to throw the circuit breakers and make sure your emergency configuration is really as functional as you had planned.

Most power hits are of short duration, but plan for two hours of battery life so that you have time to shut down machines properly in the event of a longer outage. Some UPSs have a serial port or Ethernet interface that you can use to initiate a graceful shutdown of noncritical machines after 5 minutes (configurable) of power outage.

Take advantage of power outages to do any 5-minute upgrades that you already have planned, such as adding a disk to a server. You're down anyway, so people expect to be inconvenienced. In some shops, an extra 5 minutes during a power outage is easier to accept than a scheduled downtime with a week's notice. If you have old machines that you think are not in use anymore, leave them turned off until someone complains. It might not be until weeks later—or never—that the "missing" machine is noticed.

See page 776 for more information about environment issues.

Cooling systems often have a notification system that can call you if the temperature gets too high. Tune the value of "too high" so that after the cooling system pages you, you have time to get in before machines start to fry; we use 76 degrees instead of 90, but live in the mountains 45 minutes away (in summer, indeterminate in winter). Keep a mechanical or battery-operated thermometer in the machine room—losing power means that you lose all those nifty electronic indicators that normally tell you the temperature.

A large U.S. government lab recently built a fancy new machine room and filled it with a 256-node Alpha cluster for running large scientific models. Everything was plugged into a UPS, and all the facilities were state of the art. Unfortunately, a minor power outage brought the center down for four hours. Why? The PC that controlled the HVAC (air conditioner) was not on the UPS. It failed and messed up the air conditioning system. Test carefully.

Miscellaneous tidbits

ISPs are failing, merging, and being acquired at a fantastic rate. These mergers have demolished many companies' carefully laid plans for maintaining redundant connections to the Internet. A post-merger ISP will often consolidate circuits that belonged to the independent companies. Customers that formerly had independent paths to the Internet may then have both connections running through a single conduit and once again be at the mercy of a single backhoe fiber cut.

When CNN or Slashdot announces that your web site is down, the same effect that makes highway traffic slow down to look at an accident at the side of the road causes your Internet traffic to increase enormously, often to the point of breaking whatever it was that you just fixed. If your web site cannot handle an increase in traffic of 25% or more, consider having your load balancing software route excess connections to a server that presents a single page that says "Sorry, we are too busy to handle your request right now."

*See page 669 for more information about **tripwire**.*

Use **tripwire** to keep abreast of what your sysadmins are doing, especially if different groups are responsible for different aspects of the same machine. Oracle database patches and OS patches can conflict with each other without either group realizing that they should ask what the other group has been up to. **tripwire** snooping is also useful if you are a sysadmin service organization and you find yourself having to clean up after a customer's somewhat clueless in-house sysadmin. It can clearly identify what has changed and when, making it easier to respond if the local sysadmin tries to blame you for his mistakes.

29.3 LEGAL ISSUES

The U.S. federal government and several states have laws regarding computer crime. At the federal level, there are two from the early 1990s and two more recent ones:

- The Federal Communications Privacy Act
- The Computer Fraud and Abuse Act
- The No Electronic Theft Act
- The Digital Millennium Copyright Act

As we start the new millennium, the big issues are the liability of sysadmins, network operators, and web hosting sites; strong cryptography for electronic commerce; copyright issues; and privacy issues.

Liability

System administrators are generally not held liable for content stored by users on the machines for which they are responsible. ISPs typically have an appropriate use policy (AUP) dictated by their upstream providers and required of their downstream customers. This "flow down" of liability assigns responsibility for users' actions to the users themselves, not to the ISP or the ISP's upstream provider. These policies have been used to attempt to control spam (unsolicited commercial email) and to protect ISPs in cases where customers stored child pornography in their accounts. Check the laws in your area; your mileage may vary.

A good example (but one that is too long to include here) is the AUP used by mibh.net before it was acquired by Metromedia Fiber Network, Inc. The AUP includes the usual lawyerish words about illegal actions, intellectual property violations, and appropriate use. It also includes a specific list of prohibited activities as well as enforcement policies, procedures for registering complaints, and a statement regarding liability. Although this AUP is no longer in use, it is the best one we have seen—a copy is available from www.admin.com.

Encryption

The need for encryption in electronic commerce and communication is clear. However, encryption is against the law in some countries. Law enforcement agencies do not want citizens to be able to store data that they (the police) cannot decrypt.

In the United States, the laws regarding encryption are changing. In the past, it was illegal to export any form of strong encryption technology. Companies had to create two versions of software that incorporated encryption: one for sale in the domestic market and a crippled version for export. The patent absurdity of this policy (the rest of the world has had cryptographic technology for a very long time) and the needs of electronic commerce eventually motivated the government to change its stance. Although the export restrictions are not yet completely gone, the situation in the United States is better than it used to be. However, the terrorist events of September 11, 2001, may reverse the U.S. government's momentum toward fewer restrictions on encryption technology.

Another side effect of the former U.S. laws is that many encryption-related software development projects are based in other countries. The IETF has done standards work in the area of end-to-end secure communications at the protocol level—the IPSEC effort—and vendors are beginning to ship systems that include it. The authentication part is typically bundled, but the encryption part is often installed separately. This architecture preserves flexibility for countries in which encryption cannot be used.

Copyright

The music and movie industries have noticed with some consternation that home computers are capable of playing music from CDs and of displaying movies on DVD. It is both an opportunity and a threat for them. The ultimate outcome will depend on whether these industries respond in a proactive or reactive way; unfortunately, they seem to be headed down the reactive path.

The DVD format uses an encryption key to scramble the contents of a disk by a technique called CSS, the Content Scrambling System. The idea was to limit the ability to play DVDs to licensed and approved players. Consumer DVD players include the appropriate decoding key, as do the software players that come with most DVD computer drives.

A student from Norway reverse-engineered the CSS encryption process and posted a program called DeCSS to the web. The program did not bypass the DVD encryption scheme; it simply used the decryption key from a legitimate Windows player to decode the DVD data stream and save it to disk so he could play it on Linux instead of having to use Windows.

The Motion Picture Association of America and the DVD Copy Control Association both filed lawsuits against numerous "distributors" of the DeCSS software; everyone whose web site linked to a copy of DeCSS was considered a distributor. The lawsuits alleged that the defendants were engaged not in theft of copyrighted materials, but in the distribution of trade secrets and "circumvention of copy protection," which was made illegal in the United States by the Digital Millennium Copyright Act of 1998. The MPAA won; DeCSS was found to be in violation of the DMCA.

Dmitry Sklyarov, a Russian computer scientist, wrote a program to convert Adobe eBooks to other formats, bypassing the restrictions that prevent copying. He worked for a company in Russia that produced a variety of format conversion and password recovery utilities. The software, Advanced eBook Processor, would have enabled conversions such as making an Adobe eBook accessible to blind users as an audio book. Dmitry visited the United States and was jailed for breaking a section of the DMCA that forbids distributing technology or information that can be helpful in bypassing technological restrictions. Although the case is still pending, he has been released from jail and allowed to return to Russia.

These legal cases offer up a steaming smorgasbord of some of the murkiest issues in computer law, so they're being watched with great interest by Electronic Frontier Foundation and computer law types. See the most excellent Openlaw DVD/DeCSS FAQ maintained by Rob Warren at www.cssfaq.org for more opinions and details.

During the prosecution of several cases under the DMCA, various loopholes and rough edges were found. These are now being "fixed" in an extension to the DMCA called the SSSCA: the Security Systems Standards and Certification Act, which is now winding its way through the U.S. Congress. This bill goes so far as to potentially ban the distribution of any source code that is covered by the GPL—such as Linux.

Under the SSSCA, it would be a civil offense to create or sell any kind of "interactive digital device" that does not include and utilize certified security technologies approved by the federal government. An interactive digital device is defined to be "any hardware or software capable of storing, retrieving, processing, performing, transmitting, receiving or copying information in digital form." Violations are federal felonies and include a fine of up to $500,000. The bill gives the computer industry a year to come up with suitable "certified security technologies." If it fails, the Department of Commerce will step in and set the standard. None of the meetings of industry participants are required to be open to the public. The proponents of the SSSCA are also trying to tie it to a trade agreement that would require other countries to enact similar legislation in order to qualify for favorable trade status.

The ACM (Association for Computing Machinery, the computer science professional society) has written a letter to Senator Hollings, the sponsor of the proposed bill, pointing out that it would prevent universities from teaching advanced Computer Science, would cripple real-time computing devices that need simple, auditable software (such as that used in air traffic control and medical monitoring), and would seriously damage the security of our Internet infrastructure. See

> http://www.acm.org/usacm/SSSCA-letter.html

for a complete copy of the ACM's letter. The EFF's (Electronic Frontier Foundation's) reaction was even stronger; see www.eff.org.

Another example of the difficulty of defining appropriate standards for copyright and intellectual property in the digital age is the case of CyberPatrol. This company makes Internet filtering software that religious groups are promoting to parents, schools, and libraries to protect children from objectionable content. A Canadian and a Swede wrote a tool called **cphack** that enabled them to decrypt the software's blocking list to see exactly which web sites were being blocked, how high the error rate was, and what nonobvious agendas might be present. They reported, for example, that anyone who criticized the software was blocked in all categories.

Mattel, which at that time owned CyberPatrol, sued the authors of the tool, claiming that the CyberPatrol license forbids reverse engineering. Mattel obtained a preliminary injunction against the distribution of the software, but unfortunately the case never came to trial; it was settled just before the trial was scheduled to start. The authors of the tool sold it to Mattel for $1 and agreed to a consent decree. It seemed that the authors had caved in (lawyers' bills aside!), but looking closely, it appeared that Mattel was attempting to assert ownership of a tool that was originally released under the GNU Public License.

Mattel hoped to use its newly acquired intellectual property rights to prevent **cphack** from being copied on the Internet (as if that would ever work). But because **cphack**'s authors released it under the GPL, unlimited distribution of the original program is permitted even if Mattel owns the copyright. Once a piece of software is publicly released under liberal terms such as those of the GPL, it can't be "unreleased."

Privacy

Privacy has always been difficult to safeguard, but with the rise of the Internet, privacy is in more danger than ever. During a recent incident at the University of Michigan, for example, the medical records of patients in the University of Michigan health care system were inadvertently published on the Internet. The data was freely available for months until a student noticed the oversight.

Another big privacy scandal, this one intentional, has involved DoubleClick.net, an advertising agency that provides many of the banner ads shown on web pages. DoubleClick promised for years that users in their system were never tracked or identified. Recently, however, they purchased a company that does data mining and began gathering data from each user that visited a web page containing a DoubleClick ad. The furor that ensued caused DoubleClick to withdraw the project for now and to hire two high-powered lawyers into "privacy" positions to find a way for DoubleClick to legally stalk the users who are subjected to their ads.

DoubleClick is small potatoes compared to a new threat to privacy from the combination of our ISPs and a company called Predictive Networks. According to the PRIVACY Forum Digest, Predictive, with help from ISPs, plans to collect the URLs you visit, the keywords you type into search engines, and other information by watching your work on the web. From this data, they will build a digital "signature" of you and use that profile to target Internet content and ads just to you.

Predictive says that your information is "anonymous" and that you can trust everyone involved: Predictive's employees, the ISPs' employees, the advertisers, the content providers—everyone. You can request a copy of your digital signature, but you might have to pay for it. You can also opt out of this "service," but your Internet connectivity through that ISP might cost more or be rescinded. As of this writing, Predictive's web site (www.predictivenetworks.com) still has no privacy policy and not much hard information about what they really do. The PRIVACY Forum Digest article (V09, #13, www.vortex.com) includes more details on their plans and on their position with respect to Internet users' privacy.

Policy enforcement

Log files may prove to you beyond a shadow of a doubt that person X did bad thing Y, but to a court it is all just hearsay evidence. Protect yourself with written policies. Log files sometimes include time stamps, which are useful but not necessarily admissible as evidence unless your computer is running the Network Time Protocol (NTP) to keep its clock synced with reality.

You may need a security policy in order to prosecute someone for misuse. It should include a statement such as this: *Unauthorized use of University computing systems may involve not only transgression of University policy but also a violation of state and federal laws. Unauthorized use is a crime and may involve criminal and civil penalties; it will be prosecuted to the full extent of the law.*

We advise you to put a warning in **/etc/motd** (the message of the day file) that advises users of your snooping policy. Ours reads:

```
Your keyboard input may be monitored in the event of a real or
perceived security incident.
```

Some connections (such as **ftp** sessions) do not see the message of the day. Users can also suppress the message by creating a file called **.hushlogin** in their home directories. You may want to ensure that users see the notification at least once by including it in the startup files you give to new users. If you require the use of **ssh** to log in (and you should), then configure **sshd.config** to always show the **motd** file.

Be sure to specify that users by the act of using their accounts acknowledge your written policy. Explain where users can get additional copies of policy documents, and post key documents on an appropriate bulletin board. Also include the specific penalty for noncompliance (deletion of the account, etc.).

Suppose something naughty is posted to news or the web from your site. If you are CompuServe (now part of AOL), this is a problem. In a case called *Cubby v. CompuServe*, something libelous was posted. The judge ruled that CompuServe was not guilty, but found the moderator of the newsgroup to which it was posted negligent. The more you try to control information, the more liable you become.

This principle is beautifully illustrated by the story of a Texas business founded by an enterprising computer science student of ours, Cheeser. He wrote Perl scripts to mine the Usenet news groups, collect naughty pictures, and build a subscription web site based on that content. He charged $12/month to subscribers and was raking in money hand over fist.

Cheeser tried to be a responsible pornographer and did not subscribe to newsgroups known to carry child pornography. He also monitored several newsgroups that were on the edge, sometimes with illegal content, sometimes not. This minimal oversight and his choice of a conservative county in Texas in which to locate his business were his downfall.

Acting on an anonymous tip (perhaps from a competitor), the local police confiscated his computers. Sure enough, they found an instance of child pornography that had been posted to one of the "safer" newsgroups. The criminal case never went to trial, but during the plea bargaining it became clear that the judge thought Cheeser was guilty—not because he had created the content, but because he was not a good enough censor. The implication was that if Cheeser had done no censoring at all, he would have been legally OK. Never censor your porn.

This principle also applies to other interactions with the outside world. From a legal standpoint, the more you monitor your users' use of the Internet, the more you may be liable for their actions or postings. If you are aware of an illegal or actionable activity, you have a legal duty to investigate it and to report your findings to Big Brother.

For this reason, some sites limit the data that they log, the length of time for which log files are kept, and the amount of log file history kept on backup tapes. Some software packages (e.g., the Squid web cache) help with the implementation of this policy by including levels of logging that help the sysadmin debug problems but do not violate users' privacy.

System administrators should be familiar with all relevant corporate or university policies and should make sure the policies are followed. Unenforced or inconsistent policies are worse than none, from both a practical and legal point of view.

Software licenses

Many sites have paid for K copies of a software package and have N copies in daily use, where K << N. Getting caught in this situation could be damaging to the company, probably more damaging than the cost of those N-minus-K other licenses. Other sites have received a demo copy of an expensive software package and hacked it (reset the date on the machine, found the license key, etc.) to make it continue working after the expiration of the demo period. How do you as a sysadmin deal with requests to violate license agreements and make copies of software on unlicensed machines? What do you do when you find that machines for which you are responsible are running pirated software? What about shareware that was never paid for?

It's a very tough call. Management will often not back you up in your requests that unlicensed copies of software be either removed or paid for. Often, it is a sysadmin who signs the agreement to remove the demo copies after a certain date, but a manager who makes the decision not to remove them.

Even if the job is the best one you've ever had, your personal and professional integrity are on the line. Fortunately, even in today's job market, quality sysadmins are in high demand and your job search will be short. We are aware of several cases in which a sysadmin's immediate manager would not deal with the situation and told the sysadmin not to rock the boat. The sysadmin then wrote a memo to the boss asking to correct the situation and documenting the number of copies of the software that were licensed and the number that were in use. The admin quoted a few phrases from the license agreement and cc'ed the president of the company and his boss' managers. In one case, this procedure worked and the sysadmin's manager was let go. In another case, the sysadmin quit when even higher management refused to do the right thing.

Unlicensed software in the Linux world of open source is less of a problem. The authors of neat software packages usually give them away. They sometimes ask for a small donation or a good music CD if you use their packages extensively.

Spam: unsolicited commercial email

Advertisers, marketing folks, and con artists have flocked to the Internet in droves to take advantage of "free" email communication. The cost of junk-mailing an ad to thousands of people is tiny compared to the cost of sending traditional paper mail, and the response rate is apparently better. This scenario creates two big losers: consumers, who have to wade through mounds of spam every day, and ISPs, who pay for the traffic on their networks.

We won't go into the technical details of spam tracing and spam fighting in detail here. That subject is covered more thoroughly in Chapter 19, *Electronic Mail*, starting on page 588. However, we will mention a few of the legal aspects.

The United States has laws, mostly at the state level, that have been used to successfully prosecute the senders of spam. In at least one case, the senders were required to pay for each piece of mail sent because the spam interfered with a business's normal operations. Unfortunately, most recipients of spam just delete it and don't bother to try to track down the spammer and retaliate.

ISPs do try to keep spammers from using their facilities, not only because of the bandwidth they use but also because the spam typically violates the appropriate use policy of their upstream provider and thus puts them in jeopardy of losing their own network connection.

You can find a useful page of links to spam-related resources and legislation at

http://www.elsop.com/wrc/nospam.htm

John Gilmore, a founder of the Electronic Frontier Foundation, holds an alternative view of spam. He feels that defense of the first amendment is much more important than fighting spam and that anyone should be able to send spam whenever they want. He has scripts that notice a single sender sending too much email and shuts them down, taking action as a receiver rather than trying to legislate what can be sent. The scripts slow down senders after 50 messages have been relayed through his open relay machine and stop them after 100.

John thinks that trying to make spam illegal is technically infeasible and is wrong; spam must be filtered out at the receiving end. He also feels that AUPs (appropriate use policies) are an illegal restraint of trade. He proposes an interesting computation of the value of various media in relation to the number of users:

- TV: the value of the network is n, the number of viewers
- Phone: the value is n^2, the number of possible pairs of participants
- Email: the value of the network is n!, the number of possible groups

Sysadmin surveys

SAGE, the System Administrators Guild associated with the USENIX Association, and SANS, the System Administration, Networking, and Security Institute, perform annual surveys focused mainly on the compensation of system administrators. The results of these surveys for 2000 (the latest available at press time) are excerpted in the next sections. The surveys do not distinguish between Linux and UNIX, but they do differentiate between UNIX and Windows.

SAGE salary survey

SAGE administered a sysadmin salary survey at its LISA conference and over the web. The full report is available from

http://www.usenix.org/sage/jobs/salary_survey/salary_survey.html

SAGE members can download an Acrobat file by supplying their membership number and password; others must register and are then emailed the file. SAGE does not sell your address but might send you information about their conferences and publications. (Actually, you can opt out of their spam when you register.)

Below are some interesting data points from the year 2000 results, which incorporated responses from over 5,000 system administrators who attended the conference or filled out the survey form on the web. Most of the respondents were full-time sysadmins who considered system administration their primary line of work. About 80% were from the United States; the remainder were from 68 different countries.

- The median salary was almost $70,000 in the United States, unless you worked for a university, where it was about $12,000 less.

- Over 60% of respondents received raises in 2000 (down from 86% in 1999), ranging from 11% for those staying in the same job to 17% for those changing jobs and employers.

- Over 70% of organizations cannot find enough sysadmins—the hunt is on.

- About half received bonuses; 15% received overtime pay.

- Salaried sysadmins work 46.7 hours per week, on average.

- The most common operating systems were (in order): Solaris (70%), Windows NT (67%), Linux (62%), and Windows 95 and 98 (49%). Most sysadmins deal with heterogeneous environments containing on average 5 different operating systems.

- Education does not correlate strongly with salary. A BS degree was only worth an additional $6K over a high school degree.

- Years of experience did correlate strongly with salary; most sysadmins had from 5–10 years experience.

- Over 75% of respondents expected to still be sysadmins in 5 years. This is a nice change; system administration used to be the bottom of the barrel job that you did while waiting to be promoted to software developer. But some folks *like* getting more context switches in a day than a developer gets in a year.

- Fewer than 9% of sysadmins were women, down from 13% in 1999. Women's salaries were about $5,000 lower than men's overall, but in the UK women's salaries were about $5,000 higher. Cool!

- Almost 50% of the sysadmins were between 25 and 35 years old, and fewer than 1% were below 20 or above 55.

- The most bothersome and problematic parts of the sysadmins' jobs were (in rank order): dealing with management, work load and hours, and office politics and bureaucracy.

When reviewing the survey form, most system administrators realized that they really did not know exactly how they spent their day. Most sites felt understaffed. It doesn't take too many whiny users for an insufficient user-to-sysadmin ratio to become oppressive.

SANS salary survey

The SANS survey for 2000 was administered over the web and included about 7,000 respondents. The SANS membership is typically less technical than the SAGE crowd, and it includes more system administrators who deal primarily with Windows desktops. The respondents were categorized as system administrators, network administrators, security administrators, database administrators, security consultants, or security auditors.

Many of the questions matched those of the SAGE survey, but direct comparisons are difficult because of the wider range of participants. Salaries were broken down by country; we have included the U.S. data in the summary that follows.

Of those completing the survey, about 50% labeled themselves as system administrators and another 24% as network administrators. The other categories were much smaller percentages. Here are some of the more interesting results:

- OS representation was about even between UNIX/Linux and Windows. Of the UNIX/Linux folks, 60% ran Solaris.

- The average salary was $65K overall: $70K for UNIX/Linux folks and $60K for Windows admins. The numbers for women were lower for both salary and raises. Security administrators did better than sysadmins, and network administrators did worse. Raises were 11% on average.

- A BS degree was worth $5K to an NT administrator and $8K to a UNIX admin; a master's degree added another $5K–$8K. Master's degree holders earned more than Ph.D.'s as system administrators.

29.4 SCOPE OF SERVICE

The services provided by an administrative support group must be clearly defined or users' expectations will not match reality. Here are some issues to consider:

- Response time
- Service during weekends and off-hours
- House calls (support for machines at home)
- Weird (one of a kind) hardware
- Ancient hardware
- Supported operating systems
- Standard configurations
- Backup tape expiration
- Special-purpose software
- Janitorial chores (cleaning screens and keyboards)

In addition to knowing what services are provided, users must also know about the priority scheme used to manage the work queue. Priority schemes always have wiggle room, but try to design one that covers most situations with few or no exceptions. Some priority-related variables are:

- The number of users affected
- The importance of the affected users
- The loudness of the affected users (squeaky wheels)
- Importance of the deadline (late homework vs. research grant proposal that partially funds the sysadmin group)

Our support group for faculty, staff, and computer science students has developed a set of documents that delineates their services, priority scheme, and contact mecha-

nisms. This group of customers contains several levels of importance and squeaki-
ness. The policy documents have been used for a few years with good, but not perfect, results. Copies are available from www.admin.com.

Users generally assume that all their important data is stored on backup tapes that
will be archived forever. But backup tapes don't last indefinitely; magnetic media
have a finite lifetime after which reading data becomes difficult. Backup tapes can
also be subpoenaed; your organization may not *want* old data to be available forever.
It's best to maintain an explicit written policy that specifies how long backups will be
kept. Such a policy helps users to have realistic expectations and protects you from
having to go too far back in time to accommodate lawyers.

In a Linux shop, every user has access to the source code and could easily build a
custom kernel for his or her own machine. You must consider this in your corporate
policy and should probably try to standardize on a few specific kernel configurations.
Otherwise, your goal of easy maintenance and scaling to grow with the organization
will meet some serious impediments. Encourage your creative, OS-hacking employees to suggest kernel modifications that they need for their work. Make them a part
of the standardization process so that you don't have to maintain separate kernels
for each engineer.

29.5 TROUBLE-REPORTING SYSTEMS

Our trouble-reporting system uses an email alias called "trouble." At one time we
were bombarded with trouble reports that were either incomplete or incomprehen-
sible. We wrote a script that asked the user specific questions, such as

- On what host does the problem occur?
- Is the problem repeatable?
- How important is it that the problem be fixed immediately?

The user rebellion started about an hour later, and within a day we had backed the
system out. Its only value seemed to be that with the furor over the script, many users
actually read the questions it was asking and the quality of our free-form trouble reports improved.

Another site dealt with this problem by sending out a message that explained what
information is important in a trouble report and showed examples of useless reports.
When a useless report was received, it was answered with an apology ("Sorry, I don't
have enough information to…") and a copy of the explanatory message. The users
caught on quickly.

You need to use some sort of trouble ticketing system or problems will either receive
five answers (the easy ones) or no answers (the hard ones). The system should log
resolved trouble messages and perhaps send a copy of the resolution to novice sysadmins and trainees. The log files become a useful source of data to mine during preparation of management reports (especially when you need to justify more administrative staff), and the copies to new sysadmins let them familiarize themselves with

your site's most common problems and their solutions. They also demonstrate the appropriate tone to use in messages to users.

Our current favorite ticketing system is **wreq** (www.math.duke.edu/~yu/wreq). **wreq** is based on **req** from the University of Maryland, to which it adds extra functionality and a web interface. It has almost as many features as the commercial offering Remedy but is easier to configure and use and easier to fit into your budget (free!).

wreq's graphs of tickets submitted, resolved, and rotting are especially useful for both sysadmins and management. They can help you detect long-term trends. **wreq**'s main disadvantages are its poor (ever-so-close to nonexistent, really) documentation and its lack of scalability.

29.6 MANAGING MANAGEMENT

It's essential for your managers to respect and support you. Management support for tough security policies is sometimes the hardest to get. Tightening security invariably means inconveniencing users, and the users usually outweigh you both in number and in whining ability. Make sure that any security change that impacts users (changing from **telnet** to **ssh**, converting from passwords to DSA keys, etc.) is announced well in advance, is well documented, and is well supported at changeover time. Documentation should be easy to understand and should provide cookbook-type recipes for dealing with the new system. Allow for extra staffing hours when you first cut over to the new system so that you can deal with the panicked users who didn't read their email or the **motd**.

Upper management often has no idea what system administrators do. Keeping a diary for a week that records what you do and how long it takes will surprise even you. This kind of documentation is essential when you campaign for additional staff or equipment. It can also be a source of power in day-to-day political squabbles. It may be wise to keep good records even in the absence of a particular goal.

Managers, especially nontechnical managers, are often way off in their estimates of the difficulty of a task or the amount of time it will take to complete. This is especially true of troubleshooting tasks.

Try to set expectations realistically. Double or triple your time estimates for large or crucial tasks. If an upgrade is done in two days instead of three, most users will thank you instead of cursing you as they might have if your estimate had been one day.

It is sometimes hard for a sysadmin to get a written policy put in place. In that case, document existing practices and policy. For example, "We have 8 licenses for Excel and 47 copies installed." Ask for money to buy more copies. If this fails, write a memo documenting the problem with a copy to upper management. Fortunately, good system administrators are in demand, so your job search should be short.

29.7   HIRING, FIRING, AND TRAINING

There are two approaches to building a staff of system administrators:

- Hire experienced people.
- Grow your own.

Experienced people usually come up to speed faster, but you always want them to unlearn certain things. To do their job, they need root access. But you do not know them and may not be willing to put your company's data in their hands immediately.

It takes quite a bit of time and effort to train a sysadmin, and production networks are not an ideal training ground. But given the right person (smart, interested, curious, careful, etc.), the end result is often better.

We have developed two evaluation tools for experienced applicants. We used to call them "tests," but have found that some institutions are not allowed to test applicants. We no longer test; we evaluate and assess.

The first not-a-test, a written evaluation, asks applicants to rate their experience and knowledge of various system and networking tasks. The scale of familiarity is 0 to 4:

- Never heard of it (0)
- Heard of it, never did it (1)
- Have done it, could do it with supervision (2)
- Could do it without supervision (3)
- Know it well, could teach someone else to do it (4)

Embedded among the questions are several ringers. For example, in the hardware section is a question about RS-232 connectors followed by one about "MX connectors."[6] These bogus questions let you measure the BS factor in an applicant's answers. A 3 on the MX connectors would be suspect. After the not-a-test, you might ask innocently, "So, what do *you* use MX connectors for?"

The second evaluation is designed for use during a telephone interview. Questions are set up to elicit quick answers from applicants who know their stuff. We score +1 for a right answer, 0 for an "I don't know," and -1 for obvious BS or typing **man xxx** in the background.

These two schemes have been quite good metrics for us. The percentage of bogus questions we use is determined by our state hiring folks; one or two questions aren't enough. Keep in mind that these assessments do not address some of the most important issues regarding prospective sysadmins:

- Will they get along with other members of the team?
- How is their user interface?
- Will they take direction?
- Are they on a growth curve with a positive slope?

---

6. MX refers to a mail exchanger record in DNS, not to a serial connector.

The evaluation assessments we use are on-line at www.admin.com. Can you find all the bogus questions?

A personal interview might answer some of these questions. A telephone conversation with references usually tells you more. Listen very carefully; many people do not like to say anything bad about a former employee or coworker, so they find clever ways to tell you (if you are listening carefully) that a potential employee has problems. Be very suspicious if the applicant does not include recent employers as references.

If you make a hiring mistake, fire early. You may miss a few late bloomers, but keeping people who are not pulling their own weight will alienate your other staff members as they take up the slack and clean up after the losers. In many organizations it is very hard to fire someone, especially after the initial evaluation period is over. Make sure that initial evaluations are taken seriously. Later, you may have to collect data showing incompetence, give formal warnings, set performance goals, and so on.

Attitude adjustment

System administrators often forget that they are service providers and that users are their customers. Many sysadmins secretly hold the opinion that the systems are theirs to play with and that users are a regrettable nuisance.

Sysadmins today are respected, treated as skilled professionals, and paid well. In the past they have been looked upon as electronic janitors several castes below developers and engineers. But their leverage (fix the compiler for one engineer and it's fixed for many more) has changed their status in most organizations. They still secretly have their clueless user awards and other types of harmless fun, but they are much more respected than they were 10 years ago. Managers would do well to ask the sysadmin staff their opinion of intended promotees; a user's interaction with the sysadmin staff is often very revealing of that user's creativity, independence, and problem-solving abilities.

Some of the qualities of a good system administrator are contradictory. A sysadmin must be brash enough to try innovative solutions when stuck on a problem but must also be careful enough not to try anything truly destructive. Interpersonal skills and problem-solving skills are both important, yet they seem to lie on orthogonal axes among many of the sysadmins we have known. One of our reviewers suggested that a "personable sysadmin" was an oxymoron.

Microsoft's "adminless" systems will never replace sysadmins—someone still has to hit <Return> or click OK and take the blame!

Operator wars

New sysadmins often become the victims of what we call "operator wars," in which more experienced users alias **ls** to **logout** in the novices' environments, send them mail bombs, and generally harass them and their inexperience. Sysadmins who forget to log out are especially tempting victims.

This phenomenon is more prevalent at universities than at commercial sites, but it probably happens everywhere to some degree. Although it seems fun, it can easily be carried too far and should be strictly discouraged. There are enough real whammos for a new sysadmin without adding more, even in jest.

Iterative refinement

A sysadmin will often think that a problem has been fixed, only to receive several more trouble reports as the task slowly gets done completely and correctly. This process can occur because the user who first reported the problem did not describe it clearly or suggested the wrong solution. Equally often, it can happen because the sysadmin did not test the solution carefully.

Some common complaints include:

- Man pages and documentation not installed for new software
- Software not installed everywhere
- Software that turns out to be owned by the sysadmin or installed with permissions that are wrong.

Testing is boring, but a busy sysadmin can cut productivity in half by skipping it. Every trouble report costs time and effort, both for users and for the sysadmin. The job is not done until all operational glitches have surfaced and been taken care of.

A common problem is that a user reports that "X doesn't work on machine Y" and the sysadmin goes to machine Y and tries command X and it works fine. The trouble report answer comes back "works for me" with a bit of an attitude attached. If the sysadmin actually tried the command as the user who submitted the report (for example, executing **sudo su** - *username* in front of the command), he might nail the exact problem on the first try. The "-" argument to **su** causes the resulting shell to use the environment of the user you are **su**ing to. Ergo, you can really reproduce the environment that was reported not to be working.

Users can become upset when a problem is not completely solved on the first attempt. Try to set their expectations appropriately. It is often useful to get the user who reported a problem to work with you in solving it, especially if the problem relates to an unfamiliar software package. You will obtain additional information, and the user will be less likely to think of your relationship as adversarial.

29.8 WAR STORIES AND ETHICS

Why ethics? A sysadmin's job involves a significant level of trust, from respecting users' privacy to protecting the company's trade secrets. Trust relationships go both downstream with your users and upstream with management. Without that trust, it's very hard for sysadmins to do their jobs well. Your personal and professional integrity are priceless; protect them as you earn the trust of your users, your peers, and your managers.

This section contains war stories that illustrate some ethical dilemmas a system administrator may face. Some of the stories are our own, and others have been harvested from external sources, perhaps N[th]-hand and perhaps not entirely in their most accurate forms.

Boss's mistake #1

A department chair incorrectly sent personnel data to the entire faculty instead of to the executive committee for which it was intended. He asked a student sysadmin who was working that weekend to edit faculty members' mailboxes and remove the message. Should the student do it? Should he refuse? Should he look at the message and decide for himself if it was really serious enough to warrant an invasion of privacy?

In this instance, the sysadmin did do as he was asked, but he demanded that the chairman send mail to the faculty members explaining what had happened. He also stipulated that there be a witness to watch him trim mailboxes and verify that he did not browse around while editing. This was a good solution and one that both the sysadmin and the chairman felt comfortable with.

Boss's mistake #2

A new secretary at a large computer manufacturer in the midwest was new to UNIX and email. At the end of her first week, she sent her boss a message about how nice the job was and how everyone had been very helpful. Her command line was something like:

```
% mail boss I like my new job, everyone is so helpful, thank you. Working
        here for you will be really fun ...
```

The boss read the mail and responded with a jokingly rude and sexist remark about the size of her breasts. Other folks responded about the need to put a carriage return between the name of the recipient and the message itself. It seems "everyone" was an alias for all employees.

A few hours later, the head sysadmin (who by that time had seen both the secretary's message and the boss's response) got a call from the boss. The boss explained that he had made a mistake (**R** instead of **r**, perhaps) and needed copies of the message removed from everyone's mailbox—with "everyone" being several thousand employees. Needless to say, the sysadmin refused. A moral decision was unnecessary: removing a message from thousands of mailboxes spread all around the world is an impossible task.

Which ones to fire

A novice sysadmin and an operator trainee discovered how to break into the Computing Center's student computers. These hosts were run by a different group that was somewhat looked down on for being too conservative. The rookies wanted to leave a back door. As they were about to edit the **/etc/passwd** file, a senior sysadmin advised them to use **vipw** instead of **vi**. The novices never used the back door, but the senior sysadmin did and was caught. Who should be fired?

Our answer would be either all three or just the senior sysadmin, who should have stopped the break-in when he became aware of it instead of aiding and abetting the installation of a back door. However, in this case the senior sysadmin was deemed too valuable to lose; the two rookies were fired instead.

We view this as a very bad management decision. If the limits of behavior are set by an employee's value rather than by a written policy that is consistently enforced, the company is vulnerable to litigation (to say nothing of disgruntled employees with assault rifles).

Engineers vs. IT department

A small company that sold computer hardware and software allowed its engineers to have the root password on nonserver machines so that they could install and remove software or perform network monitoring and testing. **sudo** was available but its use was not mandated.

When the company upgraded from Solaris to Linux boxes, the IT department decided not to hand out the root password anymore. One of the engineers needed root access to do some network monitoring and testing on a Linux system. He called IT for the password and was told that they no longer gave it out, but that IT would do whatever was needed as root. He then asked the IT representative to log in to his machine and make a small fix. While the sysadmin was logged in to the box on the engineer's desk, he **su**ed to root to make the necessary changes. The engineer ran a sniffer on a nearby Solaris machine and obtained the root password, which he used from then on to do his work. He also shared the password with the other engineers who needed it. The situation was never mentioned to the IT group.

There are several issues here. The engineer did need the root password or **sudo** to do his work. There were no written policies regarding the root password or sniffing on the local network. The sysadmin should never have trusted his local network and typed the root password in the clear across it.

These issues were never resolved. The IT group never discovered that the engineers had hijacked the root password and were using it regularly. The engineers never misused it. All the more reason for sysadmins to use **ssh** consistently (even on local connections) and to review their log files!

Horndog Joe

Joe, a new sysadmin at a major computer manufacturer, was infatuated with the receptionist and asked her out for a date. She always went out with newcomers once, to show them around and welcome them to the area. Joe asked her out again but she refused. A week or so later, she mentioned to one of the senior sysadmins that the machine always told her she had new mail even when she didn't. Hmmm. The senior sysadmin checked log files and found that Joe was reading the receptionist's mail. What should he do?

- Fire Joe?
- Give him a strong talking to?
- Give him a mild talking to?
- Nothing?

The right answer is actually a question: Is there a written policy that says, "Don't read other people's email?" The answer was no. Management opted for a strong talking to.

A few weeks later, it happened again. This time it seemed to be a different person reading the mail, Tom. The senior sysadmin called Tom into his office and confronted him with the evidence. But Tom was at a basketball game when the log files showed that the access had occurred.

Upon further investigation and after backtracking through several machines, the sysadmin discovered that Joe was the true culprit once again. Half an hour later, Joe was fired and the contents of his desk were on the curb.

A policy that allows for one warning is a license to steal until caught.

Wedding invitations

A sysadmin who was getting married and hadn't finished all the preparations for the wedding gave his best man (a sysadmin from another site) the key to his office and the root password to his workstation. The friend was to go into work and make last-minute place cards for the tables at the reception. This incident violated lots of local policies and was noticed by other sysadmins because the common practice was to use the **sudo** command instead of logging in as root or using **su**.

The root password was the same on all machines, so the visitor had actually been given the password and physical access to the entire site. But no damage was done.

The circumstances seemed special, but written policy was violated. The employee was a valuable member of the staff. What to do? He was somewhat reluctantly fired with cause; he fought it and lost.

Pornographic GIF images

A student's high school buddy came down to visit the computer lab during the summer. The student showed his friend how to view GIF files and showed him the location of a few "interesting" ones. He installed the friend at the last workstation at the back of the room and then worked on his homework. When they were done, they left.

Some time later (days, probably) the dean of engineering, accompanied by the basketball coach, was showing a promising recruit from Texas (a woman) around the campus. The dean had a key to the labs and so instead of entering as the students do, with an access card, he entered at the back of the lab with his key.

The first workstation they saw was the one on which the friend had viewed GIFs. And thanks to the magic of screen savers, when the mouse was moved, a sexually explicit photograph appeared on the screen. Needless to say, the dean and the basketball coach were furious; the student thought it was no big deal. The dean demanded that all GIFs be removed from university-owned computers and that the student who left it on the screen be expelled from school.

Our policy agreement, which the student had signed, said that you should not display pictures on your screen that would offend other people. The end result was that the student lost his login for a semester. The policy agreement was reviewed by the lawyers (who upheld the computer science department's side, not the dean's), and the whole incident was handled within the department. We apologized to the recruit.

Migrating data

A small Colorado business used a local service firm for hardware and software support. One evening, their system administrator was swapping out a disk on which the bearings were going bad. The service firm had supplied not only the replacement disk but also a large scratch disk so that the transfer could be made without going to tape and back again. The sysadmin installed the replacement disk and the scratch disk and rebooted.

He was surprised when the workstation booted from the replacement disk and complained that the clock was 297 days off. Should he wipe the disk immediately? Should he look at the data? Should he just return the disk to the service provider? His first instinct was to wipe the disk without looking at it, but after some reflection it seemed better to check and see whose data it was so that the service provider could determine how it had slipped out with data on it.

A quick scan of the **passwd** file showed that the disk had previously belonged to this very same company. It contained not only the root partition with encrypted passwords, but also the company's development databases and new products. In short, a large part of the assets of the company, a bit out of date, had arrived from the service provider on a replacement disk. When asked, the service provider admitted that the way they tested disks was to copy data from one to another, regardless of what data happened to be on the source disk.

This incident illustrates a problem that is obvious with hindsight and also hard to fix. Whose responsibility is the data on a broken disk? It cannot always be wiped before being returned for repair. Service providers (and probably more importantly, peripheral resellers) do not necessarily see your data as valuable; they see only a broken or breaking disk.

As sysadmins, we are used to protecting our backup tapes. Broken disks are taken for granted, and they shouldn't be. Whenever possible, a disk with valuable data should be wiped (a low-level format and verify should do it) before being returned for repair or trade-in. If it's too broken to reformat, make sure your service provider knows that it contains sensitive data that you would like deleted. Consider putting statements about your data in the contract with a repair service provider.

It is probably worthwhile to ask your service providers about their policy regarding customers' data. When they admit that they don't have one, act very surprised and shocked.

High-security U.S. government sites (defense installations, especially) are sometimes forbidden to let any computer equipment off-site, ever. If it breaks, they have to buy a new one. It may sound paranoid, but as this story illustrates, it is not without basis. (The policy even applies to components such as CPU boards that wouldn't normally retain data.)

Bill must die!

A student left himself logged in on a machine in the computer science undergraduate lab when he went to his teaching assistant's office to pick up a document. While he was gone, someone typed in a mail message to president@whitehouse.gov that made death threats against then President Clinton. The Secret Service called the next morning.

The student was a foreigner who had served in his country's militia as an encryption expert. He had also neglected to mention to the local system administrators that he received an acknowledgment from the White House for mail he had not sent. Things did not look good.

The system administrators spent the weekend collecting log files and card access records to determine what had happened. Luckily, the log files provided enough circumstantial evidence to convince the Secret Service that the student had probably been the victim of a prank.

The student's command history file (**~/.history**, which included time stamps) verified that he was a regular user of **pine** and **vi**. But the offending message had been sent with **emacs**, with a sizable period of inactivity before and after the event. Most users cling tenaciously to one editor and mail program, so the discrepancy was highly suggestive of a compromised account.

As it turns out, threatening the president of the United States is a felony. Even though the foreign student was exonerated, the Secret Service investigation continued. The event occurred a second time. It was again a forgery, but the log files gave us enough information to identify who we thought was sending the messages. The Secret Service never told us whether they pursued the person whose name we gave to them.

We now recommend that students use **xlock**[7] when they leave their terminals unattended. We have modified **xlock** to log the user out after a period of inactivity so that students can't hoard the good machines in the lab.

Second-hand stories from the World Trade Center

We've heard some instructive stories that dealt with the September 11, 2001, attack on the World Trade Center. Unfortunately, the sysadmins that "owned" these stories were unable to obtain their management's permission to share them. Rather than give up, we here include some second- and third-hand stories that may not be 100% true. They are certainly not the last word, but are interesting nonetheless.

---

7. **xlock** is a locking screen saver program for X Windows that requires you to type your password or the root password to unlock the screen.

One ISP routed all their calls and network traffic through a facility located in one of the smaller buildings of the World Trade Center complex. The ISP's building survived the attack, and the facility continued to operate under power from emergency generators (though it had trouble dissipating heat once the building's air conditioning had been disabled). Unfortunately, the ISP's staff were unable to enter the site to refill the generators' fuel tanks. Moral: make sure you have at least a few days' worth of generating capacity available for sustained emergency situations.

Another organization located in one of the WTC towers once maintained its disaster recovery facility in the other tower. Fortunately, the company rethought its definition of "off-site" before the attack. A third organization was able to recover because all of its critical data was replicated to multiple devices in multiple locations, mirrored synchronously over Fibre Channel. However, this particular organization lost a lot of paper documents—not everything was computerized.

CNN's web site experienced traffic on September 11th that defied the measuring abilities of CNN's load monitors. The telephone system in New York City was overloaded, and TV stations that had broadcast from antennas atop the WTC were knocked out. Everyone turned to the Internet and pummeled cnn.com. The site was at first overwhelmed by the load. After trying to cope for a while by moving servers around, CNN eventually reduced the complexity of its home page to a single image and plain text with no links. After a couple of hours, the site was up again and handling the load.

29.9 LOCAL DOCUMENTATION

Documentation is often pushed down in the priority queue in favor of "real work." It's quite easy to defer documentation because at the moment you should be writing it, you remember how to do the task in question and have no need for a cheat sheet. Any administration group that includes students probably has serious documentation problems.

Local documentation serves many purposes. Have you ever walked into a machine room needing to reboot one server, only to face racks and racks of hardware, all alike, all different, and all unlabeled? Or had to install a piece of hardware that you've handled before, but all you can remember about the chore was that it was hard to figure out? Or gone through hours of localizing a new machine to fit your environment, only to realize that you have forgotten a couple of crucial steps?

Local documentation should be kept in a well-defined spot, perhaps **/usr/local/doc**. Some documentation is most appropriate as a paper booklet or as a sign taped to a piece of hardware.

Major servers should be labeled with the hostname, boot instructions, architecture, and any special instructions needed to reboot the machine. The hostname should be readable from across the room. Be sure to keep a copy of the information on all these little sticky labels with your central records or inventory data.

Also tape the hostname to other pieces of hardware that are associated with each machine: disk drives, modems, printers, tape drives, etc. If the host is an important citizen (for example, a major server or a crucial router), include the location of its circuit breaker. If a floppy disk or flash memory card is required for bootstrapping, point to its location. Major file servers should have information about disk device names, partition tables, mount points, and the locations of backup superblocks readily available. Tape the information to the disk drives themselves or store it in a well-known location in the machine room.

Tape drives should be labeled with the device files and commands needed to access them. It's also a good idea to list the type of tapes the drive requires, the nearest place to buy them, and even the approximate price.

Printers should be labeled with their names, brief printing instructions, and the hosts that they depend on. Printers often come with network interfaces and are full citizens of the network, but they may depend on a Linux host for spooling and configuration.

Network wiring must be scrupulously documented. Label all cables, identify patch panels and wall outlets, and mark network devices. Always make it easy for your wiring technician to keep the documentation up to date; keep a pencil and forms hanging on the wall of the wiring closet so that it's painless to note that a cable moved from one device to another. Later, you should transfer this data to on-line storage.

A **diary** file associated with each machine that documents major events in its life (upgrades, hardware repairs, major software installations, and crashes, for example) provides a central place to review the history and status of a machine. You can point an email alias at the file so that the diary can be carbon-copied on mail sent among sysadmins. This is perhaps the most painless and least organized way of keeping records, but its simplicity makes it easier to enforce.

It's a good idea to prepare a printed document that you can give to new users. It should document local customs, procedures for reporting problems, the names and locations of printers, your backup and downtime schedules, and so on. This type of document can save an enormous amount of sysadmin or user services time. You should also make the information available on the web. A printed document is more likely to be read by new users, but a web page is easier to refer to at the time questions arise. Do both.

In addition to documenting your local computing environment, you may want to prepare some introductory material about Linux. Such material is essential in a university environment in which the user community is transient and often Linux-illiterate. We have printed one-page crib sheets about the **vi** editor, email, logging in and out, the X Windows environment, and the use of man pages.

29.10 PROCUREMENT

At many sites, the system administration team and the purchasing team are totally separate. This is bad.

Sysadmins need to know about any new hardware that's being ordered in order to verify that it fits the current infrastructure and can be supported. They also need to be able to influence the specifications that go into purchase requests. Sysadmins can often provide good information about the competence of vendors (especially third-party resellers) and the reliability of certain types of equipment.

A system administrator's participation is especially valuable in organizations that by default must buy from the lowest bidder (for example, government institutions and state universities). Most purchasing systems allow you to specify evaluation criteria. Be sure to include escape clauses such as "must be compatible with existing environment" or "must be able to run XYZ software package well."

The incremental cost of adding a workstation is not constant. Is it the 60th of that architecture or the first? Does it have enough local disk for the system files? Does it have enough memory to run today's bloated applications? Is there a spare network port to plug it into? Will it be in an area of the building that is accessible to the network? Is it a completely new OS?

Questions like these tend to emphasize a more fundamental question: Do you stay stagnant and buy equipment from your current vendor, or do you try the latest whizzy toy from a startup that might shake the world or might be out of business in a year? The nature of your organization may answer this one. It's not a simple yes or no; you must often make a complex tradeoff between the latest and greatest equipment and the machines that you are comfortable with and understand.

If you are allowed to negotiate with vendors (officially or otherwise) you can often do much better than your purchasing department. Don't be shy about quoting prices from other vendors for comparable equipment or inflating the size of expected purchases for the coming year. After all, the sales people have inflated the value of their product. Being able to get an order out fast is useful at a bean counting boundary such as the end of a fiscal quarter or year. When you submit orders in the last week of a company's accounting period, you can often obtain a sizable additional discount just to make a department's quota look better. Another bargain time is just before or just after new models are introduced; vendors want to reduce their inventory of the older products. This kind of vendor bashing is common at universities and may or may not be appropriate at companies and government institutions. But it is fun.

29.11 DECOMMISSIONING HARDWARE

Retiring a computer used to be a painful ordeal. Stubborn users wouldn't let go; weaning required them to learn a new system or convert to new applications. But since cheap Intel/PC hardware has become the standard architecture base, retiring ancient machines just means adding more memory or replacing the CPU board. The user interface remains the same; everything just gets faster.

A related problem at universities involves donations from businesses that would like to get a tax deduction. Often, the right answer is, "No thanks, we don't need 2,000 nine-track tapes and racks to put them in." One university in Budapest was given an IBM mainframe several years ago. Instead of saying no and buying fast PCs, they dedicated their whole budget to shipping and electrical wiring the first year and maintenance in following years. Status just isn't worth it. On the other hand, many universities establish strong relationships with their local computer industry and get lots of valuable hardware donated—it's just last year's model. Consider total cost of ownership and know when to say "No, thanks."

If you are a company and have surplus computer gear, consider donating it to your local schools or colleges; they often do not have the budget to keep their labs current and may welcome your older PCs.

29.12 ORGANIZATIONS, CONFERENCES, AND OTHER RESOURCES

Several UNIX and Linux support groups—both general and vendor-specific—exist to help you network with other people that are using the same software. Table 29.1 presents a brief list of organizations. Plenty of national and regional groups exist that are not listed in this table.

Table 29.1   Linux and UNIX organizations

Name	URL	What it is
LPI	www.lpi.org	Linux Professional Institute
LI	www.li.org	Linux International
USENIX	www.usenix.org	UNIX users group, quite technical
SAGE	www.sage.org	The System Administrators Guild associated with USE-NIX; holds the LISA conference each year
SANS	www.sans.org	Runs sysadmin and security conferences; less technical than SAGE with a focus on tutorials
AUUG	www.auug.org.au	Australian UNIX Users Group, covers both technical and managerial aspects of computing
SAGE-AU	www.sage-au.org.au	Australian SAGE, holds yearly conferences in Oz

Some of the organizations hold conferences on Linux-related topics, although most conferences are broader than just Linux or UNIX and include tracks and events for Windows, too. Linux International and the Linux Professional Institute promote Linux in various ways—LI through marketing efforts to bring Linux into the business community (and to fund some of the open source development efforts) and LPI through its Linux system administrator certification program.

LI's web site has some good fodder for managers who are reluctant to use open source operating systems. They sponsor a Linux booth at several trade shows, including LinuxWorld, Linux Expo, and CeBit. LI is also leading an internationalization project to bring all the world's character sets to Linux. Their summer internship program matches students with Linux developers to give the students hands-on experience writing production-quality code.

USENIX, an organization of users of Linux, UNIX, and other open source operating systems, holds one general conference and several specialized (smaller) conferences or workshops each year. The general conference has a parallel track devoted to open systems that features ongoing OS development in the Linux and BSD communities. In 2000 and 2001, USENIX joined forces with the Linux community to sponsor ALS, the Atlanta/Annual Linux Showcase meeting, a week-long conference devoted to Linux. The big event for sysadmins is the USENIX LISA (Large Installation System Administration) conference held every fall. Trade shows are often associated with these conferences.

Many local areas have regional Linux user groups, some affiliated with USENIX and some not. The local groups usually have monthly meetings, local or visiting speakers, and pizza and beer before or after the meetings. It's a good way to network with other Linux sysadmins in your area.

The biggest Linux trade show is the LinuxWorld Expo conference and exposition, which is held twice a year in the United States and occasionally in Europe and Asia. The most recent U.S. conferences were held in New York and California.

The premier trade show for the networking industry is Interop; its tutorial series is also of high quality and is not UNIX-specific. Interop used to be an annual event that was eagerly awaited by techies and vendors alike. Interops now happens several times a year—a traveling network circus, so to speak. The salaries of tutorial speakers have been cut in half, but the quality of the tutorials seems to have survived.

LPI: the Linux Professional Institute

The LPI provides Linux certification. That is, it administers tests that measure a sysadmin's competence and knowledge of various Linux tasks. Three levels of certification are available, each of which consists of a two-part test. The tests so far (Levels 1 and 2) are in a multiple-choice format and are administered over the web by Vue Electronic Testing Service (www.vue.com/lpi).

Level 1 seems to cover Linux power user commands and very basic sysadmin tasks. Level 2 is more in depth and includes networking. Level 3 is defined but has not yet been fully developed (as of early 2002).

The LPI web site (www.lpi.org) outlines the kinds of knowledge expected at each level of certification and provides sample questions from each of the tests.

Certification is important and hard to do well. System administration is a hands-on type of science (or is it an art?). A multiple-choice test, while easy to administer and grade, is not very good at measuring the problem-solving skills that are the hallmark of a good sysadmin. We hope that Level 3 of the LPI suite will involve a hands-on lab component, more like the Cisco CCIE certification than the Microsoft MCSE exam.

SAGE: the System Administrators Guild

SAGE, USENIX's System Administrators Guild, is the first international organization for system administrators. It promotes system administration as a profession by sponsoring conferences and informal programs. See www.sage.org for all the details.

SAGE has just launched a sysadmin certification program that is a bit behind the Linux certification timeline. The www.sagecert.org web site has all the details. Their Junior System Administration exam, cSAGE, is now available; it requires 1–3 years of experience as a sysadmin. The exam is in two parts: a core component that is platform- and vendor-neutral, and then a more specific module that can be targeted to a particular system or vendor. The entire exam takes about four hours.

Another SAGE activity that's under development is a mentoring program in which senior sysadmins would work to improve the skills of folks who are trying to enter the profession. Mentors typically work one-on-one with their trainees once or twice a week.

A more formal educational activity involves the members of the SAGE community who teach university classes in system administration. This group exchanges and shares assignments and teaching ideas via the sysadm-education mailing list. To subscribe, send mail to majordomo@maillist.peak.org and include the text "subscribe sysadm-education" in the body of your message.

The USENIX and SAGE newsletter *;login:* is produced by both organizations; it contains administrative news, tips, reviews, and announcements of interest to sysadmins. SAGE has also produced a series of short, focused booklets that are available for a small fee ($10 for members; ~$15 for nonmembers). New booklets are free if you are a SAGE member when they're first published. Here is the current list.

- *Job Descriptions for System Administrators*, edited by Tina Darmohray
- *A Guide to Developing Computing Policy Documents*, edited by Barbara Dijker
- *System Security: A Management Perspective*, by David Oppenheimer et al.
- *Educating and Training System Administrators: A Survey*, by David Kuncicky and Bruce Wynn
- *Hiring System Administrators*, by Gretchen Phillips
- *A System Administrator's Guide to Auditing*, by Geoff Halprin
- *System and Network Administration for Higher Reliability*, by John Sellens

SAGE, together with USENIX, its parent organization, puts on the LISA conference each fall and sometimes a network administration conference in the spring. The LISA conference is the biggest, best, most technical, and most focused of the conferences aimed at system and network administrators. It's held each fall and typically includes three days of tutorials and three days of technical sessions, invited talks, and help sessions. Occasionally, one-day workshops on special topics run in parallel. For information, send mail to conference@usenix.org or see www.usenix.org.

In addition to the original SAGE, several national and regional groups have been formed to help sysadmins interact more regularly with their peers. As of this writing, the national groups are SAGE-AU in Australia; SAGE-WISE in Wales, Ireland, Scotland, and England; and SAGE-PT in Portugal. Contact information for the regional groups can be found at the www.usenix.org/sage/locals.

SANS: the System Administration, Networking, and Security Institute

SANS, which is described on page 685, provides a certification program in the security space. The exams are well respected and involve both multiple choice questions and lab exercises. There are three levels: general security (GSEC), a second tier covering five topics (firewalls and VPNs, hacker exploits and incident handling, intrusion detection, UNIX security, and Windows security), and a final level labeled Security Engineer. Certification is valid for only 2–3 years, so you must keep up with recent developments and recertify to stay current.

The SAGE, LPI, and SANS certification programs are new enough that their certificates are not yet standard requirements for employment as a system administrator or security professional.

Mailing lists and web resources

Sysadmins have access to a huge variety of mailing lists and web search engines. We list some of our favorites in Chapter 1, *Where to Start*. In addition, an extensive list of Linux-related mailing lists is available from www.linux.org/docs/lists.html. There are also mailing lists that focus on particular distributions; Table 29.2 shows some specifics for our example distributions.

Table 29.2   Distribution-specific mailing lists

Distro	List names[a]	URLs
Red Hat	redhat-*xxx*	www.redhat.com/support/mailing-lists
SuSE	suse-*xxx*	www.suse.com/support/mailinglists
Debian	debian-*xxx*	www.debian.org/MailingLists/subscribe and lists.debian.org

a. The *xxx* fields in the list names have many possible values and depend on the subjects you are interested in. These distributions don't have sysadmin-specific lists, but several lists touch on sysadmin topics.

Printed resources

The best resources for administrators in the printed realm (aside from this book :-) are the O'Reilly series of books. The series began with *UNIX in a Nutshell* over 20 years ago and now includes a separate volume on just about every important Linux and UNIX subsystem and command. The series also includes books on the Internet, Windows, and other non-UNIXy topics. All the books are reasonably priced, timely, and focused. Tim O'Reilly has become quite interested in the open source movement and runs a yearly conference on this topic as well as conferences on Perl, Java, and TCL/Tk. See www.oreilly.com for more information.

29.13 STANDARDS

The standardization process helps us in some cases (modems from different manufacturers can talk to each other) and hurts us in others (OSI protocols, millions of dollars down the drain). Standards committees should codify and formalize existing practice, not invent.

Standards are intended to level the playing field and make it possible for customers to buy compatible products from competing vendors. Some of the parties involved in the standardization process really do just want to codify existing practice. Others have a more political purpose: to delay a competitor or to reduce the amount of work required to bring their own company's products into conformance.

Government organizations are often the biggest procurers of standards-based systems and applications. The use of standards allows them to buy competitively without favoring a particular brand. However, some cynics have called standards a non-monetary trade barrier—companies slow down the standards process until their products catch up.

There are several standards bodies, both formal and informal. Each has different rules for membership, voting, and clout. From a system or network administrator's perspective, the most important bodies are the Free Standards Group's LSB (Linux Standard Base), POSIX (pronounced PAHZ-icks, Portable Operating System Interfaces) and the IETF (the Internet Engineering Task Force, described on page 239).

LSB: the Linux Standard Base

The Free Standards Group is a nonprofit organization that promotes open source standards—in particular, the Linux standardization effort. Currently about 20 corporations contribute to the effort, including major manufacturers such as Compaq, Hewlett-Packard, IBM, and Silicon Graphics. Major distributors such as Red Hat, SuSE, Debian, Mandrake, Caldera, and Turbolinux also participate.[8] The goal is to make it easier for third-party software developers to build a software product for Linux and have that be one product, not 20 or 50 slightly different variations of the same product.

The list of items being threaded through the standards process includes:

- Library interfaces, including X11
- Binary formats
- Dynamic linking mechanisms
- Package formats
- Syntax of commands and utilities
- The shell
- Logins, UIDs, and GIDs
- Filesystem hierarchy, including the structure of **/dev** and **/proc**
- Startup files

---

8. Twenty sets of folks, many of them competitors, all trying to agree on standards for the penguin—sounds like a daunting task.

As of this writing, LSB for IA-32 architecture standards are at version 1.1.0 draft-1 and the IA-64 architecture effort is at version 0.5.0. See www.linuxbase.org for the current status of the project as well as the draft specifications and test suites.

POSIX

POSIX, an offshoot of the IEEE that charges for copies of their standards, has engaged itself for the last several years in defining a general standard for UNIX. Their major effort in the past has been focused on the commands and system call or library interfaces. Linux is POSIX compliant and tracks the POSIX standards.

29.14 SAMPLE DOCUMENTS

Several of the policy or procedure documents referred to in this chapter are available from www.admin.com. Table 29.3 lists the docs and their corresponding contents.

Table 29.3   Policy and procedure documents at www.admin.com

Document	Contents
ugrad.policy	Undergraduate lab user policy agreement
grad.policy	Faculty and graduate student user policy agreement
sysadmin.policy	Sysadmin policy agreement
services	CSOPS services, policies, and priorities
hiring.quiz1	"Rate your experience" quiz
hiring.quiz2	Administrative knowledge quiz
localization	Localization checklist
amanda	Checklist for client backups with Amanda
tcp-wrappers	Checklist for installing TCP wrappers
mibh-aup	Example of a good Acceptable Use Policy

29.15 RECOMMENDED READING

BURGESS, MARK S. *Principles of Network and System Administration.* New York, NY: Wiley. 2000.

LIMONCELLI, THOMAS A., AND CHRISTINE HOGAN. *The Practice of System and Network Administration.* Reading, MA: Addison Wesley. 2001.

BURGESS, MARK. "Computer Immunology." LISA 1998 proceedings.

SAN DIEGO SUPERCOMPUTER CENTER. Local policies, standards, and procedures. http://security.sdsc.edu/help/SGs.shtml

EATON, DAVID W. "comp.software.config-mgmt FAQ, part 3." http://www.iac.honeywell.com/Pub/Tech/CM/PMTools.html

This FAQ contains a summary of trouble ticketing systems, including many commercial ones we had never heard of. It seems to be well maintained but didn't contain any of our favorites.

HARROW, JEFFREY R., AND COMPAQ COMPUTER CORPORATION. *The Rapidly Changing Face of Computing* (periodical). http://www.compaq.com/rcfoc

This regularly updated site contains some interesting articles about technology-related issues. It's a combination of news and editorial content.

29.16 EXERCISES

★ **E29.1** Reread your site's user agreement. What are the main issues that it covers? Are there any topics that should be added?

★ **E29.2** Who are some of the current major corporate supporters of Linux? What are their interests and motivations? What sort of contributions are they making?

★ **E29.3** You are cleaning up after a disk crash and notice files in the **lost+found** directory. When you investigate further, you find that some of the files are mail messages that were sent between two students who are setting up a back door around the department firewall to archive MP3 files on the main data server. What should you do?

★★ **E29.4** Evaluate your site's local documentation for new users, sysadmins, standard procedures, and emergencies.

★★ **E29.5** In a trenchant essay, forecast the future of Linux over the next five years. How will the current development and distribution models hold up over time? What will be the long-term impact of the adoption of Linux by hardware vendors?

Colophon

This book was produced with Microsoft Windows 98 and 2000. Unfortunately, application software for Linux still has a long way to go before it can compete with the offerings available on Windows and MacOS.

We used Adobe FrameMaker for layout, with Adobe Illustrator and Adobe Photoshop for graphics and illustrations. We also used Adobe Acrobat throughout the production process. It allowed us to distribute chapters and graphic files to many different people without worrying about fonts or application compatibility. We delivered the final manuscript as an Acrobat file, too.

Tyler Curtain drew the cartoons using pen and ink. We scanned them on a desktop scanner, cleaned them up in Photoshop, and converted them to PostScript artwork with Adobe Streamline.

The body text is Minion Multiple Master, designed by Robert Slimbach. Headings, tables, and illustrations are set in Myriad Multiple Master by Robert Slimbach and Carol Twombly.

The "code" font is PMN Caecilia, designed by Peter Matthias Noordzij. We searched for a long time for a fixed-width font that looked similar to Courier but lacked Courier's many typesetting problems. We couldn't find one. We finally settled on this proportional font and used tabs to line up columns of output. This approach works pretty well, but Caecilia is missing some of the characters needed for technical typesetting, and its italic version is noticeably slimmer than its roman.

The lack of good fonts for this application represents a sizable hole in an otherwise saturated and commodified typeface market. Type designers take note!

Index

We have alphabetized files under their last components. And in most cases, *only* the last component is listed. For example, to find index entries relating to the **/etc/passwd** file, look under **passwd**. Our friendly Linux distributors have forced our hand by hiding standard files in new and inventive directories on each system.

About the Authors

Evi Nemeth has retired from the computer science faculty at the University of Colorado but still dabbles in network research at CAIDA, the Cooperative Association for Internet Data Analysis at the San Diego Supercomputer Center. She is currently exploring the Caribbean on her new toy, a 40-foot sailboat named Wonderland.

evi@cs.colorado.edu

Garth Snyder has worked at NeXT and Sun and holds a degree in Electrical Engineering from Swarthmore College. He is currently an MD/MBA candidate at the University of Rochester.

snyderga@simon.rochester.edu

Trent R. Hein is the co-founder of Applied Trust Engineering, a company which provides network infrastructure security and performance consulting services. Trent holds a BS in Computer Science from the University of Colorado.

trent@atrust.com